FINANCIAL ACCOUNTING

Tools for Business Decision Making

Paul D. Kimmel PhD, CPA
Associate Professor of Accounting
University of Wisconsin—Milwaukee
Milwaukee, Wisconsin

Jerry J. Weygandt PhD, CPA
Arthur Andersen Alumni Professor of Accounting
University of Wisconsin
Madison, Wisconsin

Donald E. Kieso PhD, CPA
KPMG Peat Marwick Emeritus Professor
  of Accountancy
Northern Illinois University
DeKalb, Illinois

John Wiley & Sons, Inc.
New York • Chichester • Weinheim
Brisbane • Singapore • Toronto

**Dedicated to
our parents and our in-laws,
and to our families,
most especially our spouses,
    Merlynn
      Enid
     Donna**

EXECUTIVE EDITOR:	Susan Elbe
SENIOR MARKETING MANAGER:	Rebecca Hope
DESIGN SUPERVISOR:	Ann Marie Renzi
SENIOR DEVELOPMENTAL EDITOR:	Nancy Perry
PHOTO EDITORS:	Elaine Paoloni, Jennifer Atkins
ILLUSTRATION EDITOR:	Anna Melhorn
PRODUCTION SERVICE:	Phyllis Niklas
COVER AND TEXT DESIGN:	Kenny Beck

This book was set in New Aster by York Graphic Services and printed and bound by Von Hoffmann Press. The cover was printed by Phoenix Color Corp.

This book is printed on acid-free paper.

The paper in this book was manufactured by a mill whose forest management programs include sustained yield harvesting of its timberlands. Sustained yield harvesting principles ensure that the numbers of trees cut each year does not exceed the amount of new growth.

Copyright © 1998 John Wiley & Sons, Inc. All rights reserved.

No part of this publication may be reproduced, stored in a retrieval system or transmitted in any form or by any means, electronic, mechanical, photocopying, recording, scanning or otherwise, except as permitted under Sections 107 or 108 of the 1976 United States Copyright Act, without either the prior written permission of the Publisher, or authorization through payment of the appropriate per-copy fee to the Copyright Clearance Center, 222 Rosewood Drive, Danvers, MA 01923, (508) 750-8400, fax (508) 750-4470. Requests to the Publisher for permission should be addressed to the Permissions Department, John Wiley & Sons, Inc., 605 Third Avenue, New York, NY 10158-0012, (212) 850-6011, fax (212) 850-6008, E-Mail: PERMREQ@WILEY.COM.

Library of Congress Cataloging in Publication Data:
Kimmel, Paul D.
    Financial accounting: tools for business decision making / Paul D. Kimmel, Jerry J. Weygandt, Donald E. Kieso.
      p.   cm.
    Includes index.
    ISBN 0-471-16919-6 (cloth: alk. paper)
    1. Accounting.   I. Weygandt, Jerry J.   II. Kieso, Donald E.
III. Title.
HF5635.K538   1997
657—dc21   97-48608
                                                                         CIP

ISBN 0-471-16919-6

Printed in the United States of America

10 9 8 7 6 5 4

ABOUT THE AUTHORS

Paul D. Kimmel, PhD, CPA, received his bachelors degree from the University of Minnesota and his doctorate in accounting from the University of Wisconsin. He is an Associate Professor at the University of Wisconsin—Milwaukee, and has public accounting experience with Deloitte & Touche (Minneapolis). He was the recipient of the UWM School of Business Advisory Council Teaching Award, the Reggie Taite Excellence in Teaching Award, and a three-time winner of the Outstanding Teaching Assistant Award at the University of Wisconsin. He is also a recipient of the Elijah Watts Sells Award for Honorary Distinction for his results on the CPA exam. He is a member of the American Accounting Association and has published articles in *Accounting Review, Accounting Horizons, Issues in Accounting Education, Journal of Accounting Education,* as well as other journals. His research interests include accounting for financial instruments and innovation in accounting education. He has published papers and given numerous talks on incorporating critical thinking into accounting education, and helped prepare a catalog of critical thinking resources for the Federated Schools of Accountancy.

Jerry J. Weygandt, PhD, CPA, is Arthur Andersen Alumni Professor of Accounting at the University of Wisconsin—Madison. He holds a PhD in accounting from the University of Illinois. Articles by Professor Weygandt have appeared in *Accounting Review, Journal of Accounting Research, Journal of Accountancy,* and other professional journals. These articles have examined such financial reporting issues as accounting for price-level adjustments, pensions, convertible securities, stock option contracts, and interim reports. He is a member of the American Accounting Association, the American Institute of Certified Public Accountants, and the Wisconsin Society of Certified Public Accountants. He has served on numerous committees of the American Accounting Association and as a member of the editorial board of *Accounting Review*. In addition, he is actively involved with the American Institute of Certified Public Accountants and has been a member of the Accounting Standards Executive Committee (AcSEC) of that organization. He has served on the FASB task force that examined the reporting issues related to "accounting for income taxes" and is presently a trustee of the Financial Accounting Foundation. Professor Weygandt has received the Chancellor's Award for Excellence in Teaching; he also has served as President and Secretary-Treasurer of the American Accounting Association. Recently he received the Wisconsin Institute of CPA's Outstanding Educator's Award and the Lifetime Achievement Award.

Donald E. Kieso, PhD, CPA, received his bachelors degree from Aurora University and his doctorate in accounting from the University of Illinois. He has served as chairman of the Department of Accountancy and is currently the KPMG Peat Marwick Emeritus Professor of Accountancy at Northern Illinois University. He has public accounting experience with Price Waterhouse & Co. (San Francisco and Chicago) and Arthur Andersen & Co. (Chicago) and research experience with the Research Division of the American Institute of Certified Public Accountants (New York). He is a recipient of NIU's Teaching Excellence Award and four Golden Apple Teaching Awards. He has served as a member of the Board of Directors of the Illinois CPA Society, the Board of Governors of the American Accounting Association's Administrators of Accounting Programs Group, AACSB's Accounting Accreditation and Visitation Committees, and the State of Illinois Comptroller's Commission, as Secretary-Treasurer of the Federation of Schools of Accountancy, and as Secretary-Treasurer of the American Accounting Association. Professor Kieso is currently serving as Vice-Chairman and member of the Board of Trustees and Executive Committee of Aurora University, as a member of the Boards of Directors of Castle BancGroup and the Sandwich State Bank, and as Treasurer and member of the Board of Directors of The Sandwich Community Hospital. From 1989 to 1993 he served as a charter member of the national Accounting Education Change Commission. In 1988 he received the Outstanding Accounting Educator Award from the Illinois CPA Society; in 1992 he received the FSA's Joseph A. Silvoso Award of Merit and the NIU Foundation's Humanitarian Award for Service to Higher Education; and in 1995 he received a Distinguished Service Award from the Illinois CPA Society.

PREFACE

In recent years accounting education has seen numerous efforts to change the way accounting is taught. These efforts reflect the demands of an ever-changing business world, opportunities created by new instructional technologies, and an increased understanding of how students learn. In this book we have drawn from what we believe to be the most promising of these innovations. Our efforts were driven by a few key beliefs:

- **"Less is more."**
  Our instructional objective is to provide students with an understanding of those concepts that are fundamental to the use of accounting. Most students will forget procedural details within a short period of time. On the other hand, concepts, if well taught, should be remembered for a lifetime. Concepts are especially important in a world where the details are constantly changing.

- **"Don't just sit there—do something."**
  Students learn best when they are actively engaged. The overriding pedagogical objective of this book is to provide students with continual opportunities for active learning. One of the best tools for active learning is strategically placed questions. Our discussions are framed by questions, often beginning with rhetorical questions and ending with review questions. Even our selection of analytical devices, called Decision Tools, is referenced using key questions to emphasize the purpose of each.

- **"I'll believe it when I see it."**
  Students will be most willing to commit time and energy to a topic when they believe that it is relevant to their future career. There is no better way to demonstrate relevance than to ground discussion in the real world. Consistent with this, we adopted a macro-approach: Chapters 1 and 2 show students how to use financial statements of real companies. By using high-profile companies like Starbucks, Microsoft, Nike, and Intel to frame our discussion of accounting issues, we demonstrate the relevance of accounting while teaching students about companies with which they have daily contact. As they become acquainted with the financial successes and failures of these companies many students will begin to follow business news more closely, making their learning a dynamic, ongoing process. We also discuss small companies like Green Mountain Coffee and Iomega to highlight the challenges faced by small companies as they try to grow big.

- **"You need to make a decision."**
  All business people must make decisions. Decision making involves critical evaluation and analysis of the information at hand, and this takes practice. We have integrated important analytical tools throughout the book. After each new decision tool is presented, we summarize the key features of that tool in a Decision Toolkit. At the end of each chapter we provide a comprehensive demonstration of an analysis of a real company using the decision tools presented in the chapter. The presentation of these tools throughout the book is logically sequenced to take full advantage of the tools presented in earlier chapters, culminating in a capstone analysis chapter.

KEY FEATURES OF EACH CHAPTER

Chapter 1, Introduction to Financial Statements. In Chapter 1, students learn about the purpose of each of the four financial statements, first using a hypothetical company (to keep things simple) and then looking at simplified statements of Starbucks Coffee (to make things real). We next discuss the importance of some basic assumptions and principles that underlie these financial statements.

Chapter 2, A Further Look at Financial Statements. In this chapter we introduce students to the components of the statements through examples of types of revenues, expenses, assets, and liabilities. Next they are given basic tools for evaluating financial statements including the current ratio, debt to total assets ratio, return on assets ratio, and current cash debt coverage ratio. The decision tools are used to evaluate two well-known electronics companies, Circuit City and Best Buy.

Chapter 3, The Accounting Information System. The purpose of this chapter and the next is to show students where the statements they learned about in Chapters 1 and 2 come from. Chapter 3 teaches students how accounting records the events that a company encounters each day. We present the necessary fundamentals of the accounting system while avoiding many mechanical aspects that are not necessary to understand the accounting process. To further integrate Chapters 3 and 4 with what students have already learned, the transactions that are analyzed are those that resulted in the financial statements presented in Chapter 1.

Chapter 4, Accrual Accounting Concepts. This chapter finishes the process started in Chapter 3. The purpose of this chapter is to demonstrate the difference between cash and accrual accounting by applying the revenue recognition and matching principles through the adjustment process. Like Chapter 3, the discussion here focuses on those aspects of the process that are fundamental to understanding statement preparation while avoiding those aspects that are not. So, for example, the *reasons* for adjustment are emphasized while presentation of the specifics of closing entries and work sheets is eliminated. A basic discussion of closing and work sheets is provided to ensure that these terms are part of a student's working vocabulary.

Chapter 5, Merchandising Operations. Chapter 5 introduces basic merchandising concepts and begins a two-chapter discussion of inventory issues. To simplify the discussion, we assume a perpetual system, thus avoiding separate accounts for purchases, freight-in, and so on. (The periodic approach is discussed in Chapter 6.) The chapter concludes with a comparison of the profitability of Kmart and Wal-Mart, employing the gross profit rate and the ratio of operating expenses to sales.

Chapter 6, Reporting and Analyzing Inventory. This chapter first introduces the periodic system of inventory accounting. Next, it presents inventory cost flow assumptions, along with a thorough discussion of the implications of the financial statement and tax effects of various cost flow assumptions. To simplify the presentation, a periodic system is assumed. Lower of cost or market is discussed at a conceptual level. The chapter concludes with an analysis of inventory. First, the inventory turnover ratios of both Kmart and Wal-Mart are discussed. Then the significant implications of the LIFO reserve are demonstrated by analyzing the inventory of Caterpillar Inc.

Chapter 7, Internal Control and Cash. First, the chapter presents general concepts and applications of internal control, with numerous references to actual cases of internal control failures (which are always of interest to students). To ensure understanding of these concepts, we then apply them to the cash account. Finally, the implications of the operating cycle and techniques of cash management are presented, including cash budgeting, the ratio of cash to daily cash expenses, and free cash flow.

Chapter 8, Reporting and Analyzing Receivables. We begin Chapter 8 by discussing the basic elements of accounts and notes receivable, including estimating bad debts and computing interest on notes. We then focus on management of receivables: (1) determining whom to extend credit to, (2) establishing a payment period, (3) monitoring collections, (4) evaluating the receivables balance, and (5) accelerating receipts. The chapter analyzes the receivables of Intel Corporation as well as discussing the implications of bad debts expense for banks.

Chapter 9, Reporting and Analyzing Long-Lived Assets. In this chapter we discuss plant assets and intangible assets. We do not discuss natural resources. The chapter begins by noting the varying significance of plant assets across different industries, discussing the recording of purchases of plant assets, and outlining the issues faced by management in the decision whether to buy or lease. In discussing depreciation, we chose to present the calculations for only the straight-line approach, since it is used by 90% of U.S. companies for financial reporting. (Calculations for other methods are presented in an appendix.) For the units-of-activity and declining-balance approaches we discuss the resulting expense and book value patterns and their implications for analysis. After discussing asset sales, impairments, and other issues, we demonstrate how to evaluate long-lived assets by comparing the average useful life, average age of plant assets, and the asset turnover ratio. Our analysis compares Southwest Airlines with Valujet.

The chapter concludes by describing aspects of accounting for intangible assets that would be important to analysts. For example, we discuss the requirement to expense research and development costs, and we illustrate how a company's choice of estimated useful life impacts its amortization expense.

Chapter 10, Reporting and Analyzing Liabilities. This chapter first discusses current liabilities and then addresses long-term liabilities. The discussion of current liabilities presents common examples—notes payable, sales taxes, payroll, payroll taxes, unearned revenues, and current maturities of long-term debt. The current liabilities material concludes with an analysis of the liquidity of Chrysler Corporation, in which we evaluate its working capital, current ratio, acid-test ratio, and available lines of credit.

The discussion of long-term liabilities begins with a thorough discussion of bond basics: why bonds are used, how bonds are issued, factors influencing bond pricing, and the various types of bonds. (Present value calculations are presented in an appendix at the end of the book.) The presentation of accounting for bonds includes a discussion of accounting for premiums and discounts using the straight-line approach. Other issues covered are contingent liabilities, lease obligations, and off-balance sheet financing. The discussion of long-term debt concludes by analyzing Chrysler's long-term debt using the debt to total assets ratio and times interest earned ratio.

Chapter 11, Reporting and Analyzing Stockholders' Equity. The chapter opens with a discussion of the pros and cons of the corporate form of organization. Reporting issues covered include the issuance and repurchase of common stock, issuance of preferred stock, and accounting for the various types of dividends. The reasons for cash dividends, stock dividends, and stock splits are discussed along with their implications for analysis. Recent dividend practices of Nike, Reebok, and other major companies are compared and contrasted. The earnings and dividend record of Nike are analyzed from the perspective of a common stock investor, using earnings per share, price-earnings ratio, return on common stockholders' equity ratio, payout ratio, and dividend yield.

Chapter 12, Reporting and Analyzing Investments. The chapter begins with a discussion of the various reasons companies purchase investment securities. The basic issues of accounting for investments in debt and stock securities are discussed, with an emphasis on why the accounting for stock investments varies depending on the percentage ownership. Consolidation accounting is discussed at a conceptual level. The implications of classifying securities as trading securities, available-for-sale, or held-to-maturity are discussed and illustrated by evaluating the investment portfolio of the bank holding company KeyCorp.

Chapter 13, Statement of Cash Flows. This chapter begins with a discussion of the purpose and usefulness of the statement of cash flows. The chapter then splits into two sections, allowing instructors the choice of emphasizing the indirect method or the direct method. Each of these sections follows a two-year progression, with the first year addressing only the most basic items affecting cash flow, and the second year adding additional items. The chapter concludes with an analysis of Microsoft's statement of cash flows employing free cash flow, the capital expenditure ratio, the current cash debt coverage ratio, cash debt coverage ratio, and cash return on sales ratio. Comparative numbers for Oracle are provided.

Chapter 14, Financial Analysis: The Big Picture. This chapter is a capstone, reinforcing an understanding of those analytical tools learned in previous chapters and demonstrating their interrelationships. Most importantly, this chapter demonstrates to students how much they have learned about using financial statement numbers to analyze a company. The chapter begins with a discussion of the importance of the concept of earning power, by contrasting net income resulting from operations with net income resulting from irregular items such as extraordinary items, discontinued operations, or accounting changes. The potential usefulness of comprehensive income is also discussed. Next, we present the analytical tools of horizontal and vertical analysis. The chapter concludes with a thorough analysis of Kellogg Company, Inc., employing the new tools learned in this chapter, as well as all tools presented in previous chapters.

PROVEN PEDAGOGICAL FRAMEWORK

In this book we have used many proven pedagogical tools to help students learn accounting concepts and apply them to decision making in the business world. This pedagogical framework emphasizes the *processes* students undergo as they learn.

Learning How to Use the Text

A **Student Owner's Manual** begins the text to help students understand the value of the pedagogical framework and how to use it. After becoming familiar with the pedagogy, students can take a **learning styles quiz** (page xxii) to help them identify how they learn best (visually, aurally, through reading and writing, kinesthetically, or through a combination of these styles). We then offer tips on in-class and at-home learning strategies, as well as help in identifying the text pedagogy that would be most useful to them for their learning style. Finally, Chapter 1 contains notes (printed in red) that explain each pedagogical element the first time it appears.

Understanding the Context

- **Study Objectives,** listed at the beginning of each chapter, form a learning framework throughout the text, with each objective repeated in the margin at the appropriate place in the main body of the chapter and again in the **Summary of Study Objectives.** Also, end-of-chapter assignment materials are linked to the Study Objectives.
- A **Chapter-Opening Vignette** presents a scenario that relates an actual business situation of a well-known company to the topic of the chapter. The vignette also serves as a recurrent example throughout the chapter. Each vignette ends with the Internet addresses of the companies cited in the story to encourage students to go on-line to get more information about these companies.
- A chapter **Preview** links the chapter-opening vignette to the major topics of the chapter. First, an introductory paragraph explains how the vignette relates to the topics to be discussed, and then a graphic outline of the chapter provides a "visual road map," useful for seeing the big picture as well as the connections between subtopics.

Learning the Material

- This book emphasizes the accounting experiences of **real companies throughout,** from chapter-opening vignettes to the chapter's last item of homework material. Details on these many features follow. In addition, every chapter uses **financial statements** from real companies. These specimen financial statements are easily identified by the company logo or related photo that appears near the statement heading.
- Continuing the real-world flavor of the book, **Business Insight** boxes in each chapter give students glimpses into how real companies make decisions using accounting information. The boxes, highlighted with striking photographs, focus on three different accounting perspectives—those of investors, managers, and international business.
- Color **illustrations** support and reinforce the concepts of the text. **Infographics** are a special type of illustration that help students visualize and apply accounting concepts to the real world. The infographics often portray important concepts in entertaining and memorable ways.
- **Before You Go On** sections occur at the end of each key topic and consist of two parts: ***Review It*** serves as a learning check within the chapter by asking students to stop and answer knowledge and comprehension questions about the material just covered. ***Do It*** is a brief demonstration problem that gives immediate practice using the material just covered. Solutions are provided to help students understand the reasoning involved in reaching an answer.
- **Helpful Hints** in the margins expand upon or help clarify concepts under discussion in the nearby text. This feature actually makes the book an Annotated *Student* Edition.
- **Alternative Terminology** notes in the margins present synonymous terms that students may come across in subsequent accounting courses and in business.
- Marginal **International Notes** provide a helpful and convenient way for instructors to begin to expose students to international issues in accounting, reporting, and decision making.
- Each chapter presents **decision tools** that are useful for analyzing the financial statement components discussed in that chapter. At the end of the text discussion relating to the decision tool, a **Decision Toolkit** summarizes the key features of that decision tool and reinforces its purpose. For example, Chapter 8 presents the receivables turnover ratio and average collection period as tools for use in analyzing receivables. At the end of that discussion the Toolkit you see at the top of page viii is shown.
- A **Using the Decision Toolkit** exercise, which follows the final Before You Go On section in the chapter, asks students to use the decision tools presented in that chapter. Students evaluate the financial situation of a real-world company, often using ratio analysis to do so. In most cases the company used in this analysis is a competitor of the example company in the chapter. For example, in Chapter 11, Nike was analyzed as the example company in the chapter discussion, so Reebok is analyzed in the Using the Decision Toolkit at the end of the chapter. Such comparisons expand and enrich the analysis and help fo-

DECISION TOOLKIT

Decision Checkpoints	Info Needed for Decision	Tool to Use for Decision	How to Evaluate Results
Are collections being made in a timely fashion?	Net credit sales and average receivables balance	Receivables turnover ratio = $\dfrac{\text{Net credit sales}}{\text{Average net receivables}}$ Average collection period = $\dfrac{365 \text{ days}}{\text{Receivables turnover ratio}}$	Average collection period should be consistent with corporate credit policy. An increase may suggest a decline in financial health of customers.

cus student attention on comparative situations that flavor real-world decision making.

Putting It Together

- At the end of each chapter, between the body of the text and the homework materials, are several useful features for review and reference: a **Summary of Study Objectives** lists the main points of the chapter; the **Decision Toolkit—A Summary** presents in one place the decision tools used throughout the chapter; and a **Glossary** of important terms gives definitions with page references to the text.
- Next, a **Demonstration Problem** gives students another opportunity to refer to a detailed solution to a representative problem before they do homework assignments. **Problem-Solving Strategies** help establish a logic for approaching similar problems and assist students in understanding the solution.

Developing Skills Through Practice

Throughout the homework material, certain questions, exercises, and problems make use of the decision tools presented in the chapter. These are marked with the icon.

- **Self-Study Questions** comprise a practice test to enable students to check their understanding of important concepts. These questions are keyed to the Study Objectives, so students can go back and review sections of the chapter in which they find they need further work.
- **Questions** provide a full review of chapter content and help students prepare for class discussions and testing situations.
- **Brief Exercises** build students' confidence and test their basic skills. Each exercise focuses on one of the Study Objectives.

- Each of the **Exercises** focuses on one or more of the Study Objectives. These tend to take a little longer to complete, and they present more of a challenge to students than Brief Exercises. The Exercises help instructors and students make a manageable transition to more challenging problems.
- **Problems** stress the applications of the concepts presented in the chapter and are paired with a set of **Alternative Problems** to give instructors greater flexibility in assigning homework. Certain problems, marked with the icon, help build business writing skills.
- Each Brief Exercise, Exercise, Problem, and Alternative Problem has a **description of the concept** covered and is keyed to the Study Objectives.

Expanding and Applying Knowledge

Broadening Your Perspective is a unique section at the end of each chapter that offers a wealth of resources to help instructors and students pull together the learning for the chapter. This section offers problems and projects for those instructors who want to broaden the learning experience by bringing in more real-world decision making and critical thinking activities.

- **Financial Reporting and Analysis** problems use financial statements of real-world companies for further practice in understanding and interpreting financial reporting. A *Financial Reporting Problem* in each chapter directs students to study various aspects of the financial statements of Starbucks Corporation, which are printed in Chapter 1 (in simplified form) and in Appendix A (in full). A *Comparative Analysis Problem* offers the opportunity to compare and contrast the financial reporting of Starbucks with a smaller competitor, Green Mountain Coffee. Since the ability to read and understand business publications is an asset over the span of one's career, **Research Cases** direct students to the *Wall Street Journal*, annual reports, or articles published in other popular business periodicals for further study and analysis of key topics. The **Interpreting Financial Statements** problems offer one or more minicases per chapter that ask students to read parts of financial statements of actual companies and use the decision tools presented in the chapter to interpret this information.

- **Critical Thinking** problems offer additional opportunities and activities. The **Management Decision Cases** help students build decision-making skills by analyzing accounting information in a less structured situation. These cases require evaluation of a manager's decision or lead to a decision among alternative courses of action. They also give practice in building business communication skills. The **Real-World Focus** problems ask students to apply concepts presented in the chapter to specific situations faced by actual companies.
- **Group Activities** present interesting in-class activities and projects to promote group cooperation. **Communication Activities** provide practice in written communication—a skill much in demand among employers. **Ethics Cases** describe typical ethical dilemmas and ask students to analyze the situation, identify the ethical issues involved, and decide on an appropriate course of action.
- **Financial Analysis on the Web** exercises guide students to Web sites from which they can mine and analyze information related to the chapter topic.

ACTIVE TEACHING AND LEARNING SUPPLEMENTARY MATERIAL

The supplementary material for students and instructors is driven by the same basic beliefs as the textbook, providing a consistent and well-integrated active learning system. This hands-on, real-world package guides *instructors* through the processes of active learning and gives them the tools to create an interactive learning environment. With its emphasis on activities, exercises, and the Internet, the package encourages *students* to take an active role in the course and prepares them for decision making in a real-world context.

Instructor's Active Teaching Aids

Instructor's Resource System on CD-ROM. Responding to the changing needs of instructors and to developments in distance learning and electronic classrooms, the supplement CD-ROM provides all the instructor support material in an electronic format that is easy to navigate and use. This CD-ROM contains all the print supplements, as well as the electronic ones, for use in the classroom, for printing out material, for uploading to your own Web site, or for downloading and modifying, thus giving you the flexibility to access and prepare the material based on your needs.

Solutions Manual. The Solutions Manual contains detailed solutions to all exercises and problems in the textbook and suggested answers to the questions and cases. Print is large and bold for easy readability in lecture settings, and instructors may duplicate any portion of the manual without paying a permissions fee. Each chapter includes an *assignment classification table*, which identifies end-of-chapter items by study objectives, and an *assignment characteristics table*, describing each problem and alternative problem and identifying difficulty level and estimated completion time. The Solutions Manual has been carefully verified by a team of independent accuracy checkers. (Also available in Word 6.0 for Windows on diskette.)

Solutions Transparencies. Packaged in an organizer box with chapter file folders, these transparencies feature detailed solutions to all exercises and problems in the textbook, and suggested answers to the Broadening Your Perspectives activities. They feature large, bold type for better projection and easy readability in large classroom settings.

Instructor's Manual. *Jessica Frazier, Eastern Kentucky University*. The Instructor's Manual is a comprehensive set of resources for preparing and presenting an active learning course. The Instructor's Manual discusses how to incorporate all the supplements, includes information on group and active learning, and has sample syllabi for use of the textbook. The Instructor's Manual also includes a series of discussions on how to incorporate ethics material, group activities, and communication activities in the course.

In addition to reading comprehension checks and short vocabulary and multiple-choice quizzes, each chapter also includes a number of activities and exercises designed to engage students in the learning process, including Research and Communication exercises, World Wide Web Research Exercises, Ethics Exercises, and International and Social Responsibility Exercises. The Web site for the text includes links for all Internet-based activities and exercises. Suggested solutions are provided where appropriate. Also included for each chapter are an *assignment classification table*; an *assignment characteristics table*; a *list of study objectives* in extra large, bold print for transparencies; and *suggestions for integrating supplements* into the classroom.

PowerPoint Presentation Material. *Jessica Frazier, Eastern Kentucky University.* This PowerPoint lecture aid contains a combination of key concepts, images, and problems from the textbook for use in the classroom. Designed according to the organization of the material in the textbook, this series of electronic transparencies can be used to reinforce accounting principles visually and graphically.

Test Bank. *Larry Falcetto, Emporia State University.* Keeping assessment consistent with the focus of the text is the main objective of this comprehensive testing package. The Test Bank features over 2,500 questions with an emphasis on concepts, decision making, and a real-world environment. Actual financial statements have been used throughout the Test Bank to provide a relevant context for questions. All questions are classified according to study objectives, learning skills, and objectives in tables at the beginning of each chapter, to make selection of exam questions easier. In addition to the examination material provided for each chapter, four comprehensive examinations covering four to five chapters are also included.

The Test Bank also includes a series of preprinted Achievement Tests for easy testing of major concepts. Each test covers two chapters from the textbook. In addition, a final exam covering all chapters in the text is included. The tests, easy to photocopy and distribute directly to students, consist of multiple-choice, matching, and true/false questions, and problems and exercises (computation and journal entries). Solutions are included at the end of each Achievement Test.

Computerized Test Bank. The Test Bank is also available for use with IBM and IBM true-compatibles running Windows 3.1 or higher. This Computerized Test Bank offers a number of valuable options that allow instructors to create multiple versions of the same test by scrambling questions; generate a large number of test questions randomly or manually; and modify and customize test questions by changing existing problems or adding your own.

Test Preparation Service. Simply call Wiley's special number (1-800-541-5602) with the questions you want on an examination. Wiley will provide a customized master exam within 24 hours. If you prefer, questions can be selected from a number of chapters.

Checklist of Key Figures. A list of key amounts for problems allows students to verify the accuracy of their answers as they work through the assignments. Available for download through our Web site at http://www.wiley.com/college/kimmel.

***Nightly Business Report* Video.** To bring the relevance of accounting into the classroom, the authors have selected a series of video clips from the *Nightly Business Report*, related to some of the actual companies discussed in the text. Each of the segments is approximately 3–5 minutes long and can be used to introduce topics to the students, enhance lecture material, and provide real-world context for related concepts. An Instructor's Manual with suggestions for integrating the material into the classroom accompanies the video.

Student Active Learning Aids

Student Workbook. The Student Workbook is a comprehensive review of accounting and a powerful tool for students to use in the classroom, guiding students through chapter content, tied to study objectives, and providing resources for use during lectures. This is an excellent resource when preparing for exams. The Student Workbook is also an active learning tool, providing students with opportunities to engage in the learning and decision-making process.

Each chapter of the Student Workbook includes study objectives and a chapter review consisting of 20–30 key points; a demonstration problem linked to study objectives in the textbook; true/false, multiple-choice, and matching questions related to key terms; and exercises linked to study objectives. Solutions to the exercises explain the hows and whys so students get immediate feedback. A chapter outline and blank working papers allow students space to take lecture notes and record problems worked in class.

Easy Accounting. *Dan Gode, University of Rochester.* Easy Accounting is a self-paced CD-ROM tutorial designed to review financial accounting concepts. It uses simple examples that have been carefully crafted to introduce concepts gradually. Throughout, the program emphasizes the logic underlying the accounting process. Easy Accounting uses interactive and graphical tools to enhance the learning process. Intuitive navigation and a powerful search mechanism allow students to easily follow the tutorial from start to finish or skip to the topics they want to complete. The discussions and examples are followed by brief, interactive problems that provide immediate feedback to the student. Built-in tools, such as an on-line financial calculator, help solve the problems.

On-Line Business Survival Guide in Accounting. The journey of 1,000 Web sites begins with one click, and this practical guide gets instructors and students on the road. The On-Line Business Survival Guide is a brief, clear introduction to using the World Wide Web as a business research tool. Starting with the basics, this manual covers everything students need to know to become master sleuths at finding critical information on the Internet. In addition, the guide provides a hands-on guide to using the *Wall Street Journal Interactive Edition*, as well as a discount offer for a subscription to the *Wall Street Journal Interactive* on-line.

Business Extra Web Site at http://www.wiley.com/college/businessextra. To complement the On-Line Business Survival Guide in Accounting, the Business Extra Web Site gives professors and students instant access to a wealth of current articles dealing with all aspects of financial accounting. The articles are organized by topic, and discussion questions follow each article. Students will find a password inside the On-Line Business Survival Guide that will give them access to the Business Extra Web Site.

Financial Accounting Web Site at http://www.wiley.com/college/kimmel. As a resource and learning tool for instructors and students, the Financial Accounting Web Site serves as a launching pad to numerous activities, resources, and related sites. Available through the Web site are links to companies discussed in the text and Instructor's Manual, additional cases and problems for students, and items such as the Checklist of Key Figures and PowerPoint Presentations for download. This site also provides a link to the Business Extra Web Site discussed above. Visit this site often for updated and new materials.

Paul D. Kimmel
Milwaukee, Wisconsin
Jerry J. Weygandt
Madison, Wisconsin
Donald E. Kieso
DeKalb, Illinois

ACKNOWLEDGMENTS

During the course of development of *Financial Accounting*, the authors benefited greatly from the input of focus group participants, manuscript reviewers, ancillary authors, and proofers. The constructive suggestions and innovative ideas of the reviewers and the creativity and accuracy of the ancillary authors and checkers is greatly appreciated.

FOCUS GROUP PARTICIPANTS AND REVIEWERS

Thomas G. Amyot, *College of Saint Rose*
Angela H. Bell, *Jacksonville State University*
G. Eddy Birrer, *Gonzaga University*
Sarah Ruth Brown, *University of North Alabama*
Judye Cadle, *Tarleton State University*
George M. Dow, *Valencia Community College—West*
Kathy J. Dow, *Salem State College*
Larry R. Falcetto, *Emporia State University*
Sheila D. Foster, *The Citadel*
Jessica J. Frazier, *Eastern Kentucky University*
David Gotlob, *Indiana University–Purdue University Fort Wayne*
Leon J. Hanouille, *Syracuse University*
Carol Olson Houston, *San Diego State University*
Robert J. Kirsch, *Southern Connecticut State University*
Frank Korman, *Mountain View College*
Jerry G. Kreuze, *Western Michigan University*
P. Merle Maddocks, *University of Alabama—Huntsville*
Gale E. Newell, *Western Michigan University*
Franklin J. Plewa, *Idaho State University*
Marc A. Rubin, *Miami University*
Ann E. Selk, *University of Wisconsin—Green Bay*
William E. Smith, *Xavier University*
Teresa A. Speck, *St. Mary's University of Minnesota*
Linda G. Wade, *Tarleton State University*
Stuart K. Webster, *University of Wyoming*

ANCILLARY AUTHORS, CONTRIBUTORS, AND PROOFERS

Thomas G. Amyot, *College of Saint Rose*—Solutions Manual Proofer
John C. Borke, *University of Wisconsin—Platteville*—Solutions Manual Proofer and Technical Advisor
Kathy J. Dow, *Salem State College*—Solutions Manual Proofer
Larry R. Falcetto, *Emporia State University*—Supplements Coordinator and Test Bank Author
Jessica J. Frazier, *Eastern Kentucky University*—Instructor's Manual and PowerPoint Author
Wayne Higley, *Buena Vista College*—Content Proofer and Technical Advisor
Martha King, *Emporia State University*—Problem Material Contributor
Mary Rozek, *University of Wisconsin—Milwaukee*—World Wide Web Problems Contributor
Ann E. Selk, *University of Wisconsin—Green Bay*—Solutions Manual Proofer
Teresa A. Speck, *St. Mary's University of Minnesota*—Solutions Manual Proofer
Dick Wasson, *Southwestern College*—Content Proofer and Technical Advisor

We appreciate the exemplary support and professional commitment given us by our solutions manual compositor Elm Street Publications (Ingrid Mount and Barb Lange), executive editor Susan Elbe, development editors Ann Torbert and Nancy Perry, supplements editor David Kear, marketing managers Wendy Goldner and Rebecca Hope, vice-president of college production and manufacturing Ann Berlin, designers Kenny Beck and Ann Marie Renzi, illustration editor Anna Melhorn, photo editor Elaine Paoloni, and production coordinator Phyllis Niklas.

We thank Starbucks Corporation and Green Mountain Coffee for permitting us the use of their 1996 Annual Reports for our specimen financial statements and accompanying notes.

Suggestions and comments from users are encouraged and appreciated. Please feel free to e-mail any one of us at account @ wiley.com.

Paul D. Kimmel
Jerry J. Weygandt
Donald E. Kieso

STUDENT OWNER'S MANUAL
How to Use the Study Aids in This Book

At the beginning of each chapter, **Study Objectives** provide you with a learning framework. Each Study Objective then reappears at the point within the chapter where the concept is discussed and is also summarized at the end of the chapter.

The **Preview** begins by linking the vignette with the major topics of the chapter. It then gives a graphic outline of major topics and subtopics that will be discussed. This narrative and visual preview give you a mental framework upon which to arrange the information you are learning.

The **Chapter-Opening Vignette** is a brief story that helps you picture how the topics of the chapter relate to the real worlds of accounting and business. Throughout the chapter, references to the vignette will help you put new ideas in context, organize them, and remember them. Each vignette ends with the **Internet addresses** of the companies cited in the story.

xiii

xiv Student Owner's Manual

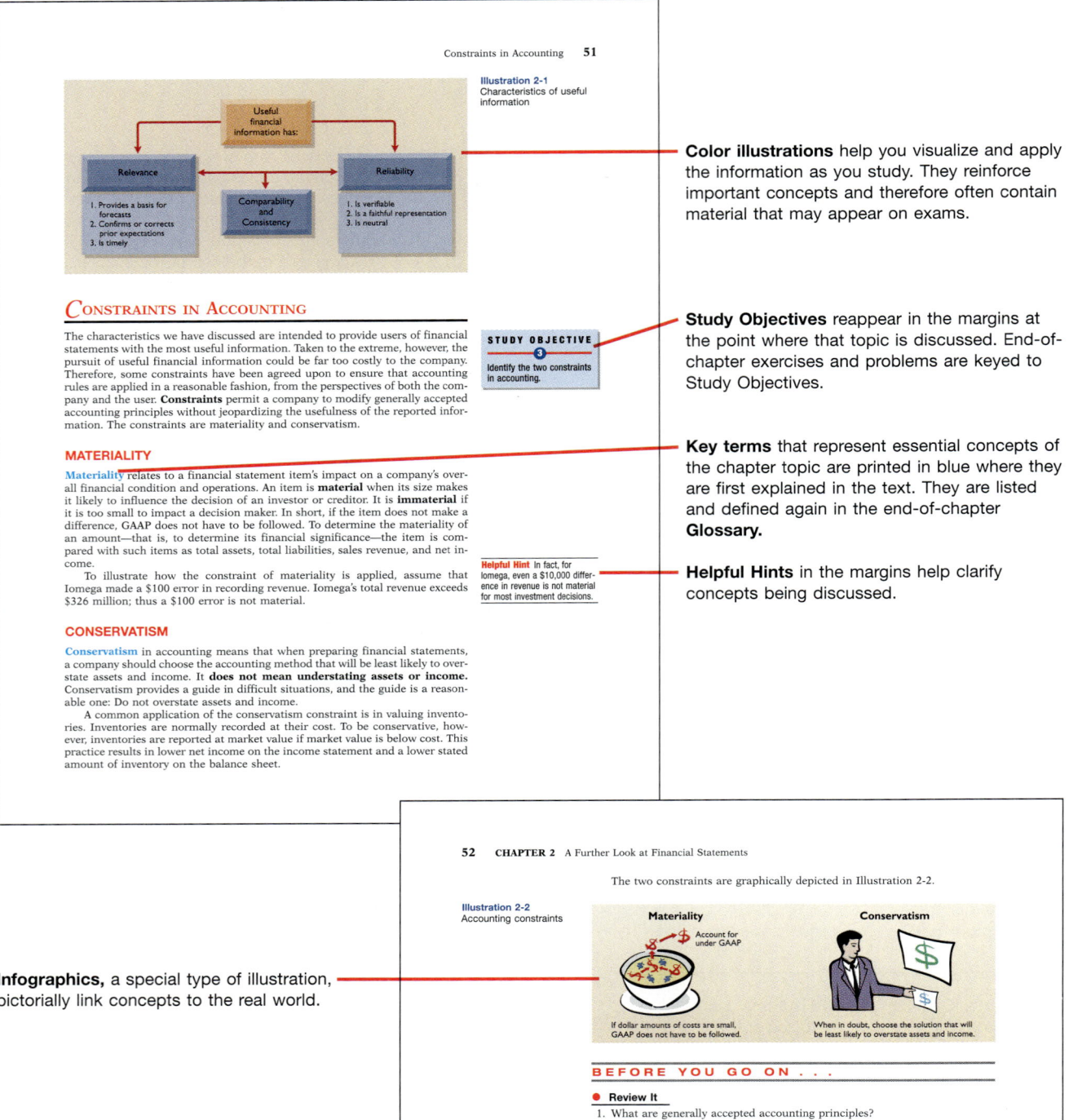

Color illustrations help you visualize and apply the information as you study. They reinforce important concepts and therefore often contain material that may appear on exams.

Study Objectives reappear in the margins at the point where that topic is discussed. End-of-chapter exercises and problems are keyed to Study Objectives.

Key terms that represent essential concepts of the chapter topic are printed in blue where they are first explained in the text. They are listed and defined again in the end-of-chapter **Glossary.**

Helpful Hints in the margins help clarify concepts being discussed.

Infographics, a special type of illustration, pictorially link concepts to the real world.

Student Owner's Manual xv

There are two primary reasons for using the single-step form: (1) A company does not realize any type of profit or income until total revenues exceed total expenses, so it makes sense to divide the statement into these two categories. (2) The form is simple and easy to read.

A second form of the income statement is the **multiple-step income statement.** The multiple-step income statement is often considered more useful because it highlights the components of net income. The Best Buy income statement in Illustration 2-4 is an example. The multiple-step income statement has three important line items: gross profit, income from operations, and net income. They are determined as follows: (1) Cost of goods sold is subtracted from sales to determine gross profit; (2) operating expenses are deducted from gross profit to determine income from operations; and (3) the results of activities not related to operations are added or subtracted to determine net income. You should note that income tax expense is reported in a separate section of the income statement before net income.

BEST BUY CO., INC.
Consolidated Income Statement
(in thousands)

	For the years ended		
	March 2, 1996	Feb. 25, 1995	Feb. 26, 1994
Revenues	$7,217,448	$5,079,557	$3,006,534
Cost of goods sold	6,280,877	4,389,164	2,549,609
Gross profit	936,571	690,393	456,925
Operating expenses			
Selling, general, and administrative expenses	813,988	568,466	379,747
Income from operations	122,583	121,927	77,178
Other expenses and losses			
Interest expense, net	43,594	27,876	8,800
Other			425
Income before income taxes	78,989	94,051	67,953
Income tax expense	30,970	36,400	26,668
Net income	$ 48,019	$ 57,651	$ 41,285

Illustration 2-4 Best Buy's income statement

Financial statements appear regularly throughout the book. Statements from real companies are usually identified by a logo or related photo. Often, numbers or categories are highlighted in red type to draw your attention to key information.

The Classified Balance Sheet 65

judged in the light of the company's earnings. ...vely stable earnings, such as public utilities, have higher debt to total assets ratios than do cyclical companies with widely fluctuating earnings, such as many high-tech companies. In later chapters you will learn additional ways to evaluate solvency.

Business Insight examples give glimpses into how real companies make decisions using accounting information. Three different icons identify three different points of view—human silhouettes for *investor perspectives,* a city skyline for *management perspectives,* and a globe for *international perspectives.*

BUSINESS INSIGHT
Investor Perspective

Debt financing differs greatly across industries and companies. Here are some debt to total assets ratios for selected companies:

	Total Debt to Total Assets As a Percent
Advanced Micro Devices	29%
General Motors Corporation	93
Roberts Pharmaceutical	23
Callaway Golf Company	19
Sears, Roebuck & Company	64
Eastman Kodak Company	83

Each chapter presents **decision tools** that help business decision makers use financial statements. At the end of the text discussion, a **Decision Toolkit** summarizes the key features of a decision tool and reviews why and how you would use it.

DECISION TOOLKIT

Decision Checkpoints	Info Needed for Decision	Tool to Use for Decision	How to Evaluate Results
Can the company meet its near-term obligations?	Current assets and current liabilities	Current ratio = Current assets / Current liabilities	Higher ratio suggests favorable liquidity.
Can the company meet its long-term obligations?	Total debt and total assets	Debt to total assets ratio = Total debt / Total assets	Lower value suggests favorable solvency.

Before You Go On sections follow each key topic. **Review It** questions prompt you to stop and review the key points you have just studied. If you cannot answer these questions, you should go back and read the section again. Brief **Do It** exercises ask you to put newly acquired knowledge to work in some form of financial statement preparation. They outline the **Reasoning** necessary to complete the exercise and show a **Solution.**

BEFORE YOU GO ON . . .

● **Review It**
1. What does a statement of stockholders' equity show?
2. What are the major sections in a classified balance sheet?
3. What is liquidity? How can it be measured?
4. What is solvency? How can it be measured?

● **Do It**
Selected financial data for Drummond Company at December 31, 1998, are as follows: cash $60,000; receivables (net) $80,000; inventory $70,000; and current liabilities $140,000. Compute the current ratio.

Reasoning: The formula for the current ratio is: Current assets ÷ Current liabilities.

Solution: The current ratio is 1.5:1 ($210,000 ÷ $140,000).

xvi Student Owner's Manual

USING THE DECISION TOOLKIT

In the opening story we noted that Iomega Corporation's stock price increased dramatically during 1995 and 1996. Many people questioned whether this increase was justified by Iomega's results. Let's look for ourselves: A simplified balance sheet and income statement for Iomega Corporation are presented in Illustrations 2-22 and 2-23.

A **Using the Decision Toolkit** exercise follows the final set of *Review It* questions in the chapter. It asks you to use information from financial statements to make financial decisions. You should think through the questions related to the decision before you study the printed **Solution.**

---

70 CHAPTER 2 A Further Look at Financial Statements

Illustration 2-23
Iomega's income statement

IOMEGA CORPORATION AND SUBSIDIARIES
Consolidated Statements of Operations
(in thousands)

	Years Ended December 31		
	1995	1994	1993
Sales	$326,225	$141,380	$147,123
Cost of sales	235,838	92,453	92,585
Gross margin	90,387	48,927	54,538
Operating expenses			
Selling, general, and administrative	57,189	36,862	38,862
Research and development	19,576	15,438	18,972
Other operating expenses	—	(2,491)	14,131
Total operating expenses	76,765	49,809	71,965
Operating income (loss)	13,622	(882)	(17,427)
Foreign currency gain (loss)	(1,243)	353	328
Interest income	537	871	620
Interest expense	(1,652)	(15)	(70)
Other income (expense)	375	(301)	2,230
Income (loss) before income taxes	11,639	26	(14,319)
Provision for income taxes	(3,136)	(1,908)	(206)
Net income (loss)	$ 8,503	$ (1,882)	$ (14,525)

Additional information: Iomega's net cash provided by operating activities was a negative $26,990 (thousand).

Instructions

Using these statements, answer the following questions:

1. Calculate the current ratio for Iomega for 1995 and 1994 and the current cash debt coverage ratio for 1995, and discuss its liquidity position.
2. Calculate the debt to total assets ratio for Iomega for 1995 and 1994 and the cash debt coverage ratio for 1995, and discuss its solvency.
3. Calculate the profit margin ratio and return on assets ratio for Iomega for 1995 and 1994, and discuss its profitability.
4. What other information would be useful in your analysis?

Solution

1. Current ratio:

    1995 ($212,132/$199,509) = 1.06:1; 1994 ($60,557/$25,739) = 2.35:1

    Iomega's liquidity declined substantially from 1994 to 1995. In 1994 there was $2.35 of current assets available to meet current liabilities. In 1995 there was only $1.06. In fact, 1995 working capital was almost negative, since current assets exceeded current liabilities by only $12,623. This should be a concern both to Iomega's short-term creditors and to its investors.

    Current cash debt coverage ratio:

    $$1995 \quad \frac{-\$26,990}{(\$199,509 + \$25,739)/2} = -.24 \text{ times}$$

    It is quite common for a company to have negative cash provided by operations in its early years. Thus, the negative current cash debt coverage

---

firms. Second, we would want to calculate additional performance measures that you will learn about in later chapters (e.g., earnings and price-earnings ratios). In addition, we would want to see of the company's statement of cash flows to assess its ability the funding required to continue to grow. We would want management discussion and analysis section of the annual management's assessment of its plans.

SUMMARY OF STUDY OBJECTIVES

❶ *Explain the meaning of generally accepted accounting principles and describe the basic objective of financial reporting.* Generally accepted accounting principles are a set of rules and practices recognized as a general guide for financial reporting purposes. The basic objective of financial reporting is to provide information that is useful for decision making.

❷ *Discuss the qualitative characteristics of accounting information.* To be judged useful, information should possess these qualitative characteristics: relevance, reliability, comparability, and consistency.

❸ *Identify the two constraints in accounting.* The major constraints are materiality and conservatism.

❹ *Distinguish between a single-step and a multiple-step income statement.* In a single-step income statement, all data are classified under two categories, revenues or expenses, and net income is determined in one step. A multiple-step income statement shows numerous steps in determining net income, including results of non-operating activities.

❺ *Identify and compute ratios for analyzing a company's profitability.* Profitability ratios, such as profit margin and return on assets, measure different aspects of the operating success of an enterprise for a given period of time.

❻ *Explain the relationship between a retained earn-*

The **Summary of Study Objectives** gives a chapter summary related to the Study Objectives located throughout the chapter. It provides you with another opportunity to review as well as to see how all the key topics within the chapter are related.

Student Owner's Manual **xvii**

At the end of each chapter, **Decision Toolkit—A Summary** reviews the contexts and techniques useful for decision making that were covered in the chapter.

The **Glossary** defines all the **key terms** and concepts introduced in the chapter.

A **Demonstration Problem** is the final step before you begin homework. **Problem-Solving Strategies** in the margins give you tips about how to approach the problem, and the **Solution** demonstrates both the form and content of complete answers.

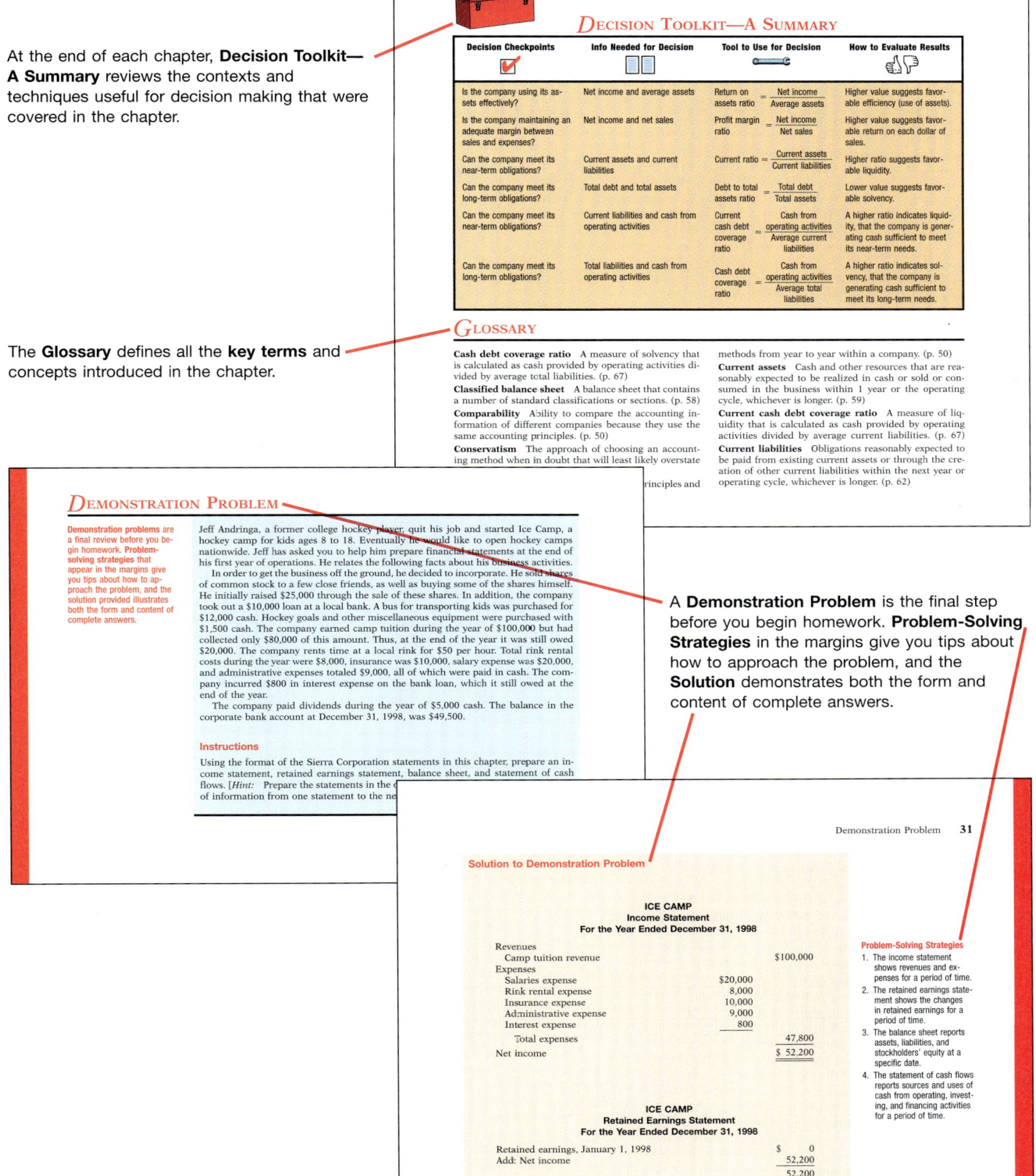

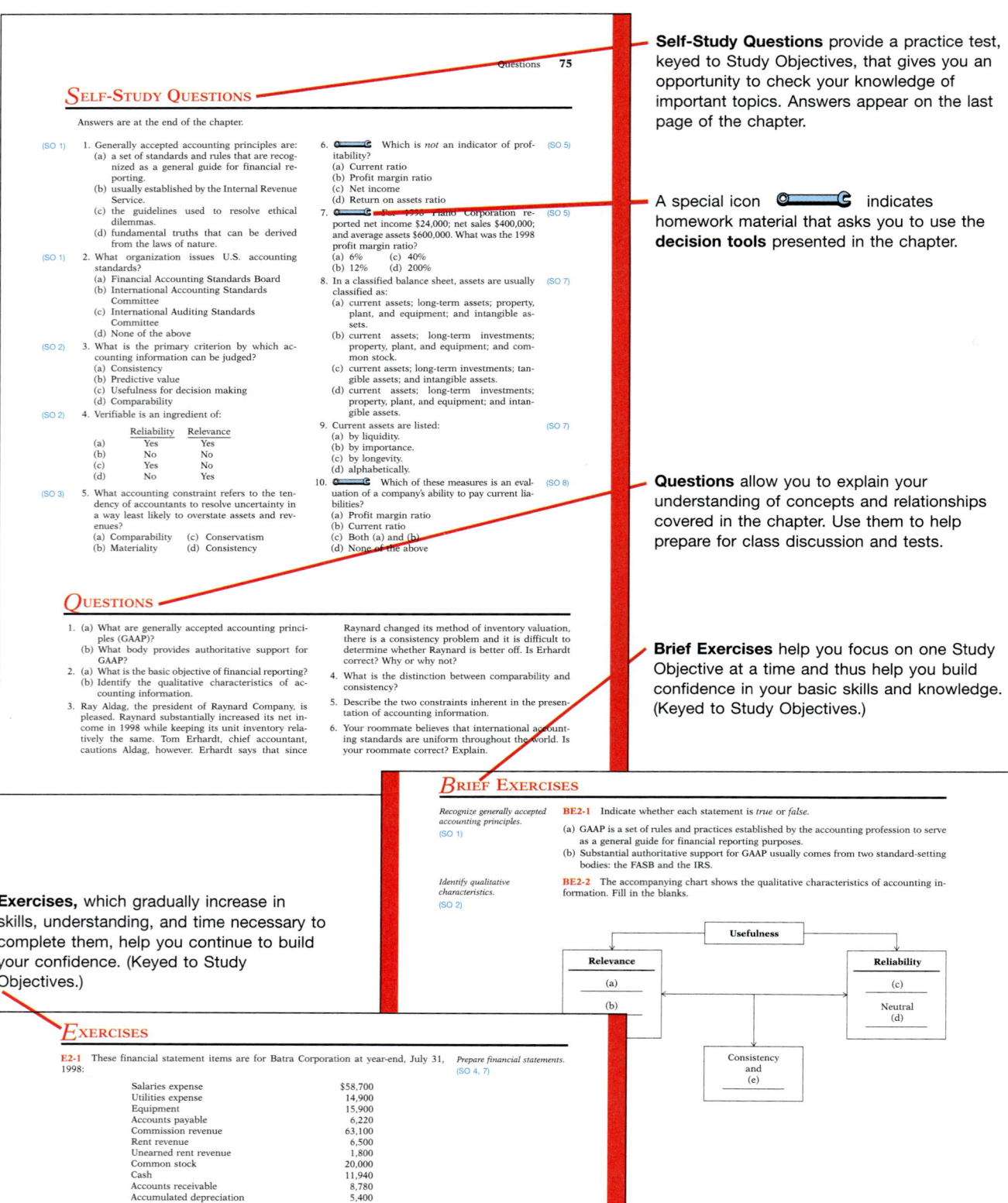

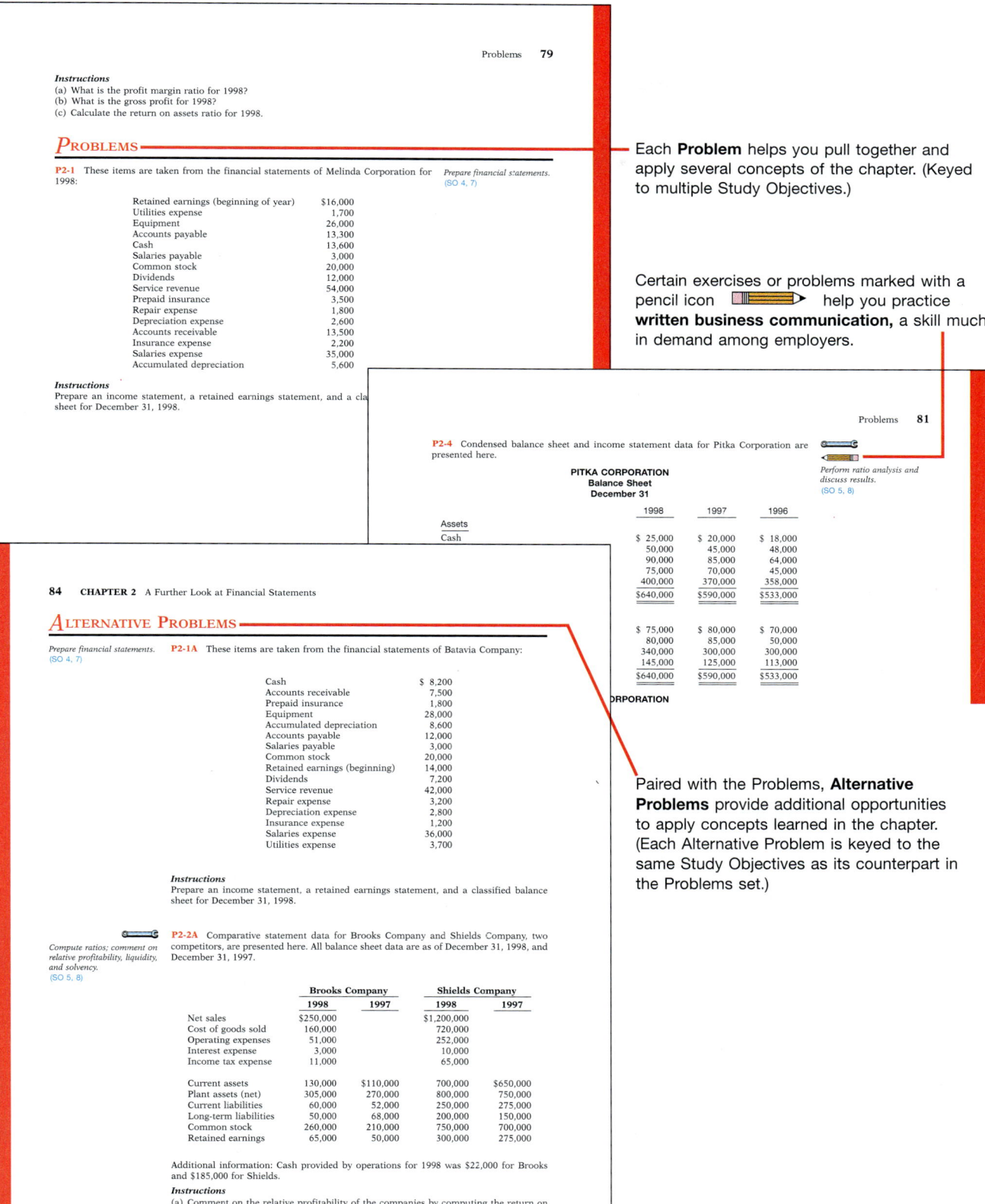

xx Student Owner's Manual

BROADENING YOUR PERSPECTIVE

FINANCIAL REPORTING AND ANALYSIS

FINANCIAL REPORTING PROBLEM: *Starbucks Corporation*

BYP2-1 The financial statements of Starbucks Corporation are presented in Appendix A at the end of this book.

Instructions
Answer the following questions using the Consolidated Balance Sheet and the Notes to Consolidated Financial Statements section.
(a) What were Starbucks' total current assets at September 29, 1996, and October 1, 1995?
(b) Are the assets included in current assets listed in the proper order? Explain.
(c) How are Starbucks' assets classified?
(d) What were Starbucks' current liabilities at September 29, 1996, and October 1, 1995?

COMPARATIVE ANALYSIS PROBLEM: *Starbucks vs. Green Mountain Coffee*

BYP2-2 The financial statements of Green Mountain Coffee are presented in Appendix B, following the financial statements for Starbucks in Appendix A.

Instructions
(a) For each company calculate the following values for 1996:
  (1) Working capital
  (2) Current ratio
  (3) Debt to total assets ratio
  (4) Profit margin ratio
  (5) Return on assets ratio
(b) Based on your findings above, discuss the relative liquidity, solvency, and profitability of the two companies.

RESEARCH CASE

BYP2-3 Several commonly available indexes enable individuals to locate articles from numerous business publications and periodicals. Articles can generally be searched for by company name or by subject matter. Four common indexes are *The Wall Street Journal Index*, *Business Abstracts* (formerly *Business Periodicals Index*), *Predicasts F&S Index*, and *ABI/Inform*.

Instructions
Use one of these resources to find a list of articles about a New York Stock Exchange company of your choosing. Choose an article from this list that you believe would be of interest to an investor or creditor of this company. Read the article and answer the fol-

> The **Broadening Your Perspective** section helps you pull together various concepts covered in the chapter and apply them to real-world business decisions.

> In the **Financial Reporting Problem** you study various aspects of the financial statements of Starbucks Corporation, which are printed in Chapter 1 (in simplified form) and in Appendix A (in full).

> A **Comparative Analysis Problem** offers the opportunity to compare and contrast the financial reporting of Starbucks with a competitor, Green Mountain Coffee, whose financial statements are printed in Chapter 1 (in simplified form) and in Appendix B (in full).

> **Research Cases** direct you to the *Wall Street Journal*, annual reports, or articles published in other popular business periodicals for further study and analysis of key topics.

INTERPRETING FINANCIAL STATEMENTS

BYP2-4 Minicase 1 *Kellogg Company*
Kellogg Company has its headquarters in Battle Creek, Michigan. The company manufactures and sells ready-to-eat breakfast cereals and convenience foods including toaster pastries and cereal bars.
Selected data from Kellogg Company's 1994 annual report follows (dollar amounts and share data in millions):

	1994	1993	1992
Net sales	$6,562.0	$6,295.4	$6,190.6
Cost of goods sold	2,950.7	2,989.0	2,987.7
Selling and administrative expense	2,448.7	2,237.5	2,140.1
Net income	705.4	680.7	431.2

> **Interpreting Financial Statements** offers minicases that ask you to read parts of financial statements of actual companies and use the decision tools presented in the chapter to interpret this information.

92 CHAPTER 2 A Further Look at Financial Statements

CRITICAL THINKING

MANAGEMENT DECISION CASE

BYP2-6 As the accountant for J. Martinez Manufacturing Inc., you have been requested to develop some key ratios from the comparative financial statements. This information is to be used to convince creditors that J. Martinez Manufacturing Inc. is liquid, solvent, and profitable, and deserves their continued support. Lenders are particularly concerned about the company's ability to continue as a going concern.
These are the data requested and the computations developed from the financial statements:

	1998	1997
Current ratio	3.1	2.1
Working capital	Up 22%	Down 7%
Debt to total assets ratio	.60	.70
Net income	Up 32%	Down 8%
Profit margin ratio	.05	.015
Return on assets ratio	.09	.04
Gross profit	Up 22%	Down 12%

Instructions
J. Martinez Manufacturing Inc. asks you to prepare brief comments stating how each of these items supports the argument that its financial health is improving. The company wishes to use these comments to support presentation of data to its creditors. You are to prepare the comments as requested, giving the implications and the limitations of each item separately, and then the collective inference that may be drawn from them about J. Martinez's financial well-being.

A REAL-WORLD FOCUS: *Bethlehem Corporation*

BYP2-7 Located in Easton, Pennsylvania, **Bethlehem Corporation** was established in 1856. Today it offers contract services for industrial products, rebuilding and remanufacturing industrial and military equipment per customer specifications and designs. The company also manufactures and sells a line of equipment used in the chemical, environmental, and food industries.
Bethlehem Corporation has a net loss for 1994 of $239,251. One reason for the loss is that Bethlehem reported a loss (and a liability) for expenses and costs associated with certain legal proceedings against Bethlehem. They have not yet lost the case, but they are anticipating losing at least some money.

Instructions
(a) Do you think that a loss such as this is relevant to users of Bethlehem's financial statements?
(b) How reliable do you think the estimate of the loss is? What information should the company use to estimate the loss?

> **Critical Thinking** offers additional opportunities and activities.

> The **Management Decision Cases** help you build decision-making skills by analyzing accounting information in a less structured situation. These cases require evaluation of a manager's decision or lead to a decision among alternative courses of action. They also give practice in building business communication skills.

> The **Real-World Focus** problems ask you to apply concepts presented in the chapter to specific situations faced by actual companies.

Student Owner's Manual   xxi

Group Activities prepare you for the business world, where you will be working with many people, by giving you practice in solving problems with colleagues.

GROUP ACTIVITY

BYP2-8 A classified balance sheet has these sections: current assets; property, plant, and equipment; long-term investments; intangible assets; current liabilities; long-term liabilities; and stockholders' equity.

Instructions
With the class divided into seven groups, each group should choose one section of the classified balance sheet. Each group is to explain its section and illustrate the section using an example from a published annual report.

COMMUNICATION ACTIVITY

BYP2-9 L. R. Stanton is the chief executive officer of Hi-Tech Electronics. Stanton is an expert engineer but a novice in accounting.

Instructions
Write a letter to L. R. Stanton that explains (a) the three main types of ratios and (b) the bases for comparison in analyzing Hi-Tech's financial statements.

Communication Activities ask you to engage in real-world business situations via written communication, a skill much in demand among employers.

ETHICS CASE

BYP2-10 As the controller of Breathless Perfume Company, you discover a significant misstatement that overstated net income in the prior year's financial statements. The misleading financial statements are contained in the company's annual report, which was issued to banks and other creditors less than a month ago. After much thought about the consequences of telling the president, Eddy Kadu, about this misstatement, you gather your courage to inform him. Eddy says, "Hey! What they don't know won't hurt them. But, just so we set the record straight, we'll adjust this year's financial statements for last year's misstatement. We can absorb that misstatement better this year than last year anyway! Just don't make that kind of mistake again."

Instructions
(a) Who are the stakeholders in this situation?
(b) What are the ethical issues?
(c) What would you do as the controller?

Through the **Ethics Cases** you will reflect on typical ethical dilemmas and decide on an appropriate course of action.

FINANCIAL ANALYSIS ON THE WEB

BYP2-11 *Purpose:* Identify summary liquidity, solvency, and profitability information about companies, and compare this information across companies in the same industry.

Address: http://biz.yahoo.com

Steps:
1. Select **Company**.
2. Type in a company name, or use index to find company name. Perform instructions (a) and (b) below.
3. Click on the company's particular industry behind the heading "Industry." Perform instructions (c) and (d).

Instructions
Answer the following questions:
(a) What was the company's current ratio, debt to equity ratio, profit margin, and return on assets?
(b) What is the company's industry?
(c) What is the name of a competitor? What is the competitor's current ratio, debt to equity ratio, profit margin, and return on assets?
(d) Based on these measures: Which company is more liquid? Which company is more solvent? Which company is more profitable?

Financial Analysis on the Web exercises guide you to Web sites where you can find and analyze information related to the chapter topic.

Answers to Self-Study Questions provide feedback on your understanding of concepts.

Answers to Self-Study Questions
1. a 2. a 3. c 4. c 5. c 6. a 7. a 8. d 9. a 10. b

HOW DO YOU LEARN BEST?

Now that you have looked at your Owner's Manual, take time to find out how you learn best. This quiz was designed to help you find out something about your preferred learning method. Research on left brain/right brain differences and also on learning and personality differences suggests that each person has preferred ways to receive and communicate information. After taking the quiz, we will help you pinpoint the study aids in this test that will help you learn the material based on your learning style.

Circle the letter of the answer that best explains your preferences. If a single answer does not match your perception, please circle two or more choices. Leave blank any question that does not apply.

1. You are about to give directions to a person. She is staying in a hotel in town and wants to visit your house. She has a rental car. Would you
   V) draw a map on paper?
   R) write down the directions (without a map)?
   A) tell her the directions?
   K) pick her up at the hotel in your car?

2. You are staying in a hotel and have a rental car. You would like to visit friends whose address/location you do not know. Would you like them to
   V) draw you a map on paper?
   R) write down the directions (without a map)?
   A) tell you the directions by phone?
   K) pick you up at the hotel in their car?

3. You have just received a copy of your itinerary for a world trip. This is of interest to a friend. Would you
   A) call her immediately and tell her about it?
   R) send her a copy of the printed itinerary?
   V) show her on a map of the world?

4. You are going to cook a dessert as a special treat for your family. Do you
   K) cook something familiar without need for instructions?
   V) thumb through the cookbook looking for ideas from the pictures?
   R) refer to a specific cookbook where there is a good recipe?
   A) ask for advice from others?

5. A group of tourists has been assigned to you to find out about national parks. Would you
   K) drive them to a national park?
   R) give them a book on national parks?
   V) show them slides and photographs?
   A) give them a talk on national parks?

6. You are about to purchase a new stereo. Other than price, what would most influence your decision?
   A) A friend talking about it.
   K) Listening to it.
   R) Reading the details about it.
   V) Its distinctive, upscale appearance.

7. Recall a time in your life when you learned how to do something like playing a new board game. (Try to avoid choosing a very physical skill, e.g., riding a bike.) How did you learn best? By
   V) visual clues—pictures, diagrams, charts?
   A) listening to somebody explaining it?
   R) written instructions?
   K) doing it?

8. Which of these games do you prefer?
   V) *Pictionary*
   R) *Scrabble*
   K) *Charades*

9. You are about to learn to use a new program on a computer. Would you
   K) ask a friend to show you?
   R) read the manual that comes with the program?
   A) telephone a friend and ask questions about it?

10. You are not sure whether a word should be spelled "dependent" or "dependant." Do you
    R) look it up in the dictionary?
    V) see the word in your mind and choose the best way it looks?
    A) sound it out in your mind?
    K) write both versions down?

11. Apart from price, what would most influence your decision to buy a particular textbook?
    K) Using a friend's copy.
    R) Skimming parts of it.
    A) A friend talking about it.
    V) It looks OK.

12. A new movie has arrived in town. What would most influence your decision to go or not to go?
    A) Friends talked about it.
    R) You read a review of it.
    V) You saw a preview of it.

13. Do you prefer a lecturer/teacher who likes to use
    R) handouts and/or a textbook?
    V) flow diagrams, charts, slides?
    K) field trips, labs, practical sessions?
    A) discussion, guest speakers?

Results: To determine your learning preference, add up the number of individual Vs, As, Rs, and Ks you have circled. Take the letter you have the greatest number of and match it to the same letter in the Learning Styles Chart. Next to each letter in the chart are suggestions that will refer you to different learning aids throughout this text.

LEARNING STYLES CHART

VISUAL

WHAT TO DO IN CLASS	WHAT TO DO WHEN STUDYING	TEXT FEATURES THAT MAY HELP YOU THE MOST	WHAT TO DO PRIOR TO AND DURING EXAMS
Underline. Use different colors. Use symbols, charts, arrangements on the page.	Use the "In Class" strategies. Reconstruct images in different ways. Redraw pages from memory. Replace words with symbols and initials.	**Vignettes** **Previews** **Infographics/Illustrations** **Photos** **Business Insights** **Decision Toolkits** **Key Terms in blue** **Words in bold** **Questions/Exercises/ Problems** **Financial Reporting and Analysis** **Financial Analysis on the Web**	Recall the "pictures of the pages." Draw, use diagrams where appropriate. Practice turning visuals back into words.

AURAL

WHAT TO DO IN CLASS	WHAT TO DO WHEN STUDYING	TEXT FEATURES THAT MAY HELP YOU THE MOST	WHAT TO DO PRIOR TO AND DURING EXAMS
Attend lectures and tutorials. Discuss topics with students. Explain new ideas to other people. Use a tape recorder. Describe overheads, pictures, and visuals to somebody not there. Leave space in your notes for later recall.	You may take poor notes because you prefer to listen. Therefore: Expand your notes. Put summarized notes on tape and listen. Read summarized notes out loud. Explain notes to another "aural" person.	**Infographics/Illustrations** **Business Insights** **Review It/Do It** **Summary of Study Objectives** **Glossary** **Demonstration Problem** **Self-Study Questions** **Questions/Exercises/ Problems** **Financial Reporting and Analysis** **Critical Thinking** **Group Activity** **Communication Activity** **Ethics Case**	Listen to your "voices" and write them down. Speak your answers. Practice writing answers to old exam questions.

Source: Adapted from Neil D. Fleming and Colleen Mills, "Not Another Inventory, Rather a Catalyst for Reflections," *To Improve the Academy,* Volume II (1992), pp. 137–155. Used by permission.

READING/WRITING

WHAT TO DO IN CLASS	WHAT TO DO WHEN STUDYING	TEXT FEATURES THAT MAY HELP YOU THE MOST	WHAT TO DO PRIOR TO AND DURING EXAMS
Use lists, headings. Use dictionaries and definitions. Use handouts and textbooks. Read. Use lecture notes.	Write out words again and again. Reread notes silently. Rewrite ideas into other words. Organize diagrams into statements.	**Study Objectives** **Previews** **Review It/Do It** **Using the Decision Toolkit** **Summary of Study Objectives** **Glossary** **Self-Study Questions** **Questions/Exercises/ Problems** **Writing Problems** **Financial Reporting and Analysis** **Critical Thinking** **Group Activity** **Communication Activity** **Ethics Case**	Practice with multiple-choice questions. Write out lists. Write paragraphs, beginnings and endings.

KINESTHETIC

WHAT TO DO IN CLASS	WHAT TO DO WHEN STUDYING	TEXT FEATURES THAT MAY HELP YOU THE MOST	WHAT TO DO PRIOR TO AND DURING EXAMS
Use all your senses. Go to labs, take field trips. Use trial-and-error methods. Listen to real-life examples. Use hands-on approach.	You may take notes poorly because topics do not seem relevant. Therefore: Put examples in note summaries. Use pictures and photos to illustrate. Talk about notes with another "kinesthetic" person.	**Vignettes** **Previews** **Infographics/Illustrations** **Decision Toolkits** **Review It/Do It** **Using the Decision Toolkit** **Summary of Study Objectives** **Demonstration Problem** **Self-Study Questions** **Questions/Exercises/ Problems** **Financial Reporting and Analysis** **Critical Thinking** **Group Activity** **Communication Activity** **Financial Reporting on the Web**	Write practice answers. Role-play the exam situation.

BRIEF CONTENTS

1 Introduction to Financial Statements 2
2 A Further Look at Financial Statements 46
3 The Accounting Information System 96
4 Accrual Accounting Concepts 148
5 Merchandising Operations 200
6 Reporting and Analyzing Inventory 238
7 Internal Control and Cash 286
8 Reporting and Analyzing Receivables 338
9 Reporting and Analyzing Long-Lived Assets 382
10 Reporting and Analyzing Liabilities 436
11 Reporting and Analyzing Stockholders' Equity 486
12 Reporting and Analyzing Investments 538
13 Statement of Cash Flows 576
14 Financial Analysis: The Big Picture 646

APPENDIXES

A Specimen Financial Statements: Starbucks Corporation A-1
B Specimen Financial Statements: Green Mountain Coffee, Inc. B-1
C Time Value of Money C-1

CONTENTS

CHAPTER 1

Introduction to Financial Statements   2
Coffee Anyone?   2

Forms of Business Organization   4

Users and Uses of Financial Information   6
Internal Users   6
External Users   6

Business Activities   7
Financing Activities   7
Investing Activities   8
Operating Activities   8

Communicating with Users   10
Income Statement   10
Retained Earnings Statement   12
Balance Sheet   12
Statement of Cash Flows   13
Interrelationships of Statements   14

A Quick Look at Starbucks' Financial Statements   16
Income Statement   16
Retained Earnings Statement   17
Balance Sheet   17
Statement of Cash Flows   19
Other Elements of an Annual Report   20

Assumptions and Principles in Financial Reporting   22
Assumptions   22
Principles   24

CHAPTER 2

A Further Look at Financial Statements   46
Just Fooling Around?   46

Section 1 Objectives of Financial Reporting   48

Characteristics of Useful Information   49
Relevance   49
Reliability   49
Comparability and Consistency   49

Constraints in Accounting   51
Materiality   51
Conservatism   51

Section 2 The Financial Statements Revisited   52

The Income Statement   52
Gross Profit   54
Operating Expenses   54
Nonoperating Activities   54
Using the Income Statement   56

The Statement of Stockholders' Equity   57

The Classified Balance Sheet   58
Current Assets   59
Long-Term Investments   60
Property, Plant, and Equipment   61
Intangible Assets   61
Current Liabilities   62
Long-Term Liabilities   62
Stockholders' Equity   63
Using a Classified Balance Sheet   63

The Statement of Cash Flows   66
Using the Statement of Cash Flows   66

CHAPTER 3

The Accounting Information System   96
Accidents Happen   96

Accounting Information System   98

Accounting Transactions   98
Analyzing Transactions   99
Summary of Transactions   103

The Account   104
Debits and Credits   104
Debit and Credit Procedures   105
Stockholders' Equity Relationships   108
Expansion of the Basic Equation   108

Steps in the Recording Process   110
The Journal   111
The Ledger   113
Chart of Accounts   113
Posting   114

The Recording Process Illustrated   114
Summary Illustration of Journalizing and Posting   120

The Trial Balance   121
Limitations of a Trial Balance   122

CHAPTER 4

Accrual Accounting Concepts   148
Timing Is Everything   148

Timing Issues   150
The Revenue Recognition Principle   151
The Matching Principle   151
Accrual Versus Cash Basis of Accounting   153

xxvi

The Basics of Adjusting Entries 154
- Types of Adjusting Entries 155
- Adjusting Entries for Prepayments 156
- Adjusting Entries for Accruals 162
- Summary of Basic Relationships 167

The Adjusted Trial Balance and Financial Statements 169
- Preparing the Adjusted Trial Balance 169
- Preparing Financial Statements 170

Closing the Books 170
- Preparing Closing Entries 171
- Preparing a Post-Closing Trial Balance 172

Summary of the Accounting Cycle 173

Appendix 4A Adjusting Entries in an Automated World—Using a Work Sheet 177

CHAPTER 5

Merchandising Operations 200
Who Doesn't Shop at Wal-Mart? 200

Merchandising Operations 202
- Operating Cycles 203
- Inventory Systems 203

Recording Purchases of Merchandise 205
- Purchase Returns and Allowances 206
- Freight Costs 207
- Purchase Discounts 207

Recording Sales of Merchandise 209
- Sales Returns and Allowances 210
- Sales Discounts 211

Income Statement Presentation 211
- Sales Revenues 211
- Gross Profit 212
- Operating Expenses 212

Evaluating Profitability 213
- Gross Profit Rate 213
- Operating Expenses to Sales Ratio 215

CHAPTER 6

Reporting and Analyzing Inventory 238
Where Is That Spare Bulldozer Blade? 238

Classifying Inventory 240

Periodic Inventory System 241
- Recording Merchandise Transactions 241
- Cost of Goods Sold 243
- Income Statement Presentation 246

Inventory Costing 248
- Specific Identification 248
- Using Assumed Cost Flow Methods 248
- Financial Statement and Tax Effects of Cost Flow Methods 253
- Using Inventory Cost Flow Methods Consistently 255

Valuing Inventory at the Lower of Cost or Market 256

Analysis of Inventory 257
- Inventory Turnover Ratio 258
- Analysts' Adjustments for LIFO Reserve 259

Appendix 6A Inventory Errors 265

Income Statement Effects 265

Balance Sheet Effects 266

CHAPTER 7

Internal Control and Cash 286
It Takes a Thief 286

Internal Control 288
- Principles of Internal Control 288
- Limitations of Internal Control 294

Cash Controls 295
- Internal Control over Cash Receipts 295
- Internal Control over Cash Disbursements 296
- Use of a Bank 298

Reporting Cash 304
- Cash Equivalents 304
- Restricted Cash 305

Managing and Monitoring Cash 306
- Basic Principles of Cash Management 306
- Cash Budgeting 308

Assessing Cash Adequacy 310
- Ratio of Cash to Daily Cash Expenses 311
- Free Cash Flow 311

Appendix 7A Operation of the Petty Cash Fund 316

Establishing the Petty Cash Fund 316

Making Payments from Petty Cash 317

Replenishing the Petty Cash Fund 318

CHAPTER 8

Reporting and Analyzing Receivables 338
How Do You Spell Relief? 338

Types of Receivables 340

Accounts Receivable 341
- Recognizing Accounts Receivable 341
- Valuing Accounts Receivable 341

Notes Receivable 347
- Determining the Maturity Date 348
- Computing Interest 348
- Recognizing Notes Receivable 349
- Valuing Notes Receivable 349

Disposing of Notes Receivable 349
Statement Presentation of Receivables 352
Managing Receivables 353
  Extending Credit 353
  Establishing a Payment Period 354
  Monitoring Collections 354
  Evaluating the Receivables Balance 356
  Accelerating Cash Receipts 358

CHAPTER 9

Reporting and Analyzing Long-Lived Assets 382

A Tale of Two Airlines 382

Section 1 Plant Assets 384

Determining the Cost of Plant Assets 385
  Land 386
  Land Improvements 387
  Buildings 387
  Equipment 387
  To Buy or Lease? 388

Accounting for Plant Assets 390
  Depreciation 390
  Expenditures During Useful Life 398
  Impairments 398
  Plant Asset Disposals 399

Analyzing Plant Assets 402
  Average Useful Life 402
  Average Age of Plant Assets 403
  Asset Turnover Ratio 405

Section 2 Intangible Assets 406

Accounting for Intangible Assets 406
Types of Intangible Assets 408
  Patents 408
  Research and Development Costs 408
  Copyrights 408
  Trademarks and Trade Names 408
  Franchises and Licenses 409
  Goodwill 409

Financial Statement Presentation of Long-Lived Assets 410

Appendix 9A Calculation of Depreciation Using Other Methods 415
Declining-Balance 415
Units-of-Activity 417

CHAPTER 10

Reporting and Analyzing Liabilities 436

Live by Debt, Die by Debt 436

Section 1 Current Liabilities 438

What Is a Current Liability? 438

Types of Current Liabilities 439
  Notes Payable 439
  Sales Taxes Payable 440
  Payroll and Payroll Taxes Payable 441
  Unearned Revenues 442
  Current Maturities of Long-Term Debt 443

Financial Statement Presentation and Analysis 444
  Presentation 444
  Analysis 444

Section 2 Long-Term Liabilities 447

Bond Basics 447
  Why Issue Bonds? 448
  Types of Bonds 449
  Issuing Procedures 449
  Bond Trading 451
  Determining the Market Value of Bonds 451

Accounting for Bond Issues 453
  Issuing Bonds at Face Value 453
  Discount or Premium on Bonds 453
  Issuing Bonds at a Discount 454
  Amortizing Bond Discount 455
  Issuing Bonds at a Premium 457
  Amortizing Bond Premium 457

Accounting for Bond Retirements 459
  Redeeming Bonds at Maturity 459
  Redeeming Bonds Before Maturity 459

Financial Statement Presentation and Analysis 460
  Presentation 460
  Analysis 461

Other Issues in Analysis 462
  Contingent Liabilities 462
  Lease Liabilities 464

CHAPTER 11

Reporting and Analyzing Stockholders' Equity 486

What's Cooking? 486

The Corporate Form of Organization 488
  Characteristics of a Corporation 489
  Forming a Corporation 492
  Stockholder Rights 492

Stock Issue Considerations 494
  Authorized Stock 494
  Issuance of Stock 494
  Par and No-Par Value Stocks 494
  Accounting for Common Stock Issues 495

Accounting for Treasury Stock 497
  Purchase of Treasury Stock 498

Preferred Stock 500

Dividend Preferences 500
Liquidation Preference 501

Dividends 502
Cash Dividends 502
Stock Dividends 504
Stock Splits 506

Retained Earnings 508
Retained Earnings Restrictions 509

Stockholders' Equity Presentation 509

Measuring Corporate Performance 511
Dividend Record 511
Earnings Performance 512

CHAPTER 12

Reporting and Analyzing Investments 538

Is There Anything Else We Can Buy? 538

Why Corporations Invest 540

Accounting for Debt Investments 542
Recording Acquisition of Bonds 543
Recording Bond Interest 543
Recording Sale of Bonds 543

Accounting for Stock Investments 544
Holdings Less Than 20% 545
Holdings Between 20% and 50% 546
Holdings of More Than 50% 547

Valuation and Reporting of Investments 550
Categories of Securities 550
Evaluating Investment Portfolio Performance 552
Balance Sheet Presentation 553
Presentation of Realized and Unrealized Gain or Loss 554
Balance Sheet 555

CHAPTER 13

Statement of Cash Flows 576

I've Got Seven Billion Dollars Burning a Hole in My Pocket! 576

The Statement of Cash Flows: Purpose and Format 578
Purpose of the Statement of Cash Flows 578
Classification of Cash Flows 579
Significant Noncash Activities 579
Format of the Statement of Cash Flows 580
The Corporate Life Cycle 582
Usefulness of the Statement of Cash Flows 583
Preparing the Statement of Cash Flows 585

Section 1 Statement of Cash Flows—Indirect Method 587

First Year of Operations—1997 587
Determining the Net Increase/Decrease in Cash (Step 1) 588
Determining Net Cash Provided/Used by Operating Activities (Step 2) 588
Determining Net Cash Provided/Used by Investing and Financing Activities (Step 3) 590
Statement of Cash Flows—1997 591

Second Year of Operations—1998 591
Determining the Net Increase/Decrease in Cash (Step 1) 592
Determining Net Cash Provided/Used by Operating Activities (Step 2) 593
Determining Net Cash Provided/Used by Investing and Financing Activities (Step 3) 594
Statement of Cash Flows—1998 595

Summary of Conversion to Net Cash Provided by Operating Activities—Indirect Method 596

Section 2 Statement of Cash Flows—Direct Method 599

First Year of Operations—1997 599
Determining the Net Increase/Decrease in Cash (Step 1) 599
Determining Net Cash Provided/Used by Operating Activities (Step 2) 600
Determining Net Cash Provided/Used by Investing and Financing Activities (Step 3) 604
Statement of Cash Flows—1997 604

Second Year of Operations—1998 605
Determining the Net Increase/Decrease in Cash (Step 1) 606
Determining Net Cash Provided/Used by Operating Activities (Step 2) 606
Determining Net Cash Provided/Used by Investing and Financing Activities (Step 3) 608
Statement of Cash Flows—1998 609

Using Cash Flows to Evaluate a Company 612
Free Cash Flow 612
Capital Expenditure Ratio 614
Assessing Liquidity, Solvency, and Profitability Using Cash Flows 615

CHAPTER 14

Financial Analysis: The Big Picture 646

They Play the Market for Fun, Profit, and an Education 646

Earning Power and Irregular Items 648
Discontinued Operations 649
Extraordinary Items 650
Changes in Accounting Principle 652
Comprehensive Income 654

Comparative Analysis 655
  Horizontal Analysis 656
  Vertical Analysis 658
Ratio Analysis 661
  Liquidity Ratios 662
  Solvency Ratios 666
  Profitability Ratios 668
Limitations of Financial Analysis 675
  Estimates 675
  Cost 675
  Alternative Accounting Methods 675
  Atypical Data 676
  Diversification 676

APPENDIX A
Specimen Financial Statements: Starbucks Corporation A-1

APPENDIX B
Specimen Financial Statements: Green Mountain Coffee, Inc. B-1

APPENDIX C
Time Value of Money C-1

Photo Credits PC-1

Company Index I-1

Subject Index I-3

CHAPTER 1

Introduction to Financial Statements

STUDY OBJECTIVES

After studying this chapter, you should be able to:

1. Describe the primary forms of business organization.
2. Identify the users and uses of accounting.
3. Explain the three principal types of business activity.
4. Describe the content and purpose of each of the financial statements.
5. Explain the meaning of assets, liabilities, and stockholders' equity, and state the basic accounting equation.
6. Describe the components that supplement the financial statements in an annual report.
7. Explain the basic assumptions and principles underlying financial statements.

Coffee Anyone?

SEATTLE, WA   Starbucks Corporation appears to have found the recipe for success. While other companies have staked their future on innovative new high-tech products, Starbucks has brewed profits from a product that has been around ever since people first started getting up to go to work. Starbucks was formed as a Seattle business in 1971 by three coffee lovers who believed they could make a living by providing good-quality coffee. The corporate name is taken from the coffee-loving first mate in Herman Melville's novel *Moby Dick*.

Starbucks' success didn't really start perking until 1987 when it was purchased by a former employee, Howard Schultz, for $4 million. How did he build an empire of 1,300 coffee shops with more than 23,000 employees and nearly $800 million in sales in such a short time? First, Schultz's entrepreneurial vision was that Starbucks should sell coffee by the cup, rather than just bags of roasted coffee beans. Second, he believed that the company would prosper more if employees shared in its success. He created a "Bean Stock" program, where all eligible full- and part-time employees receive ownership in the company through rights to purchase stock. A third factor in Starbucks' success has been aggressive but careful planning. Each year Starbucks set what many outsiders considered unrealistic growth targets—and has always met them. To sustain this rapid growth, the Starbucks team has made many decisions: where to locate, whether to buy or rent properties, how to finance current operations and expansion, and what new products to sell.

By 1992 Starbucks' expansion goals had outstripped its available resources. To continue to open new shops and develop new products such as coffee-flavored premium ice cream, it needed more cash. So in 1992 the company raised $28 million in cash by selling shares of stock to the public. Since going public, Starbucks has enjoyed annual sales growth greater than 70%. Net income in 1996 was six times that of 1992, and the company's stock price has soared.

To acquire financing, Starbucks communicates its past performance and its plans for the future to lenders and investors. Financial information is a critical input to both the internal decisions made by management and the external decisions made by investors. Accounting is the primary source of financial information for both managers and investors.

On the World Wide Web
Starbucks Corporation:
http://www.Starbucks.com

Every chapter-opening vignette ends with the **Internet addresses** of the companies cited in the story to help you connect with these real businesses and explore them further.

PREVIEW OF CHAPTER 1

The preview describes the purpose of the chapter and outlines the major topics and subtopics you will find in it.

How do you start a business? How do you make it grow into a widely recognized brand name like Starbucks? How do you determine whether your business is making or losing money? When you need to expand your operations, where do you get money to finance expansion—should you borrow, should you issue stock, should you use your own funds? How do you convince lenders to lend you money or investors to buy your stock? Success in business requires making countless decisions, and decisions require financial information.

The purpose of this chapter is to show you what role accounting plays in providing financial information. The content and organization of the chapter are as follows:

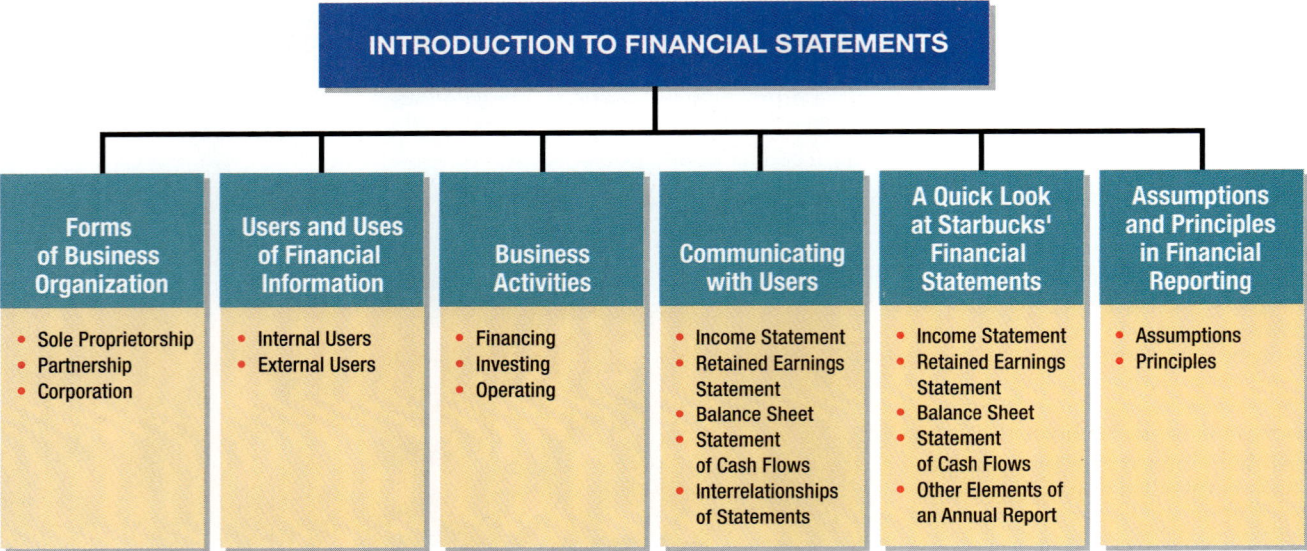

FORMS OF BUSINESS ORGANIZATION

STUDY OBJECTIVE 1

Describe the primary forms of business organization.

Terms that represent essential concepts of the chapter topic are printed in blue where they are first explained in the text. They are listed and defined again in the **glossary** at the end of the chapter.

Suppose you graduate with a marketing degree and open your own marketing agency. One of your initial decisions is what organizational form your business will have. You have three choices—sole proprietorship, partnership, or corporation. A business owned by one person is a **sole proprietorship.** A business owned by more than one person is a **partnership.** A business organized as a separate legal entity owned by stockholders is a **corporation.** Illustration 1-1 highlights these three types of organizations and the advantages of each.

You will probably choose the sole proprietorship form for your marketing agency. It is **simple to set up** and **gives you control** over the business. Small owner-operated businesses such as barber shops, law offices, and auto repair shops are often sole proprietorships, as are farms and small retail stores.

Another possibility is for you to join forces with other individuals to form a partnership. Partnerships often are formed because one individual does not have

4

Illustrations like this one convey information in pictorial form to help you visualize and apply the ideas as you study.

Illustration 1-1 Forms of business organization

enough economic resources to initiate or expand the business, or because **partners bring unique skills or resources** to the partnership. You and your partners should formalize your duties and contributions in a written partnership agreement. Partnerships are often used to organize retail and service-type businesses, including professional practices (lawyers, doctors, architects, and certified public accountants).

As a third alternative, you might organize as a corporation. In a corporation you receive shares of stock to indicate your ownership interest. Buying stock in a corporation is often more attractive than investing in a partnership because shares of stock are **easy to sell** (transfer ownership). Selling a proprietorship or partnership interest is much more involved. Many individuals can become **stockholders** by investing small amounts of money. Therefore, it is **easier for corporations to raise funds.** Successful corporations often have thousands of stockholders, and their stock is traded on organized stock exchanges like the New York Stock Exchange. Many businesses start as sole proprietorships or partnerships and eventually incorporate.

Other factors to consider in deciding which organizational form to choose are **taxes and legal liability.** If you choose a sole proprietorship or partnership, you generally receive favorable tax treatment relative to a corporation. However, a disadvantage of proprietorships and partnerships is that proprietors and partners are personally liable for all debts of the business, whereas corporate stockholders are not. In other words, corporate stockholders generally pay higher taxes but have no personal liability. We will discuss these issues in more depth in a later chapter.

Although the combined number of proprietorships and partnerships in the United States is more than five times the number of corporations, the revenue produced by corporations is eight times greater. Most of the largest enterprises in the United States—for example, Coca Cola, Exxon, General Motors, Citicorp, and Pacific Gas and Electric—are corporations. Because the majority of U.S. business is transacted by corporations, the emphasis in this book is on the corporate form of organization.

Alternative Terminology
Stockholders are sometimes called **shareholders.**

Alternative Terminology notes present synonymous terms that you may come across in practice.

Users and Uses of Financial Information

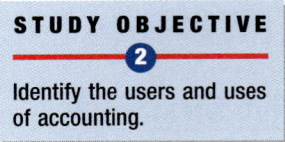

STUDY OBJECTIVE 2
Identify the users and uses of accounting.

The purpose of financial information is to provide inputs for decision making. **Accounting** is the information system that identifies, records, and communicates the economic events of an organization to interested users. Many people have an interest in knowing about the ongoing activities of the business. These people are **users** of accounting information. Users can be divided broadly into two groups: internal users and external users.

INTERNAL USERS

Internal users of accounting information are managers who plan, organize, and run a business. These include **marketing managers, production supervisors, finance directors, and company officers.** In running a business, managers must answer many important questions, as shown in Illustration 1-2.

Illustration 1-2

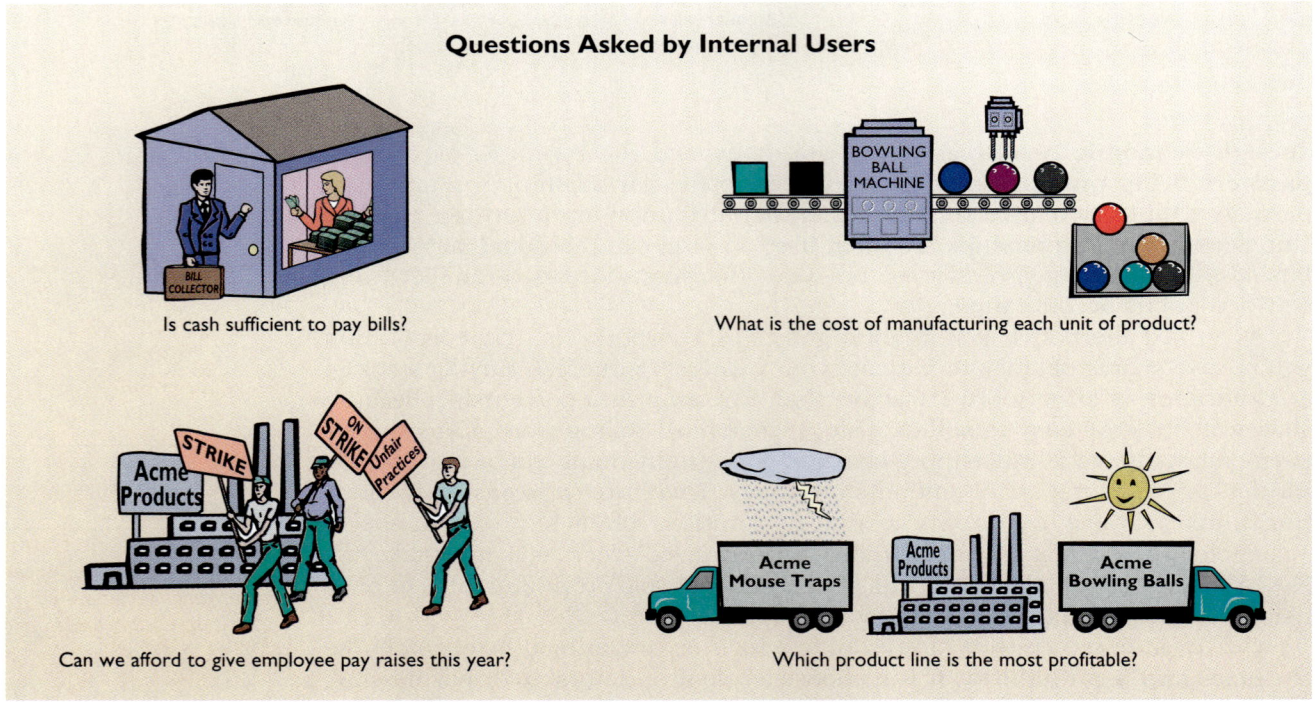

Questions Asked by Internal Users

To answer these and other questions, you need detailed information on a timely basis. For internal users, accounting provides internal reports, such as financial comparisons of operating alternatives, projections of income from new sales campaigns, and forecasts of cash needs for the next year. In addition, summarized financial information is presented in the form of financial statements.

EXTERNAL USERS

There are several types of **external users** of accounting information. **Investors** (owners) use accounting information to make decisions to buy, hold, or sell stock. **Creditors** such as suppliers and bankers use accounting information to evaluate the risks of granting credit or lending money. Some questions that may be asked by investors and creditors about a company are shown in Illustration 1-3.

Illustration 1-3

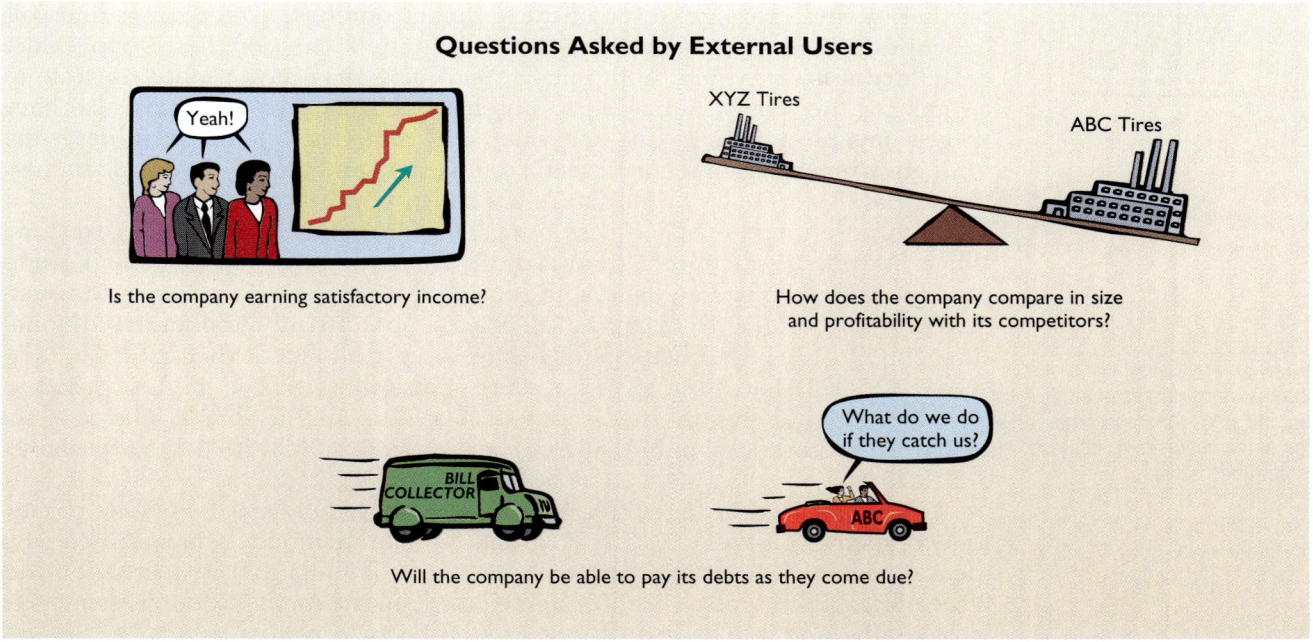

The information needs and questions of other external users vary considerably. **Taxing authorities,** such as the Internal Revenue Service, want to know whether the company complies with the tax laws. **Regulatory agencies,** such as the Securities and Exchange Commission or the Federal Trade Commission, want to know whether the company is operating within prescribed rules. **Customers** are interested in whether a company will continue to honor product warranties and otherwise support its product lines. **Labor unions** want to know whether the owners have the ability to pay increased wages and benefits. **Economic planners** use accounting information to analyze and forecast economic activity.

BUSINESS ACTIVITIES

All businesses are involved in three types of activity—financing, investing, and operating. For example, the founders of Starbucks needed financing to start their business. Some of their **financing** came from personal savings, and some came from outside sources like banks. The cash obtained was then **invested** in the equipment necessary to run their business, such as roasting equipment and delivery trucks. Once this equipment was in place, the founders could begin the **operating** activities of roasting and selling coffee beans.

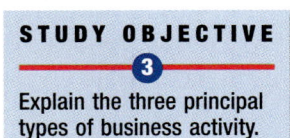

STUDY OBJECTIVE 3
Explain the three principal types of business activity.

The **accounting information system** keeps track of the results of each of the various business activities—financing, investing, and operating. Let's look in more detail at each type of business activity.

FINANCING ACTIVITIES

It takes money to make money. The two primary sources of outside funds for corporations are borrowing money and selling shares of stock.

For example, Starbucks may borrow money in a variety of ways. It can take out a loan at a bank, borrow directly from investors by issuing debt securities

8 CHAPTER 1 Introduction to Financial Statements

Financing

called bonds, or borrow money from its suppliers by purchasing goods on credit. Persons or entities to whom Starbucks owes money are its **creditors.** Creditors' claims on the business—in the form of debt and other obligations—are called **liabilities.** Specific names are given to different types of liabilities, depending on their source. Starbucks, for instance, might purchase coffee beans and coffee cups on credit from suppliers; the obligations to pay for these supplies are called **accounts payable.** Additionally, Starbucks may have a **note payable** to a bank for the money borrowed to purchase delivery trucks. It may also have **wages payable** to employees, and **sales and real estate taxes payable** to the local government. Debt securities sold to investors and due to be repaid at a particular date some years in the future are called **bonds payable.**

A corporation may also obtain funds by selling shares of stock to investors. When Starbucks was initially founded, the shares were issued to a small group of individuals who had an interest in starting the business. However, as the business grew, it became necessary to sell shares more broadly to obtain additional financing. In 1992 Starbucks sold its shares to the public for the first time. It issued 1,815,000 shares for $15.43 a share. **Common stock** is the term used to describe the total amount paid in by stockholders for the shares. The cash received from Starbucks' public sale of shares was $28,005,450 (1,815,000 shares × $15.43).

Helpful Hint Corporations may issue several classes of stock, but the stock that represents the primary ownership interest is **common stock.**

The claims of creditors differ from those of stockholders. If you loan money to a company, you are one of its creditors. In loaning money, you specify a payment schedule (for example, payment at the end of 3 months). As a creditor, you have a legal right to be paid at the agreed time. In the event of nonpayment, you may legally force the company to sell its property to pay its debts. The law requires that creditor claims be paid before ownership claims.

Owners, on the other hand, have no claim to corporate resources until the claims of creditors are satisfied. If you buy a company's stock instead of loaning it money, you have no right to expect any payments until all of its creditors are paid. Payments to stockholders are called **dividends.** Many corporations pay dividends on a regular basis as long as there is sufficient cash to cover expected payments to creditors. Also, once stock is issued, the corporation has no obligation to buy it back, whereas debt obligations must be repaid.

INVESTING ACTIVITIES

Once Starbucks obtained financing, it bought the resources it needed to operate. Resources owned by a business are called **assets.** For example, computers, delivery trucks, furniture, and buildings are assets.

Investing

Alternative Terminology Property, plant, and equipment is sometimes called **fixed assets.**

Different types of assets are given different names. For instance, if Starbucks sells goods to a customer and does not receive cash immediately, then Starbucks has a right to expect payment from that customer in the future. This right to receive money in the future is called an **account receivable.** Goods available for future sales, like coffee beans, are assets called **inventory.** Starbucks' roasting equipment is an asset referred to as **property, plant, and equipment.** And, finally, a very important asset to Starbucks or any other business is **cash.**

OPERATING ACTIVITIES

Once a business has the assets it needs to get started, it can begin its operations. Starbucks is in the business of selling all things that smell, look, or taste like coffee. It sells coffee, coffee beans, coffee cups, coffee grinders, coffee filters, and coffee thermoses. In short, if it has anything to do with coffee, Starbucks sells it. We call the sale of these products revenues. In accounting language, **revenues** are the increase in assets arising from the sale of a product or service. For example, Starbucks records revenue when it sells a coffee product and receives either cash or an account receivable.

Revenues arise from different sources and are identified by various names depending on the nature of the business. For instance, Starbucks' primary source of revenue is the sale of coffee products. However, it also generates interest revenue on debt securities held as investments. Sources of revenue common to many businesses are **sales revenue, service revenue, and interest revenue.**

Operating

Before Starbucks can sell a single cup of Komodo Dragon Blend, Decaf Mocha Java, or Yukon Blend it must buy coffee, roast coffee, transport coffee, and brew coffee. It also incurs more mundane costs like salaries, rents, and utilities. All of these costs, referred to as expenses, are necessary to sell the product. In accounting language, expenses are the cost of assets consumed or services used in the process of generating revenues.

Expenses take many forms and are identified by various names depending on the type of asset consumed or service used. For example, Starbucks keeps track of these types of expenses: **cost of sales** (such as cost of raw coffee beans and cost of processing), **store operating expense** (such as wages of store employees, rent, and electric, gas, and water costs incurred at stores), **general and administrative expense** (such as advertising costs, salaries of administrative staff, and telephone and heat costs incurred at the corporate office), and **interest expense** (amounts of interest paid on various debts).

Starbucks compares the revenues of a period with the expenses of that period to determine whether it earned a profit. When revenues exceed expenses, net income results. When expenses exceed revenues, a net loss results.

BEFORE YOU GO ON . . .

● Review It

1. What are the three forms of business organization and the advantages of each?
2. What are the two primary categories of users of financial information? Give examples of each.
3. What are the three types of business activity?
4. What are assets, liabilities, common stock, revenues, expenses, and net income?

● Do It

Classify each item as an asset, liability, common stock, revenue, or expense.

Cost of using property   Issuance of ownership shares
Service revenue   Truck purchased
Notes payable   Amounts owed to suppliers

Reasoning: Accounting classifies items by their economic characteristics. Proper classification of items is critical if accounting is to provide useful information.

Solution:

Cost of using property is classified as expense.
Service revenue is classified as revenue.
Notes payable are classified as liabilities.
Issuance of ownership shares is classified as common stock.
Truck purchased is classified as an asset.
Amounts owed to suppliers are classified as liabilities.

Review It questions at the end of major text sections prompt you to stop and review the key points you have just studied. Sometimes Review It questions stand alone; other times they are accompanied by practice exercises. The Do It exercises, like the one here, ask you to put newly acquired knowledge to work in some form of financial statement preparation. They outline the reasoning necessary to complete the exercise and show a solution.

10　CHAPTER 1　Introduction to Financial Statements

COMMUNICATING WITH USERS

STUDY OBJECTIVE 4
Describe the content and purpose of each of the financial statements.

Assets, liabilities, expenses, and revenues are of interest to users of accounting information. For business purposes, it is customary to arrange this information in the format of four different **financial statements,** which form the backbone of financial accounting. To present a picture at a point in time of what your business owns (its assets) and what it owes (its liabilities), you would present a **balance sheet.** To show how successfully your business performed during a period of time, you would report its revenues and expenses in the **income statement.** To indicate how much of previous income was distributed to you and the other owners of your business in the form of dividends, and how much was retained in the business to allow for future growth, you would present a **retained earnings statement.** And finally, of particular interest to your bankers and other creditors, you would present a **statement of cash flows** to show where your business obtained cash during a period of time and how that cash was used.

To introduce you to these statements, we have prepared the financial statements for a marketing agency, Sierra Corporation, in Illustration 1-4. Take some time now to acquaint yourself with their general formats and categories in preparation for the more detailed discussion that follows.

INCOME STATEMENT

Helpful Hint The heading of every income statement identifies the company, the type of statement, and the time period covered by the statement. Sometimes another line is added to indicate the unit of measure; when it is used, this fourth line usually indicates that the data are presented "in thousands" or "in millions."

The purpose of the income statement is to report the success or failure of the company's operations for a period of time. To indicate that Sierra's income statement reports the results of operations for a **period of time,** the income statement is dated "For the Month Ended October 31, 1998." The income statement lists the company's revenues followed by its expenses. Finally, the net income (or net loss) is determined by deducting expenses from revenues. This result is the famed "bottom line" often referred to in business.

Why are financial statement users interested in the bottom line? Investors buy and sell stock based on their beliefs about the future performance of a company. If you believe that Sierra will be even more successful in the future, and that this success will translate into a higher stock price you should buy Sierra's stock. Therefore, investors are interested in a company's past net income because it provides a source of information about future net income. Similarly, creditors also use the income statement to predict the future. When a bank loans money to a company it does so with the belief that it will be repaid in the future. If it didn't think it was going to be repaid, it wouldn't loan the money. Therefore, prior to making the loan the bank loan officer must try to predict whether the company will be profitable enough to repay its loan.

Note that the issuance of stock and dividend distributions are not used in determining net income. For example, $10,000 of cash received from issuing new stock was not treated as revenue by Sierra Corporation, and dividends paid of $500 were not regarded as a business expense.

Each chapter presents useful information about how decision makers use financial statements. Decision Toolkits summarize discussions of key decision-making contexts and techniques.

DECISION TOOLKIT

Decision Checkpoints	Info Needed for Decision	Tool to Use for Decision	How to Evaluate Results
Are the company's operations profitable?	Income statement	The income statement reports on the success or failure of the company's operations by reporting its revenues and expenses.	If the company's revenue exceeds its expenses, it will report net income; otherwise it will report a net loss.

Illustration 1-4 Sierra Corporation's financial statements

SIERRA CORPORATION
Income Statement
For the Month Ended October 31, 1998

Revenues		
Service revenue		$10,600
Expenses		
Salaries expense	$5,200	
Supplies expense	1,500	
Rent expense	900	
Insurance expense	50	
Interest expense	50	
Depreciation expense	40	
Total expenses		7,740
Net income		**$ 2,860**

Helpful Hint Note that final sums are double-underlined, and negative amounts are presented in parentheses.

SIERRA CORPORATION
Retained Earnings Statement
For the Month Ended October 31, 1998

Retained earnings, October 1	$ 0
Add: Net income	2,860
	2,860
Less: Dividends	500
Retained earnings, October 31	**$2,360**

SIERRA CORPORATION
Balance Sheet
October 31, 1998

Assets

Cash	**$15,200**
Accounts receivable	200
Advertising supplies	1,000
Prepaid insurance	550
Office equipment, net (LESS ACCmt depr)	4,960
Total assets	$21,910

Liabilities and Stockholders' Equity

Liabilities		
Notes payable		$ 5,000
Accounts payable		2,500
Interest payable		50
Unearned revenue		800
Salaries payable		1,200
Total liabilities		9,550
Stockholders' equity		
Common stock		10,000
Retained earnings		2,360
Total stockholders' equity		12,360
Total liabilities and stockholders' equity		$21,910

Helpful Hint The arrows in this illustration show interrelationships of the four financial statements.

SIERRA CORPORATION
Statement of Cash Flows
For the Month Ended October 31, 1998

Cash flows from operating activities		
Cash receipts from operating activities	$11,200	
Cash payments for operating activities	(5,500)	
Net cash provided by operating activities		$ 5,700
Cash flows from investing activities		
Purchased office equipment	(5,000)	
Net cash used by investing activities		(5,000)
Cash flows from financing activities		
Issuance of common stock	10,000	
Issued note payable	5,000	
Payment of dividend	(500)	
Net cash provided by financing activities		14,500
Net increase in cash		15,200
Cash at beginning of period		0
Cash at end of period		**$15,200**

RETAINED EARNINGS STATEMENT

If Sierra is profitable, at the end of each period it must decide what portion of profits to pay to shareholders in dividends. In theory it could pay all of its current-period profits, but few companies choose to do this. Why? Because they want to retain part of the profits in the business to allow for further expansion. High-growth companies, for example, often choose to pay no dividends. **Retained earnings** is the net income retained in the corporation.

The **retained earnings statement** shows the amounts and causes of changes in retained earnings during the period. The time period is the same as that covered by the income statement. The beginning retained earnings amount is shown on the first line of the statement. Then net income is added and dividends are deducted to calculate the retained earnings at the end of the period. If a company has a net loss, it is deducted (rather than added) in the retained earnings statement.

By monitoring the retained earnings statement, users of financial statements learn a great deal about management's dividend payment philosophy. Some investors seek companies that pay high dividends, whereas others seek companies that pay lower dividends, and instead reinvest to increase the company's growth potential. Lenders monitor their corporate customers' dividend payments because any money paid in dividends reduces a company's ability to repay its debts.

Helpful Hint The heading of this statement identifies the company, the type of statement, and the time period covered by the statement.

DECISION TOOLKIT

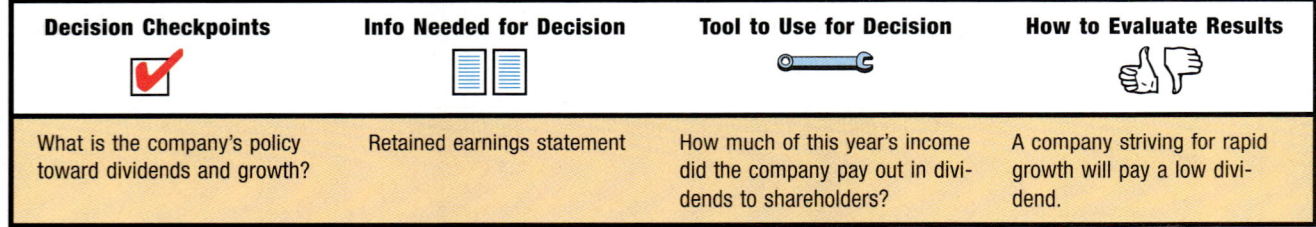

Decision Checkpoints	Info Needed for Decision	Tool to Use for Decision	How to Evaluate Results
What is the company's policy toward dividends and growth?	Retained earnings statement	How much of this year's income did the company pay out in dividends to shareholders?	A company striving for rapid growth will pay a low dividend.

BALANCE SHEET

The **balance sheet** reports assets and claims to those assets at a specific **point in time**. These claims are subdivided into two categories: claims of creditors and claims of owners. As noted earlier, claims of creditors are called **liabilities**. Claims of owners are called **stockholders' equity.** This relationship is shown in equation form in Illustration 1-5. This equation is referred to as the **basic accounting equation.**

STUDY OBJECTIVE 5
Explain the meaning of assets, liabilities, and stockholders' equity, and state the basic accounting equation.

Illustration 1-5 Basic accounting equation

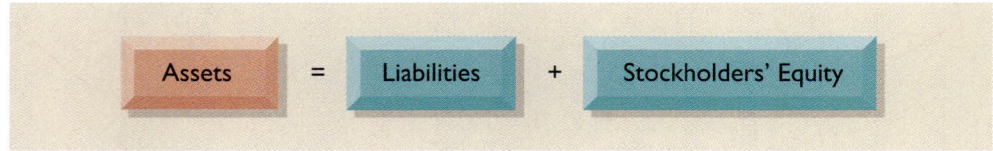

This relationship is where the name "balance sheet" comes from. Assets must be in balance with the claims to the assets.

As you can see from looking at Sierra's balance sheet in Illustration 1-4, assets are listed first, followed by liabilities and stockholders' equity. Stockholders' equity is comprised of two parts: (1) common stock and (2) retained earnings. As noted earlier, common stock results when the company sells new shares of stock in exchange for cash or other assets. Retained earnings is the net income retained in the corporation. Sierra has common stock of $10,000 and retained earnings of $2,360, for total stockholders' equity of $12,360.

Creditors use the balance sheet as another source of information to determine the likelihood that they will be repaid. They carefully evaluate the nature of a company's assets and liabilities. For example, does the company have assets that could be easily sold to repay its debts? Managers use the balance sheet to determine whether inventory is adequate to support future sales and whether cash on hand is sufficient for immediate cash needs. Managers also look at the relationship between debt and stockholders' equity to determine whether they have the best proportion of debt and common stock financing.

Helpful Hint The heading of a balance sheet must identify the company, the statement, and the date.

DECISION TOOLKIT

Decision Checkpoints	Info Needed for Decision	Tool to Use for Decision	How to Evaluate Results
Does the company rely primarily on debt or stockholders' equity to finance its assets?	Balance sheet	The balance sheet reports the company's resources and claims to those resources. There are two types of claims: liabilities and stockholders' equity.	Compare the amount of debt versus the amount of stockholders' equity to determine whether the company relies more on creditors or owners for its financing.

STATEMENT OF CASH FLOWS

The primary purpose of a **statement of cash flows** is to provide financial information about the cash receipts and cash payments of a business for a specific period of time. To help investors, creditors, and others in their analysis of a company's cash position, the statement of cash flows reports the cash effects of a company's: (1) operating activities, (2) investing activities, and (3) financing activities. In addition, the statement shows the net increase or decrease in cash during the period, and the cash amount at the end of the period.

Users are interested in the statement of cash flows because they want to know what is happening to a company's most important resource. The statement of cash flows provides answers to these simple but important questions:

Where did cash come from during the period?
How was cash used during the period?
What was the change in the cash balance during the period?

The statement of cash flows for Sierra, in Illustration 1-4, shows that cash increased $15,200 during the year. This increase resulted because operating activities (services to clients) increased cash $5,700, and financing activities increased cash $14,500. Investing activities used $5,000 of cash for the purchase of equipment.

14 CHAPTER 1 Introduction to Financial Statements

DECISION TOOLKIT

Decision Checkpoints	Info Needed for Decision	Tool to Use for Decision	How to Evaluate Results
Does the company generate sufficient cash from operations to fund its investing activities?	Statement of cash flows	The statement of cash flows shows the amount of cash provided or used by operating activities, investing activities, and financing activities.	Compare the amount of cash provided by operating activities with the amount of cash used by investing activities. Any deficiency in cash from operating activities must be made up with cash from financing activities.

INTERRELATIONSHIPS OF STATEMENTS

Because the results on some statements are used as inputs to other statements, the statements are interrelated. These interrelationships are evident in Sierra's statements in Illustration 1-4.

1. The retained earnings statement is dependent on the results of the income statement. Sierra reported net income of $2,860 for the period. This amount is added to the beginning amount of retained earnings as part of the process of determining ending retained earnings.
2. The balance sheet and retained earnings statement are interrelated because the ending amount of $2,360 on the retained earnings statement is reported as the retained earnings amount on the balance sheet.
3. The statement of cash flows and the balance sheet are also interrelated. The statement of cash flows shows how the cash account changed during the period by showing the amount of cash at the beginning of the period, the sources and uses of cash during the period, and the $15,200 of cash at the end of the period. The ending amount of cash shown on the statement of cash flows must agree with the amount of cash on the balance sheet.

Study these interrelationships carefully. To prepare financial statements you must understand the sequence in which these amounts are determined, and how each statement impacts the next.

BEFORE YOU GO ON . . .

● **Review It**

1. What questions might each of these decision makers have that could be answered by financial information: bank loan officer, stock investor, labor union president, and federal bank regulator?
2. What are the content and purpose of each statement: income statement, balance sheet, retained earnings statement, and statement of cash flows?

● **Do It**

CSU Corporation began operations on January 1, 1998. The following information is available for CSU Corporation on December 31, 1998: service revenue $17,000; accounts receivable $4,000; accounts payable $2,000; building rental expense $9,000; notes payable $5,000; common stock $10,000; retained earnings ?; equipment $16,000; insurance expense $1,000; supplies $1,800; supplies expense $200; cash $2,000; dividends $0. Prepare an income statement, a retained earnings statement, and a balance sheet using this information.

Reasoning: An income statement reports the success or failure of a company's operations for a period of time. A retained earnings statement shows the amounts and causes of changes in retained earnings during the period. A balance sheet presents the assets and claims to those assets of a company at a specific point in time.

Solution:

CSU CORPORATION
Income Statement
For the Year Ended December 31, 1998

Revenues		
Service revenue		$17,000
Expenses		
Rent expense	$9,000	
Insurance expense	1,000	
Supplies expense	200	
Total expenses		10,200
Net income		$ 6,800

CSU CORPORATION
Retained Earnings Statement
For the Year Ended December 31, 1998

Retained earnings, January 1	$ 0
Add: Net income	6,800
	6,800
Less: Dividends	0
Retained earnings, December 31	$6,800

CSU CORPORATION
Balance Sheet
December 31, 1998

Assets

Cash	$ 2,000
Accounts receivable	4,000
Supplies	1,800
Equipment	16,000
Total assets	$23,800

Liabilities and Stockholders' Equity

Liabilities	
Accounts payable	$ 2,000
Notes payable	5,000
Total liabilities	7,000
Stockholders' equity	
Common stock	10,000
Retained earnings	6,800
Total stockholders' equity	16,800
Total liabilities and stockholders' equity	$23,800

16 CHAPTER 1 Introduction to Financial Statements

A Quick Look at Starbucks' Financial Statements

The same relationships that you observed among the financial statements of Sierra Corporation are evident in the 1996 financial statements of Starbucks, which are presented in Illustrations 1-6 through 1-9. We have simplified the financial statements to assist your learning—but they may still look complicated to you. Do not be alarmed by their seeming complexity. (If you could already read and understand them, there would be little reason to take this course, except possibly to add a high grade to your transcript—which we hope you'll do anyway.) By the end of the book, you'll have a great deal of experience in reading and understanding financial statements such as these.

Before we dive in, we need to explain four points:

1. Note that numbers are reported in thousands on Starbucks' financial statements—that is, the last three 000s are omitted. Thus, Starbucks' net income in 1996 is $42,128,000 not $42,128.
2. Starbucks, like most companies, presents its financial statements for more than one year. Financial statements that report information for more than one period are called **comparative statements.** Comparative statements allow users to compare the financial position of the business at the end of an accounting period with that of previous periods.
3. Every set of financial statements is accompanied by explanatory notes and supporting schedules that are an integral part of the statements. These notes and schedules clarify information presented in the financial statements, as well as expanding upon it where additional detail is needed.
4. Many companies choose December 31 as their accounting year-end, although an increasing number of companies are choosing dates other than December 31. In the notes to its financial statements, Starbucks states that its accounting year-end is the Sunday closest to September 30 of each year. Consequently, its year-end does not fall on the same date each year. It was October 3 in 1993, October 2 in 1994, October 1 in 1995, and September 29 in 1996. As a consequence, for Starbucks, 1993 had 53 weeks, whereas 1994, 1995, and 1996 had 52 weeks.

Business Insight examples provide interesting information about actual accounting situations in business.

BUSINESS INSIGHT
Management Perspective

Why do companies choose the particular year-ends that they do? For example, why doesn't every company use December 31 as the accounting year-end? Many companies choose to end their accounting year when inventory or operations are at a low. This is advantageous because compiling accounting information requires much time and effort by managers, so they would rather do it when they aren't as busy operating the business. Also, inventory is easier and less costly to count when it is low. Some companies whose year-ends differ from December 31 are Delta Air Lines, June 30; Walt Disney Productions, September 30; Kmart Corp., January 31; and Dunkin' Donuts, Inc., October 31.

INCOME STATEMENT

Starbucks' income statement is presented in Illustration 1-6. The format of Starbucks' income statement differs from that of Sierra Corporation.[1] Starbucks first

---

[1] The pros and cons of alternative formats for the income statement are discussed in the next chapter.

A Quick Look at Starbucks' Financial Statements

STARBUCKS CORPORATION
Income Statement
For the years ended September 29, 1996,
October 1, 1995, and October 2, 1994
(in thousands)

	Sept. 29, 1996	Oct. 1, 1995	Oct. 2, 1994
Net revenues	$696,481	$465,213	$284,923
Cost of goods sold	335,800	211,279	130,324
Store operating expenses	210,693	148,757	90,087
Other operating expenses	19,787	13,932	8,698
Depreciation and amortization	35,950	22,486	12,535
General and administrative expenses	37,258	28,643	19,981
Operating income	56,993	40,116	23,298
Interest revenue	11,029	6,792	2,130
Interest expense	(8,739)	(3,765)	(3,807)
Gain on sale of investment in Noah's	9,218		
Other expenses and losses			(3,867)
Earnings before income taxes	68,501	43,143	17,754
Income taxes	26,373	17,041	7,548
Net income	$ 42,128	$ 26,102	$ 10,206

Illustration 1-6
Starbucks' income statement

Financial statements of real companies, like these, are accompanied by either a company logo or an associated photograph.

presents revenues and expenses directly related to operating the business (in the first seven lines, through "Operating income"); then it presents nonoperating revenues and expenses. For 1996 Starbucks reports net revenues of $696,481,000, then subtracts a variety of expenses directly related to operating the business (cost of goods sold, store operating expenses, and administrative expenses), to arrive at operating income of $56,993,000. It then reports interest revenue (receipts of interest from various investments in debt securities) of $11,029,000, interest expense (payments of interest on debt) of $8,739,000, and other gains and losses to arrive at earnings before taxes of $68,501,000. After subtracting income tax expense of $26,373,000, the company had a net income of $42,128,000. This represented a 61% increase over the results of the previous year.

Helpful Hint The percentage change in any amount from one year to the next is calculated as follows:

$$\frac{\text{Change during period}}{\text{Previous value}}$$

Thus, the percentage change in income is

$$\frac{\text{Change in income}}{\text{Previous year's income}}$$

RETAINED EARNINGS STATEMENT

Starbucks presents information about its retained earnings in the retained earnings statement in Illustration 1-7 (on the next page). (Many companies present the changes in retained earnings in a broader report called the Statement of Shareholders' Equity.) Find the line "Retained earnings, October 1, 1995," and you will see that beginning retained earnings was $46,552,000 for the year ended September 29, 1996. Note that this agrees with the balance in retained earnings on the October 1, 1995, balance sheet (Illustration 1-8). As we proceed down the retained earnings statement, the next figure is net income of $42,128,000. Starbucks paid no dividends. The ending balance of retained earnings, after adjustments for other items, is $90,351,000. Find this amount of retained earnings near the bottom of Starbucks' balance sheet for September 29, 1996.

BALANCE SHEET

As shown in Starbucks' balance sheet in Illustration 1-8, Starbucks' assets include the kinds previously mentioned in our discussion of Sierra Corporation, such as cash, inventories, and property, plant, and equipment, plus other types

Illustration 1-7
Starbucks' retained earnings statement

STARBUCKS CORPORATION
Retained Earnings Statement
For the years ended September 29, 1996, October 1, 1995, and October 2, 1994
(in thousands)

Retained earnings, October 4, 1993	$10,329
Dividends	(270)
Net income	10,206
Other adjustments	(228)
Retained earnings, October 2, 1994	20,037
Net income	26,102
Other adjustments	413
Retained earnings, October 1, 1995	46,552
Net income	42,128
Other adjustments	1,671
Retained earnings, September 29, 1996	**$90,351**

Illustration 1-8
Starbucks' balance sheet

STARBUCKS CORPORATION
Balance Sheets
September 29, 1996, and October 1, 1995
(in thousands)

	Sept. 29, 1996	Oct. 1, 1995
Assets		
Current assets		
Cash and cash equivalents	$126,215	$ 20,944
Short-term investments	103,221	41,507
Accounts and notes receivable	17,621	9,852
Inventories	83,370	123,657
Prepaid expenses and other current assets	9,114	9,390
Total current assets	339,541	205,350
Long-term investments	4,401	11,628
Property, plant, and equipment, net	369,477	244,728
Other assets	13,194	6,472
Total assets	$726,613	$468,178
Liabilities and Stockholders' Equity		
Current liabilities		
Accounts payable	$ 38,034	$ 28,668
Accrued compensation and related costs	15,001	12,786
Accrued interest payable	3,004	650
Other liabilities and accrued expenses	45,052	28,942
Total current liabilities	101,091	71,046
Long-term debt	173,862	84,901
Total liabilities	274,953	155,947
Stockholders' equity		
Common stock: authorized, 150,000,000 shares; issued and outstanding, 77,583,868 and 70,956,990 shares	361,309	265,679
Retained earnings	**90,351**	46,552
Total stockholders' equity	451,660	312,231
Total liabilities and stockholders' equity	$726,613	$468,178

of assets that we will discuss in later chapters, such as prepaid expenses. Similarly, its liabilities include accounts payable as well as items not yet discussed, such as accrued compensation. Starbucks' balance sheet shows that assets increased substantially from an October 1, 1995, balance of $468,178,000 to a September 29, 1996, balance of $726,613,000. Not all asset categories increased at an equal rate, however. For instance, short-term investments more than doubled, while prepaid expenses were level. As you learn more about financial statements, we will discuss how to interpret these changes.

STATEMENT OF CASH FLOWS

Starbucks' cash increased $105,271,000 from 1995 to 1996. Starbucks' balance sheet shows that cash was $20,944,000 on October 1, 1995 and $126,215,000 on September 29, 1996, an increase of $105,271,000. The reasons for this increase can be determined by examining the statement of cash flows in Illustration 1-9. This statement presents the sources and uses of cash for Starbucks during the period. Starbucks is trying to grow very rapidly; thus, it spent considerable cash during the period on investments in new assets. For example, it spent $167,246,000 on new property, plant, and equipment. In total it spent a net $211,179,000 on new assets in order to expand. Note that its cash provided by operations, $136,679,000, was not sufficient to finance this expansion. These

Illustration 1-9
Starbucks' statement of cash flows

STARBUCKS CORPORATION
Statement of Cash Flows
For the years ended September 29, 1996, October 1, 1995, and October 2, 1994
(in thousands)

	Sept. 29, 1996	Oct. 1, 1995	Oct. 2, 1994
Operating activities			
Cash receipts from operating activities	$688,712	$460,757	$282,626
Cash payments for operating activities	552,033	448,206	282,053
Net cash provided by operating activities	136,679	12,551	573
Investing activities			
Purchase of short-term investments	(178,643)	(136,256)	(106,118)
Sale of short-term investments	17,144	27,702	73,701
Maturity of short-term investments	103,056	74,808	100,103
Purchase of long-term investments	(6,040)	(12,484)	(300)
Sale of long-term investments	20,550		
Additions to property, plant, and equipment and other	(167,246)	(130,540)	(87,092)
Net cash used by investing activities	(211,179)	(176,770)	(19,706)
Financing activities			
Issuance of short-term debt	3,096	1,180	5,736
Issuance of long-term debt	160,975		
Issuance of notes payable		19,000	
Repayment of notes payable		(19,000)	(1,600)
Issuance of common stock	16,575	175,718	6,290
Other	(875)	(129)	(5)
Net cash provided by financing activities	179,771	176,769	10,421
Increase (decrease) in cash and cash equivalents	105,271	12,550	(8,712)
Cash and cash equivalents			
Beginning of year	20,944	8,394	17,106
End of year	$126,215	$ 20,944	$ 8,394

amounts are consistent with what might be expected of a company during its growth stage. In order to expand, the company needs to invest in plant and equipment, but the cash provided by its current operations is not sufficient to support this growth. Thus, it must borrow or issue stock. An examination of the financing activities shows that the company received $179,771,000 in cash from new financing. For example, it generated $160,975,000 by issuing long-term debt. The net result of the sources and uses of cash during the year was the cash increase of $105,271,000.

OTHER ELEMENTS OF AN ANNUAL REPORT

STUDY OBJECTIVE 6
Describe the components that supplement the financial statements in an annual report.

U.S. companies that are publicly traded must provide their shareholders with an **annual report** each year. The annual report always includes the financial statements introduced in this chapter. In addition, the annual report includes other important sources of information such as a management discussion and analysis section, notes to the financial statements, and an independent auditor's report. No analysis of a company's financial situation and prospects is complete without a review of each of these items.

Management Discussion and Analysis

The **management discussion and analysis (MD&A)** section covers three financial aspects of a company: its ability to pay near-term obligations, its ability to fund operations and expansion, and its results of operations. Management must highlight favorable or unfavorable trends and identify significant events and uncertainties that affect these three factors. This discussion obviously involves a number of subjective estimates and opinions. Excerpts from the MD&A section of Starbucks' annual report are presented in Illustration 1-10.

Illustration 1-10
Starbucks' management discussion and analysis

STARBUCKS CORPORATION
Management's Discussion and Analysis
of Financial Condition and Results of Operations

Starbucks presently derives approximately 86% of net revenues from its Company-operated retail stores. The Company's specialty sales operations, which include sales to wholesale customers, licensees, and joint ventures, accounted for approximately 11% of net revenues in fiscal 1996. Direct response operations account for the remainder of net revenues.

The Company's net revenues have increased from $284.9 million in fiscal 1994 to $696.5 million in fiscal 1996, due primarily to the Company's store expansion program and comparable store sales increases. Comparable store sales increased by 9% and 7% in fiscal 1995 and 1996, respectively. As part of its expansion strategy of clustering stores in existing markets, Starbucks has experienced a certain level of cannibalization of existing stores by new stores as the store concentration has increased, but management believes such cannibalization has been justified by the incremental sales and return on new store investment. The Company anticipates that this cannibalization, as well as increased competition and other factors, may continue to put downward pressure on its comparable store sales growth in future periods.

Notes to the Financial Statements

The **notes to the financial statements** provide additional details about the items presented in the main body of the statements. Information in the notes does not have to be quantifiable (numeric). Examples of notes are descriptions of the accounting policies and methods used in preparing the statements, explanations of uncertainties and contingencies, and statistics and details too voluminous to be included in the statements. The notes are essential to understanding a company's performance and position.

Illustration 1-11 is an excerpt from the notes to Starbucks' financial statements. It describes the methods that Starbucks uses to account for store pre-opening expenses.

STARBUCKS CORPORATION
Notes to Financial Statements

Store pre-opening expenses
Costs incurred in connection with start-up and promotion of new store openings are expensed as incurred.

Illustration 1-11 Notes to Starbucks' financial statements

Auditor's Report

Another important source of information is the **auditor's report.** An **auditor** is an accounting professional who conducts an independent examination of the accounting data presented by a company. Only accountants who meet certain criteria, **Certified Public Accountants (CPAs),** may perform audits. If the auditor is satisfied that the financial statements present the financial position, results of operations, and cash flows in accordance with generally accepted accounting principles, then an **unqualified opinion** is expressed. If the auditor expresses anything other than an unqualified opinion, then the financial statements should be used only with caution. That is, without an unqualified opinion, we cannot have complete confidence that the financial statements give an accurate picture of the company's financial health.

Illustration 1-12 is the auditor's report from Starbucks' 1996 annual report.

STARBUCKS CORPORATION
Auditor's Report

We have audited the accompanying consolidated balance sheets of Starbucks Corporation and subsidiaries (the Company) as of September 29, 1996, and October 1, 1995, and the related consolidated statements of earnings, shareholders' equity, and cash flows for each of the three years in the period ended September 29, 1996. These financial statements are the responsibility of the Company's management. Our responsibility is to express an opinion on these financial statements based on our audits.

We conducted our audits in accordance with generally accepted auditing standards. Those standards require that we plan and perform the audit to obtain reasonable assurance about whether the financial statements are free of material misstatement. An audit includes examining, on a test basis, evidence supporting the amounts and disclosures in the financial statements. An audit also includes assessing the accounting principles used and significant estimates made by management, as well as evaluating the overall financial statement presentation. We believe that our audits provide a reasonable basis for our opinion.

In our opinion, such consolidated financial statements present fairly, in all material respects, the financial position of Starbucks Corporation and subsidiaries as of September 29, 1996, and October 1, 1995, and the results of their operations and their cash flows for each of the three years in the period ended September 29, 1996, in conformity with generally accepted accounting principles.

Deloitte & Touche LLP

Deloitte & Touche LLP
Seattle, Washington
November 22, 1996

Illustration 1-12 Auditor's report

Assumptions and Principles in Financial Reporting

STUDY OBJECTIVE 7
Explain the basic assumptions and principles underlying financial statements.

Preparation of financial statements relies on some key assumptions and principles. It is helpful to look at some of these now that we have begun to see how accounting can be used to convey financial information to decision makers. The assumptions and principles form a foundation for financial reporting that we will refer to throughout the book.

ASSUMPTIONS

Monetary Unit Assumption

First let's talk about the assumptions. In looking at Starbucks' financial statements you will notice that everything is stated in terms of dollars. The **monetary unit assumption** requires that only those things that can be expressed in money are included in the accounting records. This might seem so obvious that it doesn't bear mentioning, but in fact it has important implications for financial reporting. Because the exchange of money is fundamental to business transactions, it makes sense that we measure a business in terms of money. However, it also means that certain important information needed by investors, creditors, and managers is not reported in the financial statements. For example, customer satisfaction is important to every business, but it is not easily quantified in dollar terms; thus it is not reported in the financial statements.

Economic Entity Assumption

The **economic entity assumption** states that every economic entity can be separately identified and accounted for. For example, suppose you are a stockholder in Starbucks. The amount of cash you have in your personal bank account and the balance owed on your personal car loan are not reported in Starbucks' balance sheet. The reason is that, for accounting purposes, you and Starbucks are separate accounting entities. In order to accurately assess Starbucks' performance and financial position it is important that we not blur it with your personal transactions, or the transactions of any other company.

BUSINESS INSIGHT
Management Perspective

A violation of the economic entity assumption contributed to the resignation by the chief executive of W. R. Grace and Company. Investors were angered to learn that company funds were allegedly used for personal medical care, a Manhattan apartment, and a personal chef for the company's chief executive. Funds were also used to support a hotel interest owned by the chief executive's son.

Source: New York Times, March 10, 1995.

Time Period Assumption

Next, notice that Starbucks' income statement, retained earnings statement, and statement of cash flows all cover periods of one year, and the balance sheet is prepared at the end of each year. The **time period assumption** states that the life of a business can be divided into artificial time periods and that useful reports covering those periods can be prepared for the business. All companies report at least annually. Many also report at least every three months (quarterly) to stockholders, and many prepare monthly statements for internal purposes.

Going Concern Assumption

The **going concern assumption** states that the business will remain in operation for the foreseeable future. Of course many businesses do fail, but in general, it is reasonable to assume that the business will continue operating. The going concern assumption underlies much of what we do in accounting. To give you just one example, if going concern is not assumed, then plant assets should be stated at their liquidation value (selling price less cost of disposal), not at their cost. Only when liquidation of the business appears likely is the going concern assumption inappropriate.

These four accounting assumptions are shown graphically in Illustration 1-13.

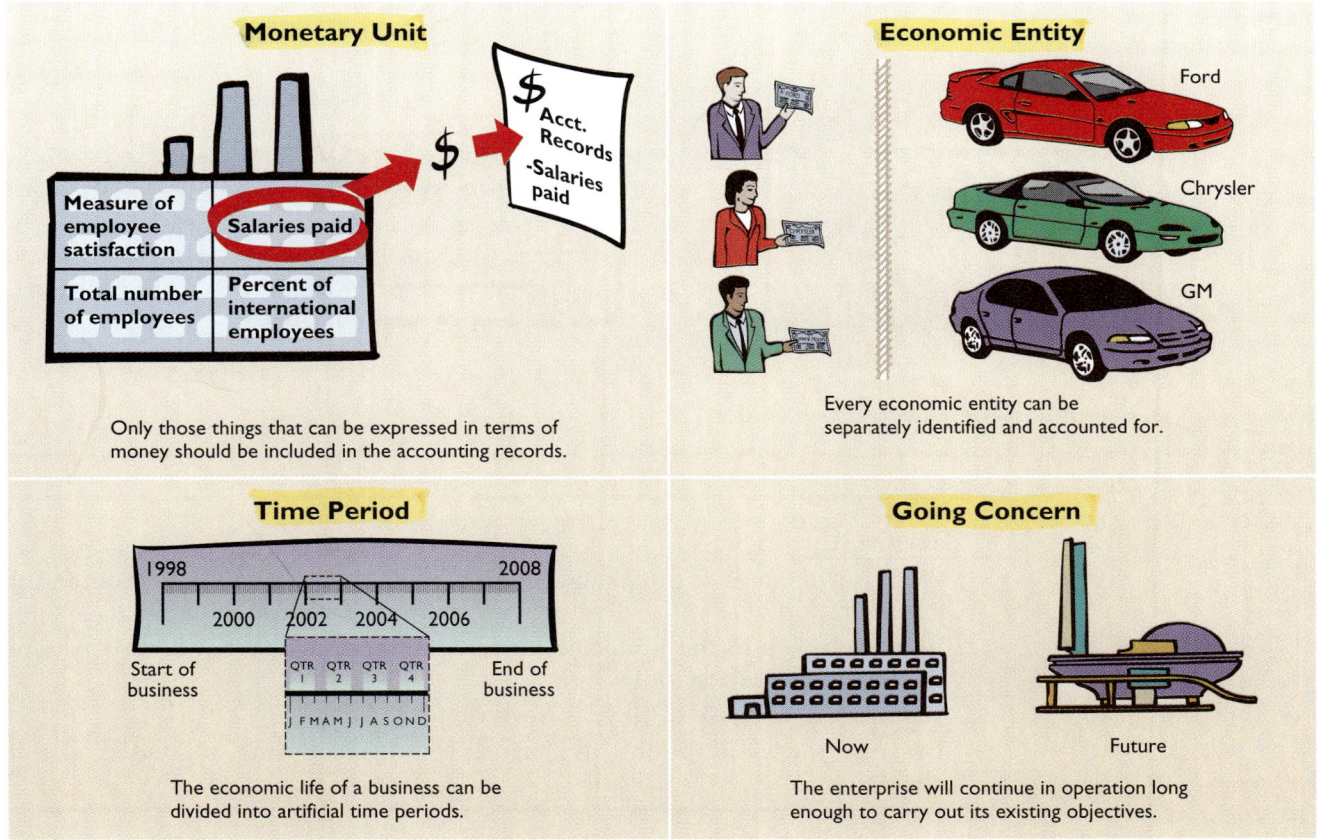

Illustration 1-13
Accounting assumptions

PRINCIPLES

Cost Principle

All of the assets on Starbucks' financial statements are recorded at the amount paid for them. The **cost principle** dictates that assets are recorded at their cost. This is true not only at the time the asset is purchased, but also over the time the asset is held. For example, if Starbucks were to purchase some land for $30,000, it would initially be reported on the balance sheet at $30,000. But what would Starbucks do if, by the end of the next year, the land had increased in value to $40,000? The answer is that under the cost principle the land would continue to be reported at $30,000. The cost principle is often criticized as being irrelevant. Critics contend that market value would be more useful to financial decision makers. Proponents of the cost principle counter that cost is the best measure because it can be easily verified from transactions between two parties, while market value is often subjective.

Helpful Hint Recently, some accounting rules have been changed, requiring that certain assets be recorded at their market value.

Full Disclosure Principle

There is important financial information that is not easily reported on the face of the statements. For example, Starbucks has debt outstanding. Investors and creditors would like to know the terms of the debt; that is, when does it mature, what is its interest rate, and is it renewable? Or Starbucks might be sued by one of its customers. Investors and creditors might not know about this lawsuit. The **full disclosure principle** requires that all circumstances and events that would make a difference to financial statement users should be disclosed. If an important item cannot reasonably be reported directly in one of the four types of financial statements, then it should be discussed in notes that accompany the statements.

These two accounting principles are shown graphically in Illustration 1-14.

Illustration 1-14
Accounting principles

BEFORE YOU GO ON . . .

● **Review It**

1. What is the intent of the management discussion and analysis section in the annual report?
2. Why are notes to the financial statements necessary? What kinds of items are included in these notes?
3. What is the purpose of the auditor's report?
4. Describe the assumptions and principles of accounting addressed in this chapter.

Using the Decision Toolkit

Green Mountain Coffee, located in Vermont, is a roaster of specialty coffees. It recently "went public" (sold its stock to the public). You are considering purchasing some of its stock, thinking that perhaps it will experience the same success as Starbucks.

Instructions

Answer these questions related to your decision whether to invest:

1. What financial statements should you request from the company?

2. What should these financial statements tell you?

3. Should you request audited financial statements? Explain.

4. Will the financial statements show the market value of Green Mountain's assets? Explain.

5. Simplified financial statements for Green Mountain Coffee are shown in Illustrations 1-15 through 1-18. What comparisons can you make between Green Mountain Coffee and Starbucks in terms of their respective results from operations and financial position?

Using the Decision Toolkit exercises, which follow the final set of Review It questions in the chapter, ask you to use information from financial statements to make financial decisions. We encourage you to think through the questions related to the decision before you study the solution.

GREEN MOUNTAIN COFFEE, INC.
Income Statement
For the years ended September 28, 1996, September 30, 1995, and September 24, 1994 (in thousands)

	Sept. 28, 1996	Sept. 30, 1995	Sept. 24, 1994
Net sales	$38,347	$34,024	$22,082
Cost of sales	22,817	21,738	13,513
Gross profit	15,530	12,286	8,569
Selling and operating expenses	10,471	9,529	8,722
General and administrative expenses	3,132	2,578	2,605
Income (loss) from operations	1,927	179	(2,758)
Other income (expense)	(21)	(24)	75
Interest expense	(422)	(399)	(232)
Income (loss) before income taxes	1,484	(244)	(2,915)
Income tax benefit (expense)	(222)	26	557
Net income (loss)	$ 1,262	$ (218)	$(2,358)

Illustration 1-15 Green Mountain Coffee's income statement

Illustration 1-16 Green Mountain Coffee's retained earnings statement

GREEN MOUNTAIN COFFEE, INC.
Retained Earnings Statement
For the years ended September 28, 1996, September 30, 1995,
and September 24, 1994 (in thousands)

Accumulated deficit, September 25, 1993	$(2,663)
Net loss	(2,358)
Accumulated deficit, September 24, 1994	(5,021)
Net loss	(218)
Accumulated deficit, September 30, 1995	(5,239)
Net income	1,262
Accumulated deficit, September 28, 1996	$(3,977)

Illustration 1-17 Green Mountain Coffee's balance sheet

GREEN MOUNTAIN COFFEE, INC.
Balance Sheet
(in thousands)

	Sept. 28, 1996	Sept. 30, 1995
Assets		
Current assets		
Cash and cash equivalents	$ 551	$ 310
Receivables, net	2,778	2,660
Inventories, net	3,276	2,766
Other current assets	1,143	492
Total current assets	7,748	6,228
Fixed assets, net	8,715	8,127
Other long-term assets, net	780	1,210
Total assets	$17,243	$15,565
Liabilities and Stockholders' Equity		
Current liabilities		
Current portion of long-term debt	$ 947	$ 618
Revolving line of credit	508	1,720
Accounts payable	3,002	2,751
Accrued payroll	480	170
Accrued expenses	264	156
Other current liabilities	114	68
Total current liabilities	5,315	5,483
Long-term debt	2,911	2,351
Other long-term obligations	144	209
Total liabilities	8,370	8,043
Stockholders' equity		
Common stock	12,850	12,761
Accumulated deficit	(3,977)	(5,239)
Total stockholders' equity	8,873	7,522
Total liabilities and stockholders' equity	$17,243	$15,565

Using the Decision Toolkit

Illustration 1-18 Green Mountain Coffee's statement of cash flows

GREEN MOUNTAIN COFFEE, INC.
Statement of Cash Flows
For the years ended September 28, 1996, September 30, 1995,
and September 24, 1994 (in thousands)

	Sept. 28, 1996	Sept. 30, 1995	Sept. 24, 1994
Operating activities			
Cash receipts from operating activities	$38,073	$32,700	$21,475
Cash payments for operating activities	34,939	32,405	25,472
Net cash provided by operating activities	3,134	295	(3,997)
Investing activities			
Purchase of property, plant, and equipment	(2,519)	(1,602)	(4,323)
Sale of property, plant, and equipment	59	0	24
Net cash used by investing activities	(2,460)	(1,602)	(4,299)
Financing activities			
Issuance of long-term debt	1,509	286	2,482
Repayment of long-term debt	(729)	(594)	(2,438)
Principal payment under capital lease obligations	(90)	(5)	0
Net change in revolving line of credit	(1,212)	1,720	(1,108)
Repayment of note payable to stockholder	0	(416)	(125)
Issuance of common stock	89	73	9,760
Net cash provided by financing activities	(433)	1,064	8,571
Increase (decrease) in cash and cash equivalents	241	(243)	275
Cash and cash equivalents Beginning of year	310	553	278
End of year	$ 551	$ 310	$ 553

Solution

1. Before you invest, you should investigate the income statement, retained earnings statement, statement of cash flows, and balance sheet.
2. You would probably be most interested in the income statement because it tells about past performance and thus gives an indication of future performance. In addition, the statement of cash flows reveals where the company is getting and spending its cash. This is especially important for a company that wants to grow. Finally, the balance sheet reveals the relationship between assets and liabilities.
3. You would want audited financial statements—statements that a CPA (certified public accountant) has examined and expressed an opinion that the statements present fairly the financial position and results of operations of the company. Investors and creditors should not make decisions without studying audited financial statements.
4. The financial statements will not show the market value of the company. As indicated, one important principle of accounting is the cost principle, which states that assets should be recorded at cost. Cost has an important advantage over other valuations: It is objective and reliable.
5. Many interesting comparisons can be made between the two companies. Green Mountain Coffee is much smaller, with total assets of $17,243,000

versus $726,613,000 for Starbucks. Also, Green Mountain Coffee has lower revenue—net sales of $38,347,000 versus $696,481,000. Green Mountain Coffee has reported net losses (rather than net income) for two of the last three years, although in 1996 it did report net income of $1,262,000. This has resulted in a negative balance (called an accumulated deficit) in its retained earnings account. In 1996 Starbucks generated cash from operating activities of $136,679,000 versus $3,134,000 for Green Mountain Coffee. If you invest in Green Mountain Coffee or loan it money, you are assuming that it will become profitable on a consistent basis. The 1996 increase in net income may, in fact, indicate a bright future—and a potentially valuable investment.

SUMMARY OF STUDY OBJECTIVES

❶ Describe the primary forms of business organization. A sole proprietorship is a business owned by one person. A partnership is a business owned by two or more people. A corporation is a separate legal entity for which evidence of ownership is provided by shares of stock.

❷ Identify the users and uses of accounting. Internal users are managers who need accounting information in planning, controlling, and evaluating business operations. The primary external users are investors and creditors. Investors (stockholders) use accounting information to help them decide whether to buy, hold, or sell shares of a company's stock. Creditors (suppliers and bankers) use accounting information to assess the risk of granting credit or loaning money to a business. Other groups who have an indirect interest in a business are taxing authorities, regulatory agencies, customers, labor unions, and economic planners.

❸ Explain the three principal types of business activity. Financing activities involve collecting the necessary funds to support the business. Investing activities involve acquiring the resources necessary to run the business. Operating activities involve putting the resources of the business into action to generate a profit.

❹ Describe the content and purpose of each of the financial statements. An income statement presents the revenues and expenses of a company for a specific period of time. A retained earnings statement summarizes the changes in retained earnings that have occurred for a specific period of time. A balance sheet reports the assets, liabilities, and stockholders' equity of a business at a specific date. A statement of cash flows summarizes information concerning the cash inflows (receipts) and outflows (payments) for a specific period of time.

❺ Explain the meaning of assets, liabilities, and stockholders' equity, and state the basic accounting equation. Assets are resources owned by a business. Liabilities are the debts and obligations of the business. Liabilities represent claims of creditors on the assets of the business. Stockholders' equity represents the claims of owners on the assets of the business. It is composed of two parts: common stock and retained earnings. The basic accounting equation is: Assets = Liabilities + Stockholders' Equity.

❻ Describe the components that supplement the financial statements in an annual report. The management discussion and analysis provide management's interpretation of the company's results and financial position as well as a discussion of plans for the future. Notes to the financial statements provide additional explanation or detail to make the financial statements more informative. The auditor's report expresses an opinion as to whether the financial statements present fairly the company's results of operations and financial position.

❼ Explain the basic assumptions and principles underlying financial statements. The monetary unit assumption requires that only transaction data capable of being expressed in terms of money be included in the accounting records of the economic entity. The economic entity assumption states that economic events can be identified with a particular unit of accountability. The time period assumption states that the economic life of a business can be divided into artificial time periods and that meaningful accounting reports can be prepared for each period. The going concern assumption states that the enterprise will continue in operation long enough to carry out its existing objectives. The cost principle states that assets should be recorded at their cost. The full disclosure principle dictates that circumstances and events that matter to financial statement users must be disclosed.

Decision Toolkit—A Summary

Decision Checkpoints	Info Needed for Decision	Tool to Use for Decision	How to Evaluate Results
Are the company's operations profitable?	Income statement	The income statement reports on the sucess or failure of the company's operations by reporting its revenues and expenses.	If the company's revenue exceeds its expenses, it will report net income; otherwise it will report a net loss.
What is the company's policy toward dividends and growth?	Retained earnings statement	How much of this year's income did the company pay out in dividends to shareholders?	A company striving for rapid growth will pay a low dividend.
Does the company rely primarily on debt or stockholders' equity to finance its assets?	Balance sheet	The balance sheet reports the company's resources and claims to those resources. There are two types of claims: liabilities and stockholders' equity.	Compare the amount of debt versus the amount of stockholders' equity to determine whether the company relies more on creditors or owners for its financing.
Does the company generate sufficient cash from operations to fund its investing activities?	Statement of cash flows	The statement of cash flows shows the amount of cash provided or used by operating activities, investing activities, and financing activities.	Compare the amount of cash provided by operating activities with the amount of cash used by investing activities. Any deficiency in cash from operating activities must be made up with cash from financing activities.

Glossary

Accounting The process of identifying, recording, and communicating the economic events of a business to interested users of the information. (p. 6)

Annual report A report prepared by corporate management that presents financial information including financial statements, notes, and the management discussion and analysis. (p. 20)

Assets Resources owned by a business. (p. 8)

Auditor's report A report prepared by an independent outside auditor stating the auditor's opinion as to the fairness of the presentation of the financial position and results of operations and their conformance with accepted accounting standards. (p. 21)

Balance sheet A financial statement that reports the assets, liabilities, and stockholders' equity at a specific date. (p. 12)

Basic accounting equation Assets = Liabilities + Stockholders' Equity. (p. 12)

Certified Public Accountant (CPA) An individual who has met certain criteria and is thus allowed to perform audits of corporations. (p. 21)

Common stock Stock representing the primary ownership interest in a corporation. In the balance sheet it represents the amount paid in by stockholders. (p. 8)

Comparative statements A presentation of the financial statements of a company for multiple years. (p. 16)

Corporation A business organized as a separate legal entity having ownership divided into transferable shares of stock. (p. 4)

Cost principle An accounting principle that states that assets should be recorded at their cost. (p. 24)

Dividends Distributions of cash or other assets from a corporation to its stockholders. (p. 8)

Economic entity assumption An assumption that economic events can be identified with a particular unit of accountability. (p. 22)

Expenses The cost of assets consumed or services used in ongoing operations to generate resources. (p. 9)

Full disclosure principle Accounting principle that dictates that circumstances and events that make a difference to financial statement users should be disclosed. (p. 24)

Going concern assumption The assumption that the enterprise will continue in operation long enough to carry out its existing objectives and commitments. (p. 23)

Income statement A financial statement that presents the revenues and expenses and resulting net income or net loss of a company for a specific period of time. (p. 10)

Liabilities The debts and obligations of a business. Liabilities represent claims of creditors on the assets of a business. (p. 8)

Management discussion and analysis (MD&A) A section of the annual report that presents management's views on the company's short-term debt paying ability, expansion, financing, and results. (p. 20)

Monetary unit assumption An assumption stating that only transaction data that can be expressed in terms of money be included in the accounting records of the economic entity. (p. 22)

Net income The amount by which revenues exceed expenses. (p. 9)

Net loss The amount by which expenses exceed revenues. (p. 9)

Notes to the financial statements Notes providing additional details about the items presented in the main body of the financial statements. (p. 20)

Partnership A business owned by more than one person. (p. 4)

Retained earnings The amount of net income kept in the corporation for future use, not distributed to stockholders as dividends. (p. 12)

Retained earnings statement A financial statement that summarizes the changes in retained earnings for a specific period of time. (p. 12)

Revenues The assets that result from the sale of a product or service. (p. 8)

Sole proprietorship A business owned by one person. (p. 4)

Statement of cash flows A financial statement that provides information about the cash inflows (receipts) and cash outflows (payments) for a specific period of time. (p. 13)

Stockholders' equity The stockholders' claim on total assets. (p. 12)

Time period assumption An accounting assumption that the economic life of a business can be divided into artificial time periods. (p. 23)

DEMONSTRATION PROBLEM

Demonstration problems are a final review before you begin homework. Problem-solving strategies that appear in the margins give you tips about how to approach the problem, and the solution provided illustrates both the form and content of complete answers.

Jeff Andringa, a former college hockey player, quit his job and started Ice Camp, a hockey camp for kids ages 8 to 18. Eventually he would like to open hockey camps nationwide. Jeff has asked you to help him prepare financial statements at the end of his first year of operations. He relates the following facts about his business activities.

In order to get the business off the ground, he decided to incorporate. He sold shares of common stock to a few close friends, as well as buying some of the shares himself. He initially raised $25,000 through the sale of these shares. In addition, the company took out a $10,000 loan at a local bank. A bus for transporting kids was purchased for $12,000 cash. Hockey goals and other miscellaneous equipment were purchased with $1,500 cash. The company earned camp tuition during the year of $100,000 but had collected only $80,000 of this amount. Thus, at the end of the year it was still owed $20,000. The company rents time at a local rink for $50 per hour. Total rink rental costs during the year were $8,000, insurance was $10,000, salary expense was $20,000, and administrative expenses totaled $9,000, all of which were paid in cash. The company incurred $800 in interest expense on the bank loan, which it still owed at the end of the year.

The company paid dividends during the year of $5,000 cash. The balance in the corporate bank account at December 31, 1998, was $49,500.

Instructions

Using the format of the Sierra Corporation statements in this chapter, prepare an income statement, retained earnings statement, balance sheet, and statement of cash flows. [*Hint:* Prepare the statements in the order stated to take advantage of the flow of information from one statement to the next, as shown in Illustration 1-4.]

Solution to Demonstration Problem

ICE CAMP
Income Statement
For the Year Ended December 31, 1998

Revenues		
Camp tuition revenue		$100,000
Expenses		
Salaries expense	$20,000	
Rink rental expense	8,000	
Insurance expense	10,000	
Administrative expense	9,000	
Interest expense	800	
Total expenses		47,800
Net income		$ 52,200

ICE CAMP
Retained Earnings Statement
For the Year Ended December 31, 1998

Retained earnings, January 1, 1998	$ 0
Add: Net income	52,200
	52,200
Less: Dividends	5,000
Retained earnings, December 31, 1998	$ 47,200

ICE CAMP
Balance Sheet
December 31, 1998

Assets

Cash	$ 49,500
Accounts receivable	20,000
Bus	12,000
Equipment	1,500
Total assets	$ 83,000

Liabilities and Stockholders' Equity

Liabilities		
Bank loan payable		$ 10,000
Interest payable		800
Total liabilities		10,800
Stockholders' equity		
Common stock		25,000
Retained earnings		47,200
Total stockholders' equity		72,200
Total liabilities and stockholders' equity		$ 83,000

Problem-Solving Strategies

1. The income statement shows revenues and expenses for a period of time.
2. The retained earnings statement shows the changes in retained earnings for a period of time.
3. The balance sheet reports assets, liabilities, and stockholders' equity at a specific date.
4. The statement of cash flows reports sources and uses of cash from operating, investing, and financing activities for a period of time.

ICE CAMP
Statement of Cash Flows
For the Year Ended December 31, 1998

Cash flows from operating activities	
Cash receipts from operating activities	$80,000
Cash payments for operating activities	(47,000)
Net cash provided by operating activities	33,000
Cash flows from investing activities	
Purchase of bus	(12,000)
Purchase of equipment	(1,500)
Net cash used by investing activities	(13,500)
Cash flows from financing activities	
Issuance of bank loan payable	10,000
Issuance of common stock	25,000
Dividends paid	(5,000)
Net cash provided by financing activities	30,000
Net increase in cash	49,500
Cash at beginning of period	0
Cash at end of period	$49,500

This would be a good time to return to the **Student Owner's Manual** at the beginning of the book (or look at it for the first time if you skipped it before) to read about the various types of homework materials that appear at the ends of chapters. Knowing the purpose of the different assignments will help you appreciate what each contributes to your accounting skills and competencies.

The tool icon indicates that an instructional activity employs one of the decision tools presented in the chapter.

The pencil icon indicates that an instructional activity requires written communication by the student.

SELF-STUDY QUESTIONS

Answers are at the end of the chapter.

(SO 1) 1. Which is *not* one of the three forms of business organization?
  (a) Sole proprietorship
  (b) Creditorship
  (c) Partnership
  (d) Corporation

(SO 1) 2. Which is an advantage of corporations relative to partnerships and sole proprietorships?
  (a) Lower taxes
  (b) Harder to transfer ownership
  (c) Reduced legal liability for investors
  (d) Most common form of organization

(SO 3) 3. Which is *not* one of the three primary business activities?
  (a) Financing
  (b) Operating
  (c) Selling
  (d) Investing

(SO 4) 4. Which statement about users of accounting information is *incorrect*?
  (a) Management is considered an internal user.
  (b) Taxing authorities are considered external users.
  (c) Present creditors are considered external users.
  (d) Regulatory authorities are considered internal users.

(SO 4) 5. Net income will result during a time period when:
  (a) assets exceed liabilities.
  (b) assets exceed revenues.
  (c) expenses exceed revenues.
  (d) revenues exceed expenses.

(SO 4) 6. What section of a cash flow statement indicates the cash spent on new equipment during the past accounting period?
  (a) The investing section
  (b) The operating section
  (c) The financing section
  (d) The cash flow statement does not give this information.

(SO 4) 7. Which financial statement reports assets, liabilities, and stockholders' equity?
  (a) Income statement
  (b) Retained earnings statement
  (c) Balance sheet
  (d) Statement of cash flows

(SO 5) 8. As of December 31, 1998, Stoneland Corporation has assets of $3,500 and stockholders' equity of $2,000. What are the liabilities for Stoneland Corporation as of December 31, 1998?
(a) $1,500 (c) $2,500
(b) $1,000 (d) $2,000

(SO 6) 9. The segment of a corporation's annual report that describes the corporation's accounting methods is the:
(a) notes to the financial statements.
(b) management discussion and analysis.
(c) auditor's report.
(d) income statement.

(SO 7) 10. The cost principle states that:
(a) assets should be recorded at cost and adjusted when the market value changes.
(b) activities of an entity should be kept separate and distinct from its owner.
(c) assets should be recorded at their cost.
(d) only transaction data capable of being expressed in terms of money should be included in the accounting records.

11. Valuing assets at their market value rather than at their cost is inconsistent with the: (SO 7)
(a) time period assumption.
(b) economic entity assumption.
(c) cost principle.
(d) All of the above

QUESTIONS

1. What are the three basic forms of business organizations?
2. What are the advantages to a business of being formed as a corporation? What are the disadvantages?
3. What are the advantages to a business of being formed as a partnership or sole proprietorship? What are the disadvantages?
4. What are the three main types of business activity? Give examples of each activity.
5. "Accounting is ingrained in our society and is vital to our economic system." Do you agree? Explain.
6. Who are the internal users of accounting data? How does accounting provide relevant data to the internal users?
7. Who are the external users of accounting data? Give examples.
8. What is the basic accounting equation?
9. What purpose does the going concern assumption serve?
10. Sue Leonard is president of Better Books. She has no accounting background. Leonard cannot understand why market value is not used as the basis for accounting measurement and reporting. Explain what basis is used and why.
11. (a) Define the terms *assets, liabilities,* and *stockholders' equity.*
    (b) What items affect stockholders' equity?
12. Which of these items are liabilities of Kool-Jewelry Stores?
    (a) Cash (f) Equipment
    (b) Accounts payable (g) Salaries payable
    (c) Dividends (h) Service revenue
    (d) Accounts receivable (i) Rent expense
    (e) Supplies
13. Listed here are some items found in the financial statements of Ruth Weber, Inc. Indicate in which financial statement(s) each item would appear.
    (a) Service revenue (d) Accounts receivable
    (b) Equipment (e) Common stock
    (c) Advertising expense (f) Wages payable
14. In February 1998 Paul Jonas invested an additional $10,000 in his business, Jonas's Pharmacy, which is organized as a corporation. Jonas's accountant recorded this receipt as an increase in cash and revenues. Is this treatment appropriate? Why or why not?
15. "A company's net income appears directly on the income statement and the retained earnings statement, and it is included indirectly in the company's balance sheet." Do you agree? Explain.
16. Hernandez Enterprises had a stockholders' equity balance of $158,000 at the beginning of the period. At the end of the accounting period, the balance was $198,000.
    (a) Assuming no additional issuances of common stock or payment of dividends during the period, what is the net income for the period?
    (b) Assuming no additional issue of common stock but dividends of $13,000 during the period, what is the net income for the period?
17. What is the purpose of the statement of cash flows?
18. What are the three main categories of the statement of cash flows? Why do you think these categories were chosen?
19. What is retained earnings? What items increase the balance in retained earnings? What items decrease the balance in retained earnings?
20. What is the importance of the economic entity assumption? Give an example of its violation.
21. What is the purpose of the management discussion and analysis (MD&A)?
22. Why is it important for financial statements to receive an unqualified auditor's opinion?
23. What types of information are presented in the notes to the financial statements?
24. Starbucks' year-end is not a fixed date; rather it can vary slightly from one year to the next. What possible problems does this pose for financial statement users?

BRIEF EXERCISES

Classify various items.
(SO 3)

BE1-1 Classify each of the following items as dividends (D), revenue (R), or expense (E).
(a) Costs incurred for advertising
(b) Assets received for services performed
(c) Costs incurred for insurance
(d) Amounts paid to employees
(e) Cash distributed to stockholders
(f) Assets received in exchange for allowing the use of our building
(g) Costs incurred for utilities used

Classify items by activity.
(SO 3)

BE1-2 Indicate in which part of the statement of cash flows each item would appear: operating activities (O), investing activities (I), or financing activities (F).
(a) Cash received from customers
(b) Cash paid to stockholders (dividends)
(c) Cash received from issuing new common stock
(d) Cash paid to suppliers
(e) Cash paid to purchase a new office building

Determine effect of transactions on stockholders' equity.
(SO 4)

BE1-3 Presented below are three transactions. Determine whether each transaction affects common stock (C), dividends (D), revenue (R), expense (E), or does not affect stockholders' equity (NSE).
(a) Paid cash to purchase equipment
(b) Received cash for services performed
(c) Paid employee salaries

Prepare a balance sheet.
(SO 4)

BE1-4 In alphabetical order below are balance sheet items for Gidget Company at December 31, 1998. Prepare a balance sheet following the format of Illustration 1-4.

Accounts payable	$90,000
Accounts receivable	$81,000
Cash	$40,500
Common stock	$31,500

Determine where items appear on financial statements.
(SO 4)

BE1-5 Indicate where each item would appear: on the income statement (IS), the balance sheet (BS), or the retained earnings statement (RE).
(a) Notes payable   (d) Cash
(b) Advertising expense   (e) Service revenue
(c) Common stock

Determine proper financial statement.
(SO 4)

BE1-6 Indicate which statement you would examine to find each of the following items: income statement (I), balance sheet (B), retained earnings statement (R), or statement of cash flows (C).
(a) Revenue during the period
(b) Supplies on hand at the end of the year
(c) Cash received from issuing new bonds during the period
(d) Total debts outstanding at the end of the period

Use basic accounting equation.
(SO 5)

BE1-7 Use the basic accounting equation to determine the missing amounts.

Assets	= Liabilities	+ Stockholders' Equity
$90,000	$50,000	(a)
(b)	$48,000	$70,000
$94,000	(c)	$72,000

Use basic accounting equation.
(SO 5)

BE1-8 Use the basic accounting equation to answer these questions:
(a) The liabilities of Hogan Company are $90,000 and the stockholders' equity is $240,000. What is the amount of Hogan Company's total assets?
(b) The total assets of Potter Company are $170,000 and its stockholders' equity is $90,000. What is the amount of its total liabilities?
(c) The total assets of Barren Co. are $700,000 and its liabilities are equal to half of its total assets. What is the amount of Barren Co.'s stockholders' equity?

BE1-9 At the beginning of the year, Lamson Company had total assets of $700,000 and total liabilities of $500,000.
(a) If total assets increased $150,000 during the year and total liabilities decreased $80,000, what is the amount of stockholders' equity at the end of the year?
(b) During the year, total liabilities increased $100,000 and stockholders' equity decreased $70,000. What is the amount of total assets at the end of the year?
(c) If total assets decreased $90,000 and stockholders' equity increased $110,000 during the year, what is the amount of total liabilities at the end of the year?

Use basic accounting equation.
(SO 5)

BE1-10 Indicate whether each of these items is an asset (A), a liability (L), or part of stockholders' equity (SE).
(a) Accounts receivable   (d) Office supplies
(b) Salaries payable   (e) Common stock
(c) Equipment   (f) Notes payable

Identify assets, liabilities, and stockholders' equity.
(SO 5)

BE1-11 Which is *not* a required part of an annual report of a publicly traded company?
(a) Statement of cash flows
(b) Notes to the financial statements
(c) Management discussion and analysis
(d) All of these are required.

Determine required part of annual report.
(SO 6)

BE1-12 The full disclosure principle dictates that:
(a) financial statements should disclose all assets at their cost.
(b) financial statements should disclose only those events that can be measured in dollars.
(c) financial statements should disclose all events and circumstances that would matter to users of financial statements.
(d) financial statements should not be relied on unless an auditor has expressed an unqualified opinion on them.

Define full disclosure principle.
(SO 7)

EXERCISES

E1-1 Here is a list of words or phrases discussed in this chapter:
1. Accounts payable   5. Corporation
2. Creditor   6. Common stock
3. Stockholder   7. Accounts receivable
4. Partnership   8. Auditor's opinion

Match words with descriptions.
(SO 1, 2, 4, 6)

Instructions
Match each word or phrase with the best description of it.
_____ (a) An expression about whether financial statements are presented in a reasonable fashion
_____ (b) A business enterprise that raises money by issuing shares of stock
_____ (c) The portion of stockholders' equity that results from receiving cash from investors
_____ (d) Obligations to suppliers of goods
_____ (e) Amounts due from customers
_____ (f) A party to whom a business owes money
_____ (g) A party that invests in common stock
_____ (h) A business that is owned jointly by two or more individuals but that does not issue stock

E1-2 This information relates to Tone Kon Co. for the year 1998:

Retained earnings, January 1, 1998	$45,000
Advertising expense	1,800
Dividends paid during 1998	5,000
Rent expense	10,400
Service revenue	50,000
Utilities expense	3,100
Salaries expense	28,000

Prepare income statement and retained earnings statement.
(SO 4)

36 CHAPTER 1 Introduction to Financial Statements

Instructions
After analyzing the data, prepare an income statement and a retained earnings statement for the year ending December 31, 1998.

Correct an incorrectly prepared balance sheet.
(SO 4)

E1-3 Kit Lucas is the bookkeeper for Aurora Company. Kit has been trying to get this balance sheet of Aurora Company to balance. It finally balanced, but now he's not sure it is correct.

AURORA COMPANY
Balance Sheet
December 31, 1998

Assets		Liabilities and Stockholders' Equity	
Cash	$16,500	Accounts payable	$20,000
Supplies	8,000	Accounts receivable	(10,000)
Equipment	46,000	Common stock	50,000
Dividends	7,000	Retained earnings	17,500
Total assets	$77,500	Total liabilities and stockholders' equity	$77,500

Instructions
Prepare a correct balance sheet.

Compute net income and prepare a balance sheet.
(SO 4)

E1-4 Deer Park Inc. is a public camping ground near the Lake Mead National Recreation Area. It has compiled the following financial information as of December 31, 1998:

Revenues during 1998: camping fees	$147,000	Market value of equipment	$140,000
Revenues during 1998: general store	40,000	Notes payable	60,000
Accounts payable	11,000	Expenses during 1998	152,000
Cash on hand	7,000	Supplies on hand	2,500
Original cost of equipment	115,500	Common stock	50,000
		Retained earnings	?

Instructions
(a) Determine net income from Deer Park Inc. for 1998.
(b) Prepare a balance sheet for Deer Park Inc. as of December 31, 1998.

Prepare an income statement.
(SO 4)

E1-5 The financial information below relates to the 1998 operations of Duchess Cruise Company:

Maintenance expense	$ 90,000	Advertising expense	$ 3,500
Property tax expense (on dock facilities)	10,000	Ticket revenue	325,000
Salaries expense	142,000		

Instructions
Prepare the 1998 income statement for Duchess Cruise Company.

Prepare a retained earnings statement.
(SO 4)

E1-6 Presented here is information for Grace Olsen Inc.:

Retained earnings, January 1, 1998	$150,000
Revenue from legal services—1998	380,000
Total expenses—1998	205,000
Dividends—1998	76,000

Instructions
Prepare the 1998 retained earnings statement for Grace Olsen Inc.

Interpret financial facts.
(SO 4)

E1-7 Consider each of the following independent situations.

(a) The retained earnings statement of Megan Corporation shows dividends of $70,000, while net income for the year was $75,000.
(b) The statement of cash flows for Nick Corporation shows that cash provided by operating activities was $10,000, cash used in investing activities was $110,000, and cash provided by financing activities was $130,000.

Instructions
For each company provide a brief discussion interpreting these financial facts. For example, you might discuss the company's financial health or its apparent growth philosophy.

E1-8 This information is for James Kirk Corporation for 1998:

Cash received from customers	$50,000
Cash dividends paid	2,000
Cash paid to suppliers	20,000
Cash paid for new equipment	40,000
Cash received from lenders	20,000

Prepare a statement of cash flows.
(SO 4)

Instructions
Prepare the 1998 statement of cash flows for James Kirk Corporation.

E1-9 Here are incomplete financial statements for Baxter, Inc.:

Calculate missing amounts.
(SO 4)

BAXTER, INC.
Balance Sheet

Assets		Liabilities and Stockholders' Equity	
Cash	$ 5,000	Liabilities	
Inventory	10,000	Accounts payable	$ 7,000
Building	50,000	Stockholders' equity	
Total assets	$65,000	Common stock	(a)
		Retained earnings	(b)
		Total liabilities and stockholders' equity	$65,000

Income Statement

Revenues	$80,000
Cost of goods sold	(c)
Administrative expenses	10,000
Net income	$ (d)

Retained Earnings Statement

Beginning retained earnings	$10,000
Net income	(e)
Dividends	5,000
Ending retained earnings	$25,000

Instructions
Calculate the missing amounts.

E1-10 Ace Cleaners Corporation has nine balance sheet items.

Classify items as assets, liabilities, and stockholders' equity.
(SO 5)

Instructions
Classify each of these items as an asset, liability, or stockholders' equity.
(a) Accounts payable (f) Notes payable
(b) Cash (g) Salaries payable
(c) Cleaning equipment (h) Common stock
(d) Cleaning supplies (i) Retained earnings
(e) Accounts receivable

E1-11 The annual report provides financial information in a variety of formats including the following:

Classify various items in an annual report.
(SO 6)

Management discussion and analysis (MD&A)
Financial statements
Notes to the financial statements
Auditor's opinion

Instructions
For each of the following, state in what area of the annual report the item would be presented. If the item would probably not be found in an annual report, state "not disclosed."

38   **CHAPTER 1**   Introduction to Financial Statements

(a) Total revenue from operating activities
(b) An independent assessment concerning whether the financial statements present a fair depiction of the company's results and financial position
(c) Management's assessment of the company's results
(d) The interest rate the company is being charged on all outstanding debts
(e) The total cumulative amount received from stockholders in exchange for common stock
(f) The names and positions of all employees hired in the last year

Identify accounting assumptions and principles.
(SO 7)

E1-12 Presented below are the assumptions and principles discussed in this chapter:
1. Full disclosure principle
2. Cost principle
3. Monetary unit assumption
4. Time period assumption
5. Going concern assumption
6. Economic entity assumption

Instructions
Identify by number the accounting assumption or principle that is described below. Do not use a number more than once.
_____ (a) Is the rationale for why plant assets are not reported at liquidation value [*Note:* Do not use the cost principle.]
_____ (b) Indicates that personal and business record-keeping should be separately maintained
_____ (c) Assumes that the dollar is the "measuring stick" used to report on financial performance
_____ (d) Separates financial information into time periods for reporting purpose
_____ (e) Indicates that market value changes subsequent to purchase are not recorded in the accounts
_____ (f) Dictates that all circumstances and events that make a difference to financial statement users should be disclosed

Identify the assumption or principle that has been violated.
(SO 7)

E1-13 Marietta Co. had three major business transactions during 1998:
(a) Merchandise inventory with a cost of $208,000 is reported at its market value of $260,000.
(b) The president of Marietta Co., George Winston, purchased a truck for personal use and charged it to his expense account.
(c) Marietta Co. wanted to make its 1998 income look better, so it added 2 more weeks to the year (a 54-week year). Previous years were 52 weeks.

Instructions
In each situation, identify the assumption or principle that has been violated, if any, and discuss what should have been done.

PROBLEMS

Prepare an income statement, retained earnings statement, and balance sheet.
(SO 4)

P1-1 On June 1 Glamor Cosmetics Co. was started with an initial investment in the company of $26,200 cash. Here are the assets and liabilities of the company at June 30, and the revenues and expenses for the month of June:

Cash	$11,000	Notes payable	$13,000
Accounts receivable	4,000	Accounts payable	1,200
Service revenue	6,500	Supplies expense	1,200
Cosmetic supplies	2,400	Gas and oil expense	800
Advertising expense	500	Utilities expense	300
Equipment	25,000		

The company issued no additional stock during June, but dividends of $1,700 were paid during the month.

Instructions
Prepare an income statement and a retained earnings statement for the month of June and a balance sheet at June 30, 1998.

P1-2 Presented below is selected financial information for Maison Corporation for December 31, 1998:

Inventory	$ 25,000
Cash paid to suppliers	80,000
Building	200,000
Common stock	50,000
Cash dividends paid	5,000
Cash paid to purchase equipment	15,000
Equipment	40,000
Revenues	100,000
Cash received from customers	90,000

Determine items included in a statement of cash flows and prepare.
(SO 4)

Instructions
Determine which items should be included in a statement of cash flows and then prepare the statement for Maison Corporation.

P1-3 GB Corporation was formed on January 1, 1998. At December 31, 1998, Guy Baker, the president and sole stockholder, decided to prepare a balance sheet, which appeared as follows:

Comment on proper accounting treatment and prepare a corrected balance sheet.
(SO 4)

GB CORPORATION
Balance Sheet
December 31, 1998

Assets		Liabilities and Stockholders' Equity	
Cash	$30,000	Accounts payable	$ 40,000
Accounts receivable	50,000	Notes payable	15,000
Inventory	20,000	Boat loan	10,000
Boat	15,000	Stockholders' equity	115,000

Guy Baker willingly admits that he is not an accountant by training. He is concerned that his balance sheet might not be correct. He has provided you with the following additional information:
1. The boat actually belongs to Guy Baker, not to GB Corporation. However, because he thinks he might take customers out on the boat occasionally, he decided to list it as an asset of the company. To be consistent he also listed as a liability of the corporation his personal loan that he took out at the bank to buy the boat.
2. The inventory was originally purchased for $10,000, but due to a surge in demand Baker now thinks he could sell it for $20,000. He thought it would be best to record it at $20,000.
3. Included in the accounts receivable balance is $5,000 that Guy Baker loaned to his brother 5 years ago. Guy included this in the receivables of GB Corporation so he wouldn't forget that his brother owes him money.

Instructions
(a) Comment on the proper accounting treatment of the three items above.
(b) Provide a corrected balance sheet for GB Corporation.

ALTERNATIVE PROBLEMS

P1-1A Aero Flying School was started on May 1 with an investment of $45,000 cash. Following are the assets and liabilities of the company on May 31, 1998, and the revenues and expenses for the month of May:

Prepare an income statement, retained earnings statement, and balance sheet.
(SO 4)

Cash	$ 7,800	Notes payable	$30,000
Accounts receivable	7,200	Rent expense	1,200
Equipment	64,000	Repair expense	400
Service revenue	9,600	Fuel expense	2,200
Advertising expense	500	Insurance expense	400
Accounts payable	800		

40 CHAPTER 1 Introduction to Financial Statements

No additional common stock was issued in May, but a dividend of $1,700 in cash was paid.

Instructions
Prepare an income statement and a retained earnings statement for the month of May and a balance sheet at May 31, 1998.

Determine items included in a statement of cash flows and prepare.
(SO 4)

P1-2A Presented below are selected financial statement items for Kennedy Corporation for December 31, 1998:

Inventory	$ 55,000
Cash paid to suppliers	70,000
Building	400,000
Common stock	20,000
Cash dividends paid	8,000
Cash paid to purchase equipment	15,000
Equipment	40,000
Revenues	200,000
Cash received from customers	120,000

Instructions
Determine which items should be included in a statement of cash flows, and then prepare the statement for Kennedy Corporation.

Comment on proper accounting treatment and prepare a corrected income statement.
(SO 4)

P1-3A Kettle Corporation was formed during 1998 by Pam Bollinger. Pam is the president and sole stockholder. At December 31, 1999, Pam prepared an income statement for Kettle Corporation. Pam is not an accountant, but she thinks she did a reasonable job preparing the income statement by looking at the financial statements of other companies. She has asked you for advice. Pam's income statement appears as follows:

KETTLE CORPORATION
Income Statement
For the Year Ended December 31, 1999

Accounts receivable	$10,000
Revenue	60,000
Rent expense	20,000
Insurance expense	3,000
Vacation expense	2,000
Net income	45,000

Pam has also provided you with these facts:
1. Included in the revenue account is $5,000 of revenue that the company earned and received payment for in 1998. She forgot to include it in the 1998 income statement, so she put it in this year's statement.
2. Pam operates her business out of the basement of her parents' home. They do not charge her anything, but she thinks that if she paid rent it would cost her about $20,000 per year. She therefore included $20,000 of rent expense in the statement.
3. To reward herself for a year of hard work, Pam went to Hawaii. She did not use company funds to pay for the trip, but she reported it as an expense on the income statement, since it was her job that made her need the vacation.

Instructions
(a) Comment on the proper accounting treatment of the three items above.
(b) Prepare a corrected income statement for Kettle Corporation.

BROADENING YOUR PERSPECTIVE

FINANCIAL REPORTING AND ANALYSIS

FINANCIAL REPORTING PROBLEM: *Starbucks Corporation*

BYP1-1 The actual financial statements of Starbucks Corporation as presented in the company's 1996 annual report are given in Illustrations 1-6 through 1-9.

Instructions

Refer to Starbucks' financial statements to answer these questions:
(a) What were Starbucks' total assets at September 29, 1996? At October 1, 1995?
(b) How much cash (and cash equivalents) did Starbucks have on September 29, 1996?
(c) What amount of accounts payable did Starbucks report on September 29, 1996? On October 1, 1995?
(d) What were Starbucks' net sales in 1994? In 1995? In 1996?
(e) What is the amount of the change in Starbucks' net income from 1995 to 1996?
(f) The accounting equation is: Assets = Liabilities + Stockholders' Equity. Replacing the words in that equation with dollar amounts, give Starbucks' accounting equation at September 29, 1996.

COMPARATIVE ANALYSIS PROBLEM: *Starbucks vs. Green Mountain Coffee*

BYP1-2 The financial statements of Green Mountain Coffee are presented in Illustrations 1-15 through 1-18, and Starbucks' financial statements are presented in Illustrations 1-6 through 1-9.

Instructions

(a) Based on the information in these financial statements, determine the following for each company.
   (1) Total assets at September 29, 1996 (Starbucks) and September 28, 1996 (Green Mountain Coffee)
   (2) Accounts receivable September 29, 1996 (Starbucks) and September 28, 1996 (Green Mountain Coffee)
   (3) Net sales for 1996
   (4) Net income for 1996
(b) What conclusions concerning the two companies can you draw from these data?

RESEARCH CASES

BYP1-3 *The Wall Street Journal* (WSJ), published weekdays by Dow Jones & Company, Inc., is a premier source of business information.

Instructions

Examine a recent copy of the WSJ and answer these questions:
(a) How many separate sections are in the WSJ? What are the contents of each section?
(b) An index of the companies referenced in each edition is given on page 2 of section B. Select a company from the index and read the associated article. What is the article about? Identify any accounting-related issues discussed in the article.

BYP1-4 Most libraries have company annual reports on file or available on microfiche.

Instructions

Obtain copies of the financial statements of two companies and answer these questions:
(a) What were the total assets, total liabilities, and total stockholders' equity at the most recent balance sheet date?
(b) Mathematically demonstrate that the basic accounting equation holds for each company.
(c) Who was the auditor of each company?
(d) What were the net sales (or revenue) and net income in the most recent income statement?

INTERPRETING FINANCIAL STATEMENTS

BYP1-5 Minicase *Med/Waste, Inc.*

Med/Waste, Inc., provides commercial cleaning and medical waste disposal services to hospitals and other large health care providers, primarily in the state of Florida. In its 1995 statement of cash flows, Med/Waste showed increases in cash from investing and financing activities and a net decrease in cash from operations. The largest sources of cash were the sale of investments and the repayment of a loan to a director.

Instructions
Answer these questions:
(a) What concerns might a creditor of Med/Waste have about this information reported in the statement of cash flows? What additional information might a creditor seek to confirm or reduce these concerns?
(b) Would an investor view this information from the statement of cash flows as negative or positive if the overall cash position improved? Explain.

CRITICAL THINKING

MANAGEMENT DECISION CASE

BYP1-6
Kelly Services, Inc., is a service company that provides personnel for temporary positions, primarily nontechnical. When a company requests assistance, Kelly matches the qualifications of its standby personnel with the requirements of the position. The companies pay Kelly Services; Kelly Services, in turn, pays the employees.

In a recent annual report, Kelly Services chronicled its contributions to community services over the past 30 years, or so. The following excerpts illustrate the variety of services provided:

1. KellyWeek, a Saint Patrick's Day customer appreciation event, originated in California. Kelly Services made donations of stationery, office decorations, and decals containing the company's name.
2. In support of Lady Bird Johnson's "Keep America Beautiful" campaign in the 1960s, the company donated, and its employees planted, gladiola gardens in cities across the United States.
3. The company initiated a holiday drawing in which thousands of customers throughout the United States and Canada nominate their favorite children's charities. Winning charities in the drawing receive a monetary donation from Kelly Services in the name of the customer.
4. KellyWeek was expanded by making donations of temporary help.
5. Kelly executives regularly volunteer their time and resources to serve as role models and mentors to youth in the Detroit area.

Instructions
Answer these questions:
(a) The economic entity assumption requires that a company keep the personal expenses of its employees separate from business expenses. Which of the activities listed above were expenses of the business, and which were personal expenses of the employees? Be specific. If part of the donation is business and part is personal, note which part is each.
(b) For those items that were company expenses, tell whether the expense was probably categorized as an advertising expense, employee wages expense, grounds maintenance expense, or charitable contribution expense. You may use any or all of the categories. Explain your answer.

A REAL-WORLD FOCUS: *Air Transportation Holding Company Inc.*

BYP1-7
Founded in 1980, **Air Transportation Holding Company** operates contract cargo shipping, specializing in small overnight deliveries throughout the eastern United States. The company flies approximately 80 routes, as specified in its contracts with Federal Express. It has hangars and maintenance facilities in North Carolina, Michigan, and South Carolina.

The specific assets, liabilities, and subdivisions of stockholders' equity of any business depend on the type of business being operated. Management of Air Transportation Holding Company explained the year's results of operations as follows: Operating expenses increased $5,498,000 (29.9%) to $23,904,000 for 1993 compared to 1992. The increase in operating expenses consisted of the following changes: Cost of flight operations increased $2,313,000 (25.7%) as a result of increases in pilot and flight personnel and costs associated with travel and landing fees, which were partially offset by decreased aircraft lease and fuel costs; maintenance expense increased $2,850,000 (42.9%) primarily as a result of increases in aircraft parts purchases and mechanic and maintenance personnel costs (due to start-up of satellite maintenance facility and the operation of additional aircraft); the general and administrative expense increase of $470,000 (17.3%) resulted from increases in operational and clerical staffing related to expansion of the aircraft fleet operated.

Instructions
(a) Recall the definition of an asset. Identify three specific types of assets owned by Air Transportation Holding Company.
(b) The preceding discussion is largely about the operating expenses of the company. Identify five expenses of operations that Air Transportation incurs.
(c) When this company renders service by providing air transportation, what stockholders' equity item is increased?

GROUP ACTIVITY

BYP1-8 Mary Company had these amounts:

Rent expense	$ 800	Utilities expense	$ 300
Notes payable	700	Accounts receivable	2,000
Cash	10,500	Telephone expense	100
Common stock	60,000	Accounts payable	3,000
Salaries expense	500	Equipment	103,000
Revenue	3,500	Retained earnings, July 1	50,000

Instructions
Your instructor will divide the class into groups of five or six students. When you are told to begin, prepare Mary Company's income statement, retained earnings statement, and balance sheet for July 31. The first group to finish with the correct statements wins!

COMMUNICATION ACTIVITY

BYP1-9 Amy Joan is the bookkeeper for Vermont Company, Inc. Amy has been trying to get the company's balance sheet to balance. She finally got it to balance, but she still isn't sure that it is correct.

VERMONT COMPANY, INC.
Balance Sheet
For the Month Ended December 31, 1998

Assets		Liabilities and Stockholders' Equity	
Equipment	$20,500	Common stock	$11,000
Cash	9,000	Accounts receivable	(3,000)
Supplies	2,000	Dividends	(2,000)
Accounts payable	(5,000)	Notes payable	10,500
Total assets	$26,500	Retained earnings	10,000
		Total liabilities and stockholders' equity	$26,500

Instructions
Explain to Amy Joan in a memo why the balance sheet is incorrect and what she should do to correct it.

ETHICS CASE

BYP1-10 After numerous campus interviews, Joe Catmus, a senior at Great Eastern College, received two office interview invitations from the Baltimore offices of two large firms. Both firms offered to cover his out-of-pocket expenses (travel, hotel, and meals). Joe scheduled the interviews for both firms on the same day, one in the morning and one in the afternoon. At the conclusion of each interview, he submitted to both firms his total out-of-pocket expenses for the trip to Baltimore: mileage $70 (280 miles at $.25), hotel $120, meals $36, and parking and tolls $18, for a total of $244. He believes this approach is appropriate. If he had made two trips, his cost would have been two times $244. He is also certain that neither firm knew he had visited the other on that same trip. Within 10 days Joe received two checks in the mail, each in the amount of $244.

Instructions
(a) Who are the stakeholders (affected parties) in this situation?
(b) What are the ethical issues?
(c) What would you do in this case?

FINANCIAL ANALYSIS ON THE WEB

BYP1-11 *Purpose:* Identify summary information about companies. This information includes basic descriptions of the company's location, activities, industry, financial health, and financial performance.

Address: http://biz.yahoo.com/i

Steps:
1. Choose **Company.**
2. Type in a company name, or use index to find company name.
3. Choose **Profile.** Perform instructions (a)–(c) below.
4. Click on the company's specific industry to identify competitors. Perform instructions (d)–(g) below.

Instructions
Answer the following questions:
(a) What was the company's net income?
(b) What was the company's total sales?
(c) What is the company's industry?
(d) What are the names of four of the company's competitors?
(e) Choose one of these competitors.
(f) What is this competitor's name? What were its sales? What was its net income?
(g) Which of these two companies is larger by size of sales? Which one reported higher net income?

Answers to Self-Study Questions
1. b 2. c 3. c 4. d 5. d 6. a 7. c 8. a 9. a 10. c
11. c

CHAPTER 2

A Further Look at Financial Statements

STUDY OBJECTIVES

After studying this chapter, you should be able to:

1. Explain the meaning of generally accepted accounting principles and describe the basic objective of financial reporting.
2. Discuss the qualitative characteristics of accounting information.
3. Identify the two constraints in accounting.
4. Distinguish between a single-step and a multiple-step income statement.
5. Identify and compute ratios for analyzing a company's profitability.
6. Explain the relationship between a retained earnings statement and a statement of stockholders' equity.
7. Identify the sections of a classified balance sheet.
8. Identify and compute ratios for analyzing a company's liquidity and solvency.
9. Identify the sections of the statement of cash flows and the purpose of each.

Just Fooling Around?

The information superhighway added a new lane recently when two brothers, Tom and David Gardner, created an online investor service called the Motley Fool. The name comes from Shakespeare's *As You Like It*. The brothers note that the fool in Shakespeare's plays was the only one who could speak unpleasant truths to kings and queens without being killed. Tom and David view themselves as 20th-century "fools," revealing the "truths" of Wall Street to the small investor, who they feel has been taken advantage of by Wall Street insiders. They provide a bulletin board service where America Online subscribers can exchange information and insights about companies that may be of interest to potential investors.

One company, Iomega, has captured the interest of Motley Fool subscribers more than all others. Iomega makes a new kind of computer disk drive called a Zip drive. In less than 1 year, Iomega's stock price soared by a multiple of 16; that is, a $1,000 investment was suddenly worth $16,000! Many people suggest that this tremendous run-up in price (one of the highest increases experienced by any U.S. company during that period) was caused by the attention the stock received on the Motley Fool bulletin board. Supporters of the Motley Fool say that this is an example of how the Internet can be used by small investors to make the kind of returns that the "big guys" make. Participants share any information they can find about the company and its product: Are Zip drive users happy with the product? How quickly are Zip drives moving off store shelves? How full is the employee parking lot at Iomega on Sundays (an indication of whether employees were working long hours to meet demand)?

Critics, however, contend that the bulletin board is nothing more than a high-tech rumor mill that has built a speculative house of cards. They suggest that, because of the fervor created by the bulletin board chatter, people paid prices for Iomega stock far greater than the underlying worth of the company. One potentially troubling aspect of the bulletin board is that participants on the board don't have to give their identities. Consequently, there is little to stop people from putting misinformation on the board to influence the price in the direction they desire.

Some critics are concerned that small investors—ironically, the very people the Gardner brothers were trying to help—will be hurt the most by misinformation.

Rather than getting swept away by rumors, investors must sort out the good information from the bad. As information services such as the Motley Fool proliferate, gathering information will become easier, and evaluating it will become the harder task.

On the World Wide Web
Iomega Corporation:
http://www.iomega.com
Motley Fool: http://fool.yahoo.com

PREVIEW OF CHAPTER 2

If you are thinking of purchasing Iomega stock, or any stock, how can you decide what the stock is worth? If you own a stock, how can you determine whether it is time to buy more stock—or time to bail out? Your decision will be influenced by a variety of considerations; one should be your careful analysis of a company's financial statements. The reason: Financial statements offer you relevant and reliable information, which will help you in your stock purchase decisions.

In this chapter we begin by looking at the objectives of financial reporting—that is, what financial reporting is supposed to accomplish. We then take a closer look at the financial statements themselves and introduce some useful ways for evaluating the information provided by the statements.

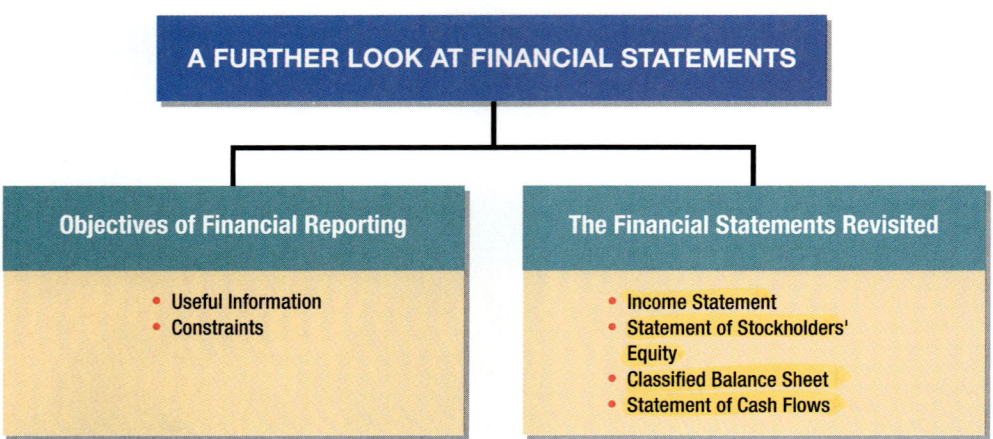

SECTION 1
OBJECTIVES OF FINANCIAL REPORTING

Financial reporting is the term used to describe all of the financial information presented by a company—both in its financial statements and in the additional disclosures you learned about in Chapter 1. For example, if you are deciding whether to invest in Iomega stock, you need financial information to help make your decision. Such information should help you understand Iomega's past financial performance and its current financial picture, and give you some idea of its future prospects. Although information found on electronic bulletin boards, like the Motley Fool, has its place, there is no substitute for careful study of the information available through traditional financial reporting channels. The primary objective of such financial reporting is to provide information useful for decision making.

Characteristics of Useful Information

How does a company like Iomega decide on the amount of financial information to disclose? In what format should its financial information be presented? How should assets, liabilities, revenues, and expenses be measured? The answers to these questions are found in accounting rules that have substantial authoritative support and are recognized as a general guide for financial reporting purposes. These rules are referred to as **generally accepted accounting principles (GAAP).** They are determined by standard-setting bodies in consultation with the accounting profession and the business community.

The primary accounting standard-setting body in the United States is the **Financial Accounting Standards Board (FASB).** The FASB's overriding criterion is that the accounting rule adopted should be the one that generates the most useful financial information for making a decision. To be useful, information should possess these qualitative characteristics: relevance, reliability, comparability, and consistency.

> **STUDY OBJECTIVE 1**
> Explain the meaning of GAAP and describe the basic objective of financial reporting.

RELEVANCE

Information of any sort is relevant if it would influence a decision. Accounting information is **relevant** if it would make a difference in a business decision. For example, when Iomega issues financial statements, the information in the statements is considered relevant because it provides a basis for forecasting Iomega's future earnings. Accounting information is also relevant to business decisions because it confirms or corrects prior expectations. Thus, Iomega's financial statements both help **predict** future events and **provide feedback** about prior expectations about the financial health of the company.

In addition, for accounting information to be relevant it must be **timely;** that is, it must be available to decision makers before it loses its capacity to influence decisions. If Iomega reported its financial information only every 5 years, the information would have limited usefulness for decision-making purposes.

> **STUDY OBJECTIVE 2**
> Discuss the qualitative characteristics of accounting information.

RELIABILITY

Reliability of information means that the information can be depended on. To be reliable, accounting information must be **verifiable**—we must be able to prove that it is free of error. Also, the information must be a **faithful representation** of what it purports to be—it must be factual. If Iomega's income statement reports sales of $5 billion when it actually had sales of only $326 million, then the statement is not a faithful representation. Finally, accounting information must be **neutral**—it cannot be selected, prepared, or presented to favor one set of interested users over another. As noted in Chapter 1, to ensure reliability, certified public accountants audit financial statements.

COMPARABILITY AND CONSISTENCY

Comparability

Let's say that you and a friend kept track of your height each year as you were growing up. If you measured your height in feet and your friend measured hers in meters, it would be difficult to compare your heights. A conversion would be

50 CHAPTER 2 A Further Look at Financial Statements

International Note

Accounting standards vary from country to country. Most countries have their own standard-setting body. This can complicate comparison of companies from different countries, such as German corporation Daimler-Benz and U.S. corporation General Motors. One group, the International Accounting Standards Committee (IASC), has been organized to try to reduce the differences in accounting practices and standards across countries.

necessary. In accounting, **comparability** results when different companies use the same accounting principles.

At one level, U.S. accounting standards are fairly comparable because they are based on certain basic principles and assumptions. These principles and assumptions allow for some variation in methods, however. For example, there are a variety of ways to report inventory. Often these different methods result in different amounts of net income. To make comparison across companies easier, each company **must disclose** the accounting methods used. From the disclosures, the external user can determine whether the financial information is comparable and try to make adjustments. Unfortunately, converting the accounting numbers of companies that use different methods is not as easy as converting your height from feet to meters.

Consistency

Users of accounting information also want to compare the same company's financial results over time. For example, to track Iomega's net income over several years, you'd need to know that the same principles have been used from year to year; otherwise, you might be "comparing apples to oranges." **Consistency** means that a company uses the same accounting principles and methods from year to year. Thus, if a company selects one inventory accounting method in the first year of operations, it is expected to continue to use that same method in succeeding years. When financial information has been reported on a consistent basis, the financial statements permit meaningful analysis of trends within a company.

BUSINESS INSIGHT
Management Perspective

There is an old story that professors often tell students about a company looking for an accountant. The company approached the first accountant and asked, "What do you believe our net income will be this year?" The accountant said, "Four million dollars." The company asked the second accountant the same question, and the answer was, "What would you like it to be?" Guess who got the job? We tell the story here because accounting principles offer flexibility, and it is important that a consistent treatment be provided from period to period. Otherwise, it would be very difficult to interpret financial statements.

A company *can* change to a new method of accounting if management can justify that the new method produces more meaningful financial information. In the year in which the change occurs, the change must be disclosed in the notes to the financial statements so that users of the statements are aware of the lack of consistency.

The characteristics that make accounting information useful are summarized in Illustration 2-1.

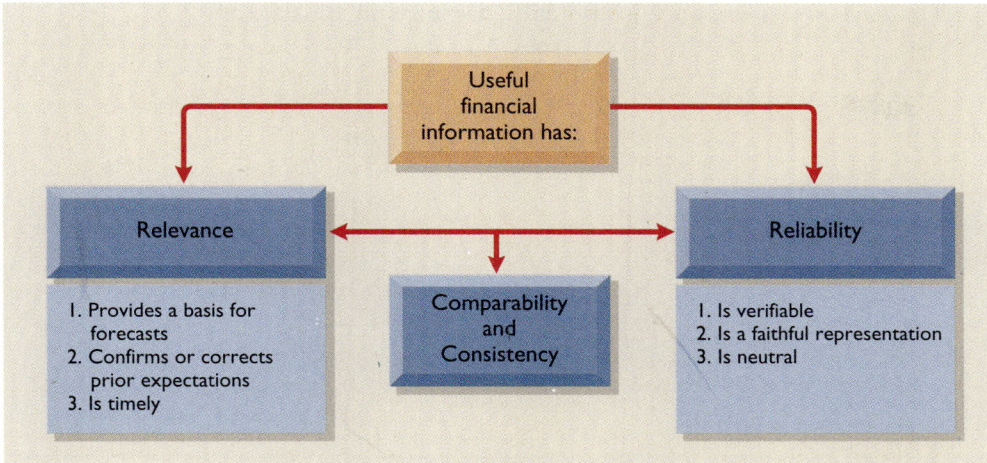

Illustration 2-1
Characteristics of useful information

CONSTRAINTS IN ACCOUNTING

The characteristics we have discussed are intended to provide users of financial statements with the most useful information. Taken to the extreme, however, the pursuit of useful financial information could be far too costly to the company. Therefore, some constraints have been agreed upon to ensure that accounting rules are applied in a reasonable fashion, from the perspectives of both the company and the user. **Constraints** permit a company to modify generally accepted accounting principles without jeopardizing the usefulness of the reported information. The constraints are materiality and conservatism.

STUDY OBJECTIVE 3
Identify the two constraints in accounting.

MATERIALITY

Materiality relates to a financial statement item's impact on a company's overall financial condition and operations. An item is **material** when its size makes it likely to influence the decision of an investor or creditor. It is **immaterial** if it is too small to impact a decision maker. In short, if the item does not make a difference, GAAP does not have to be followed. To determine the materiality of an amount—that is, to determine its financial significance—the item is compared with such items as total assets, total liabilities, sales revenue, and net income.

To illustrate how the constraint of materiality is applied, assume that Iomega made a $100 error in recording revenue. Iomega's total revenue exceeds $326 million; thus a $100 error is not material.

Helpful Hint In fact, for Iomega, even a $10,000 difference in revenue is not material for most investment decisions.

CONSERVATISM

Conservatism in accounting means that when preparing financial statements, a company should choose the accounting method that will be least likely to overstate assets and income. It **does not mean understating assets or income.** Conservatism provides a guide in difficult situations, and the guide is a reasonable one: Do not overstate assets and income.

A common application of the conservatism constraint is in valuing inventories. Inventories are normally recorded at their cost. To be conservative, however, inventories are reported at market value if market value is below cost. This practice results in lower net income on the income statement and a lower stated amount of inventory on the balance sheet.

Illustration 2-2
Accounting constraints

BEFORE YOU GO ON . . .

● **Review It**

1. What are generally accepted accounting principles?
2. What is the basic objective of financial information?
3. What qualitative characteristics make accounting information useful?
4. What are the materiality constraint and the conservatism constraint?

SECTION 2
THE FINANCIAL STATEMENTS REVISITED

In Chapter 1 we briefly introduced the four financial statements. In this section we examine each statement more carefully, illustrating how these statements accomplish their intended objectives. For illustrative purposes we use Best Buy Co., Inc., one of the nation's largest sellers of home electronics. In Chapter 1 we presented the statements of Sierra Corporation, which, being an advertising agency, is referred to as a *service* corporation. In contrast, Best Buy sells electronic appliances such as stereos and TVs. Companies that sell goods are called *merchandisers.* You may notice a number of differences between the statements of a service corporation and those of a merchandiser, especially in the income statement. These differences will be discussed further in Chapter 5.

*T*HE INCOME STATEMENT

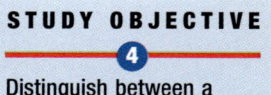

STUDY OBJECTIVE 4
Distinguish between a single-step and a multiple-step income statement.

Two forms of the income statement are widely used by companies. One is the **single-step income statement.** The statement is so named because only one step, subtracting total expenses from total revenues, is required in determining net income (or net loss). In a single-step statement, all data are classified into two categories: (1) **revenues,** which include both operating revenues and nonoperating revenues and gains (for example, interest revenue and gain on sale of equipment); and (2) **expenses,** which include cost of goods sold, operating expenses, and nonoperating expenses and losses (for example, interest expense, loss on sale of equipment, or income tax expense). A condensed single-step statement for Best Buy is shown in Illustration 2-3.

Illustration 2-3 Single-step income statement

BEST BUY CO., INC.
Income Statement
For the Year Ended March 2, 1996
(in thousands)

Revenues		
Net sales		$7,217,448
Expenses		
Cost of goods sold	$6,280,877	
Selling, general, and administrative expenses	813,988	
Interest expense, net	43,594	
Income tax expense	30,970	
Total expenses		7,169,429
Net income		$ 48,019

There are two primary reasons for using the single-step form: (1) A company does not realize any type of profit or income until total revenues exceed total expenses, so it makes sense to divide the statement into these two categories. (2) The form is simple and easy to read.

A second form of the income statement is the **multiple-step income statement.** The multiple-step income statement is often considered more useful because it highlights the components of net income. The Best Buy income statement in Illustration 2-4 is an example. The multiple-step income statement has three important line items: gross profit, income from operations, and net income. They are determined as follows: (1) Cost of goods sold is subtracted from sales to determine gross profit; (2) operating expenses are deducted from gross profit to determine income from operations; and (3) the results of activities not related to operations are added or subtracted to determine net income. You should note that income tax expense is reported in a separate section of the income statement before net income.

BEST BUY CO., INC.
Consolidated Income Statement
(in thousands)

	For the years ended		
	March 2, 1996	Feb. 25, 1995	Feb. 26, 1994
Revenues	$7,217,448	$5,079,557	$3,006,534
Cost of goods sold	6,280,877	4,389,164	2,549,609
Gross profit	936,571	690,393	456,925
Operating expenses			
Selling, general, and administrative expenses	813,988	568,466	379,747
Income from operations	122,583	121,927	77,178
Other expenses and losses			
Interest expense, net	43,594	27,876	8,800
Other			425
Income before income taxes	78,989	94,051	67,953
Income tax expense	30,970	36,400	26,668
Net income	$ 48,019	$ 57,651	$ 41,285

Illustration 2-4 Best Buy's income statement

GROSS PROFIT

Cost of goods sold is deducted from sales revenue to determine **gross profit.** As shown in Illustration 2-4, Best Buy had a gross profit of $936,571,000 in 1996. Gross profit represents the **merchandising profit** of a company—quite simply, the difference between what the company paid for its inventory and what it sold it for. It is not a measure of the overall profitability of a company because operating expenses have not been deducted. Nevertheless, the amount and trend of gross profit are closely watched by management and other interested parties. Comparisons of current gross profit with past amounts and with those in the industry indicate the effectiveness of a company's purchasing and pricing policies.

OPERATING EXPENSES

Operating expenses are the next component in a multiple-step income statement. At Best Buy, operating expenses were $813,988,000 in 1996. The company's income from operations is determined by subtracting operating expenses from gross profit. Thus, income from operations was $122,583,000 in 1996, as shown in Illustration 2-4.

Subgrouping of Operating Expenses

Sometimes, operating expenses are subdivided into selling expenses and administrative expenses (as shown in the income statement in Illustration 2-6 on page 55). **Selling expenses** are those associated with making sales. They include advertising expenses as well as expenses of completing the sale, such as delivery and shipping expenses. **Administrative expenses** relate to general operating activities such as human resources management, accounting, and store security.

Alternative Terminology
Administrative expenses are sometimes called **general expenses.**

NONOPERATING ACTIVITIES

Nonoperating activities consist of various revenues and expenses and gains and losses that are unrelated to the company's main line of operations. When nonoperating items are included, the label **Income from operations** (or Operating income) precedes them. This clearly identifies the results of the company's normal operations, an amount determined by subtracting cost of goods sold and operating expenses from net sales. The results of nonoperating activities are shown in **Other revenues and gains** and **Other expenses and losses.** Examples of each are listed in Illustration 2-5.

Illustration 2-5 Other items of nonoperating activities

Other Revenues and Gains	Other Expenses and Losses
Interest revenue from notes receivable and marketable securities	Interest expense on notes and loans payable
Dividend revenue from investments in capital stock	Casualty losses from recurring causes, such as vandalism and accidents
Rent revenue from subleasing a portion of the store	Loss from the sale or abandonment of property, plant, and equipment
Gain from the sale of property, plant, and equipment	Loss from strikes by employees and suppliers

The distinction between operating and nonoperating activities is crucial to many external users of financial data. This is because operating income is viewed as sustainable and therefore long term, and nonoperating is viewed as nonrecurring and therefore short term.

BUSINESS INSIGHT
Investor Perspective

It was once reported that a large cinema chain in North America was selling some of its assets and counting the gains as part of operating income. As a result, operating losses were being offset by these gains. Because of unfavorable press reaction to this practice, the company revised its financial statements. By not counting its nonrecurring items as part of operating income, the company changed its first-quarter results from $24.9 million operating income to a $22.6 million loss. Although the net income figure didn't change, investors were able to see that income was derived from selling *assets* rather than from selling *movie tickets*. Thus, with this new information, investors were able to make a more informed decision about the company's earnings.

The nonoperating activities are reported in the income statement immediately after the operating activities. Included among these activities in Illustration 2-4 for Best Buy is net interest expense of $43,594,000 for 1996. The amount remaining, after adding the operating and nonoperating sections together, is Best Buy's net income of $48,019,000 for 1996. Note that the net income in Illustrations 2-3 and 2-4 are the same; the difference in the two income statements is the amount of detail displayed.

In Illustration 2-6 we have provided the multiple-step income statement of a hypothetical company. This statement provides more detail than that of Best Buy.

For homework problems, the multiple-step form of the income statement should be used unless the requirements state otherwise.

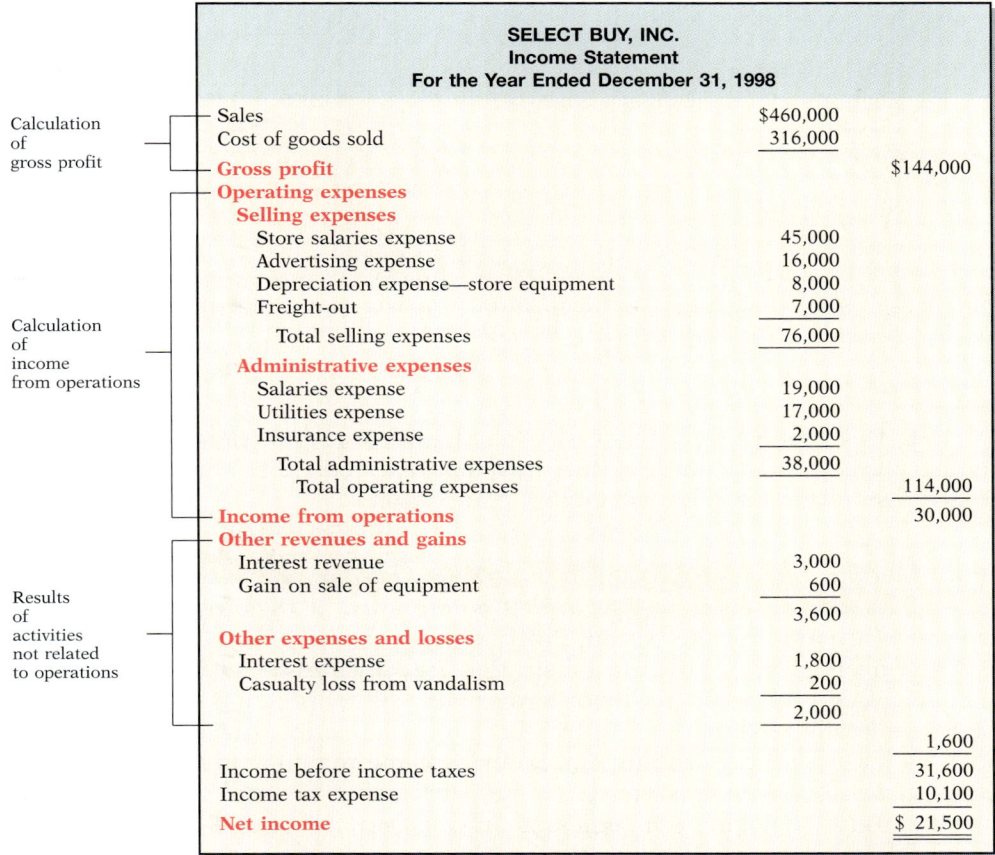

Illustration 2-6 Multiple-step income statement

USING THE INCOME STATEMENT

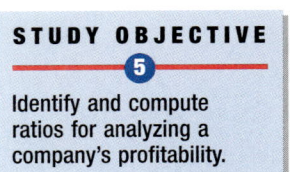

STUDY OBJECTIVE 5
Identify and compute ratios for analyzing a company's profitability.

In this section we will evaluate the profitability of Best Buy. To help in this evaluation, we will use **ratio analysis.** Ratio analysis is a technique for expressing relationships among selected financial statement data.

Profitability

Profitability ratios measure the income or operating success of a company for a given period of time. We will look at two examples of profitability ratios: return on assets and profit margin.

Return on Assets. An overall measure of profitability is the **return on assets ratio.** This ratio is computed by dividing net income by average assets. Average assets are commonly calculated by adding the beginning and ending values of assets and dividing by 2. The return on assets ratio indicates the amount of net income generated by each dollar invested in assets. Thus, the higher the return on assets, the more profitable the company. A simplified 1996 income statement for Best Buy was presented in Illustration 2-4. The 1996 and 1995 return on assets of Best Buy, Circuit City (a Best Buy competitor), and industry averages are presented in Illustration 2-7.

Illustration 2-7 Return on assets ratio

$$\text{RETURN ON ASSETS RATIO} = \frac{\text{NET INCOME}}{\text{AVERAGE ASSETS}}$$

	1996	1995
Best Buy (numbers in millions)	$\frac{\$48}{[(\$1{,}891 + \$1{,}507)/2]^*} = 2.8\%$	$\frac{\$58}{[(\$1{,}507 + \$952)/2]^*} = 4.7\%$
Circuit City	7.9%	9.4%
Industry average	8.7%	7.1%

*Amounts of average assets are taken from Best Buy's balance sheet (Illustration 2-11). Also note that amounts in the ratio calculations have been rounded. Total assets in 1994 were $952 million.

Best Buy's return on assets in 1996 and 1995 are significantly less than the industry averages and are less than half that of Circuit City. Thus, Best Buy is clearly less profitable than its primary competitor.

Profit Margin. The **profit margin ratio** measures the percentage of each dollar of sales that results in net income. It is computed by dividing net income by net sales (revenue) for the period. Profit margins for Best Buy, Circuit City, and industry averages are shown in Illustration 2-8. Businesses with high turnover, such as grocery stores (Safeway or Kroger) and discount stores (Kmart or Wal-Mart), generally experience low profit margins, whereas low-turnover businesses, such as jewelry stores (Tiffany & Co.) or airplane manufacturers (Boeing Aircraft), have high profit margins.

Best Buy's profit margin is less than one-third of Circuit City's. In other words, for each dollar of sales, Circuit City generates three times more profit.

Illustration 2-8 Profit margin ratio

$$\text{PROFIT MARGIN RATIO} = \frac{\text{NET INCOME}}{\text{NET SALES}}$$

	1996	1995
Best Buy (numbers in millions)	$\frac{\$48}{\$7,217} = 0.67\%$	$\frac{\$58}{\$5,080} = 1.1\%$
Circuit City	2.6%	3.0%
Industry average	2.5%	3.3%

DECISION TOOLKIT

Decision Checkpoints	Info Needed for Decision	Tool to Use for Decision	How to Evaluate Results
Is the company using its assets effectively?	Net income and average assets	Return on assets ratio = $\frac{\text{Net income}}{\text{Average assets}}$	Higher value suggests favorable efficiency (use of assets).
Is the company maintaining an adequate margin between sales and expenses?	Net income and net sales	Profit margin ratio = $\frac{\text{Net income}}{\text{Net sales}}$	Higher value suggests favorable return on each dollar of sales.

BEFORE YOU GO ON . . .

● **Review It**

1. How does a single-step income statement differ from a multiple-step income statement?
2. What are nonoperating activities and how are they reported in the income statement?
3. What are profitability ratios? Explain the return on assets ratio and the profit margin ratio.

THE STATEMENT OF STOCKHOLDERS' EQUITY

As discussed in Chapter 1, the retained earnings statement describes the changes in retained earnings during the year. This statement adds net income and then subtracts dividends from the beginning retained earnings to arrive at ending retained earnings.

Recall, however, that stockholders' equity is comprised of two parts: retained earnings and common stock. Therefore, the stockholders' equity of most companies is affected by factors other than just changes in retained earnings. For example, the company may issue or retire shares of common stock. Most companies, therefore, use what is called a **statement of stockholders' equity,** rather than a retained earnings statement, so that they can report **all** changes in stockholders' equity accounts. Illustration 2-9 is a simplified statement of stockholders' equity for Best Buy.

STUDY OBJECTIVE 6

Explain the relationship between a retained earnings statement and a statement of stockholders' equity.

58 CHAPTER 2 A Further Look at Financial Statements

BEST BUY CO., INC.
Statement of Stockholders' Equity
(in thousands)

	Common Stock	Retained Earnings
Balances at February 27, 1993	$138,300	$ 43,983
Issuance of common stock	87,876	
Net income		41,285
Balances at February 26, 1994	226,176	85,268
Issuance of common stock	7,027	
Net income		57,651
Balances at February 25, 1995	233,203	142,919
Issuance of common stock	7,473	
Net income		48,019
Balances at March 2, 1996	$240,676	$190,938

Illustration 2-9 Best Buy's statement of stockholders' equity

One very important point that we learn from examining this statement is that Best Buy has paid no dividends during the last 3 years. Best Buy's lenders would be particularly interested in this fact; if Best Buy were paying dividends, doing so would reduce the company's ability to pay its debts. Another fact that we learn from this statement is that common stock increased because of the issuance of new shares of stock during this 3-year period.

THE CLASSIFIED BALANCE SHEET

STUDY OBJECTIVE 7
Identify the sections of a classified balance sheet.

The balance sheet presents a snapshot of a company's financial position at a point in time. To improve users' understanding of a company's financial position, companies often group similar assets and similar liabilities together. This is useful because it tells you that items within a group have similar economic characteristics. A **classified balance sheet** generally contains the standard classifications listed in Illustration 2-10.

Illustration 2-10 Standard balance sheet classifications

Assets	Liabilities and Stockholders' Equity
Current assets	Current liabilities
Long-term investments	Long-term liabilities
Property, plant, and equipment	Stockholders' equity
Intangible assets	

These groupings help readers determine such things as (1) whether the company has enough assets to pay its debts as they come due and (2) the claims of short- and long-term creditors on the company's total assets. Many of these groupings can be seen in the balance sheet of Best Buy shown in Illustration 2-11. Each of the groupings is explained next.

The Classified Balance Sheet

BEST BUY CO., INC.
Consolidated Balance Sheets
(in thousands)

	March 2, 1996	Feb. 25, 1995
Assets		
Current assets		
Cash and cash equivalents	$ 86,445	$ 144,700
Receivables	121,438	84,440
Recoverable costs from developed properties	126,237	86,222
Merchandise inventories	1,201,142	907,677
Prepaid expenses and other current assets	25,281	17,628
Total current assets	1,560,543	1,240,667
Property, plant, and equipment	443,715	325,593
Less: Accumulated depreciation	132,676	88,116
Net property and equipment	311,039	237,477
Other assets	19,250	28,981
Total assets	$1,890,832	$1,507,125
Liabilities and Stockholders' Equity		
Current liabilities		
Accounts payable	$ 673,852	$ 395,337
Obligations under financing arrangements	93,951	81,755
Accrued salaries and related expenses	26,890	23,785
Accrued liabilities	125,582	77,102
Deferred service plan revenue and warranty reserve	30,845	24,942
Accrued income taxes	0	14,979
Current portion of long-term debt	23,568	13,718
Total current liabilities	974,688	631,618
Long-term liabilities		
Deferred service plan revenue and warranty reserve, long-term	48,243	42,138
Long-term debt	436,287	457,247
Total liabilities	1,459,218	1,131,003
Stockholders' equity		
Common stock, $.10 par value	240,676	233,203
Retained earnings	190,938	142,919
Total stockholders' equity	431,614	376,122
Total liabilities and stockholders' equity	$1,890,832	$1,507,125

Illustration 2-11 Best Buy's balance sheet

CURRENT ASSETS

Current assets are assets that are expected to be converted to cash or used in the business within a relatively short period of time. Best Buy had current assets of $1,560,543,000 in 1996. For most businesses the cutoff for classification as current assets is 1 year from the balance sheet date. For example, accounts receivable are included in current assets because they will be converted to cash through collection within 1 year. Supplies is a current asset because we expect that it will be used in the business within 1 year. However, as noted in the business insight at the top of the next page, some businesses use a period longer than 1 year as the cutoff.

60 CHAPTER 2 A Further Look at Financial Statements

BUSINESS INSIGHT
Management Perspective

Some companies use a period longer than 1 year to classify assets and liabilities as current because they have an operating cycle longer than 1 year. The **operating cycle** of a company is the average time that it takes to go from cash to cash in producing revenues. For example, if your business sells TVs, your operating cycle would be the average length of time it would take for you to purchase your inventory, sell it, and then collect cash from your customers. For most businesses this cycle takes less than a year, so they use a 1-year cutoff. But, for some businesses, such as vineyards or airplane manufacturers, this period may be longer than a year. Except where noted, we will assume that 1 year is used to determine whether an asset or liability is current or long-term.

Common types of current assets are (1) cash, (2) marketable securities, such as U.S. government bonds held as a temporary (short-term) investment, (3) receivables (notes receivable, accounts receivable, and interest receivable), (4) inventories, and (5) prepaid expenses (insurance and supplies). On the balance sheet, these items are listed in the order in which they are expected to be converted into cash. This arrangement is shown in Illustration 2-12 for UAL, Inc. (United Airlines).

UNITED AIRLINES

UAL, INC.
Balance Sheet (partial)
(in thousands)

Current assets	
Cash	$ 52,368
Marketable securities	389,862
Receivables	721,479
Aircraft fuel, spare parts, and supplies	178,840
Prepaid expenses	83,662
Total current assets	$1,426,211

Illustration 2-12 Current assets section

A company's current assets are important in assessing its short-term debt-paying ability, as explained later in the chapter.

LONG-TERM INVESTMENTS

Alternative Terminology
Long-term investments are often just referred to as investments.

Long-term investments are generally investments in stocks and bonds of other corporations that are normally held for many years. Best Buy reports no long-term investments on its balance sheet. Deluxe Check Printers Incorporated reported long-term investments in its balance sheet as shown in Illustration 2-13.

DELUXE CHECK PRINTERS INCORPORATED	
Balance Sheet (partial)	
Long-term investments	
Investment in stock of Data Card Corporation	$20,468,000
Other long-term investments	16,961,000
	$37,429,000

Illustration 2-13 Long-term investments section

PROPERTY, PLANT, AND EQUIPMENT

Property, plant, and equipment are assets with relatively long useful lives that are used in operating the business. This category includes land, buildings, machinery and equipment, delivery equipment, and furniture. Best Buy reported property, plant, and equipment of $443,715,000 in 1996. **Depreciation** is the practice of allocating the cost of assets to a number of years, rather than simply expensing the full purchase price of the asset in the year of purchase. Assets that the company depreciates should be reported on the balance sheet at cost less accumulated depreciation. Best Buy reported accumulated depreciation of $132,676,000 in 1996. The accumulated depreciation account shows the total amount of depreciation taken over the *life of the asset*. The use of an accumulated depreciation account is shown for Delta Air Lines in Illustration 2-14.

Alternative Terminology Property, plant, and equipment is sometimes called **fixed assets.**

▲ **Delta Air Lines**

DELTA AIR LINES, INC.		
Balance Sheet (partial)		
(in thousands)		
Property, plant, and equipment		
Flight equipment	$3,985,796	
Less: Accumulated depreciation	1,713,059	
		$2,272,737
Ground equipment	865,628	
Less: Accumulated depreciation	325,618	
		540,010
		$2,812,747

Illustration 2-14 Property, plant, and equipment section

INTANGIBLE ASSETS

Many companies have assets that cannot be seen yet often are very valuable. These assets are referred to as intangible assets. **Intangible assets** are noncurrent assets that do not have physical substance. They include patents, copyrights, and trademarks or trade names that give the company **exclusive right** of use for a specified period of time. Best Buy does not report any intangible assets. Illustration 2-15 shows how Brunswick Corporation reported its intangible assets.

Helpful Hint Sometimes intangible assets are reported under a broader heading called **Other assets.**

BRUNSWICK CORPORATION	
Balance Sheet (partial)	
Intangible assets	
Patents, trademarks, and other intangibles	$10,460,000

Illustration 2-15 Intangible assets section

CURRENT LIABILITIES

In the liabilities and stockholders' equity section of the balance sheet, the first grouping is current liabilities. **Current liabilities** are obligations that are to be paid within the coming year. Common examples are accounts payable, wages payable, bank loans payable, interest payable, taxes payable, and current maturities of long-term obligations (payments to be made within the next year on long-term obligations). Best Buy reported seven different types of current liabilities, for a total of $974,688,000 in 1996.

Within the current liabilities section, notes payable is usually listed first, followed by accounts payable. Other items are then listed in any order. The current liabilities section adapted from the balance sheet of UAL, Inc. (United Airlines) is shown in Illustration 2-16.

Illustration 2-16 Current liabilities section

✈ UNITED AIRLINES

UAL, INC.
Balance Sheet (partial)
(in thousands)

Current liabilities	
Notes payable	$ 297,518
Accounts payable	382,967
Current maturities of long-term obligations	81,525
Unearned ticket revenue	432,979
Salaries and wages payable	435,622
Taxes payable	80,390
Other current liabilities	240,652
Total current liabilities	$1,951,653

LONG-TERM LIABILITIES

Obligations expected to be paid after 1 year are classified as long-term liabilities. Liabilities in this category include bonds payable, mortgages payable, long-term notes payable, lease liabilities, and pension liabilities. Many companies report long-term debt maturing after 1 year as a single amount in the balance sheet and show the details of the debt in notes that accompany the financial statements. Others list the various types of long-term liabilities. Best Buy reported liabilities related to warranties of $48,243,000 and long-term debt of $436,287,000 in 1996. In its balance sheet, Consolidated Freightways, Inc., reported long-term liabilities as shown in Illustration 2-17.

Illustration 2-17 Long-term liabilities section

CONSOLIDATED FREIGHTWAYS, INC.
Balance Sheet (partial)
(in thousands)

Long-term liabilities	
Bank notes payable	$10,000
Mortgage payable	2,900
Bonds payable	53,422
Other long-term debt	9,597
Total long-term liabilities	$75,919

STOCKHOLDERS' EQUITY

Stockholders' equity is divided into two parts: common stock and retained earnings. Investments of assets in the business by the stockholders are recorded as common stock. Income retained for use in the business is recorded as retained earnings. These two parts are combined and reported as **stockholders' equity** on the balance sheet. In its balance sheet, Best Buy reported common stock of $240,676,000 and retained earnings of $190,938,000 in 1996.

Alternative Terminology
Common stock is sometimes called **capital stock.**

USING A CLASSIFIED BALANCE SHEET

You can learn a lot about a company's financial health by evaluating the relationship between its various assets and liabilities.

STUDY OBJECTIVE 8
Identify and compute ratios for analyzing a company's liquidity and solvency.

Liquidity

Suppose you are a banker considering lending money to Best Buy, or you are a computer manufacturer interested in selling it computers. You would be very concerned about Best Buy's liquidity—its ability to pay obligations that are expected to become due within the next year or operating cycle. You would look very closely at the relationship of its current assets to current liabilities.

Working Capital. One measure of liquidity is working capital, which is the excess of current assets over current liabilities. When working capital is positive, there is greater likelihood that the company will pay its liabilities. When the reverse is true, short-term creditors may not be paid, and the company may ultimately be forced into bankruptcy.

Current Ratio. Liquidity ratios measure the short-term ability of the enterprise to pay its maturing obligations and to meet unexpected needs for cash. One liquidity ratio is the current ratio, which is computed by dividing current assets by current liabilities.

The current ratio is a more dependable indicator of liquidity than working capital. Two companies with the same amount of working capital may have significantly different current ratios. The 1996 and 1995 current ratios for Best Buy, for Circuit City, and industry averages are shown in Illustration 2-18.

$$\text{CURRENT RATIO} = \frac{\text{CURRENT ASSETS}}{\text{CURRENT LIABILITIES}}$$

	1996	1995
Best Buy (numbers in millions)	$\frac{\$1,561}{\$975} = 1.60:1$	$\frac{\$1,241}{\$632} = 1.96:1$
Circuit City	2.09:1	1.96:1
Industry average	1.9:1	2.10:1

Illustration 2-18 Current ratio

What does the ratio actually mean? The 1996 ratio of 1.60:1 means that for every dollar of current liabilities, Best Buy has $1.60 of current assets. Best Buy's current ratio has decreased in the current year. Also, compared to the industry average of 1.9:1, and Circuit City's 2.09:1 current ratio, Best Buy's liquidity may be a concern.

The current ratio is only one measure of liquidity. It does not take into account the **composition** of the current assets. For example, a satisfactory current ratio does not disclose the fact that a portion of the current assets may be tied up in slow-moving inventory. The composition of the assets matters because a dollar of cash is more readily available to pay the bills than is a dollar of inventory. During 1996 Best Buy's cash balance declined while its merchandise inventory increased substantially. If inventory increased because the company is having difficulty selling its inventory, then the current ratio might not fully reflect the reduction in Best Buy's liquidity. In a later chapter you will learn additional ways to analyze a company's liquidity position.

Solvency

Now suppose that instead of being a short-term creditor, you are interested in either buying Best Buy's stock or extending the company a long-term loan. Long-term creditors and stockholders are interested in a company's long-run **solvency**—its ability to pay interest as it comes due and to repay the face value of the debt at maturity. **Solvency ratios** measure the ability of the enterprise to survive over a long period of time. The debt to total assets ratio is one source of information about debt-paying ability.

Debt to Total Assets Ratio. The **debt to total assets ratio** measures the percentage of assets financed by creditors rather than stockholders. Financing provided by creditors is more risky than financing provided by stockholders because debt must be repaid at specific points in time, whether the company is performing well or not. Thus, the higher the percentage of debt financing, the riskier the company. The debt to total assets ratio is computed by dividing total debt (both current and long-term liabilities) by total assets. The higher the percentage of debt to total assets, the greater the risk that the company may be unable to pay its debts as they come due. The ratios of debt to total assets for Best Buy, for Circuit City, and industry averages are presented in Illustration 2-19.

Helpful Hint Some users evaluate solvency using a ratio of debt divided by stockholders' equity. The higher this ratio, the lower is a company's solvency.

Illustration 2-19 Debt to total assets ratio

$$\text{DEBT TO TOTAL ASSETS RATIO} = \frac{\text{TOTAL DEBT}}{\text{TOTAL ASSETS}}$$

	1996	1995
Best Buy (numbers in millions)	$\frac{\$1,459}{\$1,891} = 77\%$	$\frac{\$1,131}{\$1,507} = 75\%$
Circuit City	58%	56%
Industry average	54%	49%

The 1996 ratio of 77% means that $.77 of every dollar invested in assets by Best Buy has been provided by Best Buy's creditors. Best Buy's ratio exceeds the industry average of 54% and the ratio of Circuit City. The higher the ratio, the lower the equity "buffer" available to creditors if the company becomes insolvent. Thus, from the creditors' point of view, a high ratio of debt to total assets is undesirable.

The adequacy of this ratio is often judged in the light of the company's earnings. Generally, companies with relatively stable earnings, such as public utilities, have higher debt to total assets ratios than do cyclical companies with widely fluctuating earnings, such as many high-tech companies. In later chapters you will learn additional ways to evaluate solvency.

BUSINESS INSIGHT
Investor Perspective

Debt financing differs greatly across industries and companies. Here are some debt to total assets ratios for selected companies:

	Total Debt to Total Assets As a Percent
Advanced Micro Devices	29%
General Motors Corporation	93
Roberts Pharmaceutical	23
Callaway Golf Company	19
Sears, Roebuck & Company	64
Eastman Kodak Company	83

DECISION TOOLKIT

Decision Checkpoints	Info Needed for Decision	Tool to Use for Decision	How to Evaluate Results
Can the company meet its near-term obligations?	Current assets and current liabilities	Current ratio = $\dfrac{\text{Current assets}}{\text{Current liabilities}}$	Higher ratio suggests favorable liquidity.
Can the company meet its long-term obligations?	Total debt and total assets	Debt to total assets ratio = $\dfrac{\text{Total debt}}{\text{Total assets}}$	Lower value suggests favorable solvency.

BEFORE YOU GO ON . . .

● **Review It**
1. What does a statement of stockholders' equity show?
2. What are the major sections in a classified balance sheet?
3. What is liquidity? How can it be measured?
4. What is solvency? How can it be measured?

● **Do It**

Selected financial data for Drummond Company at December 31, 1998, are as follows: cash $60,000; receivables (net) $80,000; inventory $70,000; and current liabilities $140,000. Compute the current ratio.

Reasoning: The formula for the current ratio is: Current assets ÷ Current liabilities.

Solution: The current ratio is 1.5:1 ($210,000 ÷ $140,000).

THE STATEMENT OF CASH FLOWS

STUDY OBJECTIVE 9

Identify the sections of the statement of cash flows and the purpose of each.

As you learned in Chapter 1, the statement of cash flows provides financial information about the sources and uses of a company's cash. Investors, creditors, and others want to know what is happening to a company's most liquid resource—its cash. In fact, many people think that "cash is king" because if a company can't generate cash, it won't survive. To aid in the analysis of cash, the statement of cash flows reports the cash effects of (1) a company's **operating activities,** (2) its **investing activities,** and (3) its **financing activities.**

Sources of cash matter. For example, you would feel much better about a company's health if you knew that its cash was generated from the operations of the business rather than borrowed. A cash flow statement provides this information. Similarly, net income does not tell you *how much* cash the firm generated from operations. The statement of cash flows can tell you that. In summary, neither the income statement nor the balance sheet can directly answer most of the important questions about cash, but the statement of cash flows does. A simplified statement of cash flows for Best Buy is provided in Illustration 2-20.

BEST BUY CO., INC.
Statement of Cash Flows
(in thousands)

	\<td colspan="3" align="center">For Fiscal Year Ending</td>
	March 2, 1996	Feb. 25, 1995	Feb. 26, 1994
Cash flows provided by operating activities			
Cash receipts from operating activities	$7,180,450	$5,048,061	$2,991,558
Cash payments for operating activities	7,080,930	5,085,472	3,117,757
Net cash provided (used) by operations	99,520	(37,411)	(126,199)
Cash flows provided by investing activities			
(Increase) decrease in property and plant	(166,216)	(204,340)	(101,412)
Other cash inflow (outflow)	7,712	(12,384)	37,914
Net cash provided (used) by investments	(158,504)	(191,956)	(63,498)
Cash flows provided by financing activities			
Issue of equity	3,133	2,366	86,513
Increase (decrease) in borrowing	(2,404)	311,829	155,918
Dividends, other distribution	0	0	0
Net cash provided (used) by financing	729	314,195	242,431
Net increase/(decrease) in cash or equivalents	(58,255)	84,828	52,734
Cash or equivalents at start of year	144,700	59,872	7,138
Cash or equivalents at year-end	$ 86,445	$ 144,700	$ 59,872

Illustration 2-20 Best Buy's statement of cash flows

USING THE STATEMENT OF CASH FLOWS

Different users have different reasons for being interested in the statement of cash flows. If you were a creditor of Best Buy (either short term or long term), you would be interested to know the source of its cash in recent years. This information would give you some indication of where it might get cash to pay you. If you have a long-term interest in Best Buy as a stockholder, you would look to the statement of cash flows for information regarding the company's ability to generate cash over the long run to meet its cash needs for growth.

Companies get cash from two sources: operating activities and financing activities. In the early years of a company's life it typically won't generate enough cash from operating activities to meet its investing needs, and so it will have to issue stock or borrow money. An established firm, however, will often be able to meet most of its cash needs with cash from operations. Best Buy's cash from operations in the previous 3 years was not sufficient to meet its investing needs. In fact, 1996 was the only one of those 3 years in which the company generated positive cash from operations. In the previous years its cash expenses had exceeded its cash revenues. Although this may happen occasionally for any company, it is not sustainable for very long, and it should be investigated by management. In order to finance its investing activities, Best Buy had to supplement its internally generated cash with cash from outside sources, by issuing new stock and by borrowing. Note that the bulk of Best Buy's cash from outside sources has come from borrowing. As noted earlier, the more a company borrows, the harder it is for the company to meet its debt obligations.

Given the liquidity and profitability concerns raised previously about Best Buy, investors and creditors would be wise to closely monitor Best Buy's cash-generating ability, to ensure that it will be able to continue to meet its obligations. Earlier we introduced you to measures of liquidity and solvency. The statement of cash flows can also be used to calculate additional measures of liquidity and solvency. The **current cash debt coverage ratio** is a measure of liquidity that is calculated as cash provided by operating activities divided by average current liabilities. It indicates the company's ability to generate sufficient cash to meet its short-term needs. The **cash debt coverage ratio** is a measure of solvency that is calculated as cash provided by operating activities divided by average total liabilities. It indicates the company's ability to generate sufficient cash to meet its long-term needs. Illustration 2-21 presents each of these measures for Best Buy and Circuit City. Industry measures are not available for these ratios.

Illustration 2-21 Current cash debt coverage ratio and cash debt coverage ratio

$$\text{CURRENT CASH DEBT COVERAGE RATIO} = \frac{\text{CASH PROVIDED BY OPERATING ACTIVITIES}}{\text{AVERAGE CURRENT LIABILITIES}}$$

	1996	1995
Best Buy (numbers in thousands)	$\frac{\$99,520}{(\$974,688 + \$631,618)/2} = .124$ times	$\frac{-\$37,411}{(\$631,618 + \$402,028)/2} = -.072$ times
Circuit City	−.072 times	.075 times

$$\text{CASH DEBT COVERAGE RATIO} = \frac{\text{CASH PROVIDED BY OPERATING ACTIVITIES}}{\text{AVERAGE TOTAL LIABILITIES}}$$

	1996	1995
Best Buy (numbers in thousands)	$\frac{\$99,520}{(\$1,459,218 + \$1,131,003)/2} = .077$ times	$\frac{-\$37,411}{(\$1,131,003 + \$641,050)/2} = -.042$ times
Circuit City	−.043 times	.048 times

68   CHAPTER 2   A Further Look at Financial Statements

Using these measures of solvency and liquidity for 1996 and 1995, neither Best Buy nor Circuit City appears very liquid or solvent. Best Buy had negative cash from operations in 1995, and Circuit City had negative cash from operations in 1996. While these negative numbers should be investigated further, they are not cause for immediate alarm. Both of these companies have been growing rapidly in recent years. It is not unusual for companies that are growing quickly to have negative cash from operations, although this is not sustainable over the long term.

DECISION TOOLKIT

Decision Checkpoints	Info Needed for Decision	Tool to Use for Decision	How to Evaluate Results
Can the company meet its near-term obligations?	Current liabilities and cash from operating activities	Current cash debt coverage ratio = $\dfrac{\text{Cash from operating activities}}{\text{Average current liabilities}}$	A higher ratio indicates liquidity, that the company is generating cash sufficient to meet its near-term needs.
Can the company meet its long-term obligations?	Total liabilities and cash from operating activities	Cash debt coverage ratio = $\dfrac{\text{Cash from operating activities}}{\text{Average total liabilities}}$	A higher ratio indicates solvency, that the company is generating cash sufficient to meet its long-term needs.

BEFORE YOU GO ON...

● **Review It**

1. What information does the statement of cash flows provide that is not available in an income statement or a balance sheet?
2. What does the current cash debt coverage ratio measure? What does the cash debt coverage ratio measure?

*U*SING THE DECISION TOOLKIT

In the opening story we noted that Iomega Corporation's stock price increased dramatically during 1995 and 1996. Many people questioned whether this increase was justified by Iomega's results. Let's look for ourselves: A simplified balance sheet and income statement for Iomega Corporation are presented in Illustrations 2-22 and 2-23.

Illustration 2-22
Iomega's balance sheet

IOMEGA CORPORATION AND SUBSIDIARIES
Consolidated Balance Sheets
(in thousands)

	December 31, 1995	December 31, 1994
Assets		
Current assets		
Cash and cash equivalents	$ 1,023	$16,861
Temporary investments	—	2,932
Trade receivables	105,955	18,892
Inventories	98,703	17,318
Other current assets	6,451	4,554
Total current assets	212,132	60,557
Property, plant, and equipment, at cost	103,149	59,193
Less: Accumulated depreciation	(49,779)	(43,917)
	53,370	15,276
Other assets	725	—
Total assets	$266,227	$75,833
Liabilities and Stockholders' Equity		
Current liabilities		
Notes payable	$ 47,640	$ —
Accounts payable	94,782	7,228
Bank overdraft	11,833	—
Accrued payroll and bonus	6,777	3,047
Deferred revenue	3,207	1,947
Accrued vacation	2,939	1,954
Accrued warranty	4,652	3,943
Other accrued liabilities	21,756	7,620
Income taxes payable	5,141	—
Current portion of capitalized lease obligations	782	—
Total current liabilities	199,509	25,739
Notes payable, net of current portion	2,551	—
Other liabilities	1,481	1,031
Total liabilities	203,541	26,770
Stockholders' equity		
Common stock	53,433	48,278
Retained earnings	9,253	785
Total stockholders' equity	62,686	49,063
Total liabilities and stockholders' equity	$266,227	$75,833

Illustration 2-23
Iomega's income statement

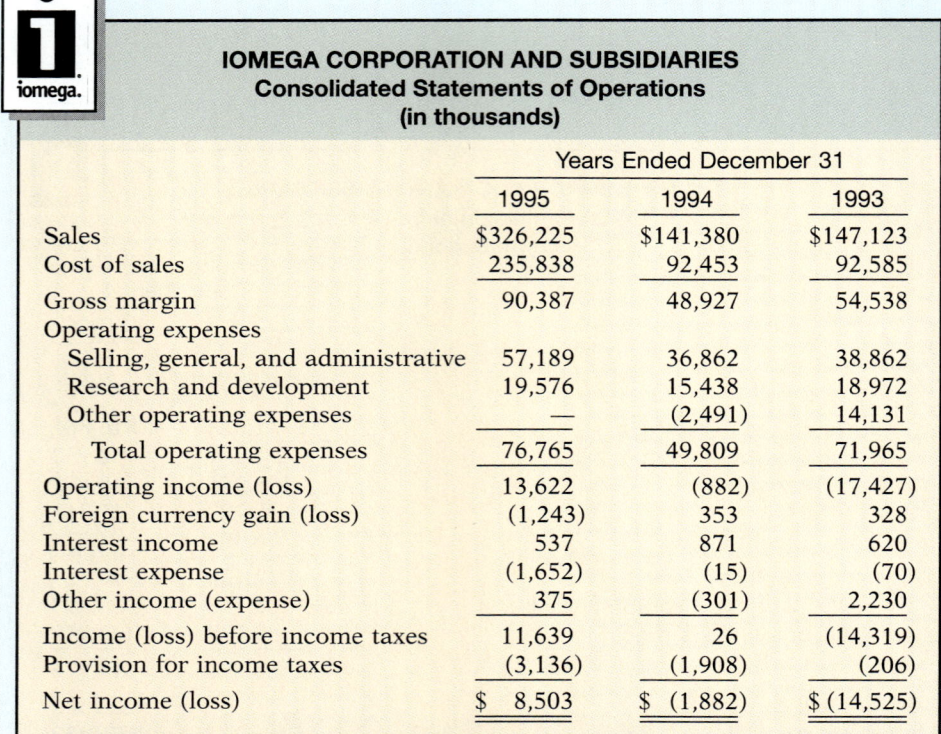

Additional information: Iomega's net cash provided by operating activities was a negative $26,990 (thousand).

Instructions

Using these statements, answer the following questions:

1. Calculate the current ratio for Iomega for 1995 and 1994 and the current cash debt coverage ratio for 1995, and discuss its liquidity position.
2. Calculate the debt to total assets ratio for Iomega for 1995 and 1994 and the cash debt coverage ratio for 1995, and discuss its solvency.
3. Calculate the profit margin ratio and return on assets ratio for Iomega for 1995 and 1994, and discuss its profitability.
4. What other information would be useful in your analysis?

Solution

1. Current ratio:

    1995 ($212,132/$199,509) = 1.06:1; 1994 ($60,557/$25,739) = 2.35:1

    Iomega's liquidity declined substantially from 1994 to 1995. In 1994 there was $2.35 of current assets available to meet current liabilities. In 1995 there was only $1.06. In fact, 1995 working capital was almost negative, since current assets exceeded current liabilities by only $12,623. This should be a concern both to Iomega's short-term creditors and to its investors.

    Current cash debt coverage ratio:

    $$1995 \quad \frac{-\$26{,}990}{(\$199{,}509 + \$25{,}739)/2} = -.24 \text{ times}$$

    It is quite common for a company to have negative cash provided by operations in its early years. Thus, the negative current cash debt coverage ratio is not alarming, although it does reinforce the concern about Iomega's liquidity.

2. Debt to total assets ratio:

   1995 ($203,541/$266,227) = 76%; 1994 ($26,770/$75,833) = 35%

   Iomega's solvency declined considerably from 1994 to 1995 as a result of a large increase in debt financing combined with a relative decline in stockholders' equity. Solvency reflects a company's ability to survive over the long term. Although it is difficult to interpret this ratio without comparative industry data, such a dramatic change might be cause for concern.

   Cash debt coverage ratio:

   $$1995 \quad \frac{-\$26,990}{(\$203,541 + \$26,770)/2} = -.234 \text{ times}$$

   The concern about Iomega's solvency is reinforced by its negative cash debt coverage ratio. While negative cash from operations is fairly common for start-up companies, it is not sustainable in the long-run. That is, if the company does not eventually attain positive cash from operations, it will fail.

3. Profit margin ratio: 1995 ($8,503/$326,225) = 2.6%; no profit margin can be calculated for 1994 since the company had a loss. Return on assets ratio: 1995 [$8,503/[($266,227 + $75,833)/2]] = 5.0%; for 1994, not enough information is available to calculate average assets. Iomega's performance has improved, given that it reported losses in both 1993 and 1994. It should be noted, however, that its return on assets of 5.0% is not particularly impressive for a firm whose stock price is going through the roof.

4. The information gathered above is useful for learning about Iomega, but it is very limited. In order to assess the performance of Iomega more fully, and to determine whether its stock price appears justified, we would want considerably more information, both financial and nonfinancial. First, we would want to have comparative information for competing firms. Second, we would want to calculate additional performance measures that you will learn about in later chapters (e.g., earnings per share and price-earnings ratios). In addition, we would want to see the details of the company's statement of cash flows to assess its ability to generate the funding required to continue to grow. We would want to read the management discussion and analysis section of the annual report to see management's assessment of its plans.

SUMMARY OF STUDY OBJECTIVES

1 *Explain the meaning of generally accepted accounting principles and describe the basic objective of financial reporting.* Generally accepted accounting principles are a set of rules and practices recognized as a general guide for financial reporting purposes. The basic objective of financial reporting is to provide information that is useful for decision making.

2 *Discuss the qualitative characteristics of accounting information.* To be judged useful, information should possess these qualitative characteristics: relevance, reliability, comparability, and consistency.

3 *Identify the two constraints in accounting.* The major constraints are materiality and conservatism.

4 *Distinguish between a single-step and a multiple-step income statement.* In a single-step income statement, all data are classified under two categories, revenues or expenses, and net income is determined in one step. A multiple-step income statement shows numerous steps in determining net income, including results of nonoperating activities.

5 *Identify and compute ratios for analyzing a company's profitability.* Profitability ratios, such as profit margin and return on assets, measure different aspects of the operating success of an enterprise for a given period of time.

6 *Explain the relationship between a retained earn-*

ings statement and a statement of stockholders' equity. The retained earnings statement presents the factors that changed the retained earnings balance during the period. A statement of stockholders' equity presents the factors that changed stockholders' equity during the period, including those that changed retained earnings. Thus, a statement of stockholders' equity is more inclusive.

7 *Identify the sections of a classified balance sheet.* In a classified balance sheet, assets are classified as current assets; long-term investments; property, plant, and equipment; or intangibles. Liabilities are classified as either current or long-term. There is also a stockholders' equity section, which shows common stock and retained earnings.

8 *Identify and compute ratios for analyzing a company's liquidity and solvency.* Liquidity ratios, such as the current ratio, measure the short-term ability of an enterprise to pay its maturing obligations and to meet unexpected needs for cash. Solvency ratios, such as the debt to total assets ratio, measure the ability of an enterprise to survive over a long period.

9 *Identify the sections of the statement of cash flows and the purpose of each.* The statement of cash flows is divided into three sections corresponding to operating activities, investing activities, and financing activities. Each section reports the sources and uses of cash from that activity.

DECISION TOOLKIT—A SUMMARY

Decision Checkpoints	Info Needed for Decision	Tool to Use for Decision	How to Evaluate Results
Is the company using its assets effectively?	Net income and average assets	Return on assets ratio = $\dfrac{\text{Net income}}{\text{Average assets}}$	Higher value suggests favorable efficiency (use of assets).
Is the company maintaining an adequate margin between sales and expenses?	Net income and net sales	Profit margin ratio = $\dfrac{\text{Net income}}{\text{Net sales}}$	Higher value suggests favorable return on each dollar of sales.
Can the company meet its near-term obligations?	Current assets and current liabilities	Current ratio = $\dfrac{\text{Current assets}}{\text{Current liabilities}}$	Higher ratio suggests favorable liquidity.
Can the company meet its long-term obligations?	Total debt and total assets	Debt to total assets ratio = $\dfrac{\text{Total debt}}{\text{Total assets}}$	Lower value suggests favorable solvency.
Can the company meet its near-term obligations?	Current liabilities and cash from operating activities	Current cash debt coverage ratio = $\dfrac{\text{Cash from operating activities}}{\text{Average current liabilities}}$	A higher ratio indicates liquidity, that the company is generating cash sufficient to meet its near-term needs.
Can the company meet its long-term obligations?	Total liabilities and cash from operating activities	Cash debt coverage ratio = $\dfrac{\text{Cash from operating activities}}{\text{Average total liabilities}}$	A higher ratio indicates solvency, that the company is generating cash sufficient to meet its long-term needs.

GLOSSARY

Cash debt coverage ratio A measure of solvency that is calculated as cash provided by operating activities divided by average total liabilities. (p. 67)

Classified balance sheet A balance sheet that contains a number of standard classifications or sections. (p. 58)

Comparability Ability to compare the accounting information of different companies because they use the same accounting principles. (p. 50)

Conservatism The approach of choosing an accounting method when in doubt that will least likely overstate assets and net income. (p. 51)

Consistency Use of the same accounting principles and methods from year to year within a company. (p. 50)

Current assets Cash and other resources that are reasonably expected to be realized in cash or sold or consumed in the business within 1 year or the operating cycle, whichever is longer. (p. 59)

Current cash debt coverage ratio A measure of liquidity that is calculated as cash provided by operating activities divided by average current liabilities. (p. 67)

Current liabilities Obligations reasonably expected to be paid from existing current assets or through the creation of other current liabilities within the next year or operating cycle, whichever is longer. (p. 62)

Current ratio A measure used to evaluate a company's liquidity and short-term debt-paying ability, computed by dividing current assets by current liabilities. (p. 63)

Debt to total assets ratio Measures the percentage of total financing provided by creditors; computed by dividing total debt by total assets. (p. 64)

Financial Accounting Standards Board (FASB) A private organization that establishes generally accepted accounting principles. (p. 49)

Generally accepted accounting principles (GAAP) A set of rules and practices, having substantial authoritative support, that are recognized as a general guide for financial reporting purposes. (p. 49)

Intangible assets Noncurrent assets that do not have physical substance. (p. 61)

Liquidity The ability of a company to pay obligations that are expected to become due within the next year or operating cycle. (p. 63)

Liquidity ratios Measures of the short-term ability of the enterprise to pay its maturing obligations and to meet unexpected needs for cash. (p. 63)

Long-term investments Generally, investments in stocks and bonds of other companies that are normally held for many years. (p. 60)

Long-term liabilities (Long-term debt) Obligations not expected to be paid within 1 year or the operating cycle. (p. 62)

Materiality The constraint of determining whether an item is large enough to likely influence the decision of an investor or creditor. (p. 51)

Operating cycle The average time required to go from cash to cash in producing revenues. (p. 60)

Profit margin ratio Measures the percentage of each dollar of sales that results in net income, computed by dividing net income by net sales. (p. 56)

Profitability ratios Measures of the income or operating success of an enterprise for a given period of time. (p. 56)

Property, plant, and equipment Assets of a relatively permanent nature that are being used in the business and are not intended for resale. (p. 61)

Ratio analysis A technique for evaluating financial statements that expresses the relationship among selected financial statement data. (p. 56)

Relevance The quality of information that indicates the information makes a difference in a decision. (p. 49)

Reliability The quality of information that gives assurance that it is free of error and bias. (p. 49)

Return on assets ratio An overall measure of profitability; computed by dividing net income by average assets. (p. 56)

Solvency The ability of a company to pay interest as it comes due and to repay the face value of debt at maturity. (p. 64)

Solvency ratios Measures of the ability of the enterprise to survive over a long period of time. (p. 64)

Statement of stockholders' equity A financial statement that presents the factors that caused stockholders' equity to change during the period, including those that caused retained earnings to change. (p. 57)

Working capital The excess of current assets over current liabilities. (p. 63)

DEMONSTRATION PROBLEM

Listed here are items taken from the income statement and balance sheet of Circuit City Corporation at February 29, 1996. Certain items have been combined for simplification.

Long-term debt, excluding current installments	$ 399,161
Cash and cash equivalents	43,704
Short-term debt	92,087
Selling, general, and administrative expenses	1,322,430
Common stock, $.50 par value	139,122
Accounts payable	604,488
Prepaid expenses and other current assets	44,395
Property and equipment, net	774,265
Cost of goods sold	5,394,293
Current portion of long-term debt	1,436
Income taxes payable	9,375
Interest expense	25,400
Deferred revenue and other long-term liabilities	231,765
Retained earnings	924,799
Merchandise inventory	1,323,183
Net sales and operating revenues	7,029,123
Net accounts and notes receivable	324,395
Provision for income taxes	107,625
Other assets	16,080
Accrued expenses and other current liabilities	123,789

Instructions

Prepare a multiple-step income statement and a classified balance sheet using the items listed. No item should be used more than once.

Solution to Demonstration Problem

CIRCUIT CITY CORPORATION
Income Statement
For the Year Ended February 29, 1996
(in thousands)

Net sales and operating revenues	$7,029,123
Cost of goods sold	5,394,293
Gross profit	1,634,830
Operating expenses	
Selling, general, and administrative expenses	1,322,430
Income from operations	312,400
Other expenses and losses	
Interest expense	25,400
Income before income taxes	287,000
Provision for income taxes	107,625
Net income	$ 179,375

CIRCUIT CITY CORPORATION
Balance Sheet
February 29, 1996
(in thousands)

Assets

Cash and cash equivalents	$ 43,704
Net accounts and notes receivable	324,395
Merchandise inventory	1,323,183
Prepaid expenses and other current assets	44,395
Total current assets	1,735,677
Property and equipment, net	774,265
Other assets	16,080
Total assets	$2,526,022

Liabilities and Stockholders' Equity

Liabilities	
Current portion of long-term debt	$ 1,436
Accounts payable	604,488
Short-term debt	92,087
Accrued expenses and other current liabilities	123,789
Income taxes payable	9,375
Total current liabilities	831,175
Long-term debt, excluding current installments	399,161
Deferred revenue and other long-term liabilities	231,765
Total liabilities	1,462,101
Stockholders' equity	
Common stock, $.50 par value	139,122
Retained earnings	924,799
Total stockholders' equity	1,063,921
Total liabilities and stockholders' equity	$2,526,022

Self-Study Questions

Answers are at the end of the chapter.

(SO 1) 1. Generally accepted accounting principles are:
(a) a set of standards and rules that are recognized as a general guide for financial reporting.
(b) usually established by the Internal Revenue Service.
(c) the guidelines used to resolve ethical dilemmas.
(d) fundamental truths that can be derived from the laws of nature.

(SO 1) 2. What organization issues U.S. accounting standards?
(a) Financial Accounting Standards Board
(b) International Accounting Standards Committee
(c) International Auditing Standards Committee
(d) None of the above

(SO 2) 3. What is the primary criterion by which accounting information can be judged?
(a) Consistency
(b) Predictive value
(c) Usefulness for decision making
(d) Comparability

(SO 2) 4. Verifiable is an ingredient of:

	Reliability	Relevance
(a)	Yes	Yes
(b)	No	No
(c)	Yes	No
(d)	No	Yes

(SO 3) 5. What accounting constraint refers to the tendency of accountants to resolve uncertainty in a way least likely to overstate assets and revenues?
(a) Comparability   (c) Conservatism
(b) Materiality   (d) Consistency

(SO 5) 6. Which is *not* an indicator of profitability?
(a) Current ratio
(b) Profit margin ratio
(c) Net income
(d) Return on assets ratio

(SO 5) 7. For 1998 Plano Corporation reported net income $24,000; net sales $400,000; and average assets $600,000. What was the 1998 profit margin ratio?
(a) 6%   (c) 40%
(b) 12%   (d) 200%

(SO 7) 8. In a classified balance sheet, assets are usually classified as:
(a) current assets; long-term assets; property, plant, and equipment; and intangible assets.
(b) current assets; long-term investments; property, plant, and equipment; and common stock.
(c) current assets; long-term investments; tangible assets; and intangible assets.
(d) current assets; long-term investments; property, plant, and equipment; and intangible assets.

(SO 7) 9. Current assets are listed:
(a) by liquidity.
(b) by importance.
(c) by longevity.
(d) alphabetically.

(SO 8) 10. Which of these measures is an evaluation of a company's ability to pay current liabilities?
(a) Profit margin ratio
(b) Current ratio
(c) Both (a) and (b)
(d) None of the above

Questions

1. (a) What are generally accepted accounting principles (GAAP)?
   (b) What body provides authoritative support for GAAP?
2. (a) What is the basic objective of financial reporting?
   (b) Identify the qualitative characteristics of accounting information.
3. Ray Aldag, the president of Raynard Company, is pleased. Raynard substantially increased its net income in 1998 while keeping its unit inventory relatively the same. Tom Erhardt, chief accountant, cautions Aldag, however. Erhardt says that since Raynard changed its method of inventory valuation, there is a consistency problem and it is difficult to determine whether Raynard is better off. Is Erhardt correct? Why or why not?
4. What is the distinction between comparability and consistency?
5. Describe the two constraints inherent in the presentation of accounting information.
6. Your roommate believes that international accounting standards are uniform throughout the world. Is your roommate correct? Explain.

76 CHAPTER 2 A Further Look at Financial Statements

7. What is meant by the term *operating cycle*?
8. Define current assets. What basis is used for ordering individual items within the current asset section?
9. Distinguish between long-term investments and property, plant, and equipment.
10. How do current liabilities differ from long-term liabilities?
11. Identify the two parts of stockholders' equity in a corporation and indicate the purpose of each.
12.
    (a) Tia Kim believes that the analysis of financial statements is directed at two characteristics of a company: liquidity and profitability. Is Tia correct? Explain.
    (b) Are short-term creditors, long-term creditors, and stockholders primarily interested in the same characteristics of a company? Explain.
13. Name ratios useful in assessing (a) liquidity, (b) solvency, and (c) profitability.
14. Tony Robins is puzzled. His company had a profit margin ratio of 10% in 1998. He feels that this is an indication that the company is doing well. Joan Graham, his accountant, says that more information is needed to determine the firm's financial well-being. Who is correct? Why?
15. What do these classes of ratios measure?
    (a) Liquidity ratios
    (b) Profitability ratios
    (c) Solvency ratios
16. Holding all other factors constant, indicate whether each of the following signals generally good or bad news about a company.
    (a) Increase in the profit margin ratio
    (b) Increase in the current ratio
    (c) Increase in the debt to total assets ratio
    (d) Decrease in the return on assets ratio
17. Which ratio or ratios from this chapter do you think should be of greatest interest to:
    (a) a pension fund considering investing in a corporation's 20-year bonds?
    (b) a bank contemplating a short-term loan?
    (c) a common stockholder?

BRIEF EXERCISES

Recognize generally accepted accounting principles.
(SO 1)

BE2-1 Indicate whether each statement is *true* or *false*.

(a) GAAP is a set of rules and practices established by the accounting profession to serve as a general guide for financial reporting purposes.
(b) Substantial authoritative support for GAAP usually comes from two standard-setting bodies: the FASB and the IRS.

Identify qualitative characteristics.
(SO 2)

BE2-2 The accompanying chart shows the qualitative characteristics of accounting information. Fill in the blanks.

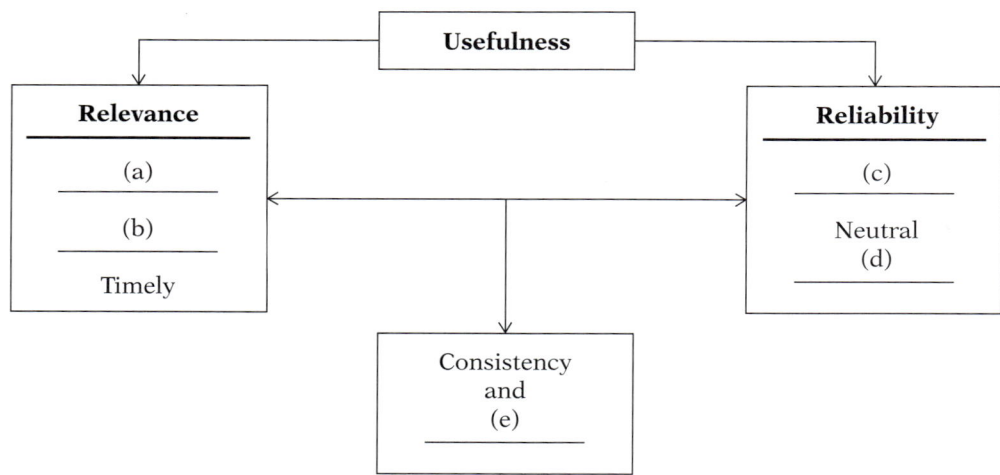

Identify qualitative characteristics.
(SO 2)

BE2-3 Given the *qualitative characteristics* of accounting established by the FASB's conceptual framework, complete each of the following statements.

(a) For information to be _____, it should have predictive or feedback value, and it must be presented on a timely basis.
(b) _____ is the quality of information that gives assurance that it is free of error and bias; it can be depended on.

(c) _____ means using the same accounting principles and methods from year to year within a company.

BE2-4 Here are some qualitative characteristics of accounting information:
1. Predictive value
2. Neutral
3. Verifiable
4. Timely

Identify qualitative characteristics.
(SO 2)

Match each qualitative characteristic to one of the following statements.
_____ (a) Accounting information should help users make predictions about the outcome of past, present, and future events.
_____ (b) Accounting information cannot be selected, prepared, or presented to favor one set of interested users over another.
_____ (c) Accounting information must be proved to be free of error and bias.
_____ (d) Accounting information must be available to decision makers before it loses its capacity to influence their decisions.

BE2-5 The Emelda Company uses these accounting practices:
(a) Inventory is reported at cost when market value is lower.
(b) Small tools are recorded as plant assets and depreciated.
(c) The income statement shows paper clips expense of $10.

Identify constraints that have been violated.
(SO 3)

Indicate the accounting constraint, if any, that has been violated by each practice.

BE2-6 A list of financial statement items for Swann Company includes the following: accounts receivable $16,500; prepaid insurance $3,600; cash $18,400; supplies $5,200; and marketable securities $8,200. Prepare the current asset section of the balance sheet listing the items in the proper sequence.

Prepare the current assets section of a balance sheet.
(SO 7)

BE2-7 These selected condensed data are taken from a recent balance sheet of Bob Evans Farms:

Calculate liquidity ratios.
(SO 8)

Cash	$ 8,241,000
Marketable securities	1,947,000
Accounts receivable	12,545,000
Inventories	14,814,000
Other current assets	5,371,000
Total current assets	$42,918,000
Total current liabilities	$44,844,000

Additional information: Current liabilities at the beginning of the year were $38,242,000, and cash provided by operations for the current year was $58,297,200.

What are (a) the working capital, (b) the current ratio, and (c) the current cash debt coverage ratio?

EXERCISES

E2-1 These financial statement items are for Batra Corporation at year-end, July 31, 1998:

Prepare financial statements.
(SO 4, 7)

Salaries expense	$58,700
Utilities expense	14,900
Equipment	15,900
Accounts payable	6,220
Commission revenue	63,100
Rent revenue	6,500
Unearned rent revenue	1,800
Common stock	20,000
Cash	11,940
Accounts receivable	8,780
Accumulated depreciation	5,400
Dividends	14,000
Depreciation expense	4,000
Retained earnings (beginning of the year)	25,200

78 CHAPTER 2 A Further Look at Financial Statements

Instructions
(a) Prepare a single-step income statement and a retained earnings statement for the year. Batra Corporation did not issue any new stock during the year.
(b) Prepare a classified balance sheet at July 31.

Prepare a classified balance sheet.
(SO 7)

E2-2 These items are taken from the financial statements of Summit's Bowling Alley at December 31, 1998:

Building	$125,800
Accounts receivable	14,520
Prepaid insurance	4,680
Cash	20,840
Equipment	62,400
Land	61,200
Insurance expense	780
Depreciation expense	5,360
Interest expense	2,600
Common stock	80,000
Retained earnings	30,000
Accumulated depreciation—building	45,600
Accounts payable	13,480
Mortgage payable	93,600
Accumulated depreciation—equipment	18,720
Interest payable	2,600
Bowling revenues	14,180

Instructions
Prepare a classified balance sheet; assume that $13,600 of the mortgage payable will be paid in 1999.

Compute liquidity ratios and compare results.
(SO 8)

E2-3 Nordstrom, Inc., operates department stores in numerous states. Selected financial statement data (in millions of dollars) for a recent year are as follows:

	End of Year	Beginning of Year
Cash and cash equivalents	$ 33	$ 91
Receivables (net)	676	586
Merchandise inventory	628	586
Prepaid expenses	61	52
Total current assets	$1,398	$1,315
Total current liabilities	$ 690	$ 627

For the year, net sales were $3,894 and cost of goods sold was $2,600.

Instructions
(a) Compute the working capital and current ratio at the beginning of the year and at the end of the current year.
(b) Did Nordstrom's liquidity improve or worsen during the year?
(c) Using the data in the chapter, compare Nordstrom's liquidity with Best Buy's.

Compute profitability ratios.
(SO 5)

E2-4 Selected comparative statement data for Mighty Products Company are presented here. All balance sheet data are as of December 31.

	1998	1997
Net sales	$800,000	$720,000
Cost of goods sold	480,000	40,000
Interest expense	7,000	5,000
Net income	56,000	42,000
Accounts receivable	120,000	100,000
Inventory	85,000	75,000
Total assets	600,000	500,000
Total common stockholders' equity	450,000	310,000

Instructions

(a) What is the profit margin ratio for 1998?
(b) What is the gross profit for 1998?
(c) Calculate the return on assets ratio for 1998.

PROBLEMS

P2-1 These items are taken from the financial statements of Melinda Corporation for 1998:

Prepare financial statements.
(SO 4, 7)

Retained earnings (beginning of year)	$16,000
Utilities expense	1,700
Equipment	26,000
Accounts payable	13,300
Cash	13,600
Salaries payable	3,000
Common stock	20,000
Dividends	12,000
Service revenue	54,000
Prepaid insurance	3,500
Repair expense	1,800
Depreciation expense	2,600
Accounts receivable	13,500
Insurance expense	2,200
Salaries expense	35,000
Accumulated depreciation	5,600

Instructions
Prepare an income statement, a retained earnings statement, and a classified balance sheet for December 31, 1998.

P2-2 Comparative financial statement data for Chen Corporation and Couric Corporation, two competitors, appear below. All balance sheet data are as of December 31, 1998, and December 31, 1997.

Compute ratios; comment on relative profitability, liquidity, and solvency.
(SO 5, 8)

	Chen Corporation		Couric Corporation	
	1998	1997	1998	1997
Net sales	$1,549,035		$339,038	
Cost of goods sold	1,080,490		238,006	
Operating expenses	302,275		79,000	
Interest expense	6,800		1,252	
Income tax expense	47,840		7,740	
Current assets	325,975	$312,410	83,336	$ 79,467
Plant assets (net)	521,310	500,000	139,728	125,812
Current liabilities	66,325	75,815	35,348	30,281
Long-term liabilities	108,500	90,000	29,620	25,000
Common stock, $10 par	500,000	500,000	120,000	120,000
Retained earnings	172,460	146,595	38,096	29,998

Additional information: Cash provided by operations for 1998 was $162,594 for Chen and $24,211 for Couric.

Instructions
(a) Comment on the relative profitability of the companies by computing the return on assets ratios and the profit margin ratios for both companies.
(b) Comment on the relative liquidity of the companies by computing working capital, the current ratios, and the current cash debt coverage ratios for both companies.
(c) Comment on the relative solvency of the companies by computing the debt to total assets ratio and the cash debt coverage ratio for each.

80 CHAPTER 2 A Further Look at Financial Statements

Compute liquidity, solvency, and profitability ratios.
(SO 5, 8)

 **P2-3** Here are the comparative statements of Magic Johnson Company:

MAGIC JOHNSON COMPANY
Income Statement
For the Years Ended December 31

	1998	1997
Net sales	$1,818,500	$1,750,500
Cost of goods sold	1,005,500	996,000
Gross profit	813,000	754,500
Selling and administrative expense	506,000	479,000
Income from operations	307,000	275,500
Other expenses and losses		
Interest expense	18,000	19,000
Income before income taxes	289,000	256,500
Income tax expense	86,700	77,000
Net income	$ 202,300	$ 179,500

MAGIC JOHNSON COMPANY
Balance Sheet
December 31

	1998	1997
Assets		
Current assets		
Cash	$ 60,100	$ 64,200
Marketable securities	54,000	50,000
Accounts receivable (net)	107,800	102,800
Inventory	123,000	115,500
Total current assets	344,900	332,500
Plant assets (net)	625,300	520,300
Total assets	$970,200	$852,800
Liabilities and Stockholders' Equity		
Current liabilities		
Accounts payable	$150,000	$145,400
Income taxes payable	43,500	42,000
Total current liabilities	193,500	187,400
Bonds payable	210,000	200,000
Total liabilities	403,500	387,400
Stockholders' equity		
Common stock ($5 par)	280,000	300,000
Retained earnings	286,700	165,400
Total stockholders' equity	566,700	465,400
Total liabilities and stockholders' equity	$970,200	$852,800

Additional information: The cash provided by operating activities for 1998 was $190,800.

Instructions
Compute these values and ratios for 1998:
(a) Working capital
(b) Current ratio
(c) Current cash debt coverage ratio
(d) Debt to total assets ratio
(e) Cash debt coverage ratio
(f) Profit margin ratio
(g) Return on assets ratio

P2-4 Condensed balance sheet and income statement data for Pitka Corporation are presented here.

Perform ratio analysis and discuss results.
(SO 5, 8)

PITKA CORPORATION
Balance Sheet
December 31

	1998	1997	1996
Assets			
Cash	$ 25,000	$ 20,000	$ 18,000
Receivables (net)	50,000	45,000	48,000
Other current assets	90,000	85,000	64,000
Investments	75,000	70,000	45,000
Plant and equipment (net)	400,000	370,000	358,000
Total assets	$640,000	$590,000	$533,000
Liabilities and Stockholders' Equity			
Current liabilities	$ 75,000	$ 80,000	$ 70,000
Long-term debt	80,000	85,000	50,000
Common stock, $10 par	340,000	300,000	300,000
Retained earnings	145,000	125,000	113,000
Total liabilities and stockholders' equity	$640,000	$590,000	$533,000

PITKA CORPORATION
Income Statement
For the Years Ended December 31

	1998	1997
Sales	$700,000	$650,000
Cost of goods sold	420,000	400,000
Gross profit	280,000	250,000
Operating expenses (including income taxes)	236,000	218,000
Net income	$ 44,000	$ 32,000

Instructions
Compute these values and ratios for 1997 and 1998:
(a) Profit margin ratio
(b) Return on assets ratio
(c) Working capital
(d) Current ratio
(e) Debt to total assets ratio
(f) Based on the ratios calculated, discuss briefly the improvement or lack thereof in financial position and operating results from 1997 to 1998 of Pitka Corporation.

P2-5 The following financial information is for Caroline Company:

Compute liquidity, solvency, and profitability ratios.
(SO 5, 8)

CAROLINE COMPANY
Balance Sheet
December 31

Assets	1998	1997
Cash	$ 70,000	$ 65,000
Short-term investments	45,000	40,000
Receivables (net)	94,000	90,000
Inventories	130,000	125,000
Prepaid expenses	25,000	23,000
Land	130,000	130,000
Building and equipment (net)	190,000	175,000
Total assets	$684,000	$648,000

82   CHAPTER 2 A Further Look at Financial Statements

Liabilities and Stockholders' Equity

Notes payable	$100,000	$100,000
Accounts payable	45,000	42,000
Accrued liabilities	40,000	40,000
Bonds payable, due 2000	150,000	150,000
Common stock, $10 par	200,000	200,000
Retained earnings	149,000	116,000
Total liabilities and stockholders' equity	$684,000	$648,000

CAROLINE COMPANY
Income Statement
For the Years Ended December 31

	1998	1997
Sales	$850,000	$790,000
Cost of goods sold	620,000	575,000
Gross profit	230,000	215,000
Operating expenses	194,000	180,000
Net income	$ 36,000	$ 35,000

Additional information: Total assets at the beginning of 1997 were $630,000, current liabilities were $155,000, and total liabilities were $305,000. Cash provided by operations for 1998 was $47,000 and for 1997 was $32,000.

Instructions
Indicate, by using ratios, the change in liquidity, solvency, and profitability of Caroline Company from 1997 to 1998.

P2-6 Selected financial data (in millions) of two intense competitors in a recent year are presented here:

Perform ratio analysis and discuss results.
(SO 5, 8)

	Kmart	Wal-Mart
Income Statement Data for Year		
Net sales	$34,025	$82,494
Cost of goods sold	25,992	65,586
Selling and administrative expenses	7,701	12,858
Interest expense	494	706
Other income (net)	572	918
Income taxes	114	1,581
Net income	$ 296	$ 2,681
Balance Sheet Data (End of Year)		
Current assets	$ 9,187	$15,338
Property, plant, and equipment (net)	7,842	17,481
Total assets	$17,029	$32,819
Current liabilities	$ 5,626	$ 9,973
Long-term debt	5,371	10,120
Total stockholders' equity	6,032	12,726
Total liabilities and stockholders' equity	$17,029	$32,819
Beginning-of-Year Balances		
Total assets	$17,504	$26,441
Total stockholders' equity	6,093	10,753

Instructions
For each company, compute these values and ratios:
(a) Working capital
(b) Current ratio
(c) Debt to total assets ratio
(d) Return on assets ratio

(e) Profit margin ratio
(f) Compare the liquidity, solvency, and profitability of the two companies.

P2-7 Here are the comparative statements of Ultra Vision Company:

Perform ratio analysis.
(SO 5, 8)

ULTRA VISION COMPANY
Income Statement
For the Year Ended December 31

	1998	1997
Net sales (all on account)	$600,000	$520,000
Expenses		
Cost of goods sold	415,000	354,000
Selling and administrative expense	120,800	114,800
Interest expense	7,200	6,000
Income tax expense	18,000	14,000
Total expenses	561,000	488,800
Net income	$ 39,000	$ 31,200

ULTRA VISION COMPANY
Balance Sheet
December 31

	1998	1997
Assets		
Current assets		
Cash	$ 21,000	$ 18,000
Marketable securities	18,000	15,000
Accounts receivable (net)	92,000	74,000
Inventory	84,000	70,000
Total current assets	$215,000	$177,000
Plant assets (net)	423,000	383,000
Total assets	$638,000	$560,000
Liabilities and Stockholders' Equity		
Current liabilities		
Accounts payable	$112,000	$110,000
Income taxes payable	23,000	20,000
Total current liabilities	135,000	130,000
Long-term liabilities		
Bonds payable	130,000	80,000
Total liabilities	265,000	210,000
Stockholders' equity		
Common stock ($5 par)	150,000	150,000
Retained earnings	223,000	200,000
Total stockholders' equity	373,000	350,000
Total liabilities and stockholders' equity	$638,000	$560,000

Instructions
Compute these values and ratios for 1998:
(a) Current ratio
(b) Working capital
(c) Debt to total assets ratio
(d) Profit margin ratio
(e) Return on assets ratio

ALTERNATIVE PROBLEMS

Prepare financial statements.
(SO 4, 7)

P2-1A These items are taken from the financial statements of Batavia Company:

Cash	$ 8,200
Accounts receivable	7,500
Prepaid insurance	1,800
Equipment	28,000
Accumulated depreciation	8,600
Accounts payable	12,000
Salaries payable	3,000
Common stock	20,000
Retained earnings (beginning)	14,000
Dividends	7,200
Service revenue	42,000
Repair expense	3,200
Depreciation expense	2,800
Insurance expense	1,200
Salaries expense	36,000
Utilities expense	3,700

Instructions
Prepare an income statement, a retained earnings statement, and a classified balance sheet for December 31, 1998.

Compute ratios; comment on relative profitability, liquidity, and solvency.
(SO 5, 8)

P2-2A Comparative statement data for Brooks Company and Shields Company, two competitors, are presented here. All balance sheet data are as of December 31, 1998, and December 31, 1997.

	Brooks Company		Shields Company	
	1998	1997	1998	1997
Net sales	$250,000		$1,200,000	
Cost of goods sold	160,000		720,000	
Operating expenses	51,000		252,000	
Interest expense	3,000		10,000	
Income tax expense	11,000		65,000	
Current assets	130,000	$110,000	700,000	$650,000
Plant assets (net)	305,000	270,000	800,000	750,000
Current liabilities	60,000	52,000	250,000	275,000
Long-term liabilities	50,000	68,000	200,000	150,000
Common stock	260,000	210,000	750,000	700,000
Retained earnings	65,000	50,000	300,000	275,000

Additional information: Cash provided by operations for 1998 was $22,000 for Brooks and $185,000 for Shields.

Instructions
(a) Comment on the relative profitability of the companies by computing the return on assets ratios and the profit margin ratios for both companies.
(b) Comment on the relative liquidity of the companies by computing working capital, the current ratios, and the current cash debt coverage ratios for both companies.
(c) Comment on the relative solvency of the companies by computing the debt to total assets ratio and the cash debt coverage ratio for each.

P2-3A The comparative statements of Marti Rosen Company are presented here:

Compute liquidity, solvency, and profitability ratios.
(SO 5, 8)

MARTI ROSEN COMPANY
Income Statement
For the Years Ended December 31

	1998	1997
Net sales	$660,000	$624,000
Cost of goods sold	440,000	405,600
Gross profit	220,000	218,400
Selling and administrative expense	143,880	149,760
Income from operations	76,120	68,640
Other expenses and losses		
Interest expense	7,920	7,200
Income before income taxes	68,200	61,440
Income tax expense	25,300	24,000
Net income	$ 42,900	$ 37,440

MARTI ROSEN COMPANY
Balance Sheet
December 31

	1998	1997
Assets		
Current assets		
Cash	$ 23,100	$ 21,600
Marketable securities	34,800	33,000
Accounts receivable (net)	106,200	93,800
Inventory	72,400	64,000
Total current assets	236,500	212,400
Plant assets (net)	465,300	459,600
Total assets	$701,800	$672,000
Liabilities and Stockholders' Equity		
Current liabilities		
Accounts payable	$134,200	$132,000
Income taxes payable	25,300	24,000
Total current liabilities	159,500	156,000
Bonds payable	132,000	120,000
Total liabilities	291,500	276,000
Stockholders' equity		
Common stock ($10 par)	140,000	150,000
Retained earnings	270,300	246,000
Total stockholders' equity	410,300	396,000
Total liabilities and stockholders' equity	$701,800	$672,000

Additional information: Cash provided by operating activities was $64,600 for 1998.

Instructions
Compute these values and ratios for 1998:
(a) Current ratio
(b) Working capital
(c) Current cash debt coverage ratio
(d) Debt to total assets ratio
(e) Cash debt coverage ratio
(f) Profit margin ratio
(g) Return on assets ratio

86 CHAPTER 2 A Further Look at Financial Statements

Perform ratio analysis and discuss results.
(SO 5, 8)

P2-4A Condensed balance sheet and income statement data for Los Colinas Corporation are presented next.

LOS COLINAS CORPORATION
Balance Sheet
December 31

	1998	1997	1996
Assets			
Cash	$ 40,000	$ 24,000	$ 20,000
Receivables (net)	70,000	45,000	48,000
Other current assets	80,000	75,000	62,000
Investments	90,000	70,000	50,000
Plant and equipment (net)	450,000	400,000	360,000
Total assets	$730,000	$614,000	$540,000
Liabilities and Stockholders' Equity			
Current liabilities	$ 98,000	$ 75,000	$ 70,000
Long-term debt	97,000	75,000	65,000
Common stock, $10 par	400,000	340,000	300,000
Retained earnings	135,000	124,000	105,000
Total liabilities and stockholders' equity	$730,000	$614,000	$540,000

LOS COLINAS CORPORATION
Income Statement
For the Years Ended December 31

	1998	1997
Sales	$660,000	$700,000
Cost of goods sold	420,000	400,000
Gross profit	240,000	300,000
Operating expenses (including income taxes)	194,000	237,000
Net income	$ 46,000	$ 63,000

Instructions
Compute these values and ratios for 1997 and 1998:
(a) Profit margin ratio   (c) Working capital
(b) Return on assets ratio   (d) Current ratio
(e) Debt to total assets ratio
(f) Based on the ratios calculated, discuss briefly the improvement or lack thereof in the financial position and operating results from 1997 to 1998 of Los Colinas.

Compute liquidity, solvency, and profitability ratios.
(SO 5, 8)

P2-5A Financial information for Star Track Company is presented here:

STAR TRACK COMPANY
Balance Sheet
December 31

	1998	1997
Assets		
Cash	$ 50,000	$ 42,000
Short-term investments	80,000	100,000
Receivables (net)	100,000	87,000
Inventories	440,000	400,000
Prepaid expenses	25,000	31,000
Land	75,000	75,000
Building and equipment (net)	570,000	500,000
Total assets	$1,340,000	$1,235,000

Liabilities and Stockholders' Equity

Notes payable	$ 125,000	$ 125,000
Accounts payable	160,000	140,000
Accrued liabilities	50,000	50,000
Bonds payable, due 2000	200,000	200,000
Common stock, $5 par	500,000	500,000
Retained earnings	305,000	220,000
Total liabilities and stockholders' equity	$1,340,000	$1,235,000

STAR TRACK COMPANY
Income Statement
For the Years Ended December 31

	1998	1997
Sales	$1,000,000	$940,000
Cost of goods sold	650,000	635,000
Gross profit	350,000	305,000
Operating expenses	235,000	215,000
Net income	$ 115,000	$ 90,000

Additional information: Total assets at the beginning of 1997 were $1,175,000, current liabilities were $300,000, and total liabilities were $500,000. Cash provided by operations was $125,000 in 1998 and $75,000 in 1997.

Instructions
Indicate, by using ratios, the change in liquidity, solvency, and profitability of Star Track Company from 1997 to 1998.

P2-6A Selected financial data (in millions) of two intense competitors in a recent year are presented here:

Perform ratio analysis and discuss results.
(SO 5, 8)

	Bethlehem Steel Corporation	Inland Steel Corporation
	Income Statement Data for Year	
Net sales	$4,819	$4,497
Cost of goods sold	4,548	3,991
Selling and administrative expense	137	265
Interest expense	46	72
Other income (net)	7	0
Income taxes	14	62
Net income	$ 81	$ 107
	Balance Sheet Data (End of Year)	
Current assets	$1,569	$1,081
Property, plant, and equipment (net)	2,759	1,610
Other assets	1,454	662
Total assets	$5,782	$3,353
Current liabilities	$1,011	$ 565
Long-term debt	3,615	2,056
Total stockholders' equity	1,156	732
Total liabilities and stockholders' equity	$5,782	$3,353
	Beginning-of-Year Balances	
Total assets	$5,877	$3,436
Total stockholders' equity	697	623

88 CHAPTER 2 A Further Look at Financial Statements

Instructions
For each company, compute these values and ratios:
(a) Working capital
(b) Current ratio
(c) Debt to total assets ratio
(d) Return on assets ratio
(e) Profit margin ratio
(f) Compare the liquidity, profitability, and solvency of the two companies.

BROADENING YOUR PERSPECTIVE

FINANCIAL REPORTING AND ANALYSIS

FINANCIAL REPORTING PROBLEM: *Starbucks Corporation*

BYP2-1 The financial statements of Starbucks Corporation are presented in Appendix A at the end of this book.

Instructions
Answer the following questions using the Consolidated Balance Sheet and the Notes to Consolidated Financial Statements section.
(a) What were Starbucks' total current assets at September 29, 1996, and October 1, 1995?
(b) Are the assets included in current assets listed in the proper order? Explain.
(c) How are Starbucks' assets classified?
(d) What were Starbucks' current liabilities at September 29, 1996, and October 1, 1995?

COMPARATIVE ANALYSIS PROBLEM: *Starbucks vs. Green Mountain Coffee*

BYP2-2 The financial statements of Green Mountain Coffee are presented in Appendix B, following the financial statements for Starbucks in Appendix A.

Instructions
(a) For each company calculate the following values for 1996:
   (1) Working capital
   (2) Current ratio
   (3) Debt to total assets ratio
   (4) Profit margin ratio
   (5) Return on assets ratio
(b) Based on your findings above, discuss the relative liquidity, solvency, and profitability of the two companies.

RESEARCH CASE

BYP2-3 Several commonly available indexes enable individuals to locate articles from numerous business publications and periodicals. Articles can generally be searched for by company name or by subject matter. Four common indexes are *The Wall Street Journal Index, Business Abstracts* (formerly *Business Periodicals Index*), *Predicasts F&S Index,* and *ABI/Inform.*

Instructions
Use one of these resources to find a list of articles about a New York Stock Exchange company of your choosing. Choose an article from this list that you believe would be of interest to an investor or creditor of this company. Read the article and answer the fol-

lowing questions. [*Note:* Your library may have either hard-copy or CD-ROM versions of these indexes.]
(a) What is the article about?
(b) What company-specific information is included in the article?
(c) Is the article related to anything you read in this chapter?
(d) Identify any accounting-related issues discussed in the article.

INTERPRETING FINANCIAL STATEMENTS

BYP2-4 Minicase 1 *Kellogg Company*
Kellogg Company has its headquarters in Battle Creek, Michigan. The company manufactures and sells ready-to-eat breakfast cereals and convenience foods including toaster pastries and cereal bars.

Selected data from Kellogg Company's 1994 annual report follows (dollar amounts and share data in millions):

	1994	1993	1992
Net sales	$6,562.0	$6,295.4	$6,190.6
Cost of goods sold	2,950.7	2,989.0	2,987.7
Selling and administrative expense	2,448.7	2,237.5	2,140.1
Net income	705.4	680.7	431.2

In its 1994 annual report, Kellogg Company outlined its plans for the future, which it described as its six "global strategies." A brief description of these plans follows.
1. Focus on the cereal and convenience food markets that are considered to be core businesses. The company has already divested seven businesses in the past three years that it considered noncore, such as the Mrs. Smith's pie business. In the coming year, Kellogg Company plans to invest more heavily in advertising in order to build brand recognition in the U.S. cereal market.
2. Continue to launch more new products.
3. Continue to be the first to introduce ready-to-eat cereals in countries around the world. Kellogg Company achieved this goal in India and the Soviet Union, and plans to achieve the goal in China.
4. Maintain or reduce present levels of capital expenditures. Kellogg Company plans to achieve this goal by using value-based management and value engineering.
5. Reduce operating costs. This measure is made necessary because of the limited ability to increase sales prices. Kellogg Company reported that cost of goods sold per kilo was virtually flat in 1994.
6. Repurchase shares of its own stock aggressively. This is done partly to improve earnings per share.

Instructions
(a) For each of the six global strategies, describe how gross profit and net income are likely to be affected.
(b) Compute the percentage change in sales, gross profit, operating costs (cost of goods sold plus selling and administrative expenses), and net income from year to year for each of the three years shown. Evaluate Kellogg Company's performance. Which trend seems to be least favorable? Do you think the global strategies described will improve that trend? Explain.

BYP2-5 Minicase 2 *Amoco Corporation*
Amoco Corporation explores for and produces crude oil and natural gas; converts crude oil into petroleum products; transports, distributes, and markets petroleum products; and produces various plastic and foam products.

Amoco's 1995 balance sheet and income statement are reproduced on the following pages.

AMOCO CORPORATION AND SUBSIDIARIES
Consolidated Statement of Financial Position (Balance Sheet)
December 31, 1995
(in millions)

Assets

Current assets	
Cash	$ 182
Marketable securities	1,212
Accounts and notes receivable, net	3,332
Inventories	1,041
Prepaid expenses and income taxes	723
Total current assets	6,490
Investments and other assets	
Investments and related advances	654
Long-term receivables and other assets	655
	1,309
Properties—at cost, less accumulated depreciation	22,046
Total assets	$29,845

Liabilities and Stockholders' Equity

Current liabilities	
Current portion of long-term obligations	$ 341
Short-term obligations	735
Accounts payable	2,822
Accrued liabilities	989
Taxes payable (including income taxes)	887
Total current liabilities	5,774
Long-term debt	
Debt	3,962
Deferred credits and other noncurrent liabilities	
Income taxes	2,745
Other	2,516
	5,261
Stockholders' equity	
Common stock	2,590
Earnings retained and invested in the business	12,258
Total stockholders' equity	14,848
Total liabilities and stockholders' equity	$29,845

AMOCO CORPORATION AND SUBSIDIARIES
Consolidated Income Statement
For the Year Ended December 31, 1995
(in millions)

Revenues	
Sales and other operating revenues	$27,066
Consumer excise taxes	3,339
Other income	599
Total revenues	31,004
Costs and expenses	
Cost of goods sold	14,140
Operating expenses	4,555
Petroleum exploration expenses, including exploratory dry holes	610
Selling and administrative expenses	2,124
Taxes other than income taxes	4,042
Depreciation expense	2,794
Interest expense	335
Total costs and expenses	28,600
Income before income taxes	2,404
Income tax expense	542
Net income	$ 1,862

The following additional information is excerpted from Amoco's 1995 annual report:

AMOCO CORPORATION AND SUBSIDIARIES
Excerpts from 1995 Annual Report

Significant spending in 1996 includes construction of a liquefied natural gas plant in Trinidad and continuation of programs in Egypt and the North Sea. . . . It is expected that the 1996 capital and exploration expenditures budget will be financed primarily by funds generated internally.

In July 1994, Amoco announced that the organizational structure of the corporation was being changed. . . . As a result of the restructuring, more than 4,000 positions have been eliminated through year-end 1995. Additional positions will be eliminated in 1996 and 1997 as a result of the ongoing process redesign. . . .

Other income in 1995 included a gain of $132 million ($83 million after tax) related to the sale of Amoco Motor Club.

The Internal Revenue Service (IRS) has challenged the application of certain foreign income taxes as credits against the corporation's U.S. taxes that otherwise would have been payable for the years 1980 through 1982. On June 18, 1992, the IRS issued a statutory Notice of Deficiency for additional taxes in the amount of $466 million, plus interest, relating to 1982. The corporation has filed a petition in the U.S. Tax Court contesting the IRS statutory Notice of Deficiency. Trial on the matter was held in April 1995, and a decision is expected in 1996.

Instructions
(a) Evaluate Amoco by calculating and evaluating the current ratio, the debt to total assets ratio, and the profit margin ratio.
(b) From the information given in the case, describe the performance you would expect from Amoco for 1996. Be specific. For example, which ratio(s) would you expect to improve? Which events are likely to affect performance?

CRITICAL THINKING

MANAGEMENT DECISION CASE

BYP2-6 As the accountant for J. Martinez Manufacturing Inc., you have been requested to develop some key ratios from the comparative financial statements. This information is to be used to convince creditors that J. Martinez Manufacturing Inc. is liquid, solvent, and profitable, and deserves their continued support. Lenders are particularly concerned about the company's ability to continue as a going concern.

These are the data requested and the computations developed from the financial statements:

	1998	1997
Current ratio	3.1	2.1
Working capital	Up 22%	Down 7%
Debt to total assets ratio	.60	.70
Net income	Up 32%	Down 8%
Profit margin ratio	.05	.015
Return on assets ratio	.09	.04
Gross profit	Up 22%	Down 12%

Instructions

J. Martinez Manufacturing Inc. asks you to prepare brief comments stating how each of these items supports the argument that its financial health is improving. The company wishes to use these comments to support presentation of data to its creditors. You are to prepare the comments as requested, giving the implications and the limitations of each item separately, and then the collective inference that may be drawn from them about J. Martinez's financial well-being.

A REAL-WORLD FOCUS: *Bethlehem Corporation*

BYP2-7 Located in Easton, Pennsylvania, **Bethlehem Corporation** was established in 1856. Today it offers contract services for industrial products, rebuilding and remanufacturing industrial and military equipment per customer specifications and designs. The company also manufactures and sells a line of equipment used in the chemical, environmental, and food industries.

Bethlehem Corporation has a net loss for 1994 of $239,251. One reason for the loss is that Bethlehem reported a loss (and a liability) for expenses and costs associated with certain legal proceedings against Bethlehem. They have not yet lost the case, but they are anticipating losing at least some money.

Instructions

(a) Do you think that a loss such as this is relevant to users of Bethlehem's financial statements?
(b) How reliable do you think the estimate of the loss is? What information should the company use to estimate the loss?
(c) Bethlehem reported a loss and a liability related to this lawsuit. Where in its financial statements would you expect to find these two amounts—that is, in what part of the income statement would the loss be presented (assuming a multiple-step income statement) and in what part of the balance sheet would the liability be presented?

GROUP ACTIVITY

BYP2-8 A classified balance sheet has these sections: current assets; property, plant, and equipment; long-term investments; intangible assets; current liabilities; long-term liabilities; and stockholders' equity.

Instructions
With the class divided into seven groups, each group should choose one section of the classified balance sheet. Each group is to explain its section and illustrate the section using an example from a published annual report.

COMMUNICATION ACTIVITY

BYP2-9 L. R. Stanton is the chief executive officer of Hi-Tech Electronics. Stanton is an expert engineer but a novice in accounting.

Instructions
Write a letter to L. R. Stanton that explains (a) the three main types of ratios and (b) the bases for comparison in analyzing Hi-Tech's financial statements.

ETHICS CASE

BYP2-10 As the controller of Breathless Perfume Company, you discover a significant misstatement that overstated net income in the prior year's financial statements. The misleading financial statements are contained in the company's annual report, which was issued to banks and other creditors less than a month ago. After much thought about the consequences of telling the president, Eddy Kadu, about this misstatement, you gather your courage to inform him. Eddy says, "Hey! What they don't know won't hurt them. But, just so we set the record straight, we'll adjust this year's financial statements for last year's misstatement. We can absorb that misstatement better this year than last year anyway! Just don't make that kind of mistake again."

Instructions
(a) Who are the stakeholders in this situation?
(b) What are the ethical issues?
(c) What would you do as the controller?

FINANCIAL ANALYSIS ON THE WEB

BYP2-11 *Purpose:* Identify summary liquidity, solvency, and profitability information about companies, and compare this information across companies in the same industry.

Address: http://biz.yahoo.com/i

Steps:
1. Select **Company.**
2. Type in a company name, or use index to find company name.
   Perform instructions (a) and (b) below.
3. Click on the company's particular industry behind the heading "Industry."
   Perform instructions (c) and (d).

Instructions
Answer the following questions:
(a) What was the company's current ratio, debt to equity ratio, profit margin, and return on assets?
(b) What is the company's industry?
(c) What is the name of a competitor? What is the competitor's current ratio, debt to equity ratio, profit margin, and return on assets?
(d) Based on these measures: Which company is more liquid? Which company is more solvent? Which company is more profitable?

CHAPTER 2 A Further Look at Financial Statements

BYP2-12 *Purpose:* This exercise is an introduction to the Big Six Accounting firms.

Addresses:

Arthur Andersen	http://www.arthurandersen.com/
Coopers & Lybrand	http://www.colybrand.com/
Deloitte & Touche	http://www.dttus.com/
Ernst & Young	http://www.ey.com/default.htm
KPMG Peat Marwick	http://www.us.kpmg.com/
Price Waterhouse	http://www.pw.com/

Steps:
1. Select a firm that is of interest to you.
2. Go to the firm's homepage.

Instructions
Answer the following questions:
(a) Name two services provided by the firm.
(b) What is the firm's total annual revenue?
(c) How many clients does it service?
(d) How many people are employed by the firm?

Answers to Self-Study Questions
1. a 2. a 3. c 4. c 5. c 6. a 7. a 8. d 9. a 10. b

CHAPTER 3

The Accounting Information System

STUDY OBJECTIVES

After studying this chapter, you should be able to:

1. Analyze the effect of business transactions on the basic accounting equation.
2. Explain what an account is and how it helps in the recording process.
3. Define debits and credits and explain how they are used to record business transactions.
4. Identify the basic steps in the recording process.
5. Explain what a journal is and how it helps in the recording process.
6. Explain what a ledger is and how it helps in the recording process.
7. Explain what posting is and how it helps in the recording process.
8. Explain the purposes of a trial balance.

Accidents Happen

How organized are you financially? Take a short quiz. Answer *yes* or *no* to each question:

- Is your wallet jammed full of gas station receipts from places you don't remember ever going?
- Does your wallet contain so many cash machine receipts that you've been declared a walking fire hazard?
- Is your wallet such a mess that it is often faster to fish for money in the crack of your car seat than to dig around in your wallet?
- Was Michael Jordan playing high school basketball the last time you balanced your checkbook?
- Have you ever been tempted to burn down your house so you don't have to try to find all of the forms, receipts, and records that you need to fill out your tax returns?

If you think it is hard to keep track of the many transactions that make up *your* life, imagine what it is like for a major corporation like Fidelity Investments, which as the largest mutual fund management firm in the world, manages more than $300 billion of investments. Millions of individuals have the bulk of their life savings invested in mutual funds. If you had your life savings invested at Fidelity Investments, you might be just slightly displeased if, when you called to find out your balance, the representative said, "You know, I kind of remember someone with a name like yours sending us some money—now what did we do with that?"

To ensure the accuracy of your balance and the security of your funds, Fidelity Investments, like all other companies large and small, relies on a sophisticated accounting information system. That's not to say that Fidelity or anybody else is error-free. In fact, if you've ever really messed up your checkbook register, you may take some comfort from one accountant's mistake at Fidelity Investments. The accountant failed to include a minus sign while doing a calculation, making what was actually a $1.3 billion loss look like a $1.3 billion gain—yes, *billion!* Fortunately, like most accounting errors, it was detected before any real harm was done.

No one expects that kind of mistake at a firm like Fidelity, which has sophisticated computer systems and top investment managers. In explaining the mistake to shareholders, a spokesperson wrote: "Some people have asked how, in this age of technology, such a mistake could be made. While many of our processes are computerized, accounting systems are complex and dictate that some steps must be handled manually by our managers and accountants, and people can make mistakes."

On the World Wide Web
Fidelity Investment:
http://www.fidelity.com

97

PREVIEW OF CHAPTER 3

As indicated in the opening story, a reliable information system is a necessity for any company. The purpose of this chapter is to explain and illustrate the features of an accounting information system. The organization and content of the chapter are as follows:

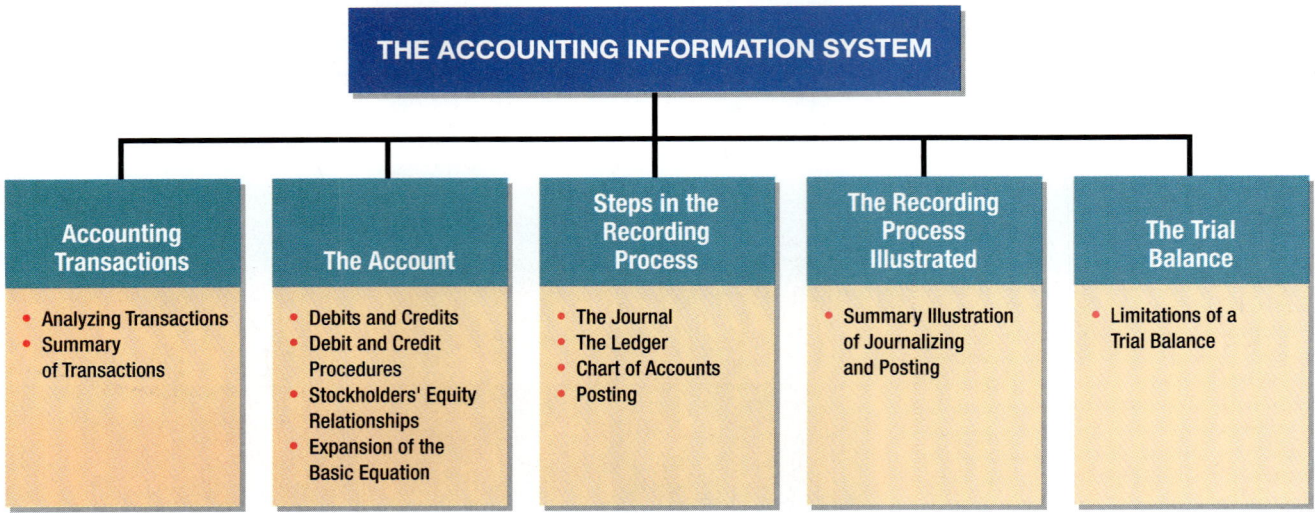

Accounting Information System

The system of collecting and processing transaction data and communicating financial information to interested parties is known as the **accounting information system.** Accounting information systems vary widely from one business to another. Factors that shape these systems are the nature of the business and the transactions in which it engages, the size of the firm, the volume of data to be handled, and the information demands that management and others place on the system.

Accounting Transactions

To use the accounting information system to develop financial statements, you need to know what economic events to recognize (record). For example, suppose General Motors hired a new employee or purchased a new computer. Are these events entered in their accounting records? Not all events are recorded and reported in the financial statements. We call economic events that require recording in the financial statements **accounting transactions.**

An accounting transaction occurs when assets, liabilities, or stockholders' equity items change as a result of some economic event. The purchase of a computer by General Motors, the payment of rent by Microsoft, and the sale of advertising space by Sierra Corporation are examples of events that change a company's assets, liabilities, or stockholders' equity. Illustration 3-1 summarizes the decision process used to decide whether or not to record economic events.

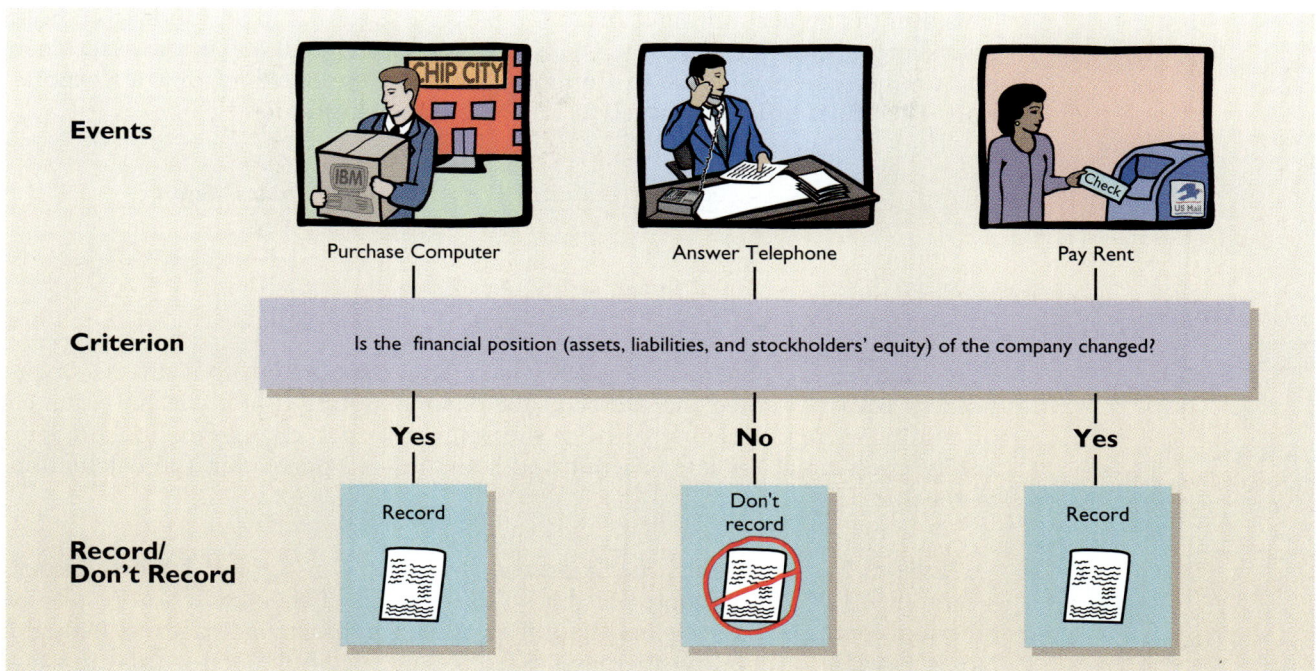

Illustration 3-1 Transaction identification process

ANALYZING TRANSACTIONS

In Chapter 1 you learned the basic accounting equation:

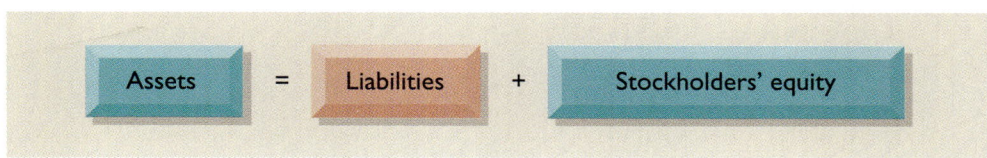

STUDY OBJECTIVE 1

Analyze the effect of business transactions on the basic accounting equation.

In this chapter you will learn how to analyze transactions in terms of their effect on assets, liabilities, and stockholders' equity. **Transaction analysis** is the process of identifying the specific effects of economic events on the accounting equation.

The accounting equation must always balance. Therefore, each transaction has a dual (double-sided) effect on the equation. For example, if an individual asset is increased, there must be a corresponding:

Decrease in another asset, *or*

Increase in a specific liability, *or*

Increase in stockholders' equity

It is quite possible that two or more items could be affected when an asset is increased. For example, if a company purchases a computer for $10,000 by paying $6,000 in cash and signing a note for $4,000, one asset (computer) increases $10,000, another asset (cash) decreases $6,000, and a liability (notes payable) increases $4,000. The result is that the accounting equation remains in balance.

Chapter 1 presented the financial statements for Sierra Corporation for its first month. To illustrate how economic events affect the accounting equation, events affecting Sierra Corporation during its first month are examined:

EVENT (1). INVESTMENT OF CASH BY STOCKHOLDERS. On October 1 cash of $10,000 is invested in the business in exchange for $10,000 of common stock.

This event is an accounting transaction because it results in an increase in both assets and stockholders' equity. There is an increase of $10,000 in the asset Cash and an increase of $10,000 in Common Stock on the books of Sierra Corporation. The effect of this transaction on the basic equation is:

	Assets	=	Liabilities	+	Stockholders' Equity	
	Cash	=			Common Stock	
(1)	+$10,000	=			+$10,000	Issued Stock

The equation is in balance. To the right of each transaction that affects stockholders' equity is noted the source of the change; in this case it was an issuance of common stock. Keeping track of the source of each change in stockholders' equity is essential for later accounting activities—in particular, the calculation of income.

EVENT (2). NOTE ISSUED IN EXCHANGE FOR CASH. On October 1 Sierra issued a 3-month, 12%, $5,000 note payable to Castle Bank. This transaction results in an equal increase in assets and liabilities: Cash (an asset) increases $5,000 and Notes Payable (a liability) increases $5,000. The specific effect of this transaction and the cumulative effect of the first two transactions are:

		Assets	=	Liabilities	+	Stockholders' Equity
		Cash	=	Notes Payable	+	Common Stock
	Old Balance	$10,000				$10,000
(2)		+5,000		+$5,000		
	New Balance	$15,000	=	$5,000	+	$10,000
				$15,000		

Observe that total assets are now $15,000 and stockholders' equity plus the new liability also total $15,000.

EVENT (3). PURCHASE OF OFFICE EQUIPMENT FOR CASH. On October 2 Sierra acquired office equipment by paying $5,000 cash to Superior Equipment Sales Co. This event is a transaction because an equal increase and decrease in Sierra's assets occur: Office Equipment (an asset) increases $5,000 and Cash (an asset) decreases $5,000:

		Assets			=	Liabilities	+	Stockholders' Equity
		Cash	+	Office Equipment	=	Notes Payable	+	Common Stock
	Old Balance	$15,000				$5,000		$10,000
(3)		−5,000		+$5,000				
	New Balance	$10,000	+	$5,000	=	$5,000	+	$10,000
		$15,000				$15,000		

The total assets are now $15,000 and stockholders' equity plus the liability also total $15,000.

EVENT (4). RECEIPT OF CASH IN ADVANCE FROM CUSTOMER. On October 2 Sierra received a $1,200 cash advance from R. Knox, a client. This event is a transaction because cash (an asset) was received for advertising services that are expected to be completed by Sierra by December 31. However, revenue should not be recorded until the work has been performed. Since the cash was received prior to performance of the service, Sierra has a liability for the work due. Cash increases by $1,200 and a liability, Unearned Service Revenue (abbreviated as Unearned Revenue), increases by an equal amount.

	Assets			=	Liabilities			+	Stockholders' Equity
	Cash	+	Office Equipment	=	Notes Payable	+	Unearned Revenue	+	Common Stock
Old Balance	$10,000		$5,000		$5,000				$10,000
(4)	+1,200						+$1,200		
New Balance	$11,200	+	$5,000	=	$5,000	+	$1,200	+	$10,000
	$16,200						$16,200		

EVENT (5). SERVICES RENDERED FOR CASH. On October 3 Sierra received $10,000 in cash from Copa Company for advertising services performed. This event is a transaction because Sierra received an asset, cash, in exchange for services. Advertising service is the principal revenue-producing activity of Sierra. **Revenue increases stockholders' equity.** Both assets and stockholders' equity are, then, increased by this transaction. Cash is increased $10,000, and Retained Earnings is increased $10,000. The new balances in the equation are:

	Assets			=	Liabilities			+	Stockholders' Equity			
	Cash	+	Office Equipment	=	Notes Payable	+	Unearned Revenue	+	Common Stock	+	Retained Earnings	
Old Balance	$11,200		$5,000		$5,000		$1,200		$10,000			
(5)	+10,000										+$10,000	Service Revenue
New Balance	$21,200	+	$5,000	=	$5,000	+	$1,200	+	$10,000	+	$10,000	
	$26,200								$26,200			

EVENT (6). PAYMENT OF RENT. On October 3 Sierra Corporation paid its office rent for the month of October in cash, $900. Rent is an expense incurred by Sierra Corporation in its effort to generate revenues. **Expenses decrease stockholders' equity.** This rent payment is a transaction because it results in a decrease in cash. It is recorded by decreasing cash and decreasing stockholders' equity (specifically, Retained Earnings) to maintain the balance of the accounting equation. To record this transaction, Cash is decreased $900 and Retained Earnings is decreased $900. The effect of these payments on the accounting equation is:

	Assets			=	Liabilities			+	Stockholders' Equity			
	Cash	+	Office Equipment	=	Notes Payable	+	Unearned Revenue	+	Common Stock	+	Retained Earnings	
Old Balance	$21,200		$5,000		$5,000		$1,200		$10,000		$10,000	
(6)	−900										−900	Rent Expense
New Balance	$20,300	+	$5,000	=	$5,000	+	$1,200	+	$10,000	+	$9,100	
	$25,300								$25,300			

EVENT (7). PURCHASE OF INSURANCE POLICY IN CASH. On October 4 Sierra paid $600 for a 1-year insurance policy that will expire next year on September 30. This event is a transaction because one asset was exchanged for another. The asset Cash is decreased $600. The asset Prepaid Insurance is increased $600 because the payment extends to more than the current month; payments of expenses that will benefit more than one accounting period are identified as prepaid expenses or prepayments. Note that the balance in total assets did not change; one asset account decreased by the same amount that another increased.

		Assets			=	Liabilities		+	Stockholders' Equity	
	Cash	+ Prepaid Insurance	+ Office Equipment		=	Notes Payable	+ Unearned Revenue	+	Common Stock	+ Retained Earnings
Old Balance	$20,300		$5,000			$5,000	$1,200		$10,000	$9,100
(7)	−600	+$600								
New Balance	$19,700 +	$600 +	$5,000		=	$5,000 +	$1,200	+	$10,000 +	$9,100
		$25,300					$25,300			

EVENT (8). PURCHASE OF SUPPLIES ON CREDIT. On October 5 Sierra purchased an estimated 3-month supply of advertising materials on account from Aero Supply for $2,500. Assets are increased by this transaction because supplies represent a resource that will be used in the process of providing services to customers. Liabilities are increased by the amount due Aero Supply. The asset Supplies is increased $2,500, and the liability Accounts Payable is increased by the same amount. The effect on the equation is:

			Assets			=		Liabilities		+ Stockholders' Equity	
	Cash	+ Supplies	+ Prepaid Insurance	+ Office Equipment		=	Notes Payable	+ Accounts Payable	+ Unearned Revenue	+ Common Stock	+ Retained Earnings
Old Balance	$19,700		$600	$5,000			$5,000		$1,200	$10,000	$9,100
(8)		+$2,500						+$2,500			
New Balance	$19,700 +	$2,500 +	$600 +	$5,000		=	$5,000 +	$2,500 +	$1,200	+ $10,000 +	$9,100
			$27,800						$27,800		

EVENT (9). HIRING OF NEW EMPLOYEES. On October 9 Sierra hired four new employees to begin work on October 15. Each employee is to receive a weekly salary of $500 for a 5-day work week, payable every 2 weeks. Employees are to receive their first paychecks on October 26. There is no effect on the accounting equation because the assets, liabilities, and stockholders' equity of the company have not changed. An accounting transaction has not occurred. At this point there is only an agreement that the employees will begin work on October 15. [See Event (11) for the first payment.]

EVENT (10). PAYMENT OF DIVIDEND. On October 20 Sierra paid a $500 dividend. Dividends are a distribution of net income and not an expense. A dividend transaction affects assets and stockholders' equity: Cash and Retained Earnings are decreased $500.

			Assets			=		Liabilities		+	Stockholders' Equity	
	Cash	+ Supplies	+ Prepaid Insurance	+ Office Equipment		=	Notes Payable	+ Accounts Payable	+ Unearned Revenue	+	Common Stock	+ Retained Earnings
Old Balance	$19,700	$2,500	$600	$5,000			$5,000	$2,500	$1,200		$10,000	$9,100
(10)	−500											−500 **Dividends**
New Balance	$19,200 +	$2,500 +	$600 +	$5,000		=	$5,000 +	$2,500 +	$1,200	+	$10,000 +	$8,600
			$27,300						$27,300			

EVENT (11). PAYMENT OF CASH FOR EMPLOYEE SALARIES. Employees have worked 2 weeks, earning $4,000 in salaries, which were paid on October 26. Salaries are an expense similar to rent because they are a cost of generating revenues. This event involving employees is a transaction because assets and stockholders' equity are affected, each by an equal amount. Thus, Cash and Retained Earnings are each decreased $4,000.

	Assets				=	Liabilities			+	Stockholders' Equity		
	Cash	+ Supplies	+ Prepaid Insurance	+ Office Equipment	=	Notes Payable	+ Accounts Payable	+ Unearned Revenue	+	Common Stock	+ Retained Earnings	
Old Balance	$19,200	$2,500	$600	$5,000		$5,000	$2,500	$1,200		$10,000	$8,600	
(11)	−4,000										−4,000	Salaries Expense
New Balance	$15,200 +	$2,500 +	$600 +	$5,000	=	$5,000 +	$2,500 +	$1,200	+	$10,000 +	$4,600	
	$23,300									$23,300		

SUMMARY OF TRANSACTIONS

The transactions of Sierra Corporation are summarized in Illustration 3-2 to show their cumulative effect on the basic accounting equation. The transaction number, the specific effects of the transaction, and the balances after each transaction are indicated. Remember that Event (9) did not result in a transaction, so no entry is included for that event. The illustration demonstrates three significant facts:

1. Each transaction is analyzed in terms of its effect on assets, liabilities, and stockholders' equity.
2. The two sides of the equation must always be equal.
3. The cause of each change in stockholders' equity must be indicated.

Illustration 3-2
Summary of transactions

	Assets				=	Liabilities			+	Stockholders' Equity		
	Cash	+ Supplies	+ Prepaid Insurance	+ Office Equipment	=	Notes Payable	+ Accounts Payable	+ Unearned Revenue	+	Common Stock	+ Retained Earnings	
(1)	+$10,000				=					+$10,000		Issued Stock
(2)	+5,000					+$5,000						
	15,000					5,000			+	10,000		
(3)	−5,000			+$5,000	=							
	10,000			+ 5,000	=	5,000			+	10,000		
(4)	+1,200				=			+$1,200				
	11,200			+ 5,000	=	5,000		+ 1,200	+	10,000		
(5)	+10,000										+$10,000	Service Revenue
	21,200			+ 5,000	=	5,000		+ 1,200	+	10,000 +	10,000	
(6)	−900				=						−900	Rent Expense
	20,300			+ 5,000	=	5,000		+ 1,200	+	10,000 +	9,100	
(7)	−600	+$600			=							
	19,700	+ 600		+ 5,000	=	5,000		+ 1,200	+	10,000 +	9,100	
(8)		+$2,500			=		+$2,500					
	19,700 +	2,500 +		600 + 5,000	=	5,000 +	2,500	+ 1,200	+	10,000 +	9,100	
(10)	−500										−500	Dividends
	19,200 +	2,500 +		600 + 5,000	=	5,000 +	2,500	+ 1,200	+	10,000 +	8,600	
(11)	−4,000										−4,000	Salaries Expense
	$15,200 +	$2,500 +	$600 +	$5,000	=	$5,000 +	$2,500 +	$1,200	+	$10,000 +	$ 4,600	
	$23,300									$23,300		

104 CHAPTER 3 The Accounting Information System

DECISION TOOLKIT

Decision Checkpoints	Info Needed for Decision	Tool to Use for Decision	How to Evaluate Results
Has an accounting transaction occurred?	Details of the event	Accounting equation	Determine the effect, if any, on assets, liabilities, and stockholders' equity.

THE ACCOUNT

STUDY OBJECTIVE 2
Explain what an account is and how it helps in the recording process.

Rather than using a tabular summary like the one in Illustration 3-2 for Sierra Corporation, an accounting information system uses accounts. An **account** is an individual accounting record of increases and decreases in a specific asset, liability, or stockholders' equity item. For example, Sierra Corporation has separate accounts for Cash, Accounts Receivable, Accounts Payable, Service Revenue, Salaries Expense, and so on. (Note that whenever we are referring to a specific account, we capitalize the name.) In its simplest form, an account consists of three parts: (1) the title of the account, (2) a left or debit side, and (3) a right or credit side. Because the alignment of these parts of an account resembles the letter T, it is referred to as a **T account.** The basic form of an account is shown in Illustration 3-3.

Illustration 3-3 Basic form of account

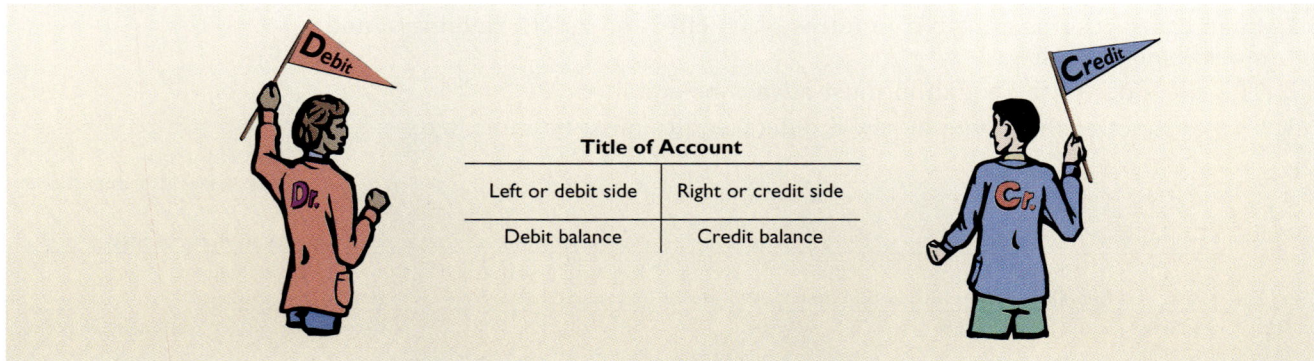

This form of account is used often throughout this book to explain basic accounting relationships.

DEBITS AND CREDITS

STUDY OBJECTIVE 3
Define debits and credits and explain how they are used to record business transactions.

The terms **debit** and **credit** mean *left* and *right,* respectively. They are commonly abbreviated as **Dr.** for debit and **Cr.** for credit. These terms **do not** mean increase or decrease. The terms *debit* and *credit* are used repeatedly in the recording process to describe where entries are made in accounts. For example, the act of entering an amount on the left side of an account is called **debiting** the account, and making an entry on the right side is **crediting** the account. When the totals of the two sides are compared, an account will have a **debit balance** if the total of the debit amounts exceeds the credits. Conversely, an account will have a **credit balance** if the credit amounts exceed the debits. Note the position of the debit or credit balances in Illustration 3-3.

The procedure of recording debits and credits in an account is shown in Illustration 3-4 for the transactions affecting the Cash account of Sierra Corporation. The data are taken from the Cash column of the tabular summary in Illustration 3-2.

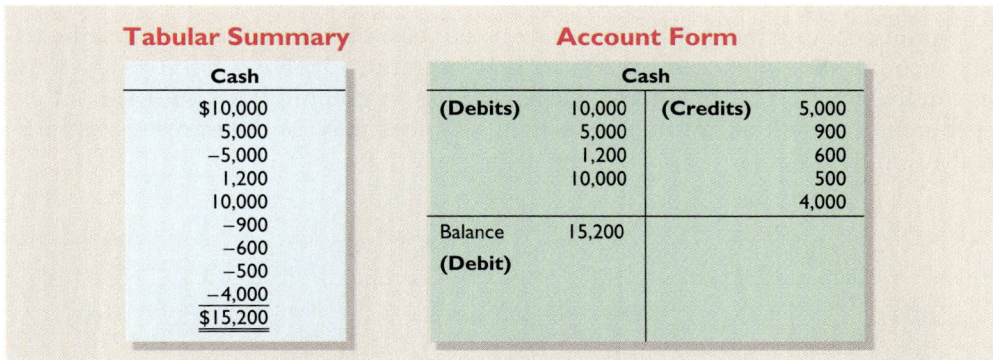

Illustration 3-4 Tabular summary and account form for Sierra Corporation's Cash account

Every positive item in the tabular summary represents a receipt of cash; every negative amount represents a payment of cash. Notice that in the account form the increases in cash are recorded as debits, and the decreases in cash are recorded as credits. Having increases on one side and decreases on the other reduces recording errors and helps in determining the totals of each side of the account as well as the balance in the account. The account balance, a debit of $15,200, indicates that Sierra Corporation had $15,200 more increases than decreases in cash (since it started with a balance of zero). That is, it has $15,200 in its Cash account.

DEBIT AND CREDIT PROCEDURES

Each transaction must affect two or more accounts to keep the basic accounting equation in balance. In other words, for each transaction, debits must equal credits. The equality of debits and credits provides the basis for the double-entry accounting system.

Under the universally used **double-entry system,** the dual (two-sided) effect of each transaction is recorded in appropriate accounts. This system provides a logical method for recording transactions. As was the case for the error in Fidelity's accounts, noted in the opening story, the double-entry system also offers a means of ensuring the accuracy of the recorded amounts. If every transaction is recorded with equal debits and credits, then the sum of all the debits to the accounts must equal the sum of all the credits. The double-entry system for determining the equality of the accounting equation is much more efficient than the plus/minus procedure used earlier. There, it was necessary after each transaction to compare total assets with total liabilities and stockholders' equity to determine the equality of the two sides of the accounting equation.

Dr./Cr. Procedures for Assets and Liabilities

In Illustration 3-4 for Sierra Corporation, increases in cash—an asset—were entered on the left side, and decreases in cash were entered on the right side. We know that both sides of the basic equation (Assets = Liabilities + Stockholders' Equity) must be equal; it therefore follows that increases and decreases in liabilities will have to be recorded *opposite from* increases and decreases in assets. Thus, increases in liabilities must be entered on the right or credit side, and decreases in liabilities must be entered on the left or debit side. The effects that debits and credits have on assets and liabilities are summarized in Illustration 3-5.

Illustration 3-5 Debit and credit effects—assets and liabilities

Debits	Credits
Increase assets	Decrease assets
Decrease liabilities	Increase liabilities

Asset accounts normally show debit balances; that is, debits to a specific asset account should exceed credits to that account. Likewise, liability accounts normally show credit balances; that is, credits to a liability account should exceed debits to that account. The normal balances may be diagrammed as in Illustration 3-6.

Illustration 3-6 Normal balances—assets and liabilities

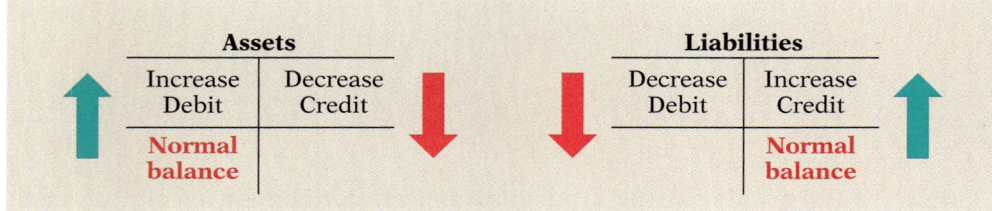

Knowing which is the normal balance in an account may help when you are trying to trace errors. For example, a credit balance in an asset account such as Land or a debit balance in a liability account such as Wages Payable would indicate errors in recording. Occasionally, however, an abnormal balance may be correct. The Cash account, for example, will have a credit balance when a company has overdrawn its bank balance (written a check that "bounced").

BUSINESS INSIGHT
Management Perspective

In automated accounting systems, the computer is programmed to flag these violations of the normal balance and to print out error or exception reports. In manual systems, careful visual inspection of the accounts is required to detect normal balance problems.

Dr./Cr. Procedures for Stockholders' Equity

The five subdivisions of stockholders' equity are: common stock, retained earnings, dividends, revenues, and expenses. In a double-entry system, accounts are kept for each of these subdivisions.

Common Stock. Common stock is issued in exchange for the stockholders' investment. The Common Stock account is increased by credits and decreased by debits. For example, when cash is invested in the business, Cash is debited and Common Stock is credited. The effects of debits and credits on the Common Stock account are shown in Illustration 3-7.

Illustration 3-7 Debit and credit effects—Common Stock

Debits	Credits
Decrease Common Stock	Increase Common Stock

The normal balance in the Common Stock account may be diagrammed as in Illustration 3-8.

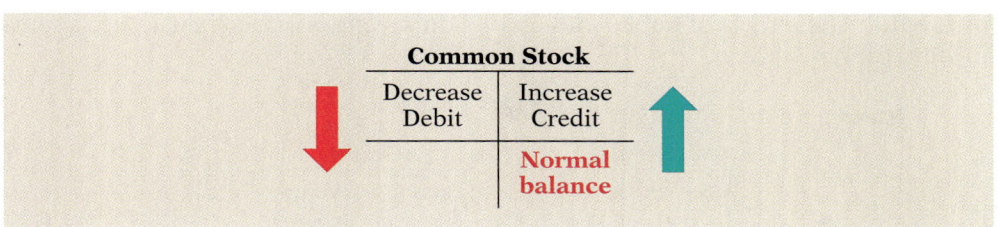

Illustration 3-8 Normal balance—Common Stock

Retained Earnings. Retained earnings is net income that is retained in the business. It represents the portion of stockholders' equity that has been accumulated through the profitable operation of the company. Retained Earnings is increased by credits (for example, net income) and decreased by debits (for example, net losses), as shown in Illustration 3-9.

Debits	Credits
Decrease Retained Earnings	Increase Retained Earnings

Illustration 3-9 Debit and credit effects—Retained Earnings

The normal balance for Retained Earnings may be diagrammed as in Illustration 3-10.

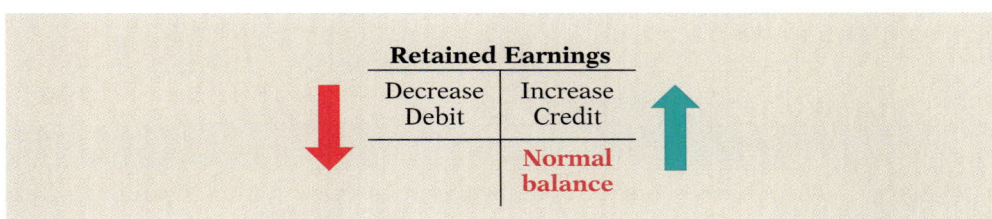

Illustration 3-10 Normal balance—Retained Earnings

Dividends. A dividend is a distribution by a corporation to its stockholders in an amount proportional to each investor's percentage ownership. The most common form of distribution is a cash dividend. Dividends result in a reduction of the stockholders' claims on retained earnings. Because dividends reduce stockholders' equity, increases in the Dividends account are recorded with debits. As shown in Illustration 3-11, the Dividends account normally has a debit balance.

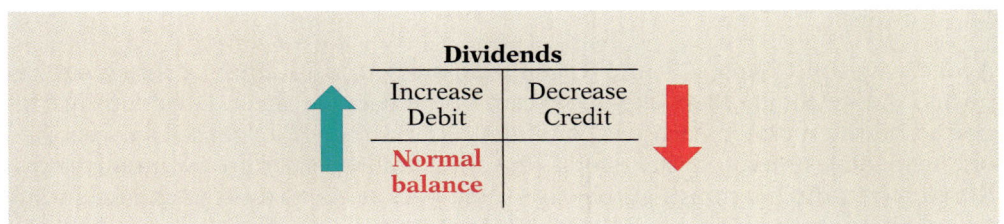

Illustration 3-11 Normal balance—Dividends

Revenues and Expenses. When revenues are earned, stockholders' equity is increased. Accordingly, **the effect of debits and credits on revenue accounts is identical to their effect on stockholders' equity.** Revenue accounts are increased by credits and decreased by debits.

On the other hand, **expenses decrease stockholders' equity.** As a result, expenses are recorded by debits. Since expenses are the negative factor in the computation of net income and revenues are the positive factor, it is logical that the increase and decrease sides of expense accounts should be the reverse of revenue accounts. Thus, expense accounts are increased by debits and decreased by credits. The effects of debits and credits on revenues and expenses are shown in Illustration 3-12.

Illustration 3-12 Debit and credit effects—revenues and expenses

Debits	Credits
Decrease revenues	Increase revenues
Increase expenses	Decrease expenses

Credits to revenue accounts should exceed debits, and debits to expense accounts should exceed credits. Thus, revenue accounts normally show credit balances, and expense accounts normally show debit balances. The normal balances may be diagrammed as in Illustration 3-13.

Illustration 3-13 Normal balances—revenues and expenses

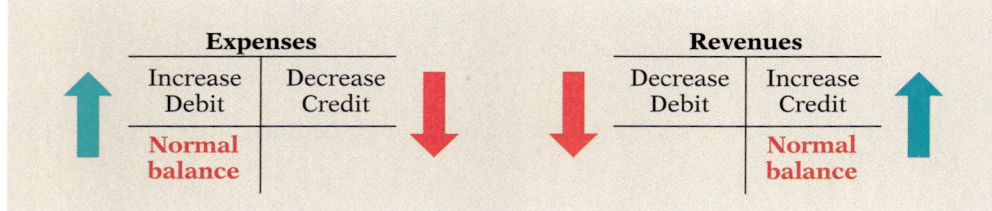

BUSINESS INSIGHT
Investor Perspective

The Chicago Cubs baseball team has these major revenue and expense accounts:

Revenues	Expenses
Admissions (ticket sales)	Players' salaries
Concessions	Administrative salaries
Television and radio	Travel
Advertising	Ballpark maintenance

STOCKHOLDERS' EQUITY RELATIONSHIPS

As indicated in Chapters 1 and 2, common stock and retained earnings are reported in the stockholders' equity section of the balance sheet. Dividends are reported on the retained earnings statement. Revenues and expenses are reported on the income statement. Dividends, revenues, and expenses are eventually transferred to retained earnings at the end of the period. As a result, a change in any one of these three items affects stockholders' equity. The relationships of the accounts affecting stockholders' equity are shown in Illustration 3-14.

EXPANSION OF THE BASIC EQUATION

You have already learned the basic accounting equation. Illustration 3-15 expands this equation to show the accounts that make up stockholders' equity. In addition, the debit/credit rules and effects on each type of account are illustrated. Study this diagram carefully. It will help you understand the fundamentals of the double-entry system. Like the basic equation, the expanded basic equation must be in balance; total debits must equal total credits.

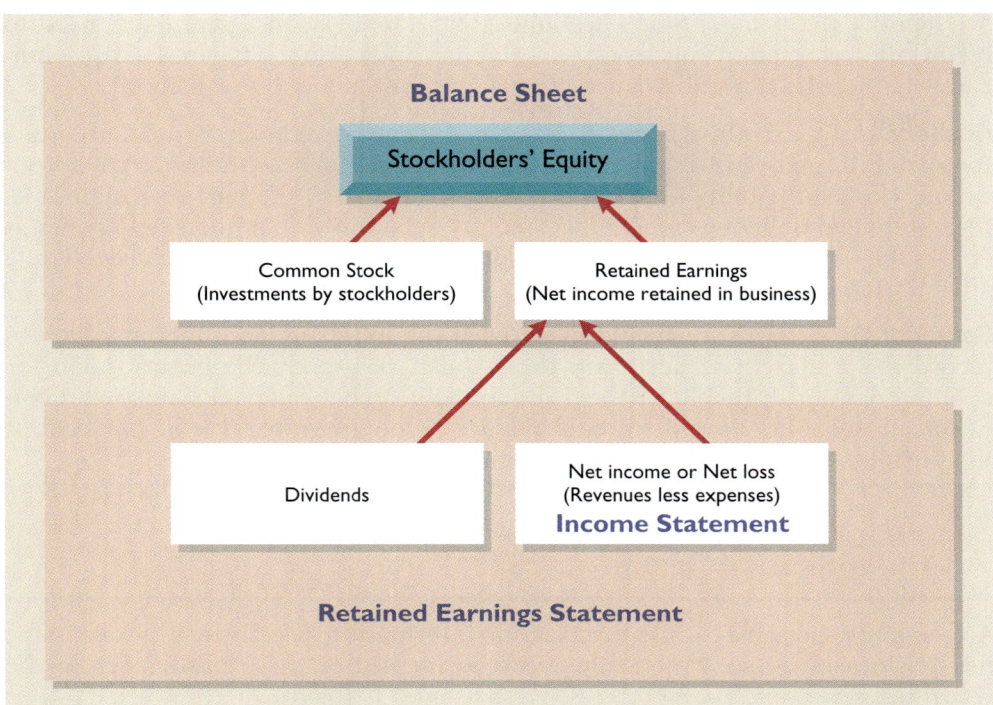

Illustration 3-14 Stockholders' equity relationships

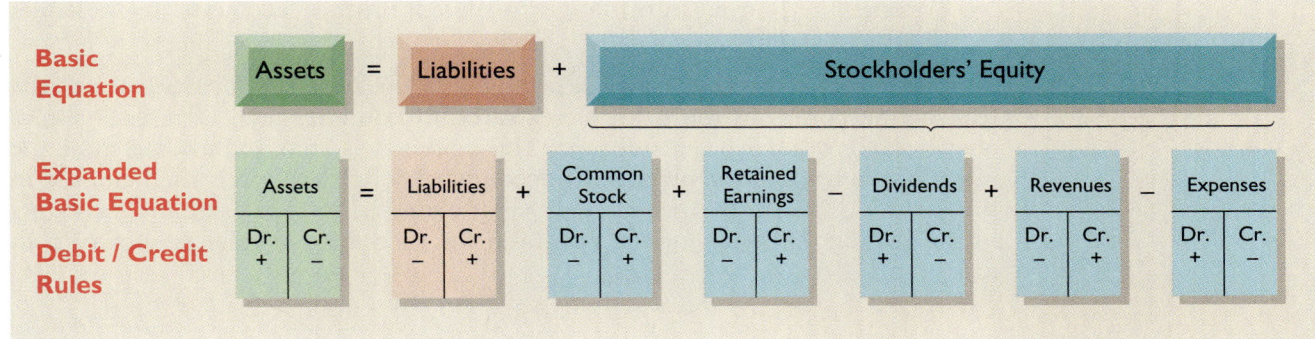

Illustration 3-15 Expansion of the basic accounting equation

BEFORE YOU GO ON . . .

● **Review It**

1. What do the terms *debit* and *credit* mean?
2. What are the debit and credit effects on assets, liabilities, and stockholders' equity?
3. What are the debit and credit effects on revenues, expenses, and dividends?
4. What are the normal balances for individual asset, liability, and stockholders' equity accounts?

● **Do It**

Kate Browne, president of Hair It Is, Inc., has just rented space in a shopping mall for the purpose of opening and operating a beauty salon. Long before opening day and before purchasing equipment, hiring assistants, and remodeling the space, Kate is strongly advised to set up a double-entry set of accounting records in which to record all of her business transactions.

Identify the balance sheet accounts that Hair It Is, Inc., will likely need to record the transactions necessary to establish and open for business. Also, indicate whether the normal balance of each account is a debit or a credit.

Reasoning: To start the business, Hair It Is, Inc., will need to have asset accounts for each different type of asset invested in the business. In addition, the corporation will need liability accounts for debts incurred by the business. Hair It Is, Inc., will need only one stockholders' equity account for common stock when it begins the business. The other stockholders' equity accounts will be needed only after business has commenced.

Solution: Hair It Is, Inc., would likely need the following accounts in which to record the transactions necessary to establish and ready the beauty salon for opening day: Cash (debit balance); Equipment (debit balance); Supplies (debit balance); Accounts Payable (credit balance); Notes Payable (credit balance), if the business borrows money; and Common Stock (credit balance).

STEPS IN THE RECORDING PROCESS

STUDY OBJECTIVE 4
Identify the basic steps in the recording process.

Although it is possible to enter transaction information directly into the accounts, few businesses do so. Practically every business uses these basic steps in the recording process:

1. Analyze each transaction in terms of its effect on the accounts.
2. Enter the transaction information in a journal.
3. Transfer the journal information to the appropriate accounts in the ledger (book of accounts).

The actual sequence of events begins with the transaction. Evidence of the transaction comes in the form of a **source document,** such as a sales slip, a check, a bill, or a cash register tape. This evidence is analyzed to determine the effect of the transaction on specific accounts. The transaction is then entered in the **journal.** Finally, the journal entry is transferred to the designated accounts in the **ledger.** The sequence of events in the recording process is shown in Illustration 3-16.

Illustration 3-16 The recording process

The basic steps in the recording process occur repeatedly in every business enterprise. The analysis of transactions has already been illustrated, and more examples of this step are given in this and later chapters. The other steps in the recording process are explained in the next sections.

THE JOURNAL

Transactions are initially recorded in chronological order in a **journal** before they are transferred to the accounts. For each transaction the journal shows the debit and credit effects on specific accounts. Companies may use various kinds of journals, but every company has the most basic form of journal, a **general journal.** The journal makes three significant contributions to the recording process:

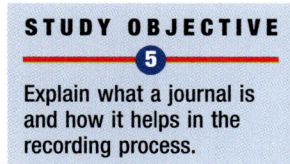

STUDY OBJECTIVE 5

Explain what a journal is and how it helps in the recording process.

1. It discloses in one place the complete effect of a transaction.
2. It provides a chronological record of transactions.
3. It helps to prevent or locate errors because the debit and credit amounts for each entry can be readily compared.

Entering transaction data in the journal is known as **journalizing.** Separate journal entries are made for each transaction. A complete entry consists of: (1) the date of the transaction, (2) the accounts and amounts to be debited and credited, and (3) a brief explanation of the transaction. To illustrate the technique of journalizing, the first three transactions of Sierra Corporation are journalized in Illustration 3-17. These transactions were: October 1, common stock was issued in exchange for $10,000 cash and $5,000 was borrowed by signing a note; October 2, office equipment was purchased for $5,000. In equation form, these transactions appeared in our earlier discussion as follows:

Assets	=	Liabilities	+	Stockholders' Equity	
Cash	=			Common Stock	
+$10,000				+$10,000	Issued Stock

Assets	=	Liabilities	+	Stockholders' Equity
Cash	=	Notes Payable		
+$5,000		+$5,000		

Assets		=	Liabilities	+	Stockholders' Equity
Cash	Office Equipment				
−$5,000	+$5,000				

Illustration 3-17
Recording transactions in journal form

GENERAL JOURNAL

Date		Account Titles and Explanation	Debit	Credit
1998 Oct.	1	Cash	10,000	
		Common Stock		10,000
		(Invested cash in business)		
	1	Cash	5,000	
		Notes Payable		5,000
		(Issued 3-month, 12% note payable for cash)		
	2	Office Equipment	5,000	
		Cash		5,000
		(Purchased office equipment for cash)		

These transactions would be recorded in the journal as in Illustration 3-17. Note the following features of the journal entries:

1. The date of the transaction is entered in the Date column.
2. The account to be debited is entered first at the left. The account to be credited is then entered on the next line, indented under the line above. The indentation differentiates debits from credits and decreases the possibility of switching the debit and credit amounts.
3. The amounts for the debits are recorded in the Debit (left) column, and the amounts for the credits are recorded in the Credit (right) column.
4. A brief explanation of the transaction is given.

It is important to use correct and specific account titles in journalizing. Since most accounts appear later in the financial statements, erroneous account titles lead to incorrect financial statements. Some flexibility exists initially in selecting account titles. The main criterion is that each title must appropriately describe the content of the account. For example, a company could use any of these account titles for recording the cost of delivery trucks: Delivery Equipment, Delivery Trucks, or Trucks. Once the company chooses the specific title to use, however, all subsequent transactions involving the account should be recorded under that account title.

BEFORE YOU GO ON . . .

● **Review It**

1. What is the correct sequence of steps in the recording process?
2. What contribution does the journal make to the recording process?
3. What are the standard form and content of a journal entry made in the general journal?

● **Do It**

The following events occurred during the first month of business of Hair It Is, Inc., Kate Browne's beauty salon:

1. Issued common stock to shareholders in exchange for $20,000 cash.
2. Purchased $4,800 of equipment on account (to be paid in 30 days).
3. Interviewed three people for the position of beautician.

In what form (type of record) should the company record these three activities? Prepare the entries to record the transactions.

Reasoning: Kate should record the transactions in a journal, which is a chronological record of the transactions. The record should be a complete and accurate representation of the transactions' effects on the assets, liabilities, and stockholders' equity of her business.

Solution: Each transaction that is recorded is entered in the general journal. The three activities are recorded as follows:

1. Cash   20,000
    Common Stock   20,000
      (Invested cash in the business)
2. Equipment   4,800
    Accounts Payable   4,800
      (Purchased equipment on account)
3. No entry because no transaction occurred.

THE LEDGER

The entire group of accounts maintained by a company is referred to collectively as the **ledger.** The ledger keeps in one place all the information about changes in specific account balances.

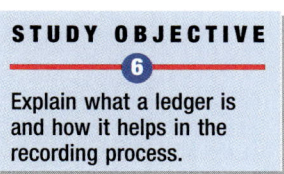

Companies may use various kinds of ledgers, but every company has a general ledger. A **general ledger** contains all the assets, liabilities, and stockholders' equity accounts, as shown in Illustration 3-18. A business can use a loose-leaf binder or card file for the ledger, with each account kept on a separate sheet or card. Most businesses today, however, use a computer disk or hard drive as the ledger. Whenever the term *ledger* is used in this textbook without additional specification, it will mean the general ledger.

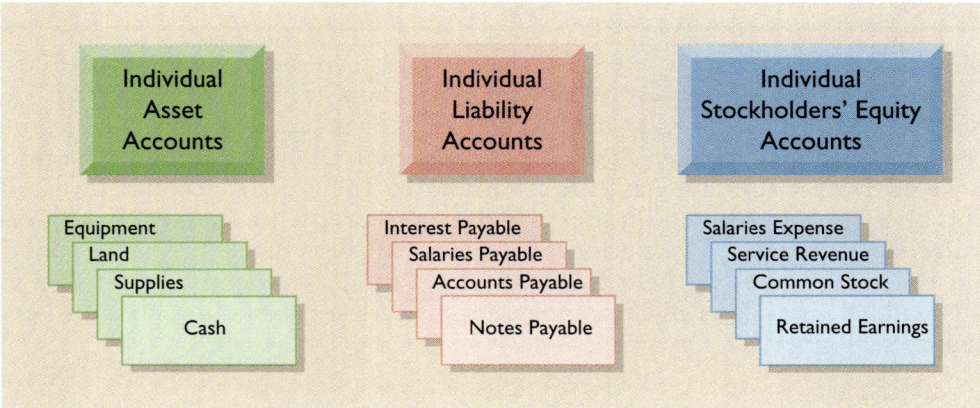

Illustration 3-18 The general ledger

CHART OF ACCOUNTS

The number and type of accounts used differ for each company, depending on the size, complexity, and type of business. For example, the number of accounts depends on the amount of detail desired by management. The management of one company may want one single account for all types of utility expense. Another may keep separate expense accounts for each type of utility expenditure, such as gas, electricity, and water. Similarly, a small corporation like Sierra Corporation will not have many accounts compared with a corporate giant like Ford Motor Company. Sierra may be able to manage and report its activities in 20 to 30 accounts, whereas Ford requires thousands of accounts to keep track of its worldwide activities.

Most companies list the accounts in a **chart of accounts.** The chart of accounts for Sierra Corporation is shown in Illustration 3-19. Accounts shown in red are used in this chapter; accounts shown in black are explained in later chapters. New accounts may be created as needed during the life of the business.

Illustration 3-19 Chart of accounts for Sierra Corporation

SIERRA CORPORATION—CHART OF ACCOUNTS

Assets	Liabilities	Stockholders' Equity	Revenues	Expenses
Cash	**Notes Payable**	**Common Stock**	**Service Revenue**	**Salaries Expense**
Accounts Receivable	**Accounts Payable**	**Retained Earnings**		Supplies Expense
Supplies	Interest Payable	**Dividends**		**Rent Expense**
Prepaid Insurance	**Unearned**	Income Summary		Insurance Expense
Office Equipment	**Service Revenue**			Interest Expense
Accumulated Depreciation—Office Equipment	Salaries Payable			Depreciation Expense

114 CHAPTER 3 The Accounting Information System

POSTING

STUDY OBJECTIVE 7
Explain what posting is and how it helps in the recording process.

The procedure of transferring journal entries to ledger accounts is called **posting.** **This phase of the recording process accumulates the effects of journalized transactions in the individual accounts.** Posting involves these steps:

1. In the ledger, enter in the appropriate columns of the debited account(s) the date and debit amount shown in the journal.
2. In the ledger, enter in the appropriate columns of the credited account(s) the date and credit amount shown in the journal.

*T*HE RECORDING PROCESS ILLUSTRATED

Illustrations 3-20 through 3-30 show the basic steps in the recording process using the October transactions of Sierra Corporation. Its accounting period is a month. A basic analysis and a debit–credit analysis precede the journalizing and posting of each transaction. Study these transaction analyses carefully. **The purpose of transaction analysis is first to identify the type of account involved and then to determine whether a debit or a credit to the account is required.** You should always perform this type of analysis before preparing a journal entry. Doing so will help you understand the journal entries discussed in this chapter as well as more complex journal entries to be described in later chapters.

Illustration 3-20
Investment of cash by stockholders

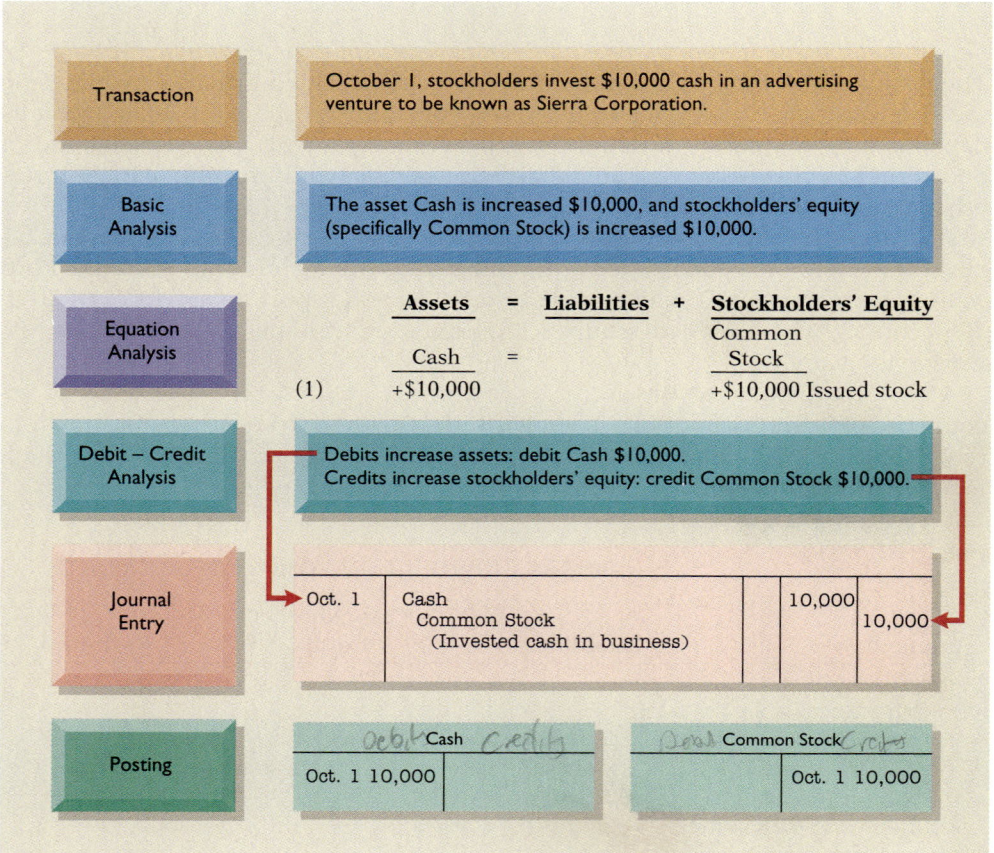

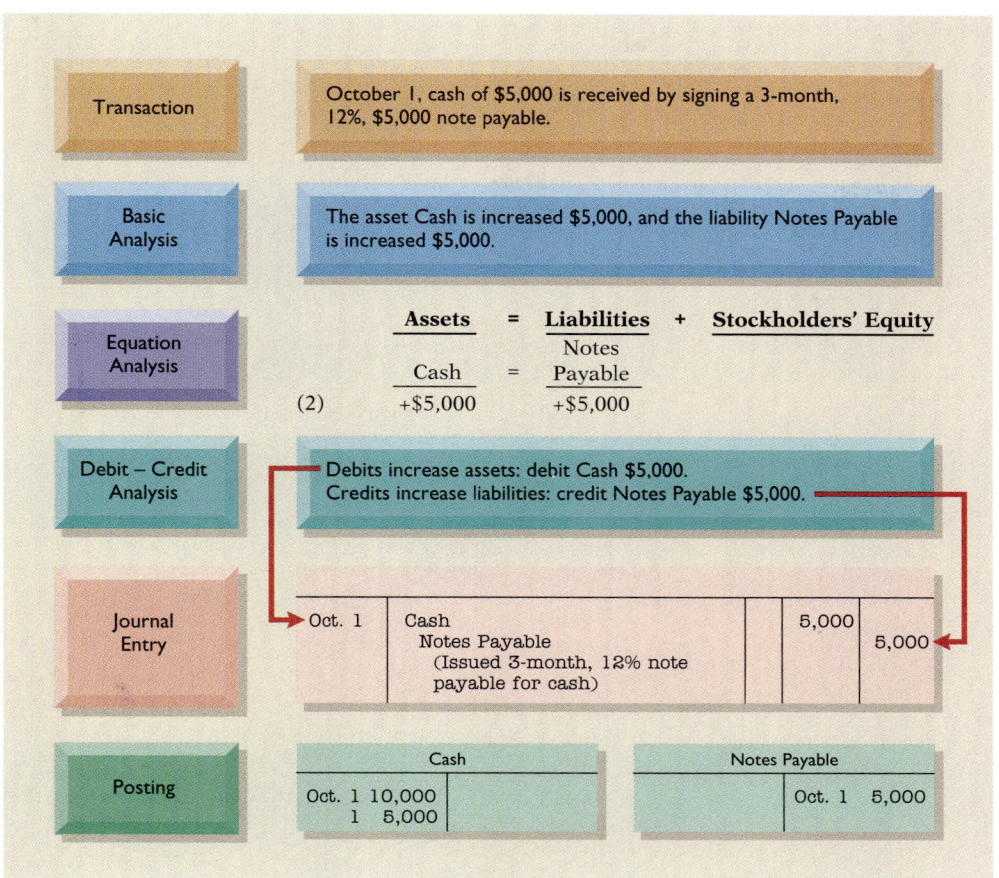

Illustration 3-21 Issue of note payable

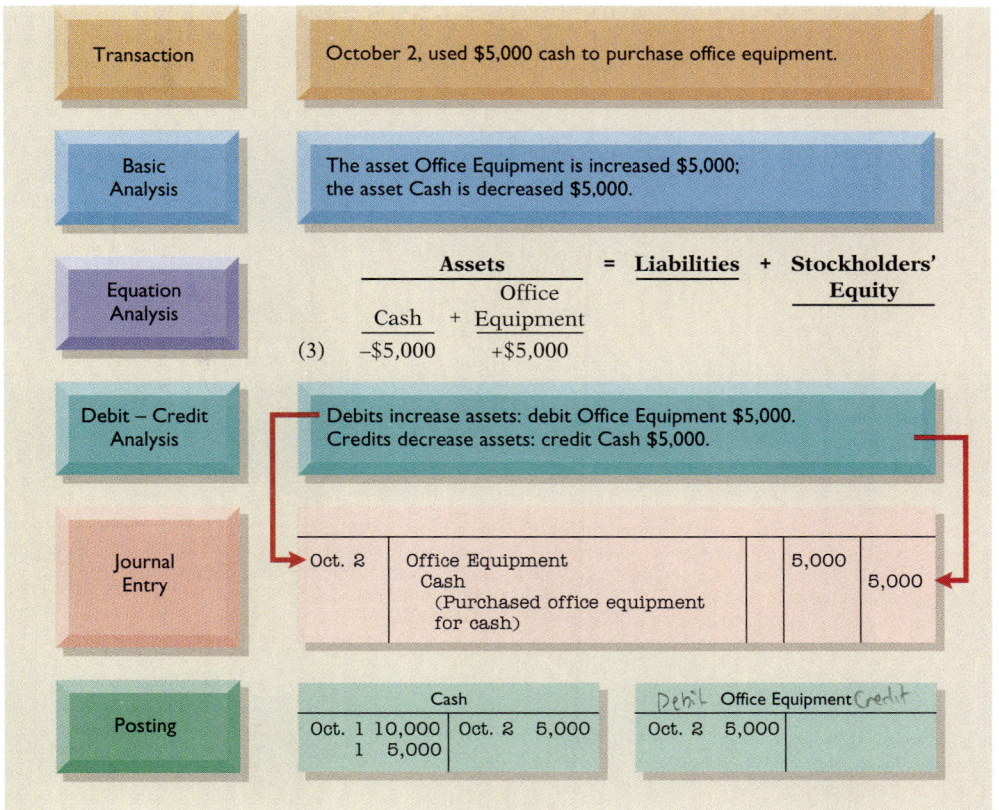

Illustration 3-22 Purchase of office equipment

115

Illustration 3-23 Receipt of cash in advance from customer

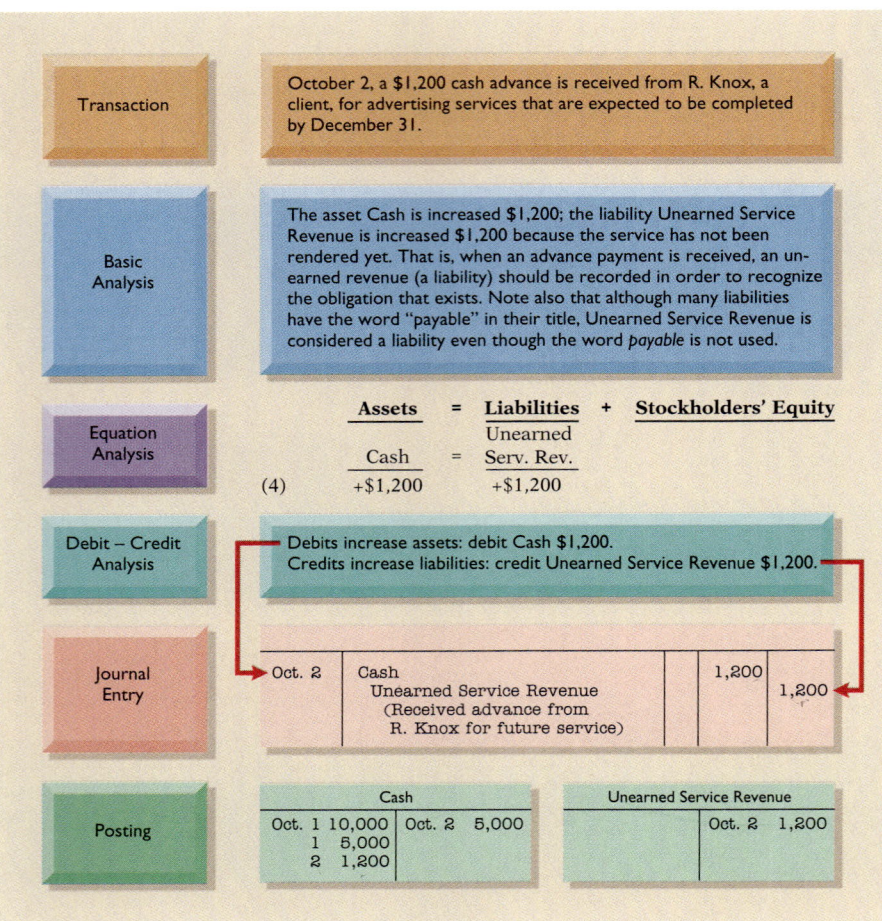

Illustration 3-24 Services rendered for cash

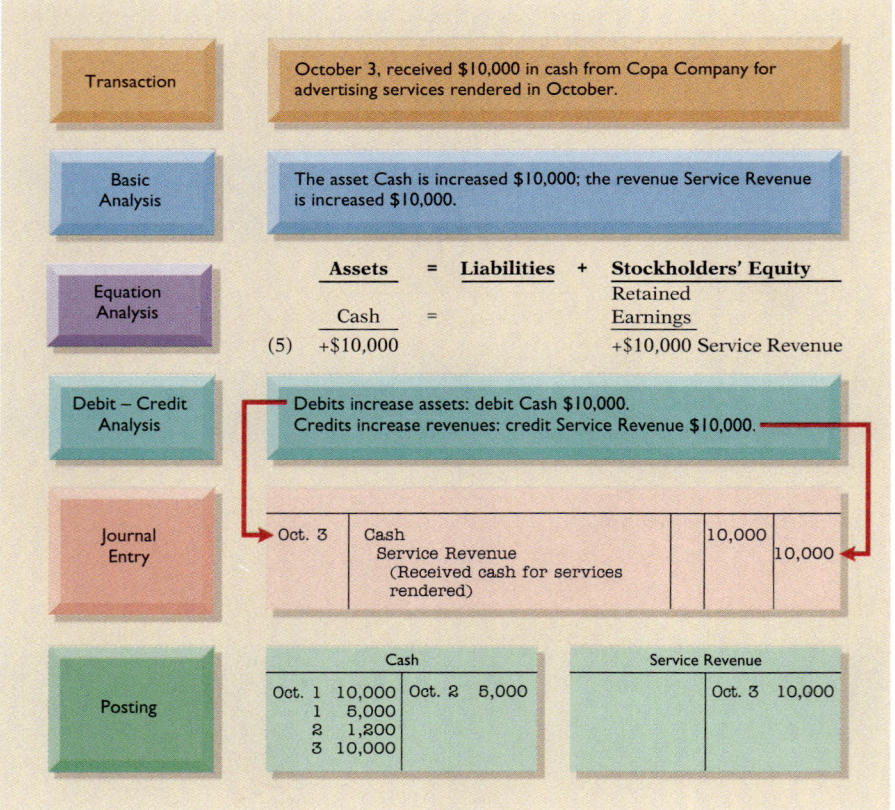

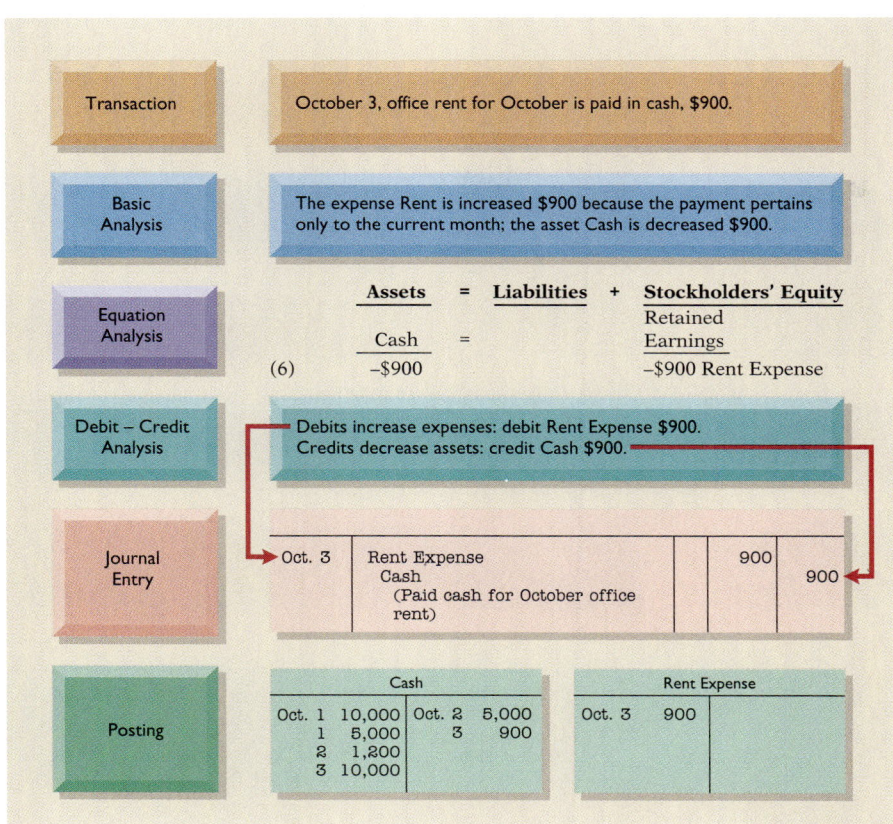

Illustration 3-25
Payment of rent in cash

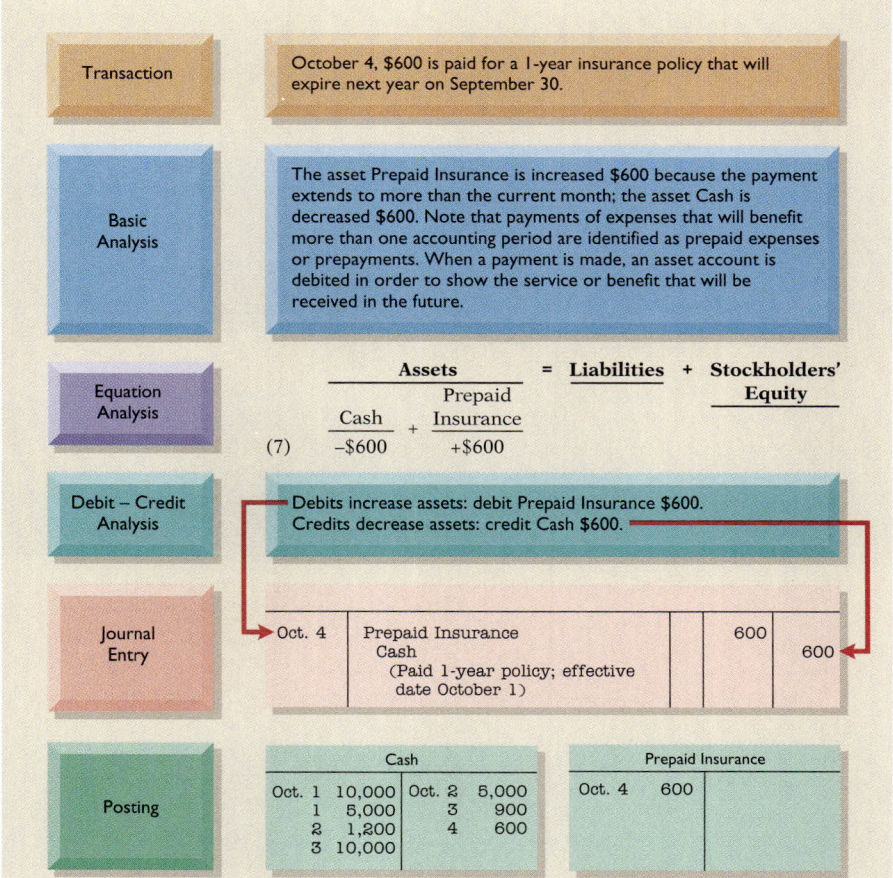

Illustration 3-26
Purchase of insurance policy in cash

Illustration 3-27
Purchase of supplies on credit

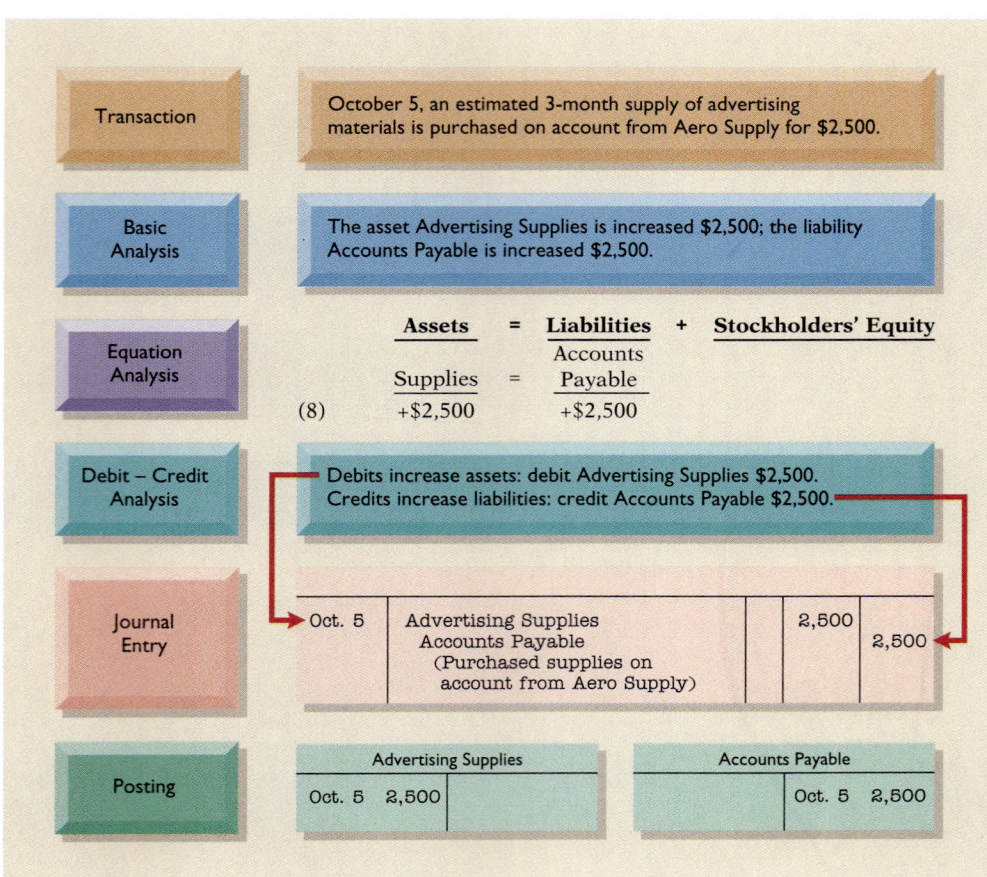

Illustration 3-28 Hiring of new employees

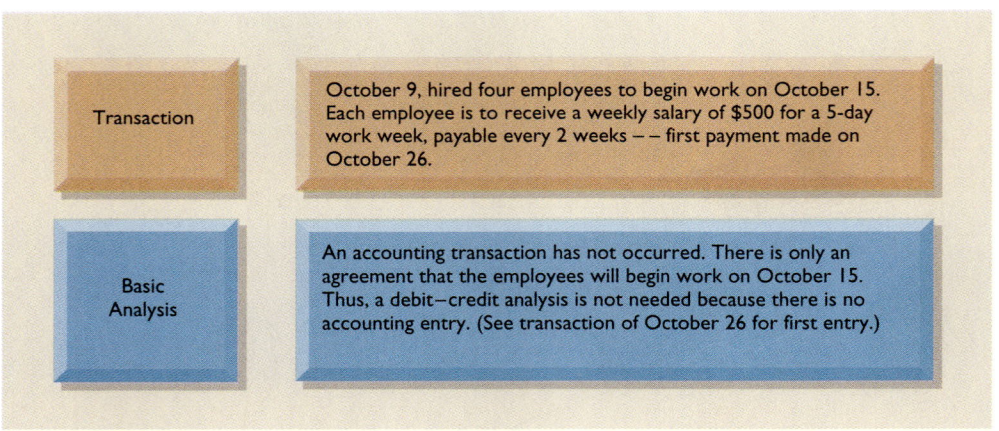

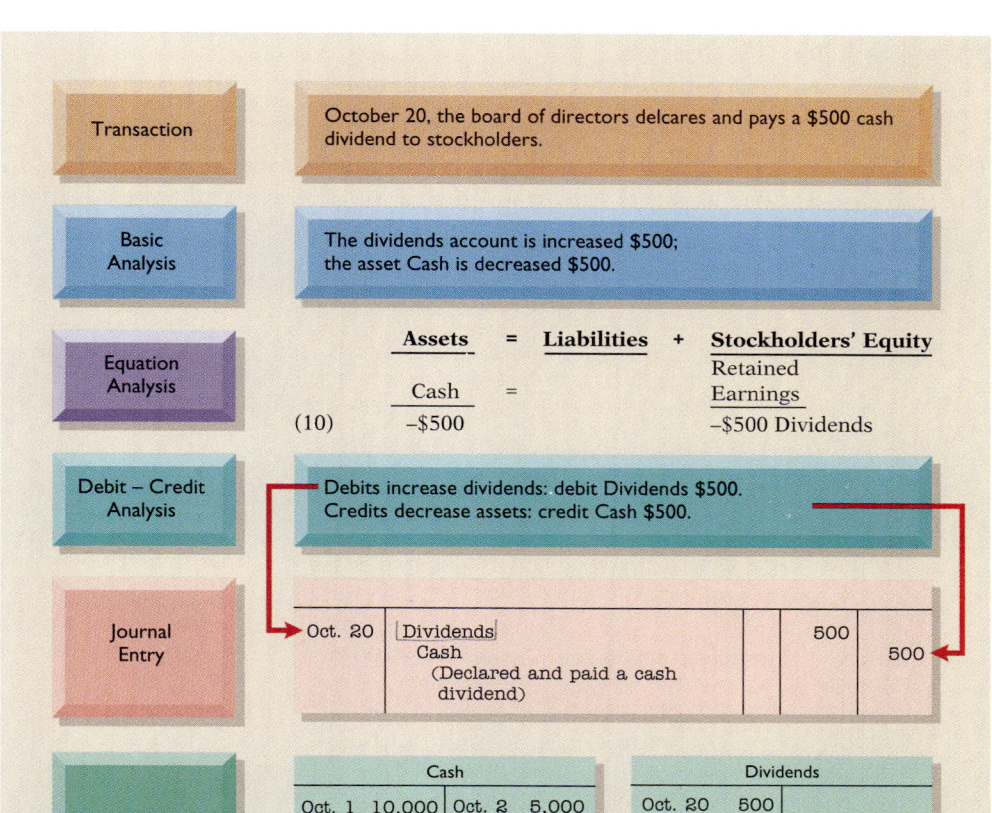

Illustration 3-29
Payment of dividend

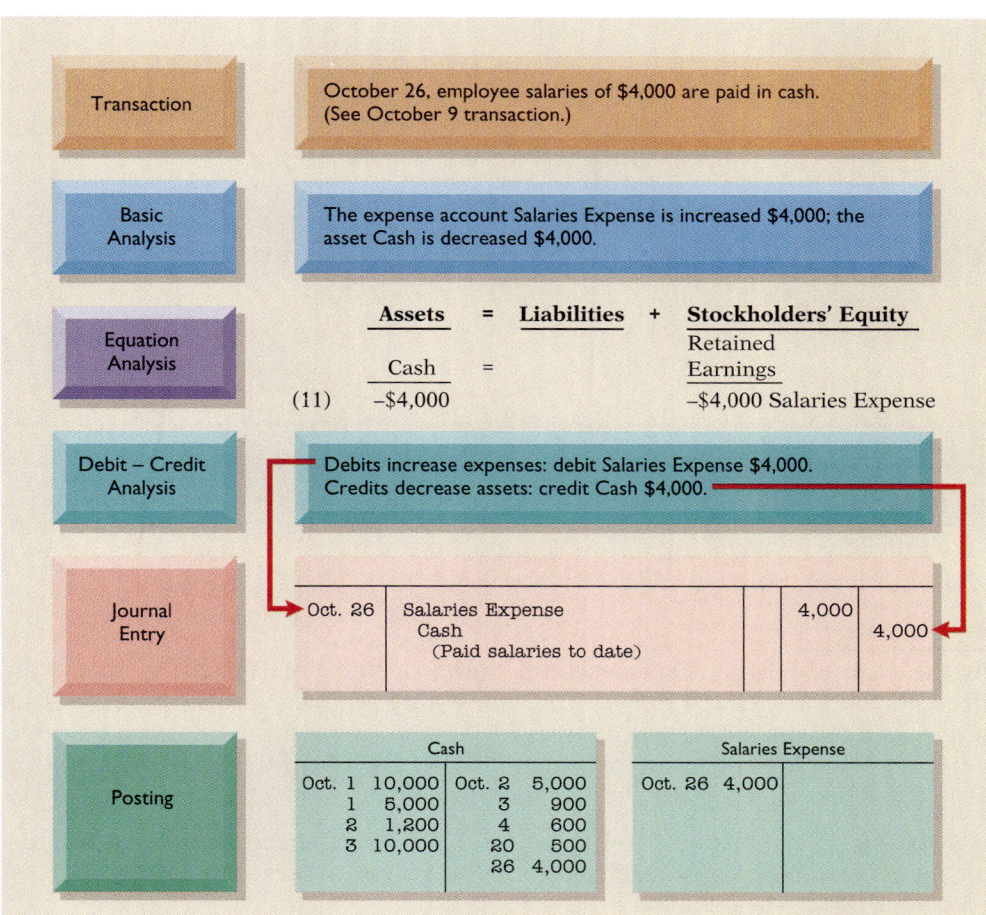

Illustration 3-30
Payment of cash for employee salaries

119

120 CHAPTER 3 The Accounting Information System

SUMMARY ILLUSTRATION OF JOURNALIZING AND POSTING

The journal for Sierra Corporation for the month of October is summarized in Illustration 3-31. The ledger is shown in Illustration 3-32 with all balances highlighted in red.

Illustration 3-31
General journal for Sierra Corporation

		GENERAL JOURNAL		
Date		Account Titles and Explanation	Debit	Credit
1998 Oct.	1	Cash	10,000	
		Common Stock		10,000
		(Invested cash in business)		
	1	Cash	5,000	
		Notes Payable		5,000
		(Issued 3-month, 12% note payable for cash)		
	2	Office Equipment	5,000	
		Cash		5,000
		(Purchased office equipment for cash)		
	2	Cash	1,200	
		Unearned Service Revenue		1,200
		(Received advance from R. Knox for future service)		
	3	Cash	10,000	
		Service Revenue		10,000
		(Received cash for services rendered)		
	3	Rent Expense	900	
		Cash		900
		(Paid cash for October office rent)		
	4	Prepaid Insurance	600	
		Cash		600
		(Paid 1-year policy; effective date October 1)		
	5	Advertising Supplies	2,500	
		Accounts Payable		2,500
		(Purchased supplies on account from Aero Supply)		
	20	Dividends	500	
		Cash		500
		(Declared and paid a cash dividend)		
	26	Salaries Expense	4,000	
		Cash		4,000
		(Paid salaries to date)		

BEFORE YOU GO ON . . .

● **Review It**

1. How does journalizing differ from posting?
2. What is the purpose of (a) the ledger and (b) a chart of accounts?

● **Do It**

In the week following her successful grand opening of Hair It Is, Inc., Kate Browne collected $2,280 in cash for hair styling services, and she paid $400 in wages and $92 for utilities. Kate recorded these transactions in a general journal and posted the entries to the general ledger. Explain the purpose and process of journalizing and posting these transactions.

Reasoning: Every business must keep track of its financial activities (receipts, payments, receivables, payables, etc.); journalizing does this. However, just

GENERAL LEDGER

Cash					Unearned Service Revenue			
Oct. 1	10,000	Oct. 2	5,000				Oct. 2	1,200
1	5,000	3	900					
2	1,200	4	600				Bal.	**1,200**
3	10,000	20	500					
		26	4,000					
Bal.	**15,200**							

Advertising Supplies				Common Stock		
Oct. 5	2,500				Oct. 1	10,000
Bal.	**2,500**				Bal.	**10,000**

Prepaid Insurance				Dividends		
Oct. 4	600			Oct. 20	500	
Bal.	**600**			Bal.	**500**	

Office Equipment				Service Revenue		
Oct. 2	5,000				Oct. 3	10,000
Bal.	**5,000**				Bal.	**10,000**

Notes Payable				Salaries Expense		
		Oct. 1	5,000	Oct. 26	4,000	
		Bal.	**5,000**	Bal.	**4,000**	

Accounts Payable				Rent Expense		
		Oct. 5	2,500	Oct. 3	900	
		Bal.	**2,500**	Bal.	**900**	

Illustration 3-32
General ledger for Sierra Corporation

recording every transaction in chronological order does not make the entries useful. To be useful, the entries need to be classified and summarized; posting the entries to specific ledger accounts does this.

Solution: The purpose of journalizing is to record every transaction in chronological order. Journalizing involves dating every transaction, measuring the dollar amount of each transaction, identifying or labeling each amount with account titles, and recording in a standard format equal debits and credits. Posting involves transferring the journalized debits and credits to specific accounts in the ledger.

THE TRIAL BALANCE

A **trial balance** is a list of accounts and their balances at a given time. Customarily, a trial balance is prepared at the end of an accounting period. The accounts are listed in the order in which they appear in the ledger, with debit balances listed in the left column and credit balances in the right column. The totals of the two columns must be equal.

The primary purpose of a trial balance is to prove the mathematical equality of debits and credits after posting. Under the double-entry system this equality will occur when the sum of the debit account balances equals the

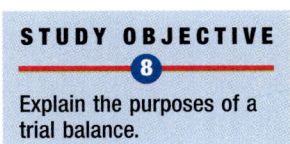

STUDY OBJECTIVE 8
Explain the purposes of a trial balance.

sum of the credit account balances. **A trial balance also uncovers errors in journalizing and posting.** For example, a trial balance may well have allowed detection of the error at Fidelity Investments discussed in the opening story. **In addition, a trial balance is useful in the preparation of financial statements,** as explained in the next chapter.

These are the procedures for preparing a trial balance:

1. List the account titles and their balances.
2. Total the debit and credit columns.
3. Verify the equality of the two columns.

The trial balance prepared from the ledger of Sierra Corporation is presented in Illustration 3-33. Note that the total debits, $28,700, equal the total credits, $28,700.

Illustration 3-33 Sierra Corporation trial balance

SIERRA CORPORATION
Trial Balance
October 31, 1998

	Debit	Credit
Cash	$15,200	
Advertising Supplies	2,500	
Prepaid Insurance	600	
Office Equipment	5,000	
Notes Payable		$ 5,000
Accounts Payable		2,500
Unearned Service Revenue		1,200
Common Stock		10,000
Dividends	500	
Service Revenue		10,000
Salaries Expense	4,000	
Rent Expense	900	
	$28,700	$28,700

LIMITATIONS OF A TRIAL BALANCE

A trial balance does not prove that all transactions have been recorded or that the ledger is correct. Numerous errors may exist even though the trial balance columns agree. For example, the trial balance may balance even when (1) a transaction is not journalized, (2) a correct journal entry is not posted, (3) a journal entry is posted twice, (4) incorrect accounts are used in journalizing or posting, or (5) offsetting errors are made in recording the amount of a transaction. In other words, as long as equal debits and credits are posted, even to the wrong account or in the wrong amount, the total debits will equal the total credits. Nevertheless, despite its limitations, the trial balance is a useful screen for finding errors and is frequently used in practice.

BEFORE YOU GO ON . . .

● **Review It**

1. What is a trial balance and how is it prepared?
2. What is the primary purpose of a trial balance?
3. What are the limitations of a trial balance?

DECISION TOOLKIT

Decision Checkpoints	Info Needed for Decision	Tool to Use for Decision	How to Evaluate Results
How do you determine that debits equal credits?	All account balances	Trial balance	List the account titles and their balances; total the debit and credit columns; verify equality.

Using the Decision Toolkit

The Kansas Farmers' Vertically Integrated Cooperative, Inc. (K-VIC), was formed by over 200 northeast Kansas farmers in the late 1980s. Its purpose is to use raw materials, primarily grain and meat products grown by K-VIC's members, to process this material into end-user food products, and to distribute the products nationally. Profits not needed for expansion or investment are returned to the members annually, on a pro-rata basis, according to the market value of the grain and meat products received from each farmer.

Assume that the following information was prepared for K-VIC's trial balance:

KANSAS FARMERS' VERTICALLY INTEGRATED COOPERATIVE, INC.
Trial Balance
December 31, 1998
(in thousands)

	Debit	Credit
Accounts Receivable	$ 712,000	
Accounts Payable		$ 37,000
Advertising and Promotion Payable		141,000
Buildings	365,000	
Cash	32,000	
Cost of Goods Sold	2,384,000	
Current Maturity of Long-Term Debt		12,000
Inventories	1,291,000	
Land	110,000	
Long-Term Debt		873,000
Machinery and Equipment	63,000	
Notes Payable to Members		495,000
Retained Earnings		822,000
Sales Revenue		3,741,000
Salaries and Wages Payable		62,000
Selling and Administrative Expense	651,000	
Trucking Expense	500,000	
	$6,108,000	$6,183,000

Because the trial balance is not in balance, you have checked with various people responsible for entering accounting data and have discovered the following:

1. The purchase of five new trucks, costing $7 million and paid for with cash, was not recorded.

2. A data entry clerk accidentally deleted the account name for an account with a credit balance of $472 million, so the amount was added to the Long-Term Debt account in the trial balance.
3. December cash sales revenue of $75 million was credited to the Sales Revenue account, but the other half of the entry was not made.
4. $50 million of selling expenses were mistakenly charged to Trucking Expense.

Instructions

Answer these questions:

(a) Which mistake or mistakes have caused the trial balance to be out of balance?
(b) Should all of the items be corrected? Explain.
(c) What is the name of the account the data entry clerk deleted?
(d) Make the necessary corrections and balance the trial balance.
(e) On your trial balance, write BAL beside the accounts that should be shown on the balance sheet and INC beside those that should be shown on the income statement.

Solution

(a) Only mistake 3 has caused the trial balance to be out of balance.
(b) All of the items should be corrected. The misclassification error (mistake 4) on the selling expense would not affect bottom line net income, but it does affect the amounts reported in the two expense accounts.
(c) There is no Common Stock account, so that must be the account that was deleted by the data entry clerk.
(d) and (e).

KANSAS FARMERS' VERTICALLY INTEGRATED COOPERATIVE, INC.
Trial Balance
December 31, 1998
(in thousands)

	Debit	Credit	
Accounts Receivable	$ 712,000		BAL
Accounts Payable		$ 37,000	BAL
Advertising and Promotion Payable		141,000	BAL
Buildings	365,000		BAL
Cash	100,000		BAL
Common Stock		472,000	BAL
Cost of Goods Sold	2,384,000		INC
Current Maturity of Long-Term Debt		12,000	BAL
Inventories	1,291,000		BAL
Land	110,000		BAL
Long-Term Debt		401,000	BAL
Machinery and Equipment	70,000		BAL
Notes Payable to Members		495,000	BAL
Retained Earnings		822,000	BAL
Sales Revenue		3,741,000	INC
Salaries and Wages Payable		62,000	BAL
Selling and Administrative Expense	701,000		INC
Trucking Expense	450,000		INC
	$6,183,000	$6,183,000	

Summary of Study Objectives

1 *Analyze the effect of business transactions on the basic accounting equation.* Each business transaction must have a dual effect on the accounting equation. For example, if an individual asset is increased, there must be a corresponding (a) decrease in another asset, or (b) increase in a specific liability, or (c) increase in stockholders' equity.

2 *Explain what an account is and how it helps in the recording process.* An account is an individual accounting record of increases and decreases in specific asset, liability, and stockholders' equity items.

3 *Define debits and credits and explain how they are used to record business transactions.* The terms *debit* and *credit* are synonymous with *left* and *right*. Assets, dividends, and expenses are increased by debits and decreased by credits. Liabilities, common stock, retained earnings, and revenues are increased by credits and decreased by debits.

4 *Identify the basic steps in the recording process.* The basic steps in the recording process are: (a) analyze each transaction in terms of its effect on the accounts, (b) enter the transaction information in a journal, and (c) transfer the journal information to the appropriate accounts in the ledger.

5 *Explain what a journal is and how it helps in the recording process.* The initial accounting record of a transaction is entered in a journal before the data are entered in the accounts. A journal (a) discloses in one place the complete effect of a transaction, (b) provides a chronological record of transactions, and (c) prevents or locates errors because the debit and credit amounts for each entry can be readily compared.

6 *Explain what a ledger is and how it helps in the recording process.* The entire group of accounts maintained by a company is referred to collectively as a ledger. The ledger keeps in one place all the information about changes in specific account balances.

7 *Explain what posting is and how it helps in the recording process.* Posting is the procedure of transferring journal entries to the ledger accounts. This phase of the recording process accumulates the effects of journalized transactions in the individual accounts.

8 *Explain the purposes of a trial balance.* A trial balance is a list of accounts and their balances at a given time. The primary purpose of the trial balance is to prove the mathematical equality of debits and credits after posting. A trial balance also uncovers errors in journalizing and posting and is useful in preparing financial statements.

Decision Toolkit—A Summary

Decision Checkpoints	Info Needed for Decision	Tool to Use for Decision	How to Evaluate Results
Has an accounting transaction occurred?	Details of the event	Accounting equation	Determine the effect, if any, on assets, liabilities, and stockholders' equity.
How do you determine that debits equal credits?	All account balances	Trial balance	List the account titles and their balances; total the debit and credit columns; verify equality.

Glossary

Account An individual accounting record of increases and decreases in specific asset, liability, and stockholders' equity items. (p. 104)

Accounting information system The system of collecting and processing transaction data and communicating financial information to interested parties. (p. 98)

Accounting transactions Events that require recording in the financial statements because they involve an exchange affecting assets, liabilities, or stockholders' equity (an external event) or because a reasonable estimate of value can be determined (an internal event). (p. 98)

126 CHAPTER 3 The Accounting Information System

Chart of accounts A list of a company's accounts. (p. 113)
Credit The right side of an account. (p. 104)
Debit The left side of an account. (p. 104)
Double-entry system A system that records the dual effect of each transaction in appropriate accounts. (p. 105)
General journal The most basic form of journal. (p. 111)
General ledger A ledger that contains all asset, liability, and stockholders' equity accounts. (p. 113)
Journal An accounting record in which transactions are initially recorded in chronological order. (p. 111)
Journalizing The procedure of entering transaction data in the journal. (p. 111)
Ledger The group of accounts maintained by a company. (p. 113)
Posting The procedure of transferring journal entries to the ledger accounts. (p. 114)
T account The basic form of an account. (p. 104)
Trial balance A list of accounts and their balances at a given time. (p. 121)

DEMONSTRATION PROBLEM

Bob Sample and other student investors opened Campus Laundry Inc. on September 1, 1998. During the first month of operations the following transactions occurred:

Sept. 1 Stockholders invested $20,000 cash in the business.
2 Paid $1,000 cash for store rent for the month of September.
3 Purchased washers and dryers for $25,000, paying $10,000 in cash and signing a $15,000 6-month, 12% note payable.
4 Paid $1,200 for 1-year accident insurance policy.
10 Received bill from the *Daily News* for advertising the opening of the laundromat, $200.
20 Declared and paid a $700 cash dividend to stockholders.
30 Determined that cash receipts for laundry fees for the month were $6,200.

The chart of accounts for the company is the same as for Sierra Corporation except for the following: Laundry Equipment and Advertising Expense.

Instructions
(a) Journalize the September transactions.
(b) Open ledger accounts and post the September transactions.
(c) Prepare a trial balance at September 30, 1998.

Problem-Solving Strategies
1. Make separate journal entries for each transaction.
2. Note that all debits precede all credit entries.
3. In journalizing, make sure debits equal credits.
4. In journalizing, use specific account titles taken from the chart of accounts.
5. Provide appropriate explanation of journal entry.
6. Arrange ledger in statement order, beginning with the balance sheet accounts.
7. Post in chronological order.
8. Prepare a trial balance, which lists accounts in the order in which they appear in the ledger.
9. List debit balances in the left column and credit balances in the right column.

Solution to Demonstration Problem

(a)
GENERAL JOURNAL

Date		Account Titles and Explanation	Debit	Credit
1998				
Sept.	1	Cash	20,000	
		Common Stock		20,000
		(Invested cash in business)		
	2	Rent Expense	1,000	
		Cash		1,000
		(Paid September rent)		
	3	Laundry Equipment	25,000	
		Cash		10,000
		Notes Payable		15,000
		(Purchased laundry equipment for cash and 6-month, 12% note payable)		
	4	Prepaid Insurance	1,200	
		Cash		1,200
		(Paid 1-year insurance policy)		

	10	Advertising Expense	200	
		Accounts Payable		200
		(Received bill from *Daily News* for advertising)		
	20	Dividends	700	
		Cash		700
		(Declared and paid a cash dividend)		
	30	Cash	6,200	
		Service Revenue		6,200
		(Received cash for laundry services rendered)		

(b) **GENERAL LEDGER**

Cash					Common Stock			
Sept. 1	20,000	Sept. 2	1,000				Sept. 1	20,000
30	6,200	3	10,000					
		4	1,200				Bal.	20,000
		20	700					
Bal.	13,300							

Prepaid Insurance				Dividends			
Sept. 4	1,200			Sept. 20	700		
Bal.	1,200			Bal.	700		

Laundry Equipment				Service Revenue			
Sept. 3	25,000					Sept. 30	6,200
Bal.	25,000					Bal.	6,200

Notes Payable				Advertising Expense			
		Sept. 3	15,000	Sept. 10	200		
		Bal.	15,000	Bal.	200		

Accounts Payable				Rent Expense			
		Sept. 10	200	Sept. 2	1,000		
		Bal.	200	Bal.	1,000		

(c)

CAMPUS LAUNDRY, INC.
Trial Balance
September 30, 1998

	Debit	Credit
Cash	$13,300	
Prepaid Insurance	1,200	
Laundry Equipment	25,000	
Notes Payable		$15,000
Accounts Payable		200
Common Stock		20,000
Dividends	700	
Service Revenue		6,200
Advertising Expense	200	
Rent Expense	1,000	
	$41,400	$41,400

128 CHAPTER 3 The Accounting Information System

SELF-STUDY QUESTIONS

Answers are at the end of the chapter.

(SO 1) 1. The effects on the basic accounting equation of performing services for cash are to:
(a) increase assets and decrease stockholders' equity.
(b) increase assets and increase stockholders' equity.
(c) increase assets and increase liabilities.
(d) increase liabilities and increase stockholders' equity.

(SO 1) 2. Genesis Company buys a $900 machine on credit. This transaction will affect the:
(a) income statement only.
(b) balance sheet only.
(c) income statement and stockholders' equity statement only.
(d) income statement, stockholders' equity statement, and balance sheet.

(SO 2) 3. Which statement about an account is *true*?
(a) In its simplest form, an account consists of two parts.
(b) An account is an individual accounting record of increases and decreases in specific asset, liability, and stockholders' equity items.
(c) There are separate accounts for specific assets and liabilities but only one account for stockholders' equity items.
(d) The left side of an account is the credit or decrease side.

(SO 3) 4. Debits:
(a) increase both assets and liabilities.
(b) decrease both assets and liabilities.
(c) increase assets and decrease liabilities.
(d) decrease assets and increase liabilities.

(SO 3) 5. A revenue account:
(a) is increased by debits.
(b) is decreased by credits.
(c) has a normal balance of a debit.
(d) is increased by credits.

(SO 3) 6. Which accounts normally have debit balances?
(a) Assets, expenses, and revenues
(b) Assets, expenses, and retained earnings
(c) Assets, liabilities, and dividends
(d) Assets, dividends, and expenses

(SO 4) 7. Which is *not* part of the recording process?
(a) Analyzing transactions
(b) Preparing a trial balance
(c) Entering transactions in a journal
(d) Posting transactions

8. Which of these statements about a journal is *false*? (SO 5)
(a) It contains only revenue and expense accounts.
(b) It provides a chronological record of transactions.
(c) It helps to locate errors because the debit and credit amounts for each entry can be readily compared.
(d) It discloses in one place the complete effect of a transaction.

9. A ledger: (SO 6)
(a) contains only asset and liability accounts.
(b) should show accounts in alphabetical order.
(c) is a collection of the entire group of accounts maintained by a company.
(d) provides a chronological record of transactions.

10. Posting: (SO 7)
(a) normally occurs before journalizing.
(b) transfers ledger transaction data to the journal.
(c) is an optional step in the recording process.
(d) transfers journal entries to ledger accounts.

11. A trial balance: (SO 8)
(a) is a list of accounts with their balances at a given time.
(b) proves the mathematical accuracy of journalized transactions.
(c) will not balance if a correct journal entry is posted twice.
(d) proves that all transactions have been recorded.

12. A trial balance will not balance if: (SO 8)
(a) a correct journal entry is posted twice.
(b) the purchase of supplies on account is debited to Supplies and credited to Cash.
(c) a $100 cash dividend is debited to Dividends for $1,000 and credited to Cash for $100.
(d) a $450 payment on account is debited to Accounts Payable for $45 and credited to Cash for $45.

QUESTIONS

1. Identify and describe the steps in the recording process.
2. Can a business enter into a transaction that affects only the left side of the basic accounting equation? If so, give an example.
3. Are the following events recorded in the accounting records? Explain your answer in each case.
   (a) A major stockholder of the company dies.
   (b) Supplies are purchased on account.
   (c) An employee is fired.
   (d) The company pays a cash dividend to its stockholders.
4. Indicate how each business transaction affects the basic accounting equation.
   (a) Paid cash for janitorial services
   (b) Purchased equipment for cash
   (c) Issued common stock to investors in exchange for cash
   (d) Paid an accounts payable in full
5. Why is an account referred to as a T account?
6. The terms *debit* and *credit* mean "increase" and "decrease," respectively. Do you agree? Explain.
7. Charles Thon, a fellow student, contends that the double-entry system means each transaction must be recorded twice. Is Charles correct? Explain.
8. Teresa Alvarez, a beginning accounting student, believes debit balances are favorable and credit balances are unfavorable. Is Teresa correct? Discuss.
9. State the rules of debit and credit as applied to (a) asset accounts, (b) liability accounts, and (c) the Common Stock account.
10. What is the normal balance for each of these accounts?
    (a) Accounts Receivable
    (b) Cash
    (c) Dividends
    (d) Accounts Payable
    (e) Service Revenue
    (f) Salaries Expense
    (g) Common Stock
11. Indicate whether each account is an asset, a liability, or a stockholders' equity account and whether it would have a normal debit or credit balance.
    (a) Accounts Receivable
    (b) Accounts Payable
    (c) Equipment
    (d) Dividends
    (e) Supplies
12. For the following transactions, indicate the account debited and the account credited.
    (a) Supplies are purchased on account.
    (b) Cash is received on signing a note payable.
    (c) Employees are paid salaries in cash.
13. For each account listed here, indicate whether it generally will have debit entries only, credit entries only, or both debit and credit entries.
    (a) Cash
    (b) Accounts Receivable
    (c) Dividends
    (d) Accounts Payable
    (e) Salaries Expense
    (f) Service Revenue
14. What are the basic steps in the recording process?
15. What are the advantages of using the journal in the recording process?
16. (a) When entering a transaction in the journal, should the debit or credit be written first?
    (b) Which should be indented, the debit or the credit?
17. (a) Can accounting transaction debits and credits be recorded directly in the ledger accounts?
    (b) What are the advantages of first recording transactions in the journal and then posting to the ledger?
18. Journalize these accounting transactions.
    (a) Doris Wang invests $9,000 in the business in exchange for common stock.
    (b) Insurance of $800 is paid for the year.
    (c) Supplies of $1,500 are purchased on account.
    (d) Cash of $7,500 is received for services rendered.
19. (a) What is a ledger?
    (b) Why is a chart of accounts important?
20. What is a trial balance and what are its purposes?
21. Kap Shin is confused about how accounting information flows through the accounting system. He believes information flows in this order:
    (a) Debits and credits are posted to the ledger.
    (b) Accounting transaction occurs.
    (c) Information is entered in the journal.
    (d) Financial statements are prepared.
    (e) Trial balance is prepared.
    Indicate to Kap the proper flow of the information.
22. Two students are discussing the use of a trial balance. They wonder whether the following errors, each considered separately, would prevent the trial balance from balancing. What would you tell them?
    (a) The bookkeeper debited Cash for $600 and credited Wages Expense for $600 for payment of wages.
    (b) Cash collected on account was debited to Cash for $900, and Service Revenue was credited for $90.

130 CHAPTER 3 The Accounting Information System

BRIEF EXERCISES

Determine effect of transaction on basic accounting equation.
(SO 1)

BE3-1 Presented here are three economic events. On a sheet of paper, list the letters (a), (b), and (c) with columns for assets, liabilities, and stockholders' equity. In each column, indicate whether the event increased (+), decreased (−), or had no effect (NE) on assets, liabilities, and stockholders' equity.
(a) Purchased supplies on account
(b) Received cash for providing a service
(c) Expenses paid in cash

Determine effect of transaction on basic accounting equation.
(SO 1)

BE3-2 Follow the same format as in BE3-1. Determine the effect on assets, liabilities, and stockholders' equity of the following three events:
(a) Issued common stock to investors in exchange for cash
(b) Paid cash dividend to stockholders
(c) Received cash from a customer who had previously been billed for services provided

Indicate debit and credit effects.
(SO 3)

BE3-3 For each of the following accounts indicate the effect of a debit or a credit on the account and the normal balance.
(a) Accounts Payable   (d) Accounts Receivable
(b) Advertising Expense   (e) Retained Earnings
(c) Service Revenue   (f) Dividends

Identify accounts to be debited and credited.
(SO 3)

BE3-4 Transactions for the H. J. Oslo Company for the month of June are presented next. Identify the accounts to be debited and credited for each transaction.
June 1 Issues common stock to investors in exchange for $2,500 cash.
      2 Buys equipment on account for $900.
      3 Pays $500 to landlord for June rent.
     12 Bills J. Kronsnoble $300 for welding work done.

Journalize transactions.
(SO 5)

BE3-5 Use the data in BE3-4 and journalize the transactions. (You may omit explanations.)

Identify steps in the recording process.
(SO 4)

BE3-6 Tage Shumway, a fellow student, is unclear about the basic steps in the recording process. Identify and briefly explain the steps in the order in which they occur.

Indicate basic debit–credit analysis.
(SO 5)

BE3-7 J. A. Norris Corporation has the following transactions during August of the current year. Indicate (a) the basic analysis and (b) the debit–credit analysis illustrated on pages 105–108.

Aug. 1 Issues shares of common stock to investors in exchange for $5,000.
      4 Pays insurance in advance for 6 months, $1,800.
     16 Receives $900 from clients for services rendered.
     27 Pays secretary $500 salary.

Journalize transactions.
(SO 5)

BE3-8 Use the data in BE3-7 and journalize the transactions. (You may omit explanations.)

Post journal entries to T accounts.
(SO 7)

BE3-9 Selected transactions for Gonzales Company are presented in journal form (without explanations). Post the transactions to T accounts.

Date		Account Title	Debit	Credit
May	5	Accounts Receivable	3,200	
		Service Revenue		3,200
	12	Cash	2,400	
		Accounts Receivable		2,400
	15	Cash	2,000	
		Service Revenue		2,000

Prepare a trial balance.
(SO 8)

BE3-10 From the ledger balances given at the top of the next page, prepare a trial balance for P. J. Carland Company at June 30, 1998. All account balances are normal.

Accounts Payable	$4,000	Service Revenue	$6,000
Cash	$3,800	Accounts Receivable	$3,000
Common Stock	$20,000	Salaries Expense	$4,000
Dividends	$1,200	Rent Expense	$1,000
Equipment	$17,000		

BE3-11 An inexperienced bookkeeper prepared the following trial balance that does not balance. Prepare a correct trial balance, assuming all account balances are normal.

Prepare a corrected trial balance.
(SO 8)

GOMEZ COMPANY
Trial Balance
December 31, 1998

	Debit	Credit
Cash	$18,800	
Prepaid Insurance		$ 3,500
Accounts Payable		3,000
Unearned Revenue	2,200	
Common Stock		10,000
Retained Earnings		7,000
Dividends		4,500
Service Revenue		25,600
Salaries Expense	18,600	
Rent Expense		2,400
	$39,600	$56,000

EXERCISES

E3-1 Selected transactions for Green Lawn Care Company, Inc., are listed here:
1. Issued common stock to investors in exchange for cash received from investors.
2. Paid monthly rent.
3. Purchased equipment on account.
4. Billed customers for services performed.
5. Paid dividend to stockholders.
6. Received cash from customers billed in (4).
7. Incurred advertising expense on account.
8. Purchased additional equipment for cash.
9. Received cash from customers when service was rendered.

Analyze the effect of transactions.
(SO 1)

Instructions
Describe the effect of each transaction on assets, liabilities, and stockholders' equity. For example, the first answer is: (1) Increase in assets and increase in stockholders' equity.

E3-2 Li Wang Computer Timeshare Company entered into these transactions during May 1998:
1. Purchased computer terminals for $19,000 from Digital Equipment on account.
2. Paid $4,000 cash for May rent on storage space.
3. Received $15,000 cash from customers for contracts billed in April.
4. Provided computer services to Brieske Construction Company for $3,000 cash.
5. Paid Southern States Power Co. $11,000 cash for energy usage in May.
6. Li Wang invested an additional $32,000 in the business in exchange for common stock of the company.
7. Paid Digital Equipment for the terminals purchased in (1).
8. Incurred advertising expense for May of $1,000 on account.

Analyze the effect of transactions on assets, liabilities, and stockholders' equity.
(SO 1)

Instructions
Indicate with the appropriate letter whether each of the transactions above results in:
(a) an increase in assets and a decrease in assets.
(b) an increase in assets and an increase in stockholders' equity.
(c) an increase in assets and an increase in liabilities.
(d) a decrease in assets and a decrease in stockholders' equity.
(e) a decrease in assets and a decrease in liabilities.

132 CHAPTER 3 The Accounting Information System

(f) an increase in liabilities and a decrease in stockholders' equity.
(g) an increase in stockholders' equity and a decrease in liabilities.

Analyze transactions and compute net income.
(SO 1)

E3-3 A tabular analysis of the transactions made by Roberta Mendez & Co. Inc. for the month of August is shown below. Each increase and decrease in stockholders' equity is explained.

	Cash	+	Accounts Receivable	+	Supplies	+	Office Equipment	=	Accounts Payable	+	Stockholders' Equity	
1.	+$15,000										+$15,000	Issued Common Stock
2.	−2,000						+$5,000		+$3,000			
3.	−750				+$750							
4.	+4,600		+$3,400								+8,000	Service Revenue
5.	−1,500								−1,500			
6.	−2,000										−2,000	Dividends
7.	−650										−650	Rent Expense
8.	+450		−450									
9.	−2,900										−2,900	Salaries Expense
10.									+500		−500	Utilities Expense

Instructions
(a) Describe each transaction.
(b) Determine how much stockholders' equity increased for the month.
(c) Compute the net income for the month.

Prepare an income statement, retained earnings statement, and balance sheet.
(SO 1)

E3-4 The tabular analysis of transactions for Roberta Mendez & Co. is presented in E3-3.

Instructions
Prepare an income statement and a retained earnings statement for August and a balance sheet at August 31, 1998.

Identify debits, credits, and normal balances.
(SO 3)

E3-5 Selected transactions for A. Mane, an interior decorator corporation, in its first month of business, are as follows:
1. Issued stock to investors for $10,000 in cash.
2. Purchased used car for $4,000 cash for use in business.
3. Purchased supplies on account for $500.
4. Billed customers $1,800 for services performed.
5. Paid $200 cash for advertising start of business.
6. Received $700 cash from customers billed in transaction (4).
7. Paid creditor $300 cash on account.
8. Paid dividends of $500 cash to stockholders.

Instructions
For each transaction indicate (a) the basic type of account debited and credited (asset, liability, stockholders' equity); (b) the specific account debited and credited (Cash, Rent Expense, Service Revenue, etc.); (c) whether the specific account is increased or decreased; and (d) the normal balance of the specific account. Use the following format, in which transaction 1 is given as an example:

	Account Debited				Account Credited			
	(a)	(b)	(c)	(d)	(a)	(b)	(c)	(d)
Trans-action	Basic Type	Specific Account	Effect	Normal Balance	Basic Type	Specific Account	Effect	Normal Balance
1	Asset	Cash	Increase	Debit	Stockholders' equity	Common Stock	Increase	Credit

Journalize transactions.
(SO 5)

E3-6 Data for A. Mane, interior decorator, are presented in E3-5.

Instructions
Journalize the transactions.

E3-7 This information relates to Marx Real Estate Agency Corporation:

Oct. 1 Lynn Marx begins business as a real estate agent with a cash investment of $13,000 in exchange for common stock of the corporation.
    2 Hires an administrative assistant.
    3 Buys office furniture for $1,900, on account.
    6 Sells a house and lot for B. Rollins; commissions due from Rollins, $3,200 (not paid by Rollins at this time).
   10 Receives cash of $140 as commissions for renting an apartment for the owner of the apartment.
   27 Pays $700 on account for the office furniture purchased on October 3.
   30 Pays the administrative assistant $960 in salary for October.

Analyze transactions and determine their effect on accounts.
(SO 3)

Instructions
Prepare the debit–credit analysis for each transaction as illustrated on pages 105–108.

E3-8 Transaction data for Marx Real Estate Agency are presented in E3-7.

Journalize transactions.
(SO 5)

Instructions
Journalize the transactions.

E3-9 Selected transactions from the journal of J. L. Kang, Inc., an investment brokerage corporation, are presented here:

Post journal entries and prepare a trial balance.
(SO 7, 8)

Date		Account Titles	Debit	Credit
Aug.	1	Cash	1,600	
		Common Stock		1,600
	10	Cash	2,400	
		Service Revenue		2,400
	12	Office Equipment	4,000	
		Cash		1,000
		Notes Payable		3,000
	25	Accounts Receivable	1,400	
		Service Revenue		1,400
	31	Cash	900	
		Accounts Receivable		900

Instructions
(a) Post the transactions to T accounts.
(b) Prepare a trial balance at August 31, 1998.

E3-10 These T accounts summarize the ledger of Lush Landscaping Company, Inc., at the end of the first month of operations:

Journalize transactions from T accounts and prepare a trial balance.
(SO 5, 8)

Cash				Unearned Revenue		
Apr. 1	9,000	Apr. 15	600		Apr. 30	800
12	900	25	1,500			
29	400					
30	800					

Accounts Receivable				Common Stock		
Apr. 7	3,200	Apr. 29	400		Apr. 1	9,000

Supplies			Service Revenue		
Apr. 4	1,800			Apr. 7	3,200
				Apr. 12	900

Accounts Payable				Salaries Expense		
Apr. 25	1,500	Apr. 4	1,800	Apr. 15	600	

134 CHAPTER 3 The Accounting Information System

Instructions
(a) Prepare the journal entries (including explanations) that resulted in the amounts posted to the account in the order they occurred.
(b) Prepare a trial balance at April 30, 1998.

Journalize transactions from T accounts and prepare a trial balance.
(SO 5, 8)

E3-11 Here is the ledger for Holly Co.:

Cash				Common Stock		
Oct. 1	4,000	Oct. 4	400		Oct. 1	4,000
10	650	12	1,500		25	2,000
10	5,000	15	250			
20	500	30	300			
25	2,000	31	500			

Accounts Receivable				Dividends	
Oct. 6	800	Oct 20	500	Oct. 30 300	
20	940				

Supplies				Service Revenue		
Oct. 4	400	Oct. 31	180		Oct. 6	800
					10	650
					20	940

Furniture			Store Wages Expense	
Oct. 3 2,000			Oct. 31 500	

Notes Payable			Supplies Expense	
	Oct. 10 5,000		Oct. 31 180	

Accounts Payable			Rent Expense	
Oct. 12 1,500	Oct. 3 2,000		Oct. 15 250	

Instructions
(a) Reproduce the journal entries for the transactions that occurred on October 1, 10, and 20 and provide explanations for each.
(b) Prepare a trial balance at October 31, 1998.

Prepare journal entries and post transactions to T accounts.
(SO 5, 7)

E3-12 Selected transactions for the Basler Corporation during its first month in business are presented below:

Sept. 1 Issued common stock in exchange for $15,000 cash received from investors.
 5 Purchased equipment for $10,000, paying $5,000 in cash and the balance on account.
 25 Paid $3,000 cash on balance owed for equipment.
 30 Paid $500 cash dividend.

Basler's chart of accounts shows: Cash, Equipment, Accounts Payable, Common Stock, and Dividends.

Instructions
(a) Journalize the transactions.
(b) Post the transactions to T accounts.

Analyze errors and their effects on trial balance.
(SO 8)

E3-13 The bookkeeper for John Castle's Equipment Repair Corporation made these errors in journalizing and posting:
1. A credit posting of $400 to Accounts Receivable was omitted.
2. A debit posting of $750 for Prepaid Insurance was debited to Insurance Expense.

3. A collection on account of $100 was journalized and posted as a debit to Cash $100 and a credit to Service Revenue $100.
4. A credit posting of $300 to Property Taxes Payable was made twice.
5. A cash purchase of supplies for $250 was journalized and posted as a debit to Supplies $25 and a credit to Cash $25.
6. A debit of $465 to Advertising Expense was posted as $456.

Instructions
For each error, indicate (a) whether the trial balance will balance; if the trial balance will not balance, indicate (b) the amount of the difference, and (c) the trial balance column that will have the larger total. Consider each error separately. Use the following form, in which error 1 is given as an example:

Error	(a) In Balance	(b) Difference	(c) Larger Column
1	No	$400	Debit

E3-14 The accounts in the ledger of Speedy Delivery Service contain the following balances on July 31, 1998:

Prepare a trial balance.
(SO 8)

Accounts Receivable	$ 8,642	Prepaid Insurance	$ 1,968
Accounts Payable	7,396	Repair Expense	961
Cash	?	Service Revenue	10,610
Delivery Equipment	49,360	Dividends	700
Gas and Oil Expense	758	Common Stock	40,000
Insurance Expense	523	Salaries Expense	4,428
Notes Payable	18,450	Salaries Payable	815
		Retained Earnings	4,636

Instructions
Prepare a trial balance with the accounts arranged as illustrated in the chapter, and fill in the missing amount for Cash.

PROBLEMS

P3-1 These November 1998 transactions affected the retained earnings account of the Larsson Corporation:

Prepare an income statement and retained earnings statement.
(SO 1)

Transaction	Amount	Description
(7)	$ 700	Property tax expense
(9)	6,000	Service revenue
(10)	350	Utilities expense
(13)	4,000	Wage expense
(16)	300	Utilities expense
(18)	1,250	Rent expense
(19)	450	Advertising expense
(22)	2,000	Service revenue
(23)	800	Dividends
(25)	600	Repair expense
(27)	400	Auto expense
(31)	9,000	Service revenue
(32)	1,600	Dividends
(33)	4,000	Wage expense
(34)	500	Utilities expense

In reviewing the account, Lars Larsson realized that the new bookkeeper had made the following error: Transaction (27) was a payment for wage expense.

Instructions

(a) Prepare an income statement for the month of November.
(b) Prepare a retained earnings statement for November, assuming that the beginning retained earnings balance was $9,500 on November 1.

Analyze transactions and compute net income.
(SO 1)

P3-2 On April 1 Laura Seall established Seall Travel Agency, Inc. These transactions were completed during the month:
1. Laura invested $20,000 cash in the company in exchange for common stock.
2. Paid $400 cash for April office rent.
3. Purchased office equipment for $2,500 cash.
4. Incurred $300 of advertising costs in the *Chicago Tribune*, on account.
5. Paid $600 cash for office supplies.
6. Earned $9,000 for services rendered: Cash of $1,000 is received from customers, and the balance of $8,000 is billed to customers on account.
7. Paid $200 cash dividends.
8. Paid *Chicago Tribune* amount due in transaction (4).
9. Paid employees' salaries, $1,200.
10. Received $8,000 in cash from customers who have previously been billed in transaction (6).

Instructions

(a) Prepare a tabular analysis of the transactions using these column headings: Cash, Accounts Receivable, Supplies, Office Equipment, Accounts Payable, Common Stock, and Retained Earnings.
(b) From an analysis of the column Retained Earnings, compute the net income or net loss for April.

Analyze transactions and prepare an income statement, retained earnings statement, and balance sheet.
(SO 1)

P3-3 Ivan Izo created a corporation providing legal services, Ivan Izo, Inc., on July 1, 1998. On July 31 the balance sheet showed: Cash $4,000; Accounts Receivable $1,500; Supplies $500; Office Equipment $5,000; Accounts Payable $4,200; Common Stock $6,500; and Retained Earnings $300. During August the following transactions occurred:
1. Collected $1,400 of accounts receivable.
2. Paid $2,700 cash on accounts payable.
3. Earned revenue of $6,400, of which $3,000 is collected in cash and the balance is due in September.
4. Purchased additional office equipment for $1,000, paying $400 in cash and the balance on account.
5. Paid salaries $1,500, rent for August $900, and advertising expenses $350.
6. Declared and paid a cash dividend of $550.
7. Received $2,000 from Standard Federal Bank; the money was borrowed on a note payable.
8. Incurred utility expenses for month on account, $250.

Instructions

(a) Prepare a tabular analysis of the August transactions beginning with July 31 balances. The column heading should be: Cash + Accounts Receivable + Supplies + Office Equipment = Notes Payable + Accounts Payable + Common Stock + Retained Earnings.
(b) Prepare an income statement for August, a retained earnings statement for August, and a balance sheet at August 31.

Journalize a series of transactions.
(SO 3, 5)

P3-4 Surepar Miniature Golf and Driving Range, Inc., was opened on March 1 by Jim McInnes. These selected events and transactions occurred during March:

Mar. 1 McInnes invested $50,000 cash in the business in exchange for common stock of the corporation.
 3 Purchased Lee's Golf Land for $38,000 cash. The price consists of land $23,000, building $9,000, and equipment $6,000. (Record this in a single entry.)
 5 Advertised the opening of the driving range and miniature golf course, paying advertising expenses of $1,600.
 6 Paid cash $1,480 for a 1-year insurance policy.
 10 Purchased golf clubs and other equipment for $1,600 from Palmer Company payable in 30 days.

18   Received golf fees of $800 in cash.
19   Sold 100 coupon books for $15.00 each. Each book contains ten coupons that enable the holder to play one round of miniature golf or to hit one bucket of golf balls.
25   Declared and paid a $500 cash dividend.
30   Paid salaries of $600.
30   Paid Palmer Company in full.
31   Received $500 of fees in cash.

Jim McInnes uses these accounts: Cash, Prepaid Insurance, Land, Buildings, Equipment, Accounts Payable, Unearned Revenue, Common Stock, Retained Earnings, Dividends, Golf Revenue, Advertising Expense, and Salaries Expense.

Instructions
Journalize the March transactions.

P3-5 Patricia Perez incorporated as a licensed architect. During the first month of the operation of her business, these events and transactions occurred:

Journalize transactions, post, and prepare a trial balance.
(SO 3, 5, 7, 8)

Apr. 1   Patricia invested $13,000 cash in exchange for common stock of the corporation.
      1   Hired a secretary-receptionist at a salary of $300 per week, payable monthly.
      2   Paid office rent for the month, $800.
      3   Purchased architectural supplies on account from Halo Company, $1,500.
     10   Completed blueprints on a carport and billed client $900 for services.
     11   Received $500 cash advance from R. Welk for the design of a new home.
     20   Received $1,500 cash for services completed and delivered to P. Donahue.
     30   Paid secretary-receptionist for the month, $1,200.
     30   Paid $600 to Halo Company on account.

Patricia uses these accounts: Cash, Accounts Receivable, Supplies, Accounts Payable, Unearned Revenue, Common Stock, Service Revenue, Salaries Expense, and Rent Expense.

Instructions
(a) Journalize the transactions.
(b) Post to the ledger T accounts.
(c) Prepare a trial balance on April 30, 1998.

P3-6 This is the trial balance of Jane's Laundry Corporation on September 30:

Journalize transactions, post, and prepare a trial balance.
(SO 3, 5, 7, 8)

JANE'S LAUNDRY
Trial Balance
September 30, 1998

	Debit	Credit
Cash	$ 8,500	
Accounts Receivable	2,200	
Supplies	1,700	
Equipment	8,000	
Accounts Payable		$ 5,000
Unearned Revenue		700
Common Stock		14,700
	$20,400	$20,400

The October transactions were as follows:

Oct. 5   Received $900 cash from customers on account.
     10   Billed customers for services performed, $5,500.
     15   Paid employee salaries, $1,200.
     17   Performed $400 of services for customers who paid in advance in August.
     20   Paid $1,600 to creditors on account.
     29   Paid a $500 cash dividend.
     31   Paid utilities, $600.

Instructions

(a) Prepare a general ledger using T accounts. Enter the opening balances in the ledger accounts as of October 1. Provision should be made for these additional accounts: Dividends, Laundry Revenue, Salaries Expense, and Utilities Expense.
(b) Journalize the transactions.
(c) Post to the ledger accounts.
(d) Prepare a trial balance on October 31, 1998.

Prepare a correct trial balance.
(SO 8)

P3-7 This trial balance of Thom Wargo Co. does not balance.

THOM WARGO CO.
Trial Balance
June 30, 1998

	Debit	Credit
Cash		$ 2,840
Accounts Receivable	$ 3,231	
Supplies	800	
Equipment	3,000	
Accounts Payable		2,666
Unearned Revenue	1,200	
Common Stock		9,000
Dividends	800	
Service Revenue		2,380
Salaries Expense	3,400	
Office Expense	910	
	$13,341	$16,886

Each of the listed accounts has a normal balance per the general ledger. An examination of the ledger and journal reveals the following errors:

1. Cash received from a customer on account was debited for $570, and Accounts Receivable was credited for the same amount. The actual collection was for $750.
2. The purchase of a typewriter on account for $340 was recorded as a debit to Supplies for $340 and a credit to Accounts Payable for $340.
3. Services were performed on account for a client for $890. Accounts Receivable was debited for $890 and Service Revenue was credited for $89.
4. A debit posting to Salaries Expense of $600 was omitted.
5. A payment on account for $206 was credited to Cash for $206 and credited to Accounts Payable for $260.
6. Payment of a $400 cash dividend to Wargo's stockholders was debited to Salaries Expense for $400 and credited to Cash for $400.

Instructions
Prepare the correct trial balance.

Journalize transactions, post, and prepare a trial balance.
(SO 3, 5, 7, 8)

P3-8 Star Theater, Inc., was recently formed by Leo Baerga. It will begin operations in March. The Star will be unique in that it will show only triple features of sequential theme movies. As of February 28, the ledger of Star showed: Cash $16,000; Land $42,000; Buildings (concession stand, projection room, ticket booth, and screen) $18,000; Equipment $16,000; Accounts Payable $12,000; and Common Stock $80,000. During the month of March the following events and transactions occurred:

Mar. 2 Acquired the three *Star Wars* movies (*Star Wars*[RM], *The Empire Strikes Back*, and *The Return of the Jedi*) to be shown for the first 3 weeks of March. The film rental was $12,000; $4,000 was paid in cash and $8,000 will be paid on March 10.
 3 Ordered the first three *Star Trek* movies to be shown the last 10 days of March. It will cost $400 per night.
 9 Received $6,500 cash from admissions.

10 Paid balance due on *Star Wars* movies rental and $3,000 on February 28 accounts payable.
11 Hired M. Brewer to operate concession stand. Brewer agrees to pay Star Theater 15% of gross receipts payable monthly.
12 Paid advertising expenses $800.
20 Received $7,200 cash from admissions.
20 Received the *Star Trek* movies and paid rental fee of $4,000.
31 Paid salaries of $3,800.
31 Received statement from M. Brewer showing gross receipts from concessions of $8,000 and the balance due to Star Theater of $1,200 for March. Brewer paid half the balance due and will remit the remainder on April 5.
31 Received $12,500 cash from admissions.

In addition to the accounts identified above, the chart of accounts includes: Accounts Receivable, Admission Revenue, Concession Revenue, Advertising Expense, Film Rental Expense, and Salaries Expense.

Instructions
(a) Using T accounts, enter the beginning balances to the ledger.
(b) Journalize the March transactions.
(c) Post the March journal entries to the ledger.
(d) Prepare a trial balance on March 31, 1998.

ALTERNATIVE PROBLEMS

P3-1A Upton Consulting Co. was started on March 1, 1998. The stockholders' equity column of the tabular summary for the month of March contained these recorded data:

Prepare an income statement and retained earnings statement.
(SO 1)

Transaction	Amount	Description
(1)	$15,000	Investment
(4)	750	Rent expense
(6)	3,250	Service revenue
(8)	400	Advertising expense
(11)	1,000	Salaries expense
(12)	2,100	Service revenue
(15)	250	Utilities expense
(18)	500	Dividends
(20)	3,200	Service revenue
(22)	200	Repair expense
(24)	1,000	Advertising expense
(27)	300	Dividends
(29)	1,100	Service revenue
(32)	900	Salaries expense
(34)	200	Property tax expense
(36)	150	Utilities expense

All data were properly recorded except the following:
1. In transaction (22), $150 of the repair expense was applicable to Michael Upton's personal residence.
2. In transaction (36), $80 was applicable to repairs on business property.

Instructions
(a) Prepare an income statement for the month of March.
(b) Prepare a retained earnings statement for March.

P3-2A Tony's Repair Shop, Inc., was started on May 1 by R. Antonio. Here is a summary of the May transactions:

Analyze transactions and compute net income.
(SO 1)

1. Invested $15,000 cash in the company in exchange for common stock.
2. Purchased equipment for $5,000 cash.
3. Paid $400 cash for May office rent.
4. Paid $500 cash for supplies.
5. Incurred $250 of advertising costs in the *Beacon News* on account.
6. Received $4,100 in cash from customers for repair service.
7. Declared and paid a $500 cash dividend.
8. Paid part-time employee salaries, $1,000.
9. Paid utility bills, $140.
10. Provided repair service on account to customers, $200.
11. Collected cash of $120 for services billed in transaction (10).

Instructions
(a) Prepare a tabular analysis of the transactions using these column headings: Cash, Accounts Receivable, Supplies, Equipment, Accounts Payable, Common Stock, and Retained Earnings. Revenue is called Service Revenue.
(b) From an analysis of the column Retained Earnings, compute the net income or net loss for May.

Analyze transactions and prepare an income statement, retained earnings statement, and balance sheet.
(SO 1)

P3-3A Donna Corso opened a veterinary business in Hills, Iowa, on August 1, 1998. On August 31 the balance sheet showed: Cash $9,000; Accounts Receivable $1,700; Supplies $600; Office Equipment $6,000; Accounts Payable $3,600; Common Stock $13,000; and Retained Earnings $700. During September the following transactions occurred:
1. Paid $3,100 cash on accounts payable.
2. Collected $1,300 of accounts receivable.
3. Purchased additional office equipment for $2,100, paying $800 in cash and the balance on account.
4. Earned revenue of $5,900, of which $2,500 is paid in cash and the balance is due in October.
5. Declared and paid a $600 cash dividend.
6. Paid salaries $700, rent for September $900, and advertising expense $100.
7. Incurred utility expenses for month on account, $170.
8. Received $7,000 from Hilldale Bank; the money was borrowed on a note payable.

Instructions
(a) Prepare a tabular analysis of the September transactions beginning with August 31 balances. The column headings should be: Cash + Accounts Receivable + Supplies + Office Equipment = Notes Payable + Accounts Payable + Common Stock + Retained Earnings.
(b) Prepare an income statement for September, a retained earnings statement for September, and a balance sheet at September 30.

Journalize a series of transactions.
(SO 3, 5)

P3-4A The Frontier Park was started on April 1 by Ed Quinn. These selected events and transactions occurred during April:

Apr. 1 Invested $60,000 cash in the business in exchange for common stock.
    4 Purchased land costing $30,000 for cash.
    8 Incurred advertising expense of $1,800 on account.
    11 Paid salaries to employees, $1,500.
    12 Hired park manager at a salary of $4,000 per month, effective May 1.
    13 Paid $1,500 for a 1-year insurance policy.
    17 Paid $600 cash dividends.
    20 Received $5,700 in cash for admission fees.
    25 Sold 100 coupon books for $25 each. Each book contains ten coupons that entitle the holder to one admission to the park.
    30 Received $5,900 in cash admission fees.
    30 Paid $700 on account for advertising incurred on April 8.

Ed Quinn uses the following accounts: Cash, Prepaid Insurance, Land, Accounts Payable, Unearned Admissions, Common Stock, Dividends, Admission Revenue, Advertising Expense, and Salaries Expense.

Instructions
Journalize the April transactions.

P3-5A Iva Holz operates an incorporated accounting practice. During the first month of operations of her business, these events and transactions occurred:

Journalize transactions, post, and prepare a trial balance.
(SO 3, 5, 7, 8)

May 1 Invested $42,000 cash in exchange for common stock of the corporation.
2 Hired a secretary-receptionist at a salary of $1,000 per month.
3 Purchased $1,200 of supplies on account from Read Supply Company.
7 Paid office rent of $900 for the month.
11 Completed a tax assignment and billed client $1,100 for services rendered.
12 Received $3,500 advance on a management consulting engagement.
17 Received cash of $1,200 for services completed for H. Arnold Co.
31 Paid secretary-receptionist $1,000 salary for the month.
31 Paid 40% of balance due Read Supply Company.

Iva uses the following chart of accounts: Cash, Accounts Receivable, Supplies, Accounts Payable, Unearned Revenue, Common Stock, Service Revenue, Salaries Expense, and Rent Expense.

Instructions
(a) Journalize the transactions.
(b) Post to the ledger T accounts.
(c) Prepare a trial balance on May 31, 1998.

P3-6A The trial balance of Sterling Dry Cleaners on June 30 is given here:

Journalize transactions, post, and prepare a trial balance.
(SO 3, 5, 7, 8)

STERLING DRY CLEANERS
Trial Balance
June 30, 1998

	Debit	Credit
Cash	$12,532	
Accounts Receivable	10,536	
Supplies	4,844	
Equipment	25,950	
Accounts Payable		$15,878
Unearned Revenue		1,730
Common Stock		36,254
	$53,862	$53,862

The July transactions were as follows:

July 8 Collected $4,936 in cash on June 30 accounts receivable.
9 Paid employee salaries, $2,100.
11 Received $4,325 in cash for services rendered.
14 Paid June 30 creditors $10,750 on account.
17 Purchased supplies on account, $554.
22 Billed customers for services rendered, $4,700.
30 Paid employee salaries $3,114, utilities $1,384, and repairs $692.
31 Paid $700 cash dividend.

Instructions
(a) Prepare a general ledger using T accounts. Enter the opening balances in the ledger accounts as of July 1. Provision should be made for the following additional accounts: Dividends, Dry Cleaning Revenue, Repair Expense, Salaries Expense, and Utilities Expense.
(b) Journalize the transactions.
(c) Post to the ledger accounts.
(d) Prepare a trial balance on July 31, 1998.

Prepare a correct trial balance.
(SO 8)

P3-7A This trial balance of Saginaw Company does not balance.

SAGINAW COMPANY
Trial Balance
May 31, 1998

	Debit	Credit
Cash	$ 5,850	
Accounts Receivable		$ 2,750
Prepaid Insurance	700	
Equipment	8,000	
Accounts Payable		4,500
Property Taxes Payable	560	
Common Stock		5,700
Retained Earnings		6,000
Service Revenue	6,690	
Salaries Expense	4,200	
Advertising Expense		1,100
Property Tax Expense	800	
	$26,800	$20,050

Your review of the ledger reveals that each account has a normal balance. You also discover the following errors:

1. The totals of the debit sides of Prepaid Insurance, Accounts Payable, and Property Tax Expense were each understated $100.
2. Transposition errors were made in Accounts Receivable and Service Revenue. Based on postings made, the correct balances were $2,570 and $6,960, respectively.
3. A debit posting to Salaries Expense of $200 was omitted.
4. A $700 cash dividend was debited to Common Stock for $700 and credited to Cash for $700.
5. A $420 purchase of supplies on account was debited to Equipment for $420 and credited to Cash for $420.
6. A cash payment of $250 for advertising was debited to Advertising Expense for $25 and credited to Cash for $25.
7. A collection from a customer for $210 was debited to Cash for $210 and credited to Accounts Payable for $210.

Instructions

Prepare the correct trial balance. [*Note:* The chart of accounts also includes the following: Dividends, Supplies, and Supplies Expense.]

Journalize transactions, post, and prepare a trial balance.
(SO 3, 5, 7, 8)

P3-8A Lake Theater, Inc., was recently begun by Frances Hill. All facilities were completed on March 31. At this time, the ledger showed: Cash $6,000; Land $10,000; Buildings (concession stand, projection room, ticket booth, and screen) $8,000; Equipment $6,000; Accounts Payable $2,000; Mortgage Payable $8,000; and Common Stock $20,000. During April, the following events and transactions occurred:

Apr. 2 Paid film rental of $800 on first movie.
 3 Ordered two additional films at $500 each.
 9 Received $1,800 cash from admissions.
 10 Made $2,000 payment on mortgage and $1,000 on accounts payable.
 11 Hired R. Thoms to operate concession stand. Thoms agrees to pay the Lake Theater 17% of gross receipts payable monthly.
 12 Paid advertising expenses, $300.
 20 Received one of the films ordered on April 3 and was billed $500. The film will be shown in April.
 25 Received $4,200 cash from admissions.
 29 Paid salaries, $1,600.

30 Received statement from R. Thoms showing gross receipts of $1,000 and the balance due to the Lake Theater of $170 for April. Thoms paid half of the balance due and will remit the remainder on May 5.
30 Prepaid $700 rental on special film to be run in May.

In addition to the accounts identified above, the chart of accounts shows: Accounts Receivable, Prepaid Rentals, Admission Revenue, Concession Revenue, Advertising Expense, Film Rental Expense, Salaries Expense.

Instructions
(a) Enter the beginning balances in the ledger T accounts as of April 1.
(b) Journalize the April transactions
(c) Post the April journal entries to the ledger T accounts.
(d) Prepare a trial balance on April 30, 1998.

BROADENING YOUR PERSPECTIVE

FINANCIAL REPORTING AND ANALYSIS

FINANCIAL REPORTING PROBLEM: *Starbucks Corporation*

BYP3-1 The financial statements of Starbucks in Appendix A at the back of this book contain the following selected accounts, all in thousands of dollars:

Accounts Payable	$ 38,034
Accounts and Notes Receivable	17,621
Interest Income	11,029
Interest Expense	8,739
Prepaid Expenses	6,534
Property, Plant, and Equipment (net)	369,477

Instructions
(a) What is the increase and decrease side for each account? What is the normal balance for each account?
(b) Identify the probable other account in the transaction and the effect on that account when:
   (1) Accounts and Notes Receivable is decreased.
   (2) Accounts Payable is decreased.
   (3) Prepaid Expenses is increased.
(c) Identify the other account(s) that ordinarily would be involved when:
   (1) Interest Expense is increased.
   (2) Property, Plant, and Equipment is increased.

COMPARATIVE ANALYSIS PROBLEM: *Starbucks vs. Green Mountain Coffee*

BYP3-2 The financial statements of Green Mountain Coffee are presented in Appendix B, following the financial statements for Starbucks in Appendix A.

Instructions
(a) Based on the information contained in these financial statements, determine the normal balance for:

Starbucks	Green Mountain Coffee
(1) Accounts Receivable	(1) Inventories
(2) Property, Plant, and Equipment	(2) Fixed Assets
(3) Accounts Payable	(3) Accrued Expenses
(4) Retained Earnings	(4) Common Stock
(5) Interest Income	(5) Interest Expense

144 CHAPTER 3 The Accounting Information System

(b) Identify the other account ordinarily involved when:
  (1) Accounts Receivable is increased.
  (2) Notes Payable is decreased.
  (3) Machinery is increased.
  (4) Interest Income is increased.

RESEARCH CASE

BYP3-3 The Enterprise Standard Industrial Classification (SIC) coding scheme, a published classification of firms into separate industries, is commonly used in practice. SIC codes permit identification of company activities on three levels of detail. Two-digit codes designate a "major group," three-digit codes designate an "industry group," and four-digit codes identify a specific "industry."

Instructions
At your library, find the *Standard Industrial Classification Manual* (published by the U.S. Government's Office of Management and Budget in 1987) and answer these questions:
(a) On what basis are SIC codes assigned to companies?
(b) Identify the major group/industry group/industry represented by these codes: 12, 271, 3571, 7033, 75, 872.
(c) Identify the SIC code for these industries:
  (1) Golfing equipment—manufacturing
  (2) Worm farms
  (3) Felt tip markers—manufacturing
  (4) Household appliance stores, electric, or gas—retail
  (5) Advertising agencies
(d) Suppose you are interested in examining several companies in the passenger airline industry. Determine the appropriate two-, three-, and four-digit SIC codes. Use *Wards Business Directory of U.S. Private and Public Companies* (Vol. 5) to compile a list of the five largest parent companies (by total sales) in the industry. [*Note:* If *Wards* is not available, alternative sources are *Standard & Poor's Register of Corporations, Directors, and Executives; Standard & Poor's Industry Surveys;* and *Dun & Bradstreet Million Dollar Directory.*]

INTERPRETING FINANCIAL STATEMENTS

BYP3-4 Minicase 1 *Bob Evans Farms, Inc.*

Bob Evans Farms, Inc., operates 354 restaurants and several food processing plants. The plants primarily process pork into sausage, some of which is used in the restaurants and some is sold to grocery stores. The food processing plants also produce "fast-food"–type frozen sandwiches, which are marketed to grocery stores.

The 1995 balance sheet of Bob Evans Farms showed a cash balance of $10 million and trade accounts receivable of $16 million. The notes to the financial statements revealed that there was a line of credit available of $63 million, of which $26 million was then outstanding.

Instructions
(a) Explain why most of the trade accounts receivable would probably not pertain to the restaurant business.
(b) What kind of individuals or companies would you expect to find in the individual accounts receivable accounts?
(c) Why might Bob Evans Farms be keeping the $10 million in cash instead of using most of it—for example, $8 million—to help pay off the line of credit debt?

BYP3-5 Minicase 2 *Chieftain International, Inc.*

Chieftain International, Inc., is an oil and natural gas exploration and production company. The company's 1994 balance sheet reported $208 million in assets with only $4.6 million in liabilities, all of which were short-term accounts payable.

During the year, Chieftain expanded its holdings of oil and gas rights, drilled 37 new wells, and invested in expensive 3-D seismic technology. The company generated $19 million cash from operating activities in 1994 and paid no dividends. It had a cash balance of $102 million at the end of the year.

Instructions
(a) Name at least two advantages to Chieftain from having no long-term debt. Can you think of disadvantages?
(b) What are some of the advantages to Chieftain from having this large a cash balance? What is a disadvantage?
(c) Why do you suppose Chieftain has the $4.6 million balance in accounts payable, since it appears that it could have made all its purchases for cash?

CRITICAL THINKING

MANAGEMENT DECISION CASE

BYP3-6 Lucy Lars operates Lucy Riding Academy, Inc. The academy's primary sources of revenue are riding fees and lesson fees, which are provided on a cash basis. Lucy also boards horses for owners, who are billed monthly for boarding fees. In a few cases, boarders pay in advance of expected use. For its revenue transactions, the academy maintains these accounts: Cash, Boarding Accounts Receivable, Unearned Revenue, Riding Revenue, Lesson Revenue, and Boarding Revenue.

The academy owns ten horses, a stable, a riding corral, riding equipment, and office equipment. These assets are accounted for in accounts Horses, Building, Riding Corral, Riding Equipment, and Office Equipment.

The academy employs stable helpers and an office employee, who receive weekly salaries. At the end of each month, the mail usually brings bills for advertising, utilities, and veterinary service. Other expenses include feed for the horses and insurance. For its expenses, the academy maintains the following accounts: Hay and Feed Supplies, Prepaid Insurance, Accounts Payable, Salaries Expense, Advertising Expense, Utilities Expense, Veterinary Expense, Hay and Feed Expense, and Insurance Expense.

Lucy Lars's sole source of personal income is dividends from the academy. Thus, the corporation declares and pays periodic dividends. To record stockholders' equity in the business and dividends, two accounts are maintained: Common Stock and Dividends.

During the first month of operations an inexperienced bookkeeper was employed. Lucy Lars asks you to review the following eight entries of the 50 entries made during the month. In each case, the explanation for the entry is correct.

May 1	Cash	15,000	
	Common Stock		15,000
	(Invested $15,000 cash in business)		
5	Cash	250	
	Riding Revenue		250
	(Received $250 cash for lesson fees)		
7	Cash	500	
	Boarding Revenue		500
	(Received $500 for boarding of horses beginning June 1)		
9	Hay and Feed Expense	1,700	
	Cash		1,700
	(Purchased estimated 2 months' supply of feed and hay for $1,700 on account)		
14	Riding Equipment	80	
	Cash		800
	(Purchased desk and other office equipment for $800 cash)		
15	Salaries Expense	400	
	Cash		400
	(Issued check to Lucy Lars for personal use)		
20	Cash	145	
	Riding Revenue		154
	(Received $154 cash for riding fees)		
31	Veterinary Expense	75	
	Accounts Payable		75
	(Received bill of $75 from veterinarian for services rendered)		

Instructions

(a) For each journal entry that is correct, so state. For each journal entry that is incorrect, prepare the entry that should have been made by the bookkeeper.
(b) Which of the incorrect entries would prevent the trial balance from balancing?
(c) What was the correct net income for May, assuming the bookkeeper reported net income of $4,500 after posting all 50 entries?
(d) What was the correct cash balance at May 31, assuming the bookkeeper reported a balance of $12,475 after posting all 50 entries?

A REAL-WORLD FOCUS: *Automated Security Holdings*

BYP3-7 *Automated Security Holdings* operates multinationally, with principal markets in the United States and the United Kingdom. The company designs, produces, installs, and maintains security systems to safeguard life and property from a wide range of hazards. The markets for these security products include commercial, industrial, and residential customers.

The following addition to the financial statements identifies a few of the accounts found in the general ledger of Automated Security Holdings:

	November 30 1993	1994
	(in thousands)	
Income Tax Payable	$ 3,929	$ 3,919
Accounts Payable	6,499	9,620
Salaries Expense	16,353	9,213
Cash	4,749	2,869
Unearned Revenue	1,211	1,434
Notes Payable	52,000	40,000
Prepaid Insurance	1,333	2,000

Instructions

(a) Identify the accounts of Automated Security Holdings that have debit balances in the trial balance.
(b) What date has Automated Security Holdings adopted for its accounting year-end?
(c) Are the accounts listed in the order in which they would appear in Automated Security Holdings' general ledger? Explain.

GROUP ACTIVITY

BYP3-8 The expanded basic accounting equation contains seven account categories: assets, liabilities, common stock, retained earnings, dividends, revenues, and expenses.

Instructions

With the class divided into seven groups, each group should choose one of the seven account categories and do these exercises.
(a) Explain the increase/decrease side of the account and the normal balance of the account.
(b) Give an example of a transaction that will result in an increase in the account category.

COMMUNICATION ACTIVITY

BYP3-9 Milly Maid Company offers home cleaning service. Two recurring transactions for the company are billing customers for services rendered and paying employee salaries. For example, on March 15 bills totaling $6,000 were sent to customers and $2,000 was paid in salaries to employees.

Instructions
Write a memorandum to your instructor that explains and illustrates the steps in the recording process for each of the March 15 transactions. Use the format illustrated in the text under the heading "The Recording Process Illustrated" (p. 114).

ETHICS CASE

BYP3-10 Mary Vonesh is the assistant chief accountant at Staples Company, a manufacturer of computer chips and cellular phones. The company presently has total sales of $20 million. It is the end of the first quarter and Mary is hurriedly trying to prepare a general ledger trial balance so that quarterly financial statements can be prepared and released to management and the regulatory agencies. The total credits on the trial balance exceed the debits by $1,000. In order to meet the 4 P.M. deadline, Mary decides to force the debits and credits into balance by adding the amount of the difference to the Equipment account. She chose Equipment because it is one of the larger account balances; percentagewise it will be the least misstated. Mary plugs the difference! She believes that the difference is quite small and will not affect anyone's decisions. She wishes that she had another few days to find the error but realizes that the financial statements are already late.

Instructions
(a) Who are the stakeholders in this situation?
(b) What ethical issues are involved?
(c) What are Mary's alternatives?

FINANCIAL ANALYSIS ON THE WEB

BYP3-11 *Purpose:* This exercise will familiarize you with skill requirements, job descriptions, and salaries for accounting careers.

Address: http://www.cob.ohio-state.edu/dept/fin/jobs/account.htm

Steps: Go to the site shown above.

Instructions
Answer the following questions:
(a) What are the three broad areas of accounting?
(b) List four skills required in these areas.
(c) How do these areas differ in required skills?
(d) Explain one of the key job functions in accounting.
(e) Based on the 1992 *Smart Money* survey, what is the salary range for a junior staff accountant with Deloitte & Touche?

Answers to Self-Study Questions
1. b   2. b   3. b   4. c   5. d   6. d   7. b   8. a   9. c   10. d   11. a   12. c

CHAPTER 4

Accrual Accounting Concepts

STUDY OBJECTIVES

After studying this chapter, you should be able to:

1. Explain the revenue recognition principle and the matching principle.
2. Differentiate between the cash basis and the accrual basis of accounting.
3. Explain why adjusting entries are needed and identify the major types of adjusting entries.
4. Prepare adjusting entries for prepayments.
5. Prepare adjusting entries for accruals.
6. Describe the nature and purpose of the adjusted trial balance.
7. Explain the purpose of closing entries.
8. Describe the required steps in the accounting cycle.

Timing Is Everything

A few simple truths:

Truth 1: Net income = Revenues − Expenses

Truth 2: In general, more net income is better than less.

Truth 3: To increase net income you must increase reported revenue or decrease reported expense.

Truth 4: Timing is everything.

So far you have learned some nice orderly rules about how to keep track of corporate transactions. Guess what? It isn't that nice and neat. In fact, it is often difficult to determine in what period some revenues and expenses should be reported. There are rules that give guidance, but occasionally these rules are overlooked, misinterpreted, or even intentionally ignored. Consider the following examples:

- Cambridge Biotech Corp., which develops vaccines and diagnostic tests for humans and animals, said that it reported revenue from transactions that "don't appear to be bona fide."
- Media Vision Technology Inc., a maker of sound and animation equipment for computers, was accused of operating a "phantom" warehouse to hide inventory for returned products already recorded as sales.
- Policy Management Systems Corp., which makes insurance software, said that it reported some sales before contracts were signed or products delivered.
- Penguin USA, a book publisher, said that it understated expenses in a number of years because it failed to report expenses for discounts given to customers for paying early.

In each case, accrual accounting concepts were violated. That is, revenues or expenses were not recorded in the proper period, which had a substantial impact on reported income.

Why might management want to report revenues or expenses in the wrong period? One *Wall Street Journal* article states

that high-tech firms have intense pressure to report higher earnings every year. If actual performance falls short of expectations, management might be tempted to bend the rules. An accounting expert suggests that investors and auditors should be suspicious of sharp increases in monthly sales at the end of each quarter or big jumps in fourth-quarter sales. Such events don't always mean management is cheating, but they are certainly worth investigating.[1]

[1] Based on Lee Burton, "Tech Concerns Fudge Figures to Buoy Stocks," *The Wall Street Journal,* May 19, 1994, p. B1.

PREVIEW OF CHAPTER 4

As indicated in the opening story, making adjustments properly is important and necessary. To do otherwise leads to a misstatement of revenues and expenses. In this chapter we introduce you to the accrual accounting concepts that make such adjustments possible.

The organization and content of the chapter are as follows:

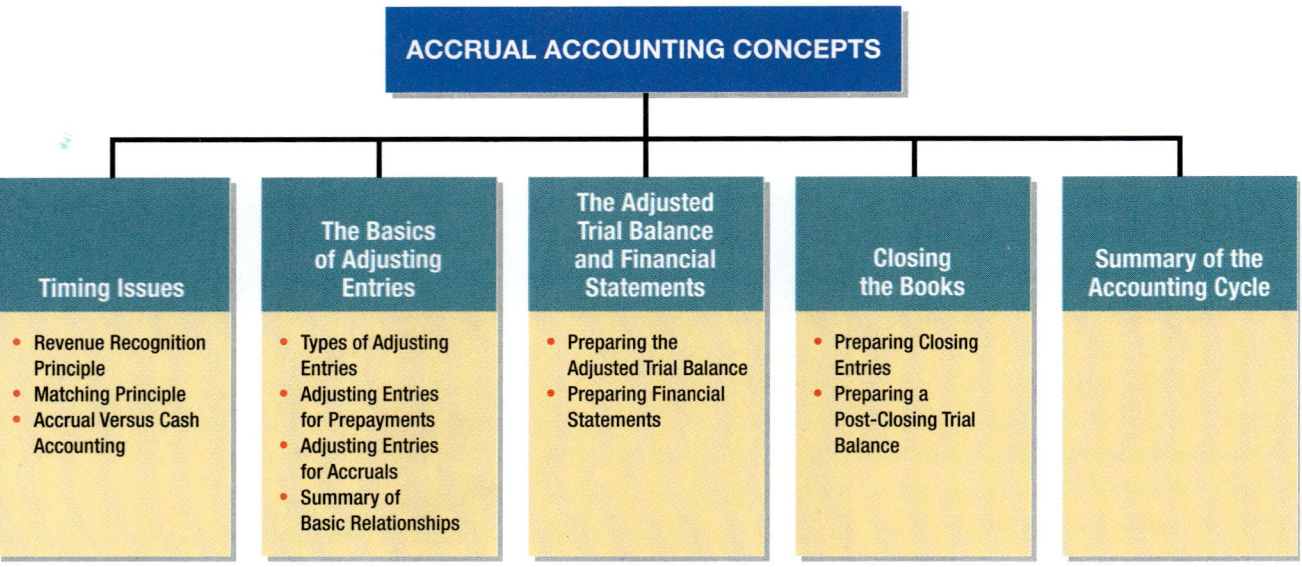

TIMING ISSUES

STUDY OBJECTIVE 1
Explain the revenue recognition principle and the matching principle.

Consider this story:

> A grocery store owner from the old country kept his accounts payable on a spindle, accounts receivable on a note pad, and cash in a cigar box. His daughter, having just passed the CPA exam, chided her father: "I don't understand how you can run your business this way. How do you know what your profits are?"
>
> "Well," the father replied, "when I got off the boat 40 years ago, I had nothing but the pants I was wearing. Today your brother is a doctor, your sister is a college professor, and you are a CPA. Your mother and I have a nice car, a well-furnished house, and a lake home. We have a good business and everything is paid for. So, you add all that together, subtract the pants, and there's your profit."

Although the old grocer may be correct in his evaluation of how to calculate income over his lifetime, most businesses need more immediate feedback about how well they are doing. For example, management usually wants monthly reports on financial results, most large corporations are required to present quarterly and annual financial statements to stockholders, and the Internal Revenue Service requires all businesses to file annual tax returns. Consequently, **accounting divides the economic life of a business into artificial time periods.** As indicated in Chapter 1, this is the **time period assumption.** Accounting time periods are generally a month, a quarter, or a year.

Helpful Hint An accounting time period that is 1 year long is called a **fiscal year.**

150

Many business transactions affect more than one of these arbitrary time periods. For example, a new building purchased by Citicorp or a new airplane purchased by Delta Air Lines will be used for many years. It doesn't make good sense to expense the full amount of the building or the airplane at the time it is purchased because each will be used for many subsequent periods. Therefore, it is necessary to determine the impact of each transaction on specific accounting periods.

Determining the amount of revenues and expenses to be reported in a given accounting period can be difficult. Proper reporting requires a thorough understanding of the nature of the company's business. Accountants have developed two principles to use as guidelines as part of generally accepted accounting principles (GAAP): the revenue recognition principle and the matching principle.

THE REVENUE RECOGNITION PRINCIPLE

The **revenue recognition principle** dictates that revenue be recognized in the accounting period in which it is earned. In a service company, revenue is considered to be earned at the time the service is performed. To illustrate, assume a dry cleaning business cleans clothing on June 30 but customers do not claim and pay for their clothes until the first week of July. Under the revenue recognition principle, revenue is earned in June when the service is performed, not in July when the cash is received. At June 30 the dry cleaner would report a receivable on its balance sheet and revenue in its income statement for the service performed.

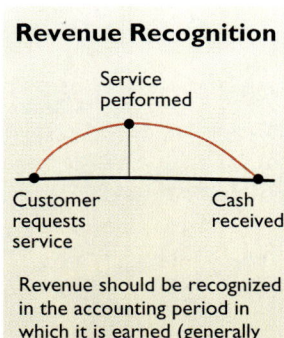

DECISION TOOLKIT

Decision Checkpoints	Info Needed for Decision	Tool to Use for Decision	How to Evaluate Results
At what point should the company record revenue?	Need to understand the nature of the company's business	Revenue should be recorded when earned. For a service business, revenue is earned when service is performed.	Recognizing revenue too early overstates current period revenue; recognizing it too late understates current period revenue.

THE MATCHING PRINCIPLE

In recognizing expenses, a simple rule is followed: "Let the expenses follow the revenues." Thus, expense recognition is tied to revenue recognition. Applied to the preceding example, this means that the salary expense incurred in performing the cleaning service on June 30 should be reported in the same period in which the service revenue is recognized. The critical issue in expense recognition is determining when the expense makes its contribution to revenue. This may or may not be the same period in which the expense is paid. If the salary incurred on June 30 is not paid until July, the dry cleaner would report salaries payable on its June 30 balance sheet. The practice of expense recognition is referred to as the **matching principle** because it dictates that efforts (expenses) be matched with accomplishments (revenues). These relationships are shown in Illustration 4-1.

Illustration 4-1 GAAP relationships in revenue and expense recognition

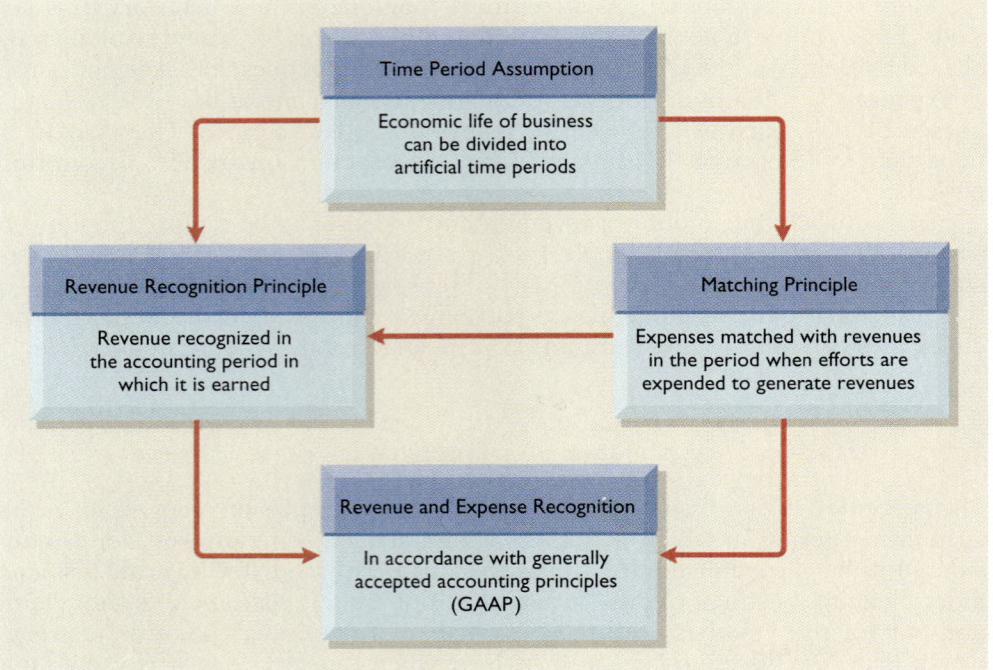

BUSINESS INSIGHT
Management Perspective

Suppose you are a filmmaker and spend $15 million to produce a film. Over what period should the $15 million be expensed? Yes, it should be expensed over the economic life of the film. But what is its economic life? The filmmaker must estimate how much revenue will be earned from box office sales, video sales, and television over a period that easily can stretch to 5 years or more. If a filmmaker allocates the cost over 5 years and the film produces revenue in the sixth year, then the matching is not correct. Furthermore, in some cases, films flop and yet the costs are still spread out over 5 years in hopes that the films will eventually succeed. For example, in the mid-1980s Orion Pictures (now bankrupt) earned $7.3 million in one year but lost $32 million the next year because it expensed 40 films that were not producing revenue. It was alleged that the company had overstated its income in earlier years because it did not expense these costs sooner. This case demonstrates the difficulty of properly matching expenses to revenues.

DECISION TOOLKIT

Decision Checkpoints	Info Needed for Decision	Tool to Use for Decision	How to Evaluate Results
At what point should the company record expenses?	Need to understand the nature of the company's business	Expenses should "follow" revenues—that is, the effort (expense) should be matched with the result (revenue).	Recognizing expenses too early overstates current period expense; recognizing it too late understates current period expense.

ACCRUAL VERSUS CASH BASIS OF ACCOUNTING

Application of the revenue recognition and matching principles results in accrual basis accounting. **Accrual basis accounting** means that transactions that change a company's financial statements are recorded **in the periods in which the events occur,** rather than in the periods in which the company receives or pays cash. For example, **using the accrual basis to determine net income means recognizing revenues when earned rather than when the cash is received, and recognizing expenses when incurred rather than when paid.**

Under **cash basis accounting,** revenue is recorded only when the cash is received, and an expense is recorded only when cash is paid. **An income statement presented under the cash basis of accounting does not satisfy generally accepted accounting principles.** Why? Because it fails to record revenue that has been earned but for which the cash has not been received, thus violating the revenue recognition principle. In addition, expenses are also not matched with earned revenues, and therefore the matching principle is violated.

Illustration 4-2 shows the relationship between accrual-based numbers and cash-based numbers, using a simple example. Suppose that you own a painting company and you paint a large building during year 1. In year 1 you incurred total expenses of $50,000, which includes the cost of the paint and your employees' salaries. Now assume that you billed your customer $80,000 at the end of year 1, but you weren't paid until year 2. On an accrual basis, you would report the revenue during the period earned—year 1—and the expenses would be matched to the period in which the revenues were earned. Thus, your net income for year 1 would be $30,000, and no revenue or expense from this project would be reported in year 2. The $30,000 of income reported for year 1 provides a useful indication of the profitability of your efforts during that period. If, instead, you were reporting on a cash basis, you would report expenses of $50,000 in year 1 and revenues of $80,000 in year 2. Net income for year 1 would be a loss of $50,000, while net income for year 2 would be $80,000. Neither of these measures is very informative about the results of your efforts during these periods.

STUDY OBJECTIVE 2
Differentiate between the cash basis and the accrual basis of accounting.

Helpful Hint Accountants are sometimes asked to convert cash-based records to the accrual basis. As you might expect, extensive adjustments to the accounting records are required for this task.

Illustration 4-2 Accrual versus cash basis accounting

	Year 1	Year 2
Activity	Purchased paint, painted building, paid employees	Received payment for work done in year 1
Accrual basis	Revenue $80,000 Expense 50,000 Net income $30,000	Revenue $ 0 Expense 0 Net income $ 0
Cash basis	Revenue $ 0 Expense 50,000 Net loss ($50,000)	Revenue $80,000 Expense 0 Net income $80,000

154 CHAPTER 4 Accrual Accounting Concepts

Although most companies use the accrual basis of accounting, some small companies use the cash basis because they often have few receivables and payables.

BUSINESS INSIGHT
Management Perspective

If you are upset about the billions of dollars of taxpayers' money needed to make good on Uncle Sam's guarantees related to the savings and loan bailout, here's one thing you might do: Suggest that your congressional representatives learn accrual accounting. Presently, the U.S. federal budget measures only cash transactions—how many dollar bills the government pays out and how many it receives in a given year. Let's say that the federal government guarantees loans made by a savings and loan. Since no cash outlay takes place initially, the budget deficit doesn't increase by a cent, even though everyone concerned knows there will be credit losses that Uncle Sam will have to make good. As a former head of the Office of Management and Budget noted, "Loan guarantees are the budget's invisible Pacmen. You can't see them now, but sooner or later they will gobble up your money."

Source: Adapted from "Phony Bookkeeping," *Forbes,* May 1990.

BEFORE YOU GO ON . . .

● **Review It**

1. What are the revenue recognition and matching principles?
2. What are the differences between the cash and accrual bases of accounting?

THE BASICS OF ADJUSTING ENTRIES

STUDY OBJECTIVE 3

Explain why adjusting entries are needed and identify the major types of adjusting entries.

In order for revenues to be recorded in the period in which they are earned, and for expenses to be recognized in the period in which they are incurred, adjusting entries are made to revenue and expense accounts at the end of the accounting period. In short, **adjusting entries are needed to ensure that the revenue recognition and matching principles are followed.**

The use of adjusting entries makes it possible to produce accurate financial statements at the end of the accounting period. Thus, the balance sheet reports appropriate assets, liabilities, and stockholders' equity at the statement date, and the income statement shows the proper net income (or loss) for the period. However, the trial balance—the first pulling together of the transaction data—may not contain up-to-date and complete data. This is true for these reasons:

1. Some events are not journalized daily because it would not be useful or efficient to do so. Examples are the use of supplies and the earning of wages by employees.
2. Some costs are not journalized during the accounting period because these costs expire with the passage of time rather than as a result of recurring daily transactions. Examples of such costs are building and equipment deterioration and rent and insurance.
3. Some items may be unrecorded. An example is a utility service bill that will not be received until the next accounting period.

Adjusting entries are required every time financial statements are prepared. An essential starting point is an analysis of each account in the trial balance to determine whether it is complete and up to date for financial statement purposes.

TYPES OF ADJUSTING ENTRIES

Adjusting entries can be classified as either prepayments or accruals. Each of these classes has two subcategories as shown in Illustration 4-3.

Prepayments:

1. **Prepaid expenses:** Expenses paid in cash and recorded as assets before they are used or consumed.
2. **Unearned revenues:** Cash received and recorded as liabilities before revenue is earned.

Accruals:

1. **Accrued revenues:** Revenues earned but not yet received in cash or recorded.
2. **Accrued expenses:** Expenses incurred but not yet paid in cash or recorded.

Illustration 4-3
Categories of adjusting entries

Specific examples and explanations of each type of adjustment are given in subsequent sections. Each example is based on the October 31 trial balance of Sierra Corporation, from Chapter 3, reproduced in Illustration 4-4. Note that Retained Earnings has been added to this trial balance with a zero balance. We will explain its use later.

SIERRA CORPORATION
Trial Balance
October 31, 1998

	Debit	Credit
Cash	$15,200	
Advertising Supplies	2,500	
Prepaid Insurance	600	
Office Equipment	5,000	
Notes Payable		$ 5,000
Accounts Payable		2,500
Unearned Revenue		1,200
Common Stock		10,000
Retained Earnings		0
Dividends	500	
Service Revenue		10,000
Salaries Expense	4,000	
Rent Expense	900	
	$28,700	$28,700

Illustration 4-4
Trial balance

It will be assumed that Sierra Corporation uses an accounting period of 1 month. Thus, monthly adjusting entries will be made. The entries will be dated October 31.

ADJUSTING ENTRIES FOR PREPAYMENTS

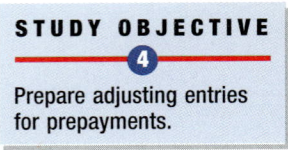

STUDY OBJECTIVE 4
Prepare adjusting entries for prepayments.

Prepayments are either prepaid expenses or unearned revenues. Adjusting entries for prepayments are required at the statement date to record the portion of the prepayment that represents the expense incurred or the revenue earned in the current accounting period. Adjusting entries for prepayments are graphically depicted in Illustration 4-5.

Illustration 4-5
Adjusting entries for prepayments

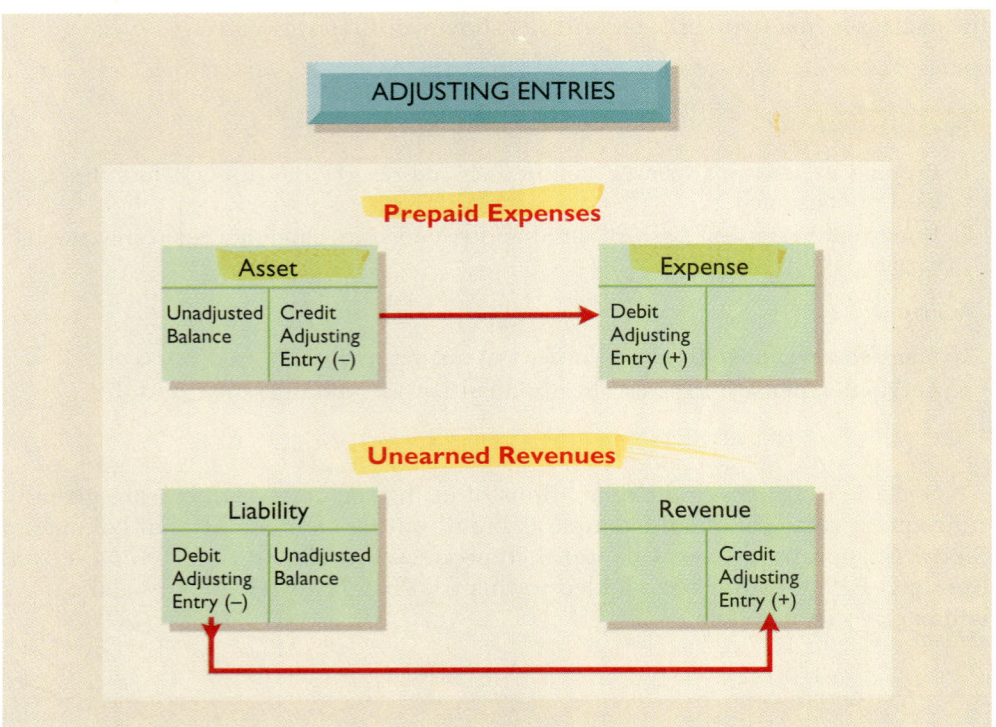

Prepaid Expenses

Payments of expenses that will benefit more than one accounting period are identified as **prepaid expenses** or **prepayments.** When such a cost is incurred, an asset account is debited to show the service or benefit that will be received in the future. Examples of common prepayments are insurance, supplies, advertising, and rent. In addition, prepayments are made when buildings and equipment are purchased.

Prepaid expenses expire either with the passage of time (e.g., rent and insurance) or through use (e.g., supplies). The expiration of these costs does not require daily entries, which would be impractical and unnecessary. Accordingly, we postpone the recognition of such cost expirations until financial statements are prepared. At each statement date, adjusting entries are made to record the expenses applicable to the current accounting period and to show the remaining amounts in the asset accounts. Prior to adjustment, assets are overstated and expenses are understated. Therefore, **an adjusting entry for prepaid expenses results in an increase (a debit) to an expense account and a decrease (a credit) to an asset account.**

Supplies. Supplies, such as paper and envelopes, generally increase (debit) an asset account when they are acquired. During the accounting period, supplies are used. Rather than record supplies expense as the supplies are used, supplies expense is recognized at the **end** of the accounting period. At that time the company must count the remaining supplies. The difference between the balance in the Supplies (asset) account and the cost of supplies on hand represents the supplies used (expense) for that period.

Recall from the facts presented in Chapter 3 that Sierra Corporation purchased advertising supplies costing $2,500 on October 5. The debit was made to the asset Advertising Supplies, and this account shows a balance of $2,500 in the October 31 trial balance. An inventory count at the close of business on October 31 reveals that $1,000 of supplies are still on hand. Thus, the cost of supplies used is $1,500 ($2,500 − $1,000). This use of supplies decreases an asset, Advertising Supplies, and decreases stockholders' equity by increasing an expense account, Advertising Supplies Expense. The use of supplies affects the accounting equation in the following way:

Supplies

Oct. 5

Supplies purchased; record asset

Oct. 31

Supplies used; record supplies expense

Assets	=	Liabilities	+	Stockholders' Equity
−$1,500				−$1,500

Oct. 31	Advertising Supplies Expense	1,500	
	Advertising Supplies		1,500
	(To record supplies used)		

After the adjusting entry is posted, the two supplies accounts, in T account form, are as in Illustration 4-6.

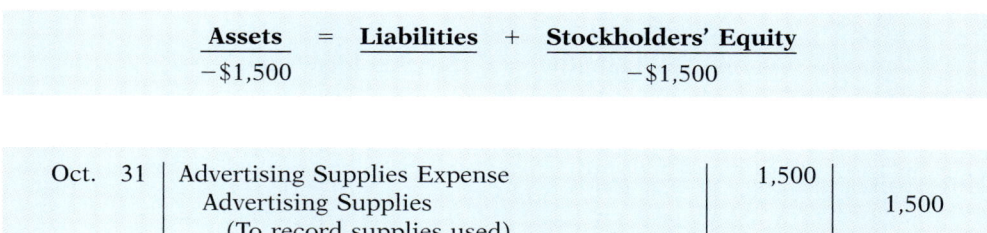

Illustration 4-6 Supplies accounts after adjustment

The asset account Advertising Supplies now shows a balance of $1,000, which is equal to the cost of supplies on hand at the statement date. In addition, Advertising Supplies Expense shows a balance of $1,500, which equals the cost of supplies used in October. **If the adjusting entry is not made, October expenses will be understated and net income overstated by $1,500. Moreover, both assets and stockholders' equity will be overstated by $1,500 on the October 31 balance sheet.**

BUSINESS INSIGHT
Management Perspective

The cost of advertising on radio, television, and magazines for burgers, bleaches, athletic shoes, and such products are sometimes considered prepayments. As a manager for Procter & Gamble noted, "If we run a long ad campaign for soap and bleach, we sometimes report the costs as prepayments if we think we'll receive sales benefits from the campaign down the road." Presently it is a judgment call whether these costs should be prepayments or expenses in the current period. Developing guidelines consistent with the matching principle is difficult. The issue is important because the outlays for advertising can be substantial. As examples, Procter & Gamble, the biggest U.S. advertiser, in a recent year spent $2.3 billion, Sears, Roebuck spent $1.5 billion, and McDonald's $760 million.

158 CHAPTER 4 Accrual Accounting Concepts

Insurance
Oct. 4
Insurance purchased; record asset

Oct. 31
Insurance expired; record insurance expense

Insurance. Companies purchase insurance to protect themselves from losses due to fire, theft, and unforeseen events. Insurance must be paid in advance, often for more than 1 year. Insurance payments (premiums) made in advance are normally recorded in the asset account Prepaid Insurance. At the financial statement date it is necessary to increase (debit) Insurance Expense and decrease (credit) Prepaid Insurance for the cost of insurance that has expired during the period.

On October 4 Sierra Corporation paid $600 for a 1-year fire insurance policy. Coverage began on October 1. The payment was recorded by increasing (debiting) Prepaid Insurance when it was paid, and this account shows a balance of $600 in the October 31 trial balance. An analysis of the policy reveals that $50 ($600/12) of insurance expires each month. The expiration of Prepaid Insurance would have the following impact on the accounting equation in October (and each of the next 11 months):

Assets	=	Liabilities	+	Stockholders' Equity
−$50				−$50

Thus, this adjusting entry is made:

Oct. 31	Insurance Expense	50	
	Prepaid Insurance		50
	(To record insurance expired)		

After the adjusting entry is posted, the accounts appear as in Illustration 4-7.

Illustration 4-7
Insurance accounts after adjustment

Prepaid Insurance			Insurance Expense	
Oct. 4 600	Oct. 31 **Adj. 50**		Oct. 31 **Adj. 50**	
Oct. 31 Bal. 550			Oct. 31 Bal. 50	

The asset Prepaid Insurance shows a balance of $550, which represents the cost that applies to the remaining 11 months of coverage. At the same time the balance in Insurance Expense is equal to the insurance cost that was used in October. If this adjustment is not made, October expenses would be understated by $50 and net income overstated by $50. Moreover, as the accounting equation shows, both assets and stockholders' equity will be overstated by $50 on the October 31 balance sheet.

Depreciation. A company typically owns a variety of assets that have long lives, such as buildings, equipment, and motor vehicles. The term of service is referred to as the useful life of the asset. Because a building is expected to provide service for many years, it is recorded as an asset, rather than an expense, on the date it is acquired. As explained in Chapter 1, such assets are recorded at cost, as required by the cost principle. According to the matching principle, a portion of this cost should then be reported as an expense during each period of the asset's useful life. Depreciation is the process of allocating the cost of an asset to expense over its useful life.

Need for Adjustment. From an accounting standpoint, the acquisition of long-lived assets is essentially a long-term prepayment for services. The need for making periodic adjusting entries for depreciation is therefore the same as described before for other prepaid expenses—that is, to recognize the cost that has been used (an expense) during the period and to report the unused cost (an asset) at the end of the period. One point is very important to understand: **Depreciation is an allocation concept, not a valuation concept.** That is, we depreciate an asset **to allocate its cost to the periods that we use it. We are not attempting to reflect the actual change in the value of the asset.**

For Sierra Corporation, assume that depreciation on the office equipment is estimated to be $480 a year, or $40 per month. This would have the following impact on the accounting equation:

Depreciation

Oct. 2

Office equipment purchased; record asset

Office Equipment
Oct $40	Nov $40	Dec $40	Jan $40
Feb $40	March $40	April $40	May $40
June $40	July $40	Aug $40	Sept $40
Depreciation = $480/year

Oct. 31
Depreciation recognized; record depreciation expense

Assets	=	Liabilities	+	Stockholders' Equity
−$40				−$40

Accordingly, depreciation for October is recognized by this adjusting entry:

Oct. 31	Depreciation Expense	40	
	Accumulated Depreciation—Office Equipment		40
	(To record monthly depreciation)		

After the adjusting entry is posted, the accounts appear as in Illustration 4-8.

Office Equipment

| Oct. 2 | 5,000 | |
| Oct. 31 | Bal. 5,000 | |

Accumulated Depreciation— Office Equipment

| | Oct. 31 | Adj. 40 |
| | Oct. 31 | Bal. 40 |

Depreciation Expense

| Oct. 31 | Adj. 40 | |
| Oct. 31 | Bal. 40 | |

Illustration 4-8
Accounts after adjustment for depreciation

The balance in the Accumulated Depreciation account will increase $40 each month.

Statement Presentation. Accumulated Depreciation—Office Equipment is a **contra asset account,** which means that it is offset against Office Equipment on the balance sheet, and its normal balance is a credit. This account is used instead of decreasing (crediting) Office Equipment in order to disclose *both* the original cost of the equipment and the total cost that has expired to date. In the balance sheet, Accumulated Depreciation—Office Equipment is deducted from the related asset account as shown in Illustration 4-9.

Office equipment	$5,000
Less: Accumulated depreciation—office equipment	40
	$4,960

Illustration 4-9 Balance sheet presentation of accumulated depreciation

The difference between the cost of any depreciable asset and its related accumulated depreciation is referred to as the **book value** of that asset. In Illustration 4-9, the book value of the equipment at the balance sheet date is $4,960. The book value and the market value of the asset are generally two different

Alternative Terminology
Book value is also referred to as **carrying value.**

values. As noted earlier, depreciation is not a matter of valuation, but a means of cost allocation.

Note also that depreciation expense identifies the portion of an asset's cost that has expired in October. The accounting equation shows that, as in the case of other prepaid adjustments, the omission of this adjusting entry would cause total assets, total stockholders' equity, and net income to be overstated and depreciation expense to be understated.

Unearned Revenues

Cash received before revenue is earned is recorded by increasing (crediting) a liability account called unearned revenues. Items like rent, magazine subscriptions, and customer deposits for future service may result in unearned revenues. Airlines such as United, American, and Delta, for instance, treat receipts from the sale of tickets as unearned revenue until the flight service is provided. Unearned revenues are the opposite of prepaid expenses. Indeed, unearned revenue on the books of one company is likely to be a prepayment on the books of the company that has made the advance payment. For example, if identical accounting periods are assumed, a landlord will have unearned rent revenue when a tenant has prepaid rent.

When the payment is received for services to be provided in a future accounting period, an unearned revenue (a liability) account should be credited to recognize the obligation that exists. Unearned revenues are subsequently earned by providing service to a customer. During the accounting period it is not practical for you to make daily entries as the revenue is earned. Instead, we delay recognition of earned revenue until the adjustment process. Then an adjusting entry is made to record the revenue that has been earned during the period and to show the liability that remains at the end of the accounting period. Typically, prior to adjustment liabilities are overstated and revenues are understated. Therefore, **the adjusting entry for unearned revenues results in a decrease (a debit) to a liability account and an increase (a credit) to a revenue account.**

Sierra Corporation received $1,200 on October 2 from R. Knox for advertising services expected to be completed by December 31. The payment was credited to Unearned Revenue, and this liability account shows a balance of $1,200 in the October 31 trial balance. From an evaluation of the work performed by Sierra for Knox during October, it is determined that $400 has been earned in October. This would affect the accounting equation in the following way:

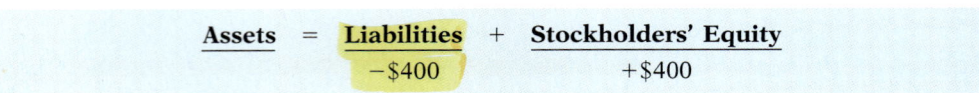

This adjusting entry is made:

Oct. 31	Unearned Service Revenue		400	
	Service Revenue			400
	(To record revenue earned)			

After the adjusting entry is posted, the accounts appear as in Illustration 4-10.

Illustration 4-10 Service revenue accounts after prepayments adjustment

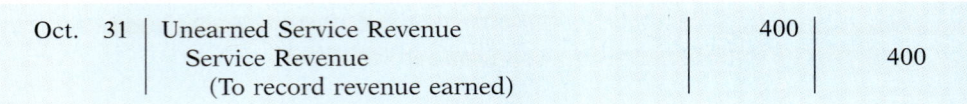

Unearned Service Revenue			Service Revenue		
Oct. 31 Adj. 400	Oct. 2	1,200		Oct. 3	10,000
				31	Adj. 400
	Oct. 31 Bal. 800			Oct. 31	Bal. 10,400

The liability Unearned Service Revenue now shows a balance of $800, which represents the remaining advertising services expected to be performed in the future. At the same time, Service Revenue shows total revenue earned in October of $10,400. If this adjustment is not made, revenues and net income will be understated by $400 in the income statement. Moreover, liabilities will be overstated and stockholders' equity will be understated by $400 on the October 31 balance sheet.

BEFORE YOU GO ON . . .

● **Review It**

1. What are the four types of adjusting entries?
2. What is the effect on assets, stockholders' equity, expenses, and net income if a prepaid expense adjusting entry is not made?
3. What is the effect on liabilities, stockholders' equity, revenues, and net income if an unearned revenue adjusting entry is not made?

● **Do It**

The ledger of Hammond, Inc., on March 31, 1998, includes these selected accounts before adjusting entries are prepared:

	Debit	Credit
Prepaid Insurance	$ 3,600	
Office Supplies	2,800	
Office Equipment	25,000	
Accumulated Depreciation—Office Equipment		$5,000
Unearned Service Revenue		9,200

An analysis of the accounts shows the following:

1. Insurance expires at the rate of $100 per month.
2. Supplies on hand total $800.
3. The office equipment depreciates $200 a month.
4. One-half of the unearned service revenue was earned in March.

Prepare the adjusting entries for the month of March.

Reasoning: In order for revenues to be recorded in the period in which they are earned and for expenses to be recognized in the period in which they are incurred, adjusting entries are made at the *end* of the accounting period. Adjusting entries for prepayments are required at the statement date to record the portion of the prepayment that represents the expense incurred or the revenue earned in the current accounting period. The failure to adjust for the prepayment leads to an overstatement of the asset or liability and a related understatement of the expense or revenue.

Solution:

1. Insurance Expense	100	
Prepaid Insurance		100
(To record insurance expired)		
2. Office Supplies Expense	2,000	
Office Supplies		2,000
(To record supplies used)		
3. Depreciation Expense	200	
Accumulated Depreciation		200
(To record monthly depreciation)		

4. Unearned Service Revenue	4,600	
Service Revenue		4,600
(To record revenue earned)		

ADJUSTING ENTRIES FOR ACCRUALS

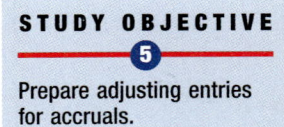

STUDY OBJECTIVE 5
Prepare adjusting entries for accruals.

The second category of adjusting entries is **accruals**. Adjusting entries for accruals are required in order to record revenues earned and expenses incurred in the current accounting period that have not been recognized through daily entries and thus are not yet reflected in the accounts. Prior to an accrual adjustment, the revenue account (and the related asset account), or the expense account (and the related liability account), are understated. Thus, the adjusting entry for accruals will **increase both a balance sheet and an income statement account.** Adjusting entries for accruals are graphically depicted in Illustration 4-11.

Illustration 4-11 Adjusting entries for accruals

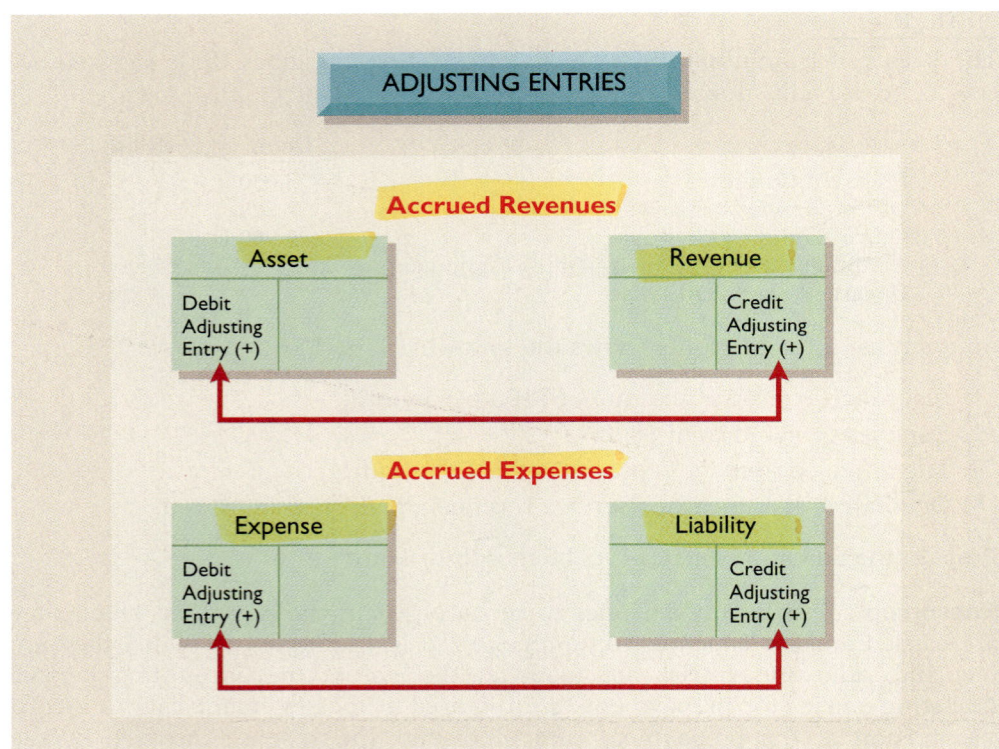

Helpful Hint For accruals, there may be no prior entry and the accounts requiring adjustment may both have zero balances prior to adjustment.

Accrued Revenues

Revenues earned but not yet received in cash or recorded at the statement date are **accrued revenues.** Accrued revenues may accumulate (accrue) with the passing of time, as in the case of interest revenue. Or they may result from services that have been performed but neither billed nor collected, as in the case of commissions and fees. The former are unrecorded because the earning of interest does not involve daily transactions; the latter may be unrecorded because only a portion of the total service has been provided and the clients won't be billed until the service has been completed.

An adjusting entry is required to show the receivable that exists at the balance sheet date and to record the revenue that has been earned during the period. Prior to adjustment both assets and revenues are understated. Accordingly, **an adjusting entry for accrued revenues results in an increase (a debit) to an asset account and an increase (a credit) to a revenue account.**

In October Sierra Corporation earned $200 for advertising services that were not billed to clients before October 31. Because these services have not been billed, they have not been recorded. Assets and stockholders' equity would be affected as follows:

Assets	=	Liabilities	+	Stockholders' Equity
+$200				+$200

Thus, this adjusting entry is made:

Oct. 31	Accounts Receivable	200	
	Service Revenue		200
	(To accrue revenue earned but not billed or collected)		

Accrued Revenues

Oct. 31

Revenue and receivable are recorded for unbilled services

Nov.

Cash is received; receivable is reduced

After the adjusting entry is posted, the accounts appear as in Illustration 4-12.

Accounts Receivable		Service Revenue	
Oct. 31 **Adj. 200**		Oct. 3 10,000	
		31 400	
		31 **Adj. 200**	
Oct. 31 Bal. 200		Oct. 31 Bal 10,600	

Illustration 4-12
Receivable and revenue accounts after accrual adjustments

The asset Accounts Receivable shows that $200 is owed by clients at the balance sheet date. The balance of $10,600 in Service Revenue represents the total revenue earned during the month ($10,000 + $400 + $200). **If the adjusting entry is not made, assets and stockholders' equity on the balance sheet, and revenues and net income on the income statement will be understated.**

In the next accounting period, the clients will be billed. When this occurs, the entry to record the billing should recognize that $200 of revenue earned in October has already been recorded in the October 31 adjusting entry. To illustrate, assume that bills totaling $3,000 are mailed to clients on November 10. Of this amount, $200 represents revenue earned in October and recorded as Service Revenue in the October 31 adjusting entry. The remaining $2,800 represents revenue earned in November. Thus, the following entry is made:

Nov. 10	Accounts Receivable	2,800	
	Service Revenue		2,800
	(To record revenue earned)		

This entry records the amount of revenue earned between November 1 and November 10. The subsequent collection of cash from clients (including the $200 earned in October) will be recorded with an increase (a debit) to Cash and a decrease (a credit) to Accounts Receivable.

Accrued Expenses

Expenses incurred but not yet paid or recorded at the statement date are called **accrued expenses.** Interest, rent, taxes, and salaries are common examples of accrued expenses. Accrued expenses result from the same factors as accrued revenues. In fact, an accrued expense on the books of one company is an accrued revenue to another company. For example, the $200 accrual of service revenue by Sierra Corporation is an accrued expense to the client that received the service.

Adjustments for accrued expenses are necessary to record the obligations that exist at the balance sheet date and to recognize the expenses that apply to the current accounting period. Prior to adjustment, both liabilities and expenses are understated. Therefore, **an adjusting entry for accrued expenses results in an increase (a debit) to an expense account and an increase (a credit) to a liability account.**

Accrued Interest. Sierra Corporation signed a 3-month note payable in the amount of $5,000 on October 1. The note requires interest at an annual rate of 12%. The amount of the interest accumulation is determined by three factors: (1) the face value of the note, (2) the interest rate, which is always expressed as an annual rate, and (3) the length of time the note is outstanding. In this instance, the total interest due on the $5,000 note at its due date 3 months in the future is $150 ($5,000 × 12% × $\frac{3}{12}$), or $50 for 1 month. The formula for computing interest and its application to Sierra Corporation for the month of October are shown in Illustration 4-13.

Illustration 4-13
Formula for computing interest

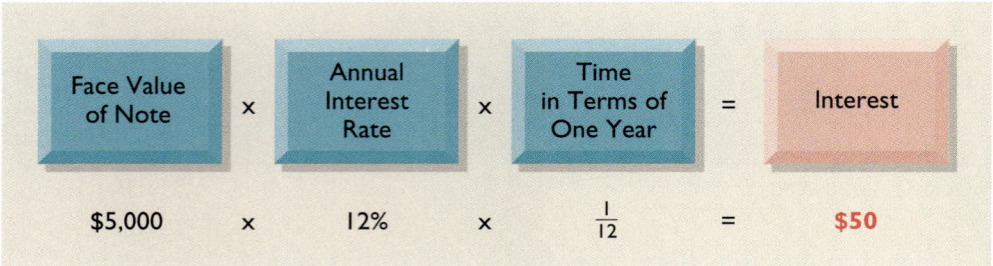

Note that the time period is expressed as a fraction of a year. The accrual of interest at October 31 would have the following impact on the accounting equation:

Assets	=	Liabilities	+	Stockholders' Equity
		+$50		−$50

This would be reflected in an accrued expense adjusting entry at October 31 as follows:

Oct. 31	Interest Expense	50	
	Interest Payable		50
	(To accrue interest on notes payable)		

After this adjusting entry is posted, the accounts appear as in Illustration 4-14.

Illustration 4-14 Interest accounts after adjustment

Interest Expense		Interest Payable	
Oct. 31 **Adj. 50**			Oct. 31 **Adj. 50**
Oct. 31 Bal. 50			Oct. 31 Bal. 50

Interest Expense shows the interest charges for the month of October. The amount of interest owed at the statement date is shown in Interest Payable. It will not be paid until the note comes due at the end of 3 months. The Interest Payable account is used, instead of crediting Notes Payable, to disclose the two different types of obligations—interest and principal—in the accounts and statements. **If this adjusting entry is not made, liabilities and interest expense will be understated, and net income and stockholders' equity will be overstated.**

Accrued Salaries. Some types of expenses, such as employee salaries and commissions, are paid for after the services have been performed. At Sierra Corporation, salaries were last paid on October 26; the next payment of salaries will not occur until November 9. As shown in the calendar, 3 working days remain in October (October 29–31).

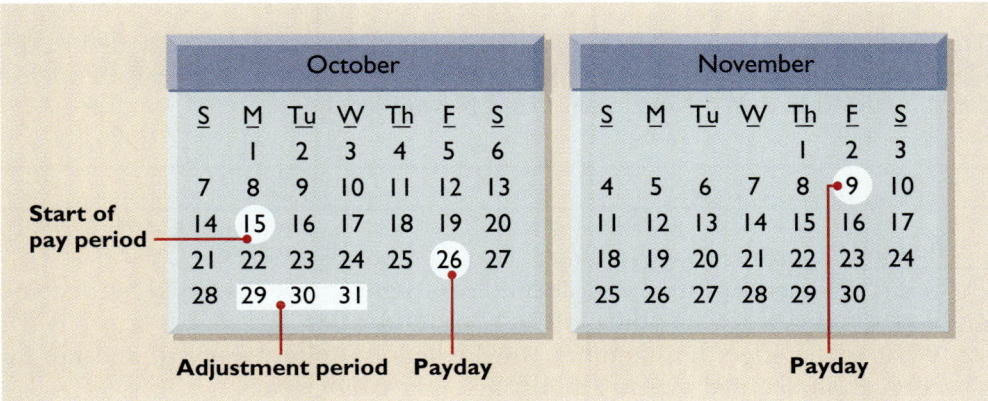

At October 31 the salaries for these days represent an accrued expense and a related liability to Sierra. The employees receive total salaries of $2,000 for a 5-day work week, or $400 per day. Thus, accrued salaries at October 31 are $1,200 ($400 × 3). This accrual increases a liability, Salaries Payable, and an expense account, Salaries Expense, and has the following impact on the accounting equation:

Assets	=	Liabilities	+	Stockholders' Equity
		+$1,200		−$1,200

The adjusting entry is:

Oct. 31	Salaries Expense	1,200	
	Salaries Payable		1,200
	(To record accrued salaries)		

After this adjusting entry is posted, the accounts are as in Illustration 4-15.

Illustration 4-15 Salary accounts after adjustment

Salaries Expense	
Oct. 26 4,000	
31 **Adj. 1,200**	
Oct. 31 Bal. 5,200	

Salaries Payable	
	Oct. 31 **Adj. 1,200**
	Oct. 31 Bal. 1,200

166　CHAPTER 4　Accrual Accounting Concepts

After this adjustment, the balance in Salaries Expense of $5,200 (13 days × $400) is the actual salary expense for October. The balance in Salaries Payable of $1,200 is the amount of the liability for salaries owed as of October 31. **If the $1,200 adjustment for salaries is not recorded, Sierra's expenses will be understated $1,200 and its liabilities will be understated $1,200.**

At Sierra Corporation, salaries are payable every 2 weeks. Consequently, the next payday is November 9, when total salaries of $4,000 will again be paid. The payment consists of $1,200 of salaries payable at October 31 plus $2,800 of salaries expense for November (7 working days as shown in the November calendar × $400). Therefore, the following entry is made on November 9:

Nov.	9	Salaries Payable	1,200	
		Salaries Expense	2,800	
		Cash		4,000
		(To record November 9 payroll)		

This entry eliminates the liability for Salaries Payable that was recorded in the October 31 adjusting entry and records the proper amount of Salaries Expense for the period between November 1 and November 9.

BEFORE YOU GO ON . . .

● **Review It**

1. What is the effect on assets, stockholders' equity, revenues, and net income if an accrued revenue adjusting entry is not made?
2. What is the effect on liabilities, stockholders' equity, expenses, and net income if an accrued expense adjusting entry is not made?

● **Do It**

Micro Computer Services Inc. began operations on August 1, 1998. At the end of August 1998, management attempted to prepare monthly financial statements. This information relates to August:

1. At August 31 the company owed its employees $800 in salaries that will be paid on September 1.
2. On August 1 the company borrowed $30,000 from a local bank on a 15-year mortgage. The annual interest rate is 10%.
3. Revenue earned but unrecorded for August totaled $1,100.

Prepare the adjusting entries needed at August 31, 1998.

Reasoning: Adjusting entries for accruals are required to record revenues earned and expenses incurred in the current accounting period that have not been recognized through daily entries. An adjusting entry for accruals will increase both a balance sheet and an income statement account.

Solution:

1. Salaries Expense		800	
Salaries Payable			800
(To record accrued salaries)			
2. Interest Expense		250	
Interest Payable			250
(To record accrued interest:			
$30,000 × 10% × $\frac{1}{12}$ = $250)			

3. Accounts Receivable		1,100	
Service Revenue			1,100
(To accrue revenue earned but not billed or collected)			

SUMMARY OF BASIC RELATIONSHIPS

Pertinent data on each of the four basic types of adjusting entries are summarized in Illustration 4-16. Take some time to study and analyze the adjusting entries. Be sure to note that **each adjusting entry affects one balance sheet account and one income statement account.**

Type of Adjustment	Accounts Before Adjustment	Adjusting Entry
Prepaid expenses	Assets overstated Expenses understated	Dr. Expenses Cr. Assets
Unearned revenues	Liabilities overstated Revenues understated	Dr. Liabilities Cr. Revenues
Accrued revenues	Assets understated Revenues understated	Dr. Assets Cr. Revenues
Accrued expenses	Expenses understated Liabilities understated	Dr. Expenses Cr. Liabilities

Illustration 4-16 Summary of adjusting entries

The journalizing and posting of adjusting entries for Sierra Corporation on October 31 are shown in Illustrations 4-17 and 4-18. When reviewing the general ledger in Illustration 4-18, note that the adjustments are highlighted in color.

GENERAL JOURNAL

Date	Account Titles and Explanation	Debit	Credit
1998	Adjusting Entries		

Oct. 31	Advertising Supplies Expense
	    Advertising Supplies
	      (To record supplies used)
		1,500	1,500

31	Insurance Expense
	    Prepaid insurance
	      (To record insurance used)
		50	50

31	Depreciation Expense
	    Accumulated Depreciation—Office Equipment
	      (To record monthly depreciation)
		40	40

31	Unearned Service Revenue
	    Service Revenue
	      (To record revenue earned)
		400	400

31	Accounts Receivable
	    Service Revenue
	      (To accrue revenue earned but not billed or collected)
		200	200

31	Interest Expense
	    Interest Payable
	      (To accrue interest on notes payable)
		50	50

31	Salaries Expense
	    Salaries Payable
	      (To record accrued salaries)
		1,200	1,200

Illustration 4-17 General journal showing adjusting entries

GENERAL LEDGER

Cash
Oct. 1	10,000		Oct. 2	5,000	
1	5,000		3	900	
2	1,200		4	600	
3	10,000		20	500	
			26	4,000	
Oct. 31 Bal. 15,200					

Accounts Receivable
Oct. 31	**200**	
Oct. 31 Bal. 200		

Advertising Supplies
Oct. 5	2,500		Oct. 31	**1,500**
Oct. 31 Bal. 1,000				

Prepaid Insurance
Oct. 4	600		Oct. 31	**50**
Oct. 31 Bal. 550				

Office Equipment
Oct. 2	5,000	
Oct. 31 Bal. 5,000		

Accumulated Depreciation—Office Equipment
	Oct. 31	**40**
	Oct. 31 Bal. 40	

Notes Payable
	Oct. 1	5,000
	Oct. 31 Bal. 5,000	

Accounts Payable
	Oct. 5	2,500
	Oct. 31 Bal. 2,500	

Interest Payable
	Oct. 31	**50**
	Oct. 31 Bal. 50	

Unearned Service Revenue
Oct. 31	**400**		Oct. 2	1,200
			Oct. 31 Bal. 800	

Salaries Payable
	Oct. 31	**1,200**
	Oct. 31 Bal. 1,200	

Common Stock
	Oct. 1	10,000
	Oct. 31 Bal. 10,000	

Retained Earnings
	Oct. 31	Bal. 0

Dividends
Oct. 20	500	
Oct. 31 Bal. 500		

Service Revenue
	Oct. 3	10,000
	31	**400**
	31	**200**
	Oct. 31 Bal. 10,600	

Salaries Expense
Oct. 26	4,000	
31	**1,200**	
Oct. 31 Bal. 5,200		

Advertising Supplies Expense
Oct. 31	**1,500**	
Oct. 31 Bal. 1,500		

Rent Expense
Oct. 3	900	
Oct. 31 Bal. 900		

Insurance Expense
Oct. 31	**50**	
Oct. 31 Bal. 50		

Interest Expense
Oct. 31	**50**	
Oct. 31 Bal. 50		

Depreciation Expense
Oct. 31	**40**	
Oct. 31 Bal. 40		

Illustration 4-18 General ledger after adjustments

The Adjusted Trial Balance and Financial Statements

After all adjusting entries have been journalized and posted, another trial balance is prepared from the ledger accounts. This trial balance is called an **adjusted trial balance.** It shows the balances of all accounts, including those that have been adjusted, at the end of the accounting period. The purpose of an adjusted trial balance is to **prove the equality** of the total debit balances and the total credit balances in the ledger after all adjustments have been made. Because the accounts contain all data that are needed for financial statements, the adjusted trial balance is the primary basis for the preparation of financial statements.

> **STUDY OBJECTIVE 6**
> Describe the nature and purpose of the adjusted trial balance.

PREPARING THE ADJUSTED TRIAL BALANCE

The adjusted trial balance for Sierra Corporation presented in Illustration 4-19 has been prepared from the ledger accounts in Illustration 4-18. To facilitate the comparison of account balances, the trial balance data, labeled "Before Adjustment" (presented earlier in Illustration 4-4), are shown alongside the adjusted data, labeled "After Adjustment." In addition, the amounts affected by the adjusting entries are highlighted in color in the "After Adjustment" columns.

Illustration 4-19 Trial balance and adjusted trial balance compared

SIERRA CORPORATION
Trial Balances
October 31, 1998

	Before Adjustment Dr.	Before Adjustment Cr.	After Adjustment Dr.	After Adjustment Cr.
Cash	$15,200		$15,200	
Accounts Receivable			200	
Advertising Supplies	2,500		1,000	
Prepaid Insurance	600		550	
Office Equipment	5,000		5,000	
Accumulated Depreciation— Office Equipment				$ 40
Notes Payable		$ 5,000		5,000
Accounts Payable		2,500		2,500
Interest Payable				50
Unearned Service Revenue		1,200		800
Salaries Payable				1,200
Common Stock		10,000		10,000
Retained Earnings		0		0
Dividends	500		500	
Service Revenue		10,000		10,600
Salaries Expense	4,000		5,200	
Advertising Supplies Expense			1,500	
Rent Expense	900		900	
Insurance Expense			50	
Interest Expense			50	
Depreciation Expense			40	
	$28,700	$28,700	$30,190	$30,190

PREPARING FINANCIAL STATEMENTS

Financial statements can be prepared directly from an adjusted trial balance. The interrelationships of data in the adjusted trial balance of Sierra Corporation are presented in Illustrations 4-20 and 4-21. As Illustration 4-20 shows, the income statement is prepared from the revenue and expense accounts; the retained earnings statement is derived from the retained earnings account, dividends account, and the net income (or net loss) shown in the income statement. As shown in Illustration 4-21, the balance sheet is then prepared from the asset and liability accounts and the ending retained earnings as reported in the retained earnings statement.

Illustration 4-20
Preparation of the income statement and retained earnings statement from the adjusted trial balance

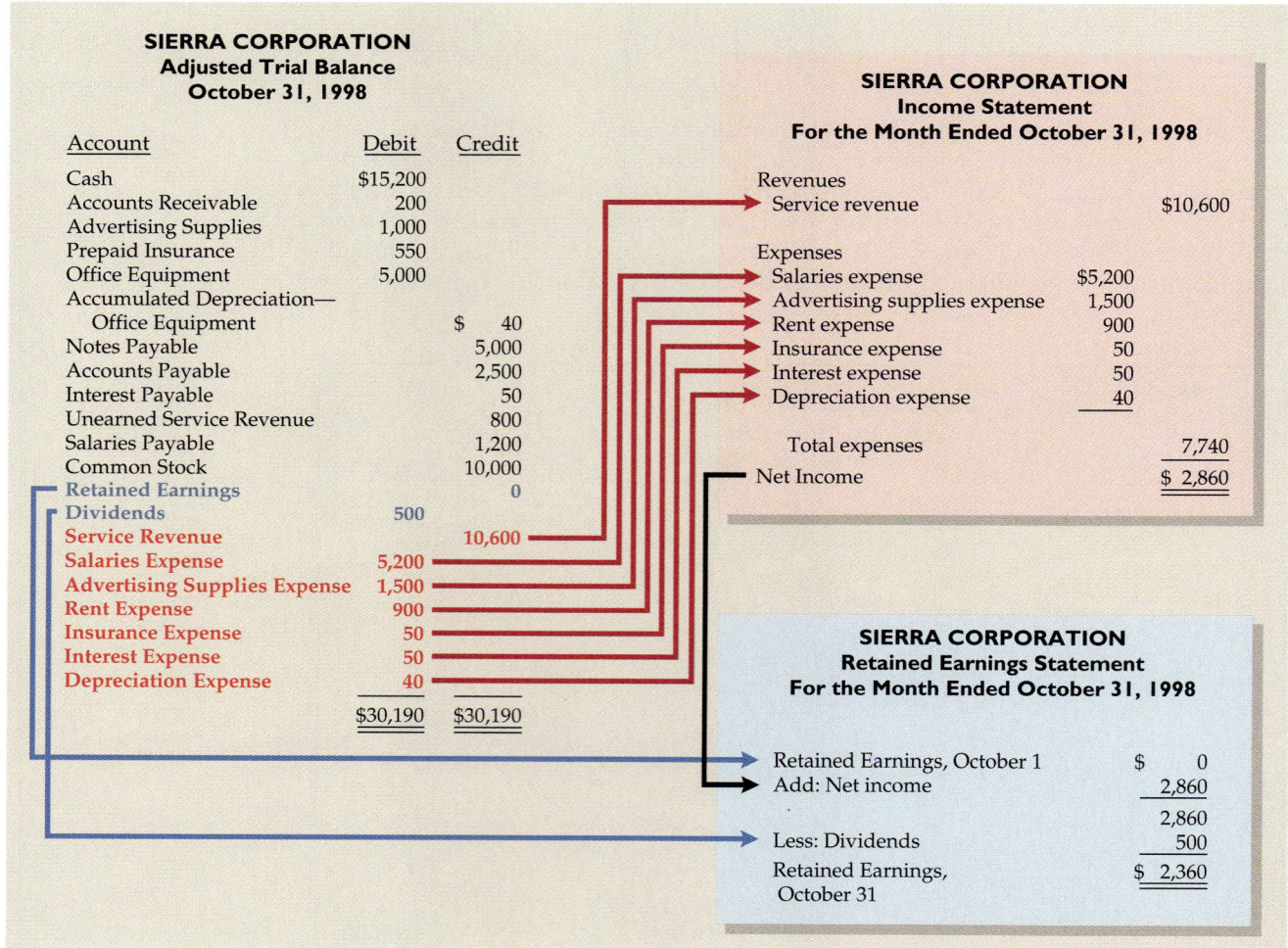

CLOSING THE BOOKS

In previous chapters you learned that revenue and expense accounts and the dividends account are subdivisions of retained earnings, which is reported in the stockholders' equity section of the balance sheet. Because revenues, expenses, and dividends relate to only a given accounting period, they are considered **temporary accounts.** In contrast, all balance sheet accounts are considered **permanent accounts** because their balances are carried forward into future accounting periods. Illustration 4-22 identifies the accounts in each category.

Alternative Terminology
Temporary accounts are sometimes called **nominal accounts,** and permanent accounts are sometimes called **real accounts.**

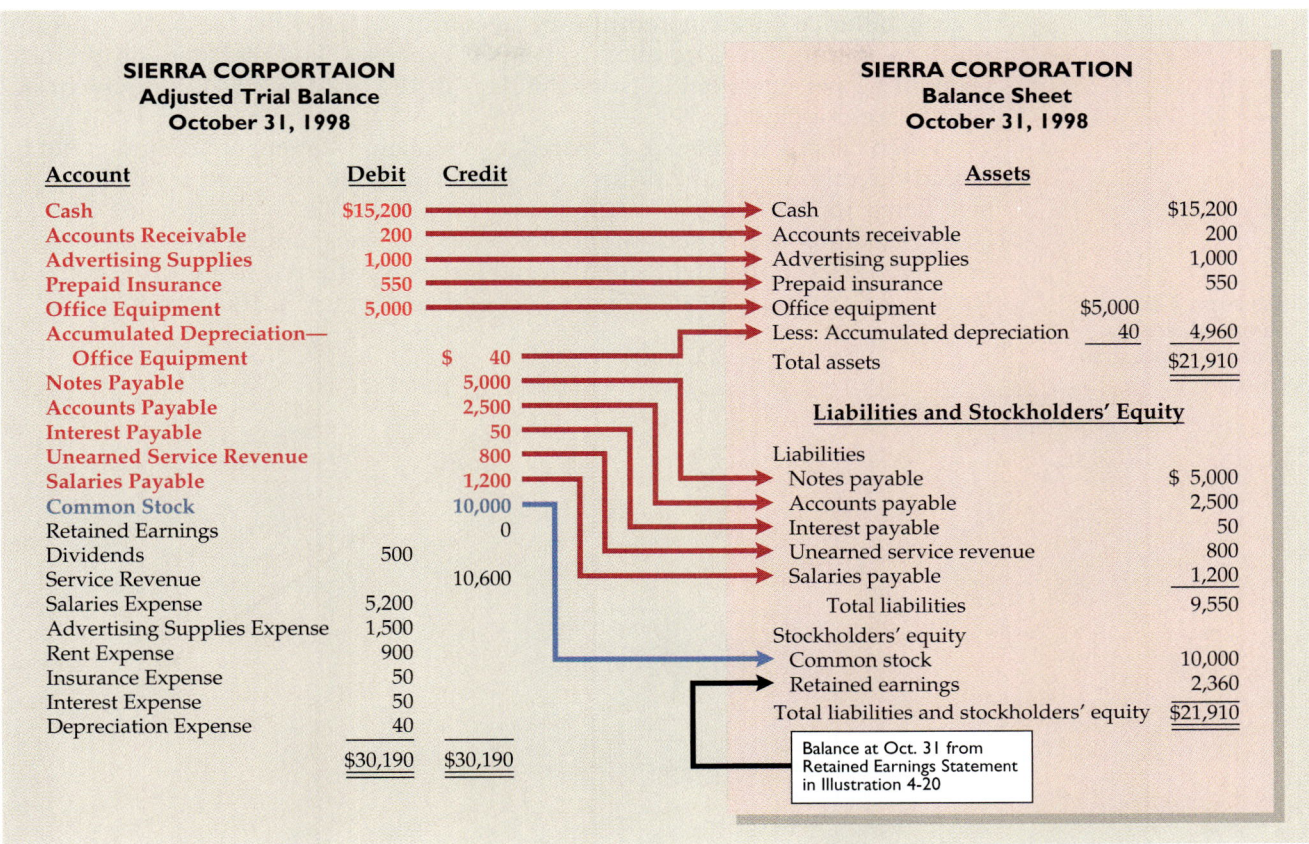

Illustration 4-21 Preparation of the balance sheet from the adjusted trial balance

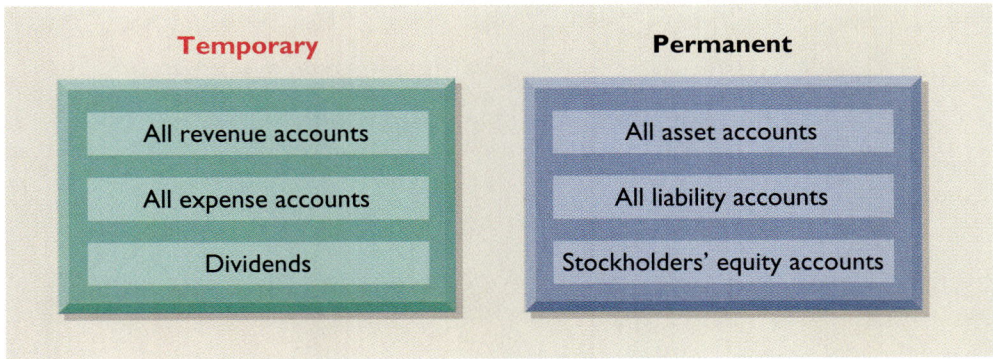

Illustration 4-22 Temporary versus permanent accounts

PREPARING CLOSING ENTRIES

At the end of the accounting period, the temporary account balances are transferred to the permanent stockholders' equity account—Retained Earnings—through the preparation of closing entries. **Closing entries** formally recognize in the ledger the transfer of net income (or net loss) and dividends to retained earnings, which will be shown in the retained earnings statement. For example, notice that in Illustration 4-21 Retained Earnings has an adjusted balance of zero. This is because it was Sierra's first year of operations. Retained Earnings started with a balance of zero, and net income has not yet been calculated and closed out to Retained Earnings. Therefore, the adjusted balance is still zero. Similarly, the zero balance does not yet reflect dividends declared during the pe-

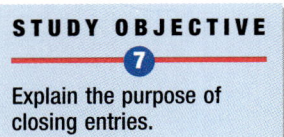

STUDY OBJECTIVE 7

Explain the purpose of closing entries.

riod, since that account has not yet been closed out either. In addition to updating Retained Earnings to its correct ending balance, closing entries produce a **zero balance in each temporary account.** As a result, these accounts are ready to accumulate data about revenues, expenses, and dividends in the next accounting period separate from the data in the prior periods. Permanent accounts are not closed.

When closing entries are prepared, each income statement account could be closed directly to Retained Earnings. However, to do so would result in excessive detail in the retained earnings account. Accordingly, the revenue and expense accounts are closed to another temporary account, **Income Summary,** and only the resulting net income or net loss is transferred from this account to Retained Earnings. The closing process is diagrammed in Illustration 4-23.

Illustration 4-23
Diagram of closing process—corporation

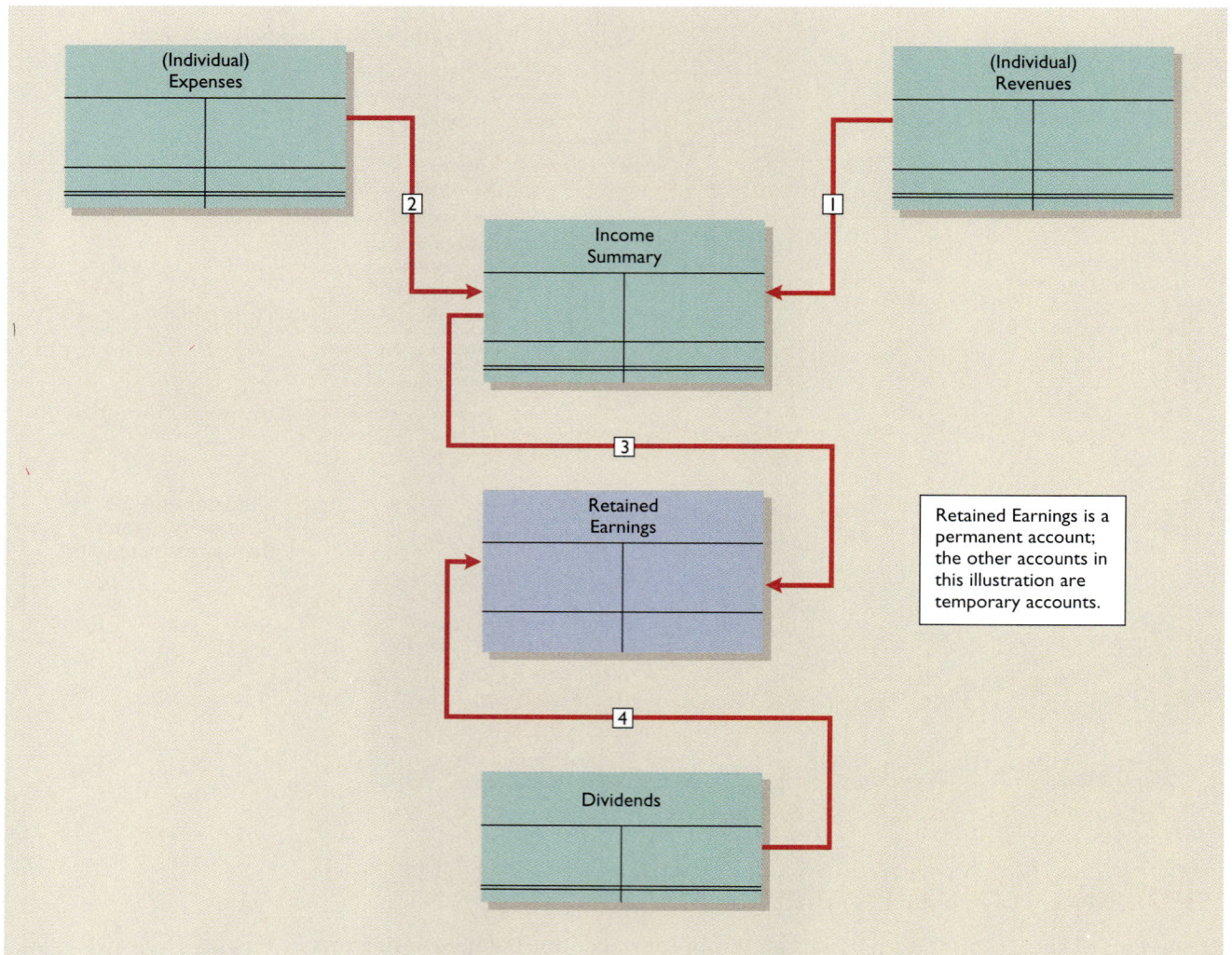

PREPARING A POST-CLOSING TRIAL BALANCE

After all closing entries are journalized and posted, another trial balance, called a **post-closing trial balance,** is prepared from the ledger. A post-closing trial balance is a list of all permanent accounts and their balances after closing entries are journalized and posted. **The purpose of this trial balance is to prove the equality of the permanent account balances that are carried forward**

into the next accounting period. Since all temporary accounts will have zero balances, **the post-closing trial balance will contain only permanent—balance sheet—accounts.**

BUSINESS INSIGHT
Management Perspective

Until Sam Walton had opened 20 Wal-Mart stores, he used what he called the "ESP method" of closing the books. ESP was a pretty basic method: If the books didn't balance, Walton calculated the amount by which they were off and entered that amount under the heading ESP—which stood for "Error Some Place." As Walton noted, "It really sped things along when it came time to close those books."

Source: Sam Walton, *Made in America* (New York: Doubleday Publishing Company, 1992), p. 53.

SUMMARY OF THE ACCOUNTING CYCLE

STUDY OBJECTIVE 8
Describe the required steps in the accounting cycle.

The required steps in the accounting cycle are shown graphically in Illustration 4-24. You can see that the cycle begins with the analysis of business transactions

Illustration 4-24
Required steps in the accounting cycle

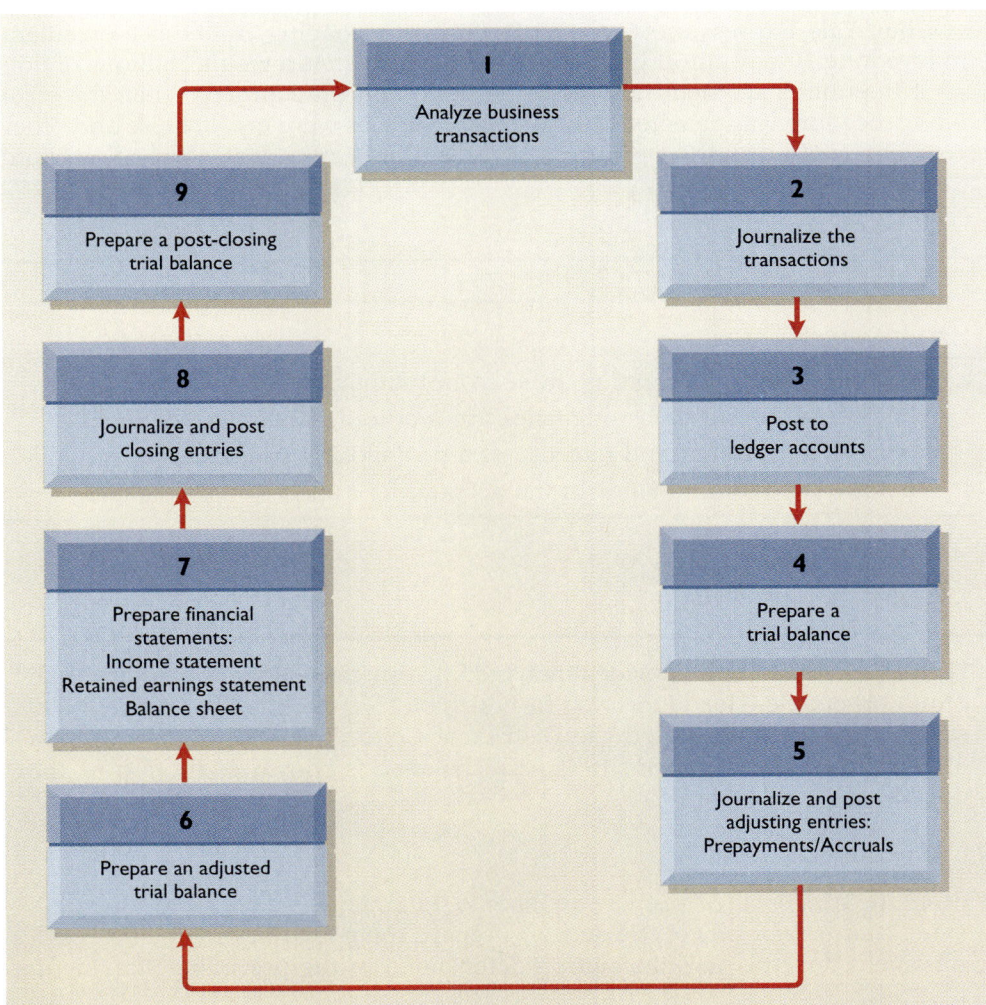

174 CHAPTER 4 Accrual Accounting Concepts

Helpful Hint Some accountants prefer to reverse certain adjusting entries at the beginning of a new accounting period. A **reversing entry** is made at the beginning of the next accounting period and is the exact opposite of the adjusting entry made in the previous period.

and ends with the preparation of a post-closing trial balance. The steps in the cycle are performed in sequence and are repeated in each accounting period.

Steps 1–3 may occur daily during the accounting period, as explained in Chapter 3. Steps 4–7 are performed on a periodic basis, such as monthly, quarterly, or annually. Steps 8 and 9, closing entries and a post-closing trial balance, are usually prepared only at the end of a company's **annual** accounting period.

BUSINESS INSIGHT
Investor Perspective

Yale Express, a short-haul trucking firm, turned over much of its cargo to local truckers to complete delivery. Yale collected the entire delivery charge and, when billed by the local trucker, remitted payment for the final phase to the local trucker. Yale used a cutoff period of 20 days into the next accounting period in making its adjusting entries for accrued liabilities. That is, it waited 20 days to receive the local truckers' bills to determine the amount of the unpaid but incurred delivery charges as of the balance sheet date.

On the other hand, Republic Carloading, a nationwide long-distance freight forwarder, frequently did not receive transportation bills from truckers to whom it passed on cargo until *months* after the year-end. In making its year-end adjusting entries, Republic waited for months in order to include all of these outstanding transportation bills.

When Yale Express merged with Republic Carloading, Yale's vice-president employed the 20-day cutoff procedure for both firms. As a result, millions of dollars of Republic's accrued transportation bills went unrecorded. When the erroneous procedure was detected and correcting entries were made, these and other errors changed a reported profit of $1.14 million into a loss of $1.88 million!

BEFORE YOU GO ON . . .

● **Review It**

1. How do permanent accounts differ from temporary accounts?
2. What four different types of entries are required in closing the books?
3. What are the content and purpose of a post-closing trial balance?
4. What are the required steps in the accounting cycle?

USING THE DECISION TOOLKIT

Humana Corporation provides managed health care services to more than 2 million people. Headquartered in Louisville, Kentucky, it has over 12,000 employees in 14 states and the District of Columbia. A simplified version of Humana's December 31, 1994, trial balance is shown at the top of the next page.

Instructions

From the trial balance, prepare an income statement, retained earnings statement, and balance sheet. Be sure to prepare them in that order, since each statement depends on information determined in the preceding statement.

HUMANA CORPORATION
Trial Balance
December 31, 1994
(in millions)

Account	Dr.	Cr.
Cash	$ 272	
Marketable Securities (current)	609	
Receivables	74	
Other Current Assets	83	
Property and Equipment, Net	317	
Marketable Securities (long-term)	322	
Other Long-Term Assets	280	
Medical Costs Payable		$ 527
Accounts Payable		233
Income Taxes Payable		56
Long-Term Debt		83
Common Stock		830
Dividends	0	
Retained Earnings		52
Revenues		3,679
Medical Cost Expense	2,918	
Selling, General, and Administrative Expense	436	
Depreciation Expense	50	
Other Expenses	18	
Income Tax Expense	81	
	$5,460	$5,460

Solution

HUMANA CORPORATION
Income Statement
For the Year Ended December 31, 1994
(in millions)

Revenues		$3,679
Medical cost expense	$2,918	
Selling, general, and administrative expense	436	
Depreciation expense	50	
Other expenses	18	
Income tax expense	81	3,503
Net income		$ 176

HUMANA CORPORATION
Retained Earnings Statement
For the Year Ended December 31, 1994
(in millions)

Beginning retained earnings	$ 52
Plus: Net income	176
Less: Dividends	0
Ending retained earnings	$228

HUMANA CORPORATION
Balance Sheet
December 31, 1994
(in millions)

Assets	
Current assets	
Cash	$ 272
Marketable securities (current)	609
Receivables	74
Other current assets	83
Total current assets	1,038
Property and equipment, net	317
Marketable securities (long-term)	322
Other long-term assets	280
Total assets	$1,957
Liabilities and Stockholders' Equity	
Liabilities	
Current liabilities	
Medical costs payable	$ 527
Accounts payable	233
Income taxes payable	56
Total current liabilities	816
Long-term debt	83
Total liabilities	899
Stockholders' equity	
Common stock	830
Retained earnings	228
Total liabilities and stockholders' equity	$1,957

SUMMARY OF STUDY OBJECTIVES

❶ Explain the revenue recognition principle and the matching principle. The revenue recognition principle dictates that revenue be recognized in the accounting period in which it is earned. The matching principle dictates that expenses be recognized when they make their contribution to revenues.

❷ Differentiate between the cash basis and the accrual basis of accounting. Accrual-based accounting means that events that change a company's financial statements are recorded in the periods in which the events occur. Under the cash basis, events are recorded only in the periods in which the company receives or pays cash.

❸ Explain why adjusting entries are needed and identify the major types of adjusting entries. Adjusting entries are made at the end of an accounting period. They ensure that revenues are recorded in the period in which they are earned and that expenses are recognized in the period in which they are incurred. The major types of adjusting entries are prepaid expenses, unearned revenues, accrued revenues, and accrued expenses.

❹ Prepare adjusting entries for prepayments. Prepayments are either prepaid expenses or unearned revenues. Adjusting entries for prepayments are required at the statement date to record the portion of the prepayment that represents the expense incurred or the revenue earned in the current accounting period.

❺ Prepare adjusting entries for accruals. Accruals are either accrued revenues or accrued expenses. Adjusting entries for accruals are required to record revenues earned and expenses incurred in the current accounting period that have not been recognized through daily entries.

6 ***Describe the nature and purpose of the adjusted trial balance.*** An adjusted trial balance is a trial balance that shows the balances of all accounts, including those that have been adjusted, at the end of an accounting period. The purpose of an adjusted trial balance is to show the effects of all financial events that have occurred during the accounting period.

7 ***Explain the purpose of closing entries.*** One purpose of closing entries is to transfer the results of operations for the period to Retained Earnings. A second purpose is that, to begin a new period, all temporary accounts (revenue accounts, expense accounts, and dividends) must start with a zero balance. To accomplish this, all temporary accounts are "closed" at the end of an accounting period. Separate entries are made to close revenues and expenses to Income Summary, Income Summary to Retained Earnings, and Dividends to Retained Earnings. Only temporary accounts are closed.

8 ***Describe the required steps in the accounting cycle.*** The required steps in the accounting cycle are: (a) analyze business transactions, (b) journalize the transactions, (c) post to ledger accounts, (d) prepare a trial balance, (e) journalize and post adjusting entries, (f) prepare an adjusted trial balance, (g) prepare financial statements, (h) journalize and post closing entries, and (i) prepare a post-closing trial balance.

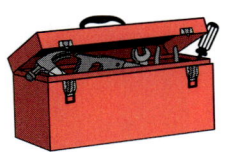

DECISION TOOLKIT—A SUMMARY

Decision Checkpoints	Info Needed for Decision	Tool to Use for Decision	How to Evaluate Results
At what point should the company record revenue?	Need to understand the nature of the company's business	Revenue should be recorded when earned. For a service business, revenue is earned when service is performed.	Recognizing revenue too early overstates current period revenue; recognizing it too late understates current period revenue.
At what point should the company record expenses?	Need to understand the nature of the company's business	Expenses should "follow" revenues—that is, the effort (expense) should be matched with the result (revenue).	Recognizing expenses too early overstates current period expense; recognizing it too late understates current period expense.

APPENDIX 4A
ADJUSTING ENTRIES IN AN AUTOMATED WORLD—USING A WORK SHEET

In the previous discussion we used T accounts and trial balances to arrive at the amounts used to prepare financial statements. Accountants frequently use a device known as a work sheet to determine these amounts. A **work sheet** is a multiple-column form that may be used in the adjustment process and in preparing financial statements. Work sheets can be prepared manually, but today most are prepared on computer spreadsheets. As its name suggests, the work sheet is a working tool or a supplementary device for the accountant. **A work sheet is not a permanent accounting record;** it is neither a journal nor a part of the general ledger. The work sheet is merely a device used to make it easier to prepare adjusting entries and the financial statements. In small companies that have relatively few accounts and adjustments, a work sheet may not be needed. In

STUDY OBJECTIVE
9
Describe the purpose and the basic form of a work sheet.

large companies with numerous accounts and many adjustments, it is almost indispensable.

The basic form of a work sheet is shown in Illustration 4A-1. Note the headings. The work sheet starts with two columns for the Trial Balance. The next two columns record all Adjustments. Next is the Adjusted Trial Balance. The last two sets of columns correspond to the Income Statement and the Balance Sheet. All items listed in the Adjusted Trial Balance columns are recorded in either the Income Statement or the Balance Sheet columns.

Illustration 4A-1 Form and procedure for a work sheet

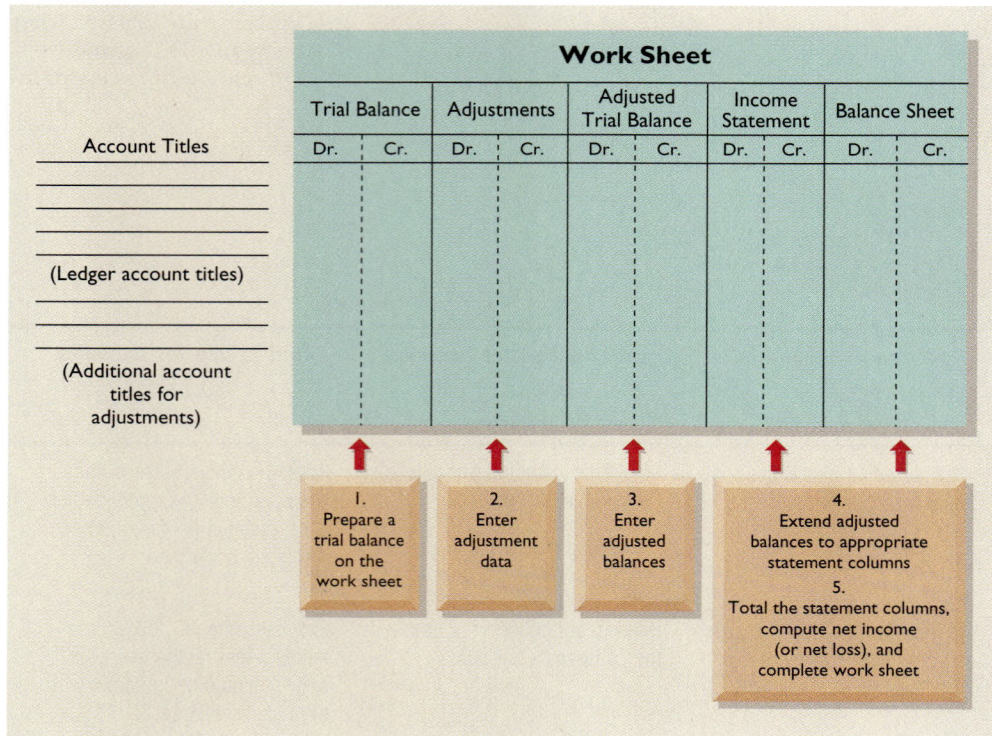

SUMMARY OF STUDY OBJECTIVE FOR APPENDIX 4A

9 *Describe the purpose and the basic form of a work sheet.* The work sheet is a device used to make it easier to prepare adjusting entries and the financial statements. It is often prepared on a computer spreadsheet. The sets of columns of the work sheet are, from left to right, the unadjusted trial balance, adjustments, adjusted trial balance, income statement, and balance sheet.

GLOSSARY

Accrual basis accounting Accounting basis in which transactions that change a company's financial statements are recorded in the periods in which the events occur, rather than in the periods in which the company receives or pays cash. (p. 153)

Accrued expenses Expenses incurred but not yet paid in cash or recorded. (p. 163)

Accrued revenues Revenues earned but not yet received in cash or recorded. (p. 162)

Adjusted trial balance A list of accounts and their balances after all adjustments have been made. (p. 169)

Adjusting entries Entries made at the end of an accounting period to ensure that the revenue recognition and matching principles are followed. (p. 154)

Book value The difference between the cost of a depreciable asset and its related accumulated depreciation. (p. 159)

Cash basis accounting An accounting basis in which revenue is recorded only when cash is received, and an expense is recorded only when cash is paid. (p. 153)

Closing entries Entries at the end of an accounting period to transfer the balances of temporary accounts to a permanent stockholders' equity account, Retained Earnings. (p. 171)

Contra asset account An account that is offset against an asset account on the balance sheet. (p. 159)

Depreciation The process of allocating the cost of an asset to expense over its useful life. (p. 158)

Fiscal year An accounting period that is 1 year long. (p. 150)

Income Summary A temporary account used in closing revenue and expense accounts. (p. 172)

Matching principle The principle that dictates that efforts (expenses) be matched with accomplishments (revenues). (p. 151)

Permanent accounts Balance sheet accounts whose balances are carried forward to the next accounting period. (p. 170)

Post-closing trial balance A list of permanent accounts and their balances after closing entries have been journalized and posted. (p. 172)

Prepaid expenses (Prepayments) Expenses paid in cash and recorded as assets before they are used or consumed. (p. 156)

Revenue recognition principle The principle that revenue be recognized in the accounting period in which it is earned. (p. 151)

Reversing entry An entry made at the beginning of the next accounting period; the exact opposite of the adjusting entry made in the previous period. (p. 174)

Temporary accounts Revenue, expense, and dividend accounts whose balances are transferred to Retained Earnings at the end of an accounting period. (p. 170)

Time period assumption An assumption that the economic life of a business can be divided into artificial time periods. (p. 150)

Unearned revenues Cash received before revenue was earned and recorded as liabilities before they are earned. (p. 160)

Useful life The length of service of a productive facility. (p. 158)

Work sheet A multiple-column form that may be used in the adjustment process and in preparing financial statements. (p. 177)

DEMONSTRATION PROBLEM

Terry Thomas and a group of investors incorporate the Green Thumb Lawn Care Corporation on April 1. At April 30 the trial balance shows the following balances for selected accounts:

Prepaid Insurance	$ 3,600
Equipment	28,000
Notes Payable	20,000
Unearned Service Revenue	4,200
Service Revenue	1,800

Analysis reveals the following additional data pertaining to these accounts:
1. Prepaid insurance is the cost of a 2-year insurance policy, effective April 1.
2. Depreciation on the equipment is $500 per month.
3. The note payable is dated April 1. It is a 6-month, 12% note.
4. Seven customers paid for the company's 6 months' lawn service package of $600 beginning in April. These customers were serviced in April.
5. Lawn services rendered other customers but not billed at April 30 totaled $1,500.

Instructions
Prepare the adjusting entries for the month of April. Show computations.

180　CHAPTER 4　Accrual Accounting Concepts

Problem-Solving Strategies
1. Note that adjustments are being made for 1 month.
2. Make computations carefully.
3. Select account titles carefully.
4. Make sure debits are made first and credits are indented.
5. Check that debits equal credits for each entry.

Solution to Demonstration Problem

GENERAL JOURNAL

Date	Account Titles and Explanation	Debit	Credit
	Adjusting Entries		
Apr. 30	Insurance Expense	150	
	Prepaid Insurance		150
	(To record insurance expired: $3,600 ÷ 24 = $150 per month)		
30	Depreciation Expense	500	
	Accumulated Depreciation—Equipment		500
	(To record monthly depreciation)		
30	Interest Expense	200	
	Interest Payable		200
	(To accrue interest on notes payable: $20,000 \times 12\% \times \frac{1}{12} = \$200$)		
30	Unearned Service Revenue	700	
	Service Revenue		700
	(To record revenue earned: $600 ÷ 6 = $100; $100 per month × 7 = $700)		
30	Accounts Receivable	1,500	
	Service Revenue		1,500
	(To accrue revenue earned but not billed or collected)		

Self-Study Questions

Answers are at the end of this chapter.

(SO 1) 1. What is the time period assumption?
(a) Revenue should be recognized in the accounting period in which it is earned.
(b) Expenses should be matched with revenues.
(c) The economic life of a business can be divided into artificial time periods.
(d) The fiscal year should correspond with the calendar year.

(SO 1) 2. Which principle dictates that efforts (expenses) be recorded with accomplishments (revenues)?
(a) Matching principle
(b) Cost principle
(c) Periodicity principle
(d) Revenue recognition principle

(SO 3) 3. Adjusting entries are made to ensure that:
(a) expenses are recognized in the period in which they are incurred.
(b) revenues are recorded in the period in which they are earned.
(c) balance sheet and income statement accounts have correct balances at the end of an accounting period.
(d) All of the above.

(SO 4, 5) 4. Each of the following is a major type (or category) of adjusting entries *except*:
(a) prepaid expenses.
(b) accrued revenues.
(c) accrued expenses.
(d) earned revenues.

(SO 5) 5. The trial balance shows Supplies $1,350 and Supplies Expense $0. If $600 of supplies are on hand at the end of the period, the adjusting entry is:
(a) Supplies   600
    Supplies Expense   600
(b) Supplies   750
    Supplies Expense   750
(c) Supplies Expense   750
    Supplies   750
(d) Supplies Expense   600
    Supplies   600

(SO 4) 6. Adjustments for unearned revenues:
(a) decrease liabilities and increase revenues.
(b) increase liabilities and increase revenues.
(c) increase assets and increase revenues.
(d) decrease revenues and decrease assets.

(SO 5) 7. Adjustments for accrued revenues:
(a) increase assets and increase liabilities.
(b) increase assets and increase revenues.
(c) decrease assets and decrease revenues.
(d) decrease liabilities and increase revenues.

(SO 5) 8. Kathy Kiska earned a salary of $400 for the last week of September. She will be paid on Octo-

ber 1. The adjusting entry for Kathy's employer at September 30 is:
(a) No entry is required.
(b) Salaries Expense 400
    Salaries Payable   400
(c) Salaries Expense 400
    Cash   400
(d) Salaries Payable 400
    Cash   400

9. Which statement is *incorrect* concerning the adjusted trial balance?
(a) An adjusted trial balance proves the equality of the total debit balances and the total credit balances in the ledger after all adjustments are made.
(b) The adjusted trial balance provides the primary basis for the preparation of financial statements.
(c) The adjusted trial balance lists the account balances segregated by assets and liabilities.
(d) The adjusted trial balance is prepared after the adjusting entries have been journalized and posted.

10. Which one of these statements about the accrual basis of accounting is *false*?
(a) Events that change a company's financial statements are recorded in the periods in which the events occur.
(b) Revenue is recognized in the period in which it is earned.
(c) This basis is in accord with generally accepted accounting principles.
(d) Revenue is recorded only when cash is received, and expense is recorded only when cash is paid.

11. Which account will have a zero balance after closing entries have been journalized and posted?
(a) Service Revenue
(b) Advertising Supplies
(c) Prepaid Insurance
(d) Accumulated Depreciation

12. Which types of accounts will appear in the post-closing trial balance?
(a) Permanent accounts
(b) Temporary accounts
(c) Accounts shown in the income statement columns of a work sheet
(d) None of the above

13. All of the following are required steps in the accounting cycle *except*:
(a) journalizing and posting closing entries.
(b) preparing an adjusted trial balance.
(c) preparing a post-closing trial balance.
(d) preparing a work sheet.

Note: All questions marked with an asterisk relate to material in Appendix 4A.

QUESTIONS

1. (a) How does the time period assumption affect an accountant's analysis of accounting transactions?
   (b) Explain the term *fiscal year*.
2. Identify and state two generally accepted accounting principles that relate to adjusting the accounts.
3. Tony Galego, a lawyer, accepts a legal engagement in March, performs the work in April, and is paid in May. If Galego's law firm prepares monthly financial statements, when should it recognize revenue from this engagement? Why?
4. In completing the engagement in question 3, Galego incurs $2,000 of expenses in March, $2,500 in April, and none in May. How much expense should be deducted from revenues in the month the revenue is recognized? Why?
5. "Adjusting entries are required by the cost principle of accounting." Do you agree? Explain.
6. Why may the financial information in a trial balance not be up to date and complete?
7. Distinguish between the two categories of adjusting entries and identify the types of adjustments applicable to each category.
8. What accounts are debited and credited in a prepaid expense adjusting entry?
9. "Depreciation is a process of valuation that results in the reporting of the fair market value of the asset." Do you agree? Explain.
10. Explain the differences between depreciation expense and accumulated depreciation.
11. Cher Company purchased equipment for $12,000. By the current balance sheet date, $7,000 had been depreciated. Indicate the balance sheet presentation of the data.
12. What accounts are debited and credited in an unearned revenue adjusting entry?
13. A company fails to recognize revenue earned but not yet received. Which of the following accounts are involved in the adjusting entry: (a) asset, (b) liability, (c) revenue, or (d) expense? For the accounts selected, indicate whether they would be debited or credited in the entry.
14. A company fails to recognize an expense incurred but not paid. Indicate which of the following accounts is debited and which is credited in the

adjusting entry: (a) asset, (b) liability, (c) revenue, or (d) expense.

15. A company makes an accrued revenue adjusting entry for $900 and an accrued expense adjusting entry for $600. How much was net income understated prior to these entries? Explain.

16. On January 9 a company pays $5,000 for salaries, of which $1,700 was reported as Salaries Payable on December 31. Give the entry to record the payment.

17. For each of the following items before adjustment, indicate the type of adjusting entry—prepaid expense, unearned revenue, accrued revenue, and accrued expense—that is needed to correct the misstatement. If an item could result in more than one type of adjusting entry, indicate each of the types.
    (a) Assets are understated.
    (b) Liabilities are overstated.
    (c) Liabilities are understated.
    (d) Expenses are understated.
    (e) Assets are overstated.
    (f) Revenue is understated.

18. One-half of the adjusting entry is given below. Indicate the account title for the other half of the entry.
    (a) Salaries Expense is debited.
    (b) Depreciation Expense is debited.
    (c) Interest Payable is credited.
    (d) Supplies is credited.
    (e) Accounts Receivable is debited.
    (f) Unearned Service Revenue is debited.

19. "An adjusting entry may affect more than one balance sheet or income statement account." Do you agree? Why or why not?

20. Why is it possible to prepare financial statements directly from an adjusted trial balance?

21.
    (a) What information do accrual basis financial statements provide that cash basis statements do not?
    (b) What information do cash basis financial statements provide that accrual basis statements do not?

22. What is the relationship, if any, between the amount shown in the adjusted trial balance column for an account and that account's ledger balance?

23. Identify the account(s) debited and credited in each of the four closing entries, assuming the company has net income for the year.

24. Describe the nature of the Income Summary account and identify the types of summary data that may be posted to this account.

25. What items are disclosed on a post-closing trial balance and what is the purpose of this work paper?

26. Which of these accounts would not appear in the post-closing trial balance? Interest Payable, Equipment, Depreciation Expense, Dividends, Unearned Service Revenue, Accumulated Depreciation—Equipment, and Service Revenue.

27. Indicate, in the sequence in which they are made, the three required steps in the accounting cycle that involve journalizing.

28. Identify, in the sequence in which they are prepared, the three trial balances that are required in the accounting cycle.

*29. What is the purpose of a work sheet?

*30. What is the basic form of a work sheet?

BRIEF EXERCISES

Indicate why adjusting entries are needed.
(SO 3)

BE4-1 The ledger of Lena Company includes the following accounts. Explain why each account may require adjustment.
(a) Prepaid Insurance
(b) Depreciation Expense
(c) Unearned Service Revenue
(d) Interest Payable

Identify the major types of adjusting entries.
(SO 3)

BE4-2 Riko Company accumulates the following adjustment data at December 31. Indicate (1) the type of adjustment (prepaid expense, accrued revenues, and so on) and (2) the status of the accounts before adjustment (overstated or understated).
(a) Supplies of $600 are on hand.
(b) Service Revenues earned but unbilled total $900.
(c) Interest of $200 has accumulated on a note payable.
(d) Rent collected in advance totaling $800 has been earned.

Prepare adjusting entry for supplies.
(SO 4)

BE4-3 Sain Advertising Company's trial balance at December 31 shows Advertising Supplies $9,700 and Advertising Supplies Expense $0. On December 31 there are $1,500 of supplies on hand. Prepare the adjusting entry at December 31 and, using T accounts, enter the balances in the accounts, post the adjusting entry, and indicate the adjusted balance in each account.

BE4-4 At the end of its first year, the trial balance of Shah Company shows Equipment $25,000 and zero balances in Accumulated Depreciation—Equipment and Depreciation Expense. Depreciation for the year is estimated to be $3,000. Prepare the adjusting entry for depreciation at December 31, post the adjustments to T accounts, and indicate the balance sheet presentation of the equipment at December 31.

Prepare adjusting entry for depreciation.
(SO 4)

BE4-5 On July 1, 1998, Bere Co. pays $15,000 to Marla Insurance Co. for a 3-year insurance contract. Both companies have fiscal years ending December 31. For Bere Co. journalize and post the entry on July 1 and the adjusting entry on December 31.

Prepare adjusting entry for prepaid expense.
(SO 4)

BE4-6 Using the data in BE4-5, journalize and post the entry on July 1 and the adjusting entry on December 31 for Marla Insurance Co. Marla uses the accounts Unearned Insurance Revenue and Insurance Revenue.

Prepare adjusting entry for unearned revenue.
(SO 4)

BE4-7 The bookkeeper for DeVoe Company asks you to prepare the following accrued adjusting entries at December 31:
(a) Interest on notes payable of $400 is accrued.
(b) Service revenue earned but unbilled totals $1,400.
(c) Salaries earned by employees of $700 have not been recorded.
Use these account titles: Service Revenue, Accounts Receivable, Interest Expense, Interest Payable, Salaries Expense, and Salaries Payable.

Prepare adjusting entries for accruals.
(SO 5)

BE4-8 The trial balance of Hoi Company includes the following balance sheet accounts. Identify the accounts that might require adjustment. For each account that requires adjustment, indicate (1) the type of adjusting entry (prepaid expenses, unearned revenues, accrued revenues, and accrued expenses) and (2) the related account in the adjusting entry.
(a) Accounts Receivable
(b) Prepaid Insurance
(c) Equipment
(d) Accumulated Depreciation—Equipment
(e) Notes Payable
(f) Interest Payable
(g) Unearned Service Revenue

Analyze accounts in an adjusted trial balance.
(SO 6)

BE4-9 The adjusted trial balance of Lumas Corporation at December 31, 1998, includes the following accounts: Retained Earnings $15,600; Dividends $6,000; Service Revenue $35,400; Salaries Expense $13,000; Insurance Expense $2,000; Rent Expense $4,000; Supplies Expense $1,500; and Depreciation Expense $1,000. Prepare an income statement for the year.

Prepare an income statement from an adjusted trial balance.
(SO 6)

BE4-10 Partial adjusted trial balance data for Lumas Corporation are presented in BE4-9. The balance in Retained Earnings is the balance as of January 1. Prepare a statement of retained earnings for the year assuming net income is $14,000.

Prepare a retained earnings statement from an adjusted trial balance.
(SO 6)

BE4-11 The following selected accounts appear in the adjusted trial balance for Khanna Company. Indicate the financial statement on which each balance would be reported.
(a) Accumulated Depreciation
(b) Depreciation Expense
(c) Retained Earnings
(d) Dividends
(e) Service Revenue
(f) Supplies
(g) Accounts Payable

Identify financial statement for selected accounts.
(SO 6)

BE4-12 Using the data in BE4-11, identify the accounts that would be included in a post-closing trial balance.

Identify post-closing trial-balance accounts.
(SO 7)

BE4-13 The required steps in the accounting cycle are listed in random order below. List the steps in proper sequence.
(a) Prepare a post-closing trial balance.
(b) Prepare an adjusted trial balance.
(c) Analyze business transactions.
(d) Prepare a trial balance.
(e) Journalize the transactions.
(f) Journalize and post closing entries.
(g) Prepare financial statements.
(h) Journalize and post adjusting entries.
(i) Post to ledger accounts.

List required steps in the accounting cycle sequence.
(SO 8)

EXERCISES

Identify accounting assumptions, principles, and constraints.
(SO 1)

E4-1 These are the assumptions, principles, and constraints discussed in this and previous chapters:
1. Economic entity assumption
2. Going concern assumption
3. Monetary unit assumption
4. Time period assumption
5. Cost principle
6. Matching principle
7. Full disclosure principle
8. Revenue recognition principle
9. Materiality
10. Conservatism

Instructions
Identify by number the accounting assumption, principle, or constraint that describes each situation below. Do not use a number more than once.

_____ (a) Is the rationale for why plant assets are not reported at liquidation value. (Do not use the cost principle.)
_____ (b) Indicates that personal and business record-keeping should be separately maintained.
_____ (c) Ensures that all relevant financial information is reported.
_____ (d) Assumes that the dollar is the "measuring stick" used to report on financial performance.
_____ (e) Requires that the operational guidelines be followed for all significant items.
_____ (f) Separates financial information into time periods for reporting purpose.
_____ (g) Requires recognition of expenses in the same period as related revenues.
_____ (h) Indicates that market value changes subsequent to purchase are not recorded in the accounts.

Identify the violated assumption, principle, or constraint.
(SO 1)

E4-2 Here are some accounting reporting situations:
(a) Tercek Company recognizes revenue at the end of the production cycle but before sale. The price of the product, as well as the amount that can be sold, is not certain.
(b) Ravine Hospital Supply Corporation reports only current assets and current liabilities on its balance sheet. Property, plant, and equipment and bonds payable are reported as current assets and current liabilities, respectively. Liquidation of the company is unlikely.
(c) Barton, Inc. is carrying inventory at its current market value of $100,000. Inventory had an original cost of $110,000.
(d) Bonilla Company is in its fifth year of operation and has yet to issue financial statements. (Do not use the full disclosure principle.)
(e) Watts Company has inventory on hand that cost $400,000. Watts reports inventory on its balance sheet at its current market value of $425,000.
(f) Steph Wolfson, president of the Classic Music Company, bought a computer for her personal use. She paid for the computer by using company funds and debited the "computers" account.

Instructions
For each situation, list the assumption, principle, or constraint that has been violated, if any. Some of these were presented in earlier chapters. List only one answer for each situation.

Identify types of adjustments and accounts before adjustment.
(SO 3, 4, 5)

E4-3 Rafael Company accumulates the following adjustment data at December 31:
(a) Service Revenue earned but unbilled totals $600.
(b) Store supplies of $300 have been used.
(c) Utility expenses of $225 are unpaid.
(d) Service revenue of $260 collected in advance has been earned.
(e) Salaries of $800 are unpaid.
(f) Prepaid insurance totaling $350 has expired.

Instructions

For each item indicate (1) the type of adjustment (prepaid expense, unearned revenue, accrued revenue, or accrued expense) and (2) the accounts before adjustment (overstatement or understatement).

E4-4 The ledger of Easy Rental Agency on March 31 of the current year includes these selected accounts before adjusting entries have been prepared:

Prepare adjusting entries from selected account data.
(SO 4, 5)

	Debits	Credits
Prepaid Insurance	$ 3,600	
Supplies	2,800	
Equipment	25,000	
Accumulated Depreciation—Equipment		$ 8,400
Notes Payable		20,000
Unearned Rent Revenue		9,300
Rent Revenue		60,000
Interest Expense	0	
Wage Expense	14,000	

An analysis of the accounts shows the following:
1. The equipment depreciates $500 per month.
2. One-third of the unearned rent revenue was earned during the quarter.
3. Interest of $600 is accrued on the notes payable.
4. Supplies on hand total $850.
5. Insurance expires at the rate of $200 per month.

Instructions

Prepare the adjusting entries at March 31, assuming that adjusting entries are made quarterly. Additional accounts are: Depreciation Expense, Insurance Expense, Interest Payable, and Supplies Expense.

E4-5 Kay Ong, D.D.S., opened an incorporated dental practice on January 1, 1998. During the first month of operations the following transactions occurred:

Prepare adjusting entries.
(SO 4, 5)

1. Performed services for patients who had dental plan insurance. At January 31, $750 of such services was earned but not yet billed to the insurance companies.
2. Utility expenses incurred but not paid prior to January 31 totaled $650.
3. Purchased dental equipment on January 1 for $80,000, paying $20,000 in cash and signing a $60,000, 3-year note payable. The equipment depreciates $400 per month. Interest is $600 per month.
4. Purchased a 1-year malpractice insurance policy on January 1 for $12,000.
5. Purchased $1,800 of dental supplies. On January 31 determined that $500 of supplies were on hand.

Instructions

Prepare the adjusting entries on January 31. Account titles are: Accumulated Depreciation—Dental Equipment, Depreciation Expense, Service Revenue, Accounts Receivable, Insurance Expense, Interest Expense, Interest Payable, Prepaid Insurance, Supplies, Supplies Expense, Utilities Expense, and Utilities Payable.

E4-6 The trial balance for Sierra Corporation is shown in Illustration 4-4. In lieu of the adjusting entries shown in the text at October 31, assume the following adjustment data:

Prepare adjusting entries.
(SO 4, 5)

1. Advertising supplies on hand at October 31 total $1,300.
2. Expired insurance for the month is $100.
3. Depreciation for the month is $50.
4. Unearned revenue earned in October totals $500.
5. Revenue earned but unbilled at October 31 is $300.
6. Interest accrued at October 31 is $70.
7. Accrued salaries at October 31 are $1,600.

Instructions

Prepare the adjusting entries for these items.

186 CHAPTER 4 Accrual Accounting Concepts

Prepare a correct income statement.
(SO 1, 4, 5, 6)

E4-7 The income statement of Weller Co. for the month of July shows net income of $1,400 based on Service Revenue $5,500; Wages Expense $2,300; Supplies Expense $1,200; and Utilities Expense $600. In reviewing the statement, you discover the following:
1. Insurance expired during July of $300 was omitted.
2. Supplies expense includes $400 of supplies that are still on hand at July 31.
3. Depreciation on equipment of $150 was omitted.
4. Accrued but unpaid wages at July 31 of $300 were not included.
5. Revenue earned but unrecorded totaled $750.

Instructions
Prepare a correct income statement for July 1998 year-end.

Analyze adjusted data.
(SO 1, 4, 5, 6)

E4-8 This is a partial adjusted trial balance of Cordero Company:

CORDERO COMPANY
Adjusted Trial Balance
January 31, 1998

	Debit	Credit
Supplies	$ 800	
Prepaid Insurance	2,400	
Salaries Payable		$ 700
Unearned Service Revenue		750
Supplies Expense	950	
Insurance Expense	400	
Salaries Expense	1,800	
Service Revenue		2,500

Instructions
Answer these questions, assuming the year begins January 1:
(a) If the amount in Supplies Expense is the January 31 adjusting entry, and $850 of supplies was purchased in January, what was the balance in Supplies on January 1?
(b) If the amount in Insurance Expense is the January 31 adjusting entry, and the original insurance premium was for 1 year, what was the total premium and when was the policy purchased?
(c) If $2,500 of salaries was paid in January, what was the balance in Salaries Payable at December 31, 1997?
(d) If $1,600 was received in January for services performed in January, what was the balance in Unearned Service Revenue at December 31, 1997?

Journalize basic transactions and adjusting entries.
(SO 4, 5, 6)

E4-9 Selected accounts of Alamo Company are shown here:

Supplies Expense		Supplies	
July 31 400		July 1 Bal. 1,100	July 31 400
		10 300	

Salaries Payable		Accounts Receivable	
	July 31 1,200	July 31 500	

Salaries Expense		Unearned Service Revenue	
July 15 1,200		July 31 800	July 1 Bal. 1,500
31 1,200			20 700

Service Revenue	
	July 14 3,000
	31 800
	31 500

Instructions
After analyzing the accounts, journalize (a) the July transactions and (b) the adjusting entries that were made on July 31. [*Hint:* July transactions were for cash.]

E4-10 The trial balances shown at the top of the next page are before and after adjustment for Apachi Company at the end of its fiscal year:

APACHI COMPANY
Trial Balance
August 31, 1998

Prepare adjusting entries from analysis of trial balances.
(SO 4, 5, 6)

	Before Adjustment Dr.	Before Adjustment Cr.	After Adjustment Dr.	After Adjustment Cr.
Cash	$10,400		$10,400	
Accounts Receivable	8,800		9,500	
Office Supplies	2,300		700	
Prepaid Insurance	4,000		2,500	
Office Equipment	14,000		14,000	
Accumulated Depreciation—Office Equipment		$ 3,600		$ 4,800
Accounts Payable		5,800		5,800
Salaries Payable		0		1,000
Unearned Rent Revenue		1,500		700
Common Stock		10,000		10,000
Retained Earnings		5,600		5,600
Service Revenue		34,000		34,700
Rent Revenue		11,000		11,800
Salaries Expense	17,000		18,000	
Office Supplies Expense	0		1,600	
Rent Expense	15,000		15,000	
Insurance Expense	0		1,500	
Depreciation Expense	0		1,200	
	$71,500	$71,500	$74,400	$74,400

Instructions
Prepare the adjusting entries that were made.

E4-11 The adjusted trial balance for Apachi Company is given in E4-10.

Prepare financial statements from adjusted trial balance.
(SO 6)

Instructions
Prepare the income and retained earnings statements for the year and the balance sheet at August 31.

PROBLEMS

P4-1 Presented below are the assumptions, principles, and constraints used in this and previous chapters.

1. Economic entity assumption
2. Going concern assumption
3. Monetary unit assumption
4. Time period assumption
5. Full disclosure principle
6. Revenue recognition principle
7. Matching principle
8. Cost principle
9. Materiality
10. Conservatism

Identify accounting assumptions, principles, and constraints.
(SO 1)

Instructions
Identify by number the accounting assumption, principle, or constraint that describes each of these situations. Do not use a number more than once.

_____ (a) Repair tools are expensed when purchased. (Do not use conservatism.)
_____ (b) Allocates expenses to revenues in proper period.
_____ (c) Assumes that the dollar is the measuring stick used to report financial information.
_____ (d) Separates financial information into time periods for reporting purposes.
_____ (e) Market value changes subsequent to purchase are not recorded in the accounts. (Do not use the revenue recognition principle.)
_____ (f) Indicates that personal and business record keeping should be separately maintained.
_____ (g) Ensures that all relevant financial information is reported.
_____ (h) Lower of cost or market is used to value inventories.

Prepare adjusting entries, post, and prepare adjusted trial balance.

(SO 4, 5, 6)

P4-2 The trial balance before adjustment of Scenic Tours at the end of its first month of operations is presented here:

SCENIC TOURS
Trial Balance
June 30, 1998

	Debit	Credit
Cash	$ 3,000	
Prepaid Insurance	7,200	
Office Equipment	1,800	
Buses	140,000	
Notes Payable		$ 62,000
Unearned Revenue		15,000
Common Stock		70,000
Tour Revenue		15,900
Salaries Expense	9,000	
Advertising Expense	800	
Gas and Oil Expense	1,100	
	$162,900	$162,900

Other data:
1. The insurance policy has a 1-year term beginning June 1, 1998.
2. The monthly depreciation is $50 on office equipment and $2,000 on buses.
3. Interest of $700 accrues on the notes payable each month.
4. Deposits of $1,500 each were received for advanced tour reservations from ten school groups. At June 30, three of these deposits have been earned.
5. Bus drivers are paid a combined total of $400 per day. At June 30, 3 days' salaries are unpaid.
6. A senior citizen's organization that had not made an advance deposit took a tour on June 30 for $1,200. This group was not billed for the services rendered until July.

Instructions
(a) Journalize the adjusting entries at June 30, 1998.
(b) Prepare a ledger using T accounts. Enter the trial balance amounts and post the adjusting entries.
(c) Prepare an adjusted trial balance at June 30, 1998.

Prepare adjusting entries, adjusted trial balance, and financial statements.

(SO 4, 5, 6)

P4-3 The River Run Motel opened for business on May 1, 1998. Here is its trial balance before adjustment on May 31:

RIVER RUN MOTEL
Trial Balance
May 31, 1998

	Debit	Credit
Cash	$ 2,500	
Prepaid Insurance	1,800	
Supplies	1,900	
Land	15,000	
Lodge	70,000	
Furniture	16,800	
Accounts Payable		$ 4,700
Unearned Rent Revenue		3,600
Mortgage Payable		35,000
Common Stock		60,000
Rent Revenue		9,200
Salaries Expense	3,000	
Utilities Expense	1,000	
Advertising Expense	500	
	$112,500	$112,500

Other data:
1. Insurance expires at the rate of $200 per month.
2. An inventory of supplies shows $1,350 of unused supplies on May 31.
3. Annual depreciation is $3,600 on the lodge and $3,000 on furniture.
4. The mortgage interest rate is 12%. (The mortgage was taken out on May 1.)
5. Unearned rent of $1,500 has been earned.
6. Salaries of $300 are accrued and unpaid at May 31.

Instructions
(a) Journalize the adjusting entries on May 31.
(b) Prepare a ledger using T accounts. Enter the trial balance amounts and post the adjusting entries.
(c) Prepare an adjusted trial balance on May 31.
(d) Prepare an income statement and a retained earnings statement for the month of May and a balance sheet at May 31.
(e) Identify which accounts should be closed on May 31.

P4-4 Ozaki Co. was organized on July 1, 1998. Quarterly financial statements are prepared. The trial balance and adjusted trial balance on September 30 are shown here:

Prepare adjusting entries, and financial statements; identify accounts to be closed.
(SO 4, 5, 6, 7)

OZAKI CO.
Trial Balance
September 30, 1998

	Unadjusted Dr.	Unadjusted Cr.	Adjusted Dr.	Adjusted Cr.
Cash	$ 6,700		$ 6,700	
Accounts Receivable	400		800	
Prepaid Rent	1,500		900	
Supplies	1,200		1,000	
Equipment	15,000		15,000	
Accumulated Depreciation—Equipment				$ 350
Notes Payable		$ 5,000		5,000
Accounts Payable		1,510		1,510
Salaries Payable				600
Interest Payable				50
Unearned Rent Revenue		900		600
Common Stock		14,000		14,000
Retained Earnings		0		0
Dividends	600		600	
Commission Revenue		14,000		14,400
Rent Revenue		400		700
Salaries Expense	9,000		9,600	
Rent Expense	900		1,500	
Depreciation Expense			350	
Supplies Expense			200	
Utilities Expense	510		510	
Interest Expense			50	
	$35,810	$35,810	$37,210	$37,210

Instructions
(a) Journalize the adjusting entries that were made.
(b) Prepare an income statement and a retained earnings statement for the 3 months ending September 30 and a balance sheet at September 30.
(c) Identify which accounts should be closed on September 30.
(d) If the note bears interest at 12%, how many months has it been outstanding?

P4-5 A review of the ledger of Montana Company at December 31, 1998, produces these data pertaining to the preparation of annual adjusting entries:

Prepare adjusting entries.
(SO 4, 5)

1. Prepaid Insurance $12,800: The company has separate insurance policies on its buildings and its motor vehicles. Policy B4564 on the building was purchased on July 1,

1997, for $9,600. The policy has a term of 3 years. Policy A2958 on the vehicles was purchased on January 1, 1998, for $4,800. This policy has a term of 2 years.
2. Unearned Subscription Revenue $49,000: The company began selling magazine subscriptions in 1998 on an annual basis. The selling price of a subscription is $50. A review of subscription contracts reveals the following:

Subscription Date	Number of Subscriptions
October 1	200
November 1	300
December 1	480
	980

3. Notes Payable, $50,000: This balance consists of a note for 6 months at an annual interest rate of 9%, dated September 1.
4. Salaries Payable $0: There are eight salaried employees. Salaries are paid every Friday for the current week. Five employees receive a salary of $600 each per week, and three employees earn $700 each per week. December 31 is a Wednesday. Employees do not work weekends. All employees worked the last 3 days of December.

Instructions
Prepare the adjusting entries at December 31, 1998.

Journalize transactions and follow through accounting cycle to preparation of financial statements.
(SO 4, 5, 6)

P4-6 On November 1, 1998, the following were the account balances of Alou Equipment Repair:

Debits		Credits	
Cash	$ 2,790	Accumulated Depreciation	$ 500
Accounts Receivable	2,510	Accounts Payable	2,100
Supplies	1,000	Unearned Service Revenue	400
Store Equipment	10,000	Salaries Payable	500
		Common Stock	10,000
		Retained Earnings	2,800
	$16,300		$16,300

During November the following summary transactions were completed:

Nov. 8 Paid $1,100 for salaries due employees, of which $600 is for November.
10 Received $1,200 cash from customers on account.
12 Received $1,400 cash for services performed in November.
15 Purchased store equipment on account $3,000.
17 Purchased supplies on account $1,500.
20 Paid creditors on account $2,500.
22 Paid November rent $300.
25 Paid salaries $1,000.
27 Performed services on account and billed customers for services rendered $700.
29 Received $550 from customers for future service.

Adjustment data:
1. Supplies on hand are valued at $1,600.
2. Accrued salaries payable are $500.
3. Depreciation for the month is $120.
4. Unearned service revenue of $300 is earned.

Instructions
(a) Enter the November 1 balances in the ledger accounts. (Use T accounts.)
(b) Journalize the November transactions.
(c) Post to the ledger accounts. Use Service Revenue, Depreciation Expense, Supplies Expense, Salaries Expense, and Rent Expense.
(d) Prepare a trial balance at November 30.

(e) Journalize and post adjusting entries.
(f) Prepare an adjusted trial balance.
(g) Prepare an income statement and a retained earnings statement for November and a balance sheet at November 30.

ALTERNATIVE PROBLEMS

P4-1A Presented here are the assumptions, principles, and constraints used in this and previous chapters:

Identify accounting assumptions, principles, and constraints.
(SO 1)

1. Economic entity assumption
2. Going concern assumption
3. Monetary unit assumption
4. Time period assumption
5. Full disclosure principle
6. Revenue recognition principle
7. Matching principle
8. Cost principle
9. Materiality
10. Conservatism

Instructions
Identify by number the accounting assumption, principle, or constraint that describes each of these situations. Do not use a number more than once.

_____ (a) Assets are not stated at their liquidation value. (Do not use the cost principle.)
_____ (b) The death of the president is not recorded in the accounts.
_____ (c) Pencil sharpeners are expensed when purchased.
_____ (d) An allowance for doubtful accounts is established. (Do not use conservatism.)
_____ (e) Each entity is kept as a unit distinct from its owner or owners.
_____ (f) Reporting must be done at defined intervals.
_____ (g) Revenue is recorded at the point of sale.
_____ (h) When in doubt, it is better to understate rather than overstate net income.
_____ (i) All important information related to inventories is presented in the footnotes or in the financial statements.

P4-2A Ortega Security Service began operations on January 1, 1998. At the end of the first year of operations, this is the trial balance before adjustment:

Prepare adjusting entries, post, and prepare adjusted trial balance.
(SO 4, 5, 6)

ORTEGA SECURITY SERVICE
Trial Balance
December 31, 1998

	Debit	Credit
Cash	$ 12,400	
Accounts Receivable	3,200	
Prepaid Insurance	3,600	
Automobiles	58,000	
Notes Payable		$ 45,000
Unearned Service Revenue		2,500
Common Stock		18,000
Service Revenue		84,000
Salaries Expense	57,000	
Repairs Expense	6,000	
Gas and Oil Expense	9,300	
	$149,500	$149,500

Other data:
1. Service revenue earned but unbilled is $1,500 at December 31.
2. Insurance coverage began on January 1 under a 2-year policy.
3. Automobile depreciation is $15,000 for the year.
4. Interest of $5,400 accrued on notes payable for the year.
5. $1,000 of the unearned service revenue has been earned.

6. Drivers' salaries total $500 per day. At December 31, 4 days' salaries are unpaid.
7. Repairs to automobiles of $650 have been incurred, but bills have not been received prior to December 31. (Use Accounts Payable.)

Instructions
(a) Journalize the annual adjusting entries at December 31, 1998.
(b) Prepare a ledger using T accounts. Enter the trial balance amounts and post the adjusting entries.
(c) Prepare an adjusted trial balance at December 31, 1998.

Prepare adjusting entries, adjusted trial balance, and financial statements.
(SO 4, 5, 6)

P4-3A Highland Cove Resort opened for business on June 1 with eight air-conditioned units. Its trial balance before adjustment on August 31 is presented here:

HIGHLAND COVE RESORT
Trial Balance
August 31, 1998

	Debit	Credit
Cash	$ 19,600	
Prepaid Insurance	5,400	
Supplies	3,300	
Land	25,000	
Cottages	125,000	
Furniture	26,000	
Accounts Payable		$ 6,500
Unearned Rent Revenue		6,800
Mortgage Payable		80,000
Common Stock		100,000
Dividends	5,000	
Rent Revenue		80,000
Salaries Expense	51,000	
Utilities Expense	9,400	
Repair Expense	3,600	
	$273,300	$273,300

Other data:
1. Insurance expires at the rate of $300 per month.
2. An inventory count on August 31 shows $700 of supplies on hand.
3. Annual depreciation is $4,800 on cottages and $2,400 on furniture.
4. Unearned rent of $5,000 was earned prior to August 31.
5. Salaries of $400 were unpaid at August 31.
6. Rentals of $800 were due from tenants at August 31. (Use Accounts Receivable.)
7. The mortgage interest rate is 12% per year. (The mortgage was taken out August 1.)

Instructions
(a) Journalize the adjusting entries on August 31 for the 3-month period June 1–August 31.
(b) Prepare a ledger using T accounts. Enter the trial balance amounts and post the adjusting entries.
(c) Prepare an adjusted trial balance on August 31.
(d) Prepare an income statement and a retained earnings statement for the 3 months ended August 31 and a balance sheet as of August 31.
(e) Identify which accounts should be closed on August 31.

P4-4A Grant Advertising Agency was founded by Thomas Grant in January 1994. Presented here are both the adjusted and unadjusted trial balances as of December 31, 1998.

GRANT ADVERTISING AGENCY
Trial Balance
December 31, 1998

	Unadjusted Dr.	Unadjusted Cr.	Adjusted Dr.	Adjusted Cr.
Cash	$ 11,000		$ 11,000	
Accounts Receivable	20,000		21,000	
Art Supplies	8,400		5,000	
Prepaid Insurance	3,350		2,500	
Printing Equipment	60,000		60,000	
Accumulated Depreciation		$ 28,000		$ 35,000
Accounts Payable		5,000		5,000
Interest Payable		0		150
Notes Payable		5,000		5,000
Unearned Advertising Revenue		7,000		5,600
Salaries Payable		0		1,800
Common Stock		20,000		20,000
Retained Earnings		5,500		5,500
Dividends	12,000		12,000	
Advertising Revenue		58,600		61,000
Salaries Expense	10,000		11,800	
Insurance Expense			850	
Interest Expense	350		500	
Depreciation Expense			7,000	
Art Supplies Expense			3,400	
Rent Expense	4,000		4,000	
	$129,100	$129,100	$139,050	$139,050

Prepare adjusting entries and financial statements; identify accounts to be closed.
(SO 4, 5, 6, 7)

Instructions
(a) Journalize the annual adjusting entries that were made.
(b) Prepare an income statement and a retained earnings statement for the year ended December 31, and a balance sheet at December 31.
(c) Identify which accounts should be closed on December 31.
(d) If the note has been outstanding 3 months, what is the annual interest rate on that note?
(e) If the company paid $13,500 in salaries in 1998, what was the balance in Salaries Payable on December 31, 1997?

P4-5A A review of the ledger of Greenberg Company at December 31, 1998, produces the following data pertaining to the preparation of annual adjusting entries:

Prepare adjusting entries.
(SO 4, 5)

1. Salaries Payable $0: There are eight salaried employees. Salaries are paid every Friday for the current week. Five employees receive a salary of $600 each per week, and three employees earn $500 each per week. December 31 is a Tuesday. Employees do not work weekends. All employees worked the last 2 days of December.
2. Unearned Rent Revenue $369,000: The company began subleasing office space in its new building on November 1. Each tenant is required to make a $5,000 security deposit that is not refundable until occupancy is terminated. At December 31 the company had the following rental contracts that are paid in full for the entire term of the lease:

Date	Term (in months)	Monthly Rent	Number of Leases
Nov. 1	6	$4,000	5
Dec. 1	6	8,500	4

3. Prepaid Advertising $13,200: This balance consists of payments on two advertising contracts. The contracts provide for monthly advertising in two trade magazines. The terms of the contracts are as follows:

Contract	Date	Amount	Number of Magazine Issues
A650	May 1	$6,000	12
B974	Sept. 1	7,200	24

The first advertisement runs in the month in which the contract is signed.

4. Notes Payable $80,000: This balance consists of a note for 1 year at an annual interest rate of 12%, dated June 1.

Instructions
Prepare the adjusting entries at December 31, 1998. Show all computations.

Journalize transactions and follow through accounting cycle to preparation of financial statements.
(SO 4, 5, 6)

P4-6A On September 1, 1998, the following were the account balances of Rijo Equipment Repair:

	Debits		Credits
Cash	$ 4,880	Accumulated Depreciation	$ 1,500
Accounts Receivable	3,520	Accounts Payable	3,400
Supplies	1,000	Unearned Service Revenue	400
Store Equipment	15,000	Salaries Payable	500
	$24,400	Common Stock	10,000
		Retained Earnings	8,600
			$24,400

During September the following summary transactions were completed:

Sept. 8 Paid $1,100 for salaries due employees, of which $600 is for September.
  10 Received $1,200 cash from customers on account.
  12 Received $3,400 cash for services performed in September.
  15 Purchased store equipment on account $3,000.
  17 Purchased supplies on account $1,500.
  20 Paid creditors $4,500 on account.
  22 Paid September rent $500.
  25 Paid salaries $1,050.
  27 Performed services on account and billed customers for services rendered $900.
  29 Received $650 from customers for future service.

Adjustment data:
1. Supplies on hand $1,800.
2. Accrued salaries payable $400.
3. Depreciation $200 per month.
4. Unearned service revenue of $350 earned.

Instructions
(a) Enter the September 1 balances in the ledger T accounts.
(b) Journalize the September transactions.
(c) Post to the ledger T accounts. Use Service Revenue, Depreciation Expense, Supplies Expense, Salaries Expense, and Rent Expense.
(d) Prepare a trial balance at September 30.
(e) Journalize and post adjusting entries.
(f) Prepare an adjusted trial balance.
(g) Prepare an income statement and a retained earnings statement for September and a balance sheet at September 30.

BROADENING YOUR PERSPECTIVE

FINANCIAL REPORTING AND ANALYSIS

FINANCIAL REPORTING PROBLEM: *Starbucks Corporation*

BYP4-1 The financial statements of Starbucks are presented in Appendix A at the end of this book.

Instructions
(a) Using the consolidated income statement and balance sheet, identify items that may result in adjusting entries for prepayments.
(b) Using the consolidated income statement, identify two items that may result in adjusting entries for accruals.
(c) What was the amount of depreciation expense for 1996 and 1995? Where was accumulated depreciation reported? Do you have any suggestions for improving Starbucks' presentation of accumulated depreciation?
(d) What has been the trend since 1994 for interest expense and interest income?
(e) What was the cash paid for interest during 1996 reported at the bottom of the Consolidated Statement of Cash Flows? What was interest expense for 1996? Where is the remainder presumably reported in the balance sheet?

COMPARATIVE ANALYSIS PROBLEM: *Starbucks vs. Green Mountain Coffee*

BYP4-2 The financial statements of Green Mountain Coffee are presented in Appendix B, following the financial statements for Starbucks in Appendix A.

Instructions
(a) Identify two accounts on Green Mountain's balance sheet that provide evidence that Green Mountain uses accrual accounting. In each case, identify the income statement account that would be affected by the adjustment process.
(b) Identify two accounts on Starbucks' balance sheet that provide evidence that Starbucks uses accrual accounting (different from the two you listed for Green Mountain). In each case, identify the income statement account that would be affected by the adjustment process.

RESEARCH CASE

BYP4-3 The March 1995 issue of *Management Review* includes an article by Barbara Ettorre entitled "How Motorola Closes Its Books in Two Days."

Instructions
Read the article and answer these questions:
(a) How often does Motorola close its books? How long did the process used to take?
(b) What was the major change Motorola initiated to shorten the closing process?
(c) What incentive does Motorola offer to ensure accurate and timely information?
(d) In a given year, how many journal entry lines does Motorola process?
(e) Provide an example of an external force that prevents Motorola from closing faster than a day and a half.
(f) According to Motorola's corporate vice-president and controller, how do external users of financial statements perceive companies that release information early?

INTERPRETING FINANCIAL STATEMENTS

BYP4-4 Minicase *Case Corporation*

Case Corporation, based in Racine, Wisconsin, manufactures farm tractors, farm equipment, and light- and medium-sized construction equipment. The company's products are distributed through both independent and company-owned distributing companies, which are located throughout the world. Case Corporation's 1995 partial income statement is shown below.

CASE CORPORATION
Income Statement (partial)
(in millions)

Revenues	
Net sales	$4,937
Interest income and other	168
	$5,105
Cost and expenses	
Cost of goods sold	3,779
Selling, general, and administrative	553
Research, development, and engineering	156
Interest expense	174
Other, net	16
	4,678
Income from operations before taxes	$ 427

Assume that this partial income statement was prepared before all adjusting entries had been made, and that the internal audit staff identified the following items that require adjustments:

1. Depreciation on the administrative offices of $13 million needs to be recorded.
2. A physical inventory determined that $1 million in office supplies had been used in 1995.
3. $4 million in salaries have been earned but not recorded. Half of this amount is for the salaries of engineering staff; the other half is for the administrative staff.
4. $3 million in insurance premiums were prepaid on May 1.
5. $7 million in prepaid rent has expired at year-end.
6. Cost of goods sold of $2 million was recorded in error as interest expense.

Instructions
(a) Make the adjusting entries required. Use standard account titles.
(b) Which of the entries is not a routine adjusting entry? Explain your answer.
(c) For each of the accounts in these adjusting entries that will be posted to Case's general ledger, tell which item on the income statement will be increased or decreased.
(d) Recast the partial income statement based on the adjusting entries prepared.

CRITICAL THINKING

MANAGEMENT DECISION CASES

BYP4-5 Holiday Travel Court was organized on April 1, 1997, by Alice Adare. Alice is a good manager but a poor accountant. From the trial balance prepared by a part-time bookkeeper, Alice prepared the following income statement for the quarter that ended March 31, 1998:

HOLIDAY TRAVEL COURT
Income Statement
For the Quarter Ended March 31, 1998

Revenues		
Rental revenues		$95,000
Operating expenses		
Advertising	$ 5,200	
Wages	29,800	
Utilities	900	
Depreciation	800	
Repairs	4,000	
Total operating expenses		40,700
Net income		$54,300

Alice knew that something was wrong with the statement because net income had never exceeded $20,000 in any one quarter. Knowing that you are an experienced accountant, she asks you to review the income statement and other data.

You first look at the trial balance. In addition to the account balances reported in the income statement, the ledger contains these selected balances at March 31, 1998:

Supplies	$ 5,200
Prepaid Insurance	7,200
Notes Payable	12,000

You then make inquiries and discover the following:
1. Rental revenues include advanced rentals for summer-month occupancy, $28,000.
2. There were $1,300 of supplies on hand at March 31.
3. Prepaid insurance resulted from the payment of a 1-year policy on January 1, 1998.
4. The mail on April 1, 1998, brought the following bills: advertising for week of March 24, $110; repairs made March 10, $260; and utilities, $180.
5. There are four employees who receive wages totaling $350 per day. At March 31, 2 days' wages have been incurred but not paid.
6. The note payable is a 3-month, 10% note dated January 1, 1998.

Instructions
(a) Prepare a correct income statement for the quarter ended March 31, 1998.
(b) Explain to Alice the generally accepted accounting principles that she did not follow in preparing her income statement and their effect on her results.

BYP4-6 Betsy and Bill Kite, local golf stars, opened Parmor Driving range on March 1, 1998, by investing $10,000 of their cash savings in the business. A caddy shack was constructed for cash at a cost of $4,000, and $800 was spent on golf balls and golf clubs. The Kites leased 5 acres of land at a cost of $1,000 per month and paid the first month's rent. During the first month, advertising costs totaled $750, of which $150 was unpaid at March 31, and $400 was paid to members of the high school golf team for retrieving golf balls. All fees from customers were deposited in the company's bank account. On March 15, a dividend of $800 in cash was paid. A $100 utility bill was received on March 31 but it was not paid. On March 31 the balance in the company's bank account was $8,550. Betsy and Bill thought they had a pretty good first month of operations. However, their estimates of profitability ranged from a loss of $1,450 to net income of $3,100.

Instructions
(a) How could the Kites have concluded that the business operated at a loss of $1,450? Was this a valid basis on which to determine net income?
(b) How could the Kites have concluded that the business operated at a net income of $3,100? [*Hint:* Prepare a balance sheet at March 31.] Was this a valid basis on which to determine net income?
(c) Without preparing an income statement, determine the actual net income for March.
(d) What were the fees earned in March?

A REAL-WORLD FOCUS: *Laser Recording Systems Incorporated*

BYP4-7 *Laser Recording Systems*, founded in 1981, produces laser disks for use in the home market. Sales since 1985 have increased approximately 15% per year. The following is an excerpt from Laser Recording Systems' 1994 financial statements (all dollar amounts are in thousands):

LASER RECORDING SYSTEMS INCORPORATED
Management Discussion

Accrued liabilities increased to $1,642 at January 31, 1994, from $138 at the end of fiscal year 1993. Compensation and related accruals increased $195 due primarily to increases in accruals for severance, vacation, commissions, and relocation expenses. Accrued professional services increased by $137 primarily as a result of legal expenses related to several outstanding contractual disputes. Other expense increased $35, of which $18 was for interest payable.

Instructions
(a) Can you tell from the above whether Laser Recording has prepaid its legal expenses and is now making an adjustment to the asset account Prepaid Legal Expenses, or whether the company is handling the legal expense via an accrued expense adjustment?
(b) Identify each of the adjustments Laser Recording is discussing as one of the four types of possible adjustments discussed in the chapter. How is net income ultimately affected by each of the adjustments?
(c) What journal entry did Laser Recording make to record its accrued interest?

GROUP ACTIVITIES

BYP4-8 These types of adjusting entries were introduced in this chapter: (1) prepaid expenses, (2) unearned revenues, (3) accrued revenues, and (4) accrued expenses.

Instructions
With the class divided into four groups, each group should choose one type of adjusting entry and report to the class on the following: (a) the status of the accounts before adjustment, (b) the debit–credit effect of the adjusting entry, and (c) the effects on the balance sheet and income statement if the adjusting entry is not made.

BYP4-9 Assume that the FASB has decided to address the problem of information overload. It has agreed to eliminate one of the principles, assumptions, constraints, or qualitative characteristics listed below. This concept will be deleted from all textbooks and will no longer be considered important in accounting literature.

Relevance	Monetary unit	Full disclosure
Reliability	Revenue recognition	Cost
Comparability and consistency	Time period	Materiality
Economic entity	Matching	Conservatism

Instructions
With the class divided into groups, each group will be assigned one or more items on the list and do these exercises:
(a) Discuss within your group why your specific concept(s) should *not* be eliminated.
(b) Pick a group leader who will present to the class the group's reasons why the FASB should not delete the group's concept(s).
(c) At the end of all presentations, the class should vote on which concept to delete.

COMMUNICATION ACTIVITIES

BYP4-10 On numerous occasions proposals have surfaced to put the federal government on the accrual basis of accounting. This is no small issue because if this basis were used, it would mean that billions in unrecorded liabilities would have to be booked and the federal deficit would increase substantially.

Instructions
(a) What is the difference between accrual basis accounting and cash basis accounting?
(b) Comment on why politicians prefer a cash basis accounting system over an accrual basis system.
(c) Write a letter to your senator explaining why you think the federal government should adopt the accrual basis of accounting.

BYP4-11 In reviewing the accounts of Marylee Co. at the end of the year, you discover that adjusting entries have not been made.

Instructions
Write a memorandum to Mary Lee Virgil, the owner of Marylee Co., that explains the nature and purpose of adjusting entries, why adjusting entries are needed, and the types of adjusting entries that may be made.

ETHICS CASE

BYP4-12 Diamond Company is a pesticide manufacturer. Its sales declined greatly this year due to the passage of legislation outlawing the sale of several of Diamond's chemical pesticides. During the coming year, Diamond will have environmentally safe and competitive replacement chemicals to replace these discontinued products. Sales in the next year are expected to greatly exceed those of any prior year. Therefore, the decline in this year's sales and profits appears to be a 1-year aberration.

Even so, the company president believes that a large dip in the current year's profits could cause a significant drop in the market price of Diamond's stock and make it a takeover target. To avoid this possibility, he urges Carol Denton, controller, in making this period's year-end adjusting entries to accrue every possible revenue and to defer as many expenses as possible. The president says to Carol, "We need the revenues this year, and next year can easily absorb expenses deferred from this year. We can't let our stock price be hammered down!" Carol didn't get around to recording the adjusting entries until January 17, but she dated the entries December 31 as if they were recorded then. Carol also made every effort to comply with the president's request.

Instructions
(a) Who are the stakeholders in this situation?
(b) What are the ethical considerations of the president's request and Carol's dating the adjusting entries December 31?
(c) Can Carol accrue revenues and defer expenses and still be ethical?

FINANCIAL ANALYSIS ON THE WEB

BYP4-13 *Purpose:* Using "Edgar Database" to locate and identify common corporate filing required by the SEC forms and their definitions.

Address: http://www.sec.gov/index.html

Steps:
1. Choose **EDGAR Database.**
2. Choose **EDGAR Form Definitions.**

Instructions
Describe the following:
(a) Prospectus   (d) 10K
(b) Schedule 14A   (e) 10Q
(c) Forms 3, 4, and 5

Answers to Self-Study Questions
1. c   2. a   3. d   4. d   5. c   6. a   7. b   8. b   9. c   10. d
11. a   12. a   13. d

CHAPTER 5

Merchandising Operations

STUDY OBJECTIVES

After studying this chapter, you should be able to:

1. Identify the differences between a service enterprise and a merchandising company.
2. Explain the recording of purchases under a perpetual inventory system.
3. Explain the recording of sales revenues under a perpetual inventory system.
4. Identify the unique features of the financial statements for a merchandising company.
5. Explain the factors affecting profitability.

Who Doesn't Shop at Wal-Mart?

In his book *The End of Work*, Jeremy Rifkin notes that until the 20th century the word *consumption* evoked negative images; to be labeled a "consumer" was an insult. (In fact, one of the deadliest diseases in history was often referred to as "consumption.") Twentieth-century merchants realized, however, that in order to prosper, they had to convince people of the need for things not previously needed. For example, General Motors made annual changes in its cars so that people would be discontented with the cars they already owned. Thus began consumerism.

Today consumption describes the U.S. lifestyle in a nutshell. We consume twice as much today per person as we did at the end of World War II. The amount of U.S. retail space per person is vastly greater than that of any other country. It appears that we live to shop. The first great retail giant was Sears, Roebuck. Started as a catalog company enabling people in rural areas to buy things by mail, it was for many years the uncontested merchandising leader. But in recent years Sears lost its edge. It didn't recognize changes in consumer shopping patterns and tastes. First it was outdone by the "blue-light special," but Kmart's time at the top was short-lived. Today the king of the shopping cart is Wal-Mart.

Wal-Mart had only 18 stores as recently as 1970. A key cause of its incredible growth is its amazing system of inventory control and distribution. Wal-Mart has a management information system that employs six satellite channels. After a decade of annual increases in earnings of 25%, the Walton family, which owns 40% of Wal-Mart, is among the wealthiest in the nation. As Wal-Mart glimmered, the fortunes of both Sears and Kmart tarnished, though each tried to remake its image and identity. Now a new round has begun. Wal-Mart's profit increases, while still a healthy 12% annually, have come down to earth. The company has actually experienced less than stellar results from some of its international holdings and stores in large cities. With unemployment rates at their lowest level in two decades and consumer confidence high, this may be the time

for either Kmart or Sears to reclaim its title as the largest satisfier of basic (and perhaps not so basic) human needs. On the other hand, a recent *Wall Street Journal* article entitled "How to Sell More to Those Who Think It's Cool to Be Frugal" suggests that consumerism as a way of life might be dying. Don't bet your wide-screen TV on it, though.

On the World Wide Web
Wal-Mart: http://www.wal-mart.com
Sears: http://www.sears.com
Kmart: http://www.kmart.com

PREVIEW OF CHAPTER 5

Wal-Mart, Kmart, and Sears are called merchandising companies because they buy and sell merchandise rather than perform services as their primary source of revenue. Merchandising companies that purchase and sell directly to consumers are called **retailers.** Merchandising companies that sell to retailers are known as **wholesalers.** For example, retailer Walgreens might buy goods from wholesaler McKesson and Robbins; retailer Office Depot might buy office supplies from wholesaler United Stationers.

Merchandising is one of the largest and most influential industries in the United States. Understanding the financial statements of these companies is important. The content and organization of the chapter are as follows:

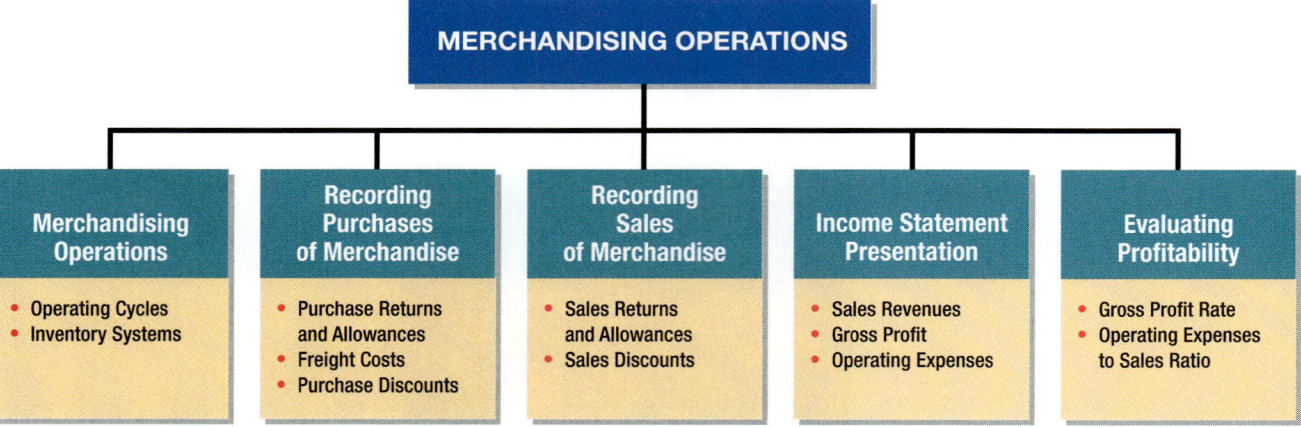

MERCHANDISING OPERATIONS

STUDY OBJECTIVE 1
Identify the differences between a service enterprise and a merchandising company.

The primary source of revenues for merchandising companies is the sale of merchandise, often referred to simply as **sales revenue** or **sales.** Expenses for a merchandising company are divided into two categories: the cost of goods sold and operating expenses.

The **cost of goods sold** is the total cost of merchandise sold during the period. This expense is directly related to the revenue recognized from the sale of goods. The income measurement process for a merchandising company is shown in Illustration 5-1. The items in the two blue boxes are unique to a merchandising company; they are not used by a service company.

Illustration 5-1 Income measurement process for a merchandising company

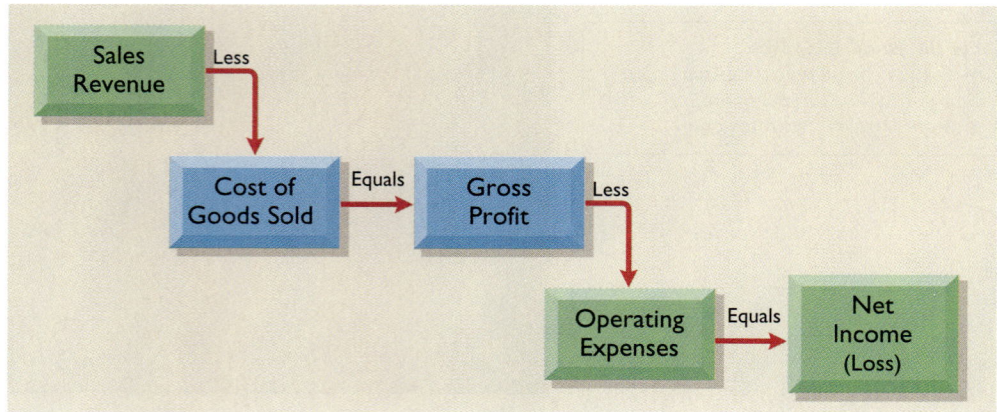

OPERATING CYCLES

The operating cycle of a merchandising company ordinarily is longer than that of a service company. The purchase of merchandise inventory and its eventual sale lengthen the cycle. Graphically, the operating cycles of service and merchandising companies can be contrasted as shown in Illustration 5-2. Note that the added asset account for a merchandising company is the Merchandise Inventory account.

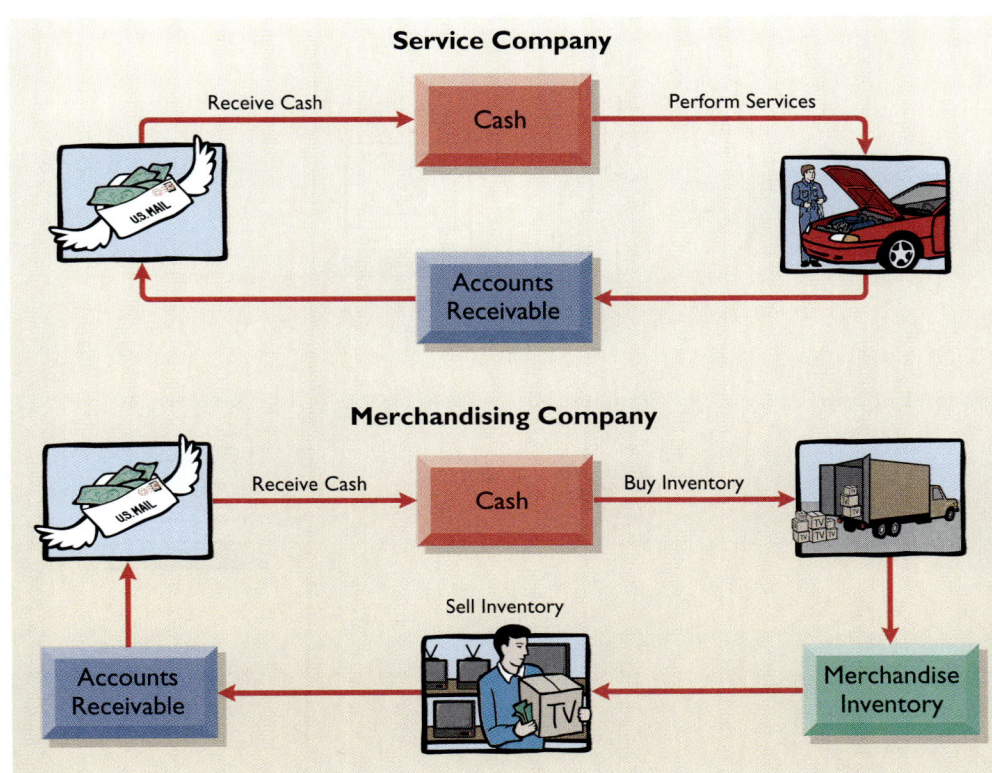

Illustration 5-2 Operating cycles for a service company and a merchandising company

INVENTORY SYSTEMS

A merchandising company keeps track of its inventory to determine what is available for sale and what has been sold. One of two systems is used to account for inventory: a **perpetual inventory system** or a **periodic inventory system.**

Perpetual System

In a **perpetual inventory system,** detailed records of the cost of each inventory purchase and sale are maintained and continuously—perpetually—show the inventory that should be on hand for every item. For example, a Ford dealership has separate inventory records for each automobile, truck, and van on its lot and showroom floor. Similarly, with the use of bar codes and optical scanners, a grocery store can keep a daily running record of every box of cereal and every jar of jelly that it buys and sells. Under a perpetual inventory system, the cost of goods sold is **determined each time a sale occurs.**

Periodic System

In a **periodic inventory system,** detailed inventory records of the goods on hand are not kept throughout the period. The cost of goods sold is **determined only at the end of the accounting period**—that is, periodically—when a physical inventory count is taken to determine the cost of goods on hand. To determine

Helpful Hint For control purposes a physical inventory count is taken under the perpetual system, even though it is not needed to determine cost of goods sold.

the cost of goods sold under a periodic inventory system, it is necessary to (1) determine the cost of goods on hand at the beginning of the accounting period, (2) add to it the cost of goods purchased, and (3) subtract the cost of goods on hand at the end of the accounting period.

Illustration 5-3 graphically compares the sequence of activities and the timing of the cost of goods sold computation under the two inventory systems.

Illustration 5-3 Comparing periodic and perpetual inventory systems

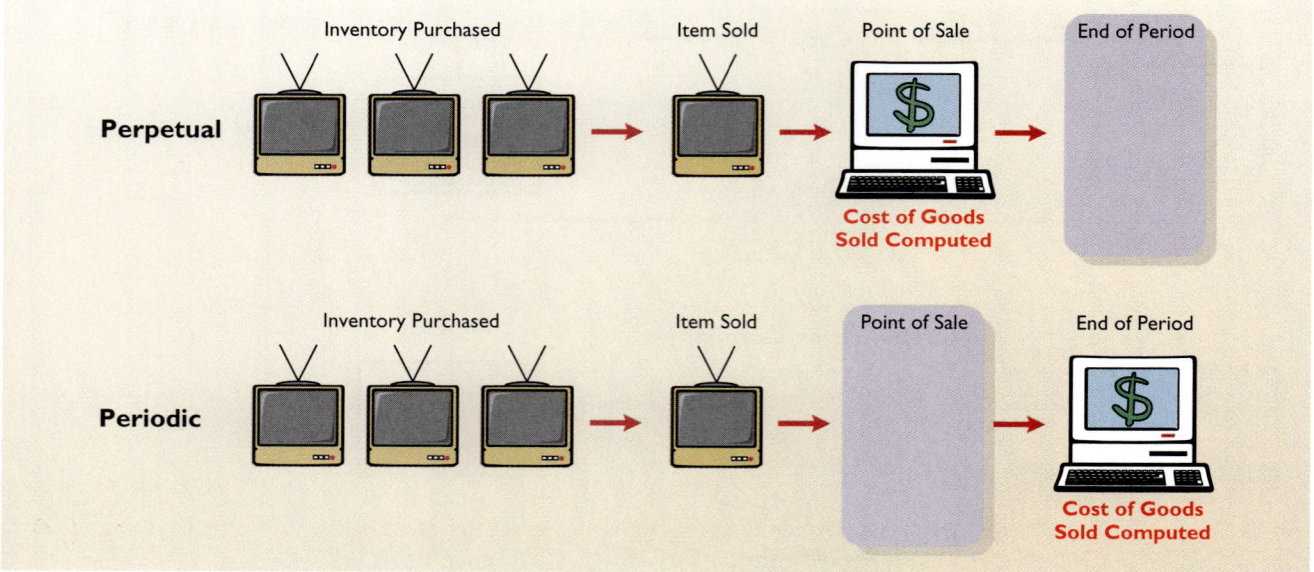

Additional Considerations

Perpetual systems have traditionally been used by companies that sell merchandise with high unit values, such as automobiles, furniture, and major home appliances. The recent widespread use of computers and electronic scanners has enabled many more companies to install perpetual inventory systems. The perpetual inventory system is so named because the accounting records continuously—perpetually—show the quantity and cost of the inventory that should be on hand at any time.

A perpetual inventory system provides better control over inventories than a periodic system. Since the inventory records show the quantities that should be on hand, the goods can be counted at any time to see whether they actually exist. Any shortages uncovered can be investigated immediately. Although a perpetual inventory system requires additional clerical work and additional cost to maintain the subsidiary records, a computerized system can minimize this cost.

Some businesses find it either unnecessary or uneconomical to invest in a computerized perpetual inventory system. Many small merchandising businesses, in particular, find that a perpetual inventory system costs more than it is worth. Managers of these businesses can control their merchandise and manage day-to-day operations without detailed inventory records by using a periodic inventory system.

Because the perpetual inventory system is growing in popularity and use, we illustrate it in this chapter. The periodic system, still widely used, is described in the next chapter.

BUSINESS INSIGHT
Investor Perspective

Investors are often eager to invest in a company that has a hot new product. However, when snowboard maker Morrow Snowboards, Inc., issued shares of stock to the public for the first time, some investors expressed reluctance to invest in Morrow because of a number of accounting control problems. To reduce investor concerns, Morrow implemented a perpetual inventory system to improve its control over inventory. In addition, it stated that it would perform a physical inventory count every quarter until it felt that the perpetual inventory system was reliable.

RECORDING PURCHASES OF MERCHANDISE

Purchases of inventory may be made for cash or on account (credit). Purchases are normally recorded when the goods are received from the seller. Every purchase should be supported by business documents that provide written evidence of the transaction. Each cash purchase should be supported by a canceled check or a cash register receipt indicating the items purchased and amounts paid. Cash purchases are recorded by an increase in Merchandise Inventory and a decrease in Cash.

Each credit purchase should be supported by a **purchase invoice,** which indicates the total purchase price and other relevant information. However, the purchaser does not prepare a separate purchase invoice. Instead, the copy of the sales invoice sent by the seller is used by the buyer as a purchase invoice. In Illustration 5-4 (page 206), for example, the sales invoice prepared by PW Audio Supply, Inc. (the seller), is used as a purchase invoice by Sauk Stereo (the buyer).

The associated entry for Sauk Stereo for the invoice from PW Audio Supply is:

May	4	Merchandise Inventory	3,800	
		Accounts Payable		3,800
		(To record goods purchased on account from PW Audio Supply)		

STUDY OBJECTIVE 2
Explain the recording of purchases under a perpetual inventory system.

Under the perpetual inventory system, purchases of merchandise for sale are recorded in the Merchandise Inventory account. Thus, Wal-Mart would increase (debit) Merchandise Inventory for clothing, sporting goods, and anything else purchased for resale to customers. Not all purchases are debited to Merchandise Inventory, however. Purchases of assets acquired for use and not for resale, such as supplies, equipment, and similar items, are recorded as increases to specific asset accounts rather than to Merchandise Inventory. For example, Wal-Mart would increase Supplies to record the purchase of materials used to make shelf signs or for cash register receipt paper.

Illustration 5-4 Sales invoice used as purchase invoice by Sauk Stereo

Helpful Hint To better understand the contents of this invoice, identify these items:
1. Seller
2. Invoice date
3. Purchaser
4. Salesperson
5. Credit terms
6. Freight terms
7. Goods sold: catalog number, description, quantity, price per unit
8. Total invoice amount

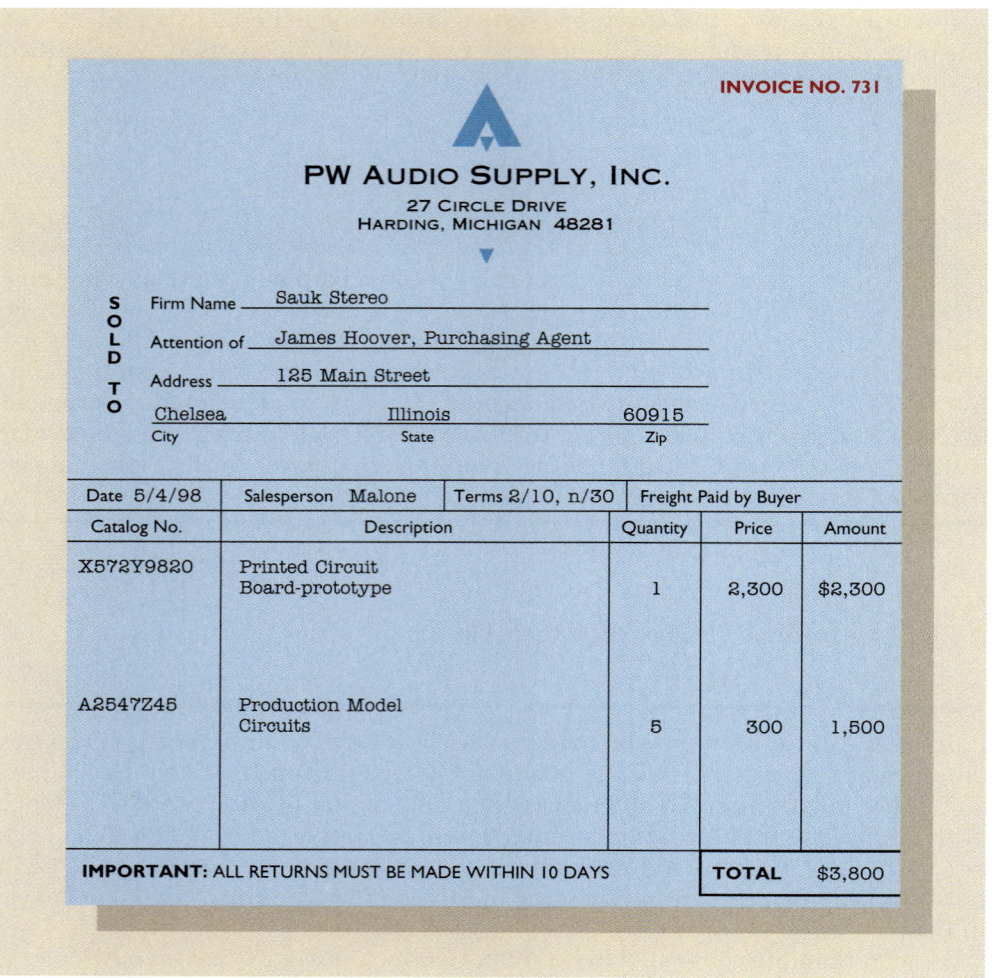

PURCHASE RETURNS AND ALLOWANCES

A purchaser may be dissatisfied with the merchandise received because the goods are damaged or defective, of inferior quality, or do not meet the purchaser's specifications. In such cases, the purchaser may return the goods to the seller for credit if the sale was made on credit, or for a cash refund if the purchase was for cash. This transaction is known as a **purchase return.** Alternatively, the purchaser may choose to keep the merchandise if the seller is willing to grant an allowance (deduction) from the purchase price. This transaction is known as a **purchase allowance.**

Assume that Sauk Stereo returned goods costing $300 to PW Audio Supply on May 8. The entry by Sauk Stereo for the returned merchandise is:

May	8	Accounts Payable	300	
		Merchandise Inventory		300
		(To record return of goods received		
		from PW Audio Supply)		

Because Sauk Stereo increased Merchandise Inventory when the goods were received, Merchandise Inventory is decreased when Sauk returns the goods.

FREIGHT COSTS

The sales invoice indicates whether the seller or the buyer pays the cost of transporting the goods to the buyer's place of business. When the buyer pays the transportation costs, these costs are considered part of the cost of purchasing inventory. As a result, the account Merchandise Inventory is increased. For example, if upon delivery of the goods on May 6, Sauk Stereo pays Acme Freight Company $150 for freight charges, the entry on Sauk's books is:

May	6	Merchandise Inventory	150	
		Cash		150
		(To record payment of freight)		

In contrast, **freight costs incurred by the seller on outgoing merchandise are an operating expense to the seller.** These costs increase an expense account titled Freight-out or Delivery Expense. For example, if the freight terms on the invoice in Illustration 5-4 had required that PW Audio Supply pay the $150 freight charges, the entry by PW Audio would be:

May	4	Freight-out	150	
		Cash		150
		(To record payment of freight on goods sold)		

When the freight charges are paid by the seller, the seller will usually establish a higher invoice price for the goods, to cover the expense of shipping.

PURCHASE DISCOUNTS

The credit terms of a purchase on account may permit the buyer to claim a cash discount for prompt payment. The buyer calls this cash discount a **purchase discount.** This incentive offers advantages to both parties: The purchaser saves money, and the seller is able to shorten the operating cycle by converting the accounts receivable into cash earlier.

The **credit terms** specify the amount of the cash discount and time period during which it is offered. They also indicate the length of time in which the purchaser is expected to pay the full invoice price. In the sales invoice in Illustration 5-4, credit terms are 2/10, n/30, which is read "two-ten, net thirty." This means that a 2% cash discount may be taken on the invoice price, less ("net of") any returns or allowances, if payment is made within 10 days of the invoice date (the **discount period**); otherwise, the invoice price, less any returns or allowances, is due 30 days from the invoice date. Alternatively, the discount period may extend to a specified number of days following the month in which the sale occurs. For example, 1/10 EOM (end of month) means that a 1% discount is available if the invoice is paid within the first 10 days of the next month.

When the seller elects not to offer a cash discount for prompt payment, credit terms will specify only the maximum time period for paying the balance due. For example, the time period may be stated as n/30, n/60, or n/10 EOM, meaning, respectively, that the net amount must be paid in 30 days, 60 days, or within the first 10 days of the next month.

When an invoice is paid within the discount period, the amount of the discount decreases Merchandise Inventory because inventory is recorded at its cost and, by paying within the discount period, the merchandiser has reduced its cost. To illustrate, assume Sauk Stereo pays the balance due of $3,500 (gross in-

Helpful Hint The term *net* in "net 30" means the remaining amount due after subtracting any sales returns and allowances and partial payments.

voice price of $3,800 less purchase returns and allowances of $300) on May 14, the last day of the discount period. The cash discount is $70 ($3,500 × 2%), and the amount of cash paid by Sauk Stereo is $3,430 ($3,500 − $70). The entry to record the May 14 payment by Sauk Stereo is:

May 14	Accounts Payable	3,500	
	Cash		3,430
	Merchandise Inventory		70
	(To record payment within discount period)		

If Sauk Stereo failed to take the discount and instead made full payment on June 3, Sauk's entry is:

June 3	Accounts Payable	3,500	
	Cash		3,500
	(To record payment with no discount taken)		

BUSINESS INSIGHT
Management Perspective

In the early 1990s, Sears wielded its retail clout by telling its suppliers that, rather than pay its obligations in the standard 30-day period, it would now pay in 60 days. This practice is often adopted by firms that are experiencing financial distress from a shortage of cash. A Sears spokesperson insisted, however, that Sears did not have cash problems but, rather, was simply utilizing "vendor-financed inventory methods to improve its return on investment." Supplier trade groups have been outspoken critics of Sears' new policy and have suggested that consumers will be the ultimate victims, because the financing costs will eventually be passed on to them.

Source: The Wall Street Journal, August 15, 1991.

A merchandising company usually should take all available discounts. For example, if Sauk Stereo takes the discount, it pays $70 less in cash. Conversely, if it forgoes the discount and invests the $3,500 in a bank savings account for 20 days at 6% interest, it will earn only $11.67 in interest. The savings obtained by taking the discount is computed as in Illustration 5-5.

Illustration 5-5 Savings obtained by taking purchase discount

Discount of 2% on $3,500	$70.00
Interest received on $3,500 (for 20 days at 6%)	11.67
Savings by taking the discount	**$58.33**

Helpful Hint So as not to miss purchase discounts, unpaid invoices should be filed by due dates. This procedure helps the purchaser remember the discount date, prevents early payment of bills, and maximizes the time that cash can be used for other purposes.

Alternatively, passing up the discount may be viewed as **paying an interest rate of 2%** for the use of $3,500 for 20 days. This is the equivalent of an annual interest rate of 36% (2% × 360/20).[1] Obviously, it would be better for Sauk Stereo to borrow at prevailing bank interest rates of 8% to 12% than to lose the discount.

---
[1] For simplicity, we use 360 days rather than 365.

DECISION TOOLKIT

Decision Checkpoints	Info Needed for Decision	Tool to Use for Decision	How to Evaluate Results
Should the company pay early to take advantage of cash discount?	Terms of purchase contract; interest rate on savings	Cash savings today versus interest revenue that could be earned	Take cash discount if discount is greater than interest revenue that would be earned if cash is not paid until the end of discount period.

BEFORE YOU GO ON . . .

● **Review It**

1. How does the measurement of net income in a merchandising company differ from that in a service enterprise?
2. In what ways is a perpetual inventory system different from a periodic system?
3. Under the perpetual inventory system, what entries are made to record purchases, purchase returns and allowances, purchase discounts, and freight costs?

RECORDING SALES OF MERCHANDISE

STUDY OBJECTIVE 3

Explain the recording of sales revenues under a perpetual inventory system.

Sales revenues, like service revenues, are recorded when earned. This is in accordance with the revenue recognition principle. Typically, sales revenues are earned when the goods are transferred from the seller to the buyer. At this point the sales transaction is completed and the sales price is established.

Sales may be made on credit or for cash. Every sales transaction should be supported by a **business document** that provides written evidence of the sale. **Cash register tapes** provide evidence of cash sales. A **sales invoice,** like the one that was shown in Illustration 5-4, provides support for a credit sale. The original copy of the invoice goes to the customer, and a copy is kept by the seller for use in recording the sale. The invoice shows the date of sale, customer name, total sales price, and other relevant information.

Two entries are made for each sale. The first entry records the sale: Assuming a cash sale, Cash is increased by a debit and Sales is increased by a credit at the selling (invoice) price of the goods. The second entry records the cost of the merchandise sold: Again assuming a cash sale, Cost of Goods Sold is increased by a debit and Merchandise Inventory is decreased by a credit for the cost of those goods. For example, assume that on May 4 PW Audio Supply has cash sales of $2,200 from merchandise having a cost of $1,400. The entries to record the day's cash sales are as follows:

May	4	Cash	2,200	
		Sales		2,200
		(To record daily cash sales)		
	4	Cost of Goods Sold	1,400	
		Merchandise Inventory		1,400
		(To record cost of merchandise sold for cash)		

For credit sales (1) Accounts Receivable is increased and Sales is increased, and (2) Cost of Goods Sold is increased and Merchandise Inventory is decreased. As a result, the Merchandise Inventory account will show at all times the amount of inventory that should be on hand. To illustrate a credit sales transaction, PW Audio Supply's sale of $3,800 on May 4 to Sauk Stereo (see Illustration 5-4) is recorded as follows (assume the merchandise cost PW Audio Supply $2,400):

May	4	Accounts Receivable	3,800	
		Sales		3,800
		(To record credit sale to Sauk Stereo per invoice #731)		
	4	Cost of Goods Sold	2,400	
		Merchandise Inventory		2,400
		(To record cost of merchandise sold on invoice #731 to Sauk Stereo)		

Helpful Hint The Sales account is credited only for sales of goods held for resale. Sales of assets not held for resale, such as equipment or land, are credited directly to the asset account.

For internal decision-making purposes, merchandising companies may use more than one sales account. For example, PW Audio Supply may decide to keep separate sales accounts for its sales of TV sets, videocassette recorders, and microwave ovens. By using separate sales accounts for major product lines, rather than a single combined sales account, company management can monitor sales trends more closely and respond in a more appropriate strategic fashion to changes in sales patterns. For example, if TV sales are increasing while microwave oven sales are decreasing, the company should reevaluate both its advertising and pricing policies on each of these items to ensure they are optimal. It should be noted that on the income statement presented to outside investors a merchandising company would normally provide only a single sales figure—the sum of all of its individual sales accounts. This is done for two reasons. First, providing detail on all of its individual sales accounts would add considerable length to its income statement. Second, companies do not want their competitors to know the details of their operating results.

SALES RETURNS AND ALLOWANCES

We now look at the "flipside" of purchase returns and allowances, which are recorded as **sales returns and allowances** on the books of the seller. PW Audio Supply's entries to record credit for returned goods involve (1) an increase in Sales Returns and Allowances and a decrease in Accounts Receivable at the $300 selling price, and (2) an increase in Merchandise Inventory (assume a $140 cost) and a decrease in Cost of Goods Sold as follows:

May	8	Sales Returns and Allowances	300	
		Accounts Receivable		300
		(To record return of goods delivered to Sauk Stereo)		
	8	Merchandise Inventory	140	
		Cost of Goods Sold		140
		(To record cost of goods returned)		

Helpful Hint Remember that the increases, decreases, and normal balances of contra accounts are the opposite of the accounts to which they correspond.

Sales Returns and Allowances is a **contra revenue account** to Sales. The normal balance of Sales Returns and Allowances is a debit. A contra account is used, instead of debiting Sales, to disclose in the accounts and in the income statement the amount of sales returns and allowances. Disclosure of this information is important to management: Excessive returns and allowances suggest inferior merchandise, inefficiencies in filling orders, errors in billing customers, and mistakes in delivery or shipment of goods. Moreover, a decrease (debit) recorded directly to Sales would obscure the relative importance of sales returns and allowances as a percentage of sales. It also could distort comparisons between total sales in different accounting periods.

> **BUSINESS INSIGHT**
> ### Investor Perspective
>
> How high is too high? Returns can become so high that it is questionable whether sales revenue should have been recognized in the first place. An example of high returns is Florafax International Inc., a floral supply company, which was alleged to ship its product without customer authorization on ten holiday occasions, including 8,562 shipments of flowers to customers for Mother's Day and 6,575 for Secretary's Day. The return rate on these shipments went as high as 69% of sales. As one employee noted: "Products went out the front door and came in the back door."

SALES DISCOUNTS

As mentioned in our discussion of purchase transactions, the seller may offer the customer a cash discount—called by the seller a **sales discount**—for the prompt payment of the balance due. Like a purchase discount, a sales discount is based on the invoice price less returns and allowances, if any. The Sales Discounts account is increased (debited) for discounts that are taken. The entry by PW Audio Supply to record the cash receipt on May 14 from Sauk Stereo within the discount period is

May 14	Cash	3,430	
	Sales Discounts	70	
	Accounts Receivable		3,500
	(To record collection within 2/10, n/30		
	discount period from Sauk Stereo)		

Like Sales Returns and Allowances, Sales Discounts is a **contra revenue account** to Sales. Its normal balance is a debit. This account is used, instead of debiting sales, to disclose the amount of cash discounts taken by customers. If the discount is not taken, PW Audio Supply increases Cash for $3,500 and decreases Accounts Receivable for the same amount at the date of collection.

INCOME STATEMENT PRESENTATION

The income statement for a merchandising company presents three amounts not shown in a service company income statement. They are: (1) sales revenues, (2) cost of goods sold, and (3) gross profit.

STUDY OBJECTIVE 4
Identify the unique features of the financial statements for a merchandising company.

SALES REVENUES

The income statement for a merchandising company typically presents gross sales revenues for the period and provides details about deductions from that total amount. As contra revenue accounts, sales returns and allowances and sales discounts are deducted from sales in the income statement to arrive at **net sales.** The sales revenues section of the income statement for PW Audio Supply is shown in Illustration 5-6.

Illustration 5-6 Statement presentation of sales revenues section

PW AUDIO SUPPLY, INC.
Income Statement (Partial)

Sales revenues		
Sales		$ 480,000
Less: Sales returns and allowances	$12,000	
Sales discounts	8,000	20,000
Net sales		**$460,000**

GROSS PROFIT

In Illustration 5-1 we saw that **cost of goods sold** is deducted from sales revenue to determine **gross profit.** Sales revenue used for this computation is **net sales,** which takes into account sales returns and allowances and sales discounts. On the basis of the sales data presented in Illustration 5-6 (net sales of $460,000) and the cost of goods sold (assume a balance of $316,000), the gross profit for PW Audio Supply is $144,000, computed as follows:

Net sales	$ 460,000
Cost of goods sold	316,000
Gross profit	**$144,000**

It is important to understand what gross profit is—and what it is not. Gross profit represents the **merchandising profit** of a company. It is *not* a measure of the overall profit of a company because operating expenses have not been deducted. Nevertheless, the amount and trend of gross profit are closely watched by management and other interested parties. Comparisons of current gross profit with past amounts and rates and with those in the industry indicate the effectiveness of a company's purchasing and pricing policies.

OPERATING EXPENSES

Operating expenses are the third component in measuring net income for a merchandising company. As indicated earlier, these expenses are similar in merchandising and service enterprises. At PW Audio Supply, operating expenses were $114,000. The firm's net income is determined by subtracting operating expenses from gross profit. Thus, net income is $30,000 as shown below:

Gross profit	$144,000
Operating expenses	114,000
Net income	$ 30,000

The net income amount is the "bottom line" of a company's income statement. Using assumed data for specific operating expenses, we can complete the income statement for PW Audio Supply as shown in Illustration 5-7.

Illustration 5-7 Income statement for a merchandising company

```
                    PW AUDIO SUPPLY, INC.
                      Income Statement
               For the Year Ended December 31, 1998
```

Sales revenues		
Sales		$480,000
Less: Sales returns and allowances	$12,000	
Sales discounts	8,000	20,000
Net sales		460,000
Cost of goods sold		316,000
Gross profit		144,000
Operating expenses		
Store salaries expense	45,000	
Rent expense	19,000	
Utilities expense	17,000	
Advertising expense	16,000	
Depreciation expense—store equipment	8,000	
Freight-out	7,000	
Insurance expense	2,000	
Total operating expenses		114,000
Net income		$ 30,000

Helpful Hint What is and is not disclosed?
1. Did company sell on credit? Yes, it had sales discounts.
2. Did company take all purchase discounts? Don't know; purchase discounts taken are not reported.

BEFORE YOU GO ON . . .

● **Review It**

1. Under the perpetual inventory system, what entries are made to record sales, sales returns and allowances, and sales discounts?
2. How are sales and contra revenue accounts reported in the income statement?
3. What is the significance of gross profit?

EVALUATING PROFITABILITY

GROSS PROFIT RATE

A company's gross profit may be expressed as a **percentage** by dividing the amount of gross profit by net sales; this is referred to as the **gross profit rate.** For PW Audio Supply the gross profit rate is 31.3% ($144,000 ÷ $460,000). The gross profit *rate* is generally considered to be more informative than the gross profit *amount* because it expresses a more meaningful (qualitative) relationship between gross profit and net sales. For example, a gross profit amount of $1,000,000 may sound impressive. But if it was the result of sales of $100,000,000, it means the company's gross profit rate was only 1%. A 1% gross profit rate is acceptable in only a few industries.

A decline in a company's gross profit rate might have several causes. The company may have begun to sell products with a lower "markup"—for example, budget blue jeans versus designer blue jeans. Increased competition may have resulted in a lower selling price. Or, the company may be forced to pay higher prices to its suppliers without being able to pass these costs on to its customers. The gross profit rates for Wal-Mart and Kmart are presented in Illustration 5-8.

STUDY OBJECTIVE 5
Explain the factors affecting profitability.

Illustration 5-8 Gross profit rate

($ in millions)	1995	1994
Wal-Mart	$19,063 / $93,627 = 20.4%	$16,908 / $82,494 = 20.5%
Kmart	$7,393 / $34,389 = 21.5%	$7,646 / $32,514 = 23.5%

GROSS PROFIT RATE = GROSS PROFIT / NET SALES

In its Management Discussion and Analysis, Kmart explained that its lower gross profit rate in 1995 was due to "aggressive clearance of discontinued inventory at stores closed during the year. The decrease also reflects a mix of both apparel and hard-line merchandise more heavily weighted toward promotional items and lower-margin merchandise." It goes on to say that the company anticipates a reduction of clearance items as well as a higher percentage of high-margin items in the future, and thus they anticipate a higher gross profit. At first glance it might be surprising that Wal-Mart has a lower gross profit rate than Kmart. It is likely, however, that this can be explained by the fact that grocery products are becoming an increasing component of Wal-Mart's sales. Grocery products tend to have very low gross profit rates. Also, Wal-Mart is expanding its warehouse-style sales in its Sam's Club stores, which are a low-margin, high-volume operation.

BUSINESS INSIGHT
Management Perspective

In a recent year Woolworth Corporation reported a gross profit rate of 32%; J. C. Penney, 31%; Best Buy, 15%; and Circuit City, 28%. Gross profit is critical. "If you don't have someone monitoring it," says one business consultant, "you are asking for instant death." A decline should trigger a search for the cause. The drop could be due to an increase in cost of goods sold or a decrease in sales revenue, either of which needs prompt attention. The change may be temporary and easily reversed, or it may signal the beginning of a bad trend.

DECISION TOOLKIT

Decision Checkpoints	Info Needed for Decision	Tool to Use for Decision	How to Evaluate Results
Is the price of goods keeping pace with changes in the cost of inventory?	Gross profit and net sales	Gross profit rate = Gross profit / Net sales	Higher ratio suggests the average margin between selling price and inventory cost is increasing. Too high a margin may result in lost sales.

OPERATING EXPENSES TO SALES RATIO

A useful measure of operating expenses is the ratio of **operating expenses to sales.** In recent years many companies have improved the efficiency of their operations, thus reducing the ratio of operating expenses to sales. As a consequence, they have increased their profitability. The record profits of many companies in the 1990s were achieved as much by reducing costs as by increasing revenues. The use of computers and changes in organizational structure have brought added efficiency. For example, one study of 1,000 companies that successfully reengineered their warehouse operations by employing new technologies found savings on labor costs averaging 25%. Epson Computers, for example, reported space savings of 50%, labor savings of 43%, and operating cost savings of 25% on their warehouses. Operating costs have been reduced to such low levels for so many companies that many investors believe further improvements in corporate profits from cost reductions will be difficult to accomplish.

The ratios of operating expenses to sales for Wal-Mart and Kmart are presented in Illustration 5-9. The ratios suggest that Wal-Mart is significantly better at controlling its operating costs than is Kmart: In 1995 Wal-Mart incurred 16 cents of operating costs for every sales dollar, whereas Kmart incurred 22 cents per sales dollar. One reason Wal-Mart has been so successful is that it has had a very lean organizational structure, with highly effective information systems that allow it to rapidly adapt to changing conditions.

$$\text{OPERATING EXPENSES TO SALES RATIO} = \frac{\text{OPERATING EXPENSES}}{\text{NET SALES}}$$

($ in millions)	1995	1994
Wal-Mart	$\frac{\$14,951}{\$93,627} = 16.0\%$	$\frac{\$12,858}{\$82,494} = 15.6\%$
Kmart	$\frac{\$7,554}{\$34,389} = 22.0\%$	$\frac{\$7,376}{\$32,514} = 22.7\%$

Illustration 5-9 Operating expenses to sales ratio

BUSINESS INSIGHT
Investor Perspective

In this chapter we have compared the gross profit rates and operating expenses to sales ratios of Kmart and Wal-Mart—two fierce competitors in the retail wars. Although such comparisons are vital to an analysis of either of these companies, we must now alert you to one problem often encountered in such comparisons: Companies do not always classify expenses in the same way. Kmart includes buying and occupancy costs in cost of goods sold, whereas Wal-Mart includes these expenses in the operating expense line item. Thus, in comparing these ratios across these two companies, we should recognize that at least some of the difference in the value of the ratios is due simply to this difference in classification. Since neither company provides sufficient detail in its footnotes to enable us to adjust the figures to similar presentation, we can at best make a rough comparison.

BEFORE YOU GO ON . . .

● **Review It**

1. How is the gross profit rate calculated? What might cause it to decline?
2. What effect does improved efficiency of operations have on the operating expenses to sales ratio?

DECISION TOOLKIT

Decision Checkpoints	Info Needed for Decision	Tool to Use for Decision	How to Evaluate Results
Is management controlling operating costs?	Net sales and operating expenses	Operating expenses to sales ratio = $\dfrac{\text{Operating expenses}}{\text{Net sales}}$	Higher value should be investigated to determine whether cost cutting is necessary.

*U*SING THE DECISION TOOLKIT

Sears is currently the number 3 retailer in the United States behind Wal-Mart and Kmart. Many analysts are suggesting that Sears has turned itself around. In 1992 it shocked and disappointed many loyal customers by closing its catalog business. In 1993 Sears closed 113 stores and eliminated 50,000 jobs. Although Sears wants to surpass Wal-Mart and Kmart, it is aiming for a different niche. It is directing itself more toward clothing and "hardline" items rather than toward being a discounter. The following financial data are available for Sears:

($ in millions)	1995	1994
Net income	$ 1,801	$ 1,454
Beginning total assets	37,312	37,911
Ending total assets	33,130	37,312
Sales	31,035	29,451
Cost of goods sold	22,866	21,568
Operating expenses	8,981	8,724

Instructions
Using the basic facts in the table, evaluate the following components of Sears's profitability for 1995 and 1994:

    Return on assets ratio
    Profit margin ratio
    Gross profit rate
    Operating expenses to sales ratio

How do Sears's gross profit rate and operating expenses to sales ratio compare to those of Wal-Mart and Kmart?

Solution

($ in millions)	1995	1994
Return on assets ratio	$\dfrac{\$1{,}801}{(\$33{,}130 + \$37{,}312)/2} = 5.1\%$	$\dfrac{\$1{,}454}{(\$37{,}312 + \$37{,}911)/2} = 3.9\%$
Profit margin ratio	$\dfrac{\$1{,}801}{\$31{,}035} = 5.8\%$	$\dfrac{\$1{,}454}{\$29{,}451} = 4.9\%$
Gross profit rate	$\dfrac{\$31{,}035 - \$22{,}866}{\$31{,}035} = 26.3\%$	$\dfrac{\$29{,}451 - \$21{,}568}{\$29{,}451} = 26.8\%$
Operating expenses to sales ratio	$\dfrac{\$8{,}981}{\$31{,}035} = 28.9\%$	$\dfrac{\$8{,}724}{\$29{,}451} = 29.6\%$

The return on assets ratio for Sears improved considerably from 1994 to 1995—from 3.9% to 5.1%, which was a 31% increase [(5.1% − 3.9%) ÷ 3.9%]. This increase was the result of a number of factors. The profit margin ratio (income per dollar of sales) increased from 4.9% to 5.8%. This can be attributed to the closing of nonprofitable stores and the liquidation of nonprofitable businesses. The gross profit rate remained relatively constant, while the operating expenses incurred per dollar of sales declined, a further indication that Sears is becoming more efficient. Thus, overall, it appears that most of its increase in profitability was the result of improved control over costs.

Sears's 1995 gross profit rate of 26.3% exceeds that of both Wal-Mart (20.4%) and Kmart (21.5%), suggesting that it can command a higher markup on its goods. However, Sears's ratio of operating expenses to sales of 28.9% suggests that it is not able to control its costs as well as Wal-Mart (16.0%) and Kmart (22.0%).

SUMMARY OF STUDY OBJECTIVES

❶ Identify the differences between a service enterprise and a merchandising company. Because of the presence of inventory, a merchandising company has sales revenue, cost of goods sold, and gross profit. To account for inventory, a merchandising company must choose between a perpetual inventory system and a periodic inventory system.

❷ Explain the recording of purchases under a perpetual inventory system. The Merchandise Inventory account is debited for all purchases of merchandise and for freight costs, and it is credited for purchase discounts and purchase returns and allowances.

❸ Explain the recording of sales revenues under a perpetual inventory system. When inventory is sold, Accounts Receivable (or Cash) is debited and Sales is credited for the selling price of the merchandise. At the same time, Cost of Goods Sold is debited and Merchandise Inventory is credited for the cost of inventory items sold. When sales revenues are recorded, entries are required for (a) cash and credit sales, (b) sales returns and allowances, and (c) sales discounts.

❹ Identify the unique features of the financial statements for a merchandising company. The income statement for a merchandising company contains three unique features: sales revenue, cost of goods sold, and gross profit. The balance sheet for a merchandiser includes merchandise inventory as part of current assets.

❺ Explain the factors affecting profitability. Profitability is affected by gross profit, as measured by the gross profit rate, and by management's ability to control costs, as measured by the ratio of operating expenses to sales.

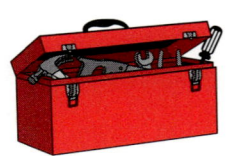

Decision Toolkit—A Summary

Decision Checkpoints	Info Needed for Decision	Tool to Use for Decision	How to Evaluate Results
Should the company pay early to take advantage of cash discount?	Terms of purchase contract; interest rate on savings	Cash savings today versus interest revenue that could be earned	Take cash discount if discount is greater than interest revenue that would be earned if cash is not paid until the end of discount period.
Is the price of goods keeping pace with changes in the cost of inventory?	Gross profit and net sales	Gross profit rate = $\dfrac{\text{Gross profit}}{\text{Net sales}}$	Higher ratio suggests the average margin between selling price and inventory cost is increasing. Too high a margin may result in lost sales.
Is management controlling operating costs?	Net sales and operating expenses	Operating expenses to sales ratio = $\dfrac{\text{Operating expenses}}{\text{Net sales}}$	Higher value should be investigated to determine whether cost cutting is necessary.

Glossary

Contra revenue account An account that is offset against a revenue account on the income statement. (p. 210)

Cost of goods sold The total cost of merchandise sold during the period. (p. 202)

Gross profit The excess of net sales over the cost of goods sold. (p. 212)

Gross profit rate Gross profit expressed as a percentage by dividing the amount of gross profit by net sales. (p. 213)

Net sales Sales less sales returns and allowances and sales discounts. (p. 212)

Operating expenses to sales ratio A measure that indicates whether a company is controlling operating expenses relative to each dollar of sales. (p. 215)

Periodic inventory system An inventory system in which detailed records are not maintained and the cost of goods sold is determined only at the end of an accounting period. (p. 203)

Perpetual inventory system A detailed inventory system in which the cost of each inventory item is maintained and the records continuously show the inventory that should be on hand. (p. 203)

Purchase discount A cash discount claimed by a buyer for prompt payment of a balance due. (p. 207)

Purchase invoice A document that supports each credit purchase. (p. 205)

Sales discount A reduction given by a seller for prompt payment of a credit sale. (p. 211)

Sales invoice A document that provides support for credit sales. (p. 209)

Sales revenue Primary source of revenue in a merchandising company. (p. 202)

Demonstration Problem

The adjusted trial balance for the year ended December 31, 1998, for Dykstra Company is shown on the next page.

Demonstration Problem

DYKSTRA COMPANY
Adjusted Trial Balance
For the Year Ended December 31, 1998

	Dr.	Cr.
Cash	$ 14,500	
Accounts Receivable	11,100	
Merchandise Inventory	29,000	
Prepaid Insurance	2,500	
Store Equipment	95,000	
Accumulated Depreciation		$ 18,000
Notes Payable		25,000
Accounts Payable		10,600
Common Stock		70,000
Retained Earnings		11,000
Dividends	12,000	
Sales		536,800
Sales Returns and Allowances	6,700	
Sales Discounts	5,000	
Cost of Goods Sold	363,400	
Freight-out	7,600	
Advertising Expense	12,000	
Store Salaries Expense	56,000	
Utilities Expense	18,000	
Rent Expense	24,000	
Depreciation Expense	9,000	
Insurance Expense	4,500	
Interest Expense	3,600	
Interest Revenue		2,500
	$673,900	$673,900

Instructions
Prepare an income statement assuming Dykstra Company does not use subgroupings for operating expenses.

Solution to Demonstration Problem

DYKSTRA COMPANY
Income Statement
For the Year Ended December 31, 1998

Sales revenues		
Sales		$536,800
Less: Sales returns and allowances	$ 6,700	
Sales discounts	5,000	11,700
Net sales		525,100
Cost of goods sold		363,400
Gross profit		161,700
Operating expenses		
Store salaries expense	56,000	
Rent expense	24,000	
Utilities expense	18,000	
Advertising expense	12,000	
Depreciation expense	9,000	
Freight-out	7,600	
Insurance expense	4,500	
Total operating expenses		131,100
Income from operations		30,600
Other revenues and gains		
Interest revenue	2,500	
Other expenses and losses		
Interest expense	3,600	1,100
Net income		$ 29,500

Problem-Solving Strategies

1. In preparing the income statement, remember that the key components are net sales, cost of goods sold, gross profit, total operating expenses, and net income (loss). These components are reported in the right-hand column of the income statement.
2. Nonoperating items follow income from operations.

Self-Study Questions

Answers are at the end of the chapter.

(SO 4) 1. Gross profit will result if:
  (a) operating expenses are less than net income.
  (b) sales revenues are greater than operating expenses.
  (c) sales revenues are greater than cost of goods sold.
  (d) operating expenses are greater than cost of goods sold.

(SO 3) 2. Which sales accounts normally have a debit balance?
  (a) Sales discounts
  (b) Sales returns and allowances
  (c) Both (a) and (b)
  (d) Neither (a) nor (b)

(SO 3) 3. A credit sale of $750 is made on June 13, terms 2/10, n/30, on which a return of $50 is granted on June 16. What amount is received as payment in full on June 23?
  (a) $700   (c) $685
  (b) $686   (d) $650

(SO 2) 4. Which of the following statements about a periodic inventory system is true?
  (a) Cost of goods sold is determined only at the end of the accounting period.
  (b) Detailed records of the cost of each inventory purchase and sale are maintained continuously.
  (c) The periodic system provides better control over inventories than a perpetual system.
  (d) The increased use of computerized systems has increased the use of the periodic system.

(SO 2) 5. Which of the following items does *not* result in an adjustment in the merchandise inventory account under a perpetual system?
  (a) A purchase of merchandise
  (b) A return of merchandise inventory to the supplier
  (c) Payment of freight costs for goods shipped to a customer
  (d) Payment of freight costs for goods received from a supplier

(SO 4) 6. If sales revenues are $400,000, cost of goods sold is $310,000, and operating expenses are $60,000, what is the gross profit?
  (a) $30,000   (c) $340,000
  (b) $90,000   (d) $400,000

(SO 4) 7. The income statement for a merchandising company shows each of these features *except:*
  (a) gross profit.
  (b) cost of goods sold.
  (c) a sales revenue section.
  (d) All of these are present.

(SO 5) 8. Which of the following would *not* affect the operating expenses to sales ratio? (Assume sales remains constant.)
  (a) An increase in advertising expense
  (b) A decrease in depreciation expense
  (c) An increase in cost of goods sold
  (d) A decrease in insurance expense

(SO 5) 9. The gross profit *rate* is equal to:
  (a) net income divided by sales.
  (b) cost of goods sold divided by sales.
  (c) sales minus cost of goods sold, divided by net sales.
  (d) sales minus cost of goods sold, divided by cost of goods sold.

(SO 5) 10. Which factor would *not* affect the gross profit rate?
  (a) An increase in the cost of heating the store
  (b) An increase in the sale of luxury items
  (c) An increase in the use of "discount pricing" to sell merchandise
  (d) An increase in the price of inventory items

Questions

1. (a) "The steps in the accounting cycle for a merchandising company are different from the steps in the accounting cycle for a service enterprise." Do you agree or disagree?
   (b) Is the measurement of net income in a merchandising company conceptually the same as in a service enterprise? Explain.

2. How do the components of revenues and expenses differ between a merchandising company and a service enterprise?

3. (a) Explain the income measurement process in a merchandising company.
   (b) How does income measurement differ between a merchandising company and a service company?

4. Chuck Rudy Co. has sales revenue of $100,000, cost of goods sold of $70,000, and operating expenses of $20,000. What is its gross profit?

5. Joan Hollins believes revenues from credit sales may be earned before they are collected in cash. Do you agree? Explain.

6. (a) What is the primary source document for recording (1) cash sales and (2) credit sales.
   (b) Using XXs for amounts, give the journal entry for each of the transactions in part (a).

7. A credit sale is made on July 10 for $900, terms 2/10, n/30. On July 12, $100 of goods are returned for credit. Give the journal entry on July 19 to record the receipt of the balance due within the discount period.

8. Goods costing $1,600 are purchased on account on July 15 with credit terms of 2/10, n/30. On July 18 a $100 credit memo is received from the supplier for damaged goods. Give the journal entry on July 24 to record payment of the balance due within the discount period.
9. Anna Ford Company reports net sales of $800,000, gross profit of $580,000, and net income of $300,000. What are its operating expenses?
10. Identify the distinguishing features of an income statement for a merchandising company.
11. Why is the normal operating cycle for a merchandising company likely to be longer than for a service company?
12. What merchandising account(s) will appear in the post-closing trial balance?
13. What types of businesses are most likely to use a perpetual inventory system?
14. What two ratios measure factors that affect profitability?
15. What factors affect a company's gross profit rate—that is, what can cause the gross profit rate to increase and what can cause it to decrease?

BRIEF EXERCISES

BE5-1 Presented here are the components in Sang Nam Company's income statement. Determine the missing amounts.

Compute missing amounts in determining net income.
(SO 4)

Sales	Cost of Goods Sold	Gross Profit	Operating Expenses	Net Income
$ 75,000	(b)	$ 43,500	(d)	$10,800
$108,000	$65,000	(c)	(e)	$29,500
(a)	$71,900	$109,600	$39,500	(f)

BE5-2 Keo Company buys merchandise on account from Mayo Company. The selling price of the goods is $900 and the cost of goods is $600. Both companies use perpetual inventory systems. Journalize the transactions on the books of both companies.

Journalize perpetual inventory entries.
(SO 2, 3)

BE5-3 Prepare the journal entries to record the following transactions on H. Hunt Company's books using a perpetual inventory system.
(a) On March 2 H. Hunt Company sold $900,000 of merchandise to B. Streisand Company, terms 2/10, n/30. The cost of the merchandise sold was $600,000.
(b) On March 6 B. Streisand Company returned $130,000 of the merchandise purchased on March 2 because it was defective. The cost of the merchandise returned was $80,000.
(c) On March 12 H. Hunt Company received the balance due from B. Streisand Company.

Journalize sales transactions.
(SO 3)

BE5-4 From the information in BE5-3, prepare the journal entries to record these transactions on B. Streisand Company's books under a perpetual inventory system.

Journalize purchase transactions.
(SO 2)

BE5-5 A. Cosby Company provides this information for the month ended October 31, 1998: sales on credit $300,000; cash sales $100,000; sales discounts $5,000; and sales returns and allowances $20,000. Prepare the sales revenues section of the income statement based on this information.

Prepare sales revenue section of income statement.
(SO 4)

BE5-6 Explain where each of these items would appear on a multiple-step income statement: gain on sale of equipment, cost of goods sold, depreciation expense, and sales returns and allowances.

Identify placement of items on a multiple-step income statement.
(SO 4)

BE5-7 Paisley Corporation reported net sales of $250,000, cost of goods sold of $100,000, operating expenses of $50,000, net income of $80,000, beginning total assets of $500,000, and ending total assets of $600,000. Calculate each of these values:
(a) Return on assets ratio
(b) Profit margin ratio
(c) Gross profit rate
(d) Operating expenses to sales ratio

Calculate profitability ratios.
(SO 5)

BE5-8 Ry Corporation reported net sales $550,000; cost of goods sold $300,000; operating expenses $150,000; and net income $70,000. Calculate these values:
(a) Profit margin ratio
(b) Gross profit rate
(c) Operating expenses to sales ratio

Calculate profitability ratios.
(SO 5)

Exercises

Journalize sales transactions.
(SO 3)

E5-1 The following transactions are for C. Pippen Company:
1. On December 3 C. Pippen Company sold $400,000 of merchandise to I. Thomas Co., terms 2/10, n/30. The cost of the merchandise sold was $320,000.
2. On December 8 I. Thomas Co. was granted an allowance of $20,000 for merchandise purchased on December 3.
3. On December 13 C. Pippen Company received the balance due from I. Thomas Co.

Instructions
(a) Prepare the journal entries to record these transactions on the books of C. Pippen Company.
(b) Assume that C. Pippen Company received the balance due from I. Thomas Co. on January 2 of the following year instead of December 13. Prepare the journal entry to record the receipt of payment on January 2.

Journalize perpetual inventory entries.
(SO 2, 3)

E5-2 On September 1 Campus Office Supply had an inventory of 30 deluxe pocket calculators at a cost of $20 each. The company uses a perpetual inventory system. During September these transactions occurred:

Sept. 6 Purchased 60 calculators at $19 each from Digital Co. for cash.
 9 Paid freight of $60 on calculators purchased from Digital Co.
 10 Returned two calculators to Digital Co. for $40 credit because they did not meet specifications.
 12 Sold 26 calculators costing $20 (including freight) for $30 each to Campus Book Store, terms n/30.
 14 Granted credit of $30 to Campus Book Store for the return of one calculator that was not ordered.
 20 Sold 30 calculators costing $20 for $30 each to Varsity Card Shop, terms n/30.

Instructions
Journalize the September transactions.

Journalize purchase transactions.
(SO 2)

E5-3 This information relates to Hans Olaf Co.:
1. On April 5 purchased merchandise from D. DeVito Company for $18,000, terms 2/10, n/30.
2. On April 6 paid freight costs of $900 on merchandise purchased from D. DeVito.
3. On April 7 purchased equipment on account for $26,000.
4. On April 8 returned damaged merchandise to D. DeVito Company and was granted a $3,000 allowance.
5. On April 15 paid the amount due to D. DeVito Company in full.

Instructions
(a) Prepare the journal entries to record the transactions listed above on the books of Hans Olaf Co.
(b) Assume that Hans Olaf Co. paid the balance due to D. DeVito Company on May 4 instead of April 15. Prepare the journal entry to record this payment.

Journalize purchase transactions.
(SO 2)

E5-4 On June 10 Pele Company purchased $5,000 of merchandise from Duvall Company, terms 2/10, n/30. Pele pays the freight costs of $300 on June 11. Damaged goods totaling $300 are returned to Duvall for credit on June 12. On June 19 Pele Company pays Duvall Company in full, less the purchase discount.

Instructions
Prepare separate entries for each transaction on the books of Pele Company.

E5-5 Presented is information related to Baja Co. for the month of January 1998:

Cost of goods sold	$208,000	Rent expense	$ 20,000
Freight-out	7,000	Sales discounts	8,000
Insurance expense	12,000	Sales returns and allowances	13,000
Salary expense	61,000	Sales	342,000

Prepare an income statement and calculate profitability ratios.
(SO 4, 5)

Instructions
(a) Prepare an income statement using the format presented on page 213. Operating expenses should not be segregated into selling and administrative expenses.
(b) Calculate these values: profit margin ratio, gross profit rate, and operating expenses to sales ratio.

E5-6 Financial information is presented here for two companies:

	Young Company	Rice Company
Sales	$90,000	?
Sales returns	?	$ 5,000
Net sales	81,000	95,000
Cost of goods sold	56,000	?
Gross profit	?	38,000
Operating expenses	15,000	?
Net income	?	15,000

Compute missing amounts and calculate profitability ratios.
(SO 4, 5)

Instructions
(a) Fill in the missing amounts. Show all computations.
(b) Calculate the profit margin ratio, gross profit rate, and operating expenses to sales ratio for each company.

E5-7 In its income statement for the year ended December 31, 1998, Chevalier Company reported the following condensed data:

Administrative expenses	$435,000	Selling expenses	$690,000
Cost of goods sold	989,000	Loss on sale of equipment	10,000
Interest expense	70,000	Net sales	2,359,000
Interest revenue	45,000		

Prepare multiple-step income statement and calculate profitability ratios.
(SO 4, 5)

Instructions
(a) Prepare a multiple-step income statement.
(b) Calculate the profit margin ratio, gross profit rate, and operating expenses to sales ratio.

E5-8 The adjusted trial balance of Cecilie Company shows these data pertaining to sales at the end of its fiscal year, October 31, 1998: Sales $900,000; Freight-out $12,000; Sales Returns and Allowances $24,000; and Sales Discounts $15,000.

Prepare sales revenue section of income statement.
(SO 4)

Instructions
Prepare the sales revenues section of the income statement.

PROBLEMS

P5-1 Eagle Hardware Store completed the following merchandising transactions in the month of May. At the beginning of May, the ledger of Eagle showed Cash of $5,000 and Common Stock of $5,000.

Journalize, post, prepare partial income statement, and calculate ratios.
(SO 2, 3, 4, 5)

May 1 Purchased merchandise on account from Depot Wholesale Supply for $5,000, terms 2/10, n/30.
 2 Sold merchandise on account for $4,000, terms 2/10, n/30. The cost of the merchandise sold was $3,000.

224 CHAPTER 5 Merchandising Operations

5   Received credit from Depot Wholesale Supply for merchandise returned $200.
9   Received collections in full, less discounts, from customers billed on sales of $4,000 on May 2.
10   Paid Depot Wholesale Supply in full, less discount.
11   Purchased supplies for cash $900.
12   Purchased merchandise for cash $2,400.
15   Received refund for poor-quality merchandise from supplier on cash purchase $230.
17   Purchased merchandise from Harlow Distributors for $1,900, terms 2/10, n/30.
19   Paid freight on May 17 purchase $250.
24   Sold merchandise for cash $6,200. The cost of the merchandise sold was $4,340.
25   Purchased merchandise from Horicon Inc. for $1,000, terms 2/10, n/30.
27   Paid Harlow Distributors in full, less discount.
29   Made refunds to cash customers for defective merchandise $100. The returned merchandise had cost $70.
31   Sold merchandise on account for $1,600, terms n/30. The cost of the merchandise sold was $1,120.

Eagle Hardware's chart of accounts includes Cash, Accounts Receivable, Merchandise Inventory, Supplies, Accounts Payable, Common Stock, Sales, Sales Returns and Allowances, Sales Discounts, and Cost of Goods Sold.

Instructions
(a) Journalize the transactions.
(b) Post the transactions to T accounts. Be sure to enter the beginning cash and common stock balances.
(c) Prepare an income statement through gross profit for the month of May.
(d) Calculate the profit margin ratio and the gross profit rate. (Assume operating expenses were $1,500.)

Journalize entries under a perpetual inventory system.
(SO 2, 3)

P5-2 Presented here are selected transactions for the Norlan Company during September of the current year. Norlan Company uses the perpetual inventory system.

Sept. 2   Purchased delivery equipment on account for $28,000.
        4   Purchased merchandise on account from Hillary Company at a cost of $60,000, terms 2/10, n/30.
        5   Paid freight charges of $2,000 on merchandise purchased from Hillary Company on September 4.
        5   Returned damaged goods costing $7,000 received from Hillary Company on September 4.
        6   Sold merchandise to Fischer Company costing $15,000 on account for $21,000, terms 1/10, n/30.
      14   Paid Hillary balance due related to September 4 transaction.
      15   Purchased supplies costing $4,000 for cash.
      16   Received balance due from Fischer Company.
      18   Purchased merchandise for cash $6,000.
      22   Sold to Waldo Company on account for $28,000 inventory costing $20,000, terms 1/10, n/30.

Instructions
Journalize the September transactions.

P5-3 Metro Department Store is located in midtown Metropolis. During the past several years, net income has been declining because suburban shopping centers have been attracting business away from city areas. At the end of the company's fiscal year on November 30, 1998, these accounts appeared in its adjusted trial balance:

Prepare financial statements and calculate profitability ratios.

(SO 4, 5)

Accounts Payable	$ 37,310
Accounts Receivable	11,770
Accumulated Depreciation—Delivery Equipment	19,680
Accumulated Depreciation—Store Equipment	41,800
Cash	8,000
Common Stock	70,000
Cost of Goods Sold	633,220
Delivery Expense	8,200
Delivery Equipment	57,000
Depreciation Expense—Delivery Equipment	4,000
Depreciation Expense—Store Equipment	9,500
Dividends	12,000
Insurance Expense	9,000
Interest Expense	8,000
Interest Revenue	5,000
Merchandise Inventory	36,200
Notes Payable	46,000
Prepaid Insurance	4,500
Property Tax Expense	3,500
Rent Expense	19,000
Retained Earnings	14,200
Salaries Expense	120,000
Sales	860,000
Sales Commissions Expense	14,000
Sales Commissions Payable	6,000
Sales Returns and Allowances	10,000
Store Equipment	125,000
Property Taxes Payable	3,500
Utilities Expense	10,600

Additional data: Notes payable are due in 2002.

Instructions
(a) Prepare a multiple-step income statement, a retained earnings statement, and a classified balance sheet.
(b) Calculate the return on assets ratio, profit margin ratio, gross profit rate, and operating expenses to sales ratio. Assume that total assets at the beginning of the year were $160,000.

P5-4 Chi Chi Ramos, a former professional golf star, operates Chi Chi's Pro Shop at Bay Golf Course. At the beginning of the current season on April 1, the ledger of Chi Chi's Pro Shop showed Cash $2,500; Merchandise Inventory $3,500; and Common Stock $6,000. The following transactions were completed during April:

Journalize, post, and prepare trial balance and partial income statement.

(SO 2, 3, 4)

Apr. 5 Purchased golf bags, clubs, and balls on account from Balata Co. $1,600, terms 2/10, n/60.
       7 Paid freight on Balata purchase $80.
       9 Received credit from Balata Co. for merchandise returned $100.
      10 Sold merchandise on account to members $900, terms n/30. The merchandise sold had a cost of $630.
      12 Purchased golf shoes, sweaters, and other accessories on account from Arrow Sportswear $660, terms 1/10, n/30.

226 CHAPTER 5 Merchandising Operations

14 Paid Balata Co. in full.
17 Received credit from Arrow Sportswear for merchandise returned $60.
20 Made sales on account to members $700, terms n/30. The cost of the merchandise sold was $490.
21 Paid Arrow Sportswear in full.
27 Granted an allowance to members for clothing that did not fit properly $30.
30 Received payments on account from members $1,100.

The chart of accounts for the pro shop includes Cash, Accounts Receivable, Merchandise Inventory, Accounts Payable, Common Stock, Sales, Sales Returns and Allowances, and Cost of Goods Sold.

Instructions
(a) Journalize the April transactions using a perpetual inventory system.
(b) Using T accounts, enter the beginning balances in the ledger accounts and post the April transactions.
(c) Prepare a trial balance on April 30, 1998.
(d) Prepare an income statement through gross profit.

Prepare a correct multiple-step income statement.
(SO 4)

P5-5 An inexperienced accountant prepared this condensed income statement for Zambrana Company, a retail firm that has been in business for a number of years.

ZAMBRANA COMPANY
Income Statement
For the Year Ended December 31, 1998

Revenues		
Net sales		$740,000
Other revenues		24,000
		764,000
Cost of goods sold		555,000
Gross profit		209,000
Operating expenses		
Selling expenses	104,000	
Administrative expenses	69,000	
		173,000
Net earnings		$ 36,000

As an experienced, knowledgeable accountant, you review the statement and determine the following facts:
1. Net sales consist of sales $800,000, less delivery expense on merchandise sold $30,000, and sales returns and allowances $30,000.
2. Other revenues consist of sales discounts $16,000 and rent revenue $8,000.
3. Selling expenses consist of salespersons' salaries $80,000; depreciation on accounting equipment $8,000; advertising $10,000; and sales commissions $6,000. The commissions represent commissions paid. At December 31, $4,000 of commissions have been earned by salespersons but have not been paid.
4. Administrative expenses consist of office salaries $27,000; dividends $4,000; utilities $12,000; interest expense $2,000; and rent $24,000, which includes prepayments totaling $6,000 for the first quarter of 1999.

Instructions
Prepare a correct detailed multiple-step income statement.

P5-6 The trial balance of Mesa Wholesale Company contained the accounts shown at December 31, the end of the company's fiscal year:

MESA WHOLESALE COMPANY
Trial Balance
December 31, 1998

	Debit	Credit
Cash	$ 33,400	
Accounts Receivable	37,600	
Merchandise Inventory	90,000	
Land	92,000	
Buildings	197,000	
Accumulated Depreciation—Buildings		$ 54,000
Equipment	83,500	
Accumulated Depreciation—Equipment		42,400
Notes Payable		50,000
Accounts Payable		37,500
Common Stock		200,000
Retained Earnings		67,800
Dividends	10,000	
Sales		902,100
Sales Discounts	4,600	
Cost of Goods Sold	709,900	
Salaries Expense	69,800	
Utilities Expense	9,400	
Repair Expense	5,900	
Gas and Oil Expense	7,200	
Insurance Expense	3,500	
	$1,353,800	$1,353,800

Journalize, post, and prepare adjusted trial balance and financial statements.
(SO 4)

Adjustment data:
1. Depreciation is $10,000 on buildings and $9,000 on equipment. (Both are administrative expenses.)
2. Interest of $7,000 is due and unpaid on notes payable at December 31.

Other data: $15,000 of the notes payable are payable next year.

Instructions
(a) Journalize the adjusting entries.
(b) Create T accounts for all accounts used in part (a). Enter the trial balance into the T accounts and post the adjusting entries.
(c) Prepare an adjusted trial balance.
(d) Prepare a multiple-step income statement and a retained earnings statement for the year, and a classified balance sheet at December 31, 1998.

ALTERNATIVE PROBLEMS

P5-1A Nisson Distributing Company completed these merchandising transactions in the month of April. At the beginning of April, the ledger of Nisson showed Cash of $9,000 and Common Stock of $9,000.

Journalize, post, prepare partial income statement, and calculate ratios.
(SO 2, 3, 4, 5)

Apr. 2 Purchased merchandise on account from Kentucky Supply Co. $4,900, terms 2/10, n/30.
   4 Sold merchandise on account $5,000, terms 2/10, n/30. The cost of the merchandise sold was $4,000.
   5 Paid $200 freight on April 4 sale.

6 Received credit from Kentucky Supply Co. for merchandise returned $300.
11 Paid Kentucky Supply Co. in full, less discount.
13 Received collections in full, less discounts, from customers billed on April 4.
14 Purchased merchandise for cash $4,400.
16 Received refund from supplier on cash purchase of April 14, $500.
18 Purchased merchandise from Pigeon Distributors $4,200, terms 2/10, n/30.
20 Paid freight on April 18 purchase $100.
23 Sold merchandise for cash $6,400. The cost of the merchandise sold was $5,120.
26 Purchased merchandise for cash $2,300.
27 Paid Pigeon Distributors in full, less discount.
29 Made refunds to cash customers for defective merchandise $90. The returned merchandise had a cost of $70.
30 Sold merchandise on account $3,700, terms n/30. The cost of the merchandise sold was $3,000.

Nisson Distributing Company's chart of accounts includes Cash, Accounts Receivable, Merchandise Inventory, Accounts Payable, Common Stock, Sales, Sales Returns and Allowances, Sales Discounts, Cost of Goods Sold, and Freight-out.

Instructions
(a) Journalize the transactions.
(b) Post the transactions to T accounts. Be sure to enter the beginning cash and common stock balances.
(c) Prepare the income statement through gross profit for the month of April.
(d) Calculate the profit margin ratio and the gross profit rate. (Assume operating expenses were $1,400.)

Journalize entries under a perpetual inventory system.
(SO 2, 3)

P5-2A Varsity Auto Sales uses a perpetual inventory system. On April 1 the new car inventory records show total inventory of $140,000 consisting of the following:

Model	Units	Unit Cost
Custom sedans	4	$14,000
Convertibles	3	16,000
Recreational vans	2	18,000

During April the following purchases and sales were made on account:

Apr. 5 Purchased three custom sedans for $14,000 each.
7 Sold two custom sedans for $18,200 each.
13 Purchased two recreational vans for $18,000 each.
17 Sold one custom sedan for $18,500.
20 Purchased two convertibles for $16,000 each.
22 Returned one convertible purchased on April 20 for $16,000 credit.
24 Sold three recreational vans for $24,000 each.
28 Sold one convertible for $21,000.

Instructions
Journalize the transactions using a perpetual inventory system.

Prepare financial statements and calculate profitability ratios.
(SO 4, 5)

P5-3A N-Mart Department Store is located near the Village Shopping Mall. At the end of the company's fiscal year on December 31, 1998, the following accounts appeared in its adjusted trial balance:

Accounts Payable	$ 89,300
Accounts Receivable	50,300
Accumulated Depreciation—Building	52,500
Accumulated Depreciation—Equipment	42,900
Building	190,000

Cash	23,000
Common Stock	150,000
Cost of Goods Sold	412,700
Depreciation Expense—Building	10,400
Depreciation Expense—Equipment	13,300
Dividends	28,000
Equipment	110,000
Insurance Expense	7,200
Interest Expense	11,000
Interest Payable	8,000
Interest Revenue	4,000
Merchandise Inventory	75,000
Mortgage Payable	80,000
Office Salaries Expense	32,000
Prepaid Insurance	2,400
Property Taxes Payable	4,800
Property Taxes Expense	4,800
Retained Earnings	26,600
Sales Salaries Expense	76,000
Sales	618,000
Sales Commissions Expense	14,500
Sales Commissions Payable	3,500
Sales Returns and Allowances	8,000
Utilities Expense	11,000

Additional data: $20,000 of the mortgage payable is due for payment next year.

Instructions
(a) Prepare a multiple-step income statement, a retained earnings statement, and a classified balance sheet.
(b) Calculate the return on assets ratio, profit margin ratio, gross profit rate, and operating expenses to sales ratio. Assume total assets at the beginning of the year were $320,000.

P5-4A Billy Jean Evert, a former professional tennis star, operates B.J.'s Tennis Shop at Jackson Lake Resort. At the beginning of the current season, the ledger of B.J.'s Tennis Shop showed Cash $2,500; Merchandise Inventory $1,700; and Common Stock $4,200. The following transactions were completed during April:

Journalize, post, and prepare trial balance and partial income statement.
(SO 2, 3, 4)

Apr. 4 Purchased racquets and balls from Robert Co. $640, terms 3/10, n/30.
6 Paid freight on Robert Co. purchase $40.
8 Sold merchandise to members $900, terms n/30. The merchandise sold cost $600.
10 Received credit of $40 from Robert Co. for a damaged racquet that was returned.
11 Purchased tennis shoes from Niki Sports for cash $300.
13 Paid Robert Co. in full.
14 Purchased tennis shirts and shorts from Martina's Sportswear $700, terms 2/10, n/60.
15 Received cash refund of $50 from Niki Sports for damaged merchandise that was returned.
17 Paid freight on Martina's Sportswear purchase $30.
18 Sold merchandise to members $800, terms n/30. The cost of the merchandise sold was $530.
20 Received $500 in cash from members in settlement of their accounts.
21 Paid Martina's Sportswear in full.
27 Granted an allowance of $30 to members for tennis clothing that did not fit properly.
30 Received cash payments on account from members $500.

The chart of accounts for the tennis shop includes Cash, Accounts Receivable, Merchandise Inventory, Accounts Payable, Common Stock, Sales, Sales Returns and Allowances, and Cost of Goods Sold.

Instructions
(a) Journalize the April transactions.
(b) Using T accounts, enter the beginning balances in the ledger accounts and post the April transactions.
(c) Prepare a trial balance on April 30, 1998.
(d) Prepare an income statement through gross profit.

Prepare a correct multiple-step income statement.
(SO 4)

P5-5A A part-time bookkeeper prepared this income statement for Tao Company for the year ending December 31, 1998:

TAO COMPANY
Income Statement
December 31, 1998

Revenues		
Sales		$702,000
Less: Freight-out	$10,000	
Sales discounts	11,300	21,300
Net sales		680,700
Other revenues (net)		1,300
Total revenues		682,000
Expenses		
Cost of goods sold		470,000
Selling expenses		100,000
Administrative expenses		50,000
Dividends		12,000
Total expenses		632,000
Net income		$ 50,000

As an experienced, knowledgeable accountant, you review the statement and determine the following facts:
1. Sales include $10,000 of deposits from customers for future sales orders.
2. Other revenues contain two items: interest expense $4,000 and interest revenue $5,300.
3. Selling expenses consist of sales salaries $76,000, advertising $10,000, depreciation on store equipment $7,500, and sales commissions expense $6,500.
4. Administrative expenses consist of office salaries $19,000; utilities expense $8,000; rent expense $16,000; and insurance expense $7,000. Insurance expense includes $1,200 of insurance applicable to 1999.

Instructions
Prepare a correct detailed multiple-step income statement.

Journalize, post, and prepare adjusted trial balance and financial statements.
(SO 4)

P5-6A The trial balance of Ivanna Fashion Center contained the following accounts at November 30, the end of the company's fiscal year:

IVANNA FASHION CENTER
Trial Balance
November 30, 1998

	Debit	Credit
Cash	$ 16,700	
Accounts Receivable	33,700	
Merchandise Inventory	45,000	
Store Supplies	5,500	
Store Equipment	85,000	
Accumulated Depreciation—Store Equipment		$ 18,000

Delivery Equipment	48,000	
Accumulated Depreciation—Delivery Equipment		6,000
Notes Payable		51,000
Accounts Payable		48,500
Common Stock		80,000
Retained Earnings		30,000
Dividends	12,000	
Sales		757,200
Sales Returns and Allowances	4,200	
Cost of Goods Sold	507,400	
Salaries Expense	140,000	
Advertising Expense	26,400	
Utilities Expense	14,000	
Repair Expense	12,100	
Delivery Expense	16,700	
Rent Expense	24,000	
	$990,700	$990,700

Adjustment data:
1. Store supplies on hand total $3,500.
2. Depreciation is $9,000 on the store equipment and $7,000 on the delivery equipment.
3. Interest of $11,000 is accrued on notes payable at November 30.

Other data: $30,000 of notes payable are due for payment next year.

Instructions
(a) Journalize the adjusting entries.
(b) Prepare T accounts for all accounts used in part (a). Enter the trial balance into the T accounts and post the adjusting entries.
(c) Prepare an adjusted trial balance.
(d) Prepare a multiple-step income statement and a retained earnings statement for the year, and a classified balance sheet at November 30, 1998.

BROADENING YOUR PERSPECTIVE

FINANCIAL REPORTING AND ANALYSIS

FINANCIAL REPORTING PROBLEM: *Starbucks Corporation*

BYP5-1 The financial statements for Starbucks are presented in Appendix A at the end of this book.

Instructions
Answer these questions using the Consolidated Income Statement:
(a) What was the percentage change in sales and in net income from 1995 to 1996?
(b) What was the profit margin ratio in each of the three years? Comment on the trend.
(c) What was Starbucks' gross profit rate in each of the three years? Comment on the trend.
(d) What was the operating expenses to sales ratio in each of the three years? Comment on any trend in this percentage.

COMPARATIVE ANALYSIS PROBLEM: *Starbucks vs. Green Mountain Coffee*

BYP5-2 The financial statements of Green Mountain Coffee are presented in Appendix B, following the financial statements for Starbucks in Appendix A.

Instructions
(a) Based on the information contained in these financial statements, determine the following values for each company:
  (1) Profit margin ratio for 1996
  (2) Gross profit for 1996
  (3) Gross profit rate for 1996
  (4) Operating income for 1996
  (5) Percentage change in operating income from 1995 to 1996
  (6) Operating expenses to sales ratio for 1996
(b) What conclusions concerning the relative profitability of the two companies can be drawn from these data?

RESEARCH CASE

BYP5-3 The April 1996 issue of the *Journal of Accountancy* includes an article by Dennis R. Beresford, L. Todd Johnson, and Cheri L. Reither entitled "Is a Second Income Statement Needed?"

Instructions
Read the article and answer these questions:
(a) On what basis would the "second income statement" be prepared? Briefly describe this basis.
(b) Why is there a perceived need for a second income statement?
(c) Identify three alternatives for reporting the proposed measure of income.

INTERPRETING FINANCIAL STATEMENTS

BYP5-4 Minicase 1 *McDonnell Douglas*

McDonnell Douglas, based in St. Louis, Missouri, describes itself in its 1994 annual report as the world's largest builder of fighter and military transport aircraft, the third largest commercial aircraft maker, and a leading producer of helicopters, missiles, and satellite launch vehicles.

The company's strategy for future growth might be described as "cautiously aggressive" because it aggressively competes in markets in which it believes that it has a competitive advantage, while it evaluates other markets carefully and then expands its product line or divests, depending upon whether it believes that it can remain or become a leading competitor.

McDonnell Douglas's 1994 income statement is reproduced here.

MCDONNELL DOUGLAS
Income Statement
For the Year Ended December 31, 1994
(in millions)

Revenues	$13,176
Costs and expenses	
Cost of products, services, and rentals	11,026
General and administrative expenses	684
Research and development	297
Interest expense	249
Total costs and expenses	12,256
Earnings before income taxes	920
Income taxes	322
Net earnings	$ 598

Instructions
(a) What account name appears to represent McDonnell Douglas's cost of goods sold account? Why do you think that company chose the account name that it did? Using that account as cost of goods sold, what is gross profit?
(b) The income statement shown is in summary form. This means that each account title listed is a summary of several other accounts. For example, the Revenue account includes such things as Commercial Aircraft Revenue, Defense Contract Revenue, and so forth, as well as any offsetting accounts such as Sales Discounts. In which summary account from the income statement would these merchandising accounts be located:
  (1) Sales returns and allowances
  (2) Merchandise inventory increases and decreases
  (3) Sales discounts
(c) The company is evaluating a divisional plant that builds satellite launch vehicles. The product line presently consists of a single vehicle, which is the only one of its kind, but competitors have built vehicles that can launch smaller satellites. The company is confident that it can produce an expanded product line, which would include both larger and smaller vehicles than the one currently made. The two choices being evaluated are: First, spend approximately $17 million in research and development to expand the product line. This cost would be considered an expense immediately. Revenue of about $100 million would be generated each year, beginning 2 years after development; it would continue at least 5 years but possibly longer. Second, sell the assets of the existing business to a competitor. This would generate a gain of $315 million next year. If the choice is made at the end of this year, how will net income be affected under each alternative? How will gross profit change? Which alternative do you recommend? Give reasons for your answer.

BYP5-5 Minicase 2 *Bob Evans Farms, Inc.*
Bob Evans Farms, Inc., operates 315 restaurants in 19 states and produces fresh and fully cooked sausage products, fresh salads, and related products distributed to grocery stores in the Midwest, Southwest, and Southeast. For a recent 3-year period Bob Evans Farms reported the following selected income statement data (in millions of dollars):

	1994	1993	1992
Sales	$699.0	$653.2	$556.3
Cost of goods sold	514.4	480.3	424.3
Selling and administrative expenses	85.0	83.6	72.0
Net income	48.2	43.1	39.3

In his letter to the stockholders, the chairman of the board and CEO made the following comments: "I am looking forward to a record-setting year at Bob Evans Farms. We have excellent leadership in place, great traditions on which to build, and the teamwork and knowledge to move ahead."

Instructions
(a) Compute the percentage change in sales and in net income from 1993 to 1994.
(b) What contribution, if any, did the company's gross profit rate make to the improved earnings?
(c) What was Bob Evans's percentage of net income to net sales in each of the three years? Comment on any trend in this percentage.
(d) Based on the trends in these ratios, does the CEO's optimism seem appropriate?

CRITICAL THINKING

MANAGEMENT DECISION CASE

BYP5-6 Three years ago Kathy Webb and her brother-in-law John Utley opened FedCo Department Store. For the first 2 years, business was good, but the following condensed income results for 1998 were disappointing:

FEDCO DEPARTMENT STORE
Income Statement
For the Year Ended December 31, 1998

Net sales	$700,000
Cost of goods sold	546,000
Gross profit	154,000
Operating expenses	
Selling expenses	100,000
Administrative expenses	25,000
	125,000
Net income	$ 29,000

Kathy believes the problem lies in the relatively low gross profit rate (gross profit divided by net sales) of 22%. John believes the problem is that operating expenses are too high. Kathy thinks the gross profit rate can be improved by making two changes: (1) Increase average selling prices by 17%; this increase is expected to lower sales volume so that total sales will increase only 6%. (2) Buy merchandise in larger quantities and take all purchase discounts; these changes are expected to increase the gross profit rate by 3%. Kathy does not anticipate that these changes will have any effect on operating expenses.

John thinks expenses can be cut by making these two changes: (1) Cut 1998 sales salaries of $60,000 in half and give sales personnel a commission of 2% of net sales. (2) Reduce store deliveries to one day per week rather than twice a week; this change will reduce 1998 delivery expenses of $30,000 by 40%. John feels that these changes will not have any effect on net sales.

Kathy and John come to you for help in deciding the best way to improve net income.

Instructions
(a) Prepare a condensed income statement for 1999 assuming (1) Kathy's changes are implemented and (2) John's ideas are adopted.
(b) What is your recommendation to Kathy and John?
(c) Prepare a condensed income statement for 1999 assuming both sets of proposed changes are made.
(d) Discuss the impact that other factors might have. For example, would increasing the quantity of inventory increase costs? Would a salary cut affect employee morale? Would decreased morale affect sales? Would decreased store deliveries decrease customer satisfaction? What other suggestions might be considered?

A REAL-WORLD FOCUS: *A. L. Laboratories*

BYP5-7 *A. L. Laboratories* is headquartered in Fort Lee, New Jersey, and also has operations in Scandinavia and Indonesia. The company develops and produces generic pharmaceuticals, specializing in both over-the-counter and prescription creams and ointments, aerosol inhalants, and liquids such as cough syrups. A significant share of its income is also derived from the development and distribution of animal health products such as food additives for poultry. The company was founded in 1975 and today has more than 2,700 employees.

Gross profit at A. L. Laboratories declined both in dollars and as a percentage of revenues. The decline was attributed to lower sales volume, customer credits associated with product recalls, inventory disposals, and the impact of higher inventory costs. In addition, the gross profit percentage declined as a result of lower production volumes.

Instructions
(a) What account is affected when A. L. Laboratories has a product recall?
(b) What factors caused gross profit to decline?
(c) What factors could cause this company to have to dispose of inventory?
(d) How would you expect the gross profit rate and operating expense ratio of a producer of generic drugs to compare with those of a name-brand producer?

Group Activity

BYP5-8 This information is taken from the accounting records of Grant Company:

Sales	$150,000
Cost of Goods Sold	90,000
Sales Discounts	8,000
Operating Expenses	30,000
Sales Returns and Allowances	10,000
Merchandise Inventory	8,000
Interest Expense	3,000
Interest Revenue	2,000

Instructions
Working in groups of four or five students, determine these values:
(a) Net sales
(b) Gross profit
(c) Income from operations
(d) Net income

Communication Activity

BYP5-9 The following situation is presented in chronological order:
1. Dexter decides to buy a surfboard.
2. He calls Surfing USA Co. to inquire about their surfboards.
3. Two days later he requests Surfing USA Co. to make him a surfboard.
4. Three days later Surfing USA Co. sends him a purchase order to fill out.
5. He sends back the purchase order.
6. Surfing USA Co. receives the completed purchase order.
7. Surfing USA Co. completes the surfboard.
8. Dexter picks up the surfboard.
9. Surfing USA Co. bills Dexter.
10. Surfing USA Co. receives payment from Dexter.

Instructions
In a memo to the president of Surfing USA Co., answer these questions:
(a) When should Surfing USA Co. record the sale?
(b) Suppose that with his purchase order, Dexter is required to make a down payment. Would that change your answer to part (a)?

Ethics Case

BYP5-10 Rita Pelzer was just hired as the assistant treasurer of Yorkshire Stores, a specialty chain store company that has nine retail stores concentrated in one metropolitan area. Among other things, the payment of all invoices is centralized in one of the departments Rita will manage. Her primary responsibility is to maintain the company's high credit rating by paying all bills when due and to take advantage of all cash discounts.

Jamie Caterino, the former assistant treasurer, who has been promoted to treasurer, is training Rita in her new duties. He instructs Rita that she is to continue the practice of preparing all checks "net of discount" and dating the checks the last day of the discount period. "But," Jamie continues, "we always hold the checks at least 4 days beyond the discount period before mailing them. That way we get another 4 days of interest on our money. Most of our creditors need our business and don't complain. And, if they scream about our missing the discount period, we blame it on the mail room or the post office. We've only lost one discount out of every hundred we take that way. I think everybody does it. By the way, welcome to our team!"

Instructions
(a) What are the ethical considerations in this case?
(b) What stakeholders are harmed or benefited?
(c) Should Rita continue the practice started by Jamie? Does she have any choice?

Financial Analysis on the Web

BYP5-11 *Purpose:* No financial decision maker should ever rely solely on the financial information reported in the annual report to make decisions. It is important to keep abreast of financial news. This activity demonstrates how to search for financial news on the Web.

Address: http://biz.yahoo.com/i

Steps:
1. Choose **Company.**
2. Type in either Pepsico Inc. or Coca-Cola.
3. Choose **News.**
4. Select an article that sounds interesting to you.

Instructions
(a) What was the source of the article? (For example, Reuters, Businesswire, Prnewswire.)
(b) Pretend that you are a personal financial planner and that one of your clients owns stock in the company. Write a brief memo to your client summarizing the article and explaining the implications of the article for their investment.

Answers to Self-Study Questions
1. c   2. c   3. b   4. a   5. c   6. b   7. d   8. c   9. c   10. a

CHAPTER 6

Reporting and Analyzing Inventory

STUDY OBJECTIVES

After studying this chapter, you should be able to:

1. Explain the recording of purchases and sales of inventory under a periodic inventory system.
2. Explain how to determine cost of goods sold under a periodic inventory system.
3. Describe the steps in determining inventory quantities.
4. Identify the unique features of the income statement for a merchandising company under a periodic inventory system.
5. Explain the basis of accounting for inventories and apply the inventory cost flow methods under a periodic inventory system.
6. Explain the financial statement and tax effects of each of the inventory cost flow assumptions.
7. Explain the lower of cost or market basis of accounting for inventories.
8. Compute and interpret the inventory turnover ratio.
9. Describe the LIFO reserve and explain its importance for comparing results of different companies.

Where Is That Spare Bulldozer Blade?

Let's talk inventory—big, bulldozer-size inventory. Caterpillar Inc. is the world's largest manufacturer of construction and mining equipment. It is also a leading producer of industrial engines. It sells its products in over 200 countries, making it one of the most successful U.S. exporters. More than 75% of its productive assets are located domestically, while 50% of its sales are foreign.

During the 1980s Caterpillar's profitability suffered, but today it enjoys record sales, profits, and growth. A big part of this turnaround can be attributed to effective management of its inventory. Imagine what a bulldozer costs. Now imagine what it costs Caterpillar to have too many bulldozers sitting around in inventory—a situation the company definitely wants to avoid. Conversely, Caterpillar must make sure it has enough inventory to meet demand. The inventory turnover ratio is one measure of inventory efficiency. Caterpillar increased its inventory turnover ratio from 4.2 in 1991 to 6.39 in 1995, which means that the average item went from being in inventory 87 days in 1991 to only 57 days in 1995.

To achieve this dramatic reduction in the amount of resources tied up in inventory, while continuing to meet customers' needs, Caterpillar used a two-pronged approach. First, it completed a factory modernization program in 1993, which dramatically increased its production efficiency. The program reduced the amount of inventory being processed at any one time by 60% and also reduced the time it takes to manufacture a part by an incredible 75%. Second, Caterpillar dramatically improved its distribution system. It ships 84,000 items daily from its 25 distribution centers strategically located around the world (10 million square feet of warehouse space—remember, we're talking bulldozers). The company guarantees that it can get any part to any customer anywhere in the world within 24 hours. In fact, its distribution system is so advanced that Caterpillar created a separate

238

unit, Caterpillar Logistics Services, that warehouses and distributes other companies' products. This unit distributes products as diverse as running shoes, computer software, and auto parts all around the world. In short, how Caterpillar manages and accounts for its inventory goes a long way in explaining how profitable it is.

On the World Wide Web
Caterpillar Inc.:
http://www.caterpillar.com

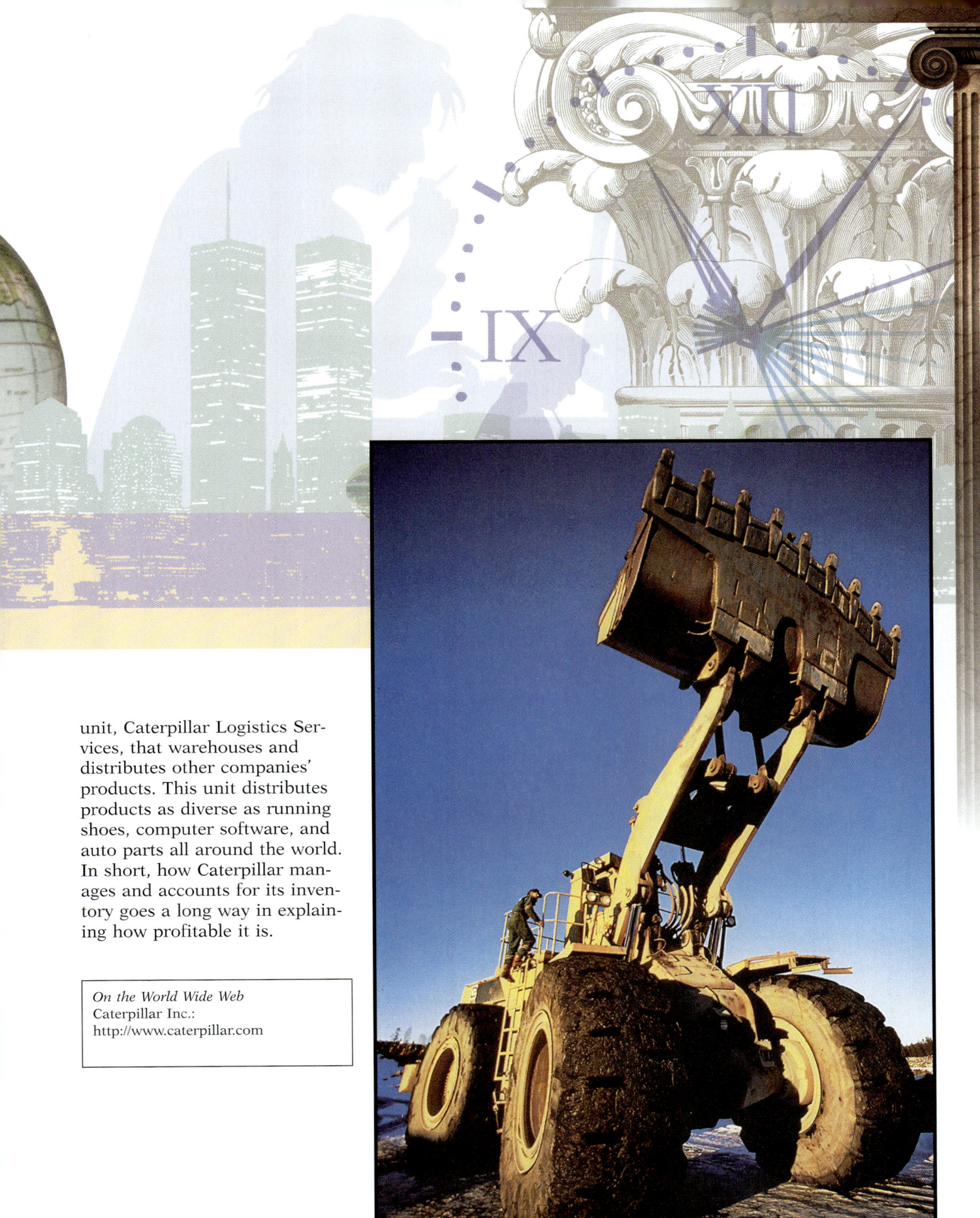

PREVIEW OF CHAPTER 6

In the previous chapter, we discussed the accounting for merchandise inventory using a perpetual inventory system. In this chapter, we explain the periodic inventory system and methods used to calculate the cost of inventory on hand at the balance sheet date. We conclude by illustrating methods for analyzing inventory.

The content and organization of this chapter are as follows:

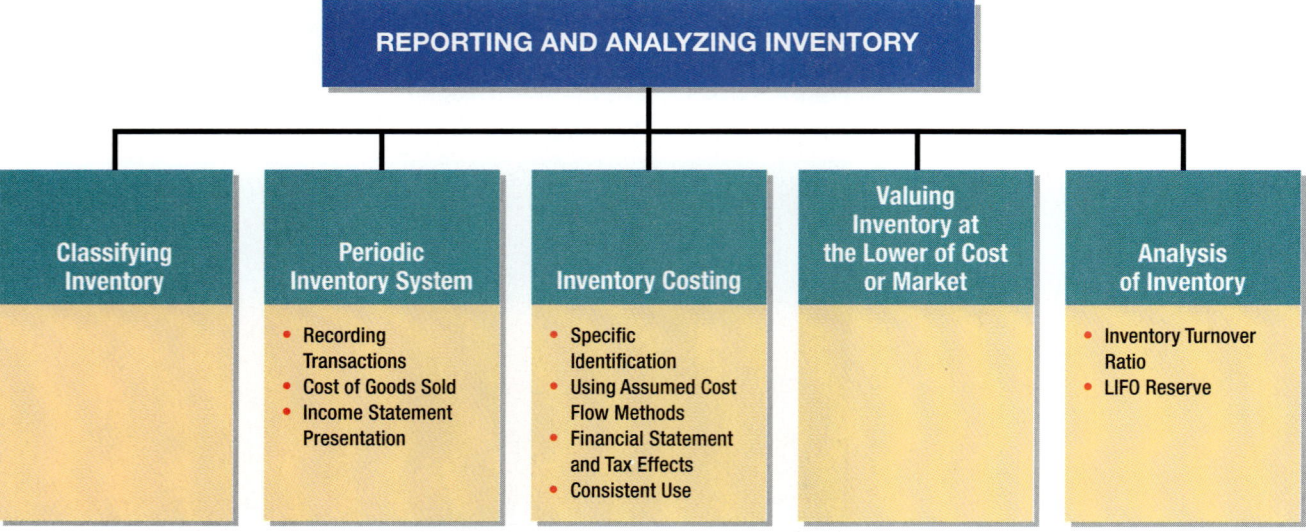

CLASSIFYING INVENTORY

How a company classifies its inventory depends on whether the firm is a merchandiser or a manufacturer. In a **merchandising** company, such as those described in Chapter 5, inventory consists of many different items. For example, in a grocery store, canned goods, dairy products, meats, and produce are just a few of the inventory items on hand. These items have two common characteristics: (1) they are owned by the company, and (2) they are in a form ready for sale to customers in the ordinary course of business. Thus, only one inventory classification, **merchandise inventory,** is needed to describe the many different items that make up the total inventory.

In a **manufacturing** company, some of its inventory may not yet be ready for sale. As a result, inventory is usually classified into three categories: finished goods, work in process, and raw materials. Finished goods inventory is manufactured items that are completed and ready for sale. Work in process is that portion of manufactured inventory that has been placed into the production process but is not yet complete. Raw materials are the basic goods that will be used in production but have not yet been placed into production. For example, General Motors classifies automobiles completed and ready for sale as **finished goods.** The automobiles on the assembly line in various stages of production are classified as **work in process.** The steel, glass, upholstery, and other components that are on hand waiting to be used in the production of automobiles are identified as **raw materials.**

Helpful Hint Regardless of the classification, all inventories are reported under Current Assets on the balance sheet.

240

By observing the levels and changes in the levels of these three inventory types, financial statement users can gain insight into management's production plans. For example, low levels of raw materials and high levels of finished goods suggest that management believes it has enough inventory on hand, and production will be slowing down—perhaps in anticipation of a recession. On the other hand, high levels of raw materials and low levels of finished goods probably indicate that management is planning to step up production.

The accounting concepts discussed in this chapter apply to the inventory classifications of both merchandising and manufacturing companies. Our focus here is on merchandise inventory.

PERIODIC INVENTORY SYSTEM

As described in Chapter 5, one of two basic systems of accounting for inventories may be used: (1) the perpetual inventory system or (2) the periodic inventory system. In Chapter 5 we focused on the characteristics of the perpetual inventory system. In this chapter we discuss and illustrate the periodic inventory system. One key difference between the two systems is the point at which cost of goods sold is computed. For a visual reminder of this difference, you may want to refer back to Illustration 5-3 on page 204.

RECORDING MERCHANDISE TRANSACTIONS

In a **periodic inventory system,** revenues from the sale of merchandise are recorded when sales are made, just as in a perpetual system. Unlike the perpetual system, however, **no attempt is made on the date of sale to record the cost of the merchandise sold.** Instead, a physical inventory count is taken at the **end of the period** to determine (1) the cost of the merchandise then on hand and (2) the cost of the goods sold during the period. And, under a periodic system, purchases of merchandise are recorded in the Purchases account rather than the Merchandise Inventory account. Also, in a periodic system, purchase returns and allowances, purchase discounts, and freight costs on purchases are recorded in separate accounts.

To illustrate the recording of merchandise transactions under a periodic inventory system, we will use purchase/sale transactions between PW Audio Supply and Sauk Stereo, Inc., as illustrated for the perpetual inventory system in Chapter 5.

> **STUDY OBJECTIVE 1**
> Explain the recording of purchases and sales of inventory under a periodic inventory system.

Recording Purchases of Merchandise

On the basis of the sales invoice (Illustration 5-4, shown on page 206) and receipt of the merchandise ordered from PW Audio Supply, Sauk Stereo records the $3,800 purchase as follows:

May	4	Purchases	3,800	
		Accounts Payable		3,800
		(To record goods purchased on account, terms 2/10, n/30)		

Purchases is a temporary account whose normal balance is a debit.

Purchase Returns and Allowances. Because $300 of merchandise received from PW Audio Supply is inoperable, Sauk Stereo returns the goods and prepares the following entry to recognize the return:

May	8	Accounts Payable	300	
		Purchase Returns and Allowances		300
		(To record return of inoperable goods purchased from PW Audio Supply)		

Purchase Returns and Allowances is a temporary account whose normal balance is a credit.

Freight Costs. When the purchaser directly incurs the freight costs, the account Freight-in (or Transportation-in) is debited. For example, if upon delivery of the goods on May 6, Sauk pays Acme Freight Company $150 for freight charges on its purchase from PW Audio Supply, the entry on Sauk's books is:

May	9	Freight-in (Transportation-in)	150	
		Cash		150
		(To record payment of freight)		

Like Purchases, Freight-in is a temporary account whose normal balance is a debit. **Freight-in is part of cost of goods purchased.** The reason is that cost of goods purchased should include any freight charges necessary to bring the goods to the purchaser. Freight costs are not subject to a purchase discount. Purchase discounts apply on the invoice cost of the merchandise.

Purchase Discounts. On May 14 Sauk Stereo pays the balance due on account to PW Audio Supply, taking the 2% cash discount allowed by PW Audio for payment within 10 days. The payment and discount are recorded by Sauk Stereo as follows:

May	14	Accounts Payable ($3,800 − $300)	3,500	
		Purchase Discounts ($3,500 × .02)		70
		Cash		3,430
		(To record payment to PW Audio Supply within the discount period)		

Purchase Discounts is a temporary account whose normal balance is a credit.

Recording Sales of Merchandise

The sale of $3,800 of merchandise to Sauk Stereo on May 4 (sales invoice No. 731, Illustration 5-4) is recorded by the seller, PW Audio Supply, as follows:

May	4	Accounts Receivable	3,800	
		Sales		3,800
		(To record credit sales per invoice #731 to Sauk Stereo)		

Sales Returns and Allowances. To record the returned goods received from Sauk Stereo on May 8, PW Audio Supply records the $300 sales return as follows:

May	8	Sales Returns and Allowances	300	
		Accounts Receivable		300
		(To record return of goods from Sauk Stereo)		

Sales Discounts. On May 15, PW Audio Supply receives payment of $3,430 on account from Sauk Stereo. PW Audio honors the 2% cash discount and records the payment of Sauk's account receivable in full as follows:

May	15	Cash	3,430	
		Sales Discount ($3,500 × .02)	70	
		Accounts Receivable ($3,800 − $300)		3,500
		(To record collection from Sauk Stereo within 2/10, n/30 discount period)		

COST OF GOODS SOLD

Under a periodic inventory system, a running account of the changes in inventory is not recorded when either purchases or sales transactions occur. Neither the daily amount of inventory of merchandise on hand nor the cost of goods sold is known. To determine the **cost of goods sold** under a periodic inventory system, it is necessary to (1) record purchases of merchandise (as shown above), (2) determine the cost of goods purchased, and (3) determine the cost of goods on hand at the beginning and end of the accounting period. The cost of goods on hand must be determined by (a) a physical inventory count and (b) an application of the cost to the items counted in the inventory.

STUDY OBJECTIVE 2

Explain how to determine cost of goods sold under a periodic inventory system.

Determining Cost of Goods Purchased

Under a periodic inventory system, various accounts, such as purchases, freight-in, purchase discounts, and purchase returns and allowances, are used to record the cost of goods purchased. (A perpetual system uses only one account, Merchandise Inventory.) These accounts, with their impact on cost of goods purchased, are listed in Illustration 6-1.

Item	Periodic Account Title	Debit or Credit Entry	Effect on Cost of Goods Purchased
Invoice price	Purchases	Debit	Increase
Freight charges paid by purchaser	Freight-in	Debit	Increase
Purchase discounts taken by purchaser	Purchase Discounts	Credit	Decrease
Purchase returns and allowances granted by seller	Purchase Returns and Allowances	Credit	Decrease

Illustration 6-1 Accounts used to record purchases of inventory

To determine cost of goods purchased we begin with **gross** purchases. This amount is then adjusted for any savings resulting from purchase discounts or any reductions due to the return of unwanted goods. The result is **net purchases.** Because freight charges are a necessary cost incurred to acquire inventory,

freight-in is added to net purchases to arrive at **cost of goods purchased.** To summarize:

1. The accounts with credit balances (Purchase Returns and Allowances and Purchase Discounts) are subtracted from Purchases to get **net purchases.**
2. Freight-in is added to net purchases to arrive at **cost of goods purchased.**

To illustrate, assume that PW Audio Supply shows these balances for the accounts above: Purchases $325,000; Purchase Returns and Allowances $10,400; Purchase Discounts $6,800; and Freight-in $12,200. Net purchases and cost of goods purchased are $307,800 and $320,000, as computed in Illustration 6-2.

Illustration 6-2 Computation of net purchases and cost of goods purchased

Purchases		$ 325,000
(1) Less: Purchase returns and allowances	$10,400	
Purchase discounts	6,800	17,200
Net purchases		307,800
(2) Add: Freight-in		12,200
Cost of goods purchased		**$320,000**

All four of the accounts used in the periodic system are temporary accounts. They are used to determine cost of goods sold. Therefore, the balances in these accounts are reduced to zero at the end of each accounting period (i.e., annually).

Determining Inventory Quantities

STUDY OBJECTIVE 3
Describe the steps in determining inventory quantities.

Companies that use a periodic inventory system take a physical inventory to determine the inventory on hand at the balance sheet date and to compute cost of goods sold. Even businesses that use a perpetual inventory system take a physical inventory. They do so to check the accuracy of the "book inventory" and to determine the amount of inventory shortage or shrinkage due to wasted raw materials, shoplifting, or employee theft.

Determining inventory quantities involves two steps: (1) taking a physical inventory of goods on hand and (2) determining the ownership of goods.

Taking a Physical Inventory. Taking a physical inventory involves actually counting, weighing, or measuring each kind of inventory on hand. In many companies, taking an inventory is a formidable task. Retailers such as Kmart, True Value Hardware, or Home Depot have thousands of different inventory items. An inventory count is generally more accurate when goods are not being sold or received during the counting. Consequently, companies often "take inventory" when the business is closed or when business is slow. Many retailers close early on a chosen day in January—after the holiday sales and returns, when inventories are at their lowest level—to count inventory. Under a periodic inventory system, the physical inventory is taken at the end of the accounting period.

After the physical inventory is taken, the quantity of each kind of inventory is listed on **inventory summary sheets.** To assure the accuracy of the summary sheets, the listing should be verified by a second employee or supervisor. Subsequently, unit costs will be applied to the quantities to determine a total cost of the inventory, which is the topic of later sections. Although taking the physical inventory may seem mechanical, an accurate inventory count is important to help companies avoid the negative consequences of poor inventory taking—incorrect financial statements and incorrect income tax returns.

BUSINESS INSIGHT
Management Perspective

Failure to observe internal control procedures over inventory contributed to the Great Salad Oil Swindle. In this case, management intentionally overstated its salad oil inventory, which was stored in large holding tanks. Three procedures contributed to overstating the oil inventory: (1) Water added to the bottom of the holding tanks caused the oil to float to the top. Inventory-taking crews who viewed the holding tanks from the top observed only salad oil, when, in fact, as much as 37 out of 40 feet of many of the holding tanks contained water. (2) The company's inventory records listed more holding tanks than it actually had. The company repainted numbers on the tanks after inventory crews examined them, so the crews counted the same tanks twice. (3) Underground pipes pumped oil from one holding tank to another during the inventory taking; therefore, the same salad oil was counted more than once. Although the salad oil swindle was unusual, it demonstrates the complexities involved in assuring that inventory is properly counted.

Determining Ownership of Goods. To determine ownership of goods, two questions must be answered: Do all of the goods included in the count belong to the company? Does the company own any goods that were not included in the count?

Goods in Transit. A complication in determining ownership is goods in transit (on board a truck, train, ship, or plane) at the end of the period. The company may have purchased goods that have not yet been received, or it may have sold goods that have not yet been delivered. To arrive at an accurate count, ownership of these goods must be determined.

Goods in transit should be included in the inventory of the company that has legal title to the goods. Legal title is determined by the terms of the sale, as shown in Illustration 6-3 and described below:

Illustration 6-3 Terms of sale

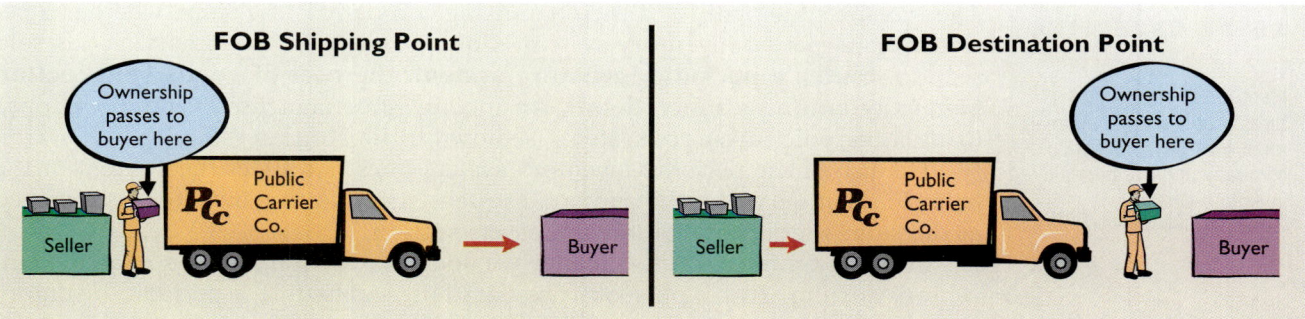

1. When the terms are **FOB (free on board) shipping point,** ownership of the goods passes to the buyer when the public carrier accepts the goods from the seller.
2. When the terms are **FOB destination,** ownership of the goods remains with the seller until the goods reach the buyer.

Consigned Goods. In some lines of business, it is customary to hold the goods of other parties and try to sell the goods for them for a fee, but without taking ownership of the goods. These are called **consigned goods.** For example, you might have a used car that you would like to sell. If you take the item to a dealer, the dealer might be willing to put the car on its lot and charge you a commission if it is sold. But under this agreement the dealer **would not take ownership** of the car, which would still belong to you. Therefore, if an inventory count were taken, the car would not be included in the dealer's inventory. Many car, boat, and antique dealers sell goods on consignment to keep their inventory costs down and to avoid the risk of purchasing an item that they won't be able to sell.

Computing Cost of Goods Sold

We have now reached the point where we can compute cost of goods sold. Doing so involves two steps:

1. Add the cost of goods purchased to the cost of goods on hand at the beginning of the period (beginning inventory) to obtain the **cost of goods available for sale.**
2. Subtract the cost of goods on hand at the end of the period (ending inventory) from the cost of goods available for sale to arrive at the **cost of goods sold.**

For PW Audio Supply the cost of goods available for sale and the cost of goods sold are $356,000 and $316,000, respectively, and the beginning and ending inventory are assumed to be $36,000 and $40,000, respectively (Illustration 6-4).

Illustration 6-4 Computation of cost of goods available for sale and cost of goods sold

Beginning inventory	$ 36,000
(1) Add: Cost of goods purchased	320,000
Cost of goods available for sale	**356,000**
(2) Less: Ending inventory	40,000
Cost of goods sold	**$316,000**

INCOME STATEMENT PRESENTATION

STUDY OBJECTIVE 4

Identify the unique features of the income statement for a merchandising company under a periodic inventory system.

The income statement for a merchandising company is the same whether a periodic or perpetual inventory system is used, except for the cost of goods sold section. **Under a periodic inventory system, the cost of goods sold section generally contains more detail.** An income statement for PW Audio Supply, using a periodic inventory system, is shown in Illustration 6-5.

The use of the periodic inventory system does not affect the content of the balance sheet. As under the perpetual system, merchandise inventory is reported at the same amount in the current assets section.

In the remainder of this chapter we address additional issues related to inventory costing. To simplify our presentation, we assume a periodic inventory accounting system.

BEFORE YOU GO ON . . .

● **Review It**

1. Discuss the three steps in determining cost of goods sold in a periodic inventory system.
2. What accounts are used in determining the cost of goods purchased?
3. In what ways is a perpetual inventory system different from a periodic inventory system?

PW AUDIO SUPPLY
Income Statement
For the Year Ended December 31, 1998

Sales revenues			
Sales			$480,000
Less: Sales returns and allowances		$ 12,000	
Sales discounts		8,000	20,000
Net sales			460,000
Cost of goods sold			
Inventory, January 1			36,000
Purchases	$325,000		
Less: Purchases returns and allowances	$10,400		
Purchase discounts	6,800	17,200	
Net purchases		307,800	
Add: Freight-in		12,200	
Cost of goods purchased			320,000
Cost of goods available for sale			356,000
Inventory, December 31			40,000
Cost of goods sold			316,000
Gross profit			144,000
Operating expenses			114,000
Net income			$ 30,000

Illustration 6-5 Income statement for a merchandising company using a periodic inventory system

Helpful Hint The far right column identifies the major subdivisions of the income statement. The next column identifies the primary items that make up cost of goods sold of $316,000; in addition, contra revenue items of $20,000 are reported. The third column explains cost of goods purchased of $320,000. The fourth column reports contra purchase items of $17,200.

● Do It

Aerosmith Company's accounting records show the following at year-end: Purchase Discounts $3,400; Freight-in $6,100; Sales $240,000; Purchases $162,500; Beginning Inventory $18,000; Ending Inventory $20,000; Sales Discounts $10,000; Purchase Returns $5,200; and Operating Expenses $57,000. Compute these amounts for Aerosmith Company:

(a) Net sales   (d) Gross profit
(b) Cost of goods purchased   (e) Net income
(c) Cost of goods sold

Reasoning: To compute the required amounts, it is important to know the relationships in measuring net income for a merchandising company. For example, it is necessary to know the difference between sales and net sales, goods available for sale and cost of goods sold, and gross profit and net income.

Solution:
(a) Net sales: Sales − Sales discounts
$240,000 − $10,000 = $230,000
(b) Cost of goods purchased:
Purchases − Purchase returns − Purchase discounts + Freight-in
$162,500 − $5,200 − $3,400 + $6,100 = $160,000
(c) Cost of goods sold:
Beginning inventory + Cost of goods purchased − Ending inventory
$18,000 + $160,000 − $20,000 = $158,000
(d) Gross profit: Net sales − Cost of goods sold
$230,000 − $158,000 = $72,000
(e) Net income: Gross profit − Operating expenses
$72,000 − $57,000 = $15,000

INVENTORY COSTING

STUDY OBJECTIVE 5

Explain the basis of accounting for inventories and apply the inventory cost flow methods under a periodic inventory system.

Purchases, purchase discounts, purchase returns and allowances, and freight-in are all costs included in the cost of goods available for sale. Cost of goods available for sale must be allocated between cost of goods sold and ending inventory at the end of the accounting period. First, the costs assignable to the ending inventory are determined. Second, the cost of the ending inventory is subtracted from the cost of goods available for sale to determine the cost of goods sold. (Refer back to Illustration 6-4 to see this computation.)

Determining ending inventory can be complicated if the units on hand for a specific item of inventory have been purchased at different prices. Assume, for example, that Crivitz TV Company purchases three 46-inch TVs at costs of $700, $750, and $800. During the year, two sets are sold at $1,200 each. Ending inventory might be $700, $750, or $800, and corresponding cost of goods sold might be $1,550 ($750 + $800), $1,500 ($700 + $800), or $1,450 ($700 + $750), respectively, depending on how Crivitz measures the cost flows of the inventory purchased and sold. In this section we discuss alternative inventory costing methods.

SPECIFIC IDENTIFICATION

If we determine that the TV in Crivitz's inventory is the one originally purchased for $750, then the ending inventory is $750 and cost of goods sold is $1,500 ($700 + $800). If Crivitz can positively identify which particular units were sold and which are still in ending inventory, it can use the **specific identification method** of inventory costing (see Illustration 6-6). In this case ending inventory and cost of goods sold are easily and accurately determined.

Illustration 6-6 Specific identification

Helpful Hint A major disadvantage of the specific identification method is that management may be able to manipulate net income through specific identification of items sold.

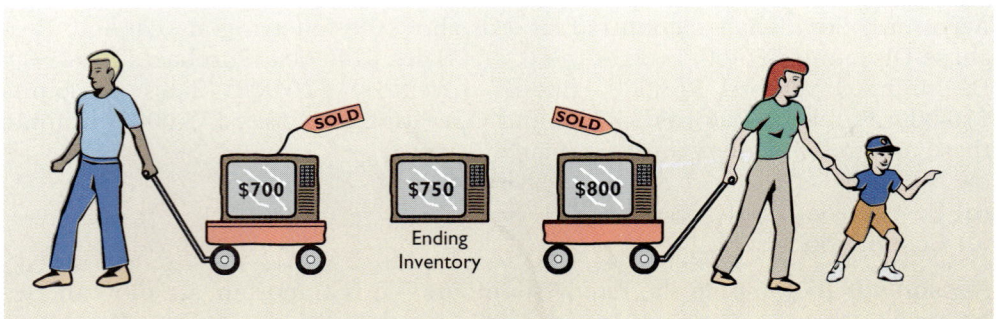

Specific identification is possible when a company sells a limited variety of high-unit-cost items that can be identified clearly from the time of purchase through the time of sale. Examples of such companies are automobile dealerships (cars, trucks, and vans), music stores (pianos and organs), and antique shops (tables and cabinets).

But what if we cannot specifically identify particular inventory units? For example, drug, grocery, and hardware stores sell thousands of relatively low-unit-cost items of inventory. These items are often indistinguishable from one another, making it impossible or impractical to track each item's cost. In that case, we must make assumptions, called **cost flow assumptions,** about which units were sold.

USING ASSUMED COST FLOW METHODS

Because specific identification is often impractical, other cost flow methods are allowed. These differ from specific identification in that they assume flows of costs that may be unrelated to the physical flow of goods. There are three assumed cost flow methods:

1. First-in, first-out (FIFO)
2. Last-in, first-out (LIFO)
3. Average cost

There is no accounting requirement that the cost flow assumption be consistent with the physical movement of the goods. The selection of the appropriate cost flow method is made by management.

To illustrate these three inventory cost flow methods, we will assume that Houston Electronics uses a periodic inventory system and has the information shown in Illustration 6-7 for its Astro condenser.

⊕ **International Note**
A survey of accounting standards in 21 major industrial countries found that all three methods were permissible. In Ireland and the U.K., LIFO is permitted only in extreme circumstances.

HOUSTON ELECTRONICS
Astro Condensers

Date	Explanation	Units	Unit Cost	Total Cost
Jan. 1	Beginning inventory	100	$10	$ 1,000
Apr. 15	Purchase	200	11	2,200
Aug. 24	Purchase	300	12	3,600
Nov. 27	Purchase	400	13	5,200
	Total	1,000		$12,000

Illustration 6-7 Cost of goods available for sale

The company had a total of 1,000 units available that it could have sold during the period. The total cost of these units was $12,000. A physical inventory at the end of the year determined that during the year 550 units were sold and 450 units were in inventory at December 31. The question then is how to determine what prices to use to value the goods sold and the ending inventory. The sum of the cost allocated to the units sold plus the cost of the units in inventory must add up to $12,000, the total cost of all goods available for sale.

First-In, First-Out (FIFO)

The **FIFO method** assumes that the **earliest goods** purchased are the first to be sold. FIFO often parallels the actual physical flow of merchandise because it generally is good business practice to sell the oldest units first. Under the FIFO method, therefore, the **costs** of the earliest goods purchased are the first to be recognized as cost of goods sold. (Note that this does not necessarily mean that the oldest units *are* sold first, but that the costs of the oldest units are recognized first. In a bin of picture hangers at the hardware store, for example, no one really knows, nor would it matter, which hangers are sold first.) The allocation of the cost of goods available for sale at Houston Electronics under FIFO is shown in Illustration 6-8 (at the top of the next page).

Note that under FIFO, since it is assumed that the first goods sold were the first goods purchased, ending inventory is based on the prices of the most recent units purchased. That is, **under FIFO, the cost of the ending inventory is obtained by taking the unit cost of the most recent purchase and working backward until all units of inventory have been costed.** In this example, the 450 units of ending inventory must be priced using the most recent prices. The last purchase was 400 units at $13 on November 27. The remaining 50 units are priced at the price of the second most recent purchase, $12, on August 24. Next, cost of goods sold is calculated by subtracting the cost of the units **not sold** (ending inventory) from the cost of all goods available for sale.

Illustration 6-8
Allocation of costs—FIFO method

Helpful Hint Note the sequencing of the allocation: (1) compute ending inventory and (2) determine cost of goods sold.

Helpful Hint Note that the ending inventory of $5,800 plus the cost of goods sold of $6,200 equals the $12,000 cost of goods available for sale.

POOL OF COSTS
COST OF GOODS AVAILABLE FOR SALE

Date	Explanation	Units	Unit Cost	Total Cost
Jan. 1	Beginning inventory	100	$10	$ 1,000
Apr. 15	Purchase	200	11	2,200
Aug. 24	Purchase	300	12	3,600
Nov. 27	Purchase	400	13	5,200
	Total	1,000		**$12,000**

STEP 1: ENDING INVENTORY

Date	Units	Unit Cost	Total Cost
Nov. 27	400	$13	$ 5,200
Aug. 24	50	12	600
Total	450		**$5,800**

STEP 2: COST OF GOODS SOLD

Cost of goods available for sale	$12,000
Less: Ending inventory	5,800
Cost of goods sold	**$ 6,200**

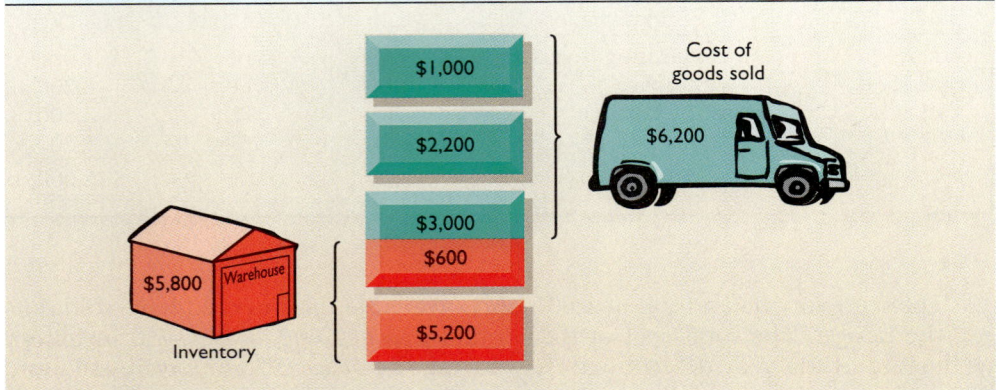

Illustration 6-9 demonstrates that cost of goods sold can also be calculated by pricing the 550 units sold using the prices of the first 550 units acquired. Note that of the 300 units purchased on August 24, only 250 units are assumed sold. This agrees with our calculation of the cost of ending inventory, where 50 of these units were assumed unsold and thus included in ending inventory.

Illustration 6-9 Proof of cost of goods sold

Date	Units	Unit Cost	Total Cost
Jan. 1	100	$10	$1,000
Apr. 15	200	11	2,200
Aug. 24	250	12	3,000
Total	550		**$6,200**

Last-In, First-Out (LIFO)

The **LIFO method** assumes that the **latest goods** purchased are the first to be sold. LIFO seldom coincides with the actual physical flow of inventory. (Exceptions include goods stored in piles, such as coal or hay, where goods are removed from the top of the pile as sold.) Under the LIFO method, the **costs** of the latest goods purchased are the first to be recognized as cost of goods sold. The allocation of the cost of goods available for sale at Houston Electronics under LIFO is shown in Illustration 6-10.

Illustration 6-10
Allocation of costs—LIFO method

POOL OF COSTS
COST OF GOODS AVAILABLE FOR SALE

Date	Explanation	Units	Unit Cost	Total Cost
Jan. 1	Beginning inventory	100	$10	$ 1,000
Apr. 15	Purchase	200	11	2,200
Aug. 24	Purchase	300	12	3,600
Nov. 27	Purchase	400	13	5,200
	Total	1,000		$12,000

STEP 1: ENDING INVENTORY

Date	Units	Unit Cost	Total Cost
Jan. 1	100	$10	$1,000
Apr. 15	200	11	2,200
Aug. 24	150	12	1,800
Total	450		$5,000

STEP 2: COST OF GOODS SOLD

Cost of goods available for sale	$12,000
Less: Ending inventory	5,000
Cost of goods sold	$ 7,000

Under LIFO, since it is assumed that the first goods sold were those that were most recently purchased, ending inventory is based on the prices of the oldest units purchased. That is, **under LIFO, the cost of the ending inventory is obtained by taking the unit cost of the earliest goods available for sale and working forward until all units of inventory have been costed.** In this example, the 450 units of ending inventory must be priced using the earliest prices. The first purchase was 100 units at $10 in the January 1 beginning inventory. Then 200 units were purchased at $11. The remaining 150 units needed are priced at $12 per unit (August 24 purchase). Next, cost of goods sold is calculated by subtracting the cost of the units **not sold** (ending inventory) from the cost of all goods available for sale.

Illustration 6-11 (at the top of the next page) demonstrates that cost of goods sold can also be calculated by pricing the 550 units sold using the prices of the last 550 units acquired. Note that of the 300 units purchased on August 24, only 150 units are assumed sold. This agrees with our calculation of the cost of ending inventory, where 150 of these units were assumed unsold and thus included in ending inventory.

Illustration 6-11 Proof of cost of goods sold

Date	Units	Unit Cost	Total Cost
Nov. 27	400	$13	$5,200
Aug. 24	150	12	1,800
Total	550		**$7,000**

Under a periodic inventory system, which we are using here, **all goods purchased during the period are assumed to be available for the first sale, regardless of the date of purchase.**

Average Cost

The **average cost method** assumes that the goods available for sale are homogeneous. Under this method, the allocation of the cost of goods available for sale is made on the basis of the **weighted average unit cost** incurred. The formula and a sample computation of the weighted average unit cost are given in Illustration 6-12.

Illustration 6-12 Formula for weighted average unit cost

The weighted average unit cost is then applied to the units on hand to determine the cost of the ending inventory. The allocation of the cost of goods available for sale at Houston Electronics using average cost is shown in Illustration 6-13.

Illustration 6-13 Allocation of costs—average cost method

POOL OF COSTS
COST OF GOODS AVAILABLE FOR SALE

Date	Explanation	Units	Unit Cost	Total Cost
Jan. 1	Beginning inventory	100	$10	$ 1,000
Apr. 15	Purchase	200	11	2,200
Aug. 24	Purchase	300	12	3,600
Nov. 27	Purchase	400	13	5,200
	Total	1,000		**$12,000**

STEP 1: ENDING INVENTORY

$12,000	÷	1,000	=	$12.00
Units		Unit Cost		Total Cost
450		$12.00		**$5,400**

STEP 2: COST OF GOODS SOLD

Cost of goods available for sale	$12,000
Less: Ending inventory	5,400
Cost of goods sold	**$ 6,600**

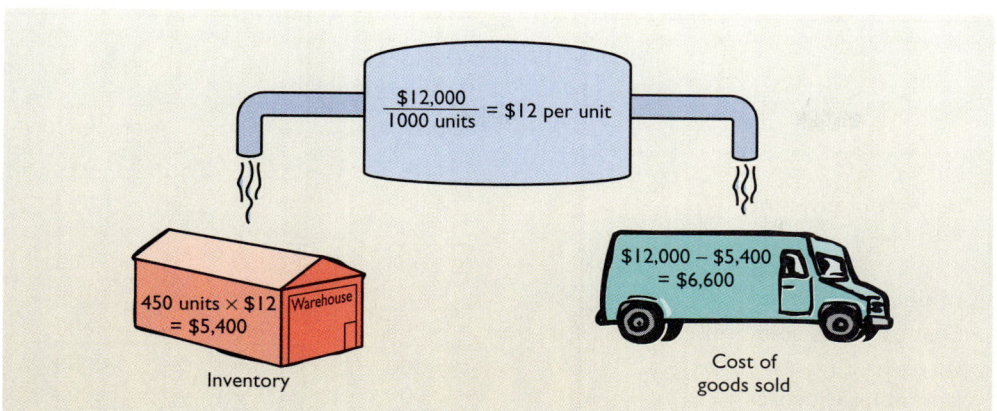

Illustration 6-13 (continued)

We can verify the cost of goods sold under this method by multiplying the units sold by the weighted average unit cost (550 × $12 = $6,600). Note that this method does not use the average of the unit costs. That average is $11.50 ($10 + $11 + $12 + $13 = $46; $46 ÷ 4). The average cost method instead uses the average **weighted** by the quantities purchased at each unit cost.

FINANCIAL STATEMENT AND TAX EFFECTS OF COST FLOW METHODS

Each of the three assumed cost flow methods is acceptable. For example, Black and Decker Manufacturing Company and Wendy's International currently use the FIFO method of inventory costing. Campbell Soup Company, Krogers, and Walgreen Drugs use LIFO for part or all of their inventory. Bristol-Myers, Starbucks, and Motorola use the average cost method. Indeed, a company may also use more than one cost flow method at the same time. Del Monte Corporation, for example, uses LIFO for domestic inventories and FIFO for foreign inventories. Illustration 6-14 shows the use of the three cost flow methods in the 600 largest U.S. companies. The reasons companies adopt different inventory cost flow methods are varied, but they usually involve one of three factors:

1. Income statement effects
2. Balance sheet effects
3. Tax effects

Income Statement Effects

To understand why companies might choose a particular cost flow method, let's examine the effects of the different cost flow assumptions on the financial statements of Houston Electronics. The condensed income statements in Illustration 6-15 (next page) assume that Houston sold its 550 units for $11,500, had operating expenses of $2,000, and is subject to an income tax rate of 30%.

Although the cost of goods available for sale ($12,000) is the same under each of the three inventory cost flow methods, both the ending inventories and costs of goods sold are different. This difference is due to the unit costs that are allocated to cost of goods sold and to ending inventory. Each dollar of difference in ending inventory results in a corresponding dollar difference in income before income taxes. For Houston, an $800 difference exists between FIFO and LIFO cost of goods sold.

STUDY OBJECTIVE 6
Explain the financial statement and tax effects of each of the inventory cost flow assumptions.

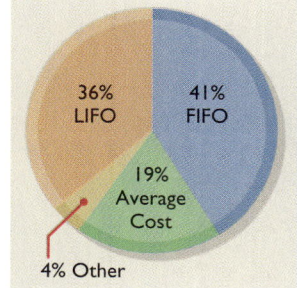

Illustration 6-14 Use of cost flow methods in major U.S. companies

Helpful Hint The management of companies in the same industry may reach different conclusions as to the most appropriate method for their respective companies.

Illustration 6-15 Comparative effects of cost flow methods

HOUSTON ELECTRONICS Condensed Income Statements	FIFO	LIFO	Average Cost
Sales	$11,500	$11,500	$11,500
Beginning inventory	1,000	1,000	1,000
Purchases	11,000	11,000	11,000
Cost of goods available for sale	12,000	12,000	12,000
Ending inventory	5,800	5,000	5,400
Cost of goods sold	6,200	7,000	6,600
Gross profit	5,300	4,500	4,900
Operating expenses	2,000	2,000	2,000
Income before income taxes	3,300	2,500	2,900
Income tax expense (30%)	990	750	870
Net income	$ 2,310	$ 1,750	$ 2,030

In periods of changing prices, the cost flow assumption can have a significant impact on income and on evaluations based on income. In a period of inflation, FIFO produces a higher net income because the lower unit costs of the first units purchased are matched against revenues. In a period of rising prices (as is the case here for Houston), FIFO reports the highest net income ($2,310) and LIFO the lowest ($1,750); average cost falls in the middle ($2,030). If prices are falling, the results from the use of FIFO and LIFO are reversed: FIFO will report the lowest net income and LIFO the highest. To management, higher net income is an advantage: It causes external users to view the company more favorably. In addition, if management bonuses are based on net income, FIFO will provide the basis for higher bonuses.

Some argue that the use of LIFO in a period of inflation enables the company to avoid reporting **paper or phantom profit** as economic gain. To illustrate, assume that Kralik Company buys 200 units of a product at $20 per unit on January 10 and 200 more on December 31 at $24 each. During the year, 200 units are sold at $30 each. The results under FIFO and LIFO are shown in Illustration 6-16.

Illustration 6-16 Income statement effects compared

	FIFO	LIFO
Sales (200 × $30)	$6,000	$6,000
Cost of goods sold	4,000 (200 × $20)	4,800 (200 × $24)
Gross profit	$2,000	$1,200

Helpful Hint The $800 is also referred to as a holding gain that is deferred under LIFO until the goods are sold.

Under LIFO, Kralik Company has recovered the current replacement cost ($4,800) of the units sold. Thus, the gross profit in economic terms is real. However, under FIFO, the company has recovered only the January 10 cost ($4,000). To replace the units sold, it must reinvest $800 (200 × $4) of the gross profit. Thus, $800 of the gross profit is said to be phantom or illusory. As a result, reported net income is also overstated in real terms.

Balance Sheet Effects

A major advantage of the FIFO method is that in a period of inflation, the costs allocated to ending inventory will approximate their current cost. For example, for Houston, 400 of the 450 units in the ending inventory are costed under FIFO at the higher November 27 unit cost of $13.

Conversely, a major shortcoming of the LIFO method is that in a period of inflation, the costs allocated to ending inventory may be significantly understated in terms of current cost. This is true for Houston, where the cost of the ending inventory includes the $10 unit cost of the beginning inventory. The understatement becomes greater over prolonged periods of inflation if the inventory includes goods purchased in one or more prior accounting periods.

Tax Effects

We have seen that both inventory on the balance sheet and net income on the income statement are higher when FIFO is used in a period of inflation. Yet, many companies have switched to LIFO. The reason is that LIFO results in the lowest income taxes (because of lower net income) during times of rising prices. For example, at Houston Electronics, income taxes are $750 under LIFO compared to $990 under FIFO. The tax saving of $240 makes more cash available for use in the business.

Helpful Hint A tax rule, often referred to as the **LIFO conformity rule**, requires that if LIFO is used for tax purposes it must also be used for financial reporting purposes. This means that if a company chooses the LIFO method to reduce its tax bills, it will also have to report lower net income in its financial statements.

DECISION TOOLKIT

Decision Checkpoints	Info Needed for Decision	Tool to Use for Decision	How to Evaluate Results
Which inventory costing method should be used?	Are prices increasing, or are they decreasing?	Income statement, balance sheet, and tax effects	Depends on objective. In a period of rising prices, income and inventory are higher and cash flow is lower under FIFO. LIFO provides opposite results. Average cost can moderate the impact of changing prices.

BUSINESS INSIGHT
Management Perspective

Most small firms use the FIFO method. But fears of rising inflation often cause many firms to switch to LIFO. For example, Chicago Heights Steel Co. in Illinois boosted cash "by 5% to 10% by lowering income taxes" when it switched to LIFO. Electronic games distributor Atlas Distributing Inc. in Chicago considered a switch "because the costs of our games, made in Japan, are rising 15% a year," says Joseph Serpico, treasurer. When inflation heats up, "the number of companies electing LIFO will rise dramatically," says William Spiro of BDO Seidman, New York.

USING INVENTORY COST FLOW METHODS CONSISTENTLY

Whatever cost flow method a company chooses, it should be used consistently from one accounting period to another. Consistent application enhances the comparability of financial statements over successive time periods. In contrast, using the FIFO method one year and the LIFO method the next year would make it difficult to compare the net incomes of the two years.

256 CHAPTER 6 Reporting and Analyzing Inventory

Helpful Hint As you learned in Chapter 2, consistency and comparability are important characteristics of accounting information.

Although consistent application is preferred, it does not mean that a company may *never* change its method of inventory costing. When a company adopts a different method, the change and its effects on net income should be disclosed in the financial statements. A typical disclosure is shown in Illustration 6-17, using information from recent financial statements of the Quaker Oats Company.

Illustration 6-17 Disclosure of change in cost flow method

> **QUAKER OATS COMPANY**
> **Notes to the Financial Statements**
>
> **Note 1:** Effective July 1, the Company adopted the LIFO cost flow assumption for valuing the majority of U.S. Grocery Products inventories. The Company believes that the use of the LIFO method better matches current costs with current revenues. The effect of this change on the current year was to decrease net income by $16.0 million.

BUSINESS INSIGHT
International Perspective

U.S. companies typically choose between LIFO and FIFO. Many choose LIFO because it reduces inventory profits and taxes. However, the international community recently considered rules that would ban LIFO entirely and force companies to use FIFO. This proposed rule was defeated, but the issue is almost certain to reappear.

The issue is sensitive. As John Wulff, controller for Union Carbide, noted, "We were in support of the international effort up until the proposal to eliminate LIFO." Wulff says that if Union Carbide had been suddenly forced to switch from LIFO to FIFO recently, its reported $632 million pretax income would have jumped by $300 million. That would have increased Carbide's income tax bill by as much as $120 million.

Do you believe that accounting principles and rules should be the same around the world?

VALUING INVENTORY AT THE LOWER OF COST OR MARKET

STUDY OBJECTIVE 7

Explain the lower of cost or market basis of accounting for inventories.

The value of the inventory of companies selling high-technology or fashion goods can drop very quickly due to changes in technology or changes in fashions. These circumstances sometimes call for inventory valuation methods other than those presented so far. For example, suppose you are the owner of a retail store that sells Compaq Desk Pro computers. During the recent 12-month period, the cost of the computers dropped $1,800 (almost 50%). At the end of your fiscal year, you have some of these computers in inventory. Do you think your inventory should be stated at cost, in accordance with the cost principle, or at its lower replacement cost?

As you probably reasoned, this situation requires a departure from the cost basis of accounting. When the value of inventory is lower than its cost, the inventory is written down to its market value. This is done by valuing the inventory at the **lower of cost or market (LCM)** in the period in which the price decline occurs. LCM is an example of the accounting concept of conservatism, which means that the best choice among accounting alternatives is the method that is least likely to overstate assets and net income.

LCM is applied to the items in inventory after one of the cost flow methods (specific identification, FIFO, LIFO, or average cost) has been used to determine cost. Under the LCM basis, market is defined as **current replacement cost**, not selling price. For a merchandising company, market is the cost of purchasing the same goods at the present time from the usual suppliers in the usual quantities. Current replacement cost is used because a decline in the replacement cost of an item usually leads to a decline in the selling price of the item.

BEFORE YOU GO ON . . .

● Review It

1. How are the three assumed cost flow methods applied in allocating cost of goods available for sale?
2. What factors should be considered by management in selecting an inventory cost flow method?
3. Which inventory cost flow method produces the highest net income in a period of rising prices? The lowest income taxes?
4. When should inventory be reported at a value other than cost?

● Do It

The accounting records of Shumway Ag Implement show these data:

Beginning inventory	4,000 units at $3
Purchases	6,000 units at $4
Sales	5,000 units at $12

Determine the cost of goods sold during the period under a periodic inventory system using (a) the FIFO method, (b) the LIFO method, and (c) the average cost method.

Reasoning: Because the units of inventory on hand and available for sale may have been purchased at different prices, a systematic method must be adopted to allocate the costs between the goods sold and the goods on hand (ending inventory).

Solution:

(a) FIFO: (4,000 @ $3) + (1,000 @ $4) = $12,000 + $4,000 = $16,000
(b) LIFO: 5,000 @ $4 = $20,000
(c) Average cost: [(4,000 @ $3) + (6,000 @ $4)] ÷ 10,000
    = ($12,000 + $24,000) ÷ 10,000
    = $3.60 per unit; 5,000 @ $3.60 = $18,000

ANALYSIS OF INVENTORY

For companies that sell goods, managing inventory levels can be one of the most critical tasks. Having too much inventory on hand costs the company money in storage costs, interest cost (on funds tied up in inventory), and costs associated with the obsolescence of technical goods (e.g., computer chips) or shifts in fashion for products like clothes. But having too little inventory on hand results in lost sales. In this section we discuss some issues related to evaluating inventory levels.

INVENTORY TURNOVER RATIO

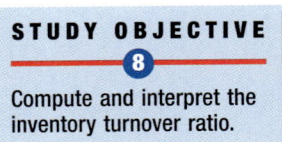

STUDY OBJECTIVE 8
Compute and interpret the inventory turnover ratio.

The **inventory turnover ratio** is calculated as cost of goods sold divided by average inventory. Its complement, **days in inventory,** indicates the average age of the inventory; it is calculated as 365 days divided by the inventory turnover ratio. Both measures indicate how quickly a company sells its goods—how many times the inventory "turns over" (is sold) during the year. High inventory turnover or low days in inventory indicates the company is tying up little of its funds in inventory—that it has a minimal amount of inventory on hand at any one time. Although minimizing the funds tied up in inventory is efficient, too high an inventory turnover ratio may indicate that the company is losing sales opportunities because of inventory shortages. Thus, management should closely monitor this ratio to achieve the best balance between too much and too little inventory.

In Chapter 5 we discussed the increasingly competitive environment of retailers like Wal-Mart and Kmart. We noted that Wal-Mart has implemented many technological innovations to improve the efficiency of its operations. Illustration 6-18 presents the inventory turnover ratios and days in inventory for Wal-Mart and Kmart, using data from the financial statements of those corporations for 1994 and 1995.

Illustration 6-18 Inventory turnover ratio and days in inventory

$$\text{INVENTORY TURNOVER RATIO} = \frac{\text{COST OF GOODS SOLD}}{\text{AVERAGE INVENTORY}}$$

$$\text{DAYS IN INVENTORY} = \frac{365}{\text{INVENTORY TURNOVER RATIO}}$$

($ in millions)		1995	1994
Wal-Mart	Inventory turnover ratio	$\frac{\$74,564}{(\$15,989 + \$14,064)/2} = 5.0$ times	$\frac{\$65,586}{(\$14,064 + \$11,014)/2} = 5.2$ times
	Days in inventory	$\frac{365 \text{ days}}{5.0} = 73$ days	$\frac{365 \text{ days}}{5.2} = 70.2$ days
Kmart	Inventory turnover ratio	$\frac{\$26,996}{(\$6,635 + \$6,853)/2} = 4.0$ times	$\frac{\$24,868}{(\$6,853 + \$7,053)/2} = 3.5$ times
	Days in inventory	$\frac{365 \text{ days}}{4.0} = 91.3$ days	$\frac{365 \text{ days}}{3.5} = 104.3$ days

The calculations in Illustration 6-18 show that Wal-Mart turns its inventory more frequently than Kmart and, consequently, the average time an item spends on a Wal-Mart shelf is shorter. This suggests that Wal-Mart is more efficient than Kmart in its inventory management. Wal-Mart's sophisticated inventory tracking and distribution system allows it to keep minimum amounts of inventory on hand, while still keeping the shelves full of what customers are looking for. In contrast, even though its inventory turnover is lower than that of Wal-Mart, Kmart has been criticized for inventory outages. However, recent improvements in Kmart's inventory tracking and distribution systems have resulted in significant improvements. It recently achieved 97% inventory stock availability, although it still had not met its goal of 98%.

BUSINESS INSIGHT
Management Perspective

As noted in the opening story, in recent years many companies, including Caterpillar, have adopted inventory management techniques to reduce the amount of inventory they have on hand. These practices are referred to as "just-in-time" inventory, or JIT. A recent *Wall Street Journal* story noted, however, that sometimes these practices can cause hardship for companies. Drops in supply and surges in the prices of oil, natural gas, corn, wheat, and coffee have left many companies that are reliant on these raw materials scrambling to find enough goods to meet their needs. By having only small amounts of inventory on hand, these companies subject themselves to much more price and supply volatility than if they held large inventories.

To reduce such volatility, many companies enter into "hedges"—financial transactions that act as a sort of insurance against big price changes. Even with hedges such as futures contracts, many times companies have to pass higher prices of commodities or raw materials on to the consumer.

Source: Aaron Lucchetti, "Low Inventories Add to Unpredictability," *The Wall Street Journal,* March 10, 1997, p. C1.

DECISION TOOLKIT

Decision Checkpoints	Info Needed for Decision	Tool to Use for Decision	How to Evaluate Results
How long is an item in inventory?	Cost of goods sold; beginning and ending inventory	Inventory turnover ratio = $\dfrac{\text{Cost of goods sold}}{\text{Average inventory}}$ Average days in inventory = $\dfrac{365 \text{ days}}{\text{Inventory turnover ratio}}$	A higher inventory turnover ratio or lower average days in inventory suggests that management is reducing the amount of inventory on hand, relative to sales.

ANALYSTS' ADJUSTMENTS FOR LIFO RESERVE

Earlier we noted that using LIFO rather than FIFO can result in significant differences in the results reported in the balance sheet and the income statement. With increasing prices, FIFO will result in higher income than LIFO. On the balance sheet, FIFO will result in higher reported inventory. The financial statement impact of using LIFO normally increases the longer a company uses LIFO.

Using different inventory cost flow assumptions complicates analysts' attempts to compare the results of firms that use different inventory methods. Fortunately, companies using LIFO are required to report the amount that inventory would increase (or occasionally decrease) if the firm had instead been using FIFO. This amount is referred to as the **LIFO reserve.** Reporting the LIFO reserve enables analysts to make adjustments to compare companies that use different cost flow methods.

Illustration 6-19 (at the top of the next page) presents an excerpt from the notes to Caterpillar's 1995 financial statements that discloses and discusses Caterpillar's LIFO reserve.

> **STUDY OBJECTIVE**
> **9**
> Describe the LIFO reserve and explain its importance for comparing results of different companies.

260 CHAPTER 6 Reporting and Analyzing Inventory

Illustration 6-19 Disclosure of LIFO reserve

> **CATERPILLAR INC.**
> **Notes to the Financial Statements**
>
> **Inventories:** The cost of inventories is determined principally by the LIFO (last-in, first-out) method of inventory valuation. LIFO was first adopted for the major portion of inventories in 1950. If the FIFO (first-in, first-out) method had been used, inventories would have been $2,103 million and $2,035 million higher than reported at December 31, 1995 and 1994, respectively.

Because Caterpillar has used LIFO for 45 years, the difference between LIFO and FIFO reported in the inventory account is very large. In fact, the 1995 LIFO reserve of $2,103 million actually exceeds total 1995 inventory of $1,921 million. Such a huge difference would clearly distort any comparisons you might try to make with one of Caterpillar's competitors that used FIFO.

To adjust Caterpillar's inventory balance you add the LIFO reserve to reported inventory, as shown in Illustration 6-20. That is, if Caterpillar used FIFO all along, its inventory would be $4,024 million rather than $1,921 million.

Illustration 6-20
Conversion of inventory from LIFO to FIFO

	(in millions)
1995 inventory using LIFO	$1,921
1995 LIFO reserve	2,103
1995 inventory assuming FIFO	**$4,024**

To adjust Caterpillar's cost of goods sold, you must subtract the $68 million change in the LIFO reserve from the reported cost of goods sold, as shown in Illustration 6-21.[1]

Illustration 6-21
Conversion of cost of goods sold from LIFO to FIFO

	(in millions)
1995 cost of goods sold using LIFO	$12,000
Less: 1995 increase in LIFO reserve	68
1995 cost of goods sold assuming FIFO	**$11,932**

The adjustment to Caterpillar's reported income in 1995 was minor. Consider, however, the impact that the inventory adjustment has on two ratios commonly used by analysts, the **current ratio** (discussed in Chapter 2) and the inventory turnover ratio, discussed earlier in this chapter. Illustration 6-22 calculates these ratios for Caterpillar under both the LIFO and FIFO cost flow assumptions. The following additional information (in millions) is used:

1994 LIFO inventory	$1,835	1995 Current assets (using LIFO inventory)	$7,647
1994 FIFO inventory	$3,870	1995 Current assets (using FIFO inventory)	$9,750
1995 Current liabilities	$6,049		

As shown in Illustration 6-22, if Caterpillar uses FIFO, its current ratio is 1.61 : 1 rather than 1.26 : 1, a 28% increase. Thus, Caterpillar's liquidity appears much stronger if a FIFO assumption is used in valuing inventories. At the same time, Caterpillar's inventory turnover ratio drops dramatically from 6.39 times to 3.02 times using the FIFO assumption. The reason: LIFO reports low inven-

---

[1]The $68 million change is determined from the information in Caterpillar's notes (Illustration 6–19)—$2,103 million less $2,035 million. In the case of a *decline* in the LIFO reserve, you would *add* the change in the reported reserve to the reported cost of goods sold.

Illustration 6-22 Impact of LIFO reserve on ratios

($ in millions)	LIFO	FIFO
Current ratio	$\dfrac{\$7{,}647}{\$6{,}049} = 1.26 : 1$	$\dfrac{\$9{,}750}{\$6{,}049} = 1.61 : 1$
Inventory turnover ratio	$\dfrac{\$12{,}000}{(\$1{,}921 + \$1{,}835)/2} = 6.39$ times	$\dfrac{\$11{,}932}{(\$4{,}024 + \$3{,}870)/2} = 3.02$ times

tory amounts (assuming increasing prices), which causes inventory turnover to be overstated. As a result, comparing Caterpillar to one of its FIFO competitors without converting its inventory will lead to distortions.

BEFORE YOU GO ON . . .

● Review It

1. What is the purpose of the inventory turnover ratio? What is the relationship between the inventory turnover ratio and average days in inventory?
2. What is the LIFO reserve? What does it tell a financial statement user?

DECISION TOOLKIT

Decision Checkpoints	Info Needed for Decision	Tool to Use for Decision	How to Evaluate Results
What is the impact of LIFO on the company's reported inventory?	LIFO reserve, cost of goods sold, ending inventory	**Inventory adjustment** LIFO Inventory + LIFO reserve = FIFO Inventory **Cost of goods sold adjustment** LIFO cost of goods sold + Change in LIFO reserve = FIFO cost of goods sold	If these adjustments are material, they can significantly affect such measures as the current ratio and the inventory turnover ratio.

USING THE DECISION TOOLKIT

Like Caterpillar, a significant portion of Manitowoc Company's earnings are derived from the sales and service of large equipment (cranes and ships). Because of the nature of its business, Manitowoc Company has traditionally been subject to extreme changes in operating performance due to fluctuations in the economy. In recent years it has acquired a number of businesses in other industries in order to dampen the impact of economic cycles on its results. As a consequence, today it operates in three separate lines of business: foodservice equipment (commercial refrigerators, freezers, and ice cube makers), cranes and related products (such as truck-mounted cranes), and marine operations (which repairs Great Lakes freshwater and saltwater ships). For 1994 the company reported net income of $14.04 million. Here is the inventory note taken from the 1994 financial statements.

262 **CHAPTER 6** Reporting and Analyzing Inventory

MANITOWOC COMPANY
Notes to the Financial Statements

Inventories: The components of inventories are summarized at December 31 as follows (in thousands):

	1994	1993
Components		
Raw materials	$11,275	$12,512
Work in process	19,463	19,262
Finished goods	20,787	24,887
Total inventories at FIFO cost	51,525	56,661
Excess of FIFO cost over LIFO value	(20,285)	(22,461)
Total inventories	$31,240	$34,200

Inventory is carried at lower of cost or market using the first-in, first-out (FIFO) method for 61% and 47% of total inventory for 1994 and 1993, respectively. The remainder of the inventory is costed using the last-in, first-out (LIFO) method.

Additional facts:

1994 Current liabilities	$ 63,610
1994 Current assets (as originally reported)	$117,657
1994 Cost of goods sold	$207,456

Instructions

Answer these questions:

1. Why does the company report its inventory in three components?
2. Why might the company use two methods (LIFO and FIFO) to account for its inventory?
3. Using the inventory note and the additional facts listed above, calculate and discuss each of the following:

   (a) 1994 and 1993 inventories assuming FIFO.
   (b) 1994 cost of goods sold assuming FIFO.
   (c) Current ratio using LIFO and current ratio assuming FIFO.
   (d) Inventory turnover ratio using LIFO and inventory turnover ratio assuming FIFO.

Solution

1. Manitowoc Company is a manufacturer, so it purchases raw materials and makes them into finished products. At the end of each period, it has some goods that have been started but are not yet complete, referred to as work in process. By reporting all three components of inventory, the company reveals important information about its inventory position. For example, if amounts of raw materials have increased significantly compared to the previous year, we might safely assume the company is planning to step up production. On the other hand, if levels of finished goods have increased relative to last year and raw materials have declined, we might conclude that sales are slowing down—that the company has too much inventory on hand and is cutting back production.

2. Companies are free to choose different cost flow assumptions for different types of inventory. A company might choose to use FIFO for a product that is expected to decrease in price over time. One common reason for choosing a method other than LIFO is that many foreign countries do not allow LIFO; thus, the company cannot use LIFO for its foreign operations.

3. (a)

	1994	1993
LIFO inventory	$31,240	$34,200
LIFO reserve	20,285	22,461
FIFO inventory	$51,525	$56,661

(b)
1994 LIFO cost of goods sold	$207,456
Change in LIFO reserve ($20,285 − $22,461)	2,176
1994 FIFO cost of goods sold	$209,632

Note that because there was a reduction of inventory during the year, the LIFO reserve actually declined. Thus, the change in the LIFO reserve is added (rather than subtracted as in the case of an increase in the LIFO reserve) to LIFO cost of goods sold to determine FIFO cost of goods sold. In the case of a reduction of inventory, cost of goods sold under FIFO actually exceeds that of LIFO.

(c) Current ratios:

LIFO	FIFO
$\dfrac{\$117{,}657}{\$63{,}610} = 1.85 : 1$	$\dfrac{\$117{,}657 + \$20{,}285}{\$63{,}610} = 2.17 : 1$

This represents a 17% increase in the current ratio [(2.17 − 1.85)/1.85].

(d) Inventory turnover ratios:

LIFO	FIFO
$\dfrac{\$207{,}456}{(\$31{,}240 + \$34{,}200)/2} = 6.34$	$\dfrac{\$209{,}632}{(\$51{,}525 + \$56{,}661)/2} = 3.88$

The inventory turnover ratio under LIFO is substantially higher than that under FIFO, even though the cost of goods sold is higher under FIFO in this case because of the inventory decline. The LIFO inventory turnover ratio is overstated because it matches a numerator calculated with current prices with a denominator calculated with old prices. The FIFO inventory turnover ratio is considered a better measure because the price mismatch has less impact.

SUMMARY OF STUDY OBJECTIVES

❶ Explain the recording of purchases and sales of inventory under a periodic inventory system. In records of purchases, entries are required for (a) cash and credit purchases, (b) purchase returns and allowances, (c) purchase discounts, and (d) freight costs. In records of sales, entries are required for (a) cash and credit sales, (b) sales returns and allowances, and (c) sales discounts.

❷ Explain how to determine cost of goods sold under a periodic inventory system. The steps in determining cost of goods sold are (a) recording the purchase of merchandise, (b) determining the cost of goods purchased, and (c) determining the cost of goods on hand at the beginning and end of the accounting period.

❸ Describe the steps in determining inventory quantities. The steps are (1) taking a physical inventory of goods on hand and (2) determining the ownership of goods in transit or on consignment.

❹ Identify the unique features of the income statement for a merchandising company under a periodic inventory system. The income statement for a merchandising company contains three features not found in a service enterprise's income statement: sales revenue, cost of goods sold, and a gross profit line. The cost of goods sold section generally shows more detail under a periodic than a perpetual inventory system by reporting beginning and ending inventories, net purchases, and total goods available for sale.

❺ Explain the basis of accounting for inventories and apply the inventory cost flow methods under a periodic inventory system. The primary basis of accounting for inventories is cost. Cost includes all expenditures necessary to acquire goods and place them in condition ready for sale. Cost of goods available for sale includes (a) cost of beginning inventory and (b) cost of goods purchased. The inventory cost flow methods are: specific identification and three assumed cost flow methods—FIFO, LIFO, and average cost.

6 *Explain the financial statement and tax effects of each of the inventory cost flow assumptions.* The cost of goods available for sale may be allocated to cost of goods sold and ending inventory by specific identification or by a method based on an assumed cost flow. When prices are rising, the first-in, first-out (FIFO) method results in lower cost of goods sold and higher net income than the average cost and the last-in, first-out (LIFO) methods. The reverse is true when prices are falling. In the balance sheet, FIFO results in an ending inventory that is closest to current value, whereas the inventory under LIFO is the farthest from current value. LIFO results in the lowest income taxes (because of lower net income).

7 *Explain the lower of cost or market basis of accounting for inventories.* The lower of cost or market (LCM) basis may be used when the current replacement cost (market) is less than cost. Under LCM, the loss is recognized in the period in which the price decline occurs.

8 *Compute and interpret the inventory turnover ratio.* The inventory turnover ratio is calculated as cost of goods sold divided by average inventory. It can be converted to average days in inventory by dividing 365 days by the inventory turnover ratio. A higher turnover ratio or lower average days in inventory suggests that management is trying to keep inventory levels low relative to its sales level.

9 *Describe the LIFO reserve and explain its importance for comparing results of different companies.* The LIFO reserve presents the difference between ending inventory using LIFO and ending inventory if FIFO were employed instead. For some companies this difference can be significant, and ignoring it can lead to inappropriate conclusions when using the current ratio or inventory turnover ratio.

DECISION TOOLKIT—A SUMMARY

Decision Checkpoints	Info Needed for Decision	Tool to Use for Decision	How to Evaluate Results
Which inventory costing method should be used?	Are prices increasing, or are they decreasing?	Income statement, balance sheet, and tax effects	Depends on objective. In a period of rising prices, income and inventory are higher and cash flow is lower under FIFO. LIFO provides opposite results. Average cost can moderate the impact of changing prices.
How long is an item in inventory?	Cost of goods sold; beginning and ending inventory	Inventory turnover ratio = $\dfrac{\text{Cost of goods sold}}{\text{Average inventory}}$ Average days in inventory = $\dfrac{365 \text{ days}}{\text{Inventory turnover ratio}}$	A higher inventory turnover ratio or lower average days in inventory suggests that management is reducing the amount of inventory on hand, relative to sales.
What is the impact of LIFO on the company's reported inventory?	LIFO reserve, cost of goods sold, ending inventory	**Inventory adjustment** LIFO Inventory + LIFO reserve = FIFO Inventory **Cost of goods sold adjustment** LIFO cost of goods sold + Change in LIFO reserve = FIFO cost of goods sold	If these adjustments are material, they can significantly affect such measures as the current ratio and the inventory turnover ratio.

APPENDIX 6A
INVENTORY ERRORS

Unfortunately, errors occasionally occur in accounting for inventory. In some cases, errors are caused by failure to count or price the inventory correctly. In other cases, errors occur because proper recognition is not given to the transfer of legal title to goods that are in transit. When errors occur, they affect both the income statement and the balance sheet.

STUDY OBJECTIVE 10
Indicate the effects of inventory errors on the financial statements.

INCOME STATEMENT EFFECTS

As you know, both the beginning and ending inventories appear in the income statement. The ending inventory of one period automatically becomes the beginning inventory of the next period. Inventory errors affect the determination of cost of goods sold and net income in two periods.

The effects on cost of goods sold can be determined by entering incorrect data in the formula in Illustration 6A-1 and then substituting the correct data.

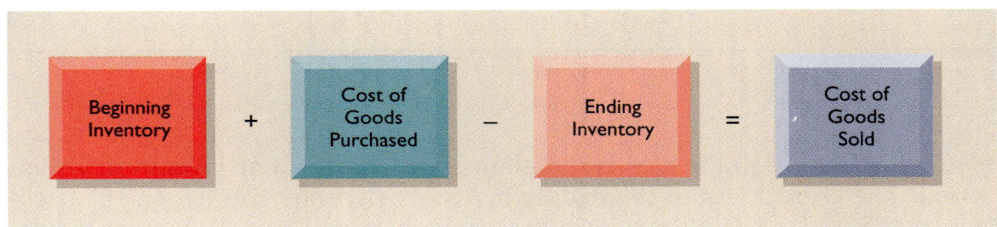

Illustration 6A-1
Formula for cost of goods sold

If beginning inventory is understated, cost of goods sold will be understated. On the other hand, understating ending inventory will overstate cost of goods sold. The effects of inventory errors on the current year's income statement are shown in Illustration 6A-2.

Inventory Error	Cost of Goods Sold	Net Income
Understate beginning inventory	Understated	Overstated
Overstate beginning inventory	Overstated	Understated
Understate ending inventory	Overstated	Understated
Overstate ending inventory	Understated	Overstated

Illustration 6A-2 Effects of inventory errors on current year's income statement

An error in the ending inventory of the current period will have a **reverse effect on net income of the next accounting period.** This is shown in Illustration 6A-3 (at the top of the next page). Note that the understatement of ending inventory in 1997 results in an understatement of beginning inventory in 1998 and an overstatement of net income in 1998.

Over the 2 years, total net income is correct because the errors offset each other. Notice that total income using incorrect data is $35,000 ($22,000 + $13,000), which is the same as the total income of $35,000 ($25,000 + $10,000) using correct data. Also note in this example that an error in the beginning in-

266 CHAPTER 6 Reporting and Analyzing Inventory

SAMPLE COMPANY
Condensed Income Statement

	1997 Incorrect		1997 Correct		1998 Incorrect		1998 Correct	
Sales		$80,000		$80,000		$90,000		$90,000
Beginning inventory	$20,000		$20,000		**$12,000**		**$15,000**	
Cost of goods purchased	40,000		40,000		68,000		68,000	
Cost of goods available for sale	60,000		60,000		80,000		83,000	
Ending inventory	**12,000**		**15,000**		23,000		23,000	
Cost of goods sold		48,000		45,000		57,000		60,000
Gross profit		32,000		35,000		33,000		30,000
Operating expenses		10,000		10,000		20,000		20,000
Net income		$22,000		$25,000		$13,000		$10,000

($3,000) Net income understated — 1997
$3,000 Net income overstated — 1998

The combined total income for the 2-year period is correct.

Illustration 6A-3 Effects of inventory errors on 2 years' income statements

ventory does not result in a corresponding error in the ending inventory for that period. The correctness of the ending inventory depends entirely on the accuracy of taking and costing the inventory at the balance sheet date under the periodic inventory system.

BUSINESS INSIGHT
Investor Perspective

Inventory fraud increases during recessions. Such fraud includes pricing inventory at amounts in excess of their actual value, or claiming to have inventory when no inventory exists. Inventory fraud is usually done to overstate ending inventory, thereby understating cost of goods sold and creating higher income.

BALANCE SHEET EFFECTS

The effect of ending inventory errors on the balance sheet can be determined by using the basic accounting equation: Assets = Liabilities + Stockholders' equity. Errors in the ending inventory have the effects shown in Illustration 6A-4.

Illustration 6A-4 Effects of ending inventory errors on balance sheet

Ending Inventory Error	Assets	Liabilities	Stockholders' Equity
Overstated	Overstated	No effect	Overstated
Understated	Understated	No effect	Understated

The effect of an error in ending inventory on the subsequent period was shown in Illustration 6A-3. Recall that if the error is not corrected, the combined total net income for the two periods would be correct. Thus, total stockholders' equity reported on the balance sheet at the end of 1998 will also be correct.

SUMMARY OF STUDY OBJECTIVE FOR APPENDIX 6A

10 *Indicate the effects of inventory errors on the financial statements.* In the income statement of the current year: (a) an error in beginning inventory will have a reverse effect on net income (overstatement of inventory results in understatement of net income, and vice versa) and (b) an error in ending inventory will have a similar effect on net income (e.g., overstatement of inventory results in overstatement of net income). If ending inventory errors are not corrected in the following period, their effect on net income for that period is reversed, and total net income for the 2 years will be correct. In the balance sheet, ending inventory errors will have the same effect on total assets and total stockholders' equity and no effect on liabilities.

GLOSSARY

Average cost method An inventory costing method that assumes that the goods available for sale are homogeneous. (p. 252)

Consigned goods Goods held for sale by one party (the consignee) although ownership of the goods is retained by another party (the consignor). (p. 246)

Cost of goods available for sale The sum of the beginning merchandise inventory and the cost of goods purchased. (p. 246)

Cost of goods purchased The sum of net purchases and freight-in. (p. 244)

Cost of goods sold The total cost of merchandise sold during the period, determined by subtracting ending inventory from the cost of goods available for sale. (p. 243)

Current replacement cost The current cost to replace an inventory item. (p. 257)

Days in inventory Measure of the average number of days inventory is held; calculated as 365 divided by inventory turnover ratio. (p. 258)

Finished goods inventory Manufactured items that are completed and ready for sale. (p. 240)

First-in, first-out (FIFO) method An inventory costing method that assumes that the costs of the earliest goods acquired are the first to be recognized as cost of goods sold. (p. 249)

FOB destination Freight terms indicating that the goods are placed free on board at the buyer's place of business, and the seller pays the freight cost; goods belong to the seller while in transit. (p. 245)

FOB shipping point Freight terms indicating that the goods are placed free on board the carrier by the seller, and the buyer pays the freight cost; goods belong to the buyer while in transit. (p. 245)

Inventory turnover ratio A ratio that measures the number of times on average the inventory sold during the period; computed by dividing cost of goods sold by the average inventory during the period. (p. 258)

Last-in, first-out (LIFO) method An inventory costing method that assumes that the costs of the latest units purchased are the first to be allocated to cost of goods sold. (p. 250)

LIFO reserve For a company using LIFO, the difference between inventory reported using LIFO and inventory using FIFO. (p. 259)

Lower of cost or market (LCM) basis (inventories) A basis whereby inventory is stated at the lower of cost or market (current replacement cost). (p. 256)

Net purchases Purchases less purchase returns and allowances and purchase discounts. (p. 243)

Periodic inventory system An inventory system in which inventoriable costs are allocated to ending inventory and cost of goods sold at the end of the period. Cost of goods sold is computed at the end of the period by subtracting the ending inventory (costs are assigned to a physical count of items on hand) from the cost of goods available for sale. (p. 241)

Raw materials Basic goods that will be used in production but have not yet been placed in production. (p. 240)

Specific identification method An actual physical flow costing method in which items still in inventory are specifically costed to arrive at the total cost of the ending inventory. (p. 248)

Weighted average unit cost Average cost that is weighted by the number of units purchased at each unit cost. (p. 252)

Work in process That portion of manufactured inventory that has begun the production process but is not yet complete. (p. 240)

Demonstration Problem

Gerald D. Englehart Company has the following inventory, purchases, and sales data for the month of March:

Inventory, March 1	200 units @ $4.00	$ 800
Purchases		
March 10	500 units @ $4.50	2,250
March 20	400 units @ $4.75	1,900
March 30	300 units @ $5.00	1,500
Sales		
March 15	500 units	
March 25	400 units	

The physical inventory count on March 31 shows 500 units on hand.

Instructions

Under a **periodic inventory system,** determine the cost of inventory on hand at March 31 and the cost of goods sold for March under (a) the first-in, first-out (FIFO) method; (b) the last-in, first-out (LIFO) method; and (c) the average cost method.

Problem-Solving Strategies

1. For FIFO, the latest costs are allocated to inventory.
2. For LIFO, the earliest costs are allocated to inventory.
3. For average costs, use a weighted average.
4. Remember, the costs allocated to cost of goods sold can be proved.
5. Total purchases are the same under all three cost flow assumptions.

Solution to Demonstration Problem

The cost of goods available for sale is $6,450:

Inventory	200 units @ $4.00	$ 800
Purchases		
March 10	500 units @ $4.50	2,250
March 20	400 units @ $4.75	1,900
March 30	300 units @ $5.00	1,500
Total cost of goods available for sale		$6,450

(a) **FIFO Method**

Ending inventory:

Date	Units	Unit Cost	Total Cost	
Mar. 30	300	$5.00	$1,500	
Mar. 20	200	4.75	950	$2,450

Cost of goods sold: $6,450 − $2,450 = $4,000

(b) **LIFO Method**

Ending inventory:

Date	Units	Unit Cost	Total Cost	
Mar. 1	200	$4.00	$ 800	
Mar. 10	300	4.50	1,350	$2,150

Cost of goods sold: $6,450 − $2,150 = $4,300

(c) **Weighted Average Cost Method**

Weighted average unit cost: $6,450 ÷ 1,400 = $4.607
Ending inventory: 500 × $4.607 = $2,303.50
Cost of goods sold: $6,450 − $2,303.50 = $4,146.50

SELF-STUDY QUESTIONS

Answers are at the end of the chapter.

(SO 1) 1. When goods are purchased for resale by a company using a periodic inventory system:
(a) purchases on account are debited to Merchandise Inventory.
(b) purchases on account are debited to Purchases.
(c) purchase returns are debited to Purchase Returns and Allowances.
(d) freight costs are debited to Purchases.

(SO 2) 2. In determining cost of goods sold:
(a) purchase discounts are deducted from net purchases.
(b) freight-out is added to net purchases.
(c) purchase returns and allowances are deducted from net purchases.
(d) freight-in is added to net purchases.

(SO 2) 3. If beginning inventory is $60,000, cost of goods purchased is $380,000, and ending inventory is $50,000, what is cost of goods sold?
(a) $390,000   (c) $330,000
(b) $370,000   (d) $420,000

(SO 3) 4. Which of the following should *not* be included in the physical inventory of a company?
(a) Goods held on consignment from another company
(b) Goods shipped on consignment to another company
(c) Goods in transit from another company shipped FOB shipping point
(d) All of the above should be included

(SO 5) 5. Kam Company has the following units and costs:

	Units	Unit Cost
Inventory, Jan. 1	8,000	$11
Purchase, June 19	13,000	12
Purchase, Nov. 8	5,000	13

If 9,000 units are on hand at December 31, what is the cost of the ending inventory under FIFO?
(a) $99,000   (c) $113,000
(b) $108,000   (d) $117,000

(SO 5) 6. From the data in question 5, what is the cost of the ending inventory under LIFO?
(a) $113,000   (c) $99,000
(b) $108,000   (d) $100,000

(SO 6) 7. In periods of rising prices, LIFO will produce:
(a) higher net income than FIFO.
(b) the same net income as FIFO.
(c) lower net income than FIFO.
(d) higher net income than average costing.

(SO 6) 8. Considerations that affect the selection of an inventory costing method do *not* include:
(a) tax effects.
(b) balance sheet effects.
(c) income statement effects.
(d) perpetual versus periodic inventory system.

(SO 7) 9. The lower of cost or market rule for inventory is an example of the application of:
(a) the conservatism constraint.
(b) the historical cost principle.
(c) the materiality constraint.
(d) the economic entity assumption.

(SO 8) 10. Which of these would cause the inventory turnover ratio to increase the most?
(a) Increasing the amount of inventory on hand
(b) Keeping the amount of inventory on hand constant but increasing sales
(c) Keeping the amount of inventory on hand constant but decreasing sales
(d) Decreasing the amount of inventory on hand and increasing sales

(SO 10) *11. Fran Company's ending inventory is understated by $4,000. The effects of this error on the current year's cost of goods sold and net income, respectively, are:
(a) understated and overstated.
(b) overstated and understated.
(c) overstated and overstated.
(d) understated and understated.

QUESTIONS

1. Goods costing $1,600 are purchased on account on July 15 with credit terms of 2/10, n/30. On July 18 a $100 credit memo is received from the supplier for damaged goods. Give the journal entry on July 24 to record payment of the balance due within the discount period assuming a periodic inventory system.

2. Identify the accounts that are added to or deducted from purchases to determine the cost of goods purchased. For each account, indicate (a) whether it is added or deducted and (b) its normal balance.

3. In the following cases, use a periodic inventory system to identify the item(s) designated by the letters X and Y.

(a) Purchases − X − Y = Net purchases
(b) Cost of goods purchased − Net purchases = X
(c) Beginning inventory + X = Cost of goods available for sale
(d) Cost of goods available for sale − Cost of goods sold = X

4. "The key to successful business operations is effective inventory management." Do you agree? Explain.

5. An item must possess two characteristics to be classified as inventory. What are these two characteristics?

6. Your friend Tom Wetzel has been hired to help take the physical inventory in Casey's Hardware Store. Explain to Tom Wetzel what this job will entail.

7. (a) Janine Company ships merchandise to Laura Corporation on December 30. The merchandise reaches the buyer on January 5. Indicate the terms of sale that will result in the goods being included in (1) Janine's December 31 inventory and (2) Laura's December 31 inventory.
   (b) Under what circumstances should Janine Company include consigned goods in its inventory?

8. Mary Ann's Hat Shop received a shipment of hats for which it paid the wholesaler $2,940. The price of the hats was $3,000, but Mary Ann's was given a $60 cash discount and required to pay freight charges of $70. In addition, Mary Ann's paid $100 to cover the travel expenses of an employee who negotiated the purchase of the hats. What amount should Mary Ann's include in inventory? Why?

9. What is the primary basis of accounting for inventories? What is the major objective in accounting for inventories?

10. Identify the distinguishing features of an income statement for a merchandising company.

11. Dave Wier believes that the allocation of cost of goods available for sale should be based on the actual physical flow of the goods. Explain to Dave why this may be both impractical and inappropriate.

12. What are the major advantage and major disadvantage of the specific identification method of inventory costing?

13. "The selection of an inventory cost flow method is a decision made by accountants." Do you agree? Explain. Once a method has been selected, what accounting requirement applies?

14. Which assumed inventory cost flow method:
    (a) usually parallels the actual physical flow of merchandise?
    (b) assumes that goods available for sale during an accounting period are homogeneous?
    (c) assumes that the latest units purchased are the first to be sold?

15. In a period of rising prices, the inventory reported in Plato Company's balance sheet is close to the current cost of the inventory, whereas York Company's inventory is considerably below its current cost. Identify the inventory cost flow method used by each company. Which company probably has been reporting the higher gross profit?

16. Shaunna Corporation has been using the FIFO cost flow method during a prolonged period of inflation. During the same time period, Shaunna has been paying out all of its net income as dividends. What adverse effects may result from this policy?

17. Lucy Ritter is studying for the next accounting midterm examination. What should Lucy know about (a) departing from the cost basis of accounting for inventories and (b) the meaning of "market" in the lower of cost or market method?

18. Rock Music Center has five CD players on hand at the balance sheet date that cost $400 each. The current replacement cost is $320 per unit. Under the lower of cost or market basis of accounting for inventories, what value should be reported for the CD players on the balance sheet? Why?

19. What cost flow assumption may be used under the lower of cost or market basis of accounting for inventories?

20. Why is it inappropriate for a company to include freight-out expense in the Cost of Goods Sold account?

21. Maureen & Nathan Company's balance sheet shows Inventories $162,800. What additional disclosures should be made?

22. Under what circumstances might the inventory turnover ratio be too high; that is, what possible negative consequences might occur?

23. What is the LIFO reserve? What are the consequences of ignoring a large LIFO reserve when analyzing a company?

*24. Mila Company discovers in 1998 that its ending inventory at December 31, 1997, was $5,000 understated. What effect will this error have on (a) 1997 net income, (b) 1998 net income, and (c) the combined net income for the 2 years?

Brief Exercises

Journalize purchase transactions.
(SO 1)

BE6-1 Prepare the journal entries to record these transactions on H. Hunt Company's books using a periodic inventory system.
(a) On March 2 H. Hunt Company purchased $900,000 of merchandise from B. Streisand Company, terms 2/10, n/30.

(b) On March 6 H. Hunt Company returned $130,000 of the merchandise purchased on March 2 because it was defective.
(c) On March 12 H. Hunt Company paid the balance due to B. Streisand Company.

BE6-2 Assume that K. Bassing Company uses a periodic inventory system and has these account balances: Purchases $400,000; Purchase Returns and Allowances $11,000; Purchase Discounts $8,000; and Freight-in $16,000. Determine net purchases and cost of goods purchased.

Compute net purchases and cost of goods purchased.
(SO 2)

BE6-3 Assume the same information as in BE6-2 and also that K. Bassing Company has beginning inventory of $60,000, ending inventory of $90,000, and net sales of $630,000. Determine the amounts to be reported for cost of goods sold and gross profit.

Compute cost of goods sold and gross profit.
(SO 2, 3)

BE6-4 Ginger Helgeson Company identifies the following items for possible inclusion in the physical inventory. Indicate whether each item should be included or excluded from the inventory taking.
(a) Goods shipped on consignment by Helgeson to another company
(b) Goods in transit from a supplier shipped FOB destination
(c) Goods sold but being held for customer pickup
(d) Goods held on consignment from another company

Identify items to be included in taking a physical inventory.
(SO 3)

BE6-5 The ledger of Wharton Company includes these items: Freight-in, Purchase Returns and Allowances, Purchases, Sales Discounts, and Purchase Discounts. Identify which items are included in calculating cost of goods available for sale.

Identify the components of cost of goods available for sale.
(SO 3)

BE6-6 In its first month of operations, Quilt Company made three purchases of merchandise in the following sequence: (1) 300 units at $6, (2) 400 units at $7, and (3) 300 units at $8. Assuming there are 400 units on hand, compute the cost of the ending inventory under (a) the FIFO method and (b) the LIFO method. Quilt uses a periodic inventory system.

Compute ending inventory using FIFO and LIFO.
(SO 5)

BE6-7 Data for Quilt Company are presented in BE6-6. Compute the cost of the ending inventory under the average cost method, assuming there are 400 units on hand.

Compute the ending inventory using average costs.
(SO 5)

BE6-8 Hawkeye Appliance Center accumulates the following cost and market data at December 31:

Determine the LCM valuation.
(SO 7)

Inventory Categories	Cost Data	Market Data
Cameras	$12,000	$10,200
Camcorders	9,000	9,500
VCRs	14,000	12,800

Compute the lower of cost or market valuation for Hawkeye's total inventory.

BE6-9 At December 31, 1998, the following information was available for Sauk Company: ending inventory $80,000; beginning inventory $60,000; cost of goods sold $210,000; and sales revenue $280,000. Calculate the inventory turnover ratio and days in inventory for Sauk Company.

Compute inventory turnover ratio and days in inventory.
(SO 8)

BE6-10 Harbor Company reported ending inventory at December 31, 1998, of $3,000,000 under the LIFO inventory method. In the notes to its financial statements, Harbor reported a LIFO reserve of $500,000 at January 1, 1998, and $700,000 at December 31, 1998. Cost of goods sold for 1998 was $8,000,000. What would Harbor Company's ending inventory and cost of goods sold have been for 1998 if it had used FIFO?

Determine ending inventory and cost of goods sold using LIFO reserve.
(SO 9)

*BE6-11 Creole Company reports net income of $90,000 in 1998. However, ending inventory was understated by $7,000. What is the correct net income for 1998? What effect, if any, will this error have on total assets as reported in the balance sheet at December 31, 1998?

Determine correct financial statement amount.
(SO 10)

EXERCISES

Journalize purchase transactions.
(SO 1)

E6-1 This information relates to Hans Olaf Co.:
1. On April 5 purchased merchandise from D. DeVito Company for $18,000, terms 2/10, net/30, FOB shipping point.
2. On April 6 paid freight costs of $900 on merhandise purchased from D. DeVito Company.
3. On April 7 purchased equipment on account for $26,000.
4. On April 8 returned damaged merchandise to D. DeVito Company and was granted a $3,000 allowance.
5. On April 15 paid the amount due to D. DeVito Company in full.

Instructions
(a) Prepare the journal entries to record these transactions on the books of Hans Olaf Co. using a periodic inventory system.
(b) Assume that Hans Olaf Co. paid the balance due to D. DeVito Company on May 4 instead of April 15. Prepare the journal entry to record this payment.

Prepare cost of goods sold section.
(SO 2)

E6-2 The trial balance of G. Garbo Company at the end of its fiscal year, August 31, 1998, includes these accounts: Merchandise Inventory $17,200; Purchases $142,400; Sales $190,000; Freight-in $4,000; Sales Returns and Allowances $3,000; Freight-out $1,000; and Purchase Returns and Allowances $2,000. The ending merchandise inventory is $26,000.

Instructions
Prepare a cost of goods sold section for the year ending August 31.

Prepare an income statement.
(SO 4)

E6-3 Presented here is information related to Baja Co. for the month of January 1998:

Freight-in	$ 10,000
Rent expense	20,000
Freight-out	7,000
Salary expense	61,000
Insurance expense	12,000
Sales discounts	8,000
Purchases	200,000
Sales returns and allowances	13,000
Purchase discounts	3,000
Sales	312,000
Purchase returns and allowances	6,000

Beginning merchandise inventory was $42,000, and ending inventory was $63,000.

Instructions
Prepare an income statement using the format presented on page 247. Operating expenses should not be divided into selling and administrative expenses.

Determine the correct inventory amount.
(SO 3)

E6-4 First Bank and Trust is considering giving Novotna Company a loan. Before doing so, they decide that further discussions with Novotna's accountant may be desirable. One area of particular concern is the inventory account, which has a year-end balance of $295,000. Discussions with the accountant reveal the following:
1. Novotna sold goods costing $35,000 to Moghul Company FOB shipping point on December 28. The goods are not expected to arrive in India until January 12. The goods were not included in the physical inventory because they were not in the warehouse.
2. The physical count of the inventory did not include goods costing $95,000 that were shipped to Novotna FOB destination on December 27 and were still in transit at year-end.
3. Novotna received goods costing $25,000 on January 2. The goods were shipped FOB shipping point on December 26 by Cellar Co. The goods were not included in the physical count.
4. Novotna sold goods costing $40,000 to Sterling of Canada FOB destination on December 30. The goods were received in Canada on January 8. They were not included in Novotna's physical inventory.

5. Novotna received goods costing $44,000 on January 2 that were shipped FOB destination on December 29. The shipment was a rush order that was supposed to arrive December 31. This purchase was included in the ending inventory of $295,000.

Instructions
Determine the correct inventory amount on December 31.

E6-5 Mawmey Inc. uses a periodic inventory system. Its records show the following for the month of May, in which 78 units were sold:

Compute inventory and cost of goods sold using FIFO and LIFO.
(SO 5)

Date	Explanation	Units	Unit Cost	Total Cost
May 1	Inventory	30	$ 8	$240
15	Purchase	25	10	250
24	Purchase	35	12	420
	Total	90		$910

Instructions
Compute the ending inventory at May 31 using the (a) FIFO and (b) LIFO method. Prove the amount allocated to cost of goods sold under each method.

E6-6 In June, Dakota Company reports the following for the month of June:

Compute inventory and cost of goods sold using FIFO and LIFO.
(SO 5)

Date	Explanation	Units	Unit Cost	Total Cost
June 1	Inventory	200	$5	$1,000
12	Purchase	300	6	1,800
23	Purchase	500	7	3,500
30	Inventory	180		

Instructions
(a) Compute the cost of the ending inventory and the cost of goods sold under (1) FIFO and (2) LIFO.
(b) Which costing method gives the higher ending inventory? Why?
(c) Which method results in the higher cost of goods sold? Why?

E6-7 Inventory data for Dakota Company are presented in E6-6.

Compute inventory and cost of goods sold using average costs.
(SO 5)

Instructions
(a) Compute the cost of the ending inventory and the cost of goods sold using the average cost method.
(b) Will the results in part (a) be higher or lower than the results under (1) FIFO and (2) LIFO?
(c) Why is the average unit cost not $6?

E6-8 This information is available for Lawrence Corporation for 1997, 1998, and 1999:

Compute inventory turnover ratio, days in inventory, and gross profit rate.
(SO 8)

	1997	1998	1999
Beginning inventory	$ 200,000	$ 300,000	$ 400,000
Ending inventory	300,000	400,000	500,000
Cost of goods sold	900,000	1,120,000	1,250,000
Sales	1,200,000	1,600,000	1,900,000

Instructions
Calculate the inventory turnover ratio, days in inventory, and gross profit rate (from Chapter 5) for Lawrence Corporation for 1997, 1998, and 1999. Comment on any trends.

*E6-9 Seles Hardware reported cost of goods sold as follows:

Determine effects of inventory errors.
(SO 10)

	1998	1999
Beginning inventory	$ 20,000	$ 30,000
Cost of goods purchased	150,000	175,000
Cost of goods available for sale	170,000	205,000
Ending inventory	30,000	35,000
Cost of goods sold	$140,000	$170,000

Seles made two errors:
1. 1998 ending inventory was overstated by $4,000.
2. 1999 ending inventory was understated by $3,000.

Instructions
Compute the correct cost of goods sold for each year.

Prepare correct income statements.
(SO 10)

*E6-10 Aruba Company reported these income statement data for a 2-year period:

	1998	1999
Sales	$210,000	$250,000
Beginning inventory	32,000	40,000
Cost of goods purchased	173,000	202,000
Cost of goods available for sale	205,000	242,000
Ending inventory	40,000	52,000
Cost of goods sold	165,000	190,000
Gross profit	$ 45,000	$ 60,000

Aruba Company uses a periodic inventory system. The inventories at January 1, 1998, and December 31, 1999, are correct. However, the ending inventory at December 31, 1998, is overstated by $6,000.

Instructions
(a) Prepare correct income statement data for the 2 years.
(b) What is the cumulative effect of the inventory error on total gross profit for the 2 years?

(c) Explain in a letter to the president of Aruba Company what has happened—that is, the nature of the error and its effect on the financial statements.

Prepare correcting entries for sales and purchases.
(SO 10)

*E6-11 An inexperienced accountant for Churchill Company made the following errors in recording merchandising transactions:
1. A $150 refund to a customer for faulty merchandise was debited to Sales $150 and credited to Cash $150.
2. A $250 credit purchase of supplies was debited to Purchases $250 and credited to Cash $250.
3. An $80 sales discount was debited to Purchase Discounts.
4. A $50 purchase return was recorded as a debit to Accounts Payable $50 and a credit to Purchases $50.
5. A cash payment of $30 for freight on merchandise purchases was debited to Purchases $300 and credited to Cash $300.

Instructions
Prepare separate correcting entries for each error, assuming that the incorrect entry is not reversed. (You may omit explanations.)

PROBLEMS

Journalize, post, and prepare trial balance and partial income statement.
(SO 1, 2, 4)

P6-1 Chi Chi Ramos, a former professional golfer, operates Chi Chi's Pro Shop at Bay Golf Course. At the beginning of the current season on April 1, the ledger of Chi Chi's Pro Shop showed Cash $2,500; Merchandise Inventory $3,500; and Common Stock $6,000. These transactions occurred during April:

Apr. 5 Purchased golf bags, clubs, and balls on account from Balata Co. $1,600, FOB shipping point, terms 2/10, n/60.
    7 Paid freight on Balata Co. purchases $80.
    9 Received credit from Balata Co. for merchandise returned $100.
    10 Sold merchandise on account to members $900, terms n/30.
    12 Purchased golf shoes, sweaters, and other accessories on account from Arrow Sportswear $660, terms 1/10, n/30.

14 Paid Balata Co. in full.
17 Received credit from Arrow Sportswear for merchandise returned $60.
20 Made sales on account to members $700, terms n/30.
21 Paid Arrow Sportswear in full.
27 Granted credit to members for clothing that did not fit $30.
30 Made cash sales $600.
30 Received payments on account from members $1,100.

The chart of accounts for the pro shop includes Cash, Accounts Receivable, Merchandise Inventory, Accounts Payable, Common Stock, Sales, Sales Returns and Allowances, Purchases, Purchase Returns and Allowances, Purchase Discounts, and Freight-in.

Instructions
(a) Journalize the April transactions using a periodic inventory system.
(b) Using T accounts, enter the beginning balances in the ledger accounts and post the April transactions.
(c) Prepare a trial balance on April 30, 1998.
(d) Prepare an income statement through Gross Profit, assuming merchandise inventory on hand at April 30 is $4,200.

P6-2 Metro Department Store is located in midtown Metropolis. During the past several years, net income has been declining because of competition from suburban shopping centers. At the end of the company's fiscal year on November 30, 1998, the following accounts appeared in its adjusted trial balance:

Prepare a multiple-step income statement.
(SO 2, 4)

Accounts Payable	$ 37,310
Accounts Receivable	11,770
Accumulated Depreciation—Delivery Equipment	19,680
Accumulated Depreciation—Store Equipment	41,800
Cash	8,000
Delivery Expense	8,200
Delivery Equipment	57,000
Depreciation Expense—Delivery Equipment	4,000
Depreciation Expense—Store Equipment	9,500
Freight-in	5,060
Common Stock	70,000
Retained Earnings	17,200
Dividends	12,000
Insurance Expense	9,000
Merchandise Inventory	34,360
Notes Payable	46,000
Prepaid Insurance	4,500
Property Tax Expense	3,500
Purchases	640,000
Purchase Discounts	7,000
Purchase Returns and Allowances	3,000
Rent Expense	19,000
Salaries Expense	120,000
Sales	860,000
Sales Commissions Expense	14,000
Sales Commissions Payable	6,000
Sales Returns and Allowances	10,000
Store Equipment	125,000
Property Taxes Payable	3,500
Utilities Expense	10,600

Additional facts:
1. Merchandise inventory at November 30, 1998, is $36,200.
2. Note that Metro Department Store uses a periodic system.

Instructions
Prepare an income statement for the year ended November 30, 1998.

276 CHAPTER 6 Reporting and Analyzing Inventory

Determine cost of goods sold and ending inventory using FIFO, LIFO, and average cost.
(SO 5, 6)

P6-3 Kane Company had a beginning inventory on January 1 of 100 units of Product SXL at a cost of $20 per unit. During the year, purchases were:

| Mar. 15 | 300 units at $24 | Sept. 4 | 300 units at $28 |
| July 20 | 200 units at $25 | Dec. 2 | 100 units at $30 |

Kane Company sold 850 units, and it uses a periodic inventory system.

Instructions
(a) Determine the cost of goods available for sale.
(b) Determine the ending inventory and the cost of goods sold under each of the assumed cost flow methods (FIFO, LIFO, and average cost). Prove the accuracy of the cost of goods sold under the FIFO and LIFO methods.
(c) Which cost flow method results in the highest inventory amount for the balance sheet? The highest cost of goods sold for the income statement?

Compute ending inventory, prepare income statements, and answer questions using FIFO and LIFO.
(SO 5, 6)

P6-4 The management of Tumatoe Inc. asks your help in determining the comparative effects of the FIFO and LIFO inventory cost flow methods. For 1998 the accounting records show these data:

Inventory, January 1 (10,000 units)	$ 35,000
Cost of 110,000 units purchased	460,000
Selling price of 95,000 units sold	665,000
Operating expenses	120,000

Units purchased consisted of 40,000 units at $4.00 on May 10; 50,000 units at $4.20 on August 15; and 20,000 units at $4.50 on November 20. Income taxes are 30%.

Instructions
(a) Prepare comparative condensed income statements for 1998 under FIFO and LIFO. (Show computations of ending inventory.)
(b) Answer the following questions for management in the form of a business letter:
  (1) Which inventory cost flow method produces the most meaningful inventory amount for the balance sheet? Why?
  (2) Which inventory cost flow method produces the most meaningful net income? Why?
  (3) Which inventory cost flow method is most likely to approximate the actual physical flow of the goods? Why?
  (4) How much more cash will be available for management under LIFO than under FIFO? Why?
  (5) How much of the gross profit under FIFO is illusionary in comparison with the gross profit under LIFO?

Compute inventory turnover ratio, days in inventory, and current ratio based on LIFO and after adjusting for LIFO reserve.
(SO 8, 9)

P6-5 This information is available for Marias Corporation for 1997, 1998, and 1999. Marias uses the LIFO inventory method.

	1997	1998	1999
Beginning inventory	$ 200,000	$ 300,000	$ 400,000
Ending inventory	300,000	400,000	500,000
Beginning LIFO reserve	150,000	170,000	200,000
Ending LIFO reserve	170,000	200,000	240,000
Current assets	500,000	600,000	700,000
Current liabilities	300,000	900,000	1,000,000
Cost of goods sold	900,000	1,120,000	1,250,000
Sales	1,200,000	1,600,000	1,900,000

Instructions
Calculate the inventory turnover ratio, days in inventory, and current ratio for Marias Corporation for 1997, 1998, and 1999 as follows:
(a) Based on LIFO
(b) After adjusting for the LIFO reserve
(c) Comment on any difference between parts (a) and (b).

ALTERNATIVE PROBLEMS

P6-1A Billy Jean Evert, a former professional tennis star, operates B.J.'s Tennis Shop at the Jackson Lake Resort. At the beginning of the current season, the ledger of B.J.'s Tennis Shop showed Cash $2,500; Merchandise Inventory $1,700; and Common Stock $4,200. These transactions were completed during April:

Journalize, post, and prepare trial balance and partial income statement.
(SO 1, 2, 4)

Apr.	4	Purchased racquets and balls from Robert Co. $640, FOB shipping point, terms 3/10, n/30.
	6	Paid freight on Robert Co. purchase $40.
	8	Sold merchandise to members $900, terms n/30.
	10	Received credit of $40 from Robert Co. for a damaged racquet that was returned.
	11	Purchased tennis shoes from Niki Sports for cash $300.
	13	Paid Robert Co. in full.
	14	Purchased tennis shirts and shorts from Martina's Sportswear $700, FOB shipping point, terms 2/10, n/60.
	15	Received cash refund of $50 from Niki Sports for damaged merchandise that was returned.
	17	Paid freight on Martina's Sportswear purchase $30.
	18	Sold merchandise to members $800, terms n/30.
	20	Received $500 in cash from members in settlement of their accounts.
	21	Paid Martina's Sportswear in full.
	27	Granted credit of $30 to members for tennis clothing that did not fit.
	30	Sold merchandise to members $900, terms n/30.
	30	Received cash payments on account from members, $500.

The chart of accounts for the tennis shop includes Cash, Accounts Receivable, Merchandise Inventory, Accounts Payable, Common Stock, Sales, Sales Returns and Allowances, Purchases, Purchase Returns and Allowances, Purchase Discounts, and Freight-in.

Instructions
(a) Journalize the April transactions using a periodic inventory system.
(b) Using T accounts, enter the beginning balances in the ledger accounts and post the April transactions.
(c) Prepare a trial balance on April 30, 1998.
(d) Prepare an income statement through Gross Profit, assuming merchandise inventory on hand at April 30 is $1,800.

P6-2A The N-Mart Department Store is located near the Village Shopping Mall. At the end of the company's fiscal year on December 31, 1998, these accounts appeared in its adjusted trial balance:

Prepare a multiple-step income statement.
(SO 2, 4)

Accounts Payable	$ 89,300
Accounts Receivable	50,300
Accumulated Depreciation—Building	52,500
Accumulated Depreciation—Equipment	42,900
Building	190,000
Cash	23,000
Depreciation Expense—Building	10,400
Depreciation Expense—Equipment	13,300
Equipment	110,000
Freight-in	3,600
Insurance Expense	7,200
Merchandise Inventory	40,500
Mortgage Payable	80,000
Office Salaries Expense	32,000
Prepaid Insurance	2,400
Property Taxes Payable	4,800
Purchases	462,000

278 CHAPTER 6 Reporting and Analyzing Inventory

Purchase Discounts	12,000
Purchase Returns and Allowances	6,400
Sales Salaries Expense	76,000
Sales	618,000
Sales Commissions Expense	14,500
Sales Commissions Payable	3,500
Sales Returns and Allowances	8,000
Common Stock	150,000
Retained Earnings	27,600
Dividends	28,000
Property Taxes Expense	4,800
Utilities Expense	11,000

Additional facts:
1. Merchandise inventory on December 31, 1998, is $75,000.
2. Note that N-Mart Department Store uses a periodic system.

Instructions
Prepare an income statement for the year ended December 31, 1998.

Determine cost of goods sold and ending inventory using FIFO, LIFO, and average cost.
(SO 5, 6)

P6-3A Steward Company had a beginning inventory of 400 units of Product MLN at a cost of $8.00 per unit. During the year, purchases were:

Feb. 20	700 units at $9		Aug. 12	300 units at $11
May 5	500 units at $10		Dec. 8	100 units at $12

Steward Company uses a periodic inventory system. Sales totaled 1,550 units.

Instructions
(a) Determine the cost of goods available for sale.
(b) Determine the ending inventory and the cost of goods sold under each of the assumed cost flow methods (FIFO, LIFO, and average cost). Prove the accuracy of the cost of goods sold under the FIFO and LIFO methods.
(c) Which cost flow method results in the lowest inventory amount for the balance sheet? The lowest cost of goods sold for the income statement?

Compute ending inventory, prepare income statements, and answer questions using FIFO and LIFO.
(SO 5, 6)

P6-4A The management of Real Novelty Inc. is reevaluating the appropriateness of using its present inventory cost flow method, which is average cost. The company requests your help in determining the results of operations for 1998 if either the FIFO or the LIFO method had been used. For 1998 the accounting records show these data:

Inventories		Purchases and Sales	
Beginning (15,000 units)	$34,000	Total net sales (225,000 units)	$865,000
Ending (20,000 units)		Total cost of goods purchased (230,000 units)	578,500

Purchases were made quarterly as follows:

Quarter	Units	Unit Cost	Total Cost
1	60,000	$2.30	$138,000
2	50,000	2.50	125,000
3	50,000	2.60	130,000
4	70,000	2.65	185,500
	230,000		$578,500

Operating expenses were $147,000, and the company's income tax rate is 30%.

Instructions
(a) Prepare comparative condensed income statements for 1998 under FIFO and LIFO. (Show computations of ending inventory.)

(b) Answer the following questions for management:
(1) Which cost flow method (FIFO or LIFO) produces the more meaningful inventory amount for the balance sheet? Why?

(2) Which cost flow method (FIFO or LIFO) produces the more meaningful net income? Why?
(3) Which cost flow method (FIFO or LIFO) is more likely to approximate the actual physical flow of goods? Why?
(4) How much more cash will be available for management under LIFO than under FIFO? Why?
(5) Will gross profit under the average cost method be higher or lower than FIFO? Than LIFO? [*Note:* It is not necessary to quantify your answer.]

P6-5A This information is available for Paisley Corporation for 1997, 1998, and 1999. Paisley uses the LIFO inventory method.

Compute inventory turnover ratio, days in inventory, and current ratio based on LIFO and after adjusting for LIFO reserve.

(SO 8, 9)

	1997	1998	1999
Beginning inventory	$ 300,000	$ 350,000	$ 500,000
Ending inventory	350,000	500,000	600,000
Beginning LIFO reserve	250,000	270,000	300,000
Ending LIFO reserve	270,000	300,000	340,000
Current assets	500,000	650,000	800,000
Current liabilities	300,000	900,000	1,000,000
Cost of goods sold	1,000,000	1,420,000	1,550,000
Sales	1,200,000	1,600,000	1,900,000

Instructions
Calculate the inventory turnover ratio, days in inventory, and current ratio for Paisley Corporation for 1997, 1998, and 1999 as follows:
(a) Based on LIFO
(b) After adjusting for the LIFO reserve
(c) Comment on any difference between parts (a) and (b).

BROADENING YOUR PERSPECTIVE

FINANCIAL REPORTING AND ANALYSIS

FINANCIAL REPORTING PROBLEM: *Starbucks Corporation*

BYP6-1 The notes that accompany a company's financial statements provide informative details that would clutter the amounts and descriptions presented in the statements. Refer to the financial statements of Starbucks and the accompanying Notes to Consolidated Financial Statements in Appendix A.

Instructions
Answer the following questions. (Give the amounts in thousands of dollars, as shown in Starbucks' annual report.)
(a) What did Starbucks report for the amount of inventories in its Consolidated Balance Sheet at September 29, 1996? At October 1, 1995?
(b) Compute the dollar amount of change and the percentage change in inventories between 1995 and 1996. Compute inventory as a percentage of current assets for 1996.
(c) How does Starbucks value its inventories? Which inventory cost flow method does Starbucks use?
(d) What are the costs of sales (cost of goods sold) reported by Starbucks for 1996, 1995, and 1994? Compute the ratio of cost of sales to net sales in 1996.

COMPARATIVE ANALYSIS PROBLEM: *Starbucks vs. Green Mountain Coffee*

BYP6-2 The financial statements of Green Mountain Coffee are presented in Appendix B, following the financial statements for Starbucks in Appendix A.

Instructions
(a) Based on the information in these financial statements, compute these 1996 values for each company:
   1. Inventory turnover ratio
   2. Days in inventory
(b) What conclusions concerning the management of the inventory can be drawn from these data?

RESEARCH CASE

BYP6-3 The September 23, 1994, edition of *The Wall Street Journal* includes an article entitled "CompUSA Auctions Notebook Computers Through Bulk Sale."

Instructions
Read the article and answer these inventory-related questions:
(a) At what amount did CompUSA estimate the retail value of the computers? What was the estimate made by one of the bidders?
(b) What was wrong with the computers?
(c) What were the rules of the auction as specified by CompUSA?
(d) CompUSA had just recorded a $3 million inventory write-down in the preceding quarter. Based on the information in the article, does it appear that additional write-downs were called for?

INTERPRETING FINANCIAL STATEMENTS

BYP6-4 Minicase 1 *Morrow Snowboards*

Snowboarding is a rapidly growing sport in the United States. Morrow Snowboards, located in Salem, Oregon, is a significant player in snowboard manufacture and sales. In 1995 Morrow announced it would sell shares of stock to the public. In its prospectus (an information-filled document that must be provided by every publicly traded U.S. firm the first time it issues shares to the public), Morrow disclosed the following information:

MORROW SNOWBOARDS
Prospectus

Uncertain Ability to Manage Growth: Since inception, the Company has experienced rapid growth in its sales, production, and employee base. These increases have placed significant demands on the Company's management, working capital, and financial and management control systems. The Company's independent auditors used management letters in connection with their audit of the fiscal years ended December 31, 1993 and 1994, and the 9-month period ended September 30, 1995, that identified certain significant deficiencies in the Company's accounting systems, procedures, and controls. To address these growth issues, the Company has, in the past 18 months, relocated its facilities and expanded production capacity, implemented a number of financial accounting control systems, and hired experienced finance, accounting, manufacturing, and marketing personnel. In the accounting area, the Company has begun implementing or improving a perpetual inventory system, a cost accounting system, written accounting policies and procedures, and a comprehensive annual capital expenditure budget. Until the Company develops a reliable perpetual inventory system, it intends to perform physical inventories on a quarterly basis. Although the Company is continuously evaluating and improving its facilities, management, and financial control systems, there can be no assurance that such improvements will meet the demands of future growth. Any inadequacies in these areas could have a material adverse effect on the Company's business, financial condition, and results of operations.

Instructions

(a) What implications does this disclosure have for someone interested in investing in Morrow Snowboards?
(b) Do you think that the price of Morrow's stock will suffer because of these admitted deficiencies in its internal controls, including its controls over inventory?
(c) Why do you think Morrow decided to disclose this negative information?
(d) List the steps that Morrow has taken to improve its control systems.
(e) Do you think that these weaknesses are unusual for a rapidly growing company?

BYP6-5 **Minicase 2** *Nike and Reebok*

Nike and Reebok compete head-to-head in the sport shoe and sport apparel business. For both companies, inventory is a significant portion of total assets. The following information was taken from each company's financial statements and notes to those financial statements.

NIKE, INC.
Notes to the Financial Statements

Inventory. Inventories are stated at the lower of cost or market. Cost is determined using the last-in, first-out (LIFO) method for substantially all U.S. inventories. International inventories are valued on a first-in, first-out (FIFO) basis.

Inventories by major classification are as follows (in thousands):

	May 31 1995	May 31 1994
Finished goods	$618,521	$465,065
Work in process	9,064	2,915
Raw materials	2,157	2,043

Other information for Nike (in thousands):

	1995	1994
Inventory	$ 629,742	$ 470,023
Cost of goods sold	2,865,280	2,301,423

REEBOK INTERNATIONAL, LTD.
Notes to the Financial Statements

Inventory. Inventory, substantially all finished goods, is recorded at the lower of cost (first-in, first-out method) or market.

Other information for Reebok (in thousands):

	1995	1994
Inventory	$ 635,012	$ 624,625
Cost of goods sold	2,114,084	1,966,138

Instructions

Address each of these questions on how these two companies manage inventory:

(a) What problems of inventory management face Nike and Reebok in the international sport apparel industry?
(b) What inventory cost flow assumptions does each company use? Why might Nike use a different approach for U.S. operations than for international operations? What are the implications of their respective cost flow assumptions for their financial statements?
(c) Nike provides more detail regarding the nature of its inventory (e.g., raw materials,

work in process, and finished goods) than does Reebok. How might this additional information be useful in evaluating Nike?

(d) Calculate and interpret the inventory turnover ratio and days in inventory for each company. Comment on how the use of different cost flow methods by the two companies affects your ability to compare their ratios.

CRITICAL THINKING

MANAGEMENT DECISION CASE

BYP6-6 Morton International, Inc., with headquarters in Chicago, Illinois, manufactures specialty chemicals, automobile airbags, and salt. During 1996, the specialty chemicals business was reorganized, and three manufacturing plants were closed. Profits were generally high, however, mostly because of an improved product mix. The automotive airbag business did very well, with sales more than 30% higher than the previous year. However, toward the end of the year, questions were being raised about the safety of airbags, and this put the future of this business in some jeopardy. The salt business had dramatically increased volume because of the demand for ice-control salt due to an unusually severe winter in the northeastern United States. However, ice-control salt has a low profit margin, and so profits were up only modestly.

The current assets portion of Morton International's balance sheet follows. Dollar amounts are in millions. Morton's fiscal year ends June 30.

Current assets	
Cash and cash equivalents	$ 71.1
Receivables, less allowance of $10.8	624.6
Deferred income tax benefits	23.6
Inventories	364.5
Prepaid expenses	112.4
Total current assets	$1,196.2

Assume that the following transactions occurred during March and April 1997:
1. Office supplies were shipped to Morton by Office Maxx, FOB destination. The goods were shipped March 30 and received March 31.
2. Morton purchased specialty plastic from Uniroyal Technology for use in airbag manufacture. The goods where shipped FOB shipping point April 1, and were received by Morton April 4.
3. Ford Motor Company purchased 10,000 airbags to be used in the manufacture of new cars. These were shipped FOB shipping point March 30, and were received by Ford April 2.
4. Bassett Furniture shipped office furniture to Morton, FOB destination, March 29. The goods were received April 3.
5. Inland Specialty Chemical shipped Morton chemicals that Morton uses in the manufacture of airbags and other items. The goods were sent FOB shipping point March 29, and were received April 1.
6. Morton purchased new automobiles for its executives from General Motors. The cars were shipped FOB destination March 19, and were received April 2.
7. Morton shipped salt to New York State Public Works, FOB Chicago, March 29. The shipment arrived in Chicago March 30 and in New York April 2.
8. Morton purchased steel, to be used in expanding its manufacturing plant, from Inland Steel, FOB Dallas. The steel was shipped March 30, arrived in Dallas April 2, and at Morton's plant April 6.
9. Morton shipped packaged salt to Associated Wholesale Grocers FOB Kansas City. The salt was shipped March 30, arrived in Kansas City April 1, and at Associated Wholesale Grocers' warehouse April 2.

Instructions
Answer the following questions:
(a) Which items would be owned by Morton International as of March 31, 1997?
(b) Which transactions involve Morton's inventory account?

A REAL-WORLD FOCUS: *General Motors Corporation*

BYP6-7 **General Motors** is the largest producer of automobiles in the world as well as the world's biggest industrial enterprise. After stumbling in the early 1990s, GM has implemented numerous cost-cutting measures, including downsizing and renegotiating contracts with suppliers. In addition, it has shifted more of its resources to the hot-selling truck market.

The annual report of General Motors Corporation disclosed the following information about its accounting for inventories:

GENERAL MOTORS CORPORATION
Notes to the Financial Statements

Note 12. Inventories
Major Classes of Inventories

	(in millions)	
	1994	1993
Productive material, work in process, and supplies	$ 5,478.3	$4,671.9
Finished product, service parts, etc.	4,649.5	3,943.2
Total	$10,127.8	$8,615.1
Memo: Increase in LIFO inventories if valued at first-in, first-out (FIFO)	$ 2,535.9	$2,519.0

Inventories are stated generally at cost, which is not in excess of market. The cost of substantially all U.S. inventories other than the inventories of Saturn Corporation (Saturn) and GMHE is determined by the last-in, first-out (LIFO) method. The cost of non-U.S., Saturn, and GMHE inventories is determined generally by FIFO or average cost methods.

Instructions
(a) What is meant by "inventories are stated generally at cost, which is not in excess of market"?
(b) The company uses LIFO for most of its inventory. What impact does this have on reported ending inventory if prices are increasing?
(c) General Motors uses different cost flow methods for different types of inventory. Why might it do this?

GROUP ACTIVITY

BYP6-8 In groups of four or five students, choose one of these inventory cost flow methods: FIFO, LIFO, average cost, specific identification.

Instructions
(a) Discuss the assumed cost flow method and its effects on the financial statements if adopted.
(b) Explain to the class how to implement the method you chose and its effects on the financial statements that you discussed earlier.

COMMUNICATION ACTIVITIES

BYP6-9 In a discussion of dramatic increases in coffee bean prices, a recent *Wall Street Journal* article noted the following fact about Starbucks:

> Before this year's bean-price hike, Starbucks added several defenses that analysts say could help it maintain earnings and revenue. The company last year began accounting for its coffee-bean purchases by taking the average price of all beans in inventory.
>
> *Source:* Aaron Lucchetti, "Crowded Coffee Market May Keep a Lid on Starbucks After Price Rise Hurt Stock," *The Wall Street Journal,* June 4, 1997, p. C1.

Prior to this change the company was using FIFO.

Instructions
Your client, the CEO of Hot Cup Coffee, Inc., read this article and wrote you an e-mail message requesting that you explain why Starbucks might have taken this action. Your response should explain what impact this change in accounting method has on earnings, why the company might want to do this, and any possible disadvantages of such a change.

*BYP6-10 You are the controller of Small Toys Inc. Joy Small, the president, recently mentioned to you that she found an error in the 1997 financial statements which she believes has corrected itself. She determined, in discussions with the purchasing department, that 1997 ending inventory was overstated by $1 million. Joy says that the 1998 ending inventory is correct, and she assumes that 1998 income is correct. Joy says to you, "What happened has happened—there's no point in worrying about it anymore."

Instructions
You conclude that Joy is incorrect. Write a brief, tactful memo to her, clarifying the situation.

ETHICS CASE

BYP6-11 Lonergan Wholesale Corp. uses the LIFO cost flow method. In the current year, profit at Lonergan is running unusually high. The corporate tax rate is also high this year, but it is scheduled to decline significantly next year. In an effort to lower the current year's net income and to take advantage of the changing income tax rate, the president of Lonergan Wholesale instructs the plant accountant to recommend to the purchasing department a large purchase of inventory for delivery 3 days before the end of the year. The price of the inventory to be purchased has doubled during the year, and the purchase will represent a major portion of the ending inventory value.

Instructions
(a) What is the effect of this transaction on this year's and next year's income statement and income tax expense? Why?
(b) If Lonergan Wholesale had been using the FIFO method of inventory costing, would the president give the same directive?
(c) Should the plant accountant order the inventory purchase to lower income? What are the ethical implications of this order?

FINANCIAL ANALYSIS ON THE WEB

BYP6-12 *Purpose:* Use a company's annual report to identify the inventory method used and analyze the effects on the income statement and balance sheet.

Address: http://www.cisco.com

Steps:
1. From Cisco System's homepage, use the **quick search,** type annual report.
2. Choose **Search.**
3. Choose **Cisco System Annual Report.**
4. Choose **Financial Review.**
5. Use the financial statements and relating notes to the financial statements to answer the questions below.

Instructions
Answer the following questions:
(a) At Cisco's fiscal year end, what was the net inventory on the balance sheet?
(b) How has this changed from the previous fiscal year end?
(c) How much of the inventory was finished goods?
(d) What inventory method do they use?

Answers to Self-Study Questions
1. b 2. d 3. a 4. a 5. c 6. d 7. c 8. d 9. a 10. d *11. b

CHAPTER 7

Internal Control and Cash

STUDY OBJECTIVES

After studying this chapter, you should be able to:

1. Identify the principles of internal control.
2. Explain the applications of internal control to cash receipts.
3. Explain the applications of internal control to cash disbursements.
4. Prepare a bank reconciliation.
5. Explain the reporting of cash.
6. Discuss the basic principles of cash management.
7. Identify the primary elements of a cash budget.
8. Identify and interpret measures that evaluate the adequacy of cash.

It Takes a Thief

HAVE YOU SEEN THIS MAN? Fifty years old, thinning brown hair, hump on back, bulbous red nose with prominent veins, and wart on upper lip, goes by the name David Shelton—and at least 14 other names. David Shelton is good at what he does. He's a thief who specializes in inside jobs. It's believed that in seven recent years, while working as a bookkeeper for small businesses, he stole at least $600,000.

Ask Celia Imperiale. She hired Mr. Shelton after he responded to an employment ad she placed for a bookkeeper. His resume boasted 20 years of experience with two different employers. He had been with his "current" employer since 1981. When Ms. Imperiale called the number of this "current" employer, she was greeted by a woman who answered with the corporate name and then was transferred to the owner of the company. The owner gave a glowing recommendation. Ms. Imperiale also tried to call the previous employer, but she couldn't find a listing. Since it had been more than 12 years since Mr. Shelton had worked there, she didn't worry about it. But the "current" reference was phony. The phone number that Ms. Imperiale called belonged to a room at a low-rent motel. The glowing reference was given by Mr. Shelton's accomplice.

Mr. Shelton was a reasonably good employee, giving Ms. Imperiale no cause for concern until the day her auditor showed up—which by coincidence was the day after the last time she saw Mr. Shelton. Mr. Shelton had stolen $44,000, mainly by pocketing cash receipts from Ms. Imperiale's three stores. He filled out a proper bank deposit slip, which she always checked. But on his way to the bank he made out a new deposit slip for 10% less than the total; then he deposited 90% and kept 10% for himself. He hid his theft by manipulating the accounting records and by not paying the company's state and federal taxes as they came due. At previous companies Mr. Shelton had pocketed money by creating phony suppliers who billed his employer for work never done. He then made out a check to the phony company and sent it to a bank account that he controlled under another phony name.

Mr. Shelton was careful to leave little evidence. He drove

nondescript cars, which he parked far away from where he both worked and lived. He didn't attend corporate social functions and was never in corporate pictures. When he left Ms. Imperiale's company, he stole all of his personnel files. Ms. Imperiale is probably still paying off the loan she had to take out to pay the back taxes that Mr. Shelton didn't pay.

Postscript: David Shelton (whose real name is Donald Peterson) was apprehended when a small business owner recognized him as one of his employees after reading about him in a *Wall Street Journal* article.

Source: Adapted from J. R. Emshwiller, "Looking for a New Bookkeeper? Beware of This One," *The Wall Street Journal,* April 19, 1994, p. B1. Reprinted by permission of *The Wall Street Journal,* © 1994 Dow Jones & Company, Inc. All Rights Reserved Worldwide.

PREVIEW OF CHAPTER 7

Cash is the lifeblood of any company. Large and small companies alike must guard it carefully. Even companies that are in every other way successful can go bankrupt if they fail to manage cash. Managers must know both how to use cash efficiently and how to protect it. Due to its liquid nature, cash is the easiest asset to steal. As the opening story suggests, a particularly difficult problem arises when a company has a dishonest employee.

In this chapter you will learn ways to reduce the risk of theft of cash and other assets, how to report cash in the financial statements, and how to manage cash through the course of the company's operating cycle. The content and organization of the chapter are as follows:

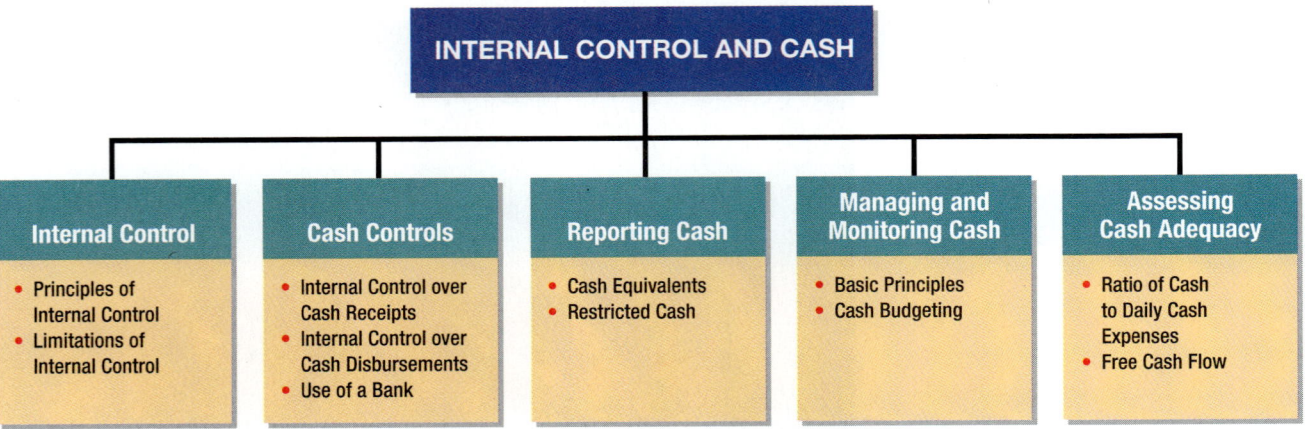

INTERNAL CONTROL

Could there be dishonest employees in the business that you own or manage? Unfortunately, the answer is yes. Situations such as the one described in the opening story emphasize the need for a good system of internal control.

Internal control consists of all the related methods and measures adopted within a business to:

1. **Safeguard its assets** from employee theft, robbery, and unauthorized use; and
2. **Enhance the accuracy and reliability of its accounting records** by reducing the risk of errors (unintentional mistakes) and irregularities (intentional mistakes and misrepresentations) in the accounting process.

All major U.S. corporations are required to maintain an adequate system of internal control. Companies that fail to comply are subject to fines, and company officers may be imprisoned.

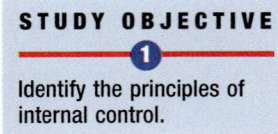

PRINCIPLES OF INTERNAL CONTROL

To safeguard assets and enhance the accuracy and reliability of its accounting records, a company follows internal control principles. The specific control measures used vary with the size and nature of the business and with management's control philosophy. However, the six principles listed in Illustration 7-1 apply to most enterprises. Each principle is explained in the following sections.

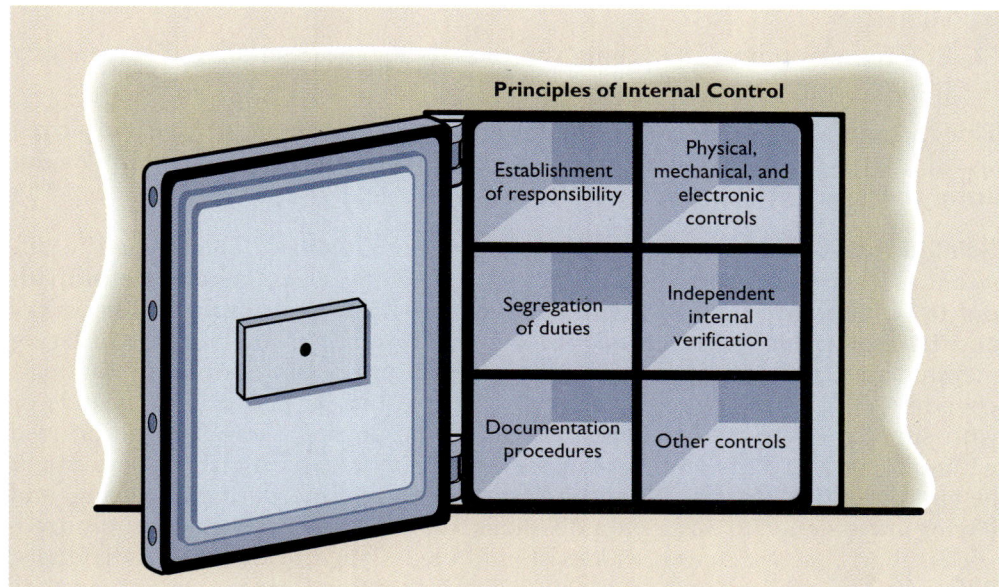

Illustration 7-1 Principles of internal control

Establishment of Responsibility

An essential characteristic of internal control is the assignment of responsibility to specific individuals. **Control is most effective when only one person is responsible for a given task.** To illustrate, assume that the cash on hand at the end of the day in a Safeway supermarket is $10 short of the cash rung up on the cash register. If only one person has operated the register, responsibility for the shortage can be assessed quickly. If two or more individuals have worked the register, however, it may be impossible to determine who is responsible for the error unless each person is assigned a separate cash drawer and register key.

Establishing responsibility includes the authorization and approval of transactions. The vice-president of sales should have the authority to establish policies for making credit sales. These policies ordinarily will require written credit department approval of credit sales.

BUSINESS INSIGHT
Investor Perspective

Poor internal controls can cost a company money even if no theft occurs. For example, it was recently reported that the share prices of two companies, Morrow Snowboards and Home Theater Products, suffered because their auditors said that the firms had inadequate internal controls. The stock prices fell because investors and creditors are uncomfortable investing in companies that don't have good internal controls. In addition, companies can even be fined for having poor internal controls. German multinational corporation Metallgesellschaft was recently fined by the Commodities Futures Trading Commission for material inadequacies in internal control systems at some of its U.S. subsidiaries.

Segregation of Duties

Segregation of duties is indispensable in a system of internal control. There are two common applications of this principle:

1. The responsibility for related activities should be assigned to different individuals.
2. The responsibility for keeping the records for an asset should be separate from the physical custody of that asset.

The rationale for segregation of duties is that the work of one employee should, without a duplication of effort, provide a reliable basis for evaluating the work of another employee.

Related Activities. There are related activities that should be assigned to different individuals in both the purchasing and selling areas. **When one individual is responsible for all of the related activities, the potential for errors and irregularities is increased.** *Related purchasing activities* include ordering merchandise, receiving goods, and paying (or authorizing payment) for merchandise. In purchasing, for example, orders could be placed with friends or with suppliers who give kickbacks. In addition, payment might be authorized without a careful review of the invoice or, even worse, fictitious invoices might be approved for payment. When the responsibilities for ordering, receiving, and paying are assigned to different individuals, the risk of such abuses is minimized.

Similarly, *related sales activities* should be assigned to different individuals. Related sales activities include making a sale, shipping (or delivering) the goods to the customer, and billing the customer. When one person is responsible for these related sales transactions, a salesperson could make sales at unauthorized prices to increase sales commissions, a shipping clerk could ship goods to himself, or a billing clerk could understate the amount billed for sales made to friends and relatives. These abuses are less likely to occur when salespersons make the sale, shipping department employees ship the goods on the basis of the sales order, and billing department employees prepare the sales invoice after comparing the sales order with the report of goods shipped.

Accountability for Assets. If accounting is to provide a valid basis of accountability for an asset, the accountant (as record keeper) should have neither physical custody of the asset nor access to it. Moreover, the custodian of the asset should not maintain or have access to the accounting records. **The custodian of the asset is not likely to convert the asset to personal use if one employee maintains the record of the asset that should be on hand and a different employee has physical custody of the asset.** The separation of accounting responsibility from the custody of assets is especially important for cash and inventories because these assets are very vulnerable to unauthorized use or misappropriation.

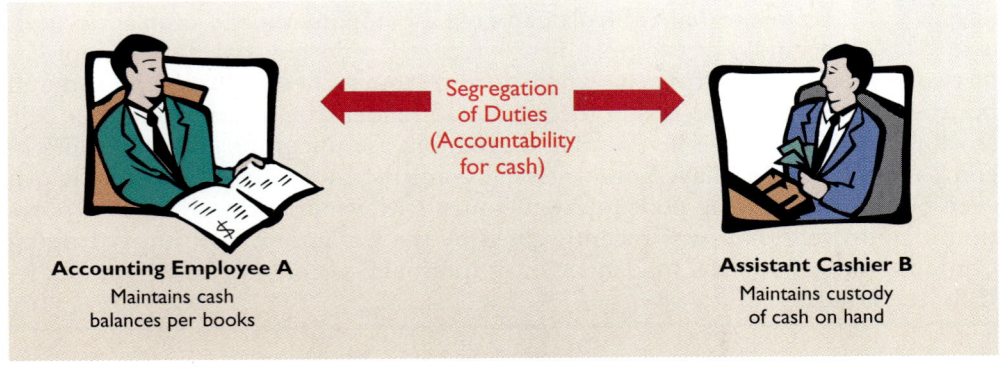

BUSINESS INSIGHT
Management Perspective

A former electronic data processing employee of Texaco, Inc., and his wife were indicted for stealing thousands of dollars from the company in an accounts payable-type fraud. The employee instructed Texaco's computer to pay his wife rent for land she allegedly leased to Texaco by assigning her an alphanumeric code as a lessor and then ordering that payments be made. The lesson here is simple: *Never* allow the same person to both authorize and pay for goods and services. Doing otherwise violates the segregation of duties principle of internal control.

Documentation Procedures

Documents provide evidence that transactions and events have occurred. For example, the shipping document indicates that the goods have been shipped, and the sales invoice indicates that the customer has been billed for the goods. By adding signatures (or initials) to the documents, the individual(s) responsible for the transaction or event can be identified.

Procedures should be established for documents. First, whenever possible, **documents should be prenumbered and all documents should be accounted for.** Prenumbering helps to prevent a transaction from being recorded more than once or, conversely, to prevent the transactions from not being recorded. Second, documents that are **source documents for accounting entries should be promptly forwarded to the accounting department to help ensure timely recording of the transaction and event.** This control measure contributes directly to the accuracy and reliability of the accounting records.

Helpful Hint An important corollary to prenumbering is that voided documents be kept until all documents are accounted for.

Physical, Mechanical, and Electronic Controls

Use of physical, mechanical, and electronic controls is essential. Physical controls relate primarily to the safeguarding of assets. Mechanical and electronic controls safeguard assets and enhance the accuracy and reliability of the accounting records. Examples of these controls are shown in Illustration 7-2.

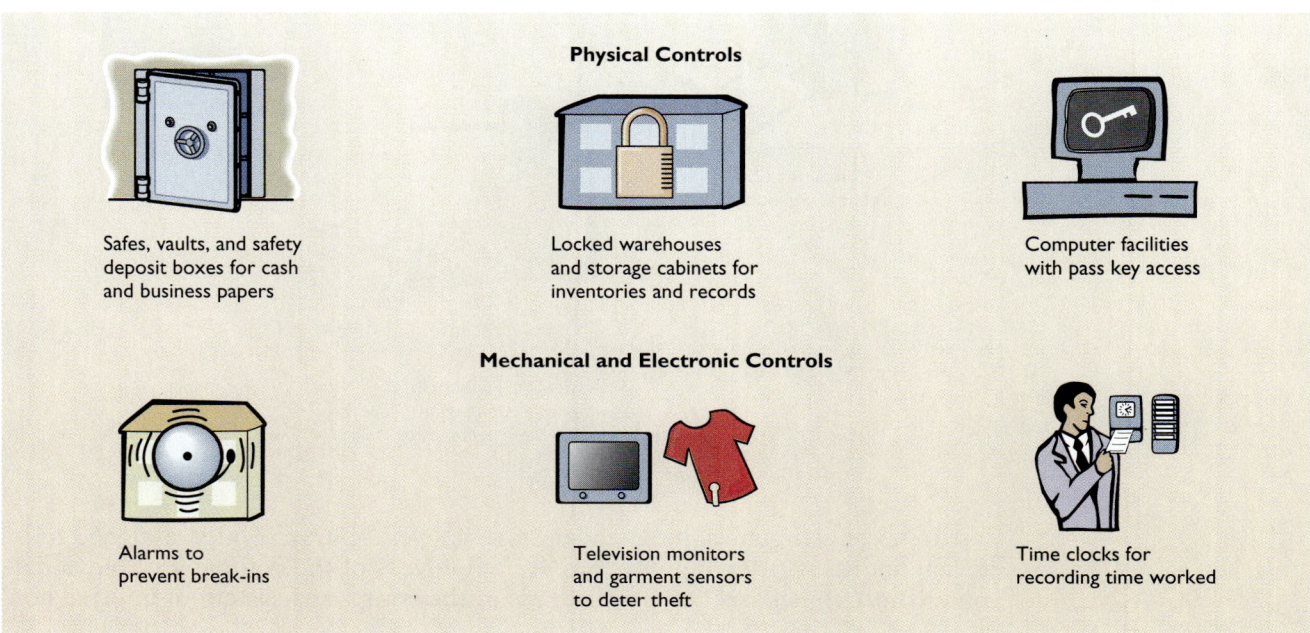

Illustration 7-2 Physical, mechanical, and electronic controls

A crucial consideration in programming computerized systems is building in controls that limit unauthorized or unintentional tampering. Entire books and movies have been produced with computer system tampering as a major theme. Most programmers would agree that tamper proofing and debugging programs are the most difficult and time-consuming phases of their jobs. Program controls built into the computer prevent intentional or unintentional errors or unauthorized access. To prevent unauthorized access, the computer system may require that passwords be entered and random personal questions be correctly answered before system access is allowed. Once access has been allowed, other program controls identify data having a value higher or lower than a predetermined amount (limit checks), validate computations (math checks), and detect improper processing order (sequence checks).

Independent Internal Verification

Most systems of internal control provide for independent internal verification. This principle involves the review, comparison, and reconciliation of data prepared by employees. Three measures are recommended to obtain maximum benefit from independent internal verification:

1. The verification should be made periodically or on a surprise basis.
2. The verification should be done by an employee who is independent of the personnel responsible for the information.
3. Discrepancies and exceptions should be reported to a management level that can take appropriate corrective action.

Independent internal verification is especially useful in comparing recorded accountability with existing assets. The reconciliation of the cash register tape with the cash in the register is an example. Another common example is the reconciliation by an independent person of the cash balance per books with the cash balance per bank. The relationship between this principle and the segregation of duties principle is shown graphically in Illustration 7-3.

Illustration 7-3 Comparison of segregation of duties principle with independent internal verification principle

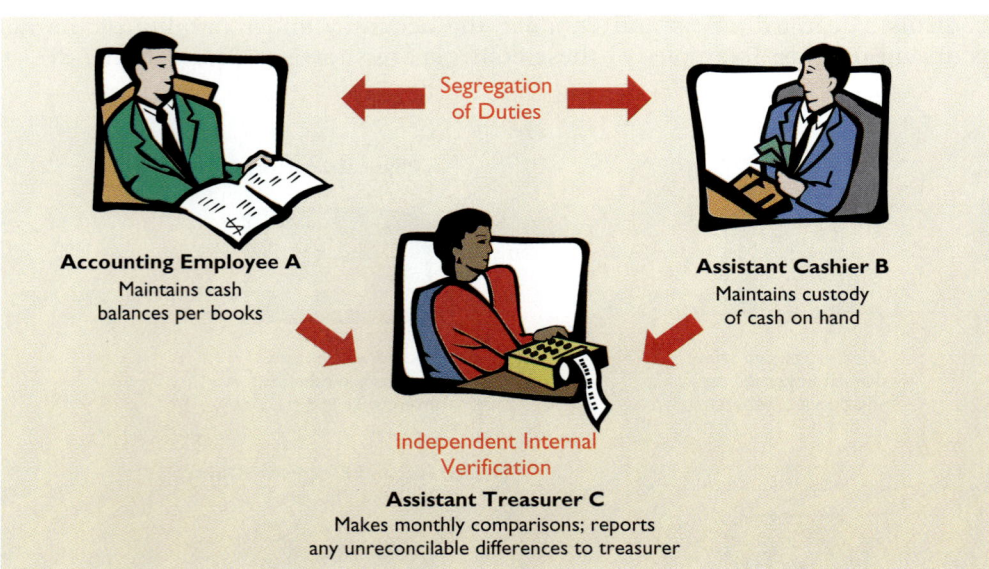

In large companies, independent internal verification is often assigned to internal auditors. **Internal auditors** are employees of the company who evaluate on a continuous basis the effectiveness of the company's system of internal control. They periodically review the activities of departments and individuals to determine whether prescribed internal controls are being followed. The importance of this function is illustrated by the number of internal auditors employed by companies. In a recent year, AT&T had 350 internal auditors, Exxon had 395, and IBM had 142.

BUSINESS INSIGHT
International Perspective

Recently Sumitomo Corporation became the fifth Japanese company to announce a huge loss, this time $1.8 billion, due to a single copper trader. Some are blaming Japanese culture because it encourages group harmony over confrontation and thus may contribute to poor internal controls. For example, good controls require that both parties to a copper trade send a confirmation slip to management to verify all trades. In Japan the counterparty to the trade often sends the confirmation slip to the trader, who then forwards it to management. Thus, it is possible for the trader to change the confirmation slip. An unethical trader could create fictitious trades to hide losses for an extended period of time or to conceal trades that are larger than allowed limits.

Source: Adapted from Sheryl Wudunn, "Big New Loss Makes Japan Look Inward," *New York Times,* June 17, 1996, p. D1.

Other Controls

Here are two other control measures:

1. **Bonding of employees who handle cash.** Bonding involves obtaining insurance protection against misappropriation of assets by dishonest employees. This measure contributes to the safeguarding of cash in two ways: First, the insurance company carefully screens all individuals before adding them to the policy and may reject risky applicants. Second, bonded employees know that the insurance company will vigorously prosecute all offenders.
2. **Rotating employees' duties and requiring employees to take vacations.** These measures are designed to deter employees from attempting any thefts, since they will not be able to permanently conceal their improper actions. Many bank embezzlements, for example, have been discovered when the perpetrator has been on vacation or assigned to a new position.

DECISION TOOLKIT

Decision Checkpoints	Info Needed for Decision	Tool to Use for Decision	How to Evaluate Results
Are the company's financial statements supported by adequate internal controls?	Auditor's report, management discussion and analysis, articles in financial press	The required measures of internal control are to (1) establish responsibility, (2) segregate duties, (3) document procedures, (4) employ physical or automated controls, and (5) use independent internal verification.	If any indication is given that these or other controls are lacking, the financial statements should be used with caution.

LIMITATIONS OF INTERNAL CONTROL

A company's system of internal control is generally designed to provide **reasonable assurance** that assets are properly safeguarded and that the accounting records are reliable. **The concept of reasonable assurance rests on the premise that the costs of establishing control procedures should not exceed their expected benefit.** To illustrate, consider shoplifting losses in retail stores. Such losses could be completely eliminated by having a security guard stop and search customers as they leave the store. Store managers have concluded, however, that the negative effects of this procedure cannot be justified. Instead, stores have attempted to "control" shoplifting losses by less costly procedures such as: (1) posting signs saying, "We reserve the right to inspect all packages" and "All shoplifters will be prosecuted," (2) using hidden TV cameras and store detectives to monitor customer activity, and (3) using sensor equipment at exits.

The **human element** is an important factor in every system of internal control. A good system can become ineffective as a result of employee fatigue, carelessness, or indifference. For example, a receiving clerk may not bother to count goods received or may just "fudge" the counts. Occasionally, two or more individuals may work together to get around prescribed controls. Such **collusion** can significantly impair the effectiveness of a system because it eliminates the protection anticipated from segregation of duties. If a supervisor and a cashier collaborate to understate cash receipts, the system of internal control may be subverted (at least in the short run). No system of internal control is perfect.

The size of the business may impose limitations on internal control. In a small company, for example, it may be difficult to apply the principles of segregation of duties and independent internal verification because of the small number of employees.

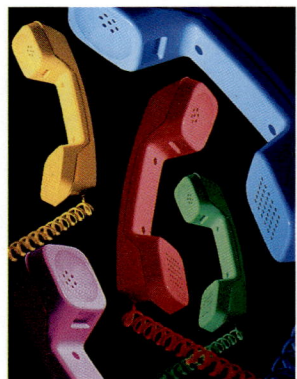

BUSINESS INSIGHT
Management Perspective

A recent study by the Association of Certified Fraud Examiners suggests that businesses with fewer than 100 employees are most at risk for employee theft. In addition, it found that the average loss per incident for small companies—$126,000—was actually higher than the average loss for larger companies. The study suggests that the high degree of trust often found in small companies makes them more vulnerable to dishonest employees. One employee intentionally asked the owner to sign checks only when the owner was extremely busy. The employee would slip in one check that was made out to himself and the owner didn't notice because he was so busy.

It has been suggested that the most important and inexpensive measure a business can take to reduce employee theft and fraud is to conduct thorough background checks. Two tips: (1) Check to see whether job applicants actually graduated from the schools they list. (2) Never use the telephone numbers for previous employers given on the reference sheet; always look them up yourself.

Source: J. R. Emshwiller, "Small Business Is the Biggest Victim of Theft by Employees, Survey Shows," *The Wall Street Journal,* October 2, 1995, p. B2.

BEFORE YOU GO ON . . .

● **Review It**
1. What are the two primary objectives of internal control?
2. Identify and describe the principles of internal control.
3. What are the limitations of internal control?

● **Do It**

Li Song owns a small retail store. Li wants to establish good internal control procedures but is confused about the difference between segregation of duties and independent internal verification. Explain the differences to Li.

Reasoning: In order to help Li, you need to thoroughly understand each principle. From this knowledge and a study of Illustration 7-3, you should be able to explain the differences between the two principles.

Solution: Segregation of duties pertains to the assignment of responsibility so that (1) the work of one employee will evaluate the work of another employee and (2) the custody of assets is separated from the records that keep track of the assets. Segregation of duties occurs daily in using assets and in executing and recording transactions. In contrast, independent internal verification involves reviewing, comparing, and reconciling data prepared by one or several employees. Independent internal verification occurs after the fact, as in reconciling cash register totals at the end of the day with cash on hand.

CASH CONTROLS

Just as cash is the beginning of a company's operating cycle, it is usually the starting point for a company's system of internal control. Cash is the one asset that is readily convertible into any other type of asset, it is easily concealed and transported, and it is highly desired. Because of these characteristics, cash is the asset most susceptible to improper diversion and use. Moreover, because of the large volume of cash transactions, numerous errors may occur in executing and recording cash transactions. To safeguard cash and to assure the accuracy of the accounting records for cash, effective internal control over cash is imperative.

Cash consists of coins, currency (paper money), checks, money orders, and money on hand or on deposit in a bank or similar depository. The general rule is that if the bank will accept it for deposit, it is cash. The application of internal control principles to cash receipts and cash disbursements is explained in the next sections.

 International Note

Other countries also have control problems. For example, a judge in France has issued a 36-page "book" detailing many of the scams that are widespread, such as kickbacks in public-works contracts, the skimming of development aid money to Africa, and bribes on arms sales.

INTERNAL CONTROL OVER CASH RECEIPTS

Cash receipts result from a variety of sources: cash sales; collections on account from customers; the receipt of interest, rents, and dividends; investments by owners; bank loans; and proceeds from the sale of noncurrent assets. The internal control principles explained earlier apply to cash receipts transactions as shown in Illustration 7-4 (at the top of the next page). As might be expected, companies vary considerably in how they apply these principles.

STUDY OBJECTIVE 2

Explain the applications of internal control to cash receipts.

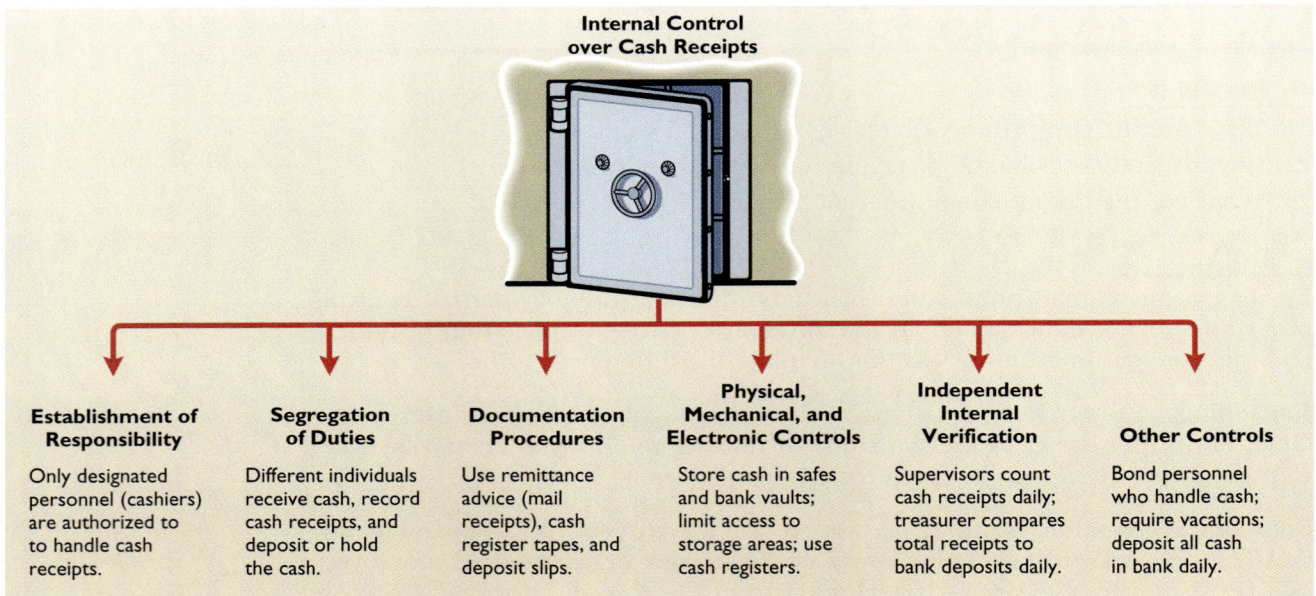

Illustration 7-4 Application of internal control principles to cash receipts

BUSINESS INSIGHT
Management Perspective

John Patterson, a young Ohio merchant, couldn't understand why his retail business didn't show a profit. There were lots of customers, but the money just seemed to disappear. Patterson suspected pilferage and sloppy bookkeeping by store clerks. Frustrated, he placed an order with a Dayton, Ohio, company for two rudimentary cash registers. A year later Patterson's store was in the black.

"What is a good thing for this little store is a good thing for every retail store in the world," he observed. A few months later, in 1884, John Patterson and his brother, Frank, bought the tiny cash register maker for $6,500. The word around Dayton was that the Patterson boys got stung.

In the following 37 years, John Patterson built National Cash Register Co. into a corporate giant. Patterson died in 1922, the year in which NCR sold its two millionth cash register. Imagine how surprised the Patterson brothers would be to see how technology has changed the cash register. One thing hasn't changed, though; the cash register is still a critical component of internal control.

Source: Wall Street Journal, January 28, 1989.

INTERNAL CONTROL OVER CASH DISBURSEMENTS

STUDY OBJECTIVE 3
Explain the applications of internal control to cash disbursements.

Cash is disbursed for a variety of reasons, such as to pay expenses and liabilities or to purchase assets. **Generally, internal control over cash disbursements is more effective when payments are made by check, rather than by cash, except for incidental amounts that are paid out of petty cash.** Payment is made by check generally only after specified control procedures have been followed. In addition, the "paid" check provides proof of payment. The principles of internal control apply to cash disbursements as shown in Illustration 7-5.

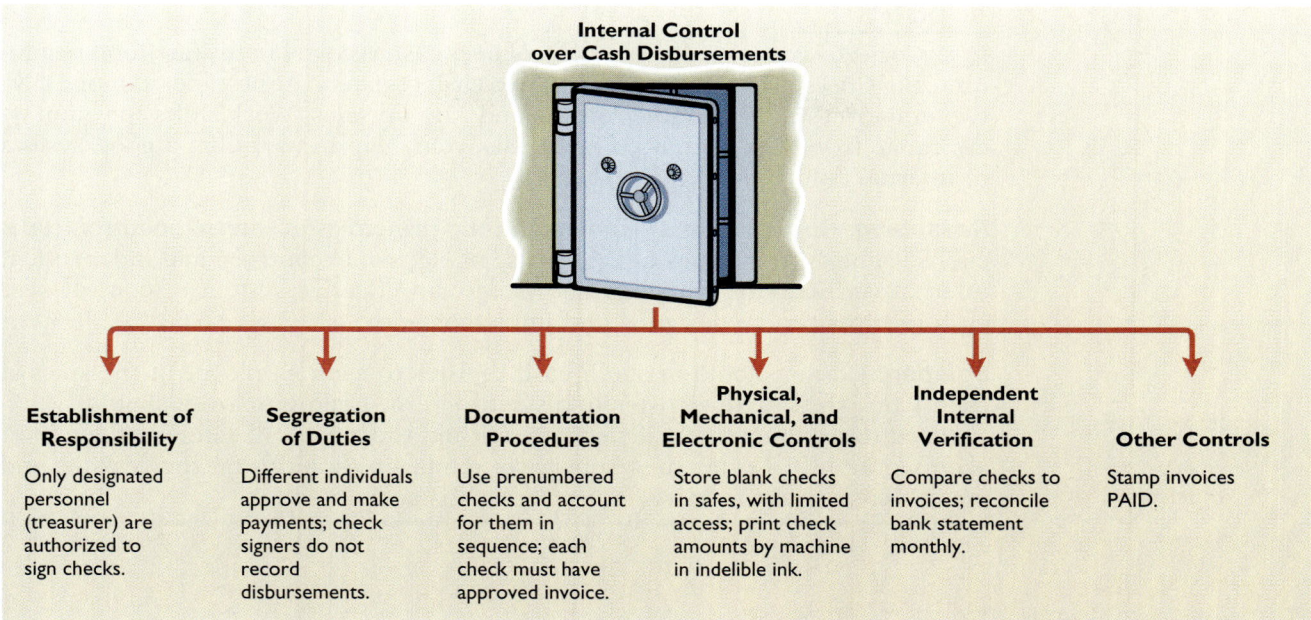

Illustration 7-5 Application of internal control principles to cash disbursements

Electronic Funds Transfer (EFT) System

To account for and control cash is an expensive and time-consuming process. For example, the cost to process a check through a bank system ranges from $.55 to $1.00 per check and is increasing. It is not surprising, therefore, that new approaches are being developed to transfer funds among parties without the use of paper (deposit tickets, checks, etc.). Such procedures, called **electronic funds transfers (EFT),** are disbursement systems that use wire, telephone, telegraph, or computer to transfer cash from one location to another. Use of EFT is quite common. For example, the authors receive no formal payroll checks from their universities, which simply send magnetic tapes to the appropriate banks for deposit. Regular payments such as those for house, car, or utilities are frequently made by EFT.

Petty Cash Fund

As you learned earlier in the chapter, better internal control over cash disbursements is possible when payments are made by check. However, using checks to pay such small amounts as those for postage due, employee working lunches, and taxi fares is both impractical and a nuisance. A common way of handling such payments, while maintaining satisfactory control, is to use a petty cash fund. A **petty cash fund** is a cash fund used to pay relatively small amounts. Information regarding the operation of a petty cash fund is provided in Appendix 7A at the end of this chapter.

BEFORE YOU GO ON . . .

● **Review It**
1. How do the principles of internal control apply to cash receipts?
2. How do the principles of internal control apply to cash disbursements?
3. What is the purpose of a petty cash fund?

● Do It

L. R. Cortez is concerned about control over cash receipts in his fast-food restaurant, Big Cheese. The restaurant has two cash registers. At no time do more than two employees take customer orders and ring up sales. Work shifts for employees range from 4 to 8 hours. Cortez asks your help in installing a good system of internal control over cash receipts.

Reasoning: Cortez needs to understand the principles of internal control, especially establishing responsibility, the use of electronic controls, and independent internal verification. With this knowledge, an effective system of control over cash receipts can be designed and implemented.

Solution: Cortez should assign a cash register to each employee at the start of each work shift, with register totals set at zero. Each employee should be instructed to use only the assigned register and to ring up all sales. At the end of each work shift, Cortez or a supervisor/manager should total the register and make a cash count to see whether all cash is accounted for.

USE OF A BANK

The use of a bank contributes significantly to good internal control over cash. A company can safeguard its cash by using a bank as a depository and clearinghouse for checks received and checks written. The use of a bank minimizes the amount of currency that must be kept on hand. In addition, the use of a bank facilitates the control of cash because a double record is maintained of all bank transactions—one by the business and the other by the bank. The asset account Cash maintained by the company is the reciprocal of the bank's liability account for that company. It should be possible to **reconcile these accounts**—make them agree—at any time.

Many companies have more than one bank account. For efficiency of operations and better control, national retailers like Wal-Mart and Kmart may have regional bank accounts. Similarly, a company such as Exxon with more than 150,000 employees may have a payroll bank account as well as one or more general bank accounts. In addition, a company may maintain several bank accounts in order to have more than one source for obtaining short-term loans when needed.

Bank Statements

Each month, the company receives from the bank a **bank statement** showing its bank transactions and balances. For example, the statement for W. A. Laird Company in Illustration 7-6 shows (1) checks paid and other debits that reduce the balance in the depositor's account, (2) deposits and other credits that increase the balance in the depositor's account, and (3) the account balance after each day's transactions. Remember that bank statements are prepared from the *bank's* perspective. Therefore, every deposit received from W. A. Laird Company by the National Bank and Trust is *credited* by the bank to W. A. Laird Company. The reverse occurs when the bank "pays" a check issued by W. A. Laird Company on its checking account balance: Payment reduces the bank's liability and is therefore *debited* to Laird's account with the bank.

All paid checks are listed in numerical sequence on the bank statement along with the date the check was paid and its amount. Upon paying a check, the bank stamps the check "paid"; a paid check is sometimes referred to as a **canceled** check. In addition, the bank includes with the bank statement memoranda explaining other debits and credits made by the bank to the depositor's account.

Helpful Hint Essentially, the bank statement is a copy of the bank's records sent to the customer for periodic review.

Illustration 7-6 Bank statement

Balance Last Statement	Deposits and Credits		Checks and Debits		Balance This Statement
	No.	Total Amount	No.	Total Amount	
13,256.90	20	34,805.10	26	32,154.55	15,907.45

CHECKS AND DEBITS			DEPOSITS AND CREDITS		DAILY BALANCE	
Date	No.	Amount	Date	Amount	Date	Amount
4-2	435	644.95	4-2	4,276.85	4-2	16,888.80
4-5	436	3,260.00	4-3	2,137.50	4-3	18,249.65
4-4	437	1,185.79	4-5	1,350.47	4-4	17,063.86
4-3	438	776.65	4-7	982.46	4-5	15,154.33
4-8	439	1,781.70	4-8	1,320.28	4-7	14,648.89
4-7	440	1,487.90	4-9 CM	1,035.00	4-8	11,767.47
4-8	441	2,420.00	4-11	2,720.00	4-9	12,802.47
4-11	442	1,585.60	4-12	757.41	4-11	13,936.87
4-12	443	1,226.00	4-13	1,218.56	4-12	13,468.28
4-29	NSF	425.60	4-27	1,545.57	4-27	13,005.45
4-29	459	1,080.30	4-29	2,929.45	4-29	14,429.00
4-30	DM	30.00	4-30	2,128.60	4-30	15,907.45
4-30	461	620.15				

Symbols: **CM** Credit Memo   **EC** Error Correction   **NSF** Not Sufficient Funds   Reconcile Your Account Promptly
DM Debit Memo   **INT** Interest Earned   **SC** Service Charge

A debit memorandum is used by the bank when a previously deposited customer's check "bounces" because of insufficient funds. In such a case, the check is marked **NSF** (not sufficient funds) by the customer's bank and is returned to the depositor's bank. The bank then debits (decreases) the depositor's account, as shown by the symbol NSF on the bank statement in Illustration 7-6, and sends the NSF check and debit memorandum to the depositor as notification of the charge. The NSF check creates an account receivable for the depositor and reduces cash in the bank account.

Reconciling the Bank Account

Because the bank and the company maintain independent records of the company's checking account, you might assume that the respective balances will always agree. In fact, the two balances are seldom the same at any given time, and it is necessary to make the balance per books agree with the balance per bank—a process called **reconciling the bank account.** The lack of agreement between the balances has two causes:

1. **Time lags** that prevent one of the parties from recording the transaction in the same period.
2. **Errors** by either party in recording transactions.

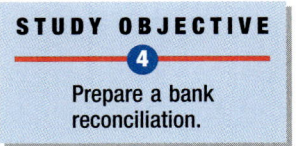

STUDY OBJECTIVE 4
Prepare a bank reconciliation.

300 CHAPTER 7 Internal Control and Cash

Time lags occur frequently. For example, several days may elapse between the time a company pays by check and the date the check is paid by the bank. Similarly, when a company uses the bank's night depository to make its deposits, there will be a difference of one day between the time the receipts are recorded by the company and the time they are recorded by the bank. A time lag also occurs whenever the bank mails a debit or credit memorandum to the company.

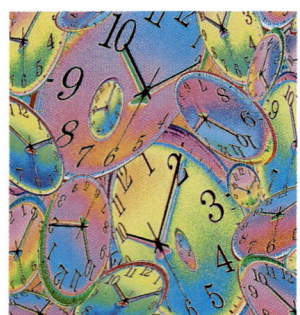

BUSINESS INSIGHT
Management Perspective

Some firms have used time lags to their advantage. For example, E. F. Hutton managers at one time overdrew their accounts by astronomical amounts—on some days the overdrafts totaled $1 billion—creating interest-free loans they could invest. The loans lasted as long as it took for the covering checks to be collected. Although not technically illegal at the time, Hutton's actions were wrong because it did not have bank permission to do so.

The incidence of errors depends on the effectiveness of the internal controls maintained by the company and the bank. Bank errors are infrequent. However, either party could inadvertently record a $450 check as $45 or $540. In addition, the bank might mistakenly charge a check drawn by C. D. Berg to the account of C. D. Burg.

Reconciliation Procedure. In reconciling the bank account, it is customary to reconcile the balance per books and balance per bank to their adjusted (correct or true) cash balances. **To obtain maximum benefit from a bank reconciliation, the reconciliation should be prepared by an employee who has no other responsibilities pertaining to cash.** When the internal control principle of independent internal verification is not followed in preparing the reconciliation, cash embezzlements may escape unnoticed. For example, in the opening story, a bank reconciliation by someone other than Mr. Shelton might have exposed his embezzlement.

The reconciliation schedule is divided into two sections, as shown in Illustration 7-7. The starting point in preparing the reconciliation is to enter the balance per bank statement and balance per books on the schedule. The following steps should reveal all the reconciling items that cause the difference between the two balances:

Helpful Hint Deposits in transit and outstanding checks are reconciling items because of time lags.

1. Compare the individual deposits on the bank statement with the deposits in transit from the preceding bank reconciliation and with the deposits per company records or copies of duplicate deposit slips. Deposits recorded by the depositor that have not been recorded by the bank represent **deposits in transit** and are added to the balance per bank.

2. Compare the paid checks shown on the bank statement or the paid checks returned with the bank statement with (a) checks outstanding from the preceding bank reconciliation and (b) checks issued by the company as recorded in the cash payments journal. Issued checks recorded by the company that have not been paid by the bank represent **outstanding checks** that are deducted from the balance per the bank.

3. Note any **errors** discovered in the foregoing steps and list them in the appropriate section of the reconciliation schedule. For example, if a paid check correctly written by the company for $195 was mistakenly recorded by the

Cash Controls **301**

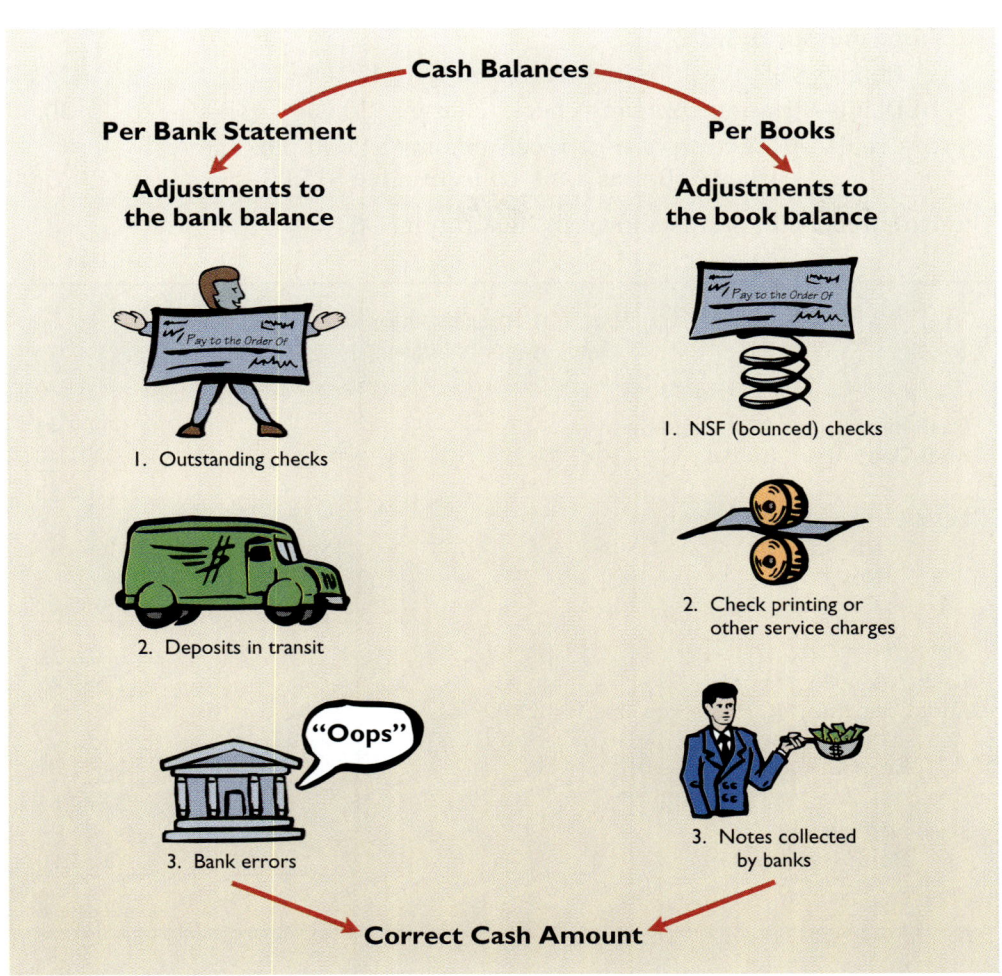

Illustration 7-7 Bank reconciliation procedures

company for $159, the error of $36 is deducted from the balance per books. All errors made by the depositor are reconciling items in determining the adjusted cash balance per books. In contrast, all errors made by the bank are reconciling items in determining the adjusted cash balance per the bank.

4. Trace **bank memoranda** to the depositor's records. Any unrecorded memoranda should be listed in the appropriate section of the reconciliation schedule. For example, a $5 debit memorandum for bank service charges is deducted from the balance per books, and a $32 credit memorandum for interest earned is added to the balance per books.

Bank Reconciliation Illustrated. The bank statement for Laird Company was shown in Illustration 7-6. It shows a balance per bank of $15,907.45 on April 30, 1998. On this date the balance of cash per books is $11,589.45. From the foregoing steps, the following reconciling items are determined:

1. **Deposits in transit:** April 30 deposit (received by bank on May 1). $2,201.40
2. **Outstanding checks:** No. 453: $3,000.00; No. 457: $1,401.30; No. 460: $1,502.70. 5,904.00
3. **Errors:** Check No. 443 was correctly written by Laird for $1,226.00 and was correctly paid by the bank. However, it was recorded for $1,262.00 by Laird Company. 36.00

Helpful Hint Note in the bank statement that checks No. 459 and 461 have been paid but check No. 460 is not listed. Thus, this check is outstanding. If a complete bank statement were provided, checks No. 453 and 457 would also not be listed. The amounts for these three checks are obtained from the company's cash payments records.

302 CHAPTER 7 Internal Control and Cash

4. **Bank memoranda:**

(a) Debit—NSF check from J. R. Baron for $425.60	425.60
(b) Debit—Printing company checks charge, $30.00	30.00
(c) Credit—Collection of note receivable for $1,000 plus interest earned $50, less bank collection fee $15.00	1,035.00

The bank reconciliation is shown in Illustration 7-8.

Illustration 7-8 Bank reconciliation

Helpful Hint The terms *adjusted balance*, *true cash balance*, and *correct cash balance* may be used interchangeably.

W. A. LAIRD COMPANY
Bank Reconciliation
April 30, 1998

Cash balance per bank statement		$15,907.45
Add: Deposits in transit		2,201.40
		18,108.85
Less: Outstanding checks		
No. 453	$3,000.00	
No. 457	1,401.30	
No. 460	1,502.70	5,904.00
Adjusted cash balance per bank		**$12,204.85**
Cash balance per books		$11,589.45
Add: Collection of note receivable for $1,000 plus interest earned $50, less collection fee $15	$1,035.00	
Error in recording check No. 443	36.00	1,071.00
		12,660.45
Less: NSF check	425.60	
Bank service charge	30.00	455.60
Adjusted cash balance per books		**$12,204.85**

BUSINESS INSIGHT
Management Perspective

Imagine reconciling a bank statement when you have an employee like Billie Hurst. She worked as a librarian at Southwest Missouri State University for 30 years, yet she never got around to cashing paychecks totalling more than $100,000 because she didn't need the money.

The 72-year-old woman got the money anyway when State Treasurer Wendell Bailey presented an $88,100.85 check to Hurst's cousin and guardian, Frances Jane Gleghorn, after a special act of the legislature made it possible to pay checks more than 5 years old.

Bailey's office said it already had reissued checks amounting to $20,024.53 for uncashed checks not more than 5 years old, bringing the total reimbursement to $108,125.38.

Hurst occasionally cashed a paycheck, Gleghorn said, but co-workers tried for years to get her to cash the rest of the checks.

Source: Bay City Times, March 24, 1989.

Entries from Bank Reconciliation. Each reconciling item in determining the **adjusted cash balance per books** should be recorded by the depositor. If these items are not journalized and posted, the Cash account will not show the correct balance. The adjusting entries for the Laird Company bank reconciliation on April 30 are as follows:

Collection of Note Receivable. This entry involves four accounts. Assuming that the interest of $50 has not been recorded and the collection fee is charged to Miscellaneous Expense, the entry is:

Apr. 30	Cash	1,035.00	
	Miscellaneous Expense	15.00	
	Notes Receivable		1,000.00
	Interest Revenue		50.00
	(To record collection of notes receivable by bank)		

Helpful Hint These entries are adjusting entries. In prior chapters, Cash was an account that did not require adjustment because a bank reconciliation had not been explained.

Book Error. An examination of the cash disbursements journal shows that check No. 443 was a payment on account to Andrea Company, a supplier. The correcting entry is:

Apr. 30	Cash	36.00	
	Accounts Payable—Andrea Company		36.00
	(To correct error in recording check No. 443)		

NSF Check. As indicated earlier, an NSF check becomes an accounts receivable to the depositor. The entry is:

Apr. 30	Accounts Receivable—J. R. Baron	425.60	
	Cash		425.60
	(To record NSF check)		

Bank Service Charges. Check printing charges (DM) and other bank service charges (SC) are debited to Miscellaneous Expense because they are usually nominal in amount. The entry is:

Apr. 30	Miscellaneous Expense	30.00	
	Cash		30.00
	(To record charge for printing company checks)		

The foregoing entries could also be combined into one compound entry.

After the entries are posted, the cash account will appear as in Illustration 7-9. The adjusted cash balance in the ledger should agree with the adjusted cash balance per books in the bank reconciliation in Illustration 7-8.

Cash

Apr. 30 Bal.	$11,589.45	Apr. 30	$425.60
30	1,035.00	30	30.00
30	36.00		
Apr. 30 Bal.	**$12,204.85**		

Illustration 7-9 Adjusted balance in cash account

What entries does the bank make? If any bank errors are discovered in preparing the reconciliation, the bank should be notified so it can make the necessary corrections on its records. The bank does not make any entries for deposits in transit or outstanding checks. Only when these items reach the bank will the bank record these items.

BEFORE YOU GO ON . . .

● **Review It**

1. Why is it necessary to reconcile a bank account?
2. What steps are involved in the reconciliation procedure?
3. What information is included in a bank reconciliation?

● **Do It**

Sally Kist owns Linen Kist Fabrics. Sally asks you to explain how the following reconciling items should be treated in reconciling the bank account at December 31: (1) a debit memorandum for an NSF check, (2) a credit memorandum for a note collected by the bank, (3) outstanding checks, and (4) a deposit in transit.

Reasoning: Sally needs to understand that one cause of a reconciling item is time lags. Items (1) and (2) are reconciling items because Linen Kist Fabrics has not yet recorded the memoranda. Items (3) and (4) are reconciling items because the bank has not recorded the transactions.

Solution: In reconciling the bank account, the reconciling items are treated by Linen Kist Fabrics as follows:

NSF check: Deducted from balance per books.
Collection of note: Added to balance per books.
Outstanding checks: Deducted from balance per bank.
Deposit in transit: Added to balance per bank.

REPORTING CASH

STUDY OBJECTIVE 5
Explain the reporting of cash.

Cash is reported in two different statements: the balance sheet and the statement of cash flows. The balance sheet reports the amount of cash available at a given point in time. The statement of cash flows shows the sources and uses of cash during a period of time. The cash flow statement was introduced in Chapters 1 and 2 and will be discussed in much detail in Chapter 13. In this section we discuss some important points regarding the presentation of cash in the balance sheet.

When presented in a balance sheet, cash on hand, cash in banks, and petty cash are often combined and reported simply as **Cash.** Because it is the most liquid asset owned by the company, cash is listed first in the current asset section of the balance sheet.

CASH EQUIVALENTS

Some companies use the designation "cash and cash equivalents" in reporting cash, as shown in Illustration 7-10 for landfill operator Addington Resources. **Cash equivalents** are short-term, highly liquid investments that are both:

1. Readily convertible to known amounts of cash, and
2. So near their maturity that their market value is relatively insensitive to changes in interest rates.

Examples of cash equivalents are Treasury bills, commercial paper (short-term corporate notes), and money market funds. All typically are purchased with cash that is in excess of immediate needs.

ADDINGTON RESOURCES, INC., AND SUBSIDIARIES
Consolidated Balance Sheets (partial)
As of December 31
(in thousands)

	1994	1993
Assets		
Current assets		
Cash and cash equivalents	$ 3,469	$ 13,744
Short-term investments	8,474	0
Net assets held for disposal	0	141,866
Accounts receivable, net	18,944	8,945
Inventories	6,495	11,803
Prepaid expenses and other	2,776	7,718
Total current assets	40,158	184,076
Property, plant, and equipment at cost	182,835	140,758
Less: Accumulated depreciation	(28,962)	(22,682)
	194,031	302,152
Assets held for sale	16,605	0
Restricted cash	4,437	2,348
Other	8,008	11,158
Total assets	$223,081	$315,658

Illustration 7-10
Balance sheets of Addington Resources

RESTRICTED CASH

A company may have cash that is not available for general use but rather is restricted for a special purpose. Cash restricted in use should be reported separately on the balance sheet as **restricted cash.** If the restricted cash is expected to be used within the next year, the amount should be reported as a current asset. When this is not the case, the restricted funds should be reported as a noncurrent asset. An example of the presentation of restricted cash is provided by the financial statements of Addington Resources in Illustration 7-10. State and local governments in which Addington operates landfills require it to put cash into a restricted fund to cover closing and clean-up costs related to landfills. The company does not have access to these funds for general use, and so they must be reported separately, rather than as part of cash and cash equivalents. Since the cash is not expected to be used within the coming year, Addington reports it among noncurrent assets.

DECISION TOOLKIT

Decision Checkpoints	Info Needed for Decision	Tool to Use for Decision	How to Evaluate Results
Is all of the company's cash available for general use?	Balance sheet and notes to financial statements	Does the company report any cash as being restricted?	A restriction on the use of cash limits management's ability to use those resources for general obligations. This might be considered when assessing liquidity.

MANAGING AND MONITORING CASH

Many companies struggle, not because they can't generate sales, but because they can't manage their cash. A real-life example of this is a clothing manufacturing company owned by Sharon McCollick. McCollick gave up a stable, high-paying marketing job with Intel Corporation to start her own company. Soon she had more orders from stores such as J. C. Penney Co. and Dayton Hudson Corporation than she could fill. Yet she found herself on the brink of financial disaster, owing three mortgage payments on her house and $2,000 to the IRS. Her company could generate sales, but it wasn't collecting cash fast enough to support its operations. The bottom line is that a business must have cash.[1]

To understand cash management, consider the operating cycle of Sharon McCollick's clothing manufacturing company. To begin it must purchase cloth. Let's assume that it purchases the cloth on credit provided by the supplier, so the company owes its supplier money. Next, employees convert the cloth to clothing. Now the company also owes its employees money. Next, it sells the clothing to retailers, on credit. McCollick's company has no money to repay suppliers or employees until its customers pay it. In a manufacturing operation there may be a significant lag between the original purchase of raw materials and the ultimate receipt of cash from customers. Managing the often precarious balance created by the ebb and flow of cash during the operating cycle is one of a company's greatest challenges. The objective is to ensure that a company has sufficient cash to meet payments as they come due, yet minimize the amount of non-revenue-generating cash on hand.

A merchandising company's operating cycle is generally shorter than a manufacturing company's, depending on how long the inventory is held for sale. The cash to cash operating cycle of a merchandising operation is shown graphically in Illustration 7-11.

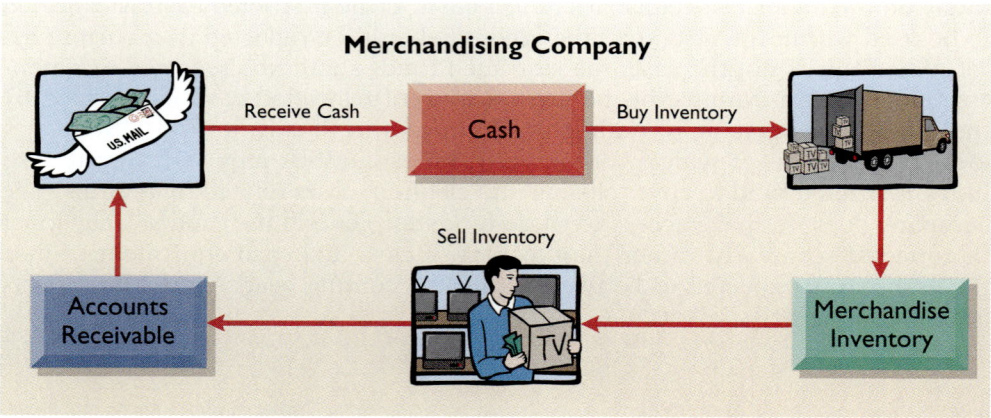

Illustration 7-11 Operating cycle of a merchandising company

BASIC PRINCIPLES OF CASH MANAGEMENT

Sharon McCollick's company, or any company, can improve its chances of having adequate cash by following five basic principles of cash management. Sticking to these principles is often difficult because other factors enter in. Thus, in

---

[1]Adapted from T. Petzinger Jr., "The Front Lines—Sharon McCollick Got Mad and Tore Down a Bank's Barriers," *The Wall Street Journal,* May 19, 1995, p. B1.

managing cash, a company must consider many factors. Management of cash is the responsibility of the company treasurer, and it is a critical job for the success of the company. The basic principles of cash management are:

1. **Increase the speed of collection on receivables.** Money owed Sharon McCollick by her customers is money that she can't use. The more quickly customers pay her, the more quickly she can use those funds. Thus, rather than have an average collection period of 30 days, she may want an average collection period of 15 days. However, any attempt to force her customers to pay earlier must be carefully weighed against the possibility that she may anger or alienate customers. Perhaps her competitors are willing to provide a 30-day grace period. As noted in Chapter 5, one common way to encourage customers to pay more quickly is to offer cash discounts for early payment under such terms as 2/10, n/30.

2. **Keep inventory levels low.** Maintaining a large inventory of cloth and finished clothing is costly. It requires that large amounts of cash be tied up, as well as warehouse space. Increasingly, firms are using techniques to reduce the inventory on hand, thus conserving their cash. Of course, if Sharon has inadequate inventory, she will lose sales. The proper level of inventory is an important decision.

3. **Delay payment of liabilities.** By keeping track of when her bills are due, Sharon McCollick's company can avoid paying bills too early. Let's say her supplier allows 30 days for payment. If she pays in 10 days, she has lost the use of cash for 20 days. Therefore, she should use the full payment period but should not "stretch" payment past the point that could damage her credit rating (and future borrowing ability). Sharon McCollick's company also should conserve cash by taking cash discounts offered by suppliers, when possible.

4. **Plan the timing of major expenditures.** To maintain operations or to grow, all companies must make major expenditures, which normally require some form of outside financing. In order to increase the likelihood of obtaining outside financing, the timing of major expenditures should be carefully considered in light of the firm's operating cycle. If at all possible, the expenditure should be made when the firm normally has excess cash—usually during the off-season.

5. **Invest idle cash.** Cash on hand earns nothing. An important part of the treasurer's job is to ensure that any excess cash is invested, even if it is only overnight. Many businesses, such as Sharon McCollick's clothing company, are seasonal. During her slow season, when she has excess cash, she should invest it. To avoid a cash crisis, however, it is very important that these investments be highly liquid and risk-free. A *liquid investment* is one with a market in which someone is always willing to buy or sell the investment. A *risk-free investment* means there is no concern that the party will default on its promise to pay its principal and interest. For example, using excess cash to purchase stock in a small company because you heard that it was probably going to increase in value in the near term is totally inappropriate. First, the stock of small companies is often illiquid. Second, if the stock suddenly decreases in value, you might be forced to sell the stock at a loss in order to pay your bills as they come due. The most common form of liquid investments are interest-paying U.S. government securities.

These five principles of cash management are summarized in Illustration 7-12 (on the next page).

 International Note

International sales complicate cash management. For example, if Nike must repay a Japanese supplier 30 days from today in Japanese yen, it will be concerned about how the exchange rate of U.S. dollars for yen might change during those 30 days. Often corporate treasurers make investments known as *hedges* to lock in an exchange rate to reduce the company's exposure to exchange rate fluctuation.

308 **CHAPTER 7** Internal Control and Cash

Illustration 7-12 Five principles of sound cash management

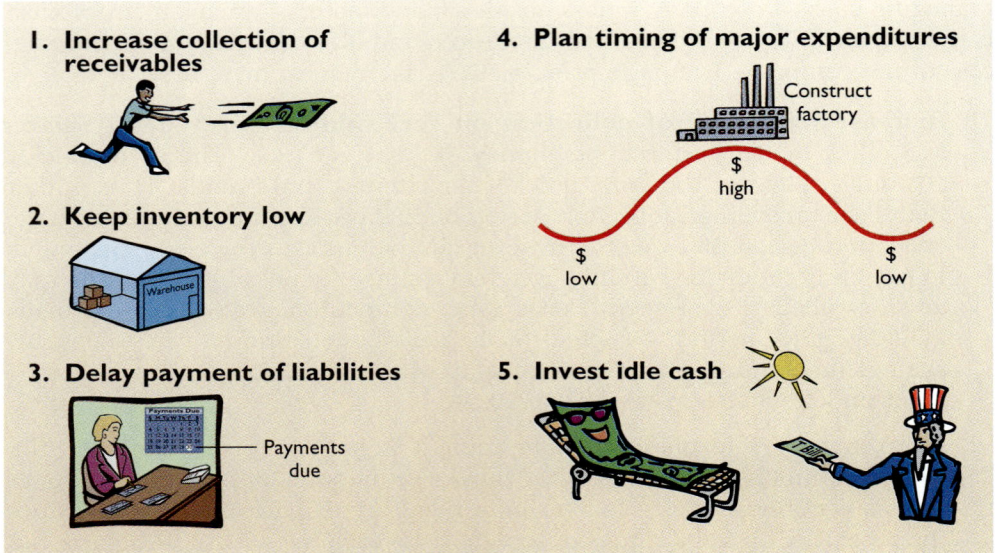

CASH BUDGETING

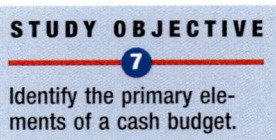

STUDY OBJECTIVE 7
Identify the primary elements of a cash budget.

Because cash is so vital in a company, **planning the company's cash needs** is a key business activity. It enables the company to plan ahead to cover possible cash shortfalls and to make investments of idle funds. The **cash budget** shows anticipated cash flows, usually over a 1- to 2-year period. In this section we introduce the basics of cash budgeting. More advanced discussion of cash budgets and budgets in general is provided in managerial accounting texts.

As shown in Illustration 7-13, the cash budget contains three sections—cash receipts, cash disbursements, and financing—and the beginning and ending cash balances.

Illustration 7-13 Basic form of a cash budget

Cash Budget	
Beginning cash balance	$X,XXX
Add: Cash receipts (itemized)	X,XXX
Total available cash	X,XXX
Less: Cash disbursements (itemized)	X,XXX
Excess (deficiency) of available cash over cash disbursements	X,XXX
Financing needed	X,XXX
Ending cash balance	$X,XXX

The **cash receipts section** includes expected receipts from the company's principal source(s) of revenue, such as cash sales and collections from customers on credit sales. This section also shows anticipated receipts of interest and dividends, and proceeds from planned sales of investments, plant assets, and the company's capital stock.

The **cash disbursements section** shows expected payments for direct materials, direct labor, manufacturing overhead, and selling and administrative expenses. This section also includes projected payments for income taxes, dividends, investments, and plant assets.

The **financing section** shows expected borrowings and the repayment of the borrowed funds plus interest. This section is needed when there is a cash deficiency or when the cash balance is less than management's minimum required balance.

Data in the cash budget must be prepared in sequence because the ending cash balance of one period becomes the beginning cash balance for the next period. Data for preparing the cash budget are obtained from other budgets and from information provided by management. In practice, cash budgets are often prepared for the year on a monthly basis.

To minimize detail, we will assume that Hayes Company prepares an annual cash budget by quarters. Preparing a cash budget requires making some assumptions. For example, the cash budget for Hayes Company is based on the company's assumptions regarding collection of accounts receivable, sales of securities, payments for materials and salaries, and purchases of property, plant, and equipment. The accuracy of the cash budget is very dependent on the accuracy of these assumptions.

The cash budget for Hayes Company is shown in Illustration 7-14. The budget indicates that $3,000 of financing will be needed in the second quarter to maintain a minimum cash balance of $15,000. Since there is an excess of available cash over disbursements of $22,500 at the end of the third quarter, the borrowing is repaid in this quarter plus $100 interest.

A cash budget contributes to more effective cash management. For example, it can show when additional financing will be necessary well before the actual need arises. Conversely, it can indicate when excess cash will be available for investments or other purposes.

Illustration 7-14 Cash budget

HAYES COMPANY
Cash Budget
For the Year Ending December 31, 1998

	Quarter 1	Quarter 2	Quarter 3	Quarter 4
Beginning cash balance	$ 38,000	$ 25,500	$ 15,000	$ 19,400
Add: Receipts				
Collections from customers	168,000	198,000	228,000	258,000
Sale of securities	2,000	0	0	0
Total receipts	170,000	198,000	228,000	258,000
Total available cash	208,000	223,500	243,000	277,400
Less: Disbursements				
Materials	23,200	27,200	31,200	35,200
Salaries	62,000	72,000	82,000	92,000
Selling and administrative expenses (excluding depreciation)	94,300	99,300	104,300	109,300
Purchase of truck	0	10,000	0	0
Income tax expense	3,000	3,000	3,000	3,000
Total disbursements	182,500	211,500	220,500	239,500
Excess (deficiency) of available cash over disbursements	25,500	12,000	22,500	37,900
Financing				
Borrowings	0	3,000	0	0
Repayments—plus $100 interest	0	0	3,100	0
Ending cash balance	$ 25,500	$ 15,000	$ 19,400	$ 37,900

DECISION TOOLKIT

Decision Checkpoints	Info Needed for Decision	Tool to Use for Decision	How to Evaluate Results
Will the company be able to meet its projected cash needs?	Cash budget (typically available only to management)	The cash budget shows projected sources and uses of cash. If cash uses exceed internal cash sources, then the company must look for outside sources.	Two issues: (1) Are management's projections reasonable? (2) If outside sources are needed, are they available?

BEFORE YOU GO ON . . .

● **Review It**

1. What are the five principal elements of sound cash management?
2. What are the three sections of the cash budget?

● **Do It**

Martian Company's management wants to maintain a minimum monthly cash balance of $15,000. At the beginning of March the cash balance is $16,500, expected cash receipts for March are $210,000, and cash disbursements are expected to be $220,000. How much cash, if any, must be borrowed to maintain the desired minimum monthly balance?

Reasoning: The best way to answer this question is to insert the dollar data into the basic form of the cash budget.

Solution:

Beginning cash balance	$ 16,500
Add: Cash receipts for March	210,000
Total available cash	226,500
Less: Cash disbursements for March	220,000
Excess of available cash over cash disbursements	6,500
Financing	**8,500**
Ending cash balance	$ 15,000

To maintain the desired minimum cash balance of $15,000, Martian Company must borrow $8,500 of cash.

ASSESSING CASH ADEQUACY

STUDY OBJECTIVE 8

Identify and interpret measures that evaluate the adequacy of cash.

The statement of cash flows provides information on net cash provided by operating activities, which is cash provided from operating activities less cash used in operating activities. Net cash provided by operating activities is a very important number because it indicates the amount of cash generated internally by operations. As illustrated in Chapter 2, net cash provided by operating activities is used to compute two ratios which measure liquidity and solvency:

Current Cash Debt Coverage Ratio

Net cash provided by operating activities / Current liabilities — Indicates whether a company can pay off its current liabilities from current operations (measures liquidity).

Cash Debt Coverage Ratio

$$\frac{\text{Net cash provided by operating activities}}{\text{Total liabilities}}$$ 	Indicates whether a company can pay off its total liabilities from current operations (measures solvency).

In this chapter, an additional tool was provided to help management better understand the company's cash situation—a cash budget. The cash budget is used to help a company anticipate possible cash shortfalls and to make investments of idle cash.

Two additional tools used to measure the adequacy of cash are (1) the ratio of cash to daily cash expenses and (2) free cash flow.

RATIO OF CASH TO DAILY CASH EXPENSES

One measure of the adequacy of cash is the **ratio of cash to daily cash expenses.** In this ratio, "cash" includes cash plus cash equivalents. It computes the number of days of cash expenses the cash on hand can cover. Cash expenses per day can be approximated by subtracting depreciation (a noncash expense) from total expenses and dividing by 365 days. (Note that this is a rough approximation that ignores many other accrual adjustments.) Dividing the balance in cash and cash equivalents by average daily cash expenses, as shown in Illustration 7-15, gives the number of days the company can operate without any additional infusion of cash.

Illustration 7-15 Ratio of cash to daily cash expenses

$$\text{CASH TO DAILY CASH EXPENSES RATIO} = \frac{\text{CASH AND CASH EQUIVALENTS}}{\text{AVERAGE DAILY CASH EXPENSES}}$$

FREE CASH FLOW

Another important analysis that helps investors and management understand a company's solvency and overall financial strength is free cash flow analysis. This analysis starts with net cash provided by operating activities and ends with **free cash flow,** which is calculated as net cash provided by operating activities less capital expenditures and dividends (Illustration 7-16).

Illustration 7-16 Free cash flow

$$\text{FREE CASH FLOW} = \text{NET CASH PROVIDED BY OPERATING ACTIVITIES} - \left(\text{CAPITAL EXPENDITURES} + \text{CASH DIVIDENDS} \right)$$

A computation of free cash flow for Elle Company is shown below:

ELLE COMPANY Free Cash Flow Analysis		
Net cash provided by operating activities		$250,000
Less: Capital expenditures	$80,000	
Dividends paid	50,000	130,000
Free cash flow		$120,000

Free cash flow is the amount of discretionary cash flow a company has for purchasing additional investments, paying its debts, or adding to its liquidity. This measure provides another assessment of a company's solvency and overall financial strength. For example, the information for Elle Company shows that it has a positive and substantial net cash provided by operating activities of $250,000. Capital spending is deducted first in the free cash flow statement to indicate it is the least discretionary expenditure a company makes. Dividends are then deducted to arrive at free cash flow. Although a company can cut its dividend, it will do so only in a financial emergency. Elle has more than sufficient cash flow to meet its dividend payments and, therefore, appears to have satisfactory solvency. In other words, Elle has discretionary cash flow to add to its liquidity, retire debt, or increase capital spending.

If Elle Company finds additional investments that are profitable, it can increase its spending without putting its dividend or basic capital spending in jeopardy. Companies that have substantial free cash flow can take advantage of profitable investments even in tough times. In addition, companies with substantial free cash flow do not have to worry about survival in poor economic times. In fact, they often fare better in poor economic times because they can take advantage of opportunities that other companies cannot.

DECISION TOOLKIT

Decision Checkpoints	Info Needed for Decision	Tool to Use for Decision	How to Evaluate Results
Does the company have adequate cash to meet its daily needs?	Cash and cash equivalents, average daily expenses	Cash to daily cash expenses ratio = $\dfrac{\text{Cash and cash equivalents}}{\text{Average daily cash expenses}}$	A low measure should be investigated. If this measure is low, additional financing may be necessary.
Does the company have any discretionary cash available?	Net cash provided by operating activities, capital expenditures, and cash dividends	Free cash flow = Net cash provided by operating activities minus capital expenditures and cash dividends	Free cash flow allows a company to buy additional investments, reduce its debts, or add to its liquidity. The greater the free cash flow, the greater its options.

Each of these measures is applied to the Harley-Davidson Corporation, as shown in Illustration 7-17. The following financial information was provided in the 1995 Harley-Davidson financial statements:

	($ in thousands)	
	1995	1994
Sales	$1,350,466	$1,158,887
Total expenses	1,237,986	1,054,615
Depreciation	42,329	32,863
Cash and cash equivalents	31,462	57,884
Cash from operating activities	169,072	82,963
Cash paid for capital expenditures	112,985	88,666
Cash paid for dividends	13,593	10,672

($ in thousands)	1995		1994	
Cash to daily cash expenses ratio	$\dfrac{\$31{,}462}{(\$1{,}237{,}986 - \$42{,}329)/365}$	= 9.60 days	$\dfrac{\$57{,}884}{(\$1{,}054{,}615 - \$32{,}863)/365}$	= 20.68 days
Free cash flow	$169,072 − $112,985 − $13,593 = $42,494		$82,963 − $88,666 − $10,672 = −$16,375	

Illustration 7-17 Harley-Davidson cash adequacy ratios

Harley-Davidson had a stronger cash balance in 1994 than in 1995. The ratio of cash to daily cash expenses indicates that at the end of 1994 its cash was sufficient to meet the needs of more than 20 days of normal activity, while in 1995 its cash balance would cover only 9.6 days of activity.

The computation of Harley's free cash flow shows that in 1995 Harley generated positive free cash flow of $42,494,000. In 1995 Harley's operating activities generated sufficient cash to cover capital expenditures and dividend payments, and gave management additional flexibility to increase capital expenditures or dividend payments or to retire its own stock or debt. However, the negative 1994 free cash flow of $16,375,000 shows that 1994 operations did not generate enough cash to cover 1994 capital expenditures and dividends.

BEFORE YOU GO ON . . .

- **Review It**
  1. What is the formula for the cash to daily cash expenses ratio? What does it tell management about the company's cash position?
  2. How is free cash flow computed?

USING THE DECISION TOOLKIT

Presented below is hypothetical financial information for the Mattel Corporation. Included in this information is financial statement data from the year ended December 31, 1998, which should be used to calculate free cash flow and the cash to daily cash expenses ratio.

Year Ended December 31, 1998
(in millions)

Net cash provided by operating activities	$325
Capital expenditures	162
Dividends paid	80
Total expenses	680
Depreciation expense	40
Cash balance	506

Also provided is projected data which is management's best estimate of its sources and uses of cash during 1999. This information should be used to prepare a cash budget for 1999.

(in millions)	
Beginning cash balance	$506
Cash collected from sales	355
Cash received from marketable securities sold	20
Cash disbursed for inventory	357
Cash disbursed for selling and administrative expense	201
Cash paid for property, plant, and equipment	45
Cash paid for taxes	17

Mattel Corporation's management believes it should maintain a balance of $400 million cash.

Instructions

(a) Using the hypothetical information presented above, prepare a cash budget for 1999 for the Mattel Corporation.
(b) Using the 1998 information presented above, calculate the cash to daily cash expenses ratio and free cash flow.
(c) Comment on Mattel's cash adequacy, and discuss steps that might be taken to improve its cash position.

Solution

(a)

MATTEL CORPORATION
Cash Budget
For the Year 1999
(in millions)

Beginning cash balance		$506
Add: Cash received during 1999		
From sales of product	$355	
From sale of marketable securities	20	375
Total cash available during first quarter		881
Less: Cash disbursements for first quarter		
Cash paid for inventory	357	
Cash paid for selling and administrative costs	201	
Cash paid for taxes	17	575
Excess of available cash over cash disbursements		306
Financing needed		94
Ending cash balance		$400

(b) To calculate the cash to daily cash expenses ratio, first approximate average daily cash expenses by total expenses minus depreciation expense divided by 365. The average daily cash expenses (in millions) is calculated as: ($680 − $40)/365 = $1.75. Next, the cash to daily cash expenses ratio is calculated as: $506/$1.75 = 289.1 days. This ratio suggests the company will have cash sufficient to cover 289 days of normal expenses.

The company's free cash flow is calculated by subtracting cash paid for dividends and capital expenditures from cash provided by operating activities:

	(in millions)	
Net cash provided by operating activities		$325
Less: Capital expenditures	$162	
Dividends paid	80	242
Free cash flow in 1998		$ 83

(c) Mattel's cash position appears adequate. It has enough cash on hand to cover 289 days, and its 1998 free cash flow was sufficient to cover its needs and provided additional cash for expansion, dividends, or other uses. In 1999 it is projecting a cash shortfall. This is not necessarily of concern, but it should be investigated. Given that its primary line of business is toys, and that most toys are sold at Christmas, we would expect Mattel's cash position to vary significantly during the course of the year. After Christmas it probably has a lot of excess cash, and earlier in the year, when it is making and selling its product but has not yet been paid, it may need to borrow to meet any temporary cash shortfalls. In the event that Mattel's management is concerned with its cash position, it could take the following steps: (1) Offer its customers cash discounts for early payment, such as 2/10, n/30. (2) Implement inventory management techniques to reduce the need for large inventories of such things as the plastics used to make its toys. (3) Carefully time payments to suppliers by keeping track of when payments are due, so as not to pay too early. (4) If it has plans for major expenditures, time those expenditures to coincide with its seasonal period of excess cash.

SUMMARY OF STUDY OBJECTIVES

❶ Identify the principles of internal control. The principles of internal control are establishment of responsibility; segregation of duties; documentation procedures; physical, mechanical, and electronic controls; independent internal verification; and other controls.

❷ Explain the applications of internal control to cash receipts. Internal controls over cash receipts include: (a) designating only personnel such as cashiers to handle cash; (b) assigning the duties of receiving cash, recording cash, and having custody of cash to different individuals; (c) obtaining remittance advices for mail receipts, cash register tapes for over-the-counter receipts, and deposit slips for bank deposits; (d) using company safes and bank vaults to store cash with access limited to authorized personnel, and using cash registers in executing over-the-counter receipts; (e) making independent daily counts of register receipts and daily comparisons of total receipts with total deposits; and (f) bonding personnel who handle cash and requiring them to take vacations.

❸ Explain the applications of internal control to cash disbursements. Internal controls over cash disbursements include: (a) having only specified individuals such as the treasurer authorized to sign checks; (b) assigning the duties of approving items for payment, paying the items, and recording the payment to different individuals; (c) using prenumbered checks and accounting for all checks, with each check supported by an approved invoice; (d) storing blank checks in a safe or vault with access restricted to authorized personnel, and using a checkwriter to imprint amounts on checks; (e) comparing each check with the approved invoice before issuing the check, and making monthly reconciliations of bank and book balances; and (f) after payment, stamping each approved invoice "paid."

❹ Prepare a bank reconciliation. In reconciling the bank account, it is customary to reconcile the balance per books and the balance per bank to their adjusted balance. The steps in determining the reconciling items are to ascertain deposits in transit, outstanding checks, errors by the depositor or the bank, and unrecorded bank memoranda.

❺ Explain the reporting of cash. Cash is listed first in the current assets section of the balance sheet. In some cases, cash is reported together with cash equivalents. Cash restricted for a special purpose is reported separately as a current asset or as a noncurrent asset depending on when the cash is expected to be used.

❻ Discuss the basic principles of cash management. (a) Increase collection of receivables, (b) keep inventory levels low, (c) delay payment of liabilities, (d) plan timing of major expenditures, and (e) invest idle cash.

❼ Identify the primary elements of a cash budget. The three main elements of a cash budget are the cash receipts section, cash disbursements section, and financing section.

❽ Identify and interpret measures that evaluate the adequacy of cash. The cash to daily cash expenses ratio indicates how many days of expenditures the current cash resources will cover. The computation of free cash flow reveals the amount of discretionary cash available.

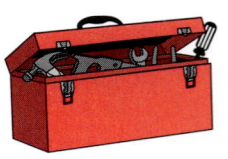

Decision Toolkit—A Summary

Decision Checkpoints	Info Needed for Decision	Tool to Use for Decision	How to Evaluate Results
Are the company's financial statements supported by adequate internal controls?	Auditor's report, management discussion and analysis, articles in financial press	The required measures of internal control are to (1) establish responsibility, (2) segregate duties, (3) document procedures, (4) employ physical or automated controls, and (5) use independent internal verification.	If any indication is given that these or other controls are lacking, the financial statements should be used with caution.
Is all of the company's cash available for general use?	Balance sheet and notes to financial statements	Does the company report any cash as being restricted?	A restriction on the use of cash limits management's ability to use those resources for general obligations. This might be considered when assessing liquidity.
Will the company be able to meet its projected cash needs?	Cash budget (typically available only to management)	The cash budget shows projected sources and uses of cash. If cash uses exceed internal cash sources, then the company must look for outside sources.	Two issues: (1) Are management's projections reasonable? (2) If outside sources are needed, are they available?
Does the company have adequate cash to meet its daily needs?	Cash and cash equivalents, average daily expenses	$$\text{Cash to daily cash expenses ratio} = \frac{\text{Cash and cash equivalents}}{\text{Average daily cash expenses}}$$	A low measure should be investigated. If this measure is low, additional financing may be necessary.
Does the company have any discretionary cash available?	Net cash provided by operating activities, capital expenditures, and cash dividends	$$\text{Free cash flow} = \text{Net cash provided by operating activities minus capital expenditures and cash dividends}$$	Free cash flow allows a company to buy additional investments, reduce its debts, or add to its liquidity. The greater the free cash flow, the greater its options.

APPENDIX 7A

OPERATION OF THE PETTY CASH FUND

STUDY OBJECTIVE 9
Explain the operation of a petty cash fund.

The operation of a petty cash fund involves (1) establishing the fund, (2) making payments from the fund, and (3) replenishing the fund.

ESTABLISHING THE PETTY CASH FUND

Two essential steps in establishing a petty cash fund are appointing a petty cash custodian who will be responsible for the fund and determining the size of the fund. Ordinarily, the amount is expected to cover anticipated disbursements for a 3- to 4-week period. When the fund is established, a check payable to the petty cash custodian is issued for the stipulated amount. If Laird Company decides to establish a $100 fund on March 1, the entry in general journal form is:

Mar.	1	Petty Cash	100.00	
		Cash		100.00
		(To establish a petty cash fund)		

Helpful Hint Petty cash funds are authorized and legitimate. In contrast, "slush" funds are unauthorized and hidden (under the table).

The check is then cashed and the proceeds are placed in a locked petty cash box or drawer. Most petty cash funds are established on a fixed amount basis. Moreover, no additional entries will be made to the Petty Cash account unless the stipulated amount of the fund is changed. For example, if Laird Company decides on July 1 to increase the size of the fund to $250, it would debit Petty Cash $150 and credit Cash $150.

MAKING PAYMENTS FROM PETTY CASH

The custodian of the petty cash fund has the authority to make payments from the fund that conform to prescribed management policies. Usually management limits the size of expenditures that may be made and does not permit use of the fund for certain types of transactions (such as making short-term loans to employees). Each payment from the fund must be documented on a prenumbered petty cash receipt (or petty cash voucher), as shown in Illustration 7A-1. Note that the signatures of both the custodian and the individual receiving payment are required on the receipt. If other supporting documents such as a freight bill or invoice are available, they should be attached to the petty cash receipt.

Helpful Hint From the standpoint of internal control, the receipt satisfies two principles: (1) establishing responsibility (signature of custodian) and (2) documentation procedures.

The receipts are kept in the petty cash box until the fund is replenished. As a result, the sum of the petty cash receipts and money in the fund should equal the established total at all times. This means that surprise counts can be made at any time by an independent person, such as an internal auditor, to determine whether the fund is being maintained intact.

No accounting entry is made to record a payment at the time it is taken from petty cash. It is considered both inexpedient and unnecessary to do so. Instead, the accounting effects of each payment are recognized when the fund is replenished.

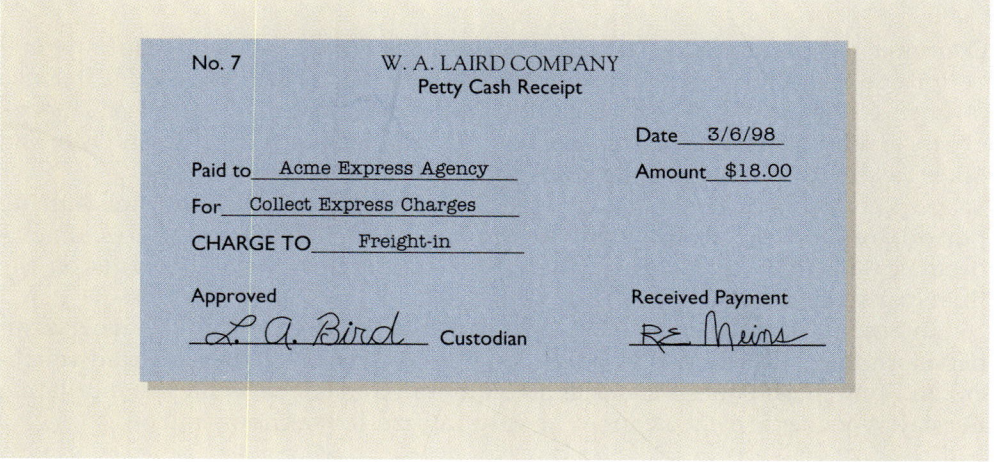

Illustration 7A-1 Petty cash receipt

Replenishing the Petty Cash Fund

Helpful Hint Replenishing involves three internal control procedures: segregation of duties, documentation procedures, and independent internal verification.

When the money in the petty cash fund reaches a minimum level, the fund is replenished. The request for reimbursement is initiated by the petty cash custodian. This individual prepares a schedule (or summary) of the payments that have been made and sends the schedule, supported by petty cash receipts and other documentation, to the treasurer's office. The receipts and supporting documents are examined in the treasurer's office to verify that they were proper payments from the fund. The treasurer then approves the request and a check is prepared to restore the fund to its established amount. At the same time, all supporting documentation is stamped "paid" so that it cannot be submitted again for payment.

To illustrate, assume that on March 15 the petty cash custodian requests a check for $87. The fund contains $13 cash and petty cash receipts for postage $44, supplies $38, and miscellaneous expenses $5. The entry, in general journal form, to record the check is:

Mar. 15	Postage Expense	44	
	Supplies	38	
	Miscellaneous Expense	5	
	Cash		87
	(To replenish petty cash fund)		

Note that the Petty Cash account is not affected by the reimbursement entry. Replenishment changes the composition of the fund by replacing the petty cash receipts with cash, but it does not change the balance in the fund.

Occasionally, in replenishing a petty cash fund it may be necessary to recognize a cash shortage or overage. To illustrate, assume in the preceding example that the custodian had only $12 in cash in the fund plus the receipts as listed. The request for reimbursement would therefore be for $88, and the following entry would be made:

Mar. 15	Postage Expense	44	
	Supplies	38	
	Miscellaneous Expense	5	
	Cash Over and Short	1	
	Cash		88
	(To replenish petty cash fund)		

Conversely, if the custodian had $14 in cash, the reimbursement request would be for $86 and Cash Over and Short would be credited for $1. A debit balance in Cash Over and Short is reported in the income statement as miscellaneous expense; a credit balance is reported as miscellaneous revenue. Cash Over and Short is closed to Income Summary at the end of the year.

A petty cash fund should be replenished **at the end of the accounting period, regardless of the cash in the fund.** Replenishment at this time is necessary in order to recognize the effects of the petty cash payments on the financial statements.

Internal control over a petty cash fund is strengthened by (1) having a supervisor make surprise counts of the fund to ascertain whether the paid vouchers and fund cash equal the designated amount and (2) canceling or mutilating the paid vouchers so they cannot be resubmitted for reimbursement.

SUMMARY OF STUDY OBJECTIVE FOR APPENDIX 7A

9 *Explain the operation of a petty cash fund.* In operating a petty cash fund, a company must establish the fund by appointing a custodian and determining the size of the fund, make payments from the fund for documented expenditures, and replenish the fund. The fund is replenished at least at the end of each accounting period, and accounting entries to record payments are made at that time.

GLOSSARY

Bank statement A statement received monthly from the bank that shows the depositor's bank transactions and balances. (p. 298)

Cash Resources that consist of coins, currency, checks, money orders, and money on hand or on deposit in a bank or similar depository. (p. 295)

Cash budget A projection of anticipated cash flows, usually over a 1- to 2-year period. (p. 308)

Cash equivalents Highly liquid investments, with maturities of 3 months or less when purchased, that can be converted to a specific amount of cash. (p. 304)

Deposits in transit Deposits recorded by the depositor that have not been recorded by the bank. (p. 300)

Electronic funds transfer (EFT) A disbursement system that uses wire, telephone, telegraph, or computer to transfer cash from one location to another. (p. 297)

Free cash flow A measure that computes the amount of discretionary cash available by subtracting capital expenditures and cash dividends from net cash provided by operating activities. (p. 311)

Internal auditors Company employees who evaluate on a continuous basis the effectiveness of the company's system of internal control. (p. 292)

Internal control The plan of organization and all the related methods and measures adopted within a business to safeguard its assets and enhance the accuracy and reliability of its accounting records. (p. 288)

NSF check A check that is not paid by a bank because of insufficient funds in a customer's bank account. (p. 299)

Outstanding checks Checks issued and recorded by a company that have not been paid by the bank. (p. 300)

Petty cash fund A cash fund used to pay relatively small amounts. (p. 297)

Ratio of cash to daily cash expenses A measure that indicates the number of days of expenses available cash can cover. Calculated as cash and cash equivalents divided by average daily expenses. (p. 311)

Restricted cash Cash that is not available for general use, but instead is restricted for a particular purpose. (p. 305)

DEMONSTRATION PROBLEM

Trillo Company's bank statement for May 1988 shows these data:

Balance May 1	$12,650	Balance May 31	$14,280
Debit memorandum:		Credit memorandum:	
NSF check	175	Collection of note receivable	505

The cash balance per books at May 31 is $13,319. Your review of the data reveals the following:

1. The NSF check was from Hup Co., a customer.
2. The note collected by the bank was a $500, 3-month, 12% note. The bank charged a $10 collection fee. No interest has been accrued.
3. Outstanding checks at May 31 total $2,410.
4. Deposits in transit at May 31 total $1,752.
5. A Trillo Company check for $352 dated May 10 cleared the bank on May 25. This check, which was a payment on account, was journalized for $325.

Instructions

(a) Prepare a bank reconciliation at May 31.
(b) Journalize the entries required by the reconciliation.

Problem-Solving Strategies
1. Follow the four steps used in reconciling items (pp. 300–301).
2. Work carefully to minimize mathematical errors in the reconciliation.
3. All entries are based on reconciling items per books.
4. Make sure the cash ledger balance after posting the reconciling entries agrees with the adjusted cash balance per books.

Solution to Demonstration Problem

(a)

Cash balance per bank statement		$14,280
Add: Deposits in transit		1,752
		16,032
Less: Outstanding checks		2,410
Adjusted cash balance per bank		$13,622
Cash balance per books		$13,319
Add: Collection of note receivable $500, plus $15 interest less collection fee $10		505
		13,824
Less: NSF check	$175	
Error in recording check	27	202
Adjusted cash balance per books		$13,622

(b)

Date	Account	Debit	Credit
May 31	Cash	505	
	Miscellaneous Expense	10	
	Notes Receivable		500
	Interest Revenue		15
	(To record collection of note by bank)		
31	Accounts Receivable—Hup Co.	175	
	Cash		175
	(To record NSF check from Hup Co.)		
31	Accounts Payable	27	
	Cash		27
	(To correct error in recording check)		

Note: All questions, exercises, and problems marked with an asterisk relate to material in Appendix 7A.

SELF-STUDY QUESTIONS

Answers are at the end of the chapter.

(SO 1) 1. Internal control is used in a business to enhance the accuracy and reliability of its accounting records and to:
(a) safeguard its assets.
(b) prevent fraud.
(c) produce correct financial statements.
(d) deter employee dishonesty.

(SO 1) 2. The principles of internal control do *not* include:
(a) establishment of responsibility.
(b) documentation procedures.
(c) management responsibility.
(d) independent internal verification.

(SO 1) 3. Physical controls do *not* include:
(a) safes and vaults to store cash.
(b) independent bank reconciliations.
(c) locked warehouses for inventories.
(d) bank safety deposit boxes for important papers.

(SO 5) 4. Which of the following items in a cash drawer at November 30 is *not* cash?
(a) Money orders
(b) Coins and currency
(c) A customer check dated December 1
(d) A customer check dated November 28

(SO 2) 5. Permitting only designated personnel such as cashiers to handle cash receipts is an application of the principle of:
(a) segregation of duties.
(b) establishment of responsibility.
(c) independent internal verification.
(d) other controls.

(SO 3) 6. The use of prenumbered checks in disbursing cash is an application of the principle of:
(a) establishment of responsibility.
(b) segregation of duties.
(c) physical, mechanical, and electronic controls.
(d) documentation procedures.

(SO 3) 7. The control features of a bank account do *not* include:
   (a) having bank auditors verify the correctness of the bank balance per books.
   (b) minimizing the amount of cash that must be kept on hand.
   (c) providing a double record of all bank transactions.
   (d) safeguarding cash by using a bank as a depository.

(SO 4) 8. In a bank reconciliation, deposits in transit are:
   (a) deducted from the book balance.
   (b) added to the book balance.
   (c) added to the bank balance.
   (d) deducted from the bank balance.

(SO 6) 9. Which of the following is *not* one of the sections of a cash budget?
   (a) Cash receipts section
   (b) Cash disbursements section
   (c) Financing section
   (d) Cash from operations section

(SO 5) 10. Which statement correctly describes the reporting of cash?
   (a) Cash cannot be combined with cash equivalents.
   (b) Restricted cash funds may be combined with Cash.
   (c) Cash is listed first in the current asset section.
   (d) Restricted cash funds cannot be reported as a current asset.

(SO 9) *11. A check is written to replenish a $100 petty cash fund when the fund contains receipts of $94 and $3 in cash. In recording the check:
   (a) Cash Over and Short should be debited for $3.
   (b) Petty Cash should be debited for $94.
   (c) Cash should be credited for $94.
   (d) Petty Cash should be credited for $3.

QUESTIONS

1. "Internal control is concerned only with enhancing the accuracy of the accounting records." Do you agree? Explain.
2. What principles of internal control apply to most business enterprises?
3. In the corner grocery store, all sales clerks make change out of one cash register drawer. Is this a violation of internal control? Why?
4. J. Duma is reviewing the principle of segregation of duties. What are the two common applications of this principle?
5. How do documentation procedures contribute to good internal control?
6. What internal control objectives are met by physical, mechanical, and electronic controls?
7. (a) Explain the control principle of independent internal verification.
   (b) What practices are important in applying this principle?
8. As the company accountant, explain these ideas to the management of Cobo Company:
   (a) The concept of reasonable assurance in internal control
   (b) The importance of the human factor in internal control
9. Midwest Inc. owns these assets at the balance sheet date:

Cash in bank—savings account	$ 5,000
Cash on hand	850
Cash refund due from the IRS	1,000
Checking account balance	12,000
Postdated checks	500

   What amount should be reported as Cash in the balance sheet?
10. What principle(s) of internal control is (are) involved in making daily cash counts of over-the-counter receipts?
11. Dent Department Stores has just installed new electronic cash registers in its stores. How do cash registers improve internal control over cash receipts?
12. At Allen Wholesale Company two mail clerks open all mail receipts. How does this strengthen internal control?
13. "To have maximum effective internal control over cash disbursements, all payments should be made by check." Is this true? Explain.
14. Handy Company's internal controls over cash disbursements provide for the treasurer to sign checks imprinted by a checkwriter after comparing the check with the approved invoice. Identify the internal control principles that are present in these controls.
15. How do these principles apply to cash disbursements:
    (a) Physical, mechanical, and electronic controls
    (b) Other controls
16. What is the essential feature of an electronic funds transfer (EFT) procedure?
17. "The use of a bank contributes significantly to good internal control over cash." Is this true? Why?
18. Paul Pascal is confused about the lack of agreement between the cash balance per books and the balance per bank. Explain the causes for the lack of agreement to Paul, and give an example of each cause.
19. Describe the basic principles of cash management.
20. Mary Mora asks your help concerning an NSF check. Explain to Mary (a) what an NSF check is, (b) how it

322 CHAPTER 7 Internal Control and Cash

is treated in a bank reconciliation, and (c) whether it will require an adjusting entry per bank.

21.
   (a) "Cash equivalents are the same as cash." Do you agree? Explain.
   (b) How should restricted cash funds be reported on the balance sheet?

22. What measures may be computed to evaluate the adequacy of cash?

*23. (a) Identify the three activities that pertain to a petty cash fund, and indicate an internal control principle that is applicable to each activity.
   (b) When are journal entries required in the operation of a petty cash fund?

BRIEF EXERCISES

Explain the importance of internal control. (SO 1)

BE7-1 Gina Milan is the new owner of Liberty Parking. She has heard about internal control but is not clear about its importance for her business. Explain to Gina the two purposes of internal control, and give her one application of each purpose for Liberty Parking.

Identify internal control principles. (SO 1)

BE7-2 The internal control procedures in Marion Company make the following provisions. Identify the principles of internal control that are being followed in each case.
(a) Employees who have physical custody of assets do not have access to the accounting records.
(b) Each month the assets on hand are compared to the accounting records by an internal auditor.
(c) A prenumbered shipping document is prepared for each shipment of goods to customers.

Identify the internal control principles applicable to cash receipts. (SO 2)

BE7-3 Tene Company has the following internal control procedures over cash receipts. Identify the internal control principle that is applicable to each procedure.
(a) All over-the-counter receipts are registered on cash registers.
(b) All cashiers are bonded.
(c) Daily cash counts are made by cashier department supervisors.
(d) The duties of receiving cash, recording cash, and having custody of cash are assigned to different individuals.
(e) Only cashiers may operate cash registers.

Identify the internal control principles applicable to cash disbursements. (SO 3)

BE7-4 Hills Company has the following internal control procedures over cash disbursements. Identify the internal control principle that is applicable to each procedure.
(a) Company checks are prenumbered.
(b) The bank statement is reconciled monthly by an internal auditor.
(c) Blank checks are stored in a safe in the treasurer's office.
(d) Only the treasurer or assistant treasurer may sign checks.
(e) Check signers are not allowed to record cash disbursement transactions.

Identify the control features of a bank account. (SO 3)

BE7-5 T. J. Boad is uncertain about the control features of a bank account. Explain the control benefits of (a) a check and (b) a bank statement.

Indicate location of reconciling items in a bank reconciliation. (SO 4)

BE7-6 The following reconciling items are applicable to the bank reconciliation for Ashley Co. Indicate how each item should be shown on a bank reconciliation.
(a) Outstanding checks
(b) Bank debit memorandum for service charge
(c) Bank credit memorandum for collecting a note for the depositor
(d) Deposit in transit

Identify reconciling items that require adjusting entries. (SO 4)

BE7-7 Using the data in BE7-6, indicate (a) the items that will result in an adjustment to the depositor's records and (b) why the other items do not require adjustment.

Prepare partial bank reconciliation. (SO 4)

BE7-8 At July 31 Dana Company has this bank information: cash balance per bank $7,420; outstanding checks $762; deposits in transit $1,700; and a bank service charge $20. Determine the adjusted cash balance per bank at July 31.

Prepare a cash budget. (SO 6)

BE7-9 The following information is available for Marais Company for the month of January: expected cash receipts $60,000; expected cash disbursements $65,000; cash balance on January 1 $12,000. Management wishes to maintain a minimum cash balance of $10,000. Prepare a basic cash budget for the month of January.

BE7-10 Tijuana Company has these cash balances: Cash in Bank $12,742; Payroll Bank Account $6,000; and Plant Expansion Fund Cash $25,000. Explain how each balance should be reported on the balance sheet.

Explain the statement presentation of cash balances.
(SO 5)

BE7-11 Kellogg Company's 1996 annual report disclosed the following financial information: net income $531 million; cash dividends $344 million; net cash provided by operating activities $712 million; and capital expenditures $307 million. Compute Kellogg Company's free cash flow for 1996.

Compute free cash flow.
(SO 8)

BE7-12 Amoco Corporation's 1996 annual report disclosed the following financial information: total expenses $33,278 million; depreciation, depletion, and amortization $2,294 million; and cash and cash equivalents $1,321 million. Compute Amoco's cash to daily cash expenses ratio.

Compute cash to daily cash expenses ratio.
(SO 8)

*BE7-13 On March 20 Gimbal's petty cash fund of $100 is replenished when the fund contains $12 in cash and receipts for postage $52, supplies $26, and travel expense $10. Prepare the journal entry to record the replenishment of the petty cash fund.

Prepare entry to replenish a petty cash fund.
(SO 9)

EXERCISES

E7-1 Joe Marino is the owner of Marino's Pizza. Marino's operates strictly on a carry-out basis. Customers pick up their orders at a counter where a clerk exchanges the pizza for cash. While at the counter, the customer can see other employees making the pizzas and the large ovens in which the pizzas are baked.

Identify the principles of internal control.
(SO 1)

Instructions
Identify the six principles of internal control and give an example of each principle that you might observe when picking up your pizza. [*Note:* It may not be possible to observe all the principles.]

E7-2 The following control procedures are used in Tolan Company for over-the-counter cash receipts:
1. Cashiers are experienced; they are not bonded.
2. All over-the-counter receipts are registered by three clerks who use a cash register with a single cash drawer.
3. To minimize the risk of robbery, cash in excess of $100 is stored in an unlocked attaché case in the stock room until it is deposited in the bank.
4. At the end of each day the total receipts are counted by the cashier on duty and reconciled to the cash register total.
5. The company accountant makes the bank deposit and then records the day's receipts.

List internal control weaknesses over cash receipts and suggest improvements.
(SO 1, 2)

Instructions
(a) For each procedure, explain the weakness in internal control and identify the control principle that is violated.
(b) For each weakness, suggest a change in procedure that will result in good internal control.

E7-3 The following control procedures are used in Ann's Boutique Shoppe for cash disbursements:
1. Each week Ann leaves 100 company checks in an unmarked envelope on a shelf behind the cash register.
2. The store manager personally approves all payments before signing and issuing checks.
3. The company checks are unnumbered.
4. After payment, bills are "filed" in a paid invoice folder.
5. The company accountant prepares the bank reconciliation and reports any discrepancies to the owner.

List internal control weaknesses for cash disbursements and suggest improvements.
(SO 3)

Instructions
(a) For each procedure, explain the weakness in internal control and identify the internal control principle that is violated.
(b) For each weakness, suggest a change in the procedure that will result in good internal control.

324 CHAPTER 7 Internal Control and Cash

Identify internal control weaknesses for cash disbursements and suggest improvements.
(SO 3)

E7-4 At O'Malley Company checks are not prenumbered because both the purchasing agent and the treasurer are authorized to issue checks. Each signer has access to unissued checks kept in an unlocked file cabinet. The purchasing agent pays all bills pertaining to goods purchased for resale. Prior to payment, the purchasing agent determines that the goods have been received and verifies the mathematical accuracy of the vendor's invoice. After payment, the invoice is filed by vendor and the purchasing agent records the payment in the cash disbursements journal. The treasurer pays all other bills following approval by authorized employees. After payment, the treasurer stamps all bills "paid," files them by payment date, and records the checks in the cash disbursements journal. O'Malley Company maintains one checking account that is reconciled by the treasurer.

Instructions
(a) List the weaknesses in internal control over cash disbursements.
(b) Write a memo indicating your recommendations for improving company procedures.

Prepare bank reconciliation and adjusting entries.
(SO 4)

E7-5 Ono LoKo is unable to reconcile the bank balance at January 31. Ono's reconciliation is shown here:

Cash balance per bank	$3,560.20
Add: NSF check	530.00
Less: Bank service charge	25.00
Adjusted balance per bank	$4,065.20
Cash balance per books	$3,875.20
Less: Deposits in transit	490.00
Add: Outstanding checks	730.00
Adjusted balance per books	$4,115.20

Instructions
(a) Prepare a correct bank reconciliation.
(b) Journalize the entries required by the reconciliation.

Determine outstanding checks.
(SO 4)

E7-6 At April 30 the bank reconciliation of Drofo Company shows three outstanding checks: No. 254 $650, No. 255 $820, and No. 257 $410. The May bank statement and the May cash payments journal are given here:

Bank Statement Checks Paid			Cash Payments Journal Checks Issued		
Date	Check No.	Amount	Date	Check No.	Amount
5/4	254	$650	5/2	258	$159
5/2	257	410	5/5	259	275
5/17	258	159	5/10	260	925
5/12	259	275	5/15	261	500
5/20	261	500	5/22	262	750
5/29	263	480	5/24	263	480
5/30	262	750	5/29	264	360

Instructions
Using step 2 in the reconciliation procedure (see page 300), list the outstanding checks at May 31.

Prepare bank reconciliation and adjusting entries.
(SO 4)

E7-7 The following information pertains to Mohammed Company:
1. Cash balance per bank, July 31, $7,463.
2. July bank service charge not recorded by the depositor $15.
3. Cash balance per books, July 31, $7,190.
4. Deposits in transit, July 31, $1,700.
5. Note for $1,200 collected for Mohammed in July by the bank, plus interest $36 less fee $20. The collection has not been recorded by Mohammed, and no interest has been accrued.
6. Outstanding checks, July 31, $772.

Instructions
(a) Prepare a bank reconciliation at July 31.
(b) Journalize the adjusting entries at July 31 on the books of Mohammed Company.

E7-8 This information relates to the Cash account in the ledger of Reston Company:

Balance September 1—$17,150; Cash deposited—$64,000
Balance September 30—$17,404; Checks written—$63,746

Prepare bank reconciliation and adjusting entries.
(SO 4)

The September bank statement shows a balance of $16,422 at September 30 and the following memoranda:

Credits			Debits	
Collection of $1,500 note plus interest $30	$1,530		NSF check: J. Hower	$410
Interest earned on checking account	45		Safety deposit box rent	30

At September 30 deposits in transit were $4,500 and outstanding checks totaled $2,383.

Instructions
(a) Prepare the bank reconciliation at September 30.
(b) Prepare the adjusting entries at September 30, assuming (1) the NSF check was from a customer on account, and (2) no interest had been accrued on the note.

E7-9 The cash records of Kuwait Company show the following:
1. The June 30 bank reconciliation indicated that deposits in transit total $850. During July the general ledger account Cash shows deposits of $15,750, but the bank statement indicates that only $15,600 in deposits were received during the month.
2. The June 30 bank reconciliation also reported outstanding checks of $920. During the month of July, Kuwait Company books show that $17,200 of checks were issued, yet the bank statement showed that $16,400 of checks cleared the bank in July.
3. In September deposits per bank statement totaled $26,700, deposits per books were $25,400, and deposits in transit at September 30 were $2,400.
4. In September cash disbursements per books were $23,700, checks clearing the bank were $25,000, and outstanding checks at September 30 were $2,100.

There were no bank debit or credit memoranda, and no errors were made by either the bank or Kuwait Company.

Compute deposits in transit and outstanding checks for two bank reconciliations.
(SO 4)

Instructions
Answer these questions:
(a) In situation 1, what were the deposits in transit at July 31?
(b) In situation 2, what were the outstanding checks at July 31?
(c) In situation 3, what were the deposits in transit at August 31?
(d) In situation 4, what were the outstanding checks at August 31?

E7-10 Hanover Company expects to have a cash balance of $46,000 on January 1, 1998. These are the relevant monthly budget data for the first 2 months of 1998:
1. Collections from customers: January $70,000; February $150,000.
2. Payments to suppliers: January $40,000; February $75,000.
3. Direct labor: January $30,000; February $40,000. Wages are paid in the month they are incurred.
4. Manufacturing overhead: January $21,000; February $30,000. These costs include depreciation of $1,000 per month. All other overhead costs are paid as incurred.
5. Selling and administrative expenses: January $14,000; February $20,000. These costs are exclusive of depreciation. They are paid as incurred.
6. Sales of marketable securities in January are expected to realize $10,000 in cash. Hanover Company has a line of credit at a local bank that enables it to borrow up to $25,000. The company wants to maintain a minimum monthly cash balance of $20,000.

Prepare cash budget for two months.
(SO 7)

Instructions
Prepare a cash budget for January and February.

E7-11 Ascend Communications, Inc. reported the following financial data in its 1996 annual report: net income $113 million; cash and cash equivalents $214 million; total expenses (not including depreciation) $256 million; net cash provided by operating activities $55 million; dividends paid, zero; and capital expenditures $39 million. Compute and comment on the following two measures of cash adequacy: (1) cash to daily cash expenses ratio and (2) free cash flow.

Compute and comment on cash to daily cash expenses ratio and free cash flow.
(SO 8)

Prepare journal entries for a petty cash fund.
(SO 9)

*E7-12 Ramona Company uses a petty cash system. The fund was established on March 1 with a balance of $100. During March the following petty cash receipts were found in the petty cash box:

Date	Receipt No.	For	Amount
Mar. 5	1	Stamp Inventory	$38
7	2	Supplies	19
9	3	Miscellaneous Expense	12
11	4	Travel Expense	24
14	5	Miscellaneous Expense	5

There was no cash over or short. The fund was replenished on March 15. On March 20 the amount in the fund was increased to $150.

Instructions
Journalize the entries in March that pertain to the operation of the petty cash fund.

PROBLEMS

Identify internal control weaknesses over cash receipts.
(SO 1, 2)

P7-1 Red River Theater is in the Red River Mall. A cashier's booth is located near the entrance to the theater. Two cashiers are employed. One works from 1:00 to 5:00 P.M., the other from 5:00 to 9:00 P.M. Each cashier is bonded. The cashiers receive cash from customers and operate a machine that ejects serially numbered tickets. The rolls of tickets are inserted and locked into the machine by the theater manager at the beginning of each cashier's shift.

After purchasing a ticket, the customer takes the ticket to a doorperson stationed at the entrance of the theater lobby some 60 feet from the cashier's booth. The doorperson tears the ticket in half, admits the customer, and returns the ticket stub to the customer. The other half of the ticket is dropped into a locked box by the doorperson.

At the end of each cashier's shift, the theater manager removes the ticket rolls from the machine and makes a cash count. The cash count sheet is initialed by the cashier. At the end of the day, the manager deposits the receipts in total in a bank night deposit vault located in the mall. In addition, the manager sends copies of the deposit slip and the initialed cash count sheets to the theater company treasurer for verification and to the company's accounting department. Receipts from the first shift are stored in a safe located in the manager's office.

Instructions
(a) Identify the internal control principles and their application to the cash receipts transactions of Red River Theater.
(b) If the doorperson and cashier decided to collaborate to misappropriate cash, what actions might they take?

Prepare bank reconciliation and adjusting entries.
(SO 4)

P7-2 On July 31, 1998, Lori Company had a cash balance per books of $6,815.30. The statement from Tri-County Bank on that date showed a balance of $7,075.80. A comparison of the bank statement with the cash account revealed the following facts:
1. The bank service charge for July was $25.
2. The bank collected a note receivable of $1,200 for Lori Company on July 15, plus $48 of interest. The bank made a $10 charge for the collection. Lori has not accrued any interest on the note.
3. The July 31 receipts of $1,819.60 were not included in the bank deposits for July. These receipts were deposited by the company in a night deposit vault on July 31.
4. Company check No. 2480 issued to J. Brokaw, a creditor, for $492 that cleared the bank in July was incorrectly entered in the cash payments journal on July 10 for $429.
5. Checks outstanding on July 31 totaled $1,480.10.
6. On July 31 the bank statement showed an NSF charge of $550 for a check received by the company from R. Close, a customer, on account.

Instructions
(a) Prepare the bank reconciliation as of July 31.
(b) Prepare the necessary adjusting entries at July 31.

P7-3 The bank portion of the bank reconciliation for London Company at October 31, 1998, is shown here:

Prepare bank reconciliation and adjusting entries from detailed data.
(SO 4)

LONDON COMPANY
Bank Reconciliation
October 31, 1998

Cash balance per bank			$12,367.90
Add: Deposits in transit			1,530.20
			13,898.10
Less: Outstanding checks			

Check Number	Check Amount	
2451	$1,260.40	
2470	720.10	
2471	844.50	
2472	426.80	
2474	1,050.00	4,301.80

Adjusted cash balance per bank $ 9,596.30

The adjusted cash balance per bank agreed with the cash balance per books at October 31. The November bank statement showed the following checks and deposits:

Bank Statement

Checks			Deposits	
Date	Number	Amount	Date	Amount
11-1	2470	$ 720.10	11-1	$ 1,530.20
11-2	2471	844.50	11-4	1,211.60
11-5	2474	1,050.00	11-8	990.10
11-4	2475	1,640.70	11-13	2,575.00
11-8	2476	2,830.00	11-18	1,472.70
11-10	2477	600.00	11-21	2,945.00
11-15	2479	1,750.00	11-25	2,567.30
11-18	2480	1,330.00	11-28	1,650.00
11-27	2481	695.40	11-30	1,186.00
11-30	2483	575.50	Total	$16,127.90
11-29	2486	900.00		
	Total	$12,936.20		

The cash records per books for November showed the following:

Cash Payments Journal

Date	Number	Amount	Date	Number	Amount
11-1	2475	$1,640.70	11-20	2483	$ 575.50
11-2	2476	2,830.00	11-22	2484	829.50
11-2	2477	600.00	11-23	2485	974.80
11-4	2478	538.20	11-24	2486	900.00
11-8	2479	1,570.00	11-29	2487	398.00
11-10	2480	1,330.00	11-30	2488	800.00
11-15	2481	695.40	Total		$14,294.10
11-18	2482	612.00			

Cash Receipts Journal

Date	Amount
11-3	$ 1,211.60
11-7	990.10
11-12	2,575.00
11-17	1,472.70
11-20	2,954.00
11-24	2,567.30
11-27	1,650.00
11-29	1,186.00
11-30	1,225.00
Total	$15,831.70

328   CHAPTER 7   Internal Control and Cash

The bank statement contained two bank memoranda:
1. A credit of $2,105.00 for the collection of a $2,000 note for London Company plus interest of $120 and less a collection fee of $15. London Company has not accrued any interest on the note.
2. A debit for the printing of additional company checks $50.00.

At November 30 the cash balance per books was $11,133.90 and the cash balance per bank statement was $17,614.60. The bank did not make any errors, but two errors were made by London Company.

Instructions
(a) Using the four steps in the reconciliation procedure described on pages 300–301, prepare a bank reconciliation at November 30.
(b) Prepare the adjusting entries based on the reconciliation. [*Note:* The correction of any errors pertaining to recording checks should be made to Accounts Payable. The correction of any errors relating to recording cash receipts should be made to Accounts Receivable.]

Prepare bank reconciliation and adjusting entries.
(SO 4)

P7-4 Mayo Company's bank statement from Lane National Bank at August 31, 1998, gives this information:

Balance, August 1	$17,400	Bank credit memoranda:	
August deposits	73,000	Collection of note receivable	
Checks cleared in August	68,660	plus $90 interest	$3,090
Balance, August 31	24,850	Interest earned	45
		Bank debit memorandum:	
		Safety deposit box rent	25

A summary of the Cash account in the ledger for August shows: Balance, August 1, $16,900; receipts $77,000; disbursements $73,570; and balance, August 31, $20,330. Analysis reveals that the only reconciling items on the July 31 bank reconciliation were a deposit in transit for $4,000 and outstanding checks of $4,500. The deposit in transit was the first deposit recorded by the bank in August. In addition, you determine that there were two errors involving company checks drawn in August: (1) a check for $400 to a creditor on account that cleared the bank in August was journalized and posted for $420, and (2) a salary check to an employee for $275 was recorded by the bank for $285.

Instructions
(a) Prepare a bank reconciliation at August 31.
(b) Journalize the adjusting entries to be made by Mayo Company at August 31. Assume the interest on the note has been accrued by the company.

Prepare cash budget for two months.
(SO 7)

P7-5 Joplin Company prepares monthly cash budgets. Here are relevant data from operating budgets for 1998:

	January	February
Sales	$360,000	$400,000
Direct materials purchases	100,000	110,000
Direct labor	80,000	95,000
Manufacturing overhead	60,000	75,000
Selling and administrative expenses	75,000	85,000

All sales are on account. Collections are expected to be 50% in the month of sale, 30% in the first month following the sale, and 20% in the second month following the sale. Forty percent (40%) of direct material purchases are paid in cash in the month of purchase, and the balance due is paid in the month following the purchase. All other items above are paid in the month incurred. Depreciation has been excluded from manufacturing overhead and selling and administrative expenses.

Other data are listed here:
1. Credit sales—November 1997, $200,000; December 1997, $280,000
2. Purchases of direct materials—December 1997, $90,000
3. Other receipts—January: collection of December 31, 1997, interest receivable $3,000; February: proceeds from sale of securities $5,000
4. Other disbursements—February: payment of $20,000 for land

The company's cash balance on January 1, 1998, is expected to be $60,000. The company wants to maintain a minimum cash balance of $50,000.

Instructions
(a) Prepare schedules for (1) expected collections from customers and (2) expected payments for direct materials purchases.
(b) Prepare a cash budget for January and February.

P7-6 MTR Company maintains a petty cash fund for small expenditures. These transactions occurred over a 2-month period:

Journalize and post petty cash fund transactions.
(SO 9)

July 1 Established the petty cash fund by writing a check on Metro Bank for $200.
15 Replenished the petty cash fund by writing a check for $194.30. On this date the fund consisted of $5.70 in cash and these petty cash receipts: freight-out $94.00, postage expense $42.40, entertainment expense $46.60, and miscellaneous expense $10.70.
31 Replenished the petty cash fund by writing a check for $192.00. At this date, the fund consisted of $8.00 in cash and these petty cash receipts: freight-out $82.10, charitable contributions expense $30.00, postage expense $47.80, and miscellaneous expense $32.10.
Aug. 15 Replenished the petty cash fund by writing a check for $188.00. On this date, the fund consisted of $12.00 in cash and these petty cash receipts: freight-out $74.40, entertainment expense $43.00, postage expense $33.00, and miscellaneous expense $38.00.
16 Increased the amount of the petty cash fund to $300 by writing a check for $100.
31 Replenished the petty cash fund by writing a check for $283.00. On this date, the fund consisted of $17 in cash and these petty cash receipts: postage expense $145.00, entertainment expense $90.60, and freight-out $45.40.

Instructions
(a) Journalize the petty cash transactions.
(b) Post to the Petty Cash account.
(c) What internal control features exist in a petty cash fund?

P7-7 Acura Company is a very profitable small business. It has not, however, given much consideration to internal control. For example, in an attempt to keep clerical and office expenses to a minimum, the company has combined the jobs of cashier and bookkeeper. As a result, Rob Rowe handles all cash receipts, keeps the accounting records, and prepares the monthly bank reconciliations.

Prepare comprehensive bank reconciliation with internal control deficiencies.
(SO 1, 2, 3, 4)

The balance per the bank statement on October 31, 1998, was $18,380. Outstanding checks were: No. 62 for $126.75, No. 183 for $150, No. 284 for $253.25, No. 862 for $190.71, No. 863 for $226.80, and No. 864 for $165.28. Included with the statement was a credit memorandum of $200 indicating the collection of a note receivable for Acura Company by the bank on October 25. This memorandum has not been recorded by Acura Company.

The company's ledger showed one cash account with a balance of $21,892.72. The balance included undeposited cash on hand. Because of the lack of internal controls, Rowe took for personal use all of the undeposited receipts in excess of $3,795.51. He then prepared the following bank reconciliation in an effort to conceal his theft of cash:

Cash balance per books, October 31		$21,892.72
Add: Outstanding checks		
No. 862	$190.71	
No. 863	226.80	
No. 864	165.28	482.79
		22,375.51
Less: Undeposited receipts		3,795.51
Unadjusted balance per bank, October 31		18,580.00
Less: Bank credit memorandum		200.00
Cash balance per bank statement, October 31		$18,380.00

330 CHAPTER 7 Internal Control and Cash

Instructions
(a) Prepare a correct bank reconciliation. [*Hint:* Deduct the amount of the theft from the adjusted balance per books.]
(b) Indicate the three ways that Rowe attempted to conceal the theft and the dollar amount involved in each method.
(c) What principles of internal control were violated in this case?

ALTERNATIVE PROBLEMS

Identify internal control principles over cash disbursements.
(SO 1, 3)

P7-1A Segal Office Supply Company recently changed its system of internal control over cash disbursements. The system includes the following features:

Instead of being unnumbered and manually prepared, all checks must now be prenumbered and written by using the new checkwriter purchased by the company. Before a check can be issued, each invoice must have the approval of Cindy Morris, the purchasing agent, and Ray Mills, the receiving department supervisor. Checks must be signed by either Frank Malone, the treasurer, or Mary Arno, the assistant treasurer. Before signing a check, the signer is expected to compare the amounts of the check with the amounts on the invoice.

After signing a check, the signer stamps the invoice "paid" and inserts within the stamp, the date, check number, and amount of the check. The "paid" invoice is then sent to the accounting department for recording.

Blank checks are stored in a safe in the treasurer's office. The combination to the safe is known by only the treasurer and assistant treasurer. Each month the bank statement is reconciled with the bank balance per books by the assistant chief accountant.

Instructions
Identify the internal control principles and their application to cash disbursements of Segal Office Supply Company.

Prepare bank reconciliation and adjusting entries.
(SO 4)

P7-2A On May 31, 1998, Maloney Company had a cash balance per books of $5,781.50. The bank statement from Community Bank on that date showed a balance of $6,804.60. A comparison of the statement with the cash account revealed the following facts:

1. The statement included a debit memo of $40 for the printing of additional company checks.
2. Cash sales of $836.15 on May 12 were deposited in the bank. The cash receipts journal entry and the deposit slip were incorrectly made for $846.15. The bank credited Maloney Company for the correct amount.
3. Outstanding checks at May 31 totaled $1,276.25, and deposits in transit were $936.15.
4. On May 18 the company issued check No. 1181 for $685 to M. Helms, on account. The check, which cleared the bank in May, was incorrectly journalized and posted by Maloney Company for $658.
5. A $2,000 note receivable was collected by the bank for Maloney Company on May 31 plus $80 interest. The bank charged a collection fee of $20. No interest has been accrued on the note.
6. Included with the cancelled checks was a check issued by Teller Company to P. Jonet for $600 that was incorrectly charged to Maloney Company by the bank.
7. On May 31 the bank statement showed an NSF charge of $700 for a check issued by W. Hoad, a customer, to Maloney Company on account.

Instructions
(a) Prepare the bank reconciliation as of May 31, 1998.
(b) Prepare the necessary adjusting entries at May 31, 1998.

P7-3A The bank portion of the bank reconciliation for Sandra Company at November 30, 1998, is shown here:

Prepare bank reconciliation and adjusting entries from detailed data.
(SO 4)

SANDRA COMPANY
Bank Reconciliation
November 30, 1998

Cash balance per bank			$14,367.90
Add: Deposits in transit			2,530.20
			16,898.10
Less: Outstanding checks			

Check Number	Check Amount
3451	$2,260.40
3470	720.10
3471	844.50
3472	1,426.80
3474	1,050.00

	6,301.80
Adjusted cash balance per bank	$10,596.30

The adjusted cash balance per bank agreed with the cash balance per books at November 30. The December bank statement showed the following checks and deposits:

Bank Statement

Checks			Deposits	
Date	Number	Amount	Date	Amount
12-1	3451	$ 2,260.40	12-1	$ 2,530.20
12-2	3471	844.50	12-4	1,211.60
12-7	3472	1,426.80	12-8	2,365.10
12-4	3475	1,640.70	12-16	2,672.70
12-8	3476	1,300.00	12-21	2,945.00
12-10	3477	2,130.00	12-26	2,567.30
12-15	3479	3,080.00	12-29	2,836.00
12-27	3480	600.00	12-30	1,025.00
12-30	3482	475.50	Total	$18,152.90
12-29	3483	1,140.00		
12-31	3485	540.80		
	Total	$15,438.70		

The cash records per books for December showed the following:

Cash Payments Journal

Date	Number	Amount	Date	Number	Amount
12-1	3475	$1,640.70	12-20	3482	$ 475.50
12-2	3476	1,300.00	12-22	3483	1,140.00
12-2	3477	2,130.00	12-23	3484	832.00
12-4	3478	538.20	12-24	3485	450.80
12-8	3479	3,080.00	12-30	3486	1,389.50
12-10	3480	600.00	Total		$14,384.10
12-17	3481	807.40			

Cash Receipts Journal

Date	Amount
12-3	$ 1,211.60
12-7	2,365.10
12-15	2,672.70
12-20	2,954.00
12-25	2,567.30
12-28	2,836.00
12-30	1,025.00
12-31	1,190.40
Total	$16,822.10

The bank statement contained two memoranda:
1. A credit of $2,145 for the collection of a $2,000 note for Sandra Company plus interest of $160 and less a collection fee of $15.00. Sandra Company has not accrued any interest on the note.
2. A debit of $547.10 for an NSF check written by A. Jordan, a customer. At December 31 the check had not been redeposited in the bank.

At December 31 the cash balance per books was $13,034.30, and the cash balance per bank statement was $18,680.00. The bank did not make any errors, but two errors were made by Sandra Company.

Instructions
(a) Using the four steps in the reconciliation procedure described on pages 300–301, prepare a bank reconciliation at December 31.
(b) Prepare the adjusting entries based on the reconciliation. [*Note:* The correction of any errors pertaining to recording checks should be made to Accounts Payable. The correction of any errors relating to recording cash receipts should be made to Accounts Receivable.]

Prepare bank reconciliation and adjusting entries.
(SO 4)

P7-4A Palmeiro Company maintains a checking account at Marine City Bank. At July 31 selected data from the ledger balance and the bank statement are as follows:

	Cash in Bank	
	Per Books	Per Bank
Balance, July 1	$17,600	$19,200
July receipts	82,000	
July credits		80,070
July disbursements	76,900	
July debits		74,740
Balance, July 31	$22,700	$24,530

Analysis of the bank data reveals that the credits consist of $78,000 of July deposits and a credit memorandum of $2,070 for the collection of a $2,000 note plus interest revenue of $70. The July debits per bank consist of checks cleared $74,700 and a debit memorandum of $40 for printing additional company checks. You also discover the following errors involving July checks: (1) a check for $230 to a creditor on account that cleared the bank in July was journalized and posted as $320, and (2) a salary check to an employee for $255 was recorded by the bank for $155. The June 30 bank reconciliation contained only two reconciling items: deposits in transit $5,000 and outstanding checks of $6,600.

Instructions
(a) Prepare a bank reconciliation at July 31.
(b) Journalize the adjusting entries to be made by Palmeiro Company at July 31. Assume the interest on the note has been accrued.

Prepare cash budget for two months.
(SO 7)

P7-5A Badger Company prepares monthly cash budgets. Here are relevant data from operating budgets for 1998:

	January	February
Sales	$350,000	$400,000
Direct materials purchases	120,000	130,000
Direct labor	80,000	95,000
Manufacturing overhead	70,000	75,000
Selling and administrative expenses	79,000	86,000

All sales are on account. Collections are expected to be 50% in the month of sale, 40% in the first month following the sale, and 10% in the second month following the sale. Fifty percent (50%) of direct material purchases are paid in cash in the month of purchase, and the balance due is paid in the month following the purchase. All other items above are paid in the month incurred except for selling and administrative expenses that includes $1,000 of depreciation per month.

Other data are listed here:
1. Credit sales—November 1997, $260,000; December 1997, $300,000.
2. Purchases of direct materials—December 1997, $100,000.
3. Other receipts—January: collection of December 31, 1997, notes receivable $15,000; February: proceeds from sale of securities $6,000
4. Other disbursements—February: $5,000 cash dividend

The company's cash balance on January 1, 1998, is expected to be $55,000. The company wants to maintain a minimum cash balance of $50,000.

Instructions
(a) Prepare schedules for (1) expected collections from customers and (2) expected payments for direct materials purchases.
(b) Prepare a cash budget for January and February.

P7-6A Dockers Company maintains a petty cash fund for small expenditures. The following transactions occurred over a 2-month period:

Journalize and post petty cash fund transactions.
(SO 9)

July 1 Established the petty cash fund by writing a check on Metro Bank for $200.
     15 Replenished the petty cash fund by writing a check for $195.00. On this date the fund consisted of $5.00 in cash and these petty cash receipts: freight-out $94.00, postage expense $42.40, entertainment expense $46.60, and miscellaneous expense $11.90.
     31 Replenished the petty cash fund by writing a check for $192.00. At this date, the fund consisted of $8.00 in cash and these petty cash receipts: freight-out $82.10, charitable contributions expense $40.00, postage expense $27.80, and miscellaneous expense $42.10.
Aug. 15 Replenished the petty cash fund by writing a check for $187.00. On this date, the fund consisted of $13.00 in cash and these petty cash receipts: freight-out $74.60, entertainment expense $43.00, postage expense $33.00, and miscellaneous expense $37.00.
     16 Increased the amount of the petty cash fund to $300 by writing a check for $100.
     31 Replenished the petty cash fund by writing a check for $283.00. On this date, the fund consisted of $17 in cash and these petty cash receipts: postage expense $140.00, travel expense $95.60, and freight-out $46.40.

Instructions
(a) Journalize the petty cash transactions.
(b) Post to the Petty Cash account.
(c) What internal control features exist in a petty cash fund?

BROADENING YOUR PERSPECTIVE

FINANCIAL REPORTING AND ANALYSIS

FINANCIAL REPORTING PROBLEM: *Starbucks Corporation*

BYP7-1 The financial statements of Starbucks are presented in Appendix A of this book, together with two reports: (1) a management report, Management's Responsibility for Financial Statements, and (2) an auditor's report, Report of Independent Auditors.

Instructions
Using the financial statements and reports, answer these questions about Starbucks' internal controls and cash:
(a) What comments, if any, concerning the company's system of internal control are included in each report?

(b) What reference, if any, is made to internal auditors in each report?
(c) What comments, if any, are made about cash in the report of the independent auditors?
(d) What data about cash and cash equivalents are shown in the consolidated balance sheet (statement of financial condition)?
(e) What activities are identified in the consolidated statement of cash flows as being responsible for the changes in cash during 1996?
(f) How are cash equivalents defined in the Notes to Consolidated Financial Statements?

COMPARATIVE ANALYSIS PROBLEM: *Starbucks vs. Green Mountain Coffee*

BYP7-2 The financial statements of Green Mountain Coffee are presented in Appendix B, following the financial statements for Starbucks in Appendix A.

Instructions
(a) Based on the information contained in these financial statements, determine each of the following for each company:
  (1) Cash and cash equivalents balance at September 28, 1996, for Green Mountain and at October 1, 1996, for Starbucks.
  (2) Increase (decrease) in cash and cash equivalents from 1995 to 1996.
  (3) Cash provided by operating activities during 1996 (from statement of cash flows).
  (4) Total assets balance at September 28, 1996, for Green Mountain and at October 1, 1996, for Starbucks.
(b) What conclusions concerning the management of cash can be drawn from these data?

RESEARCH CASE

BYP7-3 The "Fortune 500" issue of *Fortune* magazine can serve as a useful reference. This annual issue of *Fortune*, which generally appears in late April or early May, contains a great deal of information regarding the largest U.S. industrial and service companies.

Instructions
Examine the most recent edition and answer these questions:
(a) Identify the three largest U.S. corporations in terms of revenues, profits, assets, market value, and number of employees.
(b) Identify the largest corporation headquartered (or operating, if needed) in your state (by total revenue). How does this corporation rank in terms of revenues, profits, assets, market value, and number of employees?

INTERPRETING FINANCIAL STATEMENTS

BYP7-4 Minicase *Microsoft, Inc.*

Microsoft is the leading developer of software in the world. To continue to be successful Microsoft must generate new products, and generating new products requires significant amounts of cash. Shown on the facing page is the current assets section of Microsoft's June 30, 1995, balance sheet and excerpts from a footnote describing the first item listed in the balance sheet, "Cash and short-term investments." Following the Microsoft data is the current assets section from Oracle, another major software developer.

Instructions
(a) What is the definition of a cash equivalent? Give some examples of cash equivalents. How do cash equivalents differ from other types of short-term investments?
(b) Comment on Microsoft's presentation of cash in its balance sheet.
(c) What problems might this presentation of cash pose for a user of Microsoft's financial statements?
(d) Compare the liquidity of Microsoft and Oracle for 1995.
(e) Is it possible to have too many liquid assets?

MICROSOFT, INC.
Balance Sheets (partial)
As of June 30
(in millions)

	1995	1994
Current assets		
Cash and short-term investments (see Note 1)	$4,750	$3,614
Accounts receivable—net of allowances of $92 and $139	581	475
Inventories	88	102
Other	201	121
Total current assets	$5,620	$4,312
Total current liabilities	$1,347	$913

Note 1:

	1995	1994
Cash and equivalents	$1,962	$1,477
Short-term investments	2,788	2,137
Cash and short-term investments	$4,750	$3,614

ORACLE
Balance Sheets (partial)
As of May 31
(in millions)

	1995	1994
Current assets		
Cash and cash equivalents	$480	$409
Short-term cash investments	106	60
Receivables	846	516
Other current assets	185	95
Total current assets	$1,617	$1,080
Current liabilities	$1,055	$682

CRITICAL THINKING

MANAGEMENT DECISION CASE

BYP7-5 The board of trustees of a local church is concerned about the internal accounting controls pertaining to the offering collections made at weekly services. They ask you to serve on a three-person audit team with the internal auditor of the university and a CPA who had just joined the church. At a meeting of the audit team and the board of trustees you learn the following:

1. The church's board of trustees has delegated responsibility for the financial management and audit of the financial records to the finance committee. This group prepares the annual budget and approves major disbursements but is not involved in collections or recordkeeping. No audit has been made in recent years because the same trusted employee has kept church records and served as financial secretary for 15 years. The church does not carry any fidelity insurance.
2. The collection at the weekly service is taken by a team of ushers who volunteer to serve for 1 month. The ushers take the collection plates to a basement office at the

rear of the church. They hand their plates to the head usher and return to the church service. After all plates have been turned in, the head usher counts the cash received. The head usher then places the cash in the church safe along with a notation of the amount counted. The head usher volunteers to serve for 3 months.
3. The next morning the financial secretary opens the safe and recounts the collection. The secretary withholds $150–$200 in cash, depending on the cash expenditures expected for the week, and deposits the remainder of the collections in the bank. To facilitate the deposit, church members who contribute by check are asked to make their checks payable to "cash."
4. Each month the financial secretary reconciles the bank statement and submits a copy of the reconciliation to the board of trustees. The reconciliations have rarely contained any bank errors and have never shown any errors per books.

Instructions
(a) Indicate the weaknesses in internal accounting control in the handling of collections.
(b) List the improvements in internal control procedures that you plan to make at the next meeting of the audit team for (1) the ushers, (2) the head usher, (3) the financial secretary, and (4) the finance committee.
(c) What church policies should be changed to improve internal control?

A REAL-WORLD FOCUS: *Alternative Distributor Corp.*

BYP7-6 *Alternative Distributor Corp.*, a distributor of groceries and related products, is headquartered in Medford, Massachusetts. It was founded in 1980 and today has seven employees and total sales of $7 million.

During its audit, Alternative Distributor Corp. was advised that existing internal controls necessary for the company to develop reliable financial statements were inadequate. The audit report stated that the current system of accounting for sales, receivables, and cash receipts constituted a material weakness. Among other items, the report focused on nontimely deposit of cash receipts, exposing Alternative Distributor to potential loss or misappropriation, excessive past due accounts receivable due to lack of collection efforts, disregard of advantages offered by vendors for prompt payment of invoices, absence of appropriate segregation of duties by personnel consistent with appropriate control objectives, inadequate procedures for applying accounting principles, lack of qualified management personnel, lack of supervision by an outside board of directors, and overall poor recordkeeping.

Instructions
Identify the principles of internal control violated by Alternative Distributor Corp.

GROUP ACTIVITY

BYP7-7 From your employment or personal experiences, think of situations in which cash has been received or disbursed.

Instructions
Form groups of five or six students.
(a) Identify the internal control principles used for cash receipts.
(b) Identify the internal control principles used for cash disbursements.
(c) Identify any weaknesses in internal control related to cash receipts and disbursements.

COMMUNICATION ACTIVITY

BYP7-8 As a new auditor for the CPA firm of Rawls, Keoto, and Landry, you have been assigned to review the internal controls over mail cash receipts of Adirondack Company. Your review reveals that checks are promptly endorsed "For Deposit Only" but no list of the checks is prepared by the person opening the mail. The mail is opened either by the cashier or by the employee who maintains the accounts receivable records. Mail receipts are deposited in the bank weekly by the cashier.

Instructions
Write a letter to L. S. Osman, owner of the Adirondack Company, explaining the weaknesses in internal control and your recommendations for improving the system.

Ethics Case

BYP7-9 You are the assistant controller in charge of general ledger accounting at Lemon Twist Bottling Company. Your company has a large loan from an insurance company. The loan agreement requires that the company's cash account balance be maintained at $200,000 or more as reported monthly. At June 30 the cash balance is $80,000, which you report to Sam Williams, the financial vice-president. Sam excitedly instructs you to keep the cash receipts book open for one additional day for purposes of the June 30 report to the insurance company. Sam says, "If we don't get that cash balance over $200,000, we'll default on our loan agreement. They could close us down and put us all out of our jobs!" Sam continues, "I talked to Grochum Distributors (one of Lemon Twist's largest customers) this morning and they said they sent us a check for $150,000 yesterday. We should receive it tomorrow. If we include just that one check in our cash balance, we'll be in the clear. It's in the mail!"

Instructions
(a) Who will suffer negative effects if you do not comply with Sam Williams's instructions? Who will suffer if you do comply?
(b) What are the ethical considerations in this case?
(c) What alternatives do you have?

Financial Analysis on the Web

BYP7-10 *Purpose:* The Financial Accounting Standards Board (FASB) is a private organization established to improve accounting standards and financial reporting. The FASB conducts extensive research before issuing a "Statement of Financial Accounting Standards," which represents an authoritative expression of generally accepted accounting principles.

Address: http://www.rutgers.edu/accounting/raw/fasb/home.htm

Steps: Visit the homepage of the FASB.

Instructions
Answer the following questions:
(a) What is the mission of the FASB?
(b) Using the table of contents, locate FASB Statement 128. What topic does Statement 128 address? What was the issue date?

Answers to Self-Study Questions
1. a 2. c 3. b 4. c 5. b 6. d 7. a 8. c 9. d 10. c
*11. a

CHAPTER 8

Reporting and Analyzing Receivables

STUDY OBJECTIVES

After studying this chapter, you should be able to:

1. Identify the different types of receivables.
2. Explain how accounts receivable are recognized in the accounts.
3. Describe the methods used to account for bad debts.
4. Compute the maturity date of and interest on notes receivable.
5. Describe the entries to record the disposition of notes receivable.
6. Explain the statement presentation of receivables.
7. Describe the principles of sound accounts receivable management.
8. Identify ratios to analyze a company's receivables.
9. Describe methods to accelerate the receipt of cash from receivables.

How Do You Spell Relief?

Fred Tarter believes that in every problem lies an opportunity—and sometimes that opportunity can mean a big profit. For example, today fewer people pay cash for their prescriptions; instead, pharmacies bill a customer's health plan for some or all of the prescription's cost. Consequently pharmacies must spend a lot of time and energy collecting cash from these health plans. This procedure is a headache for pharmacies because there are 4,500 different health plans in the United States. Also, it often leaves pharmacies with too many receivables and not enough cash. Their suppliers want to be paid within 15 days, but their receivables are outstanding for 30 and often 60 days.

Enter Fred Tarter. Having recently sold his advertising agency, Fred had some spare time and money on his hands. While reading a pharmacy trade journal, he learned of the pharmacies' headache. To Fred this problem spelled opportunity.

Fred found out that 56,000 pharmacies are connected by computer to a claims processing business. Fred's idea was this: Taking advantage of this network, he would purchase pharmacy receivables, charging a fee of 1.4% to 2%. Pharmacies would be willing to pay this because they would get their cash sooner and save the headache of having to collect the accounts. Fred would then use these receivables as backing to raise new money so he could buy more receivables.

Based on this idea, Fred started a company called the Pharmacy Fund in 1993. By 1996 over 500 small pharmacies were selling their receivables to his company. The Pharmacy Fund establishes a computer link with each pharmacy, which allows it to buy the receivables at the end of each day and credit the pharmacy's account immediately. Thus, rather than having to wait weeks to receive its cash from insurance companies, the pharmacy gets its cash the same day as the sale. The Pharmacy Fund's customers say that this has solved their cash-flow problems, reduced their overhead costs, and allowed them to automate their billing and record-keeping. Using these

338

receivables as backing, the Pharmacy Fund raised additional financing of $80 million in 1996 and an even larger amount in 1997. This financing will allow the Pharmacy Fund to buy the receivables of up to 5,000 additional pharmacies.

Other investors are interested in getting in on this action. Nursing home receivables or home health care receivables have been mentioned as other possibilities. Fred Tarter has already identified his next opportunity—a target some would say is a "natural" for him: dentistry receivables. (Get it? Tarter—dentistry. We'll stick to accounting jokes from now on!)

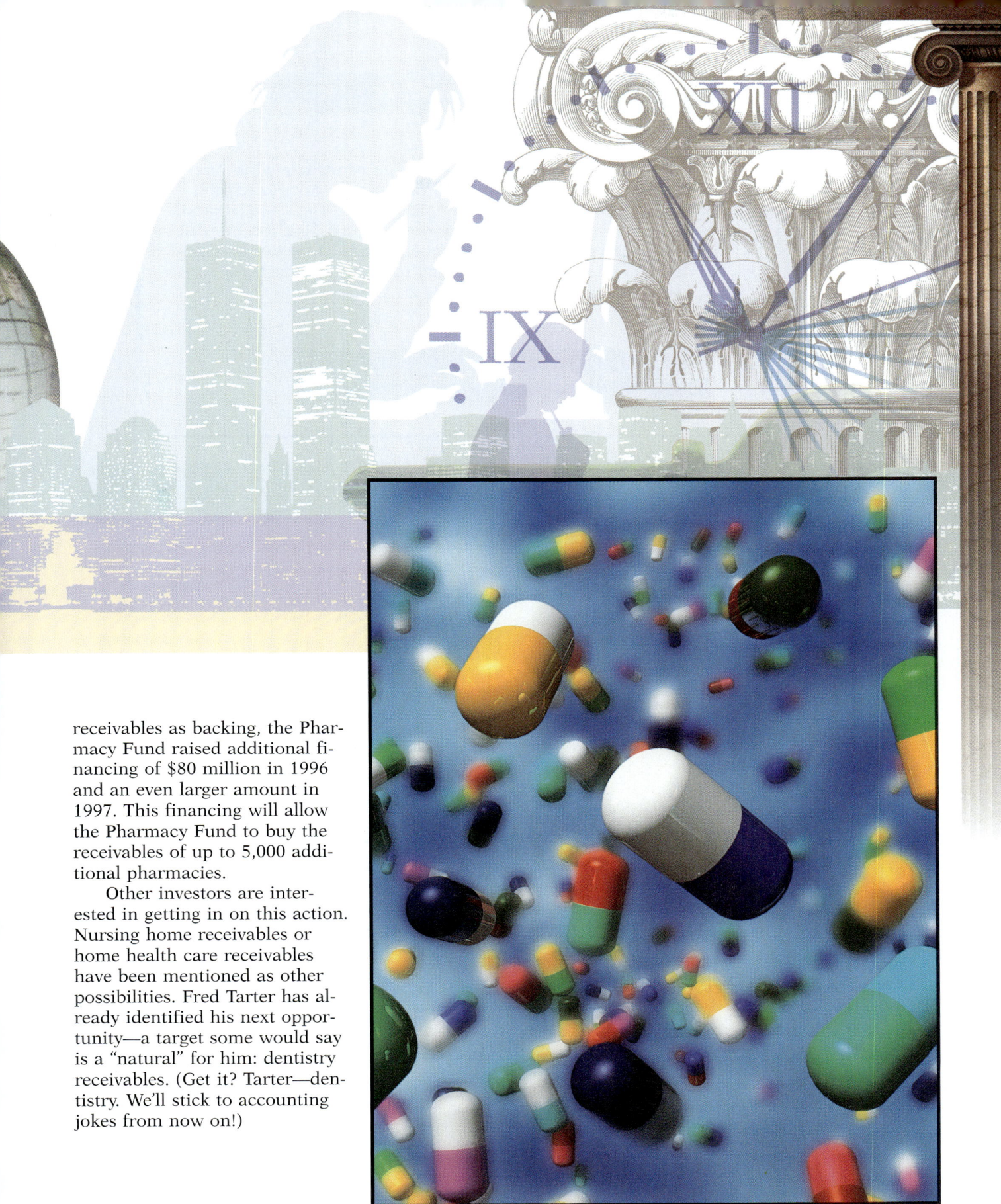

PREVIEW OF CHAPTER 8

In this chapter we discuss some of the decisions related to reporting and analyzing receivables. As indicated in the opening story, receivables are a significant asset on the books of many pharmacies. The same situation also occurs for many other companies, because a significant portion of sales are done on credit in the United States. As a consequence, companies must pay close attention to their receivables balances and manage them carefully.

The organization and content of the chapter are as follows:

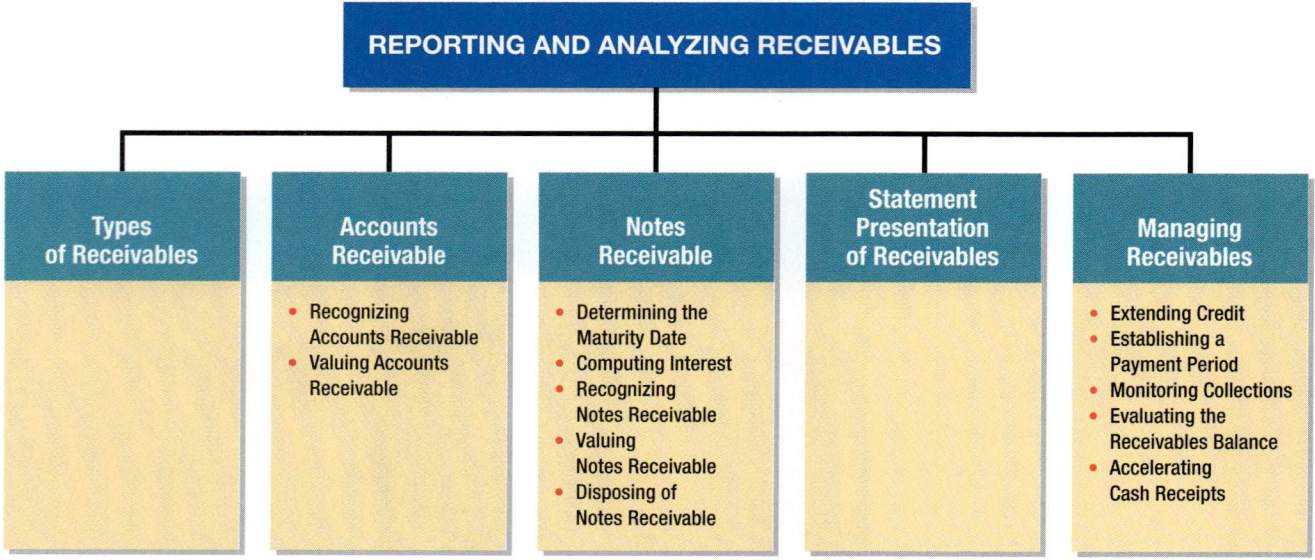

TYPES OF RECEIVABLES

STUDY OBJECTIVE 1
Identify the different types of receivables.

The term **receivables** refers to amounts due from individuals and companies. Receivables are claims that are expected to be collected in cash. The management of receivables is a very important activity for any company that sells goods on credit. Receivables are important because they represent one of a company's most liquid assets. For many companies receivables are also one of the largest assets. For example, Illustration 8-1 lists receivables as a percentage of total assets for five well-known companies in a recent year.

Illustration 8-1 Receivables as a percentage of assets

Company	Receivables as a Percentage of Total Assets
Ford Motor Company	63%
General Mills	11
Minnesota Mining and Manufacturing Company (3M)	17
Scotts Co.	22
Intel Corporation	18

The relative significance of a company's receivables as a percentage of its assets differs depending on its industry, the time of year, whether it extends long-term financing, and its credit policies. To reflect important differences among receivables, they are frequently classified as (1) accounts, (2) notes, and (3) other.

Accounts receivable are amounts owed by customers on account. They result from the sale of goods and services. These receivables generally are expected to be collected within 30 to 60 days. They are usually the most significant type of claim held by a company.

Notes receivable represent claims for which formal instruments of credit are issued as evidence of the debt. The credit instrument normally requires the debtor to pay interest and extends for time periods of 60–90 days or longer. Notes and accounts receivable that result from sales transactions are often called **trade receivables.**

Other receivables include nontrade receivables such as interest receivable, loans to company officers, advances to employees, and income taxes refundable. These are unusual; therefore, they are generally classified and reported as separate items in the balance sheet.

ACCOUNTS RECEIVABLE

Two accounting problems associated with accounts receivable are:

1. Recognizing accounts receivable.
2. Valuing accounts receivable.

A third issue, accelerating cash receipts from receivables, is discussed later in the chapter.

RECOGNIZING ACCOUNTS RECEIVABLE

Initial recognition of accounts receivable is relatively straightforward. For a service organization, a receivable is recorded when service is provided on account. For a merchandiser, accounts receivable are recorded at the point of sale of merchandise on account. When a merchandiser sells goods, both Accounts Receivable and Sales are increased.

Receivables also are reduced as a result of sales discounts and sales returns. The seller may offer terms that encourage early payment by providing a discount. For example, terms of 2/10, n/30 provide the buyer with a 2% discount if paid within 10 days. If the buyer chooses to pay within the discount period, the seller's accounts receivable is reduced. Also, the buyer might find some of the goods unacceptable and choose to return the unwanted goods. For example, if merchandise with a selling price of $100 is returned, the seller reduces Accounts Receivable by $100 upon receipt of the returned merchandise.

STUDY OBJECTIVE 2
Explain how accounts receivable are recognized in the accounts.

VALUING ACCOUNTS RECEIVABLE

Once receivables are recorded in the accounts, the next question is: How should receivables be reported in the financial statements? They are reported on the balance sheet as an asset, but determining the **amount** to report is sometimes difficult because some receivables will become uncollectible. To ensure that receivables are not overstated on the balance sheet, they are stated at their cash (net) realizable value. **Cash (net) realizable value** is the net amount expected to be received in cash; it excludes amounts that the company estimates it will not collect. Receivables are therefore reduced by estimated uncollectible receivables on the balance sheet.

STUDY OBJECTIVE 3
Describe the methods used to account for bad debts.

The income statement is also affected by the amount of uncollectibles. An expense for estimated uncollectibles is recorded to make certain that expenses are not understated and are matched with related sales revenue. This expense is reported on the income statement as **bad debts expense.**

Although each customer must satisfy the credit requirements of the seller before the credit sale is approved, inevitably some accounts receivable become uncollectible. For example, one of your customers may not be able to pay because it experienced a decline in sales due to a downturn in the economy. Similarly, individuals may be laid off from their jobs or be faced with unexpected hospital bills. Credit losses are debited to Bad Debts Expense (or Uncollectible Accounts Expense). Such losses are considered a normal and necessary risk of doing business on a credit basis.

Two methods are used in accounting for uncollectible accounts: (1) the allowance method and (2) the direct write-off method. Each of these methods is explained in the following sections.

Allowance Method for Uncollectible Accounts

Helpful Hint In this context, *material* means significant or important.

The **allowance method** is required for financial reporting purposes when bad debts are material in amount. It has three essential features:

1. Uncollectible accounts receivable are **estimated** and **matched against sales** in the same accounting period in which the sales occurred.
2. Estimated uncollectibles are recorded as an increase (a debit) to Bad Debts Expense and an increase (a credit) to Allowance for Doubtful Accounts (a contra asset account) through an adjusting entry at the end of each period.
3. Actual uncollectibles are debited to Allowance for Doubtful Accounts and credited to Accounts Receivable at the time the specific account is written off as uncollectible.

Recording Estimated Uncollectibles. To illustrate the allowance method, assume that Hampson Furniture has credit sales of $1,200,000 in 1998, of which $200,000 remains uncollected at December 31. The credit manager estimates that $12,000 of these sales will prove uncollectible. The adjusting entry to record the estimated uncollectibles is:

Dec. 31	Bad Debts Expense	12,000	
	Allowance for Doubtful Accounts		12,000
	(To record estimate of uncollectible accounts)		

Bad Debts Expense is reported in the income statement as an operating expense (usually as a selling expense). Thus, the estimated uncollectibles are matched with sales in 1998 because the expense is recorded in the same year the sales are made.

Allowance for Doubtful Accounts shows the estimated amount of claims on customers that are expected to become uncollectible in the future. A contra account is used instead of a direct credit to Accounts Receivable because we do not know which customers will not pay. The credit balance in the allowance account will absorb the specific write-offs when they occur. It is deducted from Accounts Receivable in the current asset section of the balance sheet as shown in Illustration 8-2.

The amount of $188,000 in Illustration 8-2 represents the expected **cash realizable value** of the accounts receivable at the statement date. **Allowance for Doubtful Accounts is not closed at the end of the fiscal year.**

Illustration 8-2 Presentation of allowance for doubtful accounts

HAMPSON FURNITURE Balance Sheet (partial)		
Current assets		
Cash		$ 14,800
Accounts receivable	$200,000	
Less: Allowance for doubtful accounts	12,000	188,000
Merchandise inventory		310,000
Prepaid expense		25,000
Total current assets		$537,800

International Note
The Finance Ministry in Japan recently noted that financial institutions should make better disclosure of bad loans. This disclosure would help depositors pick healthy banks.

Recording the Write-off of an Uncollectible Account. Companies use various methods of collecting past-due accounts, such as letters, calls, and legal action. When all means of collecting a past-due account have been exhausted and collection appears impossible, the account should be written off. To prevent premature or unauthorized write-offs, each write-off should be formally approved in writing by authorized management personnel. To maintain good internal control, authorization to write off accounts should not be given to someone who also has daily responsibilities related to cash or receivables.

To illustrate a receivables write-off, assume that the vice-president of finance of Hampson Furniture authorizes a write-off of the $500 balance owed by R. A. Ware on March 1, 1999. The entry to record the write-off is:

Mar. 1	Allowance for Doubtful Accounts	500	
	Accounts Receivable—R. A. Ware		500
	(Write-off of R. A. Ware account)		

Bad Debts Expense is not increased when the write-off occurs. **Under the allowance method, every bad debt write-off is debited to the allowance account and not to Bad Debts Expense.** A debit to Bad Debts Expense would be incorrect because the expense has already been recognized, when the adjusting entry was made for estimated bad debts. Instead, the entry to record the write-off of an uncollectible account reduces both Accounts Receivable and the Allowance for Doubtful Accounts. After posting, the general ledger accounts will appear as in Illustration 8-3.

Illustration 8-3 General ledger balances after write-off

Accounts Receivable				Allowance for Doubtful Accounts			
Jan. 1 Bal.	200,000	Mar. 1	**500**	Mar. 1	**500**	Jan. 1 Bal.	12,000
Mar. 1 Bal.	199,500					Mar. 1	11,500

A write-off affects only balance sheet accounts. Cash realizable value in the balance sheet, therefore, remains the same, as shown in Illustration 8-4.

Illustration 8-4 Cash realizable value comparison

	Before Write-off	After Write-off
Accounts receivable	$ 200,000	$ 199,500
Allowance for doubtful accounts	12,000	11,500
Cash realizable value	**$188,000**	**$188,000**

BUSINESS INSIGHT
International Perspective

Many investors are eager to buy shares of Chinese companies. Analysts advise caution, however, because tight credit in China is making it hard for many companies to collect their receivables. Thus, a significant number of transactions booked as sales will never be collected. Under Chinese accounting practices, bad debt write-offs are rare, and so some companies have 2-year-old receivables on their books. Even those Chinese companies that follow international standards are not required to write off an account until it is 1 year old.

Recovery of an Uncollectible Account. Occasionally, a company collects from a customer after the account has been written off as uncollectible. Two entries are required to record the recovery of a bad debt: (1) The entry made in writing off the account is reversed to reinstate the customer's account. (2) The collection is journalized in the usual manner. To illustrate, assume that on July 1, R. A. Ware pays the $500 amount that had been written off on March 1. These are the entries:

	(1)		
July 1	Accounts Receivable—R. A. Ware	500	
	Allowance for Doubtful Accounts		500
	(To reverse write-off of R. A. Ware account)		
	(2)		
1	Cash	500	
	Accounts Receivable—R. A. Ware		500
	(To record collection from R. A. Ware)		

Helpful Hint Like the write-off, a recovery does not involve the income statement.

Note that the recovery of a bad debt, like the write-off of a bad debt, affects only balance sheet accounts. The net effect of the two entries above is an increase in Cash and an increase in Allowance for Doubtful Accounts for $500. Accounts Receivable and the Allowance for Doubtful Accounts both increase in entry (1) for two reasons: First, the company made an error in judgment when it wrote off the account receivable. Second, R. A. Ware did pay, and therefore the Accounts Receivable account should show this collection for possible future credit purposes.

Estimating the Allowance. For Hampson Furniture in Illustration 8-2, the amount of the expected uncollectibles was given. However, in "real life," companies must estimate that amount if they use the allowance method. Frequently the allowance is estimated as a percentage of the outstanding receivables.

Under the **percentage of receivables basis,** management establishes a percentage relationship between the amount of receivables and expected losses from uncollectible accounts. A schedule (often called an **aging schedule**) is prepared in which customer balances are classified by the length of time they have been unpaid. Because of its emphasis on time, the analysis is often called **aging the accounts receivable.**

After the accounts are arranged by age, the expected bad debt losses are determined by applying percentages based on past experience to the totals of each category. The longer a receivable is past due, the less likely it is to be collected.

As a result, the estimated percentage of uncollectible debts increases as the number of days past due increases. An aging schedule for Dart Company is shown in Illustration 8-5. Note the increasing uncollectible percentages from 2% to 40%.

Illustration 8-5 Aging schedule

Customer	Total	Not Yet Due	1–30	31–60	61–90	Over 90
T. E. Adert	$ 600		$ 300		$ 200	$ 100
R. C. Bortz	300	$ 300				
B. A. Carl	450		200	$ 250		
O. L. Diker	700	500			200	
T. O. Ebbet	600			300		300
Others	36,950	26,200	5,200	2,450	1,600	1,500
	$39,600	$27,000	$5,700	$3,000	$2,000	$1,900
Estimated percentage uncollectible		2%	4%	10%	20%	40%
Total estimated bad debts	$ 2,228	$ 540	$ 228	$ 300	$ 400	$ 760

Total estimated bad debts for Dart Company ($2,228) represent the existing customer claims expected to become uncollectible in the future. Thus, this amount represents the **required balance** in Allowance for Doubtful Accounts at the balance sheet date. Accordingly, **the amount of the bad debt adjusting entry is the difference between the required balance and the existing balance in the allowance account.** If the trial balance shows Allowance for Doubtful Accounts with a credit balance of $528, then an adjusting entry for $1,700 ($2,228 − $528) is necessary:

Dec. 31	Bad Debts Expense	1,700	
	Allowance for Doubtful Accounts		1,700
	(To adjust allowance account to total estimated uncollectibles)		

After the adjusting entry is posted, the accounts of Dart Company will appear as in Illustration 8-6.

Illustration 8-6 Bad debt accounts after posting

Bad Debts Expense		Allowance for Doubtful Accounts	
Dec. 31 Adj. 1,700			Bal. 528
			Dec. 31 Adj. 1,700
			Bal. 2,228

An important aspect of accounts receivable management is simply maintaining a close watch. Studies have shown that accounts more than 60 days past due lose approximately 50% of their value if no payment activity occurs within the next 30 days. For each additional 30 days that pass, the collectible value halves once again.

Occasionally the allowance account will have a **debit balance** prior to adjustment because write-offs during the year have **exceeded** previous provisions for bad debts. In such a case, **the debit balance is added to the required balance** when the adjusting entry is made. Thus, if there had been a $500 debit balance in the allowance account before adjustment, the adjusting entry would have been for $2,728 ($2,228 + $500) to arrive at a credit balance of $2,228.

The percentage of receivables basis provides an estimate of the cash realizable value of the receivables. It also provides a reasonable matching of expense to revenue.

DECISION TOOLKIT

Decision Checkpoints	Info Needed for Decision	Tool to Use for Decision	How to Evaluate Results
Is the amount of past due accounts increasing? Which accounts require management's attention?	List of outstanding receivables and their due dates	Prepare an aging schedule showing the receivables in various stages: outstanding 0–30 days, 30–60 days, 60–90 days, and over 90 days.	Accounts in the older categories require follow-up: letters, phone calls, and possible renegotiation of terms.

Direct Write-off Method for Uncollectible Accounts

Under the **direct write-off method,** bad debt losses are not estimated, and no allowance account is used. When a particular account is determined to be uncollectible, the loss is charged to Bad Debts Expense. Assume, for example, that Warden Co. writes off M. E. Doran's $200 balance as uncollectible on December 12. The entry is:

Dec. 12	Bad Debts Expense	200	
	Accounts Receivable—M. E. Doran		200
	(To record write-off of M. E. Doran		
	account)		

When this method is used, bad debts expense will show only actual losses from uncollectibles. Accounts receivable will be reported at its gross amount.

Under the direct write-off method, bad debts expense is often recorded in a period different from the period in which the revenue was recorded. Thus, no attempt is made to match bad debts expense to sales revenues in the income statement or to show the cash realizable value of the accounts receivable in the balance sheet. **Consequently, unless bad debt losses are insignificant, the direct write-off method is not acceptable for financial reporting purposes.**

BEFORE YOU GO ON . . .

● **Review It**

1. How are accounts receivable recognized in the accounts?
2. To maintain adequate internal controls over receivables, who should authorize receivables write-offs?
3. What are the essential features of the allowance method?
4. What is the primary criticism of the direct write-off method?

● **Do It**

Brule Corporation has been in business for 5 years. The ledger at the end of the current year shows: Accounts Receivable $30,000; Sales $180,000; and Allowance for Doubtful Accounts with a debit balance of $2,000. Bad debts are estimated to be 10% of accounts receivable. Prepare the entry necessary to adjust the Allowance for Doubtful Accounts.

Reasoning: Receivables are to be reported at their cash (net) realizable value—that is, the amount the company expects to collect in cash. This amount excludes any amount the company does not expect it will collect. The estimated uncollectible amount should be recorded in an allowance account.

Solution: The following entry should be made to bring the balance in the Allowance for Doubtful Accounts up to a balance of $3,000 (.1 × $30,000):

	Bad Debts Expense	5,000	
	Allowance for Doubtful Accounts		5,000
	(To record estimate of		
	uncollectible accounts)		

Helpful Hint The debit to Bad Debts Expense is calculated as follows:

Allowance for Doubtful Accounts

2,000	5,000
	3,000

NOTES RECEIVABLE

Credit may also be granted in exchange for a formal credit instrument known as a promissory note. A **promissory note** is a written promise to pay a specified amount of money on demand or at a definite time. Promissory notes may be used (1) when individuals and companies lend or borrow money, (2) when the amount of the transaction and the credit period exceed normal limits, and (3) in settlement of accounts receivable.

In a promissory note, the party making the promise to pay is called the **maker;** the party to whom payment is to be made is called the **payee.** The payee may be specifically identified by name or may be designated simply as the bearer of the note.

In the note shown in Illustration 8-7, Brent Company is the maker and Wilma Company is the payee. To the Wilma Company, the promissory note is a note receivable; to the Brent Company, the note is a note payable.

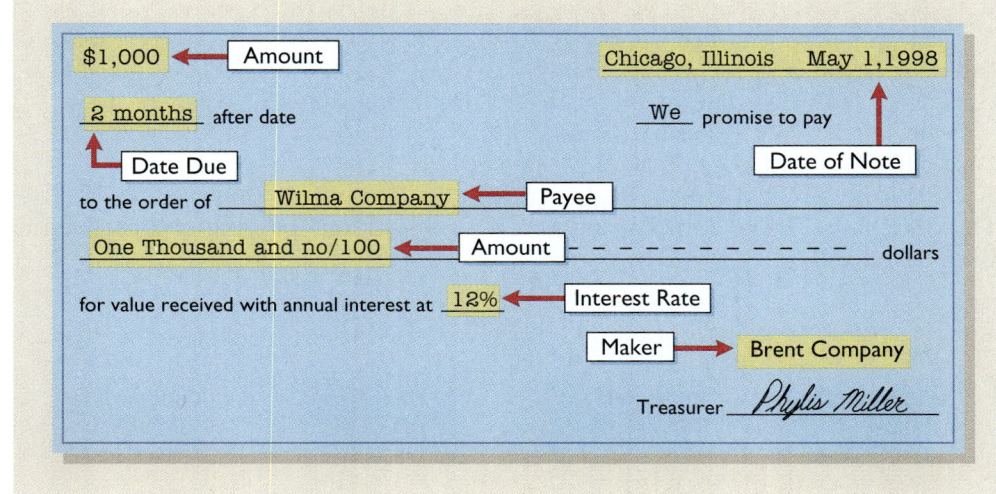

Illustration 8-7
Promissory note

Helpful Hint Who are the two key parties to a note, and what entry does each party make when the note is issued?
Answer:
1. The maker, Brent Company, credits Notes Payable.
2. The payee, Wilma Company, debits Notes Receivable.

Notes receivable give the holder a stronger legal claim to assets than accounts receivable. Like accounts receivable, notes receivable can be readily sold to another party. Promissory notes are negotiable instruments (as are checks), which means that, when sold, they can be transferred to another party by endorsement.

Notes receivable are frequently accepted from customers who need to extend the payment of an outstanding account receivable and are often required from high-risk customers. In some industries (e.g., the pleasure and sport boat industry) all credit sales are supported by notes. The majority of notes, however, originate from lending transactions. There are three basic issues in accounting for notes receivable:

1. Recognizing notes receivable.
2. Valuing notes receivable.
3. Disposing of notes receivable.

We will look at each of these issues, but first we need to consider two issues that did not apply to accounts receivable: determining the maturity date and computing interest.

DETERMINING THE MATURITY DATE

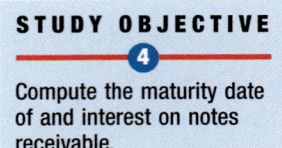

STUDY OBJECTIVE 4
Compute the maturity date of and interest on notes receivable.

When the life of a note is expressed in terms of months, the due date is found by counting the months from the date of issue. For example, the maturity date of a 3-month note dated May 1 is August 1. A note drawn on the last day of a month matures on the last day of a subsequent month; that is, a July 31 note due in 2 months matures on September 30. When the due date is stated in terms of days, it is necessary to count the exact number of days to determine the maturity date. In counting, **the date the note is issued is omitted but the due date is included.** For example, the maturity date of a 60-day note dated July 17 is September 15, computed as in Illustration 8-8.

Illustration 8-8 Computation of maturity date

Term of note		60
July (31 − 17)	14	
August	31	45
Maturity date, September		**15**

The due date (maturity date) of a promissory note may be stated in one of three ways: on a specific date ("July 23, 1998"), at the end of a stated period ("one year from the date of the note"), or on demand.

COMPUTING INTEREST

The basic formula for computing interest on an interest-bearing note is given in Illustration 8-9.

Illustration 8-9 Formula for computing interest

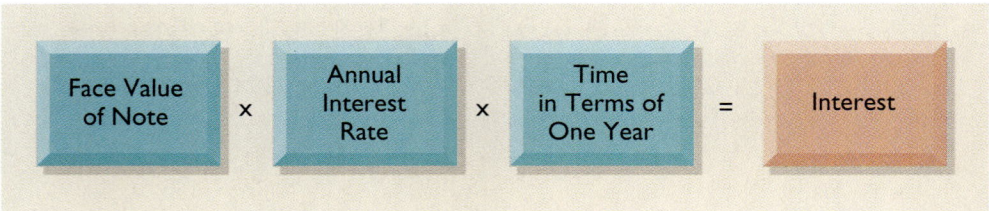

The interest rate specified on the note is an **annual** rate of interest. The time factor in the computation expresses the fraction of a year that the note is outstanding. When the maturity date is stated in days, the time factor is frequently the number of days divided by 360. When the due date is stated in months, the time factor is the number of months divided by 12. The computation of interest is shown in Illustration 8-10.

Terms of Note	Interest Computation
	Face × Rate × Time = Interest
$ 730, 18%, 120 days	$ 730 × 18% × 120/360 = $ 43.80
$1,000, 15%, 6 months	$1,000 × 15% × 6/12 = $ 75.00
$2,000, 12%, 1 year	$2,000 × 12% × 1/1 = $240.00

Illustration 8-10
Computation of interest

There are different ways to calculate interest. For example, the computation in Illustration 8-10 assumed 360 days for the year. Many financial institutions use 365 days to compute interest. (For homework problems, assume 360 days.)

RECOGNIZING NOTES RECEIVABLE

To illustrate the basic entry for notes receivable, we will use Brent Company's $1,000, 2-month, 12% promissory note dated May 1. Assuming that the note was written to settle an open account, we record this entry for the receipt of the note by Wilma Company:

May 1	Notes Receivable	1,000	
	Accounts Receivable—Brent Company		1,000
	(To record acceptance of Brent Company note)		

The note receivable is recorded at its **face value,** the value shown on the face of the note. No interest revenue is reported when the note is accepted because the revenue recognition principle does not recognize revenue until earned. Interest is earned (accrued) as time passes.

If a note is exchanged for cash, the entry is a debit to Notes Receivable and a credit to Cash in the amount of the loan.

VALUING NOTES RECEIVABLE

Like accounts receivable, short-term notes receivable are reported at their **cash (net) realizable value.** The notes receivable allowance account is Allowance for Doubtful Accounts. Valuing short-term notes receivable is the same as valuing accounts receivable. The computations and estimations involved in determining cash realizable value and in recording the proper amount of bad debts expense and related allowance are similar.

Long-term notes receivable, however, pose additional estimation problems. As an example, we need only look at the problems a number of large U.S. banks are having in collecting their receivables. Loans to less-developed countries are particularly worrisome. Developing countries need loans for development but often find repayment difficult. U.S. loans (notes) to less-developed countries at one time totaled approximately $135 billion. In Brazil alone, Citibank at one time had loans equivalent to 80% of its stockholders' equity; Chemical Bank had 77% of its equity lent out in Mexico. Determining the proper allowance is understandably difficult for these types of long-term receivables.

DISPOSING OF NOTES RECEIVABLE

Notes may be held to their maturity date, at which time the face value plus accrued interest is due. In some situations, the maker of the note defaults and appropriate adjustment must be made. In other situations, similar to accounts receivable, the holder of the note speeds up the conversion to cash by selling the receivables. The entries for honoring and dishonoring notes are illustrated next.

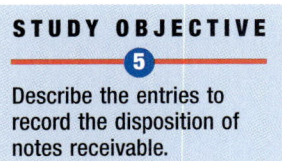

STUDY OBJECTIVE 5
Describe the entries to record the disposition of notes receivable.

Honor of Notes Receivable

A note is **honored** when it is paid in full at its maturity date. For each interest-bearing note, the amount due at maturity is the face value of the note plus interest for the length of time specified on the note.

To illustrate, assume that Wolder Co. lends Higley Inc. $10,000 on June 1, accepting a 4-month, 9% interest note. In this situation, interest is $300 ($10,000 × 9% × $\frac{4}{12}$); the amount due, the maturity value, is $10,300. To obtain payment, Wolder (the payee) must present the note either to Higley Inc. (the maker) or to the maker's agent, such as a bank. If Wolder presents the note to Higley Inc. on October 1, the maturity date, the entry by Wolder to record the collection is:

Helpful Hint How many days of interest should be accrued at September 30 for a 90-day note issued on August 16? *Answer:* 45 days (15 days in August plus 30 days in September).

Oct. 1	Cash	10,300	
	Notes Receivable		10,000
	Interest Revenue		300
	(To record collection of Higley Inc. note and interest)		

If Wolder Co. prepares financial statements as of September 30, it is necessary to accrue interest. In this case, the adjusting entry by Wolder is for 4 months, or $300, as shown below:

Sept. 30	Interest Receivable	300	
	Interest Revenue		300
	(To accrue 4 months' interest on Higley note)		

When interest has been accrued, it is necessary to credit Interest Receivable at maturity. The entry by Wolder to record the honoring of the Higley note on October 1 is:

Oct. 1	Cash	10,300	
	Notes Receivable		10,000
	Interest Receivable		300
	(To record collection of Higley Inc. note and interest)		

In this case, Interest Receivable is credited because the receivable was established in the adjusting entry.

BUSINESS INSIGHT
International Perspective

At one time, the debt owed by various governments to banks worldwide exceeded $1.3 trillion. (A trillion is a lot of money—enough to give every man, woman, and child in the world approximately $250 each.) Why was such a huge volume of loans made in the first place? The reasons are numerous, but the three major ones are: (1) the goal to provide stability to these governments and thereby increase trade, (2) the belief that governments would never default on payment, and (3) the desire by banks to increase their income by lending to various countries. Yet many countries are finding it difficult to repay their loans, and the long-term success of the lending banks will depend partly on the ability to collect their notes receivable. Various plans are being implemented to solve the international debt problem. These plans range from reducing or forgiving the debt to restructuring loans and encouraging even more lending.

Dishonor of Notes Receivable

A **dishonored note** is a note that is not paid in full at maturity. A dishonored note receivable is no longer negotiable; however, the payee still has a claim against the maker of the note. Therefore, the Notes Receivable account is usually transferred to an Account Receivable.

To illustrate, assume that Higley Inc. on October 1 indicates that it cannot pay at the present time. The entry to record the dishonor of the note depends on whether eventual collection is expected. If Wolder Co. expects eventual collection, the amount due (face value and interest) on the note is recorded as an increase (a debit) to Accounts Receivable. Wolder Co. would make the following entry at the time the note is dishonored (assuming no previous accrual of interest):

Oct. 1	Accounts Receivable	10,300	
	Notes Receivable		10,000
	Interest Revenue		300
	(To record the dishonor of the note)		

If there is no hope of collection, the face value of the note should be written off by decreasing (debiting) the Allowance for Doubtful Accounts. No interest revenue would be recorded because collection will not occur.

BEFORE YOU GO ON . . .

● **Review It**

1. What is the basic formula for computing interest?
2. At what value are notes receivable reported on the balance sheet?
3. Explain the difference between honoring and dishonoring a note receivable.

● **Do It**

Gambit Stores accepts from Leonard Co. a $3,400, 90-day, 12% note dated May 10 in settlement of Leonard's overdue open account. What is the maturity date of the note? What entry is made by Gambit at the maturity date, assuming Leonard pays the note and interest in full at that time?

Reasoning: When the due date is stated in terms of days, it is necessary to count the exact number of days to determine the maturity date. The date the note is issued is omitted from the count, but the due date is included. The entry to record interest at maturity in this solution assumes that no interest is previously accrued on this note.

Solution: The maturity date is August 8, computed as follows:

Term of note		90 days
May (31 − 10)	21	
June	30	
July	31	82
Maturity date, August		8

The interest payable at maturity date is $102, computed as follows:

$$\text{Face} \times \text{Rate} \times \text{Time} = \text{Interest}$$
$$\$3,400 \times 12\% \times \frac{90}{360} = \$102$$

352 CHAPTER 8 Reporting and Analyzing Receivables

This entry is recorded by Gambit Stores at the maturity date:

Cash	3,502	
Notes Receivable		3,400
Interest Revenue		102
(To record collection of Leonard note and interest)		

STATEMENT PRESENTATION OF RECEIVABLES

STUDY OBJECTIVE 6
Explain the statement presentation of receivables.

Each of the major types of receivables should be identified in the balance sheet or in the notes to the financial statements. Short-term receivables are reported in the current asset section of the balance sheet below temporary investments. Temporary investments appear before short-term receivables because these investments are nearer to cash. Both the gross amount of receivables and the allowance for doubtful accounts should be reported. Illustration 8-11 shows the current asset presentation of receivables for CPC International Inc. Note that notes receivable are listed before accounts receivable because notes are more easily converted to cash.

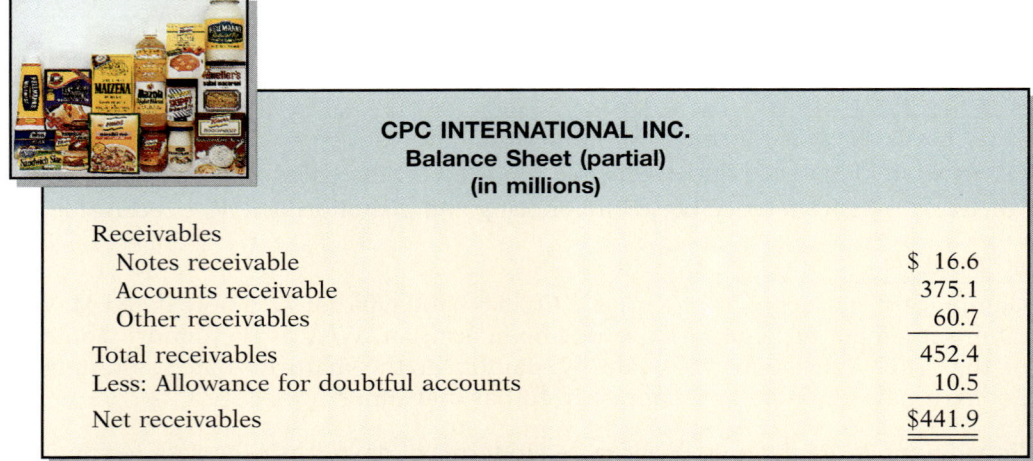

Illustration 8-11
Balance sheet presentation of receivables

In the income statement, Bad Debts Expense is reported as selling expenses in the operating expenses section. Interest Revenue is shown under Other Revenues and Gains in the nonoperating section of the income statement.

If a company has significant risk of uncollectible accounts or other problems with its receivables, it is required to discuss this possibility in the notes to the financial statements.

BEFORE YOU GO ON . . .

● **Review It**
1. Explain where receivables are reported on the balance sheet and in what order.
2. Where are Bad Debts Expense and Interest Revenue reported on the income statement?

Managing Receivables

Managing accounts receivable involves five steps:

1. Determine to whom to extend credit.
2. Establish a payment period.
3. Monitor collections.
4. Evaluate the receivables balance.
5. Accelerate cash receipts from receivables when necessary.

> **STUDY OBJECTIVE 7**
> Describe the principles of sound accounts receivable management.

EXTENDING CREDIT

A critical part of managing receivables is determining who should be extended credit and who should not. Many companies increase sales by being generous with their credit policy, but they may end up extending credit to risky customers who do not pay. If the credit policy is too tight, you will lose sales; if it is too loose, you may sell to "deadbeats" who will pay either very late or not at all. One CEO noted that prior to getting his credit and collection department in order, his salespeople had 300 square feet of office space per person, while the people in credit and collections had six people crammed into a single 300-square-foot space. Although this arrangement boosted sales, it had very expensive consequences in bad debts expense.

Certain steps can be taken to help minimize losses as credit standards are relaxed. Risky customers might be required to provide letters of credit or bank guarantees. Then if the customer does not pay, the bank that provided the guarantee will. Particularly risky customers might be required to pay cash on delivery. In addition, you should ask potential customers for references from banks and suppliers to determine their payment history. It is important to check these references on potential new customers as well as periodically to check the financial health of continuing customers. Many resources are available for investigating customers. For example, *The Dun & Bradstreet Reference Book of American Business* lists millions of companies and provides credit ratings for many of them.

BUSINESS INSIGHT
Management Perspective

Give the man credit. Like most of us, John Galbreath receives piles of unsolicited, "preapproved" credit card applications in the mail. Galbreath doesn't just toss them out, though. In April he filled out a credit card application on which he stated he was 97 years old and had no income, no telephone, and no Social Security number. In a space inviting him to let the credit card company pay off his other credit card balances, Galbreath said he owed money to the Mafia.

Back came a credit card and a letter welcoming John to the fold with a $1,500 credit limit. Galbreath had requested the card under a false name, John C. Reath, an alias under which he had received two other credit cards—earning exemplary credit. John C. Reath might be a bit "long in the tooth," but it seems he paid his bills on time.

Source: "Forbes Informer," edited by Kate Bohner Lewis, *Forbes,* August 14, 1995, p. 19. Reprinted by permission of FORBES Magazine © Forbes Inc., 1995.

ESTABLISHING A PAYMENT PERIOD

Companies that extend credit should determine a required payment period and communicate that policy to their customers. It is important to make sure that your company's payment period is consistent with that of your competitors. For example, if you decide to require payment within 15 days, but your competitors require payment within 45 days, you may lose sales to your competitor. However, as noted in Chapter 5, you might allow up to 45 days to pay but offer a sales discount for people paying within 15 days to match competitors' terms but encourage prompt payment of accounts.

MONITORING COLLECTIONS

One initial step that can be taken to monitor receivables is to calculate a company's **credit risk ratio,** which is found by dividing the Allowance for Doubtful Accounts by Accounts Receivable, as shown in Illustration 8-12:

Illustration 8-12 Credit risk ratio

$$\text{CREDIT RISK RATIO} = \frac{\text{ALLOWANCE FOR DOUBTFUL ACCOUNTS}}{\text{ACCOUNTS RECEIVABLE}}$$

Changes in this ratio over time may suggest that a company's overall credit risk is increasing or decreasing, and differences across companies may suggest differences in each company's overall credit risk.

The credit risk ratio for Intel Corporation and comparative industry data are shown in Illustration 8-13:

Illustration 8-13 Credit risk ratio comparison

($ in millions)	1995	1994
Intel Corporation	$\frac{\$57}{\$3{,}173} = 1.79\%$	$\frac{\$32}{\$2{,}010} = 1.59\%$
Industry average	2.93%	3.37%

Intel's credit risk ratio was 1.79% in 1995 and 1.59% in 1994. Intel's ratios compared favorably with the industry averages of 2.93% for 1995 and 3.37% for 1994.

Preparation of the accounts receivable aging schedule was discussed on page 345. An accounts receivable aging schedule should be prepared at least monthly. In addition to estimating the allowance for bad debts, the aging schedule has other uses to management. It aids estimation of the timing of future cash inflows, which is very important to the treasurer's efforts to prepare a cash budget. It provides information about the overall collection experience of the company and identifies problem accounts. Problem accounts need to be pursued with phone calls, letters, and occasionally legal action. Sometimes special arrangements must be made with problem accounts. For example, it was recently reported that Intel Corporation (a major manufacturer of computer chips) required that Packard Bell (one of the largest U.S. sellers of personal computers) give it an interest-bearing note receivable in exchange for its past-due account receivable owed to Intel. This was cause for concern within the investment community, first because it suggested that Packard Bell was in trouble, and second because of the impact on Intel's accounts receivable, since Packard Bell is one of its largest customers.

BUSINESS INSIGHT
Investor Perspective

Changes in bad debts expense can be big news for investors. When Bank of New York recently announced a $350 million increase in its allowance for bad debts, the stock market reacted by sending the bank's stock price down by nearly 5%. Small investors were very angry because the news was first reported to a group of 90 large investors in a conference call before the market closed for the day, and then it was reported in a press release to the general public after the market closed. Share prices of many other large banks also declined that day because the market was anticipating that they too would soon announce increases in their allowance for bad debts.

Recently, four major banks had the following allowances for bad debts as a percentage of outstanding loans:

Citicorp	3.24%
Bank of New York	2.01%
Bank America	2.29%
Chase Manhattan	2.24%

DECISION TOOLKIT

Decision Checkpoints	Info Needed for Decision	Tool to Use for Decision	How to Evaluate Results
Is the company's credit risk increasing?	Allowance for doubtful accounts and accounts receivable	Credit risk ratio = Allowance for doubtful accounts / Accounts receivable	Increase in ratio may suggest increased credit risk, requiring evaluation of credit policies.

If a company has significant concentrations of credit risk, it is required to discuss this risk in the notes to its financial statements. A **concentration of credit risk** is a threat of nonpayment from a single customer or class of customers that could adversely affect the financial health of the company. An excerpt from the credit risk note from the 1995 annual report of Intel Corporation is shown in Illustration 8-14 (at the top of the next page). In addition to discussing Intel's credit exposure, including a reference to its granting of a loan to "one of the Company's five largest customers," the note provides a brief discussion of Intel's credit policy. The $400 million account receivable, converted to a note receivable, that was due from Packard Bell represented 13% of the December 30, 1995, receivables balance.

356 CHAPTER 8 Reporting and Analyzing Receivables

INTEL CORPORATION
Notes to the Financial Statements

Concentration of credit risk: During 1995, the Company experienced an increase in its concentration of credit risk due to increasing trade receivables from sales to manufacturers of microcomputer systems. The Company's five largest customers accounted for approximately 33% of net revenues for 1995. At December 30, 1995, these customers accounted for approximately 34% of net accounts receivable. A portion of the receivable balance from one of the Company's five largest customers has been converted into a loan. The total amount receivable from this customer was approximately $400 million at December 30, 1995.

The Company endeavors to keep pace with the evolving computer industry and has adopted credit policies and standards intended to accommodate industry growth and inherent risk. Management believes that credit risks are moderated by the diversity of its end customers and geographic sales areas. Intel performs ongoing credit evaluations of its customers' financial condition and requires collateral as deemed necessary.

Illustration 8-14 Note on concentration of credit risk

DECISION TOOLKIT

Decision Checkpoints	Info Needed for Decision	Tool to Use for Decision	How to Evaluate Results
Does the company have significant concentrations of credit risk?	Note to the financial statements on concentrations of credit risk	If risky credit customers are identified, the financial health of those customers should be evaluated to gain an independent assessment of the potential for a material credit loss.	If a material loss appears likely, the potential negative impact of that loss on the company should be carefully evaluated, along with the adequacy of the allowance for doubtful accounts.

EVALUATING THE RECEIVABLES BALANCE

STUDY OBJECTIVE 8

Identify ratios to analyze a company's receivables.

Investors and managers keep a watchful eye on the relationship among sales, accounts receivable, and cash collections. If sales increase, then accounts receivable are also expected to increase. But a disproportionate increase in accounts receivable might signal trouble. Perhaps the company increased its sales by loosening its credit policy, and these receivables may be difficult or impossible to collect. Such receivables are considered less liquid. Recall that liquidity is measured by how quickly certain assets can be converted to cash. The ratio used to assess the liquidity of the receivables is the **receivables turnover ratio.** This ratio measures the number of times, on average, receivables are collected during the period. The receivables turnover ratio is computed by dividing net credit sales (net sales less cash sales) by the average net receivables during the year. Unless seasonal factors are significant, **average** receivables outstanding can be computed from the beginning and ending balances of the net receivables.[1]

The receivables turnover ratio for Intel Corporation and comparative industry data are shown in Illustration 8-15.

---

[1] If seasonal factors are significant, the average receivables balance might be determined by using monthly amounts.

RECEIVABLES TURNOVER RATIO =	$\dfrac{\text{NET CREDIT SALES}}{\text{AVERAGE NET RECEIVABLES}}$	
($ in millions)	1995	1994
Intel Corporation	$\dfrac{\$16{,}202}{(\$3{,}116 + \$1{,}978)/2} = 6.36$ times	$\dfrac{\$11{,}521}{(\$1{,}978 + \$1{,}448)/2} = 6.73$ times
Industry average	6.33 times	6.28 times

Illustration 8-15 Receivables turnover ratio

This calculation assumes that all sales are credit sales and uses the ending balance of net receivables of $1,448 million from December 31, 1993. It also assumes sales and net accounts receivable data (in millions) as follows:

	1995	1994
Sales	$16,202	$11,521
Accounts receivable	3,116	1,978

Intel's receivables turnover ratio was 6.36 in 1995. This turnover compared favorably with the industry average of 6.33. The turnover ratio declined somewhat relative to the 1994 ratio of 6.73. This decline can be explained primarily by the large outstanding balance of the Packard Bell receivable that Intel continued to hold in its accounts receivable account. Without the $400 million Packard Bell balance, Intel's receivables turnover ratio would have been 6.9.

BUSINESS INSIGHT
Management Perspective

In some cases, receivables turnover may be misleading. Some companies, especially large retail chains, encourage credit and revolving charge sales, and they slow collections in order to earn a healthy return on the outstanding receivables in the form of interest at rates of 18% to 22%. This may explain why J. C. Penney's turnover is only 4.1 times. In general, however, the faster the turnover, the greater the reliance that can be placed on the current ratio for assessing liquidity.

A popular variant of the receivables turnover ratio is to convert it into an **average collection period** in terms of days. This is done by dividing the receivables turnover ratio into 365 days. For example, 365 days divided by Intel's 1995 receivables turnover of 6.36 times results in an average collection period of approximately 57.4 days. This means that Intel collects its receivables, on average, every 57 days, or approximately every 8 weeks. The average collection period is frequently used to assess the effectiveness of a company's credit and collection policies. The general rule is that the collection period should not greatly exceed the credit term period (i.e., the time allowed for payment).

DECISION TOOLKIT

Decision Checkpoints	Info Needed for Decision	Tool to Use for Decision	How to Evaluate Results
Are collections being made in a timely fashion?	Net credit sales and average receivables balance	Receivables turnover ratio = $\dfrac{\text{Net credit sales}}{\text{Average net receivables}}$ Average collection period = $\dfrac{365 \text{ days}}{\text{Receivables turnover ratio}}$	Average collection period should be consistent with corporate credit policy. An increase may suggest a decline in financial health of customers.

ACCELERATING CASH RECEIPTS

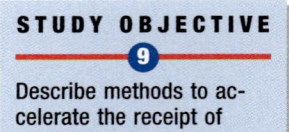

STUDY OBJECTIVE 9
Describe methods to accelerate the receipt of cash from receivables.

In the normal course of events, accounts receivable are collected in cash and removed from the books. However, as credit sales and receivables have grown in size and significance, the "normal course of events" has changed. Two common expressions apply to the collection of receivables: (1) Time is money—that is, waiting for the normal collection process costs money. (2) A bird in the hand is worth two in the bush—that is, getting the cash now is better than getting it later or not at all. Therefore, in order to accelerate the receipt of cash from receivables, companies frequently sell their receivables to another company for cash, thereby shortening the cash-to-cash operating cycle.

There are three reasons for the sale of receivables. The first is their size. In recent years, **for competitive reasons, sellers (retailers, wholesalers, and manufacturers) often have provided financing to purchasers of their goods.** For example, many major companies in the automobile, truck, industrial and farm equipment, computer, and appliance industries have created companies that accept responsibility for accounts receivable financing. General Motors has General Motors Acceptance Corp. (GMAC), Sears has Sears Roebuck Acceptance Corp. (SRAC), Ford has Ford Motor Credit Corp. (FMCC), and Chrysler has Chrysler Finance Corporation (CFC). These companies are referred to as **captive finance companies** because they are wholly owned by the company making the product. The purpose of captive financing companies is to encourage the sale of their product by assuring financing to buyers. However, the parent companies involved do not necessarily want to hold large amounts of receivables.

Second, **receivables may be sold because they may be the only reasonable source of cash.** When money is tight, companies may not be able to borrow money in the usual credit markets. If money is available, the cost of borrowing may be prohibitive.

A final reason for selling receivables is that **billing and collection are often time-consuming and costly.** As a result, it is often easier for a retailer to sell the receivable to another party that has expertise in billing and collection matters. Credit card companies such as MasterCard, VISA, American Express, and Diners Club specialize in billing and collecting accounts receivable.

Sale of Receivables to a Factor

A common way to accelerate receivables collection is a sale to a factor. A **factor** is a finance company or bank that buys receivables from businesses for a fee and then collects the payments directly from the customers. Factoring was traditionally associated with the textiles, apparel, footwear, furniture, and home furnishing industries. As you learned in the opening story, it has now spread to other types of businesses and is a multibillion dollar business. For example, Sears, Roebuck & Co. once sold $14.8 billion of customer accounts receivable. Similarly, Chemical Bank sold many of its receivables, transforming them into securities. Chemical packaged and sold $850 million of balances outstanding on its consumer credit cards, transforming them into two 2- to 3-year trusts.

BUSINESS INSIGHT
Management Perspective

"They're the devil in disguise," is how CEO Barry Weinstein describes factors. Unable to raise capital from bankers or outside investors, Weinstein turned to factoring receivables. The arrangement was pricey: The factor charged interest of 5% a month, to a maximum of 13% of the total invoice, on any uncollected invoices that were factored. The deal became an endless cycle. Soon Weinstein was factoring all new invoices to get the cash to pay the interest on the older factored invoices.

Source: Inc., July 1994, p. 97.

Factoring arrangements vary widely, but typically the factor charges a commission. It ranges from 1% to 3% of the amount of receivables purchased. To illustrate, assume that Hendredon Furniture factors $600,000 of receivables to Federal Factors, Inc. Federal Factors assesses a service charge of 2% of the amount of receivables sold. The following journal entry records the sale by Hendredon Furniture:

Cash	588,000	
Service Charge Expense (2% × $600,000)	12,000	
Accounts Receivable		600,000
(To record the sale of accounts receivable)		

If the company usually sells its receivables, the service charge expense incurred by Hendredon Furniture is recorded as selling expense. If receivables are sold infrequently, this amount may be reported under Other Expenses and Losses in the income statement.

National Credit Card Sales

Approximately 1 billion credit cards were estimated to be in use recently—more than three credit cards for every man, woman, and child in this country. A common type of credit card is a national credit card such as VISA, MasterCard, and American Express. Three parties are involved when national credit cards are used in making retail sales: (1) the credit card issuer, who is independent of the retailer, (2) the retailer, and (3) the customer. **A retailer's acceptance of a national credit card is another form of selling—(factoring)—the receivable by the retailer.**

The use of national credit cards translates to more sales with zero bad debts for the retailer. Both are powerful reasons for a retailer to accept such cards. The major advantages of national credit cards to the retailer are shown in Illustration 8-16 (page 360). In exchange for these advantages, the retailer pays the credit card issuer a fee of 2% to 6% of the invoice price for its services.

360 CHAPTER 8 Reporting and Analyzing Receivables

Illustration 8-16 Advantages of credit cards to the retailer

BUSINESS INSIGHT
Management Perspective

Interest rates on most credit cards are quite high, averaging approximately 18.8%. As a result, consumers are often looking for companies that charge lower rates. But be careful: Some companies offer lower interest rates but have eliminated the standard 25-day grace period before finance charges are incurred. Other companies encourage consumers to get more in debt by advertising that only a $1 minimum payment is due on a $1,000 account balance. They, of course, earn more interest! Chase Manhattan Corp. markets a credit card that allows cardholders to skip a payment twice a year. However, the outstanding balance continues to incur interest. Other credit card companies calculate finance charges initially on 2-month, rather than 1-month averages, a practice that often translates into higher interest charges. In short, read the fine print! Because of rising competition among banks to issue MasterCard and VISA credit cards, recent interest rates ranged from 9.5% with annual fees (of $18 to $35) to 21% with no annual fees.

Source: The Wall Street Journal, February 21, 1992, and *Fortune,* November 28, 1994.

VISA and MasterCard Sales. Sales resulting from the use of VISA and MasterCard are considered cash sales by the retailer. These cards are issued by banks. Upon receipt of credit card sales slips from a retailer, the bank immediately adds the amount to the seller's bank balance. These credit card sales slips are therefore recorded in the same manner as checks deposited from a cash sale. The banks that issue these cards generally charge a fee of 2% to 4% of the credit card sales slips for this service. To illustrate, Anita Ferreri purchases $1,000 of compact discs for her restaurant from Karen Kerr Music Co., and she charges this amount on her VISA First Bank Card. The service fee that First Bank charges Karen Kerr Music is 3%. The entry by Karen Kerr Music to record this transaction is:

Cash	970	
Service Charge Expense	30	
Sales		1,000
(To record VISA credit card sales)		

The basic principles of managing accounts receivable are summarized in Illustration 8-17.

Illustration 8-17 Managing receivables

BEFORE YOU GO ON . . .

● **Review It**

1. What is meant by a concentration of credit risk?
2. What is the interpretation of the receivables turnover ratio and the average collection period?

3. Why do companies sell their receivables?
4. For whom is the service charge on a credit card sale an expense?

● **Do It**

Peter M. Dell Wholesalers Co. has been expanding faster than it can raise capital. According to its local banker, the company has reached its debt ceiling. Dell's customers are slow in paying (60–90 days), but its suppliers (creditors) are demanding 30-day payment. Dell has a cash flow problem.

Dell needs to raise $120,000 in cash to safely cover next Friday's employee payroll. Dell's present balance of outstanding receivables totals $750,000. What might Dell do to alleviate this cash crunch? Record the entry that Dell would make when it raises the needed cash.

Reasoning: One source of immediate cash at a competitive cost is the sale of receivables to a factor. Rather than waiting until it can collect receivables, Dell may raise immediate cash by selling its receivables. The last thing Dell (or any employer) wants to do is miss a payroll.

Solution: If Dell Co. factors $125,000 of its accounts receivable at a 1% service charge, this entry would be made:

Cash	123,750	
Service Charge Expense	1,250	
Accounts Receivable		125,000
(To record sale of receivables to factor)		

USING THE DECISION TOOLKIT

The following information was taken from the 1995 financial statements of AMD (formerly Advanced Micro Devices), Intel's primary competitor in providing microprocessors for personal computers.

AMD
Selected Financial Information
(in millions)

	1995		1994	
Sales		$2,430		$2,134
Current assets				
Cash and cash equivalents		$ 113		$ 85
Short-term investments		377		293
Accounts receivable	$286		$347	
Allowance for doubtful accounts	10		10	
Net accounts receivable		276		337
Inventories		155		129
Other current assets		176		143
Total current assets		$1,097		$ 987
Total current liabilities		$ 622		$ 592

Notes to the Financial Statements

Note 4: Concentrations of Credit Risk Financial instruments that potentially subject the company to concentrations of credit risk consist primarily of cash equivalents, short-term investments, trade receivables, and financial instruments used in hedging activities.

Concentrations of credit risk with respect to trade receivables are limited because a large number of geographically diverse customers make up the company's customer base, thus spreading the trade credit risk. The company controls credit risk through credit approvals, credit limits, and monitoring procedures. The company performs in-depth credit evaluations of all new customers and requires letters of credit, bank guarantees, and advance payments, if deemed necessary. Bad debt expenses have not been material.

Instructions

Using that information and data from Intel's 1995 financial statements, comment on AMD's accounts receivable management and liquidity relative to that of Intel, with consideration given to (1) the credit risk ratio, (2) the current ratio, and (3) the receivables turnover ratio and average collection period. Intel's credit risk ratio and current ratio were 1.79% and 2.24:1, respectively. The other ratios were calculated earlier in the chapter.

Solution

1. Here are the credit risk ratios of Intel and AMD:

Intel	AMD
$\dfrac{\$57}{\$3{,}173} = 1.79\%$	$\dfrac{\$10}{\$286} = 3.5\%$

   AMD's note on credit risk does not suggest significant exposure to any troubled firms, even though it is nearly double Intel's.

2. Here is the current ratio (Current assets ÷ Current liabilities) for each company:

Intel	AMD
$\dfrac{\$8{,}097}{\$3{,}619} = 2.24:1$	$\dfrac{\$1{,}097}{\$622} = 1.76:1$

   This suggests that Intel is substantially more liquid than AMD.

3. The receivables turnover ratio and average collection period for AMD are given next:

	Intel	AMD
Receivables turnover ratio	6.36 times	$\dfrac{\$2{,}430}{(\$276 + \$337)/2} = 7.93$ times
Average collection period	57.4 days	$\dfrac{365}{7.93} = 46.0$ days

   AMD's receivables turnover ratio of 7.93 compared to Intel's 6.36, and its average collection days of 46.0 versus Intel's 57.4, suggest that AMD is able to collect from its customers much more rapidly. As noted previously, even disregarding Intel's troubled receivable from Packard Bell, Intel's receivables turnover ratio and average collection period would still have been only 6.9 and 52.9 days, respectively. AMD's more rapid collection of receivables may compensate in part for its lower current ratio. That is, since it can turn its receivables into cash more quickly, its receivables appear to be more liquid than those of Intel.

However, there may be another explanation for this difference. Sales at Intel grew by 41% during 1995, whereas at AMD they grew at only 14%. In an environment of rapidly increasing sales, the denominator (average receivables) may not be representative of what the actual average receivables were during the year. Thus, Intel's collection rate might actually not be as bad, relative to AMD, as this ratio suggests.

SUMMARY OF STUDY OBJECTIVES

❶ Identify the different types of receivables. Receivables are frequently classified as accounts, notes, and other. Accounts receivable are amounts owed by customers on account. Notes receivable represent claims that are evidenced by formal instruments of credit. Other receivables include nontrade receivables such as interest receivable, loans to company officers, advances to employees, and income taxes refundable.

❷ Explain how accounts receivable are recognized in the accounts. Accounts receivable are recorded at invoice price. They are reduced by Sales Returns and Allowances. Cash discounts reduce the amount received on accounts receivable.

❸ Describe the methods used to account for bad debts. The two methods of accounting for uncollectible accounts are the allowance method and the direct write-off method. The percentage of receivables basis is used to estimate uncollectible accounts in the allowance method. It emphasizes the cash realizable value of the accounts receivable. An aging schedule is frequently used with this basis.

❹ Compute the maturity date of and interest on notes receivable. The maturity date of a note must be computed unless the due date is specified or the note is payable on demand. For a note stated in months, the maturity date is found by counting the months from the date of issue. For a note stated in days, the number of days is counted, omitting the issue date and including the due date. The formula for computing interest is: Face value × Interest rate × Time.

❺ Describe the entries to record the disposition of notes receivable. Notes can be held to maturity, at which time the face value plus accrued interest is due and the note is removed from the accounts. In many cases, however, similar to accounts receivable, the holder of the note speeds up the conversion by selling the receivable to another party. In some situations, the maker of the note dishonors the note (defaults), and the note is written off.

❻ Explain the statement presentation of receivables. Each major type of receivable should be identified in the balance sheet or in the notes to the financial statements. Short-term receivables are considered current assets. The gross amount of receivables and allowance for doubtful accounts should be reported. Bad debts and service charge expenses are reported in the income statement as operating (selling) expenses, and interest revenue is shown as other revenues and gains in the nonoperating section of the statement. Accounts receivable may be evaluated for liquidity by computing the receivables turnover ratio and the average collection period.

❼ Describe the principles of sound accounts receivable management. To properly manage receivables, management must (a) determine to whom to extend credit, (b) determine a payment period, (c) monitor collections, (d) evaluate the receivables balance, and (e) accelerate cash receipts from receivables when necessary.

❽ Identify ratios to analyze a company's receivables. The receivables turnover ratio and the average collection period both are useful in analyzing management's effectiveness in managing receivables. The accounts receivable aging schedule also provides useful information.

❾ Describe methods to accelerate the receipt of cash from receivables. If the company needs additional cash resources, management can accelerate the collection of cash from receivables by selling (factoring) its receivables or by allowing customers to pay with bank credit cards.

Decision Toolkit—A Summary

Decision Checkpoints	Info Needed for Decision	Tool to Use for Decision	How to Evaluate Results
Is the amount of past due accounts increasing? Which accounts require management's attention?	List of outstanding receivables and their due dates	Prepare an aging schedule showing the receivables in various stages: outstanding 0–30 days, 30–60 days, 60–90 days, and over 90 days.	Accounts in the older categories require follow-up: letters, phone calls, and possible renegotiation of terms.
Is the company's credit risk increasing?	Allowance for doubtful accounts and accounts receivable	$\text{Credit risk ratio} = \dfrac{\text{Allowance for doubtful accounts}}{\text{Accounts receivable}}$	Increase in ratio may suggest increased credit risk, requiring evaluation of credit policies.
Does the company have significant concentrations of credit risk?	Note to the financial statements on concentrations of credit risk	If risky credit customers are identified, the financial health of those customers should be evaluated to gain an independent assessment of the potential for a material credit loss.	If a material loss appears likely, the potential negative impact of that loss on the company should be carefully evaluated, along with the adequacy of the allowance for doubtful accounts.
Are collections being made in a timely fashion?	Net credit sales and average receivables balance	$\text{Receivables turnover ratio} = \dfrac{\text{Net credit sales}}{\text{Average net receivables}}$ $\text{Average collection period} = \dfrac{365\text{ days}}{\text{Receivables turnover ratio}}$	Average collection period should be consistent with corporate credit policy. An increase may suggest a decline in financial health of customers.

Glossary

Accounts receivable Amounts owed by customers on account. (p. 341)

Aging the accounts receivable The analysis of customer balances by the length of time they have been unpaid. (p. 344)

Allowance method A method of accounting for bad debts that involves estimating uncollectible accounts at the end of each period. (p. 342)

Average collection period The average amount of time that a receivable is outstanding, calculated by dividing 365 days by the receivables turnover ratio. (p. 357)

Bad debts expense An expense to record uncollectible receivables. (p. 342)

Cash (net) realizable value The net amount expected to be received in cash. (p. 341)

Concentration of credit risk The threat of nonpayment from a single customer or class of customers that could adversely affect the financial health of the company. (p. 355)

Credit risk ratio A measure of the risk that a company's customers may not pay their accounts, calculated as the Allowance for Doubtful Accounts divided by Accounts Receivable. (p. 354)

Direct write-off method A method of accounting for bad debts that involves expensing accounts at the point they are determined to be uncollectible. (p. 346)

Dishonored note A note that is not paid in full at maturity. (p. 351)

Factor A finance company or bank that buys receivables from businesses for a fee and then collects the payments directly from the customers. (p. 358)

Maker The party in a promissory note who is making the promise to pay. (p. 347)

Notes receivable Claims for which formal instruments of credit are issued as evidence of the debt. (p. 341)

Payee The party to whom payment of a promissory note is to be made. (p. 347)

Percentage of receivables basis Management establishes a percentage relationship between the amount of receivables and the expected losses from uncollectible accounts. (p. 344)

Promissory note A written promise to pay a specified amount of money on demand or at a definite time. (p. 347)

Receivables Amounts due from individuals and companies that are expected to be collected in cash. (p. 340)

Receivables turnover ratio A measure of the liquidity of receivables, computed by dividing net credit sales by average net receivables. (p. 356)

Trade receivables Notes and accounts receivable that result from sales transactions. (p. 341)

DEMONSTRATION PROBLEM

Presented here are selected transactions related to B. Dylan Corp:

Mar.	1	Sold $20,000 of merchandise to Potter Company, terms 2/10, n/30.
	11	Received payment in full from Potter Company for balance due.
	12	Accepted Juno Company's $20,000, 6-month, 12% note for balance due.
	13	Made B. Dylan Corp. credit card sales for $13,200.
	15	Made VISA credit sales totaling $6,700. A 5% service fee is charged by VISA.
Apr.	11	Sold accounts receivable of $8,000 to Harcot Factor. Harcot Factor assesses a service charge of 2% of the amount of receivables sold.
	13	Received collections of $8,200 on B. Dylan Corp. credit card sales and added finance charges of 1.5% to the remaining balances.
May	10	Wrote off as uncollectible $16,000 of accounts receivable. B. Dylan Corp. uses the percentage of receivables basis to estimate bad debts.
June	30	The balance in accounts receivable at the end of the first 6 months is $200,000 and the bad debt percentage is 10%. At June 30 the credit balance in the allowance account prior to adjustment is $3,500.
July	16	One of the accounts receivable written off in May pays the amount due, $4,000, in full.

Instructions
Prepare the journal entries for the transactions.

Problem-Solving Strategies
1. Accounts receivable are generally recorded at invoice price.
2. Sales returns and allowances and cash discounts reduce the amount received on accounts receivable.
3. When accounts receivable are sold, a service charge expense is incurred by the seller.
4. Bad debts expense is an adjusting entry.
5. The percentage of receivables basis considers any existing balance in the allowance account.
6. Write-offs of accounts receivable affect only balance sheet accounts.

Solution to Demonstration Problem

Mar.	1	Accounts Receivable—Potter Company	20,000	
		Sales		20,000
		(To record sales on account)		
	11	Cash	19,600	
		Sales Discounts (2% × $20,000)	400	
		Accounts Receivable—Potter Company		20,000
		(To record collection of accounts receivable)		
	12	Notes Receivable	20,000	
		Accounts Receivable—Juno Company		20,000
		(To record acceptance of Juno Company note)		
	13	Accounts Receivable	13,200	
		Sales		13,200
		(To record company credit card sales)		
	15	Cash	6,365	
		Service Charge Expense (5% × $6,700)	335	
		Sales		6,700
		(To record credit card sales)		

Apr. 11	Cash		7,840	
	Service Charge Expense (2% × $8,000)		160	
	Accounts Receivable			8,000
	(To record sale of receivables to factor)			
13	Cash		8,200	
	Accounts Receivable			8,200
	(To record collection of accounts receivable)			
	Accounts Receivable			
	[($13,200 − $8,200) × 1.5%]		75	
	Interest Revenue			75
	(To record finance charges assessed on factored receivables)			
May 10	Allowance for Doubtful Accounts		16,000	
	Accounts Receivable			16,000
	(To record write-off of accounts receivable)			
June 30	Bad Debts Expense			
	[($200,000 × 10%) − $3,500]		16,500	
	Allowance for Doubtful Accounts			16,500
	(To record estimate of uncollectible accounts)			
July 16	Accounts Receivable		4,000	
	Allowance for Doubtful Accounts			4,000
	(To reverse write-off of accounts receivable)			
	Cash		4,000	
	Accounts Receivable			4,000
	(To record collection of accounts receivable)			

SELF-STUDY QUESTIONS

Answers are at the end of the chapter.

(SO 2) 1. Jones Company on June 15 sells merchandise on account to Bullock Co. for $1,000, terms 2/10, n/30. On June 20 Bullock Co. returns merchandise worth $300 to Jones Company. On June 24 payment is received from Bullock Co. for the balance due. What is the amount of cash received?
    (a) $700   (c) $686
    (b) $680   (d) None of the above

(SO 3) 2. Net credit sales for the month are $800,000. The accounts receivable balance is $160,000. The allowance is calculated as 7.5% of the receivables balance using the percentage of receivables basis. If the Allowance for Doubtful Accounts has a credit balance of $5,000 before adjustment, what is the balance after adjustment?
    (a) $12,000   (c) $17,000
    (b) $7,000   (d) $31,000

3. In 1998 D. H. Lawrence Company had net credit (SO 3) sales of $750,000. On January 1, 1998, Allowance for Doubtful Accounts had a credit balance of $18,000. During 1998, $30,000 of uncollectible accounts receivable were written off. Past experience indicates that the allowance should be 10% of the balance in receivables (percentage of receivables basis). If the accounts receivable balance at December 31 was $200,000, what is the required adjustment to the Allowance for Doubtful Accounts at December 31, 1998?
    (a) $20,000   (c) $32,000
    (b) $75,000   (d) $30,000

4. An analysis and aging of the accounts receiv- (SO 3) able of Machiavelli Company at December 31 reveal these data:

368 CHAPTER 8 Reporting and Analyzing Receivables

Accounts Receivable $800,000
Allowance for Doubtful Accounts per
  books before adjustment (credit) 50,000
Amounts expected to become
  uncollectible 65,000

What is the cash realizable value of the accounts receivable at December 31, after adjustment?
(a) $685,000   (c) $800,000
(b) $750,000   (d) $735,000

(SO 4) 5. Which of these statements about promissory notes is *incorrect*?
(a) The party making the promise to pay is called the maker.
(b) The party to whom payment is to be made is called the payee.
(c) A promissory note is not a negotiable instrument.
(d) A promissory note is more liquid than an accounts receivable.

(SO 9) 6. Which of these statements about VISA credit card sales is *incorrect*?
(a) The credit card issuer conducts the credit investigation of the customer.
(b) The retailer is not involved in the collection process.
(c) The retailer must wait to receive payment from the issuer.
(d) The retailer receives cash more quickly than it would from individual customers.

(SO 9) 7. Morgan Retailers accepted $50,000 of Citibank VISA credit card charges for merchandise sold on July 1. Citibank charges 4% for its credit card use. The entry to record this transaction by Morgan Retailers will include a credit to Sales of $50,000 and a debit(s) to:
(a) Cash $48,000 and Service Charge Expense $2,000.
(b) Accounts Receivable $48,000 and Service Charge Expense $2,000.
(c) Cash $50,000.
(d) Accounts Receivable $50,000.

8. Sorenson Co. accepts a $1,000, 3-month, 12% (SO 4) promissory note in settlement of an account with Parton Co. The entry to record this transaction is:
(a) Notes Receivable   1,030
      Accounts Receivable   1,030
(b) Notes Receivable   1,000
      Accounts Receivable   1,000
(c) Notes Receivable   1,000
      Sales   1,000
(d) Notes Receivable   1,020
      Accounts Receivable   1,020

9. Schlicht Co. holds Osgrove Inc.'s $10,000, 120- (SO 5) day, 9% note. The entry made by Schlicht Co. when the note is collected, assuming no interest has been accrued, is:
(a) Cash   10,300
      Notes Receivable   10,300
(b) Cash   10,000
      Notes Receivable   10,000
(c) Accounts Receivable   10,300
      Notes Receivable   10,000
      Interest Revenue   300
(d) Cash   10,300
      Notes Receivable   10,000
      Interest Revenue   300

10. Moore Corporation had net credit (SO 8) sales during the year of $800,000 and cost of goods sold of $500,000. The balance in receivables at the beginning of the year was $100,000 and at the end of the year was $150,000. What was the receivables turnover ratio?
(a) 6.4   (b) 8.0   (c) 5.3   (d) 4.0

11. Hoffman Corporation sells its goods (SO 8) on terms of 2/10, n/30. It has a receivables turnover ratio of 7. What is its average collection period (days)?
(a) 2,555   (b) 30   (c) 52   (d) 210

Questions

1. What is the difference between an account receivable and a note receivable?
2. What are some common types of receivables other than accounts receivable or notes receivable?
3. What are the essential features of the allowance method of accounting for bad debts?
4. Soo Eng cannot understand why the cash realizable value does not decrease when an uncollectible account is written off under the allowance method. Clarify this point for Soo Eng.
5. Kersee Company has a credit balance of $3,200 in Allowance for Doubtful Accounts. The total estimated uncollectibles under the percentage of receivables basis is $5,800. Prepare the adjusting entry.
6. How are bad debts accounted for under the direct write-off method? What are the disadvantages of this method?
7. Your roommate is uncertain about the advantages of a promissory note. Compare the advantages of a note receivable with those of an accounts receivable.
8. How may the maturity date of a promissory note be stated?
9. Indicate the maturity date of each of the following promissory notes:

Date of Note	Terms
(a) March 13	One year after date of note
(b) May 4	3 months after date
(c) June 10	30 days after date
(d) July 2	60 days after date

10. Compute the missing amounts for each of the following notes:

Principal	Annual Interest Rate	Time	Total Interest
(a)	9%	120 days	$360
$30,000	10%	3 years	(d)
$60,000	(b)	5 months	$2,500
$50,000	11%	(c)	$1,375

11. May Company dishonors a note at maturity. What actions by May may occur with the dishonoring of the note?

12. Paula Company has accounts receivable and notes receivable. How should the receivables be reported on the balance sheet?

13. What are the steps to good receivables management?

14. How might a company monitor the risk related to its accounts receivable?

15. What is meant by a concentration of credit risk?

16. If the receivables turnover ratio is 7.15 and average net receivables during the period is $210,000, what is the amount of net credit sales for the period?

17. Allmar Company accepts both its own credit cards and national credit cards. What are the advantages of accepting both types of cards?

18. An article recently appeared in *The Wall Street Journal* indicating that companies are selling their receivables at a record rate. Why are companies selling their receivables?

19. Southern Textiles decides to sell $700,000 of its accounts receivable to First Central Factors Inc. First Central Factors assesses a service charge of 2% of the amount of receivables sold. Prepare the journal entry that Southern Textiles makes to record this sale.

BRIEF EXERCISES

BE8-1 Presented below are three receivables transactions. Indicate whether these receivables are reported as accounts receivable, notes receivable, or other receivables on a balance sheet.
(a) Advanced $10,000 to an employee
(b) Received a promissory note of $57,000 for services performed
(c) Sold merchandise on account for $60,000 to a customer

Identify different types of receivables.
(SO 1)

BE8-2 Record the following transactions on the books of Essex Co.:
(a) On July 1 Essex Co. sold merchandise on account to Cambridge Inc. for $14,000, terms 2/10, n/30.
(b) On July 8 Cambridge Inc. returned merchandise worth $3,800 to Essex Co.
(c) On July 11 Cambridge Inc. paid for the merchandise.

Record basic accounts receivable transactions.
(SO 2)

BE8-3 During its first year of operations, Wendy Company had credit sales of $3,000,000, of which $600,000 remained uncollected at year-end. The credit manager estimates that $40,000 of these receivables will become uncollectible.
(a) Prepare the journal entry to record the estimated uncollectibles.
(b) Prepare the current asset section of the balance sheet for Wendy Company, assuming that in addition to the receivables it has cash of $90,000, merchandise inventory of $130,000, and prepaid expenses of $13,000.
(c) Calculate the credit risk ratio, receivables turnover ratio, and average collection period. Assume net receivables 1 year before were $500,000.

Prepare entry for estimated uncollectibles and classifications, and compute ratios.
(SO 3, 6, 8)

BE8-4 At the end of 1998, Searcy Co. has accounts receivable of $700,000 and an allowance for doubtful accounts of $54,000. On January 24, 1999, it is learned that the company's receivable from Hutley Inc. is not collectible and therefore management authorizes a write-off of $8,000.
(a) Prepare the journal entry to record the write-off.
(b) What is the cash realizable value of the accounts receivable (1) before the write-off and (2) after the write-off?

Prepare entry for write-off, and determine cash realizable value.
(SO 3)

BE8-5 Assume the same information as BE8-4 and that on March 4, 1999, Searcy Co. receives payment of $8,000 in full from Hutley Co. Prepare the journal entries to record this transaction.

Prepare entries for collection of bad debt write-off.
(SO 3)

370 CHAPTER 8 Reporting and Analyzing Receivables

Prepare entry using percentage of receivables method.
(SO 3)

BE8-6 Massey Co. uses the percentage of receivables basis to record bad debts expense and concludes that 1% of accounts receivable will become uncollectible. Accounts receivable are $500,000 at the end of the year, and the allowance for doubtful accounts has a credit balance of $3,000.
(a) Prepare the adjusting journal entry to record bad debts expense for the year.
(b) If the allowance for doubtful accounts had a debit balance of $800 instead of a credit balance of $3,000, determine the amount to be reported for bad debts expense.

Compute maturity date and interest on note.
(SO 4)

BE8-7 Presented below are three promissory notes. Determine the missing amounts.

Date of Note	Terms	Maturity Date	Principal	Annual Interest Rate	Total Interest
April 1	60 days	(a)	$900,000	10%	(e)
July 2	30 days	(b)	79,000	(d)	$592.50
March 7	6 months	(c)	56,000	12%	(f)

Prepare entry for note receivable exchanged for accounts receivable.
(SO 4)

BE8-8 On January 10, 1998, Raja Co. sold merchandise on account to R. Opal for $12,000, terms n/30. On February 9 R. Opal gave Raja Co. a 10% promissory note in settlement of this account. Prepare the journal entry to record the sale and the settlement of the accounts receivable.

Analyze accounts receivable.
(SO 8)

BE8-9 The financial statements of Minnesota Mining and Manufacturing Company (3M) report net sales of $9.4 billion. Accounts receivable are $1.6 billion at the beginning of the year and $1.4 billion at the end of the year. Compute 3M's receivables turnover ratio. Compute 3M's average collection period for accounts receivable in days.

Prepare entries for credit card sale and sale of accounts receivable.
(SO 9)

BE8-10 Consider these transactions:
(a) St. Pierre Restaurant accepted a VISA card in payment of a $100 lunch bill. The bank charges a 3% fee. What entry should St. Pierre make?
(b) Mayfield Company sold its accounts receivable of $70,000. What entry should Mayfield make, given a service charge of 3% on the amount of receivables sold?

EXERCISES

Prepare entries for recognizing accounts receivable.
(SO 2)

E8-1 On January 6 Nicklaus Co. sells merchandise on account to Watson Inc. for $4,000, terms 2/10, n/30. On January 16 Watson pays the amount due.

Instructions
Prepare the entries on Nicklaus Co.'s books to record the sale and related collection.

Prepare entries for recognizing accounts receivable.
(SO 2)

E8-2 On January 10 Margaret Giger uses her Salizar Co. credit card to purchase merchandise from Salizar Co. for $11,000. On February 10 Giger is billed for the amount due of $11,000. On February 12 Giger pays $5,000 on the balance due. On March 10 Giger is billed for the amount due, including interest at 2% per month on the unpaid balance as of February 12.

Instructions
Prepare the entries on Salizar Co.'s books related to the transactions that occurred on January 10, February 12, and March 10.

Prepare entries to record allowance for doubtful accounts.
(SO 3)

E8-3 The ledger of the Patillo Company at the end of the current year shows Accounts Receivable $80,000; Credit Sales $940,000; and Sales Returns and Allowances $40,000.

Instructions
(a) If Allowance for Doubtful Accounts has a credit balance of $800 in the trial balance, journalize the adjusting entry at December 31, assuming bad debts are expected to be 10% of accounts receivable.
(b) If Allowance for Doubtful Accounts has a debit balance of $500 in the trial balance, journalize the adjusting entry at December 31, assuming bad debts are expected to be 8% of accounts receivable.

E8-4 Grevina Company has accounts receivable of $92,500 at March 31, 1998. An analysis of the accounts shows these amounts:

Determine bad debt expense, and prepare the adjusting entry.
(SO 3)

Month of Sale	Balance, March 31 1998	1997
March	$65,000	$75,000
February	12,600	8,000
December and January	8,500	2,400
November and October	6,400	1,100
	$92,500	$86,500

Credit terms are 2/10, n/30. At March 31, 1998, there is a $1,600 credit balance in Allowance for Doubtful Accounts prior to adjustment. The company uses the percentage of receivables basis for estimating uncollectible accounts. The company's estimates of bad debts are as follows:

Age of Accounts	Estimated Percentage Uncollectible
Current	2.0%
1–30 days past due	10.0
31–90 days past due	30.0
Over 90 days	50.0

Instructions
(a) Determine the total estimated uncollectibles.
(b) Prepare the adjusting entry at March 31, 1998, to record bad debts expense.
(c) Discuss the implications of the changes in the aging schedule from 1997 to 1998.

E8-5 On December 31, 1998, when its Allowance for Doubtful Accounts had a debit balance of $1,000, Lisa Ceja Co. estimates that 12% of its accounts receivable balance of $60,000 will become uncollectible and records the necessary adjustment to the Allowance for Doubtful Accounts. On May 11, 1999, Lisa Ceja Co. determined that Robert Worthy's account was uncollectible and wrote off $900. On June 12, 1999, Worthy paid the amount previously written off.

Prepare entry for estimated uncollectibles, write-off, and recovery.
(SO 3)

Instructions
Prepare the journal entries on December 31, 1998, May 11, 1999, and June 12, 1999.

E8-6 On March 3 Soyka Appliances sells $900,000 of its receivables to Potter Factors Inc. Potter Factors Inc. assesses a finance charge of 3% of the amount of receivables sold.

Prepare entry for sale of accounts receivable.
(SO 9)

Instructions
Prepare the entry on Soyka Appliances' books to record the sale of the receivables.

E8-7 On May 10 Monee Company sold merchandise for $3,000 and accepted the customer's First Business Bank MasterCard. At the end of the day, the First Business Bank MasterCard receipts were deposited in the company's bank account. First Business Bank charges a 4% service charge for credit card sales.

Prepare entry for credit card sale.
(SO 9)

Instructions
Prepare the entry on Monee Company's books to record the sale of merchandise.

E8-8 On July 4 Robyn's Restaurant accepts a VISA card for a $300 dinner bill. VISA charges a 3% service fee.

Prepare entry for credit card sale.
(SO 9)

Instructions
Prepare the entries on Robyn's books related to the transaction.

E8-9 Indiana Supply Co. has the following transactions related to notes receivable during the last 2 months of the year:

Prepare entries for notes receivable transactions.
(SO 4, 5)

Nov. 1 Loaned $24,000 cash to A. Gomez on a 1-year, 10% note.
Dec. 11 Sold goods to R. Wright, Inc., receiving a $3,600, 90-day, 12% note.
   16 Received a $4,000, 6-month, 12% note on account from B. Barnes.
   31 Accrued interest revenue on all notes receivable.

Instructions
Journalize the transactions for Indiana Supply Co.

372 CHAPTER 8 Reporting and Analyzing Receivables

Journalize notes receivable transactions.
(SO 4, 5)

E8-10 These transactions took place for Rather Co.:

1998

May 1 Received a $6,000, 1-year, 10% note on account from T. Jones.
Dec. 31 Accrued interest revenue on the T. Jones note.

1999

May 1 Received principal plus interest on the T. Jones note. (No interest has been accrued in 1999.)

Instructions
Record the transactions in the general journal.

Prepare entries for dishonor of notes receivable.
(SO 4, 5)

E8-11 On May 2 P. Brey Company lends $4,000 to Feingold Inc., issuing a 6-month, 10% note. At the maturity date, November 2, Feingold indicates that it cannot pay.

Instructions
(a) Prepare the entry to record the dishonor of the note, assuming that P. Brey Company expects collection will occur.
(b) Prepare the entry to record the dishonor of the note, assuming that P. Brey Company does not expect collection in the future.

PROBLEMS

Prepare journal entries related to bad debt expense, and compute ratios.
(SO 2, 3, 8)

P8-1 At December 31, 1998, Trisha Underwood Imports reported this information on its balance sheet:

Accounts receivable $1,000,000
Less: Allowance for doubtful accounts 60,000

During 1999 the company had the following transactions related to receivables:
1. Sales on account $2,600,000
2. Sales returns and allowances 40,000
3. Collections of accounts receivable 2,300,000
4. Write-offs of accounts receivable deemed uncollectible 80,000
5. Recovery of bad debts previously written off as uncollectible 25,000

Instructions
(a) Prepare the journal entries to record each of these five transactions. Assume that no cash discounts were taken on the collections of accounts receivable.
(b) Enter the January 1, 1999, balances in Accounts Receivable and Allowance for Doubtful Accounts, post the entries to the two accounts (use T accounts), and determine the balances.
(c) Prepare the journal entry to record bad debts expense for 1999, assuming that aging the accounts receivable indicates that estimated bad debts are $70,000.
(d) Compute the receivables turnover ratio and average collection period.

Compute bad debt amounts.
(SO 3)

P8-2 Here is information related to Aris Company for 1998:

Total credit sales $1,800,000
Accounts receivable at December 31 600,000
Bad debts written off 26,000

Instructions
(a) What amount of bad debts expense will Aris Company report if it uses the direct write-off method of accounting for bad debts?
(b) Assume that Aris Company decides to estimate its bad debts expense based on 4% of accounts receivable. What amount of bad debts expense will Aris Company record if the Allowance for Doubtful Accounts has a credit balance of $4,000?
(c) Assume the same facts as in part (b), except that there is a $2,000 debit balance in Allowance for Doubtful Accounts. What amount of bad debts expense will Aris record?
(d) What is the weakness of the direct write-off method of reporting bad debts expense?

P8-3 This is an aging schedule for Boitano Company:

Customer	Total	Not Yet Due	\multicolumn{4}{c}{Number of Days Past Due}
			1–30	31–60	61–90	Over 90
Aber	$ 20,000		$ 9,000	$11,000		
Bohr	30,000	$ 30,000				
Case	50,000	15,000	5,000		$30,000	
Datz	38,000					$38,000
Others	120,000	92,000	15,000	13,000		
	$258,000	$137,000	$29,000	$24,000	$30,000	$38,000
Estimated percentage uncollectible		3%	6%	12%	24%	50%
Total estimated bad debts	$ 34,930	$ 4,110	$ 1,740	$ 2,880	$ 7,200	$19,000

At December 31, 1998, the unadjusted balance in Allowance for Doubtful Accounts is a credit of $9,000.

Instructions
(a) Journalize and post the adjusting entry for bad debts at December 31, 1998. (Use T accounts.)
(b) Journalize and post to the allowance account these 1999 events and transactions:
   (1) March 1, an $800 customer balance originating in 1998 is judged uncollectible.
   (2) May 1, a check for $800 is received from the customer whose account was written off as uncollectible on March 1.
(c) Journalize the adjusting entry for bad debts at December 31, 1999, assuming that the unadjusted balance in Allowance for Doubtful Accounts is a debit of $1,100 and the aging schedule indicates that total estimated bad debts will be $27,100.

P8-4 Carlo Fassi Co. uses 8% of the accounts receivable balance to determine its allowance for bad debts for the period. At the beginning of the current period, Fassi had Allowance for Doubtful Accounts of $10,000 (credit). During the period, it had net credit sales of $900,000 and wrote off as uncollectible accounts receivable of $6,000. However, one of the accounts written off as uncollectible in the amount of $3,000 was recovered before the end of the current period. At the end of the period it had a balance in its accounts receivable account of $225,000.

Instructions
(a) Prepare the entry to record bad debts expense for the current period.
(b) Prepare the entry to record the write-off of uncollectible accounts during the current period.
(c) Prepare the entries to record the recovery of the uncollectible accounts during the current period.
(d) Determine the ending balance in Allowance for Doubtful Accounts.

P8-5 The Bon Ton Company closes its books on July 31. On June 30 the Notes Receivable account balance is $19,800. Notes Receivable include the following:

Date	Maker	Face Value	Term	Interest Rate
May 21	Alder Inc.	$6,000	60 days	12%
May 25	Dorn Co.	4,800	60 days	11%
June 30	MJH Corp.	9,000	6 months	9%

During July the following transactions were completed:

July 5 Made sales of $6,200 on Bon Ton credit cards.
   14 Made sales of $700 on VISA credit cards. The credit card service charge is 3%.
   20 Received payment in full from Alder Inc. on the amount due.
   25 Received notice that Dorn Co. note has been dishonored. (Assume that Dorn Co. is expected to pay in the future.)

Journalize transactions related to bad debts.
(SO 2, 3)

Prepare entries to record transactions related to bad debts.
(SO 2, 3)

Prepare entries for various credit card and notes receivable transactions.
(SO 2, 4, 5, 6, 9)

374　CHAPTER 8　Reporting and Analyzing Receivables

Instructions
(a) Journalize the July transactions and the July 31 adjusting entry for accrued interest receivable. (Interest is computed using 360 days.)
(b) Enter the balances at July 1 in the receivable accounts and post the entries to all of the receivable accounts. (Use T accounts.)
(c) Show the balance sheet presentation of the receivable accounts at July 31.

Journalize various receivables transactions.
(SO 2, 4, 5)

P8-6 On January 1, 1998, Comaneci Company had Accounts Receivable $54,200 and Allowance for Doubtful Accounts $4,700. Comaneci Company prepares financial statements annually. During the year the following selected transactions occurred:

Jan.	5	Sold $6,000 of merchandise to Garth Brooks Company, terms n/30.
Feb.	2	Accepted a $6,000, 4-month, 12% promissory note from Garth Brooks Company for balance due.
	12	Sold $7,200 of merchandise to Gage Company and accepted Gage's $7,200, 2-month, 10% note for the balance due.
	26	Sold $5,000 of merchandise to Mathias Co., terms n/10.
Apr.	5	Accepted a $5,000, 3-month, 8% note from Mathias Co. for balance due.
	12	Collected Gage Company note in full.
June	2	Collected Garth Brooks Company note in full.
July	5	Mathias Co. dishonors its note of April 5. It is expected that Mathias will eventually pay the amount owed.
	15	Sold $3,000 of merchandise to Tritt Inc. and accepted Tritt's $3,000, 3-month, 12% note for the amount due.
Oct.	15	The Tritt Inc. note was dishonored. Tritt Inc. is bankrupt, and there is no hope of future settlement.

Instructions
Journalize the transactions.

Calculate and interpret various ratios
(SO 7, 8)

P8-7 Presented here is basic financial information (in thousands) from the 1995 annual reports of Nike and Reebok:

	Nike	Reebok
Sales	$4,760,834	$3,481,450
Allowance for doubtful accounts, Jan. 1	28,291	44,862
Allowance for doubtful accounts, Dec. 31	32,663	46,401
Accounts receivable balance (gross), Jan. 1	1,085,900	552,964
Accounts receivable balance (gross), Dec. 31	731,973	577,337

Instructions
(a) Calculate the receivables turnover ratio and average collection period for both companies. Comment on the difference in their collection experiences.
(b) Calculate the January 1 and December 31 ratio of allowance for doubtful accounts to gross accounts receivable for each company. Comment on any apparent differences in their credit-granting practices.

ALTERNATIVE PROBLEMS

Prepare journal entries related to bad debt expense, and compute ratios.
(SO 2, 3, 8)

P8-1A At December 31, 1998, Bordeaux Inc. reported this information on its balance sheet:

Accounts receivable	$960,000
Less: Allowance for doubtful accounts	70,000

During 1999 the company had the following transactions related to receivables:
1. Sales on account　　　　　　　　　　　　　　　　　　　　　　　　　$3,200,000
2. Sales returns and allowances　　　　　　　　　　　　　　　　　　　　　50,000
3. Collections of accounts receivable　　　　　　　　　　　　　　　　　2,800,000
4. Write-offs of accounts receivable deemed uncollectible　　　　　　　　　90,000
5. Recovery of bad debts previously written off as uncollectible　　　　　　35,000

Alternative Problems   375

Instructions

(a) Prepare the journal entries to record each of these five transactions. Assume that no cash discounts were taken on the collections of accounts receivable.
(b) Enter the January 1, 1999, balances in Accounts Receivable and Allowance for Doubtful Accounts, post the entries to the two accounts (use T accounts), and determine the balances.
(c) Prepare the journal entry to record bad debts expense for 1999, assuming that aging the accounts receivable indicates that expected bad debts are $100,000.
(d) Compute the receivables turnover ratio and average collection period.

P8-2A Here is information related to Volkov Company for 1998:

Compute bad debt amounts.
(SO 3)

Total credit sales	$2,000,000
Accounts receivable at December 31	800,000
Bad debts written off	36,000

Instructions

(a) What amount of bad debts expense will Volkov Company report if it uses the direct write-off method of accounting for bad debts?
(b) Assume that Volkov Company decides to estimate its bad debts expense based on 5% of accounts receivable. What amount of bad debts expense will Volkov Company record if it has an Allowance for Doubtful Accounts credit balance of $3,000?
(c) Assume the same facts as in part (b), except that there is a $3,000 debit balance in Allowance for Doubtful Accounts. What amount of bad debts expense will Volkov record?
(d) What is the weakness of the direct write-off method of reporting bad debts expense?

P8-3A Presented here is an aging schedule for Deep Canyon Company:

Journalize transactions related to bad debts.
(SO 2, 3)

Customer	Total	Not Yet Due	\multicolumn{4}{c}{Number of Days Past Due}
			1–30	31–60	61–90	Over 90
Anita	$ 22,000		$10,000	$12,000		
Barry	40,000	$ 40,000				
Chagnon	57,000	16,000	6,000		$35,000	
David	34,000					$34,000
Others	126,000	96,000	16,000	14,000		
	$279,000	$152,000	$32,000	$26,000	$35,000	$34,000
Estimated percentage uncollectible		4%	7%	13%	25%	50%
Total estimated bad debts	$ 37,450	$ 6,080	$ 2,240	$ 3,380	$ 8,750	$17,000

At December 31, 1998, the unadjusted balance in Allowance for Doubtful Accounts is a credit of $10,000.

Instructions

(a) Journalize and post the adjusting entry for bad debts at December 31, 1998. (Use T accounts.)
(b) Journalize and post to the allowance account these 1999 events and transactions:
 (1) March 31, an $800 customer balance originating in 1998 is judged uncollectible.
 (2) May 31, a check for $800 is received from the customer whose account was written off as uncollectible on March 31.
(c) Journalize the adjusting entry for bad debts on December 31, 1999, assuming that the unadjusted balance in Allowance for Doubtful Accounts is a debit of $800 and the aging schedule indicates that total estimated bad debts will be $28,300.

P8-4A Huang Co. uses 8% of the accounts receivable balance to determine its bad debts expense for the period. At the beginning of the current period, Huang had an Allowance for Doubtful Accounts of $9,000 (credit). During the period, it had net sales of $800,000 and wrote off as uncollectible accounts receivable of $7,000. However, one of the accounts

Prepare entries to record transactions related to bad debts.
(SO 2, 3)

written off as uncollectible in the amount of $4,000 was recovered before the end of the current period. At the end of the period it had a balance in its accounts receivable account of $250,000.

Instructions
(a) Prepare the entry to record bad debts expense for the current period.
(b) Prepare the entry to record the write-off of uncollectible accounts during the current period.
(c) Prepare the entries to record the recovery of the uncollectible account during the current period.
(d) Determine the ending balance in Allowance for Doubtful Accounts.

Prepare entries for various credit card and notes receivable transactions.
(SO 2, 4, 5, 6, 9)

P8-5A Selica Company closes its books on October 31. On September 30 the Notes Receivable account balance is $23,400. Notes Receivable include the following:

Date	Maker	Face Value	Term	Interest Rate
Aug. 16	Foran Inc.	$ 8,000	60 days	12%
Aug. 25	Drexler Co.	5,200	2 months	12%
Sept. 30	MGH Corp.	10,200	6 months	9%

Interest is computed using a 360-day year. During October the following transactions were completed:

Oct. 7 Made sales of $6,900 on Selica Credit cards.
     12 Made sales of $750 on VISA credit cards. The credit card service charge is 4%.
     15 Received payment in full from Foran Inc. on the amount due.
     25 Received notice that Drexler Co. note has been dishonored. (Assume that Drexler Co. is expected to pay in future.)

Instructions
(a) Journalize the October transactions and the October 31 adjusting entry for accrued interest receivable.
(b) Enter the balances at October 1 in the receivable accounts and post the entries to all of the receivable accounts. (Use T accounts.)
(c) Show the balance sheet presentation of the receivable accounts at October 31.

Journalize various receivables transactions.
(SO 2, 4, 5)

P8-6A On January 1, 1998, Ricardo Company had Accounts Receivable $146,000; Notes Receivable $15,000; and Allowance for Doubtful Accounts $13,200. The note receivable is from Annabelle Company. It is a 4-month, 12% note dated December 31, 1997. Uptown Company prepares financial statements annually. During the year the following selected transactions occurred:

Jan. 5 Sold $12,000 of merchandise to George Company, terms n/15.
     20 Accepted George Company's $12,000, 3-month, 9% note for balance due.
Feb. 18 Sold $8,000 of merchandise to Swaim Company and accepted Swaim's $8,000, 6-month, 10% note for the amount due.
Apr. 20 Collected George Company note in full.
     30 Received payment in full from Annabelle Company on the amount due.
May 25 Accepted Avery Inc.'s $7,000, 3-month, 8% note in settlement of a past-due balance on account.
Aug. 18 Received payment in full from Swaim Company on note due.
     25 The Avery Inc. note was dishonored. Avery Inc. is not bankrupt and future payment is anticipated.
Sept. 1 Sold $10,000 of merchandise to Young Company and accepted a $10,000, 6-month, 10% note for the amount due.

Instructions
Journalize the transactions.

Calculate and interpret various ratios.
(SO 7, 8)

P8-7A Presented here is basic financial information from the 1995 annual reports of Goodyear Tire and Rubber Co. and Cooper Tire and Rubber Co.:

	Goodyear (in millions)	Cooper (in thousands)
Sales	$13,165.9	$1,494,622
Allowance for doubtful accounts, Jan. 1	54	3,600
Allowance for doubtful accounts, Dec. 31	56.2	3,600
Accounts receivable balance (gross), Jan. 1	1,578.7	224,837
Accounts receivable balance (gross), Dec. 31	1,671.2	260,649

Instructions
(a) Calculate the receivables turnover ratio and average collection period for both companies. Comment on the difference in their collection experiences.
(b) Calculate the January 1 and December 31 ratio of allowance for doubtful accounts to gross accounts receivable for each company. Comment on any apparent differences in their credit-granting practices.

BROADENING YOUR PERSPECTIVE

FINANCIAL REPORTING AND ANALYSIS

FINANCIAL REPORTING PROBLEM: *Starbucks Corporation*

BYP8-1 This information was extracted from recent annual reports of Starbucks Corporation:

	1996	1995	1994	1993
Net revenues	$696,481	$465,213	$284,923	$176,541
Accounts receivable	17,621	9,852	5,394	2,862

Instructions
(a) Assuming that all sales are credit sales, calculate the receivables turnover ratio and average collection period for Starbucks for 1996, 1995, and 1994.
(b) What factors might explain the changes in the values calculated in part (a)?
(c) The following quote is taken from the Management Discussion and Analysis of the 1996 annual report:

> Starbucks presently derives approximately 86% of net revenues from its Company-operated retail stores. The Company's specialty sales operations, which include sales to wholesale customers, licensees, and joint ventures, accounted for approximately 11% of net revenues in fiscal 1996. Direct response operations (mail order) account for the remainder of net revenues.

What implications does this sales mix have for the calculations you made in part (a)? What are the implications for Starbucks' accounts receivable management?

COMPARATIVE ANALYSIS PROBLEM: *Starbucks vs. Green Mountain Coffee*

BYP8-2 The financial statements of Green Mountain Coffee are presented in Appendix B, following the financial statements for Starbucks in Appendix A.

Instructions
(a) Based on the information contained in these financial statements, compute the following fiscal-year 1996 values for each company:
   (1) Receivables turnover ratio. (Assume all sales were credit sales.)
   (2) Average collection period for receivables.

(b) What conclusions concerning the management of accounts receivable can be drawn from these data?
(c) Green Mountain Coffee and Starbucks are competitors, but they have quite different approaches to selling. Green Mountain Coffee sells 75% of its coffee wholesale, 15% retail, and 10% direct mail. Starbucks sells 86% of its coffee retail, 11% wholesale, and 3% direct mail. What are the implications of these different sales practices for the importance of accounts receivable management to each company? What differences between the types of sales of the two companies makes direct comparison of these ratios difficult? How might your answers in parts (a) and (b) be changed by this information concerning each company's sales practices?

RESEARCH CASE

BYP8-3 The May 6, 1996, issue of *Forbes* includes an article by Matthew Schifrin and Howard Rudnitsky entitled "Rx for Receivables."

Instructions
Read the article and answer these questions:
(a) Why has the pharmacy business moved from a cash-based business to a receivables-based business?
(b) What is the economic motivation for pharmacies to sell their receivables?
(c) What is the economic motivation for the Pharmacy Fund to purchase the receivables?

INTERPRETING FINANCIAL STATEMENTS

BYP8-4 Minicase *Sears, Roebuck & Co.*
Sears is one of the world's largest retailers. It is also a huge provider of credit through its Sears credit card. Revenue generated from credit operations was $3.9 billion in 1995. The rate of interest Sears earns on outstanding receivables varies from 10% to 21% in the United States to up to 28% in Canada. Managing these receivables is critical to the performance of the corporation. One aspect of receivables management is that in some instances, to acquire cash when needed, the company will sell its receivables. At December 31, 1995, Sears had sold $4.55 billion of its receivables.

The following information (in millions) was available in Sears' 1995 financial statements:

	1995	1994	1993
Accounts receivable (gross)	$20,949	$19,033	$15,906
Allowance for doubtful accounts	843	832	810
Merchandise sales	31,035	29,451	27,420
Credit revenues	3,890	3,574	3,020
Bad debts expense	826	698	821

Instructions
(a) Discuss whether the sale of receivables by Sears represents a significant portion of its receivables. Why might Sears have sold these receivables? As an investor, what concerns might you have about these sales?
(b) Calculate and discuss the receivables turnover ratio and average collection period for Sears for 1995 and 1994.
(c) Do you think Sears provided credit as a revenue-generating activity or as a convenience for its customers?
(d) Compute the ratio of bad debts expense to merchandise sales for 1995 and 1994. Did this ratio improve or worsen? What considerations should Sears make in deciding whether it wants to have liberal or conservative credit-granting policies?

CRITICAL THINKING

MANAGEMENT DECISION CASES

BYP8-5 Johanna and Jake Berkvom own Campus Fashions. From its inception Campus Fashions has sold merchandise on either a cash or credit basis, but no credit cards have been accepted. During the past several months, the Berkvoms have begun to question their credit-sales policies. First, they have lost some sales because they refuse to accept credit cards. Second, representatives of two metropolitan banks have convinced them to accept their national credit cards. One bank, City National Bank, has stated that (1) its credit card fee is 4% and (2) it pays the retailer 96 cents on each $1 of sales within 3 days of receiving the credit card billings.

The Berkvoms decide that they should determine the cost of carrying their own credit sales. From the accounting records of the past 3 years they accumulate these data:

	1998	1997	1996
Net credit sales	$500,000	$600,000	$400,000
Collection agency fees for slow-paying customers	2,450	2,500	1,600
Salary of part-time accounts receivable clerk	3,800	3,800	3,800

Credit and collection expenses as a percentage of net credit sales are as follows: uncollectible accounts 1.6%, billing and mailing costs .5%, and credit investigation fee on new customers .15%.

Johanna and Jake also determine that the average accounts receivable balance outstanding during the year is 5% of net credit sales. The Berkvoms estimate that they could earn an average of 10% annually on cash invested in other business opportunities.

Instructions
(a) Prepare a tabulation for each year showing total credit and collection expenses in dollars and as a percentage of net credit sales.
(b) Determine the net credit and collection expenses in dollars and as a percentage of sales after considering the revenue not earned from other investment opportunities. [*Note:* The income lost on the cash held by the bank for 3 days is considered to be immaterial.]
(c) Discuss both the financial and nonfinancial factors that are relevant to the decision.

BYP8-6 Arvada Company sells office equipment and supplies to many organizations in the city and surrounding area on contract terms of 2/10, n/30. In the past, more than 75% of the credit customers have taken advantage of the discount by paying within 10 days of the invoice date.

The number of customers taking the full 30 days to pay has increased within the last year. Current indications are that less than 60% of the customers are now taking the discount. Bad debts as a percentage of gross credit sales have risen from the 1.5% provided in past years to about 4% in the current year.

The controller has responded to a request from the finance committee for more information on the collections of accounts receivable with the report reproduced here.

ARVADA COMPANY
Accounts Receivable Collections
May 31, 1999

The fact that some credit accounts will prove uncollectible is normal. Annual bad debt write-offs have been 1.5% of gross credit sales over the past 5 years. During the last fiscal year, this percentage increased to slightly less than 4%. The current Accounts Receivable balance is $1,400,000. The condition of this balance in terms of age and probability of collection is as follows:

Proportion of Total	Age Categories	Probability of Collection
66%	Not yet due	99%
16	Less than 30 days past due	96
9	30 to 60 days past due	95
5	61 to 120 days past due	91
3	121 to 180 days past due	75
1	Over 180 days past due	20

The Allowance for Doubtful Accounts had a credit balance of $29,500 on June 1, 1998. Total gross credit sales for the 1998–99 fiscal year amounted to $2,800,000. Write-offs of bad accounts during the year totaled $96,000.

Instructions

(a) Prepare an accounts receivable aging schedule for Arvada Company using the age categories identified in the controller's report to the finance committee showing:
   (1) The amount of accounts receivable outstanding for each age category and in total
   (2) The estimated amount that is uncollectible for each category and in total
(b) Compute the amount of the year-end adjustment necessary to bring Allowance for Doubtful Accounts to the balance indicated by the age analysis. Then prepare the necessary journal entry to adjust the accounting records.
(c) Assume a recessionary environment with tight credit and high interest rates.
   (1) Identify steps Arvada Company might take to improve the accounts receivable situation.
   (2) Evaluate each step identified in terms of the risks and costs involved.

A REAL-WORLD FOCUS: *Art World Industries, Inc.*

BYP8-7 *Art World Industries, Inc.,* was incorporated in 1986 in Delaware, although it is located in Los Angeles. The company employs 25 people to print, publish, and sell limited-edition graphics and reproductive prints in the wholesale market.

The operating expenses for the year ended August 1994 for Art World Industries, Inc., include bad debts expense of $6,715.50. The balance sheet shows an allowance for doubtful accounts of $175,477. The allowance was set up against certain Japanese accounts receivable that average more than 1 year in age. The Japanese acknowledge the amount due, but with the slow economy in Japan lack the resources to pay at this time.

Instructions
(a) Which basis for estimating uncollectible accounts does Art World Industries use?
(b) When Art World makes its adjusting entry to record bad debts expense, must it consider a previous existing balance in the Allowance for Doubtful Accounts?
(c) Explain the difference between the direct write-off and percentage of receivables methods. Based on Art World's disclosure above, what important factor would you have to consider in arriving at appropriate percentages to apply for the percentage of receivables method?

GROUP ACTIVITY

BYP8-8 Sherie Mitchell, controller for S & J Mitchell Co., provides you with the following list of accounts receivable that were written off during the current year:

Date	Customer	Amount
Feb. 26	Kadlec Corp.	$ 8,700
Apr. 17	Lois Hamilton Shops	13,219
June 30	Ilsa Kosinski Co.	5,500
Oct. 4	Eleanor Schewe	3,187

S & J Mitchell Co. follows the policy of debiting Bad Debts Expense as accounts are written off. Sherie Mitchell maintains that this practice is appropriate for financial statement purposes because the Internal Revenue Service will not accept other methods for recognizing bad debts.

All of S & J Mitchell's sales are on a 30-day credit basis. Sales for the current year total $2,470,000. Accounts receivable at the end of the year total $980,000. Experience has determined that bad debts losses approximate 5% of the accounts receivable balance.

Instructions
In groups of four or five students, answer these questions:
(a) Do you agree or disagree with S & J Mitchell's policy concerning recognition of bad debts? Why or why not?
(b) By what amount would net income differ if bad debts expense were computed using the percentage of receivables approach?

Communication Activity

BYP8-9 Sara Joy Corporation is a recently formed business selling the "World's Best Doormat." The corporation is selling doormats faster than Sara Joy can make them. It has been selling the product on a credit basis, telling customers to "pay when they can." Oddly, even though sales are tremendous, the company is having trouble paying its bills.

Instructions
Write a memo to the president of Sara Joy Corporation discussing these questions:
(a) What steps should be taken to improve its ability to pay its bills?
(b) What accounting steps should be taken to measure its success in improving collections, and in recording its collection success?
(c) If the corporation is still unable to pay its bills, what additional steps can be taken with its receivables to ease its liquidity problems?

Ethics Case

BYP8-10 Shirt Co. is a subsidiary of Clothes Corp. The controller believes that the yearly allowance for doubtful accounts for Shirt Co. should be 2% of net credit sales. The president of Shirt Co., nervous that the parent company might expect the subsidiary to sustain its 10% growth rate, suggests that the controller increase the allowance for doubtful accounts to 4%. The president thinks that the lower net income, which reflects a 6% growth rate, will be a more sustainable rate for Shirt Co.

Instructions
(a) Who are the stakeholders in this case?
(b) Does the president's request pose an ethical dilemma for the controller?
(c) Should the controller be concerned with Shirt Co.'s growth rate in estimating the allowance? Explain your answer.

Financial Analysis on the Web

BYP8-11 *Purpose:* The Security Exchange Act of 1934 requires any firm that is listed on one of the national exchanges to file annual reports (form 10-K), financial statements, and quarterly reports (form 10-Q) with the SEC. This exercise demonstrates how to search and access available SEC filings through the Internet.

Address: http://biz.yahoo.com/i (May use SEC address instead.)

Steps:
1. Choose **Company**.
2. Type in a company's name, or use index to find a company name.
3. Choose **SEC Filings**.

Instructions
Answer the following questions:
(a) Which SEC filings were available for the company you selected?
(b) In the company's annual report, what was one key point discussed in the "Management's Discussion and Analysis of Results of Operations and Financial Condition"?
(c) What was the net income for the period selected?

Answers to Self-Study Questions
1. c   2. a   3. c   4. d   5. c   6. c   7. a   8. b   9. d   10. a
11. c

CHAPTER 9

Reporting and Analyzing Long-Lived Assets

STUDY OBJECTIVES

After studying this chapter, you should be able to:

1. Describe how the cost principle applies to plant assets.
2. Explain the concept of depreciation.
3. Compute periodic depreciation using the straight-line method, and contrast its expense pattern with those of other methods.
4. Describe the procedure for revising periodic depreciation.
5. Explain how to account for the disposal of plant assets.
6. Describe methods for evaluating the use of plant assets.
7. Identify the basic issues related to reporting intangible assets.
8. Indicate how long-lived assets are reported on the balance sheet.

A Tale of Two Airlines

So, you're interested in starting a new business. Have you given any thought to the airline industry? Your only experience with airlines is as a passenger? Don't let that stop you, advises Ray Novelli. Novelli's airline, Presidential Air, was one of 30 new airlines that entered the U.S. market in a recent 30-month period—one per month.

The impetus behind all these upstarts is the tremendous success of two discount, no-frills airlines: Southwest Airlines and Valujet. Valujet, which was started with a $3.4-million investment, grew to be worth $630 million in its first 3 years. What is interesting is the different approach taken by these two airlines to arrive at their success.

Southwest Airlines' fleet is composed of primarily sleek, new, highly efficient planes requiring little maintenance. The average age of its planes is 8.3 years, the lowest in the industry. To be able to afford new planes, Southwest had to be very patient in its growth goals. Over a 22-year period, Southwest has risen to the number 8 spot in size for U.S. airlines—and to even higher rankings in on-time performance, customer service, and baggage handling.

Valujet, on the other hand, opted for old planes, known in the industry as Zombies, which are 25 to 30 years old and cost less than a tenth of the purchase price of a new plane. The average age of a Valujet plane is 26.3 years, the highest in the industry. This practice of buying older planes allowed Valujet to add one or two planes a month to its fleet—an unheard-of expansion. Valujet started with two planes and within a year and a half had 36 planes. By comparison, it took Southwest Airlines 10 years to acquire that many planes. For a while there was a surplus of these old planes on the market, until Valujet enjoyed such tremendous success that seemingly everyone wanted to buy or lease old planes to start an airline.

However, a terrible crash in May 1996 in Florida focused the spotlight on Valujet and called into question the wisdom of relying on old planes. Although the cause of the crash appears to have been unrelated to the age of its planes, in the aftermath of the crash Valujet has struggled to survive under the weight of both government scrutiny and lack of customer confidence. The crash heightened awareness of the age of the U.S. fleet as well as the importance of ongoing maintenance. Whether this spells the end for new discount startups remains to be seen.

Postscript: Presidential Air went out of business in April 1996. Also, in the face of continuing financial problems, in July 1997 Valujet announced its intention to merge with AirWays Corp. and to take the name of its airline, AirTran Airways. Perhaps you should proceed with caution in planning the startup of your own airline!

On the World Wide Web
Southwest Airlines:
http://www.southwestair.com
Valujet: http://www.airtran.com

PREVIEW OF CHAPTER 9

Is Valujet's approach to buying equipment really the "right formula," or is it a recipe for disaster? For airlines and many other companies, making the right decisions regarding long-lived assets is critical because these assets represent huge investments. Management must make many ongoing decisions—what to acquire and when, how to finance the assets, how to account for them, and when to dispose of them.

In this chapter we address these and other issues surrounding long-lived assets. Our discussion of long-lived assets is presented in two parts: plant assets and intangible assets. *Plant assets* are the property, plant, and equipment (physical assets) that commonly come to mind when we think of a company. However, companies also have many important *intangible assets*. These are assets such as copyrights and patents that lack physical substance but can be extremely valuable and vital to a company's success.

The content and organization of this chapter are as follows:

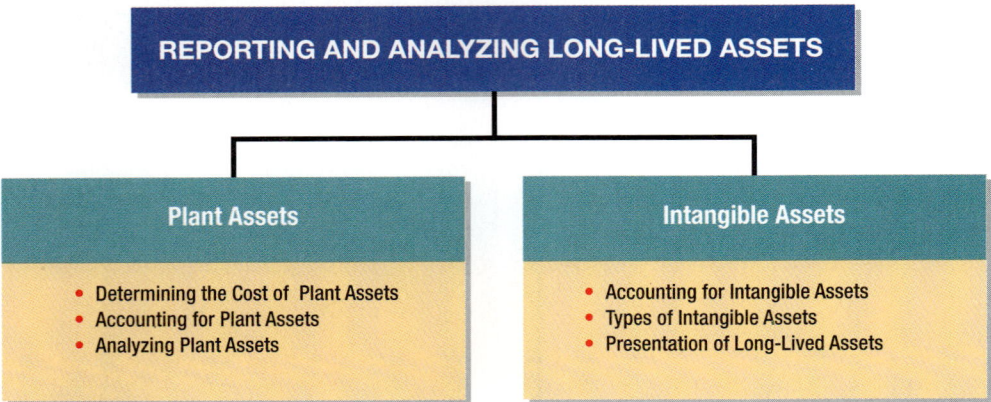

SECTION 1
PLANT ASSETS

Plant assets are resources that have physical substance (a definite size and shape), are used in the operations of a business, and are not intended for sale to customers. They are called various names—property, plant, and equipment; plant and equipment; and fixed assets—but the term we use most often in this chapter is plant assets. By whatever name, these assets are generally long-lived and are expected to provide services to the company for a number of years. Except for land, plant assets decline in service potential (value) over their useful lives.

The acquisition of plant assets is critical to the success of nearly all businesses because these resources determine the company's capacity and therefore its ability to satisfy customers. With too few planes, for example, Valujet and Southwest Airlines will lose customers to their competitors, but with too many planes, they will be flying with a lot of empty seats. Management must constantly monitor its needs and acquire assets accordingly. Failure to do so results in lost business opportunities or inefficient use of existing assets and is likely to show up eventually in poor financial results, problems for management, and declining interest among investors.

It is also important for a business enterprise to (1) keep assets in good operating condition, (2) replace worn-out or outdated facilities, and (3) expand its productive resources as needed. The decline of rail travel in the United States can be traced in part to the failure of railroad companies to perform the first two operations. Conversely, the growth of air travel in this country can be attributed in part to the general willingness of airline companies to follow these essential guidelines.

Many companies have substantial investments in plant assets. In public utility companies, for example, plant assets often represent more than 75% of total assets. Recently plant assets were more than 80% of Consolidated Edison's total assets and 92% of Pennsylvania Power & Light Company's. Illustration 9-1 shows the percentages of plant assets in relation to total assets in some other companies.

McDonald's	86%	Southwest Airlines	85%
Marriott Corporation	63%	General Motors Corporation	37%
Caterpillar	26%	Wal-Mart	44%

Illustration 9-1 Percentages of plant assets in relation to total assets

Plant assets are often subdivided into four classes:

1. Land, such as a building site.
2. Land improvements, such as driveways, parking lots, fences, and underground sprinkler systems.
3. Buildings, such as stores, offices, factories, and warehouses.
4. Equipment, such as store check-out counters, cash registers, coolers, office furniture, factory machinery, and delivery equipment.

DETERMINING THE COST OF PLANT ASSETS

Plant assets are recorded at cost in accordance with the **cost principle** of accounting. Thus, the planes at Valujet and Southwest Airlines are recorded at cost. **Cost consists of all expenditures necessary to acquire the asset and make it ready for its intended use.** For example, the purchase price, freight costs paid by the purchaser, and installation costs are all considered part of the cost of factory machinery.

The determination of which costs to include in a plant asset account and which costs not to include is very important. If a cost is not included in a plant asset account, then it must be expensed immediately. Such costs are referred to as **revenue expenditures.** On the other hand, costs that are not expensed immediately but are instead included in a plant asset account are referred to as **capital expenditures.** This distinction is important because it has immediate, and often material, implications for the income statement. Some companies, in order to boost current income, have been known to improperly capitalize expenditures that should have been expensed. For example, suppose that $1,000 of maintenance costs incurred at the end of the year are improperly capitalized to a building account; that is, they are included in the asset account Buildings rather than being expensed immediately. If the cost of the building is being allocated as an expense (depreciated) over a 40-year life, then the maintenance cost of $1,000 will be incorrectly spread across 40 years instead of being ex-

STUDY OBJECTIVE 1
Describe how the cost principle applies to plant assets.

International Note
The United Kingdom is flexible regarding asset valuation. Companies revalue to fair value when they believe this information is more relevant. Switzerland and the Netherlands also permit revaluations.

pensed in the current year. Current-year expenses will be understated by $1,000, and current-year income will be overstated by $1,000. Thus, determining which costs to capitalize and which to expense is very important.

BUSINESS INSIGHT
Investor Perspective

Once a star on Wall Street, Chambers Development, a waste management company, saw its stock price plummet in 1992 when it announced that its earnings over a 5-year period were overstated by $362 million because it had improperly capitalized costs that should have been expensed. For example, Chambers had capitalized $162 million that it had paid in dumping fees at landfill sites.

Cost is measured by the cash paid in a cash transaction or by the **cash equivalent price** paid when noncash assets are used in payment. **The cash equivalent price is equal to the fair market value of the asset given up or the fair market value of the asset received, whichever is more clearly determinable.** Once cost is established, it becomes the basis of accounting for the plant asset over its useful life. Current market or replacement values are not used after acquisition. The application of the cost principle to each of the major classes of plant assets is explained in the following sections.

LAND

The cost of land includes (1) the cash purchase price, (2) closing costs such as title and attorney's fees, (3) real estate brokers' commissions, and (4) accrued property taxes and other liens on the land assumed by the purchaser. For example, if the cash price is $50,000 and the purchaser agrees to pay accrued taxes of $5,000, the cost of the land is $55,000.

All necessary costs incurred in making land **ready for its intended use** increase (debit) the Land account. When vacant land is acquired, its cost includes expenditures for clearing, draining, filling, and grading. If the land has a building on it that must be removed to make the site suitable for construction of a new building, all demolition and removal costs, less any proceeds from salvaged materials, are chargeable to the Land account. To illustrate, assume that Hayes Manufacturing Company acquires real estate at a cash cost of $100,000. The property contains an old warehouse that is razed at a net cost of $6,000 ($7,500 in costs less $1,500 proceeds from salvaged materials). Additional expenditures are for the attorney's fee $1,000 and the real estate broker's commission $8,000. Given these factors, the cost of the land is $115,000, computed as shown in Illustration 9-2.

Illustration 9-2 Computation of cost of land

Land	
Cash price of property	$ 100,000
Net removal cost of warehouse	6,000
Attorney's fee	1,000
Real estate broker's commission	8,000
Cost of land	**$115,000**

When the acquisition is recorded, Land is debited for $115,000 and Cash is credited for $115,000.

LAND IMPROVEMENTS

The cost of land improvements includes all expenditures necessary to make the improvements ready for their intended use. For example, the cost of a new company parking lot includes the amount paid for paving, fencing, and lighting. These improvements have limited useful lives, and their maintenance and replacement are the responsibility of the company. Thus, these costs are debited to Land Improvements and are expensed over the useful lives of the improvements.

BUILDINGS

All necessary expenditures relating to the purchase or construction of a building are charged to the Buildings account. When a building is purchased, such costs include the purchase price, closing costs (attorney's fees, title insurance, etc.), and real estate broker's commission. Costs to make the building ready for its intended use consist of expenditures for remodeling rooms and offices and replacing or repairing the roof, floors, electrical wiring, and plumbing.

When a new building is constructed, its cost consists of the contract price plus payments made by the owner for architects' fees, building permits, and excavation costs. In addition, interest costs incurred to finance the project are included in the cost of the asset when a significant period of time is required to get the asset ready for use. In these circumstances, interest costs are considered as necessary as materials and labor. However, the inclusion of interest costs in the cost of a constructed building is **limited to the construction period.** When construction has been completed, subsequent interest payments on funds borrowed to finance the construction are recorded as increases (debits) to Interest Expense.

EQUIPMENT

The cost of equipment consists of the cash purchase price, sales taxes, freight charges, and insurance during transit paid by the purchaser. It also includes expenditures required in assembling, installing, and testing the unit. However, motor vehicle licenses and accident insurance on company trucks and cars are treated as expenses as they are incurred because they represent annual recurring expenditures and do not benefit future periods. Two criteria apply in determining the cost of equipment: (1) the frequency of the cost—one time or recurring and (2) the benefit period—the life of the asset or 1 year.

To illustrate, assume that Lenard Company purchases a delivery truck at a cash price of $22,000. Related expenditures are for sales taxes $1,320, painting and lettering $500, motor vehicle license $80, and a 3-year accident insurance policy $1,600. The cost of the delivery truck is $23,820, computed as shown in Illustration 9-3.

Delivery Truck	
Cash price	$ 22,000
Sales taxes	1,320
Painting and lettering	500
Cost of delivery truck	**$23,820**

Illustration 9-3 Computation of cost of delivery truck

The cost of a motor vehicle license is treated as an expense, and the cost of an insurance policy is considered a prepaid asset. Thus, the entry to record the purchase of the truck and related expenditures is as follows:

Delivery Truck	23,820	
License Expense	80	
Prepaid Insurance	1,600	
Cash		25,500
(To record purchase of delivery truck and related expenditures)		

For another example, assume Merten Company purchases factory machinery at a cash price of $50,000. Related expenditures are for sales taxes $3,000, insurance during shipping $500, and installation and testing $1,000. The cost of the factory machinery is $54,500, computed as in Illustration 9-4.

Illustration 9-4 Computation of cost of factory machinery

Factory Machinery	
Cash price	$ 50,000
Sales taxes	3,000
Insurance during shipping	500
Installation and testing	1,000
Cost of factory machinery	**$54,500**

Thus, the entry to record the purchase and related expenditures is as follows:

Factory Machinery	54,500	
Cash		54,500
(To record purchase of factory machinery and related expenditures)		

TO BUY OR LEASE?

In this chapter we focus on assets that are purchased, but we want to expose you briefly to an alternative to purchasing—leasing. In a lease, a party that owns an asset (the **lessor**) agrees to allow another party (the **lessee**) to use the asset for an agreed period of time at an agreed price. These are some advantages of leasing an asset versus purchasing it:

1. **Reduced risk of obsolescence.** Frequently, lease terms allow the party using the asset (the lessee) to exchange the asset for a more modern one if it becomes outdated. This is much easier than trying to sell an obsolete asset.
2. **Low down payment.** To purchase an asset most companies must borrow money, which usually requires a down payment of at least 20%. Leasing an asset requires little or no down payment.
3. **Shared tax advantages.** Startup companies typically do not make much money in their early years, and so they have little need for the tax deductions available from owning an asset. In a lease, the lessor gets the tax advantage because it owns the asset. It often will pass these tax savings on to the lessee in the form of lower lease payments.
4. **Assets and liabilities not reported.** Many companies prefer to keep assets and especially liabilities off of their books. Certain types of leases, called **operating leases,** allow the lessee to account for the transaction as a rental with neither an asset nor a liability recorded.

Airlines often choose to lease many of their airplanes in long-term lease agreements. In its 1995 financial statements, Southwest Airlines stated that it leased 100 of its 224 planes under operating leases. Because operating leases are accounted for as a rental, these 100 planes did not show up on its balance sheet.

Under another type of lease, a **capital lease,** both the asset and the liability are shown on the balance sheet. For the lessee under a capital lease, long-term lease agreements are accounted for in a way that is very similar to purchases: On the lessee's balance sheet, the leased item is shown as an asset and the obligation owed to the lessor is shown as a liability. The leased asset is depreciated by the lessee in a manner similar to purchased assets. About 10% of the 124 planes that *are* listed as assets on Southwest Airlines' balance sheet are leased planes that are accounted for as capital leases. Additional discussion about leasing is presented in Chapter 10 on liabilities.

BUSINESS INSIGHT
Management Perspective

As an excellent example of the magnitude of leasing, leased planes account for nearly 40% of the U.S. fleet of commercial airlines. The reasons for leasing include favorable tax treatment, increased flexibility, and low airline income. As passenger volume is expected to double in the next 20 years, some industry analysts estimate that approximately $400 billion in airplanes will be needed, and it is anticipated that much of the financing will be done through leasing. Leasing is particularly attractive to lessors because airplanes have relatively long lives, a ready secondhand market, and a significant resale value. Or take the commercial truck fleet—over one-third of heavy-duty trucks are presently leased.

BEFORE YOU GO ON . . .

● **Review It**
1. What are plant assets? What are the major classes of plant assets? At what value should plant assets be recorded?
2. What are revenue expenditures? What are capital expenditures?
3. What are the primary advantages of leasing?

● **Do It**

Assume that a delivery truck is purchased for $15,000 cash plus sales taxes of $900 and delivery costs to the dealer of $500. The buyer also pays $200 for painting and lettering, $600 for an annual insurance policy, and $80 for a motor vehicle license. Explain how each of these costs is accounted for.

Reasoning: The cost principle applies to all expenditures made in order to get delivery equipment ready for its intended use. The principle does not apply to operating costs incurred during the useful life of the equipment, such as gas and oil, motor tuneups, licenses, and insurance.

Solution: The first four payments ($15,000, $900, $500, and $200) are considered to be expenditures necessary to make the truck ready for its intended use. Thus, the cost of the truck is $16,600. The payments for insurance and the license are considered to be operating expenses incurred during the useful life of the asset.

Accounting for Plant Assets

DEPRECIATION

STUDY OBJECTIVE 2
Explain the concept of depreciation.

As explained in Chapter 4, **depreciation** is the process of allocating to expense the cost of a plant asset over its useful (service) life in a rational and systematic manner. Such cost allocation is designed to properly match expenses with revenues in accordance with the matching principle. (See Illustration 9-5.)

Illustration 9-5 Depreciation as an allocation concept

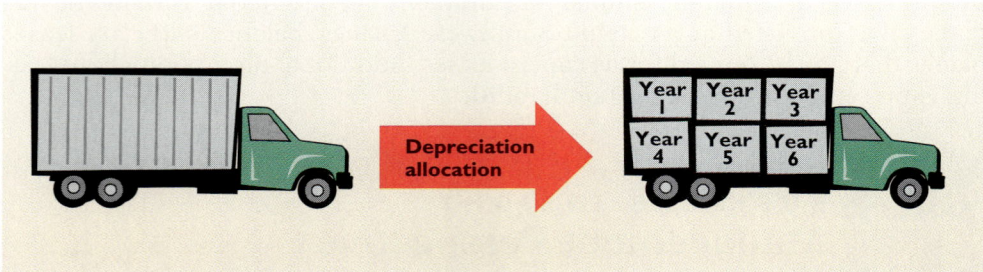

It is important to understand that **depreciation is a process of cost allocation, not a process of asset valuation.** No attempt is made to measure the change in an asset's market value during ownership because plant assets are not held for resale. Thus, the **book value**—cost less accumulated depreciation—of a plant asset may differ significantly from its **market value.** In fact, if an asset is fully depreciated, it can have zero book value but still have a significant market value.

Helpful Hint Remember that depreciation is the process of allocating cost over the useful life of an asset. It is not a measure of value.

Depreciation applies to three classes of plant assets: land improvements, buildings, and equipment. Each of these classes is considered to be a **depreciable asset** because the usefulness to the company and the revenue-producing ability of each class decline over the asset's useful life. Depreciation does not apply to land because its usefulness and revenue-producing ability generally remain intact as long as the land is owned. In fact, in many cases, the usefulness of land increases over time because of the scarcity of good sites. Thus, **land is not a depreciable asset.**

Helpful Hint Land does not depreciate because it does not wear out.

During a depreciable asset's useful life its revenue-producing ability declines because of **wear and tear.** A delivery truck that has been driven 100,000 miles will be less useful to a company than one driven only 800 miles. Similarly, trucks and cars exposed to snow and salt deteriorate faster than equipment that is not exposed to these elements.

A decline in revenue-producing ability may also occur because of **obsolescence.** Obsolescence is the process by which an asset becomes out of date before it physically wears out. The rerouting of major airlines from Chicago's Midway Airport to Chicago-O'Hare International Airport because Midway's runways were too short for jumbo jets is an example. Similarly, many companies have replaced their computers long before they had originally planned to do so because improvements in new computers made their old computers obsolete.

Recognizing depreciation for an asset does not result in the accumulation of cash for replacement of the asset. The balance in Accumulated Depreciation represents the total amount of the asset's cost that has been charged to expense to date; **it is not a cash fund.**

Factors in Computing Depreciation

Three factors affect the computation of depreciation, as shown in Illustration 9-6:

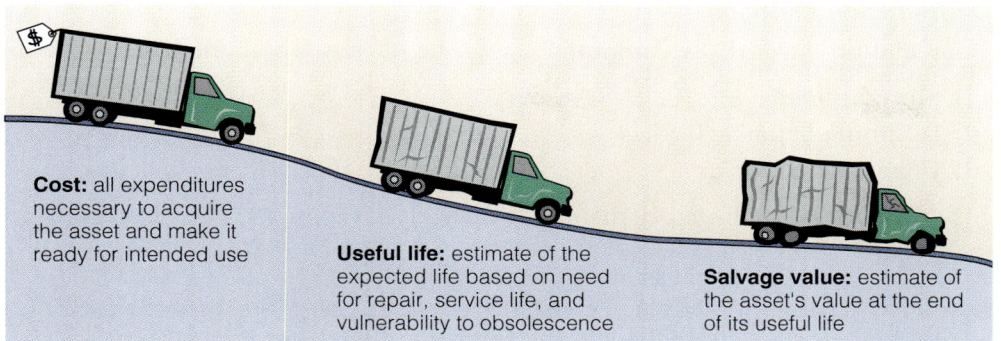

Illustration 9-6 Three factors in computing depreciation

1. **Cost.** Considerations that affect the cost of a depreciable asset have been explained earlier in this chapter. Remember that plant assets are recorded at cost, in accordance with the cost principle.
2. **Useful life.** Useful life is an estimate of the expected productive life, also called service life, of the asset. Useful life may be expressed in terms of time, units of activity (such as machine hours), or units of output. Useful life is an estimate. In making the estimate, management considers such factors as the intended use of the asset, repair and maintenance policies, and vulnerability of the asset to obsolescence. The company's past experience with similar assets is often helpful in deciding on expected useful life.
3. **Salvage value.** Salvage value is an estimate of the asset's value at the end of its useful life. The value may be based on the asset's worth as scrap or salvage or on its expected trade-in value. Like useful life, salvage value is an estimate. In making the estimate, management considers how it plans to dispose of the asset and its experience with similar assets.

BUSINESS INSIGHT
Management Perspective

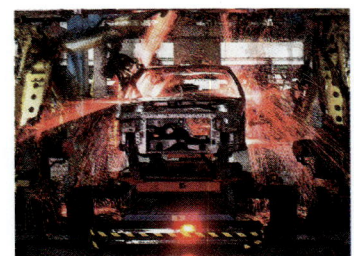

Not all companies use the same useful life. Compare the useful lives used by The Big Three automakers, for example. At one time General Motors depreciated its machinery over 10 years, compared to Ford's 12 years and Chrysler's 11 years. General Motors also depreciated its buildings over 28 years, while Ford used 30 years and Chrysler used 26 years. General Motors depreciated its dies and equipment used to manufacture car bodies about twice as fast as Ford and three times as fast as Chrysler. Now GM has changed its policy and aligned itself with its competitors by applying more liberal depreciation policies that have increased annual income. Should companies in the same industry be required to use the same useful life for the same type of assets?

BEFORE YOU GO ON . . .

● **Review It**

1. What is the relationship, if any, of depreciation to (a) cost allocation, (b) asset valuation, and (c) cash accumulation?
2. Explain the factors that affect the computation of depreciation.

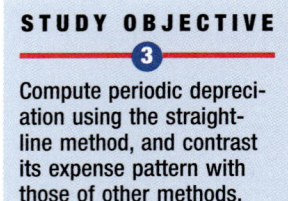

STUDY OBJECTIVE 3

Compute periodic depreciation using the straight-line method, and contrast its expense pattern with those of other methods.

Depreciation Methods

Depreciation is generally computed using one of these three methods:

1. Straight-line
2. Declining-balance
3. Units-of-activity

Like the alternative inventory methods discussed in Chapter 6, each method is acceptable under generally accepted accounting principles. Management selects the method it believes best measures an asset's contribution to revenue over its useful life. Once a method is chosen, it should be applied consistently over the useful life of the asset. Consistency enhances the comparability of financial statements.

Depreciation affects the balance sheet through accumulated depreciation, which is reported as a deduction from plant assets. It affects the income statement through depreciation expense. Illustration 9-7 shows the distribution of the *primary* depreciation methods in 600 of the largest U.S. companies. Clearly, straight-line depreciation is the most widely used approach. In fact, because some companies use more than one method, it can actually be said that straight-line depreciation is used for some or all of the depreciation taken by more than 90% of U.S. companies. For this reason, we illustrate procedures for straight-line depreciation and discuss the alternative approaches only at a conceptual level. This coverage introduces you to the basic idea of depreciation as an allocation concept without entangling you in too much procedural detail. (Also, note that many hand-held calculators are preprogrammed to perform the basic depreciation methods.) Details on the alternative approaches are presented in Appendix 9A to this chapter (page 415).

Our illustration of depreciation methods, both here and in Appendix 9A, is based on the following data relating to a small delivery truck purchased by Bill's Pizzas on January 1, 1998:

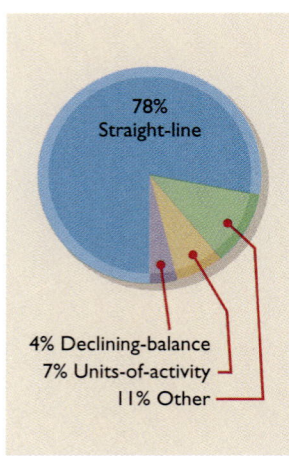

Illustration 9-7 Use of depreciation methods in major U.S. companies

Cost	$13,000
Expected salvage value	$1,000
Estimated useful life (in years)	5
Estimated useful life (in miles)	100,000

Straight-Line. Under the **straight-line method,** depreciation is the same for each year of the asset's useful life. It is measured solely by the passage of time. Management must choose the useful life of an asset based on its own expectations and experience. To compute the annual depreciation expense, it is necessary to determine depreciable cost. **Depreciable cost,** which represents the total amount subject to depreciation, is calculated as the cost of the asset less its salvage value. Depreciable cost is then divided by the asset's useful life to determine **depreciation expense.** The computation of depreciation expense in the first year for Bill's Pizzas' delivery trucks is shown in Illustration 9-8.

Alternatively, we can compute an annual *rate* at which the delivery truck is being depreciated. In this case, the rate is 20% (100% ÷ 5 years). When an annual rate is used under the straight-line method, the percentage rate is applied to the depreciable cost of the asset, as shown in the **depreciation schedule** in Illustration 9-9.

Note that the depreciation expense of $2,400 is the same each year, and that the book value at the end of the useful life is equal to the estimated $1,000 salvage value.

What happens when an asset is purchased **during** the year, rather than on January 1, as in our example? In that case, it is necessary to **prorate the annual depreciation** for the proportion of a year used. If Bill's Pizzas had pur-

Accounting for Plant Assets   **393**

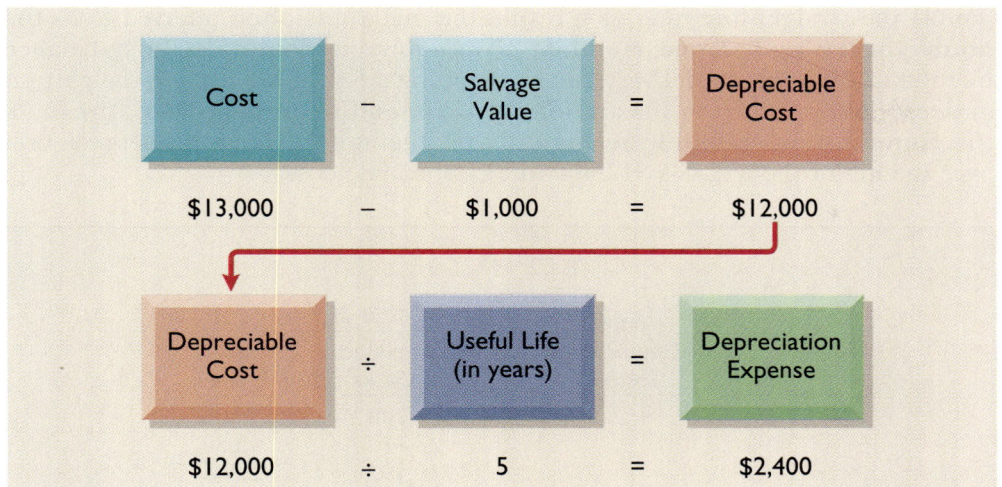

Illustration 9-8 Formula for straight-line method

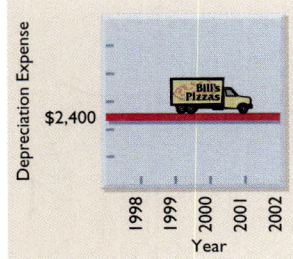

Illustration 9-9 Straight-line depreciation schedule

	BILL'S PIZZAS				
	Computation		Annual	End of Year	
Year	Depreciable Cost	× Depreciation Rate	= Depreciation Expense	Accumulated Depreciation	Book Value
1998	$12,000	20%	**$2,400**	$ 2,400	$10,600*
1999	12,000	20	**2,400**	4,800	8,200
2000	12,000	20	**2,400**	7,200	5,800
2001	12,000	20	**2,400**	9,600	3,400
2002	12,000	20	**2,400**	12,000	**1,000**
		Total	$12,000		

*$13,000 − $2,400

chased the delivery truck on April 1, 1998, the depreciation for 1998 would be $1,800 ($12,000 × 20% × $\frac{9}{12}$ of a year).

As indicated earlier, the straight-line method predominates in practice. For example, such large companies as Campbell Soup, Marriott Corporation, and General Mills use the straight-line method. It is simple to apply, and it matches expenses with revenues appropriately when the use of the asset is reasonably uniform throughout the service life. The types of assets that give equal benefits over useful life generally are those for which daily use does not affect productivity. Examples are office furniture and fixtures, buildings, warehouses, and garages for motor vehicles.

Declining-Balance. The **declining-balance method** is called an "accelerated method" because it results in more depreciation in the early years of an asset's life than does the straight-line approach. However, because the total amount of depreciation (the depreciable cost) taken over an asset's life is the same no matter what approach is used, the declining-balance method produces a decreasing annual depreciation expense over the useful life of the asset. That is, in early years it will exceed straight-line, but in later years it will be less than straight-line. Managers might choose an accelerated approach if they think that an asset's utility will decline very quickly.

The declining-balance approach can be applied at different rates, which result in varying speeds of depreciation. A common declining-balance rate is double the straight-line rate. As a result, the method is often referred to as the **double-declining-balance method.** If we apply the double-declining-balance method to Bill's Pizzas' delivery truck, assuming a 5-year life, we get the pattern of depreciation shown in Illustration 9-10. **Appendix 9A, page 416, presents the computations behind these numbers.** Again, note that total depreciation over the life of the truck is $12,000, the depreciable cost.

Illustration 9-10
Declining-balance depreciation schedule

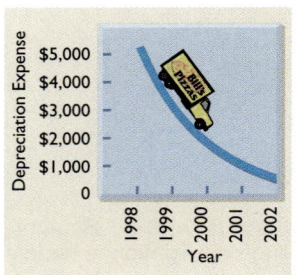

		BILL'S PIZZAS	
	Annual	End of Year	
	Depreciation	Accumulated	Book
Year	Expense	Depreciation	Value
1998	$ 5,200	$ 5,200	$7,800
1999	3,120	8,320	4,680
2000	1,872	10,192	2,808
2001	1,123	11,315	1,685
2002	685	12,000	1,000
Total	$12,000		

Units-of-Activity. Under the **units-of-activity method,** instead of expressing the asset's life as a time period, useful life is expressed in terms of the total units of production or the use expected from the asset. The units-of-activity method is ideally suited to factory machinery: Production can be measured in terms of units of output or in terms of machine hours used in operating the machinery. It is also possible to use the method for such items as delivery equipment (miles driven) and airplanes (hours in use). The units-of-activity method is generally not suitable for such assets as buildings or furniture because depreciation for these assets is a function more of time than of use.

Applying the units-of-activity method to the delivery truck owned by Bill's Pizzas, we first must know some basic information. Bill's expects to be able to drive the truck a total of 100,000 miles. If we assume that the mileage occurs in the given pattern over the 5-year life, depreciation in each year is shown in Illustration 9-11. **The computations used to arrive at these results are presented in Appendix 9A, page 417.**

Illustration 9-11 Units-of-activity depreciation schedule

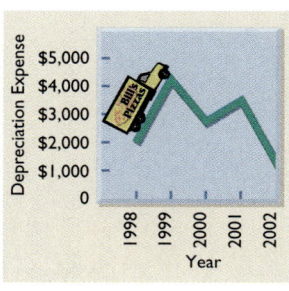

			BILL'S PIZZAS	
	Units of	Annual	End of Year	
	Activity	Depreciation	Accumulated	Book
Year	(miles)	Expense	Depreciation	Value
1998	15,000	$ 1,800	$ 1,800	$11,200
1999	30,000	3,600	5,400	7,600
2000	20,000	2,400	7,800	5,200
2001	25,000	3,000	10,800	2,200
2002	10,000	1,200	12,000	1,000
Total	100,000	$12,000		

As the name implies, under units-of-activity depreciation, the amount of depreciation is proportional to the activity that took place during that period. For example, the delivery truck was driven twice as many miles in 1999 as in 1998, and depreciation was exactly twice as much in 1999 as it was in 1998.

Management's Choice: Comparison of Methods

Illustration 9-12 presents a comparison of annual and total depreciation expense for Bill's Pizzas under the three methods.

Year	Straight-Line	Declining-Balance	Units-of-Activity
1998	$ 2,400	$ 5,200	$ 1,800
1999	2,400	3,120	3,600
2000	2,400	1,872	2,400
2001	2,400	1,123	3,000
2002	2,400	685	1,200
	$12,000	**$12,000**	**$12,000**

Illustration 9-12
Comparison of depreciation methods

Periodic depreciation varies considerably among the methods, but total depreciation is the same for the 5-year period. Each method is acceptable in accounting because each recognizes the decline in service potential of the asset in a rational and systematic manner. The depreciation expense pattern under each method is presented graphically in Illustration 9-13.

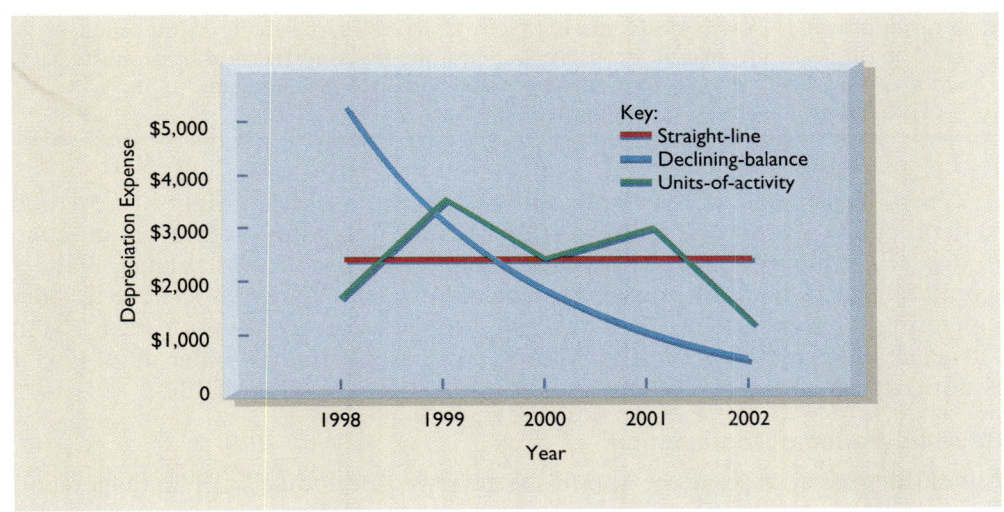

Illustration 9-13
Patterns of depreciation

Depreciation and Income Taxes

The Internal Revenue Service (IRS) allows corporate taxpayers to deduct depreciation expense when computing taxable income. However, the tax regulations of the IRS do not require the taxpayer to use the same depreciation method on the tax return that is used in preparing financial statements. Consequently, many large corporations use straight-line depreciation in their financial statements to maximize net income, and at the same time they use a special accelerated-depreciation method on their tax returns to minimize their income taxes. For tax purposes, taxpayers must use on their tax returns either the straight-line method or a special accelerated-depreciation method called the **Modified Accelerated Cost Recovery System** (MACRS).

Helpful Hint Depreciation per GAAP is usually different from depreciation per IRS rules.

 International Note
In Germany, tax laws have a strong influence on financial accounting. Depreciation expense determined by the tax code must also be used for preparing financial statements.

Depreciation Disclosure in the Notes

The choice of depreciation method must be disclosed in a company's financial statements or in related notes that accompany the statements. Illustration 9-14 shows the "property and equipment" notes from the financial statements of Valujet and Southwest Airlines.

Illustration 9-14
Disclosure of depreciation policies

VALUJET
Notes to the Financial Statements

Property and equipment Property and equipment is stated on the basis of cost. Flight equipment is depreciated to its residual values, estimated at 20%, using the straight-line method over seven to ten years. Other property and equipment is depreciated over three years.

SOUTHWEST AIRLINES
Notes to the Financial Statements

Property and equipment Depreciation is provided by the straight-line method to residual values over periods ranging from 15 to 20 years for flight equipment and 3 to 30 years for ground property and equipment. Amortization of property under capital leases is on a straight-line basis over the lease term and is included in depreciation expense.

From these notes we learn that both companies use the straight-line method to depreciate their planes. Southwest Airlines also uses the straight-line method to depreciate planes that it leases rather than purchases. At first glance, Valujet would appear to be more conservative than Southwest Airlines because it is depreciating its planes over a 7- to 10-year life, whereas Southwest uses a 15- to 20-year life. Recall, however, that Valujet purchases primarily older planes, so it is not surprising that the company is using a shorter estimated life.

Revising Periodic Depreciation

STUDY OBJECTIVE 4
Describe the procedure for revising periodic depreciation.

Annual depreciation expense should be reviewed periodically by management. If wear and tear or obsolescence indicates that annual depreciation is inadequate or excessive, the depreciation expense amount should be changed.

When a change in an estimate is required, the change is made in **current and future years but not to prior periods.** Thus, when a change is made, (1) there is no correction of previously recorded depreciation expense, and (2) depreciation expense for current and future years is revised. The rationale for this treatment is that continual restatement of prior periods would adversely affect the user's confidence in financial statements.

Significant changes in estimates must be disclosed in the financial statements. Although a company may have a legitimate reason for changing an estimated life, financial statement users should be aware that some companies might change an estimate simply to achieve financial statement goals. For example, extending an asset's estimated life reduces depreciation expense and increases current period income.

Two recent examples of changes in depreciation estimates that substantially increased income occurred in the airline industry, as shown in the excerpts from financial statements in Illustration 9-15.

Illustration 9-15
Disclosures of changes in depreciation estimates

TRANS WORLD AIRLINES INC.
Notes to the Financial Statements

Effective January 1, 1990, the estimated depreciable service lives of four MD-80 and two DC9-30 aircraft owned by TWA were extended and the residual values adjusted to more fairly reflect the remaining operational life of these aircraft which were acquired in TWA's 1986 acquisition of Ozark Holdings, Inc. Such change resulted in an approximate increase in average depreciable lives of five years for the four owned MD-80 aircraft and ten years for the two owned DC9-30 aircraft. The provision for depreciation expense in 1990 was reduced approximately $2,600,000 because of this change in estimate.

DELTA AIR LINES
Management Discussion and Analysis

Fiscal 1993 results were positively impacted by changes in two accounting estimates. Effective April 1, 1993, Delta revised its depreciation policy by increasing the estimated useful lives of substantially all of its flight equipment from 15 to 20 years and reducing residual values from 10% to 5% of cost. This change reduced depreciation expense by $34.3 million in fiscal 1993, and is expected to reduce depreciation expense by an estimated $126 million in fiscal 1994.

Both airlines were operating at losses at the time of these changes. Whether these changes are reasonable depends on the accuracy of their assumptions regarding these planes. Our opening story suggests that although many planes are lasting a long time, recent safety concerns might ground many old planes.

BEFORE YOU GO ON...

● **Review It**

1. Why is depreciation an allocation concept rather than a valuation concept?
2. What is the formula for computing annual depreciation under the straight-line method?
3. How do the depreciation methods differ in their effects on annual depreciation over the useful life of an asset?
4. Are revisions of periodic depreciation made to prior periods? Explain.

● **Do It**

On January 1, 1998, Iron Mountain Ski Corporation purchased a new snow grooming machine for $50,000. The machine is estimated to have a 10-year life with a $2,000 salvage value. What journal entry would Iron Mountain Ski Corporation make at December 31, 1998, if it uses the straight-line method of depreciation?

Reasoning: Depreciation is an allocation concept. Under straight-line depreciation an equal amount of the depreciable cost is allocated to each period.

Solution:

$$\text{Depreciation expense} = \frac{\text{Cost} - \text{Salvage value}}{\text{Useful life}} = \frac{\$50,000 - \$2,000}{10} = \$4,800$$

The entry to record the first year's depreciation would be:

Dec. 31	Depreciation Expense	4,800	
	Accumulated Depreciation		4,800
	(To record annual depreciation on snow grooming machine)		

EXPENDITURES DURING USEFUL LIFE

During the useful life of a plant asset, a company may incur costs for ordinary repairs, additions, and improvements. **Ordinary repairs** are expenditures to maintain the operating efficiency and expected productive life of the unit. They usually are fairly small amounts that occur frequently throughout the service life. Motor tune-ups and oil changes, the painting of buildings, and the replacing of worn-out gears on factory machinery are examples. They are debited to Repair (or Maintenance) Expense as incurred. Because they are immediately charged against revenues as an expense, these costs are **revenue expenditures.**

Additions and improvements are costs incurred to increase the operating efficiency, productive capacity, or expected useful life of the plant asset. These expenditures are usually material in amount and occur infrequently during the period of ownership. Expenditures for additions and improvements increase the company's investment in productive facilities and are generally debited to the plant asset affected. Accordingly, they are **capital expenditures.** The accounting for capital expenditures varies depending on the nature of the expenditure.

Helpful Hint These expenditures occur after all costs have been incurred to make the asset ready for its intended use when it was acquired.

Northwest Airlines recently spent $120 million to spruce up 40 DC9-30 jets. The improvements were designed to extend the lives of the planes, meet stricter government noise limits, and save money. The capital expenditure was expected to extend the life of the jets by 10 to 15 years and save about $560 million over the cost of buying new planes. The DC9 jets now have an average age of 24 years.

IMPAIRMENTS

As noted earlier, the book value of plant assets is rarely the same as the market value. In instances where the market value of a plant asset declines substantially, its market value may be materially below book value. This may happen because a machine has become obsolete, or the market for the product made by the machine has dried up or has become very competitive. A **permanent decline** in the market value of an asset is referred to as an **impairment.** In order that the asset is not overstated on the books, it is written down to its new market value during the year in which the decline in value occurs. In the past, some companies delayed recording losses on impairments until a year when it was "convenient" to do so—when the impact on the firm's reported results was minimized. For example, if a firm has record profits in one year, it can then afford to write down some of its bad assets without hurting its reported results too much. The practice of timing the recognition of gains and losses to achieve certain income results is known as **earnings management.** A recent FASB standard requires immediate recognition of these write-downs in order to reduce the practice of earnings management.

Write-downs can create problems for users of financial statements. Critics of write-downs note that after a firm writes down assets, its depreciation expense will be lower in all subsequent periods. Some firms intentionally write down assets in bad years, when they are going to report low results anyway. Then in subsequent years, when the company recovers, its results will look even better because of lower depreciation expense.

BUSINESS INSIGHT
Investor Perspective

In recent years companies such as IBM, 3M, Westinghouse, and Digital Equipment Corporation have reported huge write-downs. These companies are quick to emphasize that these are "nonrecurring events"; that is, they are one-time charges and thus do not represent a recurring drag on future earnings. However, a number of large firms have reported large write-downs in multiple years, which makes analysts suspicious. After one of IBM's recent write-downs, one analyst recommended not buying IBM stock because, with such frequent write-downs, "What confidence do we have the same will not happen again?"

Source: F. R. Bleakley, "New Write-offs Mostly Please Investors," *The Wall Street Journal,* December 21, 1995, p. C1.

PLANT ASSET DISPOSALS

Companies dispose of plant assets that are no longer useful to them. Illustration 9-16 shows the three ways in which plant asset disposals are made.

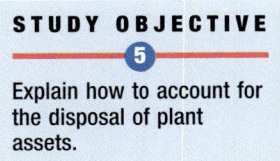

STUDY OBJECTIVE 5

Explain how to account for the disposal of plant assets.

Illustration 9-16
Methods of plant asset disposal

Whatever the disposal method, the company must determine the book value of the plant asset at the time of disposal. Recall that the book value is the difference between the cost of the plant asset and the accumulated depreciation to date. If the disposal occurs at any time during the year, depreciation for the fraction of the year to the date of disposal must be recorded. The book value is then eliminated by reducing (debiting) Accumulated Depreciation for the total depreciation associated with that asset to the date of disposal and reducing (crediting) the asset account for the cost of the asset.

Sale of Plant Assets

In a disposal by sale, the book value of the asset is compared with the proceeds received from the sale. If the proceeds from the sale exceed the book value of the plant asset, a **gain on disposal** occurs. If the proceeds from the sale are less than the book value of the plant asset sold, a **loss on disposal** occurs.

400 CHAPTER 9 Reporting and Analyzing Long-Lived Assets

Only by coincidence will the book value and the fair market value of the asset be the same at the time the asset is sold. Gains and losses on sales of plant assets are therefore quite common. As an example, Delta Air Lines, Inc., reported a $94,343,000 gain on the sale of five Boeing B-727-200 aircraft and five Lockheed L-1011-1 aircraft.

Gain on Sale. To illustrate a gain on sale of plant assets, assume that on July 1, 1998, Wright Company sells office furniture for $16,000 cash. The office furniture originally cost $60,000 and as of January 1, 1998, had accumulated depreciation of $41,000. Depreciation for the first 6 months of 1998 is $8,000. The entry to record depreciation expense and update accumulated depreciation to July 1 is as follows:

July 1	Depreciation Expense	8,000	
	Accumulated Depreciation—Office Furniture		8,000
	(To record depreciation expense for the first 6 months of 1998)		

After the accumulated depreciation balance is updated, a gain on disposal of $5,000 is computed as shown in Illustration 9-17.

Illustration 9-17
Computation of gain on disposal

Cost of office furniture		$60,000
Less: Accumulated depreciation ($41,000 + $8,000)		49,000
Book value at date of disposal		11,000
Proceeds from sale		16,000
Gain on disposal of plant asset		**$ 5,000**

The entry to record the sale and the gain on sale of the plant asset is as follows:

July 1	Cash	16,000	
	Accumulated Depreciation—Office Furniture	49,000	
	Office Furniture		60,000
	Gain on Disposal		5,000
	(To record sale of office furniture at a gain)		

The gain on disposal of the plant asset is reported in the Other Revenues and Gains section of the income statement.

Loss on Sale. Assume that instead of selling the office furniture for $16,000, Wright sells it for $9,000. In this case, a loss of $2,000 is computed as in Illustration 9-18.

Illustration 9-18
Computation of loss on disposal

Cost of office furniture	$60,000
Less: Accumulated depreciation	49,000
Book value at date of disposal	11,000
Proceeds from sale	9,000
Loss on disposal of plant asset	**$ 2,000**

The entry to record the sale and the loss on sale of the plant asset is as follows:

July 1	Cash	9,000	
	Accumulated Depreciation—Office Furniture	49,000	
	Loss on Disposal	2,000	
	Office Furniture		60,000
	(To record sale of office furniture at a loss)		

The loss on disposal of the plant asset is reported in the Other Expenses and Losses section of the income statement.

Retirement of Plant Assets

Some assets are simply retired by the company at the end of their useful life rather than sold. For example, some productive assets used in manufacturing may have very specific uses and consequently have no ready market when the company no longer needs them. In this case the asset is simply retired.

Retirement of an asset is recorded as a special case of a sale where no cash is received. Accumulated Depreciation is decreased (debited) for the full amount of depreciation taken over the life of the asset. The asset account is reduced (credited) for the original cost of the asset. The loss (a gain is not possible on a retirement) is equal to the asset's book value on the date of retirement.[1]

BEFORE YOU GO ON . . .

● **Review It**

1. What is the difference between an ordinary repair and an addition or improvement? Why is this distinction important to financial reporting?
2. What is an impairment? In what way do some critics suggest that companies manage their earnings through the write-downs associated with impairments?
3. What is the proper accounting for sales and retirements of plant assets?

● **Do It**

Overland Trucking has an old truck that cost $30,000 and has accumulated depreciation of $16,000. Assume two different situations: (1) The company sells the old truck for $17,000 cash. (2) The truck is worthless, so the company simply retires it. What entry should Overland use to record each scenario?

Reasoning: Gains and losses on the sale or retirement of plant assets are determined by the difference between the book value and the fair market value of the company's asset.

Solution:

1. Sale of truck for cash:

Cash		17,000	
Accumulated Depreciation—Truck		16,000	
Truck			30,000
Gain on Disposal [$17,000 − ($30,000 − $16,000)]			3,000
(To record sale of truck at a gain)			

---

[1]The accounting for exchanges is discussed in more advanced courses.

2. Retirement of truck:

Accumulated Depreciation—Truck	16,000	
Loss on Disposal	14,000	
Truck		30,000
(To record retirement of truck at a loss)		

Analyzing Plant Assets

STUDY OBJECTIVE 6

Describe methods for evaluating the use of plant assets.

The presentation of financial statement information about plant assets enables decision makers to analyze the company's use of its plant assets. Illustration 9-19 presents information from the financial statements of Valujet and Southwest Airlines. We will use three measures to analyze plant assets: average useful life, average age of plant assets, and asset turnover ratio.

Illustration 9-19 Financial facts for Valujet and Southwest Airlines

($ in thousands)	Valujet	Southwest Airlines
Total cost of plant assets—1995	$215,789	$3,784,388
Total cost of plant assets—1994	75,566	3,342,801
Accumulated depreciation—1995	18,834	1,005,081
Accumulated depreciation—1994	3,687	837,838
Depreciation expense	15,147	156,771
Total assets—1995	346,741	3,256,122
Total assets—1994	173,039	2,823,071
Net sales	367,757	2,872,751

AVERAGE USEFUL LIFE

By selecting a longer estimated useful life, a company spreads the cost of its plant assets over a longer period of time. As a result, the amount of depreciation expense reported in each period is lower and net income is higher. A more conservative company will choose a shorter estimated useful life and will have a lower reported net income.

    In the notes to financial statements, many companies are not very precise about the estimated useful life of specific assets. For example, a common disclosure might read, "Plant assets are depreciated using the straight-line method over estimated useful lives ranging from 5 to 40 years." This statement makes it difficult to determine whether a company is using a conservative approach for depreciation. It is unclear, for example, how many assets are being depreciated using short lives and how many using long lives. To overcome this problem, we can estimate the **average useful life** of plant assets for a company and compare it to that of its competitors. The average useful life is estimated by dividing the average cost of plant assets (property, plant, and equipment) by the depreciation expense.

Illustration 9-20 presents a computation of the average useful life used by Valujet and by Southwest Airlines.

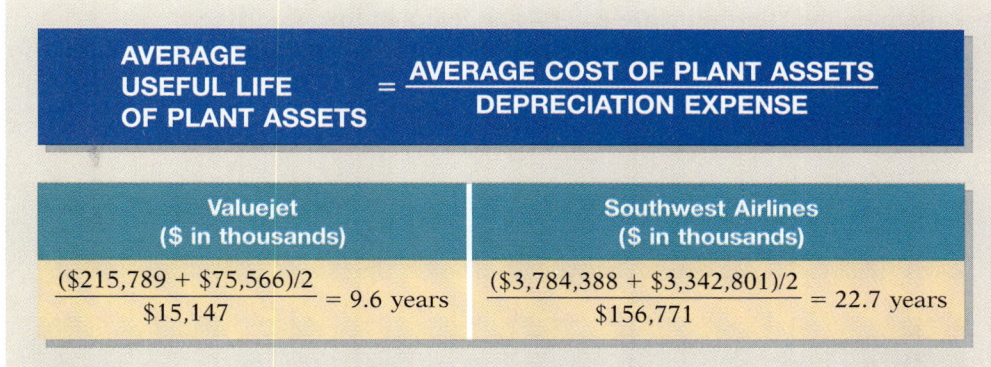

Illustration 9-20
Average useful life of plant assets

The estimate of each company's average useful life is consistent with the information published in their notes. Although both airlines depreciate some assets over a 3-year life, the majority of their assets are depreciated over longer lives. We recommend that, when analyzing a company, you use the estimate of the average useful life only as a check on the company's published depreciable lives. It is a rough approximation at best but can be useful when a company does not provide detailed disclosures for specific assets.

Helpful Hint Illustration 9-14 shows that Valujet depreciates its planes over 7 to 10 years, and Southwest uses a 15- to 20-year life. Also, Valujet depreciates its other property and equipment over a 3-year period, while Southwest uses a range of 3 to 30 years.

DECISION TOOLKIT

Decision Checkpoints	Info Needed for Decision	Tool to Use for Decision	How to Evaluate Results
Is the company's estimated useful life for depreciation reasonable?	Estimated useful life of assets from notes to financial statements of this company and its competitors	If the company's estimated useful life significantly exceeds that of competitors or does not seem reasonable in light of the circumstances, the reason for the difference should be investigated. If notes do not provide sufficient detail, average useful life can be estimated as: $$\text{Average useful life} = \frac{\text{Average cost of plant assets}}{\text{Depreciation expense}}$$	Too high an estimated useful life will result in understating depreciation expense and overstating net income.

AVERAGE AGE OF PLANT ASSETS

Because most companies use straight-line depreciation in their financial reporting, it is easy to estimate the average age of plant assets. For example, if XYZ Co. has depreciation expense of $10,000 and accumulated depreciation of $30,000, the **average age of plant assets** is 3 years ($30,000 ÷ $10,000). As a result, comparing the average age of plant assets gives an indication of the potential effectiveness of a company's plant assets relative to others in the industry. Consider the importance of new equipment to a hospital or new planes to an airline. Not only are newer planes more fuel efficient but they also require less maintenance and they are safer—key features for an airline.

The average age of plant assets can be approximated using the formula in Illustration 9-21.

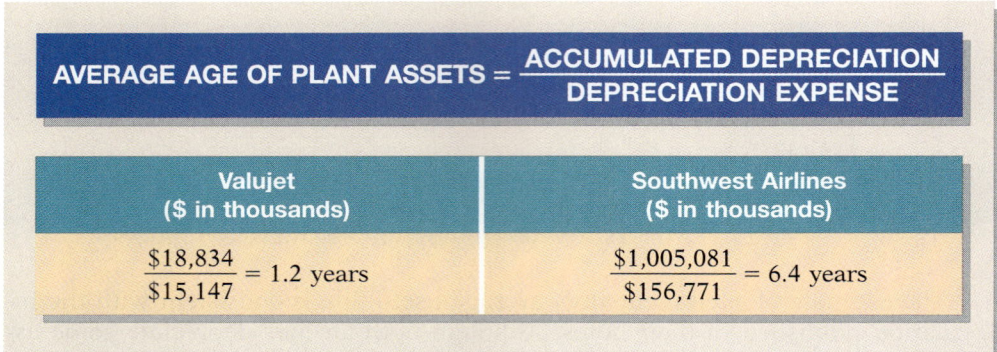

Illustration 9-21
Average age of plant assets

Neither airline provides information by major class of asset for depreciation; as a consequence, we cannot refine our estimate. If, for example, they provided information on planes and buildings separately, we could calculate each and have a more precise estimate of the average age of planes and of buildings. Given the information available, we can calculate only the average age of plant assets in general (see Illustration 9-21 for Valujet and Southwest Airlines for 1995). These numbers suggest that the average age of a Valujet plane is 1.2 years and the average age of a Southwest Airlines plane is 6.4 years. From this one might conclude that Valujet planes are substantially newer than those of Southwest. But we know from the opening story that Valujet has the oldest fleet of any major airline—with an average plane age of 26 years—whereas Southwest has the newest fleet. What is wrong with our estimate?

Our estimate of average age is wrong because this ratio does not work when a company purchases *used* assets. The figure of 1.2 years tells us that Valujet has *owned this asset* for 1.2 years. If it had been purchased new, it would be 1.2 years old. However, if it was 24 years old when purchased, it would now be 25.2 years old. This is an important lesson: Never use ratios unless you fully understand their strengths and weaknesses. Ratios can be very informative but also very misleading.

DECISION TOOLKIT

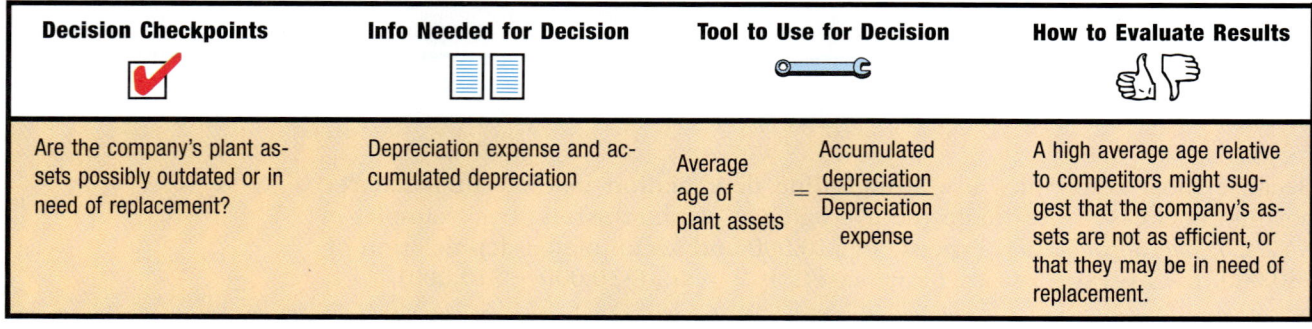

ASSET TURNOVER RATIO

The **asset turnover ratio** indicates how efficiently a company is able to generate sales with a given amount of assets—that is, how many dollars of sales are generated by each dollar invested in assets. When we compare two firms in the same industry, the one with the higher asset turnover ratio is operating more efficiently; it is generating more sales per dollar invested in assets.

The asset turnover ratios for Valujet and Southwest Airlines for 1995 are computed in Illustration 9-22.

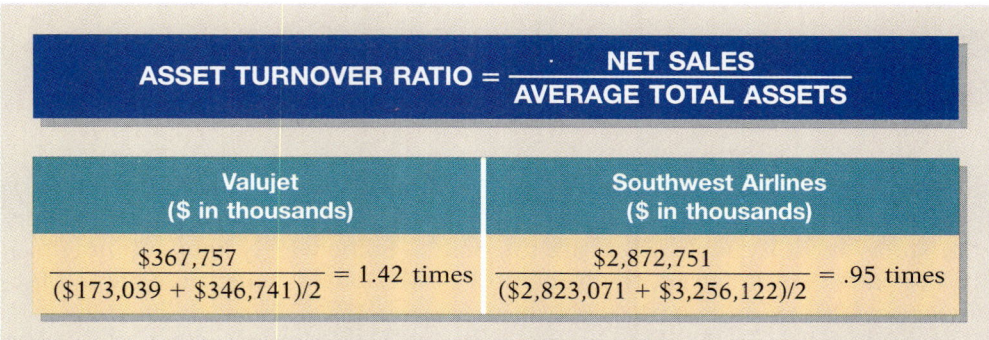

Illustration 9-22 Asset turnover ratio

The asset turnover ratios mean that for each dollar invested in assets, Valujet generates sales of $1.42 and Southwest $.95. Valujet is more successful in generating sales per dollar invested in assets, perhaps due in part to its decision to buy older planes.

For a complete picture, one would want to also look at the companies' profit margin ratios. Valujet's decision to use old planes might mean that it incurs more costs per dollar of sales (for things like additional fuel and repairs), which would result in lower profit per dollar of sales, as measured by the profit margin ratio. Although Valujet's asset turnover ratio is better than Southwest's, both compare favorably to the industry average for airlines of .7 times. Clearly, these airlines' ability to generate a lot of sales from a relatively small amount of assets is a big reason these two upstarts have been so successful.

Asset turnover ratios vary considerably among industries. For example, a large utility company like Union Electric Company (St. Louis) has a ratio of .36, and the large grocery chain Great Atlantic and Pacific Tea (A&P) has a ratio of 3.6. Asset turnover ratios, therefore, are only comparable within—not between—industries.

DECISION TOOLKIT

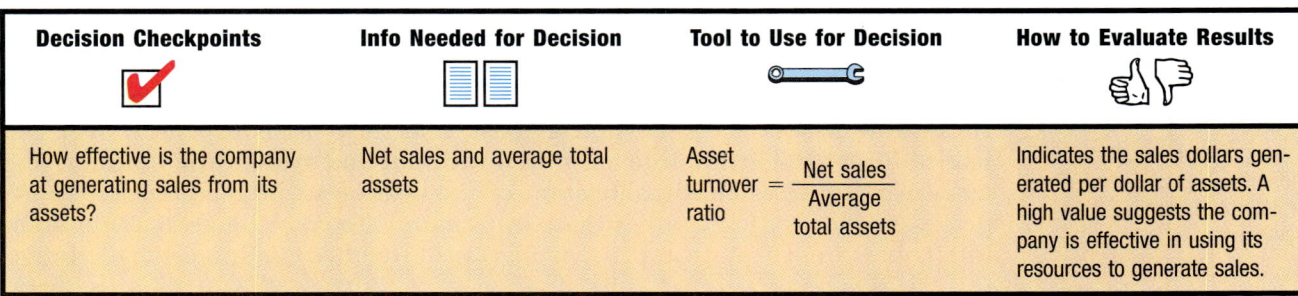

406 CHAPTER 9 Reporting and Analyzing Long-Lived Assets

> **BEFORE YOU GO ON...**
>
> ● **Review It**
> 1. What is the purpose of the computation of the average age of plant assets? How is it calculated?
> 2. What is the purpose of the asset turnover ratio? How is it computed?

SECTION 2
INTANGIBLE ASSETS

Intangible assets are rights, privileges, and competitive advantages that result from ownership of long-lived assets that do not possess physical substance. Many companies' most valuable assets are intangible. Some widely known intangibles are the patents of Polaroid, the franchises of McDonald's, the trade name Macintosh, and Nike's trademark "swoosh."

As you will learn in this section, although financial statements do report many intangibles, many other financially significant intangibles are not reported. To give an example, according to its 1996 financial statements, Microsoft had a net book value of $5.3 billion. But its *market* value—the total market price of all its shares on that same date—was roughly $57 billion. Thus, its actual market value was more than $50 billion greater than what its balance sheet said the company was worth. It is not uncommon for a company's reported book value to differ from its market value because balance sheets are reported at historical cost. But such an extreme difference seriously diminishes the usefulness of the balance sheet to decision makers. In the case of Microsoft, the difference is due to unrecorded intangibles. For many high-tech or so-called intellectual property companies, most of their value is from intangibles, many of which are not reported under current accounting rules.

Intangibles may be evidenced by contracts, licenses, and other documents. Intangibles may arise from these sources:

1. Government grants such as patents, copyrights, franchises, trademarks, and trade names.
2. Acquisition of another business in which the purchase price includes a payment for goodwill.
3. Private monopolistic arrangements arising from contractual agreements, such as franchises and leases.

ACCOUNTING FOR INTANGIBLE ASSETS

STUDY OBJECTIVE 7
Identify the basic issues related to reporting intangible assets.

Intangible assets are recorded at cost, and this cost is expensed **over the useful life of the intangible asset in a rational and systematic manner.** The term used to describe the allocation of the cost of an intangible asset to expense is **amortization,** rather than *depreciation*. To record amortization of an intangible, amortization expense is increased (debited) and the specific intangible asset account is decreased (credited). (Unlike depreciation, no contra account, such as Accumulated Amortization, is used.) Amortization expense is classified as an **operating expense** in the income statement. At disposal, the book value of the intangible asset is eliminated, and a gain or loss, if any, is recorded.

The amortization period of an intangible asset cannot be longer than 40 years. Even if the useful life of an intangible is 60 years, for example, it must be written off over 40 years. Conversely, if the useful life is less than 40 years, the useful life is used as the amortization period. This rule helps ensure that all intangibles, especially those with indeterminable lives, will be written off in a reasonable time.

Intangible assets are typically amortized on a straight-line basis. For example, the legal life of a patent is 17 years. **The cost of a patent should be amortized over its 17-year life or its useful life, whichever is shorter.** To illustrate the computation of patent amortization, assume that National Labs purchases a patent at a cost of $60,000. If the useful life of the patent is estimated to be 8 years, the annual amortization expense is $7,500 ($60,000 ÷ 8). The following entry records the annual amortization:

Dec. 31	Patent Expense	7,500	
	Patent		7,500
	(To record patent amortization)		

When analyzing a company that has significant intangibles, the reasonableness of the estimated useful life should be evaluated. In determining useful life, the company should consider obsolescence, inadequacy, and other factors; these may cause a patent or other intangible to become economically ineffective before the end of its legal life. For example, suppose a computer hardware manufacturer obtained a patent on a new computer chip that it had developed. The legal life of the patent is 17 years. From experience, we know that the useful life of a computer chip is not more than 4 to 5 years, and sometimes less. Because new superior chips are developed so rapidly, existing chips become obsolete. Consequently, we would question the amortization expense of a company if it amortized its patent on a computer chip for longer than a 5-year period. Amortizing an intangible over a period that is too long will understate amortization expense, overstate the company's net income, and overstate its assets.

DECISION TOOLKIT

Decision Checkpoints	Info Needed for Decision	Tool to Use for Decision	How to Evaluate Results
Is the company's amortization of intangibles reasonable?	Estimated useful life of intangibles from notes to financial statements of this company and its competitors	If the company's estimated useful life significantly exceeds that of competitors or does not seem reasonable in light of the circumstances, the reason for the difference should be investigated.	Too high an estimated useful life will result in understating amortization expense and overstating net income.

Types of Intangible Assets

PATENTS

A **patent** is an exclusive right issued by the United States Patent Office that enables the recipient to manufacture, sell, or otherwise control an invention for a period of 17 years from the date of the grant. **The initial cost of a patent is the cash or cash equivalent price paid to acquire the patent.**

The saying "A patent is only as good as the money you're prepared to spend defending it" is very true. Most patents are subject to some type of litigation by competitors. A well-known example is the patent infringement suit won by Polaroid against Eastman Kodak in protecting its patent on instant cameras. If the owner incurs legal costs in successfully defending the patent in an infringement suit, such costs are considered necessary to establish the validity of the patent. Thus, **they are added to the Patent account and amortized over the remaining life of the patent.**

Helpful Hint Patent infringement suits are expensive. One recent estimate of median cost of a patent case for each side was $280,000 through discovery and $580,000 through trial.

RESEARCH AND DEVELOPMENT COSTS

Research and development costs are expenditures that may lead to patents, copyrights, new processes, and new products. Many companies spend considerable sums of money on research and development in an ongoing effort to develop new products or processes. For example, in a recent year IBM spent over $2.5 billion on research and development. There are uncertainties in identifying the extent and timing of the future benefits of these expenditures. As a result, research and development costs are **usually recorded as an expense when incurred,** whether the research and development is successful or not.

To illustrate, assume that Laser Scanner Company spent $3 million on research and development that resulted in two highly successful patents. The R&D costs, however, cannot be included in the cost of the patent. Rather, they are recorded as an expense when incurred.

Many disagree with this accounting approach. They argue that to expense these costs leads to understated assets and net income. Others, however, argue that capitalizing these costs would lead to highly speculative assets on the balance sheet. Who is right is difficult to determine.

Helpful Hint Research and development costs are not intangible costs, but because these expenditures may lead to patents and copyrights, we discuss them in this section.

International Note Many factors, including differences in accounting treatment of R&D, contribute to differences in R&D expenditures across nations. R&D as a percentage of gross domestic product in 1994 was 2.6% in the United States, 2.4% in France, 2.5% in Germany, 3% in Japan, and 1.8% in Korea.

COPYRIGHTS

Copyrights are granted by the federal government, giving the owner the exclusive right to reproduce and sell an artistic or published work. Copyrights extend for the life of the creator plus 50 years. The cost of the copyright consists of the **cost of acquiring and defending it.** The cost may be only the $10 fee paid to the U.S. Copyright Office, or it may amount to a great deal more if a copyright infringement suit is involved. The useful life of a copyright generally is significantly shorter than its legal life.

TRADEMARKS AND TRADE NAMES

A **trademark** or **trade name** is a word, phrase, jingle, or symbol that distinguishes or identifies a particular enterprise or product. Trade names like

Wheaties, Trivial Pursuit, Sunkist, Kleenex, Coca-Cola, Big Mac, and Jeep create immediate product identification and generally enhance the sale of the product. The creator or original user may obtain the exclusive legal right to the trademark or trade name by registering it with the U.S. Patent Office. Such registration provides 20 years' protection and may be renewed indefinitely as long as the trademark or trade name is in use.

If the trademark or trade name is purchased, the cost is the purchase price. If it is developed by the enterprise itself, the cost includes attorney's fees, registration fees, design costs, successful legal defense costs, and other expenditures directly related to securing it.

As with other intangibles, the cost of trademarks and trade names must be amortized over the shorter of its useful life or 40 years. Because of the uncertainty involved in estimating the useful life, the cost is frequently amortized over a much shorter period.

FRANCHISES AND LICENSES

When you drive down the street in your Trans-Am purchased from a General Motors dealer, fill up your tank at the corner Standard Oil station, eat lunch at Wendy's, and make plans to vacation at a Club Med resort, you are dealing with franchises. A **franchise** is a contractual arrangement under which the franchisor grants the franchisee the right to sell certain products, to render specific services, or to use certain trademarks or trade names, usually within a designated geographic area.

Another type of franchise, granted by a governmental body, permits the enterprise to use public property in performing its services. Examples are the use of city streets for a bus line or taxi service; the use of public land for telephone, electric, and cable television lines; and the use of airwaves for radio or TV broadcasting. Such operating rights are referred to as **licenses.**

Franchises and licenses may be granted for a definite period of time, an indefinite period, or perpetual. **When costs can be identified with the acquisition of the franchise or license, an intangible asset should be recognized.** Annual payments made under a franchise agreement should be recorded as **operating expenses** in the period in which they are incurred. In the case of a limited life, the cost of a franchise (or license) should be amortized as operating expense over the useful life. If the life is indefinite or perpetual, the cost may be amortized over a reasonable period not to exceed 40 years.

BUSINESS INSIGHT
Investor Perspective

King World's most valuable asset is the right to license television shows such as "Wheel of Fortune," "Jeopardy," "The Oprah Winfrey Show," and "Inside Edition." Almost 90% of its $396.4 million in a recent year came from the fees associated with the rights to license agreements on these intangible assets.

GOODWILL

Usually the largest intangible asset that appears on a company's balance sheet is goodwill. **Goodwill** represents the value of all favorable attributes that relate to a business enterprise. These include exceptional management, desirable location, good customer relations, skilled employees, high-quality products, fair pricing policies, and harmonious relations with labor unions. Goodwill is therefore unusual: Unlike other assets such as investments, plant assets, and even other intangibles, which can be sold *individually* in the marketplace, goodwill can be identified only with the business *as a whole*.

If goodwill can be identified only with the business as a whole, how can it be determined? Certainly, many business enterprises have many of the factors cited above (exceptional management, desirable location, and so on). However, to determine the amount of goodwill in these situations would be difficult and very subjective. In other words, to recognize goodwill without an exchange transaction would lead to subjective valuations that do not contribute to the reliability of financial statements. **Therefore, goodwill is recorded only when there is an exchange transaction that involves the purchase of an entire business. When an entire business is purchased, goodwill is the excess of cost over the fair market value of the net assets (assets less liabilities) acquired.**

In recording the purchase of a business, the net assets are shown at their fair market values, cash is credited for the purchase price, and the difference is recorded as the cost of goodwill.

BUSINESS INSIGHT
International Perspective

Does the amortization requirement for goodwill create a disadvantage for U.S. companies? British companies, for example, do not have to amortize goodwill against earnings. Rather, they bypass the income statement completely and charge goodwill directly to stockholders' equity. For example, Pillsbury was purchased by Grand Met, a British firm. Many complained that U.S. companies were reluctant to bid for Pillsbury because it would mean that they would have to record a large amount of goodwill, which would substantially depress income in the future. What should be done when accounting practices are different among countries and perhaps give one country a competitive edge?

FINANCIAL STATEMENT PRESENTATION OF LONG-LIVED ASSETS

STUDY OBJECTIVE 8
Indicate how long-lived assets are reported on the balance sheet.

Usually plant assets are shown in the financial statements under Property, Plant, and Equipment, and intangibles are shown separately under Intangible Assets. Illustration 9-23 is adapted from Owens-Illinois' balance sheet.

OWENS-ILLINOIS, INC.
Partial Balance Sheet
(in millions)

Property, plant, and equipment		
Buildings and equipment, at cost	$2,207.1	
Less: Accumulated depreciation	1,229.0	$ 978.1
Intangibles		
Patents		410.0
Total		$1,388.1

Illustration 9-23 Presentation of property, plant, and equipment and intangible assets

Intangibles do not use a contra asset account like the contra asset account Accumulated Depreciation used for plant assets. Instead, the amortization of these accounts is charged directly against the account.

Either within the balance sheet or in the notes, there should be disclosure of the balances of the major classes of assets, such as land, buildings, and equipment, and accumulated depreciation by major classes or in total. In addition, the depreciation and amortization methods used should be described and the amount of depreciation and amortization expense for the period disclosed.

BEFORE YOU GO ON . . .

● **Review It**
1. Identify the major types of intangible assets and the proper accounting for them.
2. Explain the accounting for research and development costs.
3. How are intangible assets presented on the balance sheet?

*U*SING THE *D*ECISION *T*OOLKIT

Roberts Pharmaceuticals Corporation, a publicly traded company since 1990, has its headquarters in Eatontown, New Jersey. It is a rapidly growing company that acquires, develops, and markets pharmaceuticals. In 1993, after reporting losses in both 1991 and 1992, it reported positive income. As of 1993 the company had acquired, rather than developed internally, a number of existing products from other companies. It reported significant intangible assets related to these acquisitions. Suppose you noticed the improvement in Roberts' operating results and were considering investing in Roberts.

Instructions

Review the excerpts shown on the following pages from the company's 1993 annual report and consider the company's sensitivity to the amortization of its intangibles and how that might affect your decision on whether to invest. Then answer these questions:

1. What percentage of total assets are intangibles as of December 31, 1993?

2. What method does the company use to amortize intangibles, and over what period are they amortized?

3. What was the company's amortization expense for the year?

4. Comment on whether, in your opinion, the company's intangibles amortization policy is reasonable.

5. What would 1993 income have been if the company had used a 15-year useful life for amortization? [*Hint:* Base your calculation on the *average* intangible assets in 1993.]

412 CHAPTER 9 Reporting and Analyzing Long-Lived Assets

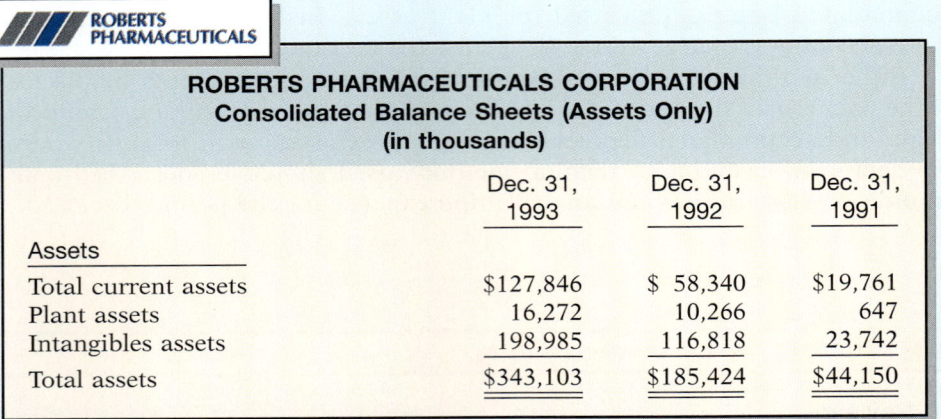

ROBERTS PHARMACEUTICALS CORPORATION
Consolidated Balance Sheets (Assets Only)
(in thousands)

	Dec. 31, 1993	Dec. 31, 1992	Dec. 31, 1991
Assets			
Total current assets	$127,846	$ 58,340	$19,761
Plant assets	16,272	10,266	647
Intangibles assets	198,985	116,818	23,742
Total assets	$343,103	$185,424	$44,150

ROBERTS PHARMACEUTICALS CORPORATION
Consolidated Statement of Operations
Years ended December 31
(in thousands)

	1993	1992	1991
Total sales and revenue	$89,657	$32,950	$13,458
Total operating costs and expenses	80,978	43,842	18,072
Operating income (loss)	8,679	(10,892)	(4,614)
Other revenues, expenses, gains, and losses	(1,451)	2,092	(512)
Net income (loss)	$ 7,228	($ 8,800)	($ 5,126)

ROBERTS PHARMACEUTICALS CORPORATION
Selected Notes to the Financial Statements

Summary of Significant Accounting Policies

Intangible assets: Intangible assets are stated at cost less accumulated amortization. Amortization is determined using the straight-line method over the estimated useful lives of the related assets which are estimated to range from ten to forty years. It is the Company's policy to periodically review and evaluate whether there has been a permanent impairment in the value of intangibles. Factors considered in the valuation include current operating results, trends, and anticipated undiscounted future cash flows.

Intangible Assets

Intangible assets consist of (in thousands):

	Dec. 31		
	1993	1992	1991
Product rights acquired	$190,496	$101,024	$22,638
Goodwill	14,834	14,760	1,161
Other assets	514	3,409	695
	205,844	119,193	24,494
Less: Accumulated amortization	6,859	2,375	752
	$198,985	$116,818	$23,742

Acquisitions

In 1992 and 1993 the Company acquired inventory, trademarks, and other rights to several products from various pharmaceutical companies. The aggregate price of these acquisitions was $78,463 and $79,939, respectively, consisting of cash and notes payable. Goodwill and other intangibles related to these acquisitions are being amortized on the straight-line basis over periods ranging from twenty-five to forty years.

Solution

1. As a percentage of the company's total assets, intangibles represent 58% ($198,985 ÷ $343,103).

2. The company uses the straight-line method to amortize intangibles. The footnotes state that they are amortized over a 10- to 40-year period.

3. The financial statements do not directly reveal the amortization expense for the year. However, from the intangibles note to the financial statements we can approximate the amortization expense by calculating the change in the accumulated amortization: $6,859 − $2,375 = $4,484.

4. This is a matter of opinion. However, one factor to consider is that Roberts is purchasing the rights to existing products, so part of their useful life may already be gone. Additionally, because of rapidly changing technology, new drugs appear to be developed at a relatively rapid rate; thus, it seems unlikely that on average drugs would have a useful life of 40 years. A 10-year life seems more appropriate.

5. In order to estimate amortization expense using a 15-year life, we would first need to calculate average intangibles for the year, to approximate the amortization:

$$\text{Average intangibles} = \frac{\$198,985 + \$116,818}{2} = \$157,902$$

Amortization over a 15-year period would be:

$$\frac{\$157,902}{15} = \$10,527$$

The reduction in income from the increased amortization would be:

$$\$10,527 - \$4,484 = \$6,043$$

Therefore, with amortization over a 15-year period, the resulting income for the year would have been only $1,185,000:

$$\$7,228 - \$6,043 = \$1,185 \quad \text{(in thousands)}$$

Conclusion: These calculations make it clear the company's income is very sensitive to the assumed useful life. Therefore, before investing, you would want to investigate further the reasonableness of the 10–40-year assumption currently being used.

SUMMARY OF STUDY OBJECTIVES

1 *Describe how the cost principle applies to plant assets.* The cost of plant assets includes all expenditures necessary to acquire the asset and make it ready for its intended use. Cost is measured by the cash or cash equivalent price paid.

2 *Explain the concept of depreciation.* Depreciation is the process of allocating to expense the cost of a plant asset over its useful (service) life in a rational and systematic manner. Depreciation is not a process of valuation, and it is not a process that results in an accumulation of cash. Depreciation is caused by wear and tear and by obsolescence.

3 *Compute periodic depreciation using the straight-line method, and contrast its expense pattern with those of other methods.* The formula for straight-line depreciation is:

$$\frac{\text{Cost} - \text{Salvage value}}{\text{Useful life (in years)}}$$

The expense patterns of the three depreciation methods are as follows:

Method	Annual Depreciation Pattern
Straight-line	Constant amount
Declining-balance	Decreasing amount
Units-of-activity	Varying amount

4 *Describe the procedure for revising periodic depreciation.* Revisions of periodic depreciation are made in present and future periods, not retroactively. The new annual depreciation is determined by dividing the depreciable cost at the time of the revision by the remaining useful life.

5 *Explain how to account for the disposal of plant assets.* The procedure for accounting for the disposal of a plant asset through sale or retirement is: (a) Eliminate the book value of the plant asset at the date of disposal. (b) Record cash proceeds, if any. (c) Account for the difference between the book value and the cash proceeds as a gain or a loss on disposal.

6 *Describe methods for evaluating the use of plant assets.* Plant assets may be analyzed using average useful life, average age, and asset turnover ratio.

7 *Identify the basic issues related to reporting intangible assets.* Intangible assets are reported at their cost less any amounts amortized. Amortization is done over the shortest of the useful life, legal life, or 40 years—usually on a straight-line basis.

8 *Indicate how long-lived assets are reported on the balance sheet.* Plant assets are usually shown under Property, Plant, and Equipment; intangibles are shown separately under Intangible Assets. Either within the balance sheet or in the notes, the balances of the major classes of assets, such as land, buildings, and equipment, and accumulated depreciation by major classes or in total are disclosed. The depreciation and amortization methods used should be described, and the amount of depreciation and amortization expense for the period should be disclosed.

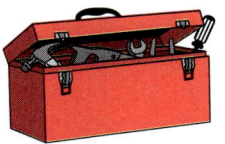

Decision Toolkit—A Summary

Decision Checkpoints	Info Needed for Decision	Tool to Use for Decision	How to Evaluate Results
Is the company's estimated useful life for depreciation reasonable?	Estimated useful life of assets from notes to financial statements of this company and its competitors	If the company's estimated useful life significantly exceeds that of competitors or does not seem reasonable in light of the circumstances, the reason for the difference should be investigated. If notes do not provide sufficient detail, average useful life can be estimated as: $$\text{Average useful life} = \frac{\text{Average cost of plant assets}}{\text{Depreciation expense}}$$	Too high an estimated useful life will result in understating depreciation expense and overstating net income.
Are the company's plant assets possibly outdated or in need of replacement?	Depreciation expense and accumulated depreciation	$$\text{Average age of plant assets} = \frac{\text{Accumulated depreciation}}{\text{Depreciation expense}}$$	A high average age relative to competitors might suggest that the company's assets are not as efficient, or that they may be in need of replacement.
How effective is the company at generating sales from its assets?	Net sales and average total assets	$$\text{Asset turnover ratio} = \frac{\text{Net sales}}{\text{Average total assets}}$$	Indicates the sales dollars generated per dollar of assets. A high value suggests the company is effective in using its resources to generate sales.
Is the company's amortization of intangibles reasonable?	Estimated useful life of intangibles from notes to financial statements of this company and its competitors	If the company's estimated useful life significantly exceeds that of competitors or does not seem reasonable in light of the circumstances, the reason for the difference should be investigated.	Too high an estimated useful life will result in understating amortization expense and overstating net income.

APPENDIX 9A

CALCULATION OF DEPRECIATION USING OTHER METHODS

In this appendix we show the calculations of the depreciation expense amounts used in the chapter for the declining-balance and units-of-activity methods.

DECLINING-BALANCE

STUDY OBJECTIVE

Compute periodic depreciation using the declining-balance method and the units-of-activity method.

The **declining-balance method** produces a decreasing annual depreciation expense over the useful life of the asset. The method is so named because the computation of periodic depreciation is based on a **declining book value** (cost less accumulated depreciation) of the asset. Annual depreciation expense is computed by multiplying the book value at the beginning of the year by the declining-balance depreciation rate. **The depreciation rate remains constant from year to year, but the book value to which the rate is applied declines each year.**

Book value for the first year is the cost of the asset because the balance in accumulated depreciation at the beginning of the asset's useful life is zero. In subsequent years, book value is the difference between cost and accumulated depreciation at the beginning of the year. **Unlike other depreciation methods, salvage value is ignored in determining the amount to which the declining-balance rate is applied.** Salvage value, however, does limit the total depreciation that can be taken. Depreciation stops when the asset's book value equals its expected salvage value.

As noted in the chapter, a common declining-balance rate is double the straight-line rate—a method often referred to as the **double-declining-balance method.** If Bill's Pizzas uses the double-declining-balance method, the depreciation rate is 40% (2 × the straight-line rate of 20%). Illustration 9A-1 presents the formula and computation of depreciation for the first year on the delivery truck.

Helpful Hint The straight-line rate is approximated as 1 ÷ Estimated life. In this case it is 1 ÷ 5 = 20%.

Illustration 9A-1
Formula for declining-balance method

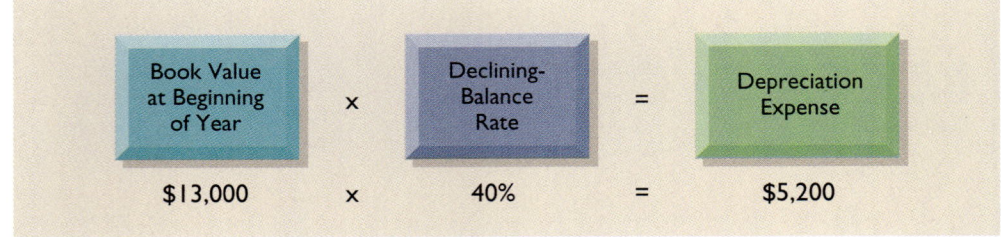

The depreciation schedule under this method is given in Illustration 9A-2.

Illustration 9A-2
Double-declining-balance depreciation schedule

Helpful Hint Book value is variable, and the depreciation rate is constant for this method.

	BILL'S PIZZAS					
	Computation			Annual	End of Year	
Year	Book Value Beginning of Year	×	Depreciation Rate	= Depreciation Expense	Accumulated Depreciation	Book Value
1998	$13,000		40%	**$5,200**	$ 5,200	$7,800*
1999	7,800		40	**3,120**	8,320	4,680
2000	4,680		40	**1,872**	10,192	2,808
2001	2,808		40	**1,123**	11,315	1,685
2002	1,685		40	**685****	12,000	**1,000**

* $13,000 − $5,200
**Computation of $674 ($1,685 × 40%) is adjusted to $685 in order for book value to equal salvage value.

Helpful Hint The method to be used for an asset that is expected to be more productive in the first half of its useful life is the declining-balance method.

You can see that the delivery equipment is 69% depreciated ($8,320 ÷ $12,000) at the end of the second year. Under the straight-line method it would be depreciated 40% ($4,800 ÷ $12,000) at that time. Because the declining-balance method produces higher depreciation expense in the early years than in the later years, it is considered an **accelerated-depreciation method.** The declining-balance method is compatible with the matching principle. The higher depreciation expense in early years is matched with the higher benefits received in these years. Conversely, lower depreciation expense is recognized in later years when the asset's contribution to revenue is less. Also, some assets lose their usefulness rapidly because of obsolescence. In these cases, the declining-balance method provides a more appropriate depreciation amount.

When an asset is purchased during the year, it is necessary to prorate the declining-balance depreciation in the first year on a time basis. For example, if Bill's Pizzas had purchased the delivery equipment on April 1, 1998, depreciation for 1998 would be $3,900 ($13,000 × 40% × $\frac{9}{12}$). The book value for computing depreciation in 1999 then becomes $9,100 ($13,000 − $3,900), and the 1999 depreciation is $3,640 ($9,100 × 40%).

UNITS-OF-ACTIVITY

Under the **units-of-activity method,** useful life is expressed in terms of the total units of production or use expected from the asset. The units-of-activity method is ideally suited to equipment whose activity can be measured in units of output, miles driven, and hours in use. The units-of-activity method is generally not suitable for assets for which depreciation is a function more of time than of use.

To use this method, the total units of activity for the entire useful life are estimated and that amount is divided into the depreciable cost to determine the depreciation cost per unit. The depreciation cost per unit is then multiplied by the units of activity during the year to give the annual depreciation. To illustrate, assume that the delivery truck of Bill's Pizzas is driven 15,000 miles in the first year. Illustration 9A-3 presents the formula and computation of depreciation expense in the first year.

Alternative Terminology Another term often used is the **units-of-production method.**

Helpful Hint Depreciation stops when the asset's book value equals its expected salvage value.

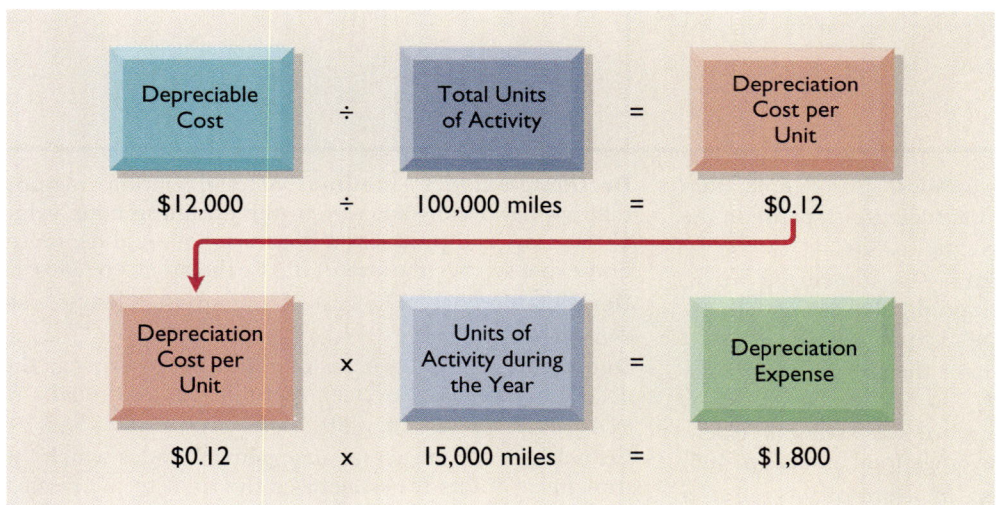

Illustration 9A-3 Formula for units-of-activity method

The depreciation schedule, using assumed mileage data, is shown in Illustration 9A-4.

Illustration 9A-4 Units-of-activity depreciation schedule

	BILL'S PIZZAS				
	Computation		Annual	End of Year	
Year	Units of Activity	× Depreciation Cost/Unit =	Depreciation Expense	Accumulated Depreciation	Book Value
1998	15,000	$.12	**$1,800**	$ 1,800	$11,200*
1999	30,000	.12	**3,600**	5,400	7,600
2000	20,000	.12	**2,400**	7,800	5,200
2001	25,000	.12	**3,000**	10,800	2,200
2002	10,000	.12	**1,200**	12,000	**1,000**

*$13,000 − $1,800

The units-of-activity method is not nearly as popular as the straight-line method, primarily because it is often difficult to make a reasonable estimate of total activity. However, this method is used by some very large companies, such as Standard Oil Company of California and Boise Cascade Corporation. When the productivity of the asset varies significantly from one period to another, the units-of-activity method results in the best matching of expenses with revenues. This method is easy to apply when assets are purchased during the year. In such a case, the productivity of the asset for the partial year is used in computing the depreciation.

SUMMARY OF STUDY OBJECTIVE FOR APPENDIX 9A

9 *Compute periodic depreciation using the declining-balance method and the units-of-activity method.* The calculation for each of these methods is shown here:

Declining-balance:

$$\text{Book value at beginning of year} \times \text{Declining-balance rate}$$

Units-of-activity:

$$\frac{\text{Depreciation cost}}{\text{Total units of activity}} = \text{Depreciation cost per unit}$$

$$\text{Depreciation cost per unit} \times \text{Units of activity during year}$$

GLOSSARY

Accelerated-depreciation method A depreciation method that produces higher depreciation expense in the early years than in the later years. (p. 416)

Additions and improvements Costs incurred to increase the operating efficiency, productive capacity, or expected useful life of a plant asset. (p. 398)

Amortization The allocation of the cost of an intangible asset to expense. (p. 406)

Asset turnover ratio Measure of sales volume, calculated as net sales divided by average total assets. (p. 405)

Average age of plant assets Measure of the age of a company's plant assets, calculated as accumulated depreciation divided by depreciation expense. (p. 403)

Average useful life A comparative measure of plant assets, calculated as the average cost of plant assets divided by depreciation expense. (p. 402)

Capital expenditures Expenditures that increase the company's investment in productive facilities. (p. 385)

Capital lease A long-term agreement allowing one party (the lessee) to use another party's asset (the lessor). The arrangement is accounted for like a purchase. (p. 389)

Cash equivalent price An amount equal to the fair market value of the asset given up or the fair market value of the asset received, whichever is more clearly determinable. (p. 386)

Copyright An exclusive right granted by the federal government allowing the owner to reproduce and sell an artistic or published work. (p. 408)

Declining-balance method A depreciation method that applies a constant rate to the declining book value of the asset and produces a decreasing annual depreciation expense over the useful life of the asset. (p. 393)

Depreciable cost The cost of a plant asset less its salvage value. (p. 392)

Depreciation The process of allocating to expense the cost of a plant asset over its useful life in a rational and systematic manner. (p. 390)

Franchise A contractual arrangement under which the franchisor grants the franchisee the right to sell certain products, to render specific services, or to use certain trademarks or trade names, usually within a designated geographic area. (p. 409)

Goodwill The value of all favorable attributes that relate to a business enterprise. (p. 409)

Impairment A permanent decline in the market value of an asset. (p. 398)

Intangible assets Rights, privileges, and competitive advantages that result from the ownership of long-lived assets that do not possess physical substance. (p. 406)

Lessee A party that has made contractual arrangements to use another party's asset without purchasing it. (p. 388)

Lessor A party that has agreed contractually to let another party use its asset. (p.388)

Licenses Operating rights to use public property, granted by a governmental agency to a business enterprise. (p. 409)

Operating lease An arrangement allowing one party (the lessee) to use the asset of another party (the lessor). The arrangement is accounted for as a rental. (p. 388)

Ordinary repairs Expenditures to maintain the operating efficiency and expected productive life of the asset. (p. 398)

Patent An exclusive right issued by the U.S. Patent Office that enables the recipient to manufacture, sell, or otherwise control an invention for a period of 17 years from the date of the grant. (p. 408)

Plant assets Tangible resources that have physical substance, are used in the operations of the business, and are not intended for sale to customers. (p. 384)

Research and development costs Expenditures that may lead to patents, copyrights, new processes, and new products. (p. 408)

Revenue expenditures Expenditures that are immediately charged against revenues as an expense. (p. 385)

Straight-line method A method in which periodic depreciation is the same for each year of the asset's useful life. (p. 392)

Trademark (trade name) A word, phrase, jingle, or symbol that distinguishes or identifies a particular enterprise or product. (p. 408)

Units-of-activity method A depreciation method in which useful life is expressed in terms of the total units of production or use expected from the asset. (p. 394)

DEMONSTRATION PROBLEM 1

DuPage Company purchased a factory machine at a cost of $18,000 on January 1, 1998. The machine was expected to have a salvage value of $2,000 at the end of its 4-year useful life. During its useful life, the machine was expected to be used 160,000 hours. Actual annual hourly use was: 1998, 40,000; 1999, 60,000; 2000, 35,000; and 2001, 25,000.

Instructions

Prepare a depreciation schedule using the straight-line method.

Solution to Demonstration Problem

DUPAGE COMPANY
Depreciation Schedule—Straight-Line Method

Year	Depreciable Cost	×	Depreciation Rate	=	Annual Depreciation Expense	Accumulated Depreciation (End of Year)	Book Value (End of Year)
1998	$16,000		25%		$4,000	$ 4,000	$14,000*
1999	16,000		25		4,000	8,000	10,000
2000	16,000		25		4,000	12,000	6,000
2001	16,000		25		4,000	16,000	2,000

*$18,000 − $4,000

Problem-Solving Strategy
Under the straight-line method, the depreciation rate is applied to depreciable cost.

DEMONSTRATION PROBLEM 2

On January 1, 1995, Skyline Limousine Co. purchased a limousine at an acquisition cost of $28,000. The vehicle has been depreciated by the straight-line method using a 4-year service life and a $4,000 salvage value. The company's fiscal year ends on December 31.

Instructions

Prepare the journal entry or entries to record the disposal of the limousine assuming that it was:
(a) Retired and scrapped with no salvage value on January 1, 1999.
(b) Sold for $5,000 on July 1, 1998.

420 CHAPTER 9 Reporting and Analyzing Long-Lived Assets

Problem-Solving Strategy
Accumulated depreciation is equal to depreciation expense per year times the number of years of use.

Solution to Demonstration Problem

(a) Jan. 1, 1999

Accumulated Depreciation—Limousine	24,000	
Loss on Disposal	4,000	
Limousine		28,000
(To record retirement of limousine)		

(b) July 1, 1998

Depreciation Expense	3,000	
Accumulated Depreciation—Limousine		3,000
(To record depreciation to date of disposal)		
Cash	5,000	
Accumulated Depreciation—Limousine	21,000	
Loss on Disposal	2,000	
Limousine		28,000
(To record sale of limousine)		

Note: All questions, exercises, and problems marked with an asterisk relate to material in Appendix 9A.

SELF-STUDY QUESTIONS

Answers are at the end of the chapter.

(SO 1) 1. Corrieten Company purchased equipment and these costs were incurred:

Cash price	$24,000
Sales taxes	1,200
Insurance during transit	200
Installation and testing	400
Total costs	$25,800

What amount should be recorded as the cost of the equipment?
(a) $24,000   (c) $25,400
(b) $25,200   (d) $25,800

(SO 1) 2. Harrington Corporation recently leased a number of trucks from Andre Corporation. In inspecting the books of Harrington Corporation, you notice that the trucks have not been recorded as assets on its balance sheet. From this you can conclude that Harrington is accounting for this transaction as a:
(a) operating lease.   (c) purchase.
(b) capital lease.   (d) None of the above

(SO 2) 3. Depreciation is a process of:
(a) valuation.   (c) cash accumulation.
(b) cost allocation.   (d) appraisal.

(SO 3) 4. Cuso Company purchased equipment on January 1, 1997, at a total invoice cost of $400,000. The equipment has an estimated salvage value of $10,000 and an estimated useful life of 5 years. What is the amount of accumulated depreciation at December 31, 1998, if the straight-line method of depreciation is used?
(a) $80,000   (c) $78,000
(b) $160,000   (d) $156,000

(SO 4) 5. When there is a change in estimated depreciation:
(a) previous depreciation should be corrected.
(b) current and future years' depreciation should be revised.
(c) only future years' depreciation should be revised.
(d) None of the above

(SO 5) 6. Additions to plant assets:
(a) are revenue expenditures.
(b) increase a Repair Expense account.
(c) increase a Purchases account.
(d) are capital expenditures.

(SO 7) 7. Pierce Company incurred $150,000 of research and development costs in its laboratory to develop a new product. It spent $20,000 in legal fees for a patent granted on January 2, 1998. On July 31, 1998, Pierce paid $15,000 for legal fees in a successful defense of the patent. What is the total amount that should be debited to Patents through July 31, 1998?
(a) $150,000   (c) $185,000
(b) $35,000   (d) Some other amount

(SO 7) 8. Indicate which one of these statements is *true*.
(a) Since intangible assets lack physical substance, they need to be disclosed only in the notes to the financial statements.
(b) Goodwill should be reported as a contra account in the Stockholders' Equity section.
(c) Totals of major classes of assets can be shown in the balance sheet, with asset details disclosed in the notes to the financial statements.
(d) Intangible assets are typically combined with plant assets and natural resources and

9. (SO 3) A company would minimize its depreciation expense in the first year of owning an asset if it:
   (a) used a high estimated life, a high salvage value, and declining-balance depreciation.
   (b) used a low estimated life, a high salvage value, and straight-line depreciation.
   (c) used a high estimated life, a high salvage value, and straight-line depreciation.
   (d) used a low estimated life, a low salvage value, and declining-balance depreciation.

10. (SO 7) If a company reports goodwill as an intangible asset on its books, what is the one thing you know with certainty?
    (a) The company is a valuable company worth investing in.
    (b) The company has a well-established brand name.
    (c) The company purchased another company.
    (d) The goodwill will generate a lot of positive business for the company for many years to come.

*11. (SO 9) Kant Enterprises purchased a truck for $11,000 on January 1, 1997. The truck will have an estimated salvage value of $1,000 at the end of 5 years. If you use the units-of-activity method, the balance in accumulated depreciation at December 31, 1998, can be computed by the following formula:
    (a) ($11,000 ÷ Total estimated activity) × Units of activity for 1998.
    (b) ($10,000 ÷ Total estimated activity) × Units of activity for 1998.
    (c) ($11,000 ÷ Total estimated activity) × Units of activity for 1997 and 1998.
    (d) ($10,000 ÷ Total estimated activity) × Units of activity for 1997 and 1998.

QUESTIONS

1. Susan Day is uncertain about how the cost principle applies to plant assets. Explain the principle to Susan.
2. How is the cost for a plant asset measured in a cash transaction? In a noncash transaction?
3. What are the primary advantages of leasing?
4. Jamie Company acquires the land and building owned by Smitt Company. What types of costs may be incurred to make the asset ready for its intended use if Jamie Company wants to use only the land? Both the land and the building?
5. In a recent newspaper release, the president of Lawsuit Company asserted that something has to be done about depreciation. The president said, "Depreciation does not come close to accumulating the cash needed to replace the asset at the end of its useful life." What is your response to the president?
6. Cecile is studying for the next accounting examination. She asks your help on two questions: (a) What is salvage value? (b) Is salvage value used in determining depreciable cost under each depreciation method? Answer Cecile's questions.
7. Contrast the straight-line method and the units-of-activity method in relation to (a) useful life and (b) the pattern of periodic depreciation over useful life.
8. Contrast the effects of the three depreciation methods on annual depreciation expense.
9. In the fourth year of an asset's 5-year useful life, the company decides that the asset will have a 6-year service life. How should the revision of depreciation be recorded? Why?
10. Distinguish between revenue expenditures and capital expenditures during an asset's useful life.
11. How is a gain or a loss on the sale of a plant asset computed?
12. Ewing Corporation owns a machine that is fully depreciated but is still being used. How should Ewing account for this asset and report it in the financial statements?
13. What are the similarities and differences between depreciation and amortization?
14. Heflin Company hires an accounting intern who says that intangible assets should always be amortized over their legal lives. Is the intern correct? Explain.
15. Goodwill has been defined as the value of all favorable attributes that relate to a business enterprise. What types of attributes could result in goodwill?
16. Bob Leno, a business major, is working on a case problem for one of his classes. In this case problem, the company needs to raise cash to market a new product it developed. Saul Cain, an engineering major, takes one look at the company's balance sheet and says, "This company has an awful lot of goodwill. Why don't you recommend that they sell some of it to raise cash?" How should Bob respond to Saul?
17. Under what conditions is goodwill recorded?
18. Often research and development costs provide companies with benefits that last a number of years. (For example, these costs can lead to the development of a patent that will increase the company's income for many years.) However, generally accepted accounting principles require that such costs be recorded as an expense when incurred. Why?
19. McDonald's Corporation reports total average assets of $14.5 billion and net sales of $9.8 billion. What is McDonald's asset turnover ratio?

20. Give an example of an industry that would be characterized by (a) a high asset turnover ratio and a low profit margin ratio, and (b) a low asset turnover ratio and a high profit margin ratio.

21. Morgan Corporation and Fairchild Corporation both operate in the same industry. Morgan uses the straight-line method to account for depreciation, whereas Fairchild uses an accelerated method. Explain what complications might arise in trying to compare the results of these two companies.

22. Lucille Corporation uses straight-line depreciation for financial reporting purposes but an accelerated method for tax purposes. Is it acceptable to use different methods for the two purposes? What is Lucille Corporation's motivation for doing this?

23. You are comparing two companies in the same industry. You have determined that Betty Corp. depreciates its plant assets over a 40-year life, whereas Herb Corp. depreciates its plant assets over a 20-year life. Discuss the implications this has for comparing the results of the two companies.

BRIEF EXERCISES

Determine the cost of land.
(SO 1)

BE9-1 These expenditures were incurred by Gene Shumway Company in purchasing land: cash price $50,000; accrued taxes $3,000; attorney's fees $2,500; real estate broker's commission $2,000; and clearing and grading $3,500. What is the cost of the land?

Determine the cost of a truck.
(SO 1)

BE9-2 Shirley Basler Company incurs these expenditures in purchasing a truck: cash price $18,000; accident insurance $2,000; sales taxes $900; motor vehicle license $100; and painting and lettering $400. What is the cost of the truck?

Compute straight-line depreciation.
(SO 3)

BE9-3 Joy Cunningham Company acquires a delivery truck at a cost of $22,000. The truck is expected to have a salvage value of $2,000 at the end of its 4-year useful life. Compute annual depreciation for the first and second years using the straight-line method.

Compute revised depreciation.
(SO 4)

BE9-4 On January 1, 1998, the Asler Company ledger shows Equipment $32,000 and Accumulated Depreciation $12,000. The depreciation resulted from using the straight-line method with a useful life of 10 years and a salvage value of $2,000. On this date the company concludes that the equipment has a remaining useful life of only 4 years with the same salvage value. Compute the revised annual depreciation.

Journalize entries for disposal of plant assets.
(SO 5)

BE9-5 Prepare journal entries to record these transactions: (a) Ruiz Company retires its delivery equipment, which cost $41,000. Accumulated depreciation is also $41,000 on this delivery equipment. No salvage value is received. (b) Assume the same information as in part (a), except that accumulated depreciation for Ruiz Company is $35,000 instead of $41,000.

Journalize entries for sale of plant assets.
(SO 5)

BE9-6 Wiley Company sells office equipment on September 30, 1998, for $21,000 cash. The office equipment originally cost $72,000 and as of January 1, 1998, had accumulated depreciation of $42,000. Depreciation for the first 9 months of 1998 is $6,250. Prepare the journal entries to (a) update depreciation to September 30, 1998, and (b) record the sale of the equipment.

Account for intangibles— patents.
(SO 6)

BE9-7 Popper Company purchases a patent for $180,000 on January 2, 1998. Its estimated useful life is 10 years.
(a) Prepare the journal entry to record patent expense for the first year.
(b) Show how this patent is reported on the balance sheet at the end of the first year.

Compute average life, average age of long-lived assets, and asset turnover ratio.
(SO 6)

BE9-8 In its 1995 annual report, McDonald's Corporation reports beginning total assets of $13.6 billion; ending total assets of $15.4 billion; property, plant, and equipment (at cost) of $17.1 billion; accumulated depreciation of $4.3 billion; depreciation expense of $620 million; and net sales of $9.8 billion.
(a) Compute the average useful life of McDonald's property, plant, and equipment.
(b) Compute the average age of McDonald's property, plant, and equipment.
(c) Compute McDonald's asset turnover ratio.

Classification of long-lived assets on balance sheet.
(SO 8)

BE9-9 This information relates to plant assets, intangibles, and research and development costs at the end of 1998 for Joker Company: buildings $800,000; accumulated depreciation—buildings $650,000; goodwill $410,000; and patent $200,000. It also spent $108,000 during the year on research and development. Prepare a partial balance sheet of Joker Company for these items.

*BE9-10 Depreciation information for Joy Cunningham Company is given in BE9-3. Assuming the declining-balance depreciation rate is double the straight-line rate, compute annual depreciation for the first and second years under the declining-balance method.

Compute declining-balance depreciation.
(SO 9)

*BE9-11 Jerry Englehart Taxi Service uses the units-of-activity method in computing depreciation on its taxicabs. Each cab is expected to be driven 120,000 miles. Taxi 10 cost $24,500 and is expected to have a salvage value of $500. Taxi 10 was driven 30,000 miles in 1997 and 20,000 miles in 1998. Compute the depreciation for each year.

Compute depreciation using units-of-activity method.
(SO 9)

EXERCISES

E9-1 The following expenditures relating to plant assets were made by John Kosinki Company during the first 2 months of 1998:
1. Paid $250 to have company name and advertising slogan painted on new delivery truck.
2. Paid $75 motor vehicle license fee on new truck.
3. Paid $850 sales taxes on new delivery truck.
4. Paid $17,500 for parking lots and driveways on new plant site.
5. Paid $5,000 of accrued taxes at time plant site was acquired.
6. Paid $8,000 for installation of new factory machinery.
7. Paid $900 for a 1-year accident insurance policy on new delivery truck.
8. Paid $200 insurance to cover possible accident loss on new factory machinery while the machinery was in transit.

Determine cost of plant acquisitions.
(SO 1)

Instructions
(a) Explain the application of the cost principle in determining the acquisition cost of plant assets.
(b) List the numbers of the foregoing transactions, and opposite each indicate the account title to which each expenditure should be debited.

E9-2 On March 1, 1998, Roy Orbis Company acquired real estate, on which it planned to construct a small office building, by paying $100,000 in cash. An old warehouse on the property was razed at a cost of $6,600; the salvaged materials were sold for $1,700. Additional expenditures before construction began included $1,100 attorney's fee for work concerning the land purchase, $4,000 real estate broker's fee, $7,800 architect's fee, and $14,000 to put in driveways and a parking lot.

Determine acquisition costs of land.
(SO 1)

Instructions
(a) Determine the amount to be reported as the cost of the land.
(b) For each cost not used in part (a), indicate the account to be debited.

E9-3 Elvis Costello Company purchased a new machine on October 1, 1998, at a cost of $96,000. The company estimated that the machine has a salvage value of $12,000. The machine is expected to be used for 84,000 working hours during its 6-year life.

Determine straight-line depreciation for partial period.
(SO 3)

Instructions
Compute the depreciation expense under the straight-line method for 1998 and 1999.

E9-4 Lindy Weink, the new controller of Waterloo Company, has reviewed the expected useful lives and salvage values of selected depreciable assets at the beginning of 1998. Here are her findings:

Compute revised annual depreciation.
(SO 3,4)

Type of Asset	Date Acquired	Cost	Accumulated Depreciation, Jan. 1, 1998	Useful Life (in years) Old	Proposed	Salvage Value Old	Proposed
Building	Jan. 1, 1992	$800,000	$114,000	40	45	$40,000	$62,000
Warehouse	Jan. 1, 1995	100,000	11,400	25	20	5,000	3,600

All assets are depreciated by the straight-line method. Waterloo Company uses a calendar year in preparing annual financial statements. After discussion, management has agreed to accept Lindy's proposed changes. (The "Proposed" useful life is total life, not remaining life.)

424 CHAPTER 9 Reporting and Analyzing Long-Lived Assets

Instructions
(a) Compute the revised annual depreciation on each asset in 1998. (Show computations.)
(b) Prepare the entry (or entries) to record depreciation on the building in 1998.

Journalize entries for disposal of plant assets.
(SO 5)

E9-5 Presented here are selected transactions for Beck Company for 1998:

Jan. 1	Retired a piece of machinery that was purchased on January 1, 1988. The machine cost $62,000 on that date and had a useful life of 10 years with no salvage value.
June 30	Sold a computer that was purchased on January 1, 1995. The computer cost $35,000 and had a useful life of 7 years with no salvage value. The computer was sold for $28,000.
Dec. 31	Discarded a delivery truck that was purchased on January 1, 1992. The truck cost $27,000 and was depreciated based on an 8-year useful life with a $3,000 salvage value.

Instructions
Journalize all entries required on the above dates, including entries to update depreciation, where applicable, on assets disposed of. Beck Company uses straight-line depreciation. (Assume depreciation is up to date as of December 31, 1997.)

Calculate average useful life, average age of plant assets, and asset turnover ratio.
(SO 6)

E9-6 During 1998 Kettle Corporation reported net sales of $2,500,000, net income of $1,500,000, and depreciation expense of $150,000. Its balance sheet reported total assets of $1,400,000, plant assets of $800,000, and accumulated depreciation—plant assets of $300,000.

Instructions
Calculate (a) average useful life of plant assets, (b) average age of plant assets, and (c) asset turnover ratio.

Prepare adjusting entries for amortization.
(SO 7)

E9-7 These are selected 1998 transactions for Graf Corporation:

| Jan. 1 | Purchased a small company and recorded goodwill of $120,000. The goodwill has a useful life of 55 years. |
| May 1 | Purchased a patent with an estimated useful life of 5 years and a legal life of 17 years for $15,000. |

Instructions
Prepare all adjusting entries at December 31 to record amortization required by the events.

Prepare entries to set up appropriate accounts for different intangibles; calculate amortization.
(SO 7)

E9-8 Collins Company, organized in 1998, has these transactions related to intangible assets in that year:

Jan. 2	Purchased patent (7-year life), $350,000.
Apr. 1	Goodwill purchased (indefinite life), $360,000.
July 1	Ten-year franchise; expiration date July 1, 2006, $450,000.
Sept. 1	Research and development costs, $185,000.

Instructions
Prepare the necessary entries to record these intangibles. All costs incurred were for cash. Make the entries as of December 31, 1998, recording any necessary amortization and indicating what the balances should be on December 31, 1998.

Answer questions of depreciation and intangibles.
(SO 2, 7)

E9-9 The questions listed below are independent of one another.

Instructions
Provide a brief answer to each question:

(a) Why should a company depreciate its buildings?
(b) How can a company have a building that has a zero reported book value but substantial market value?
(c) What are some examples of intangibles that you might find on your college campus?

(d) Give some examples of company or product trademarks or trade names. Are trade names and trademarks reported on a company's balance sheet?

*E9-10 Interstate Bus Lines uses the units-of-activity method in depreciating its buses. One bus was purchased on January 1, 1998, at a cost of $108,000. Over its 4-year useful life, the bus is expected to be driven 100,000 miles. Salvage value is expected to be $8,000.

Compute depreciation under units-of-activity method.
(SO 9)

Instructions
(a) Compute the depreciation cost per unit.
(b) Prepare a depreciation schedule assuming actual mileage was: 1998, 28,000; 1999, 30,000; 2000, 25,000; and 2001, 17,000.

*E9-11 Basic information relating to a new machine purchased by Elvis Costello Company is presented in E9-3.

Compute declining-balance and units-of-activity depreciation.
(SO 9)

Instructions
Using the facts presented in E9-3, compute depreciation using the following methods in the year indicated:
(a) Declining-balance using double the straight-line rate for 1998 and 1999
(b) Units-of-activity for 1998, assuming machine usage was 1,700 hours

PROBLEMS

P9-1 Jay Weiseman Company was organized on January 1. During the first year of operations, the following plant asset expenditures and receipts were recorded in random order:

Determine acquisition costs of land and building.
(SO 1)

Debits

1. Cost of real estate purchased as a plant site (land $100,000 and building $25,000)	$125,000
2. Installation cost of fences around property	4,000
3. Cost of demolishing building to make land suitable for construction of new building	13,000
4. Excavation costs for new building	20,000
5. Accrued real estate taxes paid at time of purchase of real estate	2,000
6. Cost of parking lots and driveways	12,000
7. Architect's fees on building plans	10,000
8. Real estate taxes paid for the current year on land	3,000
9. Full payment to building contractor	600,000
	$789,000

Credits

10. Proceeds from salvage of demolished building	$2,500

Instructions
Analyze the foregoing transactions using the following table column headings. Enter the number of each transaction in the Item column, and enter the amounts in the appropriate columns. For amounts in the Other Accounts column, also indicate the account title.

Item	Land	Building	Other Accounts

P9-2 At December 31, 1997, Jerry Hamsmith Corporation reported these plant assets:

Journalize equipment transactions related to purchase, sale, and retirement.
(SO 5, 8)

Land		$ 3,000,000
Buildings	$26,500,000	
Less: Accumulated depreciation—buildings	12,100,000	14,400,000
Equipment:	40,000,000	
Less: Accumulated depreciation—equipment	5,000,000	35,000,000
Total plant assets		$52,400,000

During 1998, the following selected cash transactions occurred:

Apr. 1	Purchased land for $2,200,000.	
May 1	Sold equipment that cost $600,000 when purchased on January 1, 1994. The equipment was sold for $350,000.	
June 1	Sold land for $1,800,000. The land cost $500,000.	
July 1	Purchased equipment for $1,200,000.	
Dec. 31	Retired equipment that cost $500,000 when purchased on December 31, 1988. No salvage value was received.	

Instructions
(a) Journalize the transactions. [*Hint:* You may wish to set up T accounts, post beginning balances, and then post 1998 transactions.] Hamsmith uses straight-line depreciation for buildings and equipment. The buildings are estimated to have a 40-year useful life and no salvage value; the equipment is estimated to have a 10-year useful life and no salvage value. Update depreciation on assets disposed of at the time of sale or retirement.
(b) Record adjusting entries for depreciation for 1998.
(c) Prepare the plant asset section of Hamsmith's balance sheet at December 31, 1998.

Journalize transactions related to diposals of plant assets.
(SO 5)

P9-3 Express Co. has delivery equipment that cost $48,000 and has been depreciated $20,000.

Instructions
Record entries for the disposal under the following assumptions:
(a) It was scrapped as having no value.
(b) It was sold for $31,000.
(c) It was sold for $18,000.

Prepare entries to record transactions related to acquisition and amortization of intangibles; prepare the intangible assets section and notes.
(SO 7, 8)

P9-4 The intangible asset section of Roberts Corporation's balance sheet at December 31, 1997, is presented here:

Patent ($60,000 cost less $6,000 amortization)	$54,000
Copyright ($36,000 cost less $14,400 amortization)	21,600
Total	$75,600

The patent was acquired in January 1997 and has a useful life of 10 years. The copyright was acquired in January 1994 and also has a useful life of 10 years. The following cash transactions may have affected intangible assets during 1998:

Jan. 2	Paid $9,000 legal costs to successfully defend the patent against infringement by another company.
Jan.–June	Developed a new product, incurring $140,000 in research and development costs. A patent was granted for the product on July 1, and its useful life is equal to its legal life.
Sept. 1	Paid $60,000 to a quarterback to appear in commercials advertising the company's products. The commercials will air in September and October.
Oct. 1	Acquired a copyright for $100,000. The copyright has a useful life of 50 years.

Instructions
(a) Prepare journal entries to record the transactions.
(b) Prepare journal entries to record the 1998 amortization expense for intangible assets.
(c) Prepare the intangible asset section of the balance sheet at December 31, 1998.
(d) Prepare the note to the financial statements on Roberts Corporation's intangible assets as of December 31, 1998.

Prepare entries to correct errors in recording and amortizing intangible assets.
(SO 7)

P9-5 Due to rapid employee turnover in the accounting department, the following transactions involving intangible assets were improperly recorded by Riley Corporation in 1998:
1. Riley developed a new manufacturing process, incurring research and development costs of $102,000. The company also purchased a patent for $37,400. In early Janu-

ary Riley capitalized $139,400 as the cost of the patents. Patent amortization expense of $8,200 was recorded based on a 17-year useful life.
2. On July 1, 1998, Riley purchased a small company and as a result acquired goodwill of $60,000. Riley recorded a half-year's amortization in 1998, based on a 50-year life ($600 amortization).

Instructions
Prepare all journal entries necessary to correct any errors made during 1998. Assume the books have not yet been closed for 1998.

P9-6 Croix Corporation and Rye Corporation, two corporations of roughly the same size, are both involved in the manufacture of canoes and sea kayaks. Each company depreciates its plant assets using the straight-line approach. An investigation of their financial statements reveals this information:

Calculate and comment on average age, average useful life of plant assets, and asset turnover ratio.
(SO 6)

	Croix Corp.	Rye Corp.
Net income	$ 400,000	$ 600,000
Sales	1,400,000	1,200,000
Total assets	2,000,000	1,500,000
Plant assets	1,500,000	800,000
Accumulated depreciation	300,000	625,000
Depreciation expense	75,000	25,000
Intangible assets (goodwill)	300,000	0
Amortization expense	60,000	0

Instructions
(a) For each company, calculate these values:
   (1) Average age of plant assets
   (2) Average useful life
   (3) Asset turnover ratio
(b) Based on your calculations in part (a), comment on the relative effectiveness of the two companies in using their assets to generate sales and produce net income. What factors complicate your ability to compare the two companies?

*P9-7 In recent years Wind Company has purchased three machines. Because of frequent employee turnover in the accounting department, a different accountant was in charge of selecting the depreciation method for each machine, and various methods have been used. Information concerning the machines is summarized in the table:

Compute depreciation under different methods.
(SO 3, 9)

Machine	Acquired	Cost	Salvage Value	Useful Life (in years)	Depreciation Method
1	Jan. 1, 1995	$ 86,000	$ 6,000	10	Straight-line
2	Jan. 1, 1996	100,000	10,000	8	Declining-balance
3	Nov. 1, 1998	78,000	6,000	6	Units-of-activity

For the declining-balance method, Wind Company uses the double-declining rate. For the units-of-activity method, total machine hours are expected to be 24,000. Actual hours of use in the first 3 years were: 1998, 4,000; 1999, 4,500; and 2000, 5,000.

Instructions
(a) Compute the amount of accumulated depreciation on each machine at December 31, 1998.
(b) If machine 2 was purchased on April 1 instead of January 1, what would be the depreciation expense for this machine in 1996? In 1997?

*P9-8 Keith Whitley Corporation purchased machinery on January 1, 1998, at a cost of $100,000. The estimated useful life of the machinery is 4 years, with an estimated residual value at the end of that period of $10,000. The company is considering different depreciation methods that could be used for financial reporting purposes.

Compute depreciation under different methods.
(SO 3, 9)

Instructions
(a) Prepare separate depreciation schedules for the machinery using the straight-line method, and the declining-balance method using double the straight-line rate. Round to the nearest dollar.

ALTERNATIVE PROBLEMS

Determine acquisition costs of land and building.
(SO 1)

P9-1A Jule Kadlec Company was organized on January 1. During the first year of operations, the following plant asset expenditures and receipts were recorded in random order:

Debits

1. Cost of real estate purchased as a plant site (land $100,000 and building $45,000)	$145,000
2. Accrued real estate taxes paid at time of purchase of real estate	2,000
3. Cost of demolishing building to make land suitable for construction of new building	12,000
4. Cost of filling and grading the land	4,000
5. Excavation costs for new building	20,000
6. Architect's fees on building plans	10,000
7. Full payment to building contractor	700,000
8. Cost of parking lots and driveways	14,000
9. Real estate taxes paid for the current year on land	5,000
	$912,000

Credits

10. Proceeds for salvage of demolished building	$3,500

Instructions
Analyze the transactions using the table column headings provided here. Enter the number of each transaction in the Item column, and enter the amounts in the appropriate columns. For amounts in the Other Accounts column, also indicate the account titles.

Item	Land	Building	Other Accounts

Journalize equipment transactions related to purchase, sale and retirement.
(SO 5, 8)

P9-2A At December 31, 1997, Yount Corporation reported these plant assets:

Land		$ 4,000,000
Buildings	$28,500,000	
Less: Accumulated depreciation—buildings	12,100,000	16,400,000
Equipment	48,000,000	
Less: Accumulated depreciation—equipment	5,000,000	43,000,000
Total plant assets		$63,400,000

During 1998, the following selected cash transactions occurred:

Apr. 1 Purchased land for $2,630,000.
May 1 Sold equipment that cost $600,000 when purchased on January 1, 1994. The equipment was sold for $370,000.
June 1 Sold land purchased on June 1, 1988, for $1,800,000. The land cost $200,000.
July 1 Purchased equipment for $1,200,000.
Dec. 31 Retired equipment that cost $500,000 when purchased on December 31, 1988. No salvage value was received.

Instructions

(a) Journalize the transactions. [*Hint:* You may wish to set up T accounts, post beginning balances, and then post 1998 transactions.] Yount uses straight-line depreciation for buildings and equipment. The buildings are estimated to have a 40-year life and no salvage value; the equipment is estimated to have a 10-year useful life and no salvage value. Update depreciation on assets disposed of at the time of sale or retirement.

(b) Record adjusting entries for depreciation for 1998.

(c) Prepare the plant asset section of Yount's balance sheet at December 31, 1998.

P9-3A Walker Co. has office furniture that cost $80,000 and has been depreciated $47,000.

Journalize transactions related to disposals of plant assets.
(SO 5)

Instructions
Record entries for the disposal under these assumptions:
(a) It was scrapped as having no value.
(b) It was sold for $21,000.
(c) It was sold for $61,000.

P9-4A The intangible asset section of the balance sheet for Eikel Company at December 31, 1997, is presented here:

Prepare entries to record transactions related to acquisition and amortization of intangibles; prepare the intangible assets section and note.
(SO 7, 8)

Patent ($70,000 cost less $7,000 amortization)	$63,000
Copyright ($48,000 cost less $19,200 amortization)	28,800
Total	$91,800

The patent was acquired in January 1997 and has a useful life of 10 years. The copyright was acquired in January 1994 and also has a useful life of 10 years. The following cash transactions may have affected intangible assets during 1998:

Jan. 2 — Paid $9,000 legal costs to successfully defend the patent against infringement by another company.

Jan.–June — Developed a new product, incurring $140,000 in research and development costs. A patent was granted for the product on July 1, and its useful life is equal to its legal life.

Sept. 1 — Paid $80,000 to an extremely large defensive lineman to appear in commercials advertising the company's products. The commercials will air in September and October.

Oct. 1 — Acquired a copyright for $80,000. The copyright has a useful life of 50 years.

Instructions
(a) Prepare journal entries to record the transactions.
(b) Prepare journal entries to record the 1998 amortization expense.
(c) Prepare the intangible asset section of the balance sheet at December 31, 1998.
(d) Prepare the notes to the financial statements on Eikel Company's intangible assets as of December 31, 1998.

P9-5A Due to rapid employee turnover in the accounting department, the following transactions involving intangible assets were improperly recorded by the Glover Company in 1998:

Prepare entries to correct errors in recording and amortizing intangible assets.
(SO 7)

1. Glover developed a new manufacturing process, incurring research and development costs of $136,000. The company also purchased a patent for $39,100. In early January Glover capitalized $175,100 as the cost of the patents. Patent amortization expense of $10,300 was recorded based on a 17-year useful life.

2. On July 1, 1998, Glover purchased a small company and as a result acquired goodwill of $76,000. Glover recorded a half-year's amortization in 1998 based on a 50-year life ($760 amortization).

Instructions
Prepare all journal entries necessary to correct any errors made during 1998. Assume the books have not yet been closed for 1998.

430 CHAPTER 9 Reporting and Analyzing Long-Lived Assets

Calculate and comment on average age, average useful life of plant assets, and asset turnover ratio.
(SO 6)

P9-6A Reggie Corporation and Newman Corporation, two corporations of roughly the same size, are both involved in the manufacture of in-line skates. Each company depreciates its plant assets using the straight-line approach. An investigation of their financial statements reveals the information:

	Reggie Corp.	Newman Corp.
Net income	$ 800,000	$1,000,000
Sales	1,600,000	1,300,000
Total assets	2,500,000	1,700,000
Plant assets	1,800,000	1,000,000
Accumulated depreciation	500,000	825,000
Depreciation expense	120,000	31,250
Intangible assets (goodwill)	300,000	0
Amortization expense	60,000	0

Instructions
(a) For each company, calculate these values:
   (1) Average age of plant assets
   (2) Average useful life
   (3) Asset turnover ratio
(b) Based on your calculations in part (a), comment on the relative effectiveness of the two companies in using their assets to generate sales and produce net income. What factors complicate your ability to compare the two companies?

Compute depreciation under different methods.
(SO 3, 9)

*P9-7A In recent years Rapid Transportation purchased three used buses. Because of frequent employee turnover in the accounting department, a different accountant selected the depreciation method for each bus and various methods have been used. Information concerning the buses is summarized in the table:

Bus	Acquired	Cost	Salvage Value	Useful Life (in years)	Depreciation Method
1	Jan. 1, 1996	$ 96,000	$ 6,000	5	Straight-line
2	Jan. 1, 1996	120,000	10,000	4	Declining-balance
3	Jan. 1, 1997	80,000	8,000	5	Units-of-activity

For the declining-balance method, Rapid Transportation uses the double-declining rate. For the units-of-activity method, total miles are expected to be 120,000. Actual miles of use in the first 3 years were: 1997, 24,000; 1998, 34,000; and 1999, 30,000.

Instructions
(a) Compute the amount of accumulated depreciation on each bus at December 31, 1998.
(b) If Bus 2 was purchased on April 1 instead of January 1, what would be the depreciation expense for this bus in 1996? In 1997?

Compute depreciation under different methods.
(SO 3, 9)

*P9-8A Scott Piper Corporation purchased machinery on January 1, 1998, at a cost of $243,000. The estimated useful life of the machinery is 5 years, with an estimated residual value at the end of that period of $12,000. The company is considering different depreciation methods that could be used for financial reporting purposes.

Instructions
(a) Prepare separate depreciation schedules for the machinery using the straight-line method, and the declining-balance method using double the straight-line rate.
(b) Which method would result in the higher reported 1998 income? In the highest total reported income over the 5-year period?
(c) Which method would result in the lower reported 1998 income? In the lowest total reported income over the 5-year period?

BROADENING YOUR PERSPECTIVE

*F*INANCIAL REPORTING AND ANALYSIS

FINANCIAL REPORTING PROBLEM: *Starbucks Corporation*

BYP9-1 Refer to the financial statements and the Notes to Consolidated Financial Statements of Starbucks, Inc., in Appendix A.

Instructions
Answer the following questions:
(a) What were the total cost and book value of property, plant, and equipment at September 29, 1996?
(b) What method or methods of depreciation are used by Starbucks for financial reporting purposes?
(c) What was the amount of depreciation and amortization expense for each of the 3 years 1994–1996?
(d) Using the statement of cash flows, what are the amounts of property, plant, and equipment purchased (capital spending) in 1996 and 1995?
(e) Read Starbucks' note on leases. Does the company primarily engage in capital leases or operating leases? What are the implications for analysis of its financial statements?

COMPARATIVE ANALYSIS PROBLEM: *Starbucks vs. Green Mountain Coffee*

BYP9-2 The financial statements of Green Mountain Coffee are presented in Appendix B, following the financial statements for Starbucks in Appendix A.

Instructions
(a) Based on the information in these financial statements, compute the following values for each company in 1996:
  (1) Average useful life of plant assets
  (2) Average age of plant assets
  (3) Asset turnover ratio
(b) What conclusions concerning the management of plant assets can be drawn from these data?

RESEARCH CASE

BYP9-3 The December 18, 1995, issue of *Forbes* includes an article by Rita Koselka entitled "Tall Story."

Instructions
Read the article and answer these questions:
(a) What is the biggest expense in running a video rental store?
(b) Over how long a period does Hollywood Entertainment Corp. depreciate its video tapes? How did the author arrive at this figure?
(c) The author asserts that, once a store is fully stocked, depreciation expense should be approximately equal to the cost of new tapes. Calculate and compare the ratios of depreciation expense to new purchases for Hollywood and Blockbuster.
(d) If Hollywood can open a new store for $400,000 or buy an existing store for $1.2 million, why might investors value Hollywood at an average of $3 million per store?

INTERPRETING FINANCIAL STATEMENTS

BYP9-4 Minicase 1 *Microsoft vs. Oracle*
As noted in the chapter, most expenditures for research and development must be expensed. One exception is that computer software companies are allowed to capitalize some

software development costs and record them as assets on their books. Any capitalized software costs are then amortized over the life of the software. The implementation of this rule differs across companies, with some capitalizing many costs and others expensing nearly all of their costs. For example, in 1995 Microsoft incurred research and development costs of $860 million and capitalized none of these costs. Oracle incurred research and development costs of $301 million and capitalized $48 million during 1995. The following additional values are available for 1995:

($ in millions)	Microsoft	Oracle
Total revenue	$5,937	$2,966
Net income	1,453	442

Instructions
(a) As you evaluate the performances of Microsoft and Oracle, what implications do their different policies on capitalization of software development expenditures have on your analysis?
(b) Which company spends a greater percentage of its revenue on developing new products? What implications might this have for the future performance of the companies?
(c) SoftKey International Inc., headquartered in Cambridge, Massachusetts, noted in its 1994 report that, beginning that year, it changed the estimated life of its computer software for amortization purposes from a 3-year life to a 12-year life. What implications does this have for the analysis of Softkey's results?

BYP9-5 **Minicase 2** *Merck vs. Johnson & Johnson*
Merck and Co., Inc., and Johnson & Johnson are two leading producers of health care products. Each has considerable assets, and each expends considerable funds each year toward the development of new products. The development of a new health care product is often very expensive and risky. New products frequently must undergo considerable testing before they are approved for distribution to the public. For example, it took Johnson & Johnson 4 years and $200 million to develop its 1-DAY ACUVUE contact lenses. Here are some basic data compiled from the 1994 financial statements of these two companies:

($ in millions)	Johnson & Johnson	Merck
Total assets	$15,668	$21,857
Total revenue	15,734	14,970
Net income	2,006	2,997
Research and development expense	1,278	1,230
Intangible assets	2,403	7,212

Instructions
(a) What kinds of intangible assets might a health care products company have? Does the composition of these intangible assets matter to investors? That is, would Merck be perceived differently if all of its intangibles were goodwill than if all of its intangibles were patents?
(b) Using the asset turnover ratio, determine which company is using its assets more effectively. [*Note:* In 1993 total assets were $19,928 million for Merck and $12,242 million for Johnson & Johnson.]
(c) Suppose the president of Merck has come to you for advice. He has noted that by eliminating research and development expenditures, the company could have reported $1.3 billion more in net income in 1994. He is frustrated because much of the research never results in a product, or the products take years to develop. He says shareholders are eager for higher returns, so he is considering eliminating research and development expenditures for at least a couple of years. What would you advise?
(d) The notes to Merck's financial statements indicate that Merck has goodwill of $4.1 billion. Where does recorded goodwill come from? Is it necessarily a good thing to have a lot of goodwill on your books?

BYP9-6 **Minicase 3** *Boeing vs. McDonnell Douglas*
Boeing and McDonnell Douglas are two leaders in the manufacture of aircraft. In 1996

Boeing announced intentions to acquire McDonnell Douglas and create one huge corporation. Competitors, primarily Airbus of Europe, are very concerned that they will not be able to compete with such a huge rival. In addition, customers are concerned that this merger will reduce the number of suppliers to a point where Boeing will be able to dictate prices. Provided below are figures taken from the 1995 financial statements of Boeing and McDonnell Douglas, which allow a comparison of the operations of the two corporations prior to their proposed merger.

($ in millions)	Boeing	McDonnell Douglas
Total revenue	$19,515	$14,322
Net income (loss)	393	(416)
Total assets	22,098	10,466
Land	404	91
Buildings and fixtures	5,791	1,647
Machinery and equipment	7,251	2,161
Total property, plant, and equipment (at cost)	13,744	3,899
Accumulated depreciation	7,288	2,541
Depreciation expense	976	196

Instructions
(a) Which company has older assets?
(b) Which company used a longer average estimated useful life for its assets?
(c) Based on the asset turnover ratio, which company uses its assets more effectively to generate sales?
(d) Besides an increase in size, what other factors might be motivating this merger?

CRITICAL THINKING

MANAGEMENT DECISION CASE

BYP9-7 Tammy Company and Hamline Company are two proprietorships that are similar in many respects except that Tammy Company uses the straight-line method and Hamline Company uses the declining-balance method at double the straight-line rate. On January 2, 1996, both companies acquired the depreciable assets listed in the table.

Asset	Cost	Salvage Value	Useful Life
Building	$320,000	$20,000	40 years
Equipment	110,000	10,000	10 years

Hamline's depreciation expense was $38,000 in 1996, $32,800 in 1997, and $28,520 in 1998. Including the appropriate depreciation charges, annual net income for the companies in the years 1996, 1997, and 1998 and total income for the 3 years were as follows:

	1996	1997	1998	Total
Tammy Company	$84,000	$88,400	$90,000	$262,400
Hamline Company	68,000	76,000	85,000	229,000

At December 31, 1998, the balance sheets of the two companies are similar except that Hamline Company has more cash than Tammy Company.

Dawna Tucci is interested in buying one of the companies, and she comes to you for advice.

Instructions
(a) Determine the annual and total depreciation recorded by Tammy during the 3 years.
(b) Assuming that Hamline Company also uses the straight-line method of depreciation instead of the declining-balance method (that is, Hamline's depreciation expense would equal Tammy's), prepare comparative income data for the 3 years.
(c) Which company should Dawna Tucci buy? Why?

A REAL-WORLD FOCUS: *Clark Equipment Company*

BYP9-8 *Clark Equipment Company* was originally formed in 1902 as a general manufacturing company. During its history it has specialized in the manufacture of drills, gears, towing tractors, and truck transmissions. Today the company operates throughout the United States and Europe in the design, manufacture, and sale of skid steer loaders, construction machinery, and transmissions for on-highway trucks and for off-highway equipment. It also is involved in a 50–50 joint venture with Volvo in the manufacture of construction equipment.

The following information relates to the plant assets of Clark Equipment Company:

($ in millions)	1994	1993
Land	$ 13.2	$ 7.4
Land improvements	8.8	5.9
Buildings	126.0	77.3
Machinery and equipment	451.7	398.4
Totals	599.7	489.0
Accumulated depreciation	315.9	272.8
Total plant assets	$283.8	$216.2

Instructions
(a) What type of costs would Clark Equipment capitalize in the land category of plant assets?
(b) Cite several possible types of land improvements that Clark Equipment might have made.
(c) What is the book value of Clark Equipment's plant assets?

GROUP ACTIVITY

*BYP9-9 With the class divided into three groups, each group should be assigned one of these depreciation methods: straight-line, units-of-activity, declining-balance.

Instructions
(a) Think of an example that would use the assigned depreciation method. Calculate depreciation for the first 2 years of useful life.
(b) Present your example to the class. Include necessary journal entries.

COMMUNICATION ACTIVITY

BYP9-10 The chapter presented some concerns regarding the current accounting standards for research and development expenditures.

Instructions
Pretend that you are either (a) the president of a company that is very dependent on ongoing research and development, writing a memo to the FASB complaining about the current accounting standards regarding research and development, or (b) the FASB member defending the current standards regarding research and development. Your letter should address these questions:

1. By requiring expensing of R&D, do you think companies will spend less on R&D? Why or why not? What are the possible implications for the competitiveness of U.S. companies?
2. If a company makes a commitment to spend money for R&D, it must believe it has future benefits. Shouldn't these costs therefore be capitalized just like the purchase of any long-lived asset that you believe will have future benefits?

Ethics Case

BYP9-11 Imporia Container Company is suffering declining sales of its principal product, nonbiodegradable plastic cartons. The president, Benny Benson, instructs his controller, John Straight, to lengthen asset lives to reduce depreciation expense. A processing line of automated plastic extruding equipment, purchased for $2.7 million in January 1998, was originally estimated to have a useful life of 8 years and a salvage value of $300,000. Depreciation has been recorded for 2 years on that basis. Benny wants the estimated life changed to 12 years total and the straight-line method continued. John is hesitant to make the change, believing it is unethical to increase net income in this manner. Benny says, "Hey, the life is only an estimate, and I've heard that our competition uses a 12-year life on their production equipment."

Instructions
(a) Who are the stakeholders in this situation?
(b) Is the proposed change in asset life unethical or simply a good business practice by an astute president?
(c) What is the effect of Benny Benson's proposed change on income before taxes in the year of change?

Financial Analysis on the Web

BYP9-12 Purpose: Use an annual report to identify a company's plant asset and the depreciation method used.

Address: http://www.reportgallery.com

Steps:
1. From Report Gallery Homepage, choose **Viewing Library.**
2. Select a particular company.
3. Choose **Annual Report.**
4. Follow instructions below.

Instructions
Answer the following questions:
(a) What is the name of the company?
(b) What is the Internet address of the annual report?
(c) At fiscal year-end, what is the net amount of its plant assets?
(d) What is the accumulated depreciation?
(e) Which method of depreciation does the company use?

Answers to Self-Study Questions
1. d   2. a   3. b   4. d   5. b   6. d   7. b   8. c   9. c   10. c
*11. d

CHAPTER 10

Reporting and Analyzing Liabilities

STUDY OBJECTIVES

After studying this chapter, you should be able to:

1. Explain a current liability and identify the major types of current liabilities.
2. Describe the accounting for notes payable.
3. Explain the accounting for other current liabilities.
4. Identify the requirements for the financial statement presentation and analysis of current liabilities.
5. Explain why bonds are issued and identify the types of bonds.
6. Prepare the entries for the issuance of bonds and interest expense.
7. Describe the entries when bonds are redeemed.
8. Identify the requirements for the financial statement presentation and analysis of long-term liabilities.

Live by Debt, Die by Debt

Debt can help a company acquire the things it needs to grow, but it is often the very thing that kills a company. A brief history of Maxwell Car Company illustrates the role of debt in the U.S. auto industry. In 1920 Maxwell Car Company was on the brink of financial ruin. Because it was axle-deep in debt and unable to pay its bills, its creditors stepped in and took over. A former General Motors executive named Walter Chrysler was hired to reorganize the company. By 1925 he had taken over the company and renamed it Chrysler. By 1933 Chrysler was booming, with sales surpassing even those of Ford. But the next few decades saw Chrysler make a series of blunders. During the 1940s, while its competitors were making yearly design changes to boost customer interest, Chrysler made no changes. During the 1960s, when customers wanted large cars, Chrysler produced small cars. During the 1970s, when customers wanted small cars, Chrysler offered big "boats." By 1980, with its creditors pounding at the gates, Chrysler was again on the brink of financial ruin.

At that point Chrysler brought in a former Ford executive named Lee Iacocca to save the company. Iacocca, considered by many as good a politician as a businessman, argued that the United States could not afford to let Chrysler fail because of the loss of jobs. He convinced the federal government to grant loan guarantees—promises that if Chrysler failed to pay its creditors, the government would pay them. Iacocca then streamlined operations and brought out some profitable products. Chrysler repaid all of its government-guaranteed loans by 1983, seven years ahead of the scheduled final payment.

Where is Chrysler today? In the 1990s Chrysler has known both feast and famine: In 1991 it operated in the red, with Iacocca leaving the company under pressure in 1992. By 1995 Chrysler was the most profitable U.S.-based car manufacturer and the envy of the entire industry.

At one time there were many U.S.-based car manufacturers; today Chrysler is one of only three, The Big Three. These companies are giants. In comparison with other U.S. corpora-

tions, The Big Three—General Motors, Ford, and Chrysler—rank, respectively, number one, two, and seven in total sales. But The Big Three have accumulated a truckload of debt on their way to getting this big. Combined, they have *$454 billion* in total outstanding liabilities. Although debt has made it possible to get so big, the Chrysler story makes it clear that debt also threatens a company's survival.

On the World Wide Web
Chrysler: http://www.chrysler.com
Ford: http://www.ford.com
General Motors: http://www.gm.com

PREVIEW OF CHAPTER 10

The opening story suggests that The Big Three—General Motors, Ford, and Chrysler—have tremendous amounts of debt. It is unlikely that they could have grown so large without this debt, but at times this debt threatens their very existence. Given this risk, why do companies borrow money? Why do they sometimes borrow short-term and other times long-term? Besides bank borrowings, what other kinds of debts does a company incur? In this chapter we address these issues.

The content and organization of the chapter are as follows:

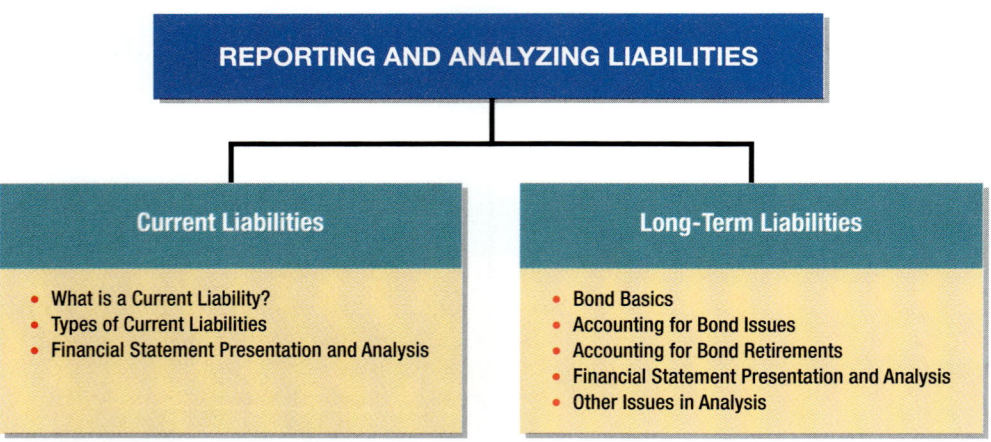

SECTION 1
CURRENT LIABILITIES

WHAT IS A CURRENT LIABILITY?

STUDY OBJECTIVE 1
Explain a current liability and identify the major types of current liabilities.

You have learned that liabilities are defined as "creditors' claims on total assets" and as "existing debts and obligations." These claims, debts, and obligations must be settled or paid at some time in the future by the transfer of assets or services. The future date on which they are due or payable (the maturity date) is a significant feature of liabilities.

As explained in Chapter 2, a **current liability** is a debt that can reasonably be expected to be paid (1) from existing current assets or through the creation of other current liabilities, and (2) within 1 year or the operating cycle, whichever is longer. Debts that do not meet both criteria are classified as **long-term liabilities.**

Financial statement users want to know whether a company's obligations are current or long-term. A company, for example, that has more current liabilities than current assets often lacks liquidity, or short-term debt-paying ability.

438

In addition, users want to know the types of liabilities a company has. If a company declares bankruptcy, a specific, predetermined order of payment to creditors exists. Thus, the amount and type of liabilities are of critical importance.

TYPES OF CURRENT LIABILITIES

The different types of current liabilities include notes payable, accounts payable, unearned revenues, and accrued liabilities such as taxes, salaries and wages, and interest. In this section we discuss a few of the common and more important types of current liabilities. All current liabilities that are material should be reported in a company's balance sheet.

Helpful Hint The entries for accounts payable and the adjusting entries for some current liabilities have been explained in previous chapters.

NOTES PAYABLE

Obligations in the form of written notes are recorded as **notes payable.** Notes payable are often used instead of accounts payable because they give the lender written documentation of the obligation in case legal remedies are needed to collect the debt. Notes payable usually require the borrower to pay interest and frequently are issued to meet short-term financing needs.

STUDY OBJECTIVE 2

Describe the accounting for notes payable.

Notes are issued for varying periods of time. **Those due for payment within 1 year of the balance sheet date are usually classified as current liabilities.** For example, recently, Chrysler reported $2.67 billion of notes payable, which it labeled "short-term debt" on its balance sheet. Most notes are interest-bearing.

To illustrate the accounting for notes payable, assume that First National Bank agrees to lend $100,000 on March 1, 1998, if Cole Williams Co. signs a $100,000, 12%, 4-month note. With an interest-bearing note, the amount of assets received when the note is issued generally equals the note's face value. Cole Williams Co. therefore will receive $100,000 cash and will make the following journal entry:

Mar. 1	Cash	100,000	
	Notes Payable		100,000
	(To record issuance of 12%, 4-month		
	note to First National Bank)		

Interest accrues over the life of the note and must be recorded periodically. If Cole Williams Co. prepares financial statements semiannually, an adjusting entry is required to recognize interest expense and interest payable of $4,000 ($100,000 × 12% × $\frac{4}{12}$) at June 30. The adjusting entry is:

June 30	Interest Expense	4,000	
	Interest Payable		4,000
	(To accrue interest for 4 months on First		
	National Bank note)		

In the June 30 financial statements, the current liability section of the balance sheet will show notes payable $100,000 and interest payable $4,000. In addition, interest expense of $4,000 will be reported under Other Expenses and Losses in the income statement. If Cole Williams Co. prepared financial statements monthly, the adjusting entry at the end of each month would have been $1,000 ($100,000 \times 12\% \times \frac{1}{12}$).

At maturity (July 1), Cole Williams Co. must pay the face value of the note ($100,000) plus $4,000 interest ($100,000 \times 12\% \times \frac{4}{12}$). The entry to record payment of the note and accrued interest is:

July 1	Notes Payable	100,000	
	Interest Payable	4,000	
	Cash		104,000
	(To record payment of First National Bank interest-bearing note and accrued interest at maturity)		

SALES TAXES PAYABLE

STUDY OBJECTIVE 3
Explain the accounting for other current liabilities.

As consumers, we are well aware that many of the products we purchase at retail stores are subject to sales taxes. The tax is expressed as a percentage of the sales price. The retailer (or selling company) collects the tax from the customer when the sale occurs and periodically (usually monthly) remits the collections to the state's department of revenue.

Helpful Hint Watch how sales are rung up at local retailers to see whether the sales tax is computed separately.

Under most state laws, the amount of the sale and the amount of the sales tax collected must be rung up separately on the cash register. (Gasoline sales are a major exception.) The cash register readings are then used to credit Sales and Sales Taxes Payable. For example, if the March 25 cash register readings for Cooley Grocery show sales of $10,000 and sales taxes of $600 (sales tax rate of 6%), the journal entry is:

Mar. 25	Cash	10,600	
	Sales		10,000
	Sales Taxes Payable		600
	(To record daily sales and sales taxes)		

When the taxes are remitted to the taxing agency, Sales Taxes Payable is decreased (debited) and Cash is decreased (credited). The company does not report sales taxes as an expense; it simply forwards the amount paid by the customer to the government. Thus, Cooley Grocery serves only as a **collection agent** for the taxing authority.

When sales taxes are not rung up separately on the cash register, total receipts are divided by 100% plus the sales tax percentage to determine sales. To illustrate, assume in our example that Cooley Grocery "rings up" total receipts of $10,600. Because the amount received from the sale is equal to the sales price 100% plus 6% of sales, or 1.06 times the sales total, we can compute sales as follows: $10,600 ÷ 1.06 = $10,000. Thus, the sales tax amount of $600 is found by either (1) subtracting sales from total receipts ($10,600 − $10,000) or (2) multiplying sales by the sales tax rate ($10,000 × 6%).

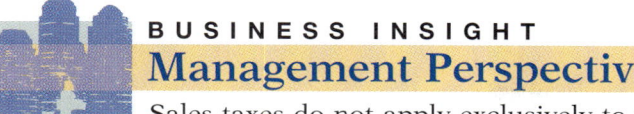

BUSINESS INSIGHT
Management Perspective

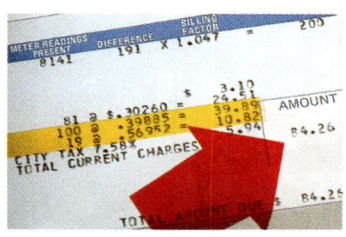

Sales taxes do not apply exclusively to retail companies. They also apply to manufacturing companies, service companies, and public utilities, and the extent of the taxes is increasing. In 1981 average total sales taxes were 6.1% in the United States. Today they are more than 8% and climbing. There are now over 9,000 state and local sales taxes, making compliance very difficult and costly. For example, American Telephone and Telegraph (AT&T) employs more than 76 full-time people to file the company's sales tax returns. They also handle the sales tax audits (at times over 200) that AT&T is undergoing at any given time.

PAYROLL AND PAYROLL TAXES PAYABLE

Every employer incurs liabilities relating to employees' salaries and wages. One is the amount of wages and salaries owed to employees—**wages and salaries payable.** Another is the amount required by law to be withheld from employees' gross pay. Until these **withholding taxes**—federal and state income taxes and Social Security taxes—are remitted to governmental taxing authorities, they are recorded as increases (credited) to appropriate liability accounts. For example, accrual and payment of a $100,000 payroll on which a corporation withholds taxes from its employees' wages and salaries would be recorded as follows:

Mar. 7	Salaries and Wages Expense	100,000	
	FICA Taxes Payable[1]		7,250
	Federal Income Taxes Payable		21,864
	State Income Taxes Payable		2,922
	Salaries and Wages Payable		67,964
	(To record payroll and withholding taxes for the week ending March 7)		
	Salaries and Wages Payable	67,964	
	Cash		67,964
	(To record payment of the March 7 payroll)		

Illustration 10-1 (page 442) summarizes the types of payroll deductions that normally occur.

Also, with every payroll, the employer incurs liabilities to pay various **payroll taxes** levied upon the employer. These payroll taxes include the employer's share of Social Security (FICA) taxes and state and federal unemployment taxes. Based on the $100,000 payroll in our example, the following entry would be made to record the employer's expense and liability for these payroll taxes:

Mar. 7	Payroll Tax Expense	13,450	
	FICA Taxes Payable		7,250
	Federal Unemployment Taxes Payable		800
	State Unemployment Taxes Payable		5,400
	(To record employer's payroll taxes on March 7 payroll)		

---

[1] Social Security taxes are commonly referred to as FICA taxes. In 1937 Congress enacted the Federal Insurance Contribution Act (FICA). As can be seen in this journal entry and the payroll tax journal entry, the employee and employer must make equal contributions to Social Security.

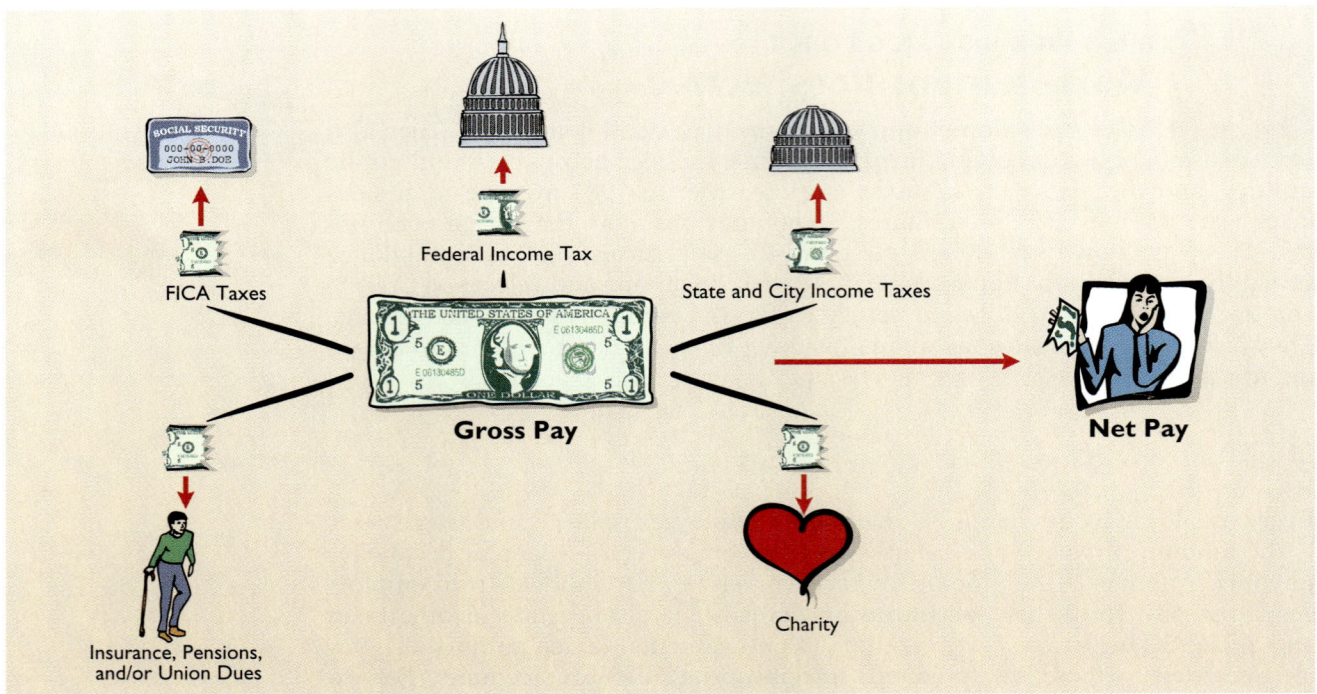

Illustration 10-1 Payroll deductions

The payroll and payroll tax liability accounts are classified as current liabilities because they must be paid to employees or remitted to taxing authorities periodically and in the near term. Taxing authorities impose substantial fines and penalties on employers if the withholding and payroll taxes are not computed correctly and paid on time.

UNEARNED REVENUES

A magazine publisher such as Sports Illustrated may receive a customer's check when magazines are ordered, and an airline company such as American Airlines often receives cash when it sells tickets for future flights. How do these companies account for unearned revenues that are received before goods are delivered or services are rendered?

1. When the advance is received, Cash is increased (debited), and a current liability account identifying the source of the unearned revenue is also increased (credited).
2. When the revenue is earned, the unearned revenue account is decreased (debited), and an earned revenue account is increased (credited).

To illustrate, assume that Superior University sells 10,000 season football tickets at $50 each for its five-game home schedule. The entry for the sales of season tickets is:

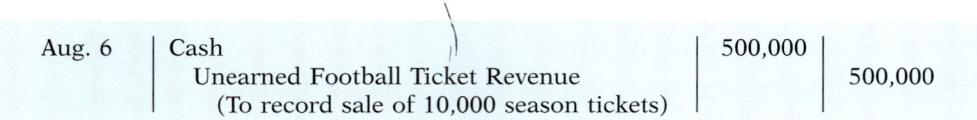

As each game is completed, this entry is made:

Sept. 7	Unearned Football Ticket Revenue	100,000	
	Football Ticket Revenue		100,000
	(To record football ticket revenues earned)		

The account Unearned Football Ticket Revenue represents unearned revenue and is reported as a current liability in the balance sheet. As revenue is earned, a transfer from unearned revenue to earned revenue occurs. Unearned revenue is material for some companies: In the airline industry, tickets sold for future flights represent almost 50% of total current liabilities. At United Airlines, unearned ticket revenue is the largest current liability, recently amounting to more than $1 billion.

Illustration 10-2 shows specific unearned and earned revenue accounts used in selected types of businesses.

Type of Business	Account Title	
	Unearned Revenue	**Earned Revenue**
Airline	Unearned Passenger Ticket Revenue	Passenger Ticket Revenue
Magazine publisher	Unearned Subscription Revenue	Subscription Revenue
Hotel	Unearned Rental Revenue	Rental Revenue

Illustration 10-2
Unearned and earned revenue accounts

CURRENT MATURITIES OF LONG-TERM DEBT

Companies often have a portion of long-term debt that comes due in the current year. As an example, assume that Wendy Construction issues a 5-year, interest-bearing $25,000 note on January 1, 1998. This note specifies that each January 1, starting January 1, 1999, $5,000 of the note should be paid. When financial statements are prepared on December 31, 1998, $5,000 should be reported as a current liability and $20,000 as a long-term liability. Current maturities of long-term debt are often identified on the balance sheet as **long-term debt due within 1 year.** At December 31, 1995, Chrysler had $1.66 billion of such debt.

It is not necessary to prepare an adjusting entry to recognize the current maturity of long-term debt. The proper statement classification of each balance sheet account is recognized when the balance sheet is prepared.

BEFORE YOU GO ON . . .

- **Review It**
  1. What are the two criteria for classifying a debt as a current liability?
  2. What are some examples of current liabilities?
  3. What are three items generally withheld from employees' wages or salaries?
  4. Identify three examples of unearned revenues.

- **Do It**

A local not-for-profit organization has asked you to act as its treasurer. Each fall the club holds a fund-raiser at which it offers space to craftspeople who bring their wares for sale. The organization charges these vendors a commission on sales and uses these collections to raise scholarship money to donate to local

444　CHAPTER 10　Reporting and Analyzing Liabilities

colleges. The organization acts as a collection agent for state sales taxes. The cash register total of $256,000 for the 4-day event includes sales taxes. The state tax rate is 6.25%, and there are no city sales taxes. Assuming that all sales were taxable, what amount of sales taxes must the organization collect from the vendors and remit to the state? How should you, as treasurer, show that tax liability in the organization's financial statements?

Reasoning: To answer the first question, you must separate the sales taxes from the total sales amount. To answer the second question, you must know how sales taxes are reported in the financial statements and whether statements will be issued before you pay the sales taxes.

Solution: First divide the total proceeds by 100% plus the sales tax percentage to find the sales amount. Then, to determine the sales taxes, subtract the sales amount from the total proceeds, *or* multiply the sales amount by the tax rate:

$$\text{Sales amount} = \$256{,}000 \div 1.0625 = \$240{,}941.18$$
$$\text{Sales taxes due} = \$256{,}000 - \$240{,}941.18 = \$15{,}058.82$$
$$\text{or}$$
$$= \$240{,}941.18 \times .0625 = \$15{,}058.82$$

If financial statements are issued before you remit the sales taxes payable, you should show sales taxes payable of $15,058.82 as a current liability. It is unlikely that you would show the sales tax liability, however, because the sales taxes should be remitted to the state as quickly as possible. You would not show the sales tax as an expense because your organization was simply a collection agent.

FINANCIAL STATEMENT PRESENTATION AND ANALYSIS

PRESENTATION

STUDY OBJECTIVE 4
Identify the requirements for the financial statement presentation and analysis of current liabilities.

Current liabilities are the first category under Liabilities on the balance sheet. Each of the principal types of current liabilities is listed separately within the category. In addition, the terms of notes payable and other pertinent information concerning the individual items are disclosed in the notes to the financial statements.

Current liabilities are seldom listed in their order of maturity because of the varying maturity dates that may exist for specific obligations such as notes payable. A more common, and entirely satisfactory, method of presenting current liabilities is to list them by **order of magnitude,** with the largest obligations first. Many companies, as a matter of custom, show current maturities of long-term debt first, regardless of amount. The adapted balance sheet of Chrysler Corp. in Illustration 10-3 shows its presentation of current liabilities.

ANALYSIS

Liquidity ratios measure the short-term ability of a company to pay its maturing obligations and to meet unexpected needs for cash. Two measures of liquidity were examined in Chapter 2: working capital (Current assets − Current liabilities) and the current ratio (Current assets ÷ Current liabilities). In this section we add a third useful measure of liquidity, the acid-test ratio.

The current ratio is a frequently used ratio, but it can be misleading. Consider the current ratio's numerator, which can include some items in current as-

Illustration 10-3
Balance sheets for Chrysler Corporation

CHRYSLER CORPORATION AND CONSOLIDATED SUBSIDIARIES
Consolidated Balance Sheets
December 31, 1995 and 1994
(in millions)

Assets	1995	1994
Current assets		
Cash and cash equivalents	$ 5,543	$ 5,145
Marketable securities	2,582	3,226
Accounts receivable, net	2,003	1,695
Inventories	4,448	3,356
Other current assets	5,256	6,549
Total current assets	19,832	19,971
Noncurrent assets	33,924	29,568
Total assets	$53,756	$49,539

Liabilities and Stockholders' Equity		
Current liabilities		
Accounts payable	$ 8,290	$ 7,826
Notes payable	2,674	4,645
Current maturities of long-term debt	1,661	811
Accrued liabilities and expenses	7,032	5,582
Total current liabilities	19,657	18,864
Long-term debt	9,858	7,650
Accrued noncurrent employee benefits	9,217	8,595
Other noncurrent liabilities	4,065	3,736
Total liabilities	42,797	38,845
Total stockholders' equity	10,959	10,694
Total liabilities and stockholders' equity	$53,756	$49,539

sets that are not very liquid. For example, when a company is having a difficult time selling its merchandise, its inventory and current ratio increase, even though its liquidity has actually declined. Similarly, prepaid expenses increase assets, but generally cannot be sold and therefore do not contribute to liquidity. Consequently, the current ratio is often supplemented with the acid-test ratio.

The **acid-test ratio** is a measure of a company's immediate short-term liquidity. It is computed by dividing the sum of cash, marketable securities (short-term), and net receivables by current liabilities. Cash, marketable securities, and net receivables are usually highly liquid compared to inventory and prepaid expenses. Thus, because it measures **immediate** liquidity, the acid-test ratio should be computed along with the current ratio. Working capital, current ratios, and acid-test ratios for Chrysler are provided in Illustration 10-4 (page 446). Industry averages are provided where available.

Chrysler's current assets nearly equal its current liabilities; thus, its current ratio is approximately 1 in both 1994 and 1995. Its working capital was, relatively speaking, very low. The industry average current ratio for manufacturers of cars and car parts is 1.6 : 1. Thus, Chrysler appears to lack liquidity. This is confirmed by the acid-test ratio. The industry average for this ratio is .7 : 1, whereas in both 1994 and 1995 Chrysler had an acid-test ratio of approximately .5 : 1.

Alternative Terminology The acid-test ratio is often referred to as the **quick ratio.**

Illustration 10-4
Liquidity measures

$$\text{WORKING CAPITAL} = \text{CURRENT ASSETS} - \text{CURRENT LIABILITIES}$$

$$\text{CURRENT RATIO} = \frac{\text{CURRENT ASSETS}}{\text{CURRENT LIABILITIES}}$$

$$\text{ACID-TEST RATIO} = \frac{\text{CASH} + \text{MARKETABLE SECURITIES (SHORT-TERM)} + \text{NET RECEIVABLES}}{\text{CURRENT LIABILITIES}}$$

($ in millions)	Chrysler 1995	Chrysler 1994	Industry Average 1995	Industry Average 1994
Working Capital	$19,832 − $19,657 = $175	$19,971 − $18,864 = $1,107	na	na
Current Ratio	$\frac{\$19,832}{\$19,657} = 1.009 : 1$	$\frac{\$19,971}{\$18,864} = 1.059 : 1$	1.6 : 1	1.3 : 1
Acid-Test Ratio	$\frac{\$5,543 + \$2,582 + \$2,003}{\$19,657} = .52 : 1$	$\frac{\$5,145 + \$3,226 + \$1,695}{\$18,864} = .53 : 1$	.7 : 1	.7 : 1

DECISION TOOLKIT

Decision Checkpoints	Info Needed for Decision	Tool to Use for Decision	How to Evaluate Results
Can the company meet its current obligations?	Cash, accounts receivable, marketable securities, and other highly liquid assets, and current liabilities	Acid-test ratio = (Cash + Marketable securities + Net receivables) / Current liabilities	Ratio should be compared to others in same industry. High ratio indicates good liquidity.

Many companies have reduced their liquid assets because they cost too much to hold. Companies that keep fewer liquid assets on hand must rely on other sources of liquidity. One such source is a bank **line of credit.** A line of credit is a prearranged agreement between a company and a lender that permits, should it be necessary, a company to borrow up to an agreed-upon amount. To the extent that its low amount of liquid assets causes a cash shortfall, a company may borrow money on its available short-term lines of credit. Therefore, given Chrysler's relatively low liquidity, adequate short-term lines of credit are critical. The debt footnote to Chrysler's 1995 financial statements discusses its available line of credit agreements (referred to in the footnote as *credit facilities*). The note, in Illustration 10-5, discusses both Chrysler and CFC (its finance division).

Illustration 10-5
Line of credit note

CHRYSLER CORPORATION
Notes to the Financial Statements

During the second quarter of 1995, CFC entered into new revolving credit facilities. The new facilities, which total $8.0 billion, consist of a $2.4 billion facility expiring in May 1996 and a $5.6 billion facility expiring in May 2000. As of December 31, 1995, no amounts were outstanding under these facilities.

At December 31, 1995, Chrysler had a $1.7 billion revolving credit agreement which expires in July 1999. None of the commitment was drawn upon at December 31, 1995.

Chrysler's available lines of credit, which total $9.7 billion, are nearly equal to the sum of its existing cash, short-term marketable securities, and net receivables. Thus, even though Chrysler has lower liquidity ratios than the industry average, its available lines of credit appear adequate to meet any short-term cash deficiency it might experience.

DECISION TOOLKIT

Decision Checkpoints	Info Needed for Decision	Tool to Use for Decision	How to Evaluate Results
Can the company obtain short-term financing when necessary?	Available lines of credit from debt note to the financial statements.	Compare available lines of credit to current liabilities. Also, evaluate liquidity ratios.	If liquidity ratios are low, then lines of credit should be high to compensate.

BEFORE YOU GO ON . . .

● **Review It**
1. In what order are current liabilities usually presented?
2. What does the acid-test ratio measure and how is it calculated?
3. What is a line of credit?

SECTION 2
LONG-TERM LIABILITIES

Long-term liabilities are obligations that are expected to be paid after 1 year. In this section we explain the accounting for the principal types of obligations reported in the long-term liability section of the balance sheet. These obligations often are in the form of bonds or long-term notes.

BOND BASICS

Bonds are a form of interest-bearing note payable issued by corporations, universities, and governmental agencies. Bonds, like common stock, are sold in small denominations (usually $1,000 or multiples of $1,000). As a result, bonds attract many investors.

STUDY OBJECTIVE 5
Explain why bonds are issued and identify the types of bonds.

WHY ISSUE BONDS?

A corporation may use long-term financing other than bonds, such as notes payable and leasing. However, these other forms of financing involve an agreement between the corporation and one individual, one company, or a financial institution. Notes payable and leasing are therefore seldom sufficient to furnish the funds needed for plant expansion and major projects like new buildings. To obtain **large amounts of long-term capital,** corporate management usually must decide whether to issue bonds or to sell common stock.

From the standpoint of the corporation seeking long-term financing, bonds offer advantages over common stock as shown in Illustration 10-6.

Illustration 10-6 Advantages of bond financing over common stock

Bond Financing	Advantages
	1. **Stockholder control is not affected.** Bondholders do not have voting rights, so current owners (stockholders) retain full control of the company.
	2. **Tax savings result.** Bond interest is deductible for tax purposes; dividends on stock are not.
	3. **Earnings per share may be higher.** Although bond interest expense reduces net income, earnings per share often is higher under bond financing because no additional shares of common stock are issued.

One commonly reported measure of corporate performance is **earnings per share**—Net income ÷ Average shares outstanding. We will discuss the pros and cons of earnings per share as a performance measure in Chapter 11. Now we focus on how earnings per share can be increased by the effective use of debt.

To illustrate the potential effect of debt on earnings per share, assume that Microsystems, Inc., is considering two plans for financing the construction of a new $5 million plant: Plan A involves issuing 200,000 shares of common stock at the current market price of $25 per share. Plan B involves issuing $5 million, 12% bonds at face value. Income before interest and taxes on the new plant will be $1.5 million; income taxes are expected to be 30%. Microsystems currently has 100,000 shares of common stock outstanding. The alternative effects on earnings per share are shown in Illustration 10-7.

Illustration 10-7 Effects on earnings per share—stocks vs. bonds

International Note
The priority of bondholders' versus stockholders' rights varies across countries. In Japan, Germany, and France stockholders and employees are given priority, with liquidation of the firm to pay creditors seen as a last resort. In Britain creditors' interests are put first; the courts are quick to give control of the firm to creditors.

	Plan A: Issue stock	Plan B: Issue bonds
Income before interest and taxes	$1,500,000	$1,500,000
Interest (12% × $5,000,000)	—	600,000
Income before income taxes	1,500,000	900,000
Income tax expense (30%)	450,000	270,000
Net income	$1,050,000	$ 630,000
Outstanding shares	300,000	100,000
Earnings per share	**$ 3.50**	**$ 6.30**

Note that with long-term debt financing (bonds) net income is $420,000 ($1,050,000 − $630,000) less. However, earnings per share is higher because there are 200,000 fewer shares of common stock outstanding.

The major disadvantage resulting from the use of bonds is that the company locks in fixed payments that must be made in good times and bad. Interest must be paid on a periodic basis, and the principal (face value) of the bonds must be paid at maturity. A company with fluctuating earnings and a relatively weak cash position may experience great difficulty in meeting interest requirements in periods of low earnings. In the extreme, this can result in bankruptcy. With common stock financing, on the other hand, the company can decide to pay low (or no) dividends if earnings are low.

TYPES OF BONDS

Bonds may have many different features. Some types of bonds commonly issued are described in the following sections.

Secured and Unsecured Bonds

Secured bonds have specific assets of the issuer pledged as collateral for the bonds. A bond secured by real estate, for example, is called a **mortgage bond.** A bond secured by specific assets set aside to retire the bonds is called a **sinking fund bond.**

Unsecured bonds are issued against the general credit of the borrower. These bonds, called **debenture bonds,** are used extensively by large corporations with good credit ratings. For example, in a recent annual report, DuPont reported more than $2 billion of debenture bonds outstanding.

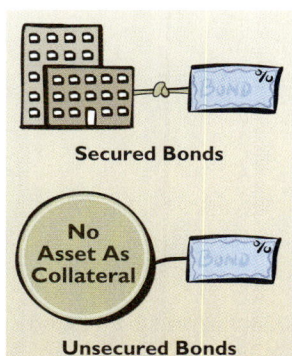

Term and Serial Bonds

Bonds that are due for payment (mature) at a single specified future date are called **term bonds.** In contrast, bonds that mature in installments are called **serial bonds.** For example, Caterpillar Inc. debentures due in 2007 are term bonds, and their debentures due between 1998 and 2007 are serial bonds.

Convertible and Callable Bonds

Bonds that can be converted into common stock at the bondholder's option are called **convertible bonds.** Bonds subject to retirement at a stated dollar amount prior to maturity at the option of the issuer are known as **callable bonds.**

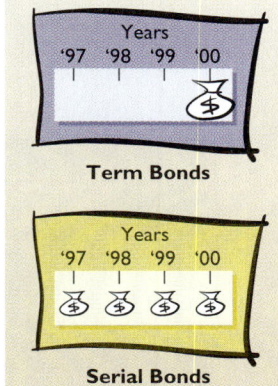

Convertible bonds have features that are attractive both to bondholders and to the issuer. The conversion often gives bondholders an opportunity to benefit if the market price of the common stock increases substantially. Furthermore, until conversion, the bondholder receives interest on the bond. For the issuer, the bonds sell at a higher price and pay a lower rate of interest than comparable debt securities that do not have a conversion option. Many corporations, such as USAir, USX Corp., and Chrysler Corporation, have convertible bonds outstanding.

ISSUING PROCEDURES

State laws grant corporations the power to issue bonds. Within the corporation, formal approval by both the board of directors and the stockholders is usually required before bonds can be issued. **In authorizing the bond issue, the board of directors must stipulate the total number of bonds to be authorized, the total face value, and the contractual interest rate.** The total bond authorization often exceeds the number of bonds originally issued. This is done intentionally to help ensure that the corporation will have the flexibility it needs to meet future cash requirements by selling more bonds.

450 CHAPTER 10 Reporting and Analyzing Liabilities

Alternative Terminology The contractual rate is often referred to as the **stated rate.**

Helpful Hint Do not confuse the terms *indenture* and *debenture.* Indenture refers to the formal bond document (contract). Debenture bonds are unsecured bonds.

The **face value** is the amount of principal due at the maturity date. The **contractual interest rate** is the rate used to determine the amount of cash interest the borrower pays and the investor receives. Usually the contractual rate is stated as an annual rate, and interest is generally paid semiannually.

The terms of the bond issue are set forth in a legal document called a **bond indenture.** In addition to the terms, the indenture summarizes the respective rights and privileges of the bondholders and their trustees, as well as the obligations and commitments of the issuing company. The **trustee** (usually a financial institution) keeps records of each bondholder, maintains custody of unissued bonds, and holds conditional title to pledged property.

After the bond indenture is prepared, **bond certificates** are printed. The indenture and the certificate are separate documents. As shown in Illustration 10-8, a **bond certificate** provides information such as the name of the issuer, the face value of the bonds, the contractual interest rate, and the maturity date of the bonds. Bonds are generally sold through an investment company that specializes in selling securities. In most cases, the issue is **underwritten** by the investment company: The company sells the bonds to the investment company, which, in turn, sells the bonds to individual investors.

Illustration 10-8 Bond certificate

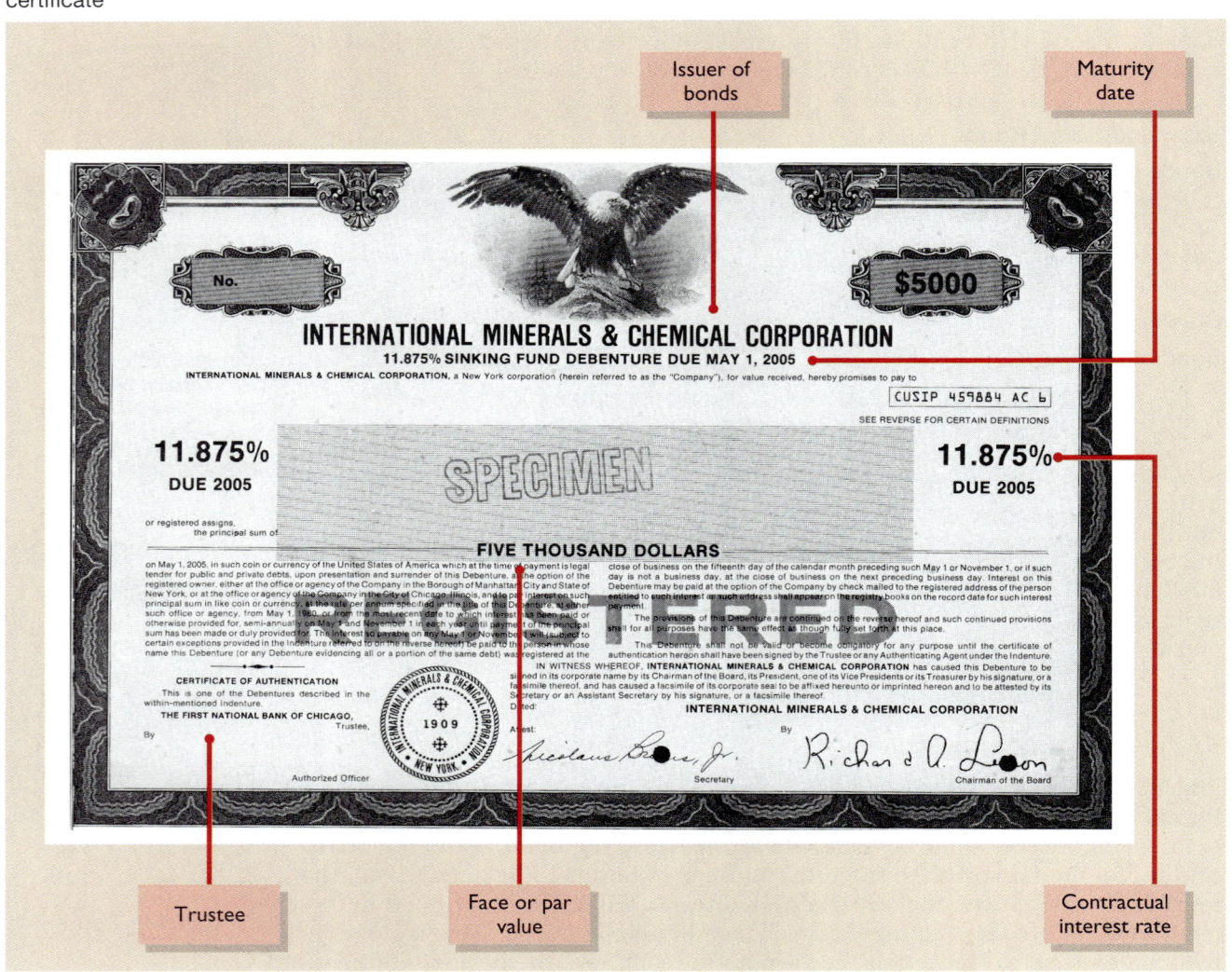

BUSINESS INSIGHT
Investor Perspective

Although bonds are generally secured by solid, substantial assets like land, buildings, and equipment, exceptions occur. For example, Trans World Airlines Inc. (TWA) at one time decided to issue $300 million of high-yielding 5-year bonds, secured by a grab-bag of assets—including some durable spare parts but also a lot of disposable items that TWA had in its warehouses, such as light bulbs and gaskets. Some called the planned TWA bonds "light bulb bonds." As one financial expert noted: "You've got to admit that some security is better than none." However, noted another, "They're digging pretty far down the barrel."

Source: The Wall Street Journal, June 2, 1989.

BOND TRADING

Corporate bonds, like capital stock, are traded on national securities markets. Thus, bondholders have the opportunity to convert their holdings into cash at any time by selling the bonds at the current market price. A corporation receives payment for its bonds (and makes journal entries to record their sale) only when it issues or buys back bonds, and when bondholders convert bonds into common stock. If a bondholder sells a bond to another investor, the issuing firm receives no further money on the transaction, **nor is the transaction journalized by the issuing corporation** (although it does keep records of the names of bondholders in some cases).

Bond prices for both new issues and existing bonds are quoted as **a percentage of the face value of the bond, which is usually $1,000.** Thus, a $1,000 bond with a quoted price of 97 means that the selling price of the bond is 97% of face value, or $970 in this case. Bond prices and trading activity are published daily in newspapers and the financial press, in the form shown in Illustration 10-9.

Bonds	Current Yield	Volume	Close	Net Change
Kmart $8\frac{3}{8}$ 17	8.4	35	$100\frac{1}{4}$	$+\frac{7}{8}$

Illustration 10-9 Market information for bonds

The information in Illustration 10-9 indicates that Kmart Corporation has outstanding $8\frac{3}{8}$%, $1,000 bonds maturing in 2017 and currently yielding an 8.4% return. In addition, 35 bonds were traded on this day, and at the close of trading, the price was $100\frac{1}{4}$% of face value, or $1,002.50. The Net Change column indicates the difference between the day's closing price and the previous day's closing price.

Helpful Hint (1) What is the price of a $1,000 bond trading at $95\frac{1}{4}$? (2) What is the price of a $1,000 bond trading at $101\frac{7}{8}$? Answers: (1) $952.50 and (2) $1,018.75.

DETERMINING THE MARKET VALUE OF BONDS

If you were an investor interested in purchasing a bond, how would you determine how much to pay? To be more specific, assume that Coronet, Inc., issues a zero-interest bond (pays no interest) with a face value of $1,000,000 due in 20 years. For this bond, the only cash you receive is $1 million at the end of 20 years. Would you pay $1 million for this bond? We hope not, because $1 mil-

452 CHAPTER 10 Reporting and Analyzing Liabilities

Same dollars at different times are not equal.

lion received 20 years from now is not the same as $1 million received today. The reason you should not pay $1 million relates to what is called the **time value of money.** If you had $1 million today, you would invest it and earn interest such that at the end of 20 years, your investment would be worth much more than $1 million. Thus, if someone is going to pay you $1 million 20 years from now, you would want to find its equivalent today, or its **present value.** In other words, you would want to determine how much must be invested today at current interest rates to have $1 million in 20 years.

The current market value (present value) of a bond is therefore a function of three factors: (1) the dollar amounts to be received, (2) the length of time until the amounts are received, and (3) the market rate of interest. The **market interest rate** is the rate investors demand for loaning funds to the corporation. The process of finding the present value is referred to as **discounting** the future amounts.

To illustrate, assume that Acropolis Company on January 1, 1998, issues $100,000 of 9% bonds, due in 5 years, with interest payable annually at year-end. The purchaser of the bonds would receive the following two cash payments: (1) **principal** of $100,000 to be paid at maturity, and (2) five $9,000 **interest payments** ($100,000 × 9%) over the term of the bonds. A time diagram depicting both cash flows is shown in Illustration 10-10.

Illustration 10-10 Time diagram depicting cash flows

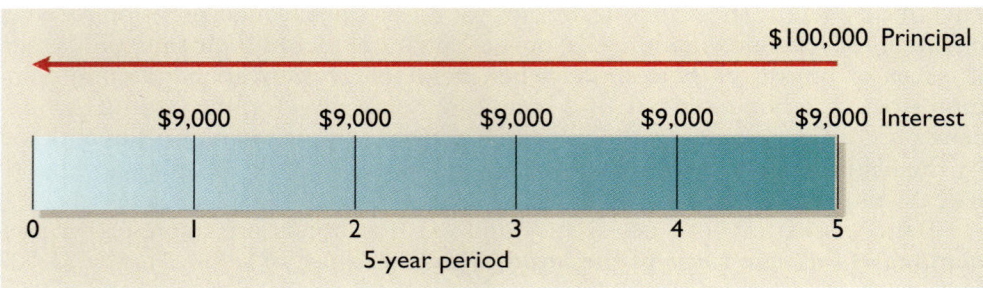

The current market value of a bond is equal to the present value of all the future cash payments promised by the bond. The present values of these amounts are listed in Illustration 10-11.

Illustration 10-11 Computing the market price of bonds

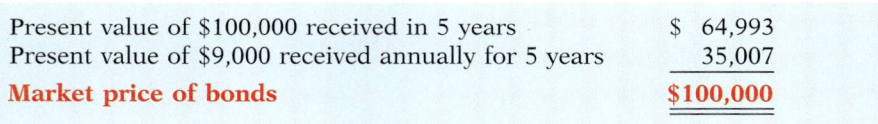

Present value of $100,000 received in 5 years	$ 64,993
Present value of $9,000 received annually for 5 years	35,007
Market price of bonds	**$100,000**

Tables are available to provide the present value numbers to be used, or these values can be determined mathematically.[2] Further discussion of the concepts and the mechanics of the time value of money computations is provided in Appendix C near the end of the book.

BEFORE YOU GO ON . . .

● **Review It**

1. What are the advantages of bond versus stock financing?
2. What are secured versus unsecured bonds, term versus serial bonds, and callable versus convertible bonds?

---

[2] For those knowledgeable in the use of present value tables, the computations in this example are: $100,000 × .64993 = $64,993 and $9,000 × 3.88965 = $35,007 (rounded).

3. Explain the terms *face value, contractual interest rate,* and *bond indenture.*
4. Explain why you would prefer to receive $1 million today rather than 5 years from now.

Accounting for Bond Issues

Bonds may be issued at face value, below face value (discount), or above face value (premium).

ISSUING BONDS AT FACE VALUE

To illustrate the accounting for bonds issued at face value, assume that Devor Corporation issues 1,000, 10-year, 9%, $1,000 bonds dated January 1, 1998, at 100 (100% of face value). The entry to record the sale is:

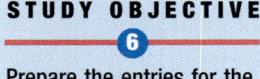

STUDY OBJECTIVE 6
Prepare the entries for the issuance of bonds and interest expense.

Jan. 1	Cash	1,000,000	
	Bonds Payable		1,000,000
	(To record sale of bonds at face value)		

Bonds payable are reported in the long-term liability section of the balance sheet because the maturity date is January 1, 2008 (more than 1 year away).

Over the term (life) of the bonds, entries are required for bond interest. Interest on bonds payable is computed in the same manner as interest on notes payable, as explained earlier. If it is assumed that interest is payable semiannually on January 1 and July 1 on the bonds described above, interest of $45,000 ($1,000,000 × 9% × $\frac{6}{12}$) must be paid on July 1, 1998. The entry for the payment, assuming no previous accrual of interest, is:

July 1	Bond Interest Expense	45,000	
	Cash		45,000
	(To record payment of bond interest)		

International Note
The use of debt financing varies considerably across countries. The amount of debt borrowed by governments can affect a country's ability to borrow funds. One measure of the degree of debt financing is the ratio of national debt to gross national product. In a 1995 survey, this ratio was 49.7%, 13%, 106.2%, and 17.1% in the United States, Australia, Belgium, and Brazil, respectively.

At December 31 an adjusting entry is required to recognize the $45,000 of interest expense incurred since July 1. The entry is:

Dec. 31	Bond Interest Expense	45,000	
	Bond Interest Payable		45,000
	(To accrue bond interest)		

Bond interest payable is classified as a current liability because it is scheduled for payment within the next year. When the interest is paid on January 1, 1999, Bond Interest Payable is decreased (debited) and Cash also is decreased (credited) for $45,000.

DISCOUNT OR PREMIUM ON BONDS

The previous illustrations assumed that the interest rates paid on bonds, often referred to as the contractual (stated) interest rate and the market (effective) interest rate, were the same. Recall that the contractual interest rate is the rate applied to the face (par) value to arrive at the interest paid in a year. The market interest rate is the rate investors demand for loaning funds to the corporation. When the contractual interest rate and the market interest rate are the same, bonds sell at face value, as illustrated above.

Helpful Hint Bond prices vary inversely with changes in the market interest rate. As market interest rates decline, bond prices will increase. When a bond is issued, if the market interest rate is below the contractual rate, the price will be higher than the face value. In the example at right, the market rate is greater than the 8% bond rate and therefore the bonds sell at a discount.

However, market interest rates change daily. They are influenced by the type of bond issued, the state of the economy, current industry conditions, and the company's individual performance. As a result, the contractual and market interest rates often differ, and therefore bonds sell below or above face value.

To illustrate, suppose that investors have one of two options: Purchase bonds that have a market rate of interest of 10% or purchase bonds that have a contractual rate of interest of 8%. Assuming that the bonds are of equal risk, investors will select the 10% investment. To make the investments equal, investors will demand a rate of return higher than the contractual interest rate on the 8% bonds. But the contractual interest rate cannot be changed, so investors will make up the difference by paying less than the face value for the bonds. In these cases, **bonds sell at a discount.** Without this discount, the 8% bonds would not be marketable until the market rate of interest fell to that level.

Conversely, if the market rate of interest is **lower** than the contractual interest rate, investors will have to pay more than face value for the bonds. That is, if the market rate of interest is 8% but the contractual interest rate on the bonds is 9%, the issuer will require more funds from the investor. In these cases, **bonds sell at a premium.** These relationships are shown graphically in Illustration 10-12.

Illustration 10-12 Interest rates and bond prices

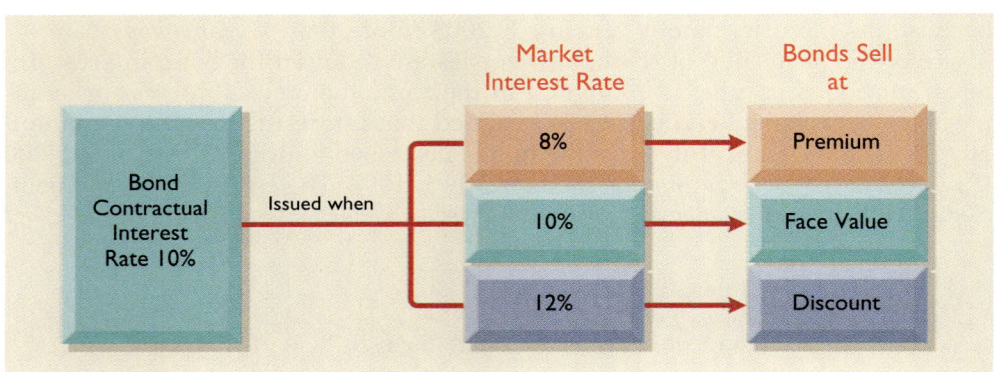

Helpful Hint Some bonds are sold at a discount by design. "Zero-coupon" bonds, which pay no interest, sell at a deep discount to face value.

Issuance of bonds at an amount different from face value is quite common. By the time a company prints the bond certificates and markets the bonds, it will be a coincidence if the market rate and the contractual rate are the same. Thus, the issuance of bonds at a discount does not mean that the financial strength of the issuer is suspect. Conversely, the sale of bonds at a premium does not indicate that the financial strength of the issuer is exceptional.

ISSUING BONDS AT A DISCOUNT

To illustrate the issuance of bonds at a discount, assume that on January 1, 1998, Candlestick, Inc., sells $1 million, 5-year, 10% bonds at 98 (98% of face value) with interest payable on July 1 and January 1. The entry to record the issuance is:

Jan. 1	Cash	980,000	
	Discount on Bonds Payable	20,000	
	Bonds Payable		1,000,000
	(To record sale of bonds at a discount)		

Although Discount on Bonds Payable has a debit balance, **it is not an asset.** Rather it is a **contra account,** which is **deducted from bonds payable** on the balance sheet as in Illustration 10-13.

Long-term liabilities		
Bonds payable	$1,000,000	
Less: Discount on bonds payable	**20,000**	$980,000

Illustration 10-13 Statement presentation of discount on bonds payable

The $980,000 represents the **carrying (or book) value** of the bonds. On the date of issue this amount equals the market price of the bonds.

Helpful Hint The carrying value (book value) of bonds issued at a discount is determined by subtracting the balance of the discount account from the balance of the Bonds Payable account.

The issuance of bonds below face value causes the total cost of borrowing to differ from the bond interest paid. That is, at maturity the issuing corporation must pay not only the contractual interest rate over the term of the bonds but also the face value (rather than the issuance price). Therefore, the difference between the issuance price and the face value of the bonds—the discount—is an **additional cost of borrowing** that should be recorded as **bond interest expense** over the life of the bonds. The total cost of borrowing $980,000 for Candlestick, Inc., is $520,000, computed as in Illustration 10-14.

Bonds Issued at a Discount	
Semiannual interest payments	
($1,000,000 × 10% × $\frac{1}{2}$ = $50,000; $50,000 × 10)	$ 500,000
Add: Bond discount ($1,000,000 − $980,000)	20,000
Total cost of borrowing	**$520,000**

Illustration 10-14 Computation of total cost of borrowing—bonds issued at discount

Alternatively, the total cost of borrowing can be determined as in Illustration 10-15.

Bonds Issued at a Discount	
Principal at maturity	$1,000,000
Semiannual interest payments ($50,000 × 10)	500,000
Cash to be paid to bondholders	1,500,000
Cash received from bondholders	980,000
Total cost of borrowing	**$ 520,000**

Illustration 10-15 Alternative computation of total cost of borrowing—bonds issued at discount

AMORTIZING BOND DISCOUNT

To comply with the matching principle, bond discount should be allocated systematically to each accounting period that benefits from the use of the cash proceeds. The **straight-line method of amortization** allocates the same amount to interest expense in each interest period. The amount is determined as shown in Illustration 10-16.

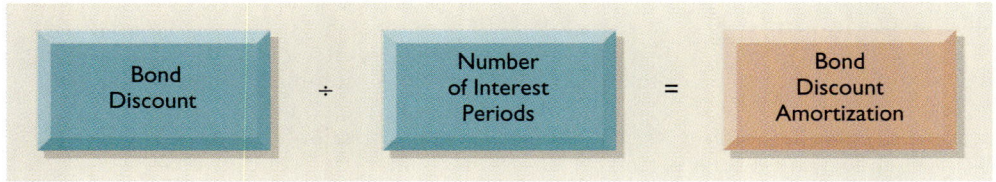

Illustration 10-16 Formula for straight-line method of bond discount amortization

In this example, the bond discount amortization is $2,000 ($20,000 ÷ 10). The entry to record the payment of bond interest and the amortization of bond discount on the first interest date (July 1, 1998) is:

Helpful Hint Note the effects of this entry: expenses increase (which reduces net income and stockholders' equity) by $52,000, assets decrease by $50,000, and liabilities increase by $2,000 (because the balance in the contra account decreases).

July 1	Bond Interest Expense	52,000	
	Discount on Bonds Payable		2,000
	Cash		50,000
	(To record payment of bond interest and amortization of bond discount)		

At December 31, the adjusting entry is:

Dec. 31	Bond Interest Expense	52,000	
	Discount on Bonds Payable		2,000
	Bond Interest Payable		50,000
	(To record accrued bond interest and amortization of bond discount)		

Alternative Terminology The amount in the Discount on Bonds Payable account is often referred to as Unamortized Discount on Bonds Payable.

Over the term of the bonds, the balance in Discount on Bonds Payable will decrease annually by the same amount until it has a zero balance at the maturity date of the bonds. Thus, the carrying value of the bonds at maturity will be equal to the face value of the bonds.

Preparing a bond discount amortization schedule, as shown in Illustration 10-17, is useful to determine interest expense, discount amortization, and the carrying value of the bond. As indicated, the interest expense recorded each period is $52,000. Also note that the carrying value of the bond increases $2,000 each period until it reaches its face value $1,000,000 at the end of period 10.

Illustration 10-17 Bond discount amortization schedule

Semiannual Interest Periods	(A) Interest To Be Paid (5% × $1,000,000)	(B) Interest Expense To Be Recorded (A) + (C)	(C) Discount Amortization ($20,000 ÷ 10)	(D) Unamortized Discount (D) − (C)	(E) Bond Carrying Value ($1,000,000 − D)
Issue date				$20,000	$ 980,000
1	$ 50,000	$ 52,000	$ 2,000	18,000	982,000
2	50,000	52,000	2,000	16,000	984,000
3	50,000	52,000	2,000	14,000	986,000
4	50,000	52,000	2,000	12,000	988,000
5	50,000	52,000	2,000	10,000	990,000
6	50,000	52,000	2,000	8,000	992,000
7	50,000	52,000	2,000	6,000	994,000
8	50,000	52,000	2,000	4,000	996,000
9	50,000	52,000	2,000	2,000	998,000
10	50,000	52,000	2,000	0	1,000,000
	$500,000	$520,000	$20,000		

Column **(A)** remains constant because the face value of the bonds ($1,000,000) is multiplied by the semiannual contractual interest rate (5%) each period.
Column **(B)** is computed as the interest paid (Column A) plus the discount amortization (Column C).
Column **(C)** indicates the discount amortization each period.
Column **(D)** decreases each period by the same amount until it reaches zero at maturity.
Column **(E)** increases each period by the amount of discount amortization until it equals the face value at maturity.

ISSUING BONDS AT A PREMIUM

The issuance of bonds at a premium can be illustrated by assuming the Candlestick, Inc., bonds described above are sold at 102 (102% of face value) rather than at 98. The entry to record the sale is:

Jan. 1	Cash	1,020,000	
	Bonds Payable		1,000,000
	Premium on Bonds Payable		20,000
	(To record sale of bonds at a premium)		

Helpful Hint Both a discount and a premium account are valuation accounts. A valuation account is one that is needed to value properly the item to which it relates. A discount account is a contra-type valuation account (its balance is deducted from Bonds Payable), whereas a premium account is an adjunct-type valuation account (its balance is added to the balance of Bonds Payable).

Premium on bonds payable is **added to bonds payable** on the balance sheet, as shown in Illustration 10-18.

Illustration 10-18 Statement presentation of bond premium

Long-term liabilities		
Bonds payable	$1,000,000	
Add: Premium on bonds payable	20,000	$1,020,000

The sale of bonds above face value causes the total cost of borrowing to be **less than the bond interest paid** because the borrower is not required to pay the bond premium at the maturity date of the bonds. Thus, the premium is considered to be **a reduction in the cost of borrowing** that reduces bond interest expense over the life of the bonds. The total cost of borrowing $1,020,000 for Candlestick, Inc., is $480,000, computed as in Illustration 10-19.

Illustration 10-19 Computation of total cost of borrowing—bonds issued at a premium

Bonds Issued at a Premium	
Semiannual interest payments	
($1,000,000 × 10% × $\frac{1}{2}$ = $50,000; $50,000 × 10)	$ 500,000
Less: Bond premium ($1,020,000 − $1,000,000)	20,000
Total cost of borrowing	**$480,000**

Alternatively, the cost of borrowing can be computed as in Illustration 10-20.

Illustration 10-20 Alternative computation of total cost of borrowing—bonds issued at a premium

Bonds Issued at a Premium	
Principal at maturity	$1,000,000
Semiannual interest payments ($50,000 × 10)	500,000
Cash to be paid to bondholders	1,500,000
Cash received from bondholders	1,020,000
Total cost of borrowing	**$ 480,000**

AMORTIZING BOND PREMIUM

The formula for determining bond premium amortization under the straight-line method is presented in Illustration 10-21.

Illustration 10-21 Formula for straight-line method of bond premium amortization

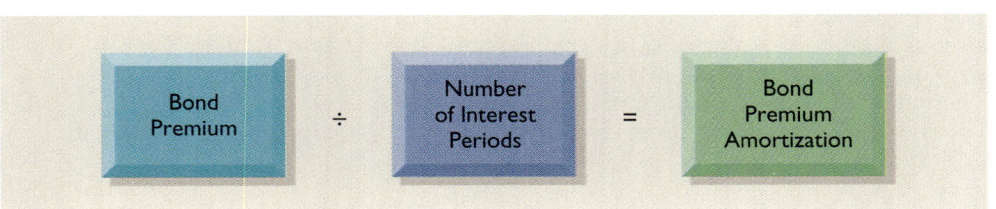

Thus, in our example, the premium amortization for each interest period is $2,000 ($20,000 ÷ 10). The entry to record the first payment of interest on July 1 is:

July 1	Bond Interest Expense	48,000	
	Premium on Bonds Payable	2,000	
	Cash		50,000
	(To record payment of bond interest and amortization of bond premium)		

At December 31, the adjusting entry is:

Dec. 31	Bond Interest Expense	48,000	
	Premium on Bonds Payable	2,000	
	Bond Interest Payable		50,000
	(To record accrued bond interest and amortization of bond premium)		

Over the term of the bonds, the balance in Premium on Bonds Payable will decrease annually by the same amount until it has a zero balance at maturity.

Preparing a bond premium amortization schedule, as shown in Illustration 10-22, is useful to determine interest expense, premium amortization, and the carrying value of the bond. As indicated, the interest expense recorded

Illustration 10-22 Bond premium amortization schedule

Semiannual Interest Periods	(A) Interest To Be Paid (5% × $1,000,000)	(B) Interest Expense To Be Recorded (A) − (C)	(C) Premium Amortization ($20,000 ÷ 10)	(D) Unamortized Premium (D) − (C)	(E) Bond Carrying Value ($1,000,000 + D)
Issue date				$20,000	$1,020,000
1	$ 50,000	$ 48,000	$ 2,000	18,000	1,018,000
2	50,000	48,000	2,000	16,000	1,016,000
3	50,000	48,000	2,000	14,000	1,014,000
4	50,000	48,000	2,000	12,000	1,012,000
5	50,000	48,000	2,000	10,000	1,010,000
6	50,000	48,000	2,000	8,000	1,008,000
7	50,000	48,000	2,000	6,000	1,006,000
8	50,000	48,000	2,000	4,000	1,004,000
9	50,000	48,000	2,000	2,000	1,002,000
10	50,000	48,000	2,000	0	1,000,000
	$500,000	$480,000	$20,000		

Column **(A)** remains constant because the face value of the bonds ($1,000,000) is multiplied by the semiannual contractual interest rate (5%) each period.
Column **(B)** is computed as the interest paid (Column A) less the premium amortization (Column C).
Column **(C)** indicates the premium amortization each period.
Column **(D)** decreases each period by the same amount until it reaches zero at maturity.
Column **(E)** decreases each period by the amount of premium amortization until it equals the face value at maturity.

each period is $48,000. Also note that the carrying value of the bond decreases $2,000 each period until it reaches its face value $1,000,000 at the end of period 10.

ACCOUNTING FOR BOND RETIREMENTS

Bonds are retired when they are purchased (redeemed) by the issuing corporation. The appropriate entries for these transactions are explained next.

REDEEMING BONDS AT MATURITY

Regardless of the issue price of bonds, the book value of the bonds at maturity will equal their face value. Assuming that the interest for the last interest period is paid and recorded separately, the entry to record the redemption of the Candlestick bonds at maturity is:

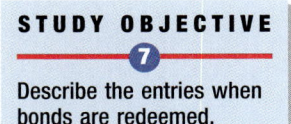

STUDY OBJECTIVE 7
Describe the entries when bonds are redeemed.

Bonds Payable	1,000,000	
Cash		1,000,000
(To record redemption of bonds at maturity)		

REDEEMING BONDS BEFORE MATURITY

Bonds may be redeemed before maturity. A company may decide to retire bonds before maturity to reduce interest cost and remove debt from its balance sheet. A company should retire debt early only if it has sufficient cash resources. When bonds are retired before maturity, it is necessary to: (1) eliminate the carrying value of the bonds at the redemption date, (2) record the cash paid, and (3) recognize the gain or loss on redemption. The carrying value of the bonds is the face value of the bonds less unamortized bond discount or plus unamortized bond premium at the redemption date.

To illustrate, assume at the end of the eighth period Candlestick, Inc., having sold its bonds at a premium, retires its bonds at 103 after paying the semiannual interest. The carrying value of the bonds at the redemption date is $1,004,000. (The calculation of this value is shown in Illustration 10-22.) The entry to record the redemption at the end of the eighth interest period (January 1, 2002) is:

Helpful Hint If a bond is redeemed prior to its maturity date and its carrying value exceeds its redemption price, will the retirement result in a gain or a loss on redemption? Answer: Gain.

Jan. 1	Bonds Payable	1,000,000	
	Premium on Bonds Payable	4,000	
	Loss on Bond Redemption	26,000	
	Cash		1,030,000
	(To record redemption of bonds at 103)		

Note that the loss of $26,000 is the difference between the cash paid of $1,030,000 and the carrying value of the bonds of $1,004,000. Losses (gains) on bond redemption are reported in a special line item at the bottom of the income statement referred to as *Extraordinary Items*. The significance of this classification is discussed in Chapter 14.

460 CHAPTER 10 Reporting and Analyzing Liabilities

BUSINESS INSIGHT
International Perspective

Now that you have read about bonds, you may be beginning to realize how significant bond financing can be. A dramatic example of bond financing—which literally changed the course of history—is seen in Britain's struggle for supremacy in the 18th and 19th centuries. With only a fraction of the population and wealth of France, Britain ultimately humbled its mightier foe through the use of bonds. Because of its effective central bank and a fair system of collecting taxes, Britain developed the capital markets that enabled its government to issue bonds. Britain was able to borrow money at almost half the cost paid by France and was able to incur more debt as a proportion of the economy than could France. Britain thus could more than match the French navy, raise an army of its own, and lavishly subsidize other armies, eventually destroying Napoleon and his threat to Europe.

Source: "How British Bonds Beat Back Bigger France," *Forbes,* March 13, 1995.

BEFORE YOU GO ON . . .

● **Review It**

1. What entry is made to record the issuance of bonds payable of $1 million at 100? At 96? At 102?
2. Why do bonds sell at a discount? At a premium? At face value?
3. Explain the accounting for redemption of bonds at maturity and before maturity by payment in cash.

● **Do It**

A bond amortization table shows (a) interest to be paid $50,000, (b) interest expense to be recorded $52,000, and (c) amortization $2,000. Answer the following questions: (1) Were the bonds sold at a premium or a discount? (2) After recording the interest expense, will the bond carrying value increase or decrease?

Reasoning: To answer the questions you need to know the effects that the amortization of bond discount and bond premium have on bond interest expense and on the carrying value of the bonds. Bond discount amortization increases both bond interest expense and the carrying value of the bonds. Bond premium amortization has the reverse effect.

Solution: The bond amortization table indicates that interest expense is $2,000 greater than the interest paid. This difference is equal to the amortization amount. Thus, the bonds were sold at a discount. The interest entry will decrease Discount on Bonds Payable and increase the carrying value of the bonds.

STUDY OBJECTIVE

Identify the requirements for the financial statement presentation and analysis of long-term liabilities.

FINANCIAL STATEMENT PRESENTATION AND ANALYSIS

PRESENTATION

Long-term liabilities are reported in a separate section of the balance sheet immediately following Current Liabilities, as shown in Illustration 10-23.

Illustration 10-23 Balance sheet presentation of long-term liabilities

PARTIAL BALANCE SHEET		
Long-term liabilities		
Bonds payable 10% due in 2009	$1,000,000	
Less: Discount on bonds payable	80,000	$ 920,000
Notes payable, 11%, due in 2015		
and secured by plant assets		500,000
Lease liability		540,000
Total long-term liabilities		$1,960,000

Alternatively, summary data may be presented in the balance sheet with detailed data (such as interest rates, maturity dates, conversion privileges, and assets pledged as collateral) shown in a supporting schedule. The current maturities of long-term debt should be reported as current liabilities if they are to be paid from current assets. This is evident on the Chrysler balance sheets in Illustration 10-3.

ANALYSIS

Solvency ratios measure the ability of a company to survive over a long period of time. The opening story in this chapter mentioned that although there once were many U.S. automobile manufacturers, only three survive today. Many of the others went bankrupt. This highlights the fact that when making a long-term loan or purchasing a company's stock, you must give consideration to a company's solvency.

To reduce the risks associated with having a large amount of debt during an economic downturn, The Big Three automobile manufacturers have taken two precautionary steps. First, all three have built up large balances of cash and cash equivalents to avoid a cash crisis. Second, recently, all three have been reluctant to build new plants or hire new workers to meet their production needs. Instead, they have asked existing workers to put in overtime. In this way, if an economic downturn follows, they avoid having to make debt payments on idle production plants, and they minimize the risk of having to lay off workers.

In an earlier chapter you learned that one measure of a company's solvency is the debt to total assets ratio. This ratio indicates the extent to which a company's debt could be repaid by liquidating its assets. Other measures can also be useful. One such measure is the **times interest earned ratio,** which provides an indication of a company's ability to meet interest payments as they come due. It is computed by dividing income before interest expense and income taxes by interest expense. It uses income before interest expense and taxes because this number best represents the amount available to cover interest.

We can use the balance sheet information in Illustration 10-3 and the additional information in Illustration 10-24 to calculate solvency ratios for Chrysler and the auto industry.

Illustration 10-24 Chrysler financial information

($ in millions)	1995	1994
Net income	$2,025	$3,713
Interest expense	995	937
Taxes	1,328	2,117

The debt to total assets ratios and times interest earned ratios for Chrysler and averages for the industry are shown in Illustration 10-25 (page 462).

462 CHAPTER 10 Reporting and Analyzing Liabilities

$$\text{DEBT TO TOTAL ASSETS RATIO} = \frac{\text{TOTAL DEBT}}{\text{TOTAL ASSETS}}$$

$$\text{TIMES INTEREST EARNED RATIO} = \frac{\text{INCOME BEFORE INTEREST EXPENSE AND INCOME TAX}}{\text{INTEREST EXPENSE}}$$

($ in millions)	Chrysler 1995	Chrysler 1994	Industry Average 1995	Industry Average 1994
Debt to Total Assets Ratio	$\frac{\$42,797}{\$53,756} = 80\%$	$\frac{\$38,845}{\$49,539} = 78\%$	83.7%	75.6%
Times Interest Earned Ratio	$\frac{\$2,025 + \$995 + \$1,328}{\$995}$ = 4.4 times	$\frac{\$3,713 + \$937 + \$2,117}{\$937}$ = 7.2 times	2.3 times	1.6 times

Illustration 10-25
Solvency ratios

The debt to total assets ratio varies across industries because different capital structures are appropriate for different industries. The debt to assets ratio for all manufacturers of cars and car parts is 83.7%. Chrysler's ratio remained relatively constant over this 2-year period, which indicates it did not change its mix between debt and equity financing. Its 1995 measure of 80% is consistent with the industry average for this measure. Chrysler's times interest earned ratio declined from 7.2 times in 1994 to 4.4 times in 1995. This decline was due to a drop in net income without an equivalent drop in interest expense. Even at its 1995 level, however, Chrysler is well above the industry average for the times interest earned ratio of 2.3. Thus, this decline should not be a concern to investors at this time.

DECISION TOOLKIT

Decision Checkpoints	Info Needed for Decision	Tool to Use for Decision	How to Evaluate Results
Can the company meet its obligations in the long term?	Interest expense and net income before interest and taxes	Times interest earned ratio = $\frac{\text{Income before interest expense and taxes}}{\text{Interest expense}}$	High ratio indicates ability to meet interest payments as scheduled.

OTHER ISSUES IN ANALYSIS

CONTINGENT LIABILITIES

Contingencies are events with uncertain outcomes. For users of financial statements, contingencies are often very important to understanding a company's financial position. A common type of contingency is lawsuits. Suppose, for example, that you were analyzing the financial statements of a cigarette manufacturer and did not consider the possible negative implications of existing unsettled lawsuits. Your analysis of the company's financial position would certainly be misleading. Other common types of contingencies are product warranties and environmental problems.

Accounting rules require that contingencies be disclosed in the footnotes, and in some cases they must be accrued as liabilities. For example, suppose that Waterford Inc. is sued by a customer for $1 million due to an injury sustained by a defective product. If at December 31 (the company's year-end) the lawsuit had not yet been resolved, how should the company account for this event? If the company can determine **a reasonable estimate** of the expected loss and if it is **probable** it will lose the suit, then the company should accrue for the loss. The loss is recorded by increasing (debiting) a loss account and increasing (crediting) a liability such as Lawsuit Liability. If *both* of these conditions are not met, then the company discloses the basic facts regarding this suit in the notes to its financial statements.

The liabilities associated with contingencies can be material. For example, Procter & Gamble is phasing out its long-time use of promotional coupons, saying that the cost was too high; Exxon was ordered to pay billions of dollars as a result of an Alaskan oil spill; and at the time this book was being written, the cigarette companies were trying to negotiate a settlement of all their lawsuits with total payments of roughly $300 billion. The notes to recent financial statements of cigarette manufacturer Phillip Morris contained four and one-half pages of discussion regarding litigation. Illustration 10-26 is an excerpt from the contingency footnote from the financial statements of Chrysler.

Illustration 10-26
Contingency footnote disclosure

CHRYSLER CORPORATION
Notes to the Financial Statements

Chrysler is subject to potential liability under governmental regulations and various claims and legal actions which are pending or may be asserted against Chrysler concerning environmental matters. . . . Although the final resolution of any such matters could have a material effect on Chrysler's consolidated operating results for the particular reporting period in which an adjustment of the estimated liability is recorded, Chrysler believes that any resulting liability should not materially affect its consolidated financial position.

The note suggests that at this time Chrysler does not have any outstanding litigation requiring accrual or disclosure. Sometimes analysts make adjustments to the financial statements for unrecorded contingencies that they feel should have been accrued for.

DECISION TOOLKIT

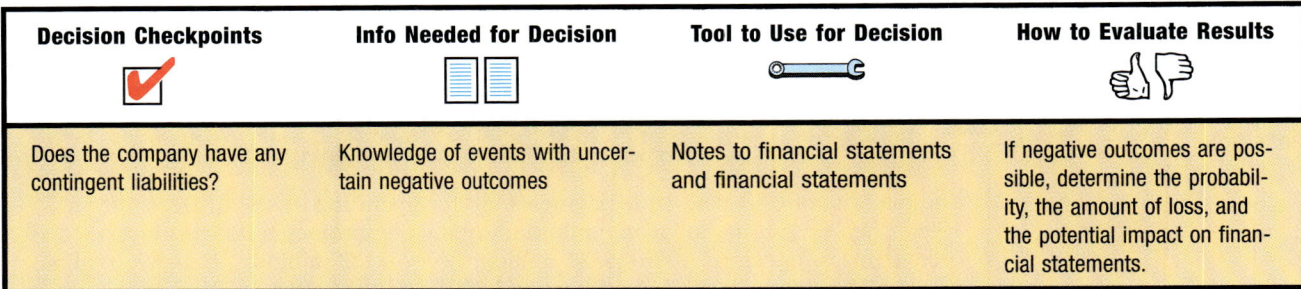

LEASE LIABILITIES

In most lease contracts, a periodic payment is made by the lessee and is recorded as rent expense in the income statement. The renting of an apartment and the rental of a car at an airport are examples of these types of leases, often referred to as **operating leases. In an operating lease the intent is temporary use of the property by the lessee with continued ownership of the property by the lessor. In some cases, however, the lease contract transfers substantially all the benefits and risks of ownership to the lessee, so that the lease is in effect a purchase of the property.** This type of lease is called a **capital lease** because the fair value of the leased asset is *capitalized* by the lessee by recording it on its balance sheet.

Accounting standards have precise criteria that determine whether a lease should be accounted for as a capital lease. The thrust of these criteria is to determine whether the lease transaction more closely resembles a purchase transaction or a rental transaction. This is determined by asking these questions:

Is it likely that the lessee will end up with the asset at the end of the lease?

Will the lessee use the asset for most of its useful life?

Will the payments made by the lessee be approximately the same as the payments it would have made if it had purchased the asset?

If the answer to any of these questions is yes, then the lease should be accounted for as a capital lease; that is, the lessee must record the asset on its books and a related liability for the lease payments. Otherwise, the lessee can account for the transaction as an operating lease, meaning that neither an asset nor liability is shown on its books.

Most lessees do not like to report leases on their balance sheets because the lease liability increases the company's total liabilities. This, in turn, may make it more difficult for the company to obtain needed funds from lenders. **As a result, companies attempt to keep leased assets and lease liabilities off the balance sheet by structuring the lease agreement to avoid meeting the criteria of a capital lease.** Then they account for most of their leases as operating leases. Recall from Chapter 9, for example, that Southwest Airlines leased half of its planes, and nearly all of these were accounted for as operating leases. Consequently, nearly half of the planes used by Southwest Airlines do not show up on its balance sheet, nor do the liabilities related to those planes. This procedure of keeping liabilities off the balance sheet is often referred to as **off-balance sheet financing.**

Critics of off-balance sheet financing contend that many operating leases represent unavoidable obligations that meet the definition of a liability, and therefore they should be reported as liabilities on the balance sheet. To reduce these concerns, companies are required to report their operating lease obligations for subsequent years in a footnote. This allows analysts and other financial statement users to adjust a company's financial statements by adding leased assets and lease liabilities if they feel that this treatment is more appropriate. The financial statement note describing Chrysler's obligations under operating leases in a recent year is presented in Illustration 10-27.

Illustration 10-27
Operating lease note

CHRYSLER CORPORATION
Notes to the Financial Statements

The majority of Chrysler's lease payments are for operating leases. At December 31, 1995, Chrysler had the following minimum rental commitments under noncancelable operating leases: 1996—$341 million; 1997—$182 million; 1998—$99 million; 1999—$77 million; 2000—$61 million; and 2001 and thereafter—$201 million.

If the time value of money is ignored, the total increase in liabilities that would result if these leases were recorded on the balance sheet is $961 million. However, this amount is immaterial relative to Chrysler's total liabilities of nearly $43 billion. Thus, the potential unrecorded off-balance sheet liabilities resulting from Chrysler's leases do not appear to be a concern.

DECISION TOOLKIT

Decision Checkpoints	Info Needed for Decision	Tool to Use for Decision	How to Evaluate Results
Does the company have significant unrecorded lease obligations?	Schedule of minimum lease payments from lease note	Compare liquidity and solvency ratios with and without unrecorded obligations included.	If ratios differ significantly after including unrecorded obligations, these obligations should not be ignored in analysis.

BEFORE YOU GO ON . . .

- **Review It**
  1. What is meant by solvency?
  2. What information does the times interest earned ratio provide, and how is the ratio calculated?
  3. Where should long-term capital lease obligations be reported in the balance sheet?
  4. What are contingent liabilities?

USING THE DECISION TOOLKIT

In recent years Ford Motor Corporation has enjoyed some tremendous successes, including its popular Taurus and Explorer vehicles. Yet observers are looking for the next big hit. Hopes are high for the new Expedition, a giant sport utility vehicle designed to compete with General Motors' large sport utility vehicles. Development of a new vehicle costs billions. A flop is financially devastating, and the financial effect is magnified if the company has large amounts of outstanding debt.

The balance sheet provides financial information for the Automotive Division of Ford Motor Co. as of December 31, 1995 and 1994. We have chosen to analyze only the Automotive Division rather than the total corporation, which includes Ford's giant financing division. In an actual analysis you would want to analyze the major divisions individually as well as the combined corporation as a whole.

Instructions

1. Evaluate Ford's liquidity using appropriate ratios and compare to those of Chrysler and to industry averages.
2. Evaluate Ford's solvency using appropriate ratios and compare to those of Chrysler and to industry averages.
3. Comment on Ford's available of lines of credit.

**FORD MOTOR COMPANY—
AUTOMOTIVE DIVISION
Balance Sheets
December 31, 1995 and 1994
(in millions)**

	1995	1994
Assets		
Cash and cash equivalents	$ 5,750	$ 4,481
Marketable securities	6,656	7,602
Accounts receivable, net	3,321	2,548
Inventories	7,162	6,487
Other current assets	4,392	5,745
Total current assets	27,281	26,863
Noncurrent assets	45,491	41,776
Total assets	$72,772	$68,639
Liabilities and Shareholders' Equity		
Current liabilities		
Accounts payable	$11,260	$10,777
Other payables	1,976	2,280
Accrued liabilities	13,392	11,943
Income taxes payable	316	316
Current maturities of long-term debt	1,832	155
Total current liabilities	28,776	25,471
Long-term debt	5,475	7,103
Other noncurrent liabilities	26,863	26,136
Total liabilities	61,114	58,710
Total shareholders' equity	11,658	9,929
Total liabilities and shareholders' equity	$72,772	$68,639
Other information		
Income before taxes	$ 3,166	$ 5,997
Interest expense	622	721
Available lines of credit (Automotive Division)	8,400	

Solution

1. Ford's liquidity can be measured using the current ratio and acid-test ratio:

	1995	1994
Current ratio	$\dfrac{\$27,281}{\$28,776} = .95:1$	$\dfrac{\$26,863}{\$25,471} = 1.05:1$
Acid-test ratio	$\dfrac{\$5,750 + \$6,656 + \$3,321}{\$28,776} = .55:1$	$\dfrac{\$4,481 + \$7,602 + \$2,548}{\$25,471} = .57:1$

Like Chrysler, Ford's current ratio hovers right around 1.0:1, and its acid-test ratio is between .5:1 and .6:1. These are increasingly common levels for large companies that have reduced the amount of cash, inventory, and receivables they hold. As noted earlier, these low measures are not necessarily cause for concern, but they do require more careful monitoring, and the company must also make sure to have other short-term financing options available, such as lines of credit.

2. Ford's solvency can be measured with the debt to total assets ratio and the times interest earned ratio:

	1995	1994
Debt to total assets ratio	$\dfrac{\$61,114}{\$72,772} = 84\%$	$\dfrac{\$58,710}{\$68,639} = 86\%$
Times interest earned ratio	$\dfrac{\$3,166 + \$622}{\$622} = 6.09$ times	$\dfrac{\$5,997 + \$721}{\$721} = 9.32$ times

Note that in this case we used the income before tax number from Ford's income statement; thus, we did not have to add back taxes. The debt to total assets ratio suggests that Ford relies slightly more on debt financing than Chrysler does, but its high value for the times interest earned ratio indicates that this debt financing in no way threatens its solvency. It is worth noting that when the automotive and financing divisions of Ford are combined, its debt to total assets ratio increases only slightly to 90%.

3. Ford has available lines of credit of $8.4 billion. This significantly improves its liquidity. It should also be noted that Ford's financing division has available lines of credit of $48 billion. Thus, the combined company has tremendous resources available to it, should it face a liquidity crunch.

SUMMARY OF STUDY OBJECTIVES

① Explain a current liability and identify the major types of current liabilities. A current liability is a debt that can reasonably be expected to be paid (a) from existing current assets or through the creation of other current liabilities, and (b) within 1 year or the operating cycle, whichever is longer. The major types of current liabilities are notes payable, accounts payable, sales taxes payable, unearned revenues, and accrued liabilities such as taxes, salaries and wages, and interest payable.

② Describe the accounting for notes payable. When a promissory note is interest-bearing, the amount of assets received upon the issuance of the note is generally equal to the face value of the note, and interest expense is accrued over the life of the note. At maturity, the amount paid is equal to the face value of the note plus accrued interest.

③ Explain the accounting for other current liabilities. Sales taxes payable are recorded at the time the related sales occur. The company serves as a collection agent for the taxing authority. Sales taxes are not an expense to the company. Until employee withholding taxes are remitted to the governmental taxing authorities, they are credited to appropriate liability accounts. Unearned revenues are initially recorded in an unearned revenue account. As the revenue is earned, a transfer from unearned revenue to earned revenue occurs. The current maturities of long-term debt should be reported as a current liability in the balance sheet.

④ Identify the requirements for the financial statement presentation and analysis of current liabilities. The nature and amount of each current liability should be reported in the balance sheet or in schedules in the notes accompanying the statements. The liquidity of a company may be analyzed by computing working capital, the current ratio, and the acid-test ratio.

⑤ Explain why bonds are issued and identify the types of bonds. Bonds may be sold to many investors, and they offer the following advantages over common stock: (a) stockholder control is not affected, (b) tax savings result, and (c) earnings per share of common stock may be higher. The following different types of bonds may be issued: secured and unsecured bonds, term and serial bonds, and convertible and callable bonds.

468 CHAPTER 10 Reporting and Analyzing Liabilities

6 *Prepare the entries for the issuance of bonds and interest expense.* When bonds are issued, Cash is debited for the cash proceeds and Bonds Payable is credited for the face value of the bonds. In addition, the accounts Premium on Bonds Payable and Discount on Bonds Payable are used to show the bond premium and bond discount, respectively. Bond discount and bond premium are amortized over the life of the bond by the straight-line method.

7 *Describe the entries when bonds are redeemed.* When bonds are redeemed at maturity, Cash is credited and Bonds Payable is debited for the face value of the bonds. When bonds are redeemed before maturity, it is necessary to (a) eliminate the carrying value of the bonds at the redemption date, (b) record the cash paid, and (c) recognize the gain or loss on redemption.

8 *Identify the requirements for the financial statement presentation and analysis of long-term liabilities.* The nature and amount of each long-term debt should be reported in the balance sheet or in schedules in the notes accompanying the statements. The long-run solvency of a company may be analyzed by computing the debt to total assets ratio and the times interest earned ratio. Other factors to consider are contingent liabilities and lease obligations.

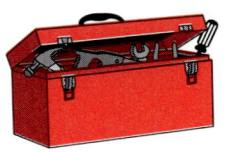

DECISION TOOLKIT—A SUMMARY

Decision Checkpoints	Info Needed for Decision	Tool to Use for Decision	How to Evaluate Results
Can the company meet its current obligations?	Cash, accounts receivable, marketable securities, and other highly liquid assets, and current liabilities	Acid-test ratio = (Cash + Marketable securities + Net receivables) / Current liabilities	Ratio should be compared to others in same industry. High ratio indicates good liquidity.
Can the company obtain short-term financing when necessary?	Available lines of credit from debt note to the financial statements	Compare available lines of credit to current liabilities. Also, evaluate liquidity ratios.	If liquidity ratios are low, then lines of credit should be high to compensate.
Can the company meet its obligations in the long term?	Interest expense and net income before interest and taxes	Times interest earned ratio = (Income before interest expense and taxes) / Interest expense	High ratio indicates ability to meet interest payments as scheduled.
Does the company have any contingent liabilities?	Knowledge of events with uncertain negative outcomes	Notes to financial statements and financial statements	If negative outcomes are possible, determine the probability, the amount of loss, and the potential impact on financial statements.
Does the company have significant unrecorded lease obligations?	Schedule of minimum lease payments from lease note	Compare liquidity and solvency ratios with and without unrecorded obligations included.	If ratios differ significantly after including unrecorded obligations, these obligations should not be ignored in analysis.

GLOSSARY

Acid-test (quick) ratio A measure of a company's immediate short-term liquidity, calculated by dividing the sum of cash, marketable securities, and net receivables by current liabilities. (p. 445)

Bond certificate A legal document that indicates the name of the issuer, the face value of the bonds, and such other data as the contractual interest rate and the maturity date of the bonds. (p. 450)

Bond indenture A legal document that sets forth the terms of the bond issue. (p. 450)

Bonds A form of interest-bearing notes payable issued by corporations, universities, and governmental entities. (p. 447)

Callable bonds Bonds that are subject to retirement at a stated dollar amount prior to maturity at the option of the issuer. (p. 449)

Capital lease A type of lease whose characteristics make it similar to a debt-financed purchase and is consequently accounted for in that fashion. (p. 464)

Contingencies Events with uncertain outcomes, such as a potential liability that may become an actual liability sometime in the future. (p. 462)

Contractual interest rate Rate used to determine the amount of interest the borrower pays and the investor receives. (p. 450)

Convertible bonds Bonds that permit bondholders to convert them into common stock at their option. (p. 449)

Current liability A debt that can reasonably be expected to be paid (1) from existing current assets or through the creation of other current liabilities, and (2) within 1 year or the operating cycle, whichever is longer. (p. 438)

Debenture bonds Bonds issued against the general credit of the borrower; also called unsecured bonds. (p. 449)

Discount (on a bond) The difference between the face value of a bond and its selling price, when a bond is sold for less than its face value. (p. 454)

Face value Amount of principal due at the maturity date of the bond. (p. 450)

Line of credit A prearranged agreement between a company and a lender that allows a company to borrow up to an agreed-upon amount. (p. 446)

Long-term liabilities Obligations expected to be paid more than 1 year in the future. (p. 447)

Market interest rate The rate investors demand for loaning funds to the corporation. (p. 452)

Mortgage bond A bond secured by real estate. (p. 449)

Notes payable An obligation in the form of a written promissory note. (p. 439)

Off-balance sheet financing The intentional effort by a company to structure its financing arrangements so as to avoid showing liabilities on its books. (p. 464)

Operating lease A contractual arrangement giving the lessee temporary use of the property with continued ownership of the property by the lessor. Accounted for as a rental. (p. 464)

Premium (on a bond) The difference between the selling price and the face value of a bond when a bond is sold for more than its face value. (p. 454)

Present value The value today of an amount to be received at some date in the future after taking into account current interest rates. (p. 452)

Secured bonds Bonds that have specific assets of the issuer pledged as collateral. (p. 449)

Serial bonds Bonds that mature in installments. (p. 449)

Sinking fund bonds Bonds secured by specific assets set aside to retire them. (p. 449)

Straight-line method of amortization A method of amortizing bond discount or bond premium that allocates the same amount to interest expense in each interest period. (p. 455)

Term bonds Bonds that mature at a single specified future date. (p. 449)

Times interest earned ratio A measure of a company's solvency, calculated by dividing income before interest expense and taxes by interest expense. (p. 461)

Unsecured bonds Bonds issued against the general credit of the borrower; also called debenture bonds. (p. 449)

Demonstration Problem

Snyder Software Inc. successfully developed a new spreadsheet program. However, to produce and market the program, the company needed $2.0 million of additional financing. On January 1, 1999, Snyder borrowed money as follows:

1. Snyder issued $500,000, 11%, 10-year bonds. The bonds sold at face value and pay semiannual interest on January 1 and July 1.
2. Snyder issued $1.0 million, 10%, 10-year bonds for $885,301. Interest is payable semiannually on January 1 and July 1. Snyder uses the straight-line method of amortization.

Instructions

(a) For the 11% bonds, prepare journal entries for these items:
 (1) The issuance of the bonds on January 1, 1999.
 (2) Interest expense on July 1 and December 31, 1999.
 (3) The payment of interest on January 1, 2000.

(b) For the 10-year, 10% bonds:
  (1) Journalize the issuance of the bonds on January 1, 1999.
  (2) Prepare the entry for the redemption of the bonds at 101 on January 1, 2002, after paying the interest due on this date. The carrying value of the bonds at the redemption date was $919,711.

Solution to Demonstration Problem

(a) (1) 1999

Jan. 1	Cash		500,000	
	Bonds Payable			500,000
	(To record issue of 11%, 10-year bonds at face value)			

(2) 1999

July 1	Bond Interest Expense		27,500	
	Cash ($500,000 × .055)			27,500
	(To record payment of semiannual interest)			
Dec. 31	Bond Interest Expense		27,500	
	Bond Interest Payable			27,500
	(To record accrual of semiannual bond interest)			

Problem-Solving Strategy
Interest expense decreases each period because the principal is decreasing each period.

(3) 2000

Jan. 1	Bond Interest Payable		27,500	
	Cash			27,500
	(To record payment of accrued interest)			

(b) (1) 1999

Jan. 1	Cash		885,301	
	Discount on Bonds Payable		114,699	
	Bonds Payable			1,000,000
	(To record issuance of bonds at a discount)			

(2) 2002

Jan. 1	Bonds Payable		1,000,000	
	Loss on Bond Redemption		90,289*	
	Discount on Bonds Payable			80,289
	Cash			1,010,000
	(To record redemption of bonds at 101)			
	*($1,010,000 − $919,711)			

SELF-STUDY QUESTIONS

Answers are at the end of the chapter.

(SO 1) 1. The time period for classifying a liability as current is 1 year or the operating cycle, whichever is:
 (a) longer. (c) probable.
 (b) shorter. (d) possible.

2. To be classified as a current liability, a debt must be expected to be paid: (SO 1)
 (a) out of existing current assets.
 (b) by creating other current liabilities.
 (c) within 2 years.
 (d) Either (a) or (b)

(SO 2) 3. Julie Gilbert Company borrows $88,500 on September 1, 1998, from Sandwich State Bank by signing an $88,500, 12%, 1-year note. What is the accrued interest at December 31, 1998?
(a) $2,655 (c) $4,425
(b) $3,540 (d) $10,620

(SO 3) 4. Reeves Company has total proceeds from sales of $4,515. If the proceeds include sales taxes of 5%, what is the amount to be credited to Sales?
(a) $4,000
(b) $4,300
(c) $4,289.25
(d) The correct answer is not given.

(SO 5) 5. What term is used for bonds that are unsecured?
(a) *Callable* bonds
(b) *Indenture* bonds
(c) *Debenture* bonds
(d) *Sinking fund* bonds

(SO 6) 6. Karson Inc. issues 10-year bonds with a maturity value of $200,000. If the bonds are issued at a premium, this indicates that:
(a) the contractual interest rate exceeds the market interest rate.
(b) the market interest rate exceeds the contractual interest rate.
(c) the contractual interest rate and the market interest rate are the same.
(d) no relationship exists between the two rates.

(SO 6) 7. On January 1 Hurley Corporation issues $500,000, 5-year, 12% bonds at 96 with interest payable on July 1 and January 1. The entry on July 1 to record payment of bond interest and the amortization of bond discount using the straight-line method will include a:
(a) debit to Interest Expense, $30,000.
(b) debit to Interest Expense, $60,000.
(c) credit to Discount on Bonds Payable, $4,000.
(d) credit to Discount on Bonds Payable, $2,000.

8. For the bonds issued in question 7, what is the carrying value of the bonds at the end of the third interest period? (SO 6)
(a) $486,000 (c) $472,000
(b) $488,000 (d) $464,000

9. Gester Corporation retires its $100,000 face value bonds at 105 on January 1, following the payment of semiannual interest. The carrying value of the bonds at the redemption date is $103,745. The entry to record the redemption will include a: (SO 7)
(a) credit of $3,745 to Loss on Bond Redemption.
(b) debit of $3,745 to Premium on Bonds Payable.
(c) credit of $1,255 to Gain on Bond Redemption.
(d) debit of $5,000 to Premium on Bonds Payable.

10. Which of the following would *not* be included in the numerator of the acid-test ratio? (SO 4)
(a) Accounts receivable
(b) Cash
(c) Marketable securities
(d) Inventory

11. Which of the following is *not* a measure of liquidity? (SO 4)
(a) Debt to total assets ratio
(b) Working capital
(c) Current ratio
(d) Acid-test ratio

12. In a recent year Kennedy Corporation had net income of $150,000, interest expense of $30,000, and tax expense of $20,000. What was Kennedy Corporation's times interest earned ratio for the year? (SO 8)
(a) 5.00 (c) 6.66
(b) 4.00 (d) 7.50

QUESTIONS

1. Li Feng believes a current liability is a debt that can be expected to be paid in 1 year. Is Li correct? Explain.

2. Rio Grande Company obtains $25,000 in cash by signing a 9%, 6-month, $25,000 note payable to First Bank on July 1. Rio Grande's fiscal year ends on September 30. What information should be reported for the note payable in the annual financial statements?

3. (a) Your roommate says, "Sales taxes are reported as an expense in the income statement." Do you agree? Explain.
   (b) Hard Walk Cafe has cash proceeds from sales of $10,400. This amount includes $400 of sales taxes. Give the entry to record the proceeds.

4. Aurora University sold 10,000 season football tickets at $90 each for its five-game home schedule. What entries should be made (a) when the tickets are sold and (b) after each game?

5. Identify three taxes commonly withheld by the employer from an employee's gross pay.

6. (a) Identify three taxes commonly paid by employers on employee's salaries and wages.
   (b) Where in the financial statements does the employer report taxes withheld from employee's pay?

7. (a) What are long-term liabilities? Give two examples.
   (b) What is a bond?

8. (a) As a source of long-term financing, what are the major advantages of bonds over common stock?
   (b) What are the major disadvantages in using bonds for long-term financing?
9. Contrast these types of bonds:
   (a) Secured and unsecured
   (b) Term and serial
   (c) Convertible and callable
10. Explain each of these important terms in issuing bonds:
    (a) Face value
    (b) Contractual interest rate
    (c) Bond indenture
    (d) Bond certificate
11. (a) What is a convertible bond?
    (b) Discuss the advantages of a convertible bond from the standpoint of the bondholders and of the issuing corporation.
12. Describe the two major obligations incurred by a company when bonds are issued.
13. Assume that Stoney Inc. sold bonds with a par value of $100,000 for $104,000. Was the market interest rate equal to, less than, or greater than the bonds' contractual interest rate? Explain.
14. Barbara Secord and Jack Dalton are discussing how the market price of a bond is determined. Barbara believes that the market price of a bond is solely a function of the amount of the principal payment at the end of the term of a bond. Is she right? Discuss.
15. If a 10%, 10-year, $600,000 bond is issued at par and interest is paid semiannually, what is the amount of the interest payment at the end of the first semiannual period?
16. If the Bonds Payable account has a balance of $900,000 and the Discount on Bonds Payable account has a balance of $40,000, what is the carrying value of the bonds?
17. Which accounts are debited and which are credited if a bond issue originally sold at a premium is redeemed before maturity at 97 immediately following the payment of interest?
18. Explain the straight-line method of amortizing discount and premium on bonds payable.
19. Jennifer Brent Corporation issues $200,000 of 8%, 5-year bonds on January 1, 1998, at 104. Assuming that the straight-line method is used to amortize the premium, what is the total amount of interest expense for 1998?
20. (a) In general, what are the requirements for the financial statement presentation of long-term liabilities?
    (b) What ratios may be computed to evaluate a company's liquidity and solvency?
21. Michael Feldman says that liquidity and solvency are the same thing. Is he correct? If not, how do they differ?
22. Tom Dodge needs a few new trucks for his business. He is considering buying the trucks but is concerned that the additional debt he will need to borrow will make his liquidity and solvency ratios look bad. What options does he have other than purchasing the assets, and how will these options affect his financial statements?
23. Lincoln Corporation has a current ratio of 1.1. Joe Investor has always been told that a corporation's current ratio should exceed 2.0. Lincoln argues that its ratio is low because it has a minimal amount of inventory on hand so as to reduce operating costs. Lincoln also points out that it has significant available lines of credit. Is Joe still correct? What other measures might he check?
24. What criteria must be met before a contingency must be recorded as a liability? How should the contingency be disclosed if the criteria are not met?
25. What is the primary difference between the nature of an operating lease and a capital lease? What is the difference in how they are recorded?
26. What are the implications for analysis if a company has significant operating leases?

BRIEF EXERCISES

Identify whether obligations are current liabilities.
(SO 1)

BE10-1 Fresno Company has these obligations at December 31: (a) a note payable for $100,000 due in 2 years, (b) a 10-year mortgage payable of $200,000 payable in ten $20,000 annual payments, (c) interest payable of $15,000 on the mortgage, and (d) accounts payable of $60,000. For each obligation, indicate whether it should be classified as a current liability.

Prepare entries for an interest-bearing note payable.
(SO 2)

BE10-2 Romez Company borrows $60,000 on July 1 from the bank by signing a $60,000, 10%, 1-year note payable. Prepare the journal entries to record (a) the proceeds of the note and (b) accrued interest at December 31, assuming adjusting entries are made only at the end of the year.

Compute and record sales taxes payable.
(SO 3)

BE10-3 Grandy Auto Supply does not segregate sales and sales taxes at the time of sale. The register total for March 16 is $9,975. All sales are subject to a 5% sales tax. Compute sales taxes payable and make the entry to record sales taxes payable and sales.

BE10-4 Outstanding University sells 3,000 season basketball tickets at $60 each for its 12-game home schedule. Give the entry to record (a) the sale of the season tickets and (b) the revenue earned by playing the first home game.

Prepare entries for unearned revenues
(SO 3)

BE10-5 Olga Inc. is considering these two alternatives to finance its construction of a new $2 million plant:
(a) Issuance of 200,000 shares of common stock at the market price of $10 per share
(b) Issuance of $2 million, 8% bonds at par
Complete the table and indicate which alternative is preferable.

Compare bond financing to stock financing.
(SO 5)

	Issue Stock	Issue Bond
Income before interest and taxes	$1,000,000	$1,000,000
Interest expense from bonds		
Income before income taxes	$	$
Income tax expense (30%)		
Net income	$	$
Outstanding shares		700,000
Earnings per share		

BE10-6 Keystone Corporation issued 1,000 9%, 5-year, $1,000 bonds dated January 1, 1998, at 100.
(a) Prepare the journal entry to record the sale of these bonds on January 1, 1998.
(b) Prepare the journal entry to record the first interest payment on July 1, 1998 (interest payable semiannually), assuming no previous accrual of interest.
(c) Prepare the adjusting journal entry on December 31, 1998, to record interest expense.

Prepare journal entries for bonds issued at face value.
(SO 6)

BE10-7 The balance sheet for Hathaway Company reports the following information on July 1, 1998:

Prepare journal entry for redemption of bonds.
(SO 7)

Long-term liabilities
    Bonds payable $1,000,000
    Less: Discount on bonds payable   60,000 $940,000

Hathaway decides to redeem these bonds at 102 after paying semiannual interest. Prepare the journal entry to record the redemption on July 1, 1998.

BE10-8 Dominic Company issues $2 million, 10-year, 9% bonds at 98, with interest payable on July 1 and January 1. The straight-line method is used to amortize bond discount.
(a) Prepare the journal entry to record the sale of these bonds on January 1, 1998.
(b) Prepare the journal entry to record interest expense and bond discount amortization on July 1, 1998, assuming no previous accrual of interest.

Prepare journal entries for bonds issued at a discount.
(SO 6)

BE10-9 Hercules Inc. issues $5 million, 5-year, 10% bonds at 103, with interest payable on July 1 and January 1. The straight-line method is used to amortize bond premium.
(a) Prepare the journal entry to record the sale of these bonds on January 1, 1998.
(b) Prepare the journal entry to record interest expense and bond premium amortization on July 1, 1998, assuming no previous accrual of interest.

Prepare journal entries for bonds issued at a premium.
(SO 6)

BE10-10 Presented here are long-term liability items for Warner Company at December 31, 1998. Prepare the long-term liabilities section of the balance sheet for Warner Company.

Prepare statement presentation of long-term liabilities.
(SO 8)

    Bonds payable, due 2001 $900,000
    Notes payable, due 2003   80,000
    Discount on bonds payable   45,000

BE10-11 Motorola's 1995 financial statements contain the following selected data (in millions):

Analyze liquidity and solvency.
(SO 4, 8)

Current assets	$10,510	Interest expense	$ 149
Total assets	22,801	Income taxes	1,001
Current liabilities	7,791	Net income	1,781
Total liabilities	11,753		
Cash	725		
Marketable securities	350		
Accounts receivable	4,081		

Compute these values:
(a) Working capital
(b) Current ratio
(c) Acid-test ratio
(d) Debt to total assets ratio
(e) Times interest earned ratio

Calculate debt to total assets ratio; discuss effect of operating leases on solvency.
(SO 8)

BE10-12 In a recent year, Southwest Airlines reported $2,893,726,000 in required payments on operating leases. If these assets had been purchased with debt, assets and liabilities would rise by approximately $1,500,000,000. Southwest's total assets in this year were $3,256,122,000 and total liabilities were $1,828,804,000.
(a) Calculate Southwest's debt to assets ratio, first using the figures reported, and then after increasing assets and liabilities for the unrecorded operating leases.
(b) Discuss the potential effect of these operating leases on your assessment of Southwest's solvency.

EXERCISES

Prepare entries for interest-bearing notes.
(SO 2)

E10-1 Cairo Company on June 1 borrows $50,000 from First Bank on a 6-month, $50,000, 12% note.

Instructions
(a) Prepare the entry on June 1.
(b) Prepare the adjusting entry on June 30.
(c) Prepare the entry at maturity (December 1), assuming monthly adjusting entries have been made through November 30.
(d) What was the total financing cost (interest expense)?

Journalize sales and related taxes.
(SO 3)

E10-2 In providing accounting services to small businesses, you encounter the following situations pertaining to cash sales:
1. Nash Company rings up sales and sales taxes separately on its cash register. On April 10 the register totals are sales $25,000 and sales taxes $1,500.
2. Pontiac Company does not segregate sales and sales taxes. Its register total for April 15 is $13,780, which includes a 6% sales tax.

Instructions
Prepare the entries to record the sales transactions and related taxes for (a) Nash Company and (b) Pontiac Company.

Journalize unearned subscription revenue.
(SO 3)

E10-3 Westland Company publishes a monthly sports magazine, *Fishing Preview*. Subscriptions to the magazine cost $24 per year. During November 1998 Westwood sells 6,000 subscriptions beginning with the December issue. Westwood prepares financial statements quarterly and recognizes subscription revenue earned at the end of the quarter. The company uses the accounts Unearned Subscription Revenue and Subscription Revenue.

Instructions
(a) Prepare the entry in November for the receipt of the subscriptions.
(b) Prepare the adjusting entry at December 31, 1998, to record subscription revenue earned in December 1998.
(c) Prepare the adjusting entry at March 31, 1999, to record subscription revenue earned in the first quarter of 1999.

Compare issuance of stock financing to issuance of bond financing.
(SO 5)

E10-4 Sundown Airlines is considering these two alternatives for financing the purchase of a fleet of airplanes:
1. Issue 60,000 shares of common stock at $45 per share. (Cash dividends have not been paid nor is the payment of any contemplated.)
2. Issue 13%, 10-year bonds at face value for $2,700,000.

It is estimated that the company will earn $900,000 before interest and taxes as a result of this purchase. The company has an estimated tax rate of 30% and has 90,000 shares of common stock outstanding prior to the new financing.

Instructions
Determine the effect on net income and earnings per share for (a) issuing stock and (b) issuing bonds.

E10-5 On January 1 Laramie Company issued $90,000, 10%, 10-year bonds at face value. Interest is payable semiannually on July 1 and January 1. Interest is not accrued on June 30.

Prepare journal entries for issuance of bonds and payment and accrual of interest.
(SO 6)

Instructions
Prepare journal entries to record these events:
(a) The issuance of the bonds
(b) The payment of interest on July 1
(c) The accrual of interest on December 31

E10-6 Pueblo Company issued $240,000, 9%, 20-year bonds on January 1, 1998, at 103. Interest is payable semiannually on July 1 and January 1. Pueblo uses straight-line amortization for bond premium or discount. Interest is not accrued on June 30.

Prepare journal entries to record issuance of bonds, payment of interest, amortization of premium, and redemption at maturity.
(SO 6, 7)

Instructions
Prepare the journal entries to record these events:
(a) The issuance of the bonds
(b) The payment of interest and the premium amortization on July 1, 1998
(c) The accrual of interest and the premium amortization on December 31, 1998
(d) The redemption of the bonds at maturity, assuming interest for the last interest period has been paid and recorded

E10-7 Cotter Company issued $180,000, 11%, 10-year bonds on December 31, 1997, for $172,000. Interest is payable semiannually on June 30 and December 31. Cotter uses the straight-line method to amortize bond premium or discount.

Prepare journal entries to record issuance of bonds, payment of interest, amortization of discount, and redemption at maturity.
(SO 6, 7)

Instructions
Prepare the journal entries to record these events:
(a) The issuance of the bonds
(b) The payment of interest and the discount amortization on June 30, 1998
(c) The payment of interest and the discount amortization on December 31, 1998
(d) The redemption of the bonds at maturity, assuming interest for the last interest period has been paid and recorded

E10-8 The situations presented here are independent.

Prepare journal entries for redemption of bonds.
(SO 7)

Instructions
For each situation prepare the appropriate journal entry for the redemption of the bonds.
(a) Ernst Corporation retired $120,000 face value, 12% bonds on June 30, 1998, at 102. The carrying value of the bonds at the redemption date was $107,500. The bonds pay semiannual interest, and the interest payment due on June 30, 1998, has been made and recorded.
(b) Young, Inc., retired $150,000 face value, 12.5% bonds on June 30, 1998, at 98. The carrying value of the bonds at the redemption date was $151,000. The bonds pay semiannual interest, and the interest payment due on June 30, 1998, has been made and recorded.

E10-9 The adjusted trial balance for Viola Corporation at the end of the current year contained these accounts:

Prepare statement presentation of long-term liabilities.
(SO 8)

Bond Interest Payable	$ 9,000
Note Payable, due 2002	59,500
Bonds Payable, due 2007	120,000
Premium on Bonds Payable	32,000

Instructions
(a) Prepare the long-term liabilities section of the balance sheet.
(b) Indicate the proper balance sheet classification for the account(s) listed above that do not belong in the long-term liabilities section.

476 CHAPTER 10 Reporting and Analyzing Liabilities

Calculate liquidity and solvency ratios; discuss impact of unrecorded obligations on liquidity and solvency.
(SO 4, 8)

E10-10 McDonald's 1995 financial statements contain the following selected data (in millions):

Current assets	$ 955.8	Interest expense	$ 340.2
Total assets	15,414.6	Income taxes	741.8
Current liabilities	1,794.9	Net income	1,427.3
Total liabilities	7,553.3		
Cash	334.8		
Accounts receivable	377.3		
Notes receivable	36.3		

Instructions

(a) Compute these values:
  (1) Working capital   (4) Debt to total assets ratio
  (2) Current ratio   (5) Times interest earned ratio
  (3) Acid-test ratio

(b) The notes to McDonald's financial statements show that during the next 5 years the company will have future minimum lease payments under operating leases of $5,542.8 million. Discuss the implications of these unrecorded obligations for the analysis of McDonald's liquidity and solvency.

Calculate current and acid-test ratios before and after paying accounts payable.
(SO 4)

E10-11 The following financial data were reported by Minnesota Mining and Manufacturing (3M) for 1996 and 1995 ($ in millions):

	1996	1995
Current assets		
Cash and cash equivalents	$ 583	$ 485
Other securities	161	287
Accounts receivable, net	2,504	2,398
Inventories	2,264	2,206
Other current assets	974	1,019
Total current assets	$6,486	$6,395
Current liabilities	$3,789	$3,724

Instructions

(a) Calculate the current and acid-test ratios for 3M for 1996 and 1995.
(b) Suppose that at the end of 1996 3M management used $500 million cash to pay off $500 million of accounts payable. How would its current ratio and acid-test ratio change?

PROBLEMS

Prepare current liability entries, adjusting entries, and current liability section.
(SO 1, 2, 3)

P10-1 On January 1, 1998, the ledger of Calcutta Company contained these liability accounts:

Accounts Payable	$42,500
Sales Taxes Payable	5,600
Unearned Service Revenue	15,000

During January the following selected transactions occurred:

Jan. 1 Borrowed $15,000 in cash from Midland Bank on a 4-month, 10%, $15,000 note.
      5 Sold merchandise for cash totaling $7,800, which includes 4% sales taxes.
     12 Provided services for customers who had made advance payments of $8,000. (Credit Service Revenue.)
     14 Paid state treasurer's department for sales taxes collected in December 1997, $5,600.
     20 Sold 500 units of a new product on credit at $52 per unit, plus 4% sales tax.
     25 Sold merchandise for cash totaling $11,440, which includes 4% sales taxes.

Instructions

(a) Journalize the January transactions.
(b) Journalize the adjusting entries at January 31 for the outstanding note payable.

(c) Prepare the current liability section of the balance sheet at January 31, 1998. Assume no change in Accounts Payable.

P10-2 The following are selected transactions of Eldorado Company, which prepares financial statements *quarterly*:

Jan. 2 Purchased merchandise on account from McCoy Company, $15,000, terms 2/10, n/30.
Feb. 1 Issued a 10%, 2-month, $15,000 note to McCoy in payment of account.
Mar. 31 Accrued interest for 2 months on McCoy note.
Apr. 1 Paid face value and interest on McCoy note.
July 1 Purchased equipment from Scottie Equipment, paying $11,000 in cash and signing a 10%, 3-month, $24,000 note.
Sept. 30 Accrued interest for 3 months on Scottie note.
Oct. 1 Paid face value and interest on Scottie note.
Dec. 1 Borrowed $10,000 from Federation Bank by issuing a 3-month, 9% interest-bearing note with a face value of $10,000.
     31 Recognized interest expense for 1 month on Federation Bank note.

Journalize and post note transactions; show balance sheet presentation.
(SO 2)

Instructions
(a) Prepare journal entries for the transactions and events.
(b) Post to the accounts Notes Payable, Interest Payable, and Interest Expense. (Use T accounts.)
(c) Show the balance sheet presentation of notes payable and interest payable at December 31.
(d) What is the total interest expense for the year?

P10-3 Beatrice Corporation sold $1,500,000, 8%, 10-year bonds on January 1, 1998. The bonds were dated January 1, 1998, and pay interest on July 1 and January 1. Beatrice Corporation uses the straight-line method to amortize bond premium or discount. Assume no interest is accrued on June 30.

Prepare journal entries to record issuance of bonds, interest, and amortization of bond premium and discount.
(SO 6, 8)

Instructions
(a) Prepare all the necessary journal entries to record the issuance of the bonds and bond interest expense for 1998, assuming that the bonds sold at 102.
(b) Prepare journal entries as in part (a) assuming that the bonds sold at 97.
(c) Show the balance sheet presentation for each bond issue at December 31, 1998.

P10-4 The following section is taken from Bermuda Corp.'s balance sheet at December 31, 1998:

Prepare journal entries to record interest payments, discount amortization, and redemption of bonds.
(SO 6, 7)

Current liabilities		
Bond interest payable (for 6 months from July 1 to December 31)		$ 132,000
Long-term liabilities		
Bonds payable, 11%, due January 1, 2009	$2,400,000	
Less: Discount on bonds payable	84,000	2,316,000

Interest is payable semiannually on January 1 and July 1. The bonds are callable on any semiannual interest date. Bermuda uses straight-line amortization for any bond premium or discount. From December 31, 1998, the bonds will be outstanding for an additional 10 years (120 months). Assume no interest is accrued on June 30.

Instructions
(Round all computations to the nearest dollar.)
(a) Journalize the payment of bond interest on January 1, 1999.
(b) Prepare the entry to amortize bond discount and to pay the interest due on July 1, 1999.
(c) Assume on July 1, 1999, after paying interest, that Bermuda Corp. calls bonds having a face value of $800,000. The call price is 102. Record the redemption of the bonds.
(d) Prepare the adjusting entry at December 31, 1999, to amortize bond discount and to accrue interest on the remaining bonds.

478 CHAPTER 10 Reporting and Analyzing Liabilities

Prepare journal entries to record issuance of bonds, interest accrual, and amortization for 2 years.

(SO 6, 8)

P10-5 Moriarity Company sold $4,000,000, 9%, 20-year bonds on January 1, 1998. The bonds were dated January 1, 1998, and pay interest on December 31 and June 30. The bonds were sold at 97. Assume no interest is accrued on June 30.

Instructions

(a) Prepare the journal entry to record the issuance of the bonds on January 1, 1998.
(b) At December 31, 1998, $6,000 of the bond discount had been amortized. Show the balance sheet presentation of the bond liability at December 31, 1998. (Assume that interest has been paid.)
(c) At December 31, 2000, when the carrying value of the bonds was $3,898,000, the company redeemed the bonds at 101. Record the redemption of the bonds assuming that interest for the year had already been paid.

ALTERNATIVE PROBLEMS

Prepare current liability entries, adjusting entries, and current liability section.

(SO 1, 2, 3)

P10-1A On January 1, 1998, the ledger of El Paso Company contained these liability accounts:

Accounts Payable	$52,000
Sales Taxes Payable	7,500
Unearned Service Revenue	16,000

During January the following selected transactions occurred:

Jan. 5 Sold merchandise for cash totaling $16,632, which includes 8% sales taxes.
12 Provided services for customers who had made advance payments of $9,000. (Credit Service Revenue.)
14 Paid state revenue department for sales taxes collected in December 1997 ($7,500).
20 Sold 500 units of a new product on credit at $50 per unit, plus 8% sales tax.
21 Borrowed $18,000 from Midland Bank on a 3-month, 10%, $18,000 note.
25 Sold merchandise for cash totaling $11,340, which includes 8% sales taxes.

Instructions

(a) Journalize the January transactions.
(b) Journalize the adjusting entries at January 31 for the outstanding notes payable.
(c) Prepare the current liability section of the balance sheet at January 31, 1998. Assume no change in accounts payable.

Journalize and post note transactions; show balance sheet presentation.

(SO 2)

P10-2A The following are selected transactions of Christianson Company, which prepares financial statements *quarterly:*

Jan. 2 Purchased merchandise on account from Thompson Company, $25,000, terms 2/10, n/30.
Feb. 1 Issued a 10%, 2-month, $25,000 note to Thompson in payment of account.
Mar. 31 Accrued interest for 2 months on Thompson note.
Apr. 1 Paid face value and interest on Thompson note.
July 1 Purchased equipment from Billie Equipment, paying $24,000 in cash and signing a 9%, 3-month, $44,000 note.
Sept. 30 Accrued interest for 3 months on Billie note.
Oct. 1 Paid face value and interest on Billie note.
Dec. 1 Borrowed $20,000 from Shoreline Bank by issuing a 3-month, 11% interest-bearing note with a face value of $20,000.
31 Recognized interest expense for 1 month on Shoreline Bank note.

Instructions

(a) Prepare journal entries for the transactions and events.
(b) Post to the accounts Notes Payable, Interest Payable, and Interest Expense. (Use T accounts.)
(c) Show the balance sheet presentation of notes payable and interest payable at December 31.
(d) What is the total interest expense for the year?

P10-3A San Diego Company sold $1,500,000, 12%, 10-year bonds on July 1, 1998. The bonds were dated July 1, 1998, and pay interest July 1 and January 1. San Diego Company uses the straight-line method to amortize bond premium or discount. Assume no interest is accrued on June 30.

Prepare journal entries to record issuance of bonds, interest, and amortization of bond premium and discount.
(SO 6, 8)

Instructions
(a) Prepare all the necessary journal entries to record the issuance of the bonds and bond interest expense for 1998, assuming that the bonds sold at 102.
(b) Prepare journal entries as in part (a) assuming that the bonds sold at 94.
(c) Show the balance sheet presentation for each bond issue at December 31, 1998.

P10-4A The following section is taken from Walenda Oil Company's balance sheet at December 31, 1998:

Prepare journal entries to record interest payments, premium amortization, and redemption of bonds.
(SO 6, 7)

Current liabilities		
Bond interest payable (for 6 months from July 1 to December 31)		$ 216,000
Long-term liabilities		
Bonds payable, 12% due January 1, 2009	$3,600,000	
Add: Premium on bonds payable	300,000	3,900,000

Interest is payable semiannually on January 1 and July 1. The bonds are callable on any semiannual interest date. Walenda uses straight-line amortization for any bond premium or discount. From December 31, 1998, the bonds will be outstanding for an additional 10 years (120 months). Assume no interest is accrued on June 30.

Instructions
(Round all computations to the nearest dollar.)
(a) Journalize the payment of bond interest on January 1, 1999.
(b) Prepare the entry to amortize bond premium and to pay the interest due on July 1, 1999.
(c) Assume on July 1, 1999, after paying interest, that Walenda Company calls bonds having a face value of $1,800,000. The call price is 101. Record the redemption of the bonds.
(d) Prepare the adjusting entry at December 31, 1999, to amortize bond premium and to accrue interest on the remaining bonds.

P10-5A Montego Electric sold $3,000,000, 10%, 20-year bonds on January 1, 1998. The bonds were dated January 1 and pay interest on July 1 and January 1. The bonds were sold at 104. Assume no interest is accrued on June 30.

Prepare journal entries to record issuance of bonds, interest accrual, and amortization for 2 years.
(SO 6, 8)

Instructions
(a) Prepare the journal entry to record the issuance of the bonds on January 1, 1998.
(b) At December 31, 1998, $6,000 of the bond premium had been amortized. Show the balance sheet presentation of the bond liability at December 31, 1998. (Assume that interest has been paid.)
(c) At December 31, 2000, when the carrying value of the bonds was $3,102,000, the company redeemed the bonds at 101. Record the redemption of the bonds assuming that interest for the year had already been paid.

BROADENING YOUR PERSPECTIVE

Financial Reporting and Analysis

FINANCIAL REPORTING PROBLEM: *Starbucks Corporation*

BYP10-1 Refer to the financial statements of Starbucks and the Notes to Consolidated Financial Statements in Appendix A.

Instructions

Answer these questions about current and contingent liabilities and payroll costs:
(a) What were Starbucks' total current liabilities at September 29, 1996? What was the increase/decrease in Starbucks' total current liabilities from the prior year?
(b) How much were the accounts payable at September 29, 1996?
(c) What were the components of total current liabilities on September 29, 1996 (other than accounts payable already discussed above)?

COMPARATIVE ANALYSIS PROBLEM: *Starbucks vs. Green Mountain Coffee*

BYP10-2 The financial statements of Green Mountain Coffee are presented in Appendix B, following the financial statements for Starbucks in Appendix A.

Instructions
(a) Based on the information contained in these financial statements, compute the following 1996 ratios for each company:
   (1) Debt to total assets
   (2) Times interest earned
(b) Starbucks reports required future operating lease payments of $364,740,000, and Green Mountain Coffee reports $5,097,000. If these transactions had instead been reported as purchases, the reported assets and liabilities of Starbucks would increase by approximately $225,000,000 and those of Green Mountain Coffee would increase by $3,500,000. Recalculate the debt to assets ratio for each company treating these transactions as purchases.
(c) What conclusions concerning the companies' long-run solvency can be drawn from these ratios? What are the implications of your findings in part (b)?

RESEARCH CASE

BYP10-3 The November 6, 1995, edition of *The Wall Street Journal* contains an article by Linda Sandler entitled "Kmart Is Pressured Over Obscure Bond 'Puts,' Which Stir Worries Amid Tough Retail Times."

Instructions
Read the article and answer these questions:
(a) What is the total dollar amount of the bond issue in question? Who purchased these bonds?
(b) What right does the "put option" give to bondholders?
(c) What amount is available under Kmart's bank lines? Why can't Kmart borrow under these lines to purchase the bonds? What is the most likely solution to the problem?
(d) Were the terms of the put bonds adequately disclosed?

INTERPRETING FINANCIAL STATEMENTS

BYP10-4 Minicase 1 *Texas Instruments*

Texas Instruments designs and produces devices that use semiconductor technology. You may have one of its calculators on your desk. Because it is in a high-tech industry, the company must constantly invest in new technology, which requires considerable financing. During 1995 Texas Instruments' current liabilities and its long-term liabilities increased by about $1 billion each. Here is additional information (in millions) from Texas Instruments' 1995 annual report:

	1995	1994
Current assets	$ 5,518	$ 4,017
Total assets	9,215	6,980
Current liabilities	3,188	2,199
Total liabilities	5,120	3,950
Stockholders' equity	4,095	3,030
Sales revenue	13,128	10,315
Income taxes	531	351
Interest expense	48	45
Net income	1,088	691

Maturities (in millions) of long-term debt due during the 4 years subsequent to December 31, 1996, are:

1997	$14	1999	$168
1998	18	2000	19

Instructions
Address each of these questions related to the liabilities of Texas Instruments:
(a) Using both working capital and the current ratio as indicators, evaluate the change in the company's liquidity from 1994 to 1995.
(b) Using both the debt to total assets ratio and the times interest earned ratio, evaluate the change in the company's solvency from 1994 to 1995.
(c) What are the implications of the information provided about the maturities of the company's long-term debt?

BYP10-5 **Minicase 2** *Northland Cranberries*
Despite being a publicly traded company only since 1987, Northland Cranberries of Wisconsin Rapids, Wisconsin, is the world's largest cranberry grower. It has engaged in an aggressive growth strategy, and as a consequence, the company has taken on significant amounts of both short-term and long-term debt. The following information is taken from recent annual reports of the company:

	1995	1994
Current assets	$ 6,745,759	$ 5,598,054
Total assets	107,744,751	83,074,339
Current liabilities	10,168,685	4,484,687
Total liabilities	73,118,204	49,948,787
Stockholders' equity	34,626,547	33,125,552
Net sales	21,783,966	18,051,355
Cost of goods sold	13,057,275	8,751,220
Interest expense	3,654,006	2,393,792
Income tax expense	1,051,000	1,917,000
Net income	1,581,707	2,942,954

Instructions
(a) Evaluate the company's liquidity by calculating and analyzing working capital and the current ratio.
(b) The following discussion of the company's liquidity was provided in the Management Discussion and Analysis section of the company's 1995 annual report. Comment on whether you agree with management's statements and what might be done to remedy the situation.
(c) Evaluate the company's solvency using the debt to total assets ratio and the times interest earned ratio.

NORTHLAND CRANBERRIES
Management Discussion and Analysis

The lower comparative current ratio at March 31, 1995, was due to $3 million of short-term borrowing then outstanding which was incurred to fund the Company's September 1994 Yellow River Marsh acquisitions. As a result of the extreme seasonality of its business, the company does not believe that its current ratio or its underlying stated working capital at its March 31, 1995, fiscal year end is a meaningful indication of the Company's liquidity. As of March 31 of each fiscal year, the Company has historically carried no significant amounts of inventories and by such date all of the Company's accounts receivable from its crop sold for processing under the supply agreements have been paid in cash, with the resulting cash received from such payments used to reduce indebtedness. The Company utilizes its revolving bank credit facility, together with cash generated from operations, to fund its working capital requirements throughout its growing season.

BYP10-6 Minicase 3 *Didde Industries, Inc.*
Presented below is the long-term debt portion of the notes to the financial statements of Didde Industries, Inc.

DIDDE INDUSTRIES, INC.
Notes to the Financial Statements

Long-Term Debt Long-term debt is summarized as follows (in thousands):

	December 31, 1998
Unsecured variable interest rate note (weighted average interest rate of 9.3% and 9.6% at December 31, 1998 and 1997, respectively) due in quarterly installments through 2000	$ 4,000
9.75% first mortgage bonds secured by a lien on phosphate rock reserves, due $7.0 million annually through 2003	40,000
8.625% to 9.875% mortgage notes secured by various distribution facilities, due monthly through 2010	13,023
Total long-term debt	57,023
Less: Current portion	15,574
	$41,449

Certain borrowings are collateralized by property, plant, and equipment. Maintenance of specified minimum working capital (current assets less liabilities) and stockholders' equity levels, and specified maximum debt ratios and investments are also required.

Long-term debt maturities for the 4 years after December 31, 1999, are $8.7 million in 2000, $8.0 million in 2001, $8.0 million in 2002, and $8.2 million in 2003.

Instructions
(a) Indicate how much long-term debt is outstanding and what different types of debt Didde Industries reports.
(b) Why do you think the loan agreement contains debt covenants requiring minimum working capital and stockholders' equity levels, and specified maximum debt ratios and maximum limits on investments?

CRITICAL THINKING

MANAGEMENT DECISION CASE

BYP10-7 On January 1, 1996, Jerry Mall Corporation issued $1,200,000 of 5-year, 8% bonds at 97; the bonds pay interest semiannually on July 1 and January 1. By January 1, 1998, the market rate of interest for bonds of risk similar to those of Jerry Mall Corporation had risen. As a result the market value of these bonds was $1,000,000 on January 1, 1998—below their carrying value. Jerry Mall, president of the company, suggests repurchasing all of these bonds in the open market at the $1,000,000 price. But to do so the company will have to issue $1,000,000 (face value) of new 10-year, 12% bonds at par. The president asks you as controller, "What is the feasibility of my proposed repurchase plan?"

Instructions
(a) What is the carrying value of the outstanding Jerry Mall Corporation 5-year bonds on January 1, 1998 (assume straight-line amortization)?
(b) Prepare the journal entry to retire the 5-year bonds on January 1, 1998. Prepare the journal entry to issue the new 10-year bonds.
(c) Prepare a short memo to the president in response to his request for advice. List the economic factors that you believe should be considered for his repurchase proposal.

A REAL-WORLD FOCUS: *Apache Corporation*

BYP10-8 *Apache Corporation* is an international, independent energy enterprise engaged in the exploration, development, production, gathering, processing, and marketing of natural gas and crude oil. Its corporate headquarters are in Houston, Texas, and it has operations in 18 states of the United States as well as Australia, the Congo, France, Myanmar, and Indonesia.

The 1994 annual report of Apache Corporation disclosed the following information:

APACHE CORPORATION
Management Discussion

In May 1994, Apache issued 9.25% bonds due 2002 in the principal amount of $100 million. The proceeds of $99 million from the offering were used to reduce bank debt, to pay off the 9.5% convertible debentures due 1996, and for general corporate purposes. In December 1994, the company privately placed 3.93% convertible notes due 1997 in the principal amount of $75 million. The notes are not redeemable before maturity and are convertible into Apache common stock at the option of the holders at any time prior to maturity, at a conversion price of $27 per share. Proceeds from the sale of the notes were used for the repayment of bank debt.

Instructions
(a) Identify the face amount, contractual interest rate, and selling price of the newly issued bonds due in 2002. Explain whether the bonds sold at a premium or a discount.
(b) For what purposes has Apache Corporation been incurring more debt?

GROUP ACTIVITIES

BYP10-9 There are six topics in the section on types of current liabilities: notes payable, sales taxes payable, payroll and payroll taxes payable, unearned revenues, current maturities of long-term debt, and contingent liabilities.

Instructions
With the class divided into six groups, each group should choose one topic and prepare a presentation to explain to the class the key points about the assigned topic.

BYP10-10 The text explains that bonds may be issued at (1) face value, (2) a discount, and (3) a premium.

Instructions
With the class divided into three groups, each group should choose one type of bond issue. Your group is to explain these topics, using dollar amounts different from those used in the text:
(a) The entry to record the sale of the bonds
(b) The entry at the end of the first interest period after the sale
(c) The financial statement presentation of the bonds and interest expense at the end of the first interest period

COMMUNICATION ACTIVITY

BYP10-11 Finn Berge, president of the Blue Marlin, is considering the issuance of bonds to finance an expansion of his business. He has asked you to (1) discuss the advantages of bonds over common stock financing, (2) indicate the type of bonds he might issue, and (3) explain the issuing procedures used in bond transactions.

Instructions
Write a memorandum to the president, answering his request.

Ethics Case

BYP10-12 Andy Vicks is the president, founder, and majority owner of Custom Medical Corporation, an emerging medical technology products company. Custom Medical is in dire need of additional capital to keep operating and to bring several promising products to final development, testing, and production. Andy, as owner of 51% of the outstanding stock, manages the company's operations. He places heavy emphasis on research and development and long-term growth. The other principal stockholder is Jill Caterino who, as a nonemployee investor, owns 40% of the stock. Jill would like to deemphasize the R&D functions and emphasize the marketing function to maximize short-run sales and profits from existing products. She believes this strategy would raise the market price of Custom Medical's stock.

All of Andy's personal capital and borrowing power are tied up in his 51% stock ownership. He knows that any offering of additional shares of stock will dilute his controlling interest because he won't be able to participate in such an issuance. Jill has money and would likely buy enough shares to gain control of Custom Medical. She then would dictate the company's future direction, even if it meant replacing Andy as president and CEO.

The company already has considerable debt. Raising additional debt will be costly, will adversely affect Custom Medical's credit rating, and will increase the company's reported losses due to the growth in interest expense. Jill and the other minority stockholders express opposition to the assumption of additional debt, fearing the company will be pushed to the brink of bankruptcy. Wanting to maintain his control and to preserve the direction of "his" company, Andy is doing everything to avoid a stock issuance and is contemplating a large issuance of bonds, even if it means the bonds are issued with a high effective-interest rate.

Instructions
(a) Who are the stakeholders in this situation?
(b) What are the ethical issues?
(c) What would you do if you were Andy?

Financial Analysis on the Web

BYP10-13 *Purpose:* Bond or debt securities pay a stated rate of interest. This rate of interest is dependent on the risk associated with the investment. Moody's Investment Service provides ratings for companies that issue debt securities.

Address: http://www.moodys.com/index.shtml

Steps: From Moody's homepage choose **SiteMap**.

Instructions
Answer the following questions:
(a) What year did Moody's introduce the first bond rating?
(b) List three basic principles Moody's uses in rating bonds.
(c) What is the definition of Moody's Aaa rating on long-term taxable debt?

BYP10-14 *Purpose:* To illustrate the time value of money. If you want to see how long it will take to reach your financial goals, try using "Investing for Kids Java Goals Calculator." (Don't be put off by the title, it's a rather interesting site.)

Address: http://tqd.advanced.org/3096/3goal.htm

Steps: Go to the site shown above.

Instructions
Your goal is to acquire $35,000 for a down payment on a house. You currently have $2,000 to invest and can contribute an additional $175 per month to reach your goal. Using the

following returns, compare the length of time it would take to reach your goal and your net investment gain.
(a) 3% (bank deposit)
(b) 5% (T-bill)
(c) 7% (T-bond)
(d) 11% (common stock)
(e) 15% (growth stock)

Answers to Self-Study Questions
1. a   2. d   3. b   4. b   5. c   6. a   7. d   8. a   9. b   10. d
11. a   12. c

CHAPTER 11

Reporting and Analyzing Stockholders' Equity

STUDY OBJECTIVES

After studying this chapter, you should be able to:

1. Identify and discuss the major characteristics of a corporation.
2. Record the issuance of common stock.
3. Explain the accounting for the purchase of treasury stock.
4. Differentiate preferred stock from common stock.
5. Prepare the entries for cash dividends and stock dividends.
6. Identify the items that affect retained earnings.
7. Prepare a comprehensive stockholders' equity section.
8. Evaluate a corporation's dividend and earnings performance from a stockholder's perspective.

What's Cooking?

Here is a riddle for you: What major U.S. corporation got its start 25 years ago with a waffle iron? Hint: It doesn't sell food. Another hint: Swoosh. Another hint: "Just do it." That's right, Nike. In 1971 Nike cofounder, Bill Bowerman, put a piece of rubber into a kitchen waffle iron, and the Waffle (trademark) sole was born. It seems fair to say that at Nike, "They don't make 'em like they used to."

Nike was cofounded by Bowerman and Phil Knight, a member of Bowerman's University of Oregon track team. Each began in the shoe business independently during the early 1960s. Bowerman got his start by making hand-crafted running shoes for his University of Oregon track team. Knight, after completing graduate school, started a small business importing low-cost, high-quality shoes from Japan. In 1964 the two joined forces, each contributing $500, and formed Blue Ribbon Sports, a partnership. At first they marketed Japanese shoes. It wasn't until 1971 that the company began manufacturing its own line of shoes. With the new shoes came a new corporate name—Nike—the Greek goddess of victory. It is hard to imagine that the company that now boasts a stable full of world-class athletes as promoters at one time had part-time employees selling shoes out of car trunks at track meets. Nike's success has been achieved through relentless innovation combined with unbridled promotion.

By 1980 Nike was sufficiently established that it was able to issue its first stock to the public. In that same year it also created a stock ownership program for its employees, allowing them to share in the company's success. Since then Nike has enjoyed phenomenal growth, with 1996 sales reaching $6.5 billion—fully $1.7 billion over 1995 sales.

Nike is not alone in its quest for the top of the sport shoe world. Reebok pushes Nike every step of the way. But recently Reebok stumbled. At the same time that Reebok shareholders watched their stock price slide, Nike shareholders watched their stock soar. Is the

race over? Probably not. The shoe market is fickle, with new styles becoming popular almost daily and vast international markets still lying untapped. Reebok's unwillingness to give up the race was boldly stated in its recent ad campaign: "This is my planet." Whether one of these two giants does eventually take control of the planet remains to be seen. Meanwhile the shareholders sit anxiously in the stands as this Olympic-size drama unfolds.

On the World Wide Web
Nike: http://www.Nike.com
Reebok: http://www.Reebok.com

PREVIEW OF CHAPTER 11

Corporations like Nike and Reebok have substantial resources at their disposal. In fact, the corporation is the dominant form of business organization in the United States in terms of sales, earnings, and number of employees. All of the 500 largest U.S. companies are corporations. In this chapter we look at the essential features of a corporation and explain the accounting for a corporation's capital stock transactions.

The content and organization of this chapter are as follows:

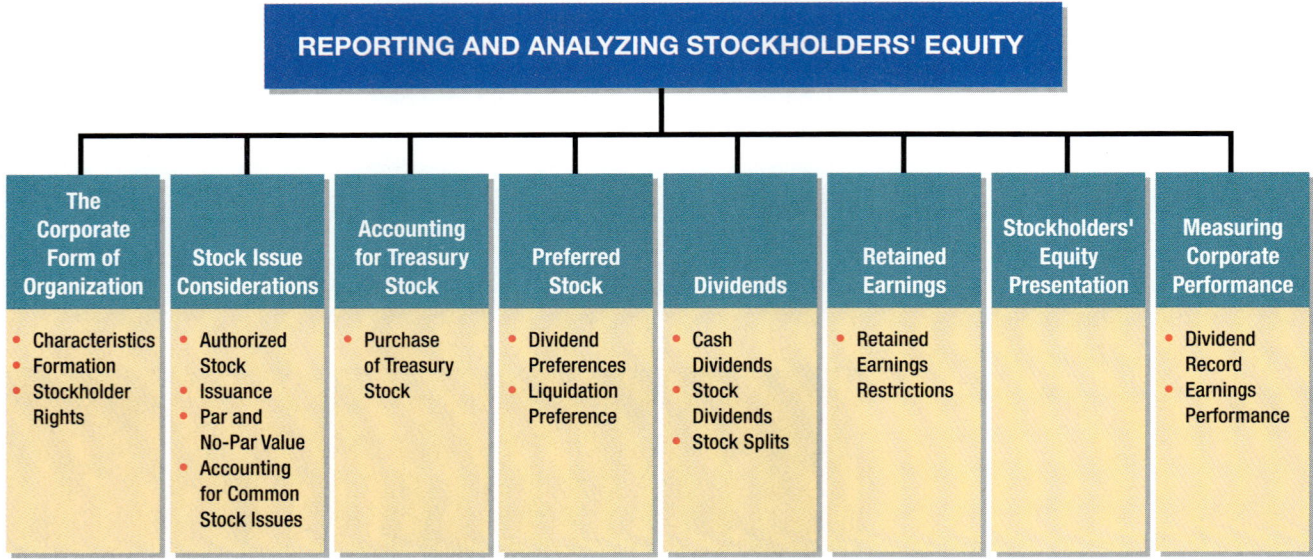

THE CORPORATE FORM OF ORGANIZATION

A corporation is created by law. As a legal entity, a **corporation** has most of the rights and privileges of a person. The major exceptions relate to privileges that can be exercised only by a living person, such as the right to vote or to hold public office. Similarly, a corporation is subject to the same duties and responsibilities as a person; for example, it must abide by the laws and it must pay taxes.

Corporations may be classified in a variety of ways. Two common classifications are **by purpose** and **by ownership.** A corporation may be organized for the purpose of making a profit (such as McDonald's or General Motors), or it may be a nonprofit charitable, medical, or educational corporation (such as the Salvation Army or the American Cancer Society).

Classification by ownership differentiates publicly held and privately held corporations. A **publicly held corporation** may have thousands of stockholders, and its stock is regularly traded on a national securities market such as the New York Stock Exchange. Examples are IBM, Caterpillar, and General Electric. In contrast, a **privately held corporation,** often referred to as a closely held corporation, usually has only a few stockholders, and it does not offer its stock for sale to the general public. Privately held companies are generally much smaller than publicly held companies, although some notable exceptions exist. Cargill Inc., a private corporation that trades in grain and other commodities, is one of the largest companies in the United States.

CHARACTERISTICS OF A CORPORATION

In 1964, when Nike's founders, Knight and Bowerman, were just getting started in the running shoe business, they formed their original organization as a partnership. In 1968 they reorganized the company as a corporation. A number of characteristics distinguish a corporation from proprietorships and partnerships. The most important of these characteristics are explained below.

STUDY OBJECTIVE 1
Identify and discuss the major characteristics of a corporation.

Separate Legal Existence

As an entity separate and distinct from its owners, the corporation acts under its own name rather than in the name of its stockholders. Nike, for example, may buy, own, and sell property, borrow money, and enter into legally binding contracts in its own name. It may also sue or be sued, and it pays its own taxes.

In contrast to a partnership, in which the acts of the owners (partners) bind the partnership, the acts of the owners (stockholders) do not bind the corporation unless such owners are agents of the corporation. For example, if you owned shares of Nike stock, you would not have the right to purchase inventory for the company unless you were designated as an agent of the corporation.

Legal existence separate from owners

Limited Liability of Stockholders

Since a corporation is a separate legal entity, creditors ordinarily have recourse only to corporate assets to satisfy their claims. The liability of stockholders is normally limited to their investment in the corporation, and creditors have no legal claim on the personal assets of the stockholders unless fraud has occurred. Thus, even in the event of bankruptcy of the corporation, stockholders' losses are generally limited to the amount of capital they have invested in the corporation.

Limited liability of stockholders

Transferable Ownership Rights

Ownership of a corporation is shown in shares of capital stock, which are transferable units. Stockholders may dispose of part or all of their interest in a corporation simply by selling their stock. In contrast to the transfer of an ownership interest in a partnership, which requires the consent of each partner, the transfer of stock is entirely at the discretion of the stockholder. It does not require the approval of either the corporation or other stockholders.

The transfer of ownership rights among stockholders normally has no effect on the operating activities of the corporation or on a corporation's assets, liabilities, and total stockholders' equity. That is, the company does not participate in the transfer of these ownership rights after the original sale of the capital stock.

Transferable ownership rights

Ability to Acquire Capital

It generally is relatively easy for a corporation to obtain capital through the issuance of stock. Buying stock in a corporation is often more attractive to an investor than investing in a partnership because a stockholder has limited liability and because shares of stock are readily transferable. Moreover, many individuals can become stockholders by investing small amounts of money. In sum, the ability of a successful corporation to obtain capital is virtually unlimited.

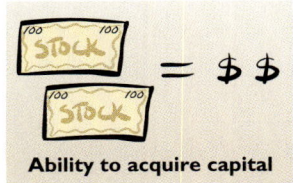
Ability to acquire capital

Continuous life

Continuous Life

The life of a corporation is stated in its charter; it may be perpetual or it may be limited to a specific number of years. If it is limited, the period of existence can be extended through renewal of the charter. Since a corporation is a separate legal entity, the life of a corporation as a going concern is separate from its owners; it is not affected by the withdrawal, death, or incapacity of a stockholder, employee, or officer. As a result, a successful corporation can have a continuous and perpetual life.

Corporation Management

Although stockholders legally own the corporation, they manage it indirectly through a board of directors they elect. Philip Knight is the chairman of Nike's board of directors. Nike's board, in turn, formulates the operating policies for the company and selects officers, such as a president and one or more vice-presidents, to execute policy and to perform daily management functions.

A typical organization chart showing the delegation of responsibility is shown in Illustration 11-1.

Illustration 11-1 Corporation organization chart

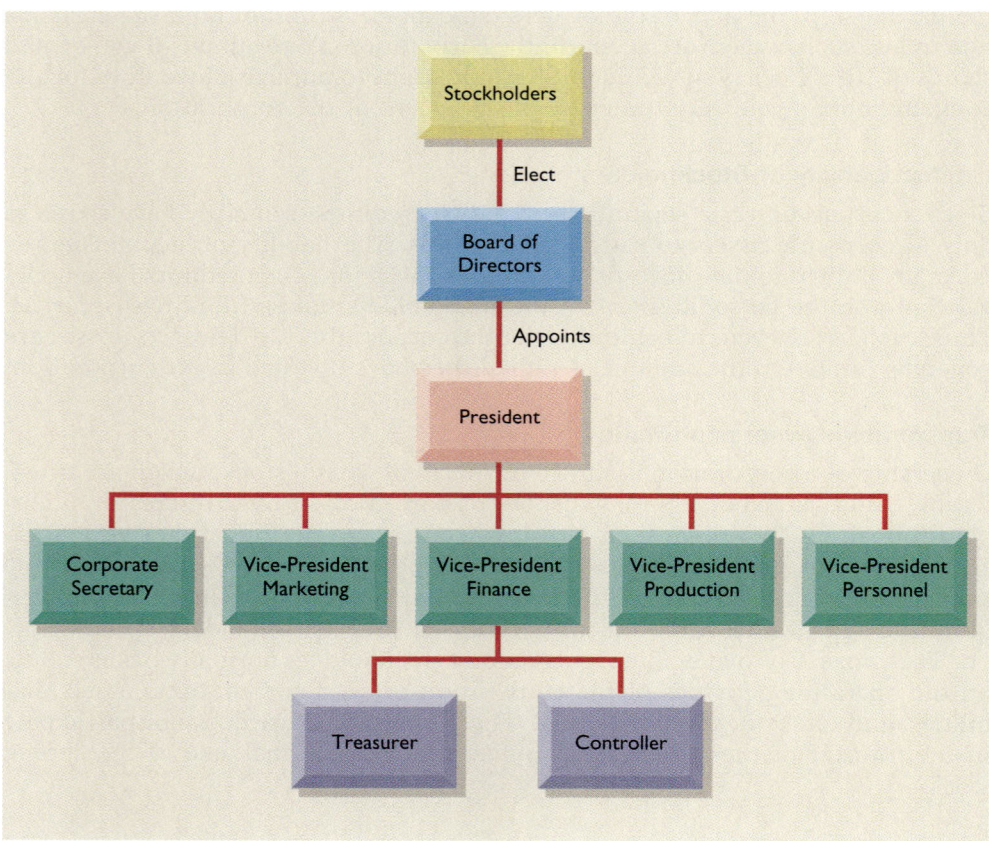

The **president** is the chief executive officer (CEO) with direct responsibility for managing the business. As the organization chart shows, the president delegates responsibility to other officers. The chief accounting officer is the **controller.** The controller's responsibilities include maintaining the accounting records and an adequate system of internal control, and preparing financial statements, tax returns, and internal reports. The **treasurer** has custody of the corporation's funds and is responsible for maintaining the company's cash position.

The organizational structure of a corporation enables a company to hire professional managers to run the business. On the other hand, some view this separation as a weakness. The separation of ownership and management prevents owners from having an active role in managing the company, which some owners like to have.

Government Regulations

A corporation is subject to numerous state and federal regulations. For example, state laws usually prescribe the requirements for issuing stock, the distributions of earnings permitted to stockholders, and the effects of retiring stock. Similarly, federal securities laws govern the sale of capital stock to the general public. Also, most publicly held corporations are required to make extensive disclosure of their financial affairs to the Securities and Exchange Commission through quarterly and annual reports. In addition, when a corporate stock is listed and traded on organized securities markets, the corporation must comply with the reporting requirements of these exchanges.

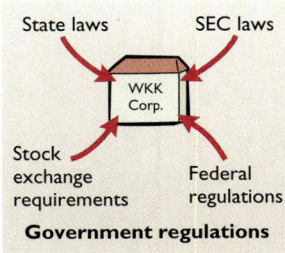

Additional Taxes

For proprietorships and partnerships, the owner's share of earnings is reported on his or her personal income tax return. Taxes are then paid by the individual on this amount. Corporations, on the other hand, must pay federal and state income taxes as a separate legal entity. These taxes are substantial: They can amount to as much as 40% of taxable income.

In addition, stockholders are required to pay taxes on cash dividends. Thus, many argue that corporate income is **taxed twice (double taxation):** once at the corporate level and again at the individual level.

The advantages and disadvantages of a corporation compared to a proprietorship and partnership are shown in Illustration 11-2.

Advantages	Disadvantages
Separate legal existence	Corporation management—separation
Limited liability of stockholders	of ownership and management
Transferable ownership rights	Government regulations
Ability to acquire capital	Additional taxes
Continuous life	
Corporation management—	
professional managers	

Illustration 11-2 Advantages and disadvantages of a corporation

DECISION TOOLKIT

Decision Checkpoints	Info Needed for Decision	Tool to Use for Decision	How to Evaluate Results
Should the company incorporate?	Capital needs, growth expectations, type of business, tax status	Corporations have limited liability, easier capital raising ability, and professional managers; but they suffer from additional taxes, government regulations, and separation of ownership from management.	Must carefully weigh the costs and benefits in light of the particular circumstances.

FORMING A CORPORATION

A corporation is formed by grant of a state charter. Regardless of the number of states in which a corporation has operating divisions, it is incorporated in only one state. It is to the company's advantage to incorporate in a state whose laws are favorable to the corporate form of business organization. For example, although General Motors has its headquarters in Michigan, it is incorporated in New Jersey. In fact, more and more corporations have been incorporating in states with rules that favor existing management. For example, Gulf Oil changed its state of incorporation to Delaware to thwart possible unfriendly takeovers. There, certain defensive tactics against takeovers can be approved by the board of directors alone, without a vote by shareholders.

Upon receipt of its charter from the state of incorporation, the corporation establishes by-laws for conducting its affairs. Corporations engaged in interstate commerce must also obtain a license from each state in which they do business. The license subjects the corporation's operating activities to the general corporation laws of the state.

STOCKHOLDER RIGHTS

When chartered, the corporation may begin selling ownership rights in the form of shares of stock. When a corporation has only one class of stock, it is identified as **common stock.** Each share of common stock gives the stockholder the ownership rights pictured in Illustration 11-3. The ownership rights of a share of stock are stated in the articles of incorporation or in the by-laws.

Illustration 11-3 Ownership rights of stockholders

Stockholders have the right:

1. To vote in election of board of directors at annual meeting. To vote on actions that require stockholder approval.

2. To share the corporate earnings through receipt of dividends.

3. To keep the same percentage ownership when new shares of stock are issued (**preemptive right**[1]).

4. To share in assets upon liquidation in proportion to their holdings. This is called a **residual claim** because owners are paid with assets that remain after all claims have been paid.

---

[1]A number of companies have eliminated the preemptive right because they believe it makes an unnecessary and cumbersome demand on management. For example, IBM, by stockholder approval, has dropped its preemptive right for stockholders.

BUSINESS INSIGHT
International Perspective

In Japan, stockholders are considered to be far less important to a corporation than employees, customers, and suppliers. Stockholders are rarely asked to vote on an issue, and the notion of bending corporate policy to favor stockholders borders on heresy. This attitude toward stockholders appears to be slowly changing, however, as influential Japanese are advocating listening to investors, raising the extremely low dividends paid by Japanese corporations, and improving disclosure of financial information.

Proof of stock ownership is evidenced by a printed or engraved form known as a **stock certificate.** As shown in Illustration 11-4, the face of the certificate shows the name of the corporation, the stockholder's name, the class and special features of the stock, the number of shares owned, and the signatures of duly authorized corporate officials. Certificates are prenumbered to facilitate their accountability; they may be issued for any quantity of shares.

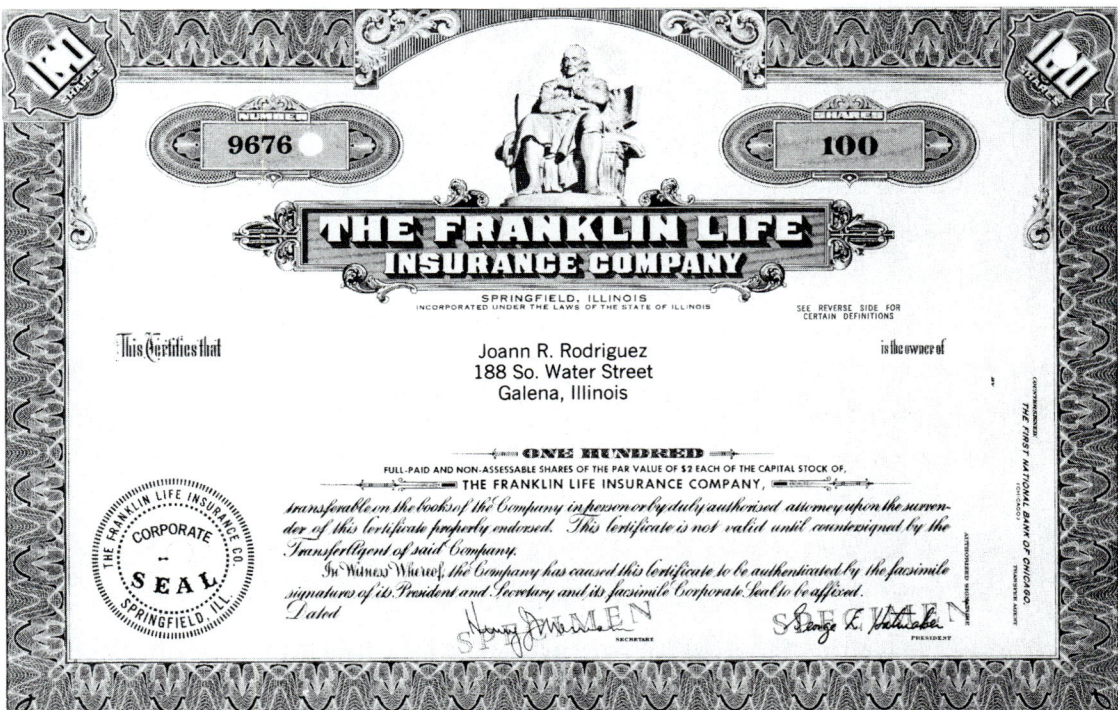

Illustration 11-4 A stock certificate

BEFORE YOU GO ON . . .

● **Review It**
1. What are the advantages and disadvantages of a corporation compared to a proprietorship and a partnership?
2. Identify the principal steps in forming a corporation.
3. What rights are inherent in owning a share of stock in a corporation?

STOCK ISSUE CONSIDERATIONS

Although Nike incorporated in 1968, it did not sell stock to the public until 1980. At that time Nike evidently decided it would benefit from the infusion of cash that a public sale of its shares would bring. When a corporation decides to issue stock, it must resolve a number of basic questions: How many shares should be authorized for sale? How should the stock be issued? At what price should the shares be issued? What value should be assigned to the stock? These questions are answered in the following sections.

AUTHORIZED STOCK

The amount of stock that a corporation is authorized to sell is indicated in its charter. If all **authorized stock** is sold, then a corporation must obtain consent of the state to amend its charter before it can issue additional shares.

The authorization of common stock does not result in a formal accounting entry because the event has no immediate effect on either corporate assets or stockholders' equity. However, disclosure of the number of shares authorized is required in the stockholders' equity section of the balance sheet.

ISSUANCE OF STOCK

International Note
U.S. and U.K. corporations raise most of their capital through millions of outside shareholders and bondholders. In contrast, companies in Germany, France, and Japan acquire financing from large banks or other institutions. Consequently, in the latter environment, shareholders are less important, and external reporting and auditing receive less emphasis.

A corporation has the choice of issuing common stock directly to investors or indirectly through an investment banking firm that specializes in bringing securities to the attention of prospective investors. Direct issue is typical in closely held companies, whereas indirect issue is customary for a publicly held corporation. New issues of stock may be offered for sale to the public through various organized U.S. securities exchanges: the New York Stock Exchange, the American Stock Exchange, and 13 regional exchanges. Stock may also be traded on the "over-the-counter" (OTC) market.

How does a corporation set the price for a new issue of stock? Among the factors to be considered are (1) the company's anticipated future earnings, (2) its expected dividend rate per share, (3) its current financial position, (4) the current state of the economy, and (5) the current state of the securities market. The calculation can be complex and is properly the subject of a finance course.

PAR AND NO-PAR VALUE STOCKS

Par value stock is capital stock that has been assigned a value per share in the corporate charter. The par value may be any amount selected by the corporation. Generally, the par value is quite low because states often levy a tax on the corporation based on its par value. For example, Reebok has a par of 1 cent, IBM has a par of $1.25, Ford Motor Company $1 par, General Motors Corporation $1.67, and PepsiCo $1\frac{2}{3}$ cents.

The significance of par value is a legal matter. Par value represents the **legal capital** per share that must be retained in the business for the protection of corporate creditors; that is, it is not available for withdrawal by stockholders. Thus, in the past, most states required the corporation to sell its shares at par or above. Today many states do not require a par value. Its usefulness as a protective device to creditors was questionable because par value was often immaterial relative to the value of the company's stock—even at the time of issue. For example, Reebok's par value is $.01 per share, yet a new issue in 1997 would have sold at a **market value** in the $30 per share range. Thus, par has no relationship with market value and in the vast majority of cases is an immaterial amount.

No-par value stock is capital stock that has not been assigned a value in the corporate charter. No-par value stock is often issued because some confusion still exists concerning par value and fair market value. If shares have no par value, then the questionable treatment of using par value as a basis for fair market value never arises. The major disadvantage of no-par stock is that some states levy a high tax on the shares issued.

No-par value stock is quite common today. For example, Nike, Procter & Gamble, and North American Van Lines all have no-par stock. In many states the board of directors is permitted to assign a **stated value** to the no-par shares, which then becomes the legal capital per share. The stated value of no-par stock may be changed at any time by action of the directors. Stated value, like par value, does not indicate or correspond to the market value of the stock. When there is no assigned stated value, the **entire proceeds received upon issuance of the stock is considered to be legal capital.**

The key point to remember is that legal capital per share always establishes the credit to the Common Stock account. The relationship of par and no-par value to legal capital is summarized in Illustration 11-5.

Stock	Legal Capital Per Share
Par value	→ Par value
No-par value with stated value	→ Stated value
No-par value without stated value	→ Entire proceeds

Illustration 11-5 Relationship of par and no-par value stock to legal capital

As will be explained later, the Common Stock account is credited for the legal capital per share each time stock is issued.

ACCOUNTING FOR COMMON STOCK ISSUES

The stockholders' equity section of a corporation's balance sheet includes: (1) **paid-in (contributed) capital** and (2) **retained earnings (earned capital).** The distinction between paid-in capital and retained earnings is important from both a legal and an economic point of view. **Paid-in capital** is the amount paid in to the corporation by stockholders in exchange for shares of ownership. *Retained earnings* is earned capital held for future use in the business. In this section we discuss the accounting for paid-in capital. In a later section we discuss retained earnings.

Let's now look at how to account for new issues of common stock. The primary objectives in accounting for the issuance of common stock are to (1) identify the specific sources of paid-in capital and (2) maintain the distinction between paid-in capital and retained earnings. As shown below, **the issuance of common stock affects only paid-in capital accounts.**

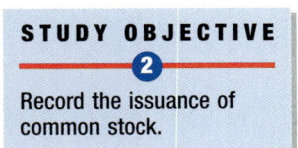

Record the issuance of common stock.

As discussed earlier, par value does not indicate a stock's market value. The cash proceeds from issuing par value stock may be equal to, greater than, or less than par value. When the issuance of common stock for cash is recorded, the par value of the shares is credited to Common Stock, and the portion of the proceeds that is above or below par value is recorded in a separate paid-in capital account.

To illustrate, assume that Hydro-Slide, Inc., issues 1,000 shares of $1 par value common stock at par for cash. The entry to record this transaction is:

Cash	1,000	
Common Stock		1,000
(To record issuance of 1,000 shares of $1 par common stock at par)		

Helpful Hint Stock is sometimes issued in exchange for services (payment to attorneys or consultants, for example) or other noncash assets (land or buildings). The accounting for such stock issues is beyond the scope of this book. Here we look at only the issuance of par value common stock in exchange for cash.

496 CHAPTER 11 Reporting and Analyzing Stockholders' Equity

If Hydro-Slide, Inc., issues an additional 1,000 shares of the $1 par value common stock for cash at $5 per share, the entry is:

Cash	5,000	
Common Stock		1,000
Paid-in Capital in Excess of Par Value		4,000
(To record issuance of 1,000 shares of common stock in excess of par)		

The total paid-in capital from these two transactions is $6,000, and the legal capital is $2,000. If Hydro-Slide, Inc., has retained earnings of $27,000, the stockholders' equity section of the balance sheet is as shown in Illustration 11-6.

Illustration 11-6 Stockholders' equity—paid-in capital in excess of par value

HYDRO-SLIDE, INC.
Partial Balance Sheet

Stockholders' equity	
Paid-in capital	
Common stock	$ 2,000
Paid-in capital in excess of par value	**4,000**
Total paid-in capital	6,000
Retained earnings	27,000
Total stockholders' equity	$33,000

Some companies issue no-par stock with a stated value. For accounting purposes, the stated value is treated in the same fashion as the par value. For example, if in our Hydro-Slide example above the stock was no-par stock with a stated value of $1, the entries would be the same as those presented for the par stock except the term "Par Value" would be replaced with "Stated Value." If a company issues no-par stock that does not have a stated value, then the full amount received is credited to the Common Stock account. In this case, there is no need for the Paid-in Capital in Excess of Stated Value account.

BUSINESS INSIGHT
Investor Perspective

The stock of publicly held companies is traded on organized exchanges at dollar prices per share established by the interaction between buyers and sellers. For each listed security the financial press reports the high and low prices of the stock during the year, the total volume of stock traded on a given day, the high and low prices for the day, and the closing market price, with the net change for the day. Nike is listed on the New York Stock Exchange. Here is a recent listing for Nike:

	52 Weeks		Sales				
Stock	High	Low	1/23	High	Low	Close	Net change
Nike	$67\frac{1}{4}$	$31\frac{3}{4}$	13714	$67\frac{7}{8}$	66	$67\frac{5}{8}$	$+1\frac{1}{2}$

These numbers indicate that the high and low market prices for the last 52 weeks have been $67\frac{1}{4}$ and $31\frac{3}{4}$; the trading volume for January 23 was 1,371,400 shares; the high, low, and closing prices for that date were $67\frac{7}{8}$, 66, and $67\frac{5}{8}$, respectively; and the net change for the day was an increase of $1\frac{1}{2}$ or $1.50 per share.

The trading of common stock on securities exchanges involves the transfer of already issued shares from an existing stockholder to another investor. Consequently, these transactions have no impact on a corporation's stockholders' equity section.

BEFORE YOU GO ON . . .

● **Review It**

1. Of what significance to a corporation is the amount of authorized stock?
2. What alternative approaches may a corporation use to sell new shares to investors?
3. Distinguish between par value and market value.
4. Explain the accounting for par and no-par common stock issued for cash.

● **Do It**

Cayman Corporation begins operations on March 1 by issuing 100,000 shares of $10 par value common stock for cash at $12 per share. Journalize the issuance of the shares.

Reasoning: In issuing shares for cash, common stock is credited for par value per share and any additional proceeds are credited to a separate paid-in capital account.

Solution:

Mar. 1	Cash	1,200,000	
	Common Stock		1,000,000
	Paid-in Capital in Excess of Par Value		200,000
	(To record issuance of 100,000 shares at $12 per share)		

ACCOUNTING FOR TREASURY STOCK

Treasury stock is a corporation's own stock that has been issued, fully paid for, reacquired by the corporation and held in its treasury for future use. A corporation may acquire treasury stock to meet any of these objectives:

1. Reissue the shares to officers and employees under bonus and stock compensation plans.
2. Increase trading of the company's stock in the securities market in the hopes of enhancing its market value.
3. Have additional shares available for use in the acquisition of other companies.
4. Reduce the number of shares outstanding and thereby increase earnings per share.

STUDY OBJECTIVE 3
Explain the accounting for the purchase of treasury stock.

Another infrequent reason for purchasing treasury shares is that management may want to eliminate hostile shareholders by buying them out.

Many corporations have treasury stock. For example, one survey of 600 companies in the United States found that 64% have treasury stock.[2] Specifically,

Helpful Hint Treasury stock is so named because the company often holds the shares in its treasury for safekeeping.

---
[2]*Accounting Trends & Techniques 1996* (New York: American Institute of Certified Public Accountants).

Kellogg Company recently reported 94.4 million treasury shares, PepsiCo 75 million, and Phillip Morris Company 82.5 million.

BUSINESS INSIGHT
Management Perspective

Both Nike and Reebok have repurchased many shares in recent years. During 1994 and 1995 Nike repurchased roughly 5 million of its shares—about 10% of those outstanding. Nike's stock price has soared since then. Thus, the stock repurchase worked out well for those investors who kept their shares. With fewer shares outstanding, the surge in Nike's profits dramatically increased the price of the remaining shares.

Reebok, in a bold (and some would say very risky) move in late 1996, bought back nearly a *third* of its shares. This decision was risky because the repurchase of shares dramatically reduced Reebok's available cash. In fact, the company borrowed significant funds to accomplish the repurchase. In a press release, management stated that it was repurchasing the shares because it believed that the stock was severely underpriced. The repurchase of so many shares was meant to signal management's belief in good future earnings. Skeptics, however, suggest that Reebok's management is repurchasing shares to make it less likely that the company will be taken over by a different company (in which case Reebok's top managers would likely lose their jobs). By depleting its cash Reebok is less likely to be acquired because acquiring companies like to purchase companies with large cash reserves so they can pay off debt used in the acquisition. Time will tell whether the Reebok investors who chose to hold onto their shares benefit as much as the Nike investors did, or whether the cash strain caused by the repurchase only magnifies Reebok's troubles.

PURCHASE OF TREASURY STOCK

The purchase of treasury stock is generally accounted for by the **cost method.** This method derives its name from the fact that the Treasury Stock account is maintained at the cost of shares purchased. None of the values (par, stated, or legal) is involved in recording treasury stock transactions. Under the cost method, **Treasury Stock is increased (debited) by the price paid to reacquire the shares; Treasury Stock decreases by the same amount when the shares are later sold.**

To illustrate, assume that on January 1, 1998, the stockholders' equity section for Mead, Inc., has 100,000 shares of $5 par value common stock outstanding (all issued at par value) and Retained Earnings of $200,000. The stockholders' equity section of the balance sheet before purchase of treasury stock is as shown in Illustration 11-7.

Illustration 11-7 Stockholders' equity with no treasury stock

MEAD, INC.
Partial Balance Sheet

Stockholders' equity	
Paid-in capital	
Common stock, $5 par value, 100,000 shares issued and outstanding	$500,000
Retained earnings	200,000
Total stockholders' equity	$700,000

On February 1, 1998, Mead acquires 4,000 shares of its stock at $8 per share. The entry is:

Feb. 1	Treasury Stock	32,000	
	Cash		32,000
	(To record purchase of 4,000 shares of treasury stock at $8 per share)		

The Treasury Stock account would increase by the cost of the shares purchased ($32,000). The original paid-in capital account, Common Stock, would not be affected because **the number of issued shares does not change.** Treasury stock is deducted from total paid-in capital and retained earnings in the stockholders' equity section of the balance sheet, as shown in Illustration 11-8 for Mead, Inc. Thus, the acquisition of treasury stock reduces stockholders' equity.

Helpful Hint Treasury Stock is a contra stockholders' equity account.

Illustration 11-8 Stockholders' equity with treasury stock

MEAD, INC.
Partial Balance Sheet

Stockholders' equity	
Paid-in capital	
Common stock, $5 par value, 100,000 shares issued and 96,000 shares outstanding	$500,000
Retained earnings	200,000
Total paid-in capital and retained earnings	700,000
Less: Treasury stock (4,000 shares)	**32,000**
Total stockholders' equity	$668,000

Both the number of shares issued (100,000) and the number in the treasury (4,000) are disclosed. The difference is the number of shares of stock outstanding (96,000). The term **outstanding stock** means the number of shares of issued stock that are being held by stockholders.

Some maintain that treasury stock should be reported as an asset because it can be sold for cash. Under this reasoning, unissued stock (stock that has been authorized but not issued) should also be shown as an asset, clearly an erroneous conclusion. Rather than being an asset, treasury stock reduces stockholder claims on corporate assets. This effect is correctly shown by reporting treasury stock as a deduction from total paid-in capital and retained earnings.

BEFORE YOU GO ON . . .

● **Review It**

1. What is treasury stock, and why do companies acquire it?
2. How is treasury stock recorded?
3. Where is treasury stock reported in the financial statements?

● **Do It**

Santa Anita Inc. purchases 3,000 shares of its $50 par value common stock for $180,000 cash on July 1. The shares are to be held in the treasury until resold. Journalize the treasury stock transaction.

Reasoning: The purchase of treasury stock is recorded at cost.

Solution:

July 1	Treasury Stock	180,000	
	Cash		180,000
	(To record the purchase of 3,000 shares at $60 per share)		

PREFERRED STOCK

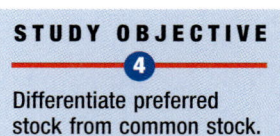

STUDY OBJECTIVE 4
Differentiate preferred stock from common stock.

To appeal to a larger segment of potential investors, a corporation may issue a class of stock in addition to common stock, called preferred stock. **Preferred stock** has contractual provisions that give it preference or priority over common stock in certain areas. Typically, preferred stockholders have a priority in relation to (1) dividends and (2) assets in the event of liquidation. However, they often do not have voting rights. Reebok has no outstanding preferred stock, while Nike has a very minor amount outstanding. A recent survey of 600 companies indicated that 25% have one or more classes of preferred stock.

Like common stock, preferred stock may be issued for cash or for noncash consideration. The entries for these transactions are similar to the entries for common stock. When a corporation has more than one class of stock, each paid-in capital account title should identify the stock to which it relates (e.g., Preferred Stock, Common Stock, Paid-in Capital in Excess of Par Value—Preferred Stock, and Paid-in Capital in Excess of Par Value—Common Stock). Assume that Stine Corporation issues 10,000 shares of $10 par value preferred stock for $12 cash per share. The entry to record the issuance is:

Cash	120,000	
Preferred Stock		100,000
Paid-in Capital in Excess of Par Value—Preferred Stock		20,000
(To record the issuance of 10,000 shares of $10 par value preferred stock)		

Preferred stock may have either a par value or no-par value. For example, Walgreen Drug Co. has $.50 par value preferred and General Motors has three classes of no-par preferred stock, each with a stated value of $100. In the stockholders' equity section of the balance sheet, preferred stock is shown first because of its dividend and liquidation preferences over common stock.

DIVIDEND PREFERENCES

As indicated before, **preferred stockholders have the right to share in the distribution of corporate income before common stockholders.** For example, if the dividend rate on preferred stock is $5 per share, common shareholders will not receive any dividends in the current year until preferred stockholders have received $5 per share. The first claim to dividends does not, however, **guarantee** dividends. Dividends depend on many factors, such as adequate retained earnings and availability of cash.

For preferred stock, the per share dividend amount is stated as a percentage of the par value of the stock or as a specified amount. For example, Crane Company specifies a $3\frac{3}{4}$% dividend on its $100 par value preferred ($100 × $3\frac{3}{4}$% = $3.75 per share), whereas Nike pays 10 cents per share on its $1 par preferred stock.

Cumulative Dividend

Preferred stock contracts often contain a **cumulative dividend** feature. This right means that preferred stockholders must be paid both current-year dividends and any unpaid prior-year dividends before common stockholders receive dividends. When preferred stock is cumulative, preferred dividends not declared in a given period are called **dividends in arrears.** To illustrate, assume that Scientific-Leasing has 5,000 shares of 7%, $100 par value cumulative preferred stock outstanding. The annual dividend is $35,000 (5,000 × $7 per share). If dividends are 2 years in arrears, preferred stockholders are entitled to receive the dividends as shown in Illustration 11-9 in the current year before any distribution may be made to common stockholders.

Dividends in arrears ($35,000 × 2)	$ 70,000
Current-year dividends	35,000
Total preferred dividends	**$105,000**

Illustration 11-9 Computation of total dividends to preferred stock

Dividends in arrears are not considered a liability. No obligation exists until a dividend is declared by the board of directors. However, the amount of dividends in arrears should be disclosed in the notes to the financial statements. Doing so enables investors to assess the potential impact of this commitment on the corporation's financial position.

Dividends cannot be paid on common stock while any dividend on preferred stock is in arrears. The cumulative feature is often critical in selling a preferred stock issue to investors. When preferred stock is noncumulative, a dividend passed in any year is lost forever. Companies that are unable to meet their dividend obligations are not looked upon favorably by the investment community. As a financial officer noted in discussing one company's failure to pay its cumulative preferred dividend for a period of time, "Not meeting your obligations on something like that is a major black mark on your record."

BUSINESS INSIGHT
Investor Perspective

Dividends in arrears can extend for fairly long periods of time. Long Island Lighting Company's directors voted at one time to make up some $390 million in preferred dividends that had been in arrears since 1984 and to resume normal quarterly preferred payments. The announcement resulted from an agreement between the company and New York State to abandon a nuclear power plant in exchange for sizable rate increases over the next 10 years.

LIQUIDATION PREFERENCE

Most preferred stocks have a preference on corporate assets if the corporation fails. This feature provides security for the preferred stockholder. The preference to assets may be for the par value of the shares or for a specified liquidating value. For example, Commonwealth Edison issued preferred stock that entitles the holders to receive $31.80 per share, plus accrued and unpaid dividends, in the event of involuntary liquidation. The liquidation preference is used in litigation pertaining to bankruptcy lawsuits involving the respective claims of creditors and preferred stockholders.

DIVIDENDS

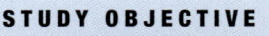

STUDY OBJECTIVE 5
Prepare the entries for cash dividends and stock dividends.

As noted earlier, a **dividend** is a distribution by a corporation to its stockholders on a pro rata basis. *Pro rata* means that if you own, say, 10% of the common shares, you will receive 10% of the dividend. Dividends can take four forms: cash, property, script (promissory note to pay cash), or stock. Cash dividends, which predominate in practice, and stock dividends, which are declared with some frequency, are the focus of our discussion.

Investors are very interested in a company's dividend practices. In the financial press, **dividends are generally reported quarterly as a dollar amount per share,** although sometimes they are reported on an annual basis. For example, Nike's **annual** dividend rate recently was 40 cents per share, whereas the recent **quarterly** rate for J.C. Penney Company was 42 cents and for PepsiCo it was 18 cents.

CASH DIVIDENDS

A **cash dividend** is a pro rata distribution of cash to stockholders. For a corporation to pay a cash dividend, it must have the following:

1. **Retained earnings.** In many states, payment of dividends from legal capital is illegal. Payment of dividends from paid-in capital in excess of par is legal in some states. **Payment of dividends from retained earnings is legal in all states.** In addition, companies are frequently constrained by agreements with their lenders to pay dividends only from retained earnings.

2. **Adequate cash.** Recently Nike had a balance in retained earnings of $1,838 million but a cash balance of only $216 million. Thus, in order to pay a dividend equal to its retained earnings, Nike would have to raise $1,622 million more in cash. It is unlikely it would do this because a dividend of this size would not be sustainable in the future (that is, Nike would not be able to pay this much in dividends in future years). In addition, such a dividend would completely deplete Nike's balance in retained earnings, so it would not be able to pay a dividend in the next year unless it had positive net income.

3. **Declared dividends.** The board of directors has full authority to determine the amount of income to be distributed in the form of dividends and the amount to be retained in the business. Dividends do not accrue like interest on a note payable, and they are not a liability until declared.

The amount and timing of a dividend are important issues for management to consider. The payment of a large cash dividend could lead to liquidity problems for the enterprise. Conversely, a small dividend or a missed dividend may cause unhappiness among stockholders who expect to receive a reasonable cash payment from the company on a periodic basis. Many companies declare and pay cash dividends quarterly. On the other hand, a number of high-growth companies pay no dividends, preferring to retain earnings and use them to finance capital expenditures.

In order to remain in business, companies must honor their interest payments to creditors, bankers, and bondholders. But the payment of dividends to stockholders is another matter. Many companies can survive, and even thrive, without such payouts. "Why give money to those strangers?" is the response of one company president. Investors must keep an eye on the company's dividend policy and understand what it may mean. For most companies, for example, regular dividend boosts in the face of irregular earnings can be a warning signal. Companies with high dividends and rising debt may be borrowing money to pay shareholders. On the other hand, low dividends may not be a negative sign because they may mean high returns through market appreciation. Presumably, investors for whom regular dividends are important tend to buy stock in companies that pay periodic dividends, and those for whom growth in the stock price (capital gains) is more important tend to buy stock in companies that retain earnings.

Entries for Cash Dividends

Three dates are important in connection with dividends: (1) the declaration date, (2) the record date, and (3) the payment date. Normally there is a time span of 2 to 4 weeks between each date. Accounting entries are required on two of the dates: the declaration date and the payment date.

On the **declaration date,** the board of directors formally declares (authorizes) the cash dividend and announces it to stockholders. The declaration of a cash dividend **commits the corporation to a binding legal obligation** that cannot be rescinded. Thus, an entry is required to recognize the decrease in retained earnings and the increase in the liability Dividends Payable. To illustrate, assume that on December 1, 1998, the directors of Media General declare a $.50 per share cash dividend on 100,000 shares of $10 par value common stock. The dividend is $50,000 (100,000 × $.50), and the entry to record the declaration is:

Declaration Date

Dec. 1	Retained Earnings	50,000	
	Dividends Payable		50,000
	(To record declaration of cash dividend)		

Dividends Payable is a current liability because it will normally be paid within the next several months. Instead of decreasing Retained Earnings, the account Dividends may be increased (debited). This account provides additional information in the ledger. For example, a company may have separate dividend accounts for each class of stock. When a dividend account is used, its balance is transferred to Retained Earnings at the end of the year by a closing entry. Consequently, the effect of the declaration is the same: Retained earnings is decreased and a current liability is increased. For homework problems, you should use the Retained Earnings account for recording dividend declarations.

The **record date** marks the time when ownership of the outstanding shares is determined for dividend purposes. The stockholders' records maintained by the corporation supply this information. The time interval between the declaration date and the record date enables the corporation to update its stock ownership records. Between the declaration date and the record date, the number of shares outstanding should remain the same. Thus, the purpose of the record date is to identify the persons or entities that will receive the dividend, not to determine the amount of the dividend liability. For Media General, the record date is December 22. No entry is required on this date because the corporation's liability recognized on the declaration date is unchanged:

Helpful Hint The record date is important in determining the dividend to be paid to each stockholder but not the total dividend.

Record Date

Dec. 22 | No entry necessary

On the **payment date,** dividend checks are mailed to the stockholders and the payment of the dividend is recorded. If January 20 is the payment date for

504 CHAPTER 11 Reporting and Analyzing Stockholders' Equity

Media General, the entry on that date is:

Payment Date

Jan. 20	Dividends Payable	50,000	
	Cash		50,000
	(To record payment of cash dividend)		

Note that payment of the dividend reduces both current assets and current liabilities but has no effect on stockholders' equity. The cumulative effect of the **declaration and payment** of a cash dividend on a company's financial statements is to **decrease both stockholders' equity and total assets.**

STOCK DIVIDENDS

A **stock dividend** is a pro rata distribution of the corporation's own stock to stockholders. Whereas a cash dividend is paid in cash, a stock dividend is paid in stock. **A stock dividend results in a decrease in retained earnings and an increase in paid-in capital.** Unlike a cash dividend, a stock dividend does not decrease total stockholders' equity or total assets.

Because a stock dividend does not result in a distribution of assets, many view it as nothing more than a publicity gesture. Stock dividends are often issued by companies that do not have adequate cash to issue a cash dividend. These companies may not want to announce that they are not going to be issuing a dividend at their normal time to do so. By issuing a stock dividend they "save face" by giving the appearance of distributing a dividend. Note that since a stock dividend neither increases nor decreases the assets in the company, investors are not receiving anything they didn't already own. In a sense it is like ordering two pieces of pie and having the host take one piece of pie and cut it into two smaller pieces. You are not better off, but you got your two pieces of pie.

To illustrate a stock dividend, assume that you have a 2% ownership interest in Cetus Inc. by virtue of owning 20 of its 1,000 shares of common stock. In a 10% stock dividend, 100 shares (1,000 × 10%) of stock would be issued. You would receive two shares (2% × 100), but your ownership interest would remain at 2% (22 ÷ 1,100). **You now own more shares of stock, but your ownership interest has not changed.** Moreover, no cash is disbursed, and no liabilities have been assumed by the corporation.

What then are the purposes and benefits of a stock dividend? Corporations generally issue stock dividends for one of the following reasons:

Helpful Hint Because of its effects, a stock dividend is also referred to as capitalizing retained earnings.

1. To satisfy stockholders' dividend expectations without spending cash.
2. To increase the marketability of its stock by increasing the number of shares outstanding and thereby decreasing the market price per share. Decreasing the market price of the stock makes it easier for smaller investors to purchase the shares.
3. To emphasize that a portion of stockholders' equity has been permanently reinvested in the business and therefore is unavailable for cash dividends.

The size of the stock dividend and the value to be assigned to each dividend share are determined by the board of directors when the dividend is declared. The per share amount must be at least equal to the par or stated value in order to meet legal requirements.

The accounting profession distinguishes between a **small stock dividend** (less than 20%–25% of the corporation's issued stock) and a **large stock dividend** (greater than 20%–25%). It recommends that the directors assign the **fair market value per share** for small stock dividends. The recommendation is based on the assumption that a small stock dividend will have little effect on the market price of the shares previously outstanding. Thus, many stockholders consider small stock dividends to be distributions of earnings equal to the fair market value of the shares distributed. The amount to be assigned for a large stock dividend is not specified by the accounting profession; however, **par or stated value per share** is normally assigned. Small stock dividends predominate in practice. Thus, we illustrate only the entries for small stock dividends.

Entries for Stock Dividends

To illustrate the accounting for stock dividends, assume that Medland Corporation has a balance of $300,000 in retained earnings and declares a 10% stock dividend on its 50,000 shares of $10 par value common stock. The current fair market value of its stock is $15 per share. The number of shares to be issued is 5,000 (10% × 50,000), and the total amount to be debited to Retained Earnings is $75,000 (5,000 × $15). The entry to record this transaction at the declaration date is:

Retained Earnings	75,000	
Common Stock Dividends Distributable		50,000
Paid-in Capital in Excess of Par Value		25,000
(To record declaration of 10% stock dividend)		

Note that at the declaration date Retained Earnings is decreased (debited) for the fair market value of the stock issued; Common Stock Dividends Distributable is increased (credited) for the par value of the dividend shares (5,000 × $10); and the excess over par (5,000 × $5) is credited to an additional paid-in capital account.

Common Stock Dividends Distributable is a stockholders' equity account; it is not a liability because assets will not be used to pay the dividend. If a balance sheet is prepared before the dividend shares are issued, the distributable account is reported in paid-in capital as an addition to common stock issued, as shown in Illustration 11-10.

MEDLAND CORPORATION
Partial Balance Sheet

Paid-in capital		
Common stock	$500,000	
Common stock dividends distributable	50,000	$550,000

Illustration 11-10 Statement presentation of common stock dividends distributable

When the dividend shares are issued, Common Stock Dividends Distributable is decreased and Common Stock is increased as follows:

Helpful Hint Note that the dividend account title is *distributable*, not *payable*.

Common Stock Dividends Distributable	50,000	
Common Stock		50,000
(To record issuance of 5,000 shares in a stock dividend)		

Effects of Stock Dividends

How do stock dividends affect stockholders' equity? They **change the composition of stockholders' equity** because a portion of retained earnings is transferred to paid-in capital. However, **total stockholders' equity remains the same.** Stock dividends also have no effect on the par or stated value per share, but the number of shares outstanding increases. These effects are shown in Illustration 11-11 for Medland Corporation.

Illustration 11-11 Stock dividend effects

	Before Dividend	After Dividend
Stockholders' equity		
Paid-in capital		
Common stock, $10 par	$500,000	$550,000
Paid-in capital in excess of par value	—	25,000
Total paid-in capital	500,000	575,000
Retained earnings	300,000	225,000
Total stockholders' equity	**$800,000**	**$800,000**
Outstanding shares	**50,000**	**55,000**

In this example, total paid-in capital is increased by $75,000 and retained earnings is decreased by the same amount. Note also that total stockholders' equity remains unchanged at $800,000.

STOCK SPLITS

A **stock split,** like a stock dividend, involves the issuance of additional shares of stock to stockholders according to their percentage ownership. However, **a stock split results in a reduction in the par or stated value per share.** The purpose of a stock split is to increase the marketability of the stock by lowering its market value per share. This, in turn, makes it easier for the corporation to issue additional stock.

The effect of a split on market value is generally inversely proportional to the size of the split. For example, after a 4-for-1 stock split, the market value of IBM stock fell from $284 to approximately $71. In announcing the split, the chief executive of IBM said, "We want to make our stock more attractive to the small investor." Similarly, on September 9, 1995, Nike announced a 2-for-1 stock split. The record date was October 9, 1995, and the payment date was October 30, 1995. Nike's stock was trading at $111 just prior to the split and at roughly $55 after the split. Within 1 year it was trading above $100 again.

Helpful Hint A stock split changes the par value per share but does not affect any balances in stockholders' equity.

In a stock split, the number of shares is increased in the same proportion that the par or stated value per share is decreased. For example, in a 2-for-1 split, one share of $10 par value stock is exchanged for two shares of $5 par value stock. **A stock split does not have any effect on total paid-in capital, retained earnings, and total stockholders' equity.** However, the number of shares outstanding increases. These effects are shown in Illustration 11-12, assuming that instead of issuing a 10% stock dividend, Medland splits its 50,000 shares of common stock on a 2-for-1 basis.

Illustration 11-12 Stock split effects

	Before Stock Split	After Stock Split
Stockholders' equity		
Paid-in capital		
Common stock	$500,000	$500,000
Paid-in capital in excess of par value	0	0
Total paid-in capital	500,000	500,000
Retained earnings	300,000	300,000
Total stockholders' equity	**$800,000**	**$800,000**
Outstanding shares	**50,000**	**100,000**

Because a stock split does not affect the balances in any stockholders' equity accounts, **it is not necessary to journalize a stock split.** Significant differences between the effects of stock splits and stock dividends are shown in Illustration 11-13.

Item	Stock Split	Stock Dividend
Total paid-in capital	No change	Increase
Total retained earnings	No change	Decrease
Total par value (common stock)	No change	Increase
Par value per share	Decrease	No change

Illustration 11-13
Effects of stock splits and stock dividends differentiated

BUSINESS INSIGHT
Management Perspective

A handful of U.S. companies have no intention of keeping their stock trading in a range accessible to mere mortals. These companies never split their stock, no matter how high their stock price gets. The king of these is investment company Berkshire Hathaway's Class A stock, which goes for a pricey $32,000—per share! The company's Class B stock is a relative bargain at roughly $1,000 per share. Other "premium" stocks are A.D. Makepeace at $9,000 and Mechanics Bank of Richmond, California, at $9,600.

Source: Bill Alpert, "Big Boppers," *Barrons*, June 24, 1996, p. 17.

BEFORE YOU GO ON . . .

● **Review It**

1. What factors affect the size of a company's cash dividend?
2. Why do companies issue stock dividends? Why do companies declare stock splits?
3. Distinguish between a small and a large stock dividend and indicate the basis for valuing each kind of dividend.
4. Contrast the effects of a small stock dividend and a 2-for-1 stock split on (a) stockholders' equity and (b) outstanding shares.

● **Do It**

Due to 5 years of record earnings at Sing CD Corporation, the market price of its 500,000 shares of $2 par value common stock tripled from $15 per share to $45. During this period, paid-in capital remained the same at $2,000,000, but retained earnings increased from $1,500,000 to $10,000,000. President Joan Elbert is considering either a 10% stock dividend or a 2-for-1 stock split. She asks you to show the before and after effects of each option on retained earnings.

Reasoning: A stock dividend decreases retained earnings and increases paid-in capital, but total stockholders' equity remains the same. A stock split changes only par value per share and the number of shares outstanding. Thus, a stock split has no effect on the retained earnings balance.

Solution: The stock dividend amount is $2,250,000 [(500,000 × 10%) × $45]. The new balance in retained earnings is $7,750,000 ($10,000,000 − $2,250,000). The retained earnings balance after the stock split is the same as it was before the split: $10,000,000. The effects in the stockholders' equity accounts are as follows:

	Original Balances	After Dividend	After Split
Paid-in capital	$ 2,000,000	$ 4,250,000	$ 2,000,000
Retained earnings	10,000,000	7,750,000	10,000,000
Total stockholders' equity	$12,000,000	$12,000,000	$12,000,000
Shares outstanding	500,000	550,000	1,000,000

RETAINED EARNINGS

STUDY OBJECTIVE 6
Identify the items that affect retained earnings.

Retained earnings is net income that is retained in the business. The balance in retained earnings is part of the stockholders' claim on the total assets of the corporation. It does not, however, represent a claim on any specific asset. Nor can the amount of retained earnings be associated with the balance of any asset account. For example, a $100,000 balance in retained earnings does not mean that there should be $100,000 in cash. The reason is that the cash resulting from the excess of revenues over expenses may have been used to purchase buildings, equipment, and other assets. Illustration 11-14 shows the amounts of retained earnings and cash in selected companies.

Illustration 11-14
Retained earnings and cash balances

	(in millions)	
Company	Retained Earnings	Cash
Circuit City Stores, Inc.	$757	$47
Nike, Inc.	$1,838	$216
Starbucks Coffee Company	$90	$229
Green Mountain Coffee, Inc.	$(4)	$.55

When expenses exceed revenues, a **net loss** results. In contrast to net income, a net loss decreases retained earnings. In closing entries a net loss is debited to the Retained Earnings account. This is done even if a debit balance results in Retained Earnings. **Net losses are not debited to paid-in capital accounts.** To do so would destroy the distinction between paid-in and earned capital. A debit balance in retained earnings, such as that of Green Mountain Coffee, is identified as a **deficit** and is reported as a deduction in the stockholders' equity section of the balance sheet, as shown in Illustration 11-15.

Illustration 11-15
Stockholders' equity with deficit

GREEN MOUNTAIN COFFEE, INC. Partial Balance Sheet (in thousands)	
Stockholders' equity	
Paid-in capital	
Common stock	$ 342
Paid-in capital in excess of par value	12,508
Total paid-in capital	$12,850
Retained earnings (deficit)	(3,977)
Total stockholders' equity	$ 8,873

RETAINED EARNINGS RESTRICTIONS

The balance in retained earnings is generally available for dividend declarations. Some companies state this fact. For example, Illustration 11-16 is from Martin Marietta Corporation's notes to its financial statements.

Illustration 11-16
Disclosure of unrestricted retained earnings

MARTIN MARIETTA CORPORATION
Notes to the Financial Statements

At December 31, retained earnings were unrestricted and available for dividend payments.

In some cases, however, there may be **retained earnings restrictions** that make a portion of the balance currently unavailable for dividends. Restrictions result from one or more of these causes: legal, contractual, or voluntary. Retained earnings restrictions are generally disclosed in the notes to the financial statements. For example, Pratt & Lambert, a leading producer of architectural finishes (paint), included the note in Illustration 11-17 in a recent financial statement.

Illustration 11-17
Disclosure of retained earnings restriction

PRATT & LAMBERT
Notes to the Financial Statements

Note D: Long-term Debt and Retained Earnings Loan agreements contain, among other covenants, a restriction on the payment of dividends, which limits future dividend payments to $20,565,000 plus 75% of future net income.

STOCKHOLDERS' EQUITY PRESENTATION

In the stockholders' equity section of the balance sheet, paid-in capital and retained earnings are reported, and the specific sources of paid-in capital are identified. Within paid-in capital, two classifications are recognized:

STUDY OBJECTIVE 7
Prepare a comprehensive stockholders' equity section.

1. **Capital stock,** which consists of preferred and common stock. Preferred stock is shown before common stock because of its preferential rights. Information about the par value, shares authorized, shares issued, and shares outstanding is reported for each class of stock.
2. **Additional paid-in capital,** which includes the excess of amounts paid in over par or stated value and paid-in capital from treasury stock.

The stockholders' equity section of the balance sheet of Graber Inc. is presented in Illustration 11-18 (page 510). Note that Common Stock Dividends Distributable is shown under Capital Stock in Paid-in Capital, and a retained earnings restriction is disclosed.

The stockholders' equity section for Graber Inc. includes most of the accounts discussed in this chapter. The disclosures pertaining to Graber's common stock indicate that 400,000 shares are issued, 100,000 shares are unissued (500,000 authorized less 400,000 issued), and 390,000 shares are outstanding (400,000 issued less 10,000 shares in treasury).

Illustration 11-18 Comprehensive stockholders' equity section

GRABER INC.
Partial Balance Sheet

Stockholders' equity		
Paid-in capital		
Capital stock		
9% Preferred stock, $100 par value, cumulative, callable at $120, 10,000 shares authorized, 6,000 shares issued and outstanding		$ 600,000
Common stock, no par, $5 stated value, 500,000 shares authorized, 400,000 shares issued, and 390,000 outstanding	$2,000,000	
Common stock dividends distributable	**50,000**	2,050,000
Total capital stock		2,650,000
Additional paid-in capital		
In excess of par value—preferred stock	30,000	
In excess of stated value—common stock	1,050,000	
Total additional paid-in capital		1,080,000
Total paid-in capital		3,730,000
Retained earnings		1,160,000
Total paid-in capital and retained earnings		4,890,000
Less: Treasury stock—common (10,000 shares)		(80,000)
Total stockholders' equity		$4,810,000

International Note

In Switzerland, there are no specific disclosure requirements for shareholders' equity. However, companies typically disclose separate categories of capital on the balance sheet.

In published annual reports, subclassifications within the stockholders' equity section are seldom presented. Moreover, the individual sources of additional paid-in capital are often combined and reported as a single amount, as shown in Illustration 11-19.

Illustration 11-19 Stockholders' equity section

KNIGHT-RIDDER INC.
Partial Balance Sheet
(in millions)

Stockholders' equity	
Common stock, $.02$\frac{1}{12}$ par value; shares authorized—250,000,000; shares issued—93,340,652	$ 1,945
Additional paid-in capital	308,320
Retained earnings	821,243
Total stockholders' equity	$1,131,508

BEFORE YOU GO ON . . .

● **Review It**

1. Identify the classifications within the paid-in capital section and the totals that are stated in the stockholders' equity section of a balance sheet.
2. How are stock dividends distributable reported in the stockholders' equity section?

Measuring Corporate Performance

Investors are interested in both a company's dividend record and its earnings performance. Although they are often parallel, that is not always the case. Thus, each should be investigated separately.

DIVIDEND RECORD

One way that companies reward stock investors for their investment is to pay them dividends. The **payout ratio** measures the percentage of earnings distributed in the form of cash dividends to common stockholders. It is computed by **dividing total cash dividends to common shareholders by net income.** Another measure, the **dividend yield,** reports the rate of return an investor earned from dividends during the year. It is computed by **dividing dividends paid per share during the year by the stock price at the end of the year.** From the information in Illustration 11-20, the payout ratios and dividend yields for Nike in 1994 and 1995 are calculated in Illustration 11-21.

> **STUDY OBJECTIVE 8**
> Evaluate a corporation's dividend and earnings performance from a stockholder's perspective.

	1995	1994
Dividends paid (in thousands)	$68,638	$59,485
Dividends paid per share	$.95	$.80
Net income (in thousands)	$399,664	$298,794
Stock price at end of year	$78.875	$59

Illustration 11-20 Nike financial information

Illustration 11-21 Nike dividend ratios

$$\text{PAYOUT RATIO} = \frac{\text{TOTAL CASH DIVIDENDS PAID ON COMMON STOCK}}{\text{NET INCOME}}$$

$$\text{DIVIDEND YIELD} = \frac{\text{DIVIDENDS PAID PER SHARE}}{\text{STOCK PRICE AT END OF YEAR}}$$

	1995	1994
Payout Ratio ($ in thousands)	$\frac{\$68,638}{\$399,664} = 17.2\%$	$\frac{\$59,485}{\$298,794} = 19.9\%$
Dividend Yield	$\frac{\$.95}{\$78.875} = 1.2\%$	$\frac{\$.80}{\$59} = 1.4\%$

Companies that have high growth rates are characterized by low payout ratios and dividend yields because they reinvest most of their net income in the business. Thus, a low payout ratio or dividend yield is not necessarily bad news. Companies, such as Nike and Reebok, that believe they have many good opportunities for growth will reinvest those funds in the company rather than pay high dividends. However, low dividend payments, or a cut in dividend payments, might signal that a company has liquidity or solvency problems and is trying to free up cash by not paying dividends. Thus, the reason for low dividend payments should be investigated.

512 CHAPTER 11 Reporting and Analyzing Stockholders' Equity

Listed in Illustration 11-22 are dividend ratios in recent years of four well-known companies.

Illustration 11-22 Variability of dividend ratios among companies

Company ($ in millions)	Payout Ratio	Dividend Yield
Microsoft	$\dfrac{0}{\$1{,}453} = 0\%$	$\dfrac{0}{\$51.625} = 0\%$
Kellogg	$\dfrac{\$328.5}{\$490.3} = 67\%$	$\dfrac{\$1.5}{\$77.25} = 1.9\%$
Sears	$\dfrac{\$475}{\$1{,}801} = 26.4\%$	$\dfrac{\$1.26}{\$39} = 3.2\%$
Johnson & Johnson	$\dfrac{\$727}{\$2{,}006} = 36.2\%$	$\dfrac{\$1.13}{\$54.75} = 2.1\%$

DECISION TOOLKIT

Decision Checkpoints	Info Needed for Decision	Tool to Use for Decision	How to Evaluate Results
What portion of its earnings does the company pay out in dividends?	Net income and total cash dividends paid on common stock	Payout ratio = $\dfrac{\text{Total cash dividends paid on common stock}}{\text{Net income}}$	A low ratio suggests that the company is retaining its earnings for investment in future growth.
What level of return can be earned on the company's dividends?	Market price of stock and dividends paid per share on common stock	Dividend yield = $\dfrac{\text{Dividends paid per share}}{\text{Stock price at year-end}}$	A high yield is attractive to investors looking for a steady investment income stream rather than stock price appreciation.

EARNINGS PERFORMANCE

Earnings per share measures the net income earned on each share of common stock. It is computed by dividing **net income** by the **average number of common shares outstanding during the year.** Stockholders usually think in terms of the number of shares they own or plan to buy or sell, so reducing net income earned to a per share amount provides a useful perspective for determining the investment return. Advanced accounting courses present more refined techniques for calculating earnings per share. For now, a basic approach is to divide earnings available to common stockholders (Net income − Preferred stock dividends) by average common shares outstanding during the year. By comparing earnings per share of a single company over time, one can evaluate its relative earnings performance from the perspective of a shareholder—that is, on a per share basis.

It is very important to note that comparisons of earnings per share across companies are **not meaningful** because of the wide variations in the numbers of shares of outstanding stock among companies and in the stock prices. Instead, in order to make a meaningful comparison of earnings across firms, we calculate the **price-earnings ratio.** The price-earnings ratio is an oft-quoted statistic that measures **the ratio of the market price of each share of common**

stock to the earnings per share. It is computed by dividing the market price per share of stock by earnings per share. The price-earnings (P-E) ratio reflects the investors' assessment of a company's future earnings. The ratio of price to earnings will be higher if investors think that current earnings levels will persist or increase than it will be if investors think that earnings will decline. A high price-earnings ratio might also indicate that a stock is priced too high and is likely to come down. From the information presented in Illustration 11-23, the earnings per share and price-earnings ratios for Nike in 1994 and 1995 are calculated in Illustration 11-24. (Note that to simplify our calculations, we assumed that any change in shares for Nike occurred in the middle of the year.)

(in thousands except per share data)	1995	1994
Net income	$399,664	$298,794
Preferred stock dividends	$30	$30
Shares outstanding at beginning of year	73,200	75,852
Shares outstanding at end of year	71,445	73,200
Market price of stock at end of year	$78.875	$59

Illustration 11-23 Nike financial information

$$\text{EARNINGS PER SHARE} = \frac{\text{NET INCOME} - \text{PREFERRED STOCK DIVIDENDS}}{\text{AVERAGE COMMON SHARES OUTSTANDING}}$$

$$\text{PRICE-EARNINGS RATIO} = \frac{\text{MARKET PRICE PER SHARE OF STOCK}}{\text{EARNINGS PER SHARE}}$$

($ in thousands)	1995	1994
Earnings per Share	$\frac{\$399,664 - \$30}{(73,200 + 71,445)/2} = \$5.53$	$\frac{\$298,794 - \$30}{(75,852 + 73,200)/2} = \$4.01$
Price-Earnings Ratio	$\frac{\$78.875}{\$5.53} = 14.26$ times	$\frac{\$59}{\$4.01} = 14.71$ times

Illustration 11-24 Nike earnings per share and price-earnings ratio

From 1994 to 1995, Nike's earnings per share increased substantially, on approximately the same number of shares, whereas its price-earnings ratio declined slightly. This decline might reflect a concern that Nike will not be able to continue its record earnings pace.

As noted, earnings per share cannot be meaningfully compared across companies. Price-earnings ratios, however, can be compared. Illustration 11-25 lists four companies and their earnings per share and price-earnings ratios for 1995 (calculated at the end of each company's fiscal year).

Company	Earnings Per Share	Price-Earnings Ratio
Microsoft	$2.32	$90.375/$2.32 = 39
Kellogg	$2.24	$77.25/$2.24 = 34.5
Sears	$4.50	$25.75/$4.5 = 5.7
General Motors	$7.21	$73.25/$7.21 = 10.2

Illustration 11-25 Variability of earnings performance ratios among companies

DECISION TOOLKIT

Decision Checkpoints	Info Needed for Decision	Tool to Use for Decision	How to Evaluate Results
How does the company's earnings performance compare with that of previous years?	Net income available to common shareholders and average common shares outstanding	Earnings per share = $\dfrac{\text{Net income} - \text{Preferred stock dividends}}{\text{Average common shares outstanding}}$	A higher measure suggests improved performance, although the number is subject to manipulation. Values should not be compared across companies.
How does the market perceive the company's prospects for future earnings?	Earnings per share and market price per share	Price-earnings ratio = $\dfrac{\text{Market price per share of stock}}{\text{Earnings per share}}$	A high ratio suggests the market has favorable expectations, although it also may suggest stock is overvalued.

Another widely used ratio that measures profitability from the common stockholders' viewpoint is **return on common stockholders' equity.** This ratio shows how many dollars of net income were earned for each dollar invested by common stockholders. It is computed by dividing net income available to common stockholders (Net income − Preferred stock dividends) by average common stockholders' equity. From the additional information in Illustration 11-26, Nike's return on common stockholders' equity ratios are calculated for 1994 and 1995 in Illustration 11-27.

Illustration 11-26 Nike financial information

($ in thousands)	1995	1994	1993
Net income	$399,664	$298,794	$365,016
Preferred stock dividends	$30	$30	$30
Common stockholders' equity	$1,964,689	$1,740,949	$1,642,819

$$\text{RETURN ON COMMON STOCKHOLDERS' EQUITY RATIO} = \dfrac{\text{NET INCOME} - \text{PREFERRED STOCK DIVIDENDS}}{\text{AVERAGE COMMON STOCKHOLDERS' EQUITY}}$$

($ in thousands)	1995	1994
Return on Common Stockholders' Equity Ratio	$\dfrac{\$399{,}664 - \$30}{(\$1{,}964{,}689 + \$1{,}740{,}949)/2} = 21.6\%$	$\dfrac{\$298{,}794 - \$30}{(\$1{,}740{,}949 + \$1{,}642{,}819)/2} = 17.7\%$

Illustration 11-27 Nike return on common stockholders' equity

From 1994 to 1995, Nike's return on common shareholders' equity increased from 17.7% to 21.6%. As a company grows larger it becomes increasingly hard to sustain such a high return. In Nike's case, since many believe the U.S. market for expensive sports shoes is saturated, it will need to grow either along new product lines, such as hiking shoes, or in new markets, such as Europe and Asia. We will talk more about factors that affect the return on common shareholders' equity in Chapter 14.

DECISION TOOLKIT

Decision Checkpoints	Info Needed for Decision	Tool to Use for Decision	How to Evaluate Results
What is the company's return on common stockholders' investment?	Earnings available to common stockholders and average common stockholders' equity	Return on common stockholders' equity ratio $= \dfrac{\text{Net income} - \text{Preferred stock dividends}}{\text{Average common stockholders' equity}}$	A high measure suggests strong earnings performance from common stockholders' perspective.

BUSINESS INSIGHT
Management Perspective

Nike's advertising success, envied throughout the business world, was recently spoofed in the humor magazine *The Onion*. The article blared, "Nike to Cease Manufacturing Products: 'From now on, we'll focus on just making ads,' says a spokesman." Another "quote" attributed to Phil Knight, Nike cofounder and CEO, was "The last few years, it became impossible to maintain our high standards of advertising while faced with the daily distractions of making sneakers. By discontinuing our entire product line, we will ensure that Nike remains the world's leader in the field of incredibly cool TV commercials well into the 21st century." Based on your understanding of accounting, how would this strategy affect Nike's return on common shareholders' equity?

Source: "Nike to Cease Manufacturing Products," *The Onion*, September 11, 1996, p. 1 (www.TheOnion.com).

BEFORE YOU GO ON . . .

● **Review It**

1. What measures can be used to evaluate a company's dividend record and how are they calculated?
2. Why should earnings per share not be compared across companies?
3. What does a high price-earnings ratio suggest about a company's future earnings potential?

USING THE DECISION TOOLKIT

During 1995 Reebok hit difficult times in which both its profits and market share declined. As a result, its stock price sagged and investors became impatient. Management believes that the future is bright for Reebok, with promises of many exciting new products, but some investors are still skeptical.

Instructions

The following facts are available for Reebok. Using this information, evaluate its (1) dividend record and (2) earnings performance, and contrast them with those for Nike for 1994 and 1995:

(in thousands except per share data)	1995	1994	1993
Dividends paid	$23,353	$24,610	$26,628
Dividends paid per share	$.30	$.30	$.30
Net income	$164,798	$254,478	$223,415
Stock price at beginning of year	$39.5	$30.0	
Preferred stock dividends	$0	$0	
Shares outstanding at beginning of year	117,156	119,902	125,574
Shares outstanding at end of year	111,015	117,156	119,902
Stock price at end of year	$28.25	$39.50	
Common stockholders' equity	$895,289	$990,505	$846,617

Solution

1. *Dividend record:* Two measures to evaluate dividend record are the payout ratio and the dividend yield. For Reebok, these measures in 1994 and 1995 are calculated as shown here:

	1995	1994
Payout ratio	$\dfrac{\$23,353}{\$164,798} = 14.2\%$	$\dfrac{\$24,610}{\$254,478} = 9.7\%$
Dividend yield	$\dfrac{\$.30}{\$28.25} = 1.1\%$	$\dfrac{\$.30}{\$39.50} = 0.8\%$

Nike's dividends paid per share have increased 15 cents from 1994 to 1995, while Reebok's remained constant. Reebok's dividend yield rose from 1994 to 1995—not because Reebok's dividend payment increased but because the price of its stock fell.

2. *Earnings performance:* There are many measures of earnings performance. Those presented in the chapter were earnings per share, the price-earnings ratio, and the return on common stockholders' equity ratio. These measures for Reebok in 1995 and 1994 are calculated as shown here:

	1995	1994
Earnings per share	$\dfrac{\$164,798 - 0}{(117,156 + 111,015)/2} = \$1.44$	$\dfrac{\$254,478 - 0}{(119,902 + 117,156)/2} = \$2.15$
Price-earnings ratio	$\dfrac{\$28.25}{\$1.44} = 19.62$	$\dfrac{\$39.50}{\$2.15} = 18.37$
Return on common stockholders' equity ratio	$\dfrac{\$164,798 - 0}{(\$895,289 + \$990,505)/2} = 17.5\%$	$\dfrac{\$254,478 - 0}{(\$990,505 + \$846,617)/2} = 27.7\%$

From 1994 to 1995 Reebok's earnings declined on both a total and per share basis. This decline was very significant and would be of obvious concern to both management and shareholders. Reebok's price-earnings ratio increased slightly, perhaps hinting that investors believe earnings will rebound somewhat in coming years. Also, compared to Nike's P-E ratio of roughly 14, Reebok seems to be high-priced; that is, Reebok's shareholders are paying more per dollar of earnings than are Nike's.

Reebok's return on common stockholders' equity declined from 27.7% to 17.5%. This is especially significant because, due to treasury stock repurchases, Reebok's common stockholders' equity declined by nearly $100 million. Because this is the denominator of the return on common stockholders' equity ratio, such a decline would normally cause an increase in the ratio. We can only wonder how low the return would have been without the treasury stock repurchases.

SUMMARY OF STUDY OBJECTIVES

❶ Identify and discuss the major characteristics of a corporation. The major characteristics of a corporation are separate legal existence, limited liability of stockholders, transferable ownership rights, ability to acquire capital, continuous life, corporation management, government regulations, and additional taxes.

❷ Record the issuance of common stock. When the issuance of common stock for cash is recorded, the par value of the shares is credited to Common Stock and the portion of the proceeds that is above or below par value is recorded in a separate paid-in capital account. When no-par common stock has a stated value, the entries are similar to those for par value stock. When no-par common stock does not have a stated value, the entire proceeds from the issue become legal capital and are credited to Common Stock.

❸ Explain the accounting for the purchase of treasury stock. The cost method is generally used in accounting for treasury stock. Under this approach, Treasury Stock is debited at the price paid to reacquire the shares.

❹ Differentiate preferred stock from common stock. Preferred stock has contractual provisions that give it priority over common stock in certain areas. Typically, preferred stockholders have a preference as to (a) dividends and (b) assets in the event of liquidation. However, they often do not have voting rights.

❺ Prepare the entries for cash dividends and stock dividends. Entries for both cash and stock dividends are required at the declaration date and the payment date. At the declaration date the entries are as follows: For a *cash dividend*—debit Retained Earnings and credit Dividends Payable; for a *small stock dividend*—debit Retained Earnings, credit Paid-in Capital in Excess of Par (or Stated) Value, and credit Common Stock Dividends Distributable. At the payment date, the entries for cash and stock dividends, respectively, are debit Dividends Payable and credit Cash, and debit Common Stock Dividends Distributable and credit Common Stock.

❻ Identify the items that affect retained earnings. Additions to retained earnings consist of net income. Deductions consist of net loss and cash and stock dividends. In some instances, portions of retained earnings are restricted, making that portion unavailable for the payment of dividends.

❼ Prepare a comprehensive stockholders' equity section. In the stockholders' equity section of the balance sheet, paid-in capital and retained earnings are reported and specific sources of paid-in capital are identified. Within paid-in capital, two classifications are shown: capital stock and additional paid-in capital. If a corporation has treasury stock, the cost of treasury stock is deducted from total paid-in capital and retained earnings to obtain total stockholders' equity.

❽ Evaluate a corporation's dividend and earnings performance from a stockholder's perspective. A company's dividend record can be evaluated by looking at what percentage of net income it chooses to pay out in dividends, as measured by the dividend payout ratio (dividends divided by net income), or it can be evaluated from the perspective of a rate of return on stockholders' investment through the dividend yield (dividends divided by stock price). Earnings performance is measured with earnings per share (net income available to common shareholders divided by average number of shares). In order to compare the relative amounts that investors are currently paying per dollar of reported earnings, the price-earnings ratio is calculated (share price divided by earnings per share). Another measure of earnings performance is the return on common stockholders' equity ratio (income available to common shareholders divided by average common shareholders' equity).

CHAPTER 11 Reporting and Analyzing Stockholders' Equity

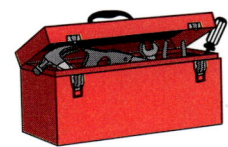

Decision Toolkit—A Summary

Decision Checkpoints	Info Needed for Decision	Tool to Use for Decision	How to Evaluate Results
Should the company incorporate?	Capital needs, growth expectations, type of business, tax status	Corporations have limited liability, easier capital raising ability, and professional managers; but they suffer from additional taxes, government regulations, and separation of ownership from management.	Must carefully weigh the costs and benefits in light of the particular circumstances.
What portion of its earnings does the company pay out in dividends?	Net income and total cash dividends paid on common stock	$$\text{Payout ratio} = \frac{\text{Total cash dividends paid on common stock}}{\text{Net income}}$$	A low ratio suggests that the company is retaining its earnings for investment in future growth.
What level of return can be earned on the company's dividends?	Market price of stock and dividends paid per share on common stock	$$\text{Dividend yield} = \frac{\text{Dividends paid per share}}{\text{Stock price at year-end}}$$	A high yield is attractive to investors looking for a steady investment income stream rather than stock price appreciation.
How does the company's earnings performance compare with that of previous years?	Net income available to common shareholders and average common shares outstanding	$$\text{Earnings per share} = \frac{\text{Net income} - \text{Preferred stock dividends}}{\text{Average common shares outstanding}}$$	A higher measure suggests improved performance, although the number is subject to manipulation. Values should not be compared across companies.
How does the market perceive the company's prospects for future earnings?	Earnings per share and market price per share	$$\text{Price-earnings ratio} = \frac{\text{Market price per share of stock}}{\text{Earnings per share}}$$	A high ratio suggests the market has favorable expectations, although it also may suggest stock is overvalued.
What is the company's return on common stockholders' investment?	Earnings available to common stockholders and average common stockholders' equity	$$\text{Return on common stockholders' equity ratio} = \frac{\text{Net income} - \text{Preferred stock dividends}}{\text{Average common stockholders' equity}}$$	A high measure suggests strong earnings performance from common stockholders' perspective.

Glossary

Authorized stock The amount of stock that a corporation is authorized to sell as indicated in its charter. (p. 494)

Cash dividend A pro rata distribution of cash to stockholders. (p. 502)

Corporation A company organized as a separate legal entity, with most of the rights and privileges of a person. Evidence of ownership is shares of stock. (p. 488)

Cumulative dividend A feature of preferred stock entitling the stockholder to receive current and unpaid prior-year dividends before common stockholders receive any dividends. (p. 501)

Declaration date The date the board of directors formally declares the dividend and announces it to stockholders. (p. 503)

Deficit A debit balance in retained earnings. (p. 508)

Dividend A distribution by a corporation to its stockholders on a pro rata (equal) basis. (p. 502)

Dividend yield A measure of the rate of return an investor earned from dividends during the year. (p. 511)

Dividends in arrears Preferred dividends that were scheduled to be declared but were not declared during a given period. (p. 501)

Earnings per share A measure of the net income earned on each share of common stock; computed by dividing net income minus preferred stock dividends by the number of average common shares outstanding during the year. (p. 512)

Legal capital The amount per share of stock that must be retained in the business for the protection of corporate creditors. (p. 494)

No-par value stock Capital stock that has not been assigned a value in the corporate charter. (p. 495)

Outstanding stock Capital stock that has been issued and is being held by stockholders. (p. 499)

Paid-in capital The amount paid in to the corporation by stockholders in exchange for shares of ownership. (p. 495)

Par value stock Capital stock that has been assigned a value per share in the corporate charter. (p. 494)

Payment date The date dividend checks are mailed to stockholders. (p. 503)

Payout ratio A measure of the percentage of earnings distributed in the form of cash dividends to common stockholders. (p. 511)

Preferred stock Capital stock that has contractual preferences over common stock in certain areas. (p. 500)

Price-earnings ratio A measure of the ratio of the market price of each share of common stock to the earnings per share; it reflects the stock market's belief about a company's future earnings potential. (p. 512)

Privately held corporation A corporation that has only a few stockholders and whose stock is not available for sale to the general public. (p. 488)

Publicly held corporation A corporation that may have thousands of stockholders and whose stock is regularly traded on a national securities market. (p. 488)

Record date The date when ownership of outstanding shares is determined for dividend purposes. (p. 503)

Retained earnings Net income that is retained in the business. (p. 508)

Retained earnings restrictions Circumstances that make a portion of retained earnings currently unavailable for dividends. (p. 509)

Return on common stockholders' equity ratio A measure of profitability from the stockholders' point of view; computed by dividing net income minus preferred stock dividends by average common stockholders' equity. (p. 514)

Stated value The amount per share assigned by the board of directors to no-par stock that becomes legal capital per share. (p. 495)

Stock dividend A pro rata distribution of the corporation's own stock to stockholders. (p. 504)

Stock split The issuance of additional shares of stock to stockholders accompanied by a reduction in the par or stated value per share. (p. 506)

Treasury stock A corporation's own stock that has been issued, fully paid for, and reacquired by the corporation but not retired. (p. 497)

Demonstration Problem

Rolman Corporation is authorized to issue 1,000,000 shares of $5 par value common stock. In its first year the company has these stock transactions:

Jan. 10   Issued 400,000 shares of stock at $8 per share.
Sept. 1   Purchased 10,000 shares of common stock for the treasury at $9 per share.
Dec. 24   Declared a cash dividend of 10 cents per share.

Instructions

(a) Journalize the transactions.
(b) Prepare the stockholders' equity section of the balance sheet assuming the company had retained earnings of $150,600 at December 31.

CHAPTER 11 Reporting and Analyzing Stockholders' Equity

Problem-Solving Strategies
1. When common stock has a par value, Common Stock is always credited for par value.
2. The Treasury Stock account is debited and credited at cost.

Solution to Demonstration Problem

(a)
Date	Account	Debit	Credit
Jan. 10	Cash	3,200,000	
	Common Stock		2,000,000
	Paid-in Capital in Excess of Par Value		1,200,000
	(To record issuance of 400,000 shares of $5 par value stock)		
Sept. 1	Treasury Stock	90,000	
	Cash		90,000
	(To record purchase of 10,000 shares of treasury stock at cost)		
Dec. 24	Retained Earnings	39,000	
	Dividends Payable		39,000
	(To record declaration of 10 cents per share cash dividend)		

ROLMAN CORPORATION
Partial Balance Sheet

(b) Stockholders' equity
  Paid-in capital
    Capital stock
      Common stock, $5 par value, 1,000,000 shares authorized, 400,000 shares issued, 390,000 outstanding $2,000,000
    Additional paid-in capital in excess of par value   1,200,000
      Total paid-in capital   3,200,000
  Retained earnings   150,600
    Total paid-in capital and retained earnings   3,350,600
  Less: Treasury stock (10,000 shares)   90,000
  Total stockholders' equity $3,260,600

SELF-STUDY QUESTIONS

Answers are at the end of the chapter.

(SO 1) 1. Which of these is *not* a major advantage of a corporation?
(a) Separate legal existence
(b) Continuous life
(c) Government regulations
(d) Transferable ownership rights

(SO 1) 2. A major disadvantage of a corporation is:
(a) limited liability of stockholders.
(b) additional taxes.
(c) transferable ownership rights.
(d) None of the above

(SO 1) 3. Which of these statements is *false*?
(a) Ownership of common stock gives the owner a voting right.
(b) The stockholders' equity section begins with paid-in capital.
(c) The authorization of capital stock does not result in a formal accounting entry.
(d) Legal capital per share applies to par value stock but not to no-par value stock.

(SO 2) 4. ABC Corporation issues 1,000 shares of $10 par value common stock at $12 per share. When the transaction is recorded, credits are made to:
(a) Common Stock $10,000 and Paid-in Capital in Excess of Stated Value $2,000.
(b) Common Stock $12,000.
(c) Common Stock $10,000 and Paid-in Capital in Excess of Par Value $2,000.
(d) Common Stock $10,000 and Retained Earnings $2,000.

(SO 7) 5. In the stockholders' equity section, the cost of treasury stock is deducted from:
(a) total paid-in capital and retained earnings.
(b) retained earnings.
(c) total stockholders' equity.
(d) common stock in paid-in capital.

(SO 4) 6. Preferred stock may have priority over common stock *except* in:
(a) dividends.
(b) assets in the event of liquidation.
(c) conversion.
(d) voting.

(SO 5) 7. Entries for cash dividends are required on the:
(a) declaration date and the record date.
(b) record date and the payment date.
(c) declaration date, record date, and payment date.
(d) declaration date and the payment date.

(SO 5) 8. Which of these statements about small stock dividends is *true*?
(a) A debit should be made to Retained Earnings for the par value of the shares issued.
(b) Market value per share should be assigned to the dividend shares.
(c) A stock dividend decreases total stockholders' equity.
(d) A stock dividend ordinarily will have no effect on total stockholders' equity.

(SO 8) 9. A high price-earnings ratio indicates:
(a) a company has strong future earnings potential.
(b) a company's stock is priced too high and is likely to come down.
(c) either (a) or (b).
(d) neither (a) nor (b).

(SO 8) 10. Herb Fischer is nearing retirement and would like to invest in a stock that will provide a good steady income supply. Herb should choose a stock with a:
(a) high current ratio.
(b) high dividend yield.
(c) high earnings per share.
(d) high price-earnings ratio.

Questions

1. Pat Kabza, a student, asks your help in understanding some characteristics of a corporation. Explain each of these to Pat:
   (a) Separate legal existence
   (b) Limited liability of stockholders
   (c) Transferable ownership rights

2. (a) Your friend T. R. Cedras cannot understand how the characteristic of corporation management is both an advantage and a disadvantage. Clarify this problem for T. R.
   (b) Identify and explain two other disadvantages of a corporation.

3. Cary Brant believes a corporation must be incorporated in the state in which its headquarters office is located. Is Cary correct? Explain.

4. What are the basic ownership rights of common stockholders in the absence of restrictive provisions?

5. A corporation has been defined as an entity separate and distinct from its owners. In what ways is a corporation a separate legal entity?

6. What are the two principal components of stockholders' equity?

7. The corporate charter of Letterman Corporation allows the issuance of a maximum of 100,000 shares of common stock. During its first 2 years of operation, Letterman sold 60,000 shares to shareholders and reacquired 7,000 of these shares. After these transactions, how many shares are authorized, issued, and outstanding?

8. Which is the better investment—common stock with a par value of $5 per share or common stock with a par value of $20 per share?

9. What factors help determine the market value of stock?

10. Why is common stock usually not issued at a price that is less than par value?

11. For what reasons might a company like IBM repurchase some of its stock (treasury stock)?

12. Wilmor, Inc., purchases 1,000 shares of its own previously issued $5 par common stock for $11,000. Assuming the shares are held in the treasury, what effect does this transaction have on (a) net income, (b) total assets, (c) total paid-in capital, and (d) total stockholders' equity?

13. (a) What are the principal differences between common stock and preferred stock?
    (b) Preferred stock may be cumulative. Discuss this feature.
    (c) How are dividends in arrears presented in the financial statements?

14. Identify the events that result in credits and debits to retained earnings.

15. Indicate how each of these accounts should be classified in the stockholders' equity section of the balance sheet:
    (a) Common stock
    (b) Paid-in capital in excess of par value
    (c) Retained earnings
    (d) Treasury stock
    (e) Paid-in capital in excess of stated value
    (f) Preferred stock

16. What three conditions must be met before a cash dividend is paid?

17. Three dates associated with Galena Company's cash dividend are May 1, May 15, and May 31. Discuss the significance of each date and give the entry at each date.

18. Contrast the effects of a cash dividend and a stock dividend on a corporation's balance sheet.

19. Jill Sims asks, "Since stock dividends don't change anything, why declare them?" What is your answer to Jill?

20. Bella Corporation has 10,000 shares of $15 par value common stock outstanding when it announces a 2-for-1 split. Before the split, the stock had a market price of $140 per share. After the split, how many

shares of stock will be outstanding, and what will be the approximate market price per share?

21. The board of directors is considering a stock split or a stock dividend. They understand that total stockholders' equity will remain the same under either action. However, they are not sure of the different effects of the two actions on other aspects of stockholders' equity. Explain the differences to the directors.

22. (a) What is the purpose of a retained earnings restriction?
(b) Identify the possible causes of retained earnings restrictions.

23. WAT Inc.'s common stock has a par value of $1 and a current market value of $15. Explain why these amounts are different.

24. What is the formula for the dividend yield and the payout ratio, and what does each indicate?

25. Matthew Dodge notes that TID Industries has an earnings per share that is double that of Derauf Inc. Therefore, he concludes that TID is a better investment. Is he correct?

26. Some investors like to buy stocks that have low price-earnings ratios. What might their logic be in doing this?

BRIEF EXERCISES

Cite advantages and disadvantages of a corporation.
(SO 1)

BE11-1 Tracy Bono is studying for her accounting midterm examination. Identify for Tracy the advantages and disadvantages of the corporate form of business organization.

Journalize issuance of par value common stock.
(SO 2)

BE11-2 On May 10 Armada Corporation issues 1,000 shares of $10 par value common stock for cash at $14 per share. Journalize the issuance of the stock.

Journalize issuance of no-par common stock.
(SO 2)

BE11-3 On June 1 Eagle Inc. issues 2,000 shares of no-par common stock at a cash price of $7 per share. Journalize the issuance of the shares.

Journalize issuance of preferred stock.
(SO 4)

BE11-4 Ozark Inc. issues 5,000 shares of $100 par value preferred stock for cash at $112 per share. Journalize the issuance of the preferred stock.

Prepare entries for a cash dividend.
(SO 5)

BE11-5 The Seabee Corporation has 10,000 shares of common stock outstanding. It declares a $1 per share cash dividend on November 1 to stockholders of record on December 1. The dividend is paid on December 31. Prepare the entries on the appropriate dates to record the declaration and payment of the cash dividend.

Prepare entries for a stock dividend.
(SO 5)

BE11-6 Satina Corporation has 100,000 shares of $10 par value common stock outstanding. It declares a 10% stock dividend on December 1 when the market value per share is $12. The dividend shares are issued on December 31. Prepare the entries for the declaration and payment of the stock dividend.

Show before and after effects of a stock dividend.
(SO 5)

BE11-7 The stockholders' equity section of Desi Corporation's balance sheet consists of common stock ($10 par) $1,000,000 and retained earnings $400,000. A 10% stock dividend (10,000 shares) is declared when the market value per share is $12. Show the before and after effects of the dividend on (a) the components of stockholders' equity and (b) the shares outstanding.

Prepare a stockholders' equity section.
(SO 7)

BE11-8 Anita Corporation has these accounts at December 31: Common Stock, $10 par, 5,000 shares issued, $50,000; Paid-in Capital in Excess of Par Value $10,000; Retained Earnings $29,000; and Treasury Stock—Common, 500 shares, $7,000. Prepare the stockholders' equity section of the balance sheet.

Calculate dividend yield at beginning and end of year; comment on implications.
(SO 8)

BE11-9 Abdella Corporation had a stock price of $25 per share at the beginning of the year and $20 per share at the end of the year. Its dividend has remained a constant $1 per share for the last 3 years. Calculate the dividend yield at the beginning and end of the year and comment on its implications for an investor interested in dividend income.

BE11-10 Paul Schwartz, president of Schwartz Corporation, believes that it is a good practice to maintain a constant payout of dividends relative to its earnings. Last year net income was $500,000, and the corporation paid $200,000 in dividends. This year, due to some unusual circumstances, the corporation had income of $2,000,000. Paul expects next year's net income to be about $600,000. What was Schwartz Corporation's payout ratio last year? If it is to maintain the same payout ratio, what amount of dividends would it pay this year? Is this necessarily a good idea—that is, what are the pros and cons of maintaining a constant payout ratio in this scenario?

Evaluate a company's dividend record.
(SO 8)

EXERCISES

E11-1 During its first year of operations, Bevis Corporation had these transactions pertaining to its common stock:

    Jan. 10 Issued 80,000 shares for cash at $5 per share.
    July 1 Issued 30,000 shares for cash at $7 per share.

Journalize issuance of common stock.
(SO 2)

Instructions
(a) Journalize the transactions, assuming that the common stock has a par value of $5 per share.
(b) Journalize the transactions, assuming that the common stock is no-par with a stated value of $1 per share.

E11-2 Santiago Co. had these transactions during the current period:

June 12 Issued 60,000 shares of $1 par value common stock for cash of $375,000.
July 11 Issued 1,000 shares of $100 par value preferred stock for cash at $105 per share.
Nov. 28 Purchased 2,000 shares of treasury stock for $80,000.

Journalize issuance of common stock and preferred stock and purchase of treasury stock.
(SO 2, 3, 4)

Instructions
Prepare the journal entries for the transactions.

E11-3 Talley Corporation is authorized to issue both preferred and common stock. The par value of the preferred is $50. During the first year of operations, the company had the following events and transactions pertaining to its preferred stock:

    Feb. 1 Issued 30,000 shares for cash at $53 per share.
    July 1 Issued 10,000 shares for cash at $57 per share.

Journalize preferred stock transactions and indicate statement presentation.
(SO 4, 7)

Instructions
(a) Journalize the transactions.
(b) Post to the stockholders' equity accounts. (Use T accounts.)
(c) Discuss the statement presentation of the accounts.

E11-4 The stockholders' equity section of Kimbria Shumway Corporation's balance sheet at December 31 is presented here:

Answer questions about stockholders' equity section.
(SO 2, 3, 4, 7)

KIMBRIA SHUMWAY CORPORATION
Partial Balance Sheet

Stockholders' equity		
Paid-in capital		
Preferred stock, cumulative, 10,000 shares authorized,		
6,000 shares issued and outstanding	$ 600,000	
Common stock, no par, 750,000 shares authorized,		
600,000 shares issued	1,800,000	
Total paid-in capital	2,400,000	
Retained earnings	1,158,000	
Total paid-in capital and retained earnings	3,558,000	
Less: Treasury stock (10,000 common shares)	(64,000)	
Total stockholders' equity	$3,494,000	

Instructions
From a review of the stockholders' equity section, answer these questions:
(a) How many shares of common stock are outstanding?
(b) Assuming there is a stated value, what is the stated value of the common stock?

524 CHAPTER 11 Reporting and Analyzing Stockholders' Equity

(c) What is the par value of the preferred stock?
(d) If the annual dividend on preferred stock is $48,000, what is the dividend rate on preferred stock?
(e) If dividends of $96,000 were in arrears on preferred stock, what would be the balance reported for retained earnings?

Prepare correct entries for capital stock transactions.
(SO 2, 3, 4)

E11-5 Anita Ferreri Corporation recently hired a new accountant with extensive experience in accounting for partnerships. Because of the pressure of the new job, the accountant was unable to review what he had learned earlier about corporation accounting. During the first month, he made the following entries for the corporation's capital stock:

May 2	Cash	144,000	
	Capital Stock		144,000
	(Issued 12,000 shares of $5 par value common stock at $12 per share)		
10	Cash	600,000	
	Capital Stock		600,000
	(Issued 10,000 shares of $50 par value preferred stock at $60 per share)		
15	Capital Stock	14,000	
	Cash		14,000
	(Purchased 1,000 shares of common stock for the treasury at $14 per share)		

Instructions
On the basis of the explanation for each entry, prepare the entries that should have been made for the capital stock transactions.

Journalize cash dividends and indicate statement presentation.
(SO 5)

E11-6 On January 1 Tarow Corporation had 75,000 shares of no-par common stock issued and outstanding. The stock has a stated value of $5 per share. During the year, the following transactions occurred:

Apr. 1 Issued 5,000 additional shares of common stock.
June 15 Declared a cash dividend of $1 per share to stockholders of record on June 30.
July 10 Paid the $1 cash dividend.
Dec. 1 Issued 2,000 additional shares of common stock.
  15 Declared a cash dividend on outstanding shares of $1.20 per share to stockholders of record on December 31.

Instructions
(a) Prepare the entries, if any, on each of the three dividend dates.
(b) How are dividends and dividends payable reported in the financial statements prepared at December 31?

Journalize stock dividends.
(SO 5)

E11-7 On January 1, 1998, Keyes Corporation had $1,500,000 of common stock outstanding that was issued at par and retained earnings of $750,000. The company issued 50,000 shares of common stock at par on July 1 and earned net income of $400,000 for the year.

Instructions
Journalize the declaration of a 10% stock dividend on December 10, 1998, for these two independent assumptions:
(a) Par value is $10 and market value is $15.
(b) Par value is $5 and market value is $20.

Compare effects of a stock dividend and a stock split.
(SO 5)

E11-8 On October 31 the stockholders' equity section of Sarah Lane Company's balance sheet consists of common stock $800,000 and retained earnings $400,000. Sarah is considering the following two courses of action: (1) declaring a 10% stock dividend on the 80,000 $10 par value shares outstanding or (2) effecting a 2-for-1 stock split that will reduce par value to $5 per share. The current market price is $15 per share.

Instructions
Prepare a tabular summary of the effects of the alternative actions on the components stockholders' equity, outstanding shares, and book value per share. Use these column headings: **Before Action, After Stock Dividend,** and **After Stock Split.**

E11-9 Before preparing financial statements for the current year, the chief accountant for Phil, Chris, and Caroline Company discovered the following errors in the accounts:

1. The declaration and payment of a $25,000 cash dividend were recorded as a debit to Interest Expense $25,000 and a credit to Cash $25,000.
2. A 10% stock dividend (1,000 shares) was declared on the $10 par value stock when the market value per share was $17. The only entry made was: Retained Earnings (Dr.) $10,000 and Dividend Payable (Cr.) $10,000. The shares have not been issued.
3. A 4-for-1 stock split involving the issue of 400,000 shares of $5 par value common stock for 100,000 shares of $20 par value common stock was recorded as a debit to Retained Earnings $2,000,000 and a credit to Common Stock $2,000,000.

Prepare correcting entries for dividends and a stock split.
(SO 5)

Instructions
Prepare the correcting entries at December 31.

E11-10 The ledger of Mintur Corporation contains these accounts: Common Stock, Preferred Stock, Treasury Stock—Common, Paid-in Capital in Excess of Par Value—Preferred Stock, Paid-in Capital in Excess of Stated Value—Common Stock, Paid-in Capital from Treasury Stock, and Retained Earnings.

Classify stockholders' equity accounts.
(SO 7)

Instructions
Classify each account using the table column headings shown here:

	Paid-in Capital			
Account	Capital Stock	Additional	Retained Earnings	Other

E11-11 The following accounts appear in the ledger of Ozabal Inc. after the books are closed at December 31:

Prepare a stockholders' equity section.
(SO 7)

Common Stock (no-par, $1 stated value, 400,000 shares authorized, 300,000 shares issued)	$ 300,000
Common Stock Dividends Distributable	75,000
Paid-in Capital in Excess of Stated Value—Common Stock	1,200,000
Preferred Stock ($5 par value, 8%, 40,000 shares authorized, 30,000 shares issued)	150,000
Retained Earnings	900,000
Treasury Stock (10,000 common shares)	60,000
Paid-in Capital in Excess of Par Value—Preferred Stock	244,000

Instructions
Prepare the stockholders' equity section at December 31, assuming $100,000 of retained earnings is restricted for plant expansion.

E11-12 This financial information is available for Mary Jo Corporation:

Calculate ratios to evaluate dividend and earnings performance.
(SO 8)

	1998	1997
Average common stockholders' equity	$1,200,000	$900,000
Dividends paid to common stockholders	50,000	30,000
Dividends paid to preferred stockholders	10,000	10,000
Net income	200,000	140,000
Market price of common stock	20	15

The average number of shares of common stock outstanding was 80,000 for 1997 and 100,000 for 1998.

Instructions
Calculate the dividend yield, payout ratio, earnings per share, price-earnings ratio, and return on common stockholders' equity ratio for 1998 and 1997.

E11-13 This financial information is available for Fountain City Corporation:

Calculate ratios to evaluate dividend and earnings performance.
(SO 8)

	1998	1997
Average common stockholders' equity	$1,800,000	$1,900,000
Dividends paid to common stockholders	90,000	70,000
Dividends paid to preferred stockholders	10,000	15,000
Net income	230,000	180,000
Market price of common stock	20	25

526 CHAPTER 11 Reporting and Analyzing Stockholders' Equity

The average number of shares of common stock outstanding was 180,000 for 1997 and 150,000 for 1998.

Instructions
Calculate the dividend yield, payout ratio, earnings per share, price-earnings ratio, and return on common stockholders' equity ratio for 1998 and 1997.

PROBLEMS

Journalize stock transactions, post, and prepare paid-in capital section.
(SO 2, 4, 7)

P11-1 Jackie Remmers Corporation was organized on January 1, 1998. It is authorized to issue 20,000 shares of 6%, $50 par value preferred stock and 500,000 shares of no-par common stock with a stated value of $1 per share. The following stock transactions were completed during the first year:

Jan. 10	Issued 100,000 shares of common stock for cash at $3 per share.
Mar. 1	Issued 10,000 shares of preferred stock for cash at $51 per share.
May 1	Issued 75,000 shares of common stock for cash at $4 per share.
Sept. 1	Issued 5,000 shares of common stock for cash at $6 per share.
Nov. 1	Issued 2,000 shares of preferred stock for cash at $53 per share.

Instructions
(a) Journalize the transactions.
(b) Post to the stockholders' equity accounts. (Use T accounts.)
(c) Prepare the paid-in capital portion of the stockholders' equity section at December 31, 1998.

Journalize transactions, post, and prepare a stockholders' equity section; calculate ratios.
(SO 2, 3, 5, 7, 8)

P11-2 The stockholders' equity accounts of Chung Corporation on January 1, 1998, were as follows:

Preferred Stock (10%, $100 par noncumulative, 5,000 shares authorized)	$ 300,000
Common Stock ($5 stated value, 300,000 shares authorized)	1,000,000
Paid-in Capital in Excess of Par Value—Preferred Stock	15,000
Paid-in Capital in Excess of Stated Value—Common Stock	400,000
Retained Earnings	488,000
Treasury Stock—Common (5,000 shares)	40,000

During 1998 the corporation had these transactions and events pertaining to its stockholders' equity:

Feb. 1	Issued 4,000 shares of common stock for $25,000.
Mar. 20	Purchased 1,000 additional shares of common treasury stock at $8 per share.
Oct. 1	Declared a 10% cash dividend on preferred stock, payable November 1.
Dec. 1	Declared a $.40 per share cash dividend to stockholders of record on December 15, payable December 31, 1998.
31	Determined that net income for the year was $215,000. At December 31 the market price of the common stock was $10 per share.

Instructions
(a) Journalize the transactions.
(b) Enter the beginning balances in the accounts and post the journal entries to the stockholders' equity accounts. (Use T accounts.)
(c) Prepare the stockholders' equity section of the balance sheet at December 31, 1998.
(d) Calculate the dividend yield, payout ratio, earnings per share, price-earnings ratio, and return on common stockholders' equity ratio.

Prepare a stockholders' equity section.
(SO 7)

P11-3 On December 31, 1997, V. Conway Company had 1,500,000 shares of $10 par common stock issued and outstanding. The stockholders' equity accounts at December 31, 1997, had the balances listed here:

Common Stock	$15,000,000
Additional Paid-in Capital	1,500,000
Retained Earnings	900,000

Transactions during 1998 and other information related to stockholders' equity accounts were as follows:

1. On January 10, 1998, Conway issued at $110 per share 100,000 shares of $100 par value, 8% cumulative preferred stock.
2. On February 8, 1998, Conway reacquired 10,000 shares of its common stock for $16 per share.
3. On June 8, 1998, Conway declared a cash dividend of $1 per share on the common stock outstanding, payable on July 10, 1998, to stockholders of record on July 1, 1998.
4. On December 15, 1998, Conway declared the yearly cash dividend on preferred stock, payable January 10, 1999, to stockholders of record on December 15, 1997.
5. Net income for the year was $3,600,000. At December 31, 1998, the market price of the common stock was $18 per share.

Instructions
Prepare the stockholders' equity section of Conway's balance sheet at December 31, 1998.

P11-4 The ledger of Reno Corporation at December 31, 1998, after the books have been closed, contains the following stockholders' equity accounts:

Reproduce retained earnings account, and prepare a stockholders' equity section.
(SO 5, 6, 7)

Preferred Stock (10,000 shares issued)	$1,000,000
Common Stock (400,000 shares issued)	2,000,000
Paid-in Capital in Excess of Par Value—Preferred Stock	200,000
Paid-in Capital in Excess of Stated Value—Common Stock	1,200,000
Common Stock Dividends Distributable	100,000
Retained Earnings	2,540,000

A review of the accounting records reveals this information:
1. Preferred stock is 10%, $100 par value, noncumulative, and callable at $125. Since January 1, 1997, 10,000 shares have been outstanding; 20,000 shares are authorized.
2. Common stock is no-par with a stated value of $5 per share; 600,000 shares are authorized.
3. The January 1 balance in Retained Earnings was $2,200,000.
4. On October 1, 100,000 shares of common stock were sold for cash at $8 per share.
5. A cash dividend of $400,000 was declared and properly allocated to preferred and common stock on November 1. No dividends were paid to preferred stockholders in 1997.
6. On December 31 a 5% common stock dividend was declared out of retained earnings on common stock when the market price per share was $7.
7. Net income for the year was $880,000.
8. On December 31, 1998, the directors authorized disclosure of a $100,000 restriction of retained earnings for plant expansion. (Use Note A.)

Instructions
(a) Reproduce the retained earnings account (T account) for the year.
(b) Prepare the stockholders' equity section of the balance sheet at December 31.

P11-5 Largent Corporation has been authorized to issue 20,000 shares of $100 par value, 10%, noncumulative preferred stock and 1,000,000 shares of no-par common stock. The corporation assigned a $2.50 stated value to the common stock. At December 31, 1998, the ledger contained the following balances pertaining to stockholders' equity:

Prepare entries for stock transactions, and prepare a stockholders' equity section.
(SO 2, 3, 4, 7)

Preferred Stock	$ 120,000
Paid-in Capital in Excess of Par Value—Preferred Stock	24,000
Common Stock	1,000,000
Paid-in Capital in Excess of Stated Value—Common Stock	2,850,000
Treasury Stock—Common (1,000 shares)	12,000
Retained Earnings	82,000

The preferred stock was issued for $144,000 cash. All common stock issued was for cash. In November 1,000 shares of common stock were purchased for the treasury at a per share cost of $12. No dividends were declared in 1998.

Instructions
(a) Prepare the journal entries for the:
   (1) Issuance of preferred stock for cash.
   (2) Issuance of common stock for cash.
   (3) Purchase of common treasury stock for cash.
(b) Prepare the stockholders' equity section of the balance sheet at December 31, 1998.

CHAPTER 11 Reporting and Analyzing Stockholders' Equity

Prepare dividend entries, prepare a stockholders' equity section, and calculate ratios.
(SO 5, 7, 8)

P11-6 On January 1, 1998, Wirth Corporation had these stockholders' equity accounts:

Common Stock ($10 par value, 80,000 shares issued and outstanding)	$800,000
Paid-in Capital in Excess of Par Value	200,000
Retained Earnings	540,000

During the year, the following transactions occurred:

Jan. 15 Declared a $1 cash dividend per share to stockholders of record on January 31, payable February 15.
Feb. 15 Paid the dividend declared in January.
Apr. 15 Declared a 10% stock dividend to stockholders of record on April 30, distributable May 15. On April 15 the market price of the stock was $13 per share.
May 15 Issued the shares for the stock dividend.
Dec. 1 Declared a $1 per share cash dividend to stockholders of record on December 15, payable January 10, 1999.
     31 Determined that net income for the year was $220,000. On December 31 the market price of the stock was $15 per share.

Instructions
(a) Journalize the transactions.
(b) Enter the beginning balances and post the entries to the stockholders' equity T accounts. [*Note:* Open additional stockholders' equity accounts as needed.]
(c) Prepare the stockholders' equity section of the balance sheet at December 31.
(d) Calculate the dividend yield, payout ratio, earnings per share, price-earnings ratio, and return on common stockholders' equity ratio.

Prepare a stockholders' equity section.
(SO 7)

P11-7 The following stockholders' equity accounts, arranged alphabetically, are in the ledger of Dublin Corporation at December 31, 1998:

Common Stock ($10 stated value)	$1,500,000
Paid-in Capital in Excess of Par Value—Preferred Stock	280,000
Paid-in Capital in Excess of Stated Value—Common Stock	900,000
Preferred Stock (8%, $100 par, noncumulative)	400,000
Retained Earnings	1,134,000
Treasury Stock—Common (8,000 shares)	88,000

Instructions
Prepare the stockholders' equity section of the balance sheet at December 31, 1998.

Prepare a stockholders' equity section.
(SO 7)

P11-8 On January 1, 1998, Cedeno Inc. had these stockholders' equity balances:

Common Stock (500,000 shares issued)	$1,000,000
Paid-in Capital in Excess of Par Value	500,000
Stock Dividends Distributable	100,000
Retained Earnings	600,000

During 1998, the following transactions and events occurred:
1. Issued 50,000 shares of $2 par value common stock as a result of a 10% stock dividend declared on December 15, 1997.
2. Issued 30,000 shares of common stock for cash at $5 per share.
3. Purchased 20,000 shares of common stock for the treasury at $6 per share.
4. Declared and paid a cash dividend of $100,000.
5. Earned net income of $300,000.

Instructions
Prepare the stockholders' equity section of the balance sheet at December 31, 1998.

ALTERNATIVE PROBLEMS

Journalize stock transactions, post, and prepare paid-in capital section.
(SO 2, 4, 7)

P11-1A Wetland Corporation was organized on January 1, 1998. It is authorized to issue 10,000 shares of 8%, $100 par value preferred stock and 500,000 shares of no-par common stock with a stated value of $2 per share. The following stock transactions were completed during the first year:

Jan. 10 Issued 80,000 shares of common stock for cash at $3 per share.
Mar. 1 Issued 5,000 shares of preferred stock for cash at $104 per share.
May 1 Issued 80,000 shares of common stock for cash at $4 per share.
Sept. 1 Issued 10,000 shares of common stock for cash at $5 per share.
Nov. 1 Issued 1,000 shares of preferred stock for cash at $108 per share.

Instructions
(a) Journalize the transactions.
(b) Post to the stockholders' equity accounts. (Use T accounts.)
(c) Prepare the paid-in capital section of stockholders' equity at December 31, 1998.

P11-2A The stockholders' equity accounts of Capozza Corporation on January 1, 1998, were as follows:

Journalize transactions, post, and prepare a stockholders' equity section; calculate ratios.
(SO 2, 3, 5, 7, 8)

Preferred Stock (12%, $50 par cumulative, 10,000 shares authorized)	$ 400,000
Common Stock ($1 stated value, 2,000,000 shares authorized)	1,000,000
Paid-in Capital in Excess of Par Value—Preferred Stock	80,000
Paid-in Capital in Excess of Stated Value—Common Stock	1,400,000
Retained Earnings	1,816,000
Treasury Stock—Common (10,000 shares)	40,000

During 1998 the corporation had these transactions and events pertaining to its stockholders' equity:

Feb. 1 Issued 20,000 shares of common stock for $100,000.
Nov. 10 Purchased 1,000 shares of common stock for the treasury at a cost of $6,000.
Nov. 15 Declared a 12% cash dividend on preferred stock, payable December 15.
Dec. 1 Declared a $.20 per share cash dividend to stockholders of record on December 15, payable December 31, 1998.
   31 Determined that net income for the year was $377,000. The market price of the common stock on this date was $9 per share.

Instructions
(a) Journalize the transactions.
(b) Enter the beginning balances in the accounts, and post the journal entries to the stockholders' equity accounts. (Use T accounts.)
(c) Prepare the stockholders' equity section of the balance sheet at December 31, 1998, including the disclosure of the preferred dividends in arrears.
(d) Calculate the dividend yield, payout ratio, earnings per share, price-earnings ratio, and return on common stockholders' equity ratio.

P11-3A On December 31, 1997, K. Schipper Company had 1,000,000 shares of $1 par common stock issued and outstanding. The stockholders' equity accounts at December 31, 1997, had the balances listed here:

Prepare a stockholders' equity section.
(SO 7)

Common Stock	$1,000,000
Additional Paid-in Capital	500,000
Retained Earnings	700,000

Transactions during 1998 and other information related to stockholders' equity accounts were as follows:

1. On January 9, 1998, Schipper issued at $6 per share 100,000 shares of $5 par value, 8% cumulative preferred stock.
2. On February 8, 1998, Schipper reacquired 10,000 shares of its common stock for $12 per share.
3. On June 10, 1998, Schipper declared a cash dividend of $1 per share on the common stock outstanding, payable on July 10, 1998, to stockholders of record on July 1, 1998.
4. On December 15, 1998, Schipper declared the yearly cash dividend on preferred stock, payable December 28, 1998 to stockholders of record on December 15, 1998.
5. Net income for the year is $2,400,000. At December 31, 1998, the market price of the common stock was $15 per share.

Instructions
Prepare the stockholders' equity section of Schipper's balance sheet at December 31, 1998.

530 CHAPTER 11 Reporting and Analyzing Stockholders' Equity

Reproduce retained earnings account, and prepare a stockholders' equity section.
(SO 5, 6, 7)

P11-4A The post-closing trial balance of Maggio Corporation at December 31, 1998, contains these stockholders' equity accounts:

Preferred Stock (15,000 shares issued)	$ 750,000
Common Stock (250,000 shares issued)	2,500,000
Paid-in Capital in Excess of Par Value—Preferred Stock	250,000
Paid-in Capital in Excess of Par Value—Common Stock	500,000
Common Stock Dividends Distributable	200,000
Retained Earnings	743,000

A review of the accounting records reveals this information:
1. Preferred stock is $50 par, 10%, and cumulative; 15,000 shares have been outstanding since January 1, 1997.
2. Authorized stock is 20,000 shares of preferred and 500,000 shares of common with a $10 par value.
3. The January 1 balance in Retained Earnings was $920,000.
4. On July 1, 20,000 shares of common stock were sold for cash at $16 per share.
5. A cash dividend of $250,000 was declared and properly allocated to preferred and common stock on October 1. No dividends were paid to preferred stockholders in 1997.
6. On December 31 an 8% common stock dividend was declared out of retained earnings on common stock when the market price per share was $16.
7. Net income for the year was $435,000.
8. On December 31, 1998, the directors authorized disclosure of a $200,000 restriction of retained earnings for plant expansion. (Use Note X.)

Instructions
(a) Reproduce the retained earnings account for the year.
(b) Prepare the stockholders' equity section of the balance sheet at December 31.

Prepare a stockholders' equity section.
(SO 7)

P11-5A The following stockholders' equity accounts, arranged alphabetically, are in the ledger of Shirley Denson Corporation at December 31, 1998:

Common Stock ($5 stated value)	$2,500,000
Paid-in Capital in Excess of Par Value—Preferred Stock	692,000
Paid-in Capital in Excess of Stated Value—Common Stock	1,500,000
Preferred Stock (8%, $50 par, noncumulative)	800,000
Retained Earnings	1,958,000
Treasury Stock—Common (10,000 shares)	130,000

Instructions
Prepare the stockholders' equity section of the balance sheet at December 31, 1998.

Prepare dividend entries, prepare a stockholders' equity section, and calculate ratios.
(SO 5, 7, 8)

P11-6A On January 1, 1998, Casey Stengel Corporation had these stockholders' equity accounts:

Common Stock ($20 par value, 60,000 shares issued and outstanding)	$1,200,000
Paid-in Capital in Excess of Par Value	200,000
Retained Earnings	500,000

During the year, the following transactions occurred:

Feb. 1 Declared a $1 cash dividend per share to stockholders of record on February 15, payable March 1.
Mar. 1 Paid the dividend declared in February.
July 1 Declared a 5% stock dividend to stockholders of record on July 15, distributable July 31. On July 1 the market price of the stock was $40 per share.
　　31 Issued the shares for the stock dividend.
Dec. 1 Declared a $2 per share dividend to stockholders of record on December 15, payable January 5, 1996.
　　31 Determined that net income for the year was $325,000. The market price of the common stock on this date was $48.

Instructions

(a) Journalize the transactions.
(b) Enter the beginning balances and post the entries to the stockholders' equity T accounts. [*Note:* Open additional stockholders' equity accounts as needed.]
(c) Prepare the stockholders' equity section of the balance sheet at December 31.
(d) Calculate the dividend yield, payout ratio, earnings per share, price-earnings ratio, and return on common stockholders' equity ratio.

BROADENING YOUR PERSPECTIVE

FINANCIAL REPORTING AND ANALYSIS

FINANCIAL REPORTING PROBLEM: *Starbucks Corporation*

BYP11-1 The stockholders' equity section of Starbucks' balance sheet is shown in the Consolidated Balance Sheet in Appendix A. You will also find data relative to this problem on other pages of the appendix.

Instructions
Answer these questions:
(a) What is the par or stated value per share of Starbucks' common stock?
(b) What percentage of Starbucks' authorized common stock was issued at September 29, 1996? (Round to the nearest full percent.)
(c) How many shares of common stock were outstanding at September 29, 1996, and at October 1, 1995?
(d) What were the high and low sale prices per share of common stock at September 29, 1996, and at October 1, 1995, as reported under Shareholder Information?
(e) Calculate the dividend yield, payout ratio, earnings per share, price-earnings ratio, and return on common stockholders' equity ratio for 1996. (Starbucks' stock price at September 29, 1996, was $35.88.)

COMPARATIVE ANALYSIS PROBLEM: *Starbucks vs. Green Mountain Coffee*

BYP11-2 The financial statements of Green Mountain Coffee are presented in Appendix B, following the financial statements for Starbucks in Appendix A.

Instructions
(a) Based on the information in these financial statements, compute the 1996 return on common stockholders' equity ratio for each company.
(b) What conclusions concerning the companies' profitability can be drawn from this ratio?

RESEARCH CASE

BYP11-3 The September 4, 1995, issue of *Fortune* includes an article by Richard D. Hylton entitled "Stock Buybacks Are Hot—Here's How You Can Cash In."

Instructions
Read the article and answer these questions:
(a) What was the total amount of announced intentions to repurchase shares of stock in 1994? What was this figure during the first 6 months of 1995?
(b) The goal of many of these repurchase programs was to increase the price of the remaining outstanding shares. Identify the three factors that will determine the impact of repurchases on share price.
(c) What did Microsoft do with the shares it repurchased? Why might it use repurchased shares for this purpose rather than issuing new shares?

INTERPRETING FINANCIAL STATEMENTS

BYP11-4 Minicase 1 *Kellogg Company*

Kellogg Company is the world's leading producer of ready-to-eat cereal products. In recent years the company has taken numerous steps aimed at improving its profitability and earnings per share. Included in these steps was the layoff of 2,000 employees—roughly 13% of Kellogg's workforce. In addition, Kellogg repurchased large amounts of its own shares: 5,684,864 in 1995; 6,194,500 in 1994; and 9,487,508 in 1993. It announced plans for significant additional repurchases in the coming year. The expenses for share repurchases were $380 million in 1995, $327 million in 1994, and $548 million in 1993—that's nearly $1.3 billion dollars over a 3-year period. The total amount expended for new property during this same period was $1.1 billion; thus, the company spent more money repurchasing stock than building the company. Also during this period the company issued $400 million in new debt. The table presents some basic facts for Kellogg Company:

	($ in millions)	
	1995	1994
Net sales	$7,003	$6,562
Net income	490	705
Total assets	3,801	4,467
Total liabilities	2,824	2,659
Common stock, $.25 par value	78	78
Capital in excess of par value	105	69
Retained earnings	3,963	3,801
Treasury stock, at cost	2,361	1,981
Preferred stock	0	0

The number of shares outstanding was 222,000,000 for 1994 and 217,000,000 for 1995.

Instructions
(a) What are some of the reasons that management purchases its own stock?
(b) What was the approximate impact on earnings per share of the common stock repurchases during this 3-year period? That is, calculate earnings per share after the share repurchases and before the repurchases for 1995. (Use the total repurchases during the 3-year period—21,366,872 shares—rounded to 21 million.)
(c) Calculate the debt to total assets ratios for 1994 and 1995 and discuss the implications of the change.

BYP11-5 Minicase 2 *Marriott Corporation*

In 1993 Marriott Corporation split into two companies: Host Marriott Corporation and Marriott International. Host Marriott retained ownership of the corporation's vast hotel and other properties, while Marriott International, rather than owning hotels, managed them. The purpose of this split was to free Marriott International from the "baggage" associated with Host Marriott, thus allowing it to be more aggressive in its pursuit of growth. The following information is provided for each corporation for 1994, their first full year operating as independent companies:

	(in millions)	
	Host Marriott	Marriott International
Sales	$1,501	$8,415
Net income	(25)	200
Total assets	3,822	3,207
Total liabilities	3,112	2,440
Stockholders' equity	710	767

Instructions
(a) The two companies were split by the issuance of shares of Marriott International to all shareholders of the previous combined company. Discuss the nature of this transaction.
(b) Calculate the debt to total assets ratio for each company.
(c) Calculate the return on assets and return on common stockholders' equity ratios for each company.

(d) The company's debtholders were fiercely opposed to the original plan to split the two companies because the original plan had Host Marriott absorbing the majority of the company's debt. They relented only when Marriott International agreed to absorb a larger share of the debt. Discuss the possible reasons the debtholders were opposed to the plan to split the company.

CRITICAL THINKING

MANAGEMENT DECISION CASE

BYP11-6 The stockholders' meeting for Mantle Corporation has been in progress for some time. The chief financial officer for Mantle is presently reviewing the company's financial statements and is explaining the items that make up the stockholders' equity section of the balance sheet for the current year. The stockholders' equity section for Mantle Corporation at December 31, 1998, is presented here:

MANTLE CORPORATION
Partial Balance Sheet

Stockholders' equity		
Paid-in capital		
Capital stock		
Preferred stock, authorized 1,000,000 shares cumulative, $100 par value, $8 per share, 6,000 shares issued and outstanding		$ 600,000
Common stock, authorized 5,000,000 shares, $1 par value, 3,000,000 shares issued and 2,700,000 outstanding		3,000,000
Total capital stock		3,600,000
Additional paid-in capital		
In excess of par value—preferred stock	$ 50,000	
In excess of par value—common stock	25,000,000	
Total additional paid-in capital		25,050,000
Total paid-in capital		28,650,000
Retained earnings		900,000
Total paid-in capital and retained earnings		29,550,000
Less: Common treasury stock (300,000 shares)		9,300,000
Total stockholders' equity		$20,250,000

A number of questions regarding the stockholders' equity section of Mantle Corporation's balance sheet have been raised at the meeting.

Instructions
Answer the following questions as if you were the chief financial officer for Mantle Corporation:
(a) "What does the cumulative provision related to the preferred stock mean?"
(b) "I thought the common stock was presently selling at $29.75, and yet the company has the stock stated at $1 per share. How can that be?"
(c) "Why is the company buying back its common stock? Furthermore, the treasury stock has a debit balance because it is subtracted from stockholders' equity. Why is treasury stock not reported as an asset if it has a debit balance?"
(d) "Why is it necessary to show additional paid-in capital? Why not just show common stock at the total amount paid in?"

A REAL-WORLD FOCUS: *Diebold, Inc.*

BYP11-7 *Diebold, Incorporated,* is a world leader in financial self-service transaction systems, security products, and customer service. The company develops, manufactures, sells, and services automated teller machines (ATMs), electronic and physical security systems, and bank facility equipment. It also designs and markets related application software and integrated systems for global financial and commercial markets. Headquartered in Canton, Ohio, Diebold has offices in five countries and manufacturing facilities in the United States and China.

The following note related to stockholders' equity was recently reported in Diebold's annual report:

DIEBOLD, INC.
Notes to the Financial Statements

On February 1, 1994, the Board of Directors declared a 3-for-2 stock split, distributed on February 22, 1994, to shareholders of record on February 10, 1994. Accordingly, all numbers of common shares, except authorized shares and treasury shares, and all per share data have been restated to reflect this stock split in addition to the 3-for-2 stock split declared on January 27, 1993, distributed on February 26, 1993, to shareholders of record on February 10, 1993.

On the basis of amounts declared and paid, the annualized quarterly dividends per share were $.80 in 1993, $.75 in 1992, and $.71 in 1991.

Instructions
(a) What is the significance of the date of record and the date of distribution?
(b) Why might Diebold have declared a 3-for-2 stock split?
(c) What impact does Diebold's stock split have on (1) total stockholders' equity, (2) total par value, and (3) outstanding shares?

A REAL-WORLD FOCUS: *Barrister Information Systems Corporation*

BYP11-8 *Barrister Information Systems Corp.* develops, assembles, markets, and services computer systems and local area networks for law firms. Headquartered in Buffalo, New York, it has offices in 19 U.S. cities.

Barrister Information Systems has two classes of preferred stock—A and C—in addition to its common stock. The 1,300 shares of Series A preferred stock are nonvoting, have a 12% cumulative dividend, have liquidation preference rights over the Series C preferred stock and the common stock, and are callable by the company at any time for $1,000 per share plus cumulative unpaid dividends. Each share of Series A preferred stock is convertible into 500 shares of common stock. As of March 31, 1993, the cumulative unpaid dividends on the Series A preferred stock totaled $254,000.

Instructions
(a) Should the $254,000 in dividends not paid be reported as a liability on the balance sheet?
(b) If the par value of the Class A preferred stock is $100 per share, what dollar amount in dividends can the shareholders expect annually on the Class A preferred stock?

GROUP ACTIVITY

BYP11-9 Companies have a variety of options with regard to actions they can take concerning common stock and dividends. For example, a company can:
(a) issue no cash dividend.　　(d) purchase treasury stock.
(b) enact a stock split.　　　　(e) issue a property dividend.
(c) issue stock dividends.　　　(f) issue large cash dividends.

The appropriateness of each of these actions depends on the circumstances faced by the company.

Instructions
In groups of five or six people, discuss what circumstances would make each of these actions appropriate. That is, for example, under what circumstances is a company likely to issue no cash dividend?

Communication Activity

BYP11-10 Louis P. Brady, your uncle, is an inventor who has decided to incorporate. Uncle Lou knows that you are an accounting major at U.N.O. In a recent letter to you, he ends with the question, "I'm filling out a state incorporation application. Can you tell me the difference among the following terms: (1) authorized stock, (2) issued stock, (3) outstanding stock, and (4) preferred stock?"

Instructions
In a brief note, differentiate for Uncle Lou the four different stock terms. Write the letter to be friendly, yet professional.

Ethics Cases

BYP11-11 The R&D division of Simplex Chemical Corp. has just developed a chemical for sterilizing the vicious Brazilian "killer bees" which are invading Mexico and the southern United States. The president of Simplex is anxious to get the chemical on the market because Simplex's profits need a boost—and his job is in jeopardy because of decreasing sales and profits. Simplex has an opportunity to sell this chemical in Central American countries, where the laws are much more relaxed than in the United States.

The director of Simplex's R&D division strongly recommends further research in the laboratory to test the side effects of this chemical on other insects, birds, animals, plants, and even humans. He cautions the president, "We could be sued from all sides if the chemical has tragic side effects that we didn't even test for in the lab." The president answers, "We can't wait an additional year for your lab tests. We can avoid losses from such lawsuits by establishing a separate wholly owned corporation to shield Simplex Chemical Corp. from such lawsuits. We can't lose any more than our investment in the new corporation, and we'll invest just the patent covering this chemical. We'll reap the benefits if the chemical works and is safe, and avoid the losses from lawsuits if it's a disaster." The following week Simplex creates a new wholly owned corporation called Zoebee Inc., sells the chemical patent to it for $10, and watches the spraying begin.

Instructions
(a) Who are the stakeholders in this situation?
(b) Are the president's motives and actions ethical?
(c) Can Simplex shield itself against losses of Zoebee Inc.?

BYP11-12 Flambeau Corporation has paid 60 consecutive quarterly cash dividends (15 years). The last 6 months have been a real cash drain on the company, however, as profit margins have been greatly narrowed by increasing competition. With a cash balance sufficient to meet only day-to-day operating needs, the president, Vince Ramsey, has decided that a stock dividend instead of a cash dividend should be declared. He tells Flambeau's financial vice-president, Janice Rahn, to issue a press release stating that the company is extending its consecutive dividend record with the issuance of a 5% stock dividend. "Write the press release convincing the stockholders that the stock dividend is just as good as a cash dividend," he orders. "Just watch our stock rise when we announce the stock dividend; it must be a good thing if that happens."

Instructions
(a) Who are the stakeholders in this situation?
(b) Is there anything unethical about President Ramsey's intentions or actions?
(c) What is the effect of a stock dividend on a corporation's stockholders' equity accounts? Which would you rather receive as a stockholder—a cash dividend or a stock dividend? Why?

Financial Analysis on the Web

BYP11-13 *Purpose:* Most publicly traded companies are analyzed by numerous analysts. These analysts often don't agree about a company's future prospects. In this exercise you will find analysts' ratings about companies and make comparisons over time and across companies in the same industry. You will also see to what extent the analysts experienced "earnings surprises." Earnings surprises can cause changes in stock prices.

Address: http://biz.yahoo.com/i

Steps:
1. Choose **Company**.
2. Choose **Industry**.
3. Select an industry.
4. Select a company.
5. Choose **Research Report**.

Instructions
Answer the following questions:
(a) How many brokers rated the company?
(b) What percentage rated it a strong buy?
(c) What was the average rating for the week?
(d) Did the average rating improve or decline relative to last week?
(e) How do the brokers rank this company among all the companies in its industry?
(f) What was the amount of the earnings surprise during the last quarter (that is, to what extent were analysts' expectations of earnings incorrect)?
(g) Are earnings expected to increase or decrease this quarter compared to last?

BYP11-14 *Purpose:* Use the stockholders' equity section of an annual report and identify the major components.

Address: http://www.reportgallery.com

Steps:
1. From Report Gallery Homepage, choose **Viewing Library**.
2. Select a particular company.
3. Choose **Annual Report**.
4. Follow instructions below.

Instructions
Answer the following questions:
(a) What is the company's name?
(b) What classes of capital stock has the company issued?
(c) For each class of stock:
   (1) How many shares are authorized, issued, and/or outstanding?
   (2) What is the par value?
(d) What are the company's retained earnings?
(e) Has the company acquired treasury stock? How many shares?

Answers to Self-Study Questions
1. c 2. b 3. d 4. c 5. a 6. d 7. d 8. b 9. c 10. b

CHAPTER 12

Reporting and Analyzing Investments

STUDY OBJECTIVES

After studying this chapter, you should be able to:

1. Identify the reasons corporations invest in stocks and debt securities.
2. Explain the accounting for debt investments.
3. Explain the accounting for stock investments.
4. Describe the purpose and usefulness of consolidated financial statements.
5. Indicate how debt and stock investments are valued and reported in the financial statements.
6. Distinguish between temporary and long-term investments.

Is There Anything Else We Can Buy?

In a rapidly changing world you must change rapidly or suffer the consequences. In business, to change means to invest. A case in point is found in the entertainment industry. Technology is bringing about new innovations so quickly that it is nearly impossible to guess which technologies will last and which will soon fade away. For example, will both satellite TV and cable TV survive, or will just one succeed, or will both be replaced by something else? If you guess (and invest) wrong, you lose. Or consider the publishing industry. Will paper newspapers and magazines be replaced by online news via the World Wide Web? If you are a publisher, you have to make your best guess about what the future holds and invest accordingly.

Time Warner Corporation lives at the center of this arena. It is not an environment for the timid, and Time Warner's philosophy is anything but timid. It might be characterized as "If we can't beat you, we will buy you." Its mantra is "invest, invest, invest." An abbreviated list of Time Warner's holdings gives an idea of its reach. Magazines: *People, Time, Life, Sports Illustrated, Fortune*. Book publishers: Time-Life Books, Book-of-the Month Club, Little, Brown & Co., Sunset Books. Music: Warner Bros., Reprise, Atlantic, Rhino, Elektra, Asylum, representing such artists as Hootie and the Blowfish, Tori Amos, Eric Clapton, and Madonna. Television and movies: Warner Bros. ("ER" and "Friends"), HBO, and movies like *Batman Forever*. Also: Six Flags Amusement Parks and partial ownership in the SEGA video game channel and Hasbro Toys. And, in 1996 Time Warner merged with Turner Broadcasting, so it now owns TNT, CNN, and Turner's incredible library of thousands of classic movies (e.g., *Gone with the Wind, The Wizard of Oz, Casablanca*). Even before the Turner merger, Time Warner owned more information and entertainment copyrights and brands than any other company in the world.

So what has Time Warner's aggressive acquisition spree meant for the bottom line? It has left Time Warner with huge debts and massive interest costs. In addition, some of the acquisitions have not come cheap, re-

sulting in large amounts of reported goodwill and goodwill amortization. As a consequence, since the merger of Time and Warner in 1988, the combined corporation has reported positive net income in only one year through 1996, and analysts predict that its losses will continue for some time longer. With so much investing by Time Warner and so little profit to show for it, one is reminded of one more of its companies, Looney Tunes cartoons—"That's all, folks."

On the World Wide Web
Time Warner Corp.:
http://www.timewarner.com

PREVIEW OF CHAPTER 12

Time Warner's management believes in a policy of aggressive growth through investing in the stock of existing companies. In addition to purchasing stock, companies also purchase other securities such as debt securities issued by corporations or by governments. Investments can be purchased for a short or long period of time, as a passive investment, or with the intent to control another company. As you will see later in the chapter, the way in which a company accounts for its investments is determined by a number of factors.

The content and organization of this chapter are as follows:

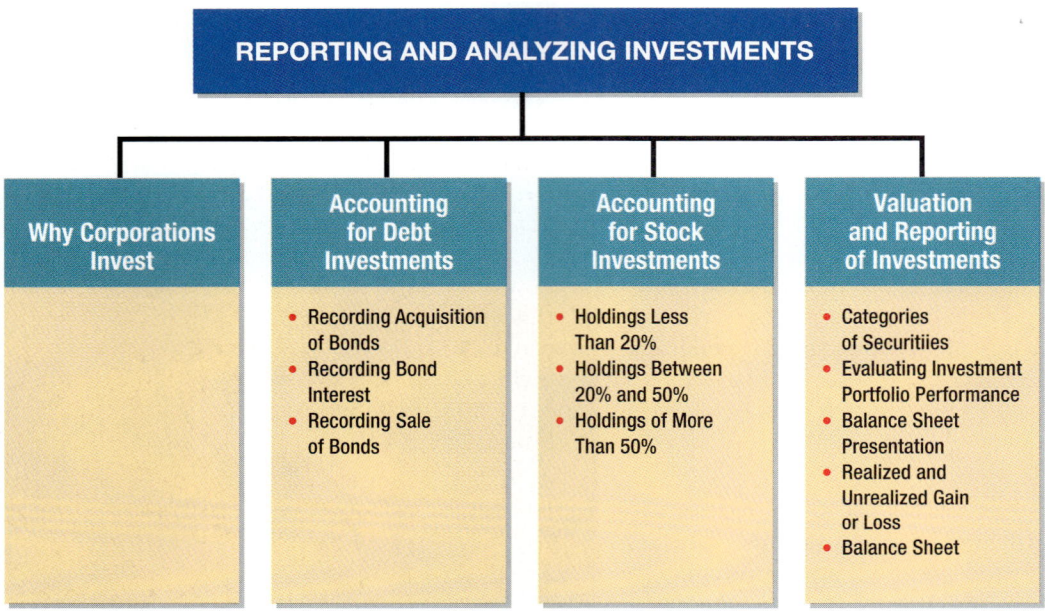

WHY CORPORATIONS INVEST

STUDY OBJECTIVE 1

Identify the reasons corporations invest in stocks and debt securities.

Corporations purchase investments in debt or equity securities generally for one of three reasons. First, a corporation may **have excess cash** that it does not need for the immediate purchase of operating assets. For example, many companies experience seasonal fluctuations in sales. A Cape Cod marina has more sales in the spring and summer than in the fall and winter, whereas the reverse is true for an Aspen ski shop. Thus, at the end of an operating cycle, many companies may have cash on hand that is temporarily idle pending the start of another operating cycle. Until the cash is needed, these companies may invest the excess funds to earn, through interest and dividends, a greater return than they would get by just holding the funds in the bank. The role played by such temporary investments in the operating cycle is depicted in Illustration 12-1.

Excess cash may also result from economic cycles. For example, when the economy is booming, General Motors generates considerable excess cash. Although it uses some of this cash to purchase new plant and equipment and pays out some of the cash in dividends, it may also invest excess cash in liquid assets in anticipation of a future downturn in the economy. It can then liquidate these investments during a recession, when sales slow down and cash is scarce.

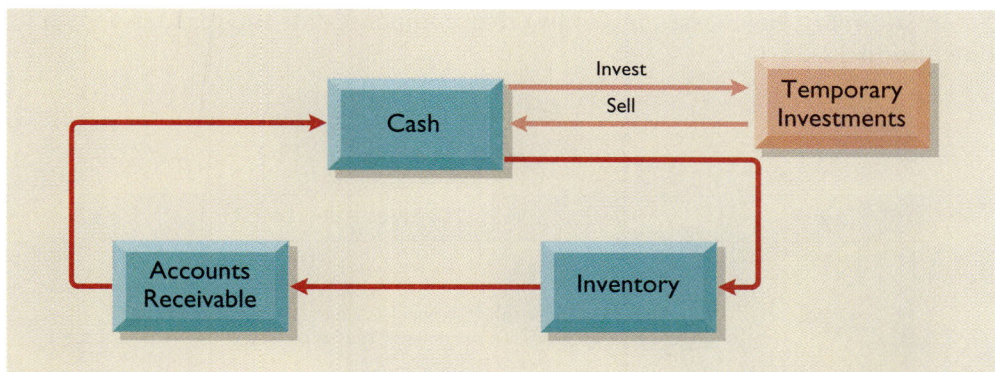

Illustration 12-1 Temporary investments and the operating cycle

When investing excess cash for short periods of time, corporations invest in low-risk, highly liquid securities—most often short-term government securities. It is generally not wise to invest short-term excess cash in shares of common stock because stock investments can experience rapid price changes. If you did invest your short-term excess cash in stock and the price of the stock declined significantly just before you needed cash again, you would be forced to sell your stock investment at a loss.

A second reason some companies such as banks purchase investments is because they generate a **significant portion of their earnings from investment income.** Although banks make most of their earnings by lending money, they also generate earnings by investing in debt and equity securities. Banks purchase investment securities because loan demand varies both seasonally and with changes in the economic climate. Thus, when loan demand is low, a bank must find other uses for its cash. Investing in securities also allows banks to diversify some of their risk. Bank regulators severely limit the ability of banks to invest in common stock; therefore, most investments held by banks are debt securities.

Pension funds and mutual funds are corporations that also regularly invest to generate earnings. However, they do so for *speculative reasons;* that is, they are speculating that the investment will increase in value and thus result in positive returns. Therefore, they invest primarily in the common stock of other corporations. These investments are passive in nature; the pension fund or mutual fund does not usually take an active role in controlling the affairs of the companies in which they invest.

A third reason why companies invest is for **strategic reasons.** A company may purchase a noncontrolling interest in another firm in a related industry in which it wishes to establish a presence. For example, Time Warner initially purchased an interest of less than 20% in Turner Broadcasting to have a stake in Turner's expanding business opportunities. Similarly, Canadian giant Seagram purchased a significant interest in Time Warner. (Thus, not even a huge corporation like Time Warner is at the top of the corporate "food chain.") Alternatively, a company can exercise some influence over one of its customers or suppliers by purchasing a significant, but not controlling, interest in that company.

A corporation may also choose to purchase a controlling interest in another company. This might be done to enter a new industry without incurring the tremendous costs and risks associated with starting from scratch. Or a company might purchase another company in its same industry. The purchase of a company that is in your industry, but involved in a different activity, is called a **vertical acquisition.** For example, Nike might purchase a chain of athletic shoe stores, such as The Athlete's Foot. In a **horizontal acquisition** you purchase a company that does the same activity as your company. For example, Nike might purchase Reebok.

542 CHAPTER 12 Reporting and Analyzing Investments

In summary, businesses invest in other companies for the reasons shown in Illustration 12-2.

Illustration 12-2 Why corporations invest

Reason	Typical Investment
To house excess cash until needed	Low-risk, high-liquidity, short-term securities such as government-issued securities
To generate earnings	Debt securities (banks and other financial institutions); and stock securities (mutual funds and pension funds)
To meet strategic goals	Stocks of companies in a related industry or in an unrelated industry that the company wishes to enter

BUSINESS INSIGHT
Investor Perspective

In the 2 months prior to approval by the federal government of the Time Warner/Turner deal, as approval appeared more certain, Time Warner's stock price increased by 30%. Although investors were applauding the strength of the combined entity, many analysts were very concerned about the mega-corporation's ability to control costs. The Time Warner deal and other acquisitions resulted in a $17.5 billion mountain of debt on Time Warner's balance sheet. Unless it can reduce this debt and control other costs, Time Warner will not return to profitability any time soon. One possible scenario is that $8 billion in debt could be taken off the books by selling the company's cable operations.

Observers were also interested to see how the two corporate cultures would merge. Ted Turner had been openly critical of Time Warner's management for running a loose ship, with far too much being spent on unnecessary extravagances such as corporate jets. Time Warner executives privately responded that if Mr. Turner was really concerned, he might consider taking a cut in his salary of $10 million a year.

STUDY OBJECTIVE 2
Explain the accounting for debt investments.

ACCOUNTING FOR DEBT INVESTMENTS

Debt investments are investments in government and corporation bonds. In accounting for debt investments, entries are required to record (1) the acquisition, (2) the interest revenue, and (3) the sale.

RECORDING ACQUISITION OF BONDS

At acquisition, the cost principle applies. Cost includes all expenditures necessary to acquire these investments, such as the price paid plus brokerage fees (commissions), if any. Assume that Kuhl Corporation acquires 50 Doan Inc. 12%, 10-year, $1,000 bonds on January 1, 1998, for $54,000, including brokerage fees of $1,000. The entry to record the investment is:

Jan. 1	Debt Investments	54,000	
	Cash		54,000
	(To record purchase of 50 Doan Inc. bonds)		

RECORDING BOND INTEREST

The bonds pay interest of $3,000 semiannually on July 1 and January 1 ($50,000 × 12% × $\frac{1}{2}$). The entry for the receipt of interest on July 1 is:

July 1	Cash	3,000	
	Interest Revenue		3,000
	(To record receipt of interest on Doan Inc. bonds)		

If Kuhl Corporation's fiscal year ends on December 31, it is necessary to accrue the interest of $3,000 earned since July 1. The adjusting entry is:

Dec. 31	Interest Receivable	3,000	
	Interest Revenue		3,000
	(To accrue interest on Doan Inc. bonds)		

Interest Receivable is reported as a current asset in the balance sheet; Interest Revenue is reported under Other Revenues and Gains in the income statement. When the interest is received on January 1, the entry is:

Jan. 1	Cash	3,000	
	Interest Receivable		3,000
	(To record receipt of accrued interest)		

A credit to Interest Revenue at this time is incorrect because the interest revenue was earned and accrued in the preceding accounting period.

RECORDING SALE OF BONDS

When the bonds are sold, it is necessary to decrease the investment account by the amount of the cost of the bonds. Any difference between the net proceeds from sale (sales price less brokerage fees) and the cost of the bonds is recorded as a gain or loss. Assume, for example, that Kuhl Corporation receives net proceeds of $58,000 on the sale of the Doan Inc. bonds on January 1, 1999, after receiving the interest due. Since the securities cost $54,000, a gain of $4,000 has been realized. The entry to record the sale is:

Helpful Hint The accounting for temporary debt investments and long-term debt investments is similar. Any exceptions are discussed in more advanced courses.

Jan. 1	Cash	58,000	
	Debt Investments		54,000
	Gain on Sale of Debt Investments		4,000
	(To record sale of Doan Inc. bonds)		

The gain on the sale of debt investments is reported under Other Revenues and Gains in the income statement.

BEFORE YOU GO ON . . .

● **Review It**

1. What are the reasons corporations invest in securities?
2. What entries are required in accounting for debt investments?

● **Do It**

Waldo Corporation had these transactions pertaining to debt investments:

Jan. 1 Purchased 30 10%, $1,000 Hillary Co. bonds for $30,000 plus brokerage fees of $900. Interest is payable semiannually on July 1 and January 1.
July 1 Received semiannual interest on Hillary Co. bonds.
July 1 Sold 15 Hillary Co. bonds for $15,000 less $400 brokerage fees.

(a) Journalize the transactions.
(b) Prepare the adjusting entry for the accrual of interest on December 31.

Reasoning: Bond investments are recorded at cost. Interest is recorded when received, accrued, or both. When bonds are sold, the investment account is credited for the cost of the bonds. Any difference between the cost and the net proceeds is recorded as a gain or loss.

Solution:

(a)
Jan. 1	Debt Investments		30,900	
	Cash			30,900
	(To record purchase of 30 Hillary Co. bonds)			

July 1	Cash		1,500	
	Interest Revenue ($30,000 × .10 × $\frac{6}{12}$)			1,500
	(To record receipt of interest on Hillary Co. bonds)			

July 1	Cash		14,600	
	Loss on Sale of Debt Investments		850	
	Debt Investments ($30,900 × $\frac{15}{30}$)			15,450
	(To record sale of 15 Hillary Co. bonds)			

(b)
Dec. 31	Interest Receivable		750	
	Interest Revenue ($15,000 × .10 × $\frac{6}{12}$)			750
	(To accrue interest on Hillary Co. bonds)			

ACCOUNTING FOR STOCK INVESTMENTS

STUDY OBJECTIVE 3

Explain the accounting for stock investments.

Stock investments are investments in the capital stock of corporations. When a company holds stock (and/or debt) of several different corporations, the group of securities is identified as an **investment portfolio.** The accounting for investments in common stock is based on the extent of the investor's influence over the operating and financial affairs of the issuing corporation (the **investee**) as shown in Illustration 12-3. In some cases, depending on the degree of investor influence, net income of the investee is considered to be income to the investor.

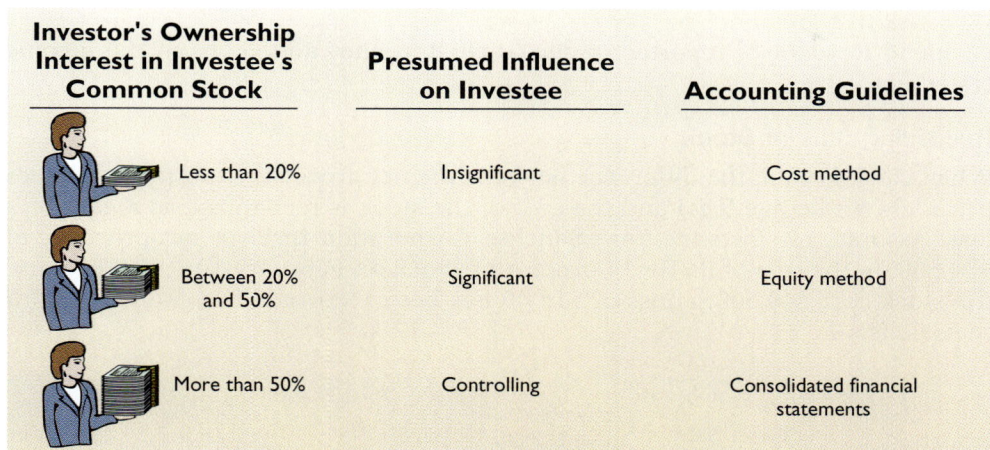

Illustration 12-3
Accounting guidelines for stock investments

The presumed influence may be negated by extenuating circumstances. For example, a company that acquires a 25% interest in another company in a "hostile" takeover may not have any significant influence over the investee.[1] In other words, companies are required to use judgment instead of blindly following the guidelines. We explain and illustrate the application of each guideline next.

HOLDINGS LESS THAN 20%

In the accounting for stock investments of less than 20%, the cost method is used. Under the **cost method,** the investment is recorded at cost, and revenue is recognized only when cash dividends are received.

Recording Acquisition of Stock

At acquisition, the cost principle applies. Cost includes all expenditures necessary to acquire these investments, such as the price paid plus brokerage fees (commissions), if any. Assume, for example, that on July 1, 1998, Sanchez Corporation acquires 1,000 shares (10% ownership) of Beal Corporation common stock at $40 per share plus brokerage fees of $500. The entry for the purchase is:

July 1	Stock Investments	40,500	
	Cash		40,500
	(To record purchase of 1,000 shares of Beal common stock)		

Recording Dividends

During the time the stock is held, entries are required for any cash dividends received. Thus, if a $2.00 per share dividend is received by Sanchez Corporation

---

[1] Among the factors that should be considered in determining an investor's influence are whether (1) the investor has representation on the investee's board of directors, (2) the investor participates in the investee's policy-making process, (3) there are material transactions between the investor and the investee, and (4) the common stock held by other stockholders is concentrated or dispersed.

on December 31, the entry is:

Dec. 31	Cash (1,000 × $2)	2,000	
	Dividend Revenue		2,000
	(To record receipt of a cash dividend)		

Dividend Revenue is reported under Other Revenues and Gains in the income statement.

Recording Sale of Stock

When stock is sold, the difference between the net proceeds from the sale (sales price less brokerage fees) and the cost of the stock is recognized as a gain or a loss. Assume, for instance, that Sanchez Corporation receives net proceeds of $39,500 on the sale of its Beal Corporation stock on February 10, 1999. Because the stock cost $40,500, a loss of $1,000 has been incurred. The entry to record the sale is:

Feb. 10	Cash	39,500	
	Loss on Sale of Stock Investments	1,000	
	Stock Investments		40,500
	(To record sale of Beal common stock)		

The loss account is reported under Other Expenses and Losses in the income statement, whereas a gain on sale is shown under Other Revenues and Gains.

HOLDINGS BETWEEN 20% AND 50%

When an investor company owns only a small portion of the shares of stock of another company (the investee), the investor cannot exercise control over the company. When an investor owns between 20% and 50% of the common stock of a corporation, however, it is generally presumed that the investor has significant influence over the financial and operating activities of the investee. The investor probably has a representative on the investee's board of directors. With a representative on the board, the investor begins to exercise some control over the investee—and the investee company in some sense really becomes part of the investor company.

    For example, even prior to purchasing all of Turner Broadcasting, Time Warner owned 20% of Turner. Because it exercised significant control over major decisions made by Turner, Time Warner used an approach called the equity method. Under the equity method, **the investor records its share of the net income of the investee in the year when it is earned.** To delay recognizing the investor's share of net income until a cash dividend is declared ignores the fact that the investor and investee are, in some sense, one company, so the investor is better off by the investee's earned income.

    Under the **equity method,** the investment in common stock is initially recorded at cost, and the investment account is **adjusted annually** to show the investor's equity in the investee. Each year, the investor (1) increases (debits) the investment account and increases (credits) revenue for its share of the investee's net income[2] and (2) decreases (credits) the investment account for the amount of dividends received. The investment account is reduced for dividends received because the net assets of the investee are decreased when a dividend is paid.

---

[2]Conversely, the investor increases (debits) a loss account and decreases (credits) the investment account for its share of the investee's net loss.

Recording Acquisition of Stock

Assume that Milar Corporation acquires 30% of the common stock of Beck Company for $120,000 on January 1, 1998. The entry to record this transaction is:

Jan. 1	Stock Investments	120,000	
	Cash		120,000
	(To record purchase of Beck common stock)		

Recording Revenue and Dividends

For 1998 Beck reports net income of $100,000 and declares and pays a $40,000 cash dividend. Milar is required to record (1) its share of Beck's income, $30,000 (30% × $100,000), and (2) the reduction in the investment account for the dividends received, $12,000 ($40,000 × 30%). The entries are:

(1)

Dec. 31	Stock Investments	30,000	
	Revenue from Investment in Beck Company		30,000
	(To record 30% equity in Beck's 1998 net income)		

(2)

Dec. 31	Cash	12,000	
	Stock Investments		12,000
	(To record dividends received)		

After the transactions for the year are posted, the investment and revenue accounts are as shown in Illustration 12-4.

Stock Investments		Revenue from Investment in Beck Company	
Jan. 1 120,000	Dec. 31 12,000		Dec. 31 **30,000**
Dec. 31 **30,000**			
Dec. 31 Bal. 138,000			

Illustration 12-4
Investment and revenue accounts after posting

During the year, the investment account has increased by $18,000. This $18,000 is Milar's 30% equity in the $60,000 increase in Beck's retained earnings ($100,000 − $40,000). In addition, Milar reports $30,000 of revenue from its investment, which is 30% of Beck's net income of $100,000. Note that the difference between reported income under the cost method and reported revenue under the equity method can be significant. For example, Milar would report only $12,000 of dividend revenue (30% × $40,000) if the cost method were used.

HOLDINGS OF MORE THAN 50%

A company that owns more than 50% of the common stock of another entity is known as the **parent company.** The entity whose stock is owned by the parent company is called the **subsidiary (affiliated) company.** Because of its stock ownership, the parent company has a **controlling interest** in the subsidiary company.

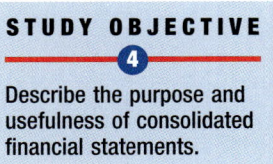

STUDY OBJECTIVE 4
Describe the purpose and usefulness of consolidated financial statements.

548 CHAPTER 12 Reporting and Analyzing Investments

Helpful Hint If the parent (A) has three wholly owned subsidiaries (B, C, and D), there are four separate legal entities but only one economic entity from the viewpoint of the shareholders of the parent company.

When a company owns more than 50% of the common stock of another company, **consolidated financial statements** are usually prepared. Consolidated financial statements present the assets and liabilities controlled by the parent company and the aggregate profitability of the subsidiary companies. They are prepared **in addition to** the financial statements for each of the individual parent and subsidiary companies. As noted earlier, prior to acquiring all of Turner Broadcasting, Time Warner accounted for its investment in Turner using the equity method. Time Warner's net investment in Turner was reported in a single line item—Other Investments. After the merger, Time Warner instead consolidated Turner's results with its own. Under this approach, the individual assets and liabilities of Turner are included with those of Time Warner; its plant and equipment are added to Time Warner's plant and equipment, its receivables are added to Time Warner's receivables, and so on.

Consolidated statements are especially useful to the stockholders, board of directors, and management of the parent company. Moreover, consolidated statements inform creditors, prospective investors, and regulatory agencies as to the magnitude and scope of operations of the companies under common control. For example, regulators and the courts undoubtedly used the consolidated statements of AT&T to determine whether a breakup of AT&T was in the public interest. Listed here are three companies that prepare consolidated statements and some of the companies they have owned. Note that one, Disney, is Time Warner's arch rival.

Beatrice Foods	American Brands, Inc.	The Walt Disney Company
Tropicana Frozen Juices	American Tobacco Company	Capital Cities/ABC, Inc.
Switzer Candy Company	Master Lock Company	Disneyland, Disney World
Samsonite Corporation	Pinkerton's Security Service	Mighty Ducks
Dannon Yogurt Company	Titleist Golf Company	Anaheim Angels
		ESPN

BUSINESS INSIGHT
Management Perspective

Time Warner, Inc., owns 100% of the common stock of Home Box Office (HBO) Corporation. The common stockholders of Time Warner elect the board of directors of the company, who, in turn, select the officers and managers of the company. The board of directors controls the property owned by the corporation, which includes the common stock of HBO. Thus, they are in a position to elect the board of directors of HBO and, in effect, control its operations. These relationships are graphically illustrated here:

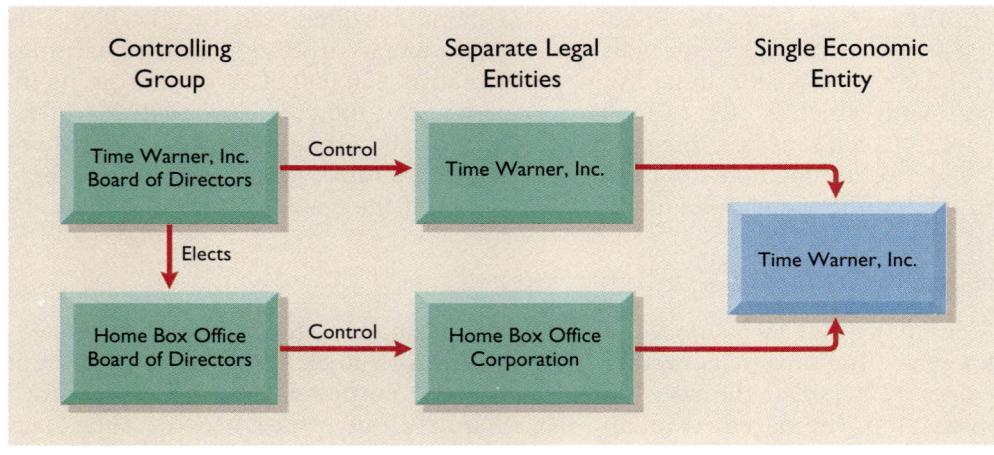

BEFORE YOU GO ON . . .

● **Review It**

1. What are the accounting entries for investments in stock with ownership of less than 20%?
2. What entries are made under the equity method when (a) the investor receives a cash dividend from the investee and (b) the investee reports net income for the year?
3. What is the purpose of consolidated financial statements?

● **Do It**

These are two independent situations:

1. Rho Jean Inc. acquired 5% of the 400,000 shares of common stock of Stillwater Corp. at a total cost of $6 per share on May 18, 1998. On August 30 Stillwater declared and paid a $75,000 dividend. On December 31 Stillwater reported net income of $244,000 for the year.
2. Debbie, Inc., obtained significant influence over North Sails by buying 40% of North Sails' 60,000 outstanding shares of common stock at a cost of $12 per share on January 1, 1998. On April 15 North Sails declared and paid a cash dividend of $45,000. On December 31 North Sails reported net income of $120,000 for the year.

Prepare all necessary journal entries for 1998 for (a) Rho Jean Inc. and (b) Debbie, Inc.

Reasoning: When an investor owns less than 20% of the common stock of another corporation, it is presumed that the investor has relatively little influence over the investee. As a result, net income earned by the investee is not considered a proper basis for recognizing income from the investment by the investor. For investments of 20%–50%, significant influence is presumed, and therefore the investor's share of the net income of the investee should be recorded.

Solution:

(a)
May 18	Stock Investments (20,000 × $6)		120,000	
	Cash			120,000
	(To record purchase of 20,000 shares of Stillwater stock)			
Aug. 30	Cash		3,750	
	Dividend Revenue ($75,000 × 5%)			3,750
	(To record receipt of cash dividend)			

(b)
Jan. 1	Stock Investments (60,000 × 40% × $12)		288,000	
	Cash			288,000
	(To record purchase of 24,000 shares of North Sails stock)			
Apr. 15	Cash		18,000	
	Stock Investments ($45,000 × 40%)			18,000
	(To record receipt of cash dividend)			
Dec. 31	Stock Investments ($120,000 × 40%)		48,000	
	Revenue from Investment in North Sails			48,000
	(To record 40% equity in North Sails' net income)			

VALUATION AND REPORTING OF INVESTMENTS

STUDY OBJECTIVE 5
Indicate how debt and stock investments are valued and reported in the financial statements.

The value of debt and stock investments may fluctuate greatly during the time they are held. For example, in one 12-month period, the stock of Digital Equipment Corporation hit a high of $76\frac{1}{2}$ and a low of $28\frac{3}{8}$. In light of such price fluctuations, how should investments be valued at the balance sheet date? Valuation could be at cost, at fair value (market value), or at the lower of cost or market value. Many people argue that fair value offers the best approach because it represents the expected cash realizable value of securities. **Fair value** is the amount for which a security could be sold in a normal market. Others counter that, unless a security is going to be sold soon, the fair value is not relevant because the price of the security will likely change again.

CATEGORIES OF SECURITIES

For purposes of valuation and reporting at a financial statement date, debt and stock investments are classified into three categories of securities:

1. **Trading securities** are securities bought and held primarily for sale in the near term to generate income on short-term price differences.
2. **Available-for-sale securities** are securities that may be sold in the future.
3. **Held-to-maturity securities** are debt securities that the investor has the intent and ability to hold to maturity.[3]

The valuation guidelines for these securities are shown in Illustration 12-5. These guidelines apply to all debt securities and all stock investments in which the holdings are less than 20%.

Illustration 12-5
Valuation guidelines

Trading Securities

Trading securities are held with the intention of selling them in a short period of time (generally less than a month). *Trading* means frequent buying and selling. As indicated in Illustration 12-5, trading securities are reported at fair value, referred to as **mark-to-market** accounting, and changes from cost are reported **as part of net income.** The changes are reported as **unrealized gains or losses** because the securities have not been sold. The unrealized gain or loss is the dif-

---
[3]This category is provided for completeness. The accounting and valuation issues related to held-to-maturity securities are discussed in more advanced accounting courses.

ference between the **total cost** of the securities in the category and their **total fair value.**

As an example, Illustration 12-6 shows the costs and fair values for investments classified as trading securities for Pace Corporation on December 31, 1998. Pace Corporation has an unrealized gain of $7,000 because total fair value ($147,000) is $7,000 greater than total cost ($140,000).

Investments	Cost	Fair Value	Unrealized Gain (Loss)
Yorkville Company bonds	$ 50,000	$ 48,000	$(2,000)
Kodak Company stock	90,000	99,000	9,000
Total	$140,000	$147,000	**$ 7,000**

Illustration 12-6 Valuation of trading securities

The fact that trading securities are a short-term investment increases the likelihood that they will be sold at fair value (the company may not be able to time their sale) and the likelihood that there will be an unrealized gain or loss. Fair value and unrealized gain or loss are recorded through an adjusting entry at the time financial statements are prepared. In the entry a valuation allowance account, Market Adjustment—Trading, is used to record the difference between the total cost and the total fair value of the securities. The adjusting entry for Pace Corporation is:

Dec. 31	Market Adjustment—Trading	7,000	
	Unrealized Gain—Income		7,000
	(To record unrealized gain on trading securities)		

Helpful Hint An unrealized gain or loss is reported in the income statement because of the likelihood that the securities will be sold at fair value since they are a short-term investment.

The use of the Market Adjustment—Trading account enables the company to maintain a record of the investment cost. Actual cost is needed to determine the gain or loss realized when the securities are sold. The Market Adjustment—Trading balance is added to the cost of the investments to arrive at a fair value for the trading securities.

The fair value of the securities is the amount reported on the balance sheet. The unrealized gain is reported on the income statement under Other Revenues and Gains. The term income is used in the account title to indicate that the gain affects net income. If the total cost of the trading securities is greater than total fair value, an unrealized loss has occurred. In such a case, the adjusting entry is a debit to Unrealized Loss—Income and a credit to Market Adjustment—Trading. The unrealized loss is reported under Other Expenses and Losses in the income statement.

The market adjustment account is carried forward into future accounting periods. No entries are made to this account during the period. At the end of each reporting period, the balance in the account is adjusted to the difference between cost and fair value at that time. The Unrealized Gain or Loss—Income account is closed at the end of the reporting period.

Available-for-Sale Securities

As indicated earlier, available-for-sale securities are held with the intent of selling them sometime in the future. If the intent is to sell the securities within the next year or operating cycle, the securities are classified as current assets in the balance sheet. Otherwise, they are classified as long-term assets in the investments section of the balance sheet.

Available-for-sale securities are also reported at fair value. The procedure for determining fair value and unrealized gain or loss for these securities is the same as that for trading securities. To illustrate, assume that Elbert Corporation has two securities that are classified as available-for-sale. Illustration 12-7 provides information on the cost, fair value, and amount of the unrealized gain or loss on December 31, 1998. For Elbert Corporation, there is an unrealized loss of $9,537 because total cost ($293,537) is $9,537 more than total fair value ($284,000).

Illustration 12-7 Valuation of available-for-sale securities

Investments	Cost	Fair Value	Unrealized Gain (Loss)
Campbell Soup Corporation 8% bonds	$ 93,537	$103,600	$10,063
Hersey Corporation stock	200,000	180,400	(19,600)
Total	$293,537	$284,000	$(9,537)

Both the adjusting entry and the reporting of the unrealized gain or loss from available-for-sale securities differ from those illustrated for trading securities. The differences result because these securities are not going to be sold in the near term. Thus, prior to actual sale there is a much greater likelihood of changes in fair value that may reverse either unrealized gains or losses. Accordingly, an unrealized gain or loss is not reported in the income statement. Instead, it is reported as **a separate component of stockholders' equity,** referred to as a **contra equity account.** In the adjusting entry, the market adjustment account is identified with available-for-sale securities, and the unrealized gain or loss account is identified with stockholders' equity. The adjusting entry for Elbert Corporation to record the unrealized loss of $9,537 is:

Helpful Hint The entry is the same regardless of whether the securities are considered temporary or long-term.

Dec. 31	Unrealized Loss—Equity	9,537	
	Market Adjustment—Available-for-Sale		9,537
	(To record unrealized loss on available-for-sale securities)		

If total fair value exceeds total cost, the adjusting entry would be recorded as an increase (debit) to the market adjustment account and an increase (a credit) to an unrealized gain account.

For available-for-sale securities, the unrealized gain or loss account is carried forward to future periods. At each future balance sheet date, it is adjusted with the market adjustment account to show the difference between cost and fair value at that time.

EVALUATING INVESTMENT PORTFOLIO PERFORMANCE

The latest accounting standards for reporting investments in debt securities and equity investments of less than 20% were introduced in 1993. These new rules were intended to improve the information provided about the performance of a company's investment portfolio. Unfortunately, even under these new standards, companies can "window-dress" their reported earnings results—that is, make net income look better than it really was.

Companies can choose which of the three categories of securities to use for an investment. Recall that gains and losses on investments classified as available-for-sale are not included in income, but rather are recorded as an adjustment to equity. If a company wanted to manage its reported income, it could simply sell those available-for-sale investments that have unrealized gains, and not sell those available-for-sale investments that have unrealized losses. By doing this, the company is deferring the losses until a later period. For example, refer back to Illustration 12-7. If Elbert Corporation wanted to increase its reported income, it could sell its investment in Campbell Soup and realize a gain of $10,063. It would then report an unrealized loss of $19,600 in the equity section of its balance sheet.

Sometimes unrealized losses on available-for-sale securities can be material. For example, in 1994 KeyCorp, a bank holding company headquartered in Cleveland, Ohio, reported net income of $853 million. However, the reduction to shareholders' equity for unrealized holding losses on available-for-sale securities was $115 million. That is, if these securities had been sold before year-end, income would have declined by $115 million. This potential loss represented 13% of net income. Similarly, in 1994 BankAmerica reported a reduction to shareholders' equity of $326 million, when net income for the year was $2,176 million. Clearly, it is important to consider the potential impact of these unrealized losses on current and future income when evaluating the performance of the company's investment portfolio.

Helpful Hint Note that even though gains and losses on held-to-maturity securities also are not reported in income until realized, a company is less likely to window-dress with these securities because penalties are associated with selling these securities prior to maturity.

DECISION TOOLKIT

Decision Checkpoints	Info Needed for Decision	Tool to Use for Decision	How to Evaluate Results
Is the company window-dressing its results by manipulating its available-for-sale portfolio?	Balance of unrealized gains and unrealized losses	Unrealized gains and losses on available-for-sale securities are not run through net income but are recorded as adjustments to stockholders' equity. A company can window-dress by selling winners and holding losers to increase reported income, or do the opposite to reduce reported income.	Window-dressing is not easy to spot: It is difficult for an outsider to determine why companies chose to either sell or hold a security. A user should evaluate a company's earnings as reported, including any unrealized gains and losses, to see total potential variation.

BEFORE YOU GO ON . . .

● **Review It**

1. What are the three categories of investment securities?
2. What are the proper valuation and reporting for each of the three categories of investment securities?
3. Explain why unrealized gains and losses on trading securities are run through the income statement, while unrealized gains and losses on available-for-sale securities are not.
4. How might a company window-dress its reported earnings using its available-for-sale securities portfolio?

BALANCE SHEET PRESENTATION

For balance sheet presentation, investments must be classified as either temporary or long-term.

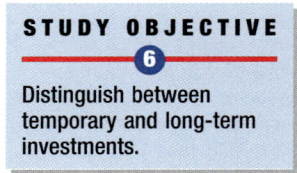

STUDY OBJECTIVE 6
Distinguish between temporary and long-term investments.

Helpful Hint Trading securities are always classified as temporary. Available-for-sale securities can be either temporary or long-term.

Temporary Investments

Temporary investments are securities held by a company that are (1) **readily marketable** and (2) **intended to be converted into cash** within the next year or operating cycle, whichever is longer. Investments that do not meet **both criteria** are classified as **long-term investments.** In a recent survey of 600 large U.S. companies, 401 reported investments in temporary securities.

Readily Marketable. **An investment is readily marketable when it can be sold easily whenever the need for cash arises.** Short-term paper[4] meets this criterion because it can be sold readily to other investors. Stocks and bonds traded on organized securities markets, such as the New York Stock Exchange, are readily marketable because they can be bought and sold daily. In contrast, there may be only a limited market for the securities issued by small corporations and no market for the securities of a privately held company.

Intent to Convert. **Intent to convert means that management intends to sell the investment within the next year or operating cycle, whichever is longer.** Generally, this criterion is satisfied when the investment is considered a resource that will be used whenever the need for cash arises. For example, a ski resort may invest idle cash during the summer months with the intent to sell the securities to buy supplies and equipment shortly before the next winter season. This investment is considered temporary even if lack of snow cancels the next ski season and eliminates the need to convert the securities into cash as intended.

Because of their high liquidity, temporary investments are listed immediately below Cash in the current asset section of the balance sheet. Temporary investments are reported at fair value. For example, Pace Corporation would report its trading securities as shown in Illustration 12-8.

Illustration 12-8
Presentation of temporary investments

PACE CORPORATION Partial Balance Sheet	
Current assets	
Cash	$21,000
Temporary investments, at fair value	60,000

Long-Term Investments

Long-term investments are generally reported in a separate section of the balance sheet immediately below Current Assets, as shown later in Illustration 12-11. Long-term investments in available-for-sale securities are reported at fair value, and investments in common stock accounted for under the equity method are reported at equity.

PRESENTATION OF REALIZED AND UNREALIZED GAIN OR LOSS

Gains and losses on investments, whether realized or unrealized, must be presented in the financial statements. In the income statement, gains and losses, as

---

[4]Short-term paper includes (1) certificates of deposits (CDs) issued by banks, (2) money market certificates issued by banks and savings and loan associations, (3) Treasury bills issued by the U.S. government, and (4) commercial paper issued by corporations with good credit ratings.

well as interest and dividend revenue, are reported in the nonoperating section under the categories listed in Illustration 12-9.

Illustration 12-9
Nonoperating items related to investments

Other Revenue and Gains	Other Expenses and Losses
Interest Revenue	Loss on Sales of Investments
Dividend Revenue	Unrealized Loss—Income
Gain on Sale of Investments	
Unrealized Gain—Income	

As indicated earlier, an unrealized gain or loss on available-for-sale securities is reported as a separate component of stockholders' equity. To illustrate, assume that Dawson Inc. has common stock of $3,000,000, retained earnings of $1,500,000, and an unrealized loss on available-for-sale securities of $100,000. The statement presentation of the unrealized loss is shown in Illustration 12-10.

Illustration 12-10
Unrealized loss in stockholders' equity section

DAWSON INC.
Partial Balance Sheet

Stockholders' equity	
Common stock	$3,000,000
Retained earnings	1,500,000
Total paid-in capital and retained earnings	4,500,000
Less: **Unrealized loss on available-for-sale securities**	(100,000)
Total stockholders' equity	$4,400,000

Note that the presentation of the loss is similar to the presentation of the cost of treasury stock in the stockholders' equity section. An unrealized gain is added in this section. Reporting the unrealized gain or loss in the stockholders' equity section serves two important purposes: (1) It reduces the volatility of net income due to fluctuations in fair value, and (2) it informs the financial statement user of the gain or loss that would occur if the securities were sold at fair value.

A new accounting standard requires that items such as this, which affect stockholders' equity but are not included in the calculation of net income, must be reported as part of a more inclusive measure called *comprehensive income*. Comprehensive income is discussed in Chapter 14.

BALANCE SHEET

Many sections of classified balance sheets have been presented in this and preceding chapters. The balance sheet in Illustration 12-11 (on the next page) includes such topics from previous chapters as the issuance of par value common stock, organization costs, restrictions of retained earnings, issuance of long-term bonds, and bond sinking funds. From this chapter, the statement includes (highlighted in red) temporary and long-term investments. The investments in temporary securities are considered trading securities; the long-term investments in stock of less than 20% owned companies are considered available-for-sale securities. Illustration 12-11 also includes a long-term investment reported at equity and descriptive notations within the statement such as the basis for valuing merchandise and two notes to the statement.

Illustration 12-11
Balance sheet

PACE CORPORATION
Balance Sheet
December 31, 1998

Assets

Current assets			
Cash			$ 21,000
Temporary investments, at fair value			**60,000**
Accounts receivable		$ 84,000	
Less: Allowance for doubtful accounts		4,000	80,000
Merchandise inventory, at FIFO cost			130,000
Prepaid insurance			23,000
Total current assets			314,000
Investments			
Bond sinking fund		100,000	
Investments in stock of less than 20% owned companies, at fair value		**50,000**	
Investment in stock of 20%–50% owned company, at equity		**150,000**	
Total investments			300,000
Property, plant, and equipment			
Land		200,000	
Buildings	$800,000		
Less: Accumulated depreciation	200,000	600,000	
Equipment	180,000		
Less: Accumulated depreciation	54,000	126,000	
Total property, plant, and equipment			926,000
Intangible assets			
Goodwill (Note 1)		170,000	
Total intangible assets			170,000
Total assets			$1,710,000

Liabilities and Stockholders' Equity

Current liabilities			
Accounts payable			$ 185,000
Bond interest payable			10,000
Federal income taxes payable			60,000
Total current liabilities			255,000
Long-term liabilities			
Bonds payable, 10%, due 2010		$ 300,000	
Less: Discount on bonds		10,000	
Total long-term liabilities			290,000
Total liabilities			545,000
Stockholders' equity			
Paid-in capital			
Common stock, $10 par value, 200,000 shares authorized, 80,000 shares issued and outstanding		800,000	
Paid-in capital in excess of par value		100,000	
Total paid-in capital		900,000	
Retained earnings (Note 2)		255,000	
Total paid-in capital and retained earnings		1,155,000	
Add: Unrealized gain on available-for-sale securities		**10,000**	
Total stockholders' equity			1,165,000
Total liabilities and stockholders' equity			$1,710,000

Note 1. Goodwill is amortized by the straight-line method over 40 years.
Note 2. Retained earnings of $100,000 is restricted for plant expansion.

BEFORE YOU GO ON . . .

● **Review It**

1. Explain where temporary and long-term investments are reported on a balance sheet.
2. Where are unrealized gains and losses from trading securities reported? Where are unrealized gains and losses from available-for-sale securities reported?

USING THE DECISION TOOLKIT

KeyCorp is an Ohio bank holding company (a corporation that owns banks). It manages $66 billion in assets, the largest of which is its loan portfolio of $47 billion. In addition to its loan portfolio, however, like other banks it has significant debt and stock investments. The nature of these investments varies from short-term to long-term and as a consequence, consistent with accounting rules, KeyCorp reports its investments in three different categories: trading, available-for-sale, and held-to-maturity. The following facts are from KeyCorp's 1995 annual report:

	($ in millions)			
	Amortized Cost	Gross Unrealized Gains	Gross Unrealized Losses	Fair Value
Trading securities	—	—	—	$ 682
Available-for-sale securities	$7,994	$112	$46	8,060
Held-to-maturity securities	1,688	51	1	1,738

Net income: $824 million

Instructions

Answer these questions:

1. Why do you suppose KeyCorp purchases investments rather than only making loans? Why does it purchase investments that vary in terms of both their maturities and their type (debt versus stock)?
2. How must KeyCorp account for its investments in each of the three categories? In what ways does classifying investments into three different categories assist investors in evaluating the profitability of a company like KeyCorp?
3. Suppose that the management of KeyCorp was not happy with its 1995 net income. What step could it have taken with its investment portfolio that definitely would have increased 1995 reported profit? How much could it have increased reported profit? Why do you suppose it chose not to do this?

Solution

1. Although banks are primarily in the business of lending money, they also need to balance their portfolio by investing in other assets. For example,

a bank may have excess cash that it has not yet loaned, which it wants to invest in very short-term liquid assets. Or it may believe that it can earn a higher rate of interest by buying long-term bonds than it can currently earn by making new loans. Or it may purchase investments for short-term speculation because it believes these investments will appreciate in value.

2. Trading securities are shown on the balance sheet at their current market value, and any unrealized gains and losses resulting from marking them to their market value are reported as income. Available-for-sale securities are reported on the balance sheet at their market value, and any unrealized gains and losses resulting from marking them to their market values are reported as a separate component of stockholders' equity on the balance sheet. Held-to-maturity securities are reported at their amortized cost; that is, they are not marked to market.

Securities are reported in three different categories to reflect the likelihood that any realized gains and losses will eventually be realized by the company. Trading securities are held for a short period; thus, if the bank has an unrealized gain on its trading security portfolio, it is likely that these securities will be sold soon and the gain will be realized. On the other hand, held-to-maturity securities are not going to be sold for a long time; thus, unrealized gains on these securities may never be realized. If securities were all grouped into a single category, the investor would not be aware of these differences in the probability of realization.

3. The answer involves selling "winner" stocks in the available-for-sale portfolio at year-end. KeyCorp could have increased reported net income by $112 million (clearly a material amount when total reported income was $824 million). Managers chose not to sell these securities because at the time (a) they felt that the securities had additional room for price appreciation, or (b) they didn't want to pay the additional taxes associated with a sale at a gain, or (c) they wanted to hold the securities because they were needed to provide the proper asset balance in their total asset portfolio, or (d) they preferred to report the gains in the next year.

SUMMARY OF STUDY OBJECTIVES

❶ Identify the reasons corporations invest in stocks and debt securities. Corporations invest for three common reasons: (a) They have excess cash either because of their operating cycle or because of economic swings; (b) they view investments as a significant revenue source; (c) they have strategic goals such as gaining control of a competitor or moving into a new line of business.

❷ Explain the accounting for debt investments. Entries for investments in debt securities are required when the bonds are purchased, interest is received or accrued, and the bonds are sold.

❸ Explain the accounting for stock investments. Entries for investments in common stock are required when the stock is purchased, dividends are received, and stock is sold. When ownership is less than 20%, the cost method is used—the investment is recorded at cost. When ownership is between 20% and 50%, the equity method should be used—the investor records its share of the net income of the investee in the year it is earned. When ownership is more than 50%, consolidated financial statements should be prepared.

❹ Describe the purpose and usefulness of consolidated financial statements. When a company owns more than 50% of the common stock of another company, consolidated financial statements are usually prepared. These statements are especially useful to the stockholders, board of directors, and management of the parent company.

❺ Indicate how debt and stock investments are valued and reported in the financial statements. Investments in debt and stock securities are classified as trading, available-for-sale, or held-to-maturity securities for valuation and reporting purposes. Trading securities are reported as current assets at fair value, with changes from cost reported in net income. Available-for-sale securities are also reported at fair value, with the changes from cost reported in stockholders' equity. Available-for-sale securities are classified as temporary or long-term depending on their expected realization.

6 *Distinguish between temporary and long-term investments.* Temporary investments are securities held by a company that are readily marketable and intended to be converted to cash within the next year or operating cycle, whichever is longer. Investments that do not meet both criteria are classified as long-term investments.

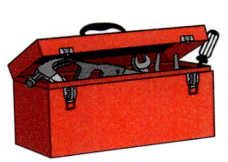

DECISION TOOLKIT—A SUMMARY

Decision Checkpoints	Info Needed for Decision	Tool to Use Decision	How to Evaluate Results
Is the company window-dressing its results by manipulating its available-for-sale portfolio?	Balance of unrealized gains and unrealized losses	Unrealized gains and losses on available-for-sale securities are not run through net income but are recorded as adjustments to stockholders' equity. A company can window-dress by selling winners and holding losers to increase reported income, or do the opposite to reduce reported income.	Window-dressing is not easy to spot: It is difficult for an outsider to determine why companies chose to either sell or hold a security. A user should evaluate a company's earnings as reported, including any unrealized gains and losses, to see total potential variation.

GLOSSARY

Available-for-sale securities Securities that may be sold in the future. (p. 550)

Consolidated financial statements Financial statements that present the assets and liabilities controlled by the parent company and the aggregate profitability of the affiliated companies. (p. 548)

Controlling interest Ownership of more than 50% of the common stock of another entity. (p. 547)

Cost method An accounting method in which the investment in common stock is recorded at cost and revenue is recognized only when cash dividends are received. (p. 545)

Debt investments Investments in government and corporation bonds. (p. 542)

Equity method An accounting method in which the investment in common stock is initially recorded at cost, and the investment account is then adjusted annually to show the investor's equity in the investee. (p. 546)

Fair value Amount for which a security could be sold in a normal market. (p. 550)

Held-to-maturity securities Debt securities that the investor has the intent and ability to hold to their maturity date. (p. 550)

Long-term investments Investments that are not readily marketable or that management does not intend to convert into cash within the next year or operating cycle, whichever is longer. (p. 554)

Mark-to-market A method of accounting for certain investments that requires that they be adjusted to their fair value at the end of each period. (p. 550)

Parent company A company that owns more than 50% of the common stock of another entity. (p. 547)

Stock investments Investments in the capital stock of corporations. (p. 544)

Subsidiary (affiliated) company A company in which more than 50% of its stock is owned by another company. (p. 547)

Temporary investments Investments that are readily marketable and intended to be converted into cash within the next year or operating cycle, whichever is longer. (p. 554)

Trading securities Securities bought and held primarily for sale in the near term to generate income on short-term price differences. (p. 550)

Demonstration Problem

In its first year of operations, DeMarco Company had these selected transactions in stock investments that are considered **trading securities:**

June 1 Purchased for cash 600 shares of Sanburg common stock at $24 per share plus $300 brokerage fees.
July 1 Purchased for cash 800 shares of Cey common stock at $33 per share plus $600 brokerage fees.
Sept. 1 Received a $1 per share cash dividend from Cey Corporation.
Nov. 1 Sold 200 shares of Sanburg common stock for cash at $27 per share less $150 brokerage fees.
Dec. 15 Received a $.50 per share cash dividend on Sanburg common stock.

Instructions

(a) Journalize the transactions.
(b) Prepare the adjusting entry at December 31 to report the securities at fair value. At December 31 the fair values per share were: Sanburg $25 and Cey $30.

Problem-Solving Strategies

1. Cost includes the price paid plus brokerage fees.
2. Gain or loss on sales is determined by the difference between net selling price and the cost of the securities.
3. The adjustment to fair value is based on the total difference between cost and fair value of the securities.

Solution to Demonstration Problem

(a)
Date	Account	Debit	Credit
June 1	Stock Investments	14,700	
	Cash [(600 × $24) + $300]		14,700
	(To record purchase of 600 shares of Sanburg common stock)		
July 1	Stock Investments	27,000	
	Cash [(800 × $33) + $600]		27,000
	(To record purchase of 800 shares of Cey common stock)		
Sept. 1	Cash	800	
	Dividend Revenue		800
	(To record receipt of $1 per share cash dividend from Cey)		
Nov. 1	Cash [(200 × $27) − $150]	5,250	
	Stock Investments (200 × $24.50)		4,900
	Gain on Sale of Stock Investments		350
	(To record sale of 200 shares of Sanburg common stock)		
Dec. 15	Cash [(600 − 200) × $.50]	200	
	Dividend Revenue		200
	(To record receipt of $.50 per share dividend from Sanburg)		

(b)
Date	Account	Debit	Credit
Dec. 31	Unrealized Loss—Income	2,800	
	Market Adjustment—Trading		2,800
	(To record unrealized loss on trading securities)		

Investment	Cost	Fair Value	Unrealized Gain (Loss)
Sanburg common stock	$ 9,800	$10,000	$ 200
Cey common stock	27,000	24,000	(3,000)
Total	$36,800	$34,000	$(2,800)

Self-Study Questions

Answers are at the end of the chapter.

(SO 2) 1. Debt investments are initially recorded at:
   (a) cost.
   (b) cost plus accrued interest.
   (c) fair value.
   (d) None of the above

(SO 2) 2. Hanes Company sells debt investments costing $26,000 for $28,000 plus accrued interest that has been recorded. In journalizing the sale, credits are:
   (a) Debt Investments and Loss on Sale of Debt Investments.
   (b) Debt Investments, Gain on Sale of Debt Investments, and Bond Interest Receivable.
   (c) Stock Investments and Bond Interest Receivable.
   (d) The correct answer is not given.

(SO 3) 3. Pryor Company receives net proceeds of $42,000 on the sale of stock investments that cost $39,500. This transaction will result in reporting in the income statement a:
   (a) loss of $2,500 under Other Expenses and Losses.
   (b) loss of $2,500 under Operating Expenses.
   (c) gain of $2,500 under Other Revenues and Gains.
   (d) gain of $2,500 under Operating Revenues.

(SO 3) 4. The equity method of accounting for long-term investments in stock should be used when the investor has significant influence over an investee and owns:
   (a) between 20% and 50% of the investee's common stock.
   (b) 20% or more of the investee's common stock.
   (c) more than 50% of the investee's common stock.
   (d) less than 20% of the investee's common stock.

(SO 4) 5. Which of these statements is *not* true? Consolidated financial statements are useful to:
   (a) determine the profitability of specific subsidiaries.
   (b) determine the aggregate profitability of enterprises under common control.
   (c) determine the breadth of a parent company's operations.
   (d) determine the full extent of aggregate obligations of enterprises under common control.

(SO 5) 6. At the end of the first year of operations, the total cost of the trading securities portfolio is $120,000 and the total fair value is $115,000. What should the financial statements show?
   (a) A reduction of an asset of $5,000 and a realized loss of $5,000
   (b) A reduction of an asset of $5,000 and an unrealized loss of $5,000 in the stockholders' equity section
   (c) A reduction of an asset of $5,000 in the current asset section and an unrealized loss of $5,000 under Other Expenses and Losses
   (d) A reduction of an asset of $5,000 in the current asset section and a realized loss of $5,000 under Other Expenses and Losses

(SO 5) 7. In the balance sheet, Unrealized Loss—Equity is reported as a:
   (a) contra asset account.
   (b) contra stockholders' equity account.
   (c) loss in the income statement.
   (d) loss in the retained earnings statement.

(SO 5) 8. If a company wants to increase its reported income by manipulating its investment accounts, which should it do?
   (a) Sell its "winner" trading securities and hold its "loser" trading securities.
   (b) Hold its "winner" trading securities and sell its "loser" trading securities.
   (c) Sell its "winner" available-for-sale securities and hold its "loser" available-for-sale securities.
   (d) Hold its "winner" available-for-sale securities and sell its "loser" available-for-sale securities.

(SO 6) 9. Temporary debt investments must be readily marketable and be expected to be sold within:
   (a) 3 months from the date of purchase.
   (b) the next year or operating cycle, whichever is shorter.
   (c) the next year or operating cycle, whichever is longer.
   (d) the operating cycle.

Questions

1. What are the reasons that corporations invest in securities?
2. (a) What is the cost of an investment in bonds?
   (b) When is interest on bonds recorded?
3. Ann Adler is confused about losses and gains on the sale of debt investments. Explain these issues to Ann:
   (a) How the gain or loss is computed
   (b) The statement presentation of gains and losses

4. Clio Company sells Cross's bonds that cost $40,000 for $45,000, including $3,000 of accrued interest. In recording the sale, Clio books a $5,000 gain. Is this correct? Explain.
5. What is the cost of an investment in stock?
6. To acquire Mega Corporation stock, R. L. Duran pays $65,000 in cash plus $1,500 broker's fees. What entry should be made for this investment, assuming the stock is readily marketable?
7. (a) When should a long-term investment in common stock be accounted for by the equity method?
   (b) When is revenue recognized under the equity method?
8. Malon Corporation uses the equity method to account for its ownership of 35% of the common stock of Flynn Packing. During 1998 Flynn reported a net income of $80,000 and declares and pays cash dividends of $10,000. What recognition should Malon Corporation give to these events?
9. What constitutes "significant influence" when an investor's financial interest is less than 50%?
10. Distinguish between the cost and equity methods of accounting for investments in stocks.
11. What are consolidated financial statements?
12. What are the valuation guidelines for investments at a balance sheet date?
13. Wendy Walner is the controller of G-Products, Inc. At December 31 the company's investments in trading securities cost $74,000 and have a fair value of $70,000. Indicate how Wendy would report these data in the financial statements prepared on December 31.
14. Using the data in question 13, how would Wendy report the data if the investment were long-term and the securities were classified as available-for-sale?
15. Reo Company's investments in available-for-sale securities at December 31 show total cost of $192,000 and total fair value of $210,000. Prepare the adjusting entry.
16. Using the data in question 15, prepare the adjusting entry assuming the securities are classified as trading securities.
17. What is the proper statement presentation of the account Unrealized Loss—Equity?
18. What purposes are served by reporting Unrealized Gains (Losses)—Equity in the stockholders' equity section?
19. Kirk Wholesale Supply owns stock in Xerox Corporation, which it intends to hold indefinitely because of some negative tax consequences if sold. Should the investment in Xerox be classified as a temporary investment? Why?

BRIEF EXERCISES

Journalize entries for debt investments.
(SO 2)

BE12-1 Phelps Corporation purchased debt investments for $41,500 on January 1, 1998. On July 1, 1998, Phelps received cash interest of $2,075. Journalize the purchase and the receipt of interest. Assume no interest has been accrued.

Journalize entries for stock investments.
(SO 3)

BE12-2 On August 1 McLain Company buys 1,000 shares of ABC common stock for $35,000 cash plus brokerage fees of $600. On December 1 the stock investments are sold for $38,000 in cash. Journalize the purchase and sale of the common stock.

Journalize transactions under the equity method.
(SO 3)

BE12-3 Harmon Company owns 30% of Hook Company. For the current year Hook reports net income of $150,000 and declares and pays a $50,000 cash dividend. Record Harmon's equity in Hook's net income and the receipt of dividends from Hook.

Prepare adjusting entry using fair value.
(SO 5)

BE12-4 Cost and fair value data for the trading securities of Michele Company at December 31, 1998, are $62,000 and $59,000, respectively. Prepare the adjusting entry to record the securities at fair value.

Indicate statement presentation using fair value.
(SO 6)

BE12-5 For the data presented in BE12-4, show the financial statement presentation of the trading securities and related accounts.

Prepare adjusting entry using fair value.
(SO 5)

BE12-6 Duggen Corporation holds available-for-sale stock securities costing $72,000 as a long-term investment. At December 31, 1998, the fair value of the securities is $65,000. Prepare the adjusting entry to record the securities at fair value.

Indicate statement presentation using fair value.
(SO 6)

BE12-7 For the data presented in BE12-6, show the financial statement presentation of the available-for-sale securities and related accounts. Assume the available-for-sale securities are noncurrent.

Prepare investments section of balance sheet.
(SO 6)

BE12-8 Saber Corporation has these long-term investments: common stock of Sword Co. (10% ownership) held as available-for-sale securities, cost $108,000, fair value $113,000; common stock of Epee Inc. (30% ownership), cost $210,000, equity $250,000; and a bond sinking fund of $150,000. Prepare the investments section of the balance sheet.

EXERCISES

E12-1 Piper Corporation had these transactions pertaining to debt investments:

Jan. 1 Purchased 60 10%, $1,000 Harris Co. bonds for $60,000 cash plus brokerage fees of $900. Interest is payable semiannually on July 1 and January 1.
July 1 Received semiannual interest on Harris Co. bonds.
July 1 Sold 30 Harris Co. bonds for $32,000 less $400 brokerage fees.

Journalize debt investment transactions, and accrue interest.
(SO 2)

Instructions
(a) Journalize the transactions.
(b) Prepare the adjusting entry for the accrual of interest at December 31.

E12-2 Malea Company had these transactions pertaining to stock investments:

Feb. 1 Purchased 800 shares of ABC common stock (2%) for $8,200 cash plus brokerage fees of $200.
July 1 Received cash dividends of $1 per share on ABC common stock.
Sept. 1 Sold 300 shares of ABC common stock for $4,000 less brokerage fees of $100.
Dec. 1 Received cash dividends of $1 per share on ABC common stock.

Journalize stock investment transactions, and explain income statement presentation.
(SO 3)

Instructions
(a) Journalize the transactions.
(b) Explain how dividend revenue and the gain (loss) on sale should be reported in the income statement.

E12-3 McCormick Inc. had these transactions pertaining to investments in common stock:

Jan. 1 Purchased 1,000 shares of Starr Corporation common stock (5%) for $70,000 cash plus $1,400 broker's commission.
July 1 Received a cash dividend of $9 per share.
Dec. 1 Sold 500 shares of Starr Corporation common stock for $37,000 cash less $800 broker's commission.
  31 Received a cash dividend of $9 per share.

Journalize transactions for investments in stock.
(SO 3)

Instructions
Journalize the transactions.

E12-4 On January 1 Ranier Corporation purchased a 25% equity investment in Bellingham Corporation for $150,000. At December 31 Bellingham declared and paid a $60,000 cash dividend and reported net income of $200,000.

Journalize and post transactions under the equity method.
(SO 3)

Instructions
(a) Journalize the transactions.
(b) Determine the amount to be reported as an investment in Bellingham stock at December 31.

E12-5 These are two independent situations:
1. Karen Cosmetics acquired 10% of the 200,000 shares of common stock of Bell Fashion at a total cost of $12 per share on March 18, 1998. On June 30 Bell declared and paid a $75,000 dividend. On December 31 Bell reported net income of $122,000 for the year. At December 31 the market price of Bell Fashion was $15 per share. The stock is classified as available-for-sale.
2. Barb, Inc., obtained significant influence over Diner Corporation by buying 30% of Diner's 30,000 outstanding shares of common stock at a total cost of $9 per share on January 1, 1998. On June 15 Diner declared and paid a cash dividend of $35,000. On December 31 Diner reported a net income of $80,000 for the year.

Journalize entries under cost and equity methods.
(SO 3)

Instructions
Prepare all the necessary journal entries for 1998 for (a) Karen Cosmetics and (b) Barb, Inc.

564 CHAPTER 12 Reporting and Analyzing Investments

Prepare adjusting entry to record fair value, and indicate statement presentation.
(SO 5, 6)

E12-6 At December 31, 1998, the trading securities for Nielson, Inc., are as follows:

Security	Cost	Fair Value
A	$17,500	$15,000
B	12,500	14,000
C	23,000	21,000
Total	$53,000	$50,000

Instructions
(a) Prepare the adjusting entry at December 31, 1998, to report the securities at fair value.
(b) Show the balance sheet and income statement presentation at December 31, 1998, after adjustment to fair value.

Prepare adjusting entry to record fair value, and indicate statement presentation.
(SO 5, 6)

E12-7 Data for investments in stock classified as trading securities are presented in E12-6. Assume instead that the investments are classified as available-for-sale securities with the same cost and fair value data. The securities are considered to be a long-term investment.

Instructions
(a) Prepare the adjusting entry at December 31, 1998, to report the securities at fair value.
(b) Show the statement presentation at December 31, 1998, after adjustment to fair value.

(c) J. Arnet, a member of the board of directors, does not understand the reporting of the unrealized gains or losses. Write a letter to Mr. Arnet explaining the reporting and the purposes it serves.

Prepare adjusting entries for fair value, and indicate statement presentation for two classes of securities.
(SO 5, 6)

E12-8 Felipe Company has these data at December 31, 1998:

Securities	Cost	Fair Value
Trading	$120,000	$125,000
Available-for-sale	100,000	90,000

The available-for-sale securities are held as a long-term investment.

Instructions
(a) Prepare the adjusting entries to report each class of securities at fair value.
(b) Indicate the statement presentation of each class of securities and the related unrealized gain (loss) accounts.

PROBLEMS

Journalize transactions, and show financial statement presentation.
(SO 2, 6)

P12-1 The following transactions related to long-term bonds occurred for Lund Corporation:

1998
Jan. 1 Purchased $50,000 RAM Corporation 10% bonds for $50,000.
July 1 Received interest on RAM bonds.
Dec. 31 Accrued interest on RAM bonds.

1999
Jan. 1 Received interest on RAM bonds.
Jan. 1 Sold $25,000 RAM bonds for $27,500.
July 1 Received interest on RAM bonds.

Instructions
(a) Journalize the transactions.
(b) Assume that the fair value of the bonds at December 31, 1998, was $57,000. These bonds are classified as available-for-sale securities. Prepare the adjusting entry to record these bonds at fair value.
(c) Show the balance sheet presentation of the bonds and interest receivable at December 31, 1998, and indicate where any unrealized gain or loss is reported in the financial statements.

P12-2 In January 1998 the management of Reed Company concludes that it has sufficient cash to purchase some temporary investments in debt and stock securities. During the year, these transactions occurred:

Feb. 1 Purchased 800 shares of IBF common stock for $32,000 plus brokerage fees of $800.
Mar. 1 Purchased 500 shares of RST common stock for $15,000 plus brokerage fees of $500.
Apr. 1 Purchased 60 $1,000, 12% CRT bonds for $60,000 plus $1,200 brokerage fees. Interest is payable semiannually on April 1 and October 1.
July 1 Received a cash dividend of $.60 per share on the IBF common stock.
Aug. 1 Sold 200 shares of IBF common stock at $42 per share less brokerage fees of $350.
Sept. 1 Received $1 per share cash dividend on the RST common stock.
Oct. 1 Received the semiannual interest on the CRT bonds.
Oct. 1 Sold the CRT bonds for $63,000 less $1,000 brokerage fees.

At December 31 the fair values of the IBF and RST common stocks were $39 and $30 per share, respectively.

Journalize investment transactions, prepare adjusting entry, and show financial statement presentation.
(SO 2, 3, 6)

Instructions
(a) Journalize the transactions and post to the accounts Debt Investments and Stock Investments. (Use the T account form.)
(b) Prepare the adjusting entry at December 31, 1998, to report the investments at fair value. All securities are considered to be trading securities.
(c) Show the balance sheet presentation of investment securities at December 31, 1998.
(d) Identify the income statement accounts and give the statement classification of each account.

P12-3 On December 31, 1997, Harmony Associates owned the following securities that are held as long-term investments:

Journalize transactions, prepare adjusting entry for stock investments, and show balance sheet presentation.
(SO 3, 5, 6)

Common Stock	Shares	Cost
A Co.	1,000	$50,000
B Co.	6,000	36,000
C Co.	1,200	24,000

On this date the total fair value of the securities was equal to its cost. The securities are not held for influence or control over the investees. In 1998 these transactions occurred:

July 1 Received $1 per share semiannual cash dividend on B Co. common stock.
Aug. 1 Received $.50 per share cash dividend on A Co. common stock.
Sept. 1 Sold 500 shares of B Co. common stock for cash at $8 per share less brokerage fees of $100.
Oct. 1 Sold 400 shares of A Co. common stock for cash at $54 per share less brokerage fees of $600.
Nov. 1 Received $1 per share cash dividend on C Co. common stock.
Dec. 15 Received $.50 per share cash dividend on A Co. common stock.
    31 Received $1 per share semiannual cash dividend on B Co. common stock.

At December 31 the fair values per share of the common stocks were: A Co. $47, B Co. $6, and C Co. $18.

Instructions
(a) Journalize the 1998 transactions and post to the account Stock Investments. (Use the T account form.)
(b) Prepare the adjusting entry at December 31, 1998, to show the securities at fair value. The stock should be classified as available-for-sale securities.
(c) Show the balance sheet presentation of the investments and the unrealized gain (loss) at December 31, 1998. At this date Harmony Associates has common stock $2,000,000 and retained earnings $1,200,000.

Prepare entries under cost and equity methods, and prepare memorandum.
(SO 3)

P12-4 Cardinal Concrete acquired 20% of the outstanding common stock of Edra Inc. on January 1, 1998, by paying $1,200,000 for 50,000 shares. Edra declared and paid an $.80 per share cash dividend on June 30 and again on December 31, 1998. Edra reported net income of $700,000 for the year.

Instructions
(a) Prepare the journal entries for Cardinal Concrete for 1998 assuming Cardinal cannot exercise significant influence over Edra. (Use the cost method.)
(b) Prepare the journal entries for Cardinal Concrete for 1998 assuming Cardinal can exercise significant influence over Edra. (Use the equity method.)
(c) The board of directors of Cardinal Concrete is confused about the differences between the cost and equity methods. Prepare a memorandum for the board that explains each method and shows in tabular form the account balances under each method at December 31, 1998.

Journalize stock transactions, and show balance sheet presentation.
(SO 3, 6)

P12-5 Here is Hi-Tech Company's portfolio of long-term available-for-sale securities at December 31, 1997:

	Cost
500 shares of Awixa Corporation common stock	$26,000
700 shares of HAL Corporation common stock	42,000
400 shares of Renda Corporation preferred stock	16,800

On December 31 the total cost of the portfolio equaled the total fair value. Hi-Tech had these transactions related to the securities during 1998:

Jan. 7 Sold 500 shares of Awixa Corporation common stock at $56 per share less brokerage fees of $700.
  10 Purchased 200 shares of $70 par value common stock of Mintor Corporation at $78 per share plus brokerage fees of $240.
  26 Received a cash dividend of $1.15 per share on HAL Corporation common stock.
Feb. 2 Received cash dividends of $.40 per share on Renda Corporation preferred stock.
  10 Sold all 400 shares of Renda Corporation preferred stock at $28 per share less brokerage fees of $180.
July 1 Received a cash dividend of $1 per share on HAL Corporation common stock.
Sept. 1 Purchased an additional 400 shares of the $70 par value common stock of Mintor Corporation at $82 per share plus brokerage fees of $400.
Dec. 15 Received a cash dividend of $1.50 per share on Mintor Corporation common stock.

At December 31, 1998, the fair values of the securities were:

HAL Corporation common stock	$64 per share
Mintor Corporation common stock	$70 per share

Hi-Tech uses separate account titles for each investment, such as Investment in HAL Corporation Common Stock.

Instructions
(a) Prepare journal entries to record the transactions.
(b) Post to the investment accounts. (Use T accounts.)
(c) Prepare the adjusting entry at December 31, 1998, to report the portfolio at fair value.
(d) Show the balance sheet presentation at December 31, 1998.

Prepare a balance sheet.
(SO 6)

P12-6 The following data, presented in alphabetical order, are taken from the records of Oklahoma Corporation:

Accounts payable	$ 240,000
Accounts receivable	110,000
Accumulated depreciation—building	180,000
Accumulated depreciation—equipment	52,000
Allowance for doubtful accounts	6,000
Bond sinking fund	360,000
Bonds payable (10%, due 2012)	400,000
Buildings	900,000
Cash	92,000

Common stock ($5 par value; 500,000 shares authorized, 300,000 shares issued)	1,500,000
Discount on bonds payable	20,000
Dividends payable	50,000
Equipment	275,000
Goodwill	200,000
Income taxes payable	120,000
Investment in Houston Inc. stock (30% ownership), at equity	240,000
Land	500,000
Merchandise inventory	170,000
Notes payable (due 1999)	70,000
Organization costs	50,000
Paid-in capital in excess of par value	200,000
Prepaid insurance	16,000
Retained earnings	300,000
Temporary stock investment, at fair value	185,000

Instructions
Prepare a balance sheet at December 31, 1998.

ALTERNATIVE PROBLEMS

P12-1A The following transactions related to long-term bonds occurred for Givarz Corporation:

Journalize transactions, and show financial statement presentation.
(SO 2, 6)

1998
Jan. 1 Purchased $100,000 Leslye Corporation 9% bonds for $100,000.
July 1 Received interest on Leslye bonds.
Dec. 31 Accrued interest on Leslye bonds.

1999
Jan. 1 Received interest on Leslye bonds.
Jan. 1 Sold $25,000 Leslye bonds for $30,500.
July 1 Received interest on Leslye bonds.

Instructions
(a) Journalize the transactions.
(b) Assume that the fair value of the bonds at December 31, 1998, was $97,000. These bonds are classified as available-for-sale securities. Prepare the adjusting entry to record these bonds at fair value.
(c) Show the balance sheet presentation of the bonds and interest receivable at December 31, 1998, and indicate where any unrealized gain or loss is reported in the financial statements.

P12-2A In January 1998 the management of Mead Company concludes that it has sufficient cash to permit some temporary investments in debt and stock securities. During the year these transactions occurred:

Journalize investment transactions, prepare adjusting entry, and show financial statement presentation.
(SO 2, 3, 6)

Feb. 1 Purchased 600 shares of CBF common stock for $31,800 plus brokerage fees of $600.
Mar. 1 Purchased 800 shares of RSD common stock for $20,000 plus brokerage fees of $400.
Apr. 1 Purchased 50 $1,000, 12% MRT bonds for $50,000 plus $1,000 brokerage fees. Interest is payable semiannually on April 1 and October 1.
July 1 Received a cash dividend of $.60 per share on the CBF common stock.
Aug. 1 Sold 200 shares of CBF common stock at $56 per share less brokerage fees of $200.
Sept. 1 Received $1 per share cash dividend on the RSD common stock.
Oct. 1 Received the semiannual interest on the MRT bonds.
Oct. 1 Sold the MRT bonds for $51,000 less $1,000 brokerage fees.

568 CHAPTER 12 Reporting and Analyzing Investments

At December 31 the fair values of the CBF and RSD common stocks were $55 and $24 per share, respectively.

Instructions
(a) Journalize the transactions and post to the accounts Debt Investments and Stock Investments. (Use the T account form.)
(b) Prepare the adjusting entry at December 31, 1998, to report the investment securities at fair value. All securities are considered to be trading securities.
(c) Show the balance sheet presentation of investment securities at December 31, 1998.
(d) Identify the income statement accounts and give the statement classification of each account.

Journalize transactions, prepare adjusting entry for stock investments, and show balance sheet presentation.
(SO 3, 5, 6)

P12-3A On December 31, 1997, Karen Associates owned the following securities that are held as long-term investments. The securities are not held for influence or control over the investee.

Common Stock	Shares	Cost
X Co.	2,000	$90,000
Y Co.	5,000	45,000
Z Co.	2,000	30,000

On this date the total fair value of the securities was equal to its cost. In 1998 these transactions occurred:

July 1 Received $1 per share semiannual cash dividend on Y Co. common stock
Aug. 1 Received $.50 per share cash dividend on X Co. common stock.
Sept. 1 Sold 700 shares of Y Co. common stock for cash at $8 per share less brokerage fees of $200.
Oct. 1 Sold 600 shares of X Co. common stock for cash at $54 per share less brokerage fees of $500.
Nov. 1 Received $1 per share cash dividend on Z Co. common stock.
Dec. 15 Received $.50 per share cash dividend on X Co. common stock.
     31 Received $1 per share semiannual cash dividend on Y Co. common stock.

At December 31 the fair values per share of the common stocks were: X Co. $48, Y Co. $8, and Z Co. $17.

Instructions
(a) Journalize the 1998 transactions and post to the account Stock Investments. (Use the T account form.)
(b) Prepare the adjusting entry at December 31, 1998, to show the securities at fair value. The stock should be classified as available-for-sale securities.
(c) Show the balance sheet presentation of the investments and the unrealized gain (loss) at December 31, 1998. At this date Karen Associates has common stock $1,500,000 and retained earnings $1,000,000.

Prepare entries under cost and equity methods, and tabulate differences.
(SO 6)

P12-4A DFM Services acquired 30% of the outstanding common stock of BNA Company on January 1, 1998, by paying $800,000 for the 40,000 shares. BNA declared and paid $.20 per share cash dividends on March 15, June 15, September 15, and December 15, 1998. BNA reported net income of $350,000 for the year.

Instructions
(a) Prepare the journal entries for DFM Services for 1998 assuming DFM cannot exercise significant influence over BNA. (Use the cost method.)
(b) Prepare the journal entries for DFM Services for 1998 assuming DFM can exercise significant influence over BNA. (Use the equity method.)
(c) In tabular form indicate the investment and income statement account balances at December 31, 1998, under each method of accounting.

Prepare a balance sheet.
(SO 6)

P12-5A The following data, presented in alphabetical order, are taken from the records of Alameda Corporation:

Accounts payable	$ 250,000
Accounts receivable	120,000
Accumulated depreciation—building	180,000

Accumulated depreciation—equipment	52,000
Allowance for doubtful accounts	6,000
Bond sinking fund	150,000
Bonds payable (10%, due 2010)	500,000
Buildings	950,000
Cash	92,000
Common stock ($10 par value; 500,000 shares authorized, 150,000 shares issued)	1,500,000
Dividends payable	80,000
Equipment	275,000
Goodwill	200,000
Income taxes payable	120,000
Investment in Dodge common stock (10% ownership), at cost	278,000
Investment in Huston common stock (30% ownership), at equity	230,000
Land	500,000
Market adjustment—available-for-sale securities (Dr.)	8,000
Merchandise inventory	170,000
Notes payable (due 1999)	70,000
Organization costs	50,000
Paid-in capital in excess of par value	200,000
Premium on bonds payable	40,000
Prepaid insurance	16,000
Retained earnings	213,000
Temporary stock investment, at fair value	180,000
Unrealized gain—available-for-sale securities	8,000

The investment in Dodge common stock is considered to be a long-term available-for-sale security.

Instructions
Prepare a balance sheet at December 31, 1998.

BROADENING YOUR PERSPECTIVE

FINANCIAL REPORTING AND ANALYSIS

FINANCIAL REPORTING PROBLEM: *Starbucks Corporation*

BYP12-1 The annual report of Starbucks is presented in Appendix A.

Instructions
Answer these questions:

(a) What information about investments is reported in the consolidated balance sheet?
(b) Based on the information in Note 3 to Starbucks' financial statements, what is the nature of Starbucks' short-term investments?
(c) What effect did interest income on investments have on Income Before Income Taxes in 1996?
(d) Judging from the statement of cash flows, did cash flows from investing activities increase or decrease in 1996, and by how much? What item changed the most?
(e) Based on the information under Liquidity and Capital Resources in Management's Discussion and Analysis of Financial Condition and Results of Operations: (1) What types of investments were made in 1996? (2) Does management expect investing activity to increase or decrease in 1997? (3) Does management expect its cash resources to be sufficient for these plans?

(f) Note 5 to Starbucks' financial statements describes a number of 50–50 joint ventures that the company has entered into. How is each of these joint ventures being accounted for? What was the effect of each of these joint ventures on 1996 net income?

COMPARATIVE ANALYSIS PROBLEM: *Starbucks vs. Green Mountain Coffee*

BYP12-2 The financial statements of Green Mountain Coffee are presented in Appendix B, following the financial statements for Starbucks in Appendix A.

Instructions
(a) Based on the information in these financial statements, determine each of the following for each company:
  (1) Cash used in (for) investing activities during 1996 (from the statement of cash flows)
  (2) Cash used for investments in joint ventures and equity investments during 1996
  (3) Total investments in joint ventures and equity investments at the end of fiscal 1996
(b) What conclusions concerning the management of investments can be drawn from these data?

RESEARCH CASE

BYP12-3 The July 6, 1995, edition of *The Wall Street Journal* includes an article by Jim Carlton and David P. Hamilton entitled "Packard Bell Sells 20% Stake to NEC for $170 Million; Deal Gives Japanese Firm Unprecedented Access to the U.S. PC Market."

Instructions
Read the article and answer these questions:
(a) Why did Packard Bell sell shares to NEC?
(b) Identify a similar transaction between two other computer companies.
(c) Under U.S. GAAP, how would NEC account for its investment in Packard Bell?
(d) Packard Bell was considering a sale of common shares to the general public. Why didn't it select this option?

INTERPRETING FINANCIAL STATEMENTS

BYP12-4 Delta Air Lines, Inc., is based in Atlanta, Georgia, and is one of the world's largest air carriers. Besides carrying passengers, Delta also provides freight and mail transportation services. Delta has service to 153 cities in 46 states and U.S. possessions, and to 44 cities in 25 foreign countries.

Here is the assets section of Delta's 1996 annual report (excluding dollar amounts):

Current assets
  Cash and cash equivalents
  Short-term investments
  Accounts receivable, net of allowance for uncollectible accounts
  Maintenance and operating supplies, at average cost
  Deferred income taxes
  Prepaid expenses and other
Property and equipment
  Flight equipment, less accumulated depreciation
  Flight equipment under capital leases, less accumulated amortization
  Ground property and equipment, less accumulated depreciation
  Advance payments for equipment
Other assets
  Marketable equity securities
  Deferred income taxes
  Investments in associated companies
  Cost in excess of net assets acquired, net of accumulated amortization
  Leasehold and operating rights, net of accumulated amortization
  Other

Delta also reported the following information concerning certain of its investments:
1. Investments in TransQuest Information Solutions (TransQuest), an information technology joint venture, is accounted for under the equity method.
2. Investments with an original maturity of 3 months or less are stated at cost, which approximates fair value.
3. Cost in excess of net assets acquired (goodwill), which is being amortized over 40 years, is related to the company's acquisition of Western Air Lines, Inc., on December 18, 1986.
4. The company's investments in Singapore Air Lines Limited are accounted for under the cost method and are classified as available-for-sale and carried at aggregate market value.
5. Cash in excess of operating requirements is invested in short-term, highly liquid investments. These investments are classified as available-for-sale and are stated at fair value.

Instructions
(a) For each item 1–5 above, determine where it should be shown on Delta's balance sheet, using the account titles listed earlier.
(b) Assume that item 2 includes an investment in IBM Corporation bonds consisting of ten bonds of $10,000 each. What accounting treatment is required for the following?
   (1) Singapore Air Lines Limited announces net income for the year of $3.15 per share. Assume that Delta holds 3,500 shares.
   (2) Western Air Lines announces a net loss of $18,000,000, or $.63 per share for the quarter.
   (3) IBM Corporation declares and pays a $.25 dividend per share.

BYP12-5 Xerox Corporation has a 50% investment interest in a joint venture with the Japanese corporation Fuji, called Fuji Xerox. Xerox accounts for this investment using the equity method. The following additional information regarding this investment was taken from Xerox's 1995 annual report:

Investment in Fuji Xerox per balance sheet	$ 1,223
Xerox's equity in Fuji Xerox net income	88
Xerox total assets	25,969
Xerox total liabilities	21,328
Fuji Xerox total assets	6,603
Fuji Xerox total liabilities	4,153

Instructions
(a) What alternative approaches are available for accounting for long-term investments in stock? Discuss whether Xerox is correct in using the equity method to account for this investment.
(b) Under the equity method, how does Xerox report its investment in Fuji Xerox? If Xerox owned a majority of Fuji Xerox, it then would have to consolidate Fuji Xerox instead of using the equity method. Discuss how this would change Xerox's financial statements. That is, in what way and how much would assets and liabilities change?
(c) The use of 50% joint ventures is becoming a fairly common practice. Why might companies like Xerox prefer to participate in a joint venture rather than own a majority share?

BYP12-6 Citicorp is one of the largest bank holding companies in the world. In addition to making loans, it has significant trading activities. During 1993, 1994, and 1995 the company reported this income information:

	($ in millions)		
	1995	1994	1993
Trading account gains and losses	$ 559	$ 158	$ 939
Gains and losses on available-for-sale securities	132	200	94
Net income	3,464	3,366	2,219

The following additional information was available regarding the company's available-for-sale portfolio:

	($ in millions)			
	Cost	Unrealized Gains	Gross Unrealized Losses	Gross Fair Value
1994	$13,176	$825	$399	$13,602
1995	18,029	829	645	18,213

Instructions
(a) Comment on the importance of securities gains and losses as a part of Citicorp's income. Does the income provided by these activities appear to be stable or volatile?
(b) Citicorp has a significant available-for-sale portfolio. How much, and by what percentage, could the company have increased its 1995 income by selling its "winners" while holding its "losers"? Why do you suppose it chose not to do this?

CRITICAL THINKING

MANAGEMENT DECISION CASE

BYP12-7 At the beginning of the question and answer portion of the annual stockholders' meeting of Revell Corporation, stockholder Carol Finstrom asks, "Why did management sell the holdings in AHM Company at a loss when this company has been very profitable during the period its stock was held by Revell?"

Since President Larry Wisdom has just concluded his speech on the recent success and bright future of Revell, he is taken aback by this question and responds, "I remember we paid $1,100,000 for that stock some years ago, and I am sure we sold that stock at a much higher price. You must be mistaken."

Finstrom retorts, "Well, right here in footnote number 7 to the annual report it shows that 240,000 shares, a 30% interest in AHM, was sold on the last day of the year. Also, it states that AHM earned $550,000 this year and paid out $150,000 in cash dividends. Further, a summary statement indicates that in past years, while Revell held AHM stock, AHM earned $1,240,000 and paid out $440,000 in dividends. Finally, the income statement for this year shows a loss on the sale of AHM stock of $180,000. So, I doubt that I am mistaken."

Red-faced, President Wisdom turns to you.

Instructions
Help out President Wisdom: What dollar amount did Revell receive upon the sale of the AHM stock? Explain why both Finstrom and Wisdom are correct.

A REAL-WORLD FOCUS: *SPS Technologies, Inc.*

BYP12-8 *SPS Technologies, Inc.,* was formed in 1903 as Standard Pressed Steel. Today the company is engaged in the design, manufacture, and marketing of high-strength mechanical fasteners, superalloys, and magnetic materials for the aerospace, automotive, and off-highway equipment industries. The company owns plants in the United States, the United Kingdom, Ireland, Australia, and Spain, and has minority interests in facilities in Brazil and India.

The following note to the financial statements appeared in a recent SPS annual report:

SPS TECHNOLOGIES, INC.,
Notes to the Financial Statements

Investments: The Company's investments in affiliates consist of a 16.75% interest in Precision Fasteners Ltd., Bombay, India; a 46.49% interest in Metalac S.A. Industria e Comercio, Sao Paulo, Brazil; a 51.0% interest in Pacific Products Limited, Guernsey, Channel Islands, United Kingdom; and a 51.0% interest in National-Arnold Magnetics Company, Adelanto, California, United States. Dividends received from these companies were $42,000, $44,000, and $66,000 in 1993, 1992, and 1991, respectively.

Instructions
(a) Do the investments in these companies represent short- or long-term investments? Are these investments in the stocks or bonds of these companies?
(b) The ownership percentages in these companies vary. Based upon the information given, which accounting method seems appropriate for each company? What other information would you like to have before deciding how to account for each investment?
(c) What is the most likely method used to account for dividends received from Precision Fasteners? From National-Arnold Magnetics Company?

GROUP ACTIVITY

BYP12-9 Finland Corporation holds a portfolio of debt and equity investments. Although some of the securities in the portfolio have declined in value, the total value of the portfolio is greater than its total cost. Finn Berge, Finland Corporation's president, has decided to classify all securities in the portfolio that have decreased in value as available-for-sale (the stock investments) or as held-to-maturity (the debt investments). He will classify all securities that have increased in value as trading securities.

Instructions
In groups of four or five discuss these issues:
(a) What impact will this classification approach have on Finland Corporation's reported results?
(b) Is this approach appropriate for classifying these securities?
(c) What are the implications of this approach for subsequent years?

COMMUNICATION ACTIVITY

BYP12-10 Chapperal Corporation has purchased two securities for its portfolio. The first is a stock investment in Sting Ray Corporation, one of its suppliers. Chapperal purchased 10% of Sting Ray with the intention of holding it for a number of years but has no intention of purchasing more shares. The second investment is a purchase of debt securities. Chapperal purchased the debt securities because its analysts believe that changes in market interest rates will cause these securities to increase in value in a short period of time. Chapperal intends to sell the securities as soon as they have increased in value.

Instructions
Write a memo to Gils Stiles, the chief financial officer, explaining how to account for each of these investments and the implications for reported income from this accounting treatment.

ETHICS CASE

BYP12-11 Scott Kreiter Financial Services Company holds a large portfolio of debt and stock securities as an investment. The total fair value of the portfolio at December 31, 1998, is greater than total cost, with some securities having increased in value and others having decreased. Vicki Lemke, the financial vice-president, and Ula Greenwood, the controller, are in the process of classifying for the first time the securities in the portfolio.

Lemke suggests classifying the securities that have increased in value as trading securities in order to increase net income for the year. She wants to classify the securities that have decreased in value as long-term available-for-sale securities so that the decreases in value will not affect 1998 net income.

Greenwood disagrees. She recommends classifying the securities that have decreased in value as trading securities and those that have increased in value as long-term available-for-sale securities. Greenwood argues that the company is having a good earnings year and that recognizing the losses now will help to smooth income for this year. Moreover, for future years, when the company may not be as profitable, the company will have built-in gains.

574 CHAPTER 12 Reporting and Analyzing Investments

Instructions
(a) Will classifying the securities as Lemke and Greenwood suggest actually affect earnings as each says it will?
(b) Is there anything unethical in what Lemke and Greenwood propose? Who are the stakeholders affected by their proposals?
(c) Assume that Lemke and Greenwood properly classify the portfolio. Assume, at year-end, that Lemke proposes to sell the securities that will increase 1998 net income, and that Greenwood proposes to sell the securities that will decrease 1998 net income. Is this unethical?

FINANCIAL ANALYSIS ON THE WEB

BYP12-12 *Purpose:* Bonds, similar to stocks, can be purchased by investors in an initial public offering or through a secondary market. Secondary markets can be reached via the Internet and provide users with investment information. Bonds Online is one site that provides a bond-specific glossary of terms.

Address: http://www.bondsonline.com

Steps:
1. From the Bonds Online homepage, choose **Bond Professor.**
2. Choose **Glossary.**

Instructions
Using the glossary, find the definition of:
(a) discount rate.
(b) capital market.
(c) rating.

Answers to Self-Study Questions
1. a   2. b   3. c   4. a   5. a   6. c   7. b   8. c   9. c

CHAPTER 13

Statement of Cash Flows

STUDY OBJECTIVES

After studying this chapter, you should be able to:

1. Indicate the primary purpose of the statement of cash flows.
2. Distinguish among operating, investing, and financing activities.
3. Explain the impact of the product life cycle on a company's cash flows.
4. Prepare a statement of cash flows using one of two approaches: (a) the indirect method or (b) the direct method.
5. Use the statement of cash flows to evaluate a company.

I've Got Seven Billion Dollars Burning a Hole in My Pocket!

Imagine starting a company in a brand new industry and growing it into one of the biggest companies in the world—in just 20 years. Imagine you are one of the richest people on the planet at age 39. Now wake up! Bill Gates, founder of software maker Microsoft Corporation, accomplished all of this and more between 1975 and 1995. It all started with MS-DOS, a software package that Gates bought from a Seattle-based programmer for $50,000. Then MS-DOS was adopted by IBM as *the* operating system for all of its personal computers. Translation: Every IBM and IBM-compatible computer *in the world* needed a copy of MS-DOS to run. The rest is history.

Although MS-DOS got the Microsoft ball rolling, in an environment that changes as fast as the computer industry, it takes continual new products to survive and thrive. To develop new products it takes cash—lots and lots of cash. And to have lots and lots of cash when you are a young company requires great cash management and careful attention to cash flows. During its early years, in order to ensure that it had enough cash to meet its needs, Microsoft employed many cash management techniques. For example, all of its employees received stock options, rather than cash, as a portion of their compensation. Stock options become valuable if Microsoft's stock price increases. By some estimates, more than 1,000 Microsoft employees have become millionaires because of these options. These and other cash management practices enabled Microsoft to build up a "war chest" of cash and short-term investments. Its 1995 statement of cash flows reported cash provided by operations of approximately $2 billion. At its fiscal year end of June 30, 1995, cash and short-term investments amounted to nearly $5 billion—65% of its total assets. At December 31, 1996, this amount had grown to nearly $7 billion. This might sound excessive, but it means that Microsoft can move quickly when it needs to—and in the computer industry speed is everything.

On the World Wide Web
Microsoft: http://www.microsoft.com

PREVIEW OF CHAPTER 13

The balance sheet, income statement, and retained earnings statement do not always show the whole picture of the financial condition of a company or institution. In fact, looking at these three financial statements of some well-known companies, a thoughtful investor might ask questions like these: How did Eastman Kodak finance cash dividends of $649 million in a year in which it earned only $17 million? How could Delta Air Lines purchase new planes that cost $900 million in a year in which it reported a net loss of $86 million? How did Kohlberg Kravis and Roberts finance its record-shattering $25 billion purchase of RJR Nabisco? Answers to these and similar questions can be found in this chapter, which presents the statement of cash flows.

The content and organization of this chapter are as follows:

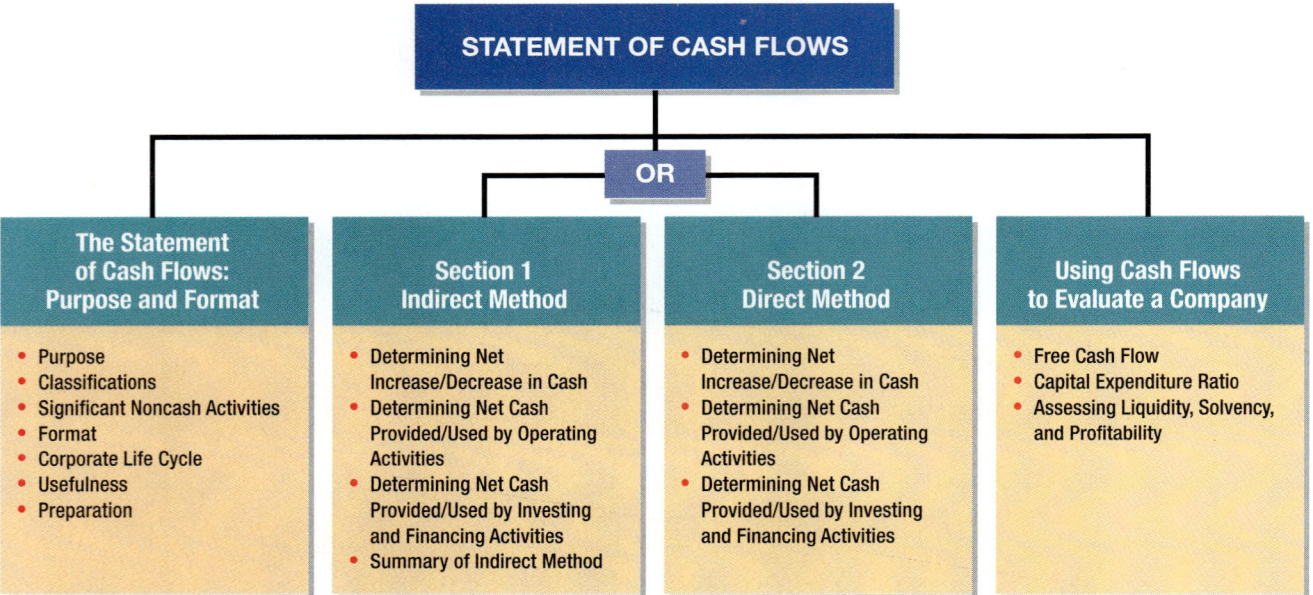

THE STATEMENT OF CASH FLOWS: PURPOSE AND FORMAT

The basic financial statements we have presented so far provide only limited information about a company's cash flows (cash receipts and cash payments). For example, comparative balance sheets show the increase in property, plant, and equipment during the year, but they do not show how the additions were financed or paid for. The income statement shows net income, but it does not indicate the amount of cash generated by operating activities. Similarly, the retained earnings statement shows cash dividends declared but not the cash dividends paid during the year. None of these statements presents a detailed summary of the **net change in cash** as a result of operating, investing, and financing activities during the period.

Helpful Hint Recall that the retained earnings statement is often presented in the statement of stockholders' equity.

STUDY OBJECTIVE 1

Indicate the primary purpose of the statement of cash flows.

PURPOSE OF THE STATEMENT OF CASH FLOWS

The primary purpose of the **statement of cash flows** is to provide information about cash receipts, cash payments, and the net change in cash resulting from the operating, investing, and financing activities of a company during the period. These activities involving cash are reported in a format that reconciles the beginning and ending cash balances.

Reporting the causes of changes in cash is useful because investors, creditors, and other interested parties want to know what is happening to a company's most liquid resource, its cash. As the opening story about Microsoft demonstrates, to understand a company's financial position it is essential to understand its cash flows. The statement of cash flows provides answers to these important questions about an enterprise:

Where did the cash come from during the period?
What was the cash used for during the period?
What was the change in the cash balance during the period?

The answers provide important clues about whether a dynamic company like Microsoft will be able to continue to thrive and invest in new ideas. The statement of cash flows also provides clues about whether a struggling company will survive or perish.

CLASSIFICATION OF CASH FLOWS

The statement of cash flows classifies cash receipts and cash payments into operating, investing, and financing activities. Transactions within each activity are as follows:

STUDY OBJECTIVE 2
Distinguish among operating, investing, and financing activities.

1. **Operating activities** include the cash effects of transactions that create revenues and expenses and thus enter into the determination of net income.
2. **Investing activities** include (a) purchasing and disposing of investments and productive long-lived assets using cash and (b) lending money and collecting the loans.
3. **Financing activities** include (a) obtaining cash from issuing debt and repaying the amounts borrowed and (b) obtaining cash from stockholders and paying them dividends.

Operating activities is the most important category because it shows the cash provided or used by company operations. This source of cash is generally considered to be the best measure of whether a company can generate sufficient cash to continue as a going concern and to expand. Illustration 13-1 (page 580) lists typical cash receipts and cash payments within each of the three activities.

Helpful Hint You determine what classification a transaction is by looking to see if it is in the list of investing activities or financing activities. If it is in neither of these lists, it is an operating activity.

As you can see, some cash flows relating to investing or financing activities are classified as operating activities. For example, receipts of investment revenue (interest and dividends) and payments of interest to lenders are classified as operating activities because these items are reported in the income statement.

Note that, generally, (1) operating activities involve income determination (income statement) items, (2) investing activities involve cash flows resulting from changes in investments and long-term asset items, and (3) financing activities involve cash flows resulting from changes in long-term liability and stockholders' equity items.

SIGNIFICANT NONCASH ACTIVITIES

Not all of a company's significant activities involve cash. Here are four examples of significant noncash activities:

1. Issuance of common stock to purchase assets
2. Conversion of bonds into common stock
3. Issuance of debt to purchase assets
4. Exchanges of plant assets

Illustration 13-1 Typical cash receipts and payments classified by activity

Types of Cash Inflows and Outflows

Operating activities
Cash inflows:
 From sale of goods or services
 From returns on loans (interest received) and on equity securities (dividends received)
Cash outflows:
 To suppliers for inventory
 To employees for services
 To government for taxes
 To lenders for interest
 To others for expenses

Investing activities
Cash inflows:
 From sale of property, plant, and equipment
 From sale of debt or equity securities of other entities
 From collection of principal on loans to other entities
Cash outflows:
 To purchase property, plant, and equipment
 To purchase debt or equity securities of other entities
 To make loans to other entities

Financing activities
Cash inflows:
 From sale of equity securities (company's own stock)
 From issuance of debt (bonds and notes)
Cash outflows:
 To stockholders as dividends
 To redeem long-term debt or reacquire capital stock

Helpful Hint Operating activities generally relate to changes in current assets and current liabilities. Investing activities generally relate to changes in investments and noncurrent assets. Financing activities relate to changes in noncurrent liabilities and stockholders' equity accounts.

Helpful Hint Do not include noncash investing and financing activities in the body of the statement of cash flows. Report this information in a separate schedule at the bottom of the statement

Significant financing and investing activities that do not affect cash are not reported in the body of the statement of cash flows. However, these activities are reported either in a separate schedule at the bottom of the statement of cash flows or in a separate note or supplementary schedule to the financial statements.

The reporting of these activities in a separate note or supplementary schedule satisfies the **full disclosure principle** because it identifies significant noncash investing and financing activities of the enterprise. In doing homework assignments you should present significant noncash investing and financing activities in a separate schedule at the bottom of the statement of cash flows. (See the lower section of Illustration 13-2 for an example.)

FORMAT OF THE STATEMENT OF CASH FLOWS

The three activities discussed above—operating, investing, and financing—plus the significant noncash investing and financing activities make up the general format of the statement of cash flows. A widely used form of the statement of cash flows is shown in Illustration 13-2.

As illustrated, the section of cash flows from operating activities always appears first, followed by the investing activities and the financing activities sections. Also, **the individual inflows and outflows from investing and financ-**

Illustration 13-2 Format of statement of cash flows

COMPANY NAME Statement of Cash Flows Period Covered		
Cash flows from operating activities		
(List of individual items)	XX	
Net cash provided (used) by operating activities		XXX
Cash flows from investing activities		
(List of individual inflows and outflows)	XX	
Net cash provided (used) by investing activities		XXX
Cash flows from financing activities		
(List of individual inflows and outflows)	XX	
Net cash provided (used) by financing activities		XXX
Net increase (decrease) in cash		XXX
Cash at beginning of period		XXX
Cash at end of period		XXX
Noncash investing and financing activities		
(List of individual noncash transactions)		XXX

Helpful Hint Indicate the classification in the statement of cash flows for each of the following: (1) Proceeds from the sale of an investment. (2) Disbursement for the purchase of treasury stock. (3) Loan to another corporation. (4) Proceeds from an insurance policy because a building was destroyed by fire. (5) Proceeds from winning a lawsuit. (6) Receipt of interest from an investment in bonds. (7) Payment of dividends. (8) Sale of merchandise for cash.
Answers:
(1) Investing   (2) Financing
(3) Investing   (4) Investing
(5) Operating   (6) Operating
(7) Financing   (8) Operating

ing activities are reported separately. Thus, the cash outflow for the purchase of property, plant, and equipment is reported separately from the cash inflow from the sale of property, plant, and equipment. Similarly, the cash inflow from the issuance of debt securities is reported separately from the cash outflow for the retirement of debt. If a company did not report the inflows and outflows separately, it would obscure the investing and financing activities of the enterprise and thus make it more difficult for the user to assess future cash flows.

The reported operating, investing, and financing activities result in net cash either **provided or used** by each activity. The net cash provided or used by each activity is totaled to show the net increase (decrease) in cash for the period. The net increase (decrease) in cash for the period is then added to or subtracted from the beginning-of-period cash balance to obtain the end-of-period cash balance. Finally, any significant noncash investing and financing activities are reported in a separate schedule at the bottom of the statement.

BUSINESS INSIGHT
Investor Perspective

Net income is not the same as net cash generated by operations. The differences are illustrated by the following results from recent annual reports for the same fiscal year ($ in millions):

Company	Net Income	Net Cash Provided by Operations
Kmart Corporation	$ 296	$ 76
Wal-Mart Stores, Inc.	2,681	2,906
Woolworth Corporation	47	(340)
J.C. Penney Company, Inc.	1,057	738
Sears Roebuck & Co.	1,454	1,930
The May Department Stores Company	782	999

Note the wide disparity among these companies that all engaged in similar types of retail merchandising.

BEFORE YOU GO ON...

● **Review It**

1. What is the primary purpose of a statement of cash flows?
2. What are the major classifications of cash flows on the statement of cash flows?
3. What are some examples of significant noncash activities?

THE CORPORATE LIFE CYCLE

STUDY OBJECTIVE 3

Explain the impact of the product life cycle on a company's cash flows.

All products go through a series of phases called the **product life cycle.** The phases (in order of their occurrence) are often referred to as the **introductory phase, growth phase, maturity phase,** and **decline phase.** The introductory phase occurs when the company is purchasing fixed assets and beginning to produce and sell. During the growth phase, the company is striving to expand its production and sales. In the maturity phase, sales and production level off. And during the decline phase, sales of the product fall due to a weakening in consumer demand.

If a company had only one product and that product was, for example, nearing the end of its salable life, we would say that the company was in the decline phase. Companies generally have more than one product, however, and not all of a company's products are in the same phase of the product life cycle at the same time. We can still characterize a company as being in one of the four phases because the majority of its products are in a particular phase.

Illustration 13-3 shows that the phase a company is in affects its cash flows. In the **introductory stage,** we expect that the company will be spending considerable amounts to purchase productive assets, but it will not be generating much (if any) cash from operations. To support its asset purchases it may have to issue stock or debt. Thus, we expect cash from operations to be negative, cash from investing to be negative, and cash from financing to be positive.

Illustration 13-3 Impact of product life cycle on cash flows

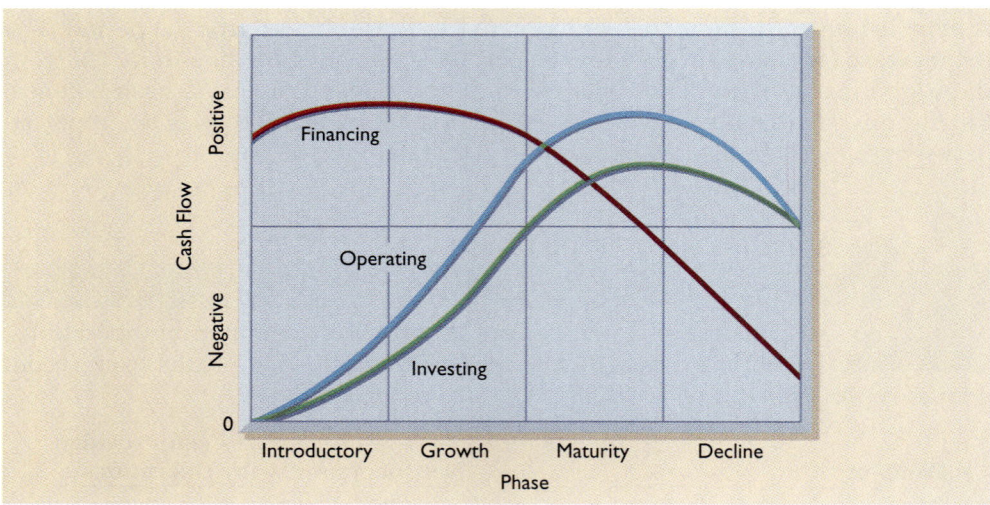

During the **growth phase,** we expect to see the company start to generate small amounts of cash from operations. Cash from operations continues to be less than net income during this phase, though, because inventory must be purchased for future projected sales. Since those sales are projected to be increasing, the size of inventory purchases must increase. Thus, less inventory will be expensed on an accrual basis than purchased on a cash basis in the growth phase.

Also, collections on accounts receivable will lag behind sales, and because sales are growing, accrual sales during a period will exceed cash collections during that period. Cash needed for asset acquisitions will continue to exceed cash provided by operations, requiring that the company make up the deficiency by issuing new stock or debt. Thus, the company continues to show negative cash from investing and positive cash from financing in the growth phase.

During the **maturity phase,** cash from operations and net income are approximately the same. Cash generated from operations exceeds investing needs. Thus, in the maturity phase the company can actually start to retire debt or buy back stock.

Finally, during the **decline phase,** cash from operations decreases. Cash from investing might actually become positive as the firm sells off excess assets, and cash from financing may be negative as the company buys back stock and retires debt.

Consider Microsoft: During its early years it had significant product development costs with little revenue. Microsoft was lucky in that its agreement with IBM to provide the operating system for IBM PCs gave it an early steady source of cash to support growth. As noted earlier, one way it conserved cash was to pay employees with stock options rather than cash. Today Microsoft could best be characterized as being between the growth and maturity phases. It continues to spend considerable amounts on research and development and investment in new assets. For the last 3 years, however, its cash from operations has exceeded its net income. Cash from operations also exceeds cash used for investing, and common stock repurchased exceeds common stock issued. For Microsoft, as for any large company, the challenge is to maintain its growth. In the software industry, where products become obsolete very quickly, the challenge is particularly great.

BUSINESS INSIGHT
Investor Perspective

Listed here are the net income, and cash from operations, investing, and financing during a recent year for some of the companies that we have discussed in previous chapters. The final column suggests their likely phase in the life cycle based on these figures.

Company ($ in millions)	Net Income	Cash Provided by Operations	Cash Provided (Used) by Investing	Cash Provided (Used) by Financing	Likely Phase in Life Cycle
Netscape	$ (3)	$ 15	$ (140)	$ 168	Introductory
Iomega	8.5	(27)	(43)	54	Introductory
Caterpillar	1,136	2,190	(1,749)	(208)	Maturity
McDonnell Douglas	(416)	869	(213)	(280)	Early Decline
Kellogg	490	1,041	(309)	(759)	Late Maturity
Southwest Airlines	183	456	(729)	415	Early Maturity
Starbucks	42	137	(211)	180	Growth

USEFULNESS OF THE STATEMENT OF CASH FLOWS

Many investors believe that "Cash is cash and everything else is accounting"; that is, cash flow is less susceptible to management manipulation and fraud than traditional accounting measures such as net income. Although we suggest that reliance on cash flows to the exclusion of accrual accounting is inappropriate, comparing cash from operations to net income can reveal important information about the "quality" of reported net income—that is, the extent to which net income provides a good measure of actual performance.

The information in a statement of cash flows should help investors, creditors, and others evaluate these aspects of the firm's financial position:

1. **The entity's ability to generate future cash flows.** By examining relationships between such items as sales and net cash provided by operating activities, or cash provided by operations and increases or decreases in cash, investors and others can predict the amounts, timing, and uncertainty of future cash flows better than from accrual-based data.

2. **The entity's ability to pay dividends and meet obligations.** Simply put, if a company does not have adequate cash, it cannot pay employees, settle debts, or pay dividends. Employees, creditors, stockholders, and customers should be particularly interested in this statement because it alone shows the flows of cash in a business.

3. **The reasons for the difference between net income and net cash provided (used) by operating activities.** Net income is important because it provides information on the success or failure of a business enterprise. However, some are critical of accrual basis net income because it requires many estimates; as a result, the reliability of the number is often challenged. Such is not the case with cash. Thus, many readers of the financial statement want to know the reasons for the difference between net income and net cash provided by operating activities. Then they can assess for themselves the reliability of the income number.

4. **The cash investing and financing transactions during the period.** By examining a company's investing activities and financing transactions, a financial statement reader can better understand *why* assets and liabilities increased or decreased during the period.

Helpful Hint Income from operations and cash flow from operating activities are different. Income from operations is based on accrual accounting; cash flow from operating activities is prepared on a cash basis.

In summary, the information in the statement of cash flows is useful in answering the following questions:

How did cash increase when there was a net loss for the period?
How were the proceeds of the bond issue used?
How was the expansion in the plant and equipment financed?
Why were dividends not increased?
How was the retirement of debt accomplished?
How much money was borrowed during the year?
Is cash flow greater or less than net income?

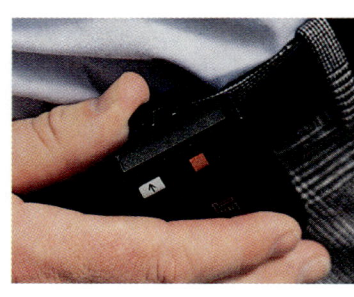

BUSINESS INSIGHT
Investor Perspective

Cash flow is also sometimes used to determine the price of a company. Page Net, a company in the telephone beeper business, had an initial public offering (IPO) in which $590 million of stock was sold. In December 1993 the stock had a market value of $1.5 billion, yet Page Net reported losses in every quarter since it went public. Its cash flow the year before the IPO was $39 million, $57 million in the IPO year, $75 million in 1992, and approximately $99 million in 1993. As one expert noted, "It is a classic example of a company valued by cash flow."

PREPARING THE STATEMENT OF CASH FLOWS

The statement of cash flows is prepared differently from the other basic financial statements. First, it is not prepared from an adjusted trial balance. Because the statement requires detailed information concerning the changes in account balances that occurred between two periods of time, an adjusted trial balance does not provide the data necessary for the statement. Second, the statement of cash flows deals with cash receipts and payments. As a result, **the accrual concept is not used in the preparation of a statement of cash flows.**

The information to prepare this statement usually comes from three sources:

1. **Comparative balance sheet.** Information in this statement indicates the amount of the changes in assets, liabilities, and stockholders' equities from the beginning to the end of the period.
2. **Current income statement.** Information in this statement helps the reader determine the amount of cash provided or used by operations during the period.
3. **Additional information.** Additional information includes transaction data that are needed to determine how cash was provided or used during the period.

Preparing the statement of cash flows from these data sources involves the three major steps explained in Illustration 13-4. First, to see where you are headed, start by identifying the change in cash during the period. Has cash increased or decreased during the year? Second, determine the net cash provided/used by operating activities. Third, determine the net cash provided/used by investing and financing activities.

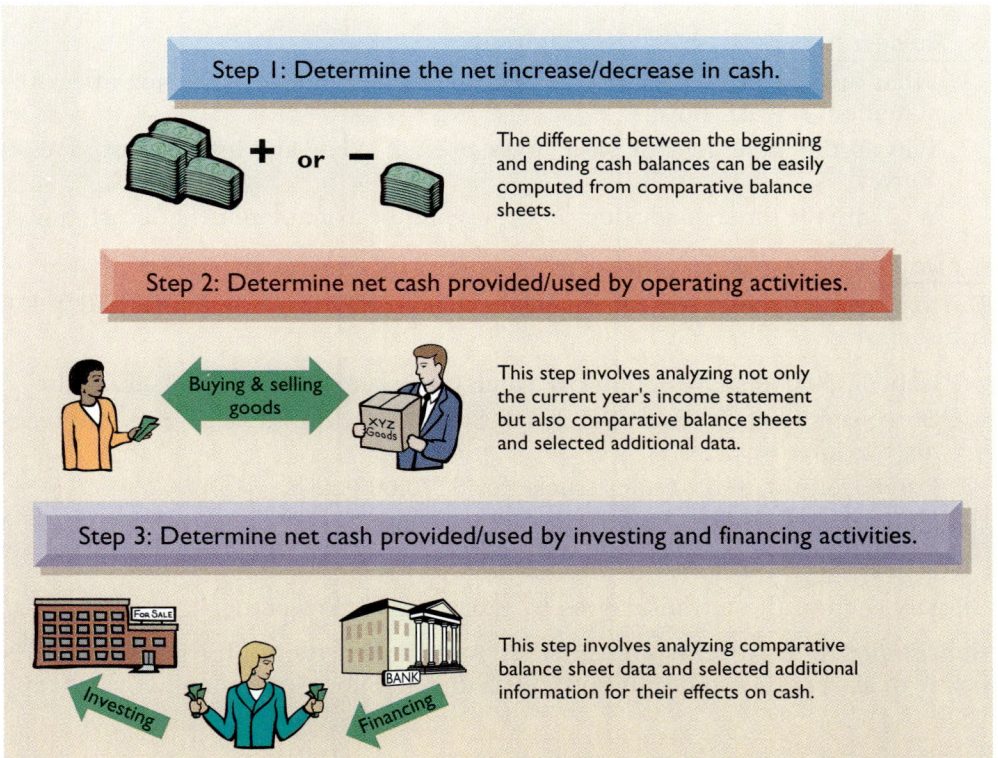

Illustration 13-4 Three major steps in preparing the statement of cash flows

Indirect and Direct Methods

In order to determine the cash provided/used by operating activities, **net income must be converted from an accrual basis to a cash basis.** This conversion may be done by either of two methods: indirect or direct. **Both methods arrive at the same total amount** for "Net cash provided by operating activities," but they differ in disclosing the items that make up the total amount. Note that the two different methods affect only the operating activities section; the investing activities and financing activities sections **are not affected by the choice of method.**

The indirect method is used extensively in practice—by about 97% of companies in a recent survey.[1] Companies favor the indirect method for three reasons: (1) It is easier to prepare, (2) it focuses on the differences between net income and net cash flow from operating activities, and (3) it tends to reveal less company information to competitors.

Others, however, favor the direct method, which is more consistent with the objective of a statement of cash flows because it shows operating cash receipts and payments. The FASB has expressed a preference for the direct method but allows the use of either method. However, when the direct method is used, the net cash flow from operating activities as computed using the indirect method must also be reported in a separate schedule.

On the following pages, in two separate sections, we describe the use of the two methods. Section 1 illustrates the indirect method, and Section 2 illustrates the direct method. These sections are independent of each other; *only one or the other* need be covered in order to understand and prepare the statement of cash flows. When you have finished the section assigned by your instructor, turn to the next topic on page 612—"Using Cash Flows to Evaluate a Company."

> **International Note**
> International accounting requirements are quite similar with regard to the cash flow statement. Here are some interesting exceptions: In Japan operating and investing activities are combined, in Australia the direct method is mandatory, and in Spain the indirect method is mandatory. Also, in a number of European and Scandinavian countries a cash flow statement is not required at all, although in practice most publicly traded companies provide one.

BEFORE YOU GO ON . . .

● **Review It**

1. What are the phases of the product life cycle, and how do they affect the statement of cash flows?
2. Why is the statement of cash flows useful? What key information does it convey?
3. What are the three major steps in the preparation of a statement of cash flows?

● **Do It**

During the first week of its existence, Plano Molding Company had these transactions:

1. Issued 100,000 shares of $5 par value common stock for $800,000 cash.
2. Borrowed $200,000 from Sandwich State Bank, signing a 5-year note bearing 8% interest.
3. Purchased two semi-trailer trucks for $170,000 cash.
4. Paid employees $12,000 for salaries and wages.
5. Collected $20,000 cash for services rendered.

Classify each of these transactions by type of cash flow activity.

Reasoning: All cash flows are classified into three activities for purposes of reporting cash inflows and outflows: operating activities, investing activities, and

---

[1] *Accounting Trends and Techniques—1996* (New York: American Institute of Certified Public Accountants, 1996).

financing activities. Operating activities include the cash effects of transactions that create revenues and expenses and thus enter into the determination of net income. Investing activities include (a) purchasing and disposing of investments and productive long-lived assets using cash and (b) lending money and collecting the loans. Financing activities include (a) obtaining cash from issuing debt and repaying the amounts borrowed and (b) obtaining cash from stockholders and providing them with a return on their investment.

Solution:
1. Financing activity
2. Financing activity
3. Investing activity
4. Operating activity
5. Operating activity

SECTION 1
STATEMENT OF CASH FLOWS—INDIRECT METHOD

To explain and illustrate the indirect method, we will use the transactions of Computer Services Company for two years: 1997 and 1998. Annual statements of cash flows will be prepared. Basic transactions will be used in the first year with additional transactions in the second year.

STUDY OBJECTIVE 4a
Prepare a statement of cash flows using the indirect method.

FIRST YEAR OF OPERATIONS—1997

Computer Services Company started on January 1, 1997, when it issued 50,000 shares of $1 par value common stock for $50,000 cash. The company rented its office space and furniture and performed consulting services throughout the first year. The comparative balance sheet for the beginning and end of 1997, showing increases or decreases, appears in Illustration 13-5.

COMPUTER SERVICES COMPANY
Comparative Balance Sheet
December 31

Assets	Dec. 31, 1997	Jan. 1, 1997	Change Increase/Decrease
Cash	$34,000	$ -0-	$34,000 increase
Accounts receivable	30,000	-0-	30,000 increase
Equipment	10,000	-0-	10,000 increase
Total	$74,000	$ -0-	
Liabilities and Stockholders' Equity			
Accounts payable	$ 4,000	$ -0-	$ 4,000 increase
Common stock	50,000	-0-	50,000 increase
Retained earnings	20,000	-0-	20,000 increase
Total	$74,000	$ -0-	

Illustration 13-5 Comparative balance sheet, 1997, with increases and decreases

Helpful Hint Note that although each of the balance sheet items increased, their individual effects are not the same. Some of these increases are cash inflows, and some are cash outflows.

Illustration 13-6 Income statement and additional information, 1997

COMPUTER SERVICES COMPANY
Income Statement
For the Year Ended December 31, 1997

Revenues	$85,000
Operating expenses	40,000
Income before income taxes	45,000
Income tax expense	10,000
Net income	$35,000

Additional information:
(a) Examination of selected data indicates that a dividend of $15,000 was declared and paid during the year.
(b) The equipment was purchased at the end of 1997. No depreciation was taken in 1997.

The income statement and additional information for Computer Services Company are shown in Illustration 13-6.

DETERMINING THE NET INCREASE/DECREASE IN CASH (STEP 1)

Helpful Hint You may wish to insert the beginning and ending cash balances and the increase/decrease in cash necessitated by these balances immediately into the statement of cash flows. The net increase/decrease is the target amount. The net cash flows from the three activities must equal the target amount.

To prepare a statement of cash flows, the first step is to **determine the net increase or decrease in cash.** This is a simple computation. For example, Computer Services Company had no cash on hand at the beginning of 1997, but had $34,000 on hand at the end of the year. Thus, the change in cash for 1997 was an increase of $34,000.

DETERMINING NET CASH PROVIDED/USED BY OPERATING ACTIVITIES (STEP 2)

To determine net cash provided by operating activities under the indirect method, **net income is adjusted for items that did not affect cash.** A useful starting point in determining net cash provided by operating activities is to understand **why** net income must be converted. Under generally accepted accounting principles, most companies use the accrual basis of accounting. As you have learned, this basis requires that revenue be recorded when earned and that expenses be recorded when incurred. Earned revenues may include credit sales that have not been collected in cash, and expenses incurred may include costs that have not been paid in cash. Under the accrual basis of accounting, net income does not indicate the net cash provided by operating activities. Therefore, under the indirect method, net income must be adjusted to convert certain items to the cash basis.

The **indirect method** (or reconciliation method) starts with net income and converts it to net cash provided by operating activities. In other words, **the indirect method adjusts net income for items that affected reported net income but did not affect cash,** as shown in Illustration 13-7. That is, noncash charges in the income statement are added back to net income and noncash credits are deducted, to compute net cash provided by operating activities.

A useful starting point in identifying the adjustments to net income is the current asset and current liability accounts other than cash. Those accounts—receivables, payables, prepayments, and inventories—should be analyzed for their effects on cash. We do that next for various accounts.

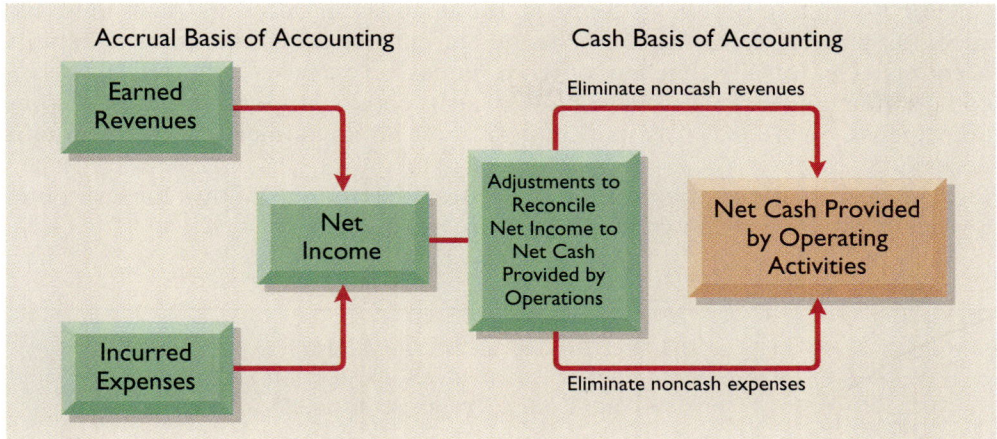

Illustration 13-7 Net income versus net cash provided by operating activities

Increase in Accounts Receivable. When accounts receivable increase during the year, revenues on an accrual basis are higher than revenues on a cash basis. In other words, operations of the period led to revenues, **but not all of these revenues resulted in an increase in cash;** some of the revenues resulted in an increase in accounts receivable.

For example, Computer Services Company, in its first year of operations, had revenues of $85,000 but collected only $55,000 in cash. Thus, on an accrual basis revenue was $85,000, but on a cash basis we would record only the $55,000 received during the period. Illustration 13-8 shows that, to convert net income to net cash provided by operating activities, the increase of $30,000 in accounts receivable must be deducted from net income.

ACCOUNTS RECEIVABLE				
Jan. 1	Balance	0	Receipts from customers	55,000
	Revenues	85,000		
Dec. 31	Balance	30,000		

Illustration 13-8 Analysis of accounts receivable

Increase in Accounts Payable. In the first year, operating expenses incurred on account were credited to Accounts Payable. When accounts payable increase during the year, operating expenses on an accrual basis are higher than they are on a cash basis. For Computer Services Company, operating expenses reported in the income statement were $40,000. However, since Accounts Payable increased $4,000, only $36,000 ($40,000 − $4,000) of the expenses were paid in cash. To convert net income to net cash provided by operating activities, the increase of $4,000 in accounts payable must be added to net income.

The T account analysis in Illustration 13-9 also indicates that payments to creditors are less than operating expenses.

ACCOUNTS PAYABLE				
Payments to creditors	36,000	Jan. 1	Balances	0
			Operating expenses	40,000
		Dec. 31	Balance	4,000

Illustration 13-9 Analysis of accounts payable

For Computer Services Company, the changes in accounts receivable and accounts payable were the only changes in current asset and current liability accounts. This means that any other revenues or expenses reported in the income statement were received or paid in cash. Thus, Computer Services' income tax expense of $10,000 was paid in cash, and no adjustment of net income is necessary.

The operating activities section of the statement of cash flows for Computer Services Company is shown in Illustration 13-10.

Illustration 13-10 Operating activities section, 1997—indirect method

COMPUTER SERVICES COMPANY
Partial Statement of Cash Flows—Indirect Method
For the Year Ended December 31, 1997

Cash flows from operating activities		
Net income		$35,000
Adjustments to reconcile net income to net cash provided by operating activities:		
Increase in accounts receivable	$(30,000)	
Increase in accounts payable	4,000	(26,000)
Net cash provided by operating activities		**$ 9,000**

DETERMINING NET CASH PROVIDED/USED BY INVESTING AND FINANCING ACTIVITIES (STEP 3)

The third and final step in preparing the statement of cash flows begins with a study of the balance sheet to determine changes in noncurrent accounts. The changes in each noncurrent account are then analyzed using selected transaction data to determine the effect, if any, the changes had on cash.

For Computer Services Company, the three noncurrent accounts are Equipment, Common Stock, and Retained Earnings, and all three have increased during the year. What caused these increases? No transaction data are given for the increases in Equipment of $10,000 and Common Stock of $50,000. When other explanations are lacking, we assume that any differences involve cash. Thus, the increase in equipment is assumed to be a purchase of equipment for $10,000 cash. This purchase is reported as a cash outflow in the investing activities section. The increase in common stock is assumed to result from the issuance of common stock for $50,000 cash. It is reported as an inflow of cash in the financing activities section of the statement of cash flows. In doing your homework, assume that **any unexplained differences in noncurrent accounts involve cash.**

The reasons for the net increase of $20,000 in the Retained Earnings account are determined by analysis. First, net income increased retained earnings by $35,000. Second, the additional information provided below the income statement in Illustration 13-6 indicates that a cash dividend of $15,000 was declared and paid. The $35,000 increase due to net income is reported in the operating activities section. The cash dividend paid is reported in the financing activities section.

This analysis can also be made directly from the Retained Earnings account in the ledger of Computer Services Company as shown in Illustration 13-11.

The $20,000 increase in Retained Earnings in 1997 is a **net** change. When a net change in a noncurrent balance sheet account has occurred during the

RETAINED EARNINGS				
Dec. 31 Cash dividend	15,000	Jan. 1 Balance		0
		Dec. 31 Net income		35,000
		Dec. 31 Balance		20,000

Illustration 13-11 Analysis of retained earnings

year, it generally is necessary to report the causes of the net change separately in the statement of cash flows.

STATEMENT OF CASH FLOWS—1997

Having completed the three steps above, we can prepare the statement of cash flows by the indirect method. The statement starts with the operating activities section, followed by the investing activities section, and then the financing activities section. The 1997 statement of cash flows for Computer Services is shown in Illustration 13-12.

COMPUTER SERVICES COMPANY
Statement of Cash Flows—Indirect Method
For the Year Ended December 31, 1997

Cash flows from operating activities		
Net income		$35,000
Adjustments to reconcile net income to net cash provided by operating activities:		
Increase in accounts receivable	$(30,000)	
Increase in accounts payable	4,000	(26,000)
Net cash provided by operating activities		9,000
Cash flows from investing activities		
Purchase of equipment		(10,000)
Net cash used by investing activities		(10,000)
Cash flows from financing activities		
Issuance of common stock	50,000	
Payment of cash dividends	(15,000)	
Net cash provided by financing activities		35,000
Net increase in cash		34,000
Cash at beginning of period		0
Cash at end of period		$34,000

Illustration 13-12 Statement of cash flows, 1997—indirect method

Computer Services Company's statement of cash flows for 1997 shows that operating activities **provided** $9,000 cash; investing activities **used** $10,000 cash; and financing activities **provided** $35,000 cash. The increase in cash of $34,000 reported in the statement of cash flows agrees with the increase of $34,000 shown as the change in the cash account in the comparative balance sheet.

SECOND YEAR OF OPERATIONS—1998

Presented in Illustrations 13-13 and 13-14 is information related to the second year of operations for Computer Services Company.

Illustration 13-13 Comparative balance sheet, 1998, with increases and decreases

COMPUTER SERVICES COMPANY
Comparative Balance Sheet
December 31

Assets	1998	1997	Change Increase/Decrease
Cash	$ 56,000	$34,000	$ 22,000 increase
Accounts receivable	20,000	30,000	10,000 decrease
Prepaid expenses	4,000	0	4,000 increase
Land	130,000	0	130,000 increase
Building	160,000	0	160,000 increase
Accumulated depreciation—building	(11,000)	0	11,000 increase
Equipment	27,000	10,000	17,000 increase
Accumulated depreciation—equipment	(3,000)	0	3,000 increase
Total	$383,000	$74,000	

Liabilities and Stockholders' Equity			
Accounts payable	$ 59,000	$ 4,000	$ 55,000 increase
Bonds payable	130,000	0	130,000 increase
Common stock	50,000	50,000	0
Retained earnings	144,000	20,000	124,000 increase
Total	$383,000	$74,000	

Illustration 13-14 Income statement and additional information, 1998

COMPUTER SERVICES COMPANY
Income Statement
For the Year Ended December 31, 1998

Revenues		$507,000
Operating expenses (excluding depreciation)	$261,000	
Depreciation expense	15,000	
Loss on sale of equipment	3,000	279,000
Income from operations		228,000
Income tax expense		89,000
Net income		$139,000

Additional information:
(a) In 1998 the company declared and paid a $15,000 cash dividend.
(b) The company obtained land through the issuance of $130,000 of long-term bonds.
(c) An office building costing $160,000 was purchased for cash; equipment costing $25,000 was also purchased for cash.
(d) During 1998 the company sold equipment with a book value of $7,000 (cost $8,000 less accumulated depreciation $1,000) for $4,000 cash.

DETERMINING THE NET INCREASE/DECREASE IN CASH (STEP 1)

To prepare a statement of cash flows from this information, the first step is to **determine the net increase or decrease in cash.** As indicated from the information presented, cash increased $22,000 ($56,000 − $34,000).

DETERMINING NET CASH PROVIDED/USED BY OPERATING ACTIVITIES (STEP 2)

As in step 2 in 1997, net income on an accrual basis must be adjusted to arrive at net cash provided/used by operating activities. Explanations for the adjustments to net income for Computer Services Company in 1998 are as follows:

Decrease in Accounts Receivable. Accounts receivable decreases during the period because cash receipts are higher than revenues reported on an accrual basis. To convert net income to net cash provided by operating activities, the decrease of $10,000 in accounts receivable must be added to net income.

Increase in Prepaid Expenses. Prepaid expenses increase during a period because cash paid for expenses is greater than expenses reported on an accrual basis. Cash payments have been made in the current period, but expenses (as charges to the income statement) have been deferred to future periods. To convert net income to net cash provided by operating activities, the increase of $4,000 in prepaid expenses must be deducted from net income. An increase in prepaid expenses results in a decrease in cash during the period.

Increase in Accounts Payable. Like the increase in 1997, the 1998 increase of $55,000 in accounts payable must be added to net income to convert to net cash provided by operating activities.

Depreciation Expense. During 1998 Computer Services Company reported depreciation expense of $15,000. Of this amount, $11,000 related to the building and $4,000 to the equipment. These two amounts were determined by analyzing the accumulated depreciation accounts as follows.

Increase in Accumulated Depreciation—Building. As shown in Illustration 13-13, this accumulated depreciation increased $11,000. This change represents the depreciation expense on the building for the year. **Because depreciation expense is a noncash charge, it is added back to net income** in order to arrive at net cash provided by operating activities.

Increase in Accumulated Depreciation—Equipment. The increase in the Accumulated Depreciation—Equipment account was $3,000. This amount does not represent the total depreciation expense for the year, though, because the additional information indicates that this account was decreased (debited $1,000) as a result of the sale of some equipment. Thus, depreciation expense for 1998 was $4,000 ($3,000 + $1,000). This amount is **added to net income** to determine net cash provided by operating activities. The T account in Illustration 13-15 provides information about the changes that occurred in this account in 1998.

Helpful Hint Whether the indirect or direct method (Section 2) is used, net cash provided by operating activities will be the same.

Helpful Hint Depreciation is similar to any other expense in that it reduces net income. It differs in that it does not involve a current cash outflow; that is why it must be added back to net income to arrive at cash provided by operations.

ACCUMULATED DEPRECIATION—EQUIPMENT				
Accumulated depreciation on equipment sold	1,000	Jan. 1 Balance		0
		Depreciation expense	4,000	
		Dec. 31 Balance		3,000

Illustration 13-15 Analysis of accumulated depreciation—equipment

Depreciation expense of $11,000 on the building plus depreciation expense of $4,000 on the equipment equals the depreciation expense of $15,000 reported on the income statement.

Other charges to expense **that do not require the use of cash,** such as the amortization of intangible assets, are treated in the same manner as deprecia-

594 CHAPTER 13 Statement of Cash Flows

tion. Depreciation and similar noncash charges are frequently listed in the statement of cash flows as the first adjustments to net income.

Loss on Sale of Equipment. On the income statement, Computer Services Company reported a $3,000 loss on the sale of equipment (book value $7,000 less cash proceeds $4,000). The loss reduced net income but **did not reduce cash.** Thus, the loss is **added to net income** in determining net cash provided by operating activities.[2]

As a result of the previous adjustments, net cash provided by operating activities is $218,000, as computed in Illustration 13-16.

Illustration 13-16 Operating activities section, 1998—indirect method

COMPUTER SERVICES COMPANY
Partial Statement of Cash Flows—Indirect Method
For the Year Ended December 31, 1998

Cash flows from operating activities		
Net income		$139,000
Adjustments to reconcile net income to net cash provided by operating activities:		
Depreciation expense	$15,000	
Loss on sale of equipment	3,000	
Decrease in accounts receivable	10,000	
Increase in prepaid expenses	(4,000)	
Increase in accounts payable	55,000	79,000
Net cash provided by operating activities		**$218,000**

Helpful Hint By custom we use the label "depreciation expense," even though the expense causes an *increase* in accumulated depreciation and could also be described as "increase in accumulated depreciation."

DETERMINING NET CASH PROVIDED/USED BY INVESTING AND FINANCING ACTIVITIES (STEP 3)

After the determination of net cash provided by operating activities, the final step involves analyzing the remaining changes in balance sheet accounts to determine net cash provided/used by investing and financing activities.

Increase in Land. As indicated from the change in the land account, land of $130,000 was purchased through the issuance of long-term bonds. Although the issuance of bonds payable for land has no effect on cash, it is a significant noncash investing and financing activity that merits disclosure. As indicated earlier, these activities are disclosed in a separate schedule at the bottom of the statement of cash flows.

Increase in Building. As indicated in the additional information, an office building was acquired using cash of $160,000. This transaction is a cash outflow reported in the investing activities section.

Increase in Equipment. The equipment account increased $17,000. Based on the additional information, this was a net increase that resulted from two transactions: (1) a purchase of equipment for $25,000 and (2) the sale of equipment costing $8,000 for $4,000. These transactions are classified as investing activities, and each transaction should be reported separately. Thus, the purchase of equipment should be reported as an outflow of cash for $25,000, and the sale should be reported as an inflow of cash for $4,000. The T account in Illustration 13-17 shows the reasons for the change in this account during the year.

---

[2] If a gain on sale occurs, a different situation results: To allow a gain to flow through to net cash provided by operating activities would be double-counting the gain—once in net income and again in the investing activities section as part of the cash proceeds from sale. As a result, a gain is deducted from net income in reporting net cash provided by operating activities.

Illustration 13-17
Analysis of equipment

EQUIPMENT			
Jan. 1 Balance	10,000	Cost of equipment sold	8,000
Purchase of equipment	25,000		
Dec. 31 Balance	27,000		

Increase in Bonds Payable. The Bonds Payable account increased $130,000. As shown in the additional information, land was acquired through the issuance of these bonds. As indicated earlier, this noncash transaction is reported in a separate schedule at the bottom of the statement.

Increase in Retained Earnings. Retained Earnings increased $124,000 during the year. This increase can be explained by two factors: (1) Net income of $139,000 increased Retained Earnings and (2) dividends of $15,000 decreased Retained Earnings. Net income is converted to net cash provided by operating activities in the operating activities section. Payment of the dividends is a **cash outflow that is reported as a financing activity.**

Helpful Hint When stocks or bonds are issued for cash, it is the amount of the issuance price (proceeds) that appears on the statement of cash flows as a financing inflow—rather than the par value of the stocks or face value of bonds.

Helpful Hint It is the *payment* of dividends, not the declaration, that appears on the statement of cash flows.

STATEMENT OF CASH FLOWS—1998

Combining the previous items, we obtain a statement of cash flows for 1998 for Computer Services Company as presented in Illustration 13-18.

Illustration 13-18 Statement of cash flows, 1998—indirect method

COMPUTER SERVICES COMPANY
Statement of Cash Flows—Indirect Method
For the Year Ended December 31, 1998

Cash flows from operating activities		
Net income		$139,000
Adjustments to reconcile net income to net cash provided by operating activities:		
Depreciation expense	$ 15,000	
Loss on sale of equipment	3,000	
Decrease in accounts receivable	10,000	
Increase in prepaid expenses	(4,000)	
Increase in accounts payable	55,000	79,000
Net cash provided by operating activities		218,000
Cash flows from investing activities		
Purchase of building	(160,000)	
Purchase of equipment	(25,000)	
Sale of equipment	4,000	
Net cash used by investing activities		(181,000)
Cash flows from financing activities		
Payment of cash dividends	(15,000)	
Net cash used by financing activities		(15,000)
Net increase in cash		22,000
Cash at beginning of period		34,000
Cash at end of period		$ 56,000
Noncash investing and financing activities		
Issuance of bonds payable to purchase land		$130,000

Helpful Hint Note that in the investing and financing activities sections, positive numbers indicate cash inflows (receipts) and negative numbers indicate cash outflows (payments).

SUMMARY OF CONVERSION TO NET CASH PROVIDED BY OPERATING ACTIVITIES—INDIRECT METHOD

As shown in the previous illustrations, the statement of cash flows prepared by the indirect method starts with net income and adds or deducts items not affecting cash, to arrive at net cash provided by operating activities. The additions and deductions consist of (1) changes in specific current assets and current liabilities and (2) noncash charges reported in the income statement. A summary of the adjustments for current assets and current liabilities is provided in Illustration 13-19.

Illustration 13-19
Adjustments for current assets and current liabilities

Current Assets and Current Liabilities	Adjustments to Convert Net Income to Net Cash Provided by Operating Activities	
	Add to Net Income	Deduct from Net Income
Accounts receivable	Decrease	Increase
Inventory	Decrease	Increase
Prepaid expenses	Decrease	Increase
Accounts payable	Increase	Decrease
Accrued expenses payable	Increase	Decrease

Adjustments for the noncash charges reported in the income statement are made as shown in Illustration 13-20.

Illustration 13-20
Adjustments for noncash charges

Noncash Charges	Adjustments to Convert Net Income to Net Cash Provided by Operating Activities
Depreciation expense	Add
Patent amortization expense	Add
Loss on sale of asset	Add

BEFORE YOU GO ON . . .

● **Review It**

1. What is the format of the operating activities section of the statement of cash flows using the indirect method?
2. Where is depreciation expense shown on a statement of cash flows using the indirect method?
3. Where are significant noncash investing and financing activities shown in a statement of cash flows? Give some examples.

● **Do It**

The following information relates to Reynolds Company. Use it to prepare a statement of cash flows using the indirect method.

Summary of Conversion to Net Cash Provided by Operating Activities—Indirect Method 597

REYNOLDS COMPANY
Comparative Balance Sheet
December 31

Assets	1998	1997	Change Increase/Decrease
Cash	$ 54,000	$ 37,000	$ 17,000 increase
Accounts receivable	68,000	26,000	42,000 increase
Inventories	54,000	0	54,000 increase
Prepaid expenses	4,000	6,000	2,000 decrease
Land	45,000	70,000	25,000 decrease
Buildings	200,000	200,000	0
Accumulated depreciation—buildings	(21,000)	(11,000)	10,000 increase
Equipment	193,000	68,000	125,000 increase
Accumulated depreciation—equipment	(28,000)	(10,000)	18,000 increase
Totals	$569,000	$386,000	

Liabilities and Stockholders' Equity			
Accounts payable	$ 23,000	$ 40,000	$ 17,000 decrease
Accrued expenses payable	10,000	0	10,000 increase
Bonds payable	110,000	150,000	40,000 decrease
Common stock ($1 par)	220,000	60,000	160,000 increase
Retained earnings	206,000	136,000	70,000 increase
Total	$569,000	$386,000	

REYNOLDS COMPANY
Income Statement
For the Year Ended December 31, 1998

Revenues		$890,000
Cost of goods sold	$465,000	
Operating expenses	221,000	
Interest expense	12,000	
Loss on sale of equipment	2,000	700,000
Income from operations		190,000
Income tax expense		65,000
Net income		$125,000

Additional information:
(a) Operating expenses include depreciation expense of $33,000.
(b) Land was sold at its book value for cash.
(c) Cash dividends of $55,000 were declared and paid in 1998.
(d) Interest expense of $12,000 was paid in cash.
(e) Equipment with a cost of $166,000 was purchased for cash. Equipment with a cost of $41,000 and a book value of $36,000 was sold for $34,000 cash.
(f) Bonds of $10,000 were redeemed at their book value for cash; bonds of $30,000 were converted into common stock.
(g) Common stock ($1 par) of $130,000 was issued for cash.
(h) Accounts payable pertain to merchandise suppliers.

CHAPTER 13 Statement of Cash Flows

Reasoning: The balance sheet and the income statement are prepared from an adjusted trial balance of the general ledger. The statement of cash flows is prepared from an analysis of the content and changes in the balance sheet and the income statement.

Helpful Hint To prepare the statement of cash flows:

1. Determine the net increase/decrease in cash.
2. Determine net cash provided/used by operating activities.
3. Determine net cash provided/used by investing and financing activities.
4. Operating activities generally relate to changes in current assets and current liabilities.
5. Investing activities generally relate to changes in noncurrent assets.
6. Financing activities generally relate to changes in noncurrent liabilities and stockholders' equity accounts.

Solution:

REYNOLDS COMPANY
Statement of Cash Flows—Indirect Method
For the Year Ended December 31, 1998

Cash flows from operating activities		
Net income		$125,000
Adjustments to reconcile net income to net cash provided by operating activities:		
Depreciation expense	$ 33,000	
Increase in accounts receivable	(42,000)	
Increase in inventories	(54,000)	
Decrease in prepaid expenses	2,000	
Decrease in accounts payable	(17,000)	
Increase in accrued expenses payable	10,000	
Loss on sale of equipment	2,000	(66,000)
Net cash provided by operating activities		59,000
Cash flows from investing activities		
Sale of land	25,000	
Sale of equipment	34,000	
Purchase of equipment	(166,000)	
Net cash used by investing activities		(107,000)
Cash flows from financing activities		
Redemption of bonds	(10,000)	
Sale of common stock	130,000	
Payment of dividends	(55,000)	
Net cash provided by financing activities		65,000
Net increase in cash		17,000
Cash at beginning of period		37,000
Cash at end of period		$ 54,000
Noncash investing and financing activities		
Conversion of bonds into common stock		$ 30,000

Note: This concludes Section 1 on preparation of the statement of cash flows using the indirect method. Unless your instructor assigns Section 2, you should turn to the concluding section of the chapter, "Using Cash Flows to Evaluate a Company," on page 612.

SECTION 2
STATEMENT OF CASH FLOWS—DIRECT METHOD

To explain and illustrate the direct method, we will use the transactions of Juarez Company for two years: 1997 and 1998. Annual statements of cash flow will be prepared. Basic transactions will be used in the first year with additional transactions in the second year.

First Year of Operations—1997

Juarez Company began business on January 1, 1997, when it issued 300,000 shares of $1 par value common stock for $300,000 cash. The company rented office and sales space along with equipment. The comparative balance sheet at the beginning and end of 1997 and the changes in each account are shown in Illustration 13-21. The income statement and additional information for Juarez Company are shown in Illustration 13-22 on page 600.

STUDY OBJECTIVE 4b
Prepare a statement of cash flows using the direct method.

Illustration 13-21 Comparative balance sheet, 1997, with increases and decreases

JUAREZ COMPANY
Comparative Balance Sheet
December 31

Assets	Dec. 31, 1997	Jan. 1, 1997	Change Increase/Decrease
Cash	$159,000	$-0-	$159,000 increase
Accounts receivable	15,000	-0-	15,000 increase
Inventory	160,000	-0-	160,000 increase
Prepaid expenses	8,000	-0-	8,000 increase
Land	80,000	-0-	80,000 increase
Total	$422,000	$-0-	
Liabilities and Stockholders' Equity			
Accounts payable	$ 60,000	$-0-	$ 60,000 increase
Accrued expenses payable	20,000	-0-	20,000 increase
Common stock	300,000	-0-	300,000 increase
Retained earnings	42,000	-0-	42,000 increase
Total	$422,000	$-0-	

The three steps cited in Illustration 13-4 on page 585 for preparing the statement of cash flows are used in the direct method.

DETERMINING THE NET INCREASE/DECREASE IN CASH (STEP 1)

The comparative balance sheet for Juarez Company shows a zero cash balance at January 1, 1997, and a cash balance of $159,000 at December 31, 1997. Therefore, the change in cash for 1997 was a net increase of $159,000.

Illustration 13-22
Income statement and additional information, 1997

JUAREZ COMPANY
Income Statement
For the Year Ended December 31, 1997

Revenues from sales	$780,000
Cost of goods sold	450,000
Gross profit	330,000
Operating expenses	170,000
Income before income taxes	160,000
Income tax expense	48,000
Net income	$112,000

Additional information:
(a) Dividends of $70,000 were declared and paid in cash.
(b) The accounts payable increase resulted from the purchase of merchandise.

DETERMINING NET CASH PROVIDED/USED BY OPERATING ACTIVITIES (STEP 2)

Under the **direct method,** net cash provided by operating activities is computed by **adjusting each item in the income statement** from the accrual basis to the cash basis. To simplify and condense the operating activities section, **only major classes of operating cash receipts and cash payments are reported.** The difference between these major classes of cash receipts and cash payments is the net cash provided by operating activities, as shown in Illustration 13-23.

Illustration 13-23 Major classes of cash receipts and payments

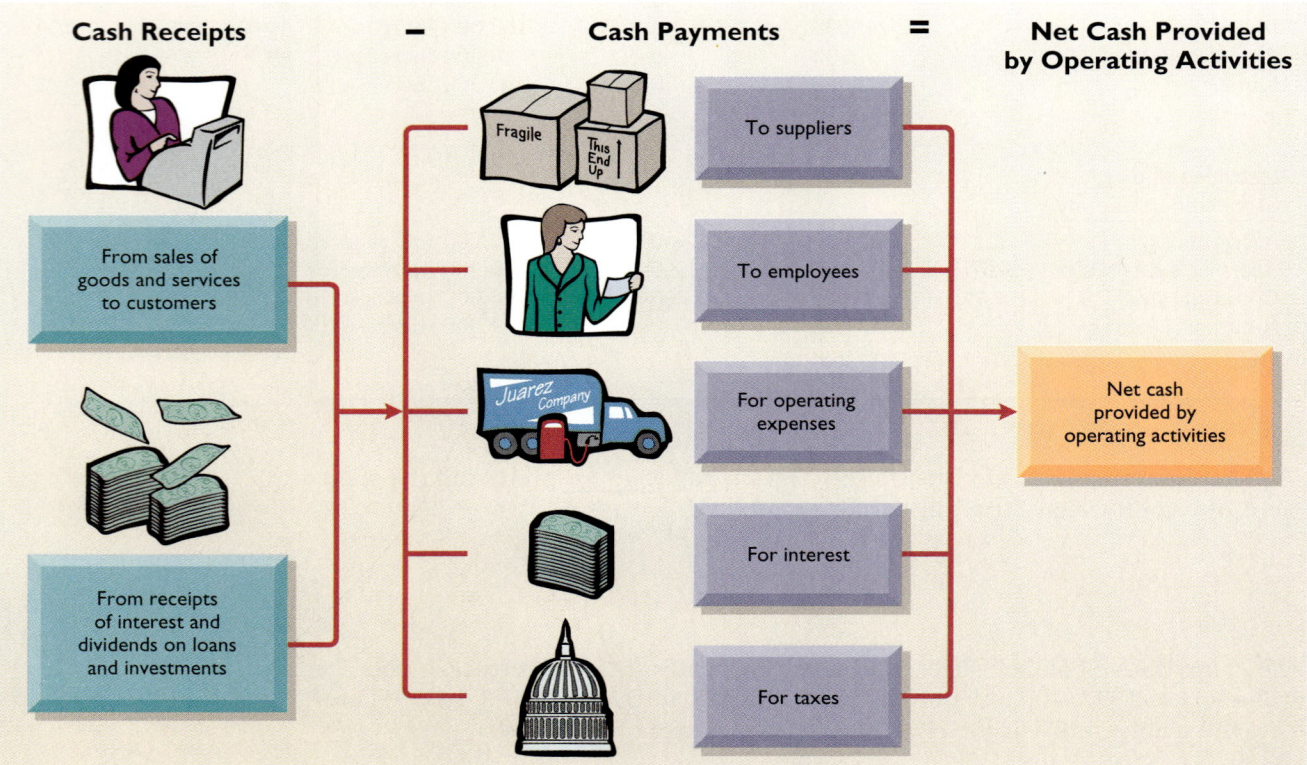

An efficient way to apply the direct method is to analyze the revenues and expenses reported in the income statement in the order in which they are listed and then determine cash receipts and cash payments related to these revenues and expenses. The direct method adjustments for Juarez Company in 1997 to determine net cash provided by operating activities are presented in the following sections.

Cash Receipts from Customers. The income statement for Juarez Company reported revenues from customers of $780,000. To determine cash receipts from customers, it is necessary to consider the change in accounts receivable during the year. When accounts receivable increase during the year, revenues on an accrual basis are higher than cash receipts from customers. In other words, operations led to increased revenues, but not all of these revenues resulted in cash receipts. To determine the amount of cash receipts, the increase in accounts receivable is deducted from sales revenues. Conversely, a decrease in accounts receivable is added to sales revenues because cash receipts from customers then exceed sales revenues.

For Juarez Company accounts receivable increased $15,000. Thus, cash receipts from customers were $765,000, computed as shown in Illustration 13-24.

Revenues from sales	$780,000
Deduct: Increase in accounts receivable	15,000
Cash receipts from customers	**$765,000**

Illustration 13-24 Computation of cash receipts from customers

Cash receipts from customers may also be determined from an analysis of the Accounts Receivable account, as shown in Illustration 13-25.

ACCOUNTS RECEIVABLE			
Jan. 1 Balance	0	Receipts from customers	765,000
Revenues from sales	780,000		
Dec. 31 Balance	15,000		

Illustration 13-25 Analysis of accounts receivable

Helpful Hint The T account shows that revenue less increase in receivables equals cash receipts.

The relationships among cash receipts from customers, revenues from sales, and changes in accounts receivable are shown in Illustration 13-26.

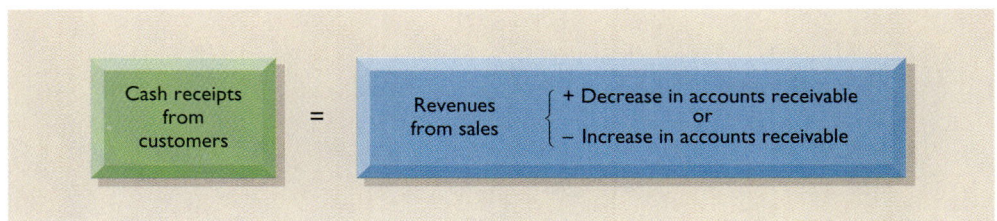

Illustration 13-26 Formula to compute cash receipts from customers—direct method

Cash Payments to Suppliers. Juarez Company reported cost of goods sold on its income statement of $450,000. To determine cash payments to suppliers, it is first necessary to find purchases for the year. To find purchases, cost of goods sold is adjusted for the change in inventory. When inventory increases during the year, it means that purchases this year exceed cost of goods sold. As a result, the increase in inventory is added to cost of goods sold to arrive at purchases.

In 1997 Juarez Company's inventory increased $160,000. Purchases, therefore, are computed as shown in Illustration 13-27.

Illustration 13-27 Computation of purchases

Cost of goods sold	$ 450,000
Add: Increase in inventory	160,000
Purchases	**$610,000**

After purchases are computed, cash payments to suppliers are determined by adjusting purchases for the change in accounts payable. When accounts payable increase during the year, purchases on an accrual basis are higher than they are on a cash basis. As a result, an increase in accounts payable is deducted from purchases to arrive at cash payments to suppliers. Conversely, a decrease in accounts payable is added to purchases because cash payments to suppliers exceed purchases. Cash payments to suppliers were $550,000, computed as in Illustration 13-28.

Illustration 13-28 Computation of cash payments to suppliers

Purchases	$ 610,000
Deduct: Increase in accounts payable	60,000
Cash payments to suppliers	**$550,000**

Cash payments to suppliers may also be determined from an analysis of the Accounts Payable account, as shown in Illustration 13-29.

Illustration 13-29 Analysis of accounts payable

ACCOUNTS PAYABLE					
Payments to suppliers	**550,000**	Jan. 1	Balance		0
			Purchases		610,000
		Dec. 31	Balance		60,000

Helpful Hint The T account shows that purchases less increase in accounts payable equals payments to suppliers.

The relationship between cash payments to suppliers, cost of goods sold, changes in inventory, and changes in account payable is shown in the formula in Illustration 13-30.

Illustration 13-30 Formula to compute cash payments to suppliers—direct method

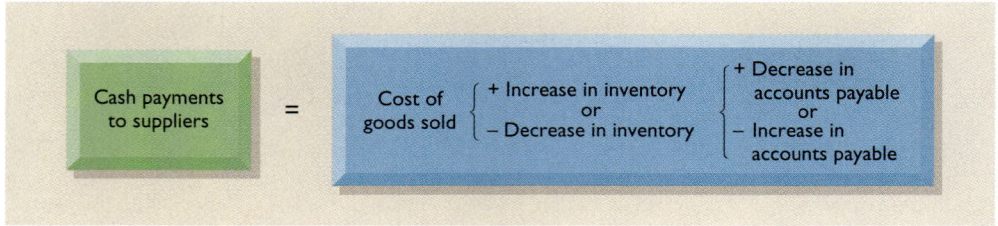

Cash Payments for Operating Expenses. Operating expenses of $170,000 were reported on Juarez Company's income statement. To determine the cash paid for operating expenses, this amount must be adjusted for any changes in prepaid expenses and accrued expenses payable. For example, when prepaid expenses increased $8,000 during the year, cash paid for operating expenses was $8,000 higher than operating expenses reported on the income statement. To convert operating expenses to cash payments for operating expenses, the increase of $8,000 must be added to operating expenses. Conversely, if prepaid expenses decrease during the year, the decrease must be deducted from operating expenses.

Operating expenses must also be adjusted for changes in accrued expenses payable. When accrued expenses payable increase during the year, operating expenses on an accrual basis are higher than they are in a cash basis. As a result, an increase in accrued expenses payable is deducted from operating expenses to arrive at cash payments for operating expenses. Conversely, a decrease in accrued expenses payable is added to operating expenses because cash payments exceed operating expenses.

Juarez Company's cash payments for operating expenses were $158,000, computed as shown in Illustration 13-31.

Helpful Hint Decrease in accounts receivable: Indicates that cash collections were greater than sales. **Increase in accounts receivable:** Indicates that sales were greater than cash collections. **Increase in prepaid expenses:** Indicates that the amount paid for the prepayments exceeded the amount that was recorded as an expense. **Decrease in prepaid expenses:** Indicates that the amount recorded as an expense exceeded the amount of cash paid for the prepayments. **Increase in accounts payable:** Indicates that expenses incurred exceed the cash paid for expenses that period.

Operating expenses	$ 170,000
Add: Increase in prepaid expenses	8,000
Deduct: Increase in accrued expenses payable	20,000
Cash payments for operating expenses	**$158,000**

Illustration 13-31
Computation of cash payments for operating expenses

The relationships among cash payments for operating expenses, changes in prepaid expenses, and changes in accrued expenses payable are shown in the formula in Illustration 13-32.

Illustration 13-32 Formula to compute cash payments for operating expenses—direct method

Cash payments for operating expenses = Operating expenses { + Increase in prepaid expense or − Decrease in prepaid expense } { + Decrease in accrued expenses payable or − Increase in accrued expenses payable }

Cash Payments for Income Taxes. The income statement for Juarez Company shows income tax expense of $48,000. This amount equals the cash paid because the comparative balance sheet indicates no income taxes payable at either the beginning or end of the year.

All of the revenues and expenses in the 1997 income statement have now been adjusted to a cash basis. The operating activities section of the statement of cash flows is presented in Illustration 13-33.

Illustration 13-33
Operating activities section—direct method

JUAREZ COMPANY
Partial Statement of Cash Flows—Direct Method
For the Year Ended December 31, 1997

Cash flows from operating activities		
Cash receipts from customers		$765,000
Cash payments:		
To suppliers	$550,000	
For operating expenses	158,000	
For income taxes	48,000	756,000
Net cash provided by operating activities		**$ 9,000**

DETERMINING NET CASH PROVIDED/USED BY INVESTING AND FINANCING ACTIVITIES (STEP 3)

Preparing the investing and financing activities sections of the statement of cash flows begins with a determination of the changes in noncurrent accounts reported in the comparative balance sheet. The change in each account is then analyzed using the additional information to determine the effect, if any, the change had on cash.

Increase in Land. No additional information is given for the increase in land. In such case, you should assume that the increase affected cash. You should make the same assumption in doing homework problems when the cause of a change in a noncurrent account is not explained. The purchase of land is an investing activity. Thus, an outflow of cash of $80,000 for the purchase of land should be reported in the investing activities section.

Increase in Common Stock. As indicated earlier, 300,000 shares of $1 par value stock were sold for $300,000 cash. The issuance of common stock is a financing activity. Thus, a cash inflow of $300,000 from the issuance of common stock is reported in the financing activities section.

Helpful Hint It is the *payment* of dividends, not the declaration, that appears on the cash flow statement.

Increase in Retained Earnings. For the Retained Earnings account, the reasons for the net increase of $42,000 are determined by analysis. First, net income increased retained earnings by $112,000. Second, the additional information indicates that a cash dividend of $70,000 was declared and paid. The adjustment of revenues and expenses to arrive at net cash provided by operations was done in step 2 earlier. The cash dividend paid is reported as an outflow of cash in the financing activities section.

This analysis can also be made directly from the Retained Earnings account in the ledger of Juarez Company, as shown in Illustration 13-34.

Illustration 13-34 Analysis of retained earnings

RETAINED EARNINGS			
Dec. 31 Cash dividend 70,000	Jan. 1 Balance		0
	Dec. 31 Net income		112,000
	Dec. 31 Balance		42,000

The $42,000 increase in Retained Earnings in 1997 is a net change. When a net change in a noncurrent balance sheet account has occurred during the year, it generally is necessary to report the individual items that cause the net change.

STATEMENT OF CASH FLOWS—1997

The statement of cash flows can now be prepared. The operating activities section is reported first, followed by the investing and financing activities sections. The statement of cash flows for Juarez Company for 1997 is presented in Illustration 13-35.

The statement of cash flows shows that operating activities **provided** $9,000 of the net increase in cash of $159,000. Financing activities **provided** $230,000 of cash, and investing activities **used** $80,000 of cash. The net increase in cash for the year of $159,000 agrees with the $159,000 increase in cash reported in the comparative balance sheet.

Illustration 13-35
Statement of cash flows, 1997—direct method

JUAREZ COMPANY Statement of Cash Flows—Direct Method For the Year Ended December 31, 1997		
Cash flows from operating activities		
Cash receipts from customers		$765,000
Cash payments:		
To suppliers	$550,000	
For operating expenses	158,000	
For income taxes	48,000	756,000
Net cash provided by operating activities		9,000
Cash flows from investing activities		
Purchase of land		(80,000)
Net cash used by investing activities		(80,000)
Cash flows from financing activities		
Issuance of common stock		300,000
Payment of cash dividend		(70,000)
Net cash provided by financing activities		230,000
Net increase in cash		159,000
Cash at beginning of period		0
Cash at end of period		$159,000

Helpful Hint Note that in the investing and financing activities sections, positive numbers indicate cash inflows (receipts) and negative numbers indicate cash outflows (payments).

SECOND YEAR OF OPERATIONS—1998

Illustrations 13-36 and 13-37 present the comparative balance sheet, the income statement, and additional information pertaining to the second year of operations for Juarez Company.

Illustration 13-36 Comparative balance sheet, 1998, with increases and decreases

JUAREZ COMPANY
Comparative Balance Sheet
December 31

Assets	1998	1997	Change Increase/Decrease
Cash	$191,000	$159,000	$ 32,000 increase
Accounts receivable	12,000	15,000	3,000 decrease
Inventory	130,000	160,000	30,000 decrease
Prepaid expenses	6,000	8,000	2,000 decrease
Land	180,000	80,000	100,000 increase
Equipment	160,000	0	160,000 increase
Accumulated depreciation—equipment	(16,000)	0	16,000 increase
Total	$663,000	$422,000	

Liabilities and Stockholders' Equity			
Accounts payable	$ 52,000	$ 60,000	$ 8,000 decrease
Accrued expenses payable	15,000	20,000	5,000 decrease
Income taxes payable	12,000	0	12,000 increase
Bonds payable	90,000	0	90,000 increase
Common stock	400,000	300,000	100,000 increase
Retained earnings	94,000	42,000	52,000 increase
Total	$663,000	$422,000	

Illustration 13-37
Income statement and additional information, 1998

JUAREZ COMPANY
Income Statement
For the Year Ended December 31, 1998

Revenues from sales		$975,000
Cost of goods sold	$660,000	
Operating expenses (excluding depreciation)	176,000	
Depreciation expense	18,000	
Loss on sale of store equipment	1,000	855,000
Income before income taxes		120,000
Income tax expense		36,000
Net income		$ 84,000

Additional information:
(a) In 1998 the company declared and paid a $32,000 cash dividend.
(b) Bonds were issued at face value for $90,000 in cash.
(c) Equipment costing $180,000 was purchased for cash.
(d) Equipment costing $20,000 was sold for $17,000 cash when the book value of the equipment was $18,000.
(e) Common stock of $100,000 was issued to acquire land.

DETERMINING THE NET INCREASE/DECREASE IN CASH (STEP 1)

The comparative balance sheet shows a beginning cash balance of $159,000 and an ending cash balance of $191,000. Thus, there was a net increase in cash in 1998 of $32,000.

DETERMINING NET CASH PROVIDED/USED BY OPERATING ACTIVITIES (STEP 2)

Cash Receipts from Customers. Revenues from sales were $975,000. Since accounts receivable decreased $3,000, cash receipts from customers were greater than sales revenues. Cash receipts from customers were $978,000, computed as shown in Illustration 13-38.

Illustration 13-38
Computation of cash receipts from customers

Revenues from sales	$ 975,000
Add: Decrease in accounts receivable	3,000
Cash receipts from customers	**$978,000**

Cash Payments to Suppliers. The conversion of cost of goods sold to purchases and purchases to cash payments to suppliers is similar to the computations made in 1997. For 1998 purchases are computed using cost of goods sold of $660,000 from the income statement and the decrease in inventory of $30,000 from the comparative balance sheet. Purchases are then adjusted by the decrease in accounts payable of $8,000. Cash payments to suppliers were $638,000, computed as in Illustration 13-39.

Illustration 13-39
Computation of cash payments to suppliers

Cost of goods sold	$ 660,000
Deduct: Decrease in inventory	30,000
Purchases	630,000
Add: Decrease in accounts payable	8,000
Cash payments to suppliers	**$638,000**

Cash Payments for Operating Expenses.

Operating expenses (exclusive of depreciation expense) for 1998 were reported at $176,000. This amount is then adjusted for changes in prepaid expenses and accrued expenses payable to arrive at cash payments for operating expenses.

As indicated from the comparative balance sheet, prepaid expenses decreased $2,000 during the year. This means that $2,000 was allocated to operating expenses (thereby increasing operating expenses), but cash payments did not increase by that amount. To arrive at cash payments for operating expenses, the decrease in prepaid expenses is deducted from operating expenses.

Accrued expenses payable decreased $5,000 during the period. As a result, cash payments were higher by $5,000 than the amount reported for operating expenses. The decrease in accrued expenses payable is added to operating expenses. Cash payments for operating expenses were $179,000, computed as shown in Illustration 13-40.

Operating expenses, exclusive of depreciation	$176,000
Deduct: Decrease in prepaid expenses	2,000
Add: Decrease in accrued expenses payable	5,000
Cash payments for operating expenses	**$179,000**

Illustration 13-40
Computation of cash payments for operating expenses

Depreciation Expense and Loss on Sale of Equipment.

Operating expenses are shown exclusive of depreciation. Depreciation expense in 1998 was $18,000. Depreciation expense is not shown on a statement of cash flows under the direct method because it is a noncash charge. If the amount for operating expenses includes depreciation expense, operating expenses must be reduced by the amount of depreciation to determine cash payments for operating expenses.

The loss on sale of store equipment of $1,000 is also a noncash charge. The loss on sale of equipment reduces net income, but it does not reduce cash. Thus, the loss on sale of equipment is not reported on a statement of cash flows prepared using the direct method.

Other charges to expense that do not require the use of cash, such as the amortization of intangible assets and depletion expense, are treated in the same manner as depreciation.

Cash Payments for Income Taxes.

Income tax expense reported on the income statement was $36,000. Income taxes payable, however, increased $12,000, which means that $12,000 of the income taxes have not been paid. As a result, income taxes paid were less than income taxes reported on the income statement. Cash payments for income taxes were therefore $24,000, as shown in Illustration 13-41.

Income tax expense	$36,000
Deduct: Increase in income taxes payable	12,000
Cash payments for income taxes	**$24,000**

Illustration 13-41
Computation of cash payments for income taxes

The relationship among cash payments for income taxes, income tax expense, and changes in income taxes payable are shown in the formula in Illustration 13-42.

Illustration 13-42 Formula to compute cash payments for income taxes—direct method

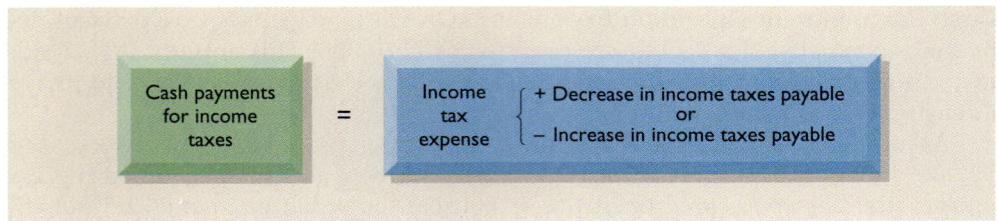

DETERMINING NET CASH PROVIDED/USED BY INVESTING AND FINANCING ACTIVITIES (STEP 3)

Increase in Land. Land increased $100,000. The additional information indicates that common stock was issued to purchase the land. Although the issuance of common stock for land has no effect on cash, it is a **significant noncash investing and financing transaction.** This transaction requires disclosure in a separate schedule at the bottom of the statement of cash flows.

Increase in Equipment. The comparative balance sheet shows that equipment increased $160,000 in 1998. The additional information in Illustration 13-37 indicates that the increase resulted from two investing transactions: (1) Equipment costing $180,000 was purchased for cash, and (2) equipment costing $20,000 was sold for $17,000 cash when its book value was $18,000. The relevant data for the statement of cash flows are the cash paid for the purchase and the cash proceeds from the sale. For Juarez Company the investing activities section will show: Purchase of equipment $180,000 as an outflow of cash, and sale of equipment $17,000 as an inflow of cash. The two amounts **should not be netted; both flows should be shown.**

The analysis of the changes in equipment should include the related Accumulated Depreciation account. These two accounts for Juarez Company are shown in Illustration 13-43.

Illustration 13-43 Analysis of equipment and related accumulated depreciation

EQUIPMENT				
Jan. 1 Balance	0	Cost of equipment sold	20,000
Cash purchase	180,000		
Dec. 31 Balance	160,000		

ACCUMULATED DEPRECIATION—EQUIPMENT				
Sale of equipment	2,000	Jan. 1 Balance	0
		Depreciation expense	18,000
		Dec. 31 Balance	16,000

Increase in Bonds Payable. Bonds Payable increased $90,000. The additional information in Illustration 13-37 indicates that bonds with a face value of $90,000 were issued for $90,000 cash. The issuance of bonds is a financing activity. For Juarez Company, there is an inflow of cash of $90,000 from the issuance of bonds payable.

Increase in Common Stock. The Common Stock account increased $100,000. As indicated in the additional information, land was acquired from the issuance of common stock. This transaction is a **significant noncash investing and financing transaction** that should be reported in a separate schedule at the bottom of the statement.

Increase in Retained Earnings. The net increase in Retained Earnings of $52,000 resulted from net income of $84,000 and the declaration and payment of a cash dividend of $32,000. **Net income is not reported in the statement of cash flows under the direct method.** Cash dividends paid of $32,000 are reported in the financing activities section as an outflow of cash.

STATEMENT OF CASH FLOWS—1998

The statement of cash flows for Juarez Company is shown in Illustration 13-44.

Illustration 13-44 Statement of cash flows, 1998—direct method

JUAREZ COMPANY
Statement of Cash Flows—Direct Method
For the Year Ended December 31, 1998

Cash flows from operating activities		
Cash receipts from customers		$978,000
Cash payments:		
To suppliers	$638,000	
For operating expenses	179,000	
For income taxes	24,000	841,000
Net cash provided by operating activities		137,000
Cash flows from investing activities		
Purchase of equipment	(180,000)	
Sale of equipment	17,000	
Net cash used by investing activities		(163,000)
Cash flows from financing activities		
Issuance of bonds payable	90,000	
Payment of cash dividends	(32,000)	
Net cash provided by financing activities		58,000
Net increase in cash		32,000
Cash at beginning of period		159,000
Cash at end of period		$191,000
Noncash investing and financing activities		
Issuance of common stock to purchase land		$100,000

BEFORE YOU GO ON . . .

● **Review It**

1. What is the format of the operating activities section of the statement of cash flows using the direct method?
2. Where is depreciation expense shown on a statement of cash flows using the direct method?
3. Where are significant noncash investing and financing activities shown on a statement of cash flows? Give some examples.

Do It

The following information relates to Reynolds Company. Use it to prepare a statement of cash flows using the direct method.

REYNOLDS COMPANY
Comparative Balance Sheet
December 31

Assets	1998	1997	Change Increase/Decrease
Cash	$ 54,000	$ 37,000	$ 17,000 increase
Accounts receivable	68,000	26,000	42,000 increase
Inventories	54,000	0	54,000 increase
Prepaid expenses	4,000	6,000	2,000 decrease
Land	45,000	70,000	25,000 decrease
Buildings	200,000	200,000	0
Accumulated depreciation—buildings	(21,000)	(11,000)	10,000 increase
Equipment	193,000	68,000	125,000 increase
Accumulated depreciation—equipment	(28,000)	(10,000)	18,000 increase
Total	$569,000	$386,000	

Liabilities and Stockholders' Equity			
Accounts payable	$ 23,000	$ 40,000	$ 17,000 decrease
Accrued expenses payable	10,000	0	10,000 increase
Bonds payable	110,000	150,000	40,000 decrease
Common stock ($1 par)	220,000	60,000	160,000 increase
Retained earnings	206,000	136,000	70,000 increase
Total	$569,000	$386,000	

REYNOLDS COMPANY
Income Statement
For the Year Ended December 31, 1998

Revenues		$890,000
Cost of goods sold	$465,000	
Operating expenses	221,000	
Interest expense	12,000	
Loss on sale of equipment	2,000	700,000
Income from operations		190,000
Income tax expense		65,000
Net income		$125,000

Additional information:
(a) Operating expenses include depreciation expense of $33,000 and charges from prepaid expenses of $2,000.
(b) Land was sold at its book value for cash.
(c) Cash dividends of $55,000 were declared and paid in 1998.
(d) Interest expense of $12,000 was paid in cash.
(e) Equipment with a cost of $166,000 was purchased for cash. Equipment with a cost of $41,000 and a book value of $36,000 was sold for $34,000 cash.
(f) Bonds of $10,000 were redeemed at their book value for cash; bonds of $30,000 were converted into common stock.
(g) Common stock ($1 par) of $130,000 was issued for cash.
(h) Accounts payable pertain to merchandise suppliers.

Reasoning: The direct method reports cash receipts less cash payments to arrive at net cash provided by operating activities.

Solution:

REYNOLDS COMPANY
Statement of Cash Flows—Direct Method
For the Year Ended December 31, 1998

Cash flows from operating activities		
Cash receipts from customers		$848,000[a]
Cash payments:		
To suppliers	$536,000[b]	
For operating expenses	176,000[c]	
For interest expense	12,000	
For income taxes	65,000	789,000
Net cash provided by operating activities		59,000
Cash flows from investing activities		
Sale of land	25,000	
Sale of equipment	34,000	
Purchase of equipment	(166,000)	
Net cash used by investing activities		(107,000)
Cash flows from financing activities		
Redemption of bonds	(10,000)	
Sale of common stock	130,000	
Payment of dividends	(55,000)	
Net cash provided by financing activities		65,000
Net increase in cash		17,000
Cash at beginning of period		37,000
Cash at end of period		$ 54,000
Noncash investing and financing activities		
Conversion of bonds into common stock		$ 30,000

Computations:
[a] $848,000 = $890,000 − $42,000
[b] $536,000 = $465,000 + $54,000 + $17,000
[c] $176,000 = $221,000 − $33,000 − $2,000 − $10,000

Technically, an additional schedule reconciling net income to net cash provided by operating activities should be presented as part of the statement of cash flows when using the direct method.

Helpful Hint To prepare the statement of cash flows:

1. Determine the net increase/decrease in cash.
2. Determine net cash provided/used by operating activities.
3. Determine net cash provided/used by investing and financing activities.
4. Operating activities generally relate to changes in current assets and current liabilities.
5. Investing activities generally relate to changes in noncurrent assets.
6. Financing activities generally relate to changes in noncurrent liabilities and stockholders' equity accounts.

Note: This concludes Section 2 on preparation of the statement of cash flows using the direct method. You should now turn to the next—and concluding—section of the chapter, "Using Cash Flows to Evaluate a Company."

USING CASH FLOWS TO EVALUATE A COMPANY

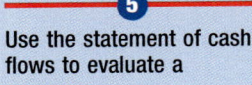

STUDY OBJECTIVE 5
Use the statement of cash flows to evaluate a company.

Traditionally, the ratios most commonly used by investors and creditors have been based on accrual accounting. In previous chapters we introduced you to some cash-based ratios that are gaining increased acceptance among analysts. In this section we review some of those measures and introduce some new ones.

FREE CASH FLOW

In the statement of cash flows, cash provided by operating activities is intended to indicate the cash-generating capability of the company. Analysts have noted, however, that **cash provided by operating activities fails to take into account that a company must invest in new fixed assets** just to maintain its current level of operations, and it must at least **maintain dividends at current levels** to satisfy investors. As discussed in Chapter 7, free cash flow is the term used to describe the cash remaining from operations after adjustment for capital expenditures and dividends.

Consider the following example: Suppose that MPC produced and sold 10,000 personal computers this year. It reported cash provided by operating activities of $100,000. In order to maintain production at 10,000 computers, MPC invested $20,000 in equipment. It chose to pay no dividends. Its free cash flow was then $80,000 ($100,000 − $20,000). The company could use this $80,000 either to purchase new assets to expand the business or to pay an $80,000 dividend and continue to produce 10,000 computers. Unfortunately, companies do not typically disclose what portion of their expenditures on fixed assets during the year was for maintaining current production levels, and what portion was for expanding production. Thus, analysts often estimate this amount by using the reported expenditures for the purchase of new fixed assets shown in the investing section of the statement of cash flows. In practice, free cash flow is often calculated with the formula in Illustration 13-45. Alternative definitions also exist.

Illustration 13-45
Free cash flow

$$\text{FREE CASH FLOW} = \text{CASH PROVIDED BY OPERATIONS} - \text{CAPITAL EXPENDITURES} - \text{DIVIDENDS PAID}$$

Illustration 13-46 provides basic information excerpted from the 1995 statement of cash flows of Microsoft Corporation.

Illustration 13-46
Microsoft cash flow information ($ in millions)

MICROSOFT CORPORATION
Partial Statement of Cash Flows
1995

Cash flows from operations		$1,990
Cash flows from investing		
Additions to property plant and equipment	$495	
Other assets	230	
Short-term investments	651	
Total cash flows from investing		(1,376)
Cash flows from financing		(138)

Microsoft's free cash flow (again noting that we do not have details to differentiate between amounts spent to maintain the current level of operations and amounts spent to expand production) is calculated as shown below in Illustration 13-47.

Cash provided by operating activities	$1,990
Less: Expenditures on property, plant, and equipment	495
Dividends paid	0
Free cash flow	$1,495

Illustration 13-47 Calculation of Microsoft's free cash flow ($ in millions)

This is a tremendous amount of cash generated in a single year. It is available for the acquisition of new assets, the retirement of stock or debt, or the payment of dividends. It should also be noted that this amount is very close to Microsoft's reported income for 1995 of $1,453 million. This lends additional credibility to Microsoft's income number as an indicator of potential future performance.

Oracle Corporation is the world's largest seller of database software and information management services. Like Microsoft, its success depends on continuing to improve its existing products while developing new products to keep pace with rapid changes in technology. Oracle's free cash flow for 1995 was $307 million. Thus, relative to a major competitor, Microsoft's free cash flow is also impressive.

DECISION TOOLKIT

Decision Checkpoints	Info Needed for Decision	Tool to Use for Decision	How to Evaluate Results
How much cash did the company generate to either expand operations or pay dividends?	Cash provided by operating activities, cash spent on fixed assets, and cash dividends. (Ideally, the measure would use cash spent to maintain the current level of operations, but that is rarely available.)	Free cash flow = Cash provided by operations − Capital expenditures − Dividends paid	Significant free cash flow indicates greater potential to finance new investment and pay additional dividends.

BUSINESS INSIGHT
Investor Perspective

Managers in some industries have long suggested that accrual-based income measures understate the true long-term potential of their companies because of what they suggest are excessive depreciation charges. For example, cable companies frequently suggested that, once they had installed a cable, it would require minimal maintenance and would guarantee the company returns for a long time to come. As a consequence, cable companies, which reported strong operating cash flows but low net income, had high stock prices because investors focused more on their cash flows from operations than on their net income. A recent *Wall Street Journal* article suggested, however, that investors have grown impatient with the cable companies and have lost faith in cash flow from operations as an indicator of cable performance. As it turns out, cable companies have had to make many expensive upgrades to previously installed cable systems.

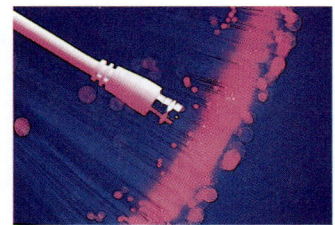

Today, after cable stock prices have fallen dramatically, cable industry analysts emphasize that either free cash flows or net income is a better indicator of a cable TV company's long-term potential than cash provided by operating activities.

Source: Susan Pulliam and Mark Robichaux, "Heard on the Street: Cash Flow Stops Propping Cable Stock," *The Wall Street Journal,* January 9, 1997, p. C1.

CAPITAL EXPENDITURE RATIO

Capital expenditures are purchases of fixed assets. In addition to free cash flows, another indicator of a company's ability to generate sufficient cash to finance new fixed assets is the **capital expenditure ratio:** cash provided by operating activities divided by capital expenditures. This measure is similar to free cash flow, except that free cash flow reveals the amount of cash available for discretionary use by management, whereas the capital expenditure ratio provides a *relative measure* of cash provided by operations compared to cash used for the purchase of productive assets. Amounts spent on capital expenditures are listed in the investing activities section of the statement of cash flows. Using the Microsoft information in Illustration 13-46, we can calculate its capital expenditure ratio as shown in Illustration 13-48.

Illustration 13-48 Capital expenditure ratio for Microsoft ($ in millions)

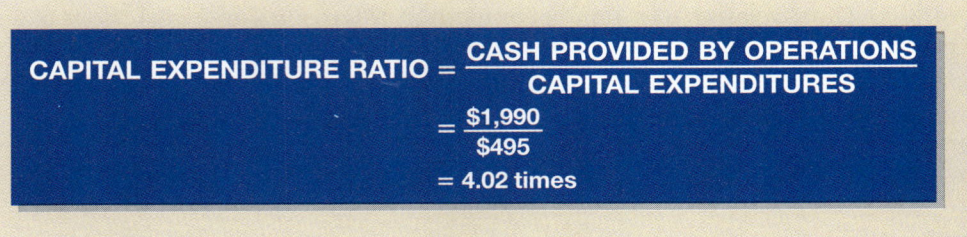

Microsoft's ratio of 4.02 times suggests that it could have purchased four times as much property, plant, and equipment as it did *without requiring any additional outside financing.* In comparison, Oracle's capital expenditure ratio for 1995 was 2.17 times. This provides additional evidence of Microsoft's superior cash-generating capability. It is important to note that this ratio will vary across industries depending on the capital intensity of the industry. That is, we would expect a manufacturing company to have a lower ratio (because by necessity it has higher capital expenditures) than a software company, which spends less of its money on fixed assets and more of its money on "intellectual" capital. This difference is evident in the Using the Decision Toolkit exercise at the end of this chapter where we evaluate two computer chip manufacturers.

DECISION TOOLKIT

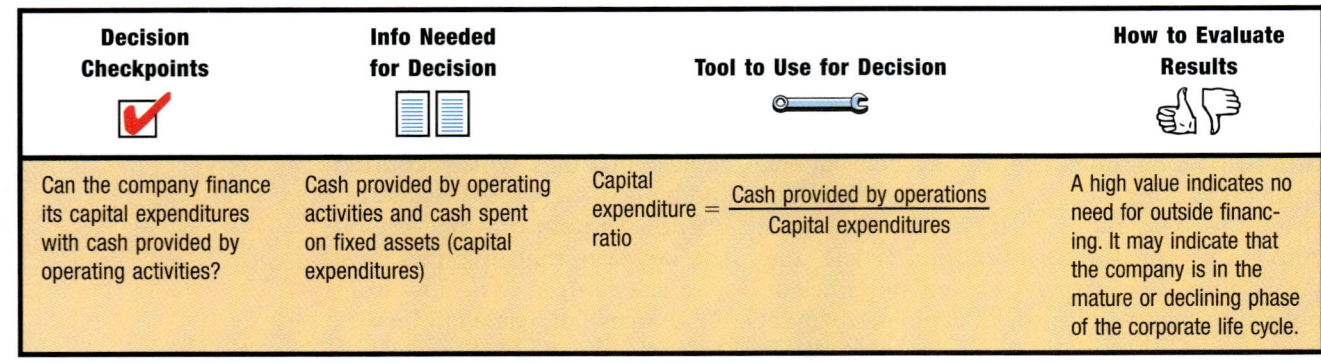

ASSESSING LIQUIDITY, SOLVENCY, AND PROFITABILITY USING CASH FLOWS

Previous chapters have presented ratios used to analyze a company's liquidity, solvency, and profitability. Those ratios used accrual-based numbers from the income statement and balance sheet. Now we introduce ratios that are *cash-based* rather than accrual-based; that is, instead of using numbers from the income statement, these ratios use numbers from the statement of cash flows.

As discussed earlier, many analysts are critical of accrual-based numbers because they feel that the adjustment process allows too much management discretion. These analysts like to supplement accrual-based analysis with measures that use the cash flow statement. One disadvantage of these measures is that, unlike the more commonly employed accrual-based measures, there are no readily available published industry averages for comparison. In the following discussion we use cash flow-based ratios to analyze Microsoft. In addition to the cash flow information provided in Illustration 13-46, we need the following information related to Microsoft in Illustration 13-49.

($ in millions)	1995	1994
Current liabilities	$1,347	$ 913
Total liabilities	1,877	913
Sales	5,937	4,649

Illustration 13-49 Additional Microsoft data

Liquidity

Liquidity is the ability of a business to meet its immediate obligations. You learned that one measure of liquidity is the *current ratio*: current assets divided by current liabilities. A disadvantage of the current ratio is that it uses year-end balances of current asset and current liability accounts, and these year-end balances may not be representative of the company's position during most of the year.

A ratio that partially corrects this problem is the **current cash debt coverage ratio:** cash provided by operating activities divided by average current liabilities. Because cash provided by operating activities involves the entire year rather than a balance at one point in time, it is often considered a better representation of liquidity on the average day. The ratio is calculated as shown in Illustration 13-50, with the ratio computed for Microsoft Corporation and comparative numbers given for Oracle. We have also provided each company's current ratio for comparative purposes.

Illustration 13-50 Current cash debt coverage ratio

$$\text{CURRENT CASH DEBT COVERAGE RATIO} = \frac{\text{CASH PROVIDED BY OPERATIONS}}{\text{AVERAGE CURRENT LIABILITIES}}$$

($ in millions)	Current cash debt coverage ratio	Current ratio
Microsoft	$\frac{\$1,990}{(\$1,347 + \$913)/2} = 1.76$ times	4.17:1
Oracle	.66 times	1.53:1

Microsoft's net cash provided by operating activities is nearly two times its average current liabilities. Oracle's ratio of .66, times, though not a cause for concern, is substantially lower than that of Microsoft. Keep in mind that Microsoft's cash position is extraordinary. For example, many companies now have current ratios in the range of 1.0. By this standard, Oracle's current ratio of 1.53:1 is respectable, but Microsoft's current ratio of 4.17:1 is nearly unheard of.

DECISION TOOLKIT

Decision Checkpoints	Info Needed for Decision	Tool to Use for Decision	How to Evaluate Results
Is the company generating sufficient cash provided by operating activities to meet its current obligations?	Cash provided by operating activities and average current liabilities	Current cash debt coverage ratio = $\dfrac{\text{Cash provided by operations}}{\text{Average current liabilities}}$	A high value suggests good liquidity. Since the numerator contains a "flow" measure, it provides a good supplement to the current ratio.

Solvency

Solvency is the ability of a company to survive over the long term. A measure of solvency that uses cash figures is the **cash debt coverage ratio:** the ratio of cash provided by operating activities to total debt as represented by average total liabilities. This ratio indicates a company's ability to repay its liabilities from cash generated from operations—that is, without having to liquidate productive assets such as property, plant, and equipment. The cash debt coverage ratios for Microsoft and Oracle for 1995 are given in Illustration 13-51. The debt to total assets ratios for each company are also provided for comparative purposes.

Illustration 13-51 Cash debt coverage ratio

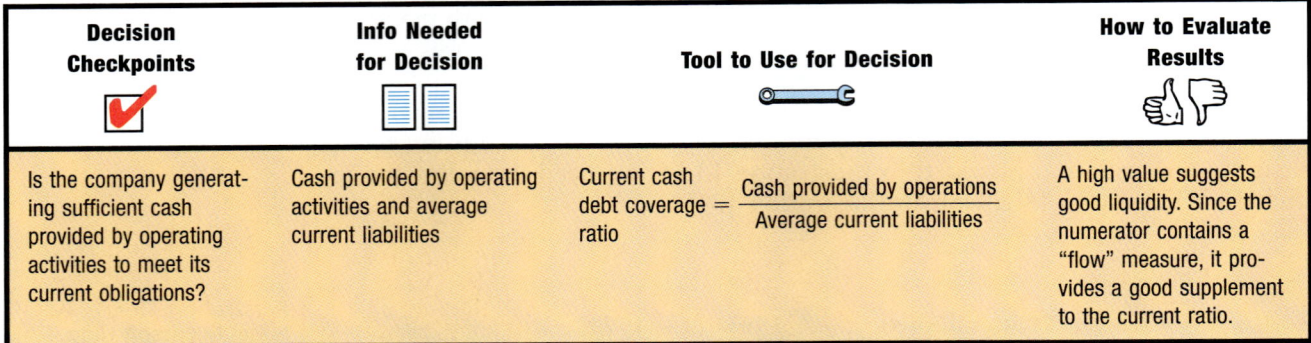

Microsoft has very low long-term obligations; thus, its cash debt coverage ratio is nearly identical to its current cash debt coverage ratio. Obviously, Microsoft is very solvent. On the other hand, Oracle has significant long-term debt, and its cash debt coverage ratio suggests that its long-term financial health needs closer monitoring than that of Microsoft. However, neither the cash nor accrual measures suggest any real cause for concern for either company.

DECISION TOOLKIT

Decision Checkpoints	Info Needed for Decision	Tool to Use for Decision	How to Evaluate Results
Is the company generating sufficient cash provided by operating activities to meet its long-term obligations?	Cash provided by operating activities and average total liabilities	Cash debt coverage ratio = $\dfrac{\text{Cash provided by operations}}{\text{Average total liabilities}}$	A high value suggests the company is solvent; that is, it will meet its obligations in the long term.

Profitability

Profitability refers to a company's ability to generate a reasonable return. Earlier chapters introduced accrual-based ratios that measures profitability, such as gross profit rate, profit margin, and return on assets. In measures of profitability the potential differences between cash accounting and accrual accounting are most pronounced. Although some differences are expected because of the difference in the timing of revenue and expense recognition under cash versus accrual accounting, significant differences should be investigated. A cash-based measure of performance is the cash return on sales ratio.

The **cash return on sales ratio** is cash provided by operating activities divided by net sales. This ratio indicates the company's ability to turn sales into dollars for the firm. A low cash return on sales ratio should be investigated because it might indicate that the firm is recognizing sales that are not really sales—that is, sales it will never collect. The cash return on sales ratios for Microsoft and Oracle for 1995 are presented in Illustration 13-52. The profit margin ratio is also presented for comparison.

Illustration 13-52 Cash return on sales ratio

$$\text{CASH RETURN ON SALES RATIO} = \dfrac{\text{CASH PROVIDED BY OPERATIONS}}{\text{NET SALES}}$$

($ in millions)	Cash return on sales ratio	Profit margin ratio
Microsoft	$\dfrac{\$1{,}990}{\$5{,}937} = 34\%$	24%
Oracle	19%	26%

Oracle's cash return on sales ratio of 19% is substantially less than Microsoft's at 34%. In addition, Oracle's cash return on sales ratio is lower than its profit margin ratio, whereas Microsoft's cash return on sales ratio is higher than its profit margin ratio. This difference should be investigated. It may simply indicate that Microsoft is more efficient in turning sales into cash. It might, on the other hand, indicate that Oracle uses more aggressive accrual accounting practices, which enable it to report higher net income. If this were the case, we might have more faith in Microsoft's long-term profitability potential than in Oracle's because Microsoft's income numbers were achieved with more conservative accounting practices. One way to determine whether this difference is cause for concern is to investigate whether it has persisted over a number of years.

618 CHAPTER 13 Statement of Cash Flows

DECISION TOOLKIT

Decision Checkpoints	Info Needed for Decision	Tool to Use for Decision	How to Evaluate Results
Are differences between cash and accrual accounting reasonable?	Cash provided by operating activities, sales, and profit margin ratio	Cash return on sales ratio = $\dfrac{\text{Cash provided by operations}}{\text{Net sales}}$	Cash return on sales ratio should be compared to profit margin ratio, and significant differences over a series of years should be investigated.

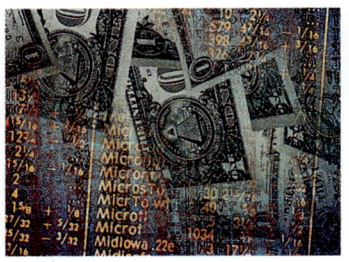

BUSINESS INSIGHT
Management Perspective

A recent *Wall Street Journal* article noted that while Microsoft's cash position is enviable, it does present some challenges; management can't find enough ways to spend the cash. For example, unlike computer chip manufacturer Intel Corporation (another huge generator of cash), Microsoft has few manufacturing costs, so it cannot spend huge sums on new plant and equipment. Microsoft's management would like to purchase other major software companies, but the federal government won't let it, for fear that it will reduce competition. (For example, the Justice Department blocked Microsoft's proposed purchase of software maker Intuit.) Instead, Microsoft is constrained to purchasing small software makers with promising new products. Ironically, even this does not use much of its cash because, first of all, the companies are small, and second, the owners of these small companies prefer to be paid with Microsoft stock rather than cash.

Microsoft's huge holdings of liquid assets could eventually hurt its stock performance. Liquid assets typically provide about a 5% return, whereas Microsoft investors are accustomed to 30% returns. If Microsoft's performance starts to decline because it can't find enough good investment projects, it should distribute cash to its shareholders in the form of dividends. One big problem: Bill Gates owns 24% of Microsoft, and the last thing he wants to do is pay personal income tax on billions of dollars of dividend income. In the early years Microsoft did not pay dividends because it wanted to conserve cash. Today it is drowning in cash but still can't pay a dividend.

Source: David Bank, "Microsoft's Problem Is What Many Firms Just Wish They Had," *The Wall Street Journal,* January 17, 1997, p. A9.

BEFORE YOU GO ON . . .

● **Review It**

1. What is the difference between cash from operations and free cash flow?
2. What does it mean if a company has negative free cash flow?
3. Why might an analyst want to supplement accrual-based ratios with cash-based ratios? What are some cash-based ratios?

Using the Decision Toolkit

Intel Corporation is the leading producer of computer chips for personal computers. It makes the hugely successful Pentium chip. Its primary competitor is AMD (formerly Advanced Micro Devices). The two are vicious competitors, with frequent lawsuits filed between them.

Instructions

Calculate the following cash-based measures for Intel, and compare them with those provided here for AMD. Financial statement data for Intel are also provided.

1. Free cash flow
2. Capital expenditure ratio
3. Current cash debt coverage ratio
4. Cash debt coverage ratio
5. Cash return on sales ratio

INTEL CORPORATION
Balance Sheet
December 31, 1995 and 1994
(in millions)

	1995	1994
Assets		
Current assets	$ 8,097	$ 6,167
Property, plant, and equipment	7,471	5,367
Long-term investments	1,653	2,127
Other assets	283	155
Total assets	$17,504	$13,816
Liabilities and Stockholders' Equity		
Current liabilities	$ 3,619	$ 3,024
Long-term debt	400	392
Other liabilities	1,345	1,133
Total liabilities	5,364	4,549
Stockholders' equity	12,140	9,267
Total liabilities and stockholders' equity	$17,504	$13,816

INTEL CORPORATION
Income Statement
For the Years Ended December 31, 1995 and 1994
(in millions)

	1995	1994
Net revenues	$16,202	$11,521
Cost of sales	7,811	5,576
Operating and administrative expenses	3,139	2,558
Operating income	5,252	3,387
Other revenues and expenses	1,686	1,099
Net income	$ 3,566	$ 2,288

INTEL CORPORATION
Statement of Cash Flows
For the Years Ended December 31, 1995 and 1994
(in millions)

	1995	1994
Net cash provided by operating activities	$4,026	$2,981
Net cash used for investing activities (see note 1)	(2,687)	(2,903)
Net cash used for financing activities	(1,056)	(557)
Net increase (decrease) in cash and cash equivalents	$ 283	$ (479)

Note 1. Cash spent on property, plant, and equipment in 1995 was $3,550. Cash paid for dividends was $116.

Here are the comparative data for AMD:

1. Free cash flow — ($3 million)
2. Capital expenditure ratio — .99 times
3. Current cash debt coverage ratio — 1.01 times
4. Cash debt coverage ratio — .75 times
5. Cash return on sales ratio — 25%

Solution

1. Intel's free cash flow is $360 million ($4,026 − $3,550 − $116), and AMD's is actually a negative $3 million. This gives Intel an advantage in ability to move quickly to invest in new projects.
2. Intel's capital expenditure ratio is 1.13 times ($4,026 ÷ $3,550), and AMD's is .99 times. This is a useful supplement to the free cash flow measure. It shows that, even though Intel appears to have considerably more ability to generate cash for capital expenditure, its cash-generating ability relative to its expenditures is not that much greater than AMD's. Note that all of these measures are well below those of Oracle and Microsoft. Manufacturing computer chips is very capital intensive, so we would expect these measures to be lower than those for software producers.

3. The current cash debt coverage ratio for Intel is calculated as:

$$\frac{\$4{,}026}{(\$3{,}619 + \$3{,}024)/2} = 1.21 \text{ times}$$

Compared to AMD's value of 1.01 times, Intel appears to be more liquid.

4. The cash debt coverage ratio for Intel is calculated as:

$$\frac{\$4{,}026}{(\$5{,}364 + \$4{,}549)/2} = .81 \text{ times}$$

Compared to AMD's value of .75 times, Intel appears to be slightly more solvent.

5. The cash return on sales ratio for Intel is calculated as:

$$\frac{\$4{,}026}{\$16{,}202} = 25\%$$

AMD's cash return on sales ratio is 25%. Thus, the two companies appear to be approximately the same in their ability to generate cash from sales.

SUMMARY OF STUDY OBJECTIVES

1 Indicate the primary purpose of the statement of cash flows. The statement of cash flows provides information about the cash receipts and cash payments of an entity during a period. A secondary objective is to provide information about the operating, investing, and financing activities of the entity during the period.

2 Distinguish among operating, investing, and financing activities. Operating activities include the cash effects of transactions that enter into the determination of net income. Investing activities involve cash flows resulting from changes in investments and long-term asset items. Financing activities involve cash flows resulting from changes in long-term liability and stockholders' equity items.

3 Explain the impact of the product life cycle on a company's cash flows. During the introductory stage, cash provided by operating activities and cash from investing are negative, whereas cash from financing is positive. During the growth stage, cash provided by operating activities becomes positive. During the maturity stage, cash provided by operating activities exceeds investing needs, so the company begins to retire debt. During the decline stage, cash provided by operating activities is reduced, cash from investing becomes positive, and cash from financing becomes more negative.

4a Prepare a statement of cash flows using the indirect method. The preparation of a statement of cash flows involves three major steps: (a) determine the net increase or decrease in cash, (b) determine net cash provided (used) by operating activities, and (c) determine net cash provided (used) by investing and financing activities. Under the indirect method, accrual-basis net income is adjusted to net cash provided by operating activities.

4b Prepare a statement of cash flows using the direct method. The preparation of the statement of cash flows involves three major steps: (a) determine the net increase or decrease in cash, (b) determine net cash provided (used) by operating activities, and (c) determine net cash provided (used) by investing and financing activities. The direct method reports cash receipts less cash payments to arrive at net cash provided by operating activities.

5 Use the statement of cash flows to evaluate a company. A number of measures can be derived by using information from the statement of cash flows as well as the other required financial statements. Free cash flow indicates the amount of cash a company generated during the current year that is available for the payment of dividends or for expansion. The capital expenditure ratio, cash provided by operating activities divided by capital expenditures, complements free cash flow by giving a relative indicator of the sufficiency of cash from operations to fund capital expenditures. Liquidity can be measured with the current cash debt coverage ratio (cash provided by operating activities divided by average current liabilities), solvency by the cash debt coverage ratio (cash provided by operating activities divided by average total liabilities), and profitability by the cash return on sales ratio (cash provided by operating activities divided by sales).

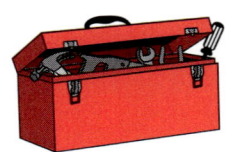

Decision Toolkit—A Summary

Decision Checkpoints	Info Needed for Decision	Tool to Use for Decision	How to Evaluate Results
How much cash did the company generate to either expand operations or pay dividends?	Cash provided by operating activities, cash spent on fixed assets, and cash dividends. (Ideally, the measure would use cash spent to maintain the current level of operations, but that is rarely available.)	Free cash flow = Cash provided by operations − Capital expenditures − Dividends paid	Significant free cash flow indicates greater potential to finance new investment and pay additional dividends.
Can the company finance its capital expenditures with cash provided by operating activities?	Cash provided by operating activities and cash spent on fixed assets (capital expenditures)	Capital expenditure ratio = $\dfrac{\text{Cash provided by operations}}{\text{Capital expenditures}}$	A high value indicates no need for outside financing. It may indicate that the company is in the mature or declining phase of the corporate life cycle.
Is the company generating sufficient cash provided by operating activities to meet its current obligations?	Cash provided by operating activities and average current liabilities	Current cash debt coverage ratio = $\dfrac{\text{Cash provided by operations}}{\text{Average current liabilities}}$	A high value suggests good liquidity. Since the numerator contains a "flow" measure, it provides a good supplement to the current ratio.
Is the company generating sufficient cash provided by operating activities to meet its long-term obligations?	Cash provided by operating activities and average total liabilities	Cash debt coverage ratio = $\dfrac{\text{Cash provided by operations}}{\text{Average total liabilities}}$	A high value suggests the company is solvent; that is, it will meet its obligations in the long term.
Are differences between cash and accrual accounting reasonable?	Cash provided by operating activities, sales, and profit margin ratio	Cash return on sales ratio = $\dfrac{\text{Cash provided by operations}}{\text{Net sales}}$	Cash return on sales ratio should be compared to profit margin ratio, and significant differences over a series of years should be investigated.

Glossary

Capital expenditure ratio A cash-based ratio that indicates the extent to which cash provided by operating activities was sufficient to fund capital expenditure (fixed asset) purchases during the year. (p. 614)

Cash debt coverage ratio A cash-basis ratio used to evaluate solvency, calculated as net cash provided by operating activities divided by average total liabilities. (p. 616)

Cash return on sales ratio A cash basis ratio used to evaluate profitability by dividing net cash provided by operating activities by sales. (p. 617)

Current cash debt coverage ratio A cash-basis ratio used to evaluate liquidity, calculated as net cash provided by operating activities divided by average current liabilities. (p. 615)

Direct method A method of determining net cash provided by operating activities by adjusting each item in the income statement from the accrual basis to the cash basis. (p. 600)

Financing activities Cash flow activities that include (a) obtaining cash from issuing debt and repaying the amounts borrowed and (b) obtaining cash from stockholders and providing them with a return on their investment. (p. 579)

Free cash flow Cash provided by operating activities adjusted for a charge for investments made to maintain the current level of operations. (p. 612)

Indirect method A method of preparing a statement of cash flows in which net income is adjusted for items that do not affect cash, to determine net cash provided by operating activities. (p. 588)

Investing activities Cash flow activities that include (a) purchasing and disposing of investments and productive long-lived assets using cash and (b) lending money and collecting on those loans. (p. 579)

Operating activities Cash flow activities that include the cash effects of transactions that create revenues and expenses and thus enter into the determination of net income. (p. 579)

Statement of cash flows A basic financial statement that provides information about the cash receipts and cash payments of an entity during a period, classified as operating, investing, and financing activities, in a format that reconciles the beginning and ending cash balances. (p. 578)

DEMONSTRATION PROBLEM

The income statement for John Kosinski Manufacturing Company contains the following condensed information:

JOHN KOSINSKI MANUFACTURING COMPANY
Income Statement
For the Year Ended December 31, 1998

Revenues		$6,583,000
Operating expenses, excluding depreciation	$4,920,000	
Depreciation expense	880,000	5,800,000
Income before income taxes		783,000
Income tax expense		353,000
Net income		$ 430,000

Included in operating expenses is a $24,000 loss resulting from the sale of machinery for $270,000 cash. Machinery was purchased at a cost of $750,000. The following balances are reported on Kosinski's comparative balance sheet at December 31:

	1998	1997
Cash	$672,000	$130,000
Accounts receivable	775,000	610,000
Inventories	834,000	867,000
Accounts payable	521,000	501,000

Income tax expense of $353,000 represents the amount paid in 1998. Dividends declared and paid in 1998 totaled $200,000.

Instructions

(a) Prepare the statement of cash flows using the indirect method.
(b) Prepare the statement of cash flows using the direct method.

Solution to Demonstration Problem

(a)

JOHN KOSINSKI MANUFACTURING COMPANY
Statement of Cash Flows—Indirect Method
For the Year Ended December 31, 1998

Cash flows from operating activities		
Net income		$ 430,000
Adjustments to reconcile net income to net cash provided by operating activities:		
Depreciation expense	$880,000	
Loss on sale of machinery	24,000	
Increase in accounts receivable	(165,000)	
Decrease in inventories	33,000	
Increase in accounts payable	20,000	792,000
Net cash provided by operating activities		1,222,000

Problem-Solving Strategy

This demonstration problem illustrates both the direct and indirect methods using the same basic data. Note the similarities and the differences between the two methods. Both methods report the same information in the investing and financing activities sections. The cash flow from operating activities section reports different information, but the amount—net cash provided by operating activities—is the same for both methods.

Cash flows from investing activities		
Sale of machinery	270,000	
Purchase of machinery	(750,000)	
Net cash used by investing activities		(480,000)
Cash flows from financing activities		
Payment of cash dividends	(200,000)	
Net cash used by financing activities		(200,000)
Net increase in cash		542,000
Cash at beginning of period		130,000
Cash at end of period		$672,000

(b)

JOHN KOSINSKI MANUFACTURING COMPANY
Statement of Cash Flows—Direct Method
For the Year Ended December 31, 1998

Cash flows from operating activities		
Cash collections from customers		$6,418,000*
Cash payments for operating expenses		4,843,000**
		1,575,000
Cash payment for income taxes		353,000
Net cash provided by operating activities		1,222,000
Cash flows from investing activities		
Sale of machinery	$270,000	
Purchase of machinery	(750,000)	
Net cash used by investing activities		(480,000)
Cash flows from financing activities		
Payment of cash dividends	(200,000)	
Net cash used by financing activities		(200,000)
Net increase in cash		542,000
Cash at beginning of period		130,000
Cash at end of period		$ 672,000

Direct Method Computations:

*Computation of cash collections from customers:

Revenues per the income statement	$6,583,000
Less increase in accounts receivable	165,000
Cash collections from customers	$6,418,000

**Computation of cash payments for operating expenses:

Operating expenses per the income statement	$4,920,000
Deduct loss from sale of machinery	(24,000)
Deduct decrease in inventories	(33,000)
Deduct increase in accounts payable	(20,000)
Cash payments for operating expenses	$4,843,000

SELF-STUDY QUESTIONS

Answers are at the end of the chapter.

(SO 1)   1. Which of the following is *incorrect* about the statement of cash flows?
    (a) It is a fourth basic financial statement.
    (b) It provides information about cash receipts and cash payments of an entity during a period.
    (c) It reconciles the ending cash account balance to the balance per the bank statement.

(SO 2) 2. The statement of cash flows classifies cash receipts and cash payments by these activities:
(a) operating and nonoperating.
(b) investing, financing, and operating.
(c) financing, operating, and nonoperating.
(d) investing, financing, and nonoperating.

(SO 2) 3. Which is an example of a cash flow from an operating activity?
(a) Payment of cash to lenders for interest
(b) Receipt of cash from the sale of capital stock
(c) Payment of cash dividends to the company's stockholders
(d) None of the above

(SO 2) 4. Which is an example of a cash flow from an investing activity?
(a) Receipt of cash from the issuance of bonds payable
(b) Payment of cash to repurchase outstanding capital stock
(c) Receipt of cash from the sale of equipment
(d) Payment of cash to suppliers for inventory

(SO 2) 5. Cash dividends paid to stockholders are classified on the statement of cash flows as:
(a) operating activities.
(b) investing activities.
(c) a combination of (a) and (b).
(d) financing activities.

(SO 2) 6. Which is an example of a cash flow from a financing activity?
(a) Receipt of cash from sale of land
(b) Issuance of debt for cash
(c) Purchase of equipment for cash
(d) None of the above

(SO 2) 7. Which of the following is *incorrect* about the statement of cash flows?
(a) The direct method may be used to report cash provided by operations.
(b) The statement shows the cash provided (used) for three categories of activity.
(c) The operating section is the last section of the statement.
(d) The indirect method may be used to report cash provided by operations.

(SO 3) 8. During the introductory phase of a company's life cycle, one would normally expect to see:
(a) negative cash from operations, negative cash from investing, and positive cash from financing.
(b) negative cash from operations, positive cash from investing, and positive cash from financing.
(c) positive cash from operations, negative cash from investing, and negative cash from financing.

(d) It provides information about the operating, investing, and financing activities of the business.

(d) positive cash from operations, negative cash from investing, and positive cash from financing.

Questions 9 and 10 apply only to the indirect method.

9. Net income is $132,000, accounts payable increased $10,000 during the year, inventory decreased $6,000 during the year, and accounts receivable increased $12,000 during the year. Under the indirect method, what is net cash provided by operations? (SO 4a)
(a) $102,000   (c) $124,000
(b) $112,000   (d) $136,000

10. Noncash charges that are added back to net income in determining cash provided by operations under the indirect method do *not* include: (SO 4a)
(a) depreciation expense.
(b) an increase in inventory.
(c) amortization expense.
(d) loss on sale of equipment.

Questions 11 and 12 apply only to the direct method.

11. The beginning balance in accounts receivable is $44,000, the ending balance is $42,000, and sales during the period are $129,000. What are cash receipts from customers? (SO 4b)
(a) $127,000   (c) $131,000
(b) $129,000   (d) $141,000

12. Which of the following items is reported on a cash flow statement prepared by the direct method? (SO 4b)
(a) Loss on sale of building
(b) Increase in accounts receivable
(c) Depreciation expense
(d) Cash payments to suppliers

13. The statement of cash flows should *not* be used to evaluate an entity's ability to: (SO 5)
(a) earn net income.
(b) generate future cash flows.
(c) pay dividends.
(d) meet obligations.

14. Free cash flow provides an indication of a company's ability to: (SO 5)
(a) generate net income.
(b) generate cash to pay dividends.
(c) generate cash to invest in new capital expenditures.
(d) both (b) and (c).

15. Which of the following ratios provides a useful comparison to the profit margin ratio? (SO 5)
(a) Capital expenditure ratio
(b) Cash return on sales ratio
(c) Cash debt coverage ratio
(d) Current cash debt coverage ratio

QUESTIONS

1. (a) What is a statement of cash flows?
   (b) Alice Weiseman maintains that the statement of cash flows is an optional financial statement. Do you agree? Explain.
2. What questions about cash are answered by the statement of cash flows?
3. Distinguish among the three activities reported in the statement of cash flows.
4. (a) What are the major sources (inflows) of cash in a statement of cash flows?
   (b) What are the major uses (outflows) of cash?
5. Why is it important to disclose certain noncash transactions? How should they be disclosed?
6. Wilma Flintstone and Barny Kublestone were discussing the format of the statement of cash flows of Rock Candy Co. At the bottom of Rock Candy's statement of cash flows was a separate section entitled "Noncash investing and financing activities." Give three examples of significant noncash transactions that would be reported in this section.
7. Why is it necessary to use comparative balance sheets, a current income statement, and certain transaction data in preparing a statement of cash flows?
8. (a) What are the phases of the corporate life cycle?
   (b) What effect does each phase have on the numbers reported in a statement of cash flows?
9. Contrast the advantages and disadvantages of the direct and indirect methods of preparing the statement of cash flows. Are both methods acceptable? Which method is preferred by the FASB? Which method is more popular?
10. When the total cash inflows exceed the total cash outflows in the statement of cash flows, how and where is this excess identified?
11. Describe the indirect method for determining net cash provided (used) by operating activities.
12. Why is it necessary to convert accrual-based net income to cash-basis income when preparing a statement of cash flows?
13. The president of Aerosmith Company is puzzled. During the last year, the company experienced a net loss of $800,000, yet its cash increased $300,000 during the same period of time. Explain to the president how this could occur.
14. Identify five items that are adjustments to convert net income to net cash provided by operating activities under the indirect method.
15. Why and how is depreciation expense reported in a statement prepared using the indirect method?
16. Why is the statement of cash flows useful?
17. During 1998 Johnny Carson Company converted $1,700,000 of its total $2,000,000 of bonds payable into common stock. Indicate how the transaction would be reported on a statement of cash flows, if at all.
18. Describe the direct method for determining net cash provided by operating activities.
19. Give the formulas under the direct method for computing (a) cash receipts from customers and (b) cash payments to suppliers.
20. Cindy Crawford Inc. reported sales of $2 million for 1998. Accounts receivable decreased $100,000 and accounts payable increased $300,000. Compute cash receipts from customers, assuming that the receivable and payable transactions related to operations.
21. In the direct method, why is depreciation expense not reported in the cash flows from operating activities section?
22. Give an example of one accrual-based ratio and one cash-based ratio to measure these characteristics of a company:
    (a) Liquidity
    (b) Solvency
    (c) Profitability

BRIEF EXERCISES

Compute cash provided by operating activities—indirect method.
(SO 4a)

BE13-1 Crystal, Inc., reported net income of $2.5 million in 1998. Depreciation for the year was $260,000, accounts receivable decreased $350,000, and accounts payable decreased $310,000. Compute net cash provided by operating activities using the indirect approach.

Compute cash provided by operating activities—indirect method.
(SO 4a)

BE13-2 The net income for Sterling Engineering Co. for 1998 was $280,000. For 1998 depreciation on plant assets was $60,000, and the company incurred a loss on sale of plant assets of $9,000. Compute net cash provided by operating activities under the indirect method.

Indicate statement presentation of selected transactions.
(SO 2)

BE13-3 Each of these items must be considered in preparing a statement of cash flows for Murphy Co. for the year ended December 31, 1998. For each item, state how it should be shown in the statement of cash flows for 1998.

(a) Issued bonds for $200,000 cash
(b) Purchased equipment for $150,000 cash
(c) Sold land costing $20,000 for $20,000 cash
(d) Declared and paid a $50,000 cash dividend

BE13-4

Answer questions related to the phases of product life cycle.
(SO 3)

(a) Why is cash from operations likely to be lower than reported net income during the growth phase?
(b) Why is cash from investing often positive during the late maturity phase and during the decline phase?

BE13-5 The comparative balance sheet for Rolex Company shows these changes in non-cash current asset accounts: accounts receivable decrease $80,000, prepaid expenses increase $12,000, and inventories increase $30,000. Compute net cash provided by operating activities using the indirect method assuming that net income is $200,000.

Compute net cash provided by operating activities—indirect method.
(SO 4a)

BE13-6 Classify each item as an operating, investing, or financing activity. Assume all items involve cash unless there is information to the contrary.
(a) Purchase of equipment   (d) Depreciation
(b) Sale of building   (e) Payment of dividends
(c) Redemption of bonds   (f) Issuance of capital stock

Classify items by activities.
(SO 2)

BE13-7 Billy Idol Corporation has accounts receivable of $14,000 at January 1, 1998, and $24,000 at December 31, 1998. Sales revenues were $480,000 for the year 1998. What is the amount of cash receipts from customers in 1998?

Compute receipts from customers—direct method.
(SO 4b)

BE13-8 Depeche Mode Corporation reported income taxes of $70,000 on its 1998 income statement and income taxes payable of $12,000 at December 31, 1997, and $9,000 at December 31, 1998. What amount of cash payments were made for income taxes during 1998?

Compute cash payments for income taxes—indirect method.
(SO 4a)

BE13-9 Excel Corporation reports operating expenses of $90,000 excluding depreciation expense of $15,000 for 1998. During the year prepaid expenses decreased $6,600 and accrued expenses payable increased $4,400. Compute the cash payments for operating expenses in 1998.

Compute cash payments for operating expenses—direct method.
(SO 4b)

BE13-10 The T accounts for Equipment and the related Accumulated Depreciation for Cindy Trevis Company at the end of 1998 are shown here:

Determine cash received from sale of equipment.
(SO 4)

Equipment				Accumulated Depreciation			
Beg. bal.	80,000	Disposals	22,000	Disposals	5,500	Beg. bal.	44,500
Acquisitions	41,600					Depr.	12,000
End. bal.	99,600					End. bal.	51,000

In addition, Cindy Trevis Company's income statement reported a loss on the sale of equipment of $6,700. What amount was reported on the statement of cash flows as "cash flow from sale of equipment"?

BE13-11 The following T account is a summary of the cash account of Anita Baker Company:

Identify financing activity transactions.
(SO 2)

Cash (Summary Form)

Balance, Jan. 1	8,000		
Receipts from customers	364,000	Payments for goods	200,000
Dividends on stock investments	6,000	Payments for operating expenses	140,000
Proceeds from sale of equipment	36,000	Interest paid	10,000
Proceeds from issuance of		Taxes paid	8,000
bonds payable	100,000	Dividends paid	40,000
Balance, Dec. 31	116,000		

628 CHAPTER 13 Statement of Cash Flows

What amount of net cash provided (used) by financing activities should be reported in the statement of cash flows?

Calculate cash-based ratios.
(SO 5)

BE13-12 Mary Jo Corporation reported cash from operations of $300,000, cash used in investing of $250,000, and cash from financing of $70,000. In addition, cash spent for fixed assets during the period was $200,000. Average current liabilities were $150,000 and average total liabilities were $225,000. No dividends were paid. Calculate these values:
(a) Free cash flow
(b) Capital expenditure ratio
(c) Current cash debt coverage ratio

Exercises

Classify transactions by type of activity.
(SO 2)

E13-1 Li Eng Corporation had these transactions during 1998:
(a) Purchased a machine for $30,000, giving a long-term note in exchange.
(b) Issued $50,000 par value common stock for cash.
(c) Collected $16,000 of accounts receivable.
(d) Declared and paid a cash dividend of $25,000.
(e) Sold a long-term investment with a cost of $15,000 for $15,000 cash.
(f) Issued $200,000 par value common stock upon conversion of bonds having a face value of $200,000.
(g) Paid $18,000 on accounts payable.

Instructions
Analyze the transactions and indicate whether each transaction resulted in a cash flow from operating activities, investing activities, financing activities, or noncash investing and financing activities.

Prepare the operating activities section—indirect method.
(SO 4a)

E13-2 Joe Pesci Company reported net income of $195,000 for 1998. Pesci also reported depreciation expense of $35,000 and a loss of $5,000 on the sale of equipment. The comparative balance sheet shows an increase in accounts receivable of $15,000 for the year, an $8,000 increase in accounts payable, and a $4,000 decrease in prepaid expenses.

Instructions
Prepare the operating activities section of the statement of cash flows for 1998. Use the indirect method.

Identify phases of product life cycle.
(SO 3)

E13-3 The information in the table is from the statement of cash flows for a company at four different points in time (A, B, C, and D). Negative values are presented in parentheses.

	Point in Time			
	A	B	C	D
Cash provided by operations	$100,000	$30,000	($60,000)	($10,000)
Cash provided by investing	30,000	25,000	(100,000)	(40,000)
Cash provided by financing	(50,000)	(110,000)	70,000	120,000
Net income	100,000	10,000	(40,000)	(5,000)

Instructions
For each point in time, state whether the company is most likely characterized as being in the introductory phase, growth phase, maturity phase, or decline phase. In each case explain your choice.

Prepare the operating activities section—indirect method.
(SO 4a)

E13-4 The current sections of Barth Inc.'s balance sheets at December 31, 1997 and 1998, are presented here:

	1998	1997
Current assets		
Cash	$105,000	$ 99,000
Accounts receivable	110,000	89,000
Inventory	171,000	186,000
Prepaid expenses	27,000	32,000
Total current assets	$413,000	$406,000

Current liabilities
Accrued expenses payable	$ 15,000	$ 5,000
Accounts payable	85,000	92,000
Total current liabilities	$100,000	$ 97,000

Barth's net income for 1998 was $122,000. Depreciation expense was $24,000.

Instructions
Prepare the net cash provided by operating activities section of Barth Inc.'s statement of cash flows for the year ended December 31, 1998, using the indirect method.

E13-5 These three accounts appear in the general ledger of Roberta Dupre Corp. during 1998:

Prepare partial statement of cash flows—indirect method.
(SO 4a)

Equipment

Date		Debit	Credit	Balance
Jan. 1	Balance			160,000
July 31	Purchase of equipment	70,000		230,000
Sept. 2	Cost of equipment constructed	53,000		283,000
Nov. 10	Cost of equipment sold		45,000	238,000

Accumulated Depreciation—Equipment

Date		Debit	Credit	Balance
Jan. 1	Balance			71,000
Nov. 10	Accumulated depreciation on equipment sold	30,000		41,000
Dec. 31	Depreciation for year		24,000	65,000

Retained Earnings

Date		Debit	Credit	Balance
Jan. 1	Balance			105,000
Aug. 23	Dividends (cash)	14,000		91,000
Dec. 31	Net income		47,000	138,000

Instructions
From the postings in the accounts, indicate how the information is reported on a statement of cash flows using the indirect method. The loss on sale of equipment was $6,000. [*Hint:* Purchase of equipment is reported in the investing activities section as a decrease in cash of $70,000.]

E13-6 Here is a comparative balance sheet for Oprah Winfrey Company:

Prepare a statement of cash flows—indirect method, and compute cash-based ratios.
(SO 4a, 5)

OPRAH WINFREY COMPANY
Comparative Balance Sheet
December 31

Assets	1998	1997
Cash	$ 63,000	$ 22,000
Accounts receivable	85,000	76,000
Inventories	180,000	189,000
Land	75,000	100,000
Equipment	260,000	200,000
Accumulated depreciation	(66,000)	(42,000)
Total	$597,000	$545,000

Liabilities and Stockholders' Equity		
Accounts payable	$ 34,000	$ 47,000
Bonds payable	150,000	200,000
Common stock ($1 par)	214,000	164,000
Retained earnings	199,000	134,000
Total	$597,000	$545,000

630 CHAPTER 13 Statement of Cash Flows

Additional information:
1. Net income for 1998 was $105,000.
2. Cash dividends of $40,000 were declared and paid.
3. Bonds payable amounting to $50,000 were redeemed for cash $50,000.
4. Common stock was issued for $50,000 cash.
5. Sales for 1998 were $978,000.

Instructions
(a) Prepare a statement of cash flows for 1998 using the indirect method.
(b) Compute these cash-basis ratios:
   (1) Current cash debt coverage
   (2) Cash return on sales
   (3) Cash debt coverage

Classify transactions by type of activity.
(SO 2)

E13-7 An analysis of comparative balance sheets, the current year's income statement, and the general ledger accounts of Pierce Brosnan Corp. uncovered the following items. Assume all items involve cash unless there is information to the contrary.
(a) Purchase of land
(b) Payment of dividends
(c) Sale of building at book value
(d) Exchange of land for patent
(e) Depreciation
(f) Redemption of bonds
(g) Receipt of interest on notes receivable
(h) Issuance of capital stock
(i) Amortization of patent
(j) Issuance of bonds for land
(k) Payment of interest on notes payable
(l) Conversion of bonds into common stock
(m) Loss on sale of land
(n) Receipt of dividends on investment in stock

Instructions
Indicate how each item should be classified in the statement of cash flows using these four major classifications: operating activity (indirect method), investing activity, financing activity, and significant noncash investing and financing activity.

Compute cash provided by operating activities—direct method.
(SO 4b)

E13-8 Kelly McGillis Company completed its first year of operations on December 31, 1998. Its initial income statement showed that Kelly McGillis had revenues of $157,000 and operating expenses of $78,000. Accounts receivable and accounts payable at year end were $42,000 and $33,000, respectively. Assume that accounts payable related to operating expenses. Ignore income taxes.

Instructions
Compute net cash provided by operating activities using the direct method.

Compute cash payments—direct method.
(SO 4b)

E13-9 The income statement for Garcia Company shows cost of goods sold $355,000 and operating expenses (exclusive of depreciation) $230,000. The comparative balance sheet for the year shows that inventory increased $6,000, prepaid expenses decreased $6,000, accounts payable (merchandise suppliers) decreased $8,000, and accrued expenses payable increased $8,000.

Instructions
Using the direct method, compute (a) cash payments to suppliers and (b) cash payments for operating expenses.

Compute cash flow from operating activities—direct method.
(SO 4b)

E13-10 The 1998 accounting records of Flypaper Airlines reveal these transactions and events:

Payment of interest	$ 6,000	Collection of accounts receivable	$180,000
Cash sales	48,000	Payment of salaries and wages	68,000
Receipt of dividend revenue	14,000	Depreciation expense	16,000
Payment of income taxes	16,000	Proceeds from sale of aircraft	812,000
Net income	38,000	Purchase of equipment for cash	22,000
Payment of accounts payable		Loss on sale of aircraft	3,000
for merchandise	90,000	Payment of dividends	14,000
Payment for land	74,000	Payment of operating expenses	20,000

Instructions

Prepare the cash flows from operating activities section using the direct method. (Not all of the items will be used.)

E13-11 The following information is taken from the 1998 general ledger of Joan Robinson Company:

Rent	Rent expense	$ 31,000
	Prepaid rent, January 1	5,900
	Prepaid rent, December 31	3,000
Salaries	Salaries expense	$ 54,000
	Salaries payable, January 1	5,000
	Salaries payable, December 31	8,000
Sales	Revenue from sales	$180,000
	Accounts receivable, January 1	12,000
	Accounts receivable, December 31	9,000

Calculate cash flows—direct method.
(SO 4b)

Instructions

In each case, compute the amount that should be reported in the operating activities section of the statement of cash flows under the direct method.

E13-12 Presented here is information for two companies in the same industry: Rita Corporation and Les Corporation:

	Rita Corporation	Les Corporation
Cash provided by operations	$200,000	$200,000
Average current liabilities	50,000	100,000
Average total liabilities	200,000	250,000
Net income	200,000	200,000
Sales	400,000	800,000

Compare two companies by using cash-based ratios.
(SO 5)

Instructions

Using the cash-based ratios presented in this chapter, compare the (a) liquidity, (b) solvency, and (c) profitability of the two companies.

PROBLEMS

P13-1 The income statement of Breckenridge Company is presented here:

Prepare the operating activities section—indirect method.
(SO 4a)

BRECKENRIDGE COMPANY
Income Statement
For the Year Ended November 30, 1998

Sales		$6,900,000
Cost of goods sold		
Beginning inventory	$1,900,000	
Purchases	4,400,000	
Goods available for sale	6,300,000	
Ending inventory	1,600,000	
Total cost of goods sold		4,700,000
Gross profit		2,200,000
Operating expenses		
Selling expenses	450,000	
Administrative expenses	700,000	1,150,000
Net income		$1,050,000

Additional information:
1. Accounts receivable decreased $300,000 during the year.
2. Prepaid expenses increased $150,000 during the year.
3. Accounts payable to suppliers of merchandise decreased $300,000 during the year.
4. Accrued expenses payable decreased $100,000 during the year.
5. Administrative expenses include depreciation expense of $60,000.

632 CHAPTER 13 Statement of Cash Flows

Prepare the operating activities section—direct method.
(SO 4b)

Instructions
Prepare the operating activities section of the statement of cash flows for the year ended November 30, 1998, for Breckenridge Company, using the indirect method.

P13-2 Data for Breckenridge Company are presented in P13-1.

Instructions
Prepare the operating activities section of the statement of cash flows using the direct method.

Prepare the operating activities section—direct method.
(SO 4b)

P13-3 Vail Company's income statement contained the condensed information below:

VAIL COMPANY
Income Statement
For the Year Ended December 31, 1998

Revenues		$840,000
Operating expenses, excluding depreciation	$624,000	
Depreciation expense	60,000	
Loss on sale of equipment	26,000	710,000
Income before income taxes		130,000
Income tax expense		40,000
Net income		$ 90,000

Vail's balance sheet contained these comparative data at December 31:

	1998	1997
Accounts receivable	$47,000	$55,000
Accounts payable	41,000	33,000
Income taxes payable	4,000	9,000

Accounts payable pertain to operating expenses.

Instructions
Prepare the operating activities section of the statement of cash flows using the direct method.

Prepare the operating activities section—indirect method.
(SO 4a)

P13-4 Data for Vail Company are presented in P13-3.

Instructions
Prepare the operating activities section of the statement of cash flows using the indirect method.

Prepare a statement of cash flows—indirect method, and compute cash-based ratios.
(SO 4a, 5)

P13-5 These are the financial statements of Patrick Swayze Company:

PATRICK SWAYZE COMPANY
Comparative Balance Sheet
December 31

Assets	1998	1997
Cash	$ 29,000	$ 13,000
Accounts receivable	28,000	14,000
Merchandise inventory	25,000	35,000
Property, plant, and equipment	60,000	78,000
Accumulated depreciation	(20,000)	(24,000)
Total	$122,000	$116,000

Liabilities and Stockholders' Equity		
Accounts payable	$ 29,000	$ 23,000
Income taxes payable	5,000	8,000
Bonds payable	27,000	33,000
Common stock	18,000	14,000
Retained earnings	43,000	38,000
Total	$122,000	$116,000

PATRICK SWAYZE COMPANY
Income Statement
For the Year Ended December 31, 1998

Sales		$220,000
Cost of goods sold		180,000
Gross profit		40,000
Selling expenses	$18,000	
Administrative expenses	6,000	24,000
Income from operations		16,000
Interest expense		2,000
Income before income taxes		14,000
Income tax expense		4,000
Net income		$ 10,000

The following additional data were provided:
1. Dividends declared and paid were $5,000.
2. During the year equipment was sold for $8,500 cash. This equipment cost $18,000 originally and had a book value of $8,500 at the time of sale.
3. All depreciation expense is in the selling expense category.
4. All sales and purchases are on account.

Instructions
(a) Prepare a statement of cash flows using the indirect method.
(b) Compute these cash-basis measures:
   (1) Current cash debt coverage ratio
   (2) Cash return on sales ratio
   (3) Cash debt coverage ratio
   (4) Free cash flow

P13-6 Data for Patrick Swayze Company are presented in P13-5. Further analysis reveals the following:
1. Accounts payable pertain to merchandise suppliers.
2. All operating expenses except for depreciation were paid in cash.

Prepare a statement of cash flows—direct method, and compute cash-based ratios.
(SO 4b, 5)

Instructions
(a) Prepare a statement of cash flows for Patrick Swayze Company using the direct method.
(b) Compute these cash-basis measures:
   (1) Current cash debt coverage ratio
   (2) Cash return on sales ratio
   (3) Cash debt coverage ratio
   (4) Free cash flow

P13-7 Condensed financial data of Fern Galenti, Inc., follow.

Prepare a statement of cash flows—indirect method.
(SO 4a)

FERN GALENTI, INC.
Comparative Balance Sheet
December 31

Assets	1998	1997
Cash	$ 97,800	$ 38,400
Accounts receivable	90,800	33,000
Inventories	112,500	102,850
Prepaid expenses	18,400	16,000
Investments	108,000	94,000
Plant assets	270,000	242,500
Accumulated depreciation	(50,000)	(52,000)
Total	$647,500	$474,750

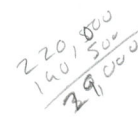

Liabilities and Stockholders' Equity		
Accounts payable	$ 92,000	$ 67,300
Accrued expenses payable	16,500	17,000
Bonds payable	85,000	110,000
Common stock	220,000	175,000
Retained earnings	234,000	105,450
Total	$647,500	$474,750

FERN GALENTI, INC.
Income Statement Data
For the Year Ended December 31, 1998

Sales		$342,780
Less:		
Cost of goods sold	$115,460	
Operating expenses, excluding depreciation	12,410	
Depreciation expense	46,500	
Income taxes	7,280	
Interest expense	2,730	
Loss on sale of plant assets	7,500	191,880
Net income		$150,900

Additional information:
1. New plant assets costing $85,000 were purchased for cash during the year.
2. Old plant assets having an original cost of $57,500 were sold for $1,500 cash.
3. Bonds matured and were paid off at face value for cash.
4. A cash dividend of $22,350 was declared and paid during the year.

Instructions
Prepare a statement of cash flows using the indirect method.

Prepare a statement of cash flows—direct method.
(SO 4b)

P13-8 Data for Fern Galenti, Inc., are presented in P13-7. Further analysis reveals that accounts payable pertain to merchandise creditors.

Instructions
Prepare a statement of cash flows for Fern Galenti, Inc., using the direct method.

Prepare a statement of cash flows—indirect method.
(SO 4a)

P13-9 This comparative balance sheet is for Cousin Tommy's Toy Company as of December 31:

COUSIN TOMMY'S TOY COMPANY
Comparative Balance Sheet
December 31

Assets	1998	1997
Cash	$ 41,000	$ 45,000
Accounts receivable	47,500	52,000
Inventory	151,450	142,000
Prepaid expenses	16,780	21,000
Land	100,000	130,000
Equipment	228,000	155,000
Accumulated depreciation—equipment	(45,000)	(35,000)
Building	200,000	200,000
Accumulated depreciation—building	(60,000)	(40,000)
Total	$679,730	$670,000

Liabilities and Stockholders' Equity		
Accounts payable	$ 43,730	$ 40,000
Bonds payable	250,000	300,000
Common stock, $1 par	200,000	150,000
Retained earnings	186,000	180,000
Total	$679,730	$670,000

Additional information:
1. Operating expenses include depreciation expense of $42,000 and charges from prepaid expenses of $4,220.
2. Land was sold for cash at book value.
3. Cash dividends of $32,000 were paid.
4. Net income for 1998 was $38,000.
5. Equipment was purchased for $95,000 cash. In addition, equipment costing $22,000 with a book value of $10,000 was sold for $8,100 cash.
6. Bonds were converted at face value by issuing 50,000 shares of $1 par value common stock.

Instructions
Prepare a statement of cash flows for the year ended December 31, 1998, using the indirect method.

ALTERNATIVE PROBLEMS

P13-1A The income statement of Tina Maria Company is presented here:

Prepare the operating activities section—indirect method.
(SO 4a)

TINA MARIA COMPANY
Income Statement
For the Year Ended December 31, 1998

Sales		$7,100,000
Cost of goods sold		
Beginning inventory	$1,700,000	
Purchases	5,430,000	
Goods available for sale	7,130,000	
Ending inventory	1,920,000	
Total cost of goods sold		5,210,000
Gross profit		1,890,000
Operating expenses		
Selling expenses	400,000	
Administrative expense	525,000	
Depreciation expense	75,000	
Amortization expense	30,000	1,030,000
Net income		$ 860,000

Additional information:
1. Accounts receivable increased $510,000 during the year.
2. Prepaid expenses increased $170,000 during the year.
3. Accounts payable to merchandise suppliers increased $50,000 during the year.
4. Accrued expenses payable decreased $180,000 during the year.

Instructions
Prepare the operating activities section of the statement of cash flows for the year ended December 31, 1998, for Tina Maria Company, using the indirect method.

P13-2A Data for Tina Maria Company are presented in P13-1A.

Prepare the operating activities section—direct method.
(SO 4b)

Instructions
Prepare the operating activities section of the statement of cash flows using the direct method.

P13-3A The income statement of Hanalei International Inc. reported the following condensed information:

636 CHAPTER 13 Statement of Cash Flows

Prepare the operating activities section—direct method.
(SO 4b)

HANALEI INTERNATIONAL INC.
Income Statement
For the Year Ended December 31, 1998

Revenues	$430,000
Operating expenses	280,000
Income from operations	150,000
Income tax expense	47,000
Net income	$103,000

Hanalei's balance sheet contained these comparative data at December 31:

	1998	1997
Accounts receivable	$50,000	$40,000
Accounts payable	30,000	41,000
Income taxes payable	6,000	4,000

Hanalei has no depreciable assets. Accounts payable pertain to operating expenses.

Instructions
Prepare the operating activities section of the statement of cash flows using the direct method.

Prepare the operating activities section—indirect method.
(SO 4a)

P13-4A Data for Hanalei International Inc. are presented in P13-3A.

Instructions
Prepare the operating activities section of the statement of cash flows using the indirect method.

Prepare a statement of cash flows—indirect method, and compute cash-based ratios.
(SO 4a, 5)

P13-5A Here are the financial statements of Sean Seymor Company:

SEAN SEYMOR COMPANY
Comparative Balance Sheet
December 31

Assets	1998		1997	
Cash		$ 26,000		$ 13,000
Accounts receivable		18,000		14,000
Merchandise inventory		38,000		35,000
Property, plant, and equipment	$70,000		$78,000	
Less accumulated depreciation	(30,000)	40,000	(24,000)	54,000
Total		$122,000		$116,000

Liabilities and Stockholders' Equity		
Accounts payable	$ 29,000	$ 33,000
Income taxes payable	15,000	20,000
Bonds payable	20,000	10,000
Common stock	25,000	25,000
Retained earnings	33,000	28,000
Total	$122,000	$116,000

SEAN SEYMOR COMPANY
Income Statement
For the Year Ended December 31, 1998

Sales		$240,000
Cost of goods sold		180,000
Gross profit		60,000
Selling expenses	$28,000	

Administrative expenses	6,000	34,000
Income from operations		26,000
Interest expense		2,000
Income before income taxes		24,000
Income tax expense		7,000
Net income		$ 17,000

The following additional data were provided:
1. Dividends of $12,000 were declared and paid.
2. During the year equipment was sold for $10,000 cash. This equipment cost $15,000 originally and had a book value of $10,000 at the time of sale.
3. All depreciation expense, $11,000, is in the selling expense category.
4. All sales and purchases are on account.
5. Additional equipment was purchased for $7,000 cash.

Instructions
(a) Prepare a statement of cash flows using the indirect method.
(b) Compute these cash-basis measures:
   (1) Current cash debt coverage ratio
   (2) Cash return on sales ratio
   (3) Cash debt coverage ratio
   (4) Free cash flow

P13-6A Data for the Sean Seymor Company are presented in P13-5A. Further analysis reveals the following:
1. Accounts payable pertains to merchandise creditors.
2. All operating expenses except for depreciation are paid in cash.

Prepare a statement of cash flows—direct method, and compute cash-based ratios.
(SO 4b, 5)

Instructions
(a) Prepare a statement of cash flows using the direct method.
(b) Compute these cash-basis measures:
   (1) Current cash debt coverage ratio
   (2) Cash return on sales ratio
   (3) Cash debt coverage ratio
   (4) Free cash flow

P13-7A Condensed financial data of Norway Company follow.

Prepare a statement of cash flows—indirect method.
(SO 4a)

NORWAY COMPANY
Comparative Balance Sheet
December 31

Assets	1998	1997
Cash	$ 96,700	$ 47,250
Accounts receivable	86,800	57,000
Inventories	121,900	102,650
Investments	84,500	87,000
Plant assets	250,000	205,000
Accumulated depreciation	(49,500)	(40,000)
Total	$590,400	$458,900
Liabilities and Stockholders' Equity		
Accounts payable	$ 52,700	$ 48,280
Accrued expenses payable	12,100	18,830
Bonds payable	100,000	70,000
Common stock	250,000	200,000
Retained earnings	175,600	121,790
Total	$590,400	$458,900

NORWAY COMPANY
Income Statement Data
For the Year Ended December 31, 1998

Sales		$297,500
Gain on sale of plant assets		8,750
		306,250
Less:		
Cost of goods sold	$99,460	
Operating expenses, excluding depreciation expense	14,670	
Depreciation expense	49,700	
Income taxes	7,270	
Interest expense	2,940	174,040
Net income		$132,210

Additional information:
1. New plant assets costing $92,000 were purchased for cash during the year.
2. Investments were sold at cost.
3. Plant assets costing $47,000 were sold for $15,550, resulting in a gain of $8,750.
4. A cash dividend of $78,400 was declared and paid during the year.

Instructions
Prepare a statement of cash flows using the indirect method.

Prepare a statement of cash flows—direct method.
(SO 4b)

P13-8A Data for Norway Company are presented in P13-7A. Further analysis reveals that accounts payable pertain to merchandise creditors.

Instructions
Prepare a statement of cash flows for Norway Company using the direct method.

Prepare a statement of cash flows—indirect method.
(SO 4a)

P13-9A Presented here is the comparative balance sheet for Cortina Company at December 31:

CORTINA COMPANY
Comparative Balance Sheet
December 31

Assets	1998	1997
Cash	$ 40,000	$ 57,000
Accounts receivable	77,000	64,000
Inventory	132,000	140,000
Prepaid expenses	12,140	16,540
Land	125,000	150,000
Equipment	200,000	175,000
Accumulated depreciation—equipment	(60,000)	(42,000)
Building	250,000	250,000
Accumulated depreciation—building	(75,000)	(50,000)
Total	$701,140	$760,540

Liabilities and Stockholders' Equity		
Accounts payable	$ 33,000	$ 45,000
Bonds payable	235,000	265,000
Common stock, $1 par	280,000	250,000
Retained earnings	153,140	200,540
Total	$701,140	$760,540

Additional information:
1. Operating expenses include depreciation expense $70,000 and charges from prepaid expenses of $4,400.
2. Land was sold for cash at cost.

3. Cash dividends of $74,290 were paid.
4. Net income for 1998 was $26,890.
5. Equipment was purchased for $65,000 cash. In addition, equipment costing $40,000 with a book value of $13,000 was sold for $14,000 cash.
6. Bonds were converted at face value by issuing 30,000 shares of $1 par value common stock.

Instructions
Prepare a statement of cash flows for 1998 using the indirect method.

BROADENING YOUR PERSPECTIVE

FINANCIAL REPORTING AND ANALYSIS

FINANCIAL REPORTING PROBLEM: *Starbucks Corporation*

Instructions

BYP13-1 Refer to the financial statements of Starbucks presented in Appendix A. Answer these questions:
(a) What was the amount of net cash provided by operating activities for the year ended September 29, 1996? For the year ended October 1, 1995? What were the primary causes of any significant changes in cash from operations between 1995 and 1996?
(b) What was the amount of increase or decrease in cash and cash equivalents for the year ended September 29, 1996? For the year ended October 1, 1995?
(c) Which method of computing net cash provided by operating activities does Starbucks use?
(d) From your analysis of the 1996 statement of cash flows, was the change in accounts and notes receivable a decrease or an increase? Was the change in inventories a decrease or an increase? Was the change in accounts payable a decrease or an increase?
(e) What was the total (net) cash used for investing activities for 1996?
(f) What was the amount of interest paid in 1996? What was the amount of income taxes paid in 1996?
(g) What significant noncash financing and investing activities did Starbucks complete in 1996?

COMPARATIVE ANALYSIS PROBLEM: *Starbucks vs. Green Mountain Coffee*

BYP13-2 The financial statements of Green Mountain Coffee are presented in Appendix B, following the financial statements for Starbucks in Appendix A.

Instructions
(a) Based on the information in these financial statements, compute these 1996 ratios for each company:
   (1) Current cash debt coverage
   (2) Cash return on sales
   (3) Cash debt coverage
(b) What conclusions concerning the management of cash can be drawn from these data?

RESEARCH CASE

BYP13-3 The March 25, 1996, issue of *Barron's* includes an article by Harry B. Ernst and Jeffrey D. Fotta entitled "Weary Bull."

Instructions
Read the article and answer these questions:
(a) The article describes a cash flow-based model used by investors. Identify the model and briefly describe its purpose.

(b) How does the model classify a firm's cash flows?
(c) Identify one way in which the cash flow classifications described in the article differ from those under GAAP.
(d) How can the model be used to predict stock prices?

INTERPRETING FINANCIAL STATEMENTS

BYP13-4 Minicase 1 *Mattel Corporation*

Mattel Corporation makes toys—some very famous toys. Among these are Barbie, Fisher-Price, Disney toys (such as Pocahontas), and Hot Wheels cars. In 1994 the company had a great year; in fact, at that point it was the best year in its history. A review of the company's balance sheet, however, reveals that the company's cash dropped from $506 million to $239 million. This drop of $267 million represented a 53% decrease in cash. The following additional information was also available from Mattel's financial statements:

	1994	1993
Cash	$ 237,002	$ 506,113
Marketable securities	20,581	17,468
Accounts receivable, net	762,024	580,313
Inventories	339,143	219,993
Prepaid expenses and other current assets	182,675	146,863
Total current assets	1,543,523	1,470,750
Total current liabilities	915,881	783,329
Cash provided (used) by operations	343,439	303,344
Cash provided (used) by investing	(526,497)	(88,804)
Cash provided (used) by financing	(86,053)	(16,369)

Instructions
(a) Discuss whether Mattel has suffered a significant reduction in its liquidity as a result of this decline in cash on hand. Use the current ratio and the current cash debt coverage ratio to support your position. [*Note:* Assume that current liabilities at December 31, 1992, were $529,389.]
(b) Using the data provided, explain why cash declined, and discuss whether this should be a concern to the company and its investors.

BYP13-5 Minicase 2 *Vermont Teddy Bear Co.*

Founded in the early 1980s, Vermont Teddy Bear Co. designs and manufactures American-made teddy bears and markets them primarily as gifts called Bear-Grams or Teddy Bear-Grams. Bear-Grams are personalized teddy bears delivered directly to the recipient for special occasions such as birthdays and anniversaries. The Shelburne, Vermont, company's primary markets are New York, Boston, and Chicago. Sales jumped dramatically in recent years, exceeding 50% increases for several consecutive years prior to 1994. Such dramatic growth has significant implications for cash flows. Here are the company's cash flow statements for 1993 and 1994:

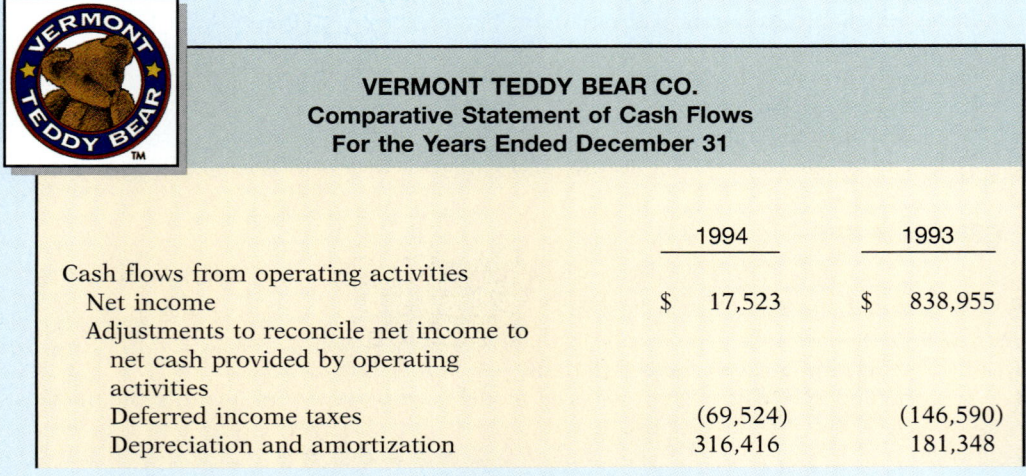

VERMONT TEDDY BEAR CO.
Comparative Statement of Cash Flows
For the Years Ended December 31

	1994	1993
Cash flows from operating activities		
Net income	$ 17,523	$ 838,955
Adjustments to reconcile net income to net cash provided by operating activities		
Deferred income taxes	(69,524)	(146,590)
Depreciation and amortization	316,416	181,348

Changes in assets and liabilities:		
Accounts receivable, trade	(38,267)	(25,947)
Inventories	(1,599,014)	(1,289,293)
Prepaid and other current assets	(444,794)	(113,205)
Deposit and other assets	(24,240)	(83,044)
Accounts payable	2,017,059	(284,567)
Accrued expenses	61,321	170,755
Accrued interest payable, debentures	—	(58,219)
Other	—	(8,960)
Income taxes payable	—	117,810
Net cash provided by (used for) operating activities	236,480	(700,957)
Net cash used for investing activities	(2,102,892)	(4,422,953)
Net cash provided by (used for) financing activities	(315,353)	9,685,435
Net change in cash and cash equivalents	($2,181,765)	$4,561,525
Other information		
Current liabilities	$ 4,055,465	$ 1,995,600
Total liabilities	4,620,085	2,184,386
Net sales	20,560,566	17,025,856

Instructions

(a) Note that net income in 1994 was only $17,523 compared to 1993 income of $838,955, but cash flow from operations was $236,480 in 1994 and a negative $700,957 in 1993. Explain the causes of this apparent paradox.

(b) Evaluate Vermont Teddy Bear's liquidity, solvency, and profitability for 1994 using cash flow-based ratios.

CRITICAL THINKING

MANAGEMENT DECISION CASE

BYP13-6 Greg Rhoda and Debra Sondgeroth are examining the following statement of cash flows for K.K. Bean Trading Company for the year ended January 31, 1998:

K.K. BEAN TRADING COMPANY
Statement of Cash Flows
For the Year Ended January 31, 1998

Sources of cash	
From sales of merchandise	$370,000
From sale of capital stock	420,000
From sale of investment (purchased below)	80,000
From depreciation	55,000
From issuance of note for truck	20,000
From interest on investments	6,000
Total sources of cash	951,000
Uses of cash	
For purchase of fixtures and equipment	340,000
For merchandise purchased for resale	258,000
For operating expenses (including depreciation)	160,000
For purchase of investment	75,000
For purchase of truck by issuance of note	20,000
For purchase of treasury stock	10,000
For interest on note payable	3,000
Total uses of cash	866,000
Net increase in cash	$ 85,000

Greg claims that K.K. Bean's statement of cash flows is an excellent portrayal of a superb first year with cash increasing $85,000. Debra replies that it was not a superb first year—but, rather, that the year was an operating failure, that the statement is presented incorrectly, and that $85,000 is not the actual increase in cash. The cash balance at the beginning of the year was $140,000.

Instructions
(a) With whom do you agree, Greg or Debra? Explain your position.
(b) Using the data provided, prepare a statement of cash flows in proper form using the indirect method. The only noncash items in the income statement are depreciation and the gain from the sale of the investment.

A REAL-WORLD FOCUS: *Praxair Incorporated*

BYP13-7 *Praxair Incorporated* was founded in 1907 as Linde-Air Products Company and was a pioneer in separating oxygen from air. It was purchased and run as a subsidiary of Union Carbide. In 1992 Praxair became an independent public company. Today the company is one of the top three largest suppliers of industrial gases worldwide. Praxair has operations in all regions of the world, with a majority of its sales occurring outside of the United States.

The following management discussion was included in Praxair's 1994 annual report:

PRAXAIR
Management Discussion and Analysis

Liquidity, Capital Resources, and Other Financial Data: In 1994 Praxair changed its presentation of the Statement of Cash Flows to the direct method to report major classes of cash receipts and payments from operations. Praxair believes the direct method more clearly presents its operating cash flows. Prior years' cash flow information has been reclassified to conform to the current year presentation.

Instructions
(a) What method has Praxair changed from?
(b) What will the newly prepared cash flow statement show that the former one did not?
(c) Will the cash flows from investing and financing appear any differently under the new method of preparation than they did under the old method?

GROUP ACTIVITY

BYP13-8 The class should be divided into groups of four or five.

Instructions
Discuss these questions: What would you expect to observe in the operating, investing, and financing sections of a statement of cash flows of:
(a) a severely financially troubled firm?
(b) a recently formed firm that is experiencing rapid growth?

COMMUNICATION ACTIVITY

BYP13-9 Arnold Byte, the owner-president of Computer Services Company, is unfamiliar with the statement of cash flows that you, as his accountant, prepared. He asks for further explanation.

Instructions
Write him a brief memo explaining the form and content of the statement of cash flows as shown in Illustration 13-12.

Ethics Case

BYP13-10 Puebla Corporation is a medium-sized wholesaler of automotive parts. It has ten stockholders who have been paid a total of $1 million in cash dividends for 8 consecutive years. The board of director's policy requires that in order for this dividend to be declared, net cash provided by operating activities as reported in Puebla's current year's statement of cash flows must exceed $1 million. President and CEO Phil Monat's job is secure so long as he produces annual operating cash flows to support the usual dividend.

At the end of the current year, controller Rick Rodgers presents president Monat with some disappointing news: The net cash provided by operating activities is calculated by the indirect method to be only $970,000. The president says to Rick, "We must get that amount above $1 million. Isn't there some way to increase operating cash flow by another $30,000?" Rick answers, "These figures were prepared by my assistant. I'll go back to my office and see what I can do." The president replies, "I know you won't let me down, Rick."

Upon close scrutiny of the statement of cash flows, Rick concludes that he can get the operating cash flows above $1 million by reclassifying a $60,000, 2-year note payable listed in the financing activities section as Proceeds from bank loan—$60,000." He will report the note instead as "Increase in payables—$60,000" and treat it as an adjustment of net income in the operating activities section. He returns to the president, saying, "You can tell the board to declare their usual dividend. Our net cash flow provided by operating activities is $1,030,000." "Good man, Rick! I knew I could count on you," exults the president.

Instructions
(a) Who are the stakeholders in this situation?
(b) Was there anything unethical about the president's actions? Was there anything unethical about the controller's actions?
(c) Are the board members or anyone else likely to discover the misclassification?

Financial Analysis on the Web

BYP13-11 *Purpose:* Locating SEC filing in Edgar Database.

Address: http://www.sec.gov/index.html

Steps:
1. From the SEC homepage, choose **Edgar Database.**
2. Choose **Search the Edgar Database.**
3. Choose **Current Event Analysis.**
4. Select a company from the Edgar Daily Report.

Instructions
Answer the following questions:
(a) What form type did you retrieve?
(b) What is the company's name?
(c) What is the Standard Industrial Classification?
(d) What period does this report cover?
(e) In what state or jurisdiction is the organization?

BYP13-12 *Purpose:* Use the Internet to view SEC filings.

Address: http://www.yahoo.com

Steps:
1. From the Yahoo homepage, choose **Stock Quotes.**
2. Enter stock symbol or use "Symbol Lookup."
3. Choose **Get Quotes.**
4. Choose **SEC filings** (this will take you to Yahoo-Edgar Online).

Instructions
Answer the following questions:
(a) What company did you select?
(b) What is its stock symbol?
(c) What other recent SEC filings are available for your viewing?
(d) Which filing is the most recent? What is the date?

Answers to Self-Study Questions
1. c 2. b 3. a 4. c 5. d 6. b 7. c 8. a 9. d
10. b 11. c 12. d 13. a 14. d 15. b

CHAPTER 14

Financial Analysis: The Big Picture

STUDY OBJECTIVES

After studying this chapter, you should be able to:

1. Understand the concept of earning power and indicate how irregular items are presented.
2. Discuss the need for comparative analysis and identify the tools of financial statement analysis.
3. Explain and apply horizontal analysis.
4. Describe and apply vertical analysis.
5. Identify and compute ratios and describe their purpose and use in analyzing a firm's liquidity, solvency, and profitability.
6. Discuss the limitations of financial statement analysis.

They Play the Market for Fun, Profit, and an Education

By day she's a trust officer at the local bank, but in her free time Betty Sinnock is the financial planner for the Beardstown Ladies—a 15-woman investment club whose success has earned it national attention and television time on "Donahue" and "20/20." The club entered the public spotlight after earning an average annual return of 23.4% on its investments during the last decade, a return many highly paid mutual fund managers did not come close to in the same period. The National Association of Investors Corporation has six times ranked the group near the top of the 11,000 investment clubs that it follows.

Do these women post a collection of impressive graduate degrees? No, this group, 12 of whom are past age 60, is largely self-educated in the ways of Wall Street. The secrets to their investment success are spelled out in a best-selling book, *The Beardstown Ladies Common-Sense Investment Guide*. A central theme of the book is this: "Women need to gain financial information—whether they be young, middle-aged, or old"; they must not "rely on others."

The group's stock-picking methodology combines sound fundamental analysis of financial data with a preference for innovative products and services. They rely heavily on information provided by the *Value Line Investment Survey* to determine whether a stock meets their criteria for safety, industry rank, and volatility. But they also look to the products they purchase themselves: If they think a new product shows promise, they analyze the company as a possible investment.

The fund's investments have made none of the women rich because each member contributes only $25 a month to the fund. But the women unanimously agree that participation in the club has been "fun" and has given them confidence in running their own personal financial affairs. As one member put it, she considers the monthly $25 as tuition toward her financial education.

On the World Wide Web
Beardstown Ladies:
http://www.outfitters.com/hnb/sinnock.html

647

PREVIEW OF CHAPTER 14

An important lesson can be learned from the Beardstown ladies: Experience is the best teacher. By now you have learned a significant amount about financial reporting by U.S. corporations. Using some of the basic decision tools presented in this book, you can perform a rudimentary analysis on any U.S. company and draw basic conclusions about its financial health. Although it would not be wise for you to bet your life savings on a company's stock relying solely on your current level of knowledge, we strongly encourage you to practice your new skills wherever possible. Only with practice will you improve your ability to interpret financial numbers.

Before unleashing you on the world of high finance, we will expose you to a few more important concepts and techniques, as well as provide you with one last comprehensive review of corporate financial statements. We use all of the decision tools presented in this text to analyze a single company—Kellogg Company, the world's leading producer of ready-to-eat cereal products.

The content and organization of this chapter are as follows:

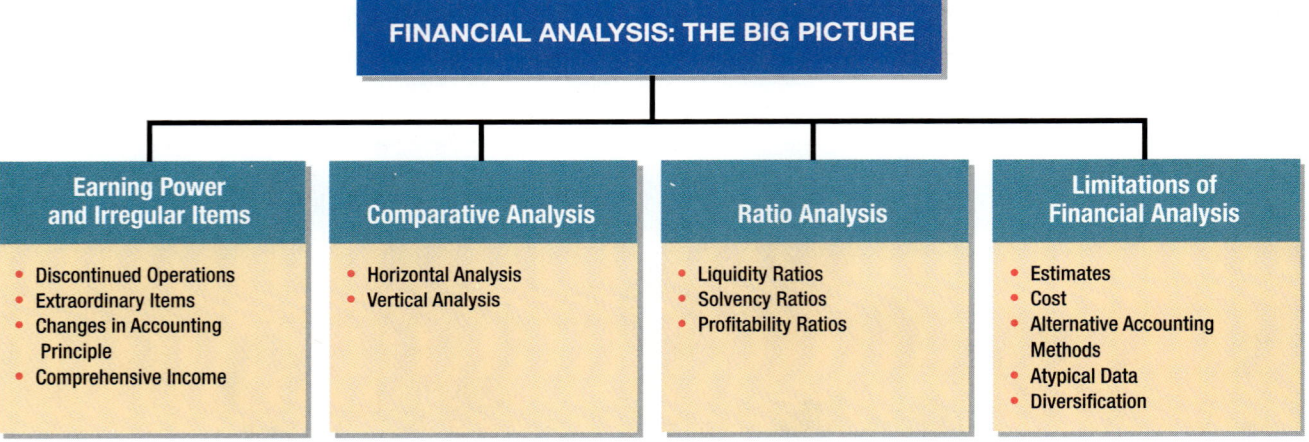

Earning Power and Irregular Items

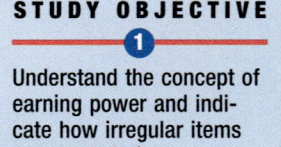

STUDY OBJECTIVE 1

Understand the concept of earning power and indicate how irregular items are presented.

Ultimately, the value of a company is a function of its future cash flows. When analysts use this year's net income to estimate future cash flows, they must make sure that this year's net income does not include irregular revenues, expenses, gains, or losses. Net income adjusted for irregular items is referred to as **earning power. Earning power is the most likely level of income to be obtained in the future—that is, to the extent this year's net income is a good predictor of future years' net income.** Earning power differs from actual net income by the amount of irregular revenues, expenses, gains, and losses included in this year's net income.

Users are interested in earning power because it helps them derive an estimate of future earnings without the "noise" of irregular items. For example, suppose Rye Corporation reports that this year's net income is $500,000 but included in that amount is a once-in-a-lifetime gain of $400,000. In estimating next year's net income for Rye Corporation, we would likely ignore this $400,000 gain and estimate that next year's net income will be in the neighborhood of $100,000.

Earning Power and Irregular Items **649**

That is, based on this year's results, the company's earning power is roughly $100,000. Therefore, identifying irregular items has important implications for using reported earnings as an input in estimating a company's value.

As an aid in the determination of earning power (or regular income), irregular items are identified by type on the income statement. Three types of irregular items are reported:

1. Discontinued operations
2. Extraordinary items
3. Changes in accounting principle

All these irregular items are reported net of income taxes; that is, the applicable income tax expense or tax savings is shown for income before income taxes and for each of the listed irregular items. The general concept is "Let the tax follow income or loss."

DISCONTINUED OPERATIONS

To downsize its operations, General Dynamics Corp. sold its missile business to Hughes Aircraft Co. for $450 million. In its income statement, General Dynamics was required to report the sale in a separate section entitled "Discontinued operations." **Discontinued operations** refer to the disposal of a significant segment of a business, such as the elimination of a major class of customers or an entire activity. Thus, the decision by Singer Co. to end its manufacture and sale of computers and the decision to close all overseas offices and terminate all foreign sales were both reported as discontinued operations. The phasing out of a model or part of a line of business, however, is *not* considered to be a disposal of a segment.

When the disposal of a significant segment occurs, the income statement should report both income from continuing operations and income (or loss) from discontinued operations. **The income (loss) from discontinued operations consists of the income (loss) from operations and the gain (loss) on disposal of the segment.** To illustrate, assume that Rozek Inc. has revenues of $2.5 million and expenses of $1.7 million from continuing operations in 1998. The company therefore has income before income taxes of $800,000. During 1998 the company discontinued and sold its unprofitable chemical division. The loss in 1998 from chemical operations (net of $60,000 taxes) was $140,000, and the loss on disposal of the chemical division (net of $30,000 taxes) was $70,000. Assuming a 30% tax rate on income before income taxes, we show the income statement presentation in Illustration 14-1.

Illustration 14-1 Statement presentation of discontinued operations

ROZEK INC.
Partial Income Statement
For the Year Ended December 31, 1998

Income before income taxes		$800,000
Income tax expense		240,000
Income from continuing operations		560,000
Discontinued operations		
Loss from operations of chemical division, net of $60,000 income tax saving	$140,000	
Loss from disposal of chemical division, net of $30,000 income tax saving	70,000	210,000
Net income		$350,000

Note that the caption "Income from continuing operations" is used and the section "Discontinued operations" is added. **Within the new section, both the operating loss and the loss on disposal are reported net of applicable income taxes.** This presentation clearly indicates the separate effects of continuing operations and discontinued operations on net income.

Besides being the world's leading cereal maker, Kellogg Company also manufactures toaster pastries, frozen waffles, cereal bars, and other convenience foods. Kellogg's products are manufactured in 20 countries on six continents and distributed in nearly 160 countries. In 1996 Kellogg did not report any discontinued operations.

DECISION TOOLKIT

Decision Checkpoints	Info Needed for Decision	Tool to Use for Decision	How to Evaluate Results
Has the company sold any major lines of business?	Discontinued operations section of income statement	Anything reported in this section indicates that the company has discontinued a major line of business.	If a major business line has been discontinued, its results in the current period should not be included in estimates of future net income.

EXTRAORDINARY ITEMS

Extraordinary items are events and transactions that meet two conditions: They are **unusual in nature** and **infrequent in occurrence.** To be considered *unusual*, the item should be abnormal and only incidentally related to the customary activities of the entity. To be regarded as *infrequent*, the event or transaction should not be reasonably expected to recur in the foreseeable future. Both criteria must be evaluated in terms of the environment in which the entity operates. Thus, Weyerhaeuser Co. reported the $36 million in damages to its timberland caused by the eruption of Mount St. Helens as an extraordinary item because the event was both unusual and infrequent. In contrast, Florida Citrus Company does not report frost damage to its citrus crop as an extraordinary item because frost damage is not viewed as infrequent. Illustration 14-2 shows the appropriate classification of extraordinary and ordinary items.

Helpful Hint Ordinary gains and losses are reported at pre-tax amounts in arriving at income before income taxes.

Extraordinary items are reported net of taxes in a separate section of the income statement immediately below discontinued operations. To illustrate, assume that in 1998 a revolutionary foreign government expropriated property held as an investment by Rozek Inc. If the loss is $70,000 before applicable income taxes of $21,000, the income statement presentation will show a deduction of $49,000, as in Illustration 14-3.

As illustrated, the caption "Income before extraordinary item" is added immediately before the listing of extraordinary items. This presentation clearly indicates the effect of the extraordinary item on net income. If there were no discontinued operations, the third line of the income statement in Illustration 14-3 would be "Income before extraordinary item."

If a transaction or event meets one, but not both, of the criteria for an extraordinary item, it should be reported in a separate line item in the upper half of the income statement, rather than being reported in the bottom half as an extraordinary item. Usually these items are reported under either "Other revenues and gains" or "Other expenses and losses" at their gross amount (not net of tax).

Earning Power and Irregular Items **651**

Extraordinary items

1. Effects of major casualties (acts of God), if rare in the area.

2. Expropriation (takeover) of property by a foreign government.

3. Effects of a newly enacted law or regulation, such as a condemnation action.

Ordinary items

1. Effects of major casualties (acts of God), frequent in the area.

2. Write-down of inventories or write-off of receivables.

3. Losses attributable to labor strikes.

4. Gains or losses from sales of property, plant, or equipment.

Illustration 14-2 Classification of extraordinary and ordinary items

This is true, for example, of gains (losses) resulting from the sale of property, plant, and equipment, as explained in Chapter 9.

Kellogg did not report any extraordinary items in its 1995 or 1996 income statements. It did, however, incur significant charges as the result of "restructuring" efforts to reduce costs. These restructuring charges did not meet the criteria required for extraordinary item classification. Instead, Kellogg reported them as "Nonrecurring charges"—of $421.8 million in 1995 and $136.1 million

Illustration 14-3 Statement presentation of extraordinary items

ROZEK INC.
Partial Income Statement
For the Year Ended December 31, 1998

Income before income taxes		$800,000
Income tax expense		240,000
Income from continuing operations		560,000
Discontinued operations		
Loss from operations of chemical division, net of $60,000 income tax saving	$140,000	
Loss from disposal of chemical division, net of $30,000 income tax saving	70,000	210,000
Income before extraordinary item		350,000
Extraordinary item		
Expropriation of investment, net of $21,000 income tax saving		**49,000**
Net income		$301,000

in 1996—in the upper half (income from operations section) of its income statement. The title "nonrecurring" suggests that the charges occur infrequently. In analyzing Kellogg's results, we must decide whether to use its income as reported, or instead to assume that these charges are, in fact, not representative of the company's future earning power. If we assume they are not representative of the company's earning power, we would add them back to net income (after consideration of their tax impact) to estimate next year's income. Since further investigation reveals that the company had similar "nonrecurring charges" in 1993, we have concluded that these charges are not as "infrequent" as the name "nonrecurring" might imply. Therefore, we use net income as it was reported by the company for all subsequent analysis.

DECISION TOOLKIT

Decision Checkpoints	Info Needed for Decision	Tool to Use for Decision	How to Evaluate Results
Has the company experienced any extraordinary events or transactions?	Extraordinary item section of income statement	Anything reported in this section indicates that the company experienced an event that was both unusual and infrequent.	These items should usually be ignored in estimating future net income.

BUSINESS INSIGHT
Management Perspective

In the recession of the early 1990s, many companies closed some of their plants and reduced the size of their work force. The costs incurred in these activities, called plant restructuring costs, are reported as Other Expenses and Losses in the income statement. These costs are not considered to be an extraordinary item because plant closings are neither unusual nor infrequent in many industries. Plant restructuring costs often have a significant effect on net income, as illustrated by the following cases:

Union Pacific Corp. $585 million after-tax charge, of which $492 million applies to the disposal of 7,100 miles of the Union Pacific Railroad.

Borden, Inc. $71.6 million before-tax charge for business reorganization costs as well as severance, relocation, and other employee-related expenses.

CHANGES IN ACCOUNTING PRINCIPLE

For ease of comparison, financial statements are expected to be prepared on a basis **consistent** with that used for the preceding period. That is, where a choice of accounting principles is available, the principle initially chosen should be applied consistently from period to period. A **change in accounting principle** occurs when the principle used in the current year is different from the one used in the preceding year. A change is permitted, when (1) management can show that the new principle is preferable to the old principle and (2) the effects of the change are clearly disclosed in the income statement. Two examples are a change in depreciation methods (such as declining-balance to straight-line) and a change in inventory costing methods (such as FIFO to average cost). The effect of a change in an accounting principle on net income can be significant. When U.S.

West, one of the six regional Bell telephone companies, changed the depreciation method for its telecommunications equipment, it posted a $3.2 billion loss (net of tax).

Sometimes a change in accounting principle is mandated by the Financial Accounting Standards Board (FASB). An example is the change in accounting for postretirement benefits other than pensions. In its income statement in the change period, Owens-Corning Fiberglas Corporation reported a charge of $227 million, net of income taxes of $117 million, under "Cumulative effect of accounting change." An accompanying note explained that the charge resulted from adopting the new standard for its domestic postretirement plans.

A change in an accounting principle affects reporting in two ways:

1. The new principle should be used in reporting the results of operations of the current year.
2. The cumulative effect of the change on all prior-year income statements should be disclosed net of applicable taxes in a special section immediately preceding Net Income.

To illustrate, we will assume that at the beginning of 1998, Rozek Inc. changes from the straight-line method to the declining-balance method for equipment purchased on January 1, 1995. The cumulative effect on prior-year income statements (statements for 1995–1997) is to increase depreciation expense and decrease income before income taxes by $24,000. If there is a 30% tax rate, the net-of-tax effect of the change is $16,800 ($24,000 × 70%). The income statement presentation is shown in Illustration 14-4.

Illustration 14-4 Statement presentation of a change in accounting principle

ROZEK INC.
Partial Income Statement
For the Year Ended December 31, 1998

Income before income taxes		$800,000
Income tax expense		240,000
Income from continuing operations		560,000
Discontinued operations		
Loss from operations of chemical division, net of $60,000 income tax saving	$140,000	
Loss from disposal of chemical division, net of $30,000 income tax saving	70,000	210,000
Income before extraordinary item and cumulative effect of change in accounting principle		350,000
Extraordinary item		
Expropriation of investment, net of $21,000 income tax saving		49,000
Cumulative effect of change in accounting principle		
Effect on prior years of change in depreciation method, net of $7,200 income tax saving		16,800
Net income		$284,200

The income statement for Rozek will also show depreciation expense for the current year. The amount is based on the new depreciation method. In this case the caption "Income before extraordinary item and cumulative effect of change in accounting principle" is inserted immediately following the section on discontinued operations. This presentation clearly indicates the cumulative effect of the change on prior years' income. If a company has neither discontinued operations nor extraordinary items, the caption "Income before cumulative effect of change in accounting principle" is used in place of "Income from continuing operations." A complete income statement showing all material items not typical of regular operations is presented in the Demonstration Problem on page 682.

Kellogg did not report any accounting changes in its 1996 financial statements. One of its primary competitors, The Quaker Oats Company, reported a net $4.1 million decrease in 1994 net income due to the adoption of a new FASB accounting standard regarding certain employee benefits. In analyzing a company, we normally suggest adding back any effect from a change in accounting principle (that is, using the amount of income before the change in accounting principle). So, for Quaker Oats, we would add back this $4.1 million to net income in evaluating its results. In this particular case, however, the $4.1 million is immaterial to Quaker Oats' financial statement because the company had net income of $189 million in 1994.

In summary, in evaluating a company, it generally makes sense to eliminate all irregular items in estimating future earning power. In some cases you must even decide whether certain information reported in the top half of the income statement should be ignored for analysis purposes, such as Kellogg's "nonrecurring" items.

DECISION TOOLKIT

Decision Checkpoints	Info Needed for Decision	Tool to Use for Decision	How to Evaluate Results
Has the company changed any of its accounting policies?	Cumulative effect of change in accounting principle section of income statement	Anything reported in this section indicates that the company has changed an accounting policy during the current year.	The cumulative effect should be ignored in estimating the future net income.

COMPREHENSIVE INCOME

Most revenues, expenses, gains, and losses recognized during the period are included in income. However, over time, specific exceptions to this general practice have developed so that certain items now bypass income and are reported directly in stockholders' equity. For example, in Chapter 12 you learned that unrealized gains and losses on available-for-sale securities are not included in income, but rather are reported in the balance sheet as adjustments to stockholders' equity.

Why are these gains and losses on available-for-sale securities excluded from net income? Because disclosing them separately (1) reduces the volatility of net income due to fluctuations in fair value, yet (2) informs the financial statement user of the gain or loss that would be incurred if the securities were sold at fair value.

Many analysts have expressed concern that the number of items that bypass the income statement has increased significantly. They feel that this has reduced the usefulness of the income statement. To address this concern, the FASB now requires that, in addition to reporting net income, a company must also report comprehensive income. **Comprehensive income** includes all changes in stockholders' equity during a period except those resulting from investments by stockholders and distributions to stockholders. A number of alternative formats for reporting comprehensive income are allowed. These formats are discussed in advanced accounting courses.

BEFORE YOU GO ON . . .

● **Review It**
1. What is earning power?
2. What are irregular items and what effect might they have on the estimation of future earnings and future cash flows?
3. What is comprehensive income?

COMPARATIVE ANALYSIS

Any item reported in a financial statement has significance: Its inclusion indicates that the item exists at a given time and in a certain quantity. For example, when Kellogg Company reports $243.8 million on its balance sheet as cash, we know that Kellogg did have cash and that the quantity was $243.8 million. But whether that represents an increase over prior years, or whether it is adequate in relation to the company's needs, cannot be determined from the amount alone. The amount must be compared with other financial data to provide more information.

Throughout this book we have relied on three types of comparisons to provide decision usefulness of financial information:

> **STUDY OBJECTIVE 2**
> Discuss the need for comparative analysis and identify the tools of financial statement analysis.

1. **Intracompany basis.** Comparisons within a company are often useful to detect changes in financial relationships and significant trends. For example, a comparison of Kellogg's current year's cash amount with the prior year's cash amount shows either an increase or a decrease. Likewise, a comparison of Kellogg's year-end cash amount with the amount of its total assets at year-end shows the proportion of total assets in the form of cash.

2. **Intercompany basis.** Comparisons with other companies provide insight into a company's competitive position. For example, Kellogg's total sales for the year can be compared with the total sales of its competitors in the breakfast cereal area, such as Quaker Oats and General Mills.

3. **Industry averages.** Comparisons with industry averages provide information about a company's relative position within the industry. For example, Kellogg's financial data can be compared with the averages for its industry compiled by financial ratings organizations such as Dun & Bradstreet, Moody's, and Standard & Poor's.

Three basic tools are used in financial statement analysis to highlight the significance of financial statement data:

1. Horizontal analysis
2. Vertical analysis
3. Ratio analysis

In previous chapters we relied primarily on ratio analysis, supplemented with some basic horizontal and vertical analysis. In the remainder of this section, we introduce some more formal forms of horizontal and vertical analysis. In the next section we review ratio analysis in some detail.

656 CHAPTER 14 Financial Analysis: The Big Picture

HORIZONTAL ANALYSIS

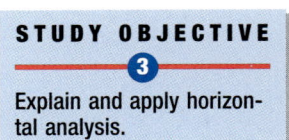

Horizontal analysis is a technique for evaluating a series of financial statement data over a period of time. Its purpose is to determine the increase or decrease that has taken place, expressed as either an amount or a percentage. For example, here are the recent net sales figures (in millions) of Kellogg Company:

1996	1995	1994	1993	1992
$6,676.6	$7,003.7	$6,562.0	$6,295.4	$6,190.6

Alternative Terminology Horizontal analysis is also often referred to as **trend analysis**.

If we assume that 1992 is the base year, we can measure all percentage increases or decreases from this base-period amount with the formula shown in Illustration 14-5.

Illustration 14-5
Horizontal analysis computation of changes since base period

$$\frac{\text{CURRENT-YEAR AMOUNT} - \text{BASE-YEAR AMOUNT}}{\text{BASE-YEAR AMOUNT}}$$

For example, we can determine that net sales for Kellogg Company increased approximately 1.7% [($6,295.4 − $6,190.6)/$6,190.6] from 1992 to 1993. Similarly, we can also determine that net sales increased by more than 7.8% [($6,676.6 − $6,190.6)/$6,190.6] from 1992 to 1996. The percentage of the base period for each of the 5 years, assuming 1992 as the base period, is shown in Illustration 14-6.

Illustration 14-6
Horizontal analysis of net sales

KELLOGG COMPANY
Net Sales (in millions)
Base Period 1992

1996	1995	1994	1993	1992
$6,676.6	$7,003.7	$6,562.0	$6,295.4	$6,190.6
107.9%	113.1%	106.0%	101.7%	100%

To further illustrate horizontal analysis, we use the financial statements of Kellogg Company. Its 2-year condensed balance sheets for 1995 and 1994 showing dollar and percentage changes are presented in Illustration 14-7.

The comparative balance sheet shows that a number of changes occurred in Kellogg's financial position from 1995 to 1996. In the assets section, current assets increased $99.8 million, or 7.0% ($99.8 ÷ $1,428.8), plant assets (net) increased $148.1, or 5.3%, and other assets increased 192.8% ($387.5 ÷ $201.0). This dramatic increase in other assets was due to trademarks, tradenames, and goodwill resulting from the purchase of the Lender's Bagels company. In the liabilities section, current liabilities increased $933.6, or 73.8%, while long-term liabilities increased $10.3, or .7%. In the stockholders' equity section, we find that retained earnings increased $214.9, or 5.7%. This suggests that the company expanded its asset base during 1996 and financed this expansion primarily by retaining income in the business and incurring short-term debt rather than assuming additional long-term debt. In addition, the company reduced its stockholders' equity 19.4% by buying treasury stock. Note that the value of treasury stock at the end of 1996 is actually more than double the value of total stock-

Illustration 14-7
Horizontal analysis of a balance sheet

KELLOGG COMPANY, INC.
Condensed Balance Sheets
December 31
(in millions)

	1996	1995	Increase (Decrease) during 1996 Amount	Percent
Assets				
Current assets	$1,528.6	$1,428.8	$ 99.8	7.0%
Plant assets (net)	2,932.9	2,784.8	148.1	5.3
Other assets	588.5	201.0	387.5	192.8
Total assets	$5,050.0	$4,414.6	$635.4	14.4%
Liabilities and Stockholders' Equity				
Current liabilities	$2,199.0	$1,265.4	$933.6	73.8%
Long-term liabilities	1,568.6	1,558.3	10.3	.7
Total liabilities	3,767.6	2,823.7	943.9	33.4
Stockholders' equity				
Common stock	201.8	183.0	18.8	10.3
Retained earnings and other	3,984.0	3,769.1	214.9	5.7
Treasury stock (cost)	(2,903.4)	(2,361.2)	542.2	23.0
Total stockholders' equity	1,282.4	1,590.9	(308.5)	(19.4)
Total liabilities and stockholders' equity	$5,050.0	$4,414.6	$635.4	14.4%

Helpful Hint It is difficult to comprehend the significance of a change when only the dollar amount of change is examined. When the change is expressed in percentage form, it is easier to grasp the true magnitude of the change.

holders' equity. This reflects the fact that Kellogg made major treasury stock repurchases over a number of years.

Presented in Illustration 14-8 is a 2-year comparative income statement of Kellogg Company for 1996 and 1995 in a condensed format.

Illustration 14-8
Horizontal analysis of an income statement

KELLOGG COMPANY, INC.
Condensed Income Statement
For the Years Ended December 31
(in millions)

	1996	1995	Increase (Decrease) during 1996 Amount	Percent
Net sales	$6,676.6	$7,003.7	($327.1)	(4.7%)
Cost of goods sold	3,122.9	3,177.7	(54.8)	(1.7)
Gross profit	3,553.7	3,826.0	(272.3)	(7.1)
Selling and administrative expenses	2,458.7	2,566.7	(108.0)	(4.2)
Nonrecurring charges	136.1	421.8	(285.7)	(67.7)
Income from operations	958.9	837.5	121.4	14.5
Interest expense	65.6	62.6	3.0	4.8
Other income (expense), net	(33.4)	21.1	(54.5)	na
Income before income taxes	859.9	796.0	63.9	8.0
Income tax expense	328.9	305.7	23.2	7.6
Net income	$ 531.0	$ 490.3	$ 40.7	8.3

Helpful Hint Note that, in a horizontal analysis, while the amount column is additive (the total is $40.7 million), the percentage column is not additive (8.3% is **not** a total).

Helpful Hint When using horizontal analysis, both dollar amount changes and percentage changes need to be examined. It is not necessarily bad if a company's earnings are growing at a declining rate. The **amount** of increase may be the same as or more than the base year, but the **percentage** change may be less because the base is greater each year.

Horizontal analysis of the income statements shows these changes:

Net sales decreased $327.1, or 4.7% ($327.1 ÷ $7,003.7).

Cost of goods sold increased $54.8, or 1.7% ($54.8 ÷ $3,177.7).

Selling and administrative expenses decreased $108.0, or 4.2% ($108.0 ÷ $2,566.7).

Overall, gross profit decreased 7.1% and net income increased 8.3%. The increase in net income can be attributed nearly entirely to the 67.7% decrease from 1995 to 1996 in the nonrecurring charges, which were due to restructuring of the company. Perhaps because of the restructuring done in 1995, some expenses, such as selling and administrative expenses, did decline during 1996. Sales also declined, however, leaving Kellogg's profit trend somewhat cloudy.

The measurement of changes from period to period in percentages is relatively straightforward and quite useful. However, complications can result in making the computations. If an item has no value in a base year or preceding year and a value in the next year, no percentage change can be computed. And if a negative amount appears in the base or preceding period and a positive amount exists the following year, or vice versa, no percentage change can be computed. For example, no percentage could be calculated for the "Other income (expense)" category in Kellogg's condensed income statement.

DECISION TOOLKIT

Decision Checkpoints	Info Needed for Decision	Tool to Use for Decision	How to Evaluate Results
How do the company's financial position and operating results compare with those of previous period?	Income statement and balance sheet	Comparative financial statements should be prepared over at least 2 years, with the first year reported being the base year. Changes in each line item relative to the base year should be presented both by amount and by percentage. This is called horizontal analysis.	Significant changes should be investigated to determine the reason for the change.

VERTICAL ANALYSIS

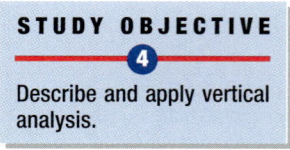

STUDY OBJECTIVE 4
Describe and apply vertical analysis.

Alternative Terminology Vertical analysis is sometimes referred to as **common-size analysis.**

Vertical analysis is a technique for evaluating financial statement data that expresses each item in a financial statement as a percent of a base amount. For example, on a balance sheet we might say that current assets are 22% of total assets (total assets being the base amount). Or on an income statement we might say that selling expenses are 16% of net sales (net sales being the base amount).

Presented in Illustration 14-9 is the comparative balance sheet of Kellogg for 1996 and 1995, analyzed vertically. The base for the asset items is **total assets**, and the base for the liability and stockholders' equity items is **total liabilities and stockholders' equity.**

In addition to showing the relative size of each category on the balance sheet, vertical analysis may show the percentage change in the individual asset, liability, and stockholders' equity items. In this case, even though current assets increased $99.8 million from 1995 to 1996, they decreased from 32.4% to 30.3% of total assets. Plant assets (net) decreased from 63.1% to 58.1% of total assets. Also, even though retained earnings increased by $214.9 million from 1995 to

Illustration 14-9
Vertical analysis of a balance sheet

KELLOGG COMPANY, INC.
Condensed Balance Sheet
December 31
(in millions)

	1996 Amount	1996 Percent	1995 Amount	1995 Percent
Assets				
Current assets	$1,528.6	30.3%	$1,428.8	32.4%
Plant assets (net)	2,932.9	58.0	2,784.8	63.0
Other assets	588.5	11.7	201.0	4.6
Total assets	$5,050.0	100.0%	$4,414.6	100.0%
Liabilities and Stockholders' Equity				
Current liabilities	$2,199.0	43.5%	$1,265.4	28.7%
Long-term liabilities	1,568.6	31.1	1,558.3	35.3
Total liabilities	3,767.6	74.6	2,823.7	64.0
Stockholders' equity				
Common stock	201.8	4.0	183.0	4.1
Retained earnings and other	3,984.0	78.9	3,769.1	85.4
Treasury stock (cost)	(2,903.4)	(57.5)	(2,361.2)	(53.5)
Total stockholders' equity	1,282.4	25.4	1,590.9	36.0
Total liabilities and stockholders' equity	$5,050.0	100.0%	$4,414.6	100.0%

1996, they decreased from 85.4% to 78.9% of total liabilities and stockholders' equity. This switch to a higher percentage of debt financing has two causes: First, current liabilities increased by $933.6 million, going from 28.7% to 43.5% of total liabilities and stockholders' equity. Second, treasury stock increased by $542.2 million, going from 53.5% to 57.5% of total liabilities and stockholders' equity. Thus, the company shifted toward a heavier reliance on debt financing both by using more short-term debt and by reducing the amount of outstanding equity.

Vertical analysis of the comparative income statements of Kellogg, shown in Illustration 14-10 on page 660, reveals that cost of goods sold **as a percentage of net sales** increased 1.4% (from 45.4% to 46.8%) and selling and administrative expenses increased .2% (from 36.6% to 36.8%). Despite these negative changes, net income as a percent of net sales increased from 7.0% to 8.0%. As shown in the horizontal analysis, Kellogg's improvement in net income relative to the prior year appears to be attributed nearly entirely to the decline in nonrecurring charges, which as a percentage of net sales declined by 4% (from 6.0% to 2.0%). As noted, because these nonrecurring charges are difficult to interpret, Kellogg's future income picture is difficult to project.

An associated benefit of vertical analysis is that it enables you to compare companies of different sizes. For example, one of Kellogg's main competitors is The Quaker Oats Company. Using vertical analysis, we can more meaningfully compare the condensed income statements of Kellogg and Quaker Oats, as shown in Illustration 14-11 (page 660).

Although Kellogg's net sales are 28% greater than the net sales of Quaker Oats, vertical analysis eliminates this difference. Kellogg's income from opera-

Illustration 14-10
Vertical analysis of an income statement

KELLOGG COMPANY, INC.
Condensed Income Statement
For the Years Ended December 31
(in millions)

	1996 Amount	1996 Percent	1995 Amount	1995 Percent
Net sales	$6,676.6	100.0%	$7,003.7	100.0%
Cost of goods sold	3,122.9	46.8	3,177.7	45.4
Gross profit	3,553.7	53.2	3,826.0	54.6
Selling and administrative expenses	2,458.7	36.8	2,566.7	36.6
Nonrecurring charges	136.1	2.0	421.8	6.0
Income from operations	958.9	14.4	837.5	12.0
Interest expense	65.6	1.0	62.6	.9
Other income (expense), net	(33.4)	.5	21.1	.3
Income before income taxes	859.9	12.9	796.0	11.4
Income tax expense	328.9	4.9	305.7	4.4
Net income	$ 531.0	8.0%	$ 490.3	7.0%

Illustration 14-11 Intercompany comparison by vertical analysis

CONDENSED INCOME STATEMENTS
For the Year Ended December 31, 1996
(in millions)

	Kellogg Company, Inc. Amount	Kellogg Company, Inc. Percent	The Quaker Oats Company Amount	The Quaker Oats Company Percent
Net sales	$6,676.6	100.0%	$5,199.0	100.0%
Cost of goods sold	3,122.9	46.8	2,807.5	54.0
Gross profit	3,553.7	53.2	2,391.5	46.0
Selling and administrative expenses	2,458.7	36.8	1,981.0	38.1
Nonrecurring (charges) gains	(136.1)	2.0	113.4	2.2
Income from operations	958.9	14.4	523.9	10.1
Other expenses and revenues (including income taxes)	427.9	6.4	276.0	5.3
Net income	$ 531.0	8.0%	$ 247.9	4.8%

tions as a percentage of net sales is 14.4%, compared to 10.1% for Quaker Oats. This difference can be attributed both to Kellogg's relative superiority in maintaining its gross profit margin (Kellogg's gross profit rate of 53.2% vs. Quaker Oats' rate of 46.0%) and to Kellogg's lower selling and administrative expense percentage (36.8% vs. 38.1%). In two areas Quaker Oats was better: Whereas Kellogg had nonrecurring losses, Quaker Oats reported nonrecurring gains, and Kellogg's other expenses were 6.4% of net sales compared to only 5.3% for Quaker Oats. However, given that neither of these items is usually very predictable over time, Kellogg's profitability picture appears more positive than that of Quaker Oats.

DECISION TOOLKIT

Decision Checkpoints	Info Needed for Decision	Tool to Use for Decision	How to Evaluate Results
How do the relationships between items in this year's financial statements compare with those of last year or those of competitors?	Income statement and balance sheet	Each line item on the income statement should be presented as a percentage of net sales, and each line item on the balance sheet should be presented as a percentage of total assets or total liabilities and stockholders' equity. These percentages should be investigated for differences either across years in the same company or in the same year across different companies. This is called vertical analysis.	Any differences either across years or between companies should be investigated to determine the cause.

BEFORE YOU GO ON...

● **Review It**

1. What different bases can be used to compare financial information?
2. What is horizontal analysis?
3. What is vertical analysis?

RATIO ANALYSIS

In previous chapters we presented many ratios used for evaluating the financial health and performance of a company. In this section we provide a comprehensive review of those ratios and discuss some important relationships among the ratios. Since earlier chapters demonstrated the calculation of each of these ratios, in this chapter we instead focus on their interpretation. Page references to prior discussions are provided if you feel you need to review any individual ratios.

For analysis of the primary financial statements, ratios can be classified into three types:

1. **Liquidity ratios:** measures of the short-term ability of the enterprise to pay its maturing obligations and to meet unexpected needs for cash
2. **Solvency ratios:** measures of the ability of the enterprise to survive over a long period of time
3. **Profitability ratios:** measures of the income or operating success of an enterprise for a given period of time

As a tool of analysis, ratios can provide clues to underlying conditions that may not be apparent from an inspection of the individual components of a particular ratio. But a single ratio by itself is not very meaningful. Accordingly, in this discussion we use the following comparisons:

1. **Intracompany comparisons** covering 2 years for Kellogg Company (using comparative financial information from Illustrations 14-9 and 14-10).
2. **Intercompany comparisons** using The Quaker Oats Company as one of Kellogg's principal competitors.

STUDY OBJECTIVE 5

Identify and compute ratios and describe their purpose and use in analyzing a firm's liquidity, solvency, and profitability.

662 CHAPTER 14 Financial Analysis: The Big Picture

3. **Industry average comparisons** based on Robert Morris Associates median ratios for manufacturers of flour and other grain mill products and comparisons with other sources. For some of the ratios that we use, industry comparisons are not available. (These are denoted "na.")

LIQUIDITY RATIOS

Liquidity ratios measure the short-term ability of the enterprise to pay its maturing obligations and to meet unexpected needs for cash. Short-term creditors such as bankers and suppliers are particularly interested in assessing liquidity. The measures that can be used to determine the enterprise's short-term debt-paying ability are the current ratio, the acid-test ratio, the current cash debt coverage ratio, the receivables turnover ratio, the average collection period, the inventory turnover ratio, and average days in inventory.

1. **Current ratio.** The current ratio expresses the relationship of current assets to current liabilities, computed by dividing current assets by current liabilities. It is widely used for evaluating a company's liquidity and short-term debt-paying ability. The 1996 and 1995 current ratios for Kellogg and comparative data are shown in Illustration 14-12.

Illustration 14-12
Current ratio

Ratio	Formula	Indicates:	Kellogg 1996	Kellogg 1995	Quaker Oats 1996	Industry 1996	Page in book
Current ratio	Current assets / Current liabilities	Short-term debt-paying ability	.70	1.13	.67	1.0	63

What do the measures actually mean? The 1996 ratio of .70 means that for every dollar of current liabilities, Kellogg has $.70 of current assets. We sometimes state such ratios as .70:1 to reinforce this interpretation. Kellogg's current ratio—and therefore its liquidity—decreased significantly in 1996. In 1995 it exceeded the industry average but in 1996 was well below the industry average, although it was approximately the same as Quaker Oats.

The current ratio is only one measure of liquidity. It does not take into account the composition of the current assets. For example, a satisfactory current ratio does not disclose that a portion of the current assets may be tied up in slow-moving inventory. A dollar of cash is more readily available to pay the bills than is a dollar's worth of slow-moving inventory. These weaknesses are addressed by the next ratio.

BUSINESS INSIGHT
Investor Perspective

The apparent simplicity of the current ratio can have real-world limitations because adding equal amounts to both the numerator and the denominator causes the ratio to decrease. Assume, for example, that a company has $2,000,000 of current assets and $1,000,000 of current liabilities; its current ratio is 2:1. If it purchases $1,000,000 of inventory on account, it will have $3,000,000 of current assets and $2,000,000 of current liabilities; its current ratio decreases to 1.5:1. If, instead, the company pays off $500,000 of its current liabilities, it will have $1,500,000 of current assets and $500,000 of current liabilities; its current ratio increases to 3:1. Thus, any trend analysis should be done with care because the ratio is susceptible to quick changes and is easily influenced by management.

2. **Acid-test ratio.** The **acid-test** or **quick ratio** is a measure of a company's immediate short-term liquidity. It is computed by dividing the sum of cash, marketable securities, and net receivables by current liabilities. Thus, it is an important complement to the current ratio. Note that it does not include inventory or prepaid expenses. Cash, marketable securities (short-term), and receivables (net) are highly liquid compared with inventory and prepaid expenses. The inventory may not be readily salable, and the prepaid expenses may not be transferable to others. The acid-test ratio for Kellogg is shown in Illustration 14-13.

Illustration 14-13
Acid-test ratio

Ratio	Formula	Indicates:	Kellogg 1996	Kellogg 1995	Quaker Oats 1996	Industry 1996	Page in book
Acid-test or quick ratio	$\text{Cash} + \dfrac{\text{Marketable securities} + \text{Net receivables}}{\text{Current liabilities}}$	Immediate short-term liquidity	.38	.64	.30	.40	445

The 1996 and 1995 acid-test ratios for Kellogg again suggest that its liquidity declined substantially during that time. Is Kellogg's 1996 acid-test ratio of .38:1 adequate? Like the current ratio, the acid-test ratio declined in 1996. However, when compared with the industry average of .40:1 and Quaker Oats' .30:1, Kellogg's acid-test ratio seems adequate.

3. **Current cash debt coverage ratio.** A disadvantage of the current and acid-test ratios is that they use year-end balances of current asset and current liability accounts. These year-end balances may not be representative of the company's current position during most of the year. A ratio that partially corrects for this problem is the ratio of net cash provided by operating activities to average current liabilities, called the **current cash debt coverage ratio.** Because it uses net cash provided by operating activities rather than a balance at one point in time, it may provide a better representation of liquidity. Kellogg's current cash debt coverage ratio is shown in Illustration 14-14.

Illustration 14-14
Current cash debt coverage ratio

Ratio	Formula	Indicates:	Kellogg 1996	Kellogg 1995	Quaker Oats 1996	Industry 1996	Page in book
Current cash debt coverage ratio	$\dfrac{\text{Cash provided by operations}}{\text{Average current liabilities}}$	Short-term debt-paying ability (cash basis)	.41	.85	.27	na	67

Like the previous measures of liquidity, this ratio decreased in 1996 for Kellogg. Is the coverage adequate? Probably so. Kellogg's operating cash flow coverage of average current liabilities is greater than Quaker Oats'. No industry comparison is available.

4. **Receivables turnover ratio.** Liquidity may be measured by how quickly certain assets can be converted to cash. Low values of the previous ratios can sometimes be compensated for if some of the company's current assets are highly liquid. How liquid, for example, are the receivables? The ratio

664 CHAPTER 14 Financial Analysis: The Big Picture

used to assess the liquidity of the receivables is the **receivables turnover ratio,** which measures the number of times, on average, receivables are collected during the period. The receivables turnover ratio is computed by dividing net credit sales (net sales less cash sales) by average net receivables during the year. The receivables turnover ratio for Kellogg is shown in Illustration 14-15.

Illustration 14-15
Receivables turnover ratio

Ratio	Formula	Indicates:	Kellogg 1996	Kellogg 1995	Quaker Oats 1996	Industry 1996	Page in book
Receivables turnover ratio	Net credit sales / Average net receivables	Liquidity of receivables	11.3	12.1	15.0	11.7	356

If we assume that all sales are credit sales, the receivables turnover ratio for Kellogg declined slightly in 1996. However, the turnover of 11.3 times compares favorably with the industry median of 11.7, even though it is well below that of 15.0 times for Quaker Oats.

BUSINESS INSIGHT
Investor Perspective

In some cases, the receivables turnover ratio may be misleading. Some companies, especially large retail chains, encourage credit and revolving charge sales, and they slow collections in order to earn a healthy return on the outstanding receivables in the form of interest at rates of 18% to 22%. In general, however, the faster the turnover, the greater the reliance that can be placed on the current and acid-test ratios for assessing liquidity.

5. **Average collection period.** A popular variant of the receivables turnover ratio converts it into an **average collection period** in days. This is done by dividing the receivables turnover ratio into 365 days. The average collection period for Kellogg is shown in Illustration 14-16.

Illustration 14-16
Average collection period

Ratio	Formula	Indicates:	Kellogg 1996	Kellogg 1995	Quaker Oats 1996	Industry 1996	Page in book
Average collection period	365 days / Receivables turnover ratio	Liquidity of receivables and collection success	32.3	30.2	24.3	31.2	357

Kellogg's 1996 receivables turnover of 11.3 times is divided into 365 days to obtain approximately 32.3 days. This means that the average collection period for receivables is 32 days, or approximately every four and one-half weeks. Analysts frequently use the average collection period to assess the effectiveness of a company's credit and collection policies. The general rule is that the collection period should not greatly exceed the credit term period (i.e., the time allowed for payment). It is interesting to note that Quaker Oats' average collection period is significantly shorter than those of Kellogg and the industry. This difference may be due to more aggressive collection practices, but it is more likely due to a difference in credit terms granted. Quaker Oats might grant more generous discounts for early payment than others in the industry.

6. **Inventory turnover ratio.** The **inventory turnover ratio** measures the number of times on average the inventory is sold during the period. Its purpose is to measure the liquidity of the inventory. The inventory turnover ratio is computed by dividing the cost of goods sold by the average inventory during the period. Unless seasonal factors are significant, average inventory can be computed from the beginning and ending inventory balances. Kellogg's inventory turnover ratio is shown in Illustration 14-17.

Illustration 14-17
Inventory turnover ratio

Ratio	Formula	Indicates:	Kellogg 1996	Kellogg 1995	Quaker Oats 1996	Industry 1996	Page in book
Inventory turnover ratio	Cost of goods sold / Average inventory	Liquidity of inventory	7.9	8.2	9.7	7.5	258

Kellogg's inventory turnover ratio declined slightly in 1996. The turnover ratio of 7.9 times is slightly higher than the industry average of 7.5 but significantly lower than Quaker Oats' 9.7. Generally, the faster the inventory turnover, the less cash is tied up in inventory and the less the chance of inventory becoming obsolete. Of course, a downside of high inventory turnover is that the company can run out of inventory when it is needed.

7. **Average days in inventory.** A variant of the inventory turnover ratio is the **average days in inventory,** which measures the average number of days it takes to sell the inventory. The average days in inventory for Kellogg is shown in Illustration 14-18.

Illustration 14-18
Average days in inventory

Ratio	Formula	Indicates:	Kellogg 1996	Kellogg 1995	Quaker Oats 1996	Industry 1996	Page in book
Average days in inventory	365 days / Inventory turnover ratio	Liquidity of inventory and inventory management	46.2	44.5	37.6	48.7	258

Kellogg's 1996 inventory turnover ratio of 7.9 divided into 365 is approximately 46.2 days. An average selling time of 46 days is roughly the same as the industry average but significantly higher than that of Quaker Oats. Some of this difference might be explained by differences in product lines across the two companies, although in many ways the types of products of these two companies are quite similar.

Inventory turnover ratios vary considerably among industries. For example, grocery store chains have a turnover of 10 times and an average selling period of 37 days. In contrast, jewelry stores have an average turnover of 1.3 times and an average selling period of 281 days. Within a company there may be significant differences in inventory turnover among different types of products. Thus, in a grocery store the turnover of perishable items such as produce, meats, and dairy products is faster than the turnover of soaps and detergents.

To conclude, all of these liquidity measures suggest that Kellogg's liquidity declined during 1996. However, its liquidity appears acceptable when compared both to that of Quaker Oats and to the industry as a whole.

SOLVENCY RATIOS

Solvency ratios measure the ability of the enterprise to survive over a long period of time. Long-term creditors and stockholders are interested in a company's long-run solvency, particularly its ability to pay interest as it comes due and to repay the face value of the debt at maturity. The debt to total assets ratio, the times interest earned ratio, and the cash debt coverage ratio provide information about debt-paying ability. In addition, free cash flow provides information about the company's solvency and its ability to pay additional dividends or invest in new projects.

8. **Debt to total assets ratio.** The **debt to total assets ratio** measures the percentage of the total assets provided by creditors. It is computed by dividing total debt (both current and long-term liabilities) by total assets. This ratio indicates the degree of leveraging; it provides some indication of the company's ability to withstand losses without impairing the interests of its creditors. The higher the percentage of debt to total assets, the greater the risk that the company may be unable to meet its maturing obligations. The lower the ratio, the more equity "buffer" is available to creditors if the company becomes insolvent. Thus, from the creditors' point of view, a low ratio of debt to total assets is usually desirable. Kellogg's debt to total assets ratio is shown in Illustration 14-19.

Illustration 14-19 Debt to total assets ratio

Ratio	Formula	Indicates:	Kellogg 1996	Kellogg 1995	Quaker Oats 1996	Industry 1996	Page in book
Debt to total assets ratio	Total debt / Total assets	Percentage of total assets provided by creditors	.75	.64	.72	.68	64

Kellogg's 1996 ratio of .75 means that creditors have provided financing sufficient to cover 75% of the company's total assets. Alternatively, it says that Kellogg would have to liquidate 75% of its assets at their book value in order to pay off all of its debts. Kellogg's 75% is above the industry average of 68% and also above the 72% ratio of Quaker Oats. Kellogg's solvency declined considerably during the year. In that time, Kellogg's use of debt financing changed in two ways: First, Kellogg significantly increased its use of short-term debt, and second, it repurchased a considerable amount of its own stock. Both these factors reduced its solvency.

The adequacy of this ratio is often judged in light of the company's earnings. Generally, companies with relatively stable earnings, such as public utilities, have higher debt to total assets ratios than cyclical companies with widely fluctuating earnings, such as many high-tech companies.

Another ratio with a similar meaning is the **debt to equity ratio.** It shows the relative use of borrowed funds (total liabilities) compared with resources invested by the owners. Because this ratio can be computed in several ways, care should be taken when making comparisons. Debt may be defined to include only the noncurrent portion of liabilities, and intangible assets may be excluded from stockholders' equity (which would equal tangible net worth). If debt and assets are defined as above (all liabilities and all assets), then when the debt to total assets ratio equals 50%, the debt to equity ratio is 1:1.

9. **Times interest earned ratio.** The **times interest earned ratio** (also called interest coverage) indicates the company's ability to meet interest payments as they come due. It is computed by dividing income before interest expense and income taxes by interest expense. Note that this ratio uses income before interest expense and income taxes because this amount represents what is available to cover interest. Kellogg's times interest earned ratio is shown in Illustration 14-20.

Illustration 14-20 Times interest earned ratio

Ratio	Formula	Indicates:	Kellogg 1996	Kellogg 1995	Quaker Oats 1996	Industry 1996	Page in book
Times interest earned ratio	Income before interest expense and income taxes / Interest expense	Ability to meet interest payments as they come due	14.1	13.7	4.9	2.8	461

For Kellogg the 1996 coverage was 14.1, which indicates that income before interest and taxes was 14.1 times the amount needed for interest expense. This was nearly three times the rate for Quaker Oats and five times the average rate for the industry. Thus, although the debt to assets ratio suggests that Kellogg relies heavily on debt financing, the times interest earned ratio suggests that the company can easily service its debt.

10. **Cash debt coverage ratio.** The ratio of net cash provided by operating activities to average total liabilities, called the **cash debt coverage ratio,** is a cash-basis measure of solvency. This ratio indicates a company's ability to repay its liabilities from cash generated from operating activities without having to liquidate the assets used in its operations. Illustration 14-21 shows Kellogg's cash debt coverage ratio.

Illustration 14-21 Cash debt coverage ratio

Ratio	Formula	Indicates:	Kellogg 1996	Kellogg 1995	Quaker Oats 1996	Industry 1996	Page in book
Cash debt coverage ratio	Cash provided by operations / Average total liabilities	Long-term debt-paying ability (cash basis)	.22	.37	.12	na	67

An industry average for this measure is not available, but Kellogg's .22 exceeded Quaker Oats' .12, although Kellogg's ratio did decline from .37 in 1995. One way of interpreting this ratio is to say that net cash generated from 1 year of operations would be sufficient to pay off 22% of Kellogg's total liabilities. If 22% of this year's liabilities were retired each year, it would take nearly 5 years to retire all of its debt, whereas it would take Quaker Oats more than 8 years to do so.

11. **Free cash flow.** One indication of a company's solvency, as well as of its ability to pay dividends or expand operations, is the amount of excess cash it generated after investing to maintain its current productive capacity and paying dividends. This amount is referred to as **free cash flow.** For example, if you generate $100,000 of cash from operations but you spend

668 CHAPTER 14 Financial Analysis: The Big Picture

$30,000 to maintain and replace your productive facilities at their current levels and pay $10,000 in dividends, you have $60,000 to use either to expand operations or to pay additional dividends.

As a practical matter, companies do not disclose what percentage of their capital expenditures were made to maintain existing production and what percentage were made to expand operations. Thus, external users normally calculate free cash flow by simply subtracting expenditures made for property, plant, and equipment (fixed assets) from cash from operations. Kellogg's free cash flow is shown in Illustration 14-22.

Illustration 14-22
Free cash flow

Ratio	Formula	Indicates:	Kellogg 1996	Kellogg 1995	Quaker Oats 1996	Industry 1996	Page in book
Free cash flow	Cash provided by operations − Capital expenditures − Dividends paid	Cash available for paying dividends or expanding operations	$60.5 (in millions)	$396.8	$10.7 (in millions)	na	311

Although Kellogg's free cash flow declined considerably from 1995 to 1996, even its 1996 amount of $60.5 million is significantly greater than Quaker Oats' $10.7 million. Kellogg has chosen to use a large portion of its free cash flow each year to repurchase its own stock.

PROFITABILITY RATIOS

Profitability ratios measure the income or operating success of an enterprise for a given period of time. A company's income, or the lack of it, affects its ability to obtain debt and equity financing, its liquidity position, and its ability to grow. As a consequence, creditors and investors alike are interested in evaluating profitability. Profitability is frequently used as the ultimate test of management's operating effectiveness. Some commonly used measures of profitability are discussed in the following pages.

Throughout this book we have introduced numerous measures of profitability. The relationships among these measures are very important. Understanding them can help management determine where to focus its efforts to improve a company's profitability. Illustration 14-23 diagrams these relationships. Our discussion of Kellogg's profitability is structured around this diagram.

Illustration 14-23
Relationships among profitability measures

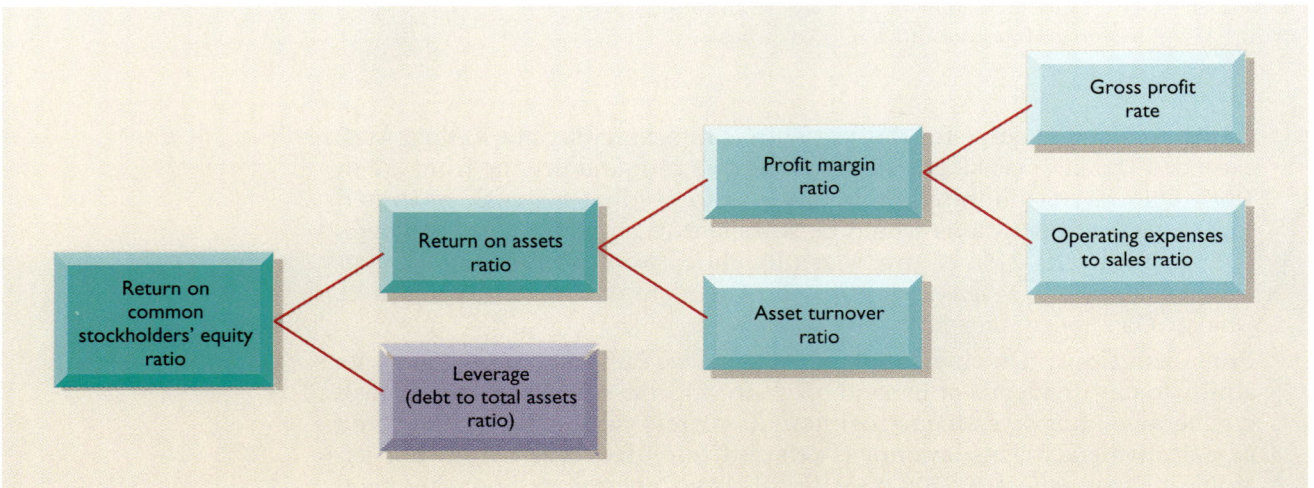

12. **Return on common stockholders' equity ratio.** A widely used measure of profitability from the common stockholder's viewpoint is the **return on common stockholders' equity ratio.** This ratio shows how many dollars of net income were earned for each dollar invested by the owners. It is computed by dividing net income minus any preferred stock dividends—that is, income available to common stockholders—by average common stockholders' equity. The return on common stockholders' equity for Kellogg is shown in Illustration 14-24.

Illustration 14-24
Return on common stockholders' equity ratio

Ratio	Formula	Indicates:	Kellogg 1996	Kellogg 1995	Quaker Oats 1996	Industry 1996	Page in book
Return on common stockholders' equity ratio	Income available to common stockholders / Average common stockholders' equity	Profitability of common stockholders' investment	.37	.29	.21	.19	514

Kellogg's 1996 rate of return on common stockholders' equity is unusually high at 37%, considering an industry average of 19% and a rate of 21% for Quaker Oats.

13. **Return on assets ratio.** The return on common stockholders' equity ratio is affected by two factors: the **return on assets ratio** and the degree of leverage. The return on assets ratio measures the overall profitability of assets in terms of the rate earned on each dollar invested in assets. It is computed by dividing net income by average total assets. Kellogg's return on assets ratio is shown in Illustration 14-25.

Illustration 14-25
Return on assets ratio

Ratio	Formula	Indicates:	Kellogg 1996	Kellogg 1995	Quaker Oats 1996	Industry 1996	Page in book
Return on assets ratio	Net income / Average total assets	Overall profitability of assets	.11	.11	.055	.14	56

Kellogg had an 11% return on assets in both 1996 and 1995. Although this rate is nearly double that of Quaker Oats, it is below the industry average.

Note that Kellogg's rate of return on stockholders' equity (37%) is substantially higher than its rate of return on assets (11%). The reason is that Kellogg has made effective use of **leverage.** **Leveraging** or **trading on the equity** at a gain means that the company has borrowed money by issuing bonds or notes at a lower rate of interest than it is able to earn by using the borrowed money. Leverage is simply trying to use money supplied by nonowners to increase the return to owners. A comparison of the rate of return on assets with the rate of interest paid for borrowed money indicates the profitability of trading on the equity. If you borrow money at 8% and your rate of return on assets is 11%, you are trading on the equity at a gain. Note, however, that trading on the equity is a two-way street; for example, if you borrow money at 11% and earn only 8% on it, you are trading on the equity at a loss. Kellogg earns more on its borrowed funds than it has to pay in interest. The notes to Kellogg's financial statements disclose that it pays interest rates of between 5% and 8% on outstanding debts, yet, as noted above, it earns 11% on each dollar invested in assets. Thus, the return to stockholders exceeds the return on the assets because of the positive benefit of leverage. Recall from our earlier discussion that Kellogg's percentage of debt financing as measured by the ratio of debt to total assets (or debt to equity) increased substantially in 1996. It appears that Kellogg's dramatic increase in return on stockholders' equity was largely a function of increased leverage.

14. **Profit margin ratio.** The return on assets ratio is affected by two factors, the first of which is the profit margin ratio. The **profit margin ratio,** or rate of return on sales, is a measure of the percentage of each dollar of sales that results in net income. It is computed by dividing net income by net sales for the period. Kellogg's profit margin ratio is shown in Illustration 14-26.

Illustration 14-26 Profit margin ratio

Ratio	Formula	Indicates:	Kellogg 1996	Kellogg 1995	Quaker Oats 1996	Industry 1996	Page in book
Profit margin ratio	Net income / Net sales	Net income generated by each dollar of sales	.08	.07	.05	.04	56

Kellogg experienced an increase in its profit margin ratio from 1995 to 1996 of 7% to 8%. Its profit margin ratio is high in comparison with the industry average of 4% and Quaker Oats' 5%.

High-volume (high inventory turnover) enterprises such as grocery stores and pharmacy chains generally experience low profit margins, whereas low-volume enterprises such as jewelry stores and airplane manufacturers have high profit margins.

15. **Asset turnover ratio.** The other factor that affects the return on assets ratio is the asset turnover ratio. The **asset turnover ratio** measures how efficiently a company uses its assets to generate sales. It is determined by dividing net sales by average total assets for the period. The resulting number shows the dollar of sales produced by each dollar invested in assets. Illustration 14-27 shows the asset turnover ratio for Kellogg.

Illustration 14-27 Asset turnover ratio

Ratio	Formula	Indicates:	Kellogg 1996	Kellogg 1995	Quaker Oats 1996	Industry 1996	Page in book
Asset turnover ratio	Net sales / Average total assets	How efficiently assets are used to generate sales	1.41	1.58	1.15	1.5	405

The asset turnover ratio shows that Kellogg generated sales of $1.41 in 1996 for each dollar it had invested in assets. The ratio declined a bit from 1995 to 1996. Kellogg's asset turnover ratio is slightly below the industry average of 1.5 times but above Quaker Oats' ratio of 1.15.

Asset turnover ratios vary considerably among industries. For example, a large utility company like Union Electric Company (St. Louis) has a ratio of .36, whereas the large grocery chain Great Atlantic and Pacific Tea (A&P) has a ratio of 3.6.

In summary, Kellogg's return on assets ratio remained unchanged from 1995 to 1996 at 11%. However, underlying this apparent stability was an increased profitability on each dollar of sales, as measured by the profit margin ratio, but a decline in the sales-generating efficiency of its assets, as measured by the asset turnover ratio. The combined effects of profit margin and asset turnover on return on assets for Kellogg can be analyzed as shown in Illustration 14-28.

Illustration 14-28
Composition of return on assets ratio

RATIOS:	PROFIT MARGIN $\frac{\text{NET INCOME}}{\text{NET SALES}}$	×	ASSET TURNOVER $\frac{\text{NET SALES}}{\text{AVERAGE TOTAL ASSETS}}$	=	RETURN ON ASSETS $\frac{\text{NET INCOME}}{\text{AVERAGE TOTAL ASSETS}}$
Kellogg					
1996	8%	×	1.41 times	=	11%
1995	7%	×	1.58 times	=	11%

16. **Gross profit rate.** Two factors strongly influence the profit margin ratio. One is the gross profit rate. The **gross profit rate** is determined by dividing gross profit (net sales less cost of goods sold) by net sales. This rate indicates a company's ability to maintain an adequate selling price above its costs. As an industry becomes more competitive, this ratio declines. For example, in the early years of the personal computer industry, gross profit rates were quite high. Today, because of dramatically increased competition and a belief that most brands of personal computers are similar in quality, gross profit rates have become relatively thin. Gross profit rates should be closely monitored over time. Illustration 14-29 shows Kellogg's gross profit rate.

Illustration 14-29
Gross profit rate

Ratio	Formula	Indicates:	Kellogg 1996	Kellogg 1995	Quaker Oats 1996	Industry 1996	Page in book
Gross profit rate	Gross profit / Net sales	Margin between selling price and cost of goods sold	.53	.55	.46	na	213

Kellogg's gross profit rate declined somewhat from 1995 to 1996 in the face of cuts in the selling price of cereal by many of its competitors. Discussion in the financial press noted that Kellogg was somewhat slow to respond to these price cuts but eventually also dropped its prices.

Much can be learned about the reasons for Kellogg's reduced profitability by reading its annual report. Consider the excerpt in Illustration 14-30 (at the top of the next page).

17. **Operating expenses to sales ratio.** This is the other factor that directly affects the profit margin ratio. Management can influence a company's profitability by maintaining adequate prices, cutting expenses, or both. The **operating expenses to sales ratio** measures the costs incurred to support each dollar of sales. It is computed by dividing operating expenses (selling

672 CHAPTER 14 Financial Analysis: The Big Picture

Illustration 14-30
Kellogg's management discussion and analysis

KELLOGG COMPANY, INC.
Management Discussion and Analysis

The Company's 1996 results were negatively impacted by competitive conditions in the U.S. ready-to-eat cereal market, in which significant price reductions were undertaken by all major competitors during the year. In an effort to improve the brand value proposition to the consumer, the Company implemented several pricing actions in 1996, most notably reductions announced June 10, 1996, averaging 19% on brands comprising approximately two-thirds of its U.S. cereal business. . . . Despite the negative impact on profitability in the short term, management believes these pricing actions are a necessary part of a long-term strategy initiated in early 1994 to improve the Company's pricing and cost structure.

Illustration 14-31
Operating expenses to sales ratio

and administrative expenses) by net sales. The operating expenses to sales ratio for Kellogg is shown in Illustration 14-31.

Ratio	Formula	Indicates:	Kellogg 1996	Kellogg 1995	Quaker Oats 1996	Industry 1996	Page in book
Operating expenses to sales ratio	Operating expenses / Net sales	The costs incurred to support each dollar of sales	.37	.37	.38	na	215

During 1995 and 1996 the financial press frequently carried stories about the cereal industry's efforts to "restructure" operations and cut expenses. Kellogg's ratio remained a constant 37% during this 2-year period. This lack of change might be explained by a couple of factors. First, it may be that the company was already cutting costs prior to 1995 and thus the ratio already reflected costs savings. Or the benefits of the restructuring efforts may not have kicked in by 1996. Of course, a third explanation exists: If you review Illustration 14-8 you will notice that Kellogg's selling and administrative expenses did decline from 1995 to 1996. However, so did its sales, leaving the ratio of operating expenses to sales roughly unchanged.

18. **Cash return on sales ratio.** The profit margin ratio discussed earlier is an accrual-based ratio using net income as a numerator. The cash-basis counterpart to that ratio is the **cash return on sales ratio,** which uses net cash provided by operating activities as the numerator and net sales as the denominator. The difference between these two ratios should be explainable as differences between accrual accounting and cash-basis accounting, such as differences in the timing of revenue and expense recognition. The cash return on sales ratio for Kellogg is shown in Illustration 14-32.

Illustration 14-32 Cash return on sales ratio

Ratio	Formula	Indicates:	Kellogg 1996	Kellogg 1995	Quaker Oats 1996	Industry 1996	Page in book
Cash return on sales ratio	Net cash provided by operations / Net sales	Net cash flow generated by each dollar of sales	.11	.15	.08	na	617

19. **Earnings per share (EPS).** Stockholders usually think in terms of the number of shares they own or plan to buy or sell. Expressing net income earned on a per share basis provides a useful perspective for determining profitability. **Earnings per share** is a measure of the net income earned on each share of common stock. It is computed by dividing net income by the number of weighted average common shares outstanding during the year. When we use "net income per share" or "earnings per share," it refers to the amount of net income applicable to each share of *common stock*. Therefore, when we compute earnings per share, if there are preferred dividends declared for the period, they must be deducted from net income to arrive at income available to the common stockholders. Kellogg's earnings per share is shown in Illustration 14-33.

Illustration 14-33
Earnings per share

Ratio	Formula	Indicates:	Kellogg 1996	Kellogg 1995	Quaker Oats 1996	Industry 1996	Page in book
Earnings per share (EPS)	Income available to common stockholders / Average number of outstanding common shares	Net income earned on each share of common stock	$2.42	$2.24	$1.80	na	513

Note that no industry average is presented in Illustration 14-33. Industry data for earnings per share are not reported, and in fact the Kellogg and Quaker Oats ratios should not be compared. Such comparisons are not meaningful because of the wide variations in the number of shares of outstanding stock among companies. Kellogg's earnings per share increased 18 cents per share in 1996. This represents an 8% increase over the 1995 EPS of $2.24.

20. **Price-earnings ratio.** The **price-earnings ratio** is an oft-quoted statistic that measures the ratio of the market price of each share of common stock to the earnings per share. The price-earnings (P-E) ratio is a reflection of investors' assessments of a company's future earnings. It is computed by dividing the market price per share of the stock by earnings per share. Kellogg's price-earnings ratio is shown in Illustration 14-34.

Illustration 14-34
Price-earnings ratio

Ratio	Formula	Indicates:	Kellogg 1996	Kellogg 1995	Quaker Oats 1996	Industry 1996	Page in book
Price-earnings ratio	Stock price / Earnings per share	Relationship between market price per share and earnings per share	27	34	19	19	513

At the end of 1996 and 1995 the market price of Kellogg's stock was 65\frac{5}{8}$ and 77\frac{2}{8}$, respectively. Quaker Oats' stock was selling for 33\frac{7}{8}$ at the end of 1996.

In 1996 each share of Kellogg's stock sold for 27 times the amount that was earned on each share. Kellogg's price-earnings ratio is higher than the industry average of 19 times but significantly lower than its previous year's ratio of 34. Quaker Oats' ratio of 19 is the same as the industry average.

674 CHAPTER 14 Financial Analysis: The Big Picture

These higher P-E ratios suggest that the market is more optimistic about Kellogg and Quaker Oats than about the other companies in the industry. However, it might also signal that their stock is overpriced. The average price-earnings ratio for the stocks that constitute the Standard and Poor's Composite 1,500 Company Index in November 1997 was an unusually high 21 times.

21. **Payout ratio.** The payout ratio measures the percentage of earnings distributed in the form of cash dividends. It is computed by dividing cash dividends paid on common stock by net income. Companies that have high growth rates are characterized by low payout ratios because they reinvest most of their net income in the business. The payout ratio for Kellogg is shown in Illustration 14-35.

Illustration 14-35
Payout ratio

Ratio	Formula	Indicates:	Kellogg 1996	Kellogg 1995	Quaker Oats 1996	Industry 1996	Page in book
Payout ratio	Cash dividends / Net income	Percentage of earnings distributed in the form of cash dividends	.65	.67	.63	.38	511

The 1996 and 1995 payout ratios for Kellogg are comparatively high when compared with the industry average of .38 but are approximately the same as that of Quaker Oats.

Management has some control over the amount of dividends paid each year, and companies are generally reluctant to reduce a dividend below the amount paid in a previous year. Therefore, the payout ratio will actually increase if a company's net income declines but the company keeps its total dividend payment the same. Of course, unless the company returns to its previous level of profitability, maintaining this higher dividend payout ratio is probably not possible over the long run. Before drawing any conclusions regarding Kellogg's dividend payout ratio, we should calculate this ratio over a longer period of time to evaluate any trends, and also try to find out whether management's philosophy regarding dividends has changed recently. The "selected financial data" section of Kellogg's Management Discussion and Analysis shows that over a 10-year period earnings per share have grown 7% per year, while dividends per share have grown 12% per year. Unless earnings growth improves, this rapid dividend growth is probably not sustainable over the long term.

BUSINESS INSIGHT
Management Perspective

Generally, companies with stable earnings have high payout ratios. For example, a utility such as Potomac Electric Company had an 86% payout ratio over a recent 5-year period, and Amoco Corporation had a 63% payout ratio over the same period. Conversely, companies that are expanding rapidly, such as Toys 'R' Us and Microsoft, have never paid a cash dividend.

In terms of the types of financial information available and the ratios used by various industries, what can be practically covered in this textbook gives you only the "Titanic approach": You are seeing only the tip of the iceberg compared to the vast databases and types of ratio analysis that are available on computers. The availability of information is not a problem. The real trick is to be discriminating enough to perform relevant analysis and select pertinent comparative data.

BEFORE YOU GO ON . . .

● **Review It**

1. What are liquidity ratios? Explain the current ratio, acid-test ratio, receivables turnover ratio, inventory turnover ratio, and current cash debt coverage ratio.
2. What are solvency ratios? Explain the debt to total assets ratio, the times interest earned ratio, and the cash debt coverage ratio.
3. What are profitability ratios? Explain the return on common stockholders' equity ratio, return on assets ratio, asset turnover ratio, cash return on sales, earnings per share, price-earnings ratio, and payout ratio.

LIMITATIONS OF FINANCIAL ANALYSIS

Significant business decisions are frequently made using one or more of the three analytical tools presented in this chapter: horizontal, vertical, and ratio analysis. You should be aware of some of the limitations of these tools and of the financial statements on which they are based.

STUDY OBJECTIVE 6
Discuss the limitations of financial statement analysis.

ESTIMATES

Financial statements contain numerous estimates. Estimates are used, for example, in determining the allowance for uncollectible receivables, periodic depreciation, the costs of warranties, and contingent losses. To the extent that these estimates are inaccurate, the financial ratios and percentages are also inaccurate.

COST

Traditional financial statements are based on cost and are not adjusted for price-level changes. Comparisons of unadjusted financial data from different periods may be rendered invalid by significant inflation or deflation. For example, a 5-year comparison of Kellogg's revenues shows a growth of 8%. But if, for example, the general price level also increased by 8%, the company's real growth would be zero. Also, some assets such as property, plant, and equipment might be many years old. The historical cost at which they are shown on the balance sheet might be significantly lower than what they could currently be sold for.

ALTERNATIVE ACCOUNTING METHODS

Variations among companies in the application of generally accepted accounting principles may hamper comparability. For example, one company may use the FIFO method of inventory costing, while another company in the same industry may use LIFO. If inventory is a significant asset to both companies, it is unlikely that their current ratios are comparable. For example, if General Motors Corporation had used FIFO instead of LIFO in valuing its inventories, its inventories would have been 26% higher, which significantly affects the current ratio (and other ratios as well).

In addition to differences in inventory costing methods, differences also exist in reporting such items as depreciation, depletion, and amortization. Although these differences in accounting methods might be detectable from reading the notes to the financial statements, adjusting the financial data to compensate for the different methods is difficult, if not impossible, in some cases.

ATYPICAL DATA

Fiscal year-end data may not be typical of a company's financial condition during the year. Firms frequently establish a fiscal year-end that coincides with the low point in their operating activity or inventory levels. Therefore, certain account balances (cash, receivables, payables, and inventories) may not be representative of the balances in the accounts during the year.

DIVERSIFICATION

Diversification in American industry also limits the usefulness of financial analysis. Many firms today are so diversified that they cannot be classified by industry. Others appear to be comparable but are not. You might think that PepsiCo, Inc., and Coca-Cola Company would be comparable as soft drink industry competitors. But are they comparable when until recently, PepsiCo, in addition to producing Pepsi-Cola, owned Pizza Hut, Kentucky Fried Chicken, Taco Bell, and Frito-Lay; and Coca-Cola, in addition to producing Coke, owns Hi-C (fruit drinks), Minute Maid (frozen juice concentrate), and Columbia Pictures (motion pictures, TV shows, and commercials)? Or, we might like to compare Kellogg to RJR Nabisco, one of its biggest competitors. But since RJR Nabisco generates a significant portion of its profits from cigarette sales, and a lot of the rest of its profits from nongrain-related products, comparisons are difficult. As a consequence, deciding what industry a company is in is actually one of the main challenges to effective evaluation of its results.

When companies have significant operations in different lines of business, they are required to report additional disclosures in a **segmental data** note to their financial statements. Segmental data include total sales, total identifiable assets, operating profit, depreciation expense, and capital expenditures by business segment. Many analysts say that the segmental information is the most important data in the financial statements because, without it, comparison of diversified companies is very difficult.

DECISION TOOLKIT

Decision Checkpoints	Info Needed for Decision	Tool to Use for Decision	How to Evaluate Results
Are efforts to evaluate the company significantly hampered by any of the common limitations of financial analysis?	Financial statements as well as a general understanding of the company and its business	The primary limitations of financial analysis are estimates, cost, alternative accounting methods, atypical data, and diversification.	If any of these factors is significant, the analysis should be relied upon with caution.

BEFORE YOU GO ON . . .

- **Review It**

  1. What are some of the limitations of financial analysis?
  2. What are the required disclosures in segmental data notes?

Using the Decision Toolkit

In analyzing a company, you should always investigate a number of years in order to determine whether the condition and performance of the company are changing. The condensed financial statements of Kellogg Company for 1994 and 1993 are presented here:

KELLOGG COMPANY, INC.
Balance Sheet
December 31
(in millions)

	1994	1993
Assets		
Current assets		
Cash and short-term investments	$ 266.3	$ 98.1
Accounts receivable (net)	564.5	536.8
Inventories	396.3	403.1
Prepaid expenses and other current assets	206.4	207.1
Total current assets	1,433.5	1,245.1
Property, plant, and equipment (net)	2,892.8	2,768.4
Intangibles and other assets	141.0	223.6
Total assets	$4,467.3	$4,237.1
Liabilities and Stockholders' Equity		
Current liabilities	$1,185.2	$1,214.6
Long-term liabilities	1,474.6	1,309.1
Stockholders' equity—common	1,807.5	1,713.4
Total liabilities and stockholders' equity	$4,467.3	$4,237.1

KELLOGG COMPANY, INC.
Income Statement
For the Years Ended December 31
(in millions)

	1994	1993
Revenues	$6,562.0	$6,295.4
Costs and expenses		
Cost of goods sold	2,950.7	2,989.0
Selling and administrative expenses	2,448.7	2,237.5
Interest expense	32.6	34.8
Total costs and expenses	5,432.0	5,261.3
Income before income taxes	1,130.0	1,034.1
Income tax expense	424.6	353.4
Net income	$ 705.4	$ 680.7

Instructions

Compute the following ratios for Kellogg for 1994 and 1993 and comment on each relative to the amounts reported in the chapter.

1. Liquidity:
   (a) Current ratio
   (b) Inventory turnover ratio (Inventory on December 31, 1992, was $416.4 million.)
2. Solvency:
   (a) Debt to total assets ratio
   (b) Times interest earned ratio
3. Profitability:
   (a) Return on common stockholders' equity ratio (Equity on December 31, 1992, was $1,945.2 million.)
   (b) Return on assets ratio (Assets on December 31, 1992, were $4,015.0 million.)
   (c) Profit margin ratio

Solution

1. Liquidity
   (a) Current ratio:

   1994: $\dfrac{\$1,433.5}{\$1,185.2} = 1.2 : 1$

   1993: $\dfrac{\$1,245.1}{\$1,214.6} = 1.0 : 1$

   (b) Inventory turnover ratio:

   1994: $\dfrac{\$2,950.7}{(\$396.3 + \$403.1)/2} = 7.4 \text{ times}$

   1993: $\dfrac{\$2,989.0}{(\$403.1 + \$416.4)/2} = 7.3 \text{ times}$

In the chapter we noted that Kellogg's liquidity as measured by the current ratio declined sharply in 1996 due to a large increase in current liabilities. Its current ratio in both 1994 and 1993 was at or above the 1996 industry average. Countering this decline in the current ratio, however, is the fact that the inventory turnover ratio in 1996 is better than it was in either 1994 or 1993. The faster that inventory turns, the more liquid it is; that is, the company can accept a lower current ratio if it can turn its inventory (and receivables) more quickly.

2. Solvency
   (a) Debt to total assets ratio:

   1994: $\dfrac{\$2,659.8}{\$4,467.3} = 59\%$

   1993: $\dfrac{\$2,523.7}{\$4,237.1} = 59\%$

   (b) Times interest earned ratio:

   1994: $\dfrac{\$705.4 + \$424.6 + \$32.6}{\$32.6} = 35.7 \text{ times}$

   1993: $\dfrac{\$680.7 + \$353.4 + \$34.8}{\$34.8} = 30.7 \text{ times}$

Kellogg's solvency as measured by the debt to total assets ratio declined in 1995 and 1996 relative to its level in 1994 and 1993. However, we can see from the 1994 and 1993 measures that the high times interest earned ratio that we observed in 1995 and 1996 was not unusual for Kellogg, but instead is about the normal measure. This consistently high times interest earned measure gives us confidence that Kellogg can meet its debt payments when due.

3. Profitability
   (a) Return on common stockholders' equity ratio:

   1994: $\dfrac{\$705.4}{(\$1{,}807.5 + \$1{,}713.4)/2} = 40\%$

   1993: $\dfrac{\$680.7}{(\$1{,}713.4 + \$1{,}945.2)/2} = 37\%$

   (b) Return on assets ratio:

   1994: $\dfrac{\$705.4}{(\$4{,}467.3 + \$4{,}237.1)/2} = 16\%$

   1993: $\dfrac{\$680.7}{(\$4{,}237.1 + \$4{,}015.0)/2} = 16\%$

   (c) Profit margin ratio:

   1994: $\dfrac{\$705.4}{\$6{,}562.0} = 11\%$

   1993: $\dfrac{\$680.7}{\$6{,}295.4} = 11\%$

We noted in the chapter that Kellogg's return on common stockholders' equity ratio was unusually high. We suggested that in 1996 Kellogg reached this high measure by increasing its leverage—that is, by trading on the equity. Note that its return on common stockholders' equity ratio was also very high back in 1994 and 1993. However, then it had much higher profit margin and return on assets ratios. By increasing its leverage, Kellogg has been able to maintain a high return on common stockholders' equity ratio, but, as we noted in the chapter, higher leverage means higher risk. That is, with higher leverage, if the company's sales turn sour, its profitability could really be hurt.

SUMMARY OF STUDY OBJECTIVES

❶ Understand the concept of earning power and indicate how irregular items are presented. Earning power refers to a company's ability to sustain its profits from operations. Irregular items—discontinued operations, extraordinary items, and changes in accounting principles—are presented on the income statement net of tax below "Income from continuing operations" to highlight their unusual nature.

❷ Discuss the need for comparative analysis and identify the tools of financial statement analysis. Comparative analysis is performed to evaluate a firm's short-term liquidity, profitability, and long-term solvency. Comparisons can detect changes in financial relationships and significant trends and provide insight into a company's competitive position and relative position in its industry. Financial statements may be analyzed horizontally, vertically, and with ratios.

❸ Explain and apply horizontal analysis. Horizontal analysis is a technique for evaluating a series of data over a period of time to determine the increase or decrease that has taken place, expressed as either an amount or a percentage.

❹ Describe and apply vertical analysis. Vertical analysis is a technique that expresses each item in a financial statement as a percentage of a relevant total or a base amount.

❺ Identify and compute ratios and describe their purpose and use in analyzing a firm's liquidity, solvency, and profitability. Financial ratios are provided in Illustrations 14-12 through 14-18 (liquidity), Illustrations 14-19 through 14-22 (solvency), and Illustrations 14-24 through 14-29, and 14-31 through 14-35 (profitability).

❻ Discuss the limitations of financial statement analysis. The usefulness of analytical tools is limited by the use of estimates, the cost basis, the application of alternative accounting methods, atypical data at year-end, and the diversification of companies.

Decision Toolkit—A Summary

Decision Checkpoints	Info Needed for Decision	Tool to Use for Decision	How to Evaluate Results
Has the company sold any major lines of business?	Discontinued operations section of income statement	Anything reported in this section indicates that the company has discontinued a major line of business.	If a major business line has been discontinued, its results in the current period should not be included in estimates of future net income.
Has the company experienced any extraordinary events or transactions?	Extraordinary item section of income statement	Anything reported in this section indicates that the company experienced an event that was both unusual and infrequent.	These items should usually be ignored in estimating future net income.
Has the company changed any of its accounting policies?	Cumulative effect of change in accounting principle section of income statement	Anything reported in this section indicates that the company has changed an accounting policy during the current year.	The cumulative effect should be ignored in estimating the future net income.
How do the company's financial position and operating results compare with those of previous period?	Income statement and balance sheet	Comparative financial statements should be prepared over at least 2 years, with the first year reported being the base year. Changes in each line item relative to the base year should be presented both by amount and by percentage. This is called horizontal analysis.	Significant changes should be investigated to determine the reason for the change.
How do the relationships between items in this year's financial statements compare with those of last year or those of competitors?	Income statement and balance sheet	Each line item on the income statement should be presented as a percentage of net sales, and each line item on the balance sheet should be presented as a percentage of total assets or total liabilities and stockholders' equity. These percentages should be investigated for differences either across years in the same company or in the same year across different companies. This is called vertical analysis.	Any differences either across years or between companies should be investigated to determine the cause.
Are efforts to evaluate the company significantly hampered by any of the common limitations of financial analysis?	Financial statements as well as a general understanding of the company and its business	The primary limitations of financial analysis are estimates, cost, alternative accounting methods, atypical data, and diversification.	If any of these factors is significant, the analysis should be relied upon with caution.

Glossary

Acid-test (quick) ratio A measure of a company's immediate short-term liquidity, computed as the sum of cash, marketable securities, and net receivables divided by current liabilities. (p. 663)

Asset turnover ratio A measure of how efficiently a company uses its assets to generate sales, computed as net sales divided by average total assets. (p. 670)

Average collection period The average number of days that receivables are outstanding, calculated as receivables turnover divided into 365 days. (p. 664)

Average days in inventory A measure of the average number of days it takes to sell the inventory, computed as inventory turnover divided into 365 days. (p. 665)

Cash debt coverage ratio A cash-basis measure used to evaluate solvency, computed as cash from operations divided by average total liabilities. (p. 667)

Cash return on sales ratio The cash-basis measure of net income generated by each dollar of sales, computed as net cash from operations divided by net sales. (p. 672)

Change in accounting principle Use of an accounting principle in the current year different from the one used in the preceding year. (p. 652)

Comprehensive income Includes all changes in stockholders' equity during a period except those resulting from investments by stockholders and distributions to stockholders. (p. 654)

Current cash debt coverage ratio A cash-basis measure of short-term debt-paying ability, computed as cash from operations divided by average current liabilities. (p. 663)

Current ratio A measure that expresses the relationship of current assets to current liabilities, calculated as current assets divided by current liabilities. (p. 662)

Debt to total assets ratio A measure of the percentage of total assets provided by creditors, computed as total debt divided by total assets. (p. 666)

Discontinued operations The disposal of a significant segment of a business. (p. 649)

Earnings per share The net income earned by each share of common stock, computed as net income divided by the weighted average common shares outstanding. (p. 673)

Extraordinary items Events and transactions that meet two conditions: (1) unusual in nature and (2) infrequent in occurrence. (p. 650)

Free cash flow The amount of cash from operations available for paying dividends or expanding operations after spending enough cash to maintain operations at their current level. (p. 667)

Gross profit rate An indicator of a company's ability to maintain an adequate selling price of goods above their cost, computed as gross profit divided by net sales. (p. 671)

Horizontal analysis A technique for evaluating a series of financial statement data over a period of time to determine the increase (decrease) that has taken place, expressed as either an amount or a percentage. (p. 656)

Inventory turnover ratio A measure of the liquidity of inventory, computed as cost of goods sold divided by average inventory. (p. 665)

Leveraging Borrowing money at a lower rate of interest than can be earned by using the borrowed money; also referred to as trading on the equity. (p. 669)

Liquidity ratios Measures of the short-term ability of the enterprise to pay its maturing obligations and to meet unexpected needs for cash. (p. 661)

Operating expenses to sales ratio A measure of the costs incurred to support each dollar of sales, computed as operating expenses divided by net sales. (p. 671)

Payout ratio A measure of the percentage of earnings distributed in the form of cash dividends, calculated as cash dividends divided by net income. (p. 674)

Price-earnings ratio A comparison of the market price of each share of common stock to the earnings per share, computed as the market price of the stock divided by earnings per share. (p. 673)

Profit margin ratio A measure of the net income generated by each dollar of sales, computed as net income divided by net sales. (p. 670)

Profitability ratios Measures of the income or operating success of an enterprise for a given period of time. (p. 661)

Quick ratio Another name for the acid-test ratio. (p. 663)

Receivables turnover ratio A measure of the liquidity of receivables, computed as net credit sales divided by average net receivables. (p. 664)

Return on assets ratio An overall measure of profitability, calculated as net income divided by average total assets. (p. 669)

Return on common stockholders' equity ratio A measure of the dollars of net income earned for each dollar invested by the owners, computed as income available to common stockholders divided by average common stockholders' equity. (p. 669)

Segmental data A required note disclosure for diversified companies in which the company reports sales, operating profit, identifiable assets, depreciation expense, and capital expenditures by major business segment. (p. 676)

Solvency ratios Measures of the ability of the enterprise to survive over a long period of time. (p. 661)

Times interest earned ratio A measure of a company's ability to meet interest payments as they come due, calculated as income before interest expense and income taxes divided by interest expense. (p. 667)

Trading on the equity Same as leveraging. (p. 669)

Vertical analysis A technique for evaluating financial statement data that expresses each item in a financial statement as a percent of a base amount. (p. 658)

Demonstration Problem

The events and transactions of Dever Corporation for the year ending December 31, 1998, resulted in these data:

Cost of goods sold	$2,600,000
Net sales	4,400,000
Other expenses and losses	9,600
Other revenues and gains	5,600
Selling and administrative expenses	1,100,000
Income from operations of plastics division	70,000
Gain on sale of plastics division	500,000
Loss from tornado disaster (extraordinary loss)	600,000
Cumulative effect of changing from straight-line depreciation to double-declining-balance (increase in depreciation expense)	300,000

Analysis reveals:

1. All items are before the applicable income tax rate of 30%.
2. The plastics division was sold on July 1.
3. All operating data for the plastics division have been segregated.

Instructions

Prepare an income statement for the year, excluding the presentation of earnings per share.

Problem-Solving Strategies
1. Remember that material items not typical of operations are reported in separate sections net of taxes.
2. Income taxes should be associated with the item that affects the taxes.
3. A corporation income statement has income tax expense when there is income before income tax.
4. All data presented in determining income before income taxes are the same as for unincorporated companies.

Solution to Demonstration Problem

DEVER CORPORATION
Income Statement
For the Year Ended December 31, 1998

Net sales		$4,400,000
Cost of goods sold		2,600,000
Gross profit		1,800,000
Selling and administrative expenses		1,100,000
Income from operations		700,000
Other revenues and gains	$ 5,600	
Other expenses and losses	9,600	4,000
Income before income taxes		696,000
Income tax expense ($696,000 × 30%)		208,800
Income from continuing operations		487,200
Discontinued operations		
Income from operations of plastics division, net of $21,000 income taxes ($70,000 × 30%)	49,000	
Gain on sale of plastics division, net of $150,000 income taxes ($500,000 × 30%)	350,000	399,000
Income before extraordinary item and cumulative effect of change in accounting principle		886,200
Extraordinary item		
Tornado loss, net of income tax saving $180,000 ($600,000 × 30%)		420,000
Cumulative effect of change in accounting principle		
Effect on prior years of change in depreciation method, net of $90,000 income tax saving ($300,000 × 30%)		210,000
Net income		$ 256,200

SELF-STUDY QUESTIONS

Answers are at the end of the chapter.

All of the Self-Study Questions in this chapter employ decision tools.

(SO 1) 1. In reporting discontinued operations, the income statement should show in a special section:
  (a) gains and losses on the disposal of the discontinued segment.
  (b) gains and losses from operations of the discontinued segment.
  (c) Neither (a) nor (b)
  (d) Both (a) and (b)

(SO 1) 2. The Candy Stick Corporation has income before taxes of $400,000 and an extraordinary loss of $100,000. If the income tax rate is 25% on all items, the income statement should show income before extraordinary items, and extraordinary items, respectively, of
  (a) $325,000 and $100,000.
  (b) $325,000 and $75,000.
  (c) $300,000 and $100,000.
  (d) $300,000 and $75,000.

(SO 2) 3. Comparisons of data within a company are an example of the following comparative basis:
  (a) industry averages.
  (b) intracompany.
  (c) intercompany.
  (d) Both (b) and (c)

(SO 3) 4. In horizontal analysis, each item is expressed as a percentage of the:
  (a) net income amount.
  (b) stockholders' equity amount.
  (c) total assets amount.
  (d) base-year amount.

(SO 4) 5. In vertical analysis, the base amount for depreciation expense is generally:
  (a) net sales.
  (b) depreciation expense in a previous year.
  (c) gross profit.
  (d) fixed assets.

(SO 4) 6. The following schedule is a display of what type of analysis?

	Amount	Percent
Current assets	$200,000	25%
Property, plant, and equipment	600,000	75%
Total assets	$800,000	

  (a) Horizontal analysis
  (b) Differential analysis
  (c) Vertical analysis
  (d) Ratio analysis

(SO 3) 7. Leland Corporation reported net sales of $300,000, $330,000, and $360,000 in the years 1996, 1997, and 1998, respectively. If 1996 is the base year, what is the trend percentage for 1998?
  (a) 77%
  (b) 108%
  (c) 120%
  (d) 130%

(SO 5) 8. Which measure is an evaluation of a firm's ability to pay current liabilities?
  (a) Acid-test ratio
  (b) Current ratio
  (c) Both (a) and (b)
  (d) None of the above

(SO 5) 9. Which measure is useful in evaluating the efficiency in managing inventories?
  (a) Inventory turnover ratio
  (b) Average days in inventory
  (c) Both (a) and (b)
  (d) None of the above

(SO 5) 10. Which of these is *not* a liquidity ratio?
  (a) Current ratio
  (b) Asset turnover ratio
  (c) Inventory turnover ratio
  (d) Receivables turnover ratio

(SO 5) 11. Plano Corporation reported net income $24,000; net sales $400,000; and average assets $600,000 for 1998. What is the 1998 profit margin?
  (a) 6%
  (b) 12%
  (c) 40%
  (d) 200%

(SO 6) 12. Which of the following is generally *not* considered to be a limitation of financial analysis?
  (a) Use of ratio analysis
  (b) Use of estimates
  (c) Use of cost
  (d) Use of alternative accounting methods

QUESTIONS

All of the Questions in this chapter employ decision tools.

1. Explain earning power. What relationship does this concept have to the treatment of irregular items on the income statement?
2. Indicate which of the following items would be reported as an extraordinary item on Fine & Fancy Food Corporation's income statement?
   (a) Loss from damages caused by a volcano eruption
   (b) Loss from the sale of temporary investments
   (c) Loss attributable to a labor strike
   (d) Loss caused when the Food and Drug Administration prohibited the manufacture and sale of a product line
   (e) Loss of inventory from flood damage because a warehouse is located on a flood plain that floods every 5 to 10 years
   (f) Loss on the write-down of outdated inventory
   (g) Loss from a foreign government's expropriation of a production facility
   (h) Loss from damage to a warehouse in southern California from a minor earthquake
3. Iron Ingots Inc. reported 1997 earnings per share of $3.26 and had no extraordinary items. In 1998 earnings per share on income before extraordinary items was $2.99, and earnings per share on net income was $3.49. Do you consider this trend to be favorable? Why or why not?
4. Rodger Robotics Inc. has been in operation for 3 years. All of its manufacturing equipment, which has a useful life of 10 to 12 years, has been depreciated on a straight-line basis. During the fourth year, Rodger Robotics changes to an accelerated depreciation method for all of its equipment.
   (a) Will Rodger Robotics post a gain or a loss on this change?
   (b) How will this change be reported?
5. (a) Tia Kim believes that the analysis of financial statements is directed at two characteristics of a company: liquidity and profitability. Is Tia correct? Explain.
   (b) Are short-term creditors, long-term creditors, and stockholders interested in primarily the same characteristics of a company? Explain.
6. (a) Distinguish among the following bases of comparison: intracompany, industry averages, and intercompany.
   (b) Give the principal value of using each of the three bases of comparison.
7. Two popular methods of financial statement analysis are horizontal analysis and vertical analysis. Explain the difference between these two methods.
8. (a) If Roe Company had net income of $540,000 in 1997 and it experienced a 24.5% increase in net income for 1998, what is its net income for 1998?
   (b) If six cents of every dollar of Roe's revenue is net income in 1997, what is the dollar amount of 1997 revenue?
9. Name the major ratios useful in assessing (a) liquidity and (b) solvency.
10. Tony Robins is puzzled. His company had a profit margin of 10% in 1998. He feels that this is an indication that the company is doing well. Joan Graham, his accountant, says that more information is needed to determine the firm's financial well-being. Who is correct? Why?
11. What does each type of ratio measure?
    (a) Liquidity ratios
    (b) Solvency ratios
    (c) Profitability ratios
12. What is the difference between the current ratio and the acid-test ratio?
13. Gerry Bullock Company, a retail store, has a receivables turnover ratio of 4.5 times. The industry average is 12.5 times. Does Bullock have a collection problem with its receivables?
14. Which ratios should be used to help answer each of these questions?
    (a) How efficient is a company in using its assets to produce sales?
    (b) How near to sale is the inventory on hand?
    (c) How many dollars of net income were earned for each dollar invested by the owners?
    (d) How able is a company to meet interest charges as they fall due?
15. The price-earnings ratio of McDonnell Douglas (aircraft builder) was 5, and the price-earnings ratio of Microsoft (computer software) was 43. Which company did the stock market favor? Explain.
16. What is the formula for computing the payout ratio? Do you expect this ratio to be high or low for a growth company?
17. Holding all other factors constant, indicate whether each of the following changes generally signals good or bad news about a company:
    (a) Increase in profit margin ratio
    (b) Decrease in inventory turnover ratio
    (c) Increase in current ratio
    (d) Decrease in earnings per share
    (e) Increase in price-earnings ratio
    (f) Increase in debt to total assets ratio
    (g) Decrease in times interest earned ratio
18. The return on assets for Windsor Corporation is 7.6%. During the same year Windsor's return on common stockholders' equity is 12.8%. What is the explanation for the difference in the two rates?
19. Which two ratios do you think should be of greatest interest in each of these cases:
    (a) A pension fund considering the purchase of 20-year bonds

(b) A bank contemplating a short-term loan
(c) A common stockholder

20. (a) What is meant by trading on the equity?
    (b) How would you determine the profitability of trading on the equity?

21. Khris Inc. has net income of $270,000, weighted average shares of common stock outstanding of 50,000 and preferred dividends for the period of $40,000. What is Khris's earnings per share of common stock? Phil Remmers, the president of Khris Inc., believes that the computed EPS of the company is high. Comment.

22. Identify and briefly explain five limitations of financial analysis.

23. Explain how the choice of one of the following accounting methods over the other raises or lowers a company's net income during a period of continuing inflation.
    (a) Use of FIFO instead of LIFO for inventory costing
    (b) Use of a 6-year life for machinery instead of a 9-year life
    (c) Use of straight-line depreciation instead of accelerated declining-balance depreciation

BRIEF EXERCISES

All of the Brief Exercises in this chapter employ decision tools.

BE14-1 On June 30 Osborn Corporation discontinued its operations in Mexico. During the year, the operating loss was $400,000 before taxes. On September 1 Osborn disposed of the Mexico facility at a pretax loss of $150,000. The applicable tax rate is 30%. Show the discontinued operations section of Osborn's income statement.

Prepare a discontinued operations section of an income statement.
(SO 1)

BE14-2 An inexperienced accountant for Lima Corporation showed the following in Lima's income statement: Income before income taxes, $300,000; Income tax expense, $72,000; Extraordinary loss from flood (before taxes), $60,000; and Net income, $168,000. The extraordinary loss and taxable income are both subject to a 30% tax rate. Prepare a corrected income statement beginning with "Income before income taxes."

Prepare a corrected income statement with an extraordinary item.
(SO 1)

BE14-3 On January 1, 1998, Shirli Inc. changed from the straight-line method of depreciation to the declining-balance method. The cumulative effect of the change was to increase the prior years' depreciation by $40,000 and 1998 depreciation by $8,000. Show the change in accounting principle section of the 1998 income statement, assuming the tax rate is 30%.

Prepare a change in accounting principles section of an income statement.
(SO 1)

BE14-4 Using these data from the comparative balance sheet of All-State Company, perform horizontal analysis.

Prepare horizontal analysis.
(SO 3)

	December 31, 1998	December 31, 1997
Accounts receivable	$ 600,000	$ 400,000
Inventory	780,000	600,000
Total assets	3,220,000	2,800,000

BE14-5 Using the data presented in BE14-4 for All-State Company, perform vertical analysis.

Prepare vertical analysis.
(SO 4)

BE14-6 Net income was $500,000 in 1996, $420,000 in 1997, and $504,000 in 1998. What is the percentage of change from (a) 1996 to 1997 and (b) 1997 to 1998? Is the change an increase or a decrease?

Calculate percentage of change.
(SO 3)

BE14-7 If Cavalier Company had net income of $672,300 in 1998 and it experienced a 25% increase in net income over 1997, what was its 1997 net income?

Calculate net income.
(SO 3)

BE14-8 Vertical analysis (common-size) percentages for Waubons Company's sales, cost of goods sold, and expenses are listed here:

Calculate change in net income.
(SO 4)

Vertical Analysis	1998	1997	1996
Sales	100.0%	100.0%	100.0%
Cost of goods sold	59.2	62.4	64.5
Expenses	25.0	26.6	29.5

Did Waubons' net income as a percent of sales increase, decrease, or remain unchanged over the 3-year period? Provide numerical support for your answer.

686 CHAPTER 14 Financial Analysis: The Big Picture

Calculate change in net income.
(SO 3)

BE14-9 Horizontal analysis (trend analysis) percentages for Tilden Company's sales, cost of goods sold, and expenses are listed here:

Horizontal Analysis	1998	1997	1996
Sales	96.2%	106.8%	100.0%
Cost of goods sold	102.0	97.0	100.0
Expenses	110.6	95.4	100.0

Explain whether Tilden's net income increased, decreased, or remained unchanged over the 3-year period.

Calculate liquidity ratios.
(SO 5)

BE14-10 These selected condensed data are taken from a recent balance sheet of Bob Evans Farms:

Cash	$ 8,241,000
Marketable securities	1,947,000
Accounts receivable	12,545,000
Inventories	14,814,000
Other current assets	5,371,000
Total current assets	$42,918,000
Total current liabilities	$44,844,000

What are the (a) current ratio and (b) acid-test ratio?

Evaluate collection of accounts receivable.
(SO 5)

BE14-11 The following data are taken from the financial statements of Diet-Mite Company:

	1998	1997
Accounts receivable (net), end of year	$ 560,000	$ 540,000
Net sales on account	5,500,000	4,100,000
Terms for all sales are 1/10, n/45.		

Compute for each year (a) the receivables turnover ratio and (b) the average collection period. What conclusions about the management of accounts receivable can be drawn from these data? At the end of 1996, accounts receivable (net) was $490,000.

Evaluate management of inventory.
(SO 5)

BE14-12 The following data were taken from the income statements of Linda Shumway Company:

	1998	1997
Sales	$6,420,000	$6,240,000
Beginning inventory	980,000	837,000
Purchases	4,640,000	4,661,000
Ending inventory	1,020,000	980,000

Compute for each year (a) the inventory turnover ratio and (b) the average days in inventory. What conclusions concerning the management of the inventory can be drawn from these data?

Calculate profitability ratios.
(SO 5)

BE14-13 Boston Patriots Corporation has net income of $15 million and net revenue of $100 million in 1998. Its assets were $12 million at the beginning of the year and $14 million at the end of the year. What are the Patriots' (a) asset turnover ratio and (b) profit margin ratio? (Round to two decimals.)

Calculate profitability ratios.
(SO 5)

BE14-14 Haymark Products Company has stockholders' equity of $400,000 and net income of $50,000. It has a payout ratio of 20% and a rate of return on assets of 16%. How much did Haymark Products pay in cash dividends, and what were its average assets?

Calculate cash-basis liquidity, profitability, and solvency ratios.
(SO 5)

BE14-15 Selected data taken from the 1998 financial statements of Shirley Denison Manufacturing Company are as follows:

Net sales for 1998	$6,860,000
Current liabilities, January 1, 1998	180,000
Current liabilities, December 31, 1998	240,000
Net cash provided by operating activities	760,000
Total liabilities, January 1, 1998	1,500,000
Total liabilities, December 31, 1998	1,300,000

Compute these ratios at December 31, 1998: (a) current cash debt coverage ratio, (b) cash return on sales ratio, and (c) cash debt coverage ratio.

EXERCISES

All of the Exercises in this chapter employ decision tools.

E14-1 The Davis Company has income from continuing operations of $240,000 for the year ended December 31, 1998. It also has the following items (before considering income taxes): (1) an extraordinary fire loss of $60,000, (2) a gain of $40,000 from the discontinuance of a division, which includes a $110,000 gain from the operation of the division and a $70,000 loss on its disposal, and (3) a cumulative change in accounting principle that resulted in an increase in the prior year's depreciation of $30,000. Assume all items are subject to income taxes at a 30% tax rate.

Prepare irregular items portion of an income statement.
(SO 1)

Instructions
Prepare Davis Company's income statement for 1998, beginning with "Income from continuing operations."

E14-2 *The Wall Street Journal* routinely publishes summaries of corporate quarterly and annual earnings reports in a feature called the "Earnings Digest." A typical "digest" report takes the following form:

Evaluate the effects of unusual or irregular items.
(SO 1, 5, 6)

ENERGY ENTERPRISES (A)

	Quarter ending July 31	
	1998	1997
Revenues	$2,049,000,000	$1,754,000,000
Net income	97,000,000	(a) 68,750,000
EPS: Net income	1.31	.93

	9 months ending July 31	
	1998	1997
Revenues	$5,578,500,000	$5,065,300,000
Extraordinary item	(b) 1,900,000	
Net income	102,700,000	(a) 33,250,000
EPS: Net income	1.39	.45

(a) Includes a net charge of $26,000,000 from loss on the sale of electrical equipment
(b) Extraordinary gain on Middle East property expropriation

The letter in parentheses following the company name indicates the exchange on which Energy Enterprises' stock is traded—in this case, the American Stock Exchange.

Instructions
Answer these questions:
(a) How was the loss on the electrical equipment reported on the income statement? Was it reported in the third quarter of 1997? How can you tell?
(b) Why did *The Wall Street Journal* list the extraordinary item separately?
(c) What is the extraordinary item? Was it included in income for the third quarter? How can you tell?
(d) Did Energy Enterprises have an operating loss in any quarter of 1997? Of 1998? How do you know?
(e) Approximately how many shares of stock were outstanding in 1998? Did the number of outstanding shares change from July 31, 1997 to July 31, 1998?
(f) As an investor, what numbers should you use to determine Energy Enterprises' profit margin ratio? Calculate the 9-month profit margin ratio for 1997 and 1998 that you consider most useful. Explain your decision.

688 CHAPTER 14 Financial Analysis: The Big Picture

Prepare horizontal analysis.
(SO 3)

E14-3 Here is financial information for Merchandise Inc.:

	December 31, 1998	December 31, 1997
Current assets	$120,000	$100,000
Plant assets (net)	400,000	330,000
Current liabilities	91,000	70,000
Long-term liabilities	144,000	95,000
Common stock, $1 par	150,000	115,000
Retained earnings	135,000	150,000

Instructions
Prepare a schedule showing a horizontal analysis for 1998 using 1997 as the base year.

Prepare vertical analysis.
(SO 4)

E14-4 Operating data for Fleetwood Corporation are presented here:

	1998	1997
Sales	$800,000	$600,000
Cost of goods sold	472,000	390,000
Selling expenses	120,000	72,000
Administrative expenses	80,000	54,000
Income tax expense	38,400	25,200
Net income	89,600	58,800

Instructions
Prepare a schedule showing a vertical analysis for 1998 and 1997.

Prepare horizontal and vertical analyses.
(SO 3, 4)

E14-5 The comparative balance sheets of Oklahoma Corporation are presented here:

OKLAHOMA CORPORATION
Comparative Balance Sheets
December 31

	1998	1997
Assets		
Current assets	$ 72,000	$ 80,000
Property, plant, and equipment (net)	99,000	90,000
Intangibles	24,000	40,000
Total assets	$195,000	$210,000
Liabilities and Stockholders' Equity		
Current liabilities	$ 40,800	$ 48,000
Long-term liabilities	138,000	150,000
Stockholders' equity	16,200	12,000
Total liabilities and stockholders' equity	$195,000	$210,000

Instructions
(a) Prepare a horizontal analysis of the balance sheet data for Oklahoma Corporation using 1997 as a base. (Show the amount of increase or decrease as well.)
(b) Prepare a vertical analysis of the balance sheet data for Oklahoma Corporation for 1998.

Prepare horizontal and vertical analyses.
(SO 3, 4)

E14-6 Here are the comparative income statements of Olympic Corporation:

OLYMPIC CORPORATION
Comparative Income Statements
For the Years Ended December 31

	1998	1997
Net sales	$550,000	$550,000
Cost of goods sold	440,000	450,000
Gross profit	$110,000	$100,000
Operating expenses	57,200	54,000
Net income	$ 52,800	$ 46,000

Instructions
(a) Prepare a horizontal analysis of the income statement data for Olympic Corporation using 1997 as a base. (Show the amounts of increase or decrease.)
(b) Prepare a vertical analysis of the income statement data for Olympic Corporation for both years.

E14-7 Nordstrom, Inc., operates department stores in numerous states. Selected financial statement data (in millions) for a recent year are presented here:

Compute liquidity ratios and compare results.
(SO 5)

	End of Year	Beginning of Year
Cash and cash equivalents	$ 33	$ 91
Receivables (net)	676	586
Merchandise inventory	628	586
Prepaid expenses	61	52
Total current assets	$1,398	$1,315
Total current liabilities	$ 690	$ 627

For the year, net sales were $3,894, cost of goods sold was $2,600, and cash from operations was $215.

Instructions
Compute the current ratio, acid-test ratio, current cash debt coverage ratio, receivables turnover ratio, average collection period, inventory turnover ratio, and average days in inventory at the end of the current year.

E14-8 Firpo Incorporated had the following transactions involving current assets and current liabilities during February 1998:

Perform current and acid-test ratio analysis.
(SO 5)

Feb. 3 Collected accounts receivable of $15,000.
　　 7 Purchased equipment for $25,000 cash.
　　11 Paid $3,000 for a 3-year insurance policy.
　　14 Paid accounts payable of $14,000.
　　18 Declared cash dividends, $6,000.

Additional information:
1. As of February 1, 1998, current assets were $140,000 and current liabilities were $50,000.
2. As of February 1, 1998, current assets included $15,000 of inventory and $5,000 of prepaid expenses.

Instructions
(a) Compute the current ratio as of the beginning of the month and after each transaction.
(b) Compute the acid-test ratio as of the beginning of the month and after each transaction.

E14-9 Georgette Company has these comparative balance sheet data:

Compute selected ratios.
(SO 5)

GEORGETTE COMPANY
Balance Sheet
December 31

	1998	1997
Cash	$ 20,000	$ 30,000
Receivables (net)	65,000	60,000
Inventories	60,000	50,000
Plant assets (net)	200,000	180,000
	$345,000	$320,000
Accounts payable	$ 50,000	$ 60,000
Mortgage payable (15%)	100,000	100,000
Common stock, $10 par	140,000	120,000
Retained earnings	55,000	40,000
	$345,000	$320,000

Additional information for 1998:
1. Net income was $25,000.
2. Sales on account were $420,000. Sales returns and allowances amounted to $20,000.
3. Cost of goods sold was $198,000.
4. Net cash provided by operating activities was $44,000.

Instructions
Compute the following ratios at December 31, 1998:
(a) Current
(b) Acid-test
(c) Receivables turnover
(d) Average collection period
(e) Inventory turnover
(f) Average days in inventory
(g) Cash return on sales
(h) Cash debt coverage
(i) Current cash debt coverage

Compute selected ratios.
(SO 5)

E14-10 Selected comparative statement data for Mighty Products Company are presented here. All balance sheet data are as of December 31.

	1998	1997
Net sales	$800,000	$720,000
Cost of goods sold	480,000	40,000
Interest expense	7,000	5,000
Net income	56,000	42,000
Accounts receivable	120,000	100,000
Inventory	85,000	75,000
Total assets	600,000	500,000
Total common stockholders' equity	450,000	310,000
Cash provided by operating activities	40,000	32,000

Instructions
Compute the following ratios for 1998:
(a) Profit margin
(b) Asset turnover
(c) Return on assets
(d) Return on common stockholders' equity
(e) Cash return on sales
(f) Gross profit rate

Compute selected ratios.
(SO 5)

E14-11 Here is the income statement for Jean LeFay, Inc:

JEAN LEFAY, INC.
Income Statement
For the Year Ended December 31, 1998

Sales	$400,000
Cost of goods sold	230,000
Gross profit	170,000
Expenses (including $20,000 interest and $24,000 income taxes)	100,000
Net income	$ 70,000

Additional information:
1. Common stock outstanding January 1, 1998, was 30,000 shares. On July 1, 1998, 10,000 more shares were issued.
2. The market price of Jean LeFay, Inc., stock was $15 in 1998.
3. Cash dividends of $21,000 were paid, $5,000 of which were to preferred stockholders.
4. Net cash provided by operating activities $98,000.

Instructions
Compute the following measures for 1998:
(a) Earnings per share
(b) Price-earnings ratio
(c) Payout ratio
(d) Times interest earned ratio
(e) Cash return on sales ratio

Compute amounts from ratios.
(SO 5)

E14-12 Shaker Corporation experienced a fire on December 31, 1998, in which its financial records were partially destroyed. It has been able to salvage some of the records and has ascertained the following balances:

	December 31, 1998	December 31, 1997
Cash	$ 30,000	$ 10,000
Receivables (net)	72,500	126,000
Inventory	200,000	180,000
Accounts payable	50,000	90,000
Notes payable	30,000	60,000
Common stock, $100 par	400,000	400,000
Retained earnings	113,500	101,000

Additional information:
1. The inventory turnover is 3.6 times.
2. The return on common stockholders' equity is 22%. The company had no additional paid-in capital.
3. The receivables turnover is 9.4 times.
4. The return on assets is 20%.
5. Total assets at December 31, 1997, were $605,000.

Instructions
Compute the following for Shaker Corporation:
(a) Cost of goods sold for 1998
(b) Net sales for 1998
(c) Net income for 1998
(d) Total assets at December 31, 1998

PROBLEMS

All of the Problems in this chapter employ decision tools.

P14-1 Here are comparative statement data for Chen Company and Couric Company, two competitors. All balance sheet data are as of December 31, 1998, and December 31, 1997.

Prepare vertical analysis and comment on profitability.
(SO 4, 5)

	Chen Company		Couric Company	
	1998	1997	1998	1997
Net sales	$1,549,035		$339,038	
Cost of goods sold	1,080,490		238,006	
Operating expenses	302,275		79,000	
Interest expense	6,800		1,252	
Income tax expense	47,840		7,740	
Current assets	325,975	$312,410	83,336	$ 79,467
Plant assets (net)	521,310	500,000	139,728	125,812
Current liabilities	66,325	75,815	35,348	30,281
Long-term liabilities	108,500	90,000	29,620	25,000
Common stock, $10 par	500,000	500,000	120,000	120,000
Retained earnings	172,460	146,595	38,096	29,998

Instructions
(a) Prepare a vertical analysis of the 1998 income statement data for Chen Company and Couric Company.
(b) Comment on the relative profitability of the companies by computing the return on assets and the return on common stockholders' equity ratios for both companies.

Compute ratios from balance sheet and income statement.
(SO 5)

P14-2 The comparative statements of Magic Johnson Company are presented here:

MAGIC JOHNSON COMPANY
Income Statement
For the Years Ended December 31

	1998	1997
Net sales	$1,818,500	$1,750,500
Cost of goods sold	1,005,500	996,000
Gross profit	813,000	754,500
Selling and administrative expenses	506,000	479,000
Income from operations	307,000	275,500
Other expenses and losses		
Interest expense	18,000	19,000
Income before income taxes	289,000	256,500
Income tax expense	86,700	77,000
Net income	$ 202,300	$ 179,500

MAGIC JOHNSON COMPANY
Balance Sheet
December 31

	1998	1997
Assets		
Current assets		
Cash	$ 60,100	$ 64,200
Marketable securities	54,000	50,000
Accounts receivable (net)	107,800	102,800
Inventory	123,000	115,500
Total current assets	344,900	332,500
Plant assets (net)	625,300	520,300
Total assets	$970,200	$852,800
Liabilities and Stockholders' Equity		
Current liabilities		
Accounts payable	$150,000	$145,400
Income taxes payable	43,500	42,000
Total current liabilities	193,500	187,400
Bonds payable	210,000	200,000
Total liabilities	403,500	387,400
Stockholders' equity		
Common stock ($5 par)	280,000	300,000
Retained earnings	286,700	165,400
Total stockholders' equity	566,700	465,400
Total liabilities and stockholders' equity	$970,200	$852,800

On July 1, 1998, 4,000 shares were repurchased and canceled. All sales were on account. Net cash provided by operating activities for 1998 was $280,000.

Instructions
Compute the following ratios for 1998:
(a) Earnings per share
(b) Return on common stockholders' equity
(c) Return on assets
(d) Current

(e) Acid-test
(f) Receivables turnover
(g) Average collection period
(h) Inventory turnover
(i) Average days in inventory
(j) Times interest earned
(k) Asset turnover
(l) Debt to total assets
(m) Current cash debt coverage
(n) Cash return on sales
(o) Cash debt coverage

P14-3 Condensed balance sheet and income statement data for Pitka Corporation are presented here:

Perform ratio analysis.
(SO 5)

PITKA CORPORATION
Balance Sheet
December 31

	1998	1997	1996
Cash	$ 25,000	$ 20,000	$ 18,000
Receivables (net)	50,000	45,000	48,000
Other current assets	90,000	85,000	64,000
Investments	75,000	70,000	45,000
Plant and equipment (net)	400,000	370,000	358,000
	$640,000	$590,000	$533,000
Current liabilities	$ 75,000	$ 80,000	$ 70,000
Long-term debt	80,000	85,000	50,000
Common stock, $10 par	340,000	300,000	300,000
Retained earnings	145,000	125,000	113,000
	$640,000	$590,000	$533,000

PITKA CORPORATION
Income Statement
For the Years Ended December 31

	1998	1997
Sales	$740,000	$700,000
Less: Sales returns and allowances	40,000	50,000
Net sales	700,000	650,000
Cost of goods sold	420,000	400,000
Gross profit	280,000	250,000
Operating expenses (including income taxes)	236,000	218,000
Net income	$ 44,000	$ 32,000

Additional information:
1. The market price of Pitka's common stock was $4.00, $5.00, and $7.95 for 1996, 1997, and 1998, respectively.
2. All dividends were paid in cash.
3. On July 1, 1997, 4,000 shares of common stock were issued.

Instructions
(a) Compute the following ratios for 1997 and 1998:
   (1) Profit margin
   (2) Gross profit
   (3) Asset turnover
   (4) Earnings per share
   (5) Price-earnings
   (6) Payout
   (7) Debt to total assets
(b) Based on the ratios calculated, discuss briefly the improvement or lack thereof in the financial position and operating results from 1997 to 1998 of Pitka Corporation.

Compute ratios; comment on overall liquidity and profitability.
(SO 5)

P14-4 This financial information is for Caroline Company:

CAROLINE COMPANY
Balance Sheet
December 31

	1998	1997
Assets		
Cash	$ 70,000	$ 65,000
Short-term investments	45,000	40,000
Receivables (net)	94,000	90,000
Inventories	130,000	125,000
Prepaid expenses	25,000	23,000
Land	130,000	130,000
Building and equipment (net)	190,000	175,000
Total assets	$684,000	$648,000
Liabilities and Stockholders' Equity		
Notes payable	$100,000	$100,000
Accounts payable	45,000	42,000
Accrued liabilities	40,000	40,000
Bonds payable, due 2000	150,000	150,000
Common stock, $10 par	200,000	200,000
Retained earnings	149,000	116,000
Total liabilities and stockholders' equity	$684,000	$648,000

CAROLINE COMPANY
Income Statement
For the Years Ended December 31

	1998	1997
Sales	$850,000	$790,000
Cost of goods sold	620,000	575,000
Gross profit	230,000	215,000
Operating expenses	194,000	180,000
Net income	$ 36,000	$ 35,000

Additional information:
1. Inventory at the beginning of 1997 was $115,000.
2. Receivables at the beginning of 1997 were $88,000.
3. Total assets at the beginning of 1997 were $630,000.
4. No common stock transactions occurred during 1997 or 1998.
5. All sales were on account.

Instructions
(a) Indicate, by using ratios, the change in liquidity and profitability of Caroline Company from 1997 to 1998. [*Note:* Not all profitability ratios can be computed nor can cash-basis ratios be computed.]
(b) Given below are three independent situations and a ratio that may be affected. For each situation, compute the affected ratio (1) as of December 31, 1998, and (2) as of December 31, 1999, after giving effect to the situation. Net income for 1999 was $40,000. Total assets on December 31, 1999, were $700,000.

Situation	Ratio
1. 18,000 shares of common stock were sold at par on July 1, 1999.	Return on common stockholders' equity
2. All of the notes payable were paid in 1999.	Debt to total assets
3. The market price of common stock was $9 and $12.80 on December 31, 1998 and 1999, respectively.	Price-earnings

P14-5 Selected financial data of two intense competitors in a recent year are presented here (in millions):

Compute selected ratios, and compare liquidity, profitability, and solvency for two companies.
(SO 5)

	Kmart Corporation	Wal-Mart Stores, Inc.
Income Statement Data for Year		
Net sales	$34,025	$82,494
Cost of goods sold	25,992	65,586
Selling and administrative expenses	7,701	12,858
Interest expense	494	706
Other income (net)	572	918
Income tax expense	114	1,581
Net income	$ 296	$ 2,681
Balance Sheet Data (End of Year)		
Current assets	$ 9,187	$15,338
Property, plant, and equipment (net)	7,842	17,481
Total assets	$17,029	$32,819
Current liabilities	$ 5,626	$ 9,973
Long-term debt	5,371	10,120
Total stockholders' equity	6,032	12,726
Total liabilities and stockholders' equity	$17,029	$32,819
Beginning-of-Year Balances		
Total assets	$17,504	$26,441
Total stockholders' equity	6,093	10,753
Other Data		
Average net receivables	$ 1,570	$ 695
Average inventory	7,317	12,539
Net cash provided by operating activities	351	3,106

Instructions

(a) For each company, compute the following ratios:
  (1) Current
  (2) Receivables turnover
  (3) Average collection period
  (4) Inventory turnover
  (5) Average days in inventory
  (6) Profit margin
  (7) Asset turnover
  (8) Return on assets
  (9) Return on common stockholders' equity
  (10) Debt to total assets
  (11) Times interest earned
  (12) Current cash debt coverage
  (13) Cash return on sales
  (14) Cash debt coverage

(b) Compare the liquidity, solvency, and profitability of the two companies.

P14-6 The comparative statements of Ultra Vision Company are presented here:

Compute numerous ratios.
(SO 5)

ULTRA VISION COMPANY
Income Statement
For Years Ended December 31

	1998	1997
Net sales (all on account)	$600,000	$520,000
Expenses		
Cost of goods sold	415,000	354,000
Selling and administrative	120,800	114,800
Interest expense	7,200	6,000
Income tax expense	18,000	14,000
Total expenses	561,000	488,800
Net income	$ 39,000	$ 31,200

696 CHAPTER 14 Financial Analysis: The Big Picture

ULTRA VISION COMPANY
Balance Sheet
December 31

	1998	1997
Assets		
Current assets		
Cash	$ 21,000	$ 18,000
Marketable securities	18,000	15,000
Accounts receivable (net)	92,000	74,000
Inventory	84,000	70,000
Total current assets	215,000	177,000
Plant assets (net)	423,000	383,000
Total assets	$638,000	$560,000
Liabilities and Stockholders' Equity		
Current liabilities		
Accounts payable	$112,000	$110,000
Income taxes payable	23,000	20,000
Total current liabilities	135,000	130,000
Long-term liabilities		
Bonds payable	130,000	80,000
Total liabilities	265,000	210,000
Stockholders' equity		
Common stock ($5 par)	150,000	150,000
Retained earnings	223,000	200,000
Total stockholders' equity	373,000	350,000
Total liabilities and stockholders' equity	$638,000	$560,000

Additional data: The common stock recently sold at $19.50 per share.

Instructions
Compute the following ratios for 1998:
(a) Current
(b) Acid-test
(c) Receivables turnover
(d) Average collection period
(e) Inventory turnover
(f) Average days in inventory
(g) Profit margin
(h) Asset turnover
(i) Return on assets
(j) Return on common stockholders' equity
(k) Earnings per share
(l) Price-earnings
(m) Payout
(n) Debt to total assets
(o) Times interest earned

Compute missing information given a set of ratios.
(SO 5)

P14-7 Presented here are an incomplete income statement and an incomplete comparative balance sheet of Vienna Corporation:

VIENNA CORPORATION
Income Statement
For the Year Ended December 31, 1998

Sales	$11,000,000
Cost of goods sold	?
Gross profit	?
Operating expenses	1,665,000
Income from operations	?
Other expenses and losses	
Interest expense	?
Income before income taxes	?
Income tax expense	560,000
Net income	$?

VIENNA CORPORATION
December 31
Balance Sheet

	1998	1997
Assets		
Current assets		
Cash	$ 450,000	$ 375,000
Accounts receivable (net)	?	950,000
Inventory	?	1,720,000
Total current assets	?	3,045,000
Plant assets (net)	4,620,000	3,955,000
Total assets	$?	$7,000,000
Liabilities and Stockholders' Equity		
Current liabilities	$?	$ 825,000
Long-term notes payable	?	2,800,000
Total liabilities	?	3,625,000
Common stock, $1 par	3,000,000	3,000,000
Retained earnings	400,000	375,000
Total stockholders' equity	3,400,000	3,375,000
Total liabilities and stockholders' equity	$?	$7,000,000

Additional information:
1. The receivables turnover for 1998 is 10 times.
2. All sales are on account.
3. The profit margin for 1998 is 14.5%.
4. Return on assets is 22% for 1998.
5. The current ratio on December 31, 1998, is 3:1.
6. The inventory turnover for 1998 is 4.8 times.

Instructions
Compute the missing information given the ratios. Show your computations. [*Note:* Start with one ratio and derive as much information as possible from it before trying another ratio. List all missing amounts under the ratio used to find the information.]

ALTERNATIVE PROBLEMS

All of the Alternative Problems in this chapter employ decision tools.

P14-1A Here are comparative statement data for Brooke Company and Shields Company, two competitors. All balance sheet data are as of December 31, 1998, and December 31, 1997.

Prepare vertical analysis and comment on profitability.
(SO 4, 5)

	Brooke Company		Shields Company	
	1998	1997	1998	1997
Net sales	$250,000		$1,200,000	
Cost of goods sold	160,000		720,000	
Operating expenses	51,000		252,000	
Interest expense	3,000		10,000	
Income tax expense	11,000		65,000	
Current assets	130,000	$110,000	700,000	$650,000
Plant assets (net)	305,000	270,000	800,000	750,000
Current liabilities	60,000	52,000	250,000	275,000
Long-term liabilities	50,000	68,000	200,000	150,000
Common stock	260,000	210,000	750,000	700,000
Retained earnings	65,000	50,000	300,000	275,000

698 CHAPTER 14 Financial Analysis: The Big Picture

Instructions
(a) Prepare a vertical analysis of the 1998 income statement data for Brooke Company and Shields Company.

(b) Comment on the relative profitability of the companies by computing the return on assets and the return on common stockholders' equity ratios for both companies.

Compute ratios from balance sheet and income statement.
(SO 5)

P14-2A The comparative statements of Marti Rosen Company are presented here:

MARTI ROSEN COMPANY
Income Statement
For the Years Ended December 31

	1998	1997
Net sales	$660,000	$624,000
Cost of goods sold	440,000	405,600
Gross profit	220,000	218,400
Selling and administrative expense	143,880	149,760
Income from operations	76,120	68,640
Other expenses and losses		
Interest expense	7,920	7,200
Income before income taxes	68,200	61,440
Income tax expense	25,300	24,000
Net income	$ 42,900	$ 37,440

MARTI ROSEN COMPANY
Balance Sheet
December 31

	1998	1997
Assets		
Current assets		
Cash	$ 23,100	$ 21,600
Marketable securities	34,800	33,000
Accounts receivable (net)	106,200	93,800
Inventory	72,400	64,000
Total current assets	236,500	212,400
Plant assets (net)	465,300	459,600
Total assets	$701,800	$672,000
Liabilities and Stockholders' Equity		
Current liabilities		
Accounts payable	$134,200	$132,000
Income taxes payable	25,300	24,000
Total current liabilities	159,500	156,000
Bonds payable	132,000	120,000
Total liabilities	291,500	276,000
Stockholders' equity		
Common stock ($10 par)	140,000	150,000
Retained earnings	270,300	246,000
Total stockholders' equity	410,300	396,000
Total liabilities and stockholders' equity	$701,800	$672,000

On July 1, 1998, 1,000 shares were repurchased and canceled. All sales were on account. Net cash provided by operating activities was $36,000.

Instructions
Compute the following ratios for 1998:
(a) Earnings per share
(b) Return on common stockholders' equity
(c) Return on assets
(d) Current
(e) Acid-test
(f) Receivables turnover
(g) Average collection period
(h) Inventory turnover
(i) Average days in inventory
(j) Times interest earned
(k) Asset turnover
(l) Debt to total assets
(m) Current cash debt coverage
(n) Cash return on sales
(o) Cash debt coverage

P14-3A These are condensed balance sheet and income statement data for Los Colinas Corporation:

Perform ratio analysis.
(SO 5)

LOS COLINAS CORPORATION
Balance Sheet
December 31

	1998	1997	1996
Cash	$ 40,000	$ 24,000	$ 20,000
Receivables (net)	70,000	45,000	48,000
Other current assets	80,000	75,000	62,000
Investments	90,000	70,000	50,000
Plant and equipment (net)	450,000	400,000	360,000
	$730,000	$614,000	$540,000
Current liabilities	$ 98,000	$ 75,000	$ 70,000
Long-term debt	97,000	75,000	65,000
Common stock, $10 par	400,000	340,000	300,000
Retained earnings	135,000	124,000	105,000
	$730,000	$614,000	$540,000

LOS COLINAS CORPORATION
Income Statement
For the Years Ended December 31

	1998	1997
Sales	$700,000	$750,000
Less: Sales returns and allowances	40,000	50,000
Net sales	660,000	700,000
Cost of goods sold	420,000	400,000
Gross profit	240,000	300,000
Operating expenses (including income taxes)	194,000	237,000
Net income	$ 46,000	$ 63,000

Additional information:
1. The market price of Los Colinas's common stock was $5.00, $4.50, and $2.30 for 1996, 1997, and 1998, respectively.
2. All dividends were paid in cash.
3. On July 1, 1997, 4,000 shares of common stock were issued, and on July 1, 1998, 6,000 shares were issued.

Instructions
(a) Compute the following ratios for 1997 and 1998:
   (1) Profit margin
   (2) Gross profit rate
   (3) Asset turnover
   (4) Earnings per share
   (5) Price-earnings
   (6) Payout
   (7) Debt to total assets

Compute ratios; comment on overall liquidity and profitability.
(SO 5)

(b) Based on the ratios calculated, discuss briefly the improvement or lack thereof in the financial position and operating results from 1997 to 1998 of Los Colinas Corporation.

P14-4A Financial information for Star Track Company is presented here:

STAR TRACK COMPANY
Balance Sheet
December 31

	1998	1997
Assets		
Cash	$ 50,000	$ 42,000
Short-term investments	80,000	100,000
Receivables (net)	100,000	87,000
Inventories	440,000	400,000
Prepaid expenses	25,000	31,000
Land	75,000	75,000
Building and equipment (net)	570,000	500,000
Total assets	$1,340,000	$1,235,000
Liabilities and Stockholders' Equity		
Notes payable	$ 125,000	$ 125,000
Accounts payable	160,000	140,000
Accrued liabilities	50,000	50,000
Bonds payable, due 2000	200,000	200,000
Common stock, $5 par	500,000	500,000
Retained earnings	305,000	220,000
Total liabilities and stockholders' equity	$1,340,000	$1,235,000

STAR TRACK COMPANY
Income Statement
For the Years Ended December 31

	1998	1997
Sales	$1,000,000	$ 940,000
Cost of goods sold	650,000	635,000
Gross profit	350,000	305,000
Operating expenses	235,000	215,000
Net income	$ 115,000	$ 90,000

Additional information:
1. Inventory at the beginning of 1997 was $350,000
2. Receivables at the beginning of 1997 were $80,000.
3. Total assets at the beginning of 1997 were $1,175,000.
4. No common stock transactions occurred during 1997 or 1998.
5. All sales were on account.

Instructions
(a) Indicate, by using ratios, the change in liquidity and profitability of Star Track Company from 1997 to 1998. [*Note:* Not all profitability ratios can be computed nor can cash-basis ratios be computed.]
(b) Given below are three independent situations and a ratio that may be affected. For each situation, compute the affected ratio (1) as of December 31, 1998, and (2) as of December 31, 1999, after giving effect to the situation. Net income for 1999 was $125,000. Total assets on December 31, 1999, were $1,500,000.

Situation	Ratio
1. 65,000 shares of common stock were sold at par on July 1, 1999.	Returns on common stockholders' equity
2. All of the notes payable were paid in 1999.	Debt to total assets
3. The market price of common stock on December 31, 1999, was $6.25. The market price on December 31, 1998, was $5.	Price-earnings

P14-5A Selected financial data of two intense competitors in a recent year are presented here (in millions):

Compute selected ratios, and compare liquidity, profitability, and solvency for two companies.

(SO 5)

	Bethlehem Steel Corporation	Inland Steel Company
Income Statement Data for Year		
Net sales	$4,819	$4,497
Cost of goods sold	4,548	3,991
Selling and administrative expenses	137	265
Interest expense	46	72
Other income (net)	7	0
Income tax expense	14	62
Net income	$ 81	$ 107
Balance Sheet Data (End of Year)		
Current assets	$1,569	$1,081
Property, plant, and equipment (net)	2,759	1,610
Other assets	1,454	662
Total assets	$5,782	$3,353
Current liabilities	$1,011	$565
Long-term debt	3,615	2,056
Total stockholders' equity	1,156	732
Total liabilities and stockholders' equity	$5,782	$3,353
Beginning-of-Year Balances		
Total assets	$5,877	$3,436
Total stockholders' equity	697	623
Other Data		
Average net receivables	$ 511	$ 515
Average inventory	868	403
Net cash provided by operating activities	90	160

Instructions

(a) For each company, compute the following ratios:
  (1) Current
  (2) Receivables turnover
  (3) Average collection period
  (4) Inventory turnover
  (5) Average days in inventory
  (6) Profit margin
  (7) Asset turnover
  (8) Return on assets
  (9) Return on common stockholders' equity
  (10) Debt to total assets
  (11) Times interest earned
  (12) Current cash debt coverage
  (13) Cash return on sales
  (14) Cash debt coverage

(b) Compare the liquidity, solvency, and profitability of the two companies.

702 CHAPTER 14 Financial Analysis: The Big Picture

BROADENING YOUR PERSPECTIVE

FINANCIAL REPORTING AND ANALYSIS

FINANCIAL REPORTING PROBLEM: *Starbucks Corporation*

BYP14-1 Your parents are considering investing in Starbucks Corporation common stock. They ask you, as an accounting expert, to make an analysis of the company for them. Fortunately, excerpts from a current annual report of Starbucks are presented in Appendix A of this textbook. Note that all dollar amounts are in thousands.

Instructions
(a) Make a 5-year trend analysis, using 1992 as the base year, of (1) net revenues and (2) operating income. Comment on the significance of the trend results.
(b) Compute for 1996 and 1995 the (1) debt to total assets ratio and (2) times interest earned ratio. How would you evaluate Starbucks' long-term solvency?
(c) Compute for 1996 and 1995 the (1) profit margin ratio, (2) asset turnover ratio, (3) return on assets ratio, and (4) return on common stockholders' equity ratio. How would you evaluate Starbucks' profitability? Total assets at October 2, 1994, were $231,421, and total stockholders' equity at October 2, 1994, was $109,898.
(d) What information outside the annual report may also be useful to your parents in making a decision about Starbucks?

COMPARATIVE ANALYSIS PROBLEM: *Starbucks vs. Green Mountain Coffee*

BYP14-2 The financial statements of Green Mountain Coffee are presented in Appendix B, following the financial statements for Starbucks in Appendix A.

Instructions
(a) Based on the information in the financial statements, determine each of the following for each company:
  (1) The percentage increase in net sales and in net income from 1995 to 1996.
  (2) The percentage increase in total assets and in total stockholders' equity from 1995 to 1996.
  (3) The earnings per share for 1996.
(b) What conclusions concerning the two companies can be drawn from these data?

RESEARCH CASE

BYP14-3 The chapter stresses the importance of comparing an individual company's financial ratios to industry norms. Robert Morris Associates (RMA), a national association of bank loan and credit officers, publishes industry-specific financial data in its *Annual Statement Studies*. This publication includes vertical analysis financial statements and various ratios classified by four-digit SIC code. [*Note:* An alternative source is Dun & Bradstreet's *Industry Norms and Key Business Ratios*.]

Obtain the 1996 edition of *Annual Statement Studies* (covering fiscal years ended April 1, 1995, through March 31, 1996) and the 1996 or 1997 annual report of Wal-Mart Stores, Inc.

Instructions
(a) Prepare a 1996 vertical analysis balance sheet and income statement for Wal-Mart.
(b) Calculate those 1996 ratios for Wal-Mart that are covered by RMA. [*Note:* The specific ratio definitions used by RMA are described in the beginning of the book. Use ending values for balance sheet items.]
(c) What is Wal-Mart's SIC code? Use your answers from parts (a) and (b) to compare Wal-Mart to the appropriate current industry data. How does Wal-Mart compare to

its competitors? [*Note:* RMA sorts current-year data by firm assets and sales, while 5 years of historical data are presented on an aggregate basis.]
(d) How many sets of financial statements did RMA use in compiling the current industry data sorted by sales?

INTERPRETING FINANCIAL STATEMENTS

BYP14-4 Minicase 1 *Manitowoc Company vs. Caterpillar Corp.*
Manitowoc Company and Caterpillar Corporation are both producers and sellers of large fixed assets. Caterpillar is substantially larger than Manitowoc. Financial information taken from each company's financial statements is provided here:

Financial Highlights	Caterpillar (in millions) 1995	1994	Manitowoc (in thousands) 1995	1994
Cash and short-term investments	$ 638	$ 419	$ 16,635	$ 16,163
Accounts receivable	4,285	4,290	51,011	29,500
Inventory	1,921	1,835	52,928	36,793
Other current assets	803	865	14,571	14,082
Current assets	7,647	7,409	135,145	96,538
Total assets	16,830	16,250	324,915	159,465
Current liabilities	6,049	5,498	110,923	54,064
Total liabilities	13,442	13,339	243,254	84,408
Total stockholders' equity	3,388	2,911	81,661	75,057
Sales	15,451		313,149	
Cost of goods sold	12,000		237,679	
Interest expense	191		1,865	
Income tax expense	501		8,551	
Net income	1,136		14,569	
Cash provided from operations	2,190		16,367	

Instructions
(a) Calculate the following liquidity ratios and discuss the relative liquidity of the two companies:
  (1) Current
  (2) Acid-test
  (3) Current cash debt coverage
  (4) Receivables turnover
  (5) Inventory turnover
(b) Calculate the following solvency ratios and discuss the relative solvency of the two companies:
  (1) Debt to total assets
  (2) Times interest earned
(c) Calculate the following profitability ratios and discuss the relative profitability of the two companies:
  (1) Asset turnover
  (2) Profit margin
  (3) Return on assets
  (4) Return on common stockholders' equity

BYP14-5 Minicase 2 *Sears, Roebuck and Co.*
The income statements, selected balance sheet information, and selected note disclosures from the annual report of Sears, Roebuck and Co. for 1993 are presented on the following pages.

SEARS

SEARS, ROEBUCK AND CO.
Consolidated Statements of Income
Years Ended December 31
(in millions except per common share data)

	1993	1992	1991
Revenues	$50,837.5	$52,344.6	$50,982.9
Expenses			
Costs and expenses	47,233.7	52,478.3	48,568.2
Restructuring (note 4)		3,108.4	
Interest	1,498.1	1,510.9	1,680.5
Total expenses	48,731.8	57,097.6	50,248.7
Operating income (loss)	2,105.7	(4,753.0)	734.2
Other income (loss)	206.0	(27.2)	129.6
Gain on the sale of subsidiaries stock	635.1	91.4	
Income (loss) before income taxes (benefit, minority interest, and equity income)	2,946.8	(4,688.8)	863.8
Income taxes (benefit)	400.9	(2,114.0)	(38.5)
Minority interest and equity in net income of unconsolidated companies	(136.9)	8.0	13.3
Income (loss) from continuing operations	2,409.1	(2,566.8)	915.6
Discontinued operations (note 3)			
Operating income, less income tax expense of $167.7, $299.2, and $231.0	240.1	507.9	363.3
Loss on disposal including income tax expense of $22.0	(64.0)		
Income (loss) before extraordinary loss and cumulative effect of accounting changes	2,585.2	(2,058.9)	1,278.9
Extraordinary loss related to the early extinguishment of debt	(210.8)		
Cumulative effect of accounting changes (note 2)		(1,873.4)	
Net income (loss)	$ 2,374.4	($3,932.3)	$ 1,278.9
Earnings (loss) per common share, after allowing for dividends on preferred shares			
Income (loss) from continuing operations	$6.22	($7.02)	$2.65
Discontinued operations	.46	1.37	1.06
Income (loss) before extraordinary loss and cumulative effect of accounting changes	6.68	(5.65)	3.71
Extraordinary loss	(.55)		
Cumulative effect of accounting changes		(5.07)	
Net income (loss)	$6.13	($10.72)	$3.71

SEARS, ROEBUCK AND CO.
Partial Balance Sheets
Years Ended December 31
(selected figures, in millions)

	1993	1992
Total assets	$90,807.8	$85,490.6
Retail customer receivables	15,905.6	13,877.6
Inventories	3,518.0	4,047.9
Total liabilities	76,809.7	74,423.2

Common shareholders' equity		
Common shares ($.75 par)	$ 293.8	$ 290.6
Capital in excess of par	2,353.8	2,194.6
Retained earnings	8,162.8	8,772.2
Less: Treasury stock (at cost)	(1,703.5)	(1,734.3)
Adjustments	995.9	(311.2)
Total common shareholders' equity	$10,102.8	$ 9,211.9

SEARS, ROEBUCK AND CO.
Notes to Financial Statements
(selected information)

Note 1. Summary of significant accounting policies
Inventories: Inventories . . . are valued primarily at the lower of cost (using the last-in, first-out or LIFO method) or market by application of internally developed price indices to estimate the effects of inflation on inventories. . . . If the first-in, first-out (FIFO) method of inventory valuation has been used instead of the LIFO method, inventories would have been $743.7 million and $738.4 million higher at December 31, 1993 and 1992, respectively.

Property and equipment: Property and equipment is stated at cost less accumulated depreciation. Depreciation is provided principally by the straight-line method over the estimated useful lives of the related assets.

Note 2. Accounting changes
Effective Jan. 1, 1992, the Company adopted SFAS No. 106, "Employers' Accounting for Postretirement Benefits Other than Pensions," and SFAS No. 112, "Employers' Accounting for Postemployment Benefits," for all domestic and foreign postretirement and postemployment benefit plans by immediately recognizing the transition amounts. The Company previously expensed the cost of these benefits, which consist of health care and life insurance, as claims were incurred.

Note 3. Discontinued operations
In May 1993, the Company entered into separate agreements to sell the Coldwell-Banker Residential business and Sears Mortgage Banking operations. A $64.0 million after-tax loss was recorded in the second quarter of 1993, primarily due to adverse income tax effects related to the sale of Sears Savings Bank. These sales were completed in the fourth quarter of 1993.

Note 4. Restructuring
The Merchandise Group recorded a pretax charge in the fourth quarter of 1992 of $2.65 billion related to discontinuing its domestic catalog operations, offering a voluntary early retirement program to certain salaried associates, closing unprofitable retail department and specialty stores, streamlining or discontinuing various unprofitable merchandise lines, and the writedown of underutilized assets to market value. Corporate also recorded a $23.8 million pretax charge related to offering termination and early retirement programs to certain associates. Additionally, Homart recorded a $326.6 million pretax write-down of land previously held for office development and selected office properties that were to be sold.

    During the first quarter of 1992, the Merchandise Group recorded a $106.0 million pretax charge for severance costs related to cost reduction programs for commission sales and headquarters staff in domestic merchandising.

    The Merchandise Group and Corporate restructuring charges and Homart [consolidated subsidiary] property write-downs amounted to a combined after-tax expense of $1.95 billion in 1992.

Instructions

(a) Calculate the following ratios for 1993 and then evaluate Sears' profitability:
  (1) Profit margin for both income from continuing operations and net income
  (2) Return on common stockholders' equity
  (3) Return on assets
  (4) Times interest earned
(b) Sears showed a loss of $1.65 billion from Hurricane Andrew in 1992. In what category does the loss appear in Sears' 1992 income statement?
(c) Sears' revenues from its merchandising operations were $26.29 billion, and its cost of sales was $18.76 billion in 1993.
  (1) Calculate Sears' inventory turnover ratio for 1993.
  (2) Suppose you wanted to compare Sears' inventory turnover ratio with that of a Canadian company, which under Canadian accounting standards must use FIFO. Would you be able to make such a comparison? If so, how?
  (3) Calculate Sears' receivables turnover ratio for 1993.
  (4) Unlike most retailers, whose fiscal year ends a month into the following year, Sear's year-end is December 31. What effect does Sears' year-end have on the inventory turnover and receivables turnover ratios?
  (5) What effect does Sears' nonstandard year-end (for a retailer) have on the comparability of Sears' ratios with those of other large retailers?
(d) Sears sold two business segments in 1993.
  (1) What did it sell and in what quarter were these sales completed?
  (2) Where does the income or loss from these sales appear on Sears' income statement?

CRITICAL THINKING

MANAGEMENT DECISION CASE

BYP14-6 You are a loan officer for Second State Bank of Port Washington. Ted Worth, President of T. Worth Corporation, has just left your office. He is interested in an 8-year loan to expand the company's operations. The borrowed funds would be used to purchase new equipment. As evidence of the company's debt-worthiness, Worth provided you with the following facts:

	1998	1997
Current ratio	3.1	2.1
Acid-test ratio	.8	1.4
Asset turnover ratio	2.8	2.2
Cash debt coverage ratio	.1	.2
Net income	Up 32%	Down 8%
Earnings per share	$3.30	$2.50

Ted Worth is a very insistent (some would say pushy) man. When you told him that you would need additional information before making your decision, he acted offended, and said, "What more could you possibly want to know?" You responded that, at a minimum, you would need complete, audited financial statements.

Instructions

(a) Explain why you would want the financial statements to be audited.
(b) Discuss the implications of the ratios provided for the lending decision you are to make. That is, does the information paint a favorable picture? Are these ratios relevant to the decision?
(c) List three other ratios that you would want to calculate for this company, and explain why you would use each.
(d) What are the limitations of ratio analysis for credit and investing decisions?

A REAL-WORLD FOCUS: *The Coca-Cola Company vs. PepsiCo, Inc.*

BYP14-7 *The Coca-Cola Company and PepsiCo, Inc.* provide refreshments to every corner of the world. Selected data from the consolidated financial statements for The Coca-Cola Company and for PepsiCo, Inc., are presented here:

	Coca-Cola	PepsiCo
Total current assets (including cash, accounts receivable, and marketable securities totaling $3,056 and $3,539, respectively)	$ 5,205	$ 5,546
Total current liabilities	6,177	5,230
Net sales	16,172	30,421
Cost of goods sold	6,167	14,886
Net income	2,554	1,606
Average receivables for the year	1,384	2,229
Average inventories for the year	1,048	1,011
Average total assets	12,947	25,112
Average common stockholders' equity	4,910	7,085
Net cash provided by operating activities	3,115	3,742
Average current liabilities	6,763	5,250
Total assets	13,873	25,432
Total liabilities	8,638	18,119
Income before income taxes	3,728	2,432
Interest expense	199	682
Cash provided by operating activities	3,115	3,742

Instructions

(a) Compute the following liquidity ratios for Coca-Cola and for PepsiCo. and comment on the relative liquidity of the two competitors:
  (1) Current
  (2) Acid-test
  (3) Receivables turnover
  (4) Average collection period
  (5) Inventory turnover
  (6) Average days in inventory
  (7) Current cash debt coverage

(b) Compute the following solvency ratios for the two companies and comment on the relative solvency of the two competitors:
  (1) Debt to total assets ratio
  (2) Times interest earned
  (3) Cash debt coverage ratio

(c) Compute the following profitability ratios for the two companies and comment on the relative profitability of the two competitors:
  (1) Profit margin
  (2) Cash return on sales
  (3) Asset turnover
  (4) Return on assets
  (5) Return on common stockholders' equity

GROUP ACTIVITY

BYP14-8 Three types of analyses are explained in the chapter: horizontal, vertical, and ratio.

Instructions
With the class divided into five groups, each group will take one of the following topics: horizontal analysis, vertical analysis, ratio analysis—liquidity, ratio analysis—solvency, and ratio analysis—profitability. For horizontal analysis and vertical analysis, the group should explain the analysis and illustrate its application to the balance sheet and income statement. For each category of ratio analysis, the group should state the formula and purpose of each ratio.

COMMUNICATION ACTIVITY

BYP14-9 L. R. Stanton is the chief executive officer of Hi-Tech Electronics. Stanton is an expert engineer but a novice in accounting. Stanton asks you, as an accounting major, to explain (a) the bases for comparison in analyzing Hi-Tech's financial statements and (b) the limitations, if any, in financial statement analysis.

Instructions
Write a memo to L. R. Stanton that explains the basis for comparison and the limitations of financial statement analysis.

ETHICS CASE

BYP14-10 Vern Fairly, president of Fairly Industries, wishes to issue a press release to bolster his company's image and maybe even its stock price, which has been gradually falling. As controller, you have been asked to provide a list of 20 financial ratios along with some other operating statistics relative to Fairly Industries' first-quarter financials and operations.

Two days after you provide the ratios and data requested, you are asked by Roberta Sanchez, the public relations director of Fairly, to prove the accuracy of the financial and operating data contained in the press release written by the president and edited by Roberta. In the news release, the president highlights the sales increase of 25% over last year's first quarter and the positive change in the current ratio from 1.5:1 last year to 3:1 this year. He also emphasizes that production was up 50% over the prior year's first quarter. You note that the release contains only positive or improved ratios and none of the negative or deteriorated ratios. For instance, no mention is made that the debt to total assets ratio has increased from 35% to 55%, that inventories are up 89%, and that although the current ratio improved, the acid-test ratio fell from 1:1 to .5:1. Nor is there any mention that the reported profit for the quarter would have been a loss had not the estimated lives of Fairly's plant and machinery been increased by 30%. Roberta emphasized, "The Pres wants this release by early this afternoon."

Instructions
(a) Who are the stakeholders in this situation?
(b) Is there anything unethical in President Fairly's actions?
(c) Should you as controller remain silent? Does Roberta have any responsibility?

FINANCIAL ANALYSIS ON THE WEB

BYP14-11 *Purpose:* Financial statements communicate to investors, creditors, and management the financial health of the organization. Companies are aware that financial statements are read by individuals who have varying degrees of understanding of financial matters. IBM's "Guide to Understanding Financials," which is located on its homepage, is one company's effort to provide online information for novice users. This guide takes an investor's approach to understanding the different financial statements.

Address: http://www.ibm.com/financialguide

Steps: Go to the above address.

Instructions
Answer the following questions:
(a) List two required elements in an annual report. List one optional element.
(b) What is the auditors' report?
(c) What financial statements are required in an annual report? What is included in the notes to the financial statements?
(d) From an investor's perspective, list two general suggestions for an approach to reviewing financial statements.

BYP14-12 *Purpose:* To understand the Management Discussion and Analysis (MD&A) section of an annual report.

Addresses: http://www.ibm.com/financialguide
http://www.yahoo.com

Steps:
1. From IBM's Financial Guide, choose **Guides Contents.**
2. Choose **Anatomy of an Annual Report.**
3. Follow instruction (a).
4. From Yahoo Homepage, choose **Stock Quotes.**
5. Enter **GE.**
6. Choose **Get Quotes.**

7. Choose **SEC filing** (this will take you to Yahoo-Edgar Online).
8. Choose **Mar. 1997 Annual Report.**
9. Follow instructions (b)–(e).

Instructions
(a) Using IBM's Financial Guide, describe the content of the Management Discussion and Analysis.
(b) In the overview section, GE's management discusses the company's performance. What were the net 1996 corporate earnings?
(c) Compare 1996 earnings with 1995 earnings.
(d) What were management's reasons for the increase in net earnings?
(e) The second part of the MD&A addresses the company's capital resources and liquidity. What was GE's debt to equity ratio in 1996?

Answers to Self-Study Questions
1. d   2. d   3. b   4. d   5. a   6. c   7. c   8. c   9. c   10. b
11. a   12. a

APPENDIX A

Specimen Financial Statements: Starbucks Corporation

*T*HE ANNUAL REPORT

Once each year a corporation communicates to its stockholders and other interested parties by issuing a complete set of audited financial statements. The **annual report,** as this communication is called, summarizes the financial results of its operations for the year and its plans for the future. Many such annual reports have become attractive, multicolored, glossy public relations ad pieces containing pictures of corporate officers and directors as well as photos and descriptions of new products and new buildings. Yet the basic function of every annual report is to report financial information, almost all of which is a product of the corporation's accounting system.

The content and organization of corporate annual reports has become fairly standardized. Excluding the public relations part of the report (pictures, products, and propaganda), the following items are the traditional financial portions of the annual report:

   Financial Highlights
   Letter to the Stockholders
   Management's Report
   Auditor's Report
   Financial Statements (and Management's Analysis)
   Notes to the Financial Statements
   Supplementary Financial Information

In this appendix we illustrate current financial reporting with a comprehensive set of corporate financial statements that are prepared in accordance with generally accepted accounting principles and audited by an international independent certified public accounting firm. We are grateful for permission to use the actual financial statements and other accompanying financial information from the annual report of a large, publicly held company, Starbucks Corporation.

Financial Highlights

The financial highlights section, called **Selected Financial Data** by Starbucks, is usually presented inside the front cover or on the first two pages of the annual report. This section generally reports the total or per share amounts for five to ten financial items for the current year and one or more previous years. Financial items from the income statement and the balance sheet that typically are presented are sales, income from continuing operations, net income, net income per share, dividends per common share, and the amount of capital expenditures. The financial highlights section from Starbucks' **Annual Report** is shown below.

Selected Financial Data

(IN THOUSANDS, EXCEPT EARNINGS PER SHARE)

The following selected financial data have been derived from the consolidated financial statements of the Company. The data set forth below should be read in conjunction with "Management's Discussion and Analysis of Financial Condition and Results of Operations" and the Company's consolidated financial statements and notes thereto.

As of and for the fiscal year ended:	Sept 29, 1996 (52 Wks)	Oct 1, 1995 (52 Wks)	Oct 2, 1994 (52 Wks)	Oct 3, 1993 (53 Wks)	Sept 27, 1992 (52 Wks)
Results of Operations Data:					
Net revenues					
Retail	$600,067	$402,655	$248,495	$153,610	$ 89,669
Specialty Sales	78,655	48,143	26,543	15,952	10,143
Direct Response	17,759	14,415	9,885	6,979	3,385
Total net revenues	696,481	465,213	284,923	176,541	103,197
Operating income	56,993	40,116	23,298	12,618	7,113
Provision for merger costs[1]	—	—	3,867	—	—
Gain on sale of investment in Noah's[2]	9,218	—	—	—	—
Net earnings	$ 42,128	$ 26,102	$ 10,206	$ 8,282	$ 4,454
Net earnings per common and common equivalent share—fully-diluted[3]	$ 0.54	$ 0.36	$ 0.17	$ 0.14	$ 0.09
Cash dividends per share	—	—	—	—	—
Balance Sheet Data:					
Working capital	$238,450	$134,304	$ 44,162	$ 42,092	$ 40,142
Total assets	726,613	468,178	231,421	201,712	91,547
Long-term debt (including current portion)	167,980	81,773	80,500	82,100	1,359
Redeemable preferred stock	—	—	—	4,944	—
Shareholders' equity	451,660	312,231	109,898	88,686	76,923

(1) Provision for merger costs reflects expenses related to the merger with The Coffee Connection, Inc. in fiscal 1994.

(2) Gain on sale of investment in Noah's of $9,218 ($5,669 after tax) results from the sale of Noah's New York Bagel, Inc. ("Noah's") stock in fiscal 1996.

(3) Earnings per share is based on the weighted average shares outstanding during the period plus, when their effect is dilutive, common stock equivalents consisting of certain shares subject to stock options. Fully-diluted earnings per share assumes conversion of the Company's convertible subordinated debentures using the "if converted" method, when such securities are dilutive, with net income adjusted for the after-tax interest expense and amortization applicable to these debentures.

Letter to the Stockholders

Nearly every annual report contains a letter to the stockholders from the Chairman of the Board or the President (or both). This letter typically discusses the company's accomplishments during the past year and highlights significant events such as mergers and acquisitions, new products, operating achievements, business philosophy, changes in officers or directors, financing commitments, expansion plans, and future prospects. The letter to the stockholders signed by Howard Schultz, Chairman of the Board and Chief Executive Officer, and Orin Smith, President and Chief Operating Officer, of Starbucks is shown below.

When we look back on the past 25 years, we are filled with a great sense of pride and gratitude for all that we have been able to accomplish. As we stand this year on the threshold of becoming a truly global brand, we want to express our enthusiasm for all that is to come.

At the end of fiscal 1993, we became the leading roaster and retailer of specialty coffee in North America, with more than 250 stores in 10 markets. Now, little more than three years later, we have firmly established our leadership position, ending fiscal 1996 with more than 1,000 retail locations in 32 markets throughout North America, and two new stores in Tokyo, Japan.

With more than 20,000 dedicated partners (employees), we are creating opportunities every day for millions of customers around the world to enjoy the Starbucks Experience. From selecting the finest arabica beans to hiring the most talented people, we are committed to applying the highest standards of quality in everything we do.

You can see it in our new store designs, which will appear this year in stores throughout North America. You can taste it in our new drinks, such as Rhumba™ Frappuccino®. You can hear it in our exclusive CDs, ranging from rhythm and blues to sounds from the '70s.

We have created an environment of constant discovery and self-renewal throughout our organization. We are gratified by the way our partners have transformed their passion for our products into a brand with depth and soul. When you walk into a Starbucks store, when you open a mail order package, when you drink our coffee on United Airlines, it is our goal to offer more than just a great cup of coffee—we want to offer a memorable experience.

Which is why we are pleased to say that with the help of our Japanese joint venture partners at SAZABY, Inc., our first stores in Tokyo, Japan opened this summer with lines around the block. We are excited about the global possibilities as more new customers embrace our business, and we know that we have many brand-building opportunities ahead of us.

In 1994, when we entered into a joint venture agreement with Pepsi-Cola to develop ready-to-drink coffee products, we knew that we wanted to redefine the category. In the spring of 1996, we launched our bottled Frappuccino™ coffee drink. After a very short testing period, we realized the enormous potential of this beverage, and we knew that we had to build new production facilities to prepare for the future of this product. We look forward to the positive reception of bottled Frappuccino when we expand the distribution nationwide in the summer of 1997. But most importantly, we knew that we had developed a platform for bigger product innovations.

Using the most sophisticated research and development technology available, we have created a coffee extract that is changing the way people think about everyday products. Early in 1996, we introduced our super-premium coffee-flavored ice creams, developed through our joint venture with Dreyer's Grand Ice Cream, Inc., which have since become the number one selling super-premium coffee-flavored ice creams in the nation.

During fiscal 1996, we installed proprietary, state-of-the-art roasting and manufacturing equipment to create a world-class manufacturing and logistics organization. We expanded our research and development efforts, building new coffee extract plants and new product development facilities. Our specialty sales and marketing team has continued to develop new channels of distribution, forming a new alliance with U.S. Office Products to sell Starbucks coffee to offices throughout the United States. And early in the first quarter of fiscal 1997, our direct response group launched a new America Online Caffè Starbucks store, which, in its previous format, had more than 600,000 visits last year.

This is not to say we haven't had our challenges, or taken risks. We had a holiday season in the first quarter that did not have the impact we had anticipated. We put our management team to the test and they demonstrated how well we can manage the company through difficult times. This team, utilizing their diverse experience, overcame significant green coffee price increases resulting from Brazilian frosts to give us a year with outstanding earnings, all the while paving the way for future growth.

With fiscal 1996 revenues of more than $696.4 million, we continue to work towards our long-term goal of becoming the most recognized and respected brand of coffee in the world. We entered several new markets this year, including Toronto, Rhode Island, North Carolina, and the overseas market of Tokyo, Japan. In fiscal 1997, we look forward to entering the new markets of Phoenix and Miami, as well as Hawaii and Singapore. At this time, we are also pleased to announce that we anticipate that cash from operations, combined with current cash and investments, will fund our core business growth in fiscal 1997.

We believe more strongly than ever that at the heart of our continuing success lie the company's two cornerstones: our coffee and our people. We were pleased to be able to grant eligible full and part-time partners stock options under our Bean Stock program again this year, which affords all partners a financial stake in our company's success. We will also be introducing a flexible benefits program in fiscal 1997, which has been created to meet the needs of our growing and diverse workforce.

Just as we tailor our benefits to our people, we design our stores to enhance our neighborhoods, and we encourage our partners to participate in events that support our communities. For the fifth consecutive year, Starbucks was also the largest corporate contributor to CARE, the international aid and development organization, whose work helps us to give back on a global level to those countries in which we do business.

Moving forward, we will continue to explore new opportunities and build value at all levels of our organization. Twenty-five years from now, when we look back again, if we can say that we grew our company with the same values and guiding principles that we embrace today, then we will know we have succeeded.

To all of you who touch Starbucks in any way, we would like to thank you for your ongoing support.

Warm regards,

Howard Schultz
chairman and chief executive officer

Orin Smith
president and chief operating officer

MANAGEMENT'S REPORT

A relatively recent addition to corporate annual reports is the statement made by management about its role in and responsibility for the accuracy and integrity of the financial statements. Starbucks' management letter is entitled **Management's Responsibility for Financial Reporting.** In it the Chairman of the Board and Chief Executive Officer along with the Chief Financial Officer and the Chief Operating Officer, on behalf of management: (1) assume primary responsibility for the financial statements and the related notes, (2) outline and assess the company's internal control system, (3) declare the financial statements in conformity with generally accepted accounting principles, and (4) comment on the audit by the certified public accountant and the composition and role of the Audit Committee of the Board of Directors. Starbucks' management report is presented below.

Management's Responsibility for Financial Reporting

(STARBUCKS CORPORATION)

The management of Starbucks Corporation is responsible for the preparation and integrity of the financial statements included in this Annual Report to Shareholders. The financial statements have been prepared in conformity with generally accepted accounting principles and include amounts based on management's best judgment where necessary. Financial information included elsewhere in this Annual Report is consistent with these financial statements.

Management maintains a system of internal controls and procedures designed to provide reasonable assurance that transactions are executed in accordance with proper authorization, that transactions are properly recorded in the Company's records, that assets are safeguarded, and that accountability for assets is maintained. The concept of reasonable assurance is based on the recognition that the cost of maintaining our system of internal accounting controls should not exceed benefits expected to be derived from the system. Internal controls and procedures are periodically reviewed and revised, when appropriate, due to changing circumstances and requirements.

Independent auditors are appointed by the Company's Board of Directors and ratified by the Company's shareholders to audit the financial statements in accordance with generally accepted auditing standards and to independently assess the fair presentation of the Company's financial position, results of operations, and cash flows. Their report appears in this Annual Report.

The Audit Committee of the Board of Directors, a majority of whom are outside directors, is responsible for monitoring the Company's accounting and reporting practices. The Audit Committee meets periodically with management and the independent auditors to ensure that each is properly discharging its responsibilities. The independent auditors have full and free access to the Committee without the presence of management to discuss the results of their audits, the adequacy of internal accounting controls, and the quality of financial reporting.

Howard Schultz
chairman and
chief executive officer

Orin Smith
president and
chief operating officer

Michael Casey
senior vice president and
chief financial officer

Auditor's Report

All publicly held corporations, as well as many other enterprises and organizations (both profit and not-for-profit, large and small) engage the services of independent certified public accountants for the purpose of obtaining an objective, expert report on their financial statements. Based on a comprehensive examination of the company's accounting system and records, and the financial statements, the outside CPA issues the auditor's report.

The standard auditor's report consists of three paragraphs: (1) an introductory paragraph, (2) a scope paragraph, and (3) the opinion paragraph. In the introductory paragraph, the auditor identifies who and what was audited and indicates the responsibilities of management and the auditor relative to the financial statements. In the scope paragraph the auditor states that the audit was conducted in accordance with generally accepted auditing standards and discusses the nature and limitations of the audit. In the opinion paragraph, the auditor expresses an informed opinion as to (1) the fairness of the financial statements and (2) their conformity with generally accepted accounting principles. The Report of Deloitte & Touche LLP appearing in Starbucks' Annual Report is shown below.

Starbucks Corporation

(SEATTLE, WASHINGTON)

We have audited the accompanying consolidated balance sheets of Starbucks Corporation and subsidiaries (the Company) as of September 29, 1996, and October 1, 1995, and the related consolidated statements of earnings, shareholders' equity, and cash flows for each of the three years in the period ended September 29, 1996. These financial statements are the responsibility of the Company's management. Our responsibility is to express an opinion on these financial statements based on our audits.

We conducted our audits in accordance with generally accepted auditing standards. Those standards require that we plan and perform the audit to obtain reasonable assurance about whether the financial statements are free of material misstatement. An audit includes examining, on a test basis, evidence supporting the amounts and disclosures in the financial statements. An audit also includes assessing the accounting principles used and significant estimates made by management, as well as evaluating the overall financial statement presentation. We believe that our audits provide a reasonable basis for our opinion.

In our opinion, such consolidated financial statements present fairly, in all material respects, the financial position of Starbucks Corporation and subsidiaries as of September 29, 1996, and October 1, 1995, and the results of their operations and their cash flows for each of the three years in the period ended September 29, 1996, in conformity with generally accepted accounting principles.

Deloitte & Touche LLP

Deloitte & Touche LLP
Seattle, Washington
November 22, 1996

The auditor's report issued on Starbucks' financial statements is "unqualified" or "clean"; that is, it contains no qualifications or exceptions. In other words, the auditor conformed completely with generally accepted auditing standards in performing the audit, and the financial statements conformed in all material respects with generally accepted accounting principles.

When the financial statements do not conform with generally accepted accounting principles, the auditor must issue a "qualified" opinion and describe the exception. If the lack of conformity with GAAP is sufficiently material, the auditor is compelled to issue an "adverse" or negative opinion. An adverse opinion means that the financial statements do not present fairly the company's financial condition and/or the results of the company's operations at the dates and for the periods reported.

In circumstances where the auditor is unable to perform all the auditing procedures necessary to reach a conclusion as to the fairness of the financial statements, a "disclaimer" must be issued. In these rare instances, the auditor must report the reason for failure to reach a conclusion on the fairness of the financial statements.

Companies strive to obtain an unqualified auditor's report. Hence, only infrequently are you likely to encounter anything other than this type of opinion on the financial statements.

Financial Statements and Accompanying Notes

The standard set of financial statements consists of: (1) a comparative income statement for three years, (2) a comparative balance sheet for two years, (3) a comparative statement of cash flows for three years, (4) a statement of retained earnings (or stockholders' equity) for three years, and (5) a set of accompanying notes that are considered an integral part of the financial statements. The auditor's report, unless stated otherwise, covers the financial statements and the accompanying notes. The financial statements and accompanying notes plus some supplementary data and analyses for Starbucks follow.

Consolidated Balance Sheets

(IN THOUSANDS, EXCEPT SHARE DATA)

	Sept 29, 1996	Oct 1, 1995
Assets		
Current Assets:		
Cash and cash equivalents	$126,215	$ 20,944
Short-term investments	103,221	41,507
Accounts and notes receivable	17,621	9,852
Inventories	83,370	123,657
Prepaid expenses and other current assets	6,534	4,768
Deferred income taxes, net	2,580	4,622
Total current assets	339,541	205,350
Joint ventures and equity investments	4,401	11,628
Property, plant, and equipment, net	369,477	244,728
Deposits and other assets	13,194	6,472
Total	$726,613	$468,178
Liabilities and Shareholders' Equity		
Current Liabilities:		
Accounts payable	$38,034	$28,668
Checks drawn in excess of bank balances	16,241	13,138
Accrued compensation and related costs	15,001	12,786
Accrued interest payable	3,004	650
Other accrued expenses	28,811	15,804
Total current liabilities	101,091	71,046
Deferred income taxes, net	7,114	3,490
Capital lease obligations	1,728	1,013
Convertible subordinated debentures	165,020	80,398
Commitments and contingencies (notes 4, 5, 8, and 12)		
Shareholders' Equity:		
Common stock–Authorized, 150,000,000 shares; issued and outstanding, 77,583,868 and 70,956,990 shares	361,309	265,679
Retained earnings, including cumulative translation adjustment of $(776) and $(435) respectively, and net unrealized holding gain on investments of $2,046 and $34, respectively	90,351	46,552
Total shareholders' equity	451,660	312,231
Total	$726,613	$468,178

Consolidated Statements of Earnings

(IN THOUSANDS, EXCEPT EARNINGS PER SHARE)

Fiscal year ended:	Sept 29, 1996	Oct 1, 1995	Oct 2, 1994
Net revenues	$696,481	$465,213	$284,923
Cost of sales and related occupancy costs	335,800	211,279	130,324
Store operating expenses	210,693	148,757	90,087
Other operating expenses	19,787	13,932	8,698
Depreciation and amortization	35,950	22,486	12,535
General and administrative expenses	37,258	28,643	19,981
Operating income	56,993	40,116	23,298
Interest income	11,029	6,792	2,130
Interest expense	(8,739)	(3,765)	(3,807)
Gain on sale of investment in Noah's	9,218	—	—
Provision for merger costs	—	—	(3,867)
Earnings before income taxes	68,501	43,143	17,754
Income taxes	26,373	17,041	7,548
Net earnings	42,128	26,102	10,206
Preferred stock dividends	—	—	270
Net earnings available to common shareholders	$ 42,128	$ 26,102	$ 9,936
Net earnings per common and common equivalent share—primary	$ 0.55	$ 0.37	$ 0.17
Net earnings per common and common equivalent share—fully-diluted	$ 0.54	$ 0.36	$ 0.17
Weighted average shares outstanding:			
Primary	76,964	71,309	59,718
Fully-diluted	80,831	71,909	59,757

Consolidated Statement of Cash Flows

(IN THOUSANDS)

Fiscal year ended:	Sept 29, 1996	Oct 1, 1995	Oct 2, 1994
Operating Activities:			
Net earnings	$ 42,128	$ 26,102	$ 10,206
Adjustments to reconcile net earnings to net cash provided (used) by operating activities:			
Depreciation and amortization	39,370	24,827	14,266
Provision for store remodels and asset disposals	412	2,745	1,333
Deferred income taxes, net	4,407	84	214
Equity in losses of investees	1,935	1,156	—
Gain on sale of investment in Noah's	(9,218)	—	—
Cash (used) provided by changes in operating assets and liabilities			
Accounts and notes receivable	(7,771)	(4,456)	(2,297)
Inventories	40,274	(67,579)	(30,079)
Prepaid expenses and other current assets	(1,769)	519	(1,813)
Accounts payable	9,291	19,590	2,389
Accrued compensation and related costs	2,208	3,717	2,944
Accrued interest payable	3,207	24	7
Other accrued expenses	12,205	5,822	3,403
Net cash provided by operating activities	136,679	12,551	573
Investing Activities:			
Purchase of short-term investments	(178,643)	(136,256)	(106,118)
Sale of short-term investments	17,144	27,702	73,701
Maturity of short-term investments	103,056	74,808	100,103
Investments in joint ventures and equity securities	(6,040)	(12,484)	(300)
Proceeds from sale of equity investments	20,550	—	—
Additions to property, plant, and equipment	(161,814)	(129,386)	(85,288)
Additions to deposits and other assets	(5,432)	(1,154)	(1,804)
Net cash used by investing activities	(211,179)	(176,770)	(19,706)
Financing Activities:			
Increase in cash provided by checks drawn in excess of bank balances	3,096	1,180	5,736
Proceeds from sale of convertible debentures	165,020	—	—
Debt issuance costs	(4,045)	—	—
Proceeds from notes payable	—	19,000	—
Principal repayments of notes payable	—	(19,000)	(1,600)
Net proceeds from sale of common stock	—	163,873	—
Proceeds from sale of common stock under employee stock purchase plan	1,735	263	—
Exercise of stock options and warrants	8,032	3,157	2,571
Tax benefit from exercise of nonqualified stock options	6,808	4,754	3,719
Payments received on subscription notes receivable	—	3,671	—
Payments on capital lease obligations	(575)	(147)	—
Debt conversion costs	(290)	—	—
Net cash provided by financing activities	179,781	176,751	10,426
Effect of exchange rate changes on cash and cash equivalents	(10)	18	(5)
Increase (decrease) in cash and cash equivalents	105,271	12,550	(8,712)
Cash and Cash Equivalents:			
Beginning of year	20,944	8,394	17,106
End of year	$126,215	$20,944	$8,394

Supplemental Disclosure of Cash Flow Information:

Cash paid during the year for:			
Interest	$ 5,630	$ 3,738	$ 3,612
Income taxes	12,127	10,761	4,565
Noncash Financing and Investing Transactions:			
Capital lease obligation incurred	$ 2,089	$ 1,522	$ —
Net unrealized holding gains (losses) on investments	2,012	141	(116)
Conversion of convertible debt into common stock, net of unamortized issue costs	79,345	100	—
Conversion of preferred stock into common stock	—	—	5,214
Preferred dividends accrued	—	—	270
Retirement of treasury stock	—	—	396

See Notes to Consolidated Financial Statements.

Consolidated Statements of Shareholders' Equity

(IN THOUSANDS, EXCEPT SHARE DATA)

	Common stock Shares	Common stock Amount	Retained earnings	Treasury stock Shares	Treasury stock Amount	Total
Balance, October 4, 1993	55,887,734	$ 78,753	$10,329	161,328	$(396)	$88,686
Exercise of stock options and warrants, including tax benefit of $3,719	1,608,548	6,290	—	—	—	6,290
Preferred dividends accrued	—	—	(270)	—	—	(270)
Conversion of redeemable preferred stock into common stock	602,034	5,214	—	—	—	5,214
Retirement of treasury stock	(161,328)	(396)	—	(161,328)	396	—
Net earnings	—	—	10,206	—	—	10,206
Unrealized holding losses, net	—	—	(116)	—	—	(116)
Translation adjustment	—	—	(112)	—	—	(112)
Balance, October 2, 1994	57,936,988	89,861	20,037	—	—	109,898
Exercise of stock options including tax benefit of $4,754	945,780	7,911	—	—	—	7,911
Sale of common stock	12,050,000	163,873	—	—	—	163,873
Payments received on stock subscription notes	—	3,671	—	—	—	3,671
Conversion of convertible debt into common stock	6,798	100	—	—	—	100
Sale of common stock under employee stock purchase plan	17,424	263	—	—	—	263
Net earnings	—	—	26,102	—	—	26,102
Unrealized holding gains, net	—	—	141	—	—	141
Translation adjustment	—	—	272	—	—	272
Balance, October 1, 1995	70,956,990	265,679	46,552	—	—	312,231
Exercise of stock options including tax benefit of $6,808	1,177,736	14,840	—	—	—	14,840
Conversions of convertible debt into common stock	5,359,769	79,055	—	—	—	79,055
Sale of common stock under employee stock purchase plan	89,373	1,735	—	—	—	1,735
Net earnings	—	—	42,128	—	—	42,128
Unrealized holding gains, net	—	—	2,012	—	—	2,012
Translation adjustment	—	—	(341)	—	—	(341)
Balance, September 29, 1996	77,583,868	$361,309	$90,351	—	$ —	$451,660

Management's Discussion and Analysis of Financial Condition and Results of Operations

General Starbucks presently derives approximately 86% of net revenues from its Company-operated retail stores. The Company's specialty sales operations, which include sales to wholesale customers, licensees, and joint ventures, accounted for approximately 11% of net revenues in fiscal 1996. Direct response operations account for the remainder of net revenues.

The Company's net revenues have increased from $284.9 million in fiscal 1994 to $696.5 million in fiscal 1996, due primarily to the Company's store expansion program and comparable store sales increases. Comparable store sales increased by 9% and 7% in fiscal 1995 and 1996, respectively. As part of its expansion strategy of clustering stores in existing markets, Starbucks has experienced a certain level of cannibalization of existing stores by new stores as the store concentration has increased, but management believes such cannibalization has been justified by the incremental sales and return on new store investment. The Company anticipates that this cannibalization, as well as increased competition and other factors, may continue to put downward pressure on its comparable store sales growth in future periods.

The Company's fiscal year ends on the Sunday closest to September 30. Fiscal years 1996, 1995, and 1994 each had 52 weeks.

The following table sets forth the percentage relationship to total net revenues, unless otherwise indicated, of certain items included in the Company's consolidated statements of earnings:

Fiscal year ended:	Sept 29, 1996 (52 Wks)	Oct 1, 1995 (52 Wks)	Oct 2, 1994 (52 Wks)
Statements of Earnings Data:			
Net revenues:			
Retail	86.2%	86.6%	87.2%
Specialty Sales	11.3	10.3	9.3
Direct Response	2.5	3.1	3.5
Total net revenues	100.0	100.0	100.0
Cost of sales and related occupancy costs	48.2	45.4	45.7
Store operating expenses[1]	35.1	36.9	36.3
Other operating expenses	2.8	3.0	3.1
Depreciation and amortization	5.2	4.8	4.4
General and administrative expenses	5.3	6.2	7.0
Operating income	8.2	8.6	8.2
Interest income	1.6	1.5	0.7
Interest expense	(1.3)	(0.8)	(1.3)
Gain on sale of investment in Noah's	1.3	0.0	0.0
Provision for merger costs	0.0	0.0	(1.4)
Earnings before income taxes	9.8	9.3	6.2
Income taxes	3.8	3.7	2.6
Net earnings	6.0%	5.6%	3.6%

(1) Shown as a percentage of retail sales.

(Results of Operations—Fiscal 1996 Compared to Fiscal 1995)

Revenues Net revenues increased 50% to $696.5 million for fiscal 1996, compared to $465.2 million for fiscal 1995. Retail sales increased 49% to $600.1 million from $402.7 million. The increase in retail sales was due primarily to the addition of new Company-operated stores. In addition, comparable store sales increased 7% for the 52 weeks ended September 29, 1996 compared to the same 52-week period in fiscal 1995. Comparable store sales increases resulted from an increase in the number of transactions combined with an increase in the average dollar value per transaction.

During fiscal 1996, the Company opened 307 Starbucks stores (including four replacement stores), converted 19 Coffee Connection stores to Starbucks stores, and closed one store. Licensees opened 26 stores. The company opened stores in several new markets including North Carolina, Rhode Island, and Ontario, Canada. The Company ended the fiscal year with 929 Company-operated stores and 75 licensed stores in North America.

Specialty Sales revenues increased 63% to $78.7 million for fiscal 1996 from $48.1 million for fiscal 1995. The increase was due primarily to the Company signing an agreement with a major U.S. airline as well as increased revenues from several hotels, a chain of wholesale clubs, office coffee distributors, and restaurants. Direct Response sales increased 23% to $17.8 million for fiscal 1996 from $14.4 million for fiscal 1995.

Costs and Expenses Cost of sales and related occupancy costs as a percentage of net revenues increased to 48.2% for fiscal 1996 compared to 45.4% for fiscal 1995. This increase was primarily the result of higher green coffee costs as a percentage of net revenues, partially offset by a shift in retail sales mix towards higher-margin products. By the end of the first quarter of fiscal 1997, the Company expects to have sold most of the higher-cost green coffees acquired subsequent to the 1994 frost in Brazil. Therefore, management expects cost of sales in fiscal 1997 to show improvement relative to fiscal 1996.

Store operating expenses as a percentage of retail sales decreased to 35.1% for fiscal 1996 from 36.9% for fiscal 1995. This improvement reflected lower retail advertising expense, store remodel expense, and pre-opening expense as a percentage of retail sales.

Other operating expenses (those associated with the Company's specialty sales and direct response operations as well as the Company's joint ventures) decreased to 2.8% of net revenues for fiscal 1996 from 3.0% for fiscal 1995 primarily from operational leverage on the Company's net revenue increase. Depreciation and amortization as a percentage of net revenues increased to 5.2% for fiscal 1996 from 4.8% for fiscal 1995. This increase was primarily the result of increased per-store buildout costs in recent years relative to earlier history. After several years of increased per-store buildout costs, average store buildout costs declined in fiscal 1996 relative to fiscal 1995.

General and administrative expenses as a percentage of net revenues were 5.3% for fiscal 1996 compared to 6.2% for fiscal 1995. This decrease as a percentage of revenues was due primarily to lower payroll-related costs and professional fees as a percentage of net revenues.

Operating Income Operating income for fiscal 1996 increased to $57.0 million (8.2% of net revenues) from $40.1 million (8.6% of net revenues) for fiscal 1995. Operating income as a percentage of net revenues decreased due to higher cost of sales and an increase in depreciation and amortization, partially offset by lower store operating expenses, general and administrative expenses, and other operating expenses as a percentage of revenues.

Interest Income Interest income for fiscal 1996 was $11.0 million compared to $6.8 million for fiscal 1995. Average investment balances were higher during fiscal 1996 as a result of proceeds from the Company's October 1995 offering of $4\frac{1}{4}$% Convertible Subordinated Debentures due 2002, which generated $161.0 million, net of issuance costs.

Gain on Sale of Investment in Noah's In March 1995, the Company invested $11.3 million in cash for shares of Noah's New York Bagel, Inc. ("Noah's") Series B Preferred Stock. On February 1, 1996, Noah's was merged with Einstein Brothers Bagels, Inc., a retailer operating primarily in the Eastern United States. In exchange for its investment in Noah's, the Company received $20.6 million in cash and recognized a $9.2 million pre-tax gain ($5.7 million, net of tax) on the transaction.

Interest Expense Interest expense for fiscal 1996 was $8.7 million compared to $3.8 million for fiscal 1995. The increase in interest expense is due to the Company's convertible subordinated debentures issued in October 1995.

Income Taxes The Company's effective tax rate for fiscal 1996 was 38.5% compared to 39.5% for fiscal 1995. The Company's fiscal 1996 effective tax rate was lower than in fiscal 1995 due primarily to changes in state tax allocations and apportionment factors as well as the implementation of tax-saving strategies. Management expects the effective tax rate may increase as the Company expands activities in higher tax jurisdictions.

(Results of Operations—Fiscal 1995 Compared to Fiscal 1994)

Revenues Net revenues increased 63% to $465.2 million for fiscal 1995, compared to $284.9 million for fiscal 1994. Retail sales increased 62% to $402.7 million from $248.5 million. The increase in retail sales was due primarily to the addition of new Company-operated stores. In addition, comparable store sales increased 9% for the 52 weeks ended October 1, 1995 compared to the same 52-week period in fiscal 1994. Comparable store sales increases resulted from an increase in the number of transactions combined with an increase in the average dollar value per transaction. The increase in average dollar value per transaction included an increase in coffee beverage and whole bean prices which took place in July 1994.

During fiscal 1995, the Company opened 230 Starbucks stores (including two replacement stores), and converted four Coffee Connection stores to Starbucks stores. Licensees opened 23 new stores. The Company opened stores in several new markets including Baltimore, Maryland; Las Vegas, Nevada; Cincinnati, Ohio; Philadelphia and Pittsburgh, Pennsylvania; and Austin, Dallas, Houston, and San Antonio, Texas. The Company ended the fiscal year with 627 Company-operated stores and 49 licensed stores. Of the Company-operated stores, 19 were operated in the Northeast as Coffee Connection stores.

Specialty Sales revenues increased 81% to $48.1 million for fiscal 1995 from $26.5 million for fiscal 1994. Increased sales to several multi-unit retailers, hotels, airlines, and a chain of wholesale clubs as well as sales to a greater number of restaurants and institutions accounted for the increase in revenues. Direct Response sales increased 46% to $14.4 million for fiscal 1995 from $9.9 million for fiscal 1994.

Costs and Expenses Cost of sales and related occupancy costs as a percentage of net revenues decreased to 45.4% for fiscal 1995 compared to 45.7% for fiscal 1994. This decrease was primarily the result of higher prices on coffee beverages and whole bean coffees, and lower packaging costs as a percentage of net revenues, partially offset by higher green coffee costs.

Store operating expenses as a percentage of retail sales increased to 36.9% for fiscal 1995 from 36.3% for fiscal 1994. This increase was primarily a result of higher retail advertising expense. Other operating expenses decreased to 3.0% of net revenues for fiscal 1995 from 3.1% for fiscal 1994. The decrease was due primarily to lower direct response promotional costs as a percentage of revenues, partially offset by start-up costs related to the Company's joint venture with Pepsi-Cola. Depreciation and amortization as a percentage of net revenues increased to 4.8% from 4.4% for fiscal 1994. This increase was primarily the result of higher store buildout and equipment costs.

General and administrative expenses as a percentage of net revenues were 6.2% for fiscal 1995 compared to 7.0% for fiscal 1994. This decrease as a percentage of revenues was due to the Company's ability to increase revenues without proportionally increasing overhead expenses.

Operating Income Operating income for fiscal 1995 increased to $40.1 million (8.6% of net revenues) from $23.3 million (8.2% of net revenues) for fiscal 1994. Operating income as a percentage of net revenues improved due to higher gross margin and lower general and administrative expenses as a percentage of revenues, partially offset by an increase in store operating expenses and depreciation and amortization as a percentage of revenues.

Interest Income Interest income for fiscal 1995 was $6.8 million compared to $2.1 million for fiscal 1994. The increase in interest income was due to higher average investment balances resulting from the Company's public offering of common stock in November 1994.

Interest Expense Interest expense for fiscal 1995 was $3.8 million, unchanged from fiscal 1994.

Income Taxes The Company's effective tax rate for fiscal 1995 was 39.5% compared to 42.5% for fiscal 1994. The Company's fiscal 1994 effective tax rate was higher than in fiscal 1995 due to one-time, non-deductible merger costs related to the Coffee Connection merger in June 1994.

(Liquidity and Capital Resources)

The Company ended fiscal 1996 with $229.4 million in total cash and short-term investments. Working capital as of September 29, 1996 totaled $238.5 million compared to $134.3 million at October 1, 1995. Cash provided by operating activities totaled $136.7 million and resulted primarily from net income before non-cash charges of $79.0 million, a $40.3 million reduction in inventories, and a $26.9 million increase in accrued liabilities and expenses.

Cash provided from financing activities for fiscal 1996 totaled $179.8 million and included net proceeds of $161.0 million from the Company's October 1995 offering of convertible subordinated debentures. Cash provided from financing activities also included cash generated from the Company's employee stock purchase plan and from the exercise of employee stock options and the related income tax benefit available to the Company upon exercise of such options. As options granted under the Company's stock option plans vest, the Company will continue to receive proceeds and a tax deduction as a result of option exercises; however, neither the amounts nor the timing thereof can be predicted.

Cash used by investing activities for fiscal 1996 totaled $211.2 million. This included capital additions to property, plant, and equipment of $161.8 million which was used to open 307 new Company-operated retail stores, remodel certain existing stores, purchase roasting and packaging equipment for the Company's roasting and distribution facilities, enhance information systems, and expand existing office space.

The Company also invested in its joint ventures. During fiscal 1996, the Company made equity investments of $2.4 million in its joint venture with SAZABY, Inc. and $2.7 million in its joint venture with Pepsi-Cola Company. The Company also made investments in and advances to its joint venture with Dreyer's Grand Ice Cream, Inc. totaling $0.9 million. The Company sold its investment in Noah's and received $20.6 million in proceeds. The Company invested excess cash in short-term investment-grade marketable debt securities.

Future cash requirements, other than normal operating expenses, are expected to consist primarily of capital expenditures related to the addition of new Company-operated retail stores. The Company also anticipates remodeling certain existing stores and incurring additional expenditures for enhancing its production capacity and information systems. While there can be no assurance that current expectations will be realized, and plans are subject to change upon further review, management expects capital expenditures for fiscal 1997 to be approximately $170 million.

The Company currently anticipates additional cash requirements of approximately $20 million for its domestic joint ventures and international expansion during fiscal 1997. In addition, under the terms of the Company's corporate office lease, the Company has agreed to provide financing to the building owner to be used exclusively for facilities and leasehold development costs to accommodate the Company. During fiscal 1996, the Company provided approximately $4.3 million under this agreement, bringing the total amount provided to date to $4.6 million as of September 29, 1996. During fiscal 1997, the Company intends to provide additional funds of approximately $3.8 million under this agreement. The maximum amount available under the agreement is $17 million. Any funds advanced by the Company will be repaid with interest over a term not to exceed 20 years.

Management believes that existing cash and investments plus cash generated from operations should be sufficient to finance capital requirements for its core businesses through fiscal 1997. Any new joint ventures, other new business opportunities, or store expansion rates substantially in excess of that presently planned may require outside funding.

(Coffee Prices, Availability, and General Risk Conditions)

Some of the information in this Annual Report, including anticipated store openings, planned capital expenditures, and trends in the Company's operations, are forward-looking statements which are subject to risks and uncertainties. Actual future results and trends may differ materially depending on a variety of factors, including, but not limited to, coffee and other raw materials prices and availability, successful execution of internal performance and expansion plans, impact of competition, availability of financing, legal proceedings, and other risks detailed in the Company's Securities and Exchange Commission filings, including the Company's Annual Report on Form 10-K for the year ended September 29, 1996.

Green coffee commodity prices are subject to substantial price fluctuations, generally a result of reports of adverse growing conditions in certain coffee-producing countries. Due to green coffee commodity price increases, the Company effected sales price increases during fiscal 1994 and 1995 to mitigate the effects of anticipated increases in its cost of goods sold. Because the Company had established fixed purchase prices for some of its supply of green coffees, the Company's margins were favorably impacted by such sales price increases during much of fiscal 1995. During the latter part of fiscal 1995 and throughout fiscal 1996, gross margins were negatively impacted relative to the prior year by the sell-through of higher-cost coffee inventories. The Company expects to have sold most of these higher-cost coffees by the end of the first quarter of fiscal 1997.

The Company enters into fixed price purchase commitments in order to secure an adequate supply of quality green coffee and fix costs for future periods. As of September 29, 1996 the Company had approximately $47 million in fixed price purchase commitments which, together with existing inventory, is expected to provide an adequate supply of green coffee well into fiscal 1997. The Company believes, based on relationships established with its suppliers in the past, that the risk of non-delivery on such purchase commitments is remote.

In addition to fluctuating coffee prices, management believes that the Company's future results of operations and earnings could be significantly impacted by other factors such as increased competition within the specialty coffee industry, the Company's ability to find optimal store locations at favorable lease rates, the increased costs associated with opening and operating retail stores in new markets, the Company's continued ability to hire, train and retain qualified personnel, and the Company's ability to obtain adequate capital to finance its planned expansion.

Due to the factors noted above, the Company's future earnings and the prices of the Company's securities may be subject to volatility. There can be no assurance that the Company will continue to generate increases in net revenues and net earnings, or growth in comparable store sales. Any variance in the factors noted above, or other areas, from what is expected by investors could have an immediate and adverse effect on the trading prices of the Company's securities.

(Seasonality and Quarterly Results)

The Company's business is subject to seasonal fluctuations. Significant portions of the Company's net revenues and profits are realized during the first quarter of the Company's fiscal year, which includes the December holiday season. In addition, quarterly results are affected by the timing of the opening of new stores, and the Company's rapid growth may conceal the impact of other seasonal influences. Because of the seasonality of the Company's business, results for any quarter are not necessarily indicative of the results that may be achieved for the full fiscal year.

(New Accounting Standard)

In October 1995, the Financial Accounting Standards Board issued Statement No. 123, "Accounting for Stock-Based Compensation". This pronouncement establishes the accounting and reporting requirements using a fair value-based method of accounting for stock-based employee compensation plans. Under the new standard, the Company may either adopt the new fair value-based measurement method or continue using the intrinsic value-based method for employee stock-based compensation and provide pro forma disclosures of net income and earnings per share as if the measurement pro-visions of SFAS No. 123 had been adopted. The Company plans to adopt only the disclosure requirements of SFAS No. 123; therefore the adoption will have no effect on the Company's consolidated net earnings or cash flows.

Notes to Consolidated Financial Statements

(YEARS ENDED SEPTEMBER 29, 1996, OCTOBER 1, 1995, AND OCTOBER 2, 1994)

Note 1: Summary of Significant Accounting Policies

Description of Business Starbucks Corporation and its subsidiaries ("Starbucks" or the "Company") purchases and roasts high-quality whole bean coffees and sells them, along with a variety of coffee beverages, pastries, confections, and coffee-related accessories and equipment, primarily through Company-operated and licensed retail stores located throughout the United States and in parts of Canada. In addition to its retail operations, the Company sells primarily whole bean coffees through a specialty sales group and a direct response operation.

Basis of Presentation The consolidated financial statements include the accounts of Starbucks Corporation and its wholly owned subsidiaries. Investments in unconsolidated joint ventures are accounted for under the equity method. Material intercompany transactions during the periods covered by these consolidated financial statements have been eliminated.

Fiscal Year End The Company's fiscal year ends on the Sunday closest to September 30. Fiscal years 1996, 1995 and 1994 each had 52 weeks.

Estimates and Assumptions The preparation of financial statements in conformity with generally accepted accounting principles requires management to make estimates and assumptions that affect the reported amounts of assets, liabilities, revenues, and expenses. Actual results may differ from these estimates.

The Coffee Connection Merger On June 2, 1994, the Company acquired all of the outstanding capital stock of The Coffee Connection, Inc., a roaster/retailer of specialty coffee on the East Coast, in exchange for newly-issued shares of the Company's common stock. The merger was accounted for as a pooling of interests for accounting and financial reporting purposes. All fees and expenses related to the merger and the consolidation of the combined companies were expensed as required under the pooling-of-interests accounting method. Such fees and expenses were approximately $3.9 million ($2.9 million after tax).

Cash and Cash Equivalents The Company considers all highly liquid instruments with a maturity of three months or less at the time of purchase to be cash equivalents.

Cash Management The Company's cash management system provides for the reimbursement of all major bank disbursement accounts on a daily basis. Checks issued but not presented for payment to the bank are reflected as "Checks drawn in excess of bank balances" in the accompanying financial statements.

Investments The Company's investments consist primarily of investment-grade marketable debt securities, all of which are classified as available-for-sale and recorded at fair value as defined below. Unrealized holding gains and losses are recorded, net of any tax effect, as a component of shareholders' equity.

Fair Value of Financial Instruments The carrying value of cash and cash equivalents approximates fair value because of the short-term maturity of those instruments. The fair value of the Company's short-term investments in marketable debt and equity securities is based upon the quoted market price on the last business day of the fiscal year plus accrued interest, if any. The fair value and amortized cost of the Company's short-term investments at September 29, 1996, were $103.2 million and $99.9 million, respectively. The fair value and amortized cost of the Company's short-term investments at October 1, 1995, were both $41.5 million. For further detail on short-term investments, see Note 3. The fair value of the Company's $4\frac{1}{4}$% Convertible Subordinated Debentures due 2002 (see Note 7) is based on the quoted NASDAQ market price on the last business day of the fiscal year. As of September 29, 1996, the fair value and principal amount of the $4\frac{1}{4}$% Convertible Subordinated Debentures due 2002 were $248.0 million and $165.0 million, respectively.

Inventories Inventories are stated at the lower of cost (primarily first-in, first-out) or market.

Property, Plant, and Equipment Property, plant, and equipment are carried at cost less accumulated depreciation and amortization. Depreciation of property, plant, and equipment, which includes amortization of assets under capital leases, is provided on the straight-line method over estimated useful lives, generally ranging from three to seven years for equipment and 40 years for buildings. Leasehold improvements are amortized over the shorter of their estimated useful lives or the related lease life, generally ten years. The portion of depreciation expense related to production and distribution facilities is included in "Cost of sales and related occupancy costs". When facts and circumstances indicate that the cost of long-lived assets may be impaired, an evaluation of recoverability is performed by comparing the carrying value of the asset to projected future cash flows. Upon indication that the carrying value of such assets may not be recoverable, the Company recognizes an impairment loss by a charge against current operations.

Hedging and Futures Contracts The Company may, from time to time, enter into futures contracts to hedge price-to-be-established coffee purchase commitments with the objective of minimizing cost risk due to market fluctuations. Any gains or losses from hedging transactions are included as part of the inventory cost. The Company did not engage in any hedging activities or futures contracts during fiscal 1996 or 1995. Hedging activities entered into during fiscal 1994 were immaterial.

Advertising The Company expenses costs of advertising the first time the advertising campaign takes place, except for direct response advertising, which is capitalized and amortized over its expected period of future benefit. Direct response advertising consists primarily of mail order catalog costs and customer retention program costs. Catalog costs are amortized over the period from the catalog mailing until the issuance of the next catalog, typically three months. Customer retention program costs are amortized over six months.

Store Preopening Expenses Costs incurred in connection with start-up and promotion of new store openings are expensed as incurred.

Rent Expense Certain of the Company's lease agreements provide for scheduled rent increases during the lease terms, or for rental payments commencing at a date other than the date of initial occupancy. Rent expenses are recognized on a straight-line basis over the terms of the leases.

Income Taxes The Company computes income taxes using the asset and liability method, under which deferred income taxes are provided for the temporary differences between the financial reporting basis and the tax basis of the Company's assets and liabilities.

Earnings per Share The computation of primary earnings per share is based on the weighted average number of shares outstanding during the period plus dilutive common stock equivalents consisting primarily of certain shares subject to stock options. The number of shares resulting from this computation for fiscal 1996, 1995, and 1994 were 76,964,000, 71,309,000, and 59,718,000, respectively.

The computation of fully-diluted earnings per share assumes conversion of the Company's convertible subordinated debentures using the "if converted" method, when such securities are dilutive, with net income adjusted for the after-tax interest expense and amortization applicable to these debentures. The number of shares resulting from this computation for fiscal 1996, 1995, and 1994 were 80,831,000, 71,909,000, and 59,757,000, respectively.

Reclassifications Certain reclassifications of prior years' balances have been made to conform to the fiscal 1996 presentation.

Note 2: Cash and Cash Equivalents

Cash and cash equivalents consist of the following (in thousands):

	Sept 29, 1996	Oct 1, 1995
Operating funds and interest-bearing deposits	$ 11,069	$10,960
Commercial paper	93,306	—
Money market funds	14,590	9,984
Local government obligations	7,060	—
U.S. government obligations	190	—
	$126,215	$20,944

Note 3: Short-term Investments

The Company's short-term investments, including aggregate fair values, cost, gross unrealized holding gains, and gross unrealized holding losses, consist of the following (in thousands):

	Fair value	Amortized cost	Gross unrealized holding gains	Gross unrealized holding losses
September 29, 1996				
Corporate debt securities	$ 33,112	$33,118	$ 11	$(17)
U.S. Government obligations	45,041	45,017	36	(12)
Commercial paper	19,958	19,959	—	(1)
Marketable equity securities	5,110	1,800	3,310	—
	$103,221	$99,894	$3,357	$(30)

	Fair value	Amortized cost	Gross unrealized holding gains	Gross unrealized holding losses
October 1, 1995				
Corporate debt securities	$19,703	$19,655	$58	$(10)
U.S. Government obligations	14,832	14,824	8	—
Commercial paper	6,972	6,972	—	—
	$41,507	$41,451	$66	$(10)

All short-term investments are classified as available-for-sale as of September 29, 1996. Marketable debt securities have remaining maturities of one year or less. The specific identification method is used to determine a cost basis for computing realized gains and losses.

On March 31, 1995, the Company invested $11.3 million in cash for shares of Noah's New York Bagel, Inc. ("Noah's") Series B Preferred Stock. On February 1, 1996, Noah's was merged with Einstein Brothers Bagels, Inc. ("Einstein"), a retailer operating primarily in the Eastern United States. In exchange for its investment in Noah's, the Company received $20.6 million in cash and recognized a $9.2 million pre-tax gain ($5.7 million net of tax) on the transaction. Concurrently, the Company purchased $1.8 million of Einstein/Noah Bagel Corporation common stock.

In fiscal 1996, 1995, and 1994, proceeds from the sale of investment securities were $17.1 million, $27.7 million, and $73.7 million, respectively. During fiscal 1996, 1995, and 1994, gross realized gains totaled $13,000, $30,000, and $167,000, respectively, and gross realized losses totaled $11,000, $62,000, and $437,000, respectively.

Note 4: Inventories

Inventories consist of the following (in thousands):

	Sept 29, 1996	Oct 1, 1995
Coffee		
Unroasted	$37,127	$ 75,975
Roasted	9,753	11,612
Other merchandise held for sale	29,518	32,731
Packaging and other supplies	6,972	3,339
	$83,370	$123,657

As of September 29, 1996, the Company had fixed price inventory purchase commitments for green coffee totaling approximately $47 million. The Company believes, based on relationships established with its suppliers in the past, that the risk of non-delivery on such purchase commitments is remote.

Note 5: Joint Ventures and Equity Investments

Joint Ventures Starbucks accounts for its joint ventures using the equity method. The Company's share of joint venture income or losses is included in "Other operating expenses."

On August 10, 1994, the Company entered into a 50/50 joint venture and partnership agreement (the "Partnership Agreement") with Pepsi-Cola Company, a division of PepsiCo, Inc., to develop ready-to-drink coffee-based beverages. During fiscal 1996, the Company modified the Partnership Agreement to revise the allocation of start-up risks and expenses between partners. The Company's investment in the joint venture was $2.6 million and $0.3 million as of September 29, 1996, and October 1, 1995, respectively. During fiscal 1996 and 1995, the Company's share of the joint venture's losses totaled $0.4 million and $1.2 million, respectively. The Company made capital contributions totaling $2.7 million and $1.2 million to the joint venture in fiscal 1996 and fiscal 1995, respectively.

On October 25, 1995, the Company signed an agreement with SAZABY Inc., a Japanese retailer and restaurateur, to form a joint venture partnership to develop Starbucks retail stores in Japan. The first two stores opened in Tokyo during the fourth quarter of fiscal 1996. The Company's investment in the joint venture was $1.7 million as of September 29, 1996. During fiscal 1996, the Company's share of the joint venture's losses totaled $0.8 million. The Company made capital contributions totaling $2.4 million to the joint venture in fiscal 1996. The Company has guaranteed loans made to the joint venture totaling 190.0 million yen ($1.8 million) as of September 29, 1996.

On October 31, 1995, the Company entered into a joint venture agreement with Dreyer's Grand Ice Cream, Inc. to develop and distribute premium coffee ice creams. The Company's investment in the joint venture was $0.1 million as of September 29, 1996. During fiscal 1996, the Company's share of the joint venture's losses totaled $0.7 million. The Company made capital contributions and advances totaling $0.9 million to the joint venture in fiscal 1996.

Equity Investments As of October 1, 1995, the Company owned a $11.3 million investment in shares of Noah's Series B Preferred Stock which was accounted for under the equity method. As discussed in Note 3, Noah's was merged with Einstein at which time the investment was sold.

Note 6: Property, Plant, and Equipment

Property, plant, and equipment are recorded at cost and consist of the following (in thousands):

	Sept 29, 1996	Oct 1, 1995
Land	$ 3,602	$ 3,602
Building	8,338	8,338
Leasehold improvements	255,567	162,948
Roasting and store equipment	120,575	82,490
Furniture, fixtures, and other	38,794	24,602
	426,876	281,980
Less accumulated depreciation and amortization	(88,003)	(52,215)
	338,873	229,765
Work in progress	30,604	14,963
	$369,477	$244,728

Note 7: Convertible Subordinated Debentures

On August 3, 1993, the Company issued $80.5 million in principal amount of $4\frac{1}{2}$% Convertible Subordinated Debentures Due 2003. During fiscal 1995, $0.1 million in principal amount of the debentures was converted into common stock. On April 12, 1996, the Company called these debentures for redemption. The total principal amount converted, net of unamortized issue costs, accrued but unpaid interest, and costs of conversion, was credited to common stock.

During the first quarter of fiscal 1996, the Company issued approximately $165.0 million in principal amount of $4\frac{1}{4}$% Convertible Subordinated Debentures Due 2002 (the "Debentures"). Net proceeds to the Company were approximately $161.0 million. Interest is payable semiannually on May 1 and November 1 of each year. The Debentures are convertible into common stock of the Company at a price of $23.25, subject to adjustment under certain conditions. The Debentures are redeemable after November 10, 1997 at the option of the Company, at specified redemption prices and subject to certain conditions. The Debentures are subordinate to all future senior indebtedness. Costs incurred in connection with the issuance of the Debentures are included in "Deposits and other assets" and are being amortized on a straight line basis over the seven-year period to maturity.

Note 8: Leases

The Company leases retail stores, roasting and distribution facilities, and office space under operating leases expiring through 2015. Most lease agreements contain renewal options and rent escalation clauses. Certain leases provide for contingent rentals based upon gross sales. The Company also leases certain computer equipment and software under agreements classified as capital leases with original lease terms ranging from two to four years.

Rental expense under these lease agreements was as follows (in thousands):

Fiscal year ended:	Sept 29, 1996	Oct 1, 1995	Oct 2, 1994
Minimum rentals	$37,527	$21,590	$11,928
Contingent rentals	1,190	1,088	1,191
	$38,717	$22,678	$13,119

Minimum future rental payments under non-cancelable lease obligations as of September 29, 1996, are as follows (in thousands):

Fiscal year ended:	Capital leases	Operating leases
1997	$1,490	$ 38,819
1998	1,173	39,013
1999	561	39,095
2000	368	38,976
2001	—	39,129
Thereafter	—	169,708
Total minimum lease payments	$3,592	$364,740
Less: Amounts representing interest and other expenses	(652)	
Present value of net minimum lease payments	2,940	
Less: Current portion	(1,212)	
Long-term capital lease obligations	$1,728	

Assets recorded under capital leases are included in "Property, plant, and equipment" within the "Furniture, fixtures, and other" category. Assets recorded under capital leases, net of accumulated amortization, totaled $3.6 million and $1.5 million at September 29, 1996, and October 1, 1995, respectively.

The Company opened a roasting and distribution facility in Pennsylvania in September 1995 (the "East Coast Plant"). Under the terms of this lease agreement, the Company has an option to purchase the land and building comprising the East Coast Plant for approximately $14 million within five years of the date of occupancy. Such option to purchase also provides that the Company may purchase, within seven years of occupancy, additional land adjacent to the East Coast Plant.

Note 9: Shareholders' Equity

In November 1994, the Company completed a public offering of 12,050,000 shares of newly-issued common stock for proceeds of approximately $163.9 million, net of expenses.

On February 28, 1996, the Company's shareholders approved an amendment to the Company's articles of incorporation increasing the number of authorized common shares from 100,000,000 to 150,000,000.

The Company has authorized 7,500,000 shares of its preferred stock, none of which is outstanding at September 29, 1996.

Note 10: Stock Options

The Company maintains several stock option plans which provide for granting incentive stock options and nonqualified stock options to employees and nonemployee directors. Stock options have been granted at prices at or above the fair market value as of the date of grant. Options vest and expire according to terms established at the grant date.

The following summarizes all stock option transactions from October 4, 1993, through September 29, 1996.

	Shares	Range of prices per share
Outstanding, October 4, 1993	6,308,646	$ 0.75–12.56
Granted	1,546,426	3.45–16.72
Exercised	(1,547,528)	0.75– 8.50
Cancelled	(189,578)	0.75–13.25
Outstanding, October 2, 1994	6,117,966	0.75–16.72
Granted	2,853,476	11.47–20.06
Exercised	(945,780)	0.75–15.00
Cancelled	(1,151,006)	1.50–13.25
Outstanding, October 1, 1995	6,874,656	0.75–20.06
Granted	2,394,617	12.81–26.94
Exercised	(1,177,736)	0.75–16.88
Cancelled	(449,158)	1.50–20.06
Outstanding, September 29, 1996	7,642,379	$ 0.75–26.94
Exercisable, September 29, 1996	3,316,967	$ 0.75–20.06

There were 5,875,009 shares of common stock reserved for future stock option grants at September 29, 1996.

In October 1995, the Financial Accounting Standards Board issued Statement No. 123, "Accounting for Stock-Based Compensation". This pronouncement establishes the accounting and reporting requirements using a fair value-based method of accounting for stock-based employee compensation plans. Under the new standard, the Company may either adopt the new fair value-based measurement method or continue using the intrinsic value-based method for employee stock-based compensation and provide pro forma disclosures of net income and earnings per share as if the measurement provisions of SFAS No. 123 had been adopted. The Company plans to adopt only the disclosure requirements of SFAS No. 123; therefore the adoption will have no effect on the Company's consolidated net earnings or cash flows.

Note 11: Income Taxes

A reconciliation of the statutory federal income tax rate with the Company's effective income tax rate is as follows:

Fiscal year ended:	Sept 29, 1996	Oct 1, 1995	Oct 2, 1994
Statutory rate	35.0%	35.0%	35.0%
State income taxes, net of federal income tax benefit	3.1	3.6	3.3
Non-deductible merger costs	—	—	3.3
Other	0.4	0.9	0.9
Effective tax rate	38.5%	39.5%	42.5%

The provision for income taxes consists of the following (in thousands):

Fiscal year ended:	Sept 29, 1996	Oct 1, 1995	Oct 2, 1994
Currently payable:			
Federal	$19,568	$14,672	$6,424
State	2,398	2,285	910
Deferred liability	4,407	84	214
	$26,373	$17,041	$7,548

Deferred income taxes (benefits) reflect the tax effect of temporary differences between the amounts of assets and liabilities for financial reporting purposes and amounts as measured for tax purposes. The tax effect of temporary differences and carryforwards that cause significant portions of deferred tax assets and liabilities are as follows (in thousands):

	Sept 29, 1996	Oct 1, 1995
Depreciation	$10,699	$ 5,779
Accrued rent	(2,839)	(1,687)
Accrued compensation and related costs	(1,219)	(927)
Inventory valuation	(832)	(1,254)
Capitalized inventory costs	(699)	(707)
Coffee Connection NOL carryforwards	(629)	(645)
Reserve for store remodels	(184)	(953)
Unrealized holding gain on investments, net	1,281	22
Other, net	(1,044)	(760)
	$ 4,534	$(1,132)

Taxes payable of $2.7 million are included in "Other accrued expenses" as of September 29, 1996, and taxes refundable of $0.5 million are included in "Prepaid expenses and other current assets" as of October 1, 1995. The Company has net operating loss carryforwards of approximately $1.6 million expiring in 2007 and 2008.

Note 12: Commitments and Contingencies

Under the amended terms of the Company's corporate office lease, the Company has agreed to provide financing to the building owner to be used exclusively for facilities and leasehold development costs to accommodate the Company. Under this agreement, the Company provided approximately $4.3 million and $0.3 million during fiscal 1996 and fiscal 1995, respectively. As of September 29, 1996, and October 1, 1995, the amounts outstanding under the agreement totaled $4.6 million and $0.3 million, respectively. These amounts are included in "Deposits and other assets" on the balance sheet. The maximum amount available under the agreement is $17.0 million. Any funds advanced by the Company will be repaid with interest at 9.5% over a term not to exceed 20 years.

In the normal course of business, the Company has various legal claims and other contingent matters outstanding. Management believes that any ultimate liability arising from these actions would not have a material adverse effect on the Company's results of operations or financial condition at September 29, 1996.

Note 13: Employee Benefit Plans

Defined Contribution Plans Starbucks maintains voluntary defined contribution profit sharing plans covering all eligible employees as defined in the plan documents. Participating employees may elect to defer and contribute a stated percentage of their compensation to the plan, not to exceed the dollar amount set by law. The Company matches 25% of each employee's contribution up to a maximum of the first 4% of each employee's compensation.

The Company's matching contributions to the plans were approximately $0.3 million, $0.3 million, and $0.1 million for fiscal 1996, 1995, and 1994, respectively.

Employee Stock Purchase Plan During fiscal 1995, the Company implemented an employee stock purchase plan. The Company's plan provides that eligible employees may contribute up to 10% of their base earnings toward the quarterly purchase of the Company's common stock. The employee's purchase price is 85% of the lesser of the fair market value of the stock on the first business day or the last business day of the quarterly offering period. No compensation expense is recorded in connection with the plan. The total number of shares issuable under the plan is 4,000,000. There were 89,373 shares issued under the plan during fiscal 1996 at prices ranging from $15.99 to $24.65. There were 17,424 shares issued under the plan during fiscal 1995 at a price of $15.09. Of the 7,944 employees eligible to participate, 1,601 were participants in the plan as of September 29, 1996.

Note 14: Related Party Transactions

An employee director of the Company serves as chairman of a wholesale customer of the Company. Sales to this customer were $22.7 million, $18.5 million, and $10.5 million for fiscal 1996, 1995, and 1994, respectively. Amounts receivable from this customer totaled $2.7 million and $1.9 million as of September 29, 1996, and October 1, 1995, respectively.

A director of the Company serves as a co-chairman and chief executive of a company which provides insurance brokerage and employee benefit consulting services to the Company. Amounts paid for those services (primarily premiums) totaled $3.8 million, $3.5 million, and $1.1 million for fiscal 1996, 1995, and 1994, respectively.

Supplementary Financial Information

In addition to the financial statements and the accompanying notes, three items of supplementary financial information typically are presented: business segment information, quarterly financial data, and stock performance information.

BUSINESS SEGMENT INFORMATION

To help financial statement users assess the performance of diversified companies that operate in several different industries and lines of business, segmented financial information is required. The required information for each significant segment includes: revenues, income from operations, capital expenditures, identifiable assets, and depreciation and amortization. This information is generally included in the form of notes and schedules in the notes accompanying the financial statements. Since Starbucks operates primarily in one line of business, it is not required to present business segment data.

QUARTERLY FINANCIAL DATA AND CAPITAL STOCK INFORMATION

Nearly all publicly held companies and many nonpublic companies issue financial information on a quarterly basis to stockholders, regulatory agencies, and others. These quarterly reports are referred to as **interim financial reports,** for which there are prescribed accounting standards. Quarterly financial data along with capital stock information are frequently summarized in the Annual Report. Starbucks summarizes its quarterly data and capital stock information as shown below.

Note 15: Quarterly Financial Information (Unaudited)

Summarized quarterly financial information for fiscal years 1996 and 1995 is as follows (in thousands, except earnings per share):

	First	Second	Third	Fourth
1996 quarter:				
Net revenues	$169,537	$153,609	$176,950	$196,385
Gross margin	83,019	76,671	93,786	107,205
Net earnings	9,566	10,391	9,446	12,725
Net earnings per common & common equivalent share— fully-diluted	$ 0.13	$ 0.14	$ 0.12	$ 0.16
1995 quarter:				
Net revenues	$115,545	$101,113	$119,174	$129,381
Gross margin	63,562	55,474	65,451	69,447
Net earnings	8,620	5,130	6,845	5,507
Net earnings per common & common equivalent share— fully-diluted	$ 0.13	$ 0.07	$ 0.09	$ 0.07

Shareholder Information

(STARBUCKS CORPORATION)

Market Information and Dividend Policy The Company's Common Stock is traded on the NASDAQ National Market System under the symbol "SBUX". The following table sets forth the quarterly high and low sale prices per share of the Common Stock as reported on the NASDAQ National Market System for each quarter during the last two fiscal years, retroactively adjusted for the two-for-one stock split on December 1, 1995.

Fiscal year ended	High	Low
September 29, 1996		
First Quarter	23\frac{1}{2}$	16\frac{15}{16}$
Second Quarter	23$\frac{5}{8}$	14$\frac{1}{2}$
Third Quarter	29$\frac{5}{8}$	24$\frac{1}{8}$
Fourth Quarter	35$\frac{7}{8}$	23
October 1, 1995		
First Quarter	14\frac{5}{8}$	10\frac{3}{4}$
Second Quarter	13$\frac{11}{16}$	11$\frac{1}{8}$
Third Quarter	18$\frac{5}{8}$	11$\frac{5}{8}$
Fourth Quarter	22$\frac{1}{8}$	17$\frac{7}{16}$

As of November 18, 1996, the approximate number of common shareholders of record was 6,710. The Company has never paid any dividends on its Common Stock. The Company presently intends to retain earnings for use in its business and therefore does not anticipate declaring a cash dividend in the near future.

Annual Meeting The Company's Annual Meeting of Shareholders will be held at 10 am (Pacific time), on Thursday, March 6, 1997 at:

Starbucks Roasting Plant
18411—77th Place South
Kent, WA 98032

Form 10-K and Quarterly Shareholder Information The Company's annual report on Form 10-K for the fiscal year ended September 29, 1996 may be obtained without charge by sending a written request to the address below.

Beginning in fiscal 1997, we will discontinue printing and mailing quarterly reports to all shareholders. Quarterly information will be available to all shareholders immediately upon its release, free of charge, via fax, by calling (800) 758-5804 extension 810887 or through access on the Internet at www.prnewswire.com. To receive a copy by mail, please send your written request to:

Investor Relations
Starbucks Corporation
P.O. Box 34067
Seattle, WA 98124-1067

We believe communicating our quarterly results in this manner will be more timely and cost-effective for our shareholders.

APPENDIX B

Specimen Financial Statements: Green Mountain Coffee

MANAGEMENT'S DISCUSSION AND ANALYSIS OF FINANCIAL CONDITION AND RESULTS OF OPERATIONS

GENERAL

For the year ended September 28, 1996, Green Mountain derived approximately 79.1% of its net sales from its wholesale operation. Green Mountain's wholesale operation sells coffee to retailers and food service concerns including supermarkets, restaurants, convenience stores, specialty food stores, hotels, universities and business offices. The Company also operated twelve retail stores and a direct mail operation, which accounted for approximately 13.0% and 7.9% of net sales, respectively, in fiscal 1996.

Cost of sales consists of the cost of raw materials including green coffee, flavorings and packaging materials, the salaries and related expenses of production and distribution personnel, depreciation on production equipment and freight and delivery expenses. Selling and operating expenses consist of expenses that directly support the sales of the Company's wholesale, retail or direct mail distribution channels, including marketing and advertising expenses, a portion of the Company's rental expense and the salaries and related expenses of employees directly supporting sales. General and administrative expenses consist of expenses incurred for corporate support and administration, including the salaries and related expenses of personnel not elsewhere categorized.

The Company's fiscal year ends on the last Saturday in September. The Company's fiscal year normally consists of 13 four-week periods with the first, second and third "quarters" ending 16 weeks, 28 weeks and 40 weeks, respectively, into the fiscal year. Fiscal 1996 and fiscal 1994 represent the years ended September 28, 1996 and September 24, 1994, respectively, and consisted of 52 weeks. Fiscal 1995 represents the year ended September 30, 1995 and consisted of 53 weeks with the fiscal fourth quarter having 13 weeks instead of the normal 12 weeks.

This document may include forward-looking statements about the Company's sales and earnings and future plans and objectives. Any such statements are subject to risks and uncertainties that could cause the actual results to vary materially. These risks include, but are not limited to, business conditions in the coffee industry and food industry in general, fluctuations in availability and cost of green coffee, economic conditions, competition, variances from budgeted sales mix and growth rates, weather and special or unusual events.

The following table sets forth certain financial data of the Company expressed as a percentage of net sales for the periods denoted below:

	Year Ended		
Statement of Operations Data:	September 28, 1996	September 30, 1995	September 24, 1994
Net sales:			
Wholesale	79.1 %	74.9 %	68.7 %
Retail	13.0 %	15.0 %	18.2 %
Catalog Sales	7.9 %	10.1 %	13.1 %
Net sales	100.0 %	100.0 %	100.0 %
Cost of sales	59.5 %	63.9 %	61.2 %
Gross profit	40.5 %	36.1 %	38.8 %
Selling and operating expenses	27.3 %	28.0 %	39.5 %
General and administrative expenses	8.2 %	7.6 %	11.8 %
Income (loss) from operations	5.0 %	0.5 %	(12.5) %
Other income (expense)	- %	- %	0.3 %
Interest expense	(1.1) %	(1.2) %	(1.0) %
Income (loss) before income taxes	3.9 %	(0.7) %	(13.2) %
Income tax benefit (expense)	(0.6) %	0.1 %	2.5 %
Net income (loss)	3.3 %	(0.6) %	(10.7) %

FISCAL 1996 VERSUS FISCAL 1995

Net sales increased by $4,323,000 or 12.7% from $34,024,000 in fiscal 1995 (a 53-week period) to $38,347,000 in fiscal 1996 (a 52-week period). On a 52-week to 52-week comparative basis, sales are estimated to have increased by 15.0% in fiscal 1996. Coffee pounds sold, excluding those sold as beverages through the Company's retail stores, increased by approximately 864,000 pounds or 19.6% from 4,408,000 pounds in fiscal 1995 to 5,272,000 pounds in fiscal 1996. On a 52-week to 52-week comparative basis, coffee pounds sold are estimated to have increased 22.0% in fiscal 1996. The difference between the percentage increase in net sales and the percentage increase in coffee pounds sold primarily relates to reductions in Green Mountain's selling prices for coffee during fiscal 1996 as a result of lower green coffee costs.

The year-to-year increase in net sales occurred primarily in the wholesale area in which net sales increased by $4,856,000 or 19.1% from $25,484,000 in fiscal 1995 to $30,340,000 in fiscal 1996. This increase resulted primarily from the year-over-year growth in the number of wholesale accounts.

Net retail sales decreased by $136,000 or 2.7% from $5,106,000 in fiscal 1995 to $4,970,000 in fiscal 1996, principally due to the closing of three espresso carts located at supermarkets during the second quarter of fiscal 1995, and the closing of an espresso cart located in Albany, New York in the first quarter of fiscal 1996. The three supermarket espresso cart locations were converted to wholesale supermarket accounts with pre-bagged, bulk and/or self-service coffee beverage displays. On a 52-week to 52-week comparative basis, retail same-store sales are estimated to have increased 3.3% in fiscal 1996.

Net direct mail sales decreased by $397,000 or 11.6% from $3,434,000 in fiscal 1995 to $3,037,000 in fiscal 1996. This decrease resulted primarily from a shift in strategy whereby the Company focused its mail order solicitations on catalog customers who more regularly buy from the Company, and decreased the number of low-margin product promotions.

Green Mountain's gross profit increased by $3,244,000 or 26.4% from $12,286,000 in fiscal 1995 to $15,530,000 in fiscal 1996. Gross profit increased by 4.4 percentage points as a percentage of net sales from 36.1% in fiscal 1995 to 40.5% in fiscal 1996. These increases were primarily attributable to the impact of lower green coffee costs.

Selling and operating expenses increased by $942,000 or 9.9% from $9,529,000 in fiscal 1995 to $10,471,000 in fiscal 1996, but decreased .7 percentage points as a percentage of net sales from 28.0% in fiscal 1995 to 27.3% in fiscal 1996. The increase in selling and operating expense includes approximately $420,000 in expenses related to the addition in fiscal 1996 of a national supermarket sales manager, a national food service and office coffee services sales manager, and eight people to the Company's direct sales force in the Boston, Connecticut and Florida markets, as well as the addition of an advertising manager and designer to the Company's corporate marketing department.

General and administrative expenses increased by $554,000 or 21.5% from $2,578,000 in fiscal 1995 to $3,132,000 in fiscal 1996 and increased .6 percentage points as a percentage of net sales from 7.6% in fiscal 1995 to 8.2% in fiscal 1996. Significant general and administrative expense increases during fiscal 1996 include: increased MIS personnel and other computer-related expenses of approximately $130,000; increased training and human resource department costs of approximately $75,000; and increased investor relations related expenses of approximately $67,000.

As a result of the foregoing, income from operations increased by $1,748,000 or 976.5% from $179,000 in fiscal 1995 to $1,927,000 in fiscal 1996, and increased 4.5 percentage points as a percentage of net sales from 0.5% in fiscal 1995 to 5.0% in fiscal 1996. The income tax benefit recognized under SFAS 109 was $26,000 in fiscal 1995 compared to income tax expense of $222,000 in fiscal 1996. The Company's effective tax rate increased from 11% in fiscal 1995 to 15% in fiscal 1996, primarily as a result of non-deductible items being a greater percentage of the net loss in fiscal 1995 compared to the percentage of net income in fiscal 1996. Net income increased by $1,480,000 from a net loss of $218,000 in fiscal 1995 to net income of $1,262,000 in fiscal 1996.

FISCAL 1995 VERSUS FISCAL 1994

Net sales increased by $11,942,000 or 54.1% from $22,082,000 in fiscal 1994 (a 52-week period) to $34,024,000 in fiscal 1995 (a 53-week period). Approximately 22 percentage points of the 54.1% full-year growth rate, or about 41% of the sales growth was due to price increases. Coffee pounds sold, excluding those sold as beverages through the Company's retail stores, increased by approximately 874,000 pounds or 24.7% from 3,534,000 pounds in fiscal 1994 to 4,408,000 pounds in fiscal 1995. On a 52-week to 52-week comparative basis, coffee pounds sold are estimated to have increased 24.7%.

The year-to-year net sales increase occurred mainly in the wholesale area in which net sales increased by $10,321,000 or 68.1% from $15,163,000 in fiscal 1994 to $25,484,000 in fiscal 1995. The wholesale net sales increase resulted primarily from increases in coffee prices to customers (approximately 44% of the 68.1% increase) related to the increased cost of green coffee, and from growth in the number of wholesale customer accounts (approximately 45% of the 68.1% increase).

Net retail sales increased $1,084,000 or 27.0% from $4,022,000 in fiscal 1994 to $5,106,000 in fiscal 1995, principally due to the opening of two new stores near the end of fiscal 1994. Net sales in the direct mail area increased $537,000 or 18.5%

from $2,897,000 in fiscal 1994 to $3,434,000 in fiscal 1995. The increase in direct mail sales resulted primarily from increases in coffee selling prices to customers, related to the increased cost of green coffee.

Gross profit increased by $3,717,000 or 43.4% from $8,569,000 in fiscal 1994 to $12,286,000 in fiscal 1995. As a percentage of net sales, gross profit decreased by 2.7 percentage points from 38.8% in fiscal 1994 to 36.1% in fiscal 1995. This decrease was due primarily to the increased cost of green coffee as a percentage of sales (i.e. Green Mountain passed on the dollar increase in green coffee, not the percentage increase) offset, in part, by lower production, distribution and delivery costs as a percentage of sales.

Selling and operating expenses increased by $807,000 or 9.3% from $8,722,000 in fiscal 1994 to $9,529,000 in fiscal 1995, primarily due to increased personnel and facility costs in fiscal 1995 related to the opening of new wholesale sales territories and retail stores during and following fiscal 1994, offset, in part, by decreased direct mail advertising expenditures. However, selling and operating expenses as a percentage of sales decreased by 11.5 percentage points from 39.5% in fiscal 1994 to 28.0% in fiscal 1995.

General and administrative expenses decreased by $27,000 or 1.0% from $2,605,000 in fiscal 1994 to $2,578,000 in fiscal 1995, and decreased by 4.2 percentage points as a percentage of net sales from 11.8% in fiscal 1994 to 7.6% in fiscal 1995. This decrease in general and administrative expenses reflects management's efforts to redeploy general and administrative personnel to more directly support the selling effort. However, general and administrative expenses as a percentage of sales increased by 3.0 percentage points for the fiscal fourth quarter from 4.5% in fiscal 1994 to 7.5% in fiscal 1995. The fiscal 1994 fourth quarter includes the impact of several short-term cost containment programs and a favorable year-end adjustment of $69,000 related to the Company's self-insured medical plan due to favorable loss experience.

As a result of the foregoing, income from operations for fiscal 1995 was $179,000 compared to a loss from operations of $2,758,000 for fiscal 1994, a $2,937,000 or 106.5% improvement. The income tax benefit recognized under SFAS 109 decreased by $531,000 or 95.3% from $557,000 in fiscal 1994 to $26,000 in fiscal 1995. The net loss decreased by $2,140,000 or 90.8% from $2,358,000 in fiscal 1994 to $218,000 in fiscal 1995.

LIQUIDITY AND CAPITAL RESOURCES

Working capital amounted to $2,433,000 and $745,000 at September 28, 1996 and September 30, 1995, respectively.

Cash used for capital expenditures aggregated $2,519,000 during fiscal 1996, and included $884,000 for equipment loaned to wholesale customers, $633,000 for production equipment, and $499,000 for computer hardware and software. During fiscal 1995, Green Mountain had capital expenditures of $1,602,000, including $961,000 for equipment on loan to wholesale customers, $333,000 for production equipment and $173,000 for computer hardware and software.

Cash used to fund the capital expenditures in fiscal 1996 was obtained from the $3,134,000 of net cash provided by operating activities. Net cash provided by operating activities reflects a $2,839,000 increase as compared to fiscal 1995, which resulted primarily from the Company's improved profitability together with the Company's efforts to control growth in accounts receivable.

The Company currently plans to make capital expenditures in fiscal 1997 of approximately $4,200,000, primarily to fund the purchase of equipment for loan to wholesale customers (approximately $2,000,000) and computer hardware and software (approximately $1,200,000). Assuming a stable mix in packaging types and sizes, management believes that it will operate at approximately 60-70% of capacity in fiscal 1997 and does not foresee significant production equipment expenditures during the year. However, management continuously reviews capital expenditure needs and actual amounts expended may differ from these estimates.

On April 12, 1996, the Company amended its credit facility with Fleet Bank - NH (Fleet). Under the revised facility, the Company borrowed $1,500,000 under a five-year term promissory note to be repaid in equal monthly principal installments. The interest rate on all term debt under the credit facility was reduced, subject to the election of the Company, to the lesser of the variable Fleet base rate (8.25% at September 28, 1996) plus 25 basis points or 275 basis points above the LIBOR rate for maturities of up to one year. The interest rate on this debt approximated 8.2% at September 28, 1996.

The interest rate of the Company's revolving line of credit under the amended Fleet credit facility was also reduced, subject to the election of the Company, to the lesser of the Fleet base rate or 250 basis points above the LIBOR rate for maturities of up to one year. The term of the revolving line of credit was also extended by one year to February 28, 1998. The outstanding balance on the revolving line of credit at September 28, 1996 was $508,000, with a total availability under the amended borrowing base formula capped at $3,000,000.

Management believes that cash flow from operations, existing cash and available borrowings under its credit facility and other sources will provide sufficient liquidity to pay all liabilities in the normal course of business, fund capital expenditures and service debt requirements for the next twelve months.

The average cost of the high quality arabica coffees the Company purchases decreased during fiscal 1996 as compared to fiscal 1995, and the Company's overall gross profit margin has improved. The Company passed the majority of such savings on to its customers through price reductions, and such price reductions had a negative impact on the Company's year-to-year percentage net sales growth rate.

The Company believes that the cost of green coffee will continue to be volatile in fiscal 1997, but expects that its average cost of green coffee in fiscal 1997 will be equivalent to, or less than, that experienced in fiscal 1996, although there can be no assurance that this will be the case. The Company believes that increases in the cost of green coffee can generally be passed on to customers or absorbed through more efficient operations, although there can be no assurance that the Company will be successful in doing so. Similarly, rapid sharp decreases in the cost of green coffee could also force the Company to lower sales prices before realizing cost reductions in its green coffee inventory. Because Green Mountain roasts over 25 different types of green coffee beans to produce its more than 70 different varieties of coffee, if one type of green coffee bean were to become unavailable or prohibitively expensive, management believes Green Mountain could substitute another type of coffee in a blend or temporarily remove that particular coffee from its product line.

DEFERRED INCOME TAXES

The Company had net deferred tax assets of $902,000 at September 28, 1996. These assets are reported net of a deferred tax asset valuation allowance at that date of $3,503,000 (including $2,681,000 primarily related to a Vermont investment tax credit which is fully reserved). The Company had income before taxes of $1,484,000 in fiscal 1996 and has been profitable in seven of its last nine fiscal quarters including the last five consecutive fiscal quarters. Presently, the Company believes that the deferred tax assets, net of deferred tax liabilities and the valuation allowance, are realizable and represent management's best estimate, based on the weight of available evidence as prescribed in SFAS 109, of the amount of deferred tax assets which most likely will be realized. However, management will continue to evaluate the amount of the valuation allowance based on near-term operating results and longer-term projections.

SEASONALITY

Historically, the Company has experienced lower net sales levels in its second fiscal quarter following high holiday-related levels in its first fiscal quarter, especially in its retail and direct mail operations. This has historically resulted in less favorable operating results during the second fiscal quarter. In addition, quarterly results may be affected by a variety of other factors, including, but not limited to, general economic trends, competition, marketing programs, weather, and special or unusual events. Because of the seasonality of the Company's business, results for any quarter are not necessarily indicative of the results that may be achieved for the full fiscal year.

REPORT OF INDEPENDENT ACCOUNTANTS

Price Waterhouse LLP

To the Board of Directors and Stockholders of Green Mountain Coffee, Inc.

In our opinion, the accompanying consolidated balance sheet and the related consolidated statements of operations, of changes in stockholders' equity and of cash flows present fairly, in all material respects, the financial position of Green Mountain Coffee, Inc. and its subsidiary at September 28, 1996 and September 30, 1995, and the results of their operations and their cash flows for each of the three years in the period ended September 28, 1996, in conformity with generally accepted accounting principles. These financial statements are the responsibility of the Company's management; our responsibility is to express an opinion on these financial statements based on our audits. We conducted our audits of these statements in accordance with generally accepted auditing standards which require that we plan and perform the audit to obtain reasonable assurance about whether the financial statements are free of material misstatement. An audit includes examining, on a test basis, evidence supporting the amounts and disclosures in the financial statements, assessing the accounting principles used and significant estimates made by management, and evaluating the overall financial statement presentation. We believe that our audits provide a reasonable basis for the opinion expressed above.

Price Waterhouse LLP

Boston, Massachusetts
November 11, 1996

APPENDIX B   Specimen Financial Statements: Green Mountain Coffee

CONSOLIDATED BALANCE SHEET

(Dollars in thousands except share data)

	September 28, 1996	September 30, 1995
ASSETS		
Current assets:		
Cash and cash equivalents	$ 551	$ 310
Receivables, less allowances of $80 at September 28, 1996 and $63 at September 30, 1995	2,778	2,660
Inventories	3,276	2,766
Other current assets	627	377
Deferred income taxes, net	516	115
Total current assets	7,748	6,228
Fixed assets, net	8,715	8,127
Other long-term assets, net	394	235
Deferred income taxes, net	386	975
	$ 17,243	$ 15,565
LIABILITIES AND STOCKHOLDERS' EQUITY		
Current liabilities:		
Current portion of long-term debt	$ 947	$ 618
Current portion of obligation under capital lease	114	68
Revolving line of credit	508	1,720
Accounts payable	3,002	2,751
Accrued payroll	480	170
Accrued expenses	264	156
Total current liabilities	5,315	5,483
Long-term debt	2,911	2,351
Obligation under capital lease	144	209
Commitments (Notes 8 and 12)		
Stockholders' equity:		
Common stock, $0.10 par value: Authorized - 10,000,000 shares; issued and outstanding - 3,417,306 shares at September 28, 1996 and 3,399,795 shares at September 30, 1995	342	340
Additional paid-in capital	12,508	12,421
Accumulated deficit	(3,977)	(5,239)
Total stockholders' equity	8,873	7,522
	$ 17,243	$ 15,565

The accompanying Notes to Consolidated Financial Statements are an integral part of these financial statements.

APPENDIX B Specimen Financial Statements: Green Mountain Coffee

CONSOLIDATED STATEMENT OF OPERATIONS

(Dollars in thousands except share data)

	Year ended		
	September 28, 1996	September 30, 1995	September 24, 1994
Net sales	$ 38,347	$ 34,024	$ 22,082
Cost of sales	22,817	21,738	13,513
Gross profit	15,530	12,286	8,569
Selling and operating expenses	10,471	9,529	8,722
General and administrative expenses	3,132	2,578	2,605
Income (loss) from operations	1,927	179	(2,758)
Other income (expense)	(21)	(24)	75
Interest expense	(422)	(399)	(232)
Income (loss) before income taxes	1,484	(244)	(2,915)
Income tax benefit (expense)	(222)	26	557
Net income (loss)	$ 1,262	$ (218)	$ (2,358)
Net income (loss) per share	$ 0.37	$ (0.06)	$ (0.70)
Weighted average shares outstanding	3,427,610	3,383,529	3,377,682

The accompanying Notes to Consolidated Financial Statements are an integral part of these financial statements.

CONSOLIDATED STATEMENT OF CHANGES IN STOCKHOLDERS' EQUITY

For the years ended September 28, 1996, September 30, 1995 and September 24, 1994
(Dollars in thousands except share data)

	Shares	Common stock	Additional paid-in capital	Accumulated deficit	Total stockholders' equity
Balance at September 25, 1993	3,376,286	$ 338	$ 12,353	$ (2,663)	$ 10,028
Additional issuance costs from initial public offering	-	-	(46)	-	(46)
Issuance of common stock under stock award plan	2,442	-	22	-	22
Issuance of common stock under employee stock purchase plan	4,757	-	21	-	21
Net loss	-	-	-	(2,358)	(2,358)
Balance at September 24, 1994	3,383,485	338	12,350	(5,021)	7,667
Issuance of common stock under employee stock purchase plan	16,310	2	71	-	73
Net loss	-	-	-	(218)	(218)
Balance at September 30, 1995	3,399,795	340	12,421	(5,239)	7,522
Issuance of common stock under employee stock purchase plan	17,511	2	87	-	89
Net income	-	-	-	1,262	1,262
Balance at September 28, 1996	3,417,306	$ 342	$ 12,508	$ (3,977)	$ 8,873

The accompanying Notes to Consolidated Financial Statements are an integral part of these financial statements

CONSOLIDATED STATEMENT OF CASH FLOWS

(Dollars in thousands)

	Year ended		
	September 28, 1996	September 30, 1995	September 24, 1994
Cash flows from operating activities:			
Net income (loss)	$ 1,262	$ (218)	$ (2,358)
Adjustments to reconcile net income (loss) to net cash provided by (used for) operating activities:			
Depreciation and amortization	2,026	1,624	1,239
Loss on disposal of fixed assets	47	15	6
Provision for (recovery of) doubtful accounts	156	157	(9)
Deferred income taxes	188	(26)	(557)
Changes in assets and liabilities:			
Receivables	(274)	(1,324)	(607)
Inventories	(510)	(359)	(981)
Other current assets	(250)	(57)	(96)
Other long-term assets, net	(180)	(97)	(103)
Accounts payable	251	758	(235)
Accrued payroll	310	(131)	70
Accrued expenses	108	(47)	(366)
Net cash provided by (used for) operating activities	3,134	295	(3,997)
Cash flows from investing activities:			
Expenditures for fixed assets	(2,519)	(1,602)	(4,323)
Proceeds from disposals of fixed assets	59	-	24
Net cash used for investing activities	(2,460)	(1,602)	(4,299)
Cash flows from financing activities:			
Proceeds from issuance of long-term debt	1,509	286	2,482
Repayment of long-term debt	(729)	(594)	(2,438)
Principal payments under capital lease obligation	(90)	(5)	-
Net change in revolving line of credit	(1,212)	1,720	(1,108)
Repayment of note payable to stockholder	-	(416)	(125)
Issuance of common stock, net of issuance costs	89	73	9,760
Net cash provided by (used for) financing activities	(433)	1,064	8,571
Net increase (decrease) in cash and cash equivalents	241	(243)	275
Cash and cash equivalents at beginning of year	310	553	278
Cash and cash equivalents at end of year	$ 551	$ 310	$ 553
Supplemental disclosures of cash flow information:			
Cash paid for interest	$ 401	$ 382	$ 224
Cash paid for income taxes	$ 5	$ 8	$ 9

The accompanying Notes to Consolidated Financial Statements are an integral part of these financial statements

1. Nature of Business and Organization

The accompanying consolidated financial statements include the accounts of Green Mountain Coffee, Inc. (the "Company") and its wholly-owned subsidiary, Green Mountain Coffee Roasters, Inc. All significant intercompany transactions and balances have been eliminated.

The Company purchases high-quality arabica coffee beans for roasting, then packages and distributes the roasted coffee primarily in the northeastern United States. The majority of the Company's revenue is derived from its wholesale operation which serves fine dining, supermarket, specialty food store, convenience store, food service, hotel, university, travel and office coffee service customers. The Company also has a direct mail operation servicing customers nationwide and currently operates twelve company-owned retail stores in Vermont, Connecticut, Illinois, Maine, Massachusetts, New Hampshire and New York.

The Company's fiscal year ends on the last Saturday in September. Fiscal 1996 and fiscal 1994 represent the years ended September 28, 1996 and September 24, 1994, respectively, and consist of 52 weeks. Fiscal 1995 represents the year ended September 30, 1995 and consists of 53 weeks.

2. Significant Accounting Policies

CASH AND CASH EQUIVALENTS

The Company considers all highly liquid investments purchased with a maturity of three months or less to be cash equivalents. Cash and cash equivalents include money market funds which are carried at cost, plus accrued interest, which approximates market. The Company does not believe that it is subject to any unusual credit and market risk.

INVENTORIES

Inventories are stated at the lower of cost or market with cost being determined by the first-in, first-out method.

OPTIONS ON FUTURES CONTRACTS

The Company enters into options contracts on coffee futures to hedge against potential increases in the price of green coffee beans. The resulting gain or loss from the sale of an option is applied to reduce or increase cost of goods sold, as applicable. For the years ended September 28, 1996, September 30, 1995 and September 24, 1994, the Company recognized gains (losses) of $(37,000), $(9,000) and $76,000, respectively, on hedging-related transactions. There were no open future contracts at September 28, 1996. Cash flows from the option transactions are classified with the related inventory.

ADVERTISING

The Company expenses the costs of advertising the first time the advertising takes place. Advertising expense totaled $1,427,000, $1,385,000 and $1,769,000 for the years ended September 28, 1996, September 30, 1995 and September 24, 1994, respectively.

FIXED ASSETS

Fixed assets are recorded at cost. Expenditures for maintenance, repairs and renewals of minor items are charged to expense as incurred. Depreciation of fixed assets is provided using the straight-line method.

Equipment under capital leases is amortized on the straight-line method over the shorter of the lease term or the estimated useful life of the equipment.

In order to facilitate sales, the Company follows an industry-wide practice of purchasing and loaning coffee brewing and related equipment to wholesale customers.

REVENUE RECOGNITION

Revenue from wholesale and mail order sales is recognized upon product shipment. Revenue from retail sales is recognized upon sale to customers.

INCOME TAXES

The Company utilizes the asset and liability method of accounting for income taxes, as set forth in Statement of Financial Accounting Standards ("SFAS") No. 109, "Accounting for Income Taxes." SFAS 109 requires the recognition of deferred tax assets and liabilities for the expected future tax consequences of temporary differences between the financial statement carrying amounts of existing assets and liabilities and their respective tax bases. Deferred tax assets and liabilities are measured using enacted tax rates in effect for the year in which those temporary differences are expected to be recovered or settled.

INCOME (LOSS) PER SHARE

Income (loss) per share is computed based upon the weighted average number of common and dilutive common equivalent shares outstanding during the year. Common equivalent shares represent the net additional shares resulting from the assumed exercise of outstanding stock options calculated using the "treasury stock" method.

STATEMENT OF CASH FLOWS

Following is a summary of noncash investing and financing activities:

During fiscal 1996, the Company financed approximately $109,000 for the purchase of five service vehicles.

During fiscal years 1996 and 1995, capital lease obligations of approximately $71,000 and $282,000 respectively, were incurred when the Company entered into leases for office and loaner equipment.

During fiscal 1995, approximately $61,000 of accrued use tax on production machinery, which had been capitalized in fiscal 1994, was reversed as a result of the State of Vermont determining that the Company qualified as a manufacturer.

FINANCIAL INSTRUMENTS

The Company enters into various types of financial instruments in the normal course of business. Fair values are estimated based on assumptions concerning the amount and timing of estimated future cash flows and assumed discount rates reflecting varying degrees of perceived risk. The fair values of cash, cash equivalents, accounts receivable, accounts payable, accrued expenses and debt approximate their carrying value at September 28, 1996.

USE OF ESTIMATES

The preparation of financial statements in conformity with generally accepted accounting principles requires management to make estimates and assumptions that affect the reported amount of assets and liabilities and disclosure of contingencies at September 28, 1996 and September 30, 1995, and the reported amounts of revenues and expenses during the three years in the period ended September 28, 1996. Actual results could differ from these estimates.

SIGNIFICANT CUSTOMER AND SUPPLY RISK

The Company has one customer which accounted for 12.1% and 10.4% of net sales in the years ended September 28, 1996 and September 30, 1995, respectively. During the year ended September 24, 1994, no customer accounted for more than 10% of the Company's net sales. Concentration of credit risk with respect to accounts receivable is limited due to the large number of customers in various industries comprising the Company's customer base. Ongoing credit evaluations of customers' payment history are performed, and collateral is not required. The Company maintains reserves for potential credit losses and such losses, in the aggregate, have not exceeded management's expectations.

The high-quality arabica coffees the Company purchases as its primary raw material are subject to supply and cost volatility caused by natural, political and other factors which typically affect agricultural products.

NEW ACCOUNTING PRONOUNCEMENT

In October 1995, the Financial Accounting Standards Board issued SFAS 123 ,"Accounting for Stock-Based Compensation." SFAS 123 establishes financial accounting and reporting standards for stock-based employee compensation plans. The statement defines a fair value based method of accounting for stock-based compensation which requires the recording of compensation expense in the financial statements. Companies electing not to adopt this fair value approach are required to disclose the effect on results of operations and earnings per share had the Company adopted the fair value approach. SFAS 123 will apply to the Company for fiscal year 1997, however, the disclosure requirement will include the effects of all awards granted in fiscal year 1996. The Company expects to retain its current method of accounting for stock-based compensation plans, and therefore, the adoption of SFAS 123 will have no impact on the Company's financial position or results of operations.

RECLASSIFICATIONS

Certain reclassifications of prior year balances have been made to conform to the current presentation.

3. Inventories

Inventories consist of the following:

	September 28, 1996	September 30, 1995
Raw materials and supplies	$ 1,291,000	$ 1,025,000
Finished goods	1,985,000	1,741,000
	$ 3,276,000	$ 2,766,000

4. Fixed Assets

Fixed assets consist of the following:

	Useful Life in Years	September 28, 1996	September 30, 1995
Leasehold improvements	5 - 10	$ 2,389,000	$ 2,150,000
Production equipment	5 - 10	4,456,000	4,095,000
Office equipment	4 - 10	3,774,000	3,186,000
Equipment on loan to wholesale customers	3 - 5	4,503,000	3,808,000
Vehicles	2 - 4	230,000	132,000
Construction-in-progress		499,000	102,000
Total fixed assets		15,851,000	13,473,000
Accumulated depreciation		(7,136,000)	(5,346,000)
		$ 8,715,000	$ 8,127,000

Included in office equipment and equipment on loan to wholesale customers at September 28, 1996 and September 30, 1995 are items recorded under a capital lease of $353,000 and $282,000 respectively. Amortization of these items is included in depreciation expense.

Depreciation expense totaled $2,005,000, $1,607,000, and $1,229,000 for the years ended September 28, 1996, September 30, 1995 and September 24, 1994, respectively.

5. Related Parties

NOTE PAYABLE TO STOCKHOLDER

At September 24, 1994, the Company had outstanding a note payable to the Company's majority stockholder totaling $416,000. The note was payable in quarterly installments of $25,000 and bore interest at 7.91%, payable monthly. The note was paid in full in April 1995. Interest paid by the Company to the majority stockholder for the years ended September 30, 1995 and September 24, 1994 was $15,000 and $36,000, respectively.

6. Income Taxes

The provision (benefit) for income taxes consists of:

	September 28, 1996	September 30, 1995	September 24, 1994
Current tax expense:			
U.S. federal	$ 447,000	$ -	$ -
State	120,000	10,000	-
Benefit of net operating loss carryforwards	(533,000)	(10,000)	-
Total current	34,000	-	-
Deferred tax expense (benefit)			
U.S. federal	515,000	(52,000)	(1,029,000)
State	(2,605,000)	(4,000)	(217,000)
Total deferred	(2,090,000)	(56,000)	(1,246,000)
Tax asset valuation allowance	2,278,000	30,000	689,000
Total tax expense (benefit)	$ 222,000	$ (26,000)	$ (557,000)

SFAS 109 is an asset and liability approach that requires the recognition of deferred tax assets and liabilities for the expected future tax consequences of events that have been recognized in the Company's financial statements or tax returns.

In estimating future tax consequences, SFAS 109 generally considers all expected future events other than enactments of changes in the tax law or rates.

Deferred tax assets (liabilities) consist of the following:

	September 28, 1996	September 30, 1995
Deferred tax assets:		
Net operating loss carryforwards	$ 1,744,000	$ 2,101,000
Investment tax credits	54,000	54,000
Vermont manufacturers investment tax credit	2,627,000	-
Section 263A adjustment	91,000	214,000
Other reserves and temporary differences	107,000	71,000
Gross deferred tax assets	4,623,000	2,440,000
Deferred tax asset valuation allowance	(3,503,000)	(1,225,000)
Deferred tax liability:		
Depreciation	(218,000)	(125,000)
Net deferred tax assets	$ 902,000	$ 1,090,000

At September 28, 1996, the Company had net operating loss carryforwards and investment tax credits for federal income tax reporting purposes of $3,599,000 and $54,000, respectively, which will expire between 1997 and 2009. In addition, in November 1996, the Company received notification from the State of Vermont that it had approved a $4,041,000 manufacturers investment tax credit pertaining to certain fixed assets purchased between July 1, 1993 and June 30, 1996, which will expire in 2005. The resulting deferred tax asset, which is fully offset by a valuation allowance, is reflected in the above table net of the federal tax effect.

Realization of the net deferred tax assets is dependent on generating sufficient taxable income prior to the expiration of the loss carryforwards. Although realization is not assured, management believes that the net deferred tax asset represents management's best estimate, based upon the weight of available evidence as prescribed in SFAS 109, of the amount which is more likely than not to be realized. If such evidence were to change, based upon near-term operating results and longer-term projections, the amount of the valuation allowance recorded against the gross deferred tax asset may be decreased or increased. Also, if certain substantial changes in the Company's ownership should occur, there would be an annual limitation on the amount of loss carryforwards which could be utilized, and restrictions on the utilization of investment tax credit carryforwards.

A reconciliation between the amount of reported income tax expense (benefit) and the amount computed using the U.S. Federal Statutory rate of 35% is as follows:

	September 28, 1996	September 30, 1995	September 24, 1994
Tax at U.S. Federal Statutory rate	$ 519,000	$ (85,000)	$(1,020,000)
Increase (decrease) in rates resulting from:			
Other nondeductible items	22,000	33,000	6,000
State taxes, net of federal benefit	(2,597,000)	(4,000)	(232,000)
Deferred tax asset valuation allowance	2,278,000	30,000	689,000
Tax at effective rates	$ 222,000	$ (26,000)	$ (557,000)

7. *Revolving Line of Credit*

The Company maintains a revolving line of credit agreement under a comprehensive credit facility ("credit facility") with Fleet Bank - NH ("Fleet"). Borrowings under the agreement are limited to $3,000,000 under a borrowing base formula and are secured by substantially all of the Company's assets. In April 1996, the Company amended the credit facility which extended the availability of the line of credit through February 28, 1998, and reduced the interest rate on the revolving line of credit, subject to the election of the Company, to the lesser of Fleet's variable base lending rate (8.25% at September 28, 1996) or 250 basis points above the LIBOR rate up to 30 days. The terms of the credit facility also provide for the maintenance of specified financial ratios and restrict certain transactions, including a prohibition from paying any dividends without prior bank approval. The Company was in compliance with these covenants at September 28, 1996.

The principal amount outstanding on the revolving line of credit at September 28, 1996 and September 30, 1995 was $508,000 and $1,720,000, respectively.

8. Long-Term Debt

	September 28, 1996	September 30, 1995
Facility and Equipment Term Loan	$ 2,827,000	$ 1,839,000
Central Vermont Economic Development Corporation Debenture	600,000	665,000
Vermont Economic Development Authority Promissory Note	182,000	222,000
Computer Equipment Installment Loans	153,000	219,000
Service Vehicle Installment Loans	96,000	24,000
	3,858,000	2,969,000
Less-current portion	947,000	618,000
	$ 2,911,000	$ 2,351,000

FACILITY AND EQUIPMENT TERM LOANS

As part of the credit facility, the Company has financed fixed asset purchases under five term loans which are secured by a senior lien on substantially all of the Company's assets and by a security interest in the fixed assets for which the borrowings are made. Under the amended credit facility, the existing equipment line of credit was eliminated and the Company borrowed an additional $1,500,000 under a new five-year promissory note to be repaid in equal monthly principal installments. The interest rate on all term loans under the credit facility was reduced to the lesser of 25 basis points above the variable Fleet base rate or 275 basis points above the LIBOR rate for maturities of up to one year (8.2% at September 28, 1996). The original terms of the loans range from 56 to 84 months and are being repaid in equal monthly payments totaling approximately $60,600 plus interest.

CENTRAL VERMONT ECONOMIC DEVELOPMENT CORPORATION DEBENTURE

The debenture from the Central Vermont Economic Development Corporation (CVEDC) is guaranteed by the U.S. Small Business Administration. The debenture term is ten years and requires equal monthly principal and interest payments of approximately $8,500 and carries a fixed interest rate of 5.812%. The debenture is secured by a secondary security interest in the related fixed assets and is guaranteed by the majority stockholder of the Company. Additional guarantees will be required of any stockholder obtaining more than 20% ownership of the Company.

VERMONT ECONOMIC DEVELOPMENT AUTHORITY PROMISSORY NOTE

The Vermont Economic Development Authority promissory note is payable in monthly principal and interest installments of approximately $4,300 over seven years, with an interest rate of 5.5%. The note is secured by a secondary security interest in the related fixed assets and contains covenants related to restrictions on prepayments of certain portions of the Company's remaining outstanding debt as defined in the underlying agreement. The Company was in compliance with these covenants at September 28, 1996.

COMPUTER EQUIPMENT INSTALLMENT LOANS

The computer equipment installment loans bear interest at 8.69%, and require monthly installments of principal and interest totaling approximately $7,600 through September 1998.

SERVICE VEHICLE INSTALLMENT LOANS

The service vehicle installment loans represent several loans to financing institutions for the purchase of service vehicles. The notes bear interest at rates between 4.8% and 7.4% and require monthly installments of principal and interest totaling approximately $3,500 through February 2000.

MATURITIES

Maturities of long-term debt for years subsequent to September 28, 1996 are as follows:

Fiscal Year	
1997	$ 947,000
1998	943,000
1999	835,000
2000	581,000
2001	314,000
Thereafter	238,000
	$ 3,858,000

9. Employee Compensation Plans

STOCK OPTION PLANS

Prior to the establishment on September 21, 1993 of the employee stock option plan (the "1993 Plan"), the Company granted to certain key management employees, individual non-qualified stock option agreements to purchase shares of the Company's common stock. All such options presently outstanding are fully vested and had an original expiration date after the fifth anniversary following the date of grant or earlier if employment terminates. Effective July 26, 1996, the term of 141,440 of such options was extended for an additional five years. The exercise price of these options exceeded the fair market value of the common stock at the date of the extension. At September 28, 1996, 212,166 options were outstanding under these individual agreements.

The 1993 Plan provides for the granting of both incentive and non-qualified stock options, with an aggregate number of 75,000 shares of common stock to be made available under the 1993 Plan. Effective July 26, 1996, and subject to approval by a majority of stockholders at the next Annual Stockholders' Meeting, the total number of shares of authorized common stock to be made available under the 1993 Plan was increased to 275,000. The option price for each incentive stock option shall not be less than the fair market value per share of common stock on the date of grant, with certain provisions which increase the option price to 110% of the fair market value of the common stock if the grantee owns in excess of 10% of the Company's common stock at the date of grant. The option price for each nonqualified stock option shall not be less than 85% of the fair market value of the common stock at the date of grant. Options under the Plan become exercisable over periods determined by the Board of Directors at a rate generally not to exceed 25% per year beginning with the first anniversary of the date of grant. At September 28, 1996 and September 30, 1995, options for 196,005 and 9,565 shares of common stock were available for grant under the plan, respectively.

On April 21, 1994, the Company entered into a marketing consulting agreement (the "Agreement") and granted 50,000 nonqualified options (separate from the 1993 Plan) to the consultant. The exercise price of the options is equal to the market value of the Company's common stock determined on the date of vesting and has an expiration date of two years following the earlier of the termination or expiration of the Agreement. Upon execution of the agreement, 20,000 of the options vested at an exercise price of $6.88 each, and 5,000 additional options were to vest at the end of each 6 month period over the term of the Agreement up to a maximum of 50,000 options in the aggregate. On October 21, 1994, 5,000 additional options vested under the Agreement at an exercise price of $6.50. The remaining 25,000 options were cancelled prior to the next scheduled vesting date as a result of the termination of the Agreement.

Option activity is summarized as follows:

	Number of shares	Option price per share
Outstanding at September 25, 1993	271,101	$ 2.55-8.02
Granted	65,000	$ 6.00-6.88
Exercised	-	-
Cancelled	(47,148)	$ 2.55
Outstanding at September 24, 1994	288,953	$ 2.55-8.02
Granted	59,684	$ 8.50
Exercised	-	-
Cancelled	(34,248)	$ 8.50
Outstanding at September 30, 1995	314,389	$ 2.55-8.50
Granted	18,400	$ 6.25-8.50
Exercised	-	-
Cancelled	(16,627)	$ 8.02-8.50
Outstanding at September 28, 1996	316,162	$ 2.55-8.50

At September 28, 1996, 60,022 of these options were not exercisable.

EMPLOYEE STOCK PURCHASE PLAN

On September 21, 1993, the Company approved the adoption of an Employee Stock Purchase Plan (the "Purchase Plan"). Under the Purchase Plan, the Company reserved 75,000 shares of common stock for purchase by eligible employees. The Purchase Plan provides for five annual offerings of 15,000 shares of common stock per offering, plus any unissued shares from prior fiscal years. Each participating employee has the option to purchase a maximum number of shares equal to 10% of the participant's base pay, divided by 85% of the market value of the common stock at such time, subject to a pro rata reduction of shares if the annual aggregate maximum number of shares offered by the Company would otherwise be exceeded. On September 24, 1994, 4,757 options were exercised under the fiscal 1994 offering, generating proceeds to the Company of $21,000. On September 30, 1995, 16,310 options were exercised under the fiscal 1995 offering, generating proceeds to the Company of $73,000. On September 28, 1996, 17,511 options were exercised under the fiscal 1996 offering, generating proceeds to the Company of $89,000.

For the fiscal 1997 offering there are outstanding options to purchase 20,273 shares under the Purchase Plan at a maximum exercise price of $6.06. The ultimate purchase price of the underlying shares of common stock is 85% of the fair market value of the common stock at the beginning or end of the fiscal year, whichever is less.

10. Defined Contribution Plan

The Company has a defined contribution plan which meets the requirements of Section 401(k) of the Internal Revenue Code. All employees of the Company with one year or more of service who are at least twenty-one years of age are eligible to participate in the plan. The plan allows employees to defer a portion of their salary on a pre-tax basis and the Company contributes 50% of amounts contributed by employees up to 5% of their salary. Company contributions to the plan amounted to $73,000, $52,000 and $29,000 for the years ended September 28, 1996, September 30, 1995 and September 24, 1994, respectively.

11. Warrants

The Company issued warrants for 100,000 shares of the Company's common stock on September 21, 1993 to its underwriter in conjunction with the Company's initial public offering. The warrants carry an exercise price of $12 per share and expire on September 21, 1998. The Company has reserved 100,000 shares of common stock in connection with these warrants.

12. Commitments

LEASES

The Company leases office and retail space, production, distribution and service facilities and certain equipment under various noncancelable operating leases, ranging from one to ten years. Property leases normally require payment of a minimum annual rental plus a pro-rata share of certain landlord operating expenses. In addition, a number of the Company's retail space leases require payment of contingent rentals based upon a percentage of sales in excess of a specified amount.

The Company has entered into a capital lease, primarily for loaner and office equipment.

Minimum future lease payments (net of committed sublease rental receipts of $33,000 for the fiscal years 1997 through 2001, and $43,000 thereafter) under noncancelable operating leases and capital leases, for years subsequent to September 28, 1996 are as follows:

Fiscal Year	Operating Leases	Capital Lease
1997	$ 1,053,000	$ 145,000
1998	941,000	145,000
1999	839,000	12,000
2000	729,000	-
2001	665,000	-
Thereafter	870,000	-
Total minimum lease payments	$ 5,097,000	302,000
Less - amount representing interest		44,000
Present value of obligations under capital lease (including current portion of $114,000)		$ 258,000

Rent expense (net of sublease income of $33,000, $30,000 and $35,000 for the years ended September 28, 1996, September 30, 1995 and September 24, 1994, respectively), under these operating leases was $991,000, $887,000 and $753,000 for the years ended September 28, 1996, September 30, 1995 and September 24, 1994, respectively.

APPENDIX C

Time Value of Money

STUDY OBJECTIVES

After studying this appendix, you should be able to:

1. Distinguish between simple and compound interest.
2. Solve for future value of a single amount.
3. Solve for future value of an annuity.
4. Identify the variables fundamental to solving present value problems.
5. Solve for present value of a single amount.
6. Solve for present value of an annuity.
7. Compute the present value of notes and bonds.

Would you rather receive $1,000 today or a year from now? You should prefer to receive the $1,000 today because you can invest the $1,000 and earn interest on it. As a result, you will have more than $1,000 a year from now. What this example illustrates is the concept of the **time value of money.** Everyone prefers to receive money today rather than in the future because of the interest factor.

NATURE OF INTEREST

Interest is payment for the use of another person's money. It is the difference between the amount borrowed or invested (called the **principal**) and the amount repaid or collected. The amount of interest to be paid or collected is usually stated as a rate over a specific period of time. The rate of interest is generally stated as an annual rate.

The amount of interest involved in any financing transaction is based on three elements:

1. **Principal (p):** The original amount borrowed or invested.
2. **Interest Rate (i):** An annual percentage of the principal.
3. **Time (n):** The number of years that the principal is borrowed or invested.

SIMPLE INTEREST

Simple interest is computed on the principal amount only. It is the return on the principal for one period. Simple interest is usually expressed as shown in Illustration C-1.

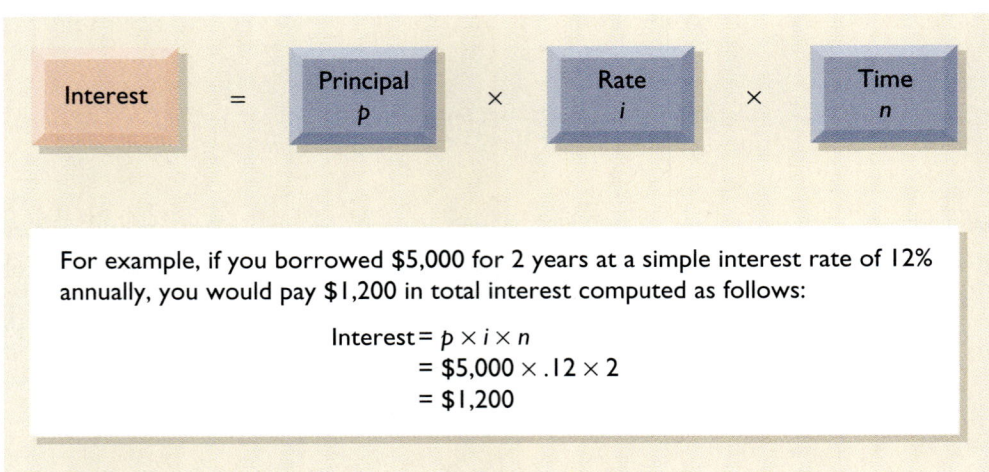

Illustration C-1 Interest computation

For example, if you borrowed $5,000 for 2 years at a simple interest rate of 12% annually, you would pay $1,200 in total interest computed as follows:

$$\text{Interest} = p \times i \times n$$
$$= \$5,000 \times .12 \times 2$$
$$= \$1,200$$

COMPOUND INTEREST

Compound interest is computed on principal **and** on any interest earned that has not been paid or withdrawn. It is the return on (or growth of) the principal for two or more time periods. Compounding computes interest not only on the principal but also on the interest earned to date on that principal, assuming the interest is left on deposit.

To illustrate the difference between simple and compound interest, assume that you deposit $1,000 in Bank One, where it will earn simple interest of 9% per year, and you deposit another $1,000 in CityCorp, where it will earn compound interest of 9% per year compounded annually. Also assume that in both cases you will not withdraw any interest until 3 years from the date of deposit. The computation of interest to be received and the accumulated year-end balances are indicated in Illustration C-2.

Illustration C-2 Simple versus compound interest

Bank One

Simple Interest Calculation	Simple Interest	Accumulated Year-end Balance
Year 1 $1,000.00 × 9%	$ 90.00	$1,090.00
Year 2 $1,000.00 × 9%	90.00	$1,180.00
Year 3 $1,000.00 × 9%	90.00	$1,270.00
	$ 270.00	

CityCorp

Compound Interest Calculation	Compound Interest	Accumulated Year-end Balance
Year 1 $1,000.00 × 9%	$ 90.00	$1,090.00
Year 2 $1,090.00 × 9%	98.10	$1,188.10
Year 3 $1,188.10 × 9%	106.93	$1,295.03
	$ 295.03	

$25.03 Difference

Note in Illustration C-2 that simple interest uses the initial principal of $1,000 to compute the interest in all 3 years. Compound interest uses the accumulated balance (principal plus interest to date) at each year-end to compute interest in the succeeding year—which explains why your compound interest account is larger.

Obviously, if you had a choice between investing your money at simple interest or at compound interest, you would choose compound interest, all other things—especially risk—being equal. In the example, compounding provides $25.03 of additional interest income. For practical purposes compounding assumes that unpaid interest earned becomes a part of the principal, and the accumulated balance at the end of each year becomes the new principal on which interest is earned during the next year.

As can be seen in Illustration C-2, you should invest your money at CityCorp, which compounds interest annually. Compound interest is used in most business situations. Simple interest is generally applicable only to short-term situations of one year or less.

SECTION 1
FUTURE VALUE CONCEPTS

FUTURE VALUE OF A SINGLE AMOUNT

The **future value of a single amount** is the value at a future date of a given amount invested assuming compound interest. For example, in Illustration C-2, $1,295.03 is the future value of the $1,000 at the end of 3 years. The $1,295.03 could be determined more easily by using the following formula:

$$FV = p \times (1 + i)^n$$

STUDY OBJECTIVE 2
Solve for future value of a single amount.

C-4 APPENDIX C Time Value of Money

Where:
FV = Future value of a single amount
p = Principal (or present value)
i = Interest rate for one period
n = Number of periods

The $1,295.03 is computed as follows:

$$FV = p \times (1 + i)^n$$
$$= \$1,000 \times (1 + i)^3$$
$$= \$1,000 \times 1.29503$$
$$= \$1,295.03$$

The 1.29503 is computed by multiplying (1.09 × 1.09 × 1.09). The amounts in this example can be depicted in the time diagram shown in Illustration C-3.

Illustration C-3 Time diagram

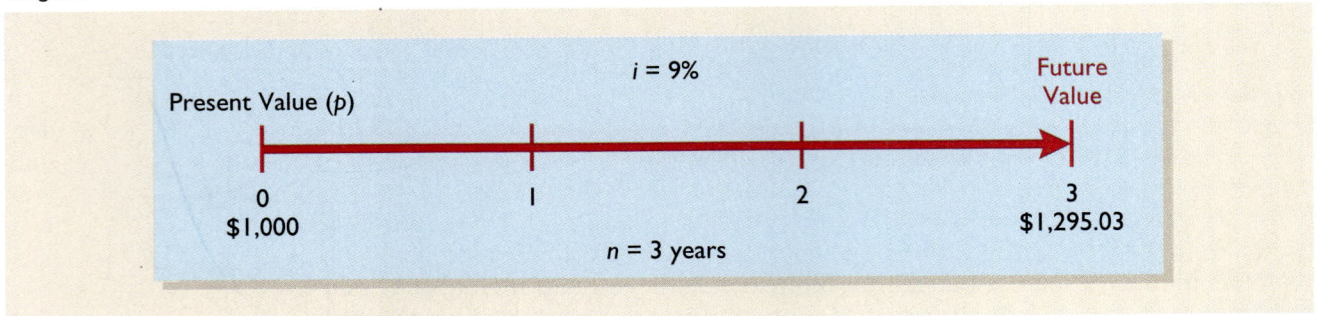

Another method that may be used to compute the future value of a single amount involves the use of a compound interest table. This table shows the future value of 1 for n periods. Table 1 is such a table.

TABLE 1 Future Value of 1

(n) Periods	4%	5%	6%	8%	9%	10%	11%	12%	15%
1	1.04000	1.05000	1.06000	1.08000	1.09000	1.10000	1.11000	1.12000	1.15000
2	1.08160	1.10250	1.12360	1.16640	1.18810	1.21000	1.23210	1.25440	1.32250
3	1.12486	1.15763	1.19102	1.25971	1.29503	1.33100	1.36763	1.40493	1.52088
4	1.16986	1.21551	1.26248	1.36049	1.41158	1.46410	1.51807	1.57352	1.74901
5	1.21665	1.27628	1.33823	1.46933	1.53862	1.61051	1.68506	1.76234	2.01136
6	1.26532	1.34010	1.41852	1.58687	1.67710	1.77156	1.87041	1.97382	2.31306
7	1.31593	1.40710	1.50363	1.71382	1.82804	1.94872	2.07616	2.21068	2.66002
8	1.36857	1.47746	1.59385	1.85093	1.99256	2.14359	2.30454	2.47596	3.05902
9	1.42331	1.55133	1.68948	1.99900	2.17189	2.35795	2.55803	2.77308	3.51788
10	1.48024	1.62889	1.79085	2.15892	2.36736	2.59374	2.83942	3.10585	4.04556
11	1.53945	1.71034	1.89830	2.33164	2.58043	2.85312	3.15176	3.47855	4.65239
12	1.60103	1.79586	2.01220	2.51817	2.81267	3.13843	3.49845	3.89598	5.35025
13	1.66507	1.88565	2.13293	2.71962	3.06581	3.45227	3.88328	4.36349	6.15279
14	1.73168	1.97993	2.26090	2.93719	3.34173	3.79750	4.31044	4.88711	7.07571
15	1.80094	2.07893	2.39656	3.17217	3.64248	4.17725	4.78459	5.47357	8.13706
16	1.87298	2.18287	2.54035	3.42594	3.97031	4.59497	5.31089	6.13039	9.35762
17	1.94790	2.29202	2.69277	3.70002	4.32763	5.05447	5.89509	6.86604	10.76126
18	2.02582	2.40662	2.85434	3.99602	4.71712	5.55992	6.54355	7.68997	12.37545
19	2.10685	2.52695	3.02560	4.31570	5.14166	6.11591	7.26334	8.61276	14.23177
20	2.19112	2.65330	3.20714	4.66096	5.60441	6.72750	8.06231	9.64629	16.36654

In Table 1, n is the number of compounding periods, the percentages are the periodic interest rates, and the 5-digit decimal numbers in the respective columns are the future value of 1 factors. In using Table 1, the principal amount is multiplied by the future value factor for the specified number of periods and interest rate. For example, the future value factor for 2 periods at 9% is 1.18810. Multiplying this factor by $1,000 equals $1,188.10, which is the accumulated balance at the end of year 2 in the CityCorp example in Illustration C-2. The $1,295.03 accumulated balance at the end of the third year can be calculated from Table 1 by multiplying the future value factor for 3 periods (1.29503) by the $1,000.

The demonstration problem in Illustration C-4 shows how to use Table 1.

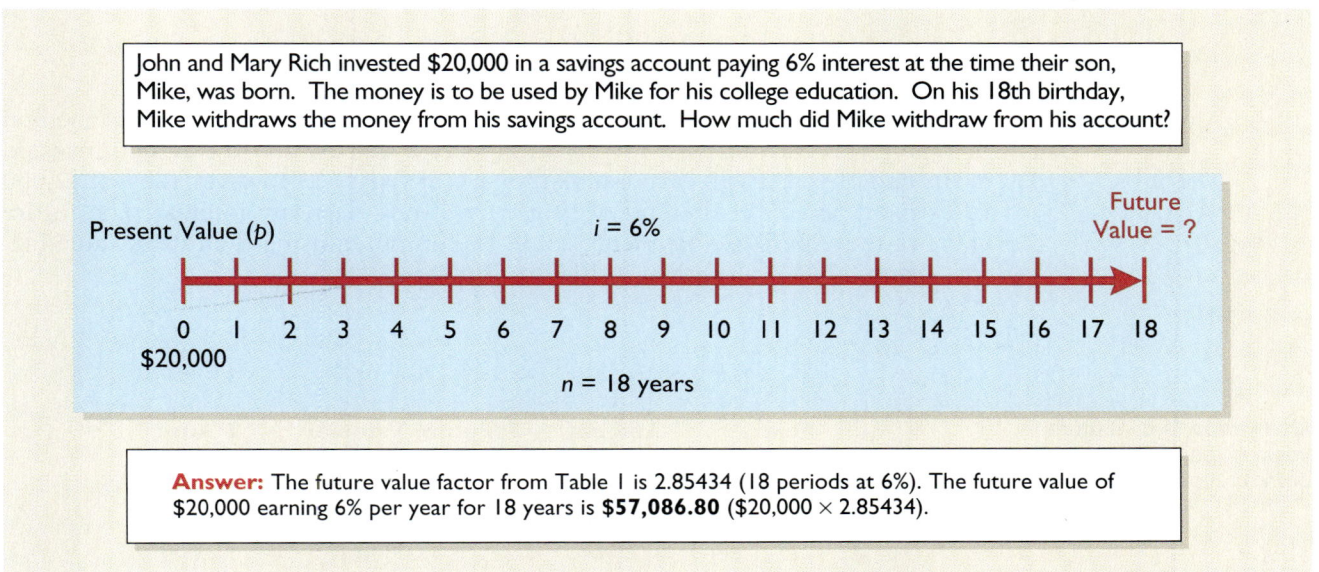

Illustration C-4
Demonstration problem—using Table 1 for *FV* of 1

Future Value of an Annuity

The preceding discussion involved the accumulation of only a single principal sum. Individuals and businesses frequently encounter situations in which a series of equal dollar amounts are to be paid or received periodically, such as loans or lease (rental) contracts. Such payments or receipts of equal dollar amounts are referred to as **annuities.** The **future value of an annuity** is the sum of all the payments (receipts) plus the accumulated compound interest on them. In computing the future value of an annuity, it is necessary to know (1) the interest rate, (2) the number of compounding periods, and (3) the amount of the periodic payments or receipts.

To illustrate the computation of the future value of an annuity, assume that you invest $2,000 at the end of each year for 3 years at 5% interest compounded annually. This situation is depicted in the time diagram in Illustration C-5.

STUDY OBJECTIVE 3
Solve for future value of an annuity.

Illustration C-5 Time diagram for a 3-year annuity

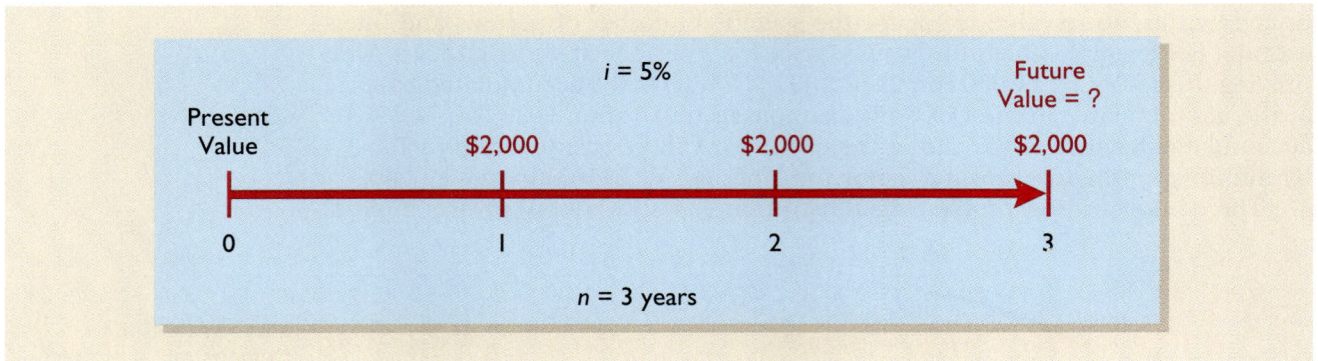

As can be seen from the preceding diagram, the $2,000 invested at the end of year 1 will earn interest for 2 years (years 2 and 3), and the $2,000 invested at the end of year 2 will earn interest for 1 year (year 3). However, the last $2,000 investment (made at the end of year 3) will not earn any interest. The future value of these periodic payments could be computed using the future value factors from Table 1, as shown in Illustration C-6.

Illustration C-6 Future value of periodic payment computation

Year Invested	Amount Invested	×	Future Value of 1 Factor at 5%	=	Future Value
1	$2,000	×	1.10250		$2,205
2	$2,000	×	1.05000		2,100
3	$2,000	×	1.00000		2,000
			3.15250		$6,305

The first $2,000 investment is multiplied by the future value factor for 2 periods (1.1025) because 2 years' interest will accumulate on it (in years 2 and 3). The second $2,000 investment will earn only 1 year's interest (in year 3) and therefore is multiplied by the future value factor for 1 year (1.0500). The final $2,000 investment is made at the end of the third year and will not earn any interest. Consequently, the future value of the last $2,000 invested is only $2,000 since it does not accumulate any interest.

This method of calculation is required when the periodic payments or receipts are not equal in each period. However, when the periodic payments (receipts) are the same in each period, the future value can be computed by using a future value of an annuity of 1 table. Table 2 is such a table.

TABLE 2   Future Value of an Annuity of 1

(n) Periods	4%	5%	6%	8%	9%	10%	11%	12%	15%
1	1.00000	1.00000	1.00000	1.00000	1.00000	1.00000	1.00000	1.00000	1.00000
2	2.04000	2.05000	2.06000	2.08000	2.09000	2.10000	2.11000	2.12000	2.15000
3	3.12160	3.15250	3.18360	3.24640	3.27810	3.31000	3.34210	3.37440	3.47250
4	4.24646	4.31013	4.37462	4.50611	4.57313	4.64100	4.70973	4.77933	4.99338
5	5.41632	5.52563	5.63709	5.86660	5.98471	6.10510	6.22780	6.35285	6.74238
6	6.63298	6.80191	6.97532	7.33592	7.52334	7.71561	7.91286	8.11519	8.75374
7	7.89829	8.14201	8.39384	8.92280	9.20044	9.48717	9.78327	10.08901	11.06680
8	9.21423	9.54911	9.89747	10.63663	11.02847	11.43589	11.85943	12.29969	13.72682
9	10.58280	11.02656	11.49132	12.48756	13.02104	13.57948	14.16397	14.77566	16.78584
10	12.00611	12.57789	13.18079	14.48656	15.19293	15.93743	16.72201	17.54874	20.30372
11	13.48635	14.20679	14.97164	16.64549	17.56029	18.53117	19.56143	20.65458	24.34928
12	15.02581	15.91713	16.86994	18.97713	20.14072	21.38428	22.71319	24.13313	29.00167
13	16.62684	17.71298	18.88214	21.49530	22.95339	24.52271	26.21164	28.02911	34.35192
14	18.29191	19.59863	21.01507	24.21492	26.01919	27.97498	30.09492	32.39260	40.50471
15	20.02359	21.57856	23.27597	27.15211	29.36092	31.77248	34.40536	37.27972	47.58041
16	21.82453	23.65749	25.67253	30.32428	33.00340	35.94973	39.18995	42.75328	55.71747
17	23.69751	25.84037	28.21288	33.75023	36.97351	40.54470	44.50084	48.88367	65.07509
18	25.64541	28.13238	30.90565	37.45024	41.30134	45.59917	50.39593	55.74972	75.83636
19	27.67123	30.53900	33.75999	41.44626	46.01846	51.15909	56.93949	63.43968	88.21181
20	29.77808	33.06595	36.78559	45.76196	51.16012	57.27500	64.20283	72.05244	102.44358

Table 2 shows the future value of 1 to be received periodically for a given number of periods. From Table 2 it can be seen that the future value of an annuity of 1 factor for 3 periods at 5% is 3.15250. The future value factor is the total of the three individual future value factors as shown in Illustration C-6. Multiplying this amount by the annual investment of $2,000 produces a future value of $6,305.

The demonstration problem in Illustration C-7 (at the top of the next page) shows how to use Table 2.

C-8 APPENDIX C Time Value of Money

Illustration C-7
Demonstration problem—using Table 2 for *FV* of an annuity of 1

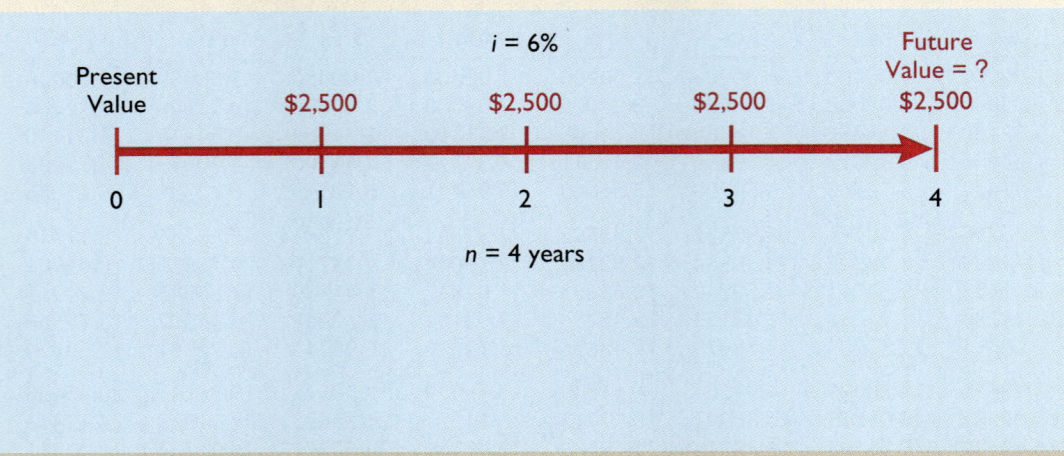

John and Char Lewis' daughter, Debra, has just started high school. They decide to start a college fund for her and will invest $2,500 in a savings account at the end of each year she is in high school (4 payments total). The account will earn 6% interest compounded annually. How much will be in the college fund at the time Debra graduates from high school?

Answer: The future value factor from Table 2 is 4.37462 (4 periods at 6%). The future value of $2,500 invested each year for 4 years at 6% interest is **$10,936.55** ($2,500 × 4.37462).

SECTION 2
PRESENT VALUE CONCEPTS

PRESENT VALUE VARIABLES

STUDY OBJECTIVE 4

Identify the variables fundamental to solving present value problems.

The **present value,** like the future value, is based on three variables: (1) the dollar amount to be received (future amount), (2) the length of time until the amount is received (number of periods), and (3) the interest rate (the discount rate). The process of determining the present value is referred to as **discounting the future amount.**

In this textbook, present value computations are used in measuring several items. For example, in Chapter 10, to determine the market price of a bond, the present value of the principal and interest payments is computed. In addition, the determination of the amount to be reported for notes payable and lease liability involves present value computations.

PRESENT VALUE OF A SINGLE AMOUNT

To illustrate present value concepts, assume that you are willing to invest a sum of money that will yield $1,000 at the end of one year. In other words, what amount would you need to invest today to have $1,000 one year from now? If you want a 10% rate of return, the investment or present value is $909.09 ($1,000 ÷ 1.10). The computation of this amount is shown in Illustration C-8.

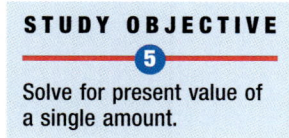

STUDY OBJECTIVE 5
Solve for present value of a single amount.

$$\text{Present Value} = \text{Future Value} \div (1 + i)^1$$
$$PV = FV \div (1 + 10\%)^1$$
$$PV = \$1{,}000 \div 1.10$$
$$PV = \$909.09$$

Illustration C-8 Present value computation—$1,000 discounted at 10% for 1 year

The future amount ($1,000), the discount rate (10%), and the number of periods (1) are known. The variables in this situation can be depicted in the time diagram in Illustration C-9.

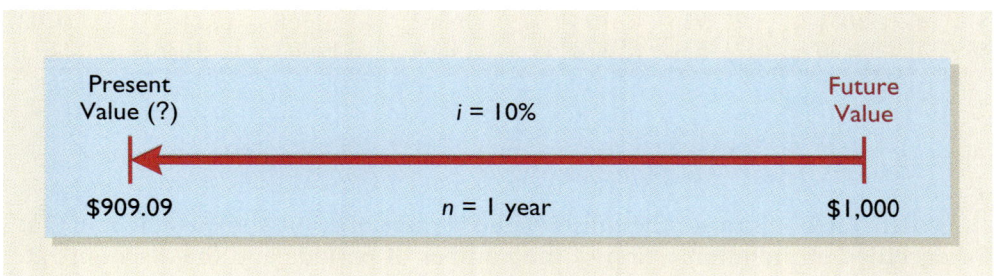

Illustration C-9 Finding present value if discounted for one period

If the single amount of $1,000 is to be received **in 2 years** and discounted at 10% [$PV = \$1{,}000 \div (1 + 10\%)^2$], its present value is $826.45 [($1,000 ÷ 1.10) ÷ 1.10], depicted as shown in Illustration C-10.

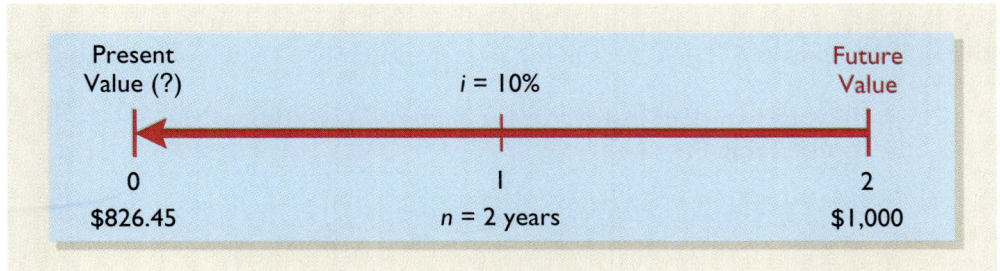

Illustration C-10 Finding present value if discounted for two periods

The present value of 1 may also be determined through tables that show the present value of 1 for n periods. In Table 3 (page C-10), n is the number of discounting periods involved. The percentages are the periodic interest rates or discount rates, and the 5-digit decimal numbers in the respective columns are the present value of 1 factors.

TABLE 3 Present Value of 1

(n) Periods	4%	5%	6%	8%	9%	10%	11%	12%	15%
1	.96154	.95238	.94340	.92593	.91743	.90909	.90090	.89286	.86957
2	.92456	.90703	.89000	.85734	.84168	.82645	.81162	.79719	.75614
3	.88900	.86384	.83962	.79383	.77218	.75132	.73119	.71178	.65752
4	.85480	.82270	.79209	.73503	.70843	.68301	.65873	.63552	.57175
5	.82193	.78353	.74726	.68058	.64993	.62092	.59345	.56743	.49718
6	.79031	.74622	.70496	.63017	.59627	.56447	.53464	.50663	.43233
7	.75992	.71068	.66506	.58349	.54703	.51316	.48166	.45235	.37594
8	.73069	.67684	.62741	.54027	.50187	.46651	.43393	.40388	.32690
9	.70259	.64461	.59190	.50025	.46043	.42410	.39092	.36061	.28426
10	.67556	.61391	.55839	.46319	.42241	.38554	.35218	.32197	.24719
11	.64958	.58468	.52679	.42888	.38753	.35049	.31728	.28748	.21494
12	.62460	.55684	.49697	.39711	.35554	.31863	.28584	.25668	.18691
13	.60057	.53032	.46884	.36770	.32618	.28966	.25751	.22917	.16253
14	.57748	.50507	.44230	.34046	.29925	.26333	.23199	.20462	.14133
15	.55526	.48102	.41727	.31524	.27454	.23939	.20900	.18270	.12289
16	.53391	.45811	.39365	.29189	.25187	.21763	.18829	.16312	.10687
17	.51337	.43630	.37136	.27027	.23107	.19785	.16963	.14564	.09293
18	.49363	.41552	.35034	.25025	.21199	.17986	.15282	.13004	.08081
19	.47464	.39573	.33051	.23171	.19449	.16351	.13768	.11611	.07027
20	.45639	.37689	.31180	.21455	.17843	.14864	.12403	.10367	.06110

When Table 3 is used, the future value is multiplied by the present value factor specified at the intersection of the number of periods and the discount rate. For example, the present value factor for 1 period at a discount rate of 10% is .90909, which equals the $909.09 ($1,000 × .90909) computed in Illustration C-8. For 2 periods at a discount rate of 10%, the present value factor is .82645, which equals the $826.45 ($1,000 × .82645) computed previously.

Note that a higher discount rate produces a smaller present value. For example, using a 15% discount rate, the present value of $1,000 due one year from now is $869.57 versus $909.09 at 10%. It should also be recognized that the further removed from the present the future value is, the smaller the present value. For example, using the same discount rate of 10%, the present value of $1,000 due in **five years** is $620.92 versus the present value of $1,000 due in **one year** is $909.09.

The following two demonstration problems (Illustrations C-11, C-12) illustrate how to use Table 3.

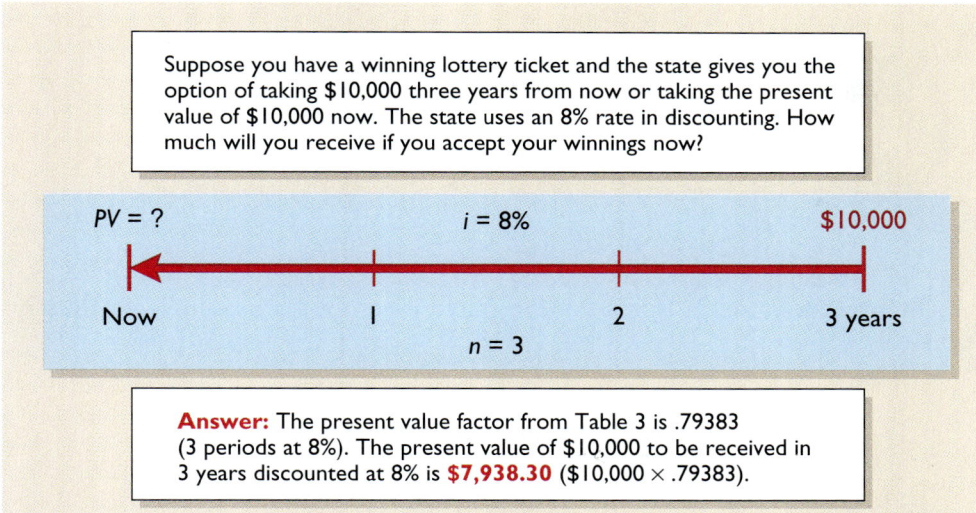

Illustration C-11
Demonstration problem—using Table 3 for *PV* of 1

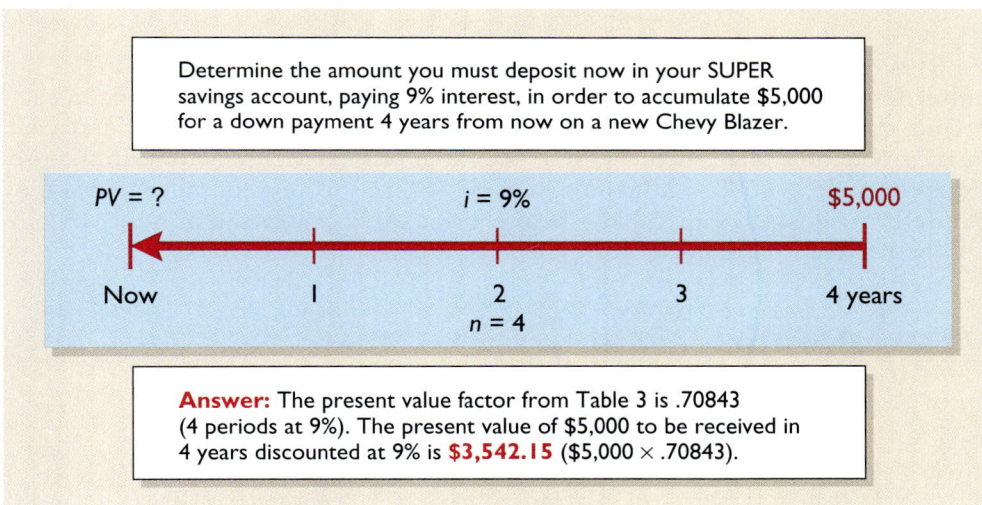

Illustration C-12
Demonstration problem—using Table 3 for *PV* of 1

PRESENT VALUE OF AN ANNUITY

The preceding discussion involved the discounting of only a single future amount. Businesses and individuals frequently engage in transactions in which a series of equal dollar amounts are to be received or paid periodically. Examples of a series of periodic receipts or payments are loan agreements, installment sales, mortgage notes, lease (rental) contracts, and pension obligations. These series of periodic receipts or payments are called **annuities.** In computing the **present value of an annuity,** it is necessary to know (1) the discount rate, (2) the number of discount periods, and (3) the amount of the periodic receipts or payments. To illustrate the computation of the present value of an annuity, assume that you will receive $1,000 cash annually for three years at a time when the discount rate is 10%. This situation is depicted in the time diagram in Illustration C-13.

STUDY OBJECTIVE 6
Solve for present value of an annuity.

C-12 APPENDIX C Time Value of Money

Illustration C-13 Time diagram for a 3-year annuity

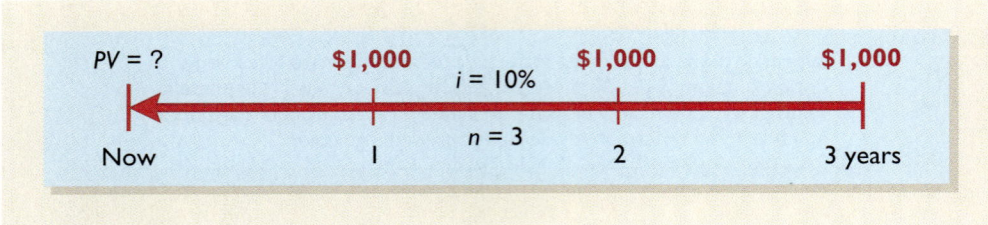

The present value in this situation may be computed as shown in Illustration C-14.

Illustration C-14 Present value of a series of future amounts computation

Future Amount	×	Present Value of 1 Factor at 10%	=	Present Value
$1,000 (One year away)		.90909		$ 909.09
1,000 (Two years away)		.82645		826.45
1,000 (Three years away)		.75132		751.32
		2.48686		$2,486.86

This method of calculation is required when the periodic cash flows are not uniform in each period. However, when the future receipts are the same in each period, there are two other ways to compute present value. First, the annual cash flow can be multiplied by the sum of the three present value factors. In the previous example, $1,000 × 2.48686 equals $2,486.86. Second, annuity tables may be used. As illustrated in Table 4 below, these tables show the present value of 1 to be received periodically for a given number of periods.

TABLE 4   Present Value of an Annuity of 1

(n) Periods	4%	5%	6%	8%	9%	10%	11%	12%	15%
1	.96154	.95238	.94340	.92593	.91743	.90909	.90090	.89286	.86957
2	1.88609	1.85941	1.83339	1.78326	1.75911	1.73554	1.71252	1.69005	1.62571
3	2.77509	2.72325	2.67301	2.57710	2.53130	2.48685	2.44371	2.40183	2.28323
4	3.62990	3.54595	3.46511	3.31213	3.23972	3.16986	3.10245	3.03735	2.85498
5	4.45182	4.32948	4.21236	3.99271	3.88965	3.79079	3.69590	3.60478	3.35216
6	5.24214	5.07569	4.91732	4.62288	4.48592	4.35526	4.23054	4.11141	3.78448
7	6.00205	5.78637	5.58238	5.20637	5.03295	4.86842	4.71220	4.56376	4.16042
8	6.73274	6.46321	6.20979	5.74664	5.53482	5.33493	5.14612	4.96764	4.48732
9	7.43533	7.10782	6.80169	6.24689	5.99525	5.75902	5.53705	5.32825	4.77158
10	8.11090	7.72173	7.36009	6.71008	6.41766	6.14457	5.88923	5.65022	5.01877
11	8.76048	8.30641	7.88687	7.13896	6.80519	6.49506	6.20652	5.93770	5.23371
12	9.38507	8.86325	8.38384	7.53608	7.16073	6.81369	6.49236	6.19437	5.42062
13	9.98565	9.39357	8.85268	7.90378	7.48690	7.10336	6.74987	6.42355	5.58315
14	10.56312	9.89864	9.29498	8.24424	7.78615	7.36669	6.98187	6.62817	5.72448
15	11.11839	10.37966	9.71225	8.55948	8.06069	7.60608	7.19087	6.81086	5.84737
16	11.65230	10.83777	10.10590	8.85137	8.31256	7.82371	7.37916	6.97399	5.95424
17	12.16567	11.27407	10.47726	9.12164	8.54363	8.02155	7.54879	7.11963	6.04716
18	12.65930	11.68959	10.82760	9.37189	8.75563	8.20141	7.70162	7.24967	6.12797
19	13.13394	12.08532	11.15812	9.60360	8.95012	8.36492	7.83929	7.36578	6.19823
20	13.59033	12.46221	11.46992	9.81815	9.12855	8.51356	7.96333	7.46944	6.25933

From Table 4 it can be seen that the present value of an annuity of 1 factor for three periods at 10% is 2.48685.[1] This present value factor is the total of the three individual present value factors, as shown in Illustration C-14. Applying this amount to the annual cash flow of $1,000 produces a present value of $2,486.85.

The following demonstration problem (Illustration C-15) illustrates how to use Table 4.

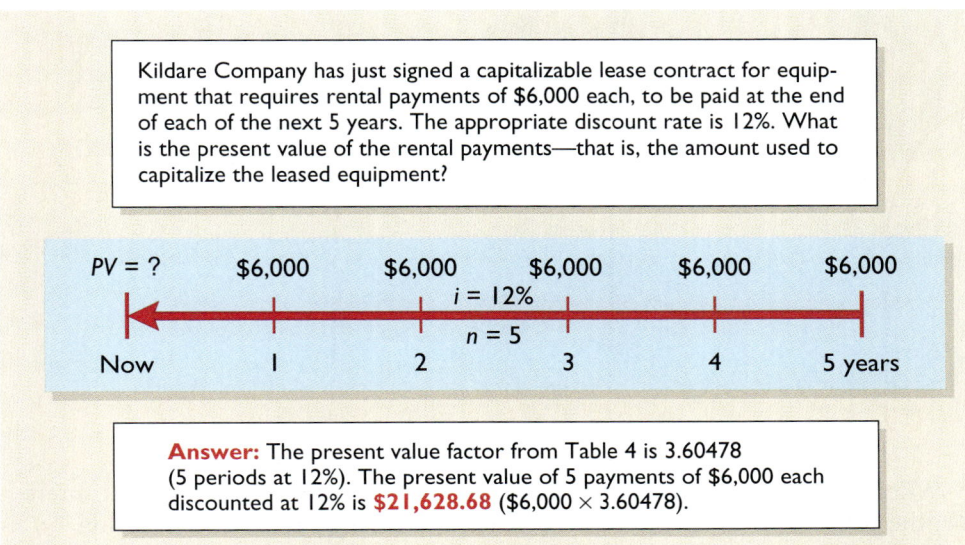

Illustration C-15
Demonstration problem—using Table 4 for *PV* of an annuity of 1

TIME PERIODS AND DISCOUNTING

In the preceding calculations, the discounting has been done on an annual basis using an annual interest rate. Discounting may also be done over shorter periods of time such as monthly, quarterly, or semiannually. When the time frame is less than one year, it is necessary to convert the annual interest rate to the applicable time frame. Assume, for example, that the investor in Illustration C-14 received $500 **semiannually** for three years instead of $1,000 annually. In this case, the number of periods becomes 6 (3 × 2), the discount rate is 5% (10% ÷ 2), the present value factor from Table 4 is 5.07569, and the present value of the future cash flows is $2,537.85 (5.07569 × $500). This amount is slightly higher than the $2,486.85 computed in Illustration C-14 because interest is computed twice during the same year; therefore interest is earned on the first half year's interest.

COMPUTING THE PRESENT VALUE OF A LONG-TERM NOTE OR BOND

The present value (or market price) of a long-term note or bond is a function of three variables: (1) the payment amounts, (2) the length of time until the amounts are paid, and (3) the discount rate. Our illustration uses a 5-year bond issue.

STUDY OBJECTIVE 7
Compute the present value of notes and bonds.

---

[1]The difference of .00001 between 2.48686 and 2.48685 is due to rounding.

C-14 APPENDIX C Time Value of Money

The first variable (dollars to be paid) is made up of two elements: (1) a series of interest payments (an annuity) and (2) the principal amount (a single sum). To compute the present value of the bond, both the interest payments and the principal amount must be discounted—two different computations. The time diagrams for a bond due in 5 years are shown in Illustration C-16.

Illustration C-16
Present value of a bond time diagram

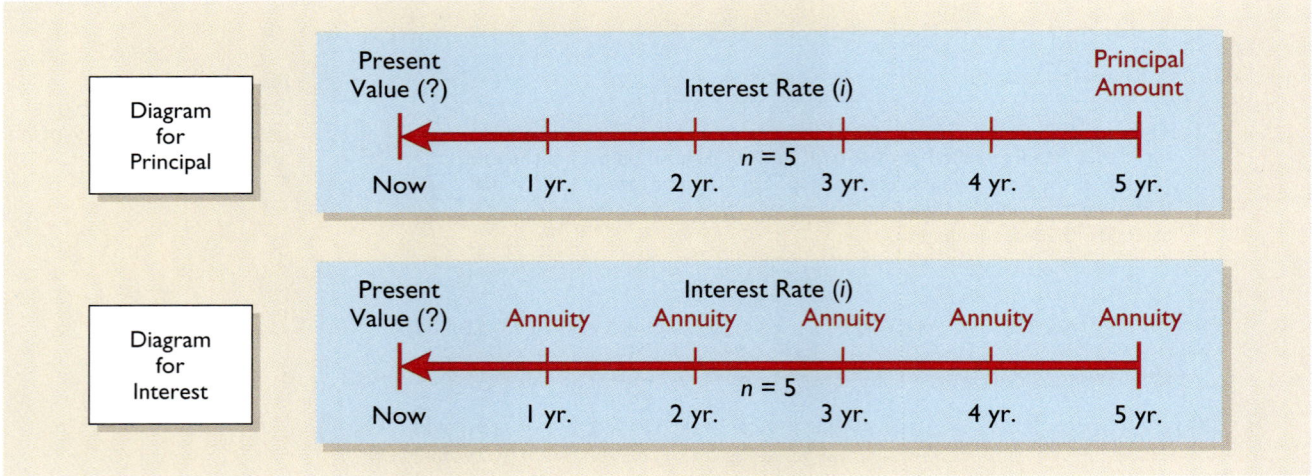

When the investor's discount rate is equal to the bond's contractual interest rate, the present value of the bonds will equal the face value of the bonds. To illustrate, assume a bond issue of 10%, 5-year bonds with a face value of $100,000 with interest payable **semiannually** on January 1 and July 1. If the discount rate is the same as the contractual rate, the bonds will sell at face value. In this case, the investor will receive (1) $100,000 at maturity and (2) a series of ten $5,000 interest payments [($100,000 × 10%) ÷ 2] over the term of the bonds. The length of time is expressed in terms of interest periods, in this case, 10, and the discount rate per interest period, 5%. The following time diagram (Illustration C-17) depicts the variables involved in this discounting situation.

Illustration C-17 Time diagram for present value of a 10%, 5-year bond paying interest semiannually

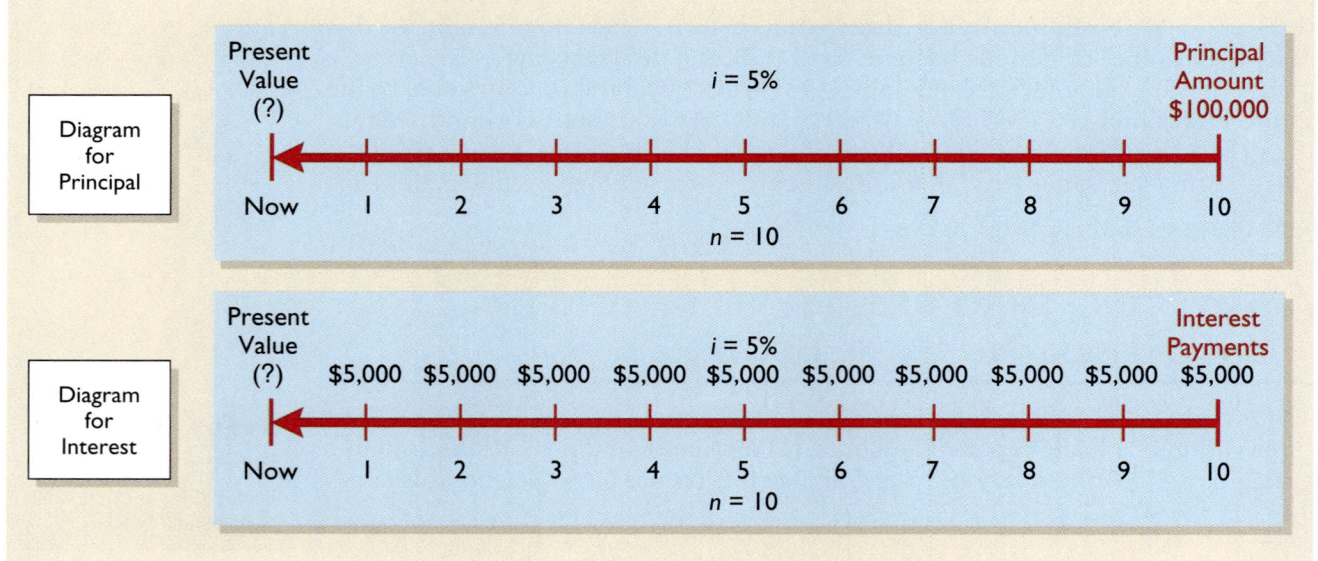

The computation of the present value of these bonds is shown in Illustration C-18.

Illustration C-18
Present value of principal and interest (face value)

10% Contractual Rate—10% Discount Rate

Present value of principal to be received at maturity
$100,000 × PV of 1 due in 10 periods at 5%
$100,000 × .61391 (Table 3) ... $ 61,391

Present value of interest to be received periodically over the term of the bonds
$5,000 × PV of 1 due periodically for 10 periods at 5%
$5,000 × 7.72173 (Table 4) ... 38,609*

Present value of bonds ... **$100,000**

*Rounded

Now assume that the investor's required rate of return is 12%, not 10%. The future amounts are again $100,000 and $5,000, respectively, but now a discount rate of 6% (12% ÷ 2) must be used. The present value of the bonds is $92,639, as computed in Illustration C-19.

Illustration C-19
Present value of principal and interest (discount)

10% Contractual Rate—12% Discount Rate

Present value of principal to be received at maturity
$100,000 × .55839 (Table 3) ... $ 55,839

Present value of interest to be received periodically over the term of the bonds
$5,000 × 7.36009 (Table 4) ... 36,800

Present value of bonds ... **$92,639**

Conversely, if the discount rate is 8% and the contractual rate is 10%, the present value of the bonds is $108,111, computed as shown in Illustration C-20.

Illustration C-20
Present value of principal and interest (premium)

10% Contractual Rate—8% Discount Rate

Present value of principal to be received at maturity
$100,000 × .67556 (Table 3) ... $ 67,556

Present value of interest to be received periodically over the term of the bonds
$5,000 × 8.11090 (Table 4) ... 40,555

Present value of bonds ... **$108,111**

The above discussion relied on present value tables in solving present value problems. Electronic hand-held calculators may also be used to compute present values without the use of these tables. Some calculators, especially the "business" or "MBA" type calculators, have present value (PV) functions that allow you to calculate present values by merely inputting the proper amount, discount rate, periods, and pressing the PV key.

Summary of Study Objectives

1 *Distinguish between simple and compound interest.* Simple interest is computed on the principal only while compound interest is computed on the principal and any interest earned that has not been withdrawn.

2 *Solve for future value of a single amount.* Prepare a time diagram of the problem. Identify the principal amount, the number of compounding periods, and the interest rate. Using the future value of 1 table, multiply the principal amount by the future value factor specified at the intersection of the number of periods and the interest rate.

3 *Solve for future value of an annuity.* Prepare a time diagram of the problem. Identify the amount of the periodic payments, the number of compounding periods, and the interest rate. Using the future value of an annuity of 1 table, multiply the amount of the payments by the future value factor specified at the intersection of the number of periods and interest rate.

4 *Identify the variables fundamental to solving present value problems.* The following three variables are fundamental to solving present value problems: (1) the future amount, (2) the number of periods, and (3) the interest rate (the discount rate).

5 *Solve for present value of a single amount.* Prepare a time diagram of the problem. Identify the future amount, the number of discounting periods, and the discount (interest) rate. Using the present value of a single amount table, multiply the future amount by the present value factor specified at the intersection of the number of periods and the discount rate.

6 *Solve for present value of an annuity.* Prepare a time diagram of the problem. Identify the future amounts (annuities), the number of discounting periods, and the discount (interest) rate. Using the present value of an annuity of 1 table, multiply the amount of the annuity by the present value factor specified at the intersection of the number of periods and the interest rate.

7 *Compute the present value of notes and bonds.* Determine the present value of the principal amount: Multiply the principal amount (a single future amount) by the present value factor (from the present value of 1 table) intersecting at the number of periods (number of interest payments) and the discount rate. Determine the present value of the series of interest payments: Multiply the amount of the interest payment by the present value factor (from the present value of an annuity of 1 table) intersecting at the number of periods (number of interest payments) and the discount rate. Add the present value of the principal amount to the present value of the interest payments to arrive at the present value of the note or bond.

Glossary

Annuity A series of equal dollar amounts to be paid or received periodically. (p. C-5)

Compound interest The interest computed on the principal and any interest earned that has not been paid or received. (p. C-2)

Discounting the future amount(s) The process of determining present value. (p. C-8)

Future value of a single amount The value at a future date of a given amount invested assuming compound interest. (p. C-3)

Future value of an annuity The sum of all the payments or receipts plus the accumulated compound interest on them. (p. C-5)

Interest Payment for the use of another's money. (p. C-2)

Present value The value now of a given amount to be invested or received in the future assuming compound interest. (p. C-8)

Present value of an annuity A series of future receipts or payments discounted to their value now assuming compound interest. (p. C-11)

Principal The amount borrowed or invested. (p. C-2)

Simple interest The interest computed on the principal only. (p. C-2)

Brief Exercises (use tables to solve exercises)

Compute the future value of a single amount.

BEC-1 Don Smith invested $5,000 at 6% annual interest, and left the money invested without withdrawing any of the interest for 10 years. At the end of the 10 years, Don withdrew the accumulated amount of money. (a) What amount did Don withdraw, assuming the investment earns simple interest? (b) What amount did Don withdraw, assuming the investment earns interest compounded annually?

BEC-2 For each of the following cases, indicate (a) to what interest rate columns and (b) to what number of periods you would refer in looking up the future value factor.

Use future value tables.

(1) In Table 1 (future value of 1):

	Annual Rate	Number of Years Invested	Compounded
Case A	6%	5	Annually
Case B	5%	3	Semiannually

(2) In Table 2 (future value of an annuity of 1):

	Annual Rate	Number of Years Invested	Compounded
Case A	5%	10	Annually
Case B	4%	6	Semiannually

BEC-3 Porter Company signed a lease for an office building for a period of 10 years. Under the lease agreement, a security deposit of $10,000 is made. The deposit will be returned at the expiration of the lease with interest compounded at 5% per year. What amount will Porter receive at the time the lease expires?

Compute the future value of a single amount.

BEC-4 Gordon Company issued $1,000,000, 10-year bonds and agreed to make annual sinking fund deposits of $80,000. The deposits are made at the end of each year into an account paying 5% annual interest. What amount will be in the sinking fund at the end of 10 years?

Compute the future value of an annuity.

BEC-5 David and Kathy Hatcher invested $5,000 in a savings account paying 6% annual interest when their daughter, Sue, was born. They also deposited $1,000 on each of her birthdays until she was 18 (including her 18th birthday). How much was in the savings account on her 18th birthday (after the last deposit)?

Compute the future value of a single amount and of an annuity.

BEC-6 Ron Watson borrowed $20,000 on July 1, 1996. This amount plus accrued interest at 6% compounded annually is to be repaid on July 1, 2001. How much will Ron have to repay on July 1, 2001?

Compute the future value of a single amount.

BEC-7 For each of the following cases, indicate (a) to what interest rate columns and (b) to what number of periods you would refer in looking up the discount rate.

Use present value tables.

(1) In Table 3 (present value of 1):

	Annual Rate	Number of Years Involved	Discounts per Year
Case A	12%	6	Annually
Case B	10%	15	Annually
Case C	8%	8	Semiannually

(2) In Table 4 (present value of an annuity of 1):

	Annual Rate	Number of Years Involved	Number of Payments Involved	Frequency of Payments
Case A	12%	20	20	Annually
Case B	10%	5	5	Annually
Case C	8%	4	8	Semiannually

BEC-8 (a) What is the present value of $10,000 due 8 periods from now, discounted at 8%?

Determine present values.

(b) What is the present value of $10,000 to be received at the end of each of 6 periods, discounted at 9%?

BEC-9 Smolinski Company is considering an investment which will return a lump sum of $500,000 five years from now. What amount should Smolinski Company pay for this investment to earn a 15% return?

Compute the present value of a single amount investment.

BEC-10 Pizzeria Company earns 11% on an investment that will return $875,000 eight years from now. What is the amount Pizzeria should invest now to earn this rate of return?

Compute the present value of a single amount investment.

APPENDIX C Time Value of Money

Compute the present value of an annuity investment.

BEC-11 Kilarny Company is considering investing in an annuity contract that will return $20,000 annually at the end of each year for 15 years. What amount should Kilarny Company pay for this investment if it earns a 6% return?

Compute the present value of an annuity investment.

BEC-12 Zarita Enterprises earns 11% on an investment that pays back $110,000 at the end of each of the next four years. What is the amount Zarita Enterprises invested to earn the 11% rate of return?

Compute the present value of bonds.

BEC-13 Hernandez Railroad Co. is about to issue $100,000 of 10-year bonds paying a 12% interest rate, with interest payable semiannually. The discount rate for such securities is 10%. How much can Hernandez expect to receive for the sale of these bonds?

Compute the present value of bonds.

BEC-14 Assume the same information as BEC-13 except that the discount rate was 12% instead of 10%. In this case, how much can Hernandez expect to receive from the sale of these bonds?

Compute the present value of a note.

BEC-15 Caledonian Taco Company receives a $50,000, 6-year note bearing interest of 11% (paid annually) from a customer at a time when the discount rate is 12%. What is the present value of the note received by Caledonian?

Compute the present value of bonds.

BEC-16 Galway Bay Enterprises issued 10%, 8-year, $2,000,000 par value bonds that pay interest semiannually on October 1 and April 1. The bonds are dated April 1, 1998, and are issued on that date. The discount rate of interest for such bonds on April 1, 1998, is 12%. What cash proceeds did Galway Bay receive from issuance of the bonds?

Compute the present value of a machine for purposes of making a purchase decision.

BEC-17 Barney Googal owns a garage and is contemplating purchasing a tire retreading machine for $16,280. After estimating costs and revenues, Barney projects a net cash flow from the retreading machine of $2,790 annually for 8 years. Barney hopes to earn a return of 11 percent on such investments. What is the present value of the retreading operation? Should Barney Googal purchase the retreading machine?

Compute the present value of a note.

BEC-18 Hung-Chao Yu Company issues a 10%, 6-year mortgage note on January 1, 1998 to obtain financing for new equipment. Land is used as collateral for the note. The terms provide for semiannual installment payments, of $112,825. What were the cash proceeds received from the issuance of the note?

Compute the maximum price to pay for a machine.

BEC-19 Ramos Company is considering purchasing equipment. The equipment will produce the following cash flows: Year 1, $30,000; Year 2, $40,000; Year 3, $50,000. Ramos requires a minimum rate of return of 15%. What is the maximum price Ramos should pay for this equipment?

Compute the interest rate on a single amount.

BEC-20 If Kerry Rodriguez invests $1,827 now and she will receive $10,000 at the end of 15 years, what annual rate of interest will Kerry earn on her investment? [*Hint:* Use Table 3.]

Compute the number of periods of a single amount.

BEC-21 Maloney Cork has been offered the opportunity of investing $24,719 now. The investment will earn 15% per year and at the end of that time will return Maloney $100,000. How many years must Maloney wait to receive $100,000? [*Hint:* Use Table 3.]

Compute the interest rate on an annuity.

BEC-22 Annie Dublin made an investment of $11,469.92. From this investment, she will receive $1,000 annually for the next 20 years starting one year from now. What rate of interest will Annie's investment be earning for her? [*Hint:* Use Table 4.]

Compute the number of periods of an annuity.

BEC-23 Andy Sanchez invests $8,851.37 now for a series of $1,000 annual returns beginning one year from now. Andy will earn a return of 8% on the initial investment. How many annual payments of $1,000 will Andy receive? [*Hint:* Use Table 4].

PHOTO CREDITS

Chapter 1
Page 3: Dave Rosenberg/Tony Stone Images/New York, Inc. Page 16: Will Crocker/The Image Bank. Pages 17, 18, 20, and 21: Index Stock. Page 22: Michael Keller/FPG International. Pages 25–27: Courtesy Green Mountain Coffee Roasters.

Chapter 2
Page 47: Jeanne Strongin. Page 50: Comstock, Inc. Pages 53, 58, 59, and 66: James Schnepf/Gamma Liaison. Page 55: Comstock, Inc. Page 60: Gary Holscher/Tony Stone Images/New York, Inc. Pages 60 and 62: Courtesy United Airlines. Page 61: Courtesy Delta Air Lines. Page 65: Vladimir Pcholkin/FPG International. Pages 69 and 70: Courtesy Iomega Corp. Page 74: Courtesy Circuit City.

Chapter 3
Page 97: SUPERSTOCK. Page 106: Vera R Storman/Tony Stone Images/New York, Inc. Page 108: Jonathan Daniel/Allsport.

Chapter 4
Page 149: John Lund/Tony Stone Images/New York, Inc. Page 152: © Orion Pictures Corporation/Jerry Ohlinger's. Page 154: Index Stock. Page 157: Romily Lockyer/The Image Bank. Page 173: Courtesy Wal-Mart Stores, Inc. Page 174: Michael Schneps. Page 175: Courtesy Humana. Page 196: Courtesy Case Corp.

Chapter 5
Page 201: Arnold Zahn /Black Star. Page 205: Courtesy Morrow Snowboards Inc. Page 208: Gregory Heisler/The Image Bank. Page 211: Lorentz Gullachsen/Tony Stone Images/New York, Inc. Page 214: Anabella Breakev/Tony Stone Images/New York, Inc. Page 215: Courtesy Wal-Mart Stores, Inc. Page 232: Courtesy McDonnell Douglas.

Chapter 6
Page 239: Terje Rakke/The Image Bank. Page 245: Luigi Giordano/The Stock Market. Page 255: Tommy Ewasko/The Image Bank. Page 256: Bob Krist/Tony Stone Images/New York, Inc. Page 259: Alvis Upitis/The Image Bank. Page 280: Courtesy Morrow Snowboards Inc. Page 283: Courtesy General Motors Corp.

Chapter 7
Page 287: Abrams/Lacagnina/The Image Bank. Page 289: Index Stock. Page 291: Mel Digiacomo/The Image Bank. Page 293: Mike Blank/Tony Stone Images/New York, Inc. Page 294: Ken Davies/Masterfile. Page 296: R. Michael Stuckey/Comstock, Inc. Page 300: J. W. Burkey/Tony Stone Images/New York, Inc. Page 302: Jay Freis/The Image Bank. Page 305: Courtesy Addington Resources. Page 334: Courtesy Microsoft. Page 335: Courtesy Oracle Corporation.

Chapter 8
Page 339: Olney/TSI Imaging/Tony Stone Images/New York, Inc. Page 344: Yann Layma/Tony Stone Images/New York, Inc. Page 352: Courtesy CPC International, Inc. Page 353: Shaun Egan/Tony Stone Images/New York, Inc. Page 355: Bob Krist/Black Star. Page 356: Courtesy Intel. Page 359: Brian Smale Photography. Pages 362 and 363: Courtesy Advanced Micro Devices, Inc.

Chapter 9
Page 383: Hank Delespinasse/The Image Bank. Page 386: David Woodfall/Tony Stone Images/New York, Inc. Page 389: Mitchell Funk/The Image Bank. Page 391: ©Frank Grant/International Stock Photo. Page 396 (top): Erik Simonsen/The Image Bank. Page 396 (bottom): J. F. Towers/The Stock Market. Page 397 (top): Courtesy TWA. Page 397 (bottom): Courtesy Delta Air Lines. Page 399: Ralph Mercer/Tony Stone Images/New York, Inc. Page 409: ©Schnepf/Gamma Liaison. Page 410: Courtesy The Pillsbury Company. Page 412: Courtesy Roberts Pharmaceuticals Corp.

Chapter 10
Page 437: Index Stock. Page 441: Marv Lyons/The Image Bank. Pages 445, 447, 463, and 464: Courtesy Chrysler Corporation. Page 451: Steven Wilkes/The Image Bank. Page 460: AKG Photo, London/Archiv/Photo Researchers. Page 466: Courtesy Ford Motor Company. Page 481: Courtesy Northland Cranberries. Page 483: Courtesy Apache Corporation.

Chapter 11
Page 487: Mike Powell/Tony Stone Images/New York, Inc. Page 493: Greg Davis/The Stock Market. Page 498: Courtesy Reebok International, Ltd. Page 501: Robert Vanmarter/Gamma Liaison. Page 507: Frank White/Gamma Liaison. Page 508: Courtesy Green Mountain Coffee Roasters. Page 510: Courtesy Knight-Ridder, Inc. Page 515: David Stewart/Tony Stone Images/New York, Inc. Page 534: Courtesy Diebold, Inc.

Chapter 12
Page 539: O'Brien/Peters/©All Action/Retna. Page 542: Steve Allen/Gamma Liaison.

PC-1

Photo Credits

Chapter 13

Page 577 (top): Wolfgang Kaehler/Corbis. Page 577 (bottom): Courtesy Microsoft. Page 581: Lance Nelson/The Stock Market. Page 584: Dick Luria/FPG International. Page 613: Rob Atkins/The Image Bank. Page 618: Index Stock. Page 619: Courtesy Intel. Page 640: Courtesy Vermont Teddy Bear Co. Page 642: Courtesy Praxair Inc.

Chapter 14

Page 647: David Miller/Courtesy Hyperion Press. Page 652: Rob Nelson/Black Star. Pages 657, 659, 660, 672, and 677: Courtesy Kellogg Company. Page 662: Nora Good/Masterfile. Page 664: Courtesy JC Penney. Page 674: Eric Sander/Gamma Liaison. Pages 704 and 705: Courtesy Sears, Roebuck and Co.

COMPANY INDEX

Addington Resources, Inc., 305
A.D. Makepeace, 507
Advanced Micro Devices, 65
AirTran Airways, 383
AirWays Corp., 383
AMD Corporation, 362–364, 619–621
American Airlines, 442
American Telephone and Telegraph (AT&T), 441
America Online, 46
Amoco Corporation, 674
Association of Certified Fraud Examiners, 294
Atlas Distributing Inc., 255

BankAmerica, 553
Bank of New York, 355
BDO Seidman, 255
Berkshire Hathaway, 507
Best Buy Co., Inc., 53, 56–57, 58, 59, 63–64, 66–68, 214
Black and Decker Manufacturing Company, 253
Boeing Aircraft, 56
Boise Cascade Corporation, 418
Borden, Inc., 652
Bristol-Myers, 253
Brunswick Corporation, 61

Callaway Golf Company, 65
Cambridge Biotech Corporation, 148
Campbell Soup Company, 253, 393, 553
Cargill Inc., 489
Caterpillar Inc., 238–239, 259–261, 449
Chambers Development, 386
Chemical Bank, 359
Chicago Cubs, 108
Chicago Heights Steel Co., 255
Chrysler Corporation, 358, 391, 436–437, 443, 444–447, 449, 461–462, 463, 464–465
Chrysler Finance Corporation (CFC), 358
Circuit City, 56–57, 63, 64, 67–68, 214
Citicorp, 5, 151
Coca Cola, 5, 676
Commonwealth Edison, 501
Consolidated Edison, 385
Consolidated Freightways, Inc., 62
CPC International Inc., 352

Daimler-Benz, 50
Dawson Inc., 555
Dayton Hudson Corporation, 306
Del Monte Corporation, 253
Delta Air Lines, 16, 61, 151, 397, 400
Deluxe Check Printers Incorporated, 60–61
Digital Equipment Corporation, 399, 550
Dun & Bradstreet, 353

Dunkin' Donuts, Inc., 16
DuPont Corporation, 449

Eastman Kodak Company, 65, 408
E.F. Hutton, 300
Elbert Corporation, 552, 553
Elle Company, 311–312
Epson Computers, 215
Exxon, 5, 49, 463

Fidelity Investments, 96–97, 122
Florafax International Inc., 211
Florida Citrus Company, 650
Ford Motor Company, 113, 358, 391, 437, 465–467, 494
Ford Motor Credit Corp. (FMCC), 358

General Dynamics Corporation, 649
General Mills, 393
General Motors Acceptance Corporation (GMAC), 358
General Motors Corporation, 5, 50, 51, 65, 98, 200, 358, 391, 398, 437, 492, 494, 500, 513
Graber Inc., 509–510
Grand Met, 410
Great Atlantic and Pacific Tea (A&P), 405, 670
Green Mountain Coffee, Inc., 25–28, 508, B1–B16
Gulf Oil Company, 492

Hammond, Inc., 161
Harley-Davidson Corporation, 312–313
Hayes Company, 309
Home Box Office (HBO) Corporation, 548
Home Theater Products, 289
Humana Corporation, 174–176

IBM Corporation, 398, 399, 408, 494, 506
Intel Corporation, 354–357, 362–364, 618, 619–621
Internal Revenue Service (IRS), 150, 395
Iomega Corporation, 46, 48, 49, 68–71

J.C. Penney, 214, 306, 357, 502

Kansas Farmers' Vertically Integrated Cooperative, Inc. (K-VIC), 123–124
Kellogg Company, 498, 513, 648, 650, 651–652, 654, 655–674, 676, 677–679
KeyCorp, 553, 557–558
King World, 409
Kmart Corporation, 16, 56, 200, 202, 213–214, 215, 216, 258, 451
Knight-Ridder Inc., 510
Kroger, 56, 253

Lender's Bagels, 656
Long Island Lighting Company, 501

I-1

I-2 Company Index

Manitowoc Company, 261–262
Marriott Corporation, 393
Martin Marietta Corporation, 509
MasterCard, 360–361
Mattel Corporation, 313–315
Maxwell Car Company, 436
McDonald's, 157
McKesson and Robbins, 202
Mead, Inc., 498–499
Mechanics Bank of Richmond, 507
Media Vision Technology, Inc., 148
Medland Corporation, 505
Metallgesellschaft, 289
Microsoft Corporation, 98, 406, 513, 576, 583, 612–613, 614, 615–618, 674
Morrow Snowboards, Inc., 205, 289
Motley Fool, 46–47
Motorola, 253

National Cash Register (NCR) Co., 296
Nike, 486–487, 489–490, 494, 495, 496, 498, 500, 502, 506, 511, 513, 514, 515
North American Van Lines, 495
Northwest Airlines, 398

Office Depot, 202
Oracle Corporation, 613, 614, 615–618
Orion Pictures, 152
Owens-Corning Fiberglas Corporation, 653
Owens-Illinois, Inc., 410

Pace Corporation, 551, 554
Pacific Gas and Electric, 5
Packard Bell, 355, 357, 363
Page Net, 584
Penguin USA, 148
Pennsylvania Power & Light Company, 385
PepsiCo, 494, 498, 502, 676
Phillip Morris Company, 463, 498
Polaroid, 408
Policy Management Systems Corporation, 148
Potomac Electric Company, 674
Pratt & Lambert, 509
Presidential Air, 382
Procter & Gamble, 157, 463, 495

Quaker Oats Company, 256, 654, 659–674

Reebok, 486–487, 494, 498, 500, 511, 515–517
Republic Carloading, 174

Reynolds Company, 597–598, 610–611
RJR Nabisco, 676
Roberts Pharmaceuticals Corporation, 65, 411–413

Safeway, 56
Sam's Club, 214
Seagram, 541
Sears Roebuck Acceptance Corp. (SRAC), 358
Sears, Roebuck & Company, 65, 157, 200, 202, 208, 216–217, 358, 359, 513
Singer Company, 649
Southwest Airlines, 382, 389, 396, 402, 403, 404, 405, 464
Sports Illustrated, 442
Standard Oil Company of California, 418
Starbucks Corporation, 2–3, 7–9, 16–21, 22–24, 259, A1–A24
Sumitomo Corporation, 293

Texaco, Inc., 291
3M Corporation, 399
Tiffany & Co., 56
Time Warner Corporation, 538–539, 541, 542, 546, 548
Toys 'R' Us, 674
Trans World Airlines (TWA), 397, 451
Turner Broadcasting, 538, 541, 542, 546, 548

Union Carbide, 256
Union Electric Company, 405, 670
Union Pacific Corporation, 652
United Airlines, 60, 62, 443
United Stationers, 202
USAir, 449
USX Corporation, 449

Value Line Investment Survey, 646
Valujet, 382–383, 396, 402, 403, 404, 405
VISA, 360–361

Walgreen Drug Company, 202, 253, 500
The Wall Street Journal, 148, 201, 259, 287, 613, 618
Wal-Mart, 56, 173, 200–201, 202, 213–214, 215, 216, 258
Walt Disney Productions, 16
Wendy's International, 253
Westinghouse, 399
Weyerhaeuser Company, 650
Woolworth Corporation, 214
W.R. Grace and Company, 22

Yale Express, 174

SUBJECT INDEX

Accelerated-depreciation methods, 416, 418
Accounting, 6, 29; constraints in, 51–52, 71; cost principle of, 385; differences in methods of, 675–676; internal controls in, 288–295
Accounting cycle, 173–174, 177
Accounting information: atypical, 676; qualitative characteristics of, 49–51, 71; segmental, 676; supplementary, A22–A24; users of, 6–7, 28
Accounting information system, 98, 125
Accounting transactions. *See* Transactions
Accounts, 104–110, 125; chart of, 113, 126; debit and credit procedures, 105–108; expanded basic equation, 108, 109; permanent, 170, 171, 172–173; stockholders' equity relationships, 108, 109; T accounts, 104; temporary, 170, 171–172
Accounts payable, 8; statement of cash flows and, 589–590, 593, 602
Accounts receivable, 8, 341–347, 365. *See also* Notes receivable; Receivables: accelerating cash receipts from, 358–361, 364; aging of, 344–345; average collection period, 357; collecting, 307, 354–356; credit card sales as, 359–361; credit policy for, 353–354; factoring, 358–359; international perspective on, 344; managing, 353–361, 364; recognizing, 341, 364; statement of cash flows and, 589, 593, 601; statement presentation of, 352, 364; turnover ratio for, 356–357; uncollectible, 342–346; valuing, 341–347
Accrual basis accounting, 153, 178. *See also* Adjusting entries: cash basis accounting vs., 153–154, 176
Accruals, 155; adjusting entries for, 162–166, 176–177
Accrued expenses, 155, 178; adjusting entries for, 163–166
Accrued interest, 164–165
Accrued revenues, 155, 178; adjusting entries for, 162–163
Accrued salaries, 165–166
Acid-test ratio, 445–446, 468, 663, 681
Activities, business, 7–9, 28
Additions and improvements, 398, 418
Adjusted balance, 302–303
Adjusted trial balance, 169–170, 177, 178; preparing, 169
Adjusting entries, 154–168, 176, 178; for accruals, 162–166; accrued expenses, 163–166; accrued revenues, 162–163; journalizing, 167; matching principle and, 151, 152, 154; posting, 168; prepaid expenses, 156–160; for prepayments, 156–162; revenue recognition principle and, 151, 152, 154; types of, 155; unearned revenues, 160–161; on work sheets, 177–178
Administrative expenses, 9, 54
Affiliated company, 547, 559
Aging schedule, 344–345
Aging the accounts receivable, 344–345, 365
Airline industry, 382–383, 389

Allowance for doubtful accounts, 342–345, 354
Allowance method, 342, 365
Allowances: purchase, 206; sales, 210–211
American Stock Exchange, 494
Amortization, 418; of bond discounts, 455–456; of bond premiums, 457–459; of intangible assets, 406–407, 410; straight-line method of, 407, 455–456, 457–459, 469
Analysis: of current liabilities, 444–447; of free cash flow, 311–313; of inventories, 257–261; of long-term liabilities, 461–462; of plant assets, 402–405, 414; ratio, 56–57, 71, 72, 73, 661–675; of transactions, 99–103, 114
Annual report, 20–21, 28, 29; for Green Mountain Coffee, Inc., B1–B16; for Starbucks Corporation, A1–A24
Annuities, C5, C11, C16; future value of, C5–C8, C16; present value of, C11–C13, C16
Assets, 8, 28, 29, 382–418. *See also* Depreciation: accountability for, 290; book value of, 159; current, 59–60; debit/credit procedures, 105–106; financial statement presentation of, 410–411; fixed, 8, 61; intangible, 61, 72, 406–410; international perspective on, 386; plant, 384–406; turnover ratio for, 405, 418; useful life of, 158
Asset turnover ratio, 405, 418, 670–671, 681
Assumed cost flow methods, 248–253, 264; adjusting for LIFO reserve, 259–261; average cost method, 252–253; FIFO (first in, first out) method, 249–250; financial statement effects, 253–255; LIFO (last in, last out) method, 250–252; tax effects, 253–255
Assumptions: cost flow, 248; economic entity, 22, 29; going concern, 23, 30; for preparing financial statements, 22–23, 28; time period, 23, 30, 150, 179
Atypical data, 676
Auditors, 21; internal, 292–293
Auditor's report, 21, 29, A6–A7
Authorized stock, 494, 518
Available-for-sale securities, 551–552, 559
Average age of plant assets, 403–404, 418
Average collection period, 357, 365, 664–665, 681
Average cost method, 267; in periodic inventory system, 252–253
Average days in inventory, 665–666, 681
Average useful life, 402–403, 418

Bad debts expense, 342, 364, 365. *See also* Uncollectible accounts
Bailey, Wendell, 302
Balance sheet, 10, 12–13, 32. *See also* Classified balance sheet: asset presentation on, 410–411, 414; common stock issues on, 495–496; comprehensive, 555–556; consolidated, 69–70, A8; cost flow method effects, 254–255; current liability presentation and analysis on, 444–447; inventory error effects on, 266–267; in-

I-3

vestments presentation on, 553–554; long-term liability presentation and analysis on, 460–462; receivables presentation on, 352, 364; for Starbucks Corporation, 18, 19, A8; stockholders' equity presentation on, 57–58, 509–510

Bank accounts: NSF (not sufficient funds) checks, 299; reconciling, 299–303, 315; service charges for, 303; statements for, 298–299

Bank memoranda, 301

Bank statements, 298–299, 319

Basic accounting equation, 12, 29, 125; expansion of, 108, 109

Beardstown Ladies, 646, 648

Bond certificates, 450, 468

Bonded employees, 293

Bond indenture, 450, 469

Bonds, 447–460, 467–468, 469; acquisition of, 543; callable, 449, 469; contractual interest rate, 450, 469; convertible, 449, 469; corporation, 542–543; debenture, 449, 469; discounts on, 453–456, 469; effect of market interest rates on, 453–454; face value of, 450, 453, 469; government, 542–543; interest on, 543; international perspectives on, 448, 453, 460; investments in, 542–544; issuing, 449–450, 453–459, 468; market value of, 451–452; mortgage, 449, 469; premiums on, 453–454, 457–459, 469; present value of, 452, C13–C15, C16; reasons for issuing, 448–449, 467; redeeming, 459, 468; sale of, 543–544; secured, 449, 469; serial, 449, 469; sinking fund, 449, 469; term, 449, 469; trading, 451; types of, 449; unsecured, 449, 469; valuation and reporting categories for, 550–552

Bonds payable, 8, 595, 608

Book value, 159, 179, 390; of bonds, 455; declining, 415–416

Bowerman, Bill, 486

Budgets, cash, 308–310

Buildings, 387, 594. *See also* Plant assets: accumulated depreciation on, 593

Business documents, 209

Businesses: operating cycle of, 60; organizational forms for, 4–5, 28; types of activities in, 7–9, 28

Business segment information, A22

Callable bonds, 449, 469

Canceled checks, 298

Capital: earned, 495; legal, 494, 519; paid-in, 495–496, 519; working, 63, 73

Capital expenditure ratio, 614, 622

Capital expenditures, 385, 398, 418; and cash flow, 614

Capital leases, 389, 418, 464, 469

Capital stock. *See* Common stock; Preferred stock

Captive finance companies, 358

Carrying value. *See* Book value

Cash, 8, 295, 319; budgeting, 308–310; determining net increase/decrease in, 588, 592, 599, 606; dividend payments and, 502; equivalents of, 304–305; from investing and financing activities, 590–591, 594–595, 604, 608–609; investing excess, 540–541; measuring the adequacy of, 310–313, 315; from operating activities, 588–589, 593–594, 600–603, 606–607; principles of managing, 306–308, 315; reporting, 304–305, 315; restricted, 305

Cash-based ratios, 615–618; cash debt coverage, 67, 72, 311, 616, 622, 667, 681; cash return on sales, 617; current cash debt coverage, 67, 72, 310, 615, 622, 663, 681

Cash basis accounting, 153–154, 176, 179

Cash budget, 308–310, 315, 319

Cash controls, 295–304. *See also* Internal control: bank accounts for, 298–304; of cash disbursements, 296–297; of cash receipts, 295–296; electronic funds transfer (EFT) systems, 297; petty cash fund, 297

Cash debt coverage ratio, 67, 72, 311, 616, 622, 667, 681

Cash disbursements: internal control over, 296–297; petty cash fund and, 317

Cash dividends, 502–504, 517, 518; entries for, 503–504

Cash equivalent price, 386, 418

Cash equivalents, 304–305, 319

Cash flows. *See also* Statement of cash flows: capital expenditure ratio and, 614; classification of, 579; company valuation by, 584, 612–618; corporate life cycle and, 582–583, 621; free cash flows, 311–313, 612–613; liquidity and, 615–616; profitability and, 617; solvency and, 616

Cash management, 306–308

Cash (net) realizable value, 341, 349, 365

Cash receipts: from customers, 601, 606; internal control over, 295–296; petty cash fund and, 317

Cash registers: for internal control, 296; tapes from, as sales receipts, 209

Cash return on sales ratio, 617, 622, 672, 681

Certificates: bond, 450, 468; stock, 493

Certified Public Accountants (CPAs), 21, 29

Change in accounting principle, 652–654, 681

Chart of accounts, 113, 126

Checks: canceled, 298; NSF (not sufficient funds), 299; outstanding, 300

Chief executive officer (CEO), 490

Chrysler, Walter, 436

Classified balance sheet, 58–65, 72; current assets, 59–60; current liabilities, 62; intangible assets, 61; long-term investments, 60–61; long-term liabilities, 62; plant assets, 61; stockholders' equity, 63; using, 63–65

Closing entries, 171, 177, 179; preparing, 171–172

Collection agents, 440

Collections. *See also* Uncollectible accounts: average collection period ratio, 357, 365, 664–665, 681; of receivables, 303, 307, 354–356

Common-size analysis, 658–660

Common stock, 8, 29, 106, 494–497. *See also* Stock: accounting for, 495–496; authorization of, 494; debit/credit rules, 106–107, 109; international perspective on, 494; issuance of, 494, 517, 604, 609; ownership rights, 492

Comparability, 49–50, 72

Comparative analysis, 655–661, 679; horizontal analysis, 656–658, 681; industry average comparisons, 655, 662; intercompany comparisons, 655, 661; intracompany comparisons, 655, 661; vertical analysis, 658–660, 681

Comparative statements, 16, 29
Compound interest, C2–C3, C16
Comprehensive balance sheet, 555–556
Comprehensive income, 654–655, 681
Concentration of credit risk, 355, 356, 363, 365
Conservatism, 51–52, 72
Consigned goods, 245–246, 267
Consistency, 50, 72
Consolidated financial statements, 548, 558, 559; for Green Mountain Coffee, Inc., B1; for Starbucks Corporation, A8–A11
Constraints in accounting, 51–52, 71
Consumerism, 200–201
Consumption, 200
Contingencies, 462–463, 469
Contingent liabilities, 462–463
Contra asset account, 159, 179
Contractual interest rate, 450, 469
Contra equity account, 552
Contra revenue account, 210, 211, 218
Contributed capital, 495
Controller, 490
Controlling interest, 547–548, 559
Convertible bonds, 449, 469
Copyrights, 61, 408, 418
Corporate capital. See Stockholders' equity
Corporations, 29, 488–493, 517, 518; advantages and disadvantages of, 491; businesses organized as, 4–5; capital acquisition, 489; cash flow data for evaluating, 612–618; characteristics of, 489–491, 517; continuous life of, 490; forming, 492; government regulations on, 491; investors' analysis of, 511–514; life cycle of, 582–583, 621; organizational structure of, 490–491; ownership rights of, 489; privately held, 488–489; publicly held, 488; reasons for investment by, 540–542, 558; separate legal existence of, 489; stockholder rights in, 492–493; taxes paid by, 491
Correct cash balance, 302
Cost flow assumptions, 248
Cost flow methods: adjusting for LIFO reserve, 259–261; assumed cost flow methods, 248–253, 264; consistent use of, 255–256; financial statement effects, 253–255; specific identification method, 248; tax effects, 255
Cost method, 498, 545
Cost of goods available for sale, 246, 267
Cost of goods purchased, 243–244, 267
Cost of goods sold, 202, 212, 218, 267; computing, 246; periodic inventory systems and, 243–246
Cost of sales, 9
Cost principle, 24, 29; bond investments and, 543; plant assets and, 385, 414; stock investments and, 545
Costs. See also Expenses: depreciable, 392; financial analysis of, 675
Credit: establishing terms for, 354; evaluating risk factors, 354–356; extending to customers, 353; lines of, 446–447, 469
Credit balance, 104
Credit cards: interest rates and terms for, 360; sales from, 359–361

Credit facilities, 446
Crediting accounts, 104; procedures for, 105–108
Creditors: claims of, 8; use of accounting information by, 6–7
Credit risk ratio, 354, 365
Credits, 104, 125, 126
Credit terms, 207
Cumulative dividends, 501, 519
Current assets, 59–60, 72; composition of, 64
Current cash debt coverage ratio, 67, 72, 310, 615, 622, 663, 681
Current liabilities, 62, 72, 438–444, 467, 469; current maturities of long-term debt, 443; financial statement presentation and analysis of, 444–447; liquidity ratios and, 444–447; notes payable, 439–440; payroll and payroll taxes payable, 441–442; sales tax payable, 440–441; types of, 439–444, 467; unearned revenues, 442–443
Current ratio, 63–64, 72, 260, 445–446, 615, 662, 681
Current replacement cost, 257, 267
Customers: cash receipts from, 601, 606; use of accounting information by, 7

Days in inventory measure, 258, 267
Debenture bonds, 449, 450, 469
Debit balance, 104
Debiting accounts, 104; procedures for, 105–108
Debits, 104, 125, 126
Debt investments, 542–544, 558, 559. See also Bonds: valuation and reporting of, 550–556, 558–559
Debt to equity ratio, 666–667
Debt to total assets ratio, 64–65, 73, 666–667, 681
Declaration date, 503, 519
Declining-balance method of depreciation, 393–394, 415–417, 418
Declining book value, 415–416
Deficit, 508, 519
Delivery expenses, 207
Deposits in transit, 300, 301, 319
Depreciable assets, 390
Depreciable cost, 392, 418
Depreciation, 179, 390–398, 414, 418; accelerated methods of, 416; adjusting entries for, 158–160; changing the method of, 652–653; declining-balance method of, 393–394, 415–417; disclosing the method of, 395–396; factors in computing, 390–391; income taxes and, 395; international perspective on, 395; methods of, 392–395; patterns of, 395; review and revision of, 396–397, 414; in statement of cash flows, 593–594, 607; straight-line method of, 392–393, 414; units-of-activity method of, 394–395, 417–418
Depreciation expense, 392
Depreciation schedule, 392
Direct method, for statement of cash flows, 586, 599–611, 621, 622
Direct write-off method, 346, 365. See also Uncollectible accounts
Disclosure: of contingencies, 463; of depreciation method, 395–396; of stockholders' equity, 510
Discontinued operations, 649–650, 681

Discounting the future amount, 452, C8, C16. *See also* Present value
Discount period, 207
Discounts: on bonds, 453–456, 469; purchase, 207–209, 242; sales, 211, 243
Dishonored notes, 351, 365
Disposal of plant assets, 399–402, 414
Diversification, 676
Dividends, 8, 29, 502–508, 518; in arrears, 501, 519; cash, 502–504, 517, 518; cumulative, 501, 519; debit/credit rules, 107, 109; declaration date, 503; payment date, 503–504; payout ratio, 511–512; percentage yield, 511–512; performance record, 511–512; preferred stock preference, 500–501; record date, 503; retained earnings and, 12; stock, 504–506, 517, 519; stock splits, 506–507
Dividend yield, 511–512, 519
Documentation procedures, 291
Double-declining-balance method of depreciation, 394, 416
Double-entry system, 105, 126
Double taxation, 491
Doubtful accounts allowance, 342–345

Earned capital, 495
Earning power, 648–649, 679
Earnings management, 398
Earnings performance, 512–514
Earnings per share (EPS), 448, 512–514, 519, 673, 681
Economic entity assumption, 22, 29
Economic planners, use of accounting information by, 7
Electronic controls, 291–292
Electronic funds transfer (EFT), 297, 319
Equipment, 387–388. *See also* Plant assets: accumulated depreciation on, 593; loss on sale of, 594, 607; purchase of, 594–595, 608
Equity method, 546, 559
Errors: bank account, 300–301, 303; inventory, 265–267
Estimates, 675
Evaluation: of companies using cash flow data, 612–618; of credit risk factors, 354–356; of investment performance, 552–553; of merchandising company profitability, 213–216
Expanded basic equation, 108, 109
Expenditure planning, 307
Expenses, 9, 29; bond interest, 455; debit/credit rules, 107–108, 109; depreciation, 392; operating, 54; recognizing, 151; on single-step income statement, 52; stockholders' equity and, 101
External users of accounting information, 6–7
Extraordinary items, 459, 650–652, 681

Face value, 349; of bonds, 450, 453, 469
Factoring, 358–359, 365
Fair value, 550, 559
Federal Trade Commission (FTC), 7
FICA (Federal Insurance Contribution Act), 441
FIFO method. *See* First in, first out (FIFO) method

Financial Accounting Standards Board (FASB), 49, 73, 653
Financial analysis, 646–680; comparative analysis, 655–661; earning power and, 648–649; horizontal analysis, 656–658; industry average comparisons, 655, 662; intercompany comparisons, 655, 661; intracompany comparisons, 655, 661; irregular items and, 648–655; limitations of, 675–676, 679; liquidity ratios, 662–666; profitability ratios, 668–674; ratio analysis, 56–57, 71, 72, 73, 661–675; solvency ratios, 666–668; vertical analysis, 658–660
Financial highlights section of annual reports, A2
Financial information. *See* Accounting information
Financial reporting, 48; characteristics of useful, 49–51; constraints in, 51–52
Financial statements, 10–15, 28, 52–71; analysis of, 646–680; asset presentation on, 410–411; assumptions for preparing, 22–23, 28; balance sheet, 12–13; classified balance sheet, 58–65; common stock issues on, 495–496; consolidated, 548, 558, 559; cost flow method effects, 253–255; current liability presentation and analysis on, 444–447; examples of, 16–21; for Green Mountain Coffee, Inc., B1–B16; income statement, 10, 52–56; interrelationships between, 14; inventory error effects on, 265–267; investments presentation on, 553–554; irregular items on, 649–655; long-term liability presentation and analysis on, 460–462; for merchandising companies, 211–213, 217; notes to, 21; preparing, 170; principles for preparing, 24, 28; receivables presentation on, 352, 364; retained earnings statement, 12; for Starbucks Corporation, 16–21, A8–A11; statement of cash flows, 13, 66–68; stockholders' equity presentation on, 57–58, 509–510; trial balance and, 122
Financing activities, 7–8, 66, 579, 580, 621, 622; net cash provided by, 590–591, 594–595, 604, 608–609
Finished goods inventory, 240, 267
First in, first out (FIFO) method, 249–250, 264, 267; financial statement effects, 253–255; international use of, 256; tax effects, 255
Fiscal year, 16, 150, 179
Fixed assets, 8, 61
FOB (free on board): destination, 245, 267; shipping point, 245, 267
Franchises, 409–410, 418
Fraud, inventory, 266
Free cash flow, 311–313, 319, 612–613, 622, 667–668, 681
Freight costs, 207, 242
Freight-in, 244
Full disclosure principle, 24, 29, 580. *See also* Disclosure
Future value, C3–C8; of an annuity, C5–C8, C16; of a single amount, C3–C5, C16

GAAP. *See* Generally accepted accounting principles
Gains: on asset disposal, 399, 400; on investments, 554–555
Galbreath, John, 353
Gardner, Tom and David, 46
Gates, Bill, 576, 618

General and administrative expenses, 9, 54
General journal, 111, 126. See also Journal
General ledger, 113, 121, 126. See also Ledger
Generally accepted accounting principles (GAAP), 49, 71, 73; matching principle and, 151, 152; revenue recognition principle and, 151, 152
Gleghorn, Frances Jane, 302
Going concern assumption, 23, 30
Goods in transit, 245
Goodwill, 409–410, 418
Gross profit, 54, 218; for merchandising companies, 212
Gross profit rate, 213–214, 218, 671, 681
Gross purchases, 243

Hedging transactions, 259
Held-to-maturity securities, 550, 559
Honored notes, 350
Horizontal acquisition, 541
Horizontal analysis, 656–658, 679, 681
Hurst, Billie, 302

Iacocca, Lee, 436
Impairments, 398–399, 418
Income: investment, 541; net, 9, 30, 581; operating, 54
Income measurement process, 202
Income statement, 10, 30, 52–56; change in accounting principle, 652–654; comprehensive income on, 654–655; cost flow method effects, 253–254; discontinued operations on, 649–650; extraordinary items on, 650–652; gross profit, 54; inventory error effects on, 265–266; irregular items on, 649–655; for merchandising companies, 211–213, 217, 246–247, 263; multiple-step, 53, 55; nonoperating activities, 54–55; operating expenses, 54; ratio analysis, 56–57; single-step, 52–53; for Starbucks Corporation, 16–17
Income Summary, 172, 179
Income taxes. See also Taxes: cash payments for, 603, 607; depreciation and, 395; withheld from wages, 441–442
Indenture, 450
Indirect method, for statement of cash flows, 586, 587–598, 621, 622–623
Industry average comparisons, 655, 662
Information. See Accounting information
Initial public offering (IPO), 584
Insurance, adjusting entries for, 158
Intangible assets, 61, 73, 406–410, 418. See also Plant assets: accounting for, 406–407; amortization of, 406–407, 410, 414; copyrights, 408; financial statement presentation of, 410–411; franchises and licenses, 409–410; goodwill, 409–410; international perspective on, 410; patents, 408; research and development costs, 408; trademarks and trade names, 408–409; types of, 408–410
Intent to convert, 554
Intercompany comparisons, 655, 661
Interest, C2, C16; accrued, 164–165; from bond investments, 543; compound, C2–C3, C16; computing for promissory notes, 348–349, 364; purchase discounts and, 208; simple, C2, C16

Interest expense, 9
Interest payments, 452
Interest rates: bond prices and, 453–454; contractual, 450; on credit cards, 360; market, 452
Interest revenue, 9
Internal auditors, 292–293, 319
Internal control, 288–295, 319. See also Cash controls: accountability for assets, 290; bank accounts for, 298–304; bonding of employees, 293; of cash receipts and disbursements, 295–298, 315; documentation procedures, 291; establishment of responsibilities, 289; independent internal verification, 292–293; international perspectives on, 293, 295; limitations of, 294; physical, mechanical, and electronic controls, 291–292; principles of, 288–293, 315; related activities and, 290; rotation of duties, 293; segregation of duties, 290
Internal users of accounting information, 6
International accounting: asset valuation and, 386; bonds and, 448, 453, 460; common stock and, 494; depreciation and, 395; intangible assets and, 410; internal controls and, 293, 295; inventory costing methods and, 256; notes receivable and, 350; plant assets and, 385, 395; stockholders' equity and, 493, 510; uncollectible accounts and, 344
International Accounting Standards Committee (IASC), 50
Intracompany comparisons, 655, 661
Inventories, 8, 238–267; analysis of, 257–261; classifying, 240–241; conservative constraint and, 51; costing methods for, 248–256, 263–264; errors in accounting for, 265–267; just-in-time practices for, 259; LIFO reserve adjustments, 259–261, 264; lower of cost or market (LCM) basis, 256–257, 264, 267; managing, 307; ownership of goods determination, 245–246; periodic system for, 203–204, 218, 241–256, 263, 267; perpetual system for, 203–205, 217, 218; physical inventory count, 244; quantity determination, 244–246, 263; turnover ratio for, 258, 260, 264, 267, 665
Inventory fraud, 266
Inventory summary sheets, 244
Inventory turnover ratio, 258, 260, 264, 267, 665, 681
Investee, 545
Investing activities, 8, 66, 579, 580, 621, 623; net cash provided by, 590–591, 594–595, 604, 608–609
Investment portfolio, 544
Investments, 538–559; available-for-sale securities, 551–552; balance sheet presentation of, 553–554; comprehensive balance sheet, 555–556; debt, 542–544, 559; evaluating performance of, 552–553; gains and losses on, 554–555; held-to-maturity securities, 550; intent to convert, 554; liquid, 307; long-term, 554, 559; readily marketable, 554; reasons for corporate, 540–542, 558; risk-free, 307; stock, 544–549; temporary, 554, 559; trading securities, 550–551; valuation and reporting of, 550–556
Investors: claims of, 8; selling shares of stock to, 8; stock prices and, 496–497; use of accounting information by, 6–7
Invoices: purchase, 205; sales, 209

I-8   Subject Index

Irregular items, 649–655, 679
Issuance: of bonds, 449–450, 453–459, 468; of stocks, 494, 517, 604, 609

Journal, 110, 111–112, 125, 126
Journalizing, 111, 126; adjusting entries, 167; illustration of, 114–121
Just-in-time (JIT) inventory, 259

Knight, Phil, 486, 490

Labor unions, use of accounting information by, 7
Land. *See also* Plant assets: costs of acquiring, 386–387, 594, 604, 608; costs of improving, 387
Last in, last out (LIFO) method, 250–252, 264, 267; financial statement effects, 253–255; international use of, 256; LIFO reserve adjustments, 259–261, 264; tax effects, 255
Lawsuits, 462–463
Lease liabilities, 464–465
Leases: capital, 389, 464, 469; operating, 388, 464, 469
Ledger, 110, 113, 121, 125, 126
Legal capital, 494, 519
Lessee, 388, 418
Lessor, 388, 418
Letters to stockholders, A3–A4
Leveraging, 669–670, 681
Liabilities, 8, 12, 28, 30, 436–468; contingent, 462–463; current, 62, 72, 438–447, 467, 469; debit/credit procedures, 105–106; delaying payment on, 307; financial statement presentation and analysis of, 444–447, 460–462; lease, 464–465; long-term, 62, 73, 438, 447–462, 469
Licenses, 409–410, 418
LIFO method. *See* Last in, last out (LIFO) method
LIFO reserve, 259–261, 264, 267
Line of credit, 446–447, 469
Liquidation preference, of preferred stock, 501
Liquid investments, 307
Liquidity, 63, 72, 73; cash-based measures of, 615
Liquidity ratios, 63–64, 73, 444–447, 661, 662–666, 681
Long-lived assets. *See also* Assets: financial statement presentation of, 410–411; intangible assets, 406–410; plant assets, 384–406
Long-term investments, 60, 73, 554, 559
Long-term liabilities, 62, 73, 438, 447–462, 469; bonds as, 447–460; computing the present value of, C13–C15; financial statement presentation and analysis of, 460–462; solvency ratios and, 461–462
Losses: on asset disposal, 399, 400–401, 594, 607; on investments, 554–555
Lower of cost or market (LCM) basis, 256–257, 264, 267

Maker (promissory note), 347, 365
Management: of cash, 306–308, 315; corporate, 490–491; of receivables, 353–361; reports by, A5
Management discussion and analysis (MD&A), 20, 30; for Starbucks Corporation, A12–A16

Manufacturing companies, inventory classification for, 240
Market interest rate, 452, 469
Market value, 390; of bonds, 451–452; of stocks, 494
Mark-to-market accounting, 550, 559
Matching principle, 151, 152, 176, 179
Materiality, 51, 73
Maturity date: for bonds, 449, 450, 459; for notes receivable, 348, 364
McCollick, Sharon, 306–307
MD&A. *See* Management discussion and analysis
Mechanical controls, 291–292
Merchandise Inventory account, 203
Merchandising companies, 52, 200–218; classifying inventory in, 240; evaluating profitability of, 213–216; freight costs, 207; gross profit, 212; gross profit rate, 213–214; income measurement process, 202; income statement for, 211–213, 217, 246–247, 263; inventory systems, 203–205; operating cycles, 203, 306; operating expenses, 212; operating expenses to sales ratio, 215; periodic inventory systems, 241–256; perpetual inventory systems, 203–215; purchase discounts, 207–209; recording purchases of merchandise, 205–209, 241–242; recording sales of merchandise, 209–211, 242–243; returns and allowances, 206, 210–211; sales discounts, 211; sales revenues, 211–212
Merchandising profit, 54, 212
Modified Accelerated Cost Recovery System (MACRS), 395
Monetary unit assumption, 22, 30
Mortgage bonds, 449, 469
Multiple-step income statement, 53, 55, 71
Mutual funds, 541

National Association of Investors Corporation, 646
Net cash. *See also* Cash: from investing and financing activities, 590–591, 594–595, 604, 608–609; from operating activities, 581, 588–590, 593–594, 600–603, 606–607
Net income, 9, 30, 581
Net loss, 9, 30, 508
Net purchases, 243–244, 267
Net sales, 212, 218; ratio of operating expenses to, 215
New York Stock Exchange, 494, 496
Nominal accounts. *See* Temporary accounts
Nonoperating activities, 54–55
Nonrecurring charges, 651–652
No-par value stock, 495, 519
Notes payable, 8, 439–440, 467, 469
Notes receivable, 341, 347–351, 365. *See also* Accounts receivable; Receivables: collecting, 303; computing the interest for, 348–349; dishonor of, 351; disposing of, 349–351; face value of, 349; honor of, 350; international perspective on, 350; maturity date for, 348, 364; recognizing, 349; valuing, 349, C13–C15, C16
Notes to the financial statements, 21, 30; for Starbucks Corporation, A16–A22
Novelli, Ray, 382
NSF (not sufficient funds) checks, 299, 303, 319

Obsolescence, 390
Off-balance sheet financing, 464, 469
Operating activities, 8–9, 66, 579, 580, 621, 623; net cash provided by, 588–590, 593–594, 600–603, 606–607
Operating cycles, 60, 73; for merchandising companies, 203, 306
Operating expenses, 54; amortization expenses as, 407; cash payments for, 602–603, 607; franchise costs as, 409–410; for merchandising companies, 202, 212; ratio of net sales to, 215
Operating expenses to sales ratio, 215, 218, 671–672, 681
Operating income, 54
Operating leases, 388, 464, 469
Order of magnitude listing, 444
Ordinary items, 651
Ordinary repairs, 398, 419
Other expenses and losses, 54
Other revenues and gains, 54
Outstanding checks, 300, 301, 319
Outstanding stock, 499, 519
Over-the-counter (OTC) market, 494
Ownership of goods, 245–246
Ownership rights, 489; common stock and, 492–493

Paid-in capital, 495–496, 519
Paper profits, 254
Parent company, 547, 559
Partnerships, 30; businesses organized as, 4–5
Par value stock, 494, 519
Patents, 61, 408, 419
Patterson, John, 296
Payee (promissory note), 347, 365
Payment date, 503–504, 519
Payout ratio, 511–512, 519, 674, 681
Payroll, 441–442
Payroll taxes, 441–442
Pension funds, 541
Percentage of receivables basis, 344, 365
Periodic inventory systems, 203–204, 218, 241–256, 263, 267; assumed cost flow methods, 248–256; cost of goods sold, 243–246; income statement, 246–247, 263; recording purchases of merchandise, 241–242, 263; recording sales of merchandise, 242–243, 263; specific identification costing method, 248
Permanent accounts, 170, 171, 179; closing entries in, 172–173
Perpetual inventory systems, 203–205, 217, 218; recording purchases of merchandise, 205–209; recording sales of merchandise, 209–211
Peterson, Donald, 287
Petty cash fund, 297, 316–318, 319; establishing, 316–317; making payments from, 317; replenishing, 318
Phantom profits, 254
Physical controls, 291–292
Physical inventory count, 244
Plant assets, 8, 61, 73, 384–406, 419. *See also* Intangible assets: accounting for, 390–402; additions and improvements, 398; analysis of, 402–405, 414; average age of, 403–404; average useful life of, 402–403; buildings, 387; classes of, 385; cost determination for, 385–389; depreciation of, 390–398; disposal of, 399–402, 414; equipment, 387–388; expenditures during useful life of, 398; financial statement presentation of, 410–411; as impairments, 398–399; international perspectives on, 385, 395; land, 386–387; land improvements, 387; leasing of, 388–389; ordinary repairs, 398; retirement of, 401; sale of, 399–401; turnover ratio for, 405
Post-closing trial balance, 172, 179; preparing, 172–173
Posting, 114, 125, 126; adjusting entries, 168
Preemptive rights, 492
Preferred stock, 500–501, 517, 519. *See also* Stock: dividend preferences, 500–501; liquidation preference, 501
Premiums, on bonds, 453–454, 457–459, 469
Prenumbering documents, 291
Prepaid expenses, 155, 179; adjusting entries for, 156–160
Prepayments, 155; adjusting entries for, 156–161, 176
Present value, 452, 469, C8–C15, C16; of an annuity, C11–C13, C16; of long-term notes/bonds, 452, C13–C15, C16; of a single amount, C9–C11, C16; time periods and, C13; variables for determining, C8, C16
President, corporate, 490
Price-earnings (P-E) ratio, 512–513, 519, 673–674, 681
Principal, C2, C16; of bonds, 452
Privately held corporations, 488–489, 519
Product life cycle, 582–583, 621
Profitability: cash-based measures of, 617; evaluating for merchandising companies, 213–216, 217
Profitability ratios, 56, 73, 661, 668–674, 681
Profit margin ratio, 56–57, 73, 670, 681
Promissory notes, 347–351, 366, 467. *See also* Notes receivable
Property, plant, and equipment. *See* Plant assets
Pro rata distribution, 502
Publicly held corporations, 488, 519
Purchase allowances, 206
Purchase discounts, 207–209, 218, 242
Purchase invoice, 205, 218
Purchase returns, 206
Purchases: cash payments for, 601–602; recording for bond investments, 543; recording with periodic inventory system, 241–247, 263; recording with perpetual inventory system, 205–209, 217

Quarterly financial data, A23
Quick ratio. *See* Acid-test ratio

Ratio analysis, 56–57, 71, 72, 73, 661–675; liquidity ratios, 661, 662–666; profitability ratios, 661, 668–674; solvency ratios, 661, 666–668
Ratios: acid-test, 445–446, 663, 681; asset turnover, 405, 670–671, 681; average collection period, 357, 365, 664–665, 681; average days in inventory, 665–666, 681; capital expenditure, 614, 622; cash-based,

615–618; cash debt coverage, 67, 72, 311, 616, 622, 667, 681; cash return on sales, 617, 622, 672, 681; cash to daily cash expenses, 311, 319; credit risk, 354; current, 63–64, 72, 260, 445–446, 615, 662, 681; current cash debt coverage, 67, 72, 310, 615, 622, 663, 681; debt to equity, 666–667; debt to total assets, 64–65, 73, 666–667, 681; earnings per share, 448, 512–514, 519, 673, 681; free cash flow, 311–313, 319, 612–613, 622, 667–668, 681; gross profit rate, 671, 681; inventory turnover, 258, 260, 264, 267, 665, 681; liquidity, 63–64, 73, 444–447, 661, 662–666, 681; operating expenses to sales, 215, 671–672, 681; payout, 511–512, 674, 681; price-earnings, 512–513, 673–674, 681; profitability, 56, 73, 661, 668–674, 681; profit margin, 56–57, 670, 681; receivables turnover, 356–357, 663–664, 681; return on assets, 56, 73, 669–670, 681; return on common stockholders' equity, 514, 669, 681; solvency, 64, 73, 461–462, 661, 666–668, 681; times interest earned, 461–462, 469, 667, 681
Raw materials, 240, 267
Readily marketable investments, 554
Real accounts. *See* Permanent accounts
Real estate tax payable, 8
Reasonable assurance, 294
Receivables, 340–365, 366. *See also* Accounts receivable; Notes receivable: accelerating cash receipts from, 358–361, 364; average collection period, 357; collecting, 307, 354–356; credit card sales as, 359–361; factoring, 358–359; managing, 353–361, 364; statement presentation of, 352, 364; turnover ratio for, 356–357, 366; types of, 340–341, 364
Receivables turnover ratio, 356–357, 366, 663–664, 681
Reconciliation of bank accounts, 299–303, 315
Record date, 503, 519
Recording process, 110–121, 125; basic steps in, 110; chart of accounts, 113; illustrated, 114–121; journal, 111–112; ledger, 113; posting procedure, 114
Redeeming bonds, 459, 468
Regulatory agencies, use of accounting information by, 7
Related activities, 290
Relevance, 49, 73
Reliability, 49, 73
Repairs, ordinary, 398
Reporting: of cash, 304–305, 315; of debt investments, 550–556, 558–559; of stock investments, 550–556, 558–559
Reports. *See also* Annual report: auditor, A6–A7; management, A5
Research and development (R&D) costs, 408, 419
Residual claims, 492
Restricted cash, 305, 319
Restructuring costs, 652
Retailers, 202
Retained earnings, 12, 30, 508–509, 519; capitalizing, 504; debit/credit rules, 107, 109; dividend payments and, 502, 517; increase in, 595, 604, 609; restrictions on, 509, 519; stockholders' equity and, 495, 508–509

Retained earnings statement, 10, 12, 28, 72; for Starbucks Corporation, 17–18
Retirement: of bonds, 459; of plant assets, 401
Return on assets ratio, 56, 73, 669–670, 681
Return on common stockholders' equity ratio, 514, 519, 669, 681
Returns: purchase, 206; sales, 210–211
Revenue expenditures, 385, 398, 419
Revenue recognition principle, 151, 152, 176, 179
Revenues, 8–9, 30; accrued, 155, 178; debit/credit rules, 107–108, 109; recognizing, 151; sales, 9, 202, 209–210, 211–212; on single-step income statement, 52; stockholders' equity and, 101; unearned, 155, 160–161, 179, 442–443
Reversing entry, 174, 179
Rifkin, Jeremy, 200
Risk-free investments, 307
Rotation of duties, 293

Salaries, accrued, 165–166
Salaries payable, 441
Sale: of bonds, 543–544; of plant assets, 399–401
Sales allowances, 210–211, 241–243
Sales discounts, 211, 218, 243
Sales invoices, 209, 218
Sales returns, 210–211, 241–243
Sales revenues, 9, 202, 218; on income statements, 211–212; recording with periodic inventory system, 242–243, 263; recording with perpetual inventory system, 209–210
Sales tax payable, 8, 440–441
Salvage value, 391, 416
Schultz, Howard, 2
Secured bonds, 449, 469
Securities. *See also* Debt investments; Stock investments: available-for-sale, 551–552, 559; held-to-maturity, 550, 559; trading, 550–551, 559
Securities and Exchange Commission (SEC), 7
Segmental data, 676, 681
Selling expenses, 54
Serial bonds, 449, 469
Serpico, Joseph, 255
Service corporations, 52
Service revenues, 9
Shareholders. *See* Stockholders
Simple interest, C2, C16
Single-step income statement, 52–53, 71
Sinking fund bonds, 449, 469
Sinnock, Betty, 646
"Slush" funds, 317
Social Security (FICA) taxes, 441
Sole proprietorships, 4, 5, 30
Solvency, 64, 72, 73; cash-based measures of, 616
Solvency ratios, 64, 73, 461–462, 661, 666–668, 681
Source document, 110
Specific identification costing method, 248, 267
Speculative investments, 541
Spiro, William, 255
Stated rate, 450

Stated value, 495, 519
Statement of cash flows, 10, 13, 30, 66–68, 72, 576–623; capital expenditure ratio and, 614; classification of cash flows, 579; corporate life cycle and, 582–583; direct method of preparing, 586, 599–611, 621, 622; evaluating a company using, 612–618, 621; financing activities and, 579, 580; format of, 580–581; free cash flow measures and, 612–613; indirect method of preparing, 586, 587–598, 621, 622–623; investing activities and, 579, 580; liquidity measures and, 615; noncash activities and, 579–580; operating activities and, 579, 580; preparation of, 585–586; profitability measures and, 617; purpose of, 578–579, 621; solvency measures and, 616; for Starbucks Corporation, 19–20, A10–A11; usefulness of, 583–584; using, 66–68
Statement of stockholders' equity, 57–58, 72, 73, A11
Stock: authorized, 494, 518; capital, 509; common, 492, 494–497; dividends from, 502–508; international perspective on, 494; investments in, 544–549; issuance of, 494, 517; no-par value, 495, 519; outstanding, 499, 519; par value, 494, 519; preferred, 500–501, 517, 519; treasury, 497–500, 517, 519; unissued, 499
Stock certificate, 493
Stock dividends, 504–506, 517, 519
Stockholders, 5, 8; claims of, 8; letters to, A3–A4; limited liability of, 489; ownership rights of, 492–493; presumed influence of, 545; stock performance information for, A23–A24
Stockholders' equity, 12, 28, 30; on classified balance sheet, 63; corporate performance and, 511–514; debit/credit procedures, 106–108; expenses and, 101; financial statement presentation of, 509–510, 517; international perspectives on, 493, 510; relationship among types of, 108, 109; retained earnings and, 495, 508–509; return on, 514; revenues and, 101; statement of, 57–58; stock dividends and, 505–506; stock splits and, 506–507; treasury stock and, 498–499
Stock investments, 544–549, 558, 559; accounting for, 544–549; acquisition of, 545, 547; consolidated financial statements, 548; controlling interest from, 547–548; cost method of recording, 545–546; dividends from, 545–546, 547; earnings performance and, 512–514; equity method of recording, 546–547; presumed influence from, 545; sale of, 546; valuation and reporting of, 550–556, 558–559
Stock splits, 506–507, 519
Store operating expense, 9
Straight-line method, 419; of amortization, 407, 455–456, 457–459, 469; of depreciation, 392–393, 414
Strategic investments, 541
Subsidiary company, 547, 559
Supplementary financial information, A22–A24
Supplies: adjusting entries for, 156–157; cash payments for, 601–602, 606

T accounts, 104, 126
Tarter, Fred, 338
Taxes. *See also* Income taxes: corporate, 491; cost flow method effects, 255; payroll, 441–442; sales, 440–441; withholding, 441–442
Taxing authorities, use of accounting information by, 7
Temporary accounts, 170, 171, 179; closing entries in, 171–172
Temporary investments, 554, 559
Term bonds, 449, 469
Theft, 286–287
Time period assumption, 23, 30, 150, 179
Times interest earned ratio, 461–462, 469, 667, 681
Time value of money, 452, C1–C16; future value concepts, C3–C8; interest and, C2–C3; present value concepts, C8–C15
Trademarks, 61, 408–409, 419
Trade names, 408–409, 419
Trade receivables, 341, 366
Trading, bond, 451
Trading on the equity, 669, 681
Trading securities, 550–551, 559
Transactions, 98–103, 125; analyzing, 99–103, 114; recording, 110, 114
Treasurer, 490
Treasury stock, 497–500, 517, 519; purchase of, 498–499
Trend analysis, 656–658
Trial balance, 121–122, 125, 126; adjusted, 169–170; example, 123–124; limitations of, 122; post-closing, 172–173
True cash balance, 302
Trustee, 450
Turner, Ted, 542
Turnover ratio: for plant assets, 405; for receivables, 356–357, 366

Uncollectible accounts: allowance method for, 342–343, 364; direct write-off method for, 346, 364; international perspective on, 344; recording the write-off of, 343; recovery of, 344
Underwriting bonds, 450
Unearned revenues, 155, 160–161, 179, 442–443
Unissued stock, 499
U.S. Copyright Office, 408
U.S. Patent Office, 408, 409
Units-of-activity method of depreciation, 394–395, 417–418, 419
Unqualified opinion, 21
Unsecured bonds, 449, 469
Useful life, 158, 179; average, 402–403; of plant assets, 391
Users of accounting information, 6–7, 28; financial statements for, 10–15

Verifiability of accounting information, 49
Vertical acquisition, 541
Vertical analysis, 658–660, 679, 681

Wages payable, 8, 441
Walton, Sam, 173
Wear and tear, 390
Weighted average unit cost, 252–253, 267
Weinstein, Barry, 359

Wholesalers, 202
Withholding taxes, 441
Working capital, 63, 73
Work in process, 240, 267
Work sheets, 179; adjusting entries prepared from, 177–178

Write-downs, 399
Writing-off bad debts: allowance method for, 342–346; direct write-off method for, 346
Wulff, John, 256

Yields, dividend, 511